di Giove Tonante

-rarsi tra i più cospicui ornati dopo che fu portati innanzi a' suoi fondamenti. 1. Colonne di marmo greco di gran mole, ch'un Abbozzo in gran parte sotto il terreno.
2 Fianco del moderno Campidoglio piantato sopra l'antico Tabulario. 3

A New Topographical Dictionary
of Ancient Rome

A New
Topographical
Dictionary

of Ancient Rome

L. Richardson, jr

The Johns Hopkins University Press
Baltimore and London

This book has been brought to publication with the generous assistance of the National Endowment for the Humanities.

The Johns Hopkins University Press
701 West 40th Street
Baltimore, Maryland 21211–2190
The Johns Hopkins Press Ltd., London

The paper used in this book meets the minimum requirements of American National Standard for Information Sciences—Permanence of Paper for Printed Library Materials, ANSI Z39.48-1984.

Library of Congress Cataloging-in-Publication Data

Richardson, Lawrence.
    A new topographical dictionary of ancient Rome / L. Richardson, Jr.
        p.   cm.
    Includes bibliographical references.
    ISBN 0-8018-4300-6 (alk. paper)
    1. Rome (Italy)—Buildings, structures, etc.—Dictionaries.
DG68.R5 1992
913.7′003—dc20   91-45046

DIS MANIBUS

M. I. R.　　C. W. M.　　F. E. B.

Contents

Illustrations

The ruins of Rome are well known. They have been drawn repeatedly, beginning in the earliest Renaissance, and since the invention of photography they have been the object of countless lenses. I am neither a draughtsman nor a photographer of any proficiency, and it would be the sheerest folly for me to try to compete with those who are so much my superiors. Fortunately Ernest Nash's *Pictorial Dictionary of Ancient Rome*[2], 2 vols. (London 1968) has appeared relatively recently, and it relieves me of much of the task of illustration. It not only presents superior photographs of every ancient monument of which substantial remains still survive but also includes a selection of drawings and plans to illuminate monuments that have been lost since the Renaissance and to elucidate points that photography cannot deal with. Everyone working with the monuments of ancient Rome must consult this admirable collection constantly. I have therefore limited the illustration of this dictionary to plans, of which Nash offers relatively few, a selection of fragments of the Marble Plan, and a few line drawings. I hope that the plans will make the text easier to understand and complement Nash's work and that the evidence of the Marble Plan will make the reader aware of the nature of much of our evidence and its virtues and shortcomings. The line drawings illustrate recent work and new discoveries.

Preface

The topographical dictionary offered in the pages that follow has been more than a decade in generation. It was begun when I was professor-in-charge of the School of Classical Studies at the American Academy in Rome in 1980. A few years earlier, in the course of directing a summer seminar for college teachers sponsored by the National Endowment for the Humanities on problems in the topography of ancient Rome, I had become acutely aware how inadequate and out of date the standard reference works on the subject had become. Then in the course of a visit to the site of Lavinium with Professor Ferdinando Castagnoli to see the newly discovered sanctuary of Minerva and the terracotta sculptures unearthed there I discussed the situation with him, for I knew he had many years earlier projected a revised version of the topographical dictionary of Samuel Ball Platner and Thomas Ashby and I was anxious to know when it might become available. And at that time he told me that his work on Lavinium had come to occupy most of his time and attention and the dictionary was still far from complete and had been put aside indefinitely. In consequence of this conversation I began to think seriously of writing such a dictionary myself, and the result is what is before the reader.

It is almost inevitable that a work of the scope of that presented here should contain at least occasional errors. It ranges in time over more than a millennium and attempts to embrace all the pertinent monuments within the sacred boundary of the world's greatest city. Consequently it calls for competence in more disciplines than almost any single scholar can command. I can only hope that the blunders the reader may find are not so egregious as to impair the book's usefulness, for like any dictionary, its primary purpose is to define the entries, to state succinctly what is and is not known about them, and to fit them into their place in a larger frame. But if the errors are not intolerable or innumerable, that is in large part owing to the help and advice I have received from many sources and many kind authorities. They are far too numerous for me to be able even to remember all of them, let alone to thank them adequately here. They are of many nationalities and ages; many of them are no longer living. But it would be invidious and ungrateful to omit the name of any. The best I can do is to tender a general heartfelt thanks to all; my appreciation is not in any way the less profound for that. The names of two, however, deserve particular commendation, Professor Fred S. Kleiner of Boston University and Professor Robert E. A. Palmer of the University of Pennsylvania. They have taught me much and saved me from countless stupidities, especially in the fields of numismatics and epigraphy. Both have read the manuscript through and made incisive observations on almost every page, correcting mistakes and omissions and improving my reading of the evidence. This is a much better book thanks to their generosity.

Most of the text was written in the libraries of the American Academy in Rome and Duke University. The staffs of these libraries have been of constant cheerful assistance and done much to make my work easier and pleasanter. I have had the benefit of the watchful eyes and willing hands of Steven M. Cerutti and John Alan Stevens in checking my references. For the production of plans and drawings I am indebted especially to the lens of Lewis Parrish and the pen of Joan Jones; other sources of the illustrations are acknowledged in the list of these. And finally, in the difficult and extended process of converting my manuscript into a finished book, I have been the grateful recipient of the expert advice and kindly forbearance of many members of the staff of the Johns Hopkins University Press, especially Jane Warth and Eric Halpern.

Introduction

The tools of the topographer of ancient Rome are very varied, everything that can be brought to bear on any historical or archaeological problem, beginning with the ancient literary sources and descending to the unearthing and analysis of any sort of physical remains. The literary sources must be evaluated, however; too often there is a tendency to take any mention of a monument at face value and out of context, and the reliability of the source is too seldom questioned, even by seasoned scholars. Inscriptions, including the stamps of ownership on lead pipes and brick-stamps, are another source of information. But the stamps on lead pipes need not always indicate ownership, and bricks are not always used within a short time of their manufacture. They may even be reused. The mutilated fragments of Forma Urbis Romae known as the Marble Plan of Rome are a marvelous help, every square inch worth study, but the plan is not meticulously drawn, and there are distortions in the surveying. Moreover, of the 712 known and catalogued fragments, many of them composed of several pieces, fewer than 50 have been positively identified and located. New joins are made from time to time, and new locations suggested or discovered. Coins showing monuments have been accorded more attention and given more weight than they deserve. As soon as a temple or other monument was decreed, it might appear on a coin and be shown in a form that had nothing to do with the ultimate reality. This is especially true of coins issued at mints other than that of Rome. Unless one knows the date of both coin and monument, a coin is almost wholly untrustworthy evidence. Even the representation of an existing building on a coin is often arbitrary, and we do not know the Roman conventions for such representations as interiors. Worse than coins are lead tesserae. However, old photographs, as well as old prints, must never be neglected. Often in the course of time the appearance of features may have changed, especially in a place as much frequented as the Forum Romanum. Sometimes this is for cosmetic reasons or convenience, sometimes because of damage, sometimes arbitrary or a mistake. In the past it was common practice to repair damaged and unstable monuments with ancient material that did not belong to these but was found nearby, a practice that is found also in antiquity. The work of the topographer is a path through a maze, beset with pitfalls and full of surprises, both pleasant and unpleasant.

There are numerous descriptions of the physical city of Rome surviving from antiquity, none of which is without value, but all of which require interpretation. None is in any sense a topographical survey. The descriptions range from Horace's poetical account of a walk through the center of the city while he is pestered by an insufferable leech and Vergil's description of Aeneas's divinely inspired, dreamlike visit to the Arcadian king Evander to attempts in Livy and Tacitus to convey the magnitude of disastrous fires, the confusion of battle, or the grandeur of ceremonies. A few merit special mention: Pliny's attempt (*HN* 3.66–67) to describe the enormous size of Rome as a metropolis by measuring the distances from the Milliarium Aureum in the Forum Romanum to the thirty-seven gates of Rome and then the length of all the streets from the same point to the limits of concentrated building and habitation; Frontinus's careful account of the water supply (*De Aquis*) with the time of construction of each new aqueduct, its volume, and the regions of the city that it served; and Strabo's attempt (5.3.7–8 [234–35]) to define Rome's magnificence as a singular combination of natural advantages, admirable organization of public works, and superb architecture. These do not convey useful information, such as can be quarried piecemeal from the works of Varro, Vitruvius, and Dionysius of Halicarnassus, but they are early attempts to treat the city as an entity, to see it as a physical organism. The antiquarians must be cited repeatedly for their interest in old and odd place-names, curious customs, and religious lore; the enormous learning of the Augustan scholar Verrius Flaccus, transmitted in abbreviated and mutilated form in the dictionary of Festus, the collection and discussion of random information of interest by Valerius Maximus and Aulus Gellius, and the erudite inventions of Macrobius and Tertullian are all important and often illuminating of what in greater writers is taken for granted. In the study of the topography of the ancient city no ancient author writing anything at all about the city can be ignored, but each individually must be carefully weighed. A scholiast will often include an explanation that he thinks is plausible, rather than something based on genuine knowledge; the scholia on Juvenal are notoriously unreliable. Or there will be information that he understands imperfectly, as is sometimes the case with Servius. But until the onset of the Middle Ages in the sixth century every scrap of writing about the city is to be prized and scrutinized, from Plautus's digression on the frequenters of the Forum Romanum to Procopius's spirited account of Belisarius's defense of Rome against the Goths. There are often nuggets of value in very unsuspected places, in Seneca's *Apocolocyntosis* and Johannes Lydus's *De Mensibus*.

The ancient sources bearing on topographical features of most of Rome have been gathered together in *Fontes ad Topographiam Veteris Urbis Romae Pertinentes* by Giuseppe Lugli in collaboration with a number of his associates and students, published from 1952 to 1969. Here, under convenient headings and with a wealth of cross references, one can find the material of every sort pertinent to any feature or monument from the general site and geography to the least dedication or image depicted on a lead tessera. No sort of evidence is neglected, and the inclusion of brick-stamps and coins, even when their pertinence is in some doubt, enhances the usefulness of this work. The abundant subheadings make reference easy, and brief footnotes provide dates and identify obscure allusions. But a few areas were not completed, and there is no discussion of these sources, or their value, when it is questionable, and inscriptions are only minimally described. The texts of authors are taken from the latest Teubner editions without apparatus, and the work is published on very poor paper with few illustrations. Consequently, it serves more as an index to the sources than a replacement for them, but as such it is tremendously valuable. Unfortunately, it was also a small edition, and it is difficult to find a copy today.

The present book is a new dictionary in the sense that every entry has been written entirely afresh and

effort has been made to take into account the results of the latest excavations and research. But significant work on the topography of the ancient city goes back as far as the Renaissance and such antiquarians and architects as Bartolomeo Marliano and Pirro Ligorio, and systematic study of the subject has been pursued since the eighteenth century. We have inherited a vast body of knowledge built up by some of the best minds in the Western world, and I have seen my task as one more of sorting and selecting than of adding. I have added where the evidence showed existing interpretations inadequate or implausible, but I have tried to refrain from speculation.

The geographical limits of this dictionary are provided by the fourteen *regiones* of the Augustan reorganization of Rome, as far as they can be determined. They are defined principally by the buildings listed for each in the regionary catalogues of the fourth century, and their outer perimeter follows approximately the line of the walls of Aurelian, except in the Transtiberim. On the left bank of the Tiber, these walls also closely follow the *octroi* (customs) boundary of the time of Commodus, which was marked by cippi and so provides a convenient definition of the city limits at the height of the empire. But on the right bank the area included within the walls was simply a wedge running to the top of the Janiculan hill to prevent any enemy from seizing that vantage point from which to bombard the city and to protect the heads of the most important Tiber bridges. Here the list of buildings given by the regionary catalogues for Regio XIV indicates an area stretching from the sanctuary of Hercules Cubans, a half-kilometer outside the Porta Portuensis on the south, to the Gaianum and Naumachia Vaticana beyond the Mausoleum Hadriani on the north, and westward to the ridge of the Janiculan hill and slope of the Vatican, including the Circus Gaii et Neronis. This is a vast area and imprecisely bounded, but although parts of it were populous, it was not rich in public buildings, so hard decisions on what to include and what to exclude do not present themselves.

Within the boundaries thus set all significant sites, monuments, and buildings from the earliest occupation of Rome to the onset of the Middle Ages in the sixth century have been included, with the exception of most Christian churches and tombs. The study of early Christian Rome is a separate discipline best left to quite different specialists, and, although I have frequently drawn on their work, I am not competent to judge it, especially in matters of liturgical importance. While this is not a dictionary exclusively of pagan Rome, it cannot cover everything, and Christian monuments have been omitted, except as they have bearing on the physical shape of pagan ones.

The most important of our sources of information,

apart from the literary sources, are the physical remains of buildings revealed in excavations. Few ancient monuments survived above ground through the centuries of neglect from the onset of the Middle Ages to the reawakening of interest in antiquity and its preservation in the Renaissance. And those that did were generally rebuilt in other architectural forms, becoming parts of towers, castles, churches, and palazzi. The rediscovery of the surviving remains in the foundations and walls of later buildings continues today, and almost no year passes without important fresh information coming to light. Apart from additions to our knowledge of architecture and city planning, excavations also yield a harvest of epigraphical material, especially inscribed pipes and brick-stamps.

Along with these one must rank other, more important inscriptions, the fragments of calendars, the various *fasti* of Rome, and the fragments of plans inscribed on marble. Inscriptions often untowardly preserve topographical information of great value. Among these pride of place must be given to the so-called Capitoline Base (*CIL* 6.975 = *ILS* 6073) now in the Palazzo dei Conservatori, an inscription of the time of Hadrian in which were listed the *magistri* of the *vici* of Rome headed with the name of each *vicus* and divided among the Augustan regiones. Unfortunately, only somewhat less than one-half the whole list survives, the magistri of Regiones I, X, XII, XIII, and XIV, but the information to be gleaned from the names of the vici is very important. Next to this we should perhaps set the decree of Tarracius Bassus, *praefectus urbi* toward the end of the fourth century, against miscreants who had cheated and usurped public benefits to their own profit. These were identified by name, together with those whom they had wronged, identified by the name of their vicus. The decree is known only in fragments, but there were multiple copies, and there are more than a dozen important fragments, which give many vicus names not exampled elsewhere (*CIL* 6.1766, 31893–901; *ILS* 6072).

The fasti are numerous, amounting to more than forty, and come from a great variety of sites, for the most part near Rome, but they are all fragmentary and of various date. The most important are the Fasti Praenestini, believed to have been compiled by Verrius Flaccus in A.D. 6–9 and displayed in the forum of Praeneste, and the Fasti Antiates Maiores, painted on plaster, of 84–55 B.C. The fasti have all been collected and handsomely published by Atilio Degrassi in *Fasti Anni Numani et Iuliani* (*Inscriptiones Italiae*, vol. 13.2) (Rome 1963), a work of the highest scholarship that includes extensive *commentarii diurni*, which bring together the literary and epigraphical sources pertaining to religious observances for each day and include modern bibliography. This supersedes Theodor Mommsen's work in *CIL* 1.2 and is a mine of information.

Of the fragments of plans on marble, the most important are those of the Forma Urbis Romae known as the Marble Plan, a map of the city drawn between A.D. 203 and 211 in the time of Septimius Severus. It was inscribed on heavy rectangular plates of marble at the scale of 1:240, and these were hung on a wall in the Templum Pacis. The wall still survives today behind the church of SS. Cosma e Damiano, and the pattern of clamps and backing can be discerned. The execution is careless and inaccurate in detail, with occasional serious errors in the surveying, but the plan is still invaluable. It showed the whole of the center of the city of Rome, many of the buildings and landmarks inscribed with their names, but it is oriented with the southeast at the top and excluded important southeastern reaches of the city, including the areas of the Baths of Caracalla and the Porta Maggiore. The bronze clamps that held it to the wall gave way in time, and the plates fell and broke at the foot of the wall. The fragments were then in large part dispersed. Their recovery began in 1562 on the initiative of Cardinal Alessandro Farnese, and the subsequent history of these, the discovery of more fragments, and their reassembly and publication by various scholars is a fascinating story in itself. They are now housed in Palazzo Braschi in Rome. The most recent publications are those by a commission of four scholars, G. Carettoni, A. M. Colini, L. Cozza, and G. Gatti, *La pianta marmorea di Roma antica*, 2 vols. (Rome 1960), and E. Rodriguez Almeida, *Forma urbis marmorea: Aggiornamento generale*, 2 vols. (Rome 1981). The first of these is a meticulous study of the monument from a great many perspectives, together with fine plates of all the fragments at large scale. The second publishes many advances made since 1960 in the joining and placing of fragments, but large numbers of fragments still remain unassigned. Moreover, it has been suspected that some fragments may belong to another, earlier version of the plan, probably Flavian in date, which raises the question whether a master plan of the city may not have been executed for Agrippa, acting as Augustus's agent, at the time of his overhauling of the water and sewer systems of Rome beginning in 33 B.C. If so, then all subsequent plans were probably based on that. In 1983, in an excavation in Via Anicia in the Transtiberim, there came to light part of a thin plate of marble showing the bank of the river and the Temple of Castor and Pollux on Circus Flaminius. This is incised at the same scale as the Marble Plan, 1:240, but much more delicately and precisely. Walls are drawn with double lines, rather than the single lines of the Marble Plan, and a range of refinements including identifications introduced. This fragment overlaps with one of the Marble Plan, and its place is certain, but it seems to have been made earlier by perhaps a century and for a different purpose. More fragments will probably come to light, and the study of the plan continues to produce new information.

From late antiquity come the two lists known as the regionary catalogues, the *Curiosum* and *Notitia*, lists of buildings and landmarks arranged according to the Augustan regiones of the city, followed by counts of buildings of various types. These are incomplete, and their purpose has been much debated. After careful study, A. Nordh concluded that the *Curiosum* was compiled in or about the time of Diocletian from public lists and/or a map of the general character of the Marble Plan and intended to be a list of the regiones of the city with the neighborhoods therein contained identified by prominent buildings or landmarks. This was then augmented by interpolations and the addition of incidental information, such as the heights of the columns of Trajan and Marcus Aurelius. At the end of the list for each regio were added certain statistics for types of buildings, amenities, and officials, some of which continue to be enigmatic today. Finally, there were appended two lists, one a compilation of significant features for the city as a whole (obelisks, bridges, hills, and so on), and the other statistical tables of buildings for the whole city. The omission of a great many famous buildings from these lists is puzzling; it is thought that perhaps it is to be laid to their not having given their name to any neighborhood. The *Notitia* was then compiled before the end of the reign of Constantine, using an early version of the *Curiosum* as basis. The *Notitia* has certain more correct readings than any of the surviving manuscripts of the *Curiosum* and omits a few of the interpolations, but contains other interpolations. The two appendices that follow these lists and are to all intents and purposes the same—the first of features most of which are omitted from the regionary lists, the other a compilation of the numbers of various sorts of buildings, many of which appear earlier in their regiones— must have been added somewhat later, the latter first, but probably neither later than the fourth century.

To the fourth century also belong the works of the Chronographer of 354 and Saint Jerome (Hieronymus). The former provides a list of the accomplishments of the kings of the early city and a list of the emperors with the remarkable events that occurred under each, beginning with Julius Caesar and extending to Licinius. Because the compiler was especially interested in building activity and such natural disasters as fires, he includes much incidental infor-

mation of value but few details. The work is included in Mommsen's *Chronica Minora* 1 (*Monumenta Germaniae Historica,* vol. 9, Berlin 1892) 141–48. The chronology of Saint Jerome—a translation into Latin of the chronology of Eusebius for the history of the world with additions extending it to A.D. 379—gives in parallel columns Eastern and Western calendars and adds events of significance in Roman history. These include much about literary figures, as well as political events, and preserve a wealth of information, not always accurate. Jerome's sources included Suetonius but are not otherwise precisely known. Because notices of significant building and catastrophes are also included, the chronicle is frequently of value for the topographer. Its latest edition is the second edition by Rudolph Helm (Eusebius, *Werke*, vol. 7, Berlin 1984).

A century later, toward the middle of the fifth century, Polemius Silvius constructed an annotated calendar, essentially Christian and astronomical, and added to it lists of landmarks *Quae sint Romae*. Apparently writing somewhere in the south of France, he relied on the work of the Chronographer of 354, or something very similar, the *Curiosum*, and other sources of the same sort. He adds to our knowledge names for monuments in use under the later empire but little else, and his list is studded with problems of every sort.

Collections of these sources, together with an assortment of others of smaller value, have been gathered together and published from time to time, as well as studies of the individual documents. The most important and accessible of such publications are those of C. L. Urlichs, *Codex Urbis Romae Topographicus* (Würzburg 1871); H. Jordan, *Topographie der Stadt Rom im Alterthum*, 2 vols. (Berlin 1871); Theodor Mommsen, *Chronica Minora* 1 (*Monumenta Germaniae Historica*, vol. 9, Berlin 1892); and R. Valentini and G. Zucchetti, *Codice topografico della città di Roma*, vol. 1 (Rome 1940). Urlich's collection is comprehensive but difficult to find, and much valuable work on the nature and quality of the texts has been done subsequently, especially by Mommsen. Jordan includes admirable discussions of certain texts that especially interested him, although the notion that the basis of the regionary catalogues was a list of the buildings that bounded each of the fourteen regions of the Augustan city, a notion prevalent everywhere in the nineteenth century, is no longer accepted. Today we depend on Valentini and Zucchetti for these; their first volume collects the most important sources from antiquity down through the sixth century, ending with Johannes Lydus and pseudo-Zaccharias. Each text is discussed in a preface and provided with an apparatus criticus and extensive annotation that takes full account of modern scholarship. The selection of literary and epigraphical material from the classical period is necessarily limited and somewhat arbitrary, but this is meant to be simply introductory. The body of the work begins with the regionary catalogues, and for these and successive documents this is now our best authority. It is referred to repeatedly here, cited as VZ.

After Constantine and the acceptance of Christianity into respectability in Rome, one begins to get Christian topographical documents, lists of the burial places of popes and martyrs, and lists of the churches and cemeteries with their respective graves. These begin in a small way with the Chronographer of 354. At first they are of small value to the topographer, because the dead were still buried beyond the pomerium, and it was there that churches dedicated to them were built. Through the Middle Ages of the sixth to ninth centuries Rome and interest in its antiquities continued to dwindle and decay. But about the time of Charlemagne we begin to feel the winds of change. An extraordinary portmanteau manuscript known as the *Codex Einsiedelnsis* (Einsiedeln no. 326) contains, among other things, a precious topographical document in five distinct parts, each written in a different hand: (1) the Einsiedeln sylloge, a collection of inscriptions, both pagan and Christian, copied from monuments, for the most part in Rome, toward the end of the eighth century; (2) the Einsiedeln itinerary, an itinerary for pilgrims arranged in eleven crossings of the city of Rome in various directions from gate to gate, with lists of the sights to be seen on either hand, as well as in the immediate path. This was composed before the creation of the Leonine city in 848–852 and after the foundation of the monastery of S. Silvestro in 752–767, so it may be placed close to the time of Charlemagne; (3) a description of the walls of Rome, offered as an appendix to the itinerary, which amounts to a statistical inventory of features such as towers and windows for the stretches of the Aurelian Walls from gate to gate at a time when they were in serious disrepair, so presumably between the time of Belisarius and the eighth century, when their repair was undertaken by four popes, Sisinnius, Gregory II, Gregory III, and Hadrian I; the most likely date for it would be early in the eighth century; (4) an appendix of the liturgical rites of Holy Week in Rome written sometime between 687 and the first years of the ninth century; and (5) an anthology of Latin poems including epitaphs of A.D. 799 and 840, originally a separate volume. It is clear that the first four parts of this miscellany were put together in Rome over a relatively short time, close to the reign of Charlemagne, most probably by a well-educated and devout cleric. The *Liber Pontificalis,* the official account of the

res gestae of the early popes in biographical form, is of varying value. The first collected edition of these lives seems to have been made under Pope Boniface II (530–532). The earliest lives are very spare and schematic. A little at a time they become richer and more informative; toward the end of the fifth century they begin to show the character of contemporary compositions. In the sixth century they focus more sharply on the politics and administration of the church. The sequel, or second edition, extending the history in similar form until the death of Pope Martin V (1431), is very uneven. Through the ninth century the lives are the work of anonymous court functionaries, compiled during the lifetime of the popes from official records and archives, and some of these (Hadrian I, Paschal I, Gregory IV) are important. In the tenth century and majority of the eleventh they are dry catalogues with occasional mention of historical events. Then, beginning with Pope Gregory VII (1073–1086), extended biographies are the work of various contemporaries, but are brought into a semblance of uniformity by the editing of twelfth-century scholars, and in such form continue until the early fifteenth century. The topographical information contained in the *Liber* is incidental, sometimes casual, but it provides much that is valuable about the transformation of the ancient pagan city into a Christian one. In modern times the *Liber* has been edited by L. Duchesne in masterly fashion (vol. 1, Paris 1886; vol. 2, Paris 1892) and by Mommsen (only vol. 1, until the death of Constantine in 715, Berlin 1898). A small section, from Pope Paschal II (1099–1118) to Pope Honorius II (1124–1130), the work of the Roman Pandolfo (ca. 1137), has been edited by J. M. March on the basis of a manuscript in Tortosa (Barcelona 1925). The significant passages for topographical studies have been excerpted by Valentini and Zucchetti, using all three important modern editions. In this dictionary citations are usually made following Duchesne (cited as LPD), as well as Valentini and Zucchetti (VZ). The significant early Christian lists, Einsiedeln material, and *Liber Pontificalis* are collected by Valentini and Zucchetti in their second volume (Rome 1942).

One of the more extraordinary productions of the twelfth-century revival of interest in antiquity is the *Mirabilia,* originally composed, as Duchesne demonstrated, by Benedetto Canonico, cantor of the basilica of S. Pietro, between 1140 and 1143. It is a guidebook for pilgrims, beginning with statistics about the fortifications of Rome, and contains lists of the principal monuments: gates, triumphal arches, hills, baths, palaces, theaters, places associated with the martyrdom of saints, and so on. The emphasis is almost equally divided between sites of religious importance and conspicuous ruins and landmarks. Into this are woven bits of history and tradition, legends, and lore of every sort. The author has let his imagination run riot at times; he is extremely ignorant about mainstream Roman history and loves the fabulous and the wonderful. But he knows the city of his own day very well and draws heavily upon that knowledge. His work is known in several versions, having been subsequently more or less elaborated to suit different audiences and successive generations. An example of this is the *Graphia Aureae Urbis* of the thirteenth century, which uses it as its central part, preceding it with foundation legends and following it with an account of the imperial administration (*dignitates*). The *Mirabilia* was enormously successful and exists in a multitude of manuscripts all over Europe. A version in the vernacular known as *Le miracole di Roma* rearranges and abbreviates it. After the invention of printing it went through numerous editions. For the study of the topography of ancient Rome it is almost worthless, but it is a curiosity of high antiquarian interest.

A work along some of the same lines is the *De Mirabilibus Urbis Romae* by Magister Gregorius, a churchman, very likely English, of the second half of the twelfth or beginning of the thirteenth century. An educated man, he wrote evidently following a pilgrimage to Rome at the instigation of, and for the edification of, his colleagues (*consodales*). He is especially impressed by statuary, but responds to the aesthetic quality of buildings as well. Unfortunately, his work is brief and unsystematic; it informs us of what there was to be seen at the time that continued to be awe-inspiring, but it does not add much to our knowledge of topography, because Gregorius's knowledge of the names and purposes of the ancient buildings was very imperfect, and at times his imagination runs wild.

Another work of Benedetto Canonico is the so-called *Ordo Romanus Benedicti,* a descriptive list of the ceremonies of the church year, especially the processions in which the pope took part, the routes these followed being given in detail that is often informative about topography, together with lists of those participating and their dress and order. This, as far as the rituals are concerned, is based on an *Ordo Romanus Antiquus* of the middle of the tenth century, but the wealth of learning, especially antiquarian lore, that Benedetto has lavished on his revisions makes it very valuable. This *Ordo* was then revised, after the return of the popes to Rome from an exile of six years, by Cencio Savelli, called Cencio Camerario, in 1188. Although he abbreviates Benedetto's *Ordo,* omitting much of topographical interest, he includes a list of 305 churches whose clerics had the right to a *presbyterium* for incense during the Easter parade from the Vatican to the Lateran. Other lists

of churches, dependent in part on this but including additions, are the catalogues of Paris (Bibliothèque de l'Arsénal, no. 526) and Turin (Biblioteca Nazionale di Torino, Lat. A, 381).

The topographical sources for the period of the eleventh to thirteenth centuries, including much material that is pertinent only to Christian and medieval Rome, such as Petrus Mallius's detailed description of the Vatican basilica and its contents and adjacencies, are collected by Valentini and Zucchetti in their third volume (Rome 1946). Here there is only incidentally information important for this dictionary.

Beginning in the fourteenth century, with the surge of humanistic interest of the early Renaissance, men such as Petrarch had an intense awareness of the former greatness of Rome, which needed expression in evocation of the physical city. By and large these were men of letters, devoted to reading Livy and Vergil, who made no attempt to fetter their imaginations with topographical exactness. They were in Rome and conjured up the ancient landscape easily. What they did not know, they made up, explaining things as logically as they could, mingling Christian elements with pagan ones. These were men such as Giovanni Cavalieri, Fazio degli Uberti, and Nicolò Signorili. Their work is seldom of real help to the modern topographer, and their mistakes are often ludicrous, but their enthusiasm for antiquity led them to copy numerous inscriptions, and sometimes their inclusion of information about the state and location of remains with relation to the landmarks of their own day is useful. Among these one must single out especially the so-called Anonymous Magliabechianus, a name given by L. Mercklin, his first modern editor, to the author of the *Tractatus de Rebus Antiquis et Situ Urbis Romae* of about 1411. His work begins with a history of the world from its beginning and is a rag bag of material drawn untidily from many sources and with many errors. He was not a learned man. In the topographical part, he is heavily dependent on the *Mirabilia* and *Graphia,* but he does include a modern designation for each ancient landmark, and this adds up to a fair coverage of the city in the early Renaissance, one of our best documents for the period.

With Poggio Bracciolini's *De Fortunae Varietate,* begun in 1431 and published in 1448, things change. He chooses, as an eloquent example of the fickleness of Fortune, the vicissitudes of the ancient city of Rome and provides a detailed description of the ruins of antiquity with precise identification of each and some indication of its glory and history. He is familiar with a great range of texts, including Frontinus's *De Aquis* and Dionysius of Halicarnassus's *Antiquitates Romanae,* and can speak with more authority than his predecessors. He has collected and studied inscriptions and knows the remains well by autopsy, having even measured the walls and counted the towers. Unfortunately, his description is abbreviated and unsystematic, but he gives a vivid picture of what remains and the state in which it appears. Within the same period appeared the truly revolutionary work of Biondo Flavio, *Roma Instaurata*, undertaken in 1444 and brought to completion in 1446. This was a systematic topography of Rome based on an extensive array of sources. The regionary catalogues and Frontinus are used properly for the first time, and postclassical sources such as the *Liber Pontificalis,* Symmachus, and Cassiodorus are not slighted, nor are the ancient churches and monasteries. His is the first attempt at a scientific topography, and he was a man of keen intelligence and lively imagination. While he was capable of egregious errors, they are the errors of a reasoning man. He is in many ways the founder of modern topography, and on his work depends much that followed in the succeeding century and a half. His book was repeatedly copied, and after the invention of printing it went through a dozen editions by the middle of the sixteenth century.

The fragmentary remnants of a still more learned work are the *Excerpta,* supposedly taken down from the lectures of Pomponio Leto, while he was showing a foreigner about the ruins of Rome. They date from late in the fifteenth century, when Leto was teaching at the Sapienza. The tour begins with the Colosseum and proceeds to the Forum Romanum and imperial fora, thence to the Campus Martius, as far as S. Maria del Popolo, and then clockwise through the hills from the Pincian to the Aventine, and finally to the Palatine and Capitoline. The work is full of current information and observation; errors are few, and speculation is almost completely lacking. It is regrettable that we do not have more from this brilliant scholar.

There follows on these the brief work of Bernardo Rucellai of the end of the fifteenth century or beginning of the sixteenth, entitled simply *De Urbe Roma.* Rucellai was a Florentine, an enthusiastic student of epigraphy and numismatics who enjoyed the friendship and advice of Donato Acciaioli, Lorenzo de'Medici, and Leon Battista Alberti and profited from their instruction, especially that of Alberti in construction. Rucellai knows the latest discoveries and has a wide knowledge of not only the sources but also the scholarship of his time, but his work is brief, and his contribution is chiefly in epigraphy. Finally, there is the *Opusculum de Mirabilibus Novae et Veteris Urbis Romae* of Francesco Albertini, begun in 1506 and finished in 1509. This contributes little or nothing to our knowledge of topography, being the work of a cleric of little scholarly proficiency; he

freely confesses that in his compilation he is heavily dependent on others, such as Pomponio Leto. But in his account of modern Rome he is very complete, beginning with the churches, which he classifies by importance, proceeding to the palaces of the popes and cardinals, then to hospitals, libraries, and other buildings of public usefulness and interest, and concluding with the works of Julius II. The works from Petrarch's in the middle of the fourteenth century to Albertini's in the early sixteenth, for the most part excerpted to emphasize the contribution to the study of topography, are assembled by Valentini and Zucchetti in their fourth and final volume (Rome 1953).

The history of the study of topography as a branch of knowledge, beginning with the humanists of the early Renaissance, is too complicated and too crowded with important figures, often in violent disagreement, to be discussed in detail here. While the disputes and feuds add much to the interest and liveliness of the field, they contribute nothing in the way of source material. The basic texts were by this time almost all generally available, and quarrels over their emendation and interpretation, although colorful and engrossing, did little to advance knowledge. Topographers such as the rivals Pirro Ligorio and Bartolomeo Marliano are worth studying for their intrinsic interest, but they do not appear as more than footnotes in modern treatises on the subject. New information of real value could only come from the physical remains themselves, and these to a very large extent lay buried. The record of those that still stood above ground was made by a succession of artists, some of them very gifted, such as Baldassare Peruzzi (1461–1536), Antonio da Sangallo il Giovane (1489–1546), Marten van Heemskerck (1498–1574), and Giovanni Antonio Dosio (ca. 1533–1609), and they have left a legacy of drawings and notebooks that enriches museum collections and provides basic information about the appearance of ruins. Often the exactness of their drawings is astonishing, but they do not cover the surviving monuments systematically, and, because the artists' interest was especially pictorial, they did not choose their views to be informative. Those who worked in architecture, such as Peruzzi and Dosio, do sometimes make exquisite drawings with plans and measured details of capitals and cornices, but these are for the most part only of familiar buildings, the Colosseum, Pantheon, and Arch of Constantine. Dosio's sketchbook, now in Berlin, was published in facsimile by Christian Hülsen in 1933; other drawings of his in the Uffizi were edited by F. Borsi and others and published as *G. A. Dosio, Roma antica* (Rome 1976). Heemskerck's sketchbooks are superb and a wonderful record of the glories of Rome in his day, including sculpture as well as architecture, modern and ancient, but they include very little in the way of plans and measurements. They have been published in facsimile by Hülsen and Hermann Egger (vol. 1, Berlin 1913; vol. 2, Berlin 1916; reprinted in Soest, Holland, 1975). Doubtless, there are still treasures of this sort yet to be discovered in private collections, but they are not apt to add much to our knowledge. Those who have contributed significantly to the study of ancient topography are Andrea Palladio (1508–1580), Étienne Du Pérac (ca. 1525–1604), and Alò Giovannoli (ca. 1550–1618).

Palladio, whose feeling for architectural volumes and vistas was probably the finest the world has ever produced, spent most of 1546 and 1547 in concentrated study of the remains of ancient architecture in Rome and its vicinity. Although he drew everything accessible with great care, he was especially drawn to the great imperial baths and the problems in vaulting and lighting that these presented, and he made studies of not only the plans of these but also all the elevations and sections that he could devise, a very complete set for almost every example. For the Baths of Caracalla, he included a number of capitals and moldings. The ground plans are almost always complete and suggest that he must have done a certain amount of discreet excavating; only occasionally does he let a plan trail off. Some of the time he must be filling in parts by conjecture, and throughout his grand bath complexes are rigidly symmetrical, but their symmetry has been borne out to be correct by modern investigations. He is our best authority for most of these now, because much has since been destroyed or built into other buildings. And in the mid-sixteenth century the ruins were still being intensively mined, not only for artistic treasures and marbles, but simply for building material. At one time he projected "books" of drawings of ancient monuments, large collections divided among the various types of buildings: arches, baths, temples, and so on, but this came to nothing. However, he did publish a small collection, *L'antichità di Roma*, in Rome in 1554, the fruit of his stay in 1546 and 1547.

In contrast, Étienne Du Pérac was a professional antiquarian, as well as a painter and architect, a Frenchman, as his name indicates, who came to Rome in the late 1550s and remained for more than twenty years, producing engravings, especially views of the remains of antique buildings in their modern setting. In this he was following in the tradition of Pirro Ligorio and Dosio, and his first great work was a panoramic bird's-eye view of the city imitating Ligorio's great panorama of 1561 showing the known ancient buildings restored to their former splendor and the lacunae filled out with suitable inventions. This, Du Pérac's monumental (1.04 m × 1.56 m) *Urbis Romae Sciographia*, was issued in

eight sheets in April 1574. To produce it he has shamelessly mined Ligorio's work, but changing enough to avoid the charge of outright plagiarism. He has reoriented a number of buildings, usually for the better, and clarified the courses of the main streets from the gates through the city, but it is perfectly clear where he has gone for inspiration and how he has worked. In the following year, 1575, he published his *Vestigi dell'antichità di Roma*, a collection of thirty-nine views of the best-known ancient monuments, bird's-eye views, somewhat simplified, with modern buildings treated so as not to distract from the ancient ones. These were provided with lengthy captions explaining them. Here, too, Du Pérac was not above using the work of his predecessors, notably Dosio's, when it was to his advantage, but much was his own, and he was a good draughtsman and a careful observer. He can often be called on for details that are preserved nowhere else. This work was a great success and went through no fewer than eight editions, the last in 1773, proof in itself of its importance.

Alò Giovannoli is different, a careful observer but an inept draughtsman, willing to draw the most unprepossessing remains of reticulate-faced walls and concrete vaulting, but incapable of conveying accurately the spatial relation of masses and the correct proportion of elements. Often one cannot tell what is ancient from what is modern in his work. But he was an indefatigable workman, and in 1616, shortly before his death, he published in Rome a small collection of views, *Vedute degli antichi vestigi di Roma*. This was followed posthumously in 1619 by *Roma antica*, a collection of 126 plates in three volumes, assembled by his friends. The fact that so many of the views are of otherwise neglected bits of antiquity and all are accompanied by extended explanatory captions makes them valuable. But their interpretation is often extremely problematical.

Systematic study of the topography of ancient Rome combining the results of excavation, both scientific and casual, with interpretation of the literary sources and the information to be gleaned from coins, inscriptions, and the Marble Plan begins in the late nineteenth century. Much had been accomplished before then, but Luigi Canina's maps of the ancient city published in 1849 and 1850 show admirably how little was known, how poorly the evidence of the Marble Plan was interpreted, and how extravagantly imagination ranged in the reconstruction of Roman grandeur. The movement toward a more rational approach was led by H. Jordan, C. Hülsen, R. Lanciani, and G. Boni. Jordan deserves special credit; his *Topographie der Stadt Rom im Alterthum* (vol. 1, parts 1 and 2, and vol. 2, Berlin 1871–85) was exemplary for method, historical perspective, and comprehensiveness, but it did not get beyond a collection of special studies. It was then taken up and completed by Hülsen (vol. 1, part 3, Berlin 1906) in a splendid survey of the city, area by area, whose composition shows the knowledge of a great scholar who devoted his life to this study. Hülsen was secretary of the Deutsches Archäologisches Institut in Rome from 1887 to 1909. Unfortunately, his knowledge of other disciplines was greater than his knowledge of architecture, and he is often a victim of the notions of the architects he employed, who were trained in the Beaux Arts tradition. Still, his advances in the study of topography were very great, and his works must still be consulted and studied. They are cited with great frequency in this dictionary. His counterpart and rival was Rodolfo Lanciani (1847?-1923), who was trained as an engineer but by the age of twenty was working as archaeologist for Prince Torlonia at Portus. In 1872 Lanciani became secretary of the Commissione Archeologica Comunale. His commentary on Frontinus, *Topografia di Roma antica, i commentarii di Frontino intorno le acque e gli acquedotti, silloge epigrafica acquaria,* originally published in the *Memorie della reale Accademia dei Lincei,* ser. 3.4, Classe di Scienze Morali (1881), was the first great work of a brilliant career that embraced topographical studies of every sort and size. In 1882 he was appointed to the chair of Roman topography at the University of Rome. He was a superb topographer and a gifted and prolific writer, although his career as a writer was curtailed by illness after 1912. Everything he wrote can be read with profit, but two works stand out in importance above the rest, his *Forma Urbis Romae,* a magnificent map of the city at a scale of 1:1000 and in great detail, with the known remains of the ancient city overlaid on the network of modern streets and buildings. The first sheet of this map was issued in 1893, and the forty-sixth and final one in 1901. It is a marvelous example of cartography, as well as an encyclopedia of topographical information, and is still an essential tool for anyone working on the ancient city. It has recently been reissued. In conjunction with this Lanciani wrote his *Storia degli scavi di Roma e notizie intorno le collezioni romane di antichità,* a collection of all the information available about excavations and discoveries in the city between A.D. 1000 and the death of Pope Clement VIII in 1605, issued in four volumes (Rome 1902–12). It was from this archive that much of the *Forma Urbis* was compiled, and it is regrettable that the collection stops in 1605, but the Herculean effort that would be required to continue it has so far been lacking. The final member of this great quartet, Giacomo Boni (1853–1925), was director of the excavations of the Forum Romanum and Palatine from 1890 to

1922 and carried out the deep explorations that brought to light the stratigraphy of the Comitium, the Sepulcretum with its early graves, the Lacus Iuturnae, and the archaic cisterns, or silos, of the Palatine, as well as the buildings buried under Domitian's Domus Augustiana. He was passionately interested in the early history of Rome and the historicity of the kings, and also in the full archaeological record of occupation and construction in the heart of the city. He was a meticulous excavator and admirably precise in recording in detail exactly what was found, and we are deeply in his debt. But he believed fervently in a Romulus we no longer accept as valid, and this colored his interpretation of his discoveries; much of his work consequently has been repeated and reinterpreted.

The following generation of scholars, many of them pupils of Lanciani, pursued by and large more specialized studies in their major publications. Thomas Ashby and Esther Van Deman exhaustively analyzed the courses and history of the aqueducts; Ian Richmond worked on a definitive publication of the Aurelian Walls and Gösta Säflund on the so-called Servian Walls; Giuseppe Lugli, who inherited Lanciani's chair at the University of Rome, took the history of Roman construction as his special province; and Herbert Bloch shaped the study of brickstamps into a fine tool. But Ashby also completed Samuel Ball Platner's *A Topographical Dictionary of Ancient Rome* (Oxford 1929) after Platner's death, which immediately became a standard reference work; Antonio Maria Colini's learned papers covered several large areas of the city, notably a long study of the remains on the Caelian; and Lugli produced a succession of works covering the general topography of Rome and bringing the coverage abreast of later developments. These begin with *I monumenti antichi di Roma e suburbio* (vol. 1, *La zona archeologica,* Rome 1930) and extend to his posthumous *Itinerario di Roma antica* (Rome 1975). Of particular interest is the map of ancient Rome in four sheets that he produced in collaboration with Italo Gismondi (Novara 1949). Despite the drawbacks of its relatively small scale (1:4000), which makes much of the representation schematic or simplified, it continues to be useful.

Lugli's successor at the University of Rome was his pupil Ferdinando Castagnoli, who devoted his early researches especially to ancient surveying and centuriation of land and town planning. Another pupil, Lucos Cozza, has made the fortifications a special field. And today there are a host of scholars of many nationalities who represent a wide range of training and a variety of points of view at work on the problems of Roman topography, some excavating, others reexcavating and restudying Boni's trenches, still others working largely at their desks. It is not possible to mention even a small number of selected names; they must be left to the bibliography for the individual entries in this dictionary. However, no one since Lugli has attempted a general survey of the state of our knowledge today. Castagnoli's surveys, *Topografia e urbanistica di Roma* (Bologna 1958) and *Topografia di Roma antica* (*Enciclopedia classica,* sez. 3.10, Turin 1957; 2d rev. ed., Turin 1980), are too concerned with the general outlines of the discipline, major complexes, and historical development of the city to give detailed attention to the individual monuments. At his death in 1988 he left an incomplete manuscript of a revision of Platner and Ashby's dictionary on which he had worked occasionally for many years. It is as a replacement for that dictionary that the present work is offered.

Bibliographical Notes
and Abbreviations

The bibliography on almost any monument of antiquity or topographical problem in Rome is enormous, and in recent years it has grown and continues to grow much more rapidly than was the case even a generation ago. It is impossible to compile anything like a complete bibliography for the topography of Rome, and even an extended bibliography of significant work on the major monuments would swell this dictionary to twice its size and materially reduce its usefulness.

Fortunately there are already good bibliographies available that make long lists of citations unnecessary and undesirable. S. B. Platner and Thomas Ashby's *A Topographical Dictionary of Ancient Rome* (London 1929) covers most of the significant work up to the time of its publication. Giuseppe Lugli et al., *Fontes ad Topographiam Veteris Urbis Romae Pertinentes,* 7 vols. (Rome 1952–69) is admirably complete for the ancient sources for most of the city. Ernest Nash, *Pictorial Dictionary of Ancient Rome²*, 2 vols. (London 1968), includes very extensive and accurate bibliography for every entry there, which means, in effect, for everything in topography that could be informatively illustrated. Ferdinando Castagnoli, *Topografia di Roma antica* (Turin 1980) is essentially a manual of bibliography, systematically arranged, somewhat selective but very full. And in recent years the Istituto di Topografia Antica of the University of Rome has undertaken to produce complete annotated bibliographies for the ancient city compiled by highly competent scholars working in the field. The first of these covers the years 1946–1961 and appears in the *Bullettino comunale (Bullettino della Commissione Archeologica del Comune di Roma)* 83 (1972–73):5–156. It was compiled by F. Castagnoli, A. M. Colini, C. Buzzetti, and G. Pisani Sartorio. The second covers the period 1961–1980 and appears in the *Bullettino comunale* 89 (1984): 305–76. The third covers the years 1981–1984 and appears in the *Bullettino comunale* 91 (1986): 141–232. For years thereafter it is proposed to issue an annual or biennial bibliography in the *Bullettino:* the first, for 1985–1986, appears in volume 92 (1987–88): 189–238.

Because every serious student of Roman topography must consult the *Bullettino comunale* regularly, almost daily, and these bibliographies are exemplary, it seems otiose to try to excerpt or repeat any part of them here; it would only encumber an already large volume. I have therefore confined the citations of modern work to those I thought particularly significant or interesting, those that presented a radically different view from that commonly accepted or that offered here, and those that are regarded as the standard treatments of various subjects and questions. For the sake of the reader's convenience, I have tried to err in giving more than seemed necessary, rather than less, but of that the reader must be the judge.

The abbreviations used in this dictionary are a combination of those recommended in the "Notes for Contributors and Abbreviations" of the *American Journal of Archaeology* and those used in the *Oxford Classical Dictionary²* (Oxford 1970), ix–xxii. However, the name of an ancient author is not abbreviated unless it is composed of more than one element, and the abbreviations of titles of ancient works have been kept to what it is hoped will leave them readily recognizable. What follows is a list of abbreviations used frequently in the dictionary. If an abbreviation is not found here, it may be assumed that it is regarded as standard and can be found by reference to the works cited above.

AA	*Archäologischer Anzeiger.*
ActaArch	*Acta archaeologica.* Copenhagen.
Act. Fr. Arv.	Henzen, W. *Acta Fratrum Arvalium Quae Supersunt.* Berlin 1874. Reprint. Berlin 1967.
AdI	*Annali dell'Istituto di Corrispondenza Archeologica.*
AE	*L'Année epigraphique.*
AJA	*American Journal of Archaeology.*
AJAH	*American Journal of Ancient History.*
Amici	Amici, C. M. *Foro di Traiano: Basilica Ulpia e biblioteche.* Rome 1982.
AnalBoll	*Analecta Bollandiana.*
AnalRom	*Analecta romana Instituti Danici.*
Anderson	Anderson, J. C., Jr. *The Historical Topography of the Imperial Fora* (Collection Latomus 182). Brussels 1984.
Anon. Magliabech.	Anonymous Magliabechianus. *Tractatus de Rebus Antiquis et Situ Urbis Romae* (VZ 4.101–50).
ANRW	Temporini, H., and W. Haase, eds. *Aufstieg und Niedergang der römischen Welt.* Berlin 1972–.
ArchCl	*Archeologia classica.*
ArchN	*Archaeological News.*
Armellini	Armellini, M. *Le chiese di Roma dal secolo IV al XIX².* Rome 1891.
ArtB	*Art Bulletin.*
Ashby 1927	Ashby, T. *The Roman Campagna in Classical Times.* London 1927. Reprint. London 1970.
Ashby 1935	Ashby, T. *The Aqueducts of Ancient Rome.* Oxford 1935.
BABesch	*Bulletin Antieke Beschaving: Annual Papers on Classical Archaeology.*
Banti	Banti, A. *I grandi bronzi imperiali.* 4 vols. Florence 1983–87.
BAR	*British Archaeological Reports: Supplementary Series, International Series.* Oxford 1975–.
BCSSA	*Bollettino del Centro di Studi per la Storia dell'Architettura.*
BdA	*Bollettino d'Arte.*
Blake 1947	Blake, M. E. *Roman Construction in Italy from the Prehistoric Period to Augustus.* Washington, D.C., 1947.
Blake 1959	Blake, M. E. *Roman Construction in Italy from Tiberius through the Flavians.* Washington, D.C. 1959.
Bloch	Bloch, H. *I bolli laterizi e la storia edilizia romana.* Rome 1938 (reprinted from *BullCom* 64 [1936]: 141–225, 65 [1937]: 83–187, 66 [1938]: 61–221).
B. M. Coins, Rom. Emp.	*British Museum Catalogue of Coins of the Roman Empire.*
B. M. Coins, Rom. Rep.	*British Museum Catalogue of Coins of the Roman Republic.*
Boatwright	Boatwright, M. T. *Hadrian and the City of Rome.* Princeton, N.J. 1987.
Boethius and Ward-Perkins	Boethius, A., and J. B. Ward-Perkins. *Etruscan and Roman Architecture.* Pelican History of Art. Harmondsworth 1970.

Broughton, *MRR*	Broughton, T. R S. *The Magistrates of the Roman Republic.* 3 vols. New York 1951–60.
Bufalini	Bufalini, L. *Roma* (plan of the city of 1551, in Frutaz, vol. 2 pls. 190–221).
BullArchCr	*Bullettino di archeologia cristiana.*
BullCom	*Bullettino della Commissione Archeologica del Comune di Roma.*
BWPr	*Winckelmannsprogramm der Archäologischen Gesellschaft zu Berlin.*
CAR	*Carta archeologica di Roma.* Florence 1962–.
CEFR 98 (1987)	*L'Urbs, espace urbain et histoire (Ier siècle av. J.C.—IIIe siècle ap. J.C.). Collection de l École Française de Rome 98.* Rome and Paris 1987.
CGL	*Corpus Glossariorum Latinorum* (= Lindsay, W. M. *Glossaria Latina.* Paris 1930).
Choisy	Choisy, A. *L'Art de bâtir chez les romains.* Paris 1873.
Chron.	*Chronographus anni 354* (in *MGH* 9.143–48).
Chron. Min.	*Chronica Minora* (in *MGH*).
CIL	*Corpus Inscriptionum Latinarum.*
Coarelli 1974	Coarelli, F. *Guida archeologica di Roma.* Verona 1974.
Coarelli 1983	Coarelli, F. *Il foro romano: Periodo arcaico.* Rome 1983.
Coarelli 1985	Coarelli, F. *Il foro romano: Periodo repubblicano e augusteo.* Rome 1985.
Coarelli 1988	Coarelli, F. *Il foro boario dalle origini alla fine della repubblica.* Rome 1988.
Cohen	Cohen, H. *Monnaies frappées sous l'empire.* 2d ed. 8 vols. Paris 1880–92.
Crema	Crema, L. *L'architettura romana* (Enciclopedia classica, sezione 3.12.1). Turin 1959.
Cur.	*Curiosum* (in Jordan 2.539–574, VZ 1.89–164).
DE	de Ruggiero, E. *Dizionario epigrafico di antichità romana.* Rome 1886–.
Degrassi	Degrassi, A. *Fasti Anni Numani et Iuliani (Inscriptiones Italiae 13.2).* Rome 1963.
Delbrück, *Hell. Bauten*	Delbrück, R. *Hellenistische Bauten in Latium.* 2 vols. Strassburg 1907–12. Reprint. Perugia 1979.
DialArch	*Dialoghi di archeologia.*
Dig.	Digesta (in *Corpus Iuris Civilis* 1).
DissPontAcc	*Dissertazioni della Pontificia Accademia Romana di Archeologia.*
D'Onofrio 1965	D'Onofrio, C. *Gli obelischi di Roma.* Rome 1965.
D'Onofrio 1972	D'Onofrio, C. *Castel S. Angelo.* Rome 1972.
Du Pérac	Du Pérac, E. *Vestigi dell'antichità di Roma.* Rome 1575.
EAA	Bianchi Bandinelli, R., and G. Pugliese Caratelli, eds. *Enciclopedia dell' arte antica.* Rome 1958–.
EE	*Ephemeris epigraphica.*
Epigraphica	*Epigraphica: Rivista italiana di epigrafia.*
FA	*Fasti archaeologici.*
Fast. Allif.	Fasti Allifani (in Degrassi, 177–84).

Fast. Amit.	Fasti Amiternini (in Degrassi, 185–200).
Fast. Ant. Mai.	Fasti Antiates Maiores (in Degrassi, 1–28).
Fast. Esquil.	Fasti Esquilini (in Degrassi, 85–89).
Fast. Maff.	Fasti Maffeiani (in Degrassi, 70–84).
Fast. Praen.	Fasti Praenestini (in Degrassi, 107–45).
Fast. Vall.	Fasti Vallenses (in Degrassi, 146–52).
Fast. Venus.	Fasti Venusini (in Degrassi, 55–62).
FGrH	Jacoby, F. *Fragmente der griechischen Historiker.* Berlin 1923–.
Forcellini	Forcellini, E. *Totius Latinitatis Lexicon.* Rev. ed., ed. F. Corradini and G. Perrin. 6 vols. Padua 1940.
Frank	Frank, T. *Roman Buildings of the Republic.* Rome 1924.
Frutaz	Frutaz, A. P. *Le piante di Roma.* 3 vols. Rome 1962.
FUR	Carettoni, G., A. M. Colini, L. Cozza, and G. Gatti. *La pianta marmorea di Roma antica (Forma Urbis Romae).* 2 vols. (text and plates). Rome 1960.
Gazzola	Gazzola, P. *Ponti romani.* 2 vols. Florence 1963.
Gnecchi	Gnecchi, F. *I medaglioni romani.* 3 vols. Milan 1912.
GV	Giuliani, C. F., and P. Verduchi. *L'area centrale del foro romano.* Florence 1987.
HCh	Hülsen, C. *Le chiese di Roma nel medio evo.* Florence 1927. Reprint. Hildesheim and New York 1975.
Heemskerck	Hülsen, C., and H. Egger. *Die römischen Skizzenbücher von Marten van Heemskerck.* 2 vols. Berlin 1913–16. Reprint. Soest, Holland 1975.
Helbig[4]	Helbig, W. *Führer durch die öffentlichen Sammlungen klassischer Altertümer in Rom.* 4th ed., ed. H. Speier. 4 vols. Tübingen 1963–72.
Henzen	Henzen, W. *Acta Fratrum Arvalium Quae Supersunt.* Berlin 1874. Reprint. Berlin 1967.
HJ	Hülsen, C., in H. Jordan. *Topographie der Stadt Rom im Alterthum.* Vol. 1.3. Berlin 1907. Reprint. Rome 1970.
Holland	Holland, L. A. *Janus and the Bridge.* Rome 1961.
Humphrey	Humphrey, J. H. *Roman Circuses: Arenas for Chariot Racing.* London 1986.
IGUR	Moretti, L. *Inscriptiones Graecae Urbis Romae.* 4 vols. Rome 1968–90.
ILLRP	Degrassi, A. *Inscriptiones Latinae Liberae Rei Publicae.* 2 vols. Florence 1957, 1963.
ILS	Dessau, H. *Inscriptiones Latinae Selectae.* 3 vols. in 5. Berlin 1892–1916. Reprint. Berlin 1962.
Iversen	Iversen, E. *Obelisks in Exile.* Vol. 1, *The Obelisks of Rome.* Copenhagen 1968.
Jordan	Jordan H. *Topographie der Stadt Rom im Alterthum.* 2 vols. in 4. Berlin 1871–1907. Reprint. Rome 1970.
JRA	*Journal of Roman Archaeology.*
JRS	*Journal of Roman Studies.*
JSAH	*Journal of the Society of Architectural Historians.*
Keil, *Gramm. Lat.*	Keil, H. *Grammatici Latini.* 8 vols. Leipzig 1855–1923.

LA   Lanciani, R. *Le acque e gli acquedotti di Roma antica (I commentarii di Frontino intorno le acque e gli acquedotti). MemLinc* 3.4 (1881): 213–616. Reprint. Rome 1975.

La grande Roma dei Tarquini   Cristofani, M. ed. *La grande Roma dei Tarquini.* Show catalogue, Rome 1990.

La Rocca 1984   La Rocca, E. *La riva a mezzaluna.* Rome 1984.

LFUR   Lanciani, R. *Forma Urbis Romae.* Milan 1893–1901.

L'Orange and von Gerkan   L'Orange, H. P., and A. von Gerkan. *Der spätantike Bildschmuck des Konstantinsbogens.* Berlin 1939.

LPD   Duchesne, L. *Liber Pontificalis.* 2 vols. Paris 1886–92.

LRE   Lanciani, R. *The Ruins and Excavations of Ancient Rome.* London 1897.

LS   Lanciani, R. *Storia degli scavi di Roma e notizie intorno le collezioni romane di antichità.* 4 vols. Rome 1902–12.

Lugli 1930   Lugli, G. *I monumenti antichi di Roma e suburbio.* Vol. 1, *La zona archeologica.* Rome 1930.

Lugli 1934   Lugli, G. *I monumenti antichi di Roma e suburbio.* Vol. 2, *Le grandi opere pubbliche.* Rome 1934.

Lugli 1938   Lugli, G. *I monumenti antichi di Roma e suburbio.* Vol. 3, *A traverso le regioni.* Rome 1938.

Lugli 1946   Lugli, G. *Roma antica: Il centro monumentale.* Rome 1946.

Lugli 1947   Lugli, G. *Monumenti minori del foro romano.* Rome 1947.

Lugli 1957   Lugli, G. *La tecnica edilizia romana.* 2 vols. Rome 1957. Reprint. London and New York 1968.

Lugli 1975   Lugli, G. *Itinerario di Roma antica.* Rome 1975.

Lugli and Gismondi   Lugli, G., and I. Gismondi. *Forma Urbis Romae Imperatorum Aetate.* Novara 1949.

MAAR   *Memoirs of the American Academy in Rome.*

MacDonald   MacDonald, W. L. *The Architecture of the Roman Empire.* Vol. 1, *An Introductory Study.* New Haven, Conn., and London 1965.

Malaise   Malaise, M. *Inventaire préliminaire des documents égyptiens découverts en Italie.* Leiden 1972.

Marchetti-Longhi   Marchetti-Longhi, G. *L'area sacra del Largo Argentina.* Rome 1960.

Mazzini   Mazzini, G. *Monete imperiali romane.* 5 vols. Milan 1957–58.

MEFRA   *Mélanges de l'École Française à Rome: Antiquité.*

MemLinc   *Memorie: Atti della Accademia Nazionale dei Lincei, Classe di scienze morali, storiche e filologiche.*

MemNap   *Memorie dell'Accademia di Archeologia, Lettere e Belle Arti di Napoli.*

MemPontAcc   *Memorie: Atti della Pontificia Accademia Romana di Archeologia.*

MGH   *Monumenta Germaniae Historica.* 15 vols. Berlin 1877–1919. Reprint. 1961.

Middleton   Middleton, J. *Ancient Rome in 1885.* Edinburgh 1885.

Migne, *PL*   Migne, J. P. *Patrologiae Cursus Completus: Series Latina.*

MonAnt   *Monumenti antichi pubblicati per cura della Accademia Nazionale dei Lincei.*

MonPiot	*Monuments Piot.*
NAkG	*Nachrichten von der Akademie der Wissenschaften in Göttingen.*
Narducci	Narducci, P. *Sulla fognatura della città di Roma.* Rome 1889.
Nash	Nash, E. *Pictorial Dictionary of Ancient Rome.* 2d ed. 2 vols. London 1968.
Neuerburg	Neuerburg, N. *L'architettura delle fontane e dei ninfei nell'Italia antica.* Naples 1965.
Nolli	Nolli, G. B. *Nuova pianta di Roma.* Rome 1748. Reprint. Rome 1932, New York 1984 (also in Frutaz, vol. 3 pls. 396–419).
Not.	*Notitia* (Jordan 2.537–74, VZ 1.164–92).
NSc	*Notizie degli scavi di antichità.*
Obsequens	Julius Obsequens. *Ab Anno Urbis Conditae DV Prodigiorum Liber.* (Included by O. Rossbach in his edition of the Epitomes of Livy, 1910.)
OpRom	*Opuscula Romana.*
Overbeck-Mau	Overbeck, J., and A. Mau. *Pompeji in seinen Gebäuden, Alterthümern und Kunstwerken.* Leipzig 1884.
PA	Platner, S. B., and T. Ashby. *A Topographical Dictionary of Ancient Rome.* London 1929. Reprint. London 1950, Rome 1965.
Pace	Pace, P. *Gli acquedotti di Roma e il De Aquaeductu di Frontino.* Rome 1983.
PAPS	*Proceedings of the American Philosophical Society.*
PBSR	*Papers of the British School at Rome.*
PECS	Stillwell, R., W. L. MacDonald, and M. H. McAllister, eds. *The Princeton Encyclopedia of Classical Sites.* Princeton, N. J. 1976.
PIR[1]	Klebs, E., and H. Dessau, eds. *Prosopographia Imperii Romani Saeculi I, II, III.* Berlin 1897–98.
PIR[2]	Groag, E. and A. Stein, eds. *Prosopographia Imperii Romani Saeculi I, II, III.* 2d ed. Berlin 1933–.
PLRE	*The Prosopography of the Later Roman Empire.* Vol. 1 (*A.D. 260–395*) by A. H. M. Jones, J. R. Martindale, and J. Morris. Cambridge 1971. Vol. 2 (*A.D. 395–527*) by J. R. Martindale. Cambridge 1980.
PP	*La parola del passato.*
PW	Pauly, A., G. Wissowa, and W. Kroll, eds. *Real-Encyclopädie der classischen Altertumswissenschaft.*
QArchEtr	*Quaderni del Centro di Studio per l'Archeologia Etrusco-italica.*
QITA	*Quaderni dell'Istituto di Topografia Antica della Università di Roma.*
RA	*Revue archéologique.*
RendAccNap	*Rendiconti dell'Accademia di Archeologia, Lettere e Belle Arti di Napoli.*
RendLinc	*Atti dell'Accademia Nazionale dei Lincei: Rendiconti.*
RendPontAcc	*Atti della Pontificia Accademia Romana di Archeologia: Rendiconti.*
RFIC	*Rivista di filologia e d'istruzione classica.*
RIC	Mattingly, H., E. A. Sydenham, and R. A. G. Carson. *The Roman Imperial Coinage.* 6 vols. London 1923–51. Rev. ed. by C. H. V. Sutherland and R. A. G. Carson. London 1984–.

Richmond	Richmond, I. A. *The City Wall of Imperial Rome*. Oxford 1930.
Riese, *Geog. Lat. Min.*	Riese, A. *Geographi Latini Minores*. Heilbronn 1878. Reprint. Hildesheim 1964.
RivFil	*Rivista di filologia e d'istruzione classica*.
RivIstArch	*Rivista dell'Istituto Nazionale d'Archeologia e Storia dell'Arte*.
RivStorAnt	*Rivista storica dell'antichità*.
Rodriguez	Rodriguez Almeida, E. *Forma urbis marmorea: Aggiornamento generale 1980*. 2 vols. (text and plates). Rome 1981.
RömMitt	*Mitteilungen des Deutschen Archäologischen Instituts, Römische Abteilung*.
Roma, archeologia nel centro (1985)	Bietti Sestieri, A. M., A. Capodiferro, G. Morganti, C. Pavolini, M. Piranomonte, and P. Scoppola, eds. *Roma, archeologia nel centro*. 2 vols. Rome 1985.
Roma medio repubblicana	Assessorato Antichità, Belle Arti e Problemi della Cultura. *Roma medio repubblicana. Aspetti culturali di Roma e del Lazio nei secoli IV e III a.C.* Show catalogue. Rome 1973.
Roma sotterranea	Luciani, R., ed. *Roma sotterranea*. Show catalogue. Rome 1984.
Roscher	Roscher, W. H., ed. *Ausführliches Lexikon der griechischen und römischen Mythologie*. 7 vols. in 10. Leipzig 1884–1937. Reprint. 1978.
Rostovtzeff, *Sylloge*	Rostovtzeff, M. I. *Tesserarum Urbis Romae et Suburbi Plumbearum Sylloge*. Saint Petersburg 1903–5.
Roullet	Roullet, A. *The Egyptian and Egyptianizing Monuments of Imperial Rome*. Leiden 1972.
Ruggiero, *Diz.*	de Ruggiero, E. *Dizionario epigrafico di antichità romane*. Rome 1886–.
Ryberg, *Archaeological Record*	Ryberg, I. S. *An Archaeological Record of Rome from the Seventh to the Second Century B.C.* Philadelphia and London 1940.
Ryberg, *Panel Reliefs*	Ryberg, I. S. *Panel Reliefs of Marcus Aurelius*. New York 1967.
Säflund	Säflund, G. *Le mura di Roma repubblicane*. Uppsala 1932.
SBHeid	*Sitzungsberichte der Heidelberger Akademie der Wissenschaften Philosophisch-historische Klasse*.
Scullard	Scullard, H. H. *Festivals and Ceremonies of the Roman Republic*. London 1981.
S.H.A.	Scriptores Historiae Augustae.
Stangl	Stangl, T. *Ciceronis Orationum Scholiastae*. Vienna 1912. Reprint. Hildesheim 1964.
StRom	*Studi romani*.
StudMisc	*Studi miscellanei: Seminario di Archeologia e Storia dell' Arte Greca e Romana dell'Università di Roma*.
TAPA	*Transactions of the American Philological Association*.
TAPS	*Transactions of the American Philosophical Society*.
Töbelmann, *Römische Gebälke*	Töbelmann, E. *Römische Gebälke*. Vol. 1 (with text by E. Fiechter and C. Hülsen). Heidelberg 1923.
Tomassetti	Tomassetti, G., and F. Tomassetti. *La campagna romana antica, medioevale e moderna*. 4 vols. Rome 1910–26. Reprint. Bologna 1976.
Urlichs	Urlichs, C. L. *Codex Urbis Romae Topographicus*. Würzburg 1871.

Van Deman — Van Deman, E. B. *The Building of the Roman Aqueducts*. Washington, D.C. 1934.

Vermaseren, *Corpus* — Vermaseren, M. J. *Corpus Inscriptionum et Monumentorum Religionis Mithriacae*. 2 vols. The Hague 1956, 1960.

VZ — Valentini, R., and G. Zucchetti, *Codice topografico della città di Roma*. 4 vols. Rome 1940–53.

Walde-Hofmann — Walde, A., and J. B. Hofmann, *Lateinisches etymologisches Wörterbuch*. 3 vols. 4th ed. Heidelberg 1965.

Wissowa, *RK* — Wissowa, G. *Religion und Kultus der Römer*. Munich 1912. Reprint. 1971.

Wurm — Wurm, H. *Baldassare Peruzzi: Architekturzeichnungen*. 2 vols. (text and plates). Tübingen 1984.

Zorzi — Zorzi, G. *I disegni delle antichità di Andrea Palladio*. Venice 1958.

ZPE — *Zeitschrift für Papyrologie und Epigraphik*.

A New Topographical Dictionary
of Ancient Rome

Acca Larentia, Ara: see **Sepulcrum Accae Larentiae.**

Ad Spem Veterem: see **Spes Vetus.**

Adonaea (Figs. 1, 2): the reconstructed name for a complex shown on a large fragment of the Marble Plan that was copied in the Codex Orsinianus before being broken up (*FUR* pl. 8) and has now been re-composed without substantial loss from four fragments (*FUR* pl. 34; Rodriguez pl. 35). This shows that the inscription reads only ADON, so the reconstruction of the name is far from certain, and it is not clear why the copyist has shown the inscription as DONAEA and relocated it. The complex itself is difficult to read, the main block consisting of a long, narrow central (?) rectangle surrounded by a single series of small units with a curvilinear side toward the rectangle and a straight back. These in turn are succeeded by parallel rows of straight lines with serifed ends, two banks of four each divided by a central aisle on either side of the rectangle. Around the square made by these run three rows of dots, closely spaced, evidently equidistant from one another in both directions. These are not apt to have been either columns or trees; perhaps, as Lloyd suggests, they are a double-aisled arbor. Beyond a wider interval comes a fourth line of dots, similarly spaced, which does seem apt to be columns, for along most of one side it is backed by a wall that would read well with the "columns" as a portico facing inward, while on the two adjacent sides the wall is continued by lines of dots that would make colonnaded approaches. If the reconstruction of the inscription is correct, there was originally an extensive addition to the right (west or south) and probably also left of what is preserved, of the character of which we are almost entirely ignorant. Because the central block represented would have covered an area of approximately 9, 200

m² and there seems to have been ample open space in the direction of the inscription (north or west), the location of this complex in Rome is especially puzzling. It can hardly be fitted anywhere within the Aurelian Walls, and the likeliest location may be toward the southeast corner of the plan, beyond the Aventine in the neighborhood of the Via Ostiensis.

The interpretation of this complex as a garden dedicated to Adonis—the files of dots representing a vine-covered arbor, the rectangle in the middle a euripus—is attractive, but we know far too little about the conventions used on the plan and too little about the design of ancient gardens to be able to interpret it convincingly. The banks of parallel lines are especially puzzling.

The suggestion that the complex at the east corner of the Palatine around the church of S. Sebastiano, commonly known as the Vigna Barberini, might be the Adonaea, or whatever else is represented on this fragment of the Marble Plan, cannot be ruled out until the area has been completely explored in excavation. The distortions produced in the composition of the plan in this neighborhood make for great uncertainty about it.

AJA 86 (1982): 95–100 (R. B. Lloyd); *MEFRA* 97 (1985): 531–32 (M. Royo), 98 (1986): 217–53 (J.-C. Grenier and F. Coarelli) 387–97 (P. Gros, M. Lenoir, et al.), 99 (1987): 481–98 (M. Lenoir et al.); *Athenaeum* 65 (1987): 244–48 (C. J. Simpson).

Adonidis Aula: a hall in the Palatine palace, presumably the Domus Augustiana, where Domitian sacrificed to Minerva and received Apollonius of Tyana (Philostratus, *VA* 7.32), but otherwise unknown.

Aedes, Aedicula, Templum, Delubrum, Fanum, Sacellum, Sacrarium, Curia, Lucus: An *aedes* is properly the place where a god resides, a temple

A

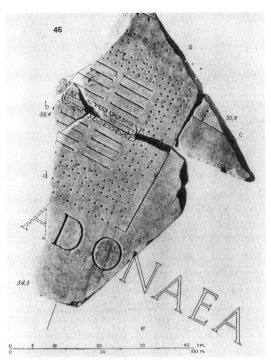

Figure 1
Adonaea,
Representation on
the Marble Plan

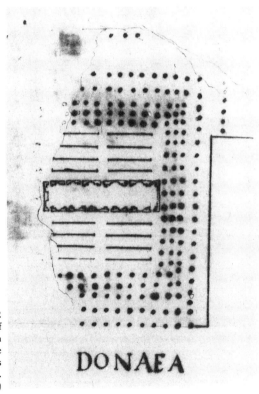

Figure 2
Adonaea, Drawing of
Its Representation on
the Marble Plan in the
Codex Orsinianus
(Cod. Vat. Lat.
3439—Fo 18r)

building, while an *aedicula* is the diminutive of this and often a smaller shrine within an aedes. A *templum* is a space defined by ritual *augurii aut auspicii causa* (Varro, *Ling.* 7.8). Most aedes were, in fact, so constituted, or stood in a precinct so constituted, but occasionally one was not. This was the case with the Temple of Vesta. And many templa did not contain an aedes; the *rostra* and *curia senatus* were always templa, but would not be considered aedes. A *delubrum* was an *area adsumpta deum causa, praeter aedem* (Varro *ap. Macrob. Sat.* 3.4.2) or an *area cum porticibus* (Probus, Keil, *Gramm. Lat.* 4.202), the temenos or templum in which an aedes stands, the altar court, but tending to be rather grand. A *fanum* was any sacred area; fanum was an inclusive term and embraced sacred groves, as well as temples (Livy 10.37.15). It is a term not much used in Rome and used especially of the cult centers of Oriental divinities and pilgrimage shrines, but it seems to have been the proper designation of Hercules Victor at Tibur. A *sacellum* is defined by Festus (422L): *sacella dicuntur loca dis sacrata sine tecto* and Trebatius (*ap. A. Gell.* 7.12.2): *sacellum est locus parvus deo sacratus cum ara;* that seems to need no further definition. A *sacrarium* is defined by Ulpian (*Dig.* 1.8.9): *sacrarium est locus in quo sacra reponuntur, quod etiam in aedificio privato esse potest;* however, in the very ancient sacrarium of Ops in the Regia there were sacrifices offered. A *curia* is defined by Varro (*Ling.* 5.155) as a place *ubi curarent sacerdotes res divinas, ut curiae veteres.* This must have been an established templum, as the refusal of seven of the curiae to allow exauguration shows. It must have contained an altar, for sacrifice was performed there for the Fordicidia, and the Curiae Veteres got to be too small to accommodate them all. However, the Curia Saliorum, the headquarters of the Salii on the Palatine, was a building containing a sacrarium in which the lituus of Romulus was kept. Presumably their records were also kept there, but whether the Salii performed any sacred rites on behalf of the people there is not known; it is presumed that they did not and that this curia was an anomaly. Finally, a *lucus* might be a grove adjoining a temple and part of its precinct, as the Lucus Iunonis Lucinae seems to have been, or a grove without a temple building but dedicated to a particular divinity, such as the Lucus Streniae. But it was especially an extraurban sanctuary, either in the near neighborhood, such as the Lucus Furrinae, or at a considerable distance, such as the Lucus Feroniae and the Grove of the Arval Brethren.

PBSR 52 (1984): 3–20 (F. Castagnoli).

Aedes Tensarum: a building on the Capitoline used to explain the location of military diplomata (*CIL*

16.4, 30), presumably the place where were kept the silver and ivory cars in which the *exuviae* (symbols) of the gods were borne to public games (cf. Festus 500–501L). It was also called the Tensarium and later, apparently after the removal of the car of Jupiter to the Circus Maximus (cf. Suetonius, *Vesp.* 5.6), Tensarium Vetus.

Aedicula: see **Aedes.**

Aedicula Capraria: a shrine listed in the regionary catalogues in Regio VII, Via Lata, probably on the Vicus Caprarius (q.v.), which would put it in the southern part of the *regio* and suggests that it was compital. Remains of it may have been a barrel-vaulted chamber discovered in 1924 at the juncture of Via delle Vergini and Via dell'Umiltà.

BullCom 53 (1925): 272–73 (E. Gatti).

Aemiliana: a district outside the pomerium (Varro, *Rust.* 3.2.6) in the southern Campus Martius. During a great fire in the Aemiliana, Claudius stationed himself in the Diribitorium (q.v.) to oversee and reward the fire fighters (Suetonius, *Claud.* 18.1). During the fire of Nero the fire, having been stopped on the sixth day at the foot of the Esquiline, broke out for a second time in the property of Tigillinus in the Aemiliana and burned in the level parts of the city with great loss of porticoes and temples (Tacitus, *Ann.* 15.40). The Aemiliana was probably the area along the Porticus Aemilia (q.v.) from the Porta Fontinalis on the shoulder of the Capitoline to the Altar of Mars, the latter probably just north of the north transept of the church of the Gesù. Others would put it along the Tiber, because of a puzzling inscription that mentioned a *navis arenaria* (*CIL* 15.7150), and derive its name from the Pons Aemilius, or properties owned by Aemilii (cf. Cicero, *Rep.* 1.9.14), but this seems very unlikely.

BullCom 85 (1976–77): 148–50 (R. E. A. Palmer, who believes that there were at least two Aemilianae in Rome); Rodriguez 115–18, 167; Coarelli 1988, 147–55.

Aeolia: a joking name for the baths of a certain Lupus, famous for their discomfort and drafts. Martial mentions them together with other buildings of which those that can be identified are in the southern Campus Martius.

Martial 2.14.12 (and cf. 1.59.3).

Aequimaelium: an open space on the slope of the Capitoline, probably adjacent to the Vicus Iugarius, believed to be the site of the house of Spurius Maelius, a rich grain dealer who aimed at monarchy. He was executed in 438 B.C., and his house was razed in perpetual memory of the heinousness of his crime. The story is told in most detail by Dionysius (Dion. Hal. 12.1.1–4.6) and in abbreviated form by many (Livy 4.16.1; Varro, *Ling.* 5.157; Cicero, *Dom.* 101; Val. Max. 6.3.1c). It was a landmark big enough to be mentioned in bounding a fire (Livy 24.47.15), a place to which Cicero would send to buy a lamb for sacrifice (*Div.* 2.39). The land immediately above it had to be terraced at public expense in 189 B.C. (Livy 38.28.3), presumably in consequence of the land slip of 192 B.C. that brought a mass of rock from the Capitoline down on the Vicus Iugarius with great loss of life (Livy 35.21.6). This puts it in the general neighborhood of the church of S. Maria della Consolazione, but one cannot be more precise. Between the Forum Romanum and the Forum Boarium, it would be a natural place for purveyors of sacrificial animals to congregate and may have been designed to accommodate them.

Aerarium Saturni: see **Saturnus, Aedes.**

Aesculapius, Aedes (Fig. 37.26): the single temple of Aesculapius known for Rome. In consequence of a plague in 293 B.C., the Sibylline Books were consulted, and the following year an embassy was sent to Epidaurus to bring the worship of the god Aesculapius to Rome. During the embassy's visit to the sanctuary a sacred serpent of great size is said to have made its way to the Roman ship and coiled up in the quarters of the leader of the embassy, Q. Ogulnius. On the arrival of the ship at Rome, the serpent abandoned the ship and swam to the Tiber island. Taking this as an omen, the Romans built the Temple of Aesculapius there and dedicated it on 1 January, the same day as the dedication of the later Temple of Vediovis on the island (Ovid, *Fast.* 1.289–94; Degrassi 388). The plague then abruptly stopped. Many sources tell the story of the serpent; it is recounted in greatest detail by Val. Max. 1.8.2 (see also Livy 10.47.6–7 and *Epit.* 11; Ovid, *Met.* 15.736–44; Pliny, *HN* 29.16 and 72; Plutarch, *Quaest. Rom.* 94; [Aur. Vict.], *De Vir. Ill.* 22).

Embellishments and restorations of the temple are poorly documented. Livy (43.4.7) records the dedication by C. Lucretius Gallus of pictures from the spoils of his conquests in Boeotia in a temple of Aesculapius in 170 B.C., but probably this was the temple of Aesculapius at Antium. Varro (*Ling.* 7.57) speaks of *equites ferentarii,* light-armed cavalry, depicted in "the old temple of Aesculapius" (*in Aesculapii aede vetere*), as though the temple had been rebuilt within memory and the painting was destroyed. Presumably it depicted some great Roman battle and was a victory dedication. Varro's phrase has led to the supposition that the temple was rebuilt about the middle of the first century B.C. Suetonius (*Aug.* 59) mentions a statue of the great Augustan physician Antonius Musa set up beside that of Aesculapius. A number of inscriptions, especially dedications to Aesculapius by grateful suppliants, are known (*CIL* 6.7–20, 30842–46; *ILS* 2092, 2101, 2194, 3833–37, 3851), but few seem to have been found in the vicinity of the church of S. Bartolomeo, which is believed to stand on the site occupied by the temple. The southeastern point of the island is revetted with travertine to imitate a ship's stern, and a staff wound with a serpent and a bust, presumably of Aesculapius, are carved in relief on the side near the stern (Nash 1.508–9). Otherwise there are no identifiable remains of the temple or its temenos. Votive material, including statuettes and parts of the human body, has been found in the Tiber in quantity; one deposit laid down deliberately near the head of the Pons Fabricius on the left bank is usually associated with the temple but might equally well, perhaps better, belong to the Temple of Apollo Medicus (see Apollo, Aedes).

RendLinc, ser. 8.26 (1971): 267–81 (M. Guarducci); P. Pensabene et al., "Terracotte votive dal Tevere" (*StMisc* 25 [Rome 1980]): passim, especially 17–20; *Athenaeum* 65 (1987): 521–27 (D. Degrassi).

Aesculetum: a grove of oaks. Pliny (*HN* 16.37) tells us that after a secession of the plebs to the Janiculum, ca. 287 B.C., because of the crushing weight of their debts and following a bitter struggle with their creditors, Q. Hortensius as dictator passed a law that *plebescita,* which earlier had not been binding on the patricians, should be binding on the whole people. This was done *in aesculeto,* and, because it was a Lex Hortensia, must have been passed in the comitia centuriata, normally assembled in the Campus Martius. The discovery of a monumental altar to the Lares dedicated by the *magistri vici Aesculeti* (*CIL* 6.30957) under Via Arenula just south of Via di S. Bartolomeo indicates the existence of this vicus nearby, probably toward the bank of the Tiber, where the Via delle Zoccolette may show its course. One side of the altar shows a Lar carrying a large branch of what is usually identified as laurel but might better be *aesculus* (cf. *BullCom* 17 [1889]: 69–72 and pl. 3). The Aesculetum might be presumed to have lain between this street and the river, but why Hortensius should have convened the comitia centuriata there remains mysterious.

CEFR 98 (1987): 62–73 (S. Panciera).

Ager, Campus, Prata: These three terms generally designate land beyond the Servian Walls. *Ager* is the territory of the city, exclusive of the city itself. In the inauguration ceremony for Numa Pompilius the augur took his station *prospectu in urbem agrumque capto* (Livy 1.18.7). *Ager Romanus* was distinguished from *ager peregrinus* but embraced all the natural features, such as rivers, lakes, and mountains. *Campus* was used for the territory near the city, just outside the walls; thus the Campus Martius and Campus Viminalis. How far it would have extended is hard to say, but probably not much more than a mile. There could also be campus inside the walls, as the campus sceleratus shows, but this was exceptional. *Prata* was a more particular term for flat land suitable for cultivation, though not necessarily under cultivation. It is rarely used for land in the near vicinity of Rome and used only of land beyond the pomerium.

Ager Albiona: see **Albionarum Lucus.**

Ager Apollinis Argentei: see **Apollo Argenteus.**

Ager L. Petilii: Land belonging to Petilius, a scriba, located *sub ianiculo,* where in 181 B.C. were found two stone chests, one said to be the sarcophagus of Numa Pompilius, the other to contain his writings (Livy 40.29.2–4; Val. Max. 1.1.12). Numa is said to have been buried across the Tiber on or under the *ianiculum* (q.v.) (Dion. Hal. 2.76.6; Plutarch, *Numa* 22.1–5), and his sarcophagus is said to have come to light after heavy rains, which suggests that the grave lay near the point where the Via Aurelia crested the hill, perhaps in the grounds of Villa Aurelia.

Ager Turax: see **Campus Tiberinus.**

Ager Vaticanus: see **Vaticanus.**

Ager Veranus: according to the *Liber Pontificalis* (LPD 1.25 [p. 155] and cf. p. 181; VZ 2.227), in A.D. 258 Saint Lawrence was martyred and buried in Via Tiburtina: *in cymiterio Cyriaces, in agrum Veranum, in crypta, III id. aug.* The name may be that of an ancient owner of the land, but it is impossible to bound the property or to identify its owner more precisely. The names Veranius and Varus were not uncommon. The site is in the basilica of S. Lorenzo fuori le Mura.

Agger: see **Murus Servii Tullii.**

Agonus: Festus (304L) says this was the original (pre-Sabine) name of the Quirinal and that the Porta Collina was once called Agonensis (Paulus *ex Fest.* 9L). Although this has been widely questioned, there is no real reason to doubt it. We know that four days in the year were *dies agonales:* 9 January, 17 March, 21 May, and 11 December. Ovid clearly had no idea what the true meaning of the word might be and offers a variety of improbable explanations (*Fast.* 1.317–32). On each of these days a ram was sacrificed in the Regia. A different god seems to have been especially honored on each occasion: Janus, Liber Pater, Vediovis (?), and Indiges. Of these, only Sol Indiges is closely associated with the Quirinal in the historical period, but they may all have been fertility festivals, and certainly these gods were very old divinities. It is possible to imagine a time when they all had places on the Quirinal, from which they were removed to make place for the Sabine divinities of Titus Tatius, as Saturn was removed from the Capitoline. Certainly throughout history the Quirinal enjoyed a peculiar attraction for cults, thanks probably to the traffic along the salt road.

Agri Novi: see **Campus Esquilinus.**

Agrippae Templum: see **Pantheon.**

Aius Locutius, Ara Saepta (Templum, Sacellum): an altar erected to the supernatural voice heard by M. Caedicius, a plebeian, from the grove of Vesta, where it came down to the Nova Via, warning of the coming of the Gauls. Caedicius heard it in 391 B.C. in the still of the night, instructing him to warn the tribuni plebis, but the warning was neglected because of his humble station. There seems to have been some difficulty in locating the exact point where it was heard, but it was described as *supra aedem Vestae*. See Livy 5.32.6, 50.5, 52.11; Cicero, *Div.* 1.101, 2.69; Plutarch, *Camil.* 30.3. Varro's account, as relayed by Aulus Gellius (16.17), placing the incident in *infima Nova Via*, cannot be right and probably is the result of corruption of the text; elsewhere (*Ling.* 5.43) Varro correctly puts the infima Nova Via at the Velabrum. Possibly Gellius, knowing that in his day the Nova Via stopped near the Altar of Aius Locutius and knowing also that the *summa Nova Via* was at the junction of this with the "Clivus Palatinus," arbitrarily altered Varro's *media* to *infima*.

Albionarum Lucus: a grove in the Albiona Ager on the right bank of the Tiber, a place in which a white heifer was sacrificed (so Paulus *ex Fest.* 4L). This is very mysterious. The area should be large, the goddesses honored important, and the sacrifice an important holiday. The uncertainty of the reading between *Albionarum* and *albinarum* is further worrisome. Paulus uses the past tense of the sacrifice, but

the present tense of the Albiona Ager. No one else mentions it.

Albula: the ancient name of the Tiber, presumably from the whitish color of the sulfur-charged waters of the Anio, which entered it just above Rome (Paulus *ex Fest.* 4L; Servius *ad Aen.* 8.332). It is unusual to find a considerable river named in the feminine in Rome, where the feminine is generally reserved for brooks and springs.

Almo Flumen: the stream known today as the Fossa Almone, Acquataccio, Travicella, and Marrana della Caffarella. It rises between the Via Appia and Via Latina and flows northwest and west, crossing the line of the Via Appia about a half-kilometer outside Porta S. Sebastiano (Porta Appia) and the Via Ostiensis about a kilometer outside Porta S. Paolo (Porta Ostiensis). It was always a considerable stream fed by numerous springs and an important tributary of the Tiber. In it, at the point where it emptied into the Tiber, the image of the Magna Mater, her *carpentum,* and her sacred implements were bathed annually on 27 March, the anniversary of her arrival in Rome. At this point the image had been transferred from ship to carpentum (Ovid, *Fast.* 4.335–40; Martial 3.47.1–2; Amm. Marc. 23.3.7).

Alta Semita (Fig. 72): presumably the street along the spine of the Quirinal on the line of modern Via del Quirinale and Via Venti Settembre that gave its name to the sixth regio of Augustan Rome in the regionary catalogues. The street ran in almost a straight line from the Porta Collina in the Servian Walls southwest to the large Hadrianic temple on Collis Salutaris below modern Piazza del Quirinale (Montecavallo). Lugli believed it there changed its name and continued as Vicus Laci Fundani, but, because in the stretch in question it was descending the series of heights at the southern end of the Quirinal known as Collis Salutaris, Collis Mucialis, and Collis Latiaris, if it had changed its name, it would have become a clivus rather than a vicus. It eventually must have linked up directly with the Vicus Iugarius, for it brought the salt-seeking traffic of the Via Salaria into Rome, and this was bound for the river and its crossing just below the Tiber island. Because the line of the salt route must be prehistoric, Alta Semita must be a very old name, and no other street in Rome is known to have been called *semita,* which is usually a footpath. The northeastern stretch just before the gate may have acquired the name Vicus Portae Collinae (*CIL* 6.450 = *ILS* 3618), though that is more likely a street running southeast from Alta Semita just inside Porta Collina.

The Augustan Regio VI known by this name was very large, including the Viminal, Quirinal, and slopes of the Pincian, together with the valleys between; but much of the northern part was taken up by horti. It seems to have been bounded by the Argiletum and Vicus Patricius on the south and southeast, the line of the Aurelian Walls, including the Castra Praetoria, on the east, northeast, and north, as far as Porta Pinciana, the ancient street following the line of modern Via di Porta Pinciana and a continuation of this running more or less due south from its termination at Via del Tritone on the west, and the line of the street isolating the imperial fora on the southwest. Its principal landmarks were the baths of Diocletian and Constantine, the Castra Praetoria, the temples of Quirinus, Salus, and Flora, and the Horti Sallustiani.

BullCom 87 (1980–81): 75–82 (E. Rodriguez-Almeida).

Amicitiae Ara: decreed by the senate in A.D. 28, together with an altar to Clementia (q.v.) (Tacitus, *Ann.* 4.74), but it is not known where it was intended to stand or whether it was ever erected.

Amphitheatrum: a building type, serving especially for the presentation of gladiatorial spectacles, apparently invented in Samnite Campania, where the tradition of gladiatorial contests was strong, essentially an oval arena surrounded on all sides by banks of seating for spectators. The main entrance was always on the long axis of the arena and led in from the exterior, so that the procession *(pompa)* with which such games began could make a grand entrance and circle the arena. The oldest amphitheater known is that of Pompeii, the date of which is disputed. It is certainly at least as old as the time of Sulla, when local magistrates were responsible for some sort of construction there. This was commemorated in an inscription in which the word for amphitheater is conspicuously absent. Instead it is recorded that the magistrates: *spectacula de sua peq. fac. coer. et coloneis locum in perpetuom deder.* (*CIL* 10.852 = *ILS* 5627). This amphitheater is without any arrangement under the arena, and the cavea is essentially a mass of earth, made by excavating the interior and piling up the earth removed from it around the circumference. Access for the spectators was mainly from a broad elevated walk around the exterior, with stairs at regular intervals leading down between sectors. Only the very privileged had a better arrangement, and that may not have been original.

In Rome the earliest amphitheater that we hear of is an invention in 53 B.C. of C. Trebonius Curio. He built two theaters with caveas that revolved, so that during the morning they could stand back to back and plays could be performed simultaneously in both, and then in the afternoon they could be wheeled about and brought together, at which time the combined orchestras became an arena (see Theatra Curionis). Whether earlier gladiatorial games had always been presented in the forum, or in some similar public space, is not known but seems likely. The earliest gladiatorial show offered in Rome was at funeral games for D. Iunius Brutus Scaeva in 264 B.C. (Val. Max. 2.4.7) and was offered in the Forum Boarium. While such games might have been put on in a theater or circus, their forming regularly a part of funeral games and triumphs argues for an informal setting. In 30/29 B.C. Statilius Taurus built the first stone amphitheater (Cass. Dio 51.23.1; Suetonius, *Aug.* 29.5, *Calig.* 18.1) in the Campus Martius; this was destroyed in the fire of Nero in A.D. 64 (Cass. Dio 62.18.2), so it must have been in the part of the Campus Martius called the Aemiliana, or its vicinity, evidently near the Capitoline Hill (Calpurnius Siculus 7.23–24). Unfortunately, we have no information about its arrangements. All that can be said is that it seems to have been used almost exclusively for gladiatorial shows and hunts. A second amphitheater begun by Caligula next to the Saepta Iulia was unfinished at his death, and the work was abandoned by Claudius (Suetonius, *Calig.* 21), and one built by Nero in A.D. 57 was of wood and evidently not intended to be permanent (Tacitus, *Ann.* 13.31.1; Suetonius, *Nero* 12.1), although some of its appointments were lavish (Pliny, *NH* 16.200, 19.24). None of these buildings seems to have been remarkable for its engineering, and while those in the Campus Martius must have been freestanding and patterned after the theaters of Pompey and Marcellus, there is no suggestion that provisions for theatrical effects were a regular concern. So also the marvels described by Corydon in Calpurnius Siculus (7.69–72) could have been arranged without sophisticated engineering. Apparently advanced showmanship with elevation of animal cages, artificial landscapes, and multiple surprises does not antedate the Flavian amphitheaters of Puteoli and Rome. It is perhaps worth noting that there was probably only a single amphitheater in Rome until the time of the construction of the Amphitheatrum Castrense in the third century.

Amphitheatrum Caligulae: an amphitheater *iuxta Saepta* begun by Caligula, but then not continued by Claudius (Suetonius, *Calig.* 21). Space for this might have been available to the east, it being quite uncertain when the Temple of Isis Campensis was built, or to the north. The former is more likely. *CIL* 6.1252 = *ILS* 205 refers to damage caused to the Aqua Virgo by Caligula; very likely this was caused by the amphitheater. The verb used is *disturbare*, which suggests demolition, and it may be that Caligula intended to route the aqueduct around his amphitheater, which would locate the latter near the northeast corner of the Saepta.

Amphitheatrum Castrense (Figs. 16, 78): the small amphitheater south of the Sessorium (q.v.) near the church of S. Croce in Gerusalemme, later included in the fortifications of Aurelian, at which time the arcades of about one-third of the outer circumference were walled up. It was a broad oval in plan, with axes of 88 m and 75.80 m, built entirely of brick-faced concrete. It originally consisted of three storeys on the exterior, and drawings of the sixteenth century still show these, but today the top storey and all but a very small part of the middle one have disappeared. We are dependent on measured drawings, especially two by Palladio (Zorzi, figs. 231–32), for information. The lowest storey is embellished with an engaged order with Corinthian capitals in brick. There are no bases, but plinths of travertine blocks. In the second storey the engaged order was replaced by pilasters, also Corinthian. In the third storey rectangular windows replaced the arcades, and the elongated pilasters of the ornamental order, also Corinthian, carried only plinthlike sections of entablature as a crowning finish. Between these were corbels for footing the masts that carried awnings for the spectators. The cavea seems to have been very narrow, restricted to a single bank of nine rows of seats, unless, as Palladio's drawing suggests, there was seating above in a *summum maenianum*. The arena was provided with chambers underneath, but there is no information about how these were arranged.

The footing of the lowest order stands high above ground level today, and it has been suggested that at the time of the building of the Aurelian Walls the ground was considerably lowered, but the brick facing descends smooth to the top of the concrete footing, showing that the level has been lowered only a foot or two around most of the circumference. There can therefore have been only a limited access, probably mainly on the axes of the amphitheater.

After much debate, scholars have now reached a general agreement that the building should be dated to the time of Elagabalus, who was responsible for a good bit of construction in this area. The complete absence of brick-stamps seems to support this date (Bloch 301–3). Its identification as the Amphitheatrum Castrense of Regio V in the regionary catalogues depends on interpreting *Castrense* as meaning "belonging to the imperial residence" but is generally accepted. PA thought it would have been unusable after the construction of the Aurelian Walls, but

there is no proof of that. If Aurelian contemplated having to defend the city seriously enough to have turned the summum maenianum into an outwork of the walls, the rest can still have continued to function as before.

RendPontAcc 8 (1955): 147–54 (A. M. Colini); Nash 1.13–16.

Amphitheatrum Flavium (Figs. 3, 4, 5): the Colosseum (a name it received only after A.D. 1000 from the nearby Colossus Solis [Neronis] [q.v.]), begun by Vespasian in the basin ringed by the Velia, Oppius, and Caelian. This was the site of an ornamental lake, one of the finest features of the Domus Aurea of Nero, probably fed by cascades down the Caelian issuing from the northeast face of the platform of the Temple of Divus Claudius, which was turned into a series of fountains and grottoes. Vespasian diverted the water to public use, drained the lake, laid a deep footing of concrete (deeper where the cavea was to stand), and set about building the world's largest and most beautiful amphitheater where the lake had been. The notion that he had to contend with a lake or pond existing here before Nero's time does not seem correct, but there was certainly water in the area, as a watercourse of some volume still runs in the lowest level of the excavations under the church of S. Clemente.

The amphitheater was remarkable for the clarity of its architectural concept, yet several emperors were involved in its construction. Vespasian carried the building to the top of the second arcade of the outer wall and the *maenianum secundum* of the seating and dedicated it before his death in 79 (Chron. 146). Titus added the third and fourth storeys of the seating and rededicated it with magnificent games lasting one hundred days in 80 (Suetonius, *Tit.* 7.3; Cass. Dio 66.25). Domitian is said to have completed the building *ad clipea*, presumably gilded bronze shields that adorned the top storey of the exterior (Chron. 146).

Nerva and Trajan made changes and additions (*CIL* 6.32254–55). It was restored by Antoninus Pius (S.H.A. *Ant. Pius* 8.2). In 217 it was struck by lightning and was so seriously damaged that it could not be used for several years (Cass. Dio 79.25.2–3). Repairs begun by Elagabalus (S.H.A. *Heliogab.* 17.8) were continued by Alexander Severus (S.H.A. *Alex. Sev.* 24.3) and seem to have continued to 238, in the time of Gordian III (S.H.A. *Max. et Balb.* 1.4). In 250 it was presumably restored by Decius after another fire caused by lightning (Hieron. *a. Abr.* 2268). It was damaged in the earthquakes of 442 (Paul. Diac., *Hist. Rom.* 13.16; *CIL* 6.32086–89 = *ILS* 5633) and 470 (*CIL* 6.32091 = *ILS* 5634, *CIL* 6.32092, 32188–89). After another earthquake

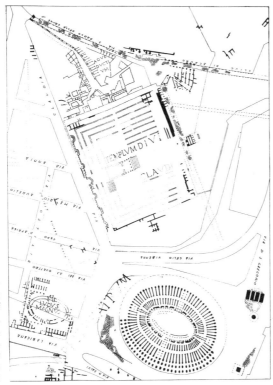

Figure 3
Amphitheatrum
Flavium, Temple of
Divus Claudius,
Ludus Magnus,
and Adjacencies,
Representation on the
Marble Plan in Relation
to Modern Streets

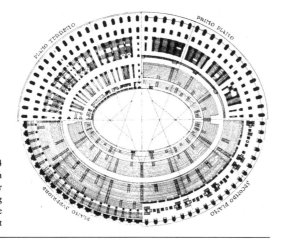

Figure 4
Amphitheatrum
Flavium, Plan in Four
Storeys, Reading
Clockwise from the
Upper Left

tury it had been reduced to more or less the state in which we see the exterior today; van Heemskerck's drawings (1: fol. 28v, 70r; 2: fol. 47r, 55r, 56v, 94v) give it its familiar appearance. Probably the plunder of the interior continued until the eighteenth century. Excavation and restoration began in the nineteenth century, but there has never been a full study of the building and the problems it presents. The north side of the exterior still stands, with thirty-two entrance arches numbered from XXIII to LIV, together with the part of the building between the façade and the travertine wall that supported the colonnade at the top of the cavea. Between this inner wall and the arena, the skeleton of the building is concrete; the two rings of radiating walls carrying sloping vaults in which the stairs to the higher parts of the cavea were arranged and on which the marble seating was supported and the heavier ring on which the podium with places for the senators and magistrates was supported survive, but this part has been stripped of the marble seating, balustrades, and whatever there was in the way of decoration and furniture.

The plan is highly logical. On the ground floor are five annular corridors, the two outermost being, in effect, a double arcade around the whole, the innermost interrupted only by four ceremonial entrances, two on the long axis for the *pompa* and performers, and two on the minor axis to the imperial box on the south side and the box for the magistrates opposite this. From these annular corridors one mounted to one's seat by stairs arranged in sets of four, a stair to a different level repeating in every fourth radial passage, except where the ceremonial entrances interrupt. Spectators were provided with tokens on which the numbers of their portal, *maenianum, vomitorium, gradus,* and *locus* appeared, and they could readily find, or be directed to, their seats. The arcades of the ground storey are decorated on the exterior with an engaged Tuscan order carrying an entablature with a continuous blank frieze and an attic of the same depth as the entablature with projections over the columns that make plinths for the order above. The ceremonial entrances are embellished with projecting pediments carried on freestanding columns and are unnumbered; the other seventy-six arches were numbered at large scale just under the architrave. The top of this storey on the exterior corresponds to that of the *maenianum primum* on the interior. The arches are 7.05 m high and 4.20 m wide. The second storey reproduces the width of the arches of the ground storey but is 2 Roman feet (0.59 m) lower. The columns are Ionic and unfluted, and a parapet ran across the base of each arch. The entablature again has a blank frieze and is surmounted by an attic similar to the one below. The top of this sto-

it was repaired by the prefect Basilius, probably consul in 508 (*CIL* 6.32094 = *ILS* 5635), for the venationes still being held there in 523 (Cassiodorus, *Var.* 5.42). The last gladiatorial games were held here in 404 (Theodoretus 5.26).

The destruction of the amphitheater seems to have begun with the earthquake during the time of Pope Leo IV (ca. 847). Its ruins were apparently then used as a shelter for a considerable community and plundered for building material. By the fourteenth cen-

rey on the exterior corresponds to that of the maenianum secundum on the interior.

The third storey reproduces the width of the arches below, but its arches are very slightly (0.05 m) lower than those of the Ionic arcade. The order is Corinthian, unfluted, and carries entablature and attic like the others, except that there is a small square window in the attic over every other arch. The arches of this storey on the exterior respond to a wall that rose 5 m above the cavea and was pierced with doors and windows to an annular corridor running just behind it. On the evidence of coins of Titus and Domitian (*B. M. Coins, Rom. Emp.* 2 pl. 50.2, 70.1; Nash 1: fig. 12), on the line of the outer wall of the second annular corridor of the ground storey was a Corinthian colonnade carrying a flat wooden roof. The columns of cipollino and granite, pieces of which are still to be seen here and there, have been assigned to the Flavian period. The fourth storey on the exterior is a solid wall decorated with Corinthian pilasters with a rectangular window between every other pair of pilasters; the coins show large round shields in the others. Just above the lintels of the windows runs a line of corbels, three in each intercolumniation, corresponding to piercings in the cornice. These braced the masts on which awnings that covered the crowd were rigged. A good bit of the cornice and low coping above it survives, though much rebuilt. The total height of the exterior is 48.50 m. It stands on a travertine podium of two steps and is surrounded by a pavement of travertine 17.50 m wide. The outer edge of this was marked by a row of travertine cippi, often erroneously said to have served in rigging the awnings, but the five remaining show no sign of this. Rather, there are holes cut on the inner face to secure a barrier that ran radially toward the amphitheater and facilitated the management of the crowds of spectators.

It is often asserted that the arches of the second and third storeys of the exterior contained statues, or statuary groups, facing to the exterior, and they are so shown on coins (and the relief of the Haterii? [Helbig[4] 1.1076]), but we must doubt that this program was ever completed, possibly ever begun. These arches in such representations are shown without the parapets that the existing arches almost all show, and no parapet is provided with a statue base. The relief of the Haterii shows a quadriga mounted over the main entrance; because this entrance has disappeared, there is no way to confirm or refute this.

In the interior the podium of the cavea was raised about 4 m above the arena and separated from it by a narrow passage paved with marble. Spectators were further protected from accident, especially with the wild beasts, by a fence inside this. Presumably the

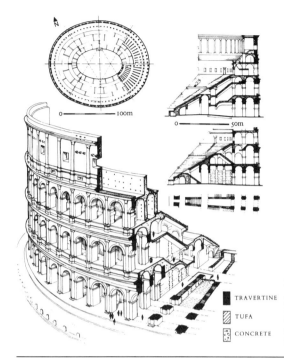

Figure 5
Amphitheatrum Flavium, Plan and Sections, Showing the Pattern of Communication

TRAVERTINE
TUFA
CONCRETE

passage was for armed guards. On the podium were the places for the chairs of distinguished spectators, assigned only to offices and collegia, not to individuals, until the time of Constantine, when they were assigned to families. Later assignment to individuals became common. The names and designations of seat holders are carved and scratched in the pavement and especially on the corona that carried a marble or bronze balustrade along the front of the podium (*CIL* 6.32099–32248; *BullCom* 8 [1880]: 236–82 [R. Lanciani]). Inscriptions in erasures of older inscriptions are common.

The podium was separated from the maenianum primum by a *balteus* or *praecinctio*. The maenianum primum had about twenty rows of seats, and the maenianum secundum had about sixteen, divided between a *maenianum superius* and a *maenianum inferius*. These were further divided into wedges (*cunei*) by stairs leading down from entrances (*vomitoria*) at mid-maenianum and at the top. These were reached by stairs in the first and second storeys, the second having a mezzanine corridor arranged over a lower interior corridor in the outer double arcade to carry traffic bound for higher levels. The *maenianum summum*, raised 5 m above the *secundum*, was *in ligneis*. Behind this was the colonnade carrying a wooden roof that made a gallery and a working platform for those who rigged the awnings. The outer corridor in the third storey had its ceiling lowered to the height of the arches of the façade and a vaulted half-storey introduced behind the entablature and attic to take the stairs serving this. It is this that the windows in the attic lit. Spectators watching from the colonnade, probably from stepped seating in wood, are shown on the coins. Along the wall behind this colonnade at least four stairs led to the roof. These were of masonry, and two have left clear prints on the wall, but, because for their installation some of the windows in the exterior wall had to be bricked up, they must be replacements for earlier wooden stairs or ladders. No spectators are shown on the roof of the colonnade on the coins, but accommodations for these may have been added later.

The arena itself is an ellipse, the long axis 86 m long, the short axis 54 m. It was floored largely with wood, sections of which could be removed for special effects. The deep substructures are complicated, their plan essentially three concentric annular passages enclosing four straight rows of cells parallel to the long axis with broad passages between and a ring of cells giving into the outermost annular passage. On the main axis there are additional large rooms in wedge-shaped annexes at either end, and there are subterranean entrances at both ends of both axes. That on the east communicated with the Ludus Magnus (q.v.). Some of these arrangements were clearly for the cages for wild animals and the elevators by which they could be hoisted into the constructions popular in the presentation of venationes. Others seem to be for machinery, cranes and catapults by which special effects were achieved. The wide central corridor was floored in part with a great framework of wooden beams, resembling a railroad, the purpose of which is obscure. There is also an extensive drainage and sewer system following the main lines of the design and emptying under Via di S. Gregorio. This part of the amphitheater has received inadequate attention as yet.

The entrance on the north seems to have been connected with the Esquiline by a portico. A broad corridor leads from it directly to the box of the magistrates and Vestals. A cryptoporticuslike passage starts not far to the east of the ceremonial entrance for the princeps on the south side and leads in the direction of the Temple of Divus Claudius on the Caelian; it is sometimes assigned to Commodus. Remains of stuccowork coffering in a poor state can be found in the vaults of the north corridor and this cryptoporticus. Whether the interior corridors were all stuccoed seems very doubtful, but there must have been a decorative finish of some sort.

The construction is of concrete, with and without brick facing, with a travertine façade and skeleton and travertine in very large blocks as high as the second storey wherever strength was required. The travertine for this work was evidently specially quarried near Tivoli and of the best quality. Where slightly less pressure had to be withstood peperino is used in the inner walls. There is also some sperone and tufa in lower parts of the inner walls. The seats were all of marble, some of it colored, but colored marble seems to have been used sparingly for such parts as the imperial box. The whole building measures 188 m on its long axis and 156 m on its cross axis.

It is shown on the Marble Plan (*FUR* pl. 19; Rodriguez pl. 11) in a number of fragments covering about one-quarter of the whole. The conventions used by the makers of the plan make it a remarkably uninformative representation. It was apparently labeled simply AMPHITHEATRUM. It is listed in the regionary catalogues in Regio III and said to have eighty-seven thousand *loca*. Modern estimates of its capacity put the maximum seating at no more than forty-five thousand.

It is the most impressive ruin in Rome, massive and awe-inspiring in its proportions and the size of the blocks of the travertine of the façade, while in the interior it has a remarkably light construction of concrete in which the stone of the *caementa* is graded according to the thrust it must bear and deliver, as in the dome of the Pantheon. As a feat of engineering it is brilliant, and that it could have been built in so short a time is amazing. That its effect as architecture should be so aesthetically satisfying, despite the great blank attic, is perhaps almost accidental and due in large part to the rhythmic play of its arcades around the oval form. This may explain why it was finally felt unnecessary to fill them with statuary.

R. Colagrossi, *L'anfiteatro flavio* (Florence and Rome 1913); G. Cozzo, *L'ingegneria romana* (Rome 1928), 203–53; Lugli 1946, 319–46 with bibliography; Nash 1.17–25; Boethius and Ward Perkins 221–24; Lugli 1975, 382–92; M. di Macco, *Il colosseo: Funzione simbolica, storica, urbana* (Rome 1971); Coarelli 1974, 166–74; *RivIstArch*, ser. 3.4 (1981): 9–69 (C. Mocchegiani Carpano and R. Luciani); *Roma sotterranea* (show catalogue, directed by R. Luciani [Rome 1985]), 108–11, 179–86 (C. Mocchegiani Carpano); *Roma: Archeologia nel centro* (Rome 1985), 1.122–46 (C. Mocchegiani Carpano et al.); *BullCom* 92 (1987–88); 323–28 (R. Rea).

Amphitheatrum Neronis: a wooden amphitheater built by Nero in A.D. 57 within the short space of a single year. It stood in the Campus Martius, and in its construction Nero evidently made use of the largest tree ever exhibited in Rome, a larch (Pliny, *HN* 16.200). It seems to have been remarkable for its blue awnings spangled with stars (Pliny, *HN* 19.24). Because it is not listed among the buildings lost in the fire of Titus (see Cass. Dio 66.24), it must have stood north or west of the Pantheon and its neighbors, perhaps a first member of the complex that included the Thermae Neronianae (q.v.).

Tacitus, *Ann.* 13.31; Suetonius, *Nero* 12; Aur. Vict., *Epit.* 5.3.

Amphitheatrum Statilii Tauri: the first stone amphitheater built in Rome, constructed at his own expense by T. Statilius Taurus, one of Octavian's most distinguished and successful generals, who had a brilliant part in the war against Sextus Pompey and at Actium and had triumphed in 34 B.C. for his successes in Africa. The amphitheater was dedicated in 29 (Cass. Dio 51.23.1; Suetonius, *Aug.* 29.5) and was destroyed in the fire of Nero in A.D. 64 (Cass. Dio 62.18.2). It stood in the Campus Martius and is listed by Strabo (5.3.8 [236]) along with the three stone theaters. But because these did not perish in that fire, the amphitheater must have stood well to the east of them in the part of Rome destroyed by the second outbreak of the fire that began in the Aemiliana (q.v.). It probably stood east of Via Lata near the south end of Piazza SS. Apostoli.

Anaglypha Traiani: see **Plutei Traiani.**

Anio Novus: the highest of all the aqueducts of Rome, begun in A.D. 38 by Caligula, at the same time as the Aqua Claudia, completed by Claudius in 52 (*CIL* 6.1256 = *ILS* 218). The water was originally taken directly from the Anio River at the forty-second milestone of the Via Sublacensis (Frontinus, *Aq.* 1.15), so it was apt to be cloudy in winter and even after summer showers. Trajan therefore ordered extension to a lake above Nero's Villa Sublacensis (Frontinus, *Aq.* 2.93), after which the water rivaled that of the Aqua Marcia in clarity and freshness and was said to exceed it in quantity. Frontinus puts the intake at 4,738 quinariae (*Aq.* 2.73), making it the most abundant of the Anio Valley aqueducts.

From the seventh milestone from the city, where it had its *piscina limaria*, Anio Novus ran on the course of the Claudia in a channel immediately over the Claudia, 609 paces on substructures, 6,491 paces on arches (Frontinus, *Aq.* 1.15). The arches ended behind the Horti Pallantiani (Frontinus, *Aq.* 1.20), and the waters were mixed at that point in a terminal piscina and distributed throughout the city in pipes, the height of the Anio Novus permitting distribution to even the highest points.

Suetonius, *Calig.* 21, *Claud.* 20; Pliny, *HN*

36.122; Frontinus, *Aq.* 1.4, 13, 15, 18–21, 2.68, 72, 73, 86, 90, 91, 93, 104, 105; Van Deman 271–330; Ashby 1935, 252–98; Pace 176–83.

Anio Vetus: the second great aqueduct of Rome, following the Appia (see Aqua Appia). The censors M'. Curius Dentatus and L.(?) Papirius Praetextatus let the contract for it in 272 B.C. and paid for it from the spoils taken from Pyrrhus (Frontinus, *Aq.* 1.6; cf. Broughton, *MRR* 1.198). The intake was above Tibur, opposite Varia (modern Vicovaro). Of its 43,000 paces only 221 ran above ground on substructures. It entered the city *ad Spem Veterem* (Porta Maggiore) and was distributed to most parts of the city, except the Palatine, Caelian, Aventine, and Circus Maximus (Frontinus, *Aq.* 2.80). Frontinus found its intake to be 4,398 quinariae (*Aq.* 2.66), but it tended to be turbid, being taken from the river, so in his reforms it was restricted to use in watering gardens and the meaner services of the city (Frontinus, *Aq.* 2.92). It was repaired by Q. Marcius Rex in 144 B.C. (Frontinus, *Aq.* 1.7; Pliny, *HN* 36.121), by Agrippa in 33 B.C. (Frontinus, *Aq.* 1.9), and by Augustus in 11–4 B.C. (Frontinus, *Aq.* 2.125). A number of the cippi of the Augustan restoration have survived (*CIL* 6.1243, cf. 31558; 14.4079, 4080, 4083, 4084). A branch of the Anio Vetus, the Specus Octavianus, inside the second milestone from the city, took part of its water to the Horti Asiniani, near the Via Nova (Frontinus, *Aq.* 1.21), but the location of this property is quite uncertain.

Frontinus, *Aq.* 1.4, 6, 7, 9, 13, 18, 21; 2.66, 67, 80, 90–92, 125; Van Deman 29–66; Ashby 1935, 54–87; Pace 121–24.

Antoninus, Templum: see **Marcus, Divus, Templum.**

Antoninus et Faustina, Templum (Fig. 48): built by Antoninus Pius in Regio IV on the north side of the Sacra Via just east of the street (Corneta?) dividing it from the Basilica Paulli (q.v.) in honor of his deified wife, who died in A.D. 141 (S.H.A. *Ant. Pius* 6.7). After his own death and deification in 161, the temple was rededicated to both (S.H.A. *Ant. Pius* 13.4). The first dedication is inscribed on the architrave and the second on the frieze, the decoration of which was chiseled away to receive it (*CIL* 6.1005 = *ILS* 348). Thereafter, it was properly known as Templum Divi Antonini et Divae Faustinae (*CIL* 6.2001). It was called Templum Faustinae (S.H.A. *Salon.* 1.4 [*Gall.* 19.4]; *Not.*) and Templum Divi Pii (S.H.A. *Carac.* 4.2). It is shown on coins of Faustina (Cohen², Faustine mère 64–71, 191–94, 253–55, 274; *RIC* 3.69–76 nos. 343, 354, 388, 396,

11

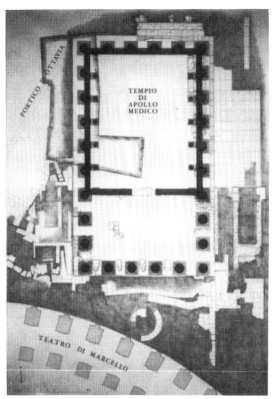

Figure 6
Temple of Apollo
(Medicus, Sosianus),
Restored Plan Showing
Actual Remains

ing cornucopias have been recovered and make reconstruction possible.

The lateral walls of the cella are of peperino ashlar masonry, built into the church of S. Lorenzo in Miranda. On the coins the temple is shown with pedimental sculptures and acroteria, but of these there is no trace today. Fragments of a colossal male and a colossal female statue were found, which are probably to be identified as the cult statues. The whole temple was revetted with marble plates simulating drafted ashlar above a plain dado that have disappeared. For the history of the church into which the temple was converted, see HCh 288–89.

HJ 8–9; *MonAnt* 23 (1914): 949–74 (A. Bartoli); PA 13–14; Lugli 1946, 220–21.

Antrum *(Not.)*, **Atrium** *(Cur.)* **Cyclopis:** listed in Regio II by the regionary catalogues, presumably a grotto or nymphaeum, perhaps embellished with sculptures of Ulysses and Polyphemus like those of Castel Gandolfo and Sperlonga (cf. *PECS,* s.v. "Alba Longa," "Sperlonga"). This apparently gave its name to a Vicus Cyclopis in Regio I *(CIL* 6.2226 = *ILS* 6077).

Aphrodision: mentioned only once, among the portents of Septimius Severus's rise to greatness. Faustina, the wife of Marcus Aurelius, is said to have prepared the wedding chamber for Septimius and Julia Domna in the Aphrodision below the Palatine (Cass. Dio 75.3.1). This might have been connected with the Temple of Venus et Roma, the Temple of Venus Obsequens, or the Temple of Venus Verticordia (see Venus et Roma, Templum; Venus Obsequens, Aedes; Venus Verticordia, Aedes).

Apollinare: an area in the Prata Flaminia that Livy (3.63.7) says was already so called before the building of the Temple of Apollo Medicus, presumably therefore coterminal with the precinct of the temple (see Apollo, Aedes).

Apollo, Aedes (Figs. 6, 7, 37.2): the only temple of Apollo in Rome before Augustus built the Temple of Apollo Palatinus (Asconius *in Cic. tog. cand.* 80–81 [Stangl 69–70]). It was vowed in 433/2 B.C. in consequence of a plague and dedicated in 431 by the consul C. Iulius (Livy 4.25.3, 4.29.7). The original dedication day was 13 July, thereafter the occasion of the Ludi Apollinares. The god very early carried the epithet Medicus. Despite variations in the wording of accounts of its location, they all point to a place between Piazza Campitelli and the Theater of Marcellus, where were unearthed substantial remains, especially of the principal façade and east

406 and 162–69 nos. 1115, 1137, 1138, 1148, 1152, 1168, 1195).

The temple was raised on a lofty podium faced with blocks of peperino finished with moldings at base and crown, with a stair extending across the whole front. In the middle of the stair are remains of an altar. A fragment of marble relief with figures of gods in archaistic style has been identified as belonging to this altar *(RendLinc* 12 [1957]: 50–57 [E. Lissi]). At the top of the stair were squarish statue bases to either side. Most of the stair has disappeared, robbed out for building material, but in 1899 the removal of the later pavement of the Sacra Via brought to light the three lowest steps of the stair, and it has since been reconstructed.

The temple was hexastyle, prostyle, with two additional columns to either side of the pronaos. The columns are monoliths of cipollino with Corinthian capitals and bases of white marble. The entablature in white marble ran down the flanks and probably around the whole building. The frieze is carved with gryphons and scrolls flanking candelabra. The cornice, fragments of which are still in place, is elaborate in the Antonine taste. Although the tympanum was dismantled and destroyed, fragments of it and of the lateral antefixes showing female figures carry-

flank. The revetment of the exterior was all in white marble, the pronaos hexastyle, pycnostyle, with three columns on each flank, the columns Corinthian with Attic bases, elegantly carved with the flutes alternately wide and narrow. The frieze is decorated with branches of laurel (?) swung between candelabra and bucrania. Around the squarish cella the order was carried engaged. The tympana were filled with an Amazonomachy of Greek workmanship of the fifth century from an unknown source. There was no stair in front, the temple being approached by two small stairs on the flanks of the pronaos. In the interior were columns of africano with figured Corinthian capitals of white marble that included tripods and serpents. They carried an entablature with a frieze showing scenes of a battle on horse and a triumph. A series of aediculae revetted with colored marble and gilded stucco surmounted by pediments alternately triangular and lunate filled the intercolumniations. The pavement was also of colored marble. Between the temple and the theater was a circular building, probably a monopteral aedicula, 5.20 m in diameter, which nearly filled the space between the two and virtually blocked traffic here.

The temple in its present state is believed to be the work of C. Sosius, consul in 32 B.C., because Pliny twice speaks of works of art in a Temple of Apollo Sosianus (*HN* 13.53, 36.28). An earlier restoration or rebuilding seems to have been carried out in 353 B.C. (Livy 7.20.9). The new dedication day was celebrated on 23 September (Degrassi 512).

This was a favorite place for meetings of the senate, especially for meeting foreign embassies and deliberating about triumphs (cf., e.g., Livy 34.43.2, 37.58.3, 39.4.1, 41.17.4; Cicero, *Fam.* 8.4.4, 8.8.6; *Att.* 15.3.1; *QFr.* 2.3.3). It was also the repository of an extraordinary collection of works of art, both paintings and sculptures, of which the most famous seems to have been a group of Niobids ascribed by some to Scopas, by others to Praxiteles (Pliny, *HN* 36.28; cf. 13.53, 35.99, 36.34–35).

In 179 B.C. the censors let the contracts for various works, especially porticoes. One or more of these is described in a corrupt passage in Livy: *aliam post navalia et ad fanum Herculis et post Spei ad Tiberim aedem Apollinis medici* (Livy 40.51.6). A single portico of such extent, or anything approaching it, is most unlikely; a portico framing part of the precinct of the temple may lie behind this corruption.

Vitruvius (3.3.4) mentions an *aedes Apollinis et Dianae* as an example of a diastyle temple. He is as likely referring to an earlier phase of this temple as to Apollo Palatinus (q.v.) although this is the only occurrence of this designation (cf. Pliny, *HN* 36.35).

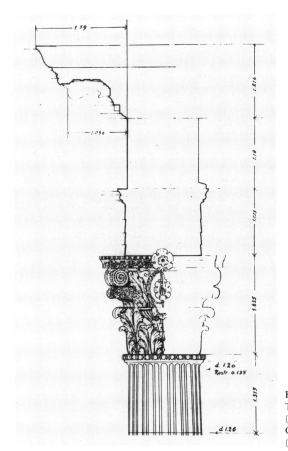

Figure 7
Temple of Apollo (Medicus, Sosianus), Order and Entablature (Architect's Drawing)

If so, this would serve to date Sosius's rebuilding of the temple to ca. 30–28 B.C.

BullCom 66 (1938): 259–60 (A. M. Colini), 68 (1940): 228–29 (A. M. Colini); Lugli 1946, 536–42; Nash 1.28–30; Lugli 1975, 285–87; *BullCom* 87 (1980–81): 57–73 (E. La Rocca); E. La Rocca, *Amazzonomachia: Le sculture frontonali del tempio di Apollo Sosiano* (Rome 1985); *BullCom* 90 (1985): 363–68 (P. Virgili).

Apollo Argenteus: The Ager Apollinis Argentei is known only from a tomb inscription found in 1729 on Monte Mario (*CIL* 6.2233 = *ILS* 4182; cf. *CIL* 6.29967). If the inscription was found more or less *in situ*, as it seems to have been, there is no way of telling how the area got its name.

Apollo Caelispex: a monument mentioned only in the regionary catalogues, listed in Regio XI between the Porta Trigemina and Hercules Olivarius, so probably in the Forum Boarium in the area between the circus brook and the Cloaca. It is identified with some probability by Coarelli as the large Apollo that came from Carthage and was set up opposite the circus (Plutarch, *Flamin*. 1.1). This would put it in the neighborhood of the carceres of the circus. He further identifies it as the Apollo shown in the Forum Boarium relief of the arch of Trajan at Beneventum, which is unlikely.

Coarelli 1988, 156–64; *JRA* 3 (1990): 240–42 (R. E. A. Palmer).

Apollo Palatinus, Aedes (also **Templum**), Augustus, *RG* 4.19, Propertius 2.31.9, et al.; **Delubrum**, Pliny, *HN* 36.24 and 32) (Fig. 63.4): the second temple to Apollo in Rome, vowed by Octavian during his campaign against Sextus Pompey in 36 B.C. and begun in that year, but completed and dedicated in 28 (Cass. Dio 53.1.3). Its dedication day was 9 October (Degrassi 518–19). It was universally admired as the most sumptuous and magnificent of all early Augustan buildings. It was built on land that had been struck by lightning (Cass. Dio 49.15.5) and therefore declared public.

It was remarkable for the porticoes connected with it, as well as the temple itself. The three cult statues were of Apollo by Scopas (Pliny, *HN* 36.25), Diana by Timotheus (Pliny, *HN* 36.32), and Latona by Cephisodotus (Pliny, *HN* 36.24; cf. 36.34–35). On the roof was a chariot of the sun and sculptures by Bupalos and Athenis (Pliny, *HN* 36.13). The doors were decorated with ivory reliefs showing the crushing of the Celtic assault on Delphi and the slaughter of the Niobids (Propertius 2.31.12–16). At the corners of the altar were four bulls by Myron (Propertius 2.31.5–8). In the temple was a collection of engraved gems dedicated by Marcellus (Pliny, *HN* 37.11).

The particulars of the architecture are not known. Servius (*ad Aen*. 8.720) says the temple was built of solid blocks of Luna marble, and it may have been diastyle (Vitruvius 3.3.4).

The temple was connected with colonnades of giallo antico in the intercolumniations of which were set statues of the fifty daughters of Danaus, with equestrian statues of their fifty bridegrooms in the open area facing them. There was also a library divided into separate sections for Greek and Latin and adorned with portraits of great men of letters. The area enclosed by these was known as the Area Apollinis, and the libraries were big enough to accommodate meetings of the senate, which met there relatively frequently (Cass. Dio 53.1.3; Suetonius, *Aug*. 29.3). The Sibylline Books were moved to this temple (Suetonius, *Aug*. 31.1; Servius *ad Aen*. 6.72) and rescued when the temple burned on 18 March 363 (Amm. Marc. 23.3.3).

Great uncertainty has reigned with respect to the location of this temple. According to one view, it should be in the Vigna Barberini, where there was certainly a major building, almost certainly a temple in a colonnaded square. But there has never been adequate exploration of this area by excavation, and its character and construction are quite unknown. A more popular view is that the temple of Apollo is the temple between the Domus Augustiana and the Scalae Caci labeled by Lanciani Aedes Iovis Propugnatoris and often called Iuppiter Victor. This is a podium of Augustan concrete approached by a long broad stair broken into successive flights, the *gradus celsi* of Ovid (*Trist*. 3.1.59). The colonnades would have framed the back and sides of a square in front of this, and the library would be the two large apsidal halls with multiple niches to the southeast. In recent excavations in the Casa di Augusto (Domus Augusti) to the northwest, evidence has come to light that strongly supports this location, though the space available must seem minimal.

Besides Palatinus, the god of this temple is also called Navalis (Propertius 4.1.3), Actius (Propertius 4.6.67), Actiacus (Ovid, *Met*. 13.715), and Rhamnusius (*Not*. Reg. X). None of these needs be a true epithet, but the last seems to require explanation. Höfer (in Roscher 4.88) hesitates between seeing it as a transference from the frequent pairing of Nemesis and Artemis and the possibility that the Apollo of Scopas that was the cult image originally came from Rhamnous. Certainly the latter is more likely to be correct.

Lugli 1946, 434–41 and 468–79; Nash 1.31–32; *RömMitt* 76 (1969): 183–204 (H. Bauer); Lugli 1975, 174–79; *AJA* 85 (1981): 335–39 (D. L. Thompson); G. Carettoni, *Das Haus des Augustus auf dem Palatin* (Mainz 1983), 9–16; *AnalRom*, suppl. 10 (1983): 21–40 (P. Zanker).

Apollo Sandaliarius: a famous and very costly statue dedicated by Augustus in Vicus Sandaliarius, presumably in a sacellum (Suetonius, *Aug*. 57.1). This was in Regio IV (*Not., Cur.*). The Vicus Sandaliarius was probably the short street running from the middle of the southeast side of the Templum Pacis almost due east to join Vicus Cuprius.

Apollo Tortor: Suetonius (*Aug*. 70.2) says that Apollo was worshiped in a certain part of Rome with this epithet, but it is not known why. It may be that he was shown here in the familiar group of the flaying of Marsyas.

Appiades: a fountain group by Stephanus in the collection of Asinius Pollio, housed in the Atrium Libertatis (Pliny, *HN* 36.33). Stephanus was Pompey's favorite sculptor, and Ovid speaks of the fountain as a neighbor of Venus Genetrix (*Ars Am.* 1.82; cf. *Rem. Am.* 660), so it may have stood against the party wall between the Atrium Libertatis and the Forum Iulium. It is presumed that the Appiades were nymphs of the Aqua Appia, but it is not clear why Stephanus should have created such a fountain.

Coarelli 1974, 106; *RömMitt* 93 (1986): 405–23 (R. B. Ulrich).

Aqua: the term used in antiquity for the whole course of any aqueduct, as well as the water that it brought to Rome. Usually its name was the name of the builder of the aqueduct (e.g., Aqua Appia) or identified the source of the water (Anio Vetus). Once it had a story attached (Aqua Virgo), and once it described the water (Aqua Tepula). Except in the immediate vicinity of the city, Roman aqueducts are underground channels ventilated by shafts at regular intervals, which also served as entrances for those who cleaned out deposits of lime and repaired the conduits, where the water flowed by gravity. Bridges and siphons are occasionally introduced to overcome geographical obstacles, but these, especially the latter, are very rare. Most of the water supply of Rome was taken from the Anio River system, with supplements from the Alban Hills, and came to Rome atop an ancient tongue of lava extending from the Alban Hills in the neighborhood of Marino. Most of these aqueducts emerged at a point known by the modern name of Le Capannelle and then were carried on arches across the last stretch of the Roman Campagna, entering Rome close to Porta Maggiore (ad Spem Veterem). These are the spectacular ruins that are justly famous as feats of engineering and architecture, especially the rusticated arches of the Aqua Claudia. Within the city for the most part they returned underground or were carried on the existing walls and bridges, so there are few dramatic stretches, except for the Neronian arches of the Claudia on the Caelian and the bridge that brought water to the Palatine. The aqueducts on the right bank of the Tiber ran almost entirely underground and so have left no dramatic remains. The water delivered by an aqueduct was measured in quinariae, an invention, according to Frontinus, of either Agrippa or Vitruvius. This was a pipe size, the diameter of the pipe being five-fourths of a digit, 2.3 cms, or slightly less than an inch.

Aqua Alexandrina (Alexandriana): an aqueduct brought in by Alexander Severus to supply his baths (S.H.A. *Alex. Sev.* 25.3; cf. Thermae Neronianae). Its springs were near Gabii, and it entered Rome at the Porta Maggiore. In the late sixteenth century its springs were used to supply the Acqua Felice. Outside the city it was identified in the seventeenth century by Adrien Azout of Rouen and mapped and described by Fabretti (*De Aquis,* 1680). Its course from the third mile of the Via Labicana on and within the city of Rome remains entirely unknown.

Van Deman 341–60; Ashby 1935, 308–15.

Aqua Alsietina: an aqueduct built by Augustus and consequently sometimes called Augusta, mainly to supply the Naumachia Augusti (q.v.). It was one of the small group of aqueducts with sources on the west side of the Tiber, drawing its water from the Lacus Alsietinus (Lago di Montignano), with additional supply from the Lacus Sabatinus (Lago di Bracciano) (Frontinus, *Aq.* 1.11, 2.71). It delivered 392 quinariae, all of which were consumed outside the city, the specus ending behind the naumachia (Frontinus, *Aq.* 2.85). It was very poor water, used only to supply the naumachia and to water gardens, except when emergency cut the lines crossing the river on bridges, when it was used to supply the Transtiberim before the building of the Aqua Traiana. Frontinus reckons its length as 22,172 paces, of which 358 paces were on arches. Remains found on the Janiculum just inside the Porta Aurelia (Porta S. Pancrazio), originally thought to belong to it (*MAAR* 6.137–46 [A. W. Van Buren]), are now believed to be channels connected with the Aqua Traiana. Frontinus's characterization of it as the lowest of the aqueducts is inaccurate.

Frontinus, *Aq.* 1.4, 11, 18, 22; 2.71, 85; Van Deman 179–86; Ashby 1935, 183–89; Nash 1.35–36; Rodriguez 144–47; Pace 147–49.

Aqua Annia: listed only in the addenda to the *Notitia* and Polemius Silvius 545 ("Anena"); evidently a corruption of *Aqua Anio* (see Anio Novus, Anio Vetus), because both Anio aqueducts are omitted from these lists.

Aqua Antoniniana: see **Aqua Marcia.**

Aqua Appia: the oldest of all the Roman aqueducts, built in 312 B.C. by the censors Appius Claudius and C. Plautius, surnamed Venox as discoverer of the springs (Livy 9.29.6). Its springs were in the Ager Lucullanus, to the left between the seventh and eighth milestones on the Via Praenestina, but they remain unidentified today. It entered the city ad Spem Veterem (see Spes Vetus) and extended to the *salinae* at Porta Trigemina at the foot of the Clivus Publicius, where it was distributed. It ran almost entirely underground for its length of 11,190 paces, only 60 paces near Porta Capena being carried on arches. It delivered 1,825 quinariae, according to Frontinus (*Aq.* 1.5, 2.65).

It was repaired by Q. Marcius Rex in 144 B.C. (Pliny, *HN* 36.121) and by Agrippa in 33 B.C. (Frontinus, *Aq.* 1.9). Near ad Spem Veterem it was joined *ad Gemellos* by a supplement constructed by Augustus and called the Aqua Augusta, which brought water from springs near the sixth milestone on the Via Praenestina near the Collatina, probably in effect doubling its supply.

The course within the city is fairly well established. From ad Spem Veterem it ran along the brow of the Caelian to the neighborhood of the Porta Capena, crossed that valley on arches and ran again underground, turning almost at right angles to run along the Aventinus Minor and Aventine above the Circus Maximus to Porta Trigemina. It was also the lowest Roman aqueduct.

Frontinus, *Aq.* 1.4–7, 9, 18, 22; 2.65, 79, 125; Van Deman 23–38; Ashby 1935, 49–54; Pace 118–20.

Aqua Attica: listed only in the addenda to the *Notitia* and Polemius Silvius 545 ("Atica"), probably a corruption of "Antiqua" and used for the Anio Vetus, which is omitted from these lists.

Aqua Aufeia (?): according to Pliny (*HN* 31.41), the original name of the Aqua Marcia. A Gens Aufeia seems attested only in Aulus Gellius 11.10.1.

Aqua Augusta (Augustea): an alternative name for the Aqua Alsietina (q.v.); also the name given the supplement of the Aqua Appia (q.v.) that joined it ad Gemellos, and the Fons Augusta of the Aqua Marcia (q.v.).

Aqua Aurelia: listed in the addenda to the *Notitia* and Polemius Silvius 545, an unidentified aqueduct or spring, just possibly the abundant spring near the summit of the Janiculum north of Via Aurelia (LA 27). But because all the identifiable items in these lists are aqueducts, it is more likely to be an alternate name for one of the more familiar ones.

Aqua Caerulea: see **Aqua Claudia.**

Aqua Cernens IIII Scari Sub Aede (Eadem Cur.): listed only in the regionary catalogues in Regio VIII after the Horrea Agrippiana and before the Atrium Caci, so possibly at least two separate landmarks and also possibly on Vicus Tuscus toward the Velabrum or on the lower slope of the Palatine, presumably a fountain or fountains, but of what form is quite uncertain. The name seems somewhat corrupted; possibly the Lacus Iuturnae (q.v.) or Statio Aquarum (q.v.) is meant. See also Quattuor Scari and Nordh's *apparatus criticus*.

Aqua Ciminia: listed in the addenda to the *Notitia* and Polemius Silvius 545. The name occurs only here, and the identification is entirely uncertain.

Aqua Claudia: the greatest of all the Roman aqueducts, begun like the Anio Novus by Caligula in A.D. 38 (Suetonius, *Calig.* 21) and completed by Claudius and dedicated 1 August 52 (Frontinus, *Aq.* 1.13). After ten years the supply is said to have failed and then been interrupted for nine years, although this has been doubted. It was restored by Vespasian in 71. Ten years later Titus and Domitian repaired it. On 3 July 88 a tunnel through Mons Aeflanus was completed. The remains themselves show repeated campaigns of repairs through the second and third centuries.

The principal springs, Caeruleus and Curtius, were 300 paces to the left of the Via Sublacensis at the thirty-eighth milestone, thus only 100 paces upstream of the springs of the Aqua Marcia and part of the same system (Frontinus, *Aq.* 1.13–14). The length of the channel is given by Frontinus (*Aq.* 1.14) as 46,406 paces, but by the Porta Maggiore inscription (*CIL* 6.1256–58 = *ILS* 218) as 45,000 paces. Its volume at intake Frontinus puts at 4,607 quinariae, second only to the Anio Novus. The Fons Augusta of the Marcia was turned into the Claudia when the Marcia was full (Frontinus, *Aq.* 2.72), but sometimes even the Claudia overflowed from its supply. It entered the city ad Spem Veterem and in its terminal piscina was mixed with the Anio Novus. Then together they were distributed to all parts of the city, even the highest (Frontinus, *Aq.* 1.18, 2.86). Outside the city from its piscina at the seventh milestone of the Via Labicana, it ran on arches that also carried the Anio Novus in a channel atop it; these are the most spectacular remains of all Roman aqueducts, the masonry revetted with great blocks of peperino, the arches rising dramatically as the spur on which they run slopes down toward the city. At the convergence of the Via Labicana and Via Praenestina, they turn to cross these in a monumental double arch finished with rusticated blocks of travertine, which was later included in the fortifications of Aurelian and became the Porta Maggiore (Porta Maior), one of the most elegant remains of antiquity.

At the Porta Maior the Neronian Arcus Caelimontani (see Arcus Neroniani) diverge to the south to carry this water to the southern and western parts of the city. The main conduit ran to a piscina *post hortos Pallantianos* (Frontinus, *Aq.* 1.20). In the Middle Ages the aqueduct was called Forma Claudiana.

Frontinus, *Aq.* 1.4, 13–15, 18–20; 2.69, 72, 76, 86, 87, 89, 91, 104, 105; Suetonius, *Calig.* 21, *Claud.* 20; Van Deman 187–270; Ashby 1935, 190–251; Nash 1.37–46; Pace 150–75.

Aqua Conclusa: in Esquiliae, known only from a single sepulchral inscription (*CIL* 6.33087 = *ILS* 8401), presumably a covered piscina, but then the possibilities are multiple. The castellum of the Claudia and Anio Novus southeast of "Minerva Medica" is certainly a possibility.

Aqua Damnata: mentioned only in the addenda to the *Notitia*. PA suggests it may be the same as the Aqua Dotraciana of Polemius Silvius 545, which is little or no help, because the lists have a common, much corrupted source. But this might be a nickname for the Aqua Alsietina (q.v.). Jordan suggests *Dotraciana* might be a corruption of *Diocletiana*, but that does little to clear matters up. Cf. *PW* 4.2059 (C. Hülsen).

Aqua Drusia: mentioned only by Polemius Silvius (546), possibly the Aqua Anio Vetus, which in the Specus Octavianus may have passed over the Arcus Drusi.

Aqua Herculea: the Rivus Herculaneus of the Aqua Marcia (q.v.).

Aqua Iovia: see **Aqua Marcia.**

Aqua Iulia: an aqueduct built by Agrippa in 33 B.C. and repaired by Augustus in 11–4 B.C. (Frontinus, *Aq.* 1.9, 2.125) and again in A.D. 14 (*CIL* 6.31563c). Its springs are about one-half mile above the Abbey of Grottaferrata. The watermen supplemented this with water from the Aqua Crabra, the main supply of Tusculum (Frontinus, *Aq.* 1.9). The length is given as 15,426½ paces, the intake as 1,206 quinariae (Frontinus, *Aq.* 1.9; 2.69); it received 162 quinariae of additional water from the Claudia and discharged 190 quinariae of water into the Tepula (Frontinus, *Aq.* 2.69). Several cippi of the aqueduct are known. A little beyond Le Capannelle, at the seventh milestone of the Via Latina, it begins to run above ground on the arches of the Marcia and goes to its terminal castellum for distribution within the city. But a branch ran to the splendid nymphaeum in Piazza Vittorio Emanuele commonly called the Trofei di Mario or Cimbrum Marii, the sort of terminal water show with which many aqueducts finished. Arches of this branch can be seen in Piazza Guglielmo Pepe.

Frontinus, *Aq.* 1.4, 9, 18, 19; 2.68, 69, 76, 83,

125; Van Deman 157–66; Ashby 1935, 161–66; Nash 1.47; *CAR* 3-G, 218 pp. 272–73; Pace 140–43. For cippi of this aqueduct, see *NSc* 1925, 51 and examples cited there.

Aqua Marcia: perhaps the most famous of all the aqueducts of Rome, built originally in 144–140 B.C. by Q. Marcius Rex, praetor urbanus, who was commissioned by the senate to repair the Aquae Appia and Anio Vetus (Pliny, *HN* 36.121; Frontinus, *Aq.* 1.7). The total cost was enormous, and the engineering was an astonishing accomplishment, because the aqueduct brought water to the top of the Capitoline. It was always considered the best water in Rome, the coldest and purest (Pliny, *HN* 31.41–42). It was repaired by Agrippa in 33 B.C. and again by Augustus in 11–4 B.C. (Frontinus, *Aq.* 1.9, 2.125); the latter work is commemorated on an archway by which it crossed the Via Tiburtina, later incorporated into the walls of Aurelian (*CIL* 6.1244 = *ILS* 98).

The springs lay 200 paces to the left of the Via Sublacensis at the thirty-eighth milestone, almost midway between the Via Sublacensis and Via Valeria. Pliny (*HN* 31.41) says that the original name of the water was Aqua Aufeia and that the spring was Fons Pitonia. Augustus added another spring, the Aqua Augusta, 800 paces farther up the Anio Valley, thus doubling the volume of the aqueduct, which Frontinus reckoned at 4,690 quinariae at the intake. The length he reckoned at 61,710½ paces, or 91.4 km (Frontinus, *Aq.* 1.7, 2.67).

In history it figures on coins of L. Marcius Philippus (*B. M. Coins, Rom. Rep.* 1.485–86, nos. 3890–95; Crawford 425). Nero outraged Rome by bathing in the springs of the Marcia (Tacitus, *Ann.* 14.22). Restorations were carried out by Titus (*CIL* 6.1246 = *ILS* 98), Hadrian, Septimius Severus in A.D. 196 (*CIL* 6.1247), and Caracalla, who claimed to have cleared the springs, made new tunnels, and added an additional spring, the Fons Antoninianus, in 212–13 (*CIL* 6.1245 = *ILS* 98).

Where it emerges from its underground channel, near the sixth milestone on the Via Latina, the Marcia was later joined by the Aqua Tepula and Aqua Iulia, which were carried in channels above it running on the same arches. This stacking is best seen where they have been sectioned where they pass through the Aurelian Walls just northeast of Porta Maggiore. The aqueduct was used in the construction of the wall from here to Porta Tiburtina, beyond which it passes underground to run to the terminal castellum inside Porta Collina, the Piscina Trium Aquarum near the north corner of the Thermae Diocletianae. Augustan cippi for this stretch with the names of all three aqueducts are numerous (cf., e.g.,

CIL 6.1249 = 31561 = *ILS* 5746). It seems to have served mainly the northern parts of the city, especially the Quirinal and Viminal hills, but was also extended to the Capitoline, probably by a siphon (Livy, *Epit.* 54; Frontinus, *Aq.* 1.7).

The Rivus Herculaneus diverged from the main line of the Aqua Marcia post Hortos Pallantianos inside the city; that is, from the castellum now built into the fifth tower of the Aurelian Walls southeast of Porta San Lorenzo. This channel ran along the brow of the Caelian, but too low to supply the hill itself with water, and emerged in a terminal castellum above Porta Capena, presumably on the Caelian side of the valley (Frontinus, *Aq.* 1.19). Here it supplied water to a considerable and populous area, including parts of Regiones I, XI, and XII. No one tells us when the Rivus Herculaneus was created, but in the general pattern of water distribution in Rome it might well be part of the original design. Later Trajan took the Marcia *amplo opere* to the Aventine (Frontinus, *Aq.* 2.87); presumably this was by siphons.

Another branch must have been taken off the Marcia to supply the Baths of Caracalla when he restored the aqueduct and added the Fons Antoninianus to its supply (*CIL* 6.1245 = *ILS* 98). This must have been taken off outside the city; PA suggests at the third milestone of the Via Latina. It crossed the Via Appia by the Arco di Druso and continued to the reservoir southwest of the baths. The supply of this Aqua Antoniniana was augmented by Diocletian, and then it took the name Forma Iovia, from his name. It is cited under that name in a variety of corruptions through the next several centuries.

Frontinus, *Aq.* 1.4, 7, 9, 12, 13, 14, 18, 19; 2.67, 68, 72, 76, 81, 87, 89, 91–3, 125; Van Deman 67–146; Ashby 1935, 88–158; Nash 1.48–50; *AJA* 87 (1983): 394 (H. B. Evans); *CAR* 3-G, 218 pp. 271–72; Pace 125–37.

Aqua Mercurii: described by Ovid (*Fast.* 5.673–74) as near the Porta Capena. He does not specify whether a spring or a stream is meant, and no one else mentions it. Merchants fetch lustral water from it for their goods and themselves, so the god may condone their dishonesty. If this is not identical with the Fons Camenarum, which is certainly unlikely, because that was always used for the chastest purposes, then perhaps the terminal fountain of the Rivus Herculaneus of the Aqua Marcia was the object of a pun. There might also have been a play on the name *Murcia,* the valley of the Circus Maximus being named Vallis Murcia, if Murcia was a water divinity, as seems likely. But it seems unlikely that there was a separate spring dedicated exclusively to Mercury.

Aqua Pinciana: known only from an inscription on a lead pipe of the time of Valentinian (*CIL* 15.7259) found in Villa Verospi, just inside Porta Salaria, presumably not a separate water, but a pipe supplying the Domus Pinciana (q.v.) with water from one of the aqueducts. Its discovery near Porta Salaria is puzzling, because one would have expected the Domus Pinciana to be supplied by the Aqua Virgo.

Aqua Sallustiana: a modern name given the brook that runs down the valley between the Quirinal and the Mons Pincius (Collis Hortulorum), occupied in the Augustan period by the Horti Sallustiani (q.v.). It was found in the excavation made for the extension of the house of Parliament (Montecitorio) in 1907–1910, flowing strong in an east/west direction (*StRom* 1 [1913]: 4–5 [G. Mancini]), and can be presumed to have emptied into the Tiber between Ponte Cavour and Ponte Umberto I, probably closer to the latter. It may well be the Spino or the Nodinus mentioned by Cicero (*Nat.D.* 3.52). It certainly never joined the Petronia Amnis in the southern Campus Martius, a notion that has distorted much of the thinking about the topography of this part of Rome in the past.

Aqua Severiana: listed in the addenda to the *Notitia* and Polemius Silvius 545, but neither the Antoniniana nor the Alexandrina, both of which are also listed, and otherwise unknown.

Aqua Tepula: the fourth aqueduct of Rome, originally constructed in 125 B.C. by the censors Cn. Servilius Caepio and L. Cassius Longinus Ravilla. The springs were in the Ager Lucullanus, two miles to the right of the Via Latina at the tenth milestone (Frontinus, *Aq.* 1.8). Beginning in 33 B.C. with the work of Agrippa, its water was mixed with that of the Aqua Iulia, and thenceforward, as perhaps earlier, it entered the city carried on the arches of the Aqua Marcia. Frontinus (*Aq.* 2.68) measured its intake as beginning at the reservoir of the Iulia, 190 quinariae; thereafter it drew 92 quinariae from the Marcia and 163 from the Anio Novus at the Horti Epaphroditiani, to make a total of 445. It took its name from the relative warmth and unpalatability of its water, and until the time of Agrippa, who improved its quality, tended to be despised.

Frontinus, *Aq.* 1.4, 8, 9, 18, 19; 2.67–69, 82, 125; Van Deman 147–56; Ashby 1935, 159–60 (and 128–58); *CAR* 3-G, 218 p. 272; Pace 138–39.

Aqua Traiana: the last of the great aqueducts of Rome, built by Trajan. It drew its water from abundant springs at the northwest point of the Lacus Sabatinus (Lago di Bracciano) and entered the city at

Porta Aurelia, on the crest of the Janiculum. Much of the ancient channel has been destroyed or confused by the rebuilding of this aqueduct by Pope Paul V in 1605 (Acqua Paola). A large castellum of this water, from which many lead pipes radiated, was found in Vigna Lais on the Via Aurelia (*CIL* 15.7369–73). The channel within the city was discovered during the excavation for the construction of the American Academy (*MAAR* 1 [1917]: 59–61 [A. W. Van Buren and G. P. Stevens]). It ran grain mills just below this on the Janiculum and delivered water to every quarter of the city. It was cut by Vitiges in the siege of Rome in 537 (Procopius, *Bell-Goth* 5.19.13) and repaired by Belisarius (*CIL* 11.3298).

Van Deman 331–40; Ashby 1935, 299–307; Nash 1.52–54.

Aqua Virgo: an aqueduct built by Agrippa and completed on 9 June 19 B.C. (Frontinus, *Aq.* 1.10), the only one entering Rome from the north. The springs were located at the eighth mile of the Via Collatina, two miles to the left of the Via Praenestina, *in agro Lucullano*. It received its name from a young girl's having shown the springs to soldiers hunting water, an incident commemorated by a picture in a shrine there (Frontinus, *Aq.* 1.10). Frontinus calculated its length as 14,105 paces, 1,240 of these being above ground, 700 on arches; its volume at intake was 2,504 quinariae (Frontinus, *Aq.* 1.10; 2.84). It was the lowest of all aqueducts, except for the Appia and the Alsietina, but supplied the crucial zones of the Collis Hortulorum (Pincian) and Campus Martius, as well as the Thermae Agrippae. It was admired for its tactile quality and considered especially suited to bathing (Pliny, *HN* 31.42). In Frontinus's day it was without a piscina (*Aq.* 1.22), but later acquired one in the Horti Lucullani. From the Horti Lucullani it ran on arches, the arch in the modern Via del Nazzareno being the one by which it crossed a side street. The arch by which it crossed the Via Lata was rebuilt as a triumphal arch to Claudius (see Arcus Claudii [2]). It ran generally south from the end of the Pincian to Piazza Trevi, then west to skirt the north end of the Saepta Iulia, where it had its castellum (Fig. 18). It was repaired by Claudius in 46 after damage caused by Caligula (*CIL* 6.1252 = *ILS* 205, and cf. *CIL* 6.1253–54, 31565, *ILS* 5747) and again by Constantine (*CIL* 6.31564 = *ILS* 702). It was repeatedly repaired during the Middle Ages and early Renaissance and is in use today, its termination being marked by the Fontana di Trevi of Niccolo Salvi (1744).

Frontinus, *Aq.* 1.4, 10, 18, 22; 2.70, 84; Van Deman 167–78; Ashby 1935, 167–82; *CAR* 2-A, 2 p. 11; Nash 1.55–56; *QITA* 5 (1968): 125–60 (L.

Quilici); Pace 144–46; J. Pinto, *The Trevi Fountain* (New Haven, Conn. 1986).

Aquaeductium (Fig. 3): an area at the end of the Caelian branch of Aqua Claudia, so named on the Marble Plan (*FUR* pl. 16; Rodriguez pl. 2). Here a street runs along the east side of the aqueduct, while to the west is a large irregular area into which projects a series of at least fifteen parallel walls of very irregular lengths perpendicular to the aqueduct and evidently abutting on it. They are not shops, but might conceivably be storage chambers or stables, because they open on what seems to be a walled yard. The remains of the aqueduct piers show that here they were built into already existing buildings.

Aqueduct: see **Aqua.**

Aquilenses: found only in the edict of Tarracius Bassus of the late fourth century, *CIL* 6.31893 = *ILS* 6072; evidently those who lived in Vicus Longi Aquilae, a district in Regio XIV listed on the Capitoline Base (*CIL* 6.975.b26 = *ILS* 6073).

Ara: Altars, both in conjunction with temples and as independent dedications, are a feature of Roman religion from the earliest times. In fact, the independent altar seems to have been the commonest expression of piety in the early period, and it does not seem to have been necessary to inaugurate a templum before dedicating an altar, although we presume that was regularly done if the altar was to be permanent. The earliest altar in Rome is supposed to be the Ara Maxima Herculis Invicti between the Circus Maximus and the Porta Trigemina. Unfortunately, we do not know the form it took, and no positive trace of it has been found. Nor do we know about the altars dedicated by Titus Tatius, of which Varro (*Ling.* 5.74) gives a list: to Ops, Flora, Vediovis and Saturn, Sol, Luna, Vulcan and Summanus, Larunda, Terminus, Quirinus, Vertumnus, the Lares, Diana and Lucina. The earliest altars we have are not extremely old; they are the U-shaped altars of which bases survive in front of the temples of Fortuna and Mater Matuta in the Area Sacra di Sant'Omobono and under the Niger Lapis. At such altars the officiating priest stood at the space between the arms of the U, so that his altar in some sense enclosed him. A row of thirteen such altars came to light recently at Lavinium (F. Castagnoli et al., *Lavinium II, le tredici are* [Rome 1975]); these run in their original construction from the mid-sixth century B.C. to the mid-fourth, after which some were reworked. The sanctuary remained in operation at least through the second century. The altars of Sant'Omobono are believed to be early fourth century in date. Because the material under the Niger Lapis was gathered together as a deposit in the fourth century, that one must be older, although the character of the molding will not allow a very early date. This form of altar continued to be used until the mid-second century, as the Capitolium of Cosa shows, and in some sense the form of the altar of the Ara Pacis Augustae continues that tradition.

The rectangular altar regularly set on axis with its temple, when there is one, with its short end toward the temple, comes in sometime in the Hellenistic period, but probably not before the First Punic War in Rome. It can be of great size and high, but is usually not, because that made working at it very difficult. Usually it does not much exceed waist height and is proportioned to this with a squarish end and the principal face about twice as long as it is high. A good example of such an altar is that in peperino of A. Postumius Albinus in front of Temple C in the Area Sacra di Largo Argentina. This is referred by Marchetti Longhi with some hesitation to the consul of 180 B.C.; he would prefer an earlier date. But the excellent letter forms are not encouraging about this, and the freshness of the altar when it was buried following the construction of Temple B, which is dated about 100 B.C., suggests, if anything, a later date. The same altar form embellished with a Doric frieze at small scale just under the crown is used for the sarcophagus of L. Cornelius Scipio Barbatus, the date of which is debated but is usually put sometime in the third century (*ILLRP* 210; Nash 2.355). He died sometime after 280. Its letter forms are less refined. This form of altar seems to have been very popular until the time of Augustus; the altar of the Temple of Apollo in Pompeii, which is generally considered Augustan, has this form.

A small wasp-waisted or hourglass-shaped altar, usually low and with a square top surface, seems to have come into use about the time of the Second Punic War. An altar of Verminus in this form in peperino was found in the Agger near Porta Collina in 1876 (Nash 2.500). It bears an inscription recording that it is a restoration by the same A. Postumius Albinus who restored the altar of Largo Argentina discussed above and according to the same law. The letter forms are also in agreement (*ILLRP* 281). A similar altar in travertine dedicated by C. Sextius Calvinus to the unknown god was found in 1829 at the west corner of the Palatine (*ILLRP* 291); Degrassi considered the dedicator likely to be the son of the consul of 124 B.C. This certainly is of a more sophisticated shape than the altar of Verminus, rectangular rather than square, and with a pulvinate crown, and the use of travertine argues for a relatively late date. Yet a third altar of this shape, again,

a restoration of an older altar, this time in lava, bears a consular date of 9 B.C. (A. E. Gordon, *Illustrated Introduction to Latin Epigraphy* [Berkeley 1983], no. 27). So the form continued to be used even under the empire, though there are few examples of it. Beginning in the time of Augustus a roughly cubical or vertically rectangular form of altar seems to have become prevalent, especially an altar with a sculptured front, or even decorated on all sides, and a pulvinate crown. One sees these especially as funerary monuments, and they persist late into the empire.

Here we may note the Ara Pacis Augustae, but only with the warning that it is, so far as we know, unique, a particular solution to a demanding problem. It owes something to the great altars of Pergamum and Priene; it also owes something to the Parthenon frieze and perhaps a little to the Altar of Pity in the agora of Athens. But it is of a very innovative design, in part harking back to the ancient U-shaped altars of early Rome, in part breaking new ground as a ianus embellished with enigmatic reliefs. It should be noted that it did not initiate a new type of monument and apparently was never meant to. In fact, it defied copying.

Finally it should be observed that round altars are very rare in Rome, almost non-existent. Certainly round altars existed, but it is questionable whether any altar connected with a temple was ever round. The round base in front of the Temple of Apollo Medicus (Sosianus), once thought to be its altar, is now considered more probably a tholus; the so-called altar of Julius Caesar in a niche in the podium in front of the Temple of Divus Iulius is unlikely to be that and certainly not the altar of the temple. A round altar is shown in a sacrifice scene on coins of Julia Domna inscribed VESTA MATER (*B. M. Coins, Rom. Emp.* 5.314 no. 716) and another on coins of Septimius Severus, again in a scene of sacrifice, this time inscribed SACRA SAECVLARIA (*B. M. Coins, Rom. Emp.* 5.325 no. 810), but the Temple of Vesta did not have an altar, only a hearth, so the former must be an altar brought in for the occasion, and at the Ludi Saeculares sacrifice seems to have been offered not on the altar of Dis and Proserpina, but on altars erected especially for the occasion. We do not have many altars surviving from antiquity other than funerary altars. Doubtless the work of iconoclastic early Christians is largely responsible for that. But the absence of round altars in Rome is so complete that it will bear thinking about.

Ara Calvini: a small altar of archaic hourglass form in travertine, found in 1829 below the west corner of the Palatine (near Sant'Anastasia), inscribed SEI DEO SEI DEIVAI SAC, with the information that it was a restoration by the praetor C. Sextius Calvinus voted by the senate. The letter forms are republican, and it is usually dated ca. 92 B.C. (*CIL* 6.110 and 30701 = *ILS* 4015; *ILLRP* 291; Lugli 1946, 401–3; Broughton *MRR* 2.18). It is now in the Antiquario Palatino.

Ara Dei Ignoti: see **Ara Calvini.**

Ara Ditis: see **Dis Pater et Proserpina, Ara.**

Ara Domitii Ahenobarbi: see **Neptunus, Aedes.**

Ara Gentis Iuliae: see **Gens Iulia, Ara.**

Ara Marmorea: known only from two inscriptions found near Porta Capena (*CIL* 6.9403 = *ILS* 7713, *CIL* 6.10020 and *IGUR* 1342); it is clear from these that it was a place designation.

Ara Martis: see **Mars, Ara.**

Ara Maxima Herculis: see **Herculis Invicti, Ara Maxima.**

Arae Incendii Neronis: altars erected by Domitian in fulfillment of a vow made after the fire of Nero *incendiorum arcendorum causa* (*CIL* 6.826, 30837- = *ILS* 4914). They probably stood along the limit of the area devastated. The inscriptions of three exist in copies. One is recorded as having been used as building material for the basilica of S. Pietro in the sixteenth century. One was found in 1618 on the southwest side of the Circus Maximus at the foot of the Aventine, where there were also some remains of steps and cippi. This, too, was used as building material for S. Pietro. The third was discovered in 1889 on the Quirinal and is under Via del Quirinale no. 30, just southwest of the church of S. Andrea al Quirinale (Fig. 72). It stood on the southeast side of Alta Semita (q.v.) in a large area sunk three steps below the level of the street, paved with travertine and marked off by travertine cippi, which are set close to the lowest step at intervals of 2.50 m.

The altar itself is a travertine box, originally faced with marble of which little remains, set 2.75 m back from the cippi and mounted on a base of two steps. It is a long rectangle, 6.25 m deep. 3.25 m wide, and 1.26 m high, lacking its crown.

Annual sacrifice was decreed on these altars on the Volcanalia, 23 August. A number of other divinities received sacrifice on that day, notably the nymphs in the Campus Martius and Quirinus *in colle*. The officiating priest was the praetor *cui haec regio sorti obvenerit*.

Degrassi 500; Nash 1.60–62.

Ara Pacis Augustae: see **Pax Augusta, Ara.**

Ara Pietatis Augustae: see **Pietas Augusta, Ara.**

Ara Saturni: see **Saturnus, Ara.**

Arbor Sancta: listed in the regionary catalogues in Regio II. The relief of the divinities of the Caelian in the Palazzo dei Conservatori (Helbig[4] 2.1806) shows the Genius Caelimontis as a bearded figure, half-nude, seated on an irregular rocky hill, embracing the trunk of a tree with his left arm. The tree's trunk is curiously twisted; to judge from its leaf, it might be a laurel. That the tree was *sancta*, rather than *sacra*, implies that it was not associated with a cult but protected for some other reason, such as its oddness. There is no more precise indication of where it grew.

Arco di Camigliano: see **Isis, Aedes** (1).

Arco della Ciambella: see **Thermae Agrippae.**

Arco di Druso: see **Arcus Traiani, Divi.**

Arco di Latrone: see **Basilica Constantini.**

Arco dei Pantani: see **Forum Augustum.**

Arco di Portogallo: a late antique arch spanning Via Lata (Via Flaminia) just south of the Ara Pacis Augustae, often called Arcus Hadriani because of two reliefs that adorned its north face, now in the Palazzo dei Conservatori (Helbig[4] 2.1447, 1800). It was demolished in 1662 by Alexander VII in order to widen the Via del Corso, but a plaque on the east side of the street just south of Via della Vite marks its location. It got its name from the residence of the Portuguese ambassador in Palazzo Fiano in the sixteenth century; earlier it was called Arcus Octaviani.

It was certainly a very late construction, as is shown by the high level of its foundations, only 2.36 m below the level of the Via del Corso, as well as by its architectural character. It was a single-fornix arch, the masonry perhaps lightly rusticated up to the springing of the arch, adorned on either side with pairs of columns of verde antico on bases of a single torus above complicated bowed plinths, the capitals composite, carrying an entablature decorated with a frieze of acanthus scrolls that broke out forward over the columns. Between the pairs of columns on the north face, at the height of the spandrels, a pair of large reliefs was let into the wall. These are now in the Palazzo dei Conservatori (Helbig[4] 2.1447, 1800). They show the apotheosis of a woman borne aloft by a winged female figure and an *allocutio* (address) to which a Genius figure attends. They are generally supposed to be Hadrianic but are so heavily restored that one cannot be certain, but some of the male heads were certainly bearded. They certainly do not belong on a triumphal arch. The arch must be regarded as a pastiche of the fourth or fifth century, using material from older buildings.

The arch is shown before demolition in important drawings of Dosio, before 1569 (Nash 1: fig. 86), Alò Giovannoli, 1615 (PA pl. 2), and R. Schenck, before 1705 (Nash 1: fig. 85), among others.

BullCom 73 (1949–50): 101–22 (S. Stucchi); Nash 1.83–87; E. La Rocca, *Rilievi storici capitolini* (Rome 1986); Boatwright 226–29.

Arcus, Fornix, Ianus: Pliny (*HN* 34.27) says that the arch was used, like the column, to lift the statues mounted on it above other mortals, that is, that as an architectural form it was essentially a base for the statuary it carried. We may doubt this, however, because its character as a passageway and/or entrance must always have been strongly felt, and it must originally have found favor principally as a memorial for a triumph. Only in a triumph could a victorious general cross the pomerium of the city without first surrendering his *imperium,* and in the republican period the line of the Servian Walls was regarded as the pomerium.

The earliest arches that we hear of are those of Stertinius of 196 B.C. (Livy 33.27.4), but there may perhaps have been earlier examples. The use of sculptures and of apotropaic devices around city gates is presumably as old, or nearly as old, as stone fortifications themselves. The Lion Gate of Mycenae belongs to the Late Bronze Age, and the gates of Hattusa in Asia Minor to the beginning of the fourteenth century B.C. In Italy the fortifications of Falerii Novi are to be dated shortly after the deduction of the Latin colony there in 241 B.C., and the Porta dell' Arco of Volterra is probably still older. Two of Stertinius's arches seem to have stood as entrances to the precincts of Fortuna and Mater Matuta in the Forum Boarium, and because propylaea have a very long history, we can with some confidence see these as simply a variation on the concept of the city gate. Probably city gates were everywhere always decked with garlands and banners to welcome the return of a successful army, and the idea of putting a crowning array of appropriate trophies atop the entrance came early. But these would have been temporary embellishments, dismantled once the celebration was over, and the idea of isolating the gate and erecting it where it would be a permanent memorial crowned with a statuary group of the triumphator in his car may not have come before the end of the Second Punic War. Duilius's great naval victories in the First

Punic War were still commemorated with columns. But the quadriga driven by Jupiter that served as the central acroterion of the Temple of Iuppiter Optimus Maximus was a creation of the late sixth century, and it seems quite likely that a combination of such a group with the Porta Triumphalis to make a suitable memorial would have suggested itself easily. The main question, where to locate such a permanent memorial, must have been more difficult, for while one can imagine that a temporary embellishment of the Porta Triumphalis in this way occurred early, it could never have been thought of as anything but temporary. While there must have been numerous entrances to sacred precincts that might have lent themselves to development in the way that Stertinius seems to have employed those of Fortuna and Mater Matuta, it is not easy to see how and when that step was taken. If Stertinius's arches were the first memorial arches in Rome, they seem to have avoided being overtly triumphal. All that Livy says is that they were surmounted by gilded statues; there is no mention or suggestion of a chariot. The arch that Scipio Africanus built in 190 B.C. (Livy 37.3.7) *in Capitolio adversus viam qua in Capitolium escenditur* was adorned with seven gilded statues and two horses; again there is no mention of a chariot. But the location of this arch in proximity to the Clivus Capitolinus, but evidently neither spanning this nor a gateway to the Area Capitolina, but rather facing the Clivus Capitolinus at a right angle to the Area Capitolina, must have been chosen to suggest a close connection with the triumph. Thereafter, down to the time of Augustus, the arches that we hear of either spanned the route followed by the triumphal procession (Fornix Fabianus, Arcus Tiberii) or were not triumphal but commemorative (Arcus Drusi). The erection of arches to Drusus and Germanicus flanking the Temple of Mars Ultor in the Forum Augustum in A.D. 19 seems to mark a new departure, and thereafter an arch might be erected almost anywhere, although proximity to the route of the triumph seems always to have been an important consideration.

There seems to be no real distinction made between an *arcus* and a *fornix.* The terms are often used interchangeably, although fornix seems always to have carried some suggestion of being an entrance, while an arcus was rather a monument. The distinction between single and triple arches also seems to have been entirely functional. While most republican arches were single, the Porta Trigemina of the Servian Walls must have been triple from the time of its construction in the first half of the fourth century, while the Arcus Gallieni is an Augustan rebuilding of the Porta Esquilina as a triple arch, and the Augustan Arco di Augusto at Fano (Fanum Fortunae) is also triple. The single-arched triumphal arch may allude to the Porta Triumphalis, but at Cosa in central Etruria the main entrance to the forum is a freestanding triple arch that may have been triumphal and is considered to date from the second quarter of the second century B.C.

Cicero says (*Nat. D.* 2.67): *transitiones perviae . . . iani nominantur*. A *ianus* is therefore distinguished from an *arcus* and a *fornix* by being double, a door at either end of a short passage. These doors might be either arched or post-and-lintel. The Ianus Geminus of the Forum Romanum must have had post-and-lintel doors at least down to the early empire, but is shown on coins of Nero (*B. M. Coins, Rom. Emp.* 1.229–31 nos. 156–67) with segmental arches over its doors. A number of Etruscan ash urns also show this form with arched doors, and the arch as a recognized tomb form must also be regarded as essentially a *ianus*. On the other hand, the ianiform enclosure of the Ara Pacis Augustae has simple post-and-lintel doors. Another form of ianus, exemplified by the Ianus Quadrifrons of the Forum Boarium, is a quadrifrontal arch. This was probably the form of the ianus of the Forum Nervae (Transitorium) and turns up with surprising frequency elsewhere in the Roman world, while the simpler ianus is extremely uncommon.

Arcus Arcadii, Honorii et Theodosii:

an arch erected by the senate after the victory of Stilicho at Pollentia in A.D. 405 (*CIL* 6.1196 = *ILS* 798) to commemorate the victories of the three emperors over the Goths, often confused with the Arcus Gratiani, Valentiniani et Theodosii nearby. One arch stood under the campanile of the church of S. Celso, the other by Sant'Orso, or Urso. S. Celso is in the Via dei Banchi Vecchi, not far from the Ponte Sant' Angelo (HCh 237.17); Sant'Orso was destroyed in 1526 to make space for an oratorio of S. Giovanni dei Fiorentini, which was in turn destroyed in 1886 for the creation of the Corso Vittorio Emanuele (HCh 501–2). The arch in question may have spanned the street through the Campus Martius leading to the Pons Neronianus. The *Mirabilia* (Jordan 2.608; VZ 3.18) lists both, describing that at S. Celso as Arcus Aureus Alexandri, and that at Sant'Orso as Theodosii et Valentiniani et Gratiani Imperatorum. The Anonymous Magliabechianus of 1410–1415 (Urlichs 153; VZ 4.117) says that the arch by S. Celso had collapsed in the time of Pope Urban V, whereas that at Sant'Orso remained whole but was not of marble and lacked its inscription. The inscription preserved in the Einsiedeln sylloge says the Arch of Arcadius, Honorius, and Theodosius was decorated with their statues and trophies. The location of the arch is quite uncertain, and even its

identification, while highly probable, is not entirely above question. Modern topographers tend to put it at the end of the Pons Neronianus, but for this there is no real warrant.

Arcus Argentariorum: see Arcus Septimii Severi (in Foro Boario).

Arcus Augusti:

an arch erected to Augustus in 19 B.C. to celebrate the return of the standards of Crassus captured by the Parthians at Carrhae (Cass. Dio 51.19.1; 54.8.3). It is explicitly stated that this stood *iuxta aedem Divi Iulii* (Schol. Veron. *ad Verg. Aen.* 7.606), and on the southwest side of the temple footings for a triple arch have come to light (Fig. 48).

This has been reconstructed by R. Gamberini Mongenet using fragments of architecture found in the vicinity and in conformance with coins of Augustus showing a triple arch of an unusual type, a lofty central arch with an inscribed attic surmounted by a quadriga flanked by lower post-and-lintel fornices to either side that are supported on columns and surmounted by triangular gables crowned by figures of barbarians offering standards to the triumphator (*B. M. Coins, Rom. Rep.* 2.50 nos. 4477–78; see also Nash 1.92–101). Other coins showing more conventional arches may allude to arches erected to Augustus elsewhere (*B. M. Coins, Rom. Rep.* 2.551 no. 310; *B. M. Coins, Rom. Emp.* 1.73–74 Aug. nos. 427–29).

If the architectural fragments assigned to this arch are correctly assigned, it was very elaborately decorated, the Doric capitals having the echinus carved with an egg molding, and the modillions treated as massed guttae. The Fasti Capitolini Consulares et Triumphales were inscribed on the reveals of this arch and not on the Regia, as had been earlier supposed. See Degrassi, *Inscript. Ital.* 13.1.1–142, especially 17–19 and pls. 8–10.

RömMitt 85 (1978): 371–84 (H.-W. Ritter); *Kaiser Augustus und die verlorene Republik* (show catalogue, Berlin 1988, Mainz 1988), 224–39 (E. Nedergaard); *JRA* 2 (1989): 198–200 (F. Kleiner).

Arcus M. Aurelii:

an arch *in Capitolio* decreed by the senate in A.D. 176 to celebrate Marcus's victories over the Germans and Sarmatians. The inscription was included in the Einsiedeln sylloge (*CIL* 6.1014 = *ILS* 374), which is the only record of this. Its location is quite uncertain. It has been supposed to be the *arcus panis aurei* of the *Mirabilia* (Jordan 2.610; VZ 3.19) and the *arcus argentariorum* of a forged bull of Pope John III (A.D. 560–573), but without real reason (Jordan 2.669). Reliefs in the Palazzo dei Conservatori (Helbig⁴ 2.1444) or others reused on the attic of the Arcus Constantini (q.v.)

may have come from this arch (I. S. Ryberg, *Panel Reliefs of Marcus Aurelius* [New York 1967], especially 84–89).

RömMitt 91 (1984): 140–205 (E. Angelicoussis).

Arcus Aureus Alexandri: see Arcus Arcadii, Honorii et Theodosii.

Arcus Iohannis Basilii or Basilidis: the medieval

name of the travertine arch by which the Aqua Claudia crossed the Via Maior (LPD 2.345), leading from the Colosseum to the Lateran. It stood roughly midway between the basilica of S. Giovanni in Laterano and SS. Quattro Coronati. It was demolished in 1604 to make space for the Via di S. Giovanni but is clearly shown on the map of Du Pérac and Latrari of 1577. It got its name from the basilica of S. Giovanni and may once have served as an entrance to the Lateran enclave. It was also sometimes called Arcus Formae in recognition of its function.

HJ 242; LS 4.134; LA 154.

Arcus Caelimontani: see Arcus Neroniani.

Arcus Claudii (1): the travertine arch, in part rus-

ticated, by which the Aqua Virgo crossed one of the side streets east of Via Lata, rebuilt in monumental form by Claudius in A.D. 46 (*CIL* 6.1252 = *ILS* 205). It is still standing at Via del Nazzareno no. 14.

HJ 457; Nash 1: fig. 52.

Arcus Claudii (2): a triumphal arch voted by the

senate to Claudius in A.D. 51/52 in commemoration of the conquest of Britain (Cass. Dio 60.22.1). Inscriptions found in the neighborhood of Palazzo Sciarra belonging to such an arch indicate that this was a monumental rebuilding of the arch by which the Aqua Virgo crossed Via Lata (*CIL* 6.920–23 = 31203–4 = *ILS* 216, 222) and that many members of the imperial household were honored by statues on the arch. Fragments of reliefs showing scenes of combat, a temple, and Vestal Virgins have also been found in the same context (*NSc* 1925, 230–33 [G. Mancini]; *RendPontAcc* 11 [1935]: 41–61 [A. M. Colini]). Some of these clearly belong with others in the Villa Medici obtained from the Capranica della Valle collection. These were long believed to belong to the Ara Pietatis Augustae (see Pietas Augusta, Ara) but are now seen as panels from the Arch of Claudius. The program of the arch would seem to have included representation of the British campaign and the victory celebration following it and is the earliest such program of panel reliefs to come down to us.

Nash 1.74–78, 102–3; *NAkG* 1976: 64–108 (H.

R. Laubscher); *RömMitt* 90 (1983): 103–9 (G. Koeppel).

Arcus Claudii (3): A number of coins of Claudius

show a triumphal arch with an inscription *de Germanis,* or the like, celebrating the victories of Claudius's generals over the Cauchi and Chatti (Cass. Dio 60.8.7; *B. M. Coins, Rom. Emp.* 1 Claudius nos. 2, 36, 95–103, 121–23, 187–91). If such an arch was ever constructed, it seems not to have been in Rome.

H.-M. von Kaenel, *Münzprägung und Münzbildnis des Claudius* (Berlin 1986), 236–39.

Arcus Constantini (Figs. 3, 16, 90): an arch erec-

ted by the senate to Constantine in A.D. 315/316 (*CIL* 6.1139 = *ILS* 694); it was especially in honor of his victory over Maxentius, as the inscription attests, but celebrated his decennalia as well. There is no mention of it in the few literary sources we have for the period. It is a triple arch at the north end of the street between the Palatine and Caelian hills on the triumphal route between the Circus Maximus and the Forum Romanum, just before the ascent to the Summa Sacra Via. The passageways and surrounding area are paved with travertine; the arch is of white marble with the addition of much colored marble, the eight Corinthian columns flanking the archways being of giallo antico, the captives in front of the attic of pavonazzetto, the tondi set in a field of porphyry, and the main cornice having a band of porphyry. Overall it measures 25.70 m wide, 21 m high, and 7.40 m deep. There is no indication of what the program of the crowning sculptures might have been.

The decorative sculptures of the arch itself are of many periods, for the most part taken from other buildings. The reliefs of the bases of the columns are Constantinian and show Victorias, legionary soldiers, and captive barbarians. So are the medallions on the ends of the arch with reliefs of the sun and the moon. And around the arch just above the side arches runs a narrow frieze with episodes of the life of Constantine exemplifying his glory and his virtues. These begin on the west end and run counterclockwise: profectio, obsidio, proelium, ingressus, oratio, and liberalitas. The Victorias and river gods filling the spandrels are also Constantinian.

The other reliefs are two in the reveals of the central arch and two at the ends of the attic showing battles between Romans and Dacians, joining fragments of a frieze believed to come from the Forum Traiani (*ArchCl* 41 [1989]: 264–83 [S. Stucchi]), eight medallions set in pairs over the side arches showing hunting and sacrifice scenes, now generally referred to the period of Hadrian but of quite uncertain original setting, and eight rectangular panels in the attic apparently belonging to the same series as three in the Palazzo dei Conservatori (Helbig⁴ 2.1444) coming from an arch erected in A.D. 176 to celebrate the victories of Marcus Aurelius over the Germans and Sarmatians. In all these reliefs, heads of Constantine and Licinius have been substituted for those of the principal figures, but there is little alteration otherwise. The Dacian captives in front of the attic are believed to come from the Forum Traiani; their heads are modern, a repair of 1732.

The arch has been much studied from many points of view. The best publication of it is that of H. P. L'Orange and A. von Gerkan, *Der spätantike Bildschmuck des Konstantinsbogen* (Berlin 1939); see also Nash 1.104–12.

Arcus Divi Constantini: see **Ianus Quadrifrons** (1).

Arcus Diocletiani: see **Arcus Novus.**

Arcus Dolabellae et Silani: an unadorned arch of travertine built in A.D. 10 by the consuls P. Cornelius Dolabella and C. Iunius Silanus (*CIL* 6.1384) *ex S.C.* It stands over the modern Via di S. Paolo della Croce, on the line of the ancient Clivus Scauri, and must have been a rebuilding of one of the gates of the Servian Walls, Porta Querquetulana (or Querquetularia) or Porta Caelimontana, more likely the latter, although no road of importance seems to have left by this gate. Nero made use of the arch in his extension of the Aqua Claudia to the Caelian, taking the aqueduct across on it in the final stretch (see Arcus Neroniani).

Nash 1.113.

Arcus Domitiani: Of the multiple arches erected by Domitian to his own glory and for the most part pulled down after his damnatio memoriae (Suetonius, *Dom.* 13; Cass. Dio 68.1.1), the only ones that seem to have left some permanent record are one on the Clivus Palatinus, of which the footings survive (*BullCom* 91.2 [1986]: 522–25 [A. Cassatella]) and his rebuilding of the Porta Carmentalis/Scelerata/Triumphalis (q.v.). This he crowned with a pair of quadrigas drawn by elephants, he himself being the charioteer (Martial 8.65). Although his statue must have been removed after his death, at least one of the quadrigae remained and is shown on the profectio panel of Marcus Aurelius on the Arch of Constantine (L'Orange and von Gerkan, pl. 47.B; I. S. Ryberg, *Panel Reliefs of Marcus Aurelius* [New York 1967], pls. 22, 26). The gate with both quadrigas appears

on Domitianic coins (*B. M. Coins, Rom. Emp.* 2 pls. 71.6, 81.1).

Coarelli 1988, 363–414.

Arcus Drusi (1): a marble arch on the Via Appia erected by the senate after 9 B.C. in memory of Drusus the Elder (Suetonius, *Claud.* 3). It was adorned with trophies. If it gave its name to the Vicus Drusianus of Regio I, it may have stood near the junction of Via Appia and Via Latina, and the Via della Ferratella, which overlies an ancient road, may give the line of the Vicus Drusianus, but this is all very doubtful. The Einsiedeln itinerary (10) lists an Arcus Recordationis near the Baths of Caracalla, which might be the Arcus Drusi (see Jordan 2.660).

F. S. Kleiner, *The Arch of Nero in Rome* (Rome 1985): 33–34.

Arcus Drusi (2): an arch decreed by the senate for Drusus the Younger after his death in A.D. 23 (Tacitus, *Ann.* 4.9; cf. 2.83). If this was ever built, we have no idea where it was located.

Arcus Drusi et Germanici: a pair of arches erected in A.D. 19 on either side of the Temple of Mars Ultor in the Forum Augustum (Fig. 36). They closed the end of the forum below the ascent to the Subura and were surmounted by statues of those honored (Tacitus, *Ann.* 2.64; cf. *CIL* 6.911, 912 = 31199, 31200). Scant remains of these were found in the excavation of the forum.

Arcus Duo: on the Capitoline, known from a military diploma that specifies its location *intro euntibus ad sinistram in muro inter duos arcus* (*CIL* 16.20). The diploma is dated to A.D. 74. Presumably entrance to the Area Capitolina is meant, but the arches cannot be identified.

Arcus Gallieni: an arch faced with travertine replacing the Porta Esquilina where the Clivus Suburanus passed through the Servian Walls in modern Via di S. Vito. The architrave bears a dedication by M. Aurelius Victor to Gallienus and Salonina (*CIL* 6.1106 = *ILS* 548), but, as has been pointed out, the architecture and construction militate against the arch's having been built at this time. The central arch is proportioned to inscription of a full circle in its opening, and the design and sobriety of the moldings suggest an early imperial date. The arch was originally a triple-fornix arch, the side arches being narrower and lower than the central one, with unfluted pilasters and simplified Corinthian capitals framing each opening. The architraves were narrow, the frieze over the central fornix was deep, and the cornice was simple. Above the cornice nothing survives. The central arch is at present 7.16 m wide, 8.80 m high, and 3.38 m deep. Gatti calculated the side arches to have been 3.45 m wide, 5.53 m high, and 2.28 m deep.

Apparently Aurelius Victor embellished the attic with a program of statuary honoring Gallienus and his house and added an ornamental frieze in metal, the clamp holes for securing this being still visible. The proportions of the arch suggest that there never was an attic.

L'urbe 2 (1937): 4.16–26 (G. Lugli); Nash 1.115–17.

Arcus Germanici (1): a marble arch *in circo Flaminio* decreed by the senate among the honors awarded Germanicus posthumously, known from the Tabula Siarensis (*ZPE* 55 [1984]: 55–82 [J. Gonzàlez]) 1.9–21. This newly discovered inscription on bronze supplements what was known already from Tacitus (*Ann.* 2.83) and other inscriptions (*CIL* 6.911 = 31199; Tabula Hebana [Ruggiero, *Diz. Epigr.* 4.740–48]). The arch was to be erected at public expense near the place *(ad eum locum)* where statues of the deified Augustus and his house had been dedicated by C. Norbanus Flaccus. It was to carry gilded figures of the nations he had conquered and an inscription commemorating his military exploits and stating that he had died in the service of the state. On the arch were to be a statue of Germanicus in a triumphal chariot with, to either side, statues of his father, Drusus Germanicus, his mother, Antonia, his wife, Agrippina, his sister, Livia (Livilla), his brother, Tiberius Germanicus (Claudius), and his sons and daughters—eleven portrait statues in all in addition to that of the triumphator. Norbanus Flaccus was consul in A.D. 15, and presumably the dedication of statues of the deified Augustus and his house was one of the honors voted close after Augustus's death. The question of where this might have been most appropriately erected is a difficult one. Presumably the program was similar to that for Germanicus and included both his natural father and his adoptive one, his mother, his wife, Livia, and his sister, Octavia, the two grandsons he had adopted, and Tiberius. This makes only seven, in addition to Augustus, but they were all adult, whereas four of the children of Germanicus were still under ten at the time of his death. Everything points to the two programs having been thought of as counterparts and to have been set complementary to each other. On the Marble Plan (*FUR* pl. 29; Rodriguez pl. 23) an arch is shown between the Porticus Octaviae and the Theatrum Marcelli. The short southeast end of the Circus Flaminius with the Theatrum Marcelli as background would have made a very appropriate lo-

cation for a statue group commemorating Augustus. Because Eugenio La Rocca has recently convincingly demonstrated that the passage between the Temple of Apollo Medicus and the Theatrum Marcelli was far too narrow to have permitted the triumphal procession to pass and that instead it must have gone through the parodoi of the theater to reach the Porta Triumphalis, this would make an appropriate location for the arch of Germanicus.

ArchCl 36 (1984): 329–32 (F. Castagnoli).

Arcus Germanici (2): see **Arcus Drusi et Germanici.**

Arcus Gordiani: see **Castra Praetoria.**

Arcus Gratiani, Valentiniani et Theodosii: built between 379 and 383 by these three emperors, *pecunia sua*, often confused with the nearby Arcus Arcadii, Honorii et Theodosii. This one stood near the church of S. Celso (HCh 237) at the approach to the Pons Aelius (Ponte Sant'Angelo) and may have served as a monumental approach to this. The inscription (*CIL* 6.1184 = *ILS* 781) states explicitly that it was designed to close the Porticus Maximae (q.v.). It is mentioned in the Einsiedeln itinerary (2.2 and 7.2), the *Mirabilia* (Jordan 2.608; VZ 3.18), and the Ordo Benedicti (Jordan 2.664 and 665). It is said to have collapsed in the time of Pope Urban V (1362–1370).

BullCom 21 (1893): 20–21 (R. Lanciani); HJ 598–99.

Arcus Hadriani: see **Arco di Portogallo.**

Arcus ad Isis: the name inscribed on the attic of an arch at the extreme left of the relief of the Haterii (Helbig[4] 1.1076). Because the buildings shown on this relief seem to have been juxtaposed arbitrarily and even their character only schematically rendered, it is impossible to make a definite identification. The arch shown is a triple-fornix arch, and the attic is crowned with a large collection of statuary, including a central quadriga flanked by pairs of captives at the foot of palm trees, flanked in turn by trophies. The arch itself has columns on plinths framing the openings and is covered with reliefs in which arms and the *instrumentum sacrum* figure prominently. A statue on a plinth fills each opening. The central one is possibly Minerva, armed, and the others are female, but not positively identifiable.

The arch has been identified as just possibly the Arco di Camigliano (or Camillo), a triple arch that led into the complex of the Iseum Campense from the east, just west of Piazza del Collegio Romano (Figs. 46, 47). Its program has been thought to be

Isiac, but the most obvious symbols are missing. The last parts of this arch were destroyed in the sixteenth century, and nothing is known to survive from it. Recently it has been proposed that it is an arch of Vespasian of uncertain location.

MemNap 24 (1906): 229–62, especially 232–33 (G. Spano); *RendPontAcc* 20 (1943–44): 124–37 (G. Gatti); Nash 1.118–19; Helbig⁴ 1.778–79 no. 1076 (H. Speier); *RömMitt* 97 (1990): 131–34 (F. S. Kleiner).

Arcus Latronis: see **Basilica Constantini.**

Arcus Lentuli et Crispini: a travertine arch erected by the consuls of A.D. 2, P. Lentulus Scipio and T. Quinctius Crispinus Valerianus (*CIL* 6.1385), between the church of S. Maria in Cosmedin and the river. The wording of the inscription is exactly that of the Arcus Dolabellae et Silani (q.v.), and it follows that this was a rebuilding of Porta Trigemina of the Servian Walls. Poggio (VZ 4.232) says it spanned the road running between the Aventine and the Tiber, so the foot of the Clivus Publicius must have been just inside the wall. Our sources do not say whether it was triple or had originally been triple, but Biondo Flavio (*Roma Instaurata* 1.20 = VZ 4.264), who saw it in ruins in the mid-fifteenth century, uses the plural.

Arcus Neroniani (Fig. 16): a branch of the Aqua Claudia (q.v.) built by Nero from Ad Spem Veterem to the Temple of Divus Claudius at the end of the Caelian, a bridge about two kilometers long, still well preserved for most of its course (Frontinus, *Aq.* 1.20; 2.76, 87). At Piazza della Navicella on the Caelian the aqueduct branched, without the introduction of a castellum, one branch carrying water to the Aventine with a termination near the church of S. Prisca (*CIL* 6.3866 = 31963 = *ILS* 5791; LA 157–58), but of this there are no remains visible today. Another branch, perhaps built by Domitian, took water from the Temple of Divus Claudius across the valley between the Caelian and Palatine to the Palatine. Of this there are spectacular remains in two tiers of arches, but a siphon was probably necessary.

The aqueduct is mentioned frequently in the postclassical period, often by the name Forma Claudiana or Forma Lateranense, sometimes simply Forma, as in the name of the church of S. Tommaso de Formis. It was repaired and kept in use well into the Middle Ages.

Archaeologia 100 (1966): 81–104 (P. K. Baillie Reynolds and T. A. Bailey); *BullCom* 86 (1978–79): 137–40 (P. Romeo); *AJA* 87 (1983): 392–99 (H. B. Evans).

Arcus Neronis: an arch decreed to Nero for Corbulo's victories in the East in A.D. 58, built in A.D. 62, and probably dismantled soon after Nero's damnatio memoriae (Tacitus, *Ann.* 13.41, 15.18). It stood *in medio Capitolini montis* and is well shown on coins of Nero (*B. M. Coins, Rom. Emp.* 1 Nero nos. 183–90, 329–34) as a single-fornix arch surmounted by a quadriga led on by Victoria and Pax. Figures of Roman soldiers at a lower level crowned the corners. The face of the arch seems to have been covered with an elaborate program of reliefs, and a large figure of Mars stood against one end.

F. S. Kleiner, *The Arch of Nero in Rome* (Rome 1985).

Arcus Novus: mentioned in the regionary catalogues in Regio VII and assigned by the Chronographer of 354 (Chron. 148) to Diocletian. This seems to have been a marble arch that spanned Via Lata at the northeast corner of the church of S. Maria in Via Lata. It was destroyed by Pope Innocent VIII (1488–1492). The last vestiges of the arch were removed in deep excavations hunting building material and antiquities in 1523 (LS 1.217–19). Fragments of a relief found here in the sixteenth century are now in Villa Medici and show that the arch was erected to commemorate the decennalia of Diocletian; these are identified by their inscriptions: VOTIS X ET XX (*CIL* 6.31383) as those that Marliano saw at S. Maria in Via Lata with other *trophaea et triumphales imagines* (*Urbis Romae Topographia* [Rome 1534], 136). This has led Kähler to identify two bases in the Boboli Gardens in Florence as coming from this arch (H. Kähler, *Zwei Sockel eines Triumphbogens im Boboligarten zu Florenz* [*BWPr* 96 (1936)]). This seems a near certainty. L. Cozza has identified three more fragments of reliefs in the Villa Medici as belonging with the VOTIS fragment (*BdA* 43 [1958]: 109–11); from subject and style, this also seems highly likely to be right. If so, the relief showed Virtus and Roman legionary soldiers celebrating the submission and pacification of the East, while female figures with mural crowns knelt in adoration of the inscription of a shield. The bases showed Victorias with palms and trophies, the Dioscuri, and bearded and trousered barbarian captives accompanied by Roman soldiers.

A considerable difference in style between the bases and the other fragments of relief indicates that the arch was, like that of Constantine, created in part *ex novo*, in part by the reuse of decorations and reliefs robbed from other monuments. The bases are probably Diocletianic, while the other fragments belong in the second century. The shield being inscribed would have been recut, as indeed it appears.

Nash 1.120–25; *NAkG* 1976: 64–108 (H. R. Laubscher).

Arcus Octaviani (1): an arch decreed to Octavian after Actium, to be erected in the forum (Cass. Dio 51.19.1). At the same time a second arch was decreed to be erected at Brundisium; evidently both were in preparation for Octavian's triumphant return. An inscription on a block of Parian marble 9 feet (2.67 m) long with a decree of public honors to Octavian and a consular date of 29 B.C. has been supposed to come from this arch (*CIL* 6.873 = *ILS* 81). It was found toward the southeast end of the forum in the sixteenth century, but the reports of its provenience are confused and contradictory, and no ancient source locates it more precisely. No other trace of it is known, but it may be shown on a denarius (*B.M. Coins, Rom. Rep.* 2:14 no. 4348).

Kaiser Augustus und die verlorene Republik (show catalogue, Berlin 1988, Mainz 1988), 224–25 (E. Nedergaard).

Arcus Octaviani (2): see **Arco di Portogallo.**

Arcus Octavii: Pliny (*HN* 36.36) says that Augustus dedicated to the honor of his father a work of Lysias, a quadriga with figures of Apollo and Diana carved from a single block of stone. This was in an aedicula adorned with columns atop an arch on the Palatine. Clearly this arch served simply as a base and was not triumphal, and the aedicula was probably more a canopy than anything else. This Lysias may be identical with the Lysias who was the son of Pyrrhandros of Chios, known from his signature on the acropolis of Lindos, but is otherwise unknown.

Historia 37 (1988): 347–51 (F. S. Kleiner).

Arcus Panis Aurei: an arch *in Capitolio* mentioned in the *Mirabilia* (Jordan 2.610; VZ 3.19), otherwise unknown, but see Arcus M. Aurelii.

Arcus Pietatis: an arch in the Campus Martius mentioned in the *Mirabilia* (Jordan 2.630; VZ 3.49) in connection with the Temple of Divus Hadrianus and the church of S. Maria in Aquiro. Other sources put it near the church of the Maddalena (Anon. Magliabech. [Urlichs 155; VZ 4.122] and a will of 1403). After a careful study of the question, Hülsen decided that it should span the Via delle Colonnelle just east of the Maddalena and be an arch that originally led from the forecourt north of the Pantheon east to the precinct of the Temple of Matidia, a passage of minor importance. He also points out that in the centuries after A.D. 1000 the name Arcus Pietatis came to be applied to several monumental arches of antiquity, including the Arch of Titus. Therefore, it is possible that we are dealing with more than one arch here, because the precincts of the temples of Divus Hadrianus and Matidia, as well as the Pantheon,

can all be presumed to have had monumental entrances. However, a monumental arch in the middle of the forecourt of the Pantheon, although proposed for the Arcus Pietatis by many, is very unlikely.

RendPontAcc 4 (1925–26): 291–303 (C. Hülsen); K. de Fine Licht, *The Rotunda in Rome* (Copenhagen 1968), 25–34.

Arcus Pompeii: an arch described by Magister Gregorius in the twelfth century (*De Mirabilibus* 24, VZ 3.161). According to him, it celebrated Pompey's triumph over Mithridates in 61 B.C. This cannot be accepted without other support; Magister Gregorius had a lively imagination and describes monuments that did not exist outside of it, such as the arch of Augustus described in great detail just before this (*De Mirabilibus* 22, VZ 3.159–60).

Arcus Recordationis: see **Arcus Drusi** (1).

Arcus Septimii Severi (Figs. 19, 40, 41): an arch in the Forum Romanum at the northwest end of the Sacra Via, in front of, but not on axis with, the Aedes Concordiae. The inscription on both sides of the attic (*CIL* 6.1033 = *ILS* 425; cf. *CIL* 6.31230) states that the arch was erected by the senate in A.D. 203 to Septimius Severus, Caracalla, and Geta in honor of conquests in the East. Later the name of Geta in the fourth line was chiseled away, and further honorific titles for Septimius and Caracalla were added in its place. The bronze letters have been robbed out, but the matrices for them survive, and the holes for clamps permit restoration of the original text in the fourth line. The arch is a triple-fornix arch of Pentelic marble on a base of travertine, which was concealed by short flights of steps leading up to the arch on the forum side. In the middle of the fourth century, the level of the forum in this area was lowered and much longer stairs were installed, but apparently in antiquity no road ever ran through the arch. Overall, the arch measures approximately 25 m wide, 23 m high, and 11.35 m deep. The central arch is 12 m high and 7 m wide; the side arches are 7.80 m high and 3 m wide. The side arches communicate with the central passage by vaulted passages; these, as well as the other passages, have coffered ceilings.

The openings are framed by fluted columns in front of pilasters with composite capitals that carry a deep entablature that breaks out from the face of the arch over them and runs around all four faces. The high plinths on which the columns are raised are embellished on the three exposed faces with reliefs showing soldiers leading captive barbarians. The spandrels are filled with river gods over the side arches and Victorias carrying trophies above figures of the seasons over the central arch. The keystones have reliefs of divinities. Just above the keystones of the side arches runs a narrow frieze showing parts of a triumphal procession, prisoners presented to the goddess Roma, groups of soldiers, carts loaded with the spoils, and allegorical figures representing provinces. Above this are four great panels showing panoramas of the campaigns in multiple registers woven together irregularly to produce a vivid confusion. These are the great glory of the arch, masterpieces of design.

The inscription fills the whole of the face of the deep attic, within which there are four vaulted chambers accessible by a stair in the southwest pier with a concealed door in the south end at the height of the springing of the side arches. The arch is shown on coins of Septimius and Caracalla surmounted by a six- or eight-horse chariot carrying Septimius Severus and Victoria and led by Caracalla and Geta (?). This group is flanked by equestrian figures facing toward the ends (Caracalla and Geta?). All trace of these has disappeared (*B. M. Coins, Rom. Emp.* 5.216n.320; *RIC* 4.124 no. 259).

L. Franchi, "Ricerche sull'arte di età severiana a Roma" (*StMisc* 4, Rome 1964), 20–32; R. Brilliant, *The Arch of Septimius Severus in the Roman Forum* (*MAAR* 29, Rome 1967); Nash 1.126–30; *RendPontAcc* 55–56 (1982–84): 299–313 (R. Nardi); *Roma, archeologia nel centro* (1985), 1.34–40 (R. Masini et al.), 41–55 (R. Nardi).

Arcus Septimii Severi (in Foro Boario), Arcus Argentariorum, Monumentum Argentariorum

(Fig. 37.18): modern names given to a post-and-lintel monumental doorway of marble on a travertine base at the southwest corner of the façade of the church of S. Giorgio in Velabro, the campanile being in part supported by one pier and encasing two of its sides in its masonry. The inscription (*CIL* 6.1035 = *ILS* 426; cf. *CIL* 6.31232) declares that it was erected in A.D. 204 by the *argentarii et negotiantes boarii huius loci qui invehent.* Here *qui invehent* is a later correction, and probably *invehent* should be *invehunt,* while *boarii* is probably only a place designation. The dedicators are probably the auctioneer/bankers and wholesale merchants of the district (see Forum Boarium), and this is probably the entrance to their collegiate schola. The dedication was made to Septimius Severus, Caracalla, Geta, Julia Domna, Fulvia Plautilla (wife of Caracalla), and Fulvius Plautianus (father-in-law of Caracalla). Following the murder of Plautianus and his damnatio memoriae in 205, his name and titles were erased; following the murder of Plautilla in 211, so were hers, and other honorific titles of Caracalla were substituted. Following the murder of Geta in 212, his name was erased and other substitutions made. The

monument is 6.15 m high and the same in width overall, the opening 3.30 m wide.

The decoration of the marble posts is very rich. The main face on the Vicus Tuscus (?) showed single large figures, bearded and togate, above small panels of animals being led to sacrifice, framed by pilasters with composite capitals. The pilasters are decorated with busts, and the inscription is flanked by reliefs of Hercules and the Genius Populi Romani. The most important reliefs are those of the reveals. They showed Septimius Severus, Julia Domna, and Geta sacrificing on a tripod on one, and Caracalla, Fulvia Plautilla, and Fulvius Plautianus on the other. As those shown suffered damnatio memoriae, their figures were chiseled away. Below the main panels were scenes of sacrifice of large cattle; above are Victorias and garlands. The pilasters on these faces are decorated with acanthus scrolls. On the visible end (west) is a group of two legionary soldiers and two Oriental captives above a panel showing a drover and below a panel of camilli flanking a thymiaterion. The north face is without reliefs or elaborate decorative carving, an indication that it was not on public view.

D. E. L. Haynes and P. E. D. Hirst, *Porta Argentariorum* (London 1939); M. Pallottino, *L'arco degli argentarii* (Rome 1946); Nash 1.88–91.

Arcus Stertinii: see **Fornices Stertinii.**

Arcus Stillans: an ancient landmark identified by the scholiast on Juvenal 3.11 as an aqueduct crossing the valley between the Caelian and Aventine on or inside Porta Capena. This would have to have been a bridge of the Aqua Marcia, although no trace of such a bridge has ever been found. The identification is then repeated in the *Mirabilia* (Jordan 2.615; VZ 3.23) of the twelfth century. But it is a misidentification to explain Juvenal's phrase *madidamque Capenam.* Marchetti Longhi (*RendPontAcc* 3 [1924–25]: 143–90) has shown that in a spurious bull of Paschal II of 1116, in which local names have been taken from authentic documents, the reference to a church *in urbe Roma ecclesiam S. Laurentii de ///// que est iuxta arcum stillantem cum omnibus pertinentiis suis et omnes curtes quas habetis in regione Schole Grece* must be to a church near the Tiber not far from the Pons Aemilius. The Arcus Stillans must then be the arch at Porta Romana (or Romanula) *ubi ex epistylio defluit aqua* (Festus 318L).

Arcus Tiberii: a single-fornix arch erected in A.D. 16 *propter aedem Saturni,* to commemorate the recovery of the standards of Varus captured by the Germans in A.D. 9 (Tacitus, *Ann.* 2.41). It stood near the northwest corner of the Basilica Iulia beside the street along the southwest side of the forum, which narrows here to accommodate it, and is represented on the Arch of Constantine (L'Orange and A. von Gerkan, pl. 14). It stood above the level of the forum and probably could be reached only by a stair of a few steps. The inscription has been recovered in fragments (*CIL* 6.906, 31422, 31575), and the concrete foundations, found in excavations in 1900, were 9 m wide and 6.30 m deep.

BullCom 31 (1903): 163–64 (D. Vaglieri); Lugli 1946, 151–52; Nash 1.131–32.

Arcus Tiberii (in Campo Martio): mentioned only by Suetonius (*Claud.* 11.3), who says a marble arch was decreed by the senate to Tiberius *iuxta* (near) the Theater of Pompey, *verum omissum,* and completed by Claudius. It is quite uncertain where it stood.

Arcus Tiburii or Diburi: evidently a corruption of the word *Divorum* (q.v.) and a medieval designation for the monumental arch by which this was entered, remains of which were still standing in the eleventh century.

RömMitt 18 (1903): 28–30 (C. Hülsen); HJ 566–67.

Arcus Titi (1) or **Arcus Vespasiani et Titi:** erected by the senate in A.D. 80–81 to commemorate the capture and destruction of Jerusalem. The inscription is preserved only in the Einsiedeln sylloge (*CIL* 6.944 = *ILS* 264), where it is reported to have been found on an arch in the Circus Maximus. There is no reason to doubt this, and the probability is that this was an arch at the apex of the sphendone of the circus.

Arcus Titi (2) (Figs. 63, 90, 92): a single-fornix arch still standing, though much restored, *in summa Sacra Via* (but probably not to be identified with the Arcus *in summa Sacra Via* shown on the relief of the Haterii in the Vatican Museum [Helbig⁴ 1.1076]). It was erected to Titus after his death, as the inscription (*CIL* 6.945 = *ILS* 265) informs us, to commemorate the capture of Jerusalem. The reliefs of the reveals show the princeps as triumphator in a quadriga and the spoils of the temple of Solomon. A relief in the crown of the coffering of the ceiling shows the apotheosis of Titus. Bronze elephants that are known to have been on the Sacra Via in A.D. 535–536 (Cassiodorus, *Var.* 10.30) very likely belonged to a quadriga showing the deified princeps in glory, an iconography familiar from coins. The arch is not mentioned in ancient literature, and in the medieval period it was built into a fortress of the Frangipani. In 1822 it was freed from the constructions around

it and restored by Valadier, the missing portions being reproduced in travertine.

The foundations rest on the pavement of the Clivus Palatinus; it has therefore been supposed that it originally stood farther north and was removed and rebuilt in its present location at the time of the construction of the Temple of Venus et Roma. However, it is more likely that it simply stands on a pre-Neronian pavement and was hemmed in by the nearby parts of the Domus Aurea. It is 13.50 m wide, 4.75 m deep, and 15.40 m high; the archway is 5.36 m wide and 8.30 m high. The whole was faced with Pentelic marble. On each side of the arch is a pair of engaged columns with fluted shafts and composite capitals, one of the earliest uses of this order. In each pier, in lieu of reliefs, is a rectangular, windowlike niche. The spandrels have reliefs of flying Victorias; the keystones show figures probably representing Virtus (toward the Colosseum) and Honos. On the frieze of the entablature running around the arch was shown the triumphal procession at small scale in very high relief. Only part of the frieze on the east face is preserved, perhaps one-quarter of the whole, but among the things shown is a river god on a ferculum, believed to represent the Jordan River. Despite its simplicity, the arch is a remarkably harmonious structure of elegant proportions, a model for single-fornix arches for the next century.

Nash 1.133–35; *RömMitt* 82 (1975): 99–116 (F. Magi); *RömMitt* 84 (1977): 331–47 (F. Magi); *BullCom* 88 (1982–83): 92–93 (E. Rodriguez Almeida); M. Pfanner, *Der Titusbogen* (Mainz 1983).

Arcus de Tosectis: the popular name for a marble arch cited by the Anonymous Magliabechianus in the early fifteenth century (Urlichs 154; VZ 4.120). It is possible that the Arcus Novus of Diocletian (see Arcus Novus) near the church of S. Maria in Via Lata is meant (HJ 470). The Arcus de Tosectis was ruinous at the time of the Anonymous Magliabechianus, and the inscription could not be made out, but he believed it was built for Antoninus Pius (see VZ 3.19–20n.6).

Arcus ad Tres Falciclas, Tripolis, and **Trofoli:** late popular names applied to the Arco di Portogallo (q.v.) found in the *Liber Pontificalis* (cf. Jordan 2.415–16).

Arcus Traiani: see **Forum Traiani.**

Arcus Divi Traiani: listed in the regionary catalogues in Regio I, perhaps the Arco di Druso just inside the Porta S. Sebastiano (Porta Appia). One notes especially the steep and strongly marked pediment thrust forward from the face of the arch and supported on freestanding columns to either side, which are Trajanic features (but see Richmond, 138–39). The Arco di Druso was built into the Aqua Alexandrina and carried the aqueduct across the Via Appia. This must be the Forma Iovia (or Iobia) of the Einsiedeln itinerary (but see *MemLinc,* ser. 3.4 [1880]: 318–19 [R. Lanciani]). If Lanciani is right that the name Iovia came to be applied to the whole system of the Marcia, that must have been later, for the itinerary distinguishes between them (see VZ 2.173).

The arch shown on coins of A.D. 104–111 (*B. M. Coins, Rom. Emp.* 3: Trajan nos. 842–46 pl. 31.6–9), often thought to be this arch, is now believed to be a Trajanic rebuilding of the entrance to the Area Capitolina, as the inscription IOM proclaims.

Nash 1.79–80.

Arcus Divi Veri (**Parthici,** *Not.*): listed in the regionary catalogues in Regio I together with the Arcus Traiani and Arcus Drusi, so probably an arch spanning the Via Appia, but nothing is known about it. A relief in the Museo Torlonia possibly showing the submission of barbarians to Lucius Verus has been associated with it (S. Reinach, *Répertoire de reliefs grecs et romains,* 3 vols. (Paris 1909–12), 1.249; F. Matz and F. von Duhn, *Antike Bildwerke in Rom* [Leipzig 1882], 3.42–43 no. 3526) but without sufficient reason. Hülsen (HJ 216) supposes the arch may have lain outside the Porta S. Sebastiano near the Almo.

Arcus Vespasiani et Titi: see **Arcus Titi** (1).

Area: see **Forum, Area, Compitum.**

Area Apollinis: listed in the regionary catalogues in Regio I. It is possibly what is shown on fragment 469 of the Marble Plan inscribed]REA APO[. This can be read as a square altar or statue base mounted on a podium approached by two flights of four steps on opposite sides, which seems to have stood in a large open area. But this fragment has recently been assigned by Rodriguez (Rodriguez 99 and pl. 14; cf. *FUR* pl. 50) to the Area Apollinis on the Palatine.

Area Calles: added by the *Notitia* to the Area Apollinis et Splenis of Regio I. The reading is very doubtful, and the monument is otherwise unknown.

Area Callisti: a place designation found inscribed on a late antique slave collar as Ara Callisti (*CIL* 15.7193). It has been supposed to be in the Transti-

berim near the church of S. Maria in Trastevere, which was founded by Pope Calixtus I in 217–222. He was believed to have been martyred in the near vicinity, and the present church of S. Callisto is thought to stand on the site of his house (HCh 234).

Area Candidi: mentioned only in the *Notitia* as a place in Regio VI, listed following X Tabernae and Gallinae Albae. It is therefore commonly put toward the south end of the Viminal near the church of S. Pudenziana (HJ 374). As an area, it should have been an open space or square, rather than a district.

Area Capitolina (Fig. 19): the precinct of the Temple of Iuppiter Optimus Maximus (Capitolinus) on the southern summit of the Capitoline Hill. It seems to have surrounded the temple and to have been irregular, created by the construction of retaining walls following the configuration of the hill and by leveling the area inside these (Livy 25.3.14; Vell. Pat. 2.3.2; A. Gellius 2.10.2). It was enlarged at least once, in 388 B.C. (Livy 6.4.12) and was regarded as an impressive accomplishment. Along the front and sides of the temple the space would have extended about 30–40 m, perhaps more in front, while in back, toward the Campus Martius, it was narrow, but sufficient for a processional way (Pliny, *HN* 8.161). Probably when other temples were added, annexes were added to accommodate them.

The principal entrance was in the middle of the southeast side, the terminus of the Clivus Capitolinus opposite the façade of the temple and the Fores Capitolini (Suetonius, *Aug.* 94.9; Tacitus, *Hist.* 3.71). The Porta Pandana (q.v.) must have been a secondary entrance, perhaps at the top of the Centum Gradus (q.v.). The area was surrounded by a wall and was closed at night and guarded by dogs under the charge of a temple attendant, in whose quarters Domitian hid when the Capitoline fell to the assault of the Vitellians (Cicero, *Rosc. Am.* 56; A. Gellius 6.1.6; Tacitus, *Hist.* 3.74). Geese sacred to Juno were also kept in the area (Cicero, *Rosc. Am.* 56; Dion. Hal. 13.7). Under the surface of the area were subterranean chambers called *favissae,* in which damaged material from the temple, old dedications, and dedications that could not be displayed were deposited (*Roma sotterranea* 271–75 [A. Cassatella]). These could not be tampered with (Paulus *ex Fest.* 78L; A. Gellius 2.10.2). Porticoes lined part of the edge of the area on the interior, at least toward the front, some of them built by Scipio Nasica as censor in 159 B.C. (Vell. Pat. 2.1.2; Tacitus, *Hist.* 3.71).

Within the Area Capitolina were numerous buildings: the Casa Romuli, the Aedes Tensarum, the Tribunal Vespasiani, Titi et Domitiani, a library and an atrium publicum, as well as several temples: of Fides, Iuppiter Feretrius, Iuppiter Custos, Iuppiter Tonans, Ops, Mars Ultor (?), Fortuna Primigenia (?), and probably Mens and Venus Erucina (qq.v.). Some of these may have stood only briefly; others were important and venerable. The Temple of Fides was probably near the southwest corner of the precinct. There were also many altars, in addition to the great altar of Jupiter: to Iuppiter Sutor, Isis et Serapis, Bellona, Genius Populi Romani (together with Felicitas and Venus Victrix), Gens Iulia, and possibly Indulgentia (qq.v.).

There were many statues of divinities in the area and in the temples (Servius *ad Aen.* 2.319). One of Jupiter of colossal size was erected by Sp. Carvilius in 293 B.C., so large that it could be seen from the precinct of Iuppiter Latiaris on the Alban Mount (Pliny, *HN* 34.34 and 43). Another mounted on a column was enlarged and turned to the east in 63 B.C. (Cicero, *Cat.* 3.20; *Div.* 1.20; Cass. Dio 37.9.1 and 34.3–4; Obsequens 61). In 305 B.C. a colossus of Hercules was dedicated there (Livy 9.44.16), and in 209 a bronze colossus of Hercules by Lysippus from Tarentum (Plutarch, *Fabius Maximus* 22.6; Pliny, *HN* 34.40; Strabo 6.3.1 [278]). There were statues of Mars (Cass. Dio 41.14.3), Liber Pater (*CIL* 16.10), Iuppiter Africus (*CIL* 16.21, 31) and Nemesis (Pliny, *HN* 11.251, 28.22). Statues of distinguished Romans were frequently erected in the area, probably both in the open area and in the various temples. Those in the open area seem to have included a set of statues of the kings of Rome and Brutus (Cass. Dio 43.45.3–4; Asconius *ad Scaur.* [Stangl 29]; Pliny, *HN* 34.22–23, 33.9–10 and 24; Appian, *BellCiv* 1.16), L. Scipio (Cicero, *Rabir.* 27; Val. Max. 2.6.2), M. Aemilius Lepidus (Val. Max. 3.1.1), the Metelli (Cicero, *Att.* 6.1.17), Q. Marcius Rex (*CIL* 16.4), T. Seius (Pliny, *HN* 18.16), Pinarius Natta (Cicero, *Div.* 2.47), Domitian (Suetonius, *Dom.* 13.2), Claudius (S.H.A. *Claud.* 3.4), Aurelian (S.H.A. *Tac.* 9.2). Periodically these became so numerous that some had to be removed; Augustus transferred a number to the Campus Martius (Suetonius, *Calig.* 34.1).

Trophies of victory (Marius: Plutarch, *Caes.* 6.1; Suetonius, *Iul.* 11; Germanicus: *CIL* 16.32) and votive offerings of every sort were thickly strewn here. A wholesale clearance of these was ordered in 179 B.C. and again under Augustus (Livy 40.51.3; Suetonius, *Calig.* 34.1). Bronze tablets containing treaties and laws and military diplomas were commonly fastened to the walls of buildings, statue bases, altars, and so forth; these must have been removed periodically. It is difficult to see how the clutter was

kept from interfering with the functioning of the temple.

Lugli 1946, 19–36.

Area Carboniana: known only in Christian sources, an area somewhere on the Caelian (Jordan 2.120; HJ 253).

Area Carruces: mentioned only in the regionary catalogues, listed in Regio I. Probably it was the square where travelers left their horse-drawn vehicles for litters. With it must have been connected the Schola Carrucarum (or better Carrucariorum), or headquarters of those engaged in transportation (cf. *Dig.* 19.2.13), known from an inscription. The whole question was carefully investigated by Schneider Graziosi (*BullCom* 40 [1912]: 204–22), who concluded that the area should lie between Porta Appia and the Temple of Mars.

Area Concordiae: see **Concordia, Aedes.**

Area Macari: known only from an inscription on a circular bronze plate: *in regione quinta in area Macari* (*CIL* 15.7174 = *ILS* 8726), so presumably somewhere on the Esquiline.

Area Palatina: an open square before the Palatine palace, where people gathered to await the Salutatio Caesaris (A. Gellius 4.1.1, 20.1.1). Because Gellius says people of every order gathered in great numbers, we must suppose it was a place of some size and perhaps given architectural definition. The only satisfactory space seems to be the level area at the top of the Clivus Palatinus leading up from Summa Sacra Via, where an area between the Domus Augustiana and Domus Tiberiana was left unencumbered to enhance the view of the façade of the Domus Augustiana (Fig. 63). The princeps might have made his appearance on the gallery above the colonnade here. It is listed in the *Notitia* for Regio X. It is probably not the area mentioned by Josephus (*AntIud* 19.223) as an open space in the palace near the public land; more probably that was an area or courtyard near the entrance to the imperial enclave (cf. Josephus, *AntIud* 19.117). There was also presumably much more public space on the Palatine in the time of Claudius than there was in the time of Antoninus Pius. Whether the Forum Palatinum of the Einsiedeln sylloge (24 = *CIL* 6.1177 = *ILS* 776) is the same as the Area Palatina is very doubtful.

HJ 66; Lugli 1946, 471–72.

Area Pannaria: mentioned only in the regionary catalogues, listed in Regio I, but probably to be connected with the Campus Lanatarius (better Lanarius?) of Regio XII. They might have been open squares on either side of the Via Appia where markets in wool and cloth were held. If so, they were of a certain antiquity, because the word *campus* usually indicates land outside the pomerium.

Area Radicaria: Marked on the Marble Plan (*FUR* pl. 15; Rodriguez pl. 1) and listed in the regionary catalogues in Regio XII, it seems to have opened off the Via Appia to the southwest, just beyond the Baths of Caracalla. It may have been isolated by streets and been, like the Area Sacra of Largo Argentina, a row of temples and dedications (less likely tombs, in view of the area left free in front of them), an interpretation that its location, a little outside Porta Capena, makes more attractive. If so, we must presume that Septimius Severus, when he created the Via Nova leading to the Septizodium, blocked off the old course of the Via Appia at various points and converted it into a minor public way giving access to public buildings and areas in the hinterland of the new artery. The epithet Radicaria is obscure; presumably it is derived from *radix*.

Area Sacra di Largo Argentina (Fig. 8): an area of the southern Campus Martius in which stands a row of temples of medium size, more or less aligned, but without other clear relationship. Because they stand between the Villa Publica (q.v.) and the Circus Flaminius, it is presumed they are on the line of the beginning of most, if not all, triumphal processions and were all the offerings of successful generals. Four temples have been uncovered, and more may extend the line to the south, even to double this number. The area is bounded on the north by the Hecatostylon (q.v.), and on the east by a portico identified by some as one of the Porticus Minuciae (q.v.), although the case is not a strong one, beyond which is another Porticus Minucia containing a large temple, presumably that of the Lares Permarini (q.v.). Just behind the temples on the west lie the annexes of the Theatrum Pompeii (q.v.), probably including the Curia Pompeii, where Caesar was murdered, but to the south there is nothing for some distance, at least as far as Piazza Costaguti.

The two northernmost of the temples were always known, remains of the northernmost, known as Temple A, having been built into the fabric of the church of S. Nicola a'Cesarini, while a few battered columns of the circular temple next to it, Temple B, could be seen in a courtyard next door. These also appear on a fragment of the Marble Plan (*FUR* pl. 32; Rodriguez pl. 28). Work here began in the summer of 1926 with the object of enlarging Via Arenula and its juncture with Corso Vittorio Emanuele and has continued intermittently ever since, although the

main work of clearing down to the ancient levels was completed and the area inaugurated as a monument by the spring of 1929.

The oldest of the temples is probably Temple A, because it seems to have begun as a small shrine on a very high platform of Grotta Oscura tufa that was subsequently enlarged in order to bring it into equal importance with Temple C. In its first phase it was prostyle, presumably tetrastyle, with a relatively shallow pronaos and a deep rectangular cella. Across the whole width of the façade a long stair of approach, calculated as eighteen steps, laid on a system of five sleeper walls, led down to a rectangular platform raised four steps above the surrounding ground level, in the center of which stood the altar, evidently rectangular, with its long axis on the axis of the temple. Little remains of the temple of this phase, especially because somewhat later the podium was remodeled and a facing in blocks of Monteverde tufa added to its top courses. This consisted of a base step with a pronounced offset, a base molding of a fine, slightly flattened, cyma recta above a high step, a plain die with wide drafted margins, and a crown molding of cyma reversa profile. Originally there was no base molding, only an offset, and the character of the crown molding is unknown. The date of the first phase is almost certainly third century B.C., whereas the facing of Monteverde tufa and the replacement of the original altar with a fine one of peperino must be second century. Later, to bring the temple into line with the architecture of Temple C, a ring of columns of Anio tufa was added to make it peripteral, hexastyle, with nine columns on the flanks. These columns have Attic bases and were probably Corinthian. At this time a new stair of approach was installed and the altar platform raised. The stair was now only ten steps high. Presumably this general raising of the level was in response to repeated flooding in the area.

Temple C, although only a little younger than Temple A and very similar to it in construction, was from the beginning a much larger edifice, although the altar platform in front of it was made to conform in size to that of Temple A, in part doubtless because of the space available. It stood on a very high platform of Grotta Oscura tufa, trimmed at the crown with a flattened cyma reversa molding, but at the base with only a simple offset. It was peripteral *sine postico* with very widely spaced columns, four on the façade, and five and an anta on each flank. The pronaos was relatively shallow, and the cella was a deep rectangle. Because there is no statue base, it is presumed that the cult image was terracotta. Originally the width of the façade was covered by the stair of approach, twenty steps in all, leading down to the altar platform, like that of Temple A lifted four steps

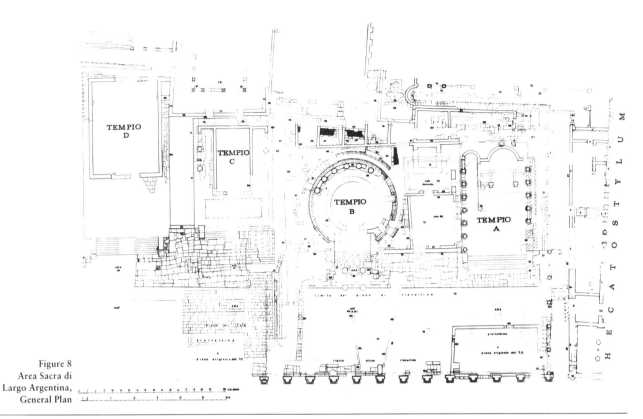

Figure 8
Area Sacra di
Largo Argentina,
General Plan

above the surrounding area. Stair and altar platform were carried on sleeper walls, and the stair is not in bond with the podium of the temple. Four clear pavements can be distinguished in the altar platform. The oldest altar stands on the second pavement; it is a fine peperino replacement installed by A. Postumius Albinus in conformance with a Lex Plaetoria (*ILLRP* 121). This was subsequently buried and preserved in excellent condition. The temple platform was emptied, but no complete account of the contents has been published. It was found that older construction in the area, notably a drain, runs obliquely under the oldest level of the altar platform. The original date of the temple is not fixed, but a date in the third century B.C. seems indicated by the material and style.

The round temple between A and C, Temple B, is much later in date. It was peripteral from the beginning, cella and peripteros walls having heavy foundations of concrete faced with fine opus incertum. Although the area under the cella was emptied to the bottom, no earlier construction was found until the original floor of this area of the time of the first construction of Temples A and C was reached, where a wall trace of blocks of cappellaccio was found aligned with those temples and cutting a chord across the cella from west to east. Its nature remains obscure. The temple itself stood on a low podium of

tufa with elaborate base and crown moldings. The eighteen columns are Corinthian, tufa shafts with Attic bases and Corinthian capitals of travertine. It is preceded by a shallow rectangular porch, only large enough to straighten the stair, and a stair calculated as having been originally of thirteen steps. To either side of the stair is added a wing from which a second wing runs out perpendicular to the stair to either side, perhaps to hold statuary or dedications, perhaps also a boundary for an altar precinct. At the time of the construction of Temple B, the level of the whole area was raised, the old altars of Temples A and C buried, and the whole repaved with tufa at a uniform level. At some later time the cella wall was destroyed, a new wall run between the columns, and an apron added to the back parts of the circumference to make an ampler podium. This work was carried out in thin slabs of tufa over a fill of rubble. At this time an immense statue base was installed, evidently to carry the great acrolithic image of a goddess of which the head, right arm, and foot were found.

In many ways Temple D, which could not be excavated completely, is the most mysterious of the four. It embraces in its podium elements of an earlier shrine with a stair descending to the level of the original construction of Temples A and C, but of this little is known, except that it was smaller than the present building. The present building dates from the time of the general pavement of the area in tufa in the first century B.C. The temple is very large, with foundations of Roman cement, and its podium is very high, approached by a stair of travertine. The pronaos is very deep, but without any trace of columns or column footings. The heavy cella walls are faced with brick and have fluted pilasters of stucco on the exterior and a line of tufa blocks along the base on the interior. There are remains of marble pavement in both pronaos and cella and a massive marble threshold for an enormous door. The size of cella and pronaos and the lack of evidence of columns suggest that the temple was hypaethral.

The area burned in the fire of Titus in A.D. 80 and was restored under Domitian. At that time the level was again raised and repaved with blocks of travertine, the last general rehandling of the precinct. Subsidiary structures were added from time to time that eventually came to fill most of the space between and behind the temples. These we can think of as sacristies and accommodations for the temple attendants. A portico of slender Ionic columns, rather widely spaced, runs along the northern flank of Temple A at a slight angle to its axis and has rooms behind it. These are all clearly of late date but replace an earlier portico to be associated with the first general pavement in tufa. Along the whole east side of the area runs a series of piers having engaged columns on their eastern faces and fluted pilasters on their western ones. There is no indication of a propylaeum or other entranceway in what has been uncovered, the stretch from the northern extremity to a point in front of the northern flank of Temple C. This portico is associated with the Domitianic pavement in travertine, but is a replacement for another associated with the pavement in tufa.

Although the dates and sequence of building in this complex are fairly well understood, the identity of the divinities to whom these temples belonged is very much disputed. Temple B is widely recognized as Lutatius Catulus's temple of Fortuna Huiusce Diei (q.v.) on the basis of evidence in Varro and appropriate form and construction. Whether the acrolith represents that goddess is debated. If the analysis of Temple D as hypaethral is correct, it seems likely to belong to Iuppiter Fulgur (q.v.). But for the older temples, A and C, there is simply no firm evidence, and a great many divinities are known to have had temples in the Campus Martius.

BullCom 60 (1932): 253–346 (G. Marchetti Longhi), 61 (1933): 163–94 (G. Marchetti Longhi), 64 (1936): 83–139 (G. Marchetti Longhi), 76 (1956–58): 45–118 (G. Marchetti Longhi), 81 (1968–69): 115–25 (I. Iacopi), 82 (1970–71): 7–62 (G. Marchetti Longhi); *MEFRA* 82 (1970): 117–58 (G. Mar-

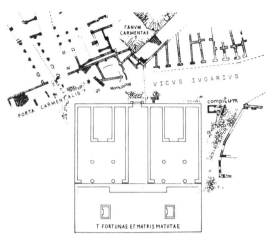

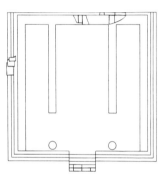

Figure 9
Area Sacra di Sant'Omobono, Plan of the Twin Temples, Final Phase

Figure 10
Area Sacra di Sant'Omobono, Plan of the Archaic Temple (Restored)

chetti Longhi); F. Coarelli, I. Kajanto, U. Nyberg, and M. Steinby, *L'area sacra di largo Argentina* (Rome 1981); *MEFRA* 97 (1986): 532–42 (M.-B. Carre and C. Virlouvet), 98 (1986): 623–41 (A. Ziolkowski).

Area Sacra di Sant'Omobono (Figs. 9, 10, 11, 37.10): an area at the foot of the Capitoline Hill on the ridge between the Forum Romanum and Forum Boarium, closer to the latter but inside the line of the Servian Walls. It is bounded on the north by the ancient Vicus Iugarius under the modern street of the same name and on the east by a street that branched from the Vicus Iugarius, which need not be of high antiquity. The other boundaries are less certain be-

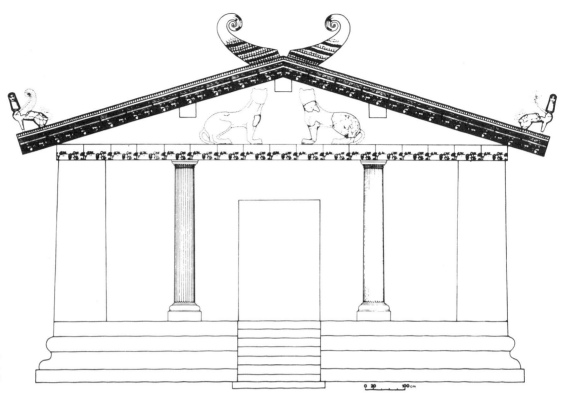

Figure 11
Area Sacra di
Sant'Omobono,
Façade of the Archaic
Temple (Restored)

cause, although the sacred precinct here is well defined, the nature of the adjacent areas is by no means entirely clear. The excavation of the area was begun in 1937 in preparation for the laying of foundations for a large government building along the east side of the Via del Teatro di Marcello (Via del Mare). With the discovery of important remains of antiquity in the area that project was abandoned and the area surrendered to archaeology, which has pushed excavation to its modern boundaries but not gone beyond these, except on the north, where the search for the Porta Carmentalis and for connection with architectural remains on the north side of the Vicus Iugarius has led to exploration under a considerable stretch of the modern street, though with inconclusive results. Ever since the discovery of this sanctuary, work has gone on there intermittently, notably in 1961–1964 and 1974–1975, when deep stratigraphic soundings were made. Although much has been written about it, its temples, and the finds, a definitive report has yet to appear.

The most important feature is a pair of single-cella temples set side by side on a large rectangular platform walled and paved with tufa. These were evidently twins throughout their history and are identified as the temples of Fortuna and Mater Matuta

(qq.v.) founded by Servius Tullius. The temples turned their backs to the Vicus Iugarius, but the precinct was entered from it by a large doorway between them. The cella of the Temple of Mater Matuta was built into the church of S. Omobono and cannot at present be studied in detail, but, because the temples were twins, the plan can be reconstructed. In their final phase, to be dated after the fire of 213 B.C. that destroyed the area from the Porta Trigemina to the Porta Carmentalis (Livy 24.47.15), each consisted of a small cella with a pronaos somewhat deeper than the cella, having two pairs of columns on the lines of the lateral walls of the cella, both cella and pronaos enclosed by a wall of tufa blocks open only in front (south). The suggestion is that the architectural form, while readily recognizable as a temple, was unusual, similar to that of the temple of the Ara della Regina at Tarquinia and the temple of Fiesole, great blank walls supporting a spreading roof over an interior with architectural arrangements much like a temple complete in itself. From the temple one descended three steps to the altar platform in front, an area much confused by repaving at various times, but preserving parts of a pair of large altars of archaic form on axis with the temples but facing east.

Deep soundings have been carried down to a

depth of more than 7 m, to virgin earth below any trace of human habitation. At least six major phases of construction are distinguished. These include: (1) a pretemple phase; (2) a first temple of the archaic period, which in the course of time underwent an important rebuilding with enlargement and renewal of the terracotta decoration; (3) a destruction layer followed by leveling, after which a deep layered fill containing heterogeneous material, some of which goes back to the Bronze Age, was laid in (this is dated to the early fourth century); (4) a construction level, the first phase of the surviving twin temples and their altars, with use of blocks of Monteverde and Anio tufa; (5) a reconstruction following a fire (almost certainly that of 213 B.C.) with repavement with flags of Monteverde tufa; and (6) an imperial repavement in travertine and rebuilding of the area with commercial establishments following abandonment of the sanctuary as a cult center.

The archaeological material recovered from the deep soundings gives precious testimony to the importance of Rome from the beginning of the Iron Age, if not earlier, as well as a wealth of decorative and votive material belonging to the temples. Objects carved in bone, ivory, and amber, as well as bronzes, have appeared, and the pottery ranges from impasto and bucchero through East Greek and Attic black figure and on through Roman wares. The temple terracottas are especially impressive and include fragments of two large felines from a pediment, archaic figured friezes, simas, and antefixes. Of particular interest are a late archaic group of Minerva and Hercules at two-thirds life-size, Hercules wearing his lion's skin as though it were a coat belted at the waist, a fine circular base of peperino, and a fragmentary inscription that has been restored as a dedication by M. Fulvius Flaccus from the spoils of Volsinii in 264 B.C. (cf. Pliny, *HN* 34.34).

BullCom 77 (1959–60): 3–143 (A. M. Colini et al.); 79 (1963–64): 3–90 (G. Colonna et al.), *QITA* 5 (1968): 63–70 (P. Somella), 71–76 (M. Torelli); Nash 1.415–17; *PP* 32 (1977): 9–128 (A. M. Colini et al.); Coarelli 1988, 205–301; *La grande Roma dei Tarquini* (1990): 111–30 (G. Pisani Sartorio, A. Sommella Mura, et al.).

Area Saturni (Fig. 19): known only from inscriptions (*CIL* 1².810 = 14.153 = *ILS* 892; *CIL* 6.1265 = *ILS* 5937; *CIL* 8.9249). The lack of space in front of the Temple of Saturn suggests that the area may have been an open space behind it, between the Vicus Iugarius and the Clivus Capitolinus, but the space between the clivus and the base of the Tabularium was also open down to the time of the building of the Temple of Vespasian. Cf. Jordan 1.2.363–65

and *CIL* 1².587, 589 = *ILS* 38 (laws that seem to have been displayed there). It was probably always a small area, but an association of *negotiatores* had their headquarters there in the late first century B.C.

Area Splenis: listed in the regionary catalogues after the Area Apollinis in Regio I and confirmed by a medieval legend in which thieves who were taking a miraculous picture of the Virgin from the ancient church of S. Sisto Vecchio on the Via Appia toward the Lateran were stopped by supernatural manifestations *ad locum qui dicitur Spleni*. There may have been a shrine to Splen as a divinity (cf. Cicero, *Nat.D.* 3.63), or there may have been a connection of the church of SS. Nereo ed Achille, Titulùs Fasciolae, across the Via Appia from S. Sisto Vecchio, with *splenium* meaning "plaster" or "bandage." In that case the Area Splenis must be sought in the immediate environs of S. Sisto.

BullCom 54 (1926): 49–53 (C. Hülsen).

Area Volcani (1): see **Volcanal.**

Area Volcani (2): listed only in the *Notitia*, in Regio IV after the Porticus Apsidata and before the Aura (Aureum Bucinum). If the sequence is significant, which is doubtful, it might be in the vicinity of the Vicus Sandaliarius, northeast of Templum Pacis.

Argeorum Sacraria (Fig. 74): twenty-seven sacraria (cf. Ulpian, *Dig.* 1.8.9.2: *sacrarium est locus in quo sacra reponuntur*) at points throughout the city of the four regions (see Regiones Quattuor). These were visited on 16 and 17 March (Ovid, *Fast.* 3.791; A. Gellius 10.15.30), though what was done there at that time is not stated. On the Ides of May they were visited again in fixed order, probably counterclockwise, by a procession in which the Flamen Dialis and Flaminica, the other chief priests, the Vestals, the praetor urbanus, and those for whom it was right (*themis:* Dion. Hal.1.38) to be present took part. This procession ended on the Pons Sublicius, and there the priests threw twenty-seven rush dolls into the Tiber (Varro, *Ling.* 7.44; Paulus *ex Fest.* 14L, 450–52L; Plutarch, *Quaest. Rom.* 32, 86; Dion. Hal. 1.38). Both the dolls and the sacraria were called Argei (Livy 1.21.5) or Argea (Paulus *ex Fest.* 14L).

In both ancient and modern times, this ceremony has excited the liveliest interest in students of Roman religion. Its foundation was ascribed by Livy to Numa, and by Dionysius to Hercules, and it was generally regarded as very old. but the partial list of sacraria, as transmitted by Varro (*Ling.* 5.45–54), cannot be older than the third century. The Latin is old-fashioned, and Varro was probably quoting from the official record of the pontifices. It is, in a slightly edited version, as follows:

Regio Suburana

1st: *In Suburanae regionis parte princeps est Caelius mons.*

4th: *Caeriolensis: quarticeps circa Minervium qua in Caelio monte itur in tabernola est.* This appears to be the neighborhood of the shrine of Minerva Capta (q.v.). The only ancient roads leading to the top of the Caelian are those leading to the Porta Caelimontana (Clivus Scauri) and to the Porta Querquetulana. This should be a minor approach, probably somewhere on the slope between the Temple of Divus Claudius and the church of SS. Quattro Coronati. The phrase *in tabernola* indicates that while the sacrarium might best be described by reference to the temple, it was independent of it.

Regio Esquilina

1st: *Oppius mons: princeps Esquilis ovis lacum* (or *lucum*) *facutalem sinistra via secundum merum est.* The Fagutal is well established to have been at the western extremity of the Oppius, near the modern church of S. Francesco di Paola. It is more likely to have been a single beech tree than a grove; the only references to a grove are late, and Festus (Paulus *ex Fest.* 77L) believed that Fagutal was the name of a sacellum of Jupiter. *Merum* is generally believed to be a corruption of *moerum (murum)*. The designation is believed to be a wall shrine.

Varro says (*Ling.* 5.49–50) that the Esquiliae, the second of Rome's early regiones, got its name either from watch posts of the king or because it was cultivated (*excultae*) by Servius Tullius. He favors the latter explanation, because the place-names are in harmony with it, and as examples he cites the *lacus . . . fagutalis* and *Larum Querquetulanum sacellum*, the *lucus Mefitis et Iunonis Lucinae*. Perhaps we should supply *aedes* before *Iunonis*. But *lacus . . . fagutalis* was altered by Pomponio Leto, Varro's first editor, to *lucus*, and he has been followed by every editor since, I believe wrongly. The reasoning behind the change is that Varro, in citing places in the list of the Argei for Regio II, is citing groves, as in citing those for Regio III, the Collina, he cites *colles*. I have no quarrel with this, but it seems to me unlikely that the copyist of the manuscript would have got the *lucus Mefitis*, about which we know from other sources, right and the *lacus fagutalis* wrong, since its name already associates it with a tree or trees. Moreover, *lucus fagutalis* amounts to a tautology.

So also in what follows: the manuscripts have *lacum fagutalem, lacum esquilinum, lacum esquilinum,* and *lacum poetelium*. For the first three there

is no justification for change, since the association with trees is already implicit in the second element, and watering places are apt to have been at least as common as groves from the very beginning and are apt to have been used as place designators from a very early period. The variation in the devices on the standards of the street fountains in Pompeii seems to have been introduced especially for this purpose. The last item, however, is puzzling; as a plebeian gentilial name Poetelius is well known in the fifth and fourth centuries B.C., but the family died out thereafter. The name might be associated with either a *lucus* or a *lacus*, but here Varro adds the particular *esquiliis* as an element of the name, making the association with trees explicit. On the face of things there is little justification for altering the manuscript readings.

3rd: *Oppius mons: terticeps cis lacum* (or *lucum*) *esquilinum; dexteriore via in tabernola est.*

4th: *Oppius mons: quarticeps cis lacum Esquilinum via dexteriore in figlinis est.* The *figlinae* should be potters' shops, or perhaps better a potter's shop, but the Esquiline was not particularly noted for the quality of its clay. It may be that the reference is to the story of the drunken potter told by Festus (468L).

5th: *Cespius mons: quinticeps cis lacum Poetelium Esquiliis est.* The plebeian Gens Poetelia produced several distinguished members in the fourth century B.C., but the name scarcely appears thereafter.

6th: *Cespius mons: sexticeps apud aedem Iunonis Lucinae, ubi aeditumus habere solet.* The location of the Temple of Iuno Lucina at the southwestern extremity of the Cispian is well known. It is more puzzling why it should be in the sacristan's lodge, or why he should occupy a sacrarium.

Regio Collina

3rd: *Collis Quirinalis: terticeps cis aedem Quirini.* If one is going counterclockwise, the first two sacraria would then presumably be on the Viminal, and one would descend Alta Semita after rounding the head of the valley between Viminal and Quirinal. The sacrarium would be east of the Temple of Quirinus.

4th: *Collis Salutaris: quarticeps adversum est †pilonar† cis aedem Salutis.* One would like to see in the corruption reference to a gateway to the Temple of Salus, because the hill is not large and the temple was its main feature.

5th: *Collis Mucialis: quinticeps apud aedem Dei Fidi; in delubro, ubi aeditumus habere solet.* (Cf. Regio Esquilina 6th.) The Temple of Semo Sancus Dius Fidius was near the Porta Sanqualis northwest of modern Piazza Magnanapoli, but no remains are known.

6th: *Collis Latiaris: sexticeps in vico Insteiano*

summo apud auguraculum aedificium solum est. The Vicus Insteius is known from a flood of water that burst forth there in 214 B.C. (Livy 24.20.8) and is probably to be located just behind the Forum Traiani. An auguraculum on the lowest lobe of the Quirinal seems incongruous; the view from it would have lain chiefly over the valley of the Forum Romanum. If, as the description seems to declare, this was the only one of the Argei that was an independent building, it is odd that it is not described in greater detail.

Regio Palatina

5th: *Germalense: quinticeps apud aedem Romuli.* This is the same as the Casa Romuli (q.v.) on the slope along the Scalae Caci (q.v.), perhaps identical with the Tugurium Faustuli. The Scalae Caci now seem positively identified, and hut foundations to the northwest of the head of these have been found, but the Casa Romuli must have been farther down the slope toward the Lupercal. Apparently the doll was kept in the hut. Because the Cermalus was only the slope of the Palatine and not a well-defined geographical entity, this designation suggests that the shrines (or dolls) served differently defined units.

6th: *Veliense: sexticeps in Velia apud aedem deum Penatium.* The Temple of the Penates seems to have disappeared in the fire of Nero and probably lay under the platform of Hadrian's Temple of Venus et Roma.

With thirteen of the twenty-seven shrines located for us, we are in a position to say something about them. They seem to have been equally distributed among the four regions, so the missing twenty-eighth must be due to some calamity or evil omen that caused it to be dropped. They are not simply places spaced out at equal intervals around the city; each has, and apparently always had, a particular location. That they are not associated with temples, so that even when they are in the charge of a sacristan it is he and not the temple that is specified, suggests that they were regarded as potentially dangerous. Moreover, some are located so vaguely that anyone at all unfamiliar with them would have difficulty finding them, and all are imprecisely enough defined that even someone familiar with the ritual might after the lapse of a year have more than a little trouble locating them. This vagueness suggests they were to some extent deliberately hidden and had to be discovered from the clues given. That the priests threw the dolls in the Tiber from the Pons Sublicius, therefore into the river at its greatest strength, suggests this was a rite of lustration, and so Plutarch (*Quaest. Rom.* 86) describes it.

Jordan 2.237–90; L. A. Holland, *Janus and the Bridge* (Rome 1961), 313–31; *PP* 26 (1971): 153–66 (G. Maddoli).

Argiletum: The main approach to the Forum Romanum on the northeast, it connected the Subura and the forum square, debouching between the Comitium and the Basilica Paulli (Fig. 39). Because the expansion of the imperial fora gradually absorbed portions of the Argiletum, it is of some importance to be able to define its beginning and end at various periods. For Livy (1.19.2) and Servius (*ad Aen.* 7.607) the Ianus Geminus stood *ad imum Argiletum* or *circa infimum Argiletum*, and a stretch of roadway with ancient paving still runs along the side of the Curia today, though in its passage through the Forum Nervae (Transitorium) its character as a road was probably obliterated. For Martial the Argiletum continued northeast of the Forum Transitorium and was a center of booksellers and cobblers (Martial 1.2.7–8, 1.3.1, 1.117.9–12, 2.17). Probably it was always the main thoroughfare of the Subura and did not lose the name Argiletum until it divided into the Clivus Suburanus and Vicus Patricius. Martial's *primae fauces Suburae* would then be the area just behind the Forum Transitorium.

Various fanciful explanations of the name Argiletum were offered in antiquity, the most popular being that it derived from a Greek scoundrel (Varro, *Ling.* 5.157; Servius *ad Aen.* 8.345). Because it was never called anything else, never via or vicus, and ran along the side of the Cloaca until the stream was culverted and put under the road in the second century B.C., the name may be connected with *argilla*.

Nash 1.151–53.

Armamentarium: an armory, evidently connected with the Colosseum, associated in the regionary catalogues with the Spoliarium (q.v.) and Samiarium (q.v.). It is listed in Regio II. Because we know that at least one of the individual gladiatorial ludi had its own armamentarium (*CIL* 6.10164 = *ILS* 5153), we should perhaps think of this as serving only for the Colosseum itself.

Armamentarium (in Castris Praetoriis): see **Castra Praetoria.**

Armilustrium: a square (Livy 27.37.4) on the Aventine where the festival of the Armilustrium was celebrated annually on 19 October. It is listed first in Regio XIII by the regionary catalogues, and by various arguments it can be shown probably to have been on the northwest corner of the hill, northwest of the church of S. Sabina. It must have contained an altar, presumably of Mars (Paulus *ex Fest.* 17L), probably at its center, and was probably bordered at least in part by a portico with square marble pillars embellished with *chutes d'armes,* two of which are in the octagonal gallery of the Uffizi in Florence (*RömMitt* 48 [1933]: 1–73 [I. W. Crous]).

The ceremony of the Armilustrium was the closing of the war season. The Salii purified the arms of the Romans by dancing with the ancilia, and trumpets were blown in accompaniment (Paulus *ex Fest.* 17L). There was a sacrifice and probably a dedication of captured arms to Mars, if there was booty. The Armilustrium square gave its name to the Vicus Armilustri, almost certainly the ancient road under the modern Via di S. Sabina.

RömMitt 48 (1933): 1–119 (I. W. Crous); Degrassi 523–24.

Arx (Figs. 19, 58): The fortified summit of the Capitoline Hill, also called Arx Capitolina (Livy 6.20.9, 28.39.15; Val. Max. 8.14.1; Tacitus, *Hist.* 3.71). Because a distinction seems frequently made between Arx and Capitoline, as, for example, *in arce aut Capitolio* (Livy 6.20.13; Val. Max. 6.3.1a), it has been supposed that the arx was the slightly higher northern height of the Capitoline Hill, and the Capitoline proper was the southern height, originally called Saturnius Mons (Varro, *Ling.* 5.42) or Tarpeius Mons (Varro, *Ling.* 5.41). But *arx* is a common noun, not a proper name, and both heights had to be provided with strong defenses to prevent an enemy from occupying either and hurling missiles from that vantage point. And the two heights must have had a single fortification system, which included the saddle between them (cf. Pliny, *HN* 16.216). This seems adequately demonstrated by the stories of the defense of the Capitoline during the siege of the Gauls and by Flavius Sabinus against the soldiers of Vitellius (Livy 5.39.9–43.3, 46.8–47.10; Tacitus, *Hist.* 3.69–73). The term *arx* would have been used especially for those parts outside the Area Capitolina but within the fortifications, but the name *arx* should not apply to the lower slopes.

The arx was the site of the house of Titus Tatius (Solinus 1.21) and that of M. Manlius Capitolinus, which was pulled down in 384 B.C. At that time it was decreed that no patrician should thenceforth live on the arx or Capitoline (Livy 5.47.8, 6.20.13). On the site of this house was later built the Temple of Iuno Moneta (see Iuno Moneta, Aedes). The only other landmark there was the Auguraculum near the brow on the southeast, an observation point where the augurs took the auspices.

In early times, when the comitia centuriata were held in the Campus Martius, sentinels were posted, and a flag was flown on the arx and on the Janiculum to guard against an unforeseen enemy attack (Cass. Dio 37.28). Servius (*ad Aen.* 8.1) also tells us

that in ancient times in periods of imminent danger there might be displayed on the Capitoline a red vexillum to summon the foot soldiers and a blue one to summon the cavalry. The custom had fallen out of use by his time, and he adds that other authorities would have it that a rose-colored vexillum was a signal of war and a white one was a signal of comitia.

In imperial times the lower slopes of the hill, except toward the Forum Romanum, were covered with commercial and residential buildings, some of them sizable insula complexes. One brought to light with the removal of the church of S. Rita de Cascia in 1927 ran to at least five storeys and extended back nearly to the Museo Capitolino. Probably such development ringed most of the hill.

Jordan 1.2.102–15; Lugli 1946, 3–53; Nash 1.506–7; *AJAH* 3 (1978): 163–78 (T. P. Wiseman).

Arx Tarpeia: an alternative name for the Arx Capitolina used by Vergil (*Aen.* 8.652) and Propertius (4.4.29).

Asinus Frictus: a place designation used in a twelfth century document to locate a church of SS. Cosma e Damiano subject to the convent of S. Erasmo, probably the same as that described in a document of 978 as *posita Romae regione II iuxta formam Claudia.* This would place it on the Caelian, and the convent lay to the west of S. Stefano Rotondo (HCh 249) and was associated with the church of S. Tomaso de Formis. It seems possible that the Asinus Frictus refers to a low passage through the aqueduct. It might even be a joking name for the Arcus Dolabellae et Silani (q.v.).

Asylum (Fig. 19): an area on the Capitoline *inter duos lucos,* in the saddle between the two crests of the hill. The identification of the two groves is entirely uncertain. The Asylum took its name from the tradition that here Romulus welcomed and accepted into citizenship in the new city all comers eager for a change in their circumstances (Livy 1.8.5–6; Dion. Hal. 2.15.3–4; Strabo 5.3.2 [230]). It was a *locus saeptus* (Cicero, *Div.* 2.40) and respected down at least to the time of the Flavian defense of the Capitol against the Vitellians (Tacitus, *Hist.* 3.71), but there seems never to have been any building there. The evidence suggests that it was a trapezoidal area immediately in front of the Palazzo del Senatore, now largely taken up by the exterior stairs of the palazzo.

Lugli 1946, 38–39.

Athenaeum: an assembly hall used especially for rhetorical and poetical declamations (S.H.A. *Pertinax* 11.3, *Alex. Sev.* 35.2, *Gordian.* 3.4) but also for other gatherings (Cass. Dio 74.17). Attached to it was a large library arranged in *cunei* (Sidon. Apoll., *Epist.* 2.9.4), perhaps like the library of Timgad. It was built by Hadrian, but there is no indication of its location in our sources. Because it was originally intended as a school of the liberal arts (Aur. Vict., *Caes.* 14.2–3), it should have been a fairly large building, and because Aurelius Victor puts it at the beginning of Hadrian's reign, we might associate it with his other early works in Rome, the Temple of Divus Traianus, the Pantheon, and the Temple of Diva Matidia. See also Atrium Minervae, for which this may be another name.

TAPS 80.2 (1990): 42–45 (R. E. A. Palmer).

Atrium: see **Domus, Insula, Atrium,** etc.

Atria Licinia: large auction halls of the time of Cicero, probably near the Forum Romanum, perhaps northeast of it (Cicero, *Quinct.* 12, 25; Servius *ad Aen.* 1.726).

Atria Septem: mentioned only by the Chronographer of 354 as buildings of Domitian, the first item in a long and very full list, followed by the Horrea Piperataria. They have not been identified.

Atrium Caci: listed in the regionary catalogues in Regio VIII following the Aquam Cernentem IIII Scaros and before the Porticus Margaritaria *(Curiosum)* and the Vicus Iugarius et Unguentarius, Graecostadium, and Porticus Margaritaria *(Notitia)*. This might indicate a place near the Porta Carmentalis.

Atrium Cyclopis: see **Antrum Cyclopis.**

Atrium Libertatis: the headquarters of the censors and a repository for their records and various laws and documents inscribed on bronze (Livy 43.16.13, 45.15.5; Granius Licinianus 28.36). It served as a place of detention for the hostages from Thurii and Tarentum in the Second Punic War (Livy 25.7.12) and was the place where the slaves of Clodius were examined prior to the trial of Milo (Cicero, *Milon.* 59). In exceptional circumstances it was used for meetings of the senate. It stood just inside the Porta Fontinalis, between this and the Forum Iulium, facing on the Clivus Argentarius (Cicero, *Att.* 4.16.14). In 193 B.C., for the convenience of the censors, a portico was built from the gate to the Altar of Mars in the Campus Martius, where the census was held (Livy 35.10.12). It was restored and enlarged in 194 B.C. (Livy 34.44.5) and rebuilt magnificently by Asinius Pollio (Suetonius, *Aug.* 29.5), who included the first public library in Rome, containing both Greek and Latin writers and busts of distinguished writers,

Varro being the only living writer represented (Pliny, *HN* 7.115). This was built from the spoils of his Illyrian campaign, for which he enjoyed a triumph (Isidore, *Orig.* 6.5.2; Ovid, *Trist.* 3.1.71–72; Pliny, *HN* 35.10). He also embellished it with his very extensive collection of sculpture, though this seems not to have been in a special gallery (Pliny, *HN* 36.23–25 and 33–34). At this time it probably covered much of the area of the Basilica Ulpia, which was in some sense a rebuilding of the atrium, commemorated by the inscription LIBERTATIS on the fragment of the Marble Plan preserving the north apse (*FUR* pl. 28; Rodriguez pl. 21). A contingent of German soldiers was housed or stationed there during the last days of Galba's reign (Tacitus, *Hist.* 1.31).

Three inscriptions of the early imperial period refer to this atrium: *CIL* 6.470 = *ILS* 3780, *CIL* 6.472 = *ILS* 274, and *CIL* 6.10025. The second of these records a restoration by Nerva. Another restoration, evidently an important one, was carried out in the sixth century under Theodoric (*CIL* 6.1794 = *ILS* 825), so at least the library appears to have kept its original name. Ovid (*Fast.* 4.621–24) is apparently mistaken in giving the dedication day as 13 April; that belongs to the Temple of Iuppiter Libertas on the Aventine (Degrassi 440).

RendLinc, ser. 8.1 (1946): 276–91 (F. Castagnoli); *MEFRA* 91 (1979): 601–22 (M. Bonnejond); Anderson 21–26.

Atrium Maenium: probably a private house, bought in 184 B.C. by Cato the Elder, together with four tabernae and the Atrium Titium as land for the Basilica Porcia. It was *in lautumiis* (see Lautumiae) on the Clivus Argentarius, probably a simple atrium house, the shops being those that would normally flank a house entrance on a busy thoroughfare. PA thinks it would have been an office or hall rather than a house, but at this date there were probably a good many private houses near the forum. See also Columna Maenia.

Livy 39.44; pseudo-Asconius *ad Cic. Div. in Caec.* 50 (Stangl 201).

Atrium Minervae: listed by the regionary catalogues in Regio VIII. Dio (51.22) says that the Chalcidicum built by Octavian in conjunction with the Curia Iulia was also called the Athenaion, and it has been proposed that Atrium Minervae is simply a translation of this, or vice versa. But the coins showing the Curia Iulia clearly show only a single hall of the general lines of the curia as rebuilt by Diocletian, with a light colonnaded porch on a high platform in front of it and extending to either side. If this is the Chalcidicum, it would never have been called an atrium. No one knows exactly what the architectural form of a chalcidicum should be, or precisely what the word means. In both the examples where we have good evidence, Leptis Magna and Pompeii, the chalcidicum is the first member of a complex to be named and seems to be a colonnaded porch of special importance (*CIL* 10.810–11 = *ILS* 3785: *chalcidicum, cryptam, porticus;* J. M. Reynolds and J. B. Ward-Perkins, *The Inscriptions of Roman Tripolitania* [Rome 1952], 324: *calchidicum et porticus et porta et via*). Therefore, all our evidence at present points to Octavian's chalcidicum's being the raised and colonnaded porch shown, which was lacking in Diocletian's building and probably suppressed at the time Domitian rebuilt the curia.

A measured drawing of the plan of the complex of the churches of S. Adriano (the Curia Diocletiani) and S. Martina by Antonio da Sangallo il Giovane shows a tripartite building, a large apsidal hall (S. Adriano), a smaller apsidal hall (SS. Luca e Martina), and an intermediate complex consisting of a long hall with a row of supports down the middle and a walled courtyard. All three members were long considered originally ancient. They are identified by Lugli (Lugli 1946, 131–38) as Curia, Atrium Minervae, and Secretarium Senatus. But we now know that the Secretarium Senatus was one of the tabernae of the Forum Iulium (L. Bonfante and H. von Heintze, eds., *In Memoriam: Otto J. Brendel* [Mainz 1976], 191–204 [E. Nash, "Secretarium Senatus"]). But study of the plan of Sangallo and the excavated remains of the Forum Iulium shows that whereas most of the walls of S. Martina have no relation to those of the Forum Iulium, those of the northeast and southeast sides were based on forum walls and very likely incorporated in their fabric remains of an ancient building aligned with the Curia above the tabernae of the forum. This suggests that Dio, being familiar only with the Domitianic rebuilding of the Curia and such modifications as were made in it and subsequently to it, did not understand the word *chalcidicum* as used in the *Res Gestae Divi Augusti* and interpreted it to mean the annexes to the curia, which were the Athenaeum of Hadrian.

On this interpretation, when the curia was rebuilt by Domitian, the chalcidicum was either suppressed or moved to the northeast end of the curia, and the Athenaeum was added by Hadrian.

Opuscula Instituti Romae Finlandiae 1 (1982): 25–40 (A. Franchetti); Anderson 49–51, 122–25.

Atrium Publicum: a building *in Capitolio* that lightning struck in 214 B.C. (Livy 24.10.9). This may be what Polybius (3.26.1) calls the treasury of the quaestors, with the information that the treaties between Rome and Carthage were kept there in his day.

Atrium Regium: mentioned only by Livy as one of the buildings lost in the fire of 210 B.C. (Livy 26.27.3, 27.11.16). Because this fire burned from the Lautumiae along the northeast side of the Forum Romanum, and the Temple of Vesta was barely saved from destruction, this is more likely to be the Regia than the Atrium Vestae.

A recent attempt to identify the Atrium Regium with the basilica of Plautus, *Curc.* 472 (*Arctos* 21 [1987]: 174–76 [E. M. Steinby]), seems unlikely to be right. It puts the *Curculio* too early, and the translation of the name into Latin between Plautus and Livy is hard to account for.

Atrium Sutorium: a building in which the Tubilustrium, the solemn purification, with sacrifice of a ewe lamb, of the trumpets used in sacred rituals, was performed on 23 March and 23 May (Degrassi 429, 460; cf. Varro, *Ling.* 6.14; Ovid, *Fast.* 3.849–50, 5.725–26; Festus 480L). There is no indication where the atrium might have been, unless the name of the Vicus Sandaliarius is a vestige of an original concentration of shoemaking and it was on or near this.

Atrium Titium: see **Atrium Maenium.**

Atrium Vestae (Figs. 12, 13): the building in which the Vestal Virgins lived (A. Gellius 1.12.9; Pliny, *Epist.* 7.19.2), except when illness forced them from it, at which time they were entrusted to the care of some reputable matron. The name was sometimes extended (cf. Ovid, *Fast.* 6.263–64) to include the group of buildings clustered around the Temple of Vesta: the Regia, the Domus Publica of the pontifex maximus (Suetonius, *Iul.* 46), and even the Lucus Vestae extending in republican times from the base of the Palatine to the Nova Via (Cicero, *Div.* 1.101). Gradually these were encroached on by other buildings or absorbed into the atrium itself, until in the early imperial period the only ones surviving were the Temple of Vesta, Regia, and Atrium, three quite separate structures. Servius's statement (*ad Aen.* 7.153) that the Temple of Vesta was not founded with inauguration, so the senate could not meet here but could meet in the Atrium Vestae, is probably only a bit of antiquarian lore, because we know of no such meeting and it seems a very unlikely place for a senate meeting.

The building, almost as large as the Basilica Iulia and much larger, one would think, than the needs of the six Vestal Virgins would require, lies between the Sacra Via and the Nova Via, south and east of the Temple of Vesta. It has a very complicated building history, modifications having been introduced in

NOVA VIA

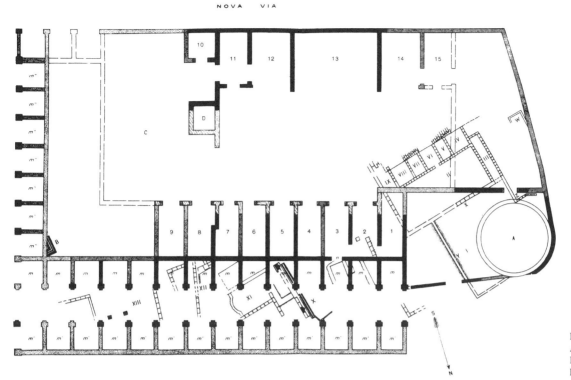

Figure 12
Atrium Vestae, Plan of
Republican and Early
Imperial Remains

nearly every generation. Of the republican period there are remains at a lower level and on a completely different orientation at an angle of nearly forty-five degrees to the walls of the imperial period. Excavations were first made in 1549, and intensive exploration of the building was conducted in 1883 and 1899–1902. New excavations were undertaken there by R. T. Scott beginning in 1987 and still continue.

Rebuilt before the fire of Nero, but part of his reorganization of the Sacra Via, the building seems to have consisted of a large rectangular court surrounded by rooms of various sizes with little intercommunication among them. The cells of the individual Vestal Virgins seem to have lain along the north side, the public rooms on the south. Presumably the court was colonnaded and contained a garden. The eastern reaches are enigmatic but seem to have been separated off from the rest. Toward the exterior was a line of tabernae opening to the exterior to the east and another opening to a portico to the north. After the fire of Nero the colonnades of the court were rebuilt and a large shallow rectangular tank installed in the middle of the open area, possibly for the breeding of fish. Most of the bank of individual cells was destroyed and replaced by a more elaborate group of rooms with a stair to an upper storey, probably leading to new living quarters. The main entrance to the atrium was made a broad door approached by a wide flight of steps at the northwest corner near the temple.

In the time of Trajan there was a very extensive renovation of the atrium. The east end of the building was reconstructed at monumental scale with a great central exedra flanked by banks of small rooms with windows to large lateral courts containing fountains. Additional rooms to north and south of the eastern court were also built, to create which several of the tabernae at the east end of the northern line and whatever was left of the eastern line were sacrificed. A number of rooms were broken up into smaller spaces, and in some places hypocausted floors and cellars were installed. One begins to see the influence of the planning of apartments of Ostian type, and probably a whole new second storey was now added.

Under Hadrian the little "Aedicula Vestae" was built west of the main entrance to the Atrium, a pretty shrine of two unfluted columns and a triangular pediment on a low base. It has been supposed that this contained a statue of Vesta, but ordinarily there seems to have been a prohibition on statues of this divinity, because she was in essence the fire itself.

Under the Severans came the last great remodeling

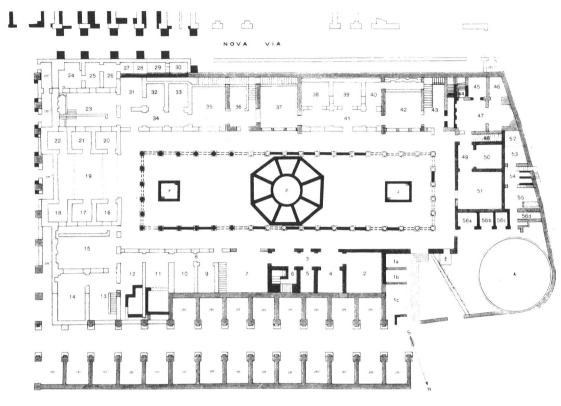

Figure 13
Atrium Vestae,
Plan after the
Severan Rebuilding

of the atrium, following a fire that destroyed part of the building in the time of Commodus. The central court was now extended to become the dominant feature for the rooms in the eastern parts as well as the western, and given colonnades of cipollino with an upper storey of breccia corallina. Later a huge central feature of octagonal shape divided into wedges around a circular center, perhaps the foundation of a pavilion or a flower bed, was also added. Small rectangular tanks to either side of this were for water and fish. A collection of statues of Virgines Vestales Maximae on inscribed pedestals stood around the court; presumably additions were made to it regularly. A statue of Nerva of the time of Trajan was also found here (*BullCom* 47 [1919]: 211–24 [C. Anti]). Six large brick arches were added about the same time to buttress the east end of the south front of the building along the Nova Via and smaller ones were added along the south part of the east front, presumably in connection with changes in the upper storey. Changes thereafter were only minor.

At no time does the Atrium Vestae seem to have included an atrium of traditional form, perhaps because it antedated the invention of that form. It is impossible to make out the usage of all but a few parts at any given period. Obviously some of the rooms were reception rooms, others for living. None seems especially designed for cult use, though many of the activities of the Vestal Virgins, such as the careful and elaborate preparation of the *mola salsa* required for every official sacrifice, presumably would have been performed here. As we see it, this is more a splendid setting for formal entertainments than anything else, the *piano nobile* of a Renaissance palazzo, fronted by and concealed behind lines of shops.

Bloch 67–85; Lugli 1946, 208–12; Nash 1.154–59; *RendPontAcc* 51–52 (1978–80): 325–55, especially 325–46 (G. Carettoni); *QArchEtr* 16 (1988): 18–26 (R. T. Scott et al.).

Auditorium Maecenatis: the modern name given a nymphaeum discovered in 1874 between Via Merulana and Via Leopardi built across the Servian Walls, therefore within the area of the Horti Maecenatis (q.v.). It is a rectangular room sunk 7 m below ground level and approached by a ramp. At the far end is an apse in which a hemicycle of six concentric steps leads up to a ring of five deep rectangular niches, while along each side wall are six larger rectangular niches. A series of orifices in the edge of the top step shows these were for a cascade, and the niches probably held fountain figures. The main room is paved with fine mosaic, and the niches are painted with landscape. The rest of the decoration is in the Third Pompeian Style. A date toward the beginning of the Christian era is indicated by the construction as well. The relation of the Servian Walls to the building remains enigmatic, but there seems clearly to have been one.

BullCom 2 (1874): 137–73 (V. Vespignani and L. Visconti); Neuerburg 204–5; Nash 1.160–63; *Roma capitale 1870–1911* (show catalogue, Venice 1983), 225–52 (S. Rizzo and C. Scondurra).

Auguraculum (1): an observation post on the Capitoline *in arce*, probably marked off by cippi, where the augurs took the auspices and from which the fetials took the *verbenae* for striking treaties. Varro (*Ling.* 7.8) gives the formula for laying out an augural templum there, and Livy (1.24) gives the formulae for investing fetials with their office. Livy (1.18.6–10) also gives a description of the ritual of augury there. Everyone specifies that it was *in arce,* but the only more precise information we get is that Claudius Centumalus's house on the Caelian obstructed the augurs' sight line and therefore had to be pulled down (Cicero, *Off.* 3.66), whereas Livy says that for the auspices Numa was seated on a stone facing south. It was always a very simple affair, the only building being a hut of thatch, presumably periodically rebuilt (Vitruvius 2.1.5). It may have lain at the head of the Sacra Via facing the Alban Mount.

AJA 82 (1978): 240–42 (L. Richardson); *BullCom* 87 (1980–81): 19–23 (G. Gianelli).

Auguraculum (2): mentioned only by Varro (*Ling.* 5.50) in his list of the Argeorum Sacraria (q.v.) as the sixth sacrarium of the Regio Collina on the Collis Latiaris, the lowest lobe of the Quirinal. The reading is corrupt, the manuscripts having *auraculum,* so there is some doubt about this, and we do not know much about the topography of the Collis Latiaris.

Auguratorium: listed by the regionary catalogues in Regio X; mentioned by the *Mirabilia* (Jordan 2.637; VZ 3.58): *ubi est S. Caesarius fuit auguratorium Caesaris.* Hülsen (HCh 232–33) locates the church of S. Caesarius in the so-called Stadium of Domitian, or Hippodromus Palatii, in the Domus Augustana. Because these are now our only sources for this landmark, they must be accepted, and any attempt to attach this to the Curia Saliorum or any other augural templum is quite futile. Our knowl-

edge of this part of the imperial palace is woefully incomplete. *CIL* 6.976 = *ILS* 317 may refer to a restoration of this building by Hadrian.

Augustus, Ara: an altar dedicated by Tiberius in Augustus's lifetime, known only from the Fasti Praenestini; the day of dedication was 17 January (Degrassi 401).

Augustus, Divus, Sacrarium: a shrine to Divus Augustus in Regio X at the site of his birthplace *ad Capita Bubula* (q.v.). It is mentioned by Suetonius (*Aug.* 5.1), who says that it existed in his day but was built only some time after Augustus's death, and in inscriptions (*CIL* 6.2329, 2330b = *ILS* 4992, 4993). It was built by Livia as Iulia Augusta (Pliny, *NH* 12.94) and after her deification rededicated by Tiberius (Cass. Dio 56.46.3) as the Templum Divi Augusti et Divae Augustae (*CIL* 6.4222 = *ILS* 4995). It was called Aedes Divorum in Palatio by the Arval Brethren (*CIL* 6.2035 = 32349, 2087, 32379) and, perhaps loosely, Caesaraeum (*CIL* 6.2104). This is probably also the Aedes Caesarum of Suetonius (*Galb.* 1) that was struck by lightning in A.D. 69, at which time all the heads fell and the scepter was dashed from the hand of Augustus.

Augustus, Divus, Templum: one of the thorniest problems in all of the topography of ancient Rome, a temple built by Tiberius (Cass.Dio 57.10.2). Tiberius either did not finish it, or finished it but did not dedicate it (Suetonius, *Tib.* 47; Tacitus, *Ann.* 6.45). It was dedicated by Caligula (Suetonius, *Calig.* 21), the day of dedication probably being 5 October, and the statue of Diva Livia was added by Claudius (Cass.Dio 60.5). It was used by Caligula as one of the supports for his famous bridge connecting the Palatine with the Capitoline (Suetonius, *Calig.* 22). It was destroyed by fire sometime before A.D. 79 (Pliny, *HN* 12.94) and evidently restored by Domitian, at which time it was connected with, or close to, a shrine of Minerva, possibly the library mentioned below (Martial 4.53.1–2; *CIL* 16.36–157, 160–89). It was extensively restored by Antoninus Pius, whose coins show it as octastyle with Corinthian capitals and containing two statues. The last mention of it is in a military diploma of A.D. 298 (*CIL* 16.156).

It is shown on coins of Caligula (*B. M. Coins, Rom. Emp.* 1 Caligula nos. 41–43, 58, 69) as hexastyle with Ionic or Corinthian columns, a sculptured pediment, and, on the roof, a central acroterion of a quadriga and lateral acroteria of Romulus with the *spolia opima* and Aeneas leading Ascanius and carrying Anchises. As rebuilt by Antoninus and shown very frequently on his coins (*B. M. Coins, Rom. Emp.* 4 Antoninus Pius nos. 916, 938–43,

1652, 1718, 1729, 2051, 2063–66, 2070, 2072, 2079, 2098), it is octastyle with Corinthian columns and the same program of acroteria.

In literature it is called Templum Augusti or Divi Augusti, except by Martial (4.53.2) and Suetonius (*Tib.* 74), who call it Templum Novum, a name that it seems to have been given early and that appears in the Acta Fratrum Arvalium (e.g., *CIL* 6.32346.10, 2041.5, 2042a.28 = *ILS* 230, *CIL* 6.2051.14), along with the variant Templum Divi Augusti Novum (*CIL* 6.2028e.12, 2044c.5, 32345). It contained a painting of Hyacinthus by Nicias of Athens (Pliny, *HN* 35.131) and other treasures (Pliny, *HN* 12.94). Connected with it was a library, the Bibliotheca Templi Divi Augusti (q.v.) or Templi Novi established by Tiberius. It is generally agreed that the large Domitianic building of brick-faced concrete often proposed to be the Temple of Augustus is rather an entrance hall to the Domus Tiberiana. The temple is presumed to lie somewhere to the west of this, behind the Basilica Iulia, in an area that has never been excavated.

BullCom 69 (1941): 29–58 (G. Lugli); Lugli 1946, 185–91; Nash 1.164; *Athenaeum* 52 (1974): 287–88 (R. E. A. Palmer).

Augustus Mons: Tacitus (*Ann.* 4.64) relates that after a fire on the Caelian had destroyed a great area, a statue of Tiberius there had miraculously remained unscathed. It was therefore proposed in the senate that the name of the Caelian be changed to Augustus. Suetonius (*Tib.* 48.1) says that Tiberius ordered this. If there was any such gesture, it was short-lived.

Aula Isiaca: a large vaulted hall discovered by Boni in 1912 under the "Basilica" in the north corner of the Domus Augustiana. It had been discovered earlier in the excavations of the Farnese family in 1724, at which time careful copies of the paintings were made, which are precious documents for the reconstruction of the decoration today. The hall is proportionately long and narrow, with one curved end, lit only through its doors and by a rectangular window high in the apsidal wall. It had a complicated architectural history, having been modified repeatedly, so the walls show construction going back to fine small reticulate facing and coming down to brick facing, the apse being a late feature. The hall was not isolated, but part of a larger complex, of which almost nothing is known. It was destroyed by the construction of a large reservoir, probably semicircular, but divided into chambers of roughly equal width by parallel walls, that is believed to belong to the Domus Transitoria of Nero. This cuts through the middle of the hall, and at this time the hall and the complex to which it belonged were buried.

The decoration, although in very poor condition today, except for some parts of the vault, is an important document for the development of the Third Pompeian Style in Rome, being an example roughly contemporary with the decorations of the house found in the gardens of Villa Farnesina known as the Casa della Farnesina. The walls are still treated architectonically with columns and pillars that rise from the dado to a deep frieze just under the vault and an elaborate central aedicula with an arched opening framing a subject picture. The rest of the wall is divided into three zones, the two lower ones being treated as a continuous wall, the upper one as space developing behind this in which we get glimpses of architecture. The continuous wall is divided between a deep lower zone painted with elaborate landscapes, some of which run behind columns, while others are marked off by them. There are also plain panels with floating erotes. Above these is a relatively deep band framed at base and top with running ornaments, the top developed as a cornice. This is embellished with a series of individually framed panels containing single figures and two-figure groups posed in artificial scrolling. All the architecture is covered with ornament and brilliantly colored in a very rich palette. Egyptianizing motifs and figures abound, especially those pertaining to the cult of Isis, hence the name given to the chamber. But the subjects of the landscapes are teasing and elusive, except for a possible disembarkation of Helen and Paris, with little that suggests Egypt. It seems unlikely that the room was actually used for cult practices.

The Aula Isiaca is usually dated to the time of Caligula, because of his known interest in the cult of Isis. However, the painting belongs rather to early than to fully developed Third Style. It is not far in character from the decorations of the Casa della Farnesina, which are usually assigned an Augustan date.

G. E. Rizzo, *Le pitture dell'Aula Isiaca di Caligola* (*Monumenti della pittura antica scoperti in Italia*, ser. 3, Roma fasc. 2 [Rome 1936]); *NSc* 25 (1971): 323–26 (G. Carettoni).

Aura: listed by the regionary catalogues in Regio IV, together with the equally mysterious Bucinum (*aureum bucinum, Not.*) and then mentioned in medieval documents that place it behind the Basilica Constantini and frequently connect it with an Arcus Aurae or Arcus Aureus that is the entrance to the Forum Transitorium east of the Temple of Minerva (see Forum Nervae). Representations of the seasons as allegorical figures are often called Horae, but there is no real support for the notion that such a statue might be meant.

HCh 177, 312, 316, 584, 596.

Aurelii: see **Sepulcrum Aureliorum.**

Aureum Bucinum: the reading of the manuscripts of the *Notitia* for Aura Bucinum in the *Curiosum* (see Aura and Bucinum).

Aventinus Mons (Fig. 14): the southernmost of the seven hills of Rome, lying southeast of the Tiber, divided into two heights, the Aventinus Maior and Aventinus Minor, or Aventine and Little Aventine (sometimes also called pseudo-Aventine), with a distinct cleft between them, down which ran the Vicus Portae Raudusculanae (Viale Aventino, Via di Porta S. Paolo). The slopes of the Aventinus Maior toward the river are precipitous, and those toward the southwest are very steep, so this hill has a very distinct geographical formation, but both heights were included in the circuit of the Servian Walls, and tradition held that Remus took his auspices for the founding of the city from the Saxum or Remoria on the Aventinus Minor. A fragment of the Acta Fratrum Arvalium (*NSc* 1914, 466, 473; *ILS* 9522) shows that in A.D. 240, though there was a distinction between the Aventinus Maior and Aventinus Minor, together they were considered a single geographical unit. Such now proves to have been the case with most of the lobes of the larger hills.

In the names given to the Augustan divisions of the city, Regio XIII is called Aventinus, while Regio XII, which includes the Aventinus Minor, is Piscina Publica, but, because both names are to be relatively late, the significance of this is minimal. Although the evidence of Ennius (Cicero, *Div.* 1.107) is equivocal, that of numerous other ancient authors seems quite unequivocal that the two parts of the Aventine were regarded as a single hill (see, e.g., Livy 1.6.4; Plutarch, *Rom.* 9.4; Paulus *ex Fest.* 344–45L).

It seems quite clear that for some reason the Aventine, though included within the circuit of the Servian Walls, was excluded from the pomerium until the time of Claudius. It was certainly not included in the city of the four regions (see Regiones Quattuor; cf. Varro, *Ling.* 5.45). The name Aventinus was provided with a number of etymologies, all fanciful, for the most part the name of a very ancient king (Livy 1.3.9; Paulus *ex Fest.* 17L; Vergil, *Aen.* 7.657 and Servius *ad Aen.* 7.657; Lydus, *Mag.* 1.34).

It appears that the Aventinus was originally *ager publicus,* as the settling there of people from the var-

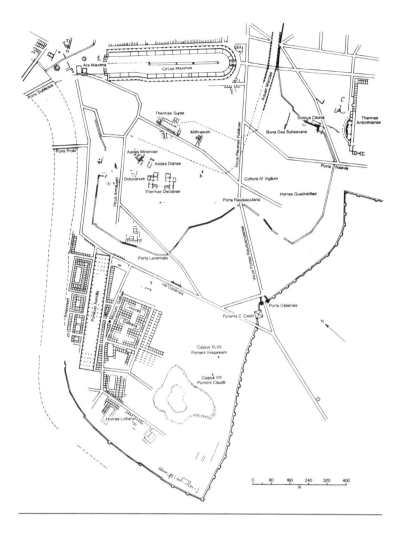

ious towns conquered by Rome shows (Livy 1.33.2; Dion. Hal. 3.43). Later parts of it were taken over unlawfully, until in 456 B.C. a Lex Icilia was passed giving it to the plebs for distribution among them (Dion. Hal. 10.31–32; Livy 3.31.1). Throughout the republic, it remained essentially a plebeian stronghold, where cults with plebeian associations found a place, but after the establishment of the empire it became a fashionable part of Rome to live in and continued so down to the late empire (see, e.g., Domus: L. Fabius Cilo, Licinius Sura, M. Valerius Bradua Mauricus).

A. Merlin, *L'Aventin dans l'antiquité* (Paris 1906).

Figure 14
Mons Aventinus, Emporium, Mons Testaceus, General Plan Showing Known Remains of Antiquity

47

B

Bacchus, Sacellum: see **Liber.**

Balineum, Balneum: see **Thermae.**

Balineum Abascanti: listed by the regionary catalogues in Regio I, but otherwise unknown. It may have been built by Domitian's freedman T. Flavius Abascantus, but the name is not uncommon.

Balnea Alexandri: baths said to have been built by Alexander Severus in all those parts of the city not provided with baths (S.H.A. *Alex. Sev.* 39).

Balineum Ampelidis: listed by the regionary catalogues in Regio XIV. It seems to have been shown on a lost fragment of the Marble Plan (*FUR* pls. 9 and 34.47; Rodriguez pl. 34.47), but not enough was preserved to give an idea of the building or any indication of its location.

Balineum Antiochiani: listed by the *Notitia* in Regio I, but otherwise unknown. PA suggests it may have been built by Flavius Antiochianus, cos. A.D. 270.

Balineum Bolani: mentioned only in the *Notitia*, listed in Regio I. PA suggests it may have been built by M. Vettius Bolanus, cos. suf. A.D. 66. His son of the same name was also consul in A.D. 111 (*PW* 2.16.1857–58; cf. *CIL* 6.65–67 = *ILS* 3500–3501).

Balineum Caenidianum: a bath created in what had been the property of Antonia Caenis, the concubine of Vespasian. It was in Villa Patrizi south of Via Nomentana, in the area now occupied by the Ministero dei Trasporti.
  MAAR 10 (1932): 73–74 (H. Sander); *RendPontAcc* 50 (1977–78): 153–54 (R. Friggeri).

Balineum Caesaris: the inscription on a fragment of the Marble Plan (*FUR* pl. 33.43; Rodriguez pl. 34.43). Its location is entirely unknown.

Balineum Charini: a bath mentioned by Martial (7.34) as the surprisingly good work of a *cinaedus* of the time of Domitian.

Balineum Claudianum: the inscription on a marble epistyle (*CIL* 6.29767) copied near the church of S. Silvestro al Quirinale and again near the Thermae Constantini. Other inscriptions relating to the Claudii come from the neighborhood (cf. Domus, Claudii), so probably this belongs here and refers to a public bath built at private expense.

Balneum Claudii Etrusci: described by Statius (*Silv.* 1.5) and praised by Martial (6.42) for the richness of the marble veneer, the clarity of the water, and the luxury and variety of the amenities offered. It was supplied by both the Aqua Virgo and the Aqua Marcia and must therefore have been in the Campus Martius, Regio VII or IX, more likely the former, but it cannot be placed more precisely.

Balneum Cotini: the inscription on a fragment of the Marble Plan (*FUR* pl. 34.48; Rodriguez pl. 34.48) now lost, and the drawing of it is uninformative.

Balineum Daphnidis: in Regio IV (*Not.*), presumably a private bath. The scholiast on Juvenal (7.233) says the Balineum Phoebi was the same as the *balneae quae Daphnes appellantur,* which might well be the same as this bath. Probably it was a much-frequented bath in the Subura, which did not have a readily accessible imperial bath complex until the building of the Baths of Titus.

Balineum Dianae (**Dianes**, *Cur.*): listed by the regionary catalogues in Regio XIV, otherwise unknown.

Balineum Fausti and **Balineum Fortunati:** mentioned by Martial (2.14.11) in a list of resorts in the southern Campus Martius, perhaps to be located south or west of the Theatrum Pompeii.

Balineum Germani: known only from a lead tessera (Rostovtzeff, *Sylloge* no. 886).

Balinea Gordiani: a few unpretentious baths that Gordian III built in different parts of the city for the use of ordinary citizens (S.H.A. *Gordian.* 32.5).

Balineum Gratiarum (**Loutron Chariton**): known from an inscription in Greek stating that it was built by Memphis and Gelasis (*IG* 14.1034, found in 1715, together with *IG* 14.1424; *IGUR* 203). This lay in a beautiful room veneered with marble and with a white marble alveus found on the Aventinus Minor facing Porta Ostiensis (*RömMitt* 2 [1894]: 332–33 [C. Hülsen]; HJ xxi and 187–88).

Balineum Grylli: mentioned twice by Martial (1.59.3, 2.14.12) in a list of buildings of which those that can be identified are in the southern Campus Martius. Apparently it was famous for being badly lit.

Balineum Iuliorum Akariorum: known only from an inscription in the Einsiedeln sylloge. The inscription (*CIL* 6.29764) is said to have been found near the Pons Gratiani (Pons Cestius).

Balineum Lupi: a bath mentioned by Martial (2.14.12; cf. 1.59.3), so notorious for its draftiness that he nicknamed it the Aeolia.

Balineum Mamertini: mentioned in the regionary catalogues, listed in Regio I. PA suggests the bath may have been built by Sex. Petronius Mamertinus, praetorian prefect A.D. 139–143.

Balneum Mercurii: known only from the Einsiedeln itinerary (9): *ibi est aqua subtus Aventinum currens scala usque in montem Aventinum et balneum Mercurii.* This puts it somewhere along the northeast slope of the Aventine above the Circus Maximus, perhaps not far from its northern extremity. Whether it was actually a bath is doubtful; a fountain seems more likely. See also Aqua Mercurii.

Balineae (and **Balneae**) **Naeratii Cerealis:** built by the consul of A.D. 358 (*CIL* 6.1744, 31916 = *ILS* 5718) and found in 1873 on the Esquiline in the modern city block north of the basilica of S. Maria Maggiore, but only hurriedly and partially excavated. Parts of the foundations and a considerable number of architectural members and sculptures were recovered (*BullCom* 2 [1874]: 84–88 [R. Lanciani]). Probably the house of the Naeratii was not far away, possibly on the Vicus Patricius (*BullCom* 33 [1905]: 294–99 [G. Gatti]).

Balneae Pallacinae: mentioned only by Cicero (*Rosc. Am.* 18). There was a Vicus Pallacinae following the line of the modern Via delle Botteghe Oscure and Via S. Marco, and this may have given its name to a district. The baths could have been almost anywhere here, because the subsoil of the Campus Martius is rich in water.

Balneum Phoebi: mentioned only by Juvenal (7.233), where possibly the name is used only *exempli gratia*. Cf. Balineum Daphnidis.

Balneum Plautini: see **Lavacrum Plautini.**

Balneum Polycleti: Porphyrion, commenting on Horace, *Ars P.* 32, says the Ludus Aemilii had been converted into the Balneum Polycleti in his day. Because Horace is talking about bronze sculpture in this passage, and the Ludus Aemilii may well have been a school for artisans in bronze, the name may have been a humorous invention at the time of the remodeling. There is no indication of where it stood.

Balneum Prisci: mentioned only in the *Notitia*, listed in Regio XIV. Lugli (Lugli 1938, 633) suggests the Balineum Ampelidis was the Balineum Ampelidis Prisci.

Balneum Scriboniolum: located in Regio XII, known from a single inscription, a slave identification, found at Grottaferrata (*CIL* 15.7188).

Balneae Seniae: known only from Cicero (*Cael.* 61–62), in which they figure in an intrigue involving delivery of poison and the laying of a trap for those involved. They seem to have been well known at the time but cannot be located. *Seniae* is unusual, not a known cognomen, and perhaps should be corrected to *Saeniae*.
   MEFRA 97 (1985): 325–28 (A. Vessilieiou).

Balneae Severi: baths built by Septimius Severus on the right bank of the Tiber near the Porta Septimiana. If the Historia Augusta (S.H.A. *Sept. Sev.* 19.5) is accurate in saying that the early collapse of the aqueduct supplying these baths prevented the public from enjoying them, it is difficult to understand why, because the proximity of the Aqua Traiana would have made substitution very easy. (See also Thermae Septimianae and Severianae). Richmond (224–26) has proposed that what is meant is that the Aurelian Walls cut through these baths, but it is hard to get this from the Latin.

Balnea Stephani: mentioned twice by Martial (11.52.4, 14.60) and said to be very close to his house (q.v.), which was on the Quirinal on a street leading from the Temple of Flora to the Capitolium Vetus (Martial 5.22.3–4). This indicates that they were somewhere along a street leading from modern Piazza Barberini to the ridge of the Quirinal, a line followed by Via delle Quattro Fontane.

Balneum qui Cognominatur Templus (in Vicum Longum): listed in the *Liber Pontificalis* (LPD 1.42.6; VZ 2.236) as among the possessions of the basilica of Saints Gervasius and Protasius, dedicated under Pope Innocent I (401–417), the present church of S. Vitale (HCh 498–99). This does not give us much to go on. Because it stood *in Vicum Longum* and not *in Vico Longo,* it must have been on a side street, and the name *Templus* is very strange.

RivStorAnt 4 (1974): 146–48 (R. E. A. Palmer).

Balneum Tigellini: a public bath evidently built by Nero's favorite. It is mentioned only by Martial (3.20.16), on a lead tessera (Rostovtzeff, *Sylloge* no. 888), and in a gloss (*CGL* 3.657.14), but there can be no doubt of its existence. Tigellinus had real estate in the Aemiliana (q.v.), so it might be there that we should look for it.

Balineum Torquati: a private bath listed by the regionary catalogues in Regio I just after the Lacus Promethei.

Balineum Vespasiani: listed by the regionary catalogues in Regio I, together with the Balineum Torquati, but otherwise unknown.

Basilica: the name given by the Romans to a type of building that became important just after the beginning of the second century after Christ, a public hall, the roof supported on columns (later often arches), in which a central nave is surrounded by one or more aisles. The nave may have its ceiling raised a second, or even third, storey on a clerestorey, and there may be a gallery over the surrounding aisle, either an open deck or a closed balcony overlooking the central nave. One side or end is regularly open to a public square, or street, and there is usually a raised tribunal at the end of the principal axis, long or short,

which is given special architectural emphasis. The successful exploitation of the form depends on comprehension of the possibilities of truss roofing to free the central area of encumbrances.

Our oldest example of such a building is that known as the hypostyle hall on Delos, very tentative and somewhat awkward in design, the clerestorey hardly more than a small square lantern over the center of the building, the surrounding aisles progressively lower as they move away from the center. It is securely dated between 210 and 207 B.C. and gives us a *terminus post quem* for all other basilicas (*Délos* 2.1, *La Salle hypostyle* [G. Leroux, 1909], 2.2, *Complement* [R. Vallois and G. Poulsen, 1914]).

In Rome there was an early basilica that had no other name, evidently a small experimental building below the Cloaca on the northeast side of the Forum Romanum in an area later covered by the southern part of the Basilica Fulvia et Aemilia (Plautus, *Curc.* 472). With the building of the Basilica Porcia in 184 B.C., basilicas began to be named, and the original basilica gave way to the Basilica Fulvia et Aemilia in 179 B.C. (Livy 40.51).

Basilicas served especially as business halls, the places where bankers set up their tables, entrepreneurs sold shares in enterprises, and the like. By the first century B.C. the tribuni plebis were accustomed to appear in the Basilica Porcia and hold audience, probably on its tribunal. Still later, under the early empire, the centumviral court met in the Basilica Iulia (Martial 6.38.5–6; Pliny, *Epist.* 5.9.1–5, 6.33.1–6), and after the time of Trajan most courts may regularly have met in basilicas. Earlier, however, religious considerations forced them to meet in the open air. The unencumbered space provided by basilicas encouraged the expansion of their use.

Roma, archeologia nel centro (1985), 1.56–66 (M. Gaggiotti).

Basilica Aemilia: see **Basilica Paulli.**

Basilica Alexandrina: a columnar hall Alexander Severus is said to have undertaken to build between the Campus Martius and the Saepta Iulia (S.H.A. *Alex. Sev.* 26.7). It was to be 100 feet (29.70 m) wide, 1,000 feet (297 m) long, and completely columnar. We are told that he was prevented from completing the project by death, but, because the Saepta was completely surrounded by a deep belt of buildings by this time, the whole project sounds fictitious.

Basilica Argentaria (Fig. 36): listed in the regionary catalogues in Regio VIII between the Cohors VI Vigilum and the Temple of Concordia. The Clivus Argentarius, though known only from medieval documents, is well identified as the road running from

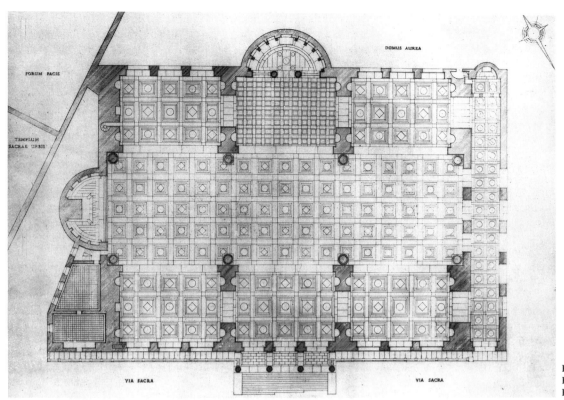

Figure 15
Basilica Constantini,
Floor Plan, Restored

the Carcer over the east shoulder of the Capitoline to the Campus Martius (VZ 1.115n.4). The Basilica Argentaria has therefore been thought to be the L-shaped arcaded hall built by Domitian and Trajan to link the west portico of Forum Iulium and Forum Traiani, the only unidentified building of importance hereabout. The floor of this hall was raised a half-dozen steps above that of the porticoes of the Forum Iulium, and the pillars were rusticated, so the building has an aesthetic distinction from its adjacent neighbors and reads as a separate entity.

MAAR 13 (1932): 219 (O. Grossi); Nash 1.430–31.

Basilica Claudii: listed by Polemius Silvius at the end of his catalogue of the eleven basilicas of Rome, but otherwise unknown.

Basilica Constantini or **Nova** (Polemius Silvius 545; *Not.* Reg. IV), **Basilica Constantiniana** (Chron. *146*; *Not.* app.) (Figs. 15, 90): begun by Maxentius, but completed by Constantine after 313 (Aur. Vict., *Caes.* 40.26) with some alteration of the program. It stands on the north side of Sacra Via, on land previously at least in part covered by Domitian's Horrea Piperataria (Chron. 146), the last of the great secular basilicas of Rome, a great shell of brick-faced concrete, which owes more in design to

the great central halls of the imperial baths than it does to classical basilicas. Although it remained in use in the Middle Ages, it had lost its proper designation by the sixth century and was called Templum Urbis Romae and Templum Romuli (LPD 1.279, 323). The south aisle and nave probably collapsed in the earthquake of Pope Leo IV in ca. 847 (LPD 2.108).

It stood on a platform of concrete raised a storey above the Sacra Via at its west end; this was 100 m long and 65 m wide. It consisted of a central nave flanked by side aisles, each divided into three equal sections communicating with the nave along their whole width and with one another by generous archways. Everything was vaulted, and all the vaults were deeply coffered in elaborate patterns of octagons, hexagons, and lozenges. The cross-vaulted roof of the great central nave, 80 m long, 25 m wide, and 35 m high, appeared supported on eight monolithic columns of Proconnesian marble, of which the sole surviving member is now in Piazza S. Maria Maggiore, taken there in 1614 (LS 2.209).

As designed by Maxentius, the entrance was to be at the east end, from a short street leading off the Sacra Via. Here a single-storey narthex, 8 m deep, preceded the building. This had five entrances to the basilica proper, three to the nave and one to each side aisle, but only two to the exterior on the east, that opposite the north aisle having been suppressed in order to preserve parts of the Domus Aurea. Another door led to the narthex at its south end. At the west end of the nave opened a vast apse, 20 m in diameter, with a half-dome; this probably became the setting of a seated colossus of Constantine. Parts of this acrolithic statue were found in 1486 and are now displayed in the courtyard of Palazzo dei Conservatori.

Constantine changed the design by adding a new entrance at the middle of the south side. Here a flight of steps led up from the Sacra Via to a shallow porch with four porphyry columns framing three double doors. Opposite this, on the short axis, he opened a second apse in the north wall, somewhat lower than that at the west end, screened from the nave by a pair of columns which must have carried a straight epistyle. In this apse a large central niche with a round head is flanked by rows of square-headed niches in two zones, four on a side, sixteen in all. Here a gallery of Constantine's lieutenants may have flanked a standing figure of the emperor. Generous round-headed windows in two zones, six to a room, lit the chambers of the side aisles, and triple-light arched windows of the type familiar from bath complexes opened in the clerestorey of the nave.

The floor was paved with colored marble in a pattern similar to that of the Pantheon. The walls were revetted with marble up to the springing of the vaults. Vaults and exterior were finished with stucco, painted and gilded. Niches for statuary abound in the interior, and presumably the exterior was similarly embellished, but we know nothing of the program.

The building was a triumph of engineering, the central nave having been the largest cross-vaulted hall in antiquity and supported by an ingenious system of flying buttresses. Stairs hidden in the thickness of the walls gave access to the roofs over the side aisles at strategic points, and stairs built into the concrete of the roofs facilitated maintenance. However, the necessity of tunneling through the concrete platform on which the basilica stands to permit a road there to continue in use (the Arcus Latronis) alarmed the builders so much that they added an enormous buttress at this point and a series of relieving arches in the superstructure above it.

The basilica was a great masterpiece and has been admired by architects and artists throughout its history. It was exhaustively studied in the High Renaissance, and its impact on such architects as Bramante, Raphael, Antonio da Sangallo, and Michelangelo was immense. Its influence on the design of the new basilica of S. Pietro is readily apparent.

PBSR 12 (1932): 1–25 (A. Minoprio); Nash 1.180–92.

Basilica Floscellaria: mentioned only in the addenda to the regionary catalogues and Polemius Silvius, without indication of its location. It was evidently a center of the flower business.

Basilica Fulvia (Fulvia et Aemilia): see **Basilica Paulli.**

Basilica Gaii et Lucii: see **Basilica Iulia.**

Basilica Hilariana: a curious building of the end of the second century after Christ discovered on the Caelian in the grounds of the military hospital in the angle between Piazza Celimontana and Via di S. Stefano Rotondo. Only a small part could be excavated, and our knowledge of it is consequently very imperfect. It was apparently half-underground; one descended a flight of twelve steps revetted with marble and came to a vestibule paved with black-and-white mosaic. This showed an eye pierced by a spear and assailed by a ring of birds and animals. Beyond it was a *tabula ansata* with the inscription: *intrantibus hic deos / propitios et basilic(ae) / Hilarianae* (CIL 6.30973a = *ILS* 3992) and a threshold with the outline of feet entering and leaving. The room to which this gave held a rectangular basin rather like an impluvium, but 0.70 m deep, and a statue base with an inscription showing that it was for a statue of M'. Poblicius Hilarus, *margaritarius,* set up by the collegium of *dendrophoroi* (CIL 6.30973b = *ILS* 4171). So the building belonged to a collegium devoted to the cults of the Magna Mater and Attis, presumably built for them by Hilarus, and this permits association of yet another inscription, *CIL* 6.641 = *ILS* 3540, with it. Its claim to being a basilica is mysterious, because it shows none of the characteristics of basilical architecture. Whether this was the schola of the collegium must remain doubtful, but seems likely.

Nash 1.183–85; *QArchEtr* 19 (1990): 72–80 (A. Corignani et al.).

Basilica Iulia: on the southwest side of the Forum Romanum between the temples of Saturn and Castor, filling this side in monumental grandeur. It was begun by Julius Caesar to replace the Basilica Sempronia of 170 B.C., probably about 54 B.C. (Cicero, *Att.* 4.16.8), paid for out of the spoils of the Gallic wars, and dedicated unfinished in 46 (Augustus, *RG* 20; Hieron. *a. Abr.* 1971). It was completed by Augustus, but then soon burned and was rebuilt in enlarged form and dedicated in the names of Gaius and Lucius Caesar in A.D. 12 (Augustus, *RG* 20; Cass.Dio 56.27.5; Suetonius, *Aug.* 29.4). It burned again in the fire of Carinus and was restored by Diocletian (Chron. 148) and restored again by Gabinius

Vettius Probianus, praefectus urbi in A.D. 416, at which time he embellished it with statues (*CIL* 6.1156 = *ILS* 722, *CIL* 6.1658, 31883 = *ILS* 9354, *CIL* 6.31884–87). Despite its rededication in the names of Gaius and Lucius, the original name persisted in use (see, e.g., Martial 6.38.6; Statius, *Silv.* 1.1.29). Part of the basilica is represented on the Marble Plan (*FUR* pl. 21; Rodriguez pl. 13).

It occupied a space 101 m long and 49 m wide, bounded on all sides by streets, fronting on the street along the southwest side of the forum, with the Vicus Iugarius and Vicus Tuscus at its ends and an unnamed street behind. The central nave, 82 m long and 16 m wide, was surrounded by two aisles, each 7.50 m wide, over which there were galleries in a second storey. These aisles were all arcaded, the façade being of blocks of white marble, while the inner rows of arcading were of concrete faced with marble. There were eighteen pillars on the long sides, and eight on the short ones. The façade was embellished with an engaged order, Tuscan on the ground storey, and unfluted Ionic above. The floor was paved with marble, colored in the nave, and white in the aisles. Because the ground sloped down from the Vicus Iugarius to the Vicus Tuscus, a gradually increasing number of steps had to be introduced to bring visitors into the basilica; these increase from one at the west end to seven at the east. Between the top of these and the façade is a narrow walk, and three steps then lead into the northern aisle, while two more lead from the outer to the inner aisle. The outer aisle on the principal façade thus has much of the character of a separate portico.

At the back of the basilica, a row of tabernae with walls of tufa and travertine responding to the pillars of the arcading opened in toward the basilica, and stairs show that there must have been another storey of such tabernae above. How accessible the flat roof over the aisle may have been is doubtful; the report that Caligula threw coins to the people from it (Suetonius, *Calig.* 37.1) need not mean it was in regular use. The roof over the central nave was a trussed gable raised on a clerestorey.

Little survives but the pavement and foundations of the arcading. Toward the northwest corner, some brick pillars and arches belong to the restoration of Diocletian. Some fragments of the architecture have been restored, but the travertine façade pillar now standing is modern and simply intended to show the architectural forms.

The basilica was especially accommodation for banking and similar business (*CIL* 6.9709 = *ILS* 7509, *CIL* 6.9711). Late in the first century after Christ it came to be used for the sessions of the centumviral court (Martial 6.38.5–6; Pliny, *Epist.* 5.9.1; Quintilian 12.5.6). We are not informed about

what other uses it may have served, but presumably the tabernae were government offices, and the use of the basilica was constant and heavy.

RendLinc, ser. 8.16 (1961): 53–60 (G. Carettoni and L. Fabbrini); *BullCom* 78 (1961–62): 37–54 (L. Fabbrini); Nash 1.186–89; Coarelli 1985, 322–24.

Basilica Iulia Aquiliana: mentioned by Vitruvius (5.1.4) as having been adapted to a long narrow site by the addition of chalcidica at either end. It has been conjectured that it was built by C. Aquillius Gallus, the great jurist, in honor of Julius Caesar, but there is no proof. More likely it was a business house built as a commercial venture; we have no indication of its location.

Basilica Iunii Bassi: on the Esquiline east of S. Maria Maggiore, built by the consul ordinarius of A.D. 331 (*CIL* 6.1737), who died in 359 (*CIL* 6.32004 = *ILS* 1286). It was in form like a Christian church, an apsidal hall with windows set high in the side walls preceded by a lower, but two-storeyed, narthex with rounded ends. It survived in good condition until the Renaissance, and Giuliano da Sangallo has left a drawing of the interior decoration that shows it to have been very rich, with marble revetment that was essentially architectonic, with pilasters dividing the walls into bays, but including figural panels of opus sectile. The marbles used were the richest in color, especially serpentine and porphyry. Of the figural panels, two showing tigers attacking calves are now on the stair of Palazzo dei Conservatori, whereas one of Hylas and one showing the consul in a biga with mounted escorts representing the four circus factions were formerly in Palazzo del Drago.

In the time of Pope Simplicius (468–483) the basilica was converted into the church of S. Andrea Catabarbara Patricia (HCh 179–81). This was absorbed into the monastery of S. Andrea in Assaio before the year 1000 and gradually abandoned. Parts of the decorations were removed in the eighteenth and nineteenth centuries, after which only naked and ruinous walls remained. These were finally destroyed in 1930 to make way for the Oriental seminary.

EAA 3, s.v. "Giunio Basso" (C. Bertelli); *RendPontAcc* 40 (1967–68): 151–70 (M. Cagiano de Azevedo); Nash 1.190–95.

Basilica Matidiae et Marcianae: The regionary catalogues list in Regio IX between the Pantheon and Templum Divi Antonini a Basilicam Matidies et Marcianes *(Not.)* or Basilicam Neptuni, Matidiaes, Marciani *(Cur.)*. It is otherwise known only from Polemius Silvius (545; VZ 1.309). We know from coins that Marciana and her daughter Matidia, grandmother and mother of Hadrian's wife, Sabina, were revered together (*B. M. Coins, Rom. Emp.* 3 Trajan no. 531) and that following their deaths they were given divine honors. Marciana was accorded by senatus consultum the car drawn by a pair of elephants in which she sits with the attributes of Ceres (*B. M. Coins, Rom. Emp.* 3 Trajan no. 655 pl. 21.9), while Matidia received by senatus consultum a building dedicated Divae Matidiae Socrui that appears on a rare bronze of Hadrian (Nash 2.37 fig. 717). This is shown as a small aedicula with two columns in which a female figure sits enthroned. It is surmounted by a triangular pediment surmounted by acroterial statues at the apex and each front corner. To either side of the aedicula on a base that is an extension of that of the aedicula, but under a slightly lower lintel, is a statue, probably female, on a high plinth. To either side of these, evidently to be read as projecting at right angles to the central group, is a portico in two storeys on a base continuous with the rest. The lower storey is columnar; the much lower attic seems not to be columnar but is difficult to read. The roofing is very uncertain. Only three bays of the flanking portico are shown to either side. It seems possible that we are intended to read this as a short section of a basilical building with small axial shrines at the ends—that to Marciana at one end, that to Matidia at the other.

In 1636, in excavations in connection with the façade of S. Ignazio, a lead pipe with the inscription *Templum Matidiae* was found (*CIL* 15.7248). This apparently belonged to a supply line from the Aqua Virgo, but its precise location and original direction can no longer be identified. It therefore serves only to put the temple in this vicinity.

On R. Lanciani's *FUR* under the southeast corner of Palazzo Serlupi is shown a paved area flanked by lines of columns with the notation *Scavi Piranesi*. C. Hülsen (HJ 575n.13) speaks of a building with granite columns, 0.90 m in diameter, and a splendid marble pavement, known from excavations of 1779, the year after Piranesi's death, but known from "Piranesi, Pantheon, Tf. 1." I have been unable to verify this. Lanciani (*BullCom* 11 [1883]: 15) mentions remains of a splendid building found in the time of Piranesi "of form and measurements as shown on my plan," as though he were then unable to cite any further source. If his drawing is accurate, the building may well have been basilical and the granite columns suggest a Hadrianic date. It is certainly the best candidate at present available for the Basilica Matidiae et Marcianae.

Nash 2.36–37; Boatwright 58–62.

Basilica Maxentii: see **Basilica Constantini.**

Basilica Neptuni (Fig. 64): listed by the *Curiosum* in Regio IX, included by Polemius Silvius, and recorded in the life of Hadrian as among his restorations (S.H.A. *Hadr.* 19.10). This is now generally accepted as identical with the Stoa of Poseidon that Dio (53.27.1) says was built by Agrippa in 25 B.C. and the Poseidonion listed as destroyed in the fire of Titus in 79 (Cass. Dio 66.24.2). It is always associated with the Pantheon, Saepta, and Baths of Agrippa and can with some confidence, although without proof, be identified as the large basilical hall between the Pantheon and the baths. Its design, like that of the Basilica Constantini, owes more to the central halls of imperial bath complexes than it does to classical basilicas. Drawings by Palladio (Zorzi, figs. 136–43) in large part confirmed by excavations show it as a large rectangular hall with wide rectangular niches at the ends and a deep semicircular niche on the north side on the short axis. The roof was cross-vaulted in three sections, supported on eight fluted columns with Corinthian capitals that carry an entablature in which the frieze is decorated with marine motifs. Smaller niches in a single zone break up the surfaces of the walls. There may have been entrances at either end, one giving directly to the Porticus Argonautarum of the Saepta, but the principal entrance was probably that connecting it to the Baths of Agrippa. There was no connection with the Pantheon. There is no indication of the purpose the building served, and the architectural form and style are Hadrianic, not Augustan.

Nash 1.196–97; *RendLinc*, ser. 8.35 (1980): 181–92 (G. Tedeschi Grisanti).

Basilica Nova: see **Basilica Constantini.**

Basilica Opimia: closely linked with the Temple of Concordia and probably built when L. Opimius rebuilt the temple in 121 B.C., perhaps only an annex of the temple. It is known only from a single mention in Varro (*Ling.* 5.156) and a couple of inscriptions of *servi publici de Basilica Opimia* (*CIL* 6.2338, 2339 = *ILS* 1969). The space available, as described by Varro, seems exiguous, and the basilica seems to have been eliminated when Tiberius rebuilt the Temple of Concordia beginning in 7 B.C. It can never have been a large building, and it must be left uncertain on which side of the Temple of Concordia it stood, although the Gradus Monetae (q.v.) make it more probable that it stood southwest of the temple.

Basilica Paulli (Fig. 39): always one of the most celebrated buildings of ancient Rome, located at the juncture of the Argiletum and the Sacra Via, balancing the Basilica Iulia on the opposite side of the

Forum Romanum, but technically in Regio IV *(Not.)*. Soundings under the floor have brought to light remains of two earlier basilicas, but the earliest of all, that mentioned by Plautus *(Curc. 472)* must have stood east of the Cloaca, because it is listed after the shrine of Cloacina in a sequence moving from west to east. This was unnamed and apparently built between 210 B.C., when fire devastated the area and there were as yet no basilicas (Livy 26.27.2–5), and the reconstruction of the Tabernae Novae in 193 by the plebeian aediles M. Iunius Brutus and L. Oppius Salinator (Livy 35.23.7; Festus 258L), because for Plautus it was not separated from the forum by a row of shops. In 179 M. Fulvius Nobilior as censor let the contract for building a basilica *post argentarias novas* (Livy 40.51.5), at which time the Cloaca must have been diverted from the so-called Braccio Morto that runs through the substructures of the basilica to the channel that runs around its west end, while the Braccio Morto was roofed and buried. Of the basilica, a foundation wall of Grotta Oscura tufa with the settings of two columns and part of a third was recovered, together with small parts of a tufa pavement, in 1946–1948. The columns were 1.10 m in diameter; the intercolumniation of 4.93–4.95 m shows that the superstructure must have been entirely of wood. This lay parallel to the northern line of columns of the nave of the imperial building, about 0.50 m south of it. Parallel to this, about 2 m south of it, a small section of a second, lighter foundation wall of similar tufa, but differing in construction, was found. Other finds included an archaic cistern with beehive-shaped dome, which had been deliberately filled with blocks of cappellaccio. Although it is not possible to reconstruct the basilica completely from these remains, one can see clearly that it had light, open architecture like the early basilicas of Cosa and Ardea. It has since been reburied, but its place is marked on the existing pavement.

In the same exploration a second foundation came to light parallel to the west colonnade of the imperial basilica, consisting of three footings for columns of blocks of Grotta Oscura tufa connected in series by somewhat lighter walls. These show columns of the same dimension as before (diameter 1.05 m), but with the astonishing intercolumniation of 5.85 m, and they have remains of a pavement of travertine slabs clearly associated with them. This must be remains of the rebuilding of L. Aemilius Paullus, of which Cicero writes indignantly in 54 B.C. *(Att. 4.16.8)*, saying that Paullus had salvaged the columns of the previous building for reuse. As Tenney Frank *(Buildings, 67)* acutely perceived, Paullus's work must have been twofold, a restoration on which he spent as little as possible and used as much of the older building as he could, and a magnificent rebuilding financed by Julius Caesar from the spoils of the Gallic wars (Plutarch, *Caes.* 29; Appian, *BellCiv* 2.26). After 54 this is always called Basilica Paulli, except once by Varro *(Ling. 6.4: Basilica Aemilia et Fulvia)* and once by Pliny referring to an event of 78 B.C. *(HN 35.13: in Basilica . . . Aemilia)*.

Between Fulvius Nobilior's original construction and Aemilius Paullus's magnificent rebuilding there is almost no record of the building. In 159 B.C. P. Cornelius Scipio Nasica installed a water clock adjacent to it (Varro, *Ling.* 6.4; Censorinus, *De Die Nat.* 23.7; Pliny, *HN* 7.215). And in 78 B.C. M. Aemilius Lepidus decorated it with *imagines clipeatae* of his ancestors (Pliny, *HN* 35.13). There is no record, literary or archaeological, of any restoration or rebuilding. By 54 it must have seemed a very antiquated and dilapidated edifice.

The rebuilding by Paullus was extravagant, and he did not live to complete it. He was proscribed by the second triumvirate, fled, and died in exile. The basilica was finished and dedicated by his son, L. Aemilius Lepidus Paullus, when he was consul in 34 (Cass. Dio 49.42). It burned in 14 B.C. and was restored by Augustus and the friends of Paullus (Cass. Dio 54.24). Later, in A.D. 22, it was restored by M. Aemilius Lepidus at his own expense (Tacitus, *Ann.* 3.72). Pliny *(HN 36.102)* considered it, the Forum Augustum, and Templum Pacis the most beautiful buildings in Rome and speaks of its Phrygian marble columns as especially beautiful. After the first century the basilica is scarcely mentioned, though it continued in use down to the early fifth century, when a fire destroyed the roof.

With the bank of tabernae that preceded it, the basilica occupied the space between the Argiletum and a small street along the west side of the Temple of Antoninus and Faustina (Corneta?) and from Sacra Via to the Macellum. The line of tabernae was still in effect a separate structure screening off the basilica proper from the forum. From the Sacra Via one mounted a flight of seven steps with a landing at halfway to a very deep arcaded portico, above which was a second arcaded storey reached by a stair at either end and from which spectators could view events in the forum. At the east end a porch a single intercolumniation wide and deep projected toward Sacra Via, a rather curious annex. Behind the arcaded portico opened the row of fifteen tabernae, three of which were really simply entrances to the basilica, while two were stairs to the gallery above. These were all given vaulted ceilings in concrete. The granite columns in the portico today do not belong to the basilica, but to a late-antique rehandling of parts of the ruin of it.

The interior was treated as a great central nave surrounded on all four sides by an aisle and with a second, narrow aisle along the north side. The columns of the nave were of africano from Teos with white marble bases and Corinthian capitals, and those of the northeast extra aisle were of cipollino. The pavement was of polychrome marble. The distribution of architectural elements, of which a great many lie scattered in the area, is disputed and awaits definitive study and publication, but above the ground storey was a second storey with columns of africano at smaller scale. Everything else seems to have been of white marble. The most interesting feature is a frieze laboriously reconstructed from a multitude of fragments showing scenes from the early history and traditions of Rome, which seems to have been part of the entablature of the lower storey of the nave (now in the Antiquarium Forense, Helbig⁴ 2.2062), while the upper had a frieze decorated with an elaborate anthemion.

The façade of the front portico on the Argiletum is preserved in a drawing by Giuliano da Sangallo (Cod. Vat. Barb. Lat. 4424, fol. 26; Nash 1.178). This shows an engaged order of very elaborate design, Doric, the columns raised on plinths, carrying an entablature in which the metopes are decorated with bucrania and paterae. Because blocks of a freestanding order of the same design are found in the area, we can presume this order was carried as a colonnade at the short ends of the basilica. The doors to the portico in the drawing have ornate frames with ornament corresponding to that found elsewhere in this building.

At the east end one mounted three steps on the line of the colonnade; at the west end the steps precede the colonnade. The approach from the north (northeast) side was originally over three steps and through a colonnade like that on the southeast; this had a travertine pavement, and the columns were closer spaced than those of the nave, some twenty-five in all with footings revetted with africano. During or after the construction of Templum Pacis and Forum Nervae the colonnade was removed and replaced by a solid wall, so that the portico became in effect a narrow extra aisle of the basilica.

Discovery in 1899 of a large inscription, a dedication to Lucius Caesar (CIL 6.36908), grandson and adoptive son of Augustus, near the southeast corner of the portico, led E. B. Van Deman to identify the little projecting porch here as the Porticus Gaii et Lucii (q.v.) mentioned by Suetonius (Aug. 29.4) and Dio (56.27.5). The inscription, though broken, is substantially complete, and it seems that it cannot be far from its original place. In this identification Van Deman was followed by Gamberini Mongenet and Nash, who slightly modified her reconstruction of

the monument to make it an arcade that ran south to join the lowest storey of the Temple of Divus Iulius. But because the Fornix Fabianus spanning the Sacra Via very near here survived at least as late as the time of Saloninus Gallienus (S.H.A. Salon. 19.4), this interpretation is questionable. Besides, one would not have expected so insignificant a building to have been dedicated to such beloved grandsons (see also Epigraphica 31 [1969]: 104–12 [S. Panciera]). One might better think that the portico in front of the Basilica Paulli was rededicated to Gaius and Lucius after the rebuilding of 14 B.C., but, as was the case with the Basilica Iulia, the older, more familiar name remained in common use and eventually drove the new name out.

NSc 1948, 111–28 (G. Carettoni); Nash 1.174–79; BCSSA 29 (1983) (A. Ghisetti Giovarina, La Basilica Emilia e la rivalutazione del dorico nel rinascimento); Coarelli 1985, 135–38, 201–9; Arctos 21 (1987): 167–84 (M. Steinby); RömMitt 94 (1987): 325–32 (M. Wegner).

Basilica Porcia: the first named basilica in Rome, built by Cato as censor in 184 B.C. (Livy 39.44.7; [Aur. Vict.], De Vir. Ill. 47) against senatorial opposition (Plutarch, Cato Mai. 19.2), the reason for which is difficult to understand. It was a small building covering the ground previously occupied by only four shops and two private (?) atria, the Atrium Maenium and Atrium Titium, in lautumiis (q.v.), therefore between the Clivus Argentarius and the Curia Hostilia, facing on the former. The tribuni plebis came to use it as their public station (Plutarch, Cato Min. 5.1; see Tabula Valeria). It burned in the conflagration caused by the pyre of Clodius in 52 B.C. (Asconius in Milon. [Stangl 32]) and was evidently then not rebuilt.

Coarelli 1985, 59–63.

Basilica Sempronia: built in 170 B.C. by the censor Ti. Sempronius Gracchus behind the Tabernae Veteres (see Tabernae Circum Forum) toward the statue of Vertumnus, on land formerly occupied by the house of Scipio Africanus, butchers' stalls, and shops (Livy 44.16.10–11). It therefore stood at the point where the Vicus Tuscus entered the Forum Romanum and must have been replaced by the Basilica Iulia. It must have been built to balance the Basilica Fulvia et Aemilia on the opposite side of the forum, and therefore was probably a sizable building from the beginning, as Livy makes it sound, but no one informs us more precisely about its size or design.

RendLinc, ser. 8.16 (1961): 53–60 (G. Carettoni and L. Fabbrini); Coarelli 1985, 138–40.

Basilica Sicinini: see **Sicininum.**

Basilica Subterranea: Discovered in 1917, thanks to the collapse of the vault of its vestibule, under the Rome/Naples railway line just outside Porta Praenestina (Porta Maggiore) along Via Praenestina, the complex consists of a steep stair of access from Via Praenestina, now replaced by a modern access, a square vestibule of small dimensions, and a rectangular basilical hall divided into three vaulted naves by two lines of three large rectangular pillars connected by heavy arches. The hall measures about 12 m long by 9 m wide, and a semicircular apse with a half-domed ceiling finishes the central nave. The floor is 7.25 m below the level of Via Praenestina. The effect is thus of great height and mystery. Illumination was provided by a large skylight in the crown of the vault of the vestibule, but torches must have been necessary in the basilica itself.

The whole, vestibule and hall, walls and ceiling, was elaborately decorated with fine stucco reliefs and painting, much of which is preserved, although little of the color survives in the hall itself. In the main room the walls and ceiling are divided into rectangular panels of many different sizes by narrow moldings; where decorated, these are worked with egg moldings. The subjects of the decoration show the greatest variety. Illustrations of myths and literature, especially plays of Euripides, are varied with genre scenes, exotic subjects such as pygmies, decorative figures and masks, and the paraphernalia of cult. The only large composition, that filling the half-dome of the apse, has been identified as Sappho throwing herself into the sea from the Leucadian rock and about to be received by a Triton, who spreads a mantle wide with both hands. Although many of the scenes remain obscure, enough are identifiable that students of religion interpret this as a cult center for a congregation of neo-Pythagoreans. Scenes related to the mysteries of Dionysus are relatively numerous. Others maintain that the hall had no religious purpose and was simply a *specus aestivus*.

The decorations of the vestibule are distinguished from those of the main hall by the use of tondos and odd shapes in the panels and heavier moldings, while the stuccowork in the side aisles is simpler and perhaps inferior to that of the main nave. The floor is paved with white mosaic with black borders that outline the walls and pillars and indicate the position of features, or furniture, now missing, and a deep space is marked off in front of the apse. A single bust in profile, poorly preserved, low on one of the pillars, may have been a portrait. There is no sign of repair or remodeling anywhere, and the suggestion is that the hall was built about the middle of the first century after Christ and used for only a short time, less than a half-century.

S. Aurigemma, *La basilica sotterranea neopitagorica di Porta Maggiore in Roma* (Rome 1961); E. H. Wedeking and B. Segall, eds., *Festschrift Eugen von Mercklin* (Stiftland 1964), 90–105 (P. Mingazzini); Nash 1.169–73; *BABesch* 45 (1970): 148–74 (F. L. Bastet).

Basilica Traiani: see **Mercati di Traiano.**

Basilica Ulpia: see **Forum Traiani.**

Basilica Vascellaria: listed in the addenda to the regionary catalogues (Vascolaria: *Cur.*) and by Polemius Silvius, but otherwise unknown. It has been suggested that this is an alternate name for the Basilica Argentaria, but that is only conjecture. Because in late antiquity there seem to have been basilicas associated with a number of trades, this might be either a market or the seat of a collegium.

Basilica Vestilia: listed in the addenda to the regionary catalogues, where there is one manuscript with the reading *vestiaria,* and there are other variants. Polemius Silvius's Basilica Hostilia is regarded as an error for Vestilia. This might be either a market hall where clothes were sold or the seat of a guild of clothes merchants.

Basis Q. Marcii Regis: the base of a statue in the Area Capitolina (q.v.) behind the Temple of Iuppiter Optimus Maximus, to which a bronze military diploma was affixed in A.D. 64 (*CIL* 16.5).

Bellona, Aedes (Figs. 17, 37.3): the principal temple of this goddess, the personification of frenzy in battle, in Rome, vowed by Appius Claudius Caecus in 296 B.C. (Livy 10.19.17; Pliny, *HN* 35.12; Ovid, *Fast.* 6.201–4; *CIL* 1² p. 192 elog. 10 = 11.1827 = *ILS* 54 = Degrassi, *Inscriptiones Italiae* 13.3.12) in a battle against the Etruscans and Samnites and dedicated on 3 June (Degrassi 464–65). Ovid (*Fast.* 6.201–4) says that it overlooked the end of the circus near at hand, and this, together with the Fasti Venusini *(ad diem),* serves to place it in the vicinity of the Circus Flaminius. From it the senators in session could hear the screams of the prisoners butchered on orders from Sulla in the Villa Publica after the battle of Porta Collina (Plutarch, *Sulla* 30.2–3; Seneca, *Clem.* 1.12.2; Cass. Dio 30–35 fr. 109.5–7). The temple has now been convincingly identified by F. Coarelli as that just east of the Temple of Apollo Medicus Sosianus, a large peripteral temple, probably hexastyle, with a deep pronaos in the Roman fashion, raised on a low podium of concrete faced with brick. It is now little more than a denuded core of concrete of the imperial period, but one can see that it was once an impressive edifice with an arcaded portico in peperino framing the precinct behind and to the east. About its earlier phases we lack information, because explorations have not been made within the concrete core of the podium.

The senate met here frequently (*CIL* 1².581 = 10.104 = *ILS* 18 = *ILLRP* 511 [SC de Bacchanalibus]; Cicero, *Verr.* 2.5.41; Plutarch, *Sulla* 7.6; Cass. Dio 50.4.5), especially, because the temple lay outside the pomerium, to receive victorious generals on their return from campaign and to consider and vote on their applications for triumphs (see, e.g., Livy 26.21.1, 28.9.5, 28.38.2, 31.47.7, etc.) and to receive foreign embassies it did not wish to have inside the pomerium (see, e.g., Livy 30.21.12, 30.40.1, 33.24.5, 42.36.2). It is mentioned in the second and third centuries, although there is no notice of its restoration (Cass. Dio 69.15.3 [70.2.2]; S.H.A. *Sept. Sev.* 22.6). Near it was a senaculum (q.v.), and between it and the Circus Flaminius, presumably within the general bounds of its precinct, was the Columna Bellica (q.v.).

Nash 1.500–501; *BullCom* 80 (1965–67): 37–72 (F. Coarelli); *RömMitt* 94 (1987): 241–65 (G. Hafner).

Bellona Insulensis, Aedes: a temple known only from a single funerary inscription from a tomb erected by Apidia Ma, who was *scapharia* of Bellona Insulensis. Here we are dealing with a shrine of Ma-Bellona on the Tiber island hitherto unknown.

RendPontAcc 43 (1970–71): 121–25 (S. Panciera).

Bellona Pulvinensis, Aedes: a shrine known only from inscriptions (*CIL* 6.490 = *ILS* 4180, *CIL* 6.2232–33 = *ILS* 4181–82) of a goddess assimilated to Bellona but probably Oriental in origin, given the epithet Pulvinensis not in allusion to the great pulvinar in the Circus Maximus, as otherwise the epithet would be shared by other divinities, but probably to a ceremonial couch on which the image of the goddess was displayed to her devotees. Her temple was in Regio VI, Alta Semita, in Vicus Bellonae, not far from the Porta Collina, and stood in a grove (*CIL* 6.2232 = *ILS* 4181, 2235). It may well have been built by Sulla as a victory monument after the battle of Porta Collina in 82 B.C. She is generally believed to be the Cappadocian goddess Ma and to have had another shrine somewhere on the Vatican Hill, perhaps not far from the Phrygianum of the Magna Mater (q.v.), whom she resembles in a number of particulars. Her worship was orgiastic, and her priests

slashed their arms in frenzy to get blood with which to sprinkle the faithful. Tombstones belonging to her priests have come to light on the Via Triumphalis on Monte Mario, which strengthens the case for location of a temple on the right bank of the Tiber (*CIL* 6.2232–33 = *ILS* 4181–82). All evidence points to a late second or third century date for these monuments, and so presumably the temple. Cf. Martial 12.57.9–11; Juvenal 6.511–21; and see Bellona, Sacellum (Enueion).

MEFRA 87 (1975): 653–65 (R. E. A. Palmer).

Bellona Rufilia, Aedes: known only from the tombstone of a priest (*CIL* 6.2234 = *ILS* 4181a) who is described as *ab Isis Serapis* and *ab aedem Bellone Rufiliae,* which seems to indicate a place in Regio III. The epithet probably refers to the name of the builder of the temple, perhaps P. Cornelius Rufinus, cos. 290, 277 B.C., after his victory over the Samnites. Because the priest is described as *fanaticus,* the divinity is to be identified as Ma-Bellona.

MEFRA 87 (1975): 653–65 (R. E. A. Palmer).

Bellona, Sacellum (Enueion): a shrine inadvertently destroyed when the temples of Isis and Serapis in Rome were destroyed in 48 B.C., at which time jars containing human flesh were discovered in it (Cass. Dio 42.26.2). This indicates that the orgiastic worship of Ma-Bellona had already been introduced into Rome, and that the exotic nature of the cult and its rites led to its confusion with the Egyptian divinities. The jars containing human flesh suggest that originally at least the cult was a mystery one confined to initiates.

Bibliotheca Apollinis Palatini (Figs. 27.15–16, 63): twin libraries, one for books in Greek and one for books in Latin, built by Augustus in conjunction with the Temple of Apollo Palatinus (see Apollo Palatinus, Aedes). They also contained a gallery of portraits of distinguished writers, probably imagines clipeatae (Tacitus, *Ann.* 2.37 and 83; *JRS* 47 [1957]: 144–46 [S. Weinstock]). The first librarian was Augustus's freedman C. Iulius Hyginus (Suetonius, *Gramm.* 20), and we have some sepulchral inscriptions of people proud of their association with the library (*CIL* 6.5188–89 = ILS 1588–89, *CIL* 6.5190–91). The libraries have been identified as twin apsidal halls along the southeast side of the precinct of Apollo adjacent to the Domus Augustiana. These are large halls preceded by a colonnade (?). The apses are shallow segmental arcs with a central niche for emphasis, and the adjoining walls are divided into bays above two shallow steps on either side. Thus they conform to the general lines of library architecture, although positive identification is impossible.

Nash 1.204–5; *AJA* 85 (1981): 335–39 (D. L. Thompson).

Bibliotheca Asinii Pollionis: the first public library in Rome, built soon after 39 B.C. by Asinius Pollio as part of the rebuilding of the Atrium Libertatis (q.v.) from the spoils of his Parthinian campaigns in Dalmatia (Ovid, *Trist.* 3.1.71–72; Pliny, *HN* 7.115; Isidore, *Orig.* 6.5.2). It contained both Greek and Latin works and was embellished with portraits of distinguished men of letters, among whom Varro was the only living person represented (Pliny, *HN* 7.115, 35.10). Whether it also contained other parts of Pollio's extensive collection of art is doubtful.

Bibliotheca Capitolina: mentioned only at its destruction in a conflagration caused by lightning in the reign of Commodus, A.D. 189 (Hieron. *a. Abr.* 2204; Orosius 7.17.3). Orosius says: *maiorum cura studioque compositam,* which is further puzzling.

Bibliotheca Divi Traiani: see **Forum Traiani.**

Bibliotheca Domus Tiberianae: see **Domus Tiberiana.**

Bibliotheca Panthei: a library built for Alexander Severus by Julius Africanus, probably an adjunct of the Thermae Alexandrinae encroaching, or opening, on the forecourt of the Pantheon in some way (*POxy* 3.39 no. 412).

Bibliotheca Porticus Octaviae: built by Octavia after the death of her son Marcellus in 23 B.C. as part of a memorial to him in the Porticus Octaviae (Ovid, *Trist.* 3.1.69–70; Plutarch, *Marc.* 30.6). The first librarian was C. Melissaeus, a freedman of Maecenas (Suetonius, *Gramm.* 21). Like other libraries of the time, it was divided between books in Greek and books in Latin (see, e.g., *CIL* 6.2347–49 = *ILS* 1970–72, *CIL* 6.4431–35, 5192). It burned in the fire of Titus in 79 (Cass. Dio 66.24.2) but was early restored by Domitian (Suetonius, *Dom.* 20); from the way Suetonius speaks, one gathers that it was considered a major loss and that the work of restoring it was a major accomplishment. Of its later history we know nothing.

Bibliotheca Templi Divi Augusti (also called **Bibliotheca Templi Novi**): a library established by Tiberius in connection with the Temple of Divus Augustus (see Augustus Divus, Aedes). For it he obtained from Syracuse the statue of Apollo Temenites, remarkable for its size and beauty, but was unable to dedicate it, being cut off by death (Suetonius, *Tib.* 74). This may be the same as the "Tuscanic" bronze Apollo 50 feet high mentioned by Pliny (*HN* 34.43) as displayed in the library. The library was probably destroyed or damaged in the fire that destroyed the Temple of Augustus shortly before 79 (Pliny, *HN* 12.94) but, if so, was restored by Domitian (Martial 12.3.7–8). From the way Martial speaks, it would appear that the books, or most of them, survived.

Bibliotheca Templi Pacis: see **Pax, Templum.**

Bibliotheca Ulpia: see **Forum Traiani.**

Bona Dea: known only from three inscriptions found near one another and close to a small aedicular shrine near the church of S. Cecilia in Trastevere in 1744 (*CIL* 6.65–67 = *ILS* 3500–3501). These inform us that a *sacrum Bonae Deae* was restored by M. Vettius Bolanus, cos. before A.D. 69, and that an image was set up to watch over an Insula Bolani (or Bolaniana) by a certain Cladus, who also made another present to the Bona Dea. From these we can gather that this was a neighborhood sanctuary of little importance, and the fact that it is not known from other sources is not surprising. Because the Bona Dea seems to have been considered especially efficacious in dealing with problems of vision, she may have had numerous neighborhood shrines (see, e.g., *CIL* 6.68, 73, 75 = *ILS* 3506, 3508, 3513).

Bona Dea Subsaxana, Aedes (Fig. 14): the principal shrine of this goddess in Rome. It stood in Regio XII *(Not., Cur.)* below the Saxum, or Remoria, where Remus was supposed to have taken his augural station preliminary to the founding of Rome (Ovid, *Fast.* 5.149–54; Festus 345L). This was the north end of the eastern part of the Aventine, the Aventinus Minor. The foundation of the temple is ascribed by Ovid (*Fast.* 5.149–54) to the senate, its dedication to Claudia, a Vestal Virgin, and the principal festival seems to have been on 1 May (Degrassi 453). Because Festus (60L) equates the early Roman goddess Bona Dea Fauna with the Greek Damia and adds that the priestess of the Bona Dea was called Damiatrix, it has been supposed that the temple might have been built after the capture of Tarentum in 272 B.C., for there was a festival called the Dameia there (see Roscher 1.1, s.v. "Damia" [R. Peter]). But the association of this temple with the legends of Hercules at the site of Rome (cf. Propertius 4.9; Macrobius, *Sat.* 1.12.27–29) makes it likely that it was very old.

The Bona Dea was unquestionably a goddess of fertility and healing with chthonic associations. She was frequently equated with Maia and the earth, sometimes with Proserpina, and called also Fauna, Ops, and Fatua. Snakes were allowed to roam free in her precinct, unharmed and harmless, and the temple attendants provided a great range of simples to those in need of medicine, both men and women, but no man was allowed inside the temple (Macrobius, *Sat.* 1.12.20–26). In 123 B.C. a Vestal Virgin, Licinia, tried to dedicate an altar, an aedicula, and a pulvinar in the precinct, but the pontifices ordered them removed (Cicero, *Dom.* 136). The temple was restored by Livia (Ovid, *Fast.* 5.157–58) and again by Hadrian (S.H.A. *Hadr.* 19.11). It was still standing in the fourth century *(Not., Cur.),* but no trace of it has come to light.

Bonus Eventus, Templum: referred to only by Ammianus Marcellinus (29.6.19), who says it was near *(prope)* the Porticus Boni Eventus (q.v.), built by Claudius, praefectus urbi in A.D. 374. The portico was evidently in the Horti Agrippae, adjacent to the west side of the Thermae Agrippae *(porticum . . . ingentem, lavacro Agrippae contiguam),* but it does not follow that the temple necessarily also was. If, however, five Corinthian capitals of extraordinary size that have turned up and been recorded in this area in the late nineteenth century are remains of the portico, its line ran northwest/southeast, and we may see the remains of ancient walls in blocks of peperino built into the foundations of S. Maria in Monterone as a likely vestige of the temple. These indicate that the temple would have faced east, away from the portico. This building seems to have been aligned with the Agrippan buildings in the neighborhood, at a slight angle to the buildings of Pompey, and so may be part of Agrippa's design. But a temple of Bonus Eventus, originally an entirely agricultural divinity (Varro, *Rust.* 1.1.6), seems rather out of place in the context of these gardens, unless it was a rebuilding of an older shrine.

Bucinum: a name listed by the regionary catalogues in Regio IV after Aura, and sometimes confused with it (Aureum Bucinum, *Not.*), and before Apollo Sandaliarius. This tends to place it in the vicinity of Templum Pacis, perhaps just behind it. It also occurs once in the *Digesta* (14.4.5.16) in the form *ad Bucinum,* as a place where a man might have a shop, as opposed to *trans Tiberim.* The word means "conch shell" and was perhaps in reference to a relief of such a shell used to identify a square or a street fountain. This would probably have been on, or just off, the Argiletum.

Busta Gallica: evidently a locus saeptus (cf. Varro, *Ling.* 5.157) explained in various ways, as a place where the Gauls cremated their dead promiscuously in a period of pestilence while they were holding the city (Livy 5.48.3), as well as a place where the Romans heaped the bones of the slaughtered Gauls after successfully retaking the city (Varro, *Ling.* 5.157). Its general location is established by Minucius's speech in Livy 22.14.11: although Camillus, after being appointed dictator and coming to Rome, might have waited in safety on the summit of the Janiculan hill, he chose that very day to descend and then crushed the Gauls *in media urbe* and *ad Busta Gallica.* Because the only bridge across the Tiber at this time was the Pons Sublicius with its bridgehead in the Forum Boarium, the Busta Gallica should be in the Forum Boarium and probably within the line of the Servian Walls, if it is *in media urbe,* although Livy may not have known where that line lay. An important inscription of the time of Sulla, *CIL* 1².809 = *ILLRP* 464, gives fragmentary information about the building and paving of streets, especially in the Forum Boarium and around the Circus Maximus, and associates the Busta Gallica with a clivus and scalae. We may then be justified in putting it in the near vicinity of S. Maria in Cosmedin. This would agree also with Varro's listing of the Doliola (q.v.) immediately after the Busta Gallica.

Caca, Sacellum: a shrine said to be of the sister of Cacus, who betrayed him in one way or another and in return was given a sacellum at which the Vestal Virgins worshiped with perennial fire. It is mentioned by Servius (*ad Aen.* 8.190) and Lactantius (*Div. Inst.* 1.20.36), but by no one else. Its importance is as elusive as its whereabouts. Many students of religion see Caca and Cacus as fire gods antedating Vesta.

Caci Scalae: see **Scalae Caci.**

Cacus (or **Cacum**): according to the *Cosmographia* (Riese, *Geog. Lat. Min.* 83) another name for the Forum Boarium: *iuxta Forum Boarium quem Cacum dicunt transiens,* but this is difficult to believe. It looks as though this were the mangled remains of a note explaining Cacus's responsibility for the name of the Forum Boarium.

Caelimontium (and **Caelemontium**): the name given to Regio II of Augustan Rome in the regionary catalogues, appearing also in *CIL* 15.7190 = *ILS* 8730. It embraced various lobes of the Caelian Hill, reaching as far as the line of the Aurelian Walls, but not much else. The name is formed like *Septimontium* and perhaps derives especially from the Porta Caelimontana of the Servian Walls. The street leading to that gate may have carried the same name and been the principal artery here, as seems attested by the epithet Caelimontienses occurring in *CIL* 6.31893 = *ILS* 6072 and *CIL* 6.31899.

Caeliolus (and **Caeliolum**): Varro (*Ling.* 5.46) says that after the Etruscan army of Caele Vibenna had been settled on the Caelian, because that situation seemed too well defended, some were moved to the Vicus Tuscus, while those who were above suspicion were settled on the Caeliolus. Martial (12.18.6) speaks of a Caelius Maior and a Caelius Minor, and Cicero (*Har. Resp.* 32) of a Caeliculus or Caeliculum. The principal lobes of the Caelian are those crowned by the Temple of Divus Claudius and the church of SS. Quattro Coronati, with a third rising east of S. Gregorio Magno. The line of the Servian Walls is very uncertain for the whole of the Caelian, but it seems likely that the Arcus Dolabellae et Silani marks one of the gates, probably the Porta Caelimontana, in which case we should be justified in identifying the street leading from this to the top of the Clivus Scauri as the main artery of this part of Rome and the lobes to either side of this as the Caelius Maior (the site of Divus Claudius) and Caelius Minor. Were we to take the line of the walls as running east along the southern brow of the hill (a more defensible line) before cutting across the waist west of the Lateran, then we should probably see the Caeliolus as the lobe of SS. Quattro Coronati.

Caelius Mons (Fig. 16): the southeasternmost of the seven hills of Rome, a long narrow tongue running from its juncture with the plateau of the Esquiline at Porta Maggiore in a gentle curve south and west and ending in lobes at the church of SS. Quattro Coronati, the Temple of Divus Claudius, and behind S. Gregorio Magno. Its length is about two kilometers, its width never more than one-half kilometer. It is separated from the Esquiline by a deepening valley, down which a watercourse runs to empty into the basin of the Colosseum (the Ceroniae); this then continued as a brook to the southwest through the valley between Palatine and Caelian and joined the brook running down the Vallis Murcia of the Circus Maximus. In its upper reaches this second brook, now called the Marrana, separates the Caelian from the surrounding country and drains its southern slopes. At its western end its draw was called the Vallis Camenarum, and through it at Porta Capena passed the

C

Figure 16
Mons Caelius, General
Plan, Showing Known
Remains of Antiquity
and Modern Streets

Via Appia. The ancient Romans distinguished a Caelius Maior and a Caelius Minor, the latter also apparently called Caeliolus (q.v.). The valley between the Caelian and the Oppius seems to have been called Subura, a duplication of the name of the valley between Esquiline and Quirinal, and in the city of the Regiones Quattuor (q.v.) the tribe of the Caelian was the Suburana (abbreviated Suc.), with the suggestion that this valley was the most populous section of the Regio.

The hill is said by Tacitus (*Ann.* 4.65) to have first been called Querquetulanus Mons (q.v.) from the oak woods covering it, but this is probably simply an extrapolation from the name of the Porta Querquetulana (q.v.) in the Servian Walls. It is said to have got the name Caelius from Caele Vibenna, an Etruscan soldier of fortune who came to the aid of one of the kings of Rome with a force of fighting men and was rewarded with citizenship and land within the city (Tacitus, *Ann.* 4.65; Varro, *Ling.* 5.46; Paulus *ex Fest.* 38L and Festus 486L; Dion. Hal. 2.36.2). There was a well-known Gens Caelia, a plebeian family, and the name is thus parallel to that of the Oppius and Cispius. Under Tiberius, in consequence of a fire and miraculous preservation of a statue of Tiberius, there was a proposal to change the name to Mons Augustus, but this never caught on (Tacitus, *Ann.* 4.64; Suetonius, *Tib.* 48.2).

Tradition varies as to which king was responsible for the addition of the Caelian to the city. We find it ascribed to Romulus (Varro, *Ling.* 5.46), Tullus Hostilius ([Aur. Vict.], *De Vir. Ill.* 4.4; Dion. Hal. 3.1.5), Ancus Marcius (Cicero, *Rep.* 2.18; Strabo 5.3.7 [234]), Tarquinius Priscus (Tacitus, *Ann.* 4.65), and Servius Tullius (*CIL* 13.1668 = *ILS* 212). When the question is so inconsequential, the divergence of authority is surprising.

The line of the Servian Walls on the Caelian is discussed under the rubric Caeliolus (q.v.). Both Caelian and Subura figured in the Septimontium (Festus 459L, 474–76L) and were thus very old parts of the city. The suggestion in Varro's story of the transference of the Caelian settlement to the Vicus Tuscus because of the strategic strength of the Caelian and distrust of the Etruscans suggests a fortified village or town, but this would probably have been palisaded at best and the defenses completely destroyed at the time of the transference.

In the Augustan redistricting of Rome, the Caelian was divided among four of the new *regiones,* the western and southern slopes falling into I, the main body of the hill into II, most of the old Subura into III, and the eastern reaches of the hill into V. It was always thickly populated under the republic, but, so far as we know, the site of no major temple or shrine, a rather remarkable circumstance. In A.D. 27 the hill was apparently devastated by fire (Tacitus, *Ann.* 4.64) and thereafter became a favorite place for the residences of the rich, but palatial houses *(domus)* rather than villas *(horti).* This character persisted at least until the end of the fourth century.

A. M. Colini, *Storia e topografia del Celio nell'antichità* (*MemPontAcc* 7 [1944]).

Caesares, Septem: known only from inscriptions at Praeneste (*CIL* 14.2886) and Reate (*CIL* 9.4680 = *ILS* 7484) but presumably indicating a district in Rome. The first is the base of a statue of a freedman of a certain Paris, in all probability the pantomimist of the reign of Nero, who was *coactor argentarius,* the second of a *vinarius, a septem Caesaribus.* With such diverse interests involved, we should look for a place of intense commercial activity, and the idea of portraits of seven Caesars in a public place suggests the neighborhood of the Mausoleum Augusti (q.v.) (but see *PAPS* 125.5 [1981]: 368–69 [R. E. A. Palmer]).

Caesarum, Aedes: see **Augustus Divus, Sacrarium.**

Calcarienses: see **[Schola] Calcariensium.**

Camellenses: a district in Rome where tradesmen were found abusing the norms of business recognized by the Romans and subject to an edict of the praefectus urbi Tarracius Bassus aimed at curbing their activities (*CIL* 6.31893 = *ILS* 6072, 31899). They are listed immediately after the Caelimontanienses, which has been taken to mean that they belonged somewhere on or near the Caelian, but, because in our main copy of this edict they are one of the first four names on the list and inscribed in letters conspicuously larger than the rest, they may have been singled out rather for the seriousness of the offenses against them.

Camenae: originally almost certainly water goddesses presiding over a spring of especially good water (Vitruvius 8.3.1; Frontinus, *Aq.* 1.4). They became assimilated to the Muses. Their spring was in a grove on the Caelian near Porta Capena (Servius *ad Aen.* 7.697), almost certainly the spring of S. Gregorio Magno, *mirabilis, immo saluberrimus fons,* which Lanciani (LFUR sheet 35) connected with a well just to the northeast of the church. The name was extended to the whole area around the spring, including the valley between the Caelian and the Aventine and a Vicus Camenarum (*CIL* 6.975 = *ILS* 6073). At the spring was a small aedicula of bronze, supposed to have been put there by Numa, which was struck by lightning and then removed to the nearby Temple of Honos et Virtus (see Honos et Virtus, Aedes) (Servius *ad Aen.* 1.8). Later still, in ca. 187 B.C., M. Fulvius Nobilior took it and put it in his Temple of Hercules Musarum (see Hercules Musarum, Aedes). The aedicula must have been replaced by a full-scale temple, for the tragic poet Accius is said to have erected a very tall statue of himself there (Pliny, *HN* 34.19; cf. Juvenal 3.13). Presumably it is the dedication of this temple that fell on 13 August and became the annual festival of the Camenae (Degrassi 494–96). Juvenal's comment on the revetting of the banks of the spring with marble and conversion of it into an artificial nymphaeum (3.17–20) is probably somewhat exaggerated.

By order of Numa, the spring of the Camenae was consecrated to the use of the Vestal Virgins, who had to sprinkle the Temple of Vesta daily with its water, which had to be fetched by hand (Plutarch, *Numa* 13.2; Festus 152L). The Vicus Camenarum of Regio I would presumably have been the street of which Lanciani (LFUR sheet 35) shows only a small portion, running slightly west of north from Porta Capena toward the Palatine.

Campus: see **Ager, Campus, Prata.**

Campus Agrippae: a considerable tract listed by the regionary catalogues in Via Lata (Regio VII), probably laid out as a park and a place where Romans liked to stroll (A. Gellius 14.5.1). It was begun by Agrippa and embellished with a portico built by his sister, Vipsania Polla, but unfinished at his death and then completed by Augustus. The Porticus Vipsania (q.v.) was still standing at the time the regionary catalogues were compiled, and Martial locates it close to a gate and with its laurels in view from his house (Martial 4.18.1–2, 1.108.3), which was on the clivus leading from the Temple of Quirinus to the Temple of Flora (see Domus Martialis). So the gate is probably the Porta Quirinalis (q.v.), and the Campus Agrippae may have extended from the street leading out through this gate (following roughly the line of Via delle Quattro Fontane) on the east, possibly as far as Via Lata on the west and Via S. Claudio on the north (along the line of the so-called Aqua Sallustiana), if the remains of a portico found just south of Via del Tritone belong to the Porticus Vipsania. On the south it may have been bounded by the line of the Servian Walls on the brow of the Quirinal, if Agrippa was allowed to include the pomerial strip within it.

Campus Boarius: known only from inscriptions (*CIL* 6.9226; cf. 1².1259 = *ILLRP* 802). Because the subject of the first inscription is described as a gatekeeper of the campus, the Forum Boarium cannot be meant. The logical place for a Campus Boarius in the vicinity of Rome would be to the east of the city, but beyond that one can say nothing.

Campus Bruttianus: mentioned in the regionary catalogues and Polemius Silvius (545), listed in Regio XIV. Because the Gens Bruttia is well known, the allusion is probably to that, rather than to the servants of magistrates (A. Gellius 10.3.19; Paulus *ex Fest.* 28L), whose interest in the right bank of the Tiber would be difficult to explain.

Campus Caelemontanus: mentioned in a single sepulchral inscription (*CIL* 6.9475). On analogy with the Campus Viminalis and Campus Esquilinus, this should be a tract of land just outside the Servian Walls at Porta Caelimontana.

Campus Codetanus: see **Codeta.**

Campus Cohortium Praetoriarum: Hülsen's reconstruction of the name for what Tacitus (*Ann.* 12.36) calls *campus, qui castra praeiacet,* a zone between the Castra Praetoriana and the Servian Walls, where only altars, dedications, and such small monuments as might suit a military drill ground have come to light (*BullCom* 4 [1876]: 175–93 [R. Lanciani]; 5 [1877]: 21–28 [R. Lanciani]).

Campus Esquilinus: a large area just outside the Porta Esquilina, which in the late republic was the great cemetery of Rome, where burial of public heroes could be made in plots assigned by decree of the senate (Cicero, *Phil.* 9.17) and slaves could be laid down beside wits and ne'er-do-wells (Horace, *Sat.* 1.8.8–16). The part between the Servian Walls and the line of the Aurelian Walls was reclaimed under Augustus and made the fifth regio of the city, Esquiliae, but under Claudius public executions were still performed in the Campus Esquilinus (Suetonius, *Claud.* 25.3; cf. Strabo 5.3.9 [237]), so the cemetery limit must simply have been moved beyond the new line. Once reclaimed, the former cemetery was regarded as a very salubrious district. Maecenas built his famous horti (see Horti Maecenatiani) there, and Propertius lived there (3.23.24, 4.8.1–2). The archaeological finds indicate that this cemetery was in use from the seventh century B.C. to the first. A gap from the end of the sixth century to the middle of the fourth, for which no burials have been recovered, is puzzling.

BullCom 42 (1914): 117–75 (G. Pinza); I. S. Ryberg, *An Archaeological Record of Rome* (Philadelphia 1940), 1–153; *Roma medio repubblicana* (show catalogue, Rome 1973), 188–233.

Campus Flaminius: evidently synonymous with Prata Flaminia (q.v.), used by Varro (*Ling.* 5.154) and explained as the site around which the Circus Flaminius was built and from which it took its name. Because we now know that the Circus Flaminius was simply a public square and not a regular circus, Varro must be rationalizing. Livy (*Epit.* 20) says that Gaius Flaminius as censor (220 B.C.) built both the Via Flaminia and the circus.

Campus Iovis: mentioned only once (S.H.A. *Pescen. Niger* 12.4) as the site of the house of Pescennius. In the absence of any corroborative evidence or reasonable explanation of the phrase, it is to be regarded as fictitious.

Campus Lanatarius: listed by the regionary catalogues in Regio XII and probably to be associated with the Area Pannaria (q.v.) of Regio I. This would have been the site of a wool market, probably outside the Servian Walls (hence *campus*), so very likely on the Via Appia, and possibly it and the Area Pannaria were on opposite sides of the road, not far from Porta Capena. It must have been relatively old to be called *campus*, and *lanatarius* may be a mistake for either *lanarius*, the form one would expect, or better *laniarius*, because butchers were to be found outside Porta Capena (*CIL* 6.167 = *ILS* 3682a = *ILLRP* 97, *CIL* 6.168 = *ILLRP* 98; Plautus, *Pseud.* 326–34).

Campus Martialis: a place on the Caelian where the Equirria were held whenever flooding of the Campus Martius prevented their being held there (Paulus *ex Fest.* 117L; Ovid, *Fast.* 3.517–22). This was probably just beyond the line of the Servian Walls and very probably the same as the Campus Caelemontanus (q.v.). If there is a memory of it preserved in the name of the medieval church of S. Gregorio in Martio, it may have lain a little to the west of the baptistery of S. Giovanni in Laterano (HCh 258–59).

Campus Martius (Figs. 17, 18): the flood plain of the Tiber north of Rome, bounded by the river on the west, by the Pincian Hill on the east, and by the Quirinal and Capitoline hills on the southeast and south. This very large tract was divided into smaller units to identify particular locations, some of them also called campus, as was the Campus Agrippae,

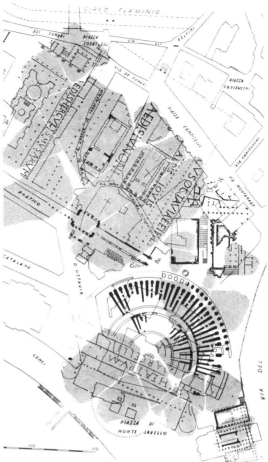

Figure 17
Southern Campus Martius, Porticus Octaviae, Porticus Philippi, Temple of Apollo Medicus, Temple of Bellona, Theatrum Marcelli, and Adjacencies, Representation on the Marble Plan in Relation to Modern Streets

others called differently, as were the Prata Flaminia, Aemiliana, and Villa Publica. In Augustus's time the Campus Martius proper seems to have begun only at the Petronia Amnis (q.v.) (Festus 296L). In the Augustan division of the city, the Campus Martius was divided between Regio VII, Via Lata, and Regio IX, Circus Flaminius, the line of division between the two being somewhat uncertain, but lying parallel to the line of the Via Flaminia and possibly along it. The topographical value of the evidence of *CIL* 6.874 = *ILS* 5935 must remain doubtful; it deals with the princeps' purchase of land from private individuals in order to make it public, but the phrase *ad camp. versus* is susceptible of more than one interpretation and is hardly likely to mean everything north of the Pantheon.

The Campus in its broadest extent stretched about two kilometers north and south from the Capitoline Hill to beyond Porta Flaminia and about the same east and west from the Quirinal hill to the Pons Ner-

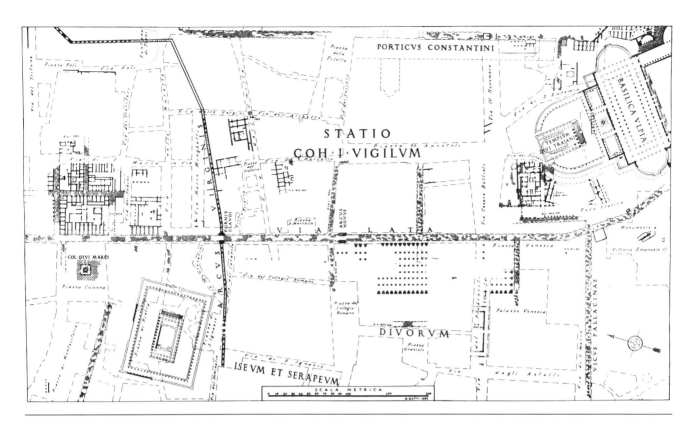

Figure 18
Campus Martius,
Area along the Southern
Stretch of Via Lata
(Via Flaminia),
Porticus Minucia
Frumentaria (?), Statio
Cohortis I Vigilum,
Temple of Divus
Hadrianus, and
Columna Marci Aurelii

onianus. It was low, its surface only 3–8 m above the Tiber, and with few, and only minor, elevations; consequently it was subject to frequent flooding. It was cut and drained by two important watercourses; one, the Petronia Amnis, ran south and west from the western slope of the Quirinal, its source being the Fons Cati (see Cati Fons), now in the courtyard of Palazzo del Quirinale. This passed along the line of Via S. Marco and Via delle Botteghe Oscure to the western end of the latter, where it turned abruptly south and emptied into the Tiber opposite the west end of the island. The other drained the valley between the Pincian and the Quirinal now marked by Via del Tritone; its ancient name is unknown, and in modern times it is usually called the Aqua Sallustiana (q.v.). Its springs were near the eastern end of Via Sallustiana, and it followed, as it does today, a roughly east-northeast/west-southwest course, emptying into the Tiber near Ponte Umberto I, opposite the Palazzo di Giustizia. There was also a swamp, the Palus Caprae, or Capreae, in the little basin now marked by the Pantheon; this may have been the source of a rivulet that followed, at least in part, the line of the runoff of the Thermae Agrippae, often called the Euripus Agrippae, running west and then northwest in an arc to empty into the Tiber just above Ponte Vittorio Emanuele. There was also a

volcanic vent of some sort from which issued hot vapor near the river just below the bend at Ponte Vittorio Emanuele; this was the origin of the Tarentum (q.v.). It has since disappeared and may have disappeared quite early. The Campus was essentially open ground, but there may have been an oak grove, the Aesculetum (q.v.), near the river at the southern end of modern Via Arenula.

The Campus Martius, often simply called Campus (see, e.g., Livy 40.52.4; Cicero, *Cat.* 2.1; Horace, *Carm.* 1.8.4, 3.1.11), was traditionally land that belonged to Tarquinius Superbus and after his expulsion was dedicated to Mars (Livy 2.5.2; Plutarch, *Poplic.* 8.1; Florus 1.3.9.1). However, there was another tradition, that the Campus had early been dedicated to Mars and had been appropriated by Tarquin, and to support this was the evidence of the existence of an Ara Martis in the Campus as early as the time of Numa (Dion. Hal. 5.13.2; Festus 204L). The former was the more popular tradition, though the latter seems sounder.

From the beginning of the republic the Campus was *ager publicus,* and only in the time of Sulla, when there was an economic crisis brought on by the Social War and the war impending with Mithridates, was part of it sold for private ownership (Orosius 5.18.27). This was the land near the Capitoline that was traditionally assigned to the members of the chief priesthoods. The name of the Prata Flaminia may reflect either a very old ownership (Livy 3.54.15, 3.63.7) or, more likely, may have been given to the area on the left bank of the Petronia Amnis after the creation of the Circus Flaminius. Gellius (7.7.4) says the Campus Tiberinus (q.v.) was the same as the Campus Martius and the gift of a Vestal Virgin, Gaia Taracia or Fufetia, to the state, but this is very doubtful, and Gellius is our only authority for it. However, certainly after Sulla and possibly before him, encroachment on the Campus by private builders was a serious problem (cf. Cicero, *Nat. D.* 2.11; *Att.* 13.33.4; Varro, *Rust.* 3.2.5). Some of these buildings may have been on land awarded the builders as an honor (cf. Servius *ad Aen.* 9.272), but others were probably simply abusive. The regionary catalogues list 3,805 insulae and 120 domus in Regio VII, as well as 2,777 insulae and 140 domus in Regio IX.

Early the Campus was regularly used as a public pasture and provided space and facilities for military drilling and athletics, including swimming (Dion. Hal. 5.13.2; Horace, *Carm.* 3.7.25–28; Vegetius 1.10). It lay outside the pomerium throughout the republic and must have been curiously gerrymandered by the surveyors of the new pomerial lines in the early empire (see Pomerium). It was not brought wholly within the pomerium until the construction of the Aurelian Walls. It therefore made an ideal place for the assembly of citizens both in their military formations as an army and in the comitia centuriata in which they voted and the census was concluded (Livy 1.44.1–2; Dion. Hal. 4.22.1–2; A. Gellius 15.27.4–5). The area in which the voting was conducted was given the humorous name Ovile, later changed to Saepta (cf. Servius *ad Ecl.* 1.33). In the buildings in the Campus, the senate accorded audiences to embassies that were forbidden entrance to the city (see, e.g., Livy 30.21.12, 33.24.5).

Besides the Altar of Mars, which must have been very ancient, we know of three other early cult centers here, the Ara Ditis et Proserpinae in the Tarentum, the Apollinare with the Temple of Apollo built in 431 B.C., and the Temple of Bellona beside the Apollinare, vowed in 296 B.C. However, the archaeological evidence from the Area Sacra of Largo Argentina proves that two of the four temples there, A and C, have a phase that goes back to the early third century at the latest, so we may presume that temples were not uncommon in the southern Campus Martius by the time of the Punic wars. Between the Punic wars and Actium, we hear of at least fifteen temples built in the Campus, most of them victory monuments, and can presume the list is far from complete.

But the evidence suggests that they were all clustered in the Prata Flaminia or close to the Petronia Amnis. Building on a large scale in the middle Campus began only with Pompey's theater and porticoes and Julius Caesar's project for the Saepta in the middle of the first century B.C. Caesar is said to have conceived the idea of enlarging the Campus by diverting the Tiber to a straightened course close under Monte Mario and the Vatican (Cicero, *Att.* 13.33.4); so far as we know, the project was never more than a proposal.

Beginning with Pompey's theater, the central Campus Martius was rapidly built up. By the end of the reign of Augustus, there can have been practically no space available in the area south and east of the Pantheon, while buildings and park associated with the Mausoleum Augusti filled the throat between the river and the Via Flaminia to the north. By the end of the reign of Hadrian, the only open space of any extent an area west of the Stadium of Domitian around which the river looped and another north of the straight street running from the vicinity of Piazza Colonna to the Pons Neronianus. This open space was probably kept free of construction as long as possible, but the second area at least was probably a park rather than playing fields and drill grounds. Strabo (5.3.8 [236]) has left a brilliant description of the Campus in his day, in which he characterizes it as the showplace *par excellence* of Rome.

With the decline of the population of Rome brought on by the removal of power to Constantinople and other centers, as well as the decline in wealth and vigor brought by the barbarian invasions, the dwindling population of Rome became concentrated more and more in and around the Campus Martius. This was the heart of the city in the Renaissance and baroque periods and still remains so to a very large degree today. New developments have produced large satellite communities of every sort, but the Campus Martius is the hub from which they radiate.

HJ 472–621; *MemLinc*, ser. 8.1 (1949): 93–193 (F. Castagnoli); Lugli 1938, 5–282; Lugli 1975, 410–77, especially 411–14; *MEFRA* 89 (1977): 807–46 (F. Coarelli); *Liverpool Classical Monthly* 4 (1979): 129–34 (T. P. Wiseman); *AnalRom*, suppl. 10 (1983): 21–40 (L. Quilici); *TAPS* 80.2 (1990): 1–64 (R. E. A. Palmer).

Campus Minor: mentioned only by Catullus (55.3), perhaps an alternate name for the part of the Campus Martius stretching from the Petronia Amnis to the Capitoline, at least part of which was also known as the Prata Flaminia (q.v.).

PBSR 48 (1980): 6–16 (T. P. Wiseman).

Campus Neronis (also **Prata Neronis**): a designation in documents of the seventh to eleventh centuries inclusive (Jordan 2.430), evidently identical with the plain of Nero of Procopius (*BellGoth* 1.19.3, 28.15, 29.22–25; 2.1.4–5, 2.19–21). It was the district on the right bank of the Tiber to which the Pons Neronianus led and where the Circus Gaii et Neronis stood, probably all the relatively flat land between the Circus Gaii et Neronis and the Tiber, and probably reaching as far east as the Mausoleum Hadriani. But in at least one source it seems restricted to the area immediately surrounding the circus (*DissPontAcc* 2.8.376 [C. Hülsen]).

Campus Octavius: listed in the addenda to the regionary catalogues and Polemius Silvius (545), but otherwise unknown.

Campus Pecuarius: listed in the appendix of the regionary catalogues and in a single inscription (*CIL* 6.9660 = *ILS* 7515), the funerary inscription of a negotiator. It probably lay close outside the Servian Walls, but everything else about it is uncertain.

Campus Sceleratus: an area in the agger just inside Porta Collina and south of Vicus Portae Collinae where Vestal Virgins who were convicted of unchastity were buried alive in a small chamber prepared for this purpose (Dion. Hal. 2.67.3–4; Plutarch, *Numa* 10.6–7; Festus 448L; Servius *ad Aen.* 11.206). The first infliction of this punishment may have been in 337 B.C. (Livy 8.15.7–8).

Campus Tiberinus: identified by Aulus Gellius (7.7.4) as an alternate name for the Campus Martius. Both Gellius and Pliny (*HN* 34.25) tell the story that the Campus Tiberinus was presented to the Roman state by a Vestal Virgin, Gaia Taracia or Fufetia. Plutarch (*Poplic.* 8.4) gives a slightly different version, in which the land donated is adjacent to the Campus Martius that belonged to Tarquinius Superbus, possibly land on the left bank of the Petronia Amnis, what was later called the Prata Flaminia. But Boehm, following the lead of Mommsen, has shown that the story of Gaia Taracia is a doublet of that of Acca Larentia and that both spring from a single root. Macrobius (*Sat.* 1.10.16) tells us that Acca left four *agri* to the Roman people, the Ager Turax, the Ager Semurius, the Ager Lintirius, and the Ager Solenius. The first and Taracia are clearly the same name.

Campus Vaticanus: used only by Cicero (*Att.* 13.33.4) in a context in which it is clear that he means the area now known as Prati di Castello. It

was probably a phrase invented for the occasion and not in general use. See Vaticanus.

Campus Viminalis Subager (for **Sub Aggere** [?]): found only in the regionary catalogues, listed in Regio V. This ought to be the area just outside the Porta Viminalis, perhaps deliberately kept free of construction for public use. The area outside Porta Viminalis has yielded very little in the way of archaeological remains in the part north of Porta Viminalis, probably because of the proximity of the Castra Praetoria. The troops quartered there must have used this as an exercise ground. But the finds are almost equally scarce in the area south of Porta Viminalis, where the Campus should lie in order to fall within Regio V. It seems not unlikely that this was a public park.

Canalis: the open channel of the Cloaca through the Forum Romanum in Plautus's day (*Curc.* 476). Livy (1.56.2) credits Tarquinius Superbus with culverting the Cloaca, but it appears rather that he dredged out its channel and confined it within walls to prevent flooding. It was probably in large part culverted in preparation for the construction of the Basilica Fulvia et Aemilia in 179 B.C. Cf. also Paulus *ex Fest.* 40L: Canalicolae forenses.

Capita Bubula, Ad: a locality in the Regio Palatina, the birthplace of Augustus (Suetonius, *Aug.* 5) near the Curiae Veteres (q.v.), because Servius (*ad Aen.* 8.361) says Augustus was born *in curiis veteribus,* therefore probably near the northeast angle of the hill. It may be that the façade of the Curiae Veteres was decorated with the skulls of the animals sacrificed there.

Capitolinus Mons (Fig. 19): the smallest of the seven hills of Rome, a ridge between the Forum Romanum and the Campus Martius with an axis lying northeast/southwest, the southwest end precipitous cliffs above the river (see Tarpeia Rupes), the northeast end dropping to a low saddle to connect with the lower heights of the Quirinal. The Capitoline proper was composed of two heights connected by a high saddle, at least part of which was known as Inter Duos Lucos, the site of modern Piazza del Campidoglio, especially the eastern part of this. The southwestern height, slightly lower than the northeastern and larger, was originally known as Mons Saturnius (Varro, *Ling.* 5.42; Festus 430L; Solinus 1.12). It was also known as Mons Tarpeius from the cliff at its southwest extremity from which criminals condemned on capital charges were hurled, the name of the Saxum Tarpeium or Rupes Tarpeia being ex-

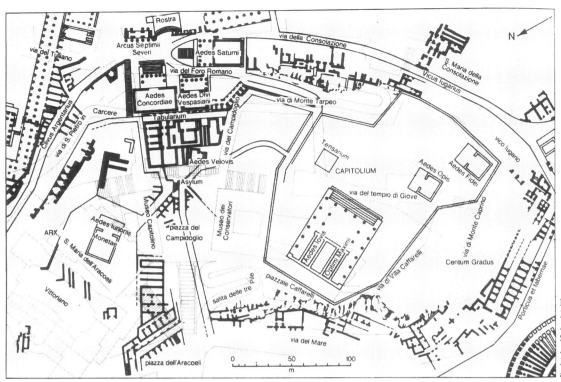

Figure 19
Mons Capitolinus and
Adjacencies, Plan
Showing Remains of
Antiquity in Relation to
Modern Streets
and Buildings

tended to both the southwest lobe and the hill as a whole (Varro, *Ling.* 5.41). After Tarquinius Priscus decided to build the temple to the Capitoline triad on the southern height and excavations were being made for the foundations of the massive temple, a human head of remarkable size and perfect preservation was discovered and taken as an omen that this would be the head of the world (Livy 1.55.5–6; Varro, *Ling.* 5.41). From this event, the epithet Capitolinus was added to the titles of Jupiter and given to the hill, being extended to include the hill as a whole, although the Area Capitolina (q.v.) was confined to the southwestern height.

Both heights must have been included in a single system of fortifications from a very early period, perhaps originally simply palisading. During the sack of the city by the Gauls in about 390 B.C., the fighting strength of Rome took refuge on the Capitoline and was able to hold it against every assault, including one by way of the Saxum Tarpeium (Livy 5.39.9–40.6, 43.1–5, 47.1–5). Propertius (4.4) would have the same state of affairs prevail during the war with Titus Tatius, which is only logical if the Capitoline was defended by the Romans. A gate in the castellum, originally called the Porta Saturnia, was later known as the Porta Pandana (Varro, *Ling.* 5.42; Solinus 1.13). It was on the Capitoline crest (Dion. Hal. 10.14.2) and was probably a postern at the top of

the Centum Gradus (q.v.). According to one story the name was changed because of an agreement Romulus made with Titus Tatius that the gate should always remain open, or always open to the Sabines (Fastus 246L, 496L). The etymology is questionable, but we must presume the gate was regularly open throughout the classical period.

It has become usual to distinguish the northeastern height by the name Arx, but arx is a common noun and should apply to everything within the system of fortifications. The very common phrase *arx et Capitolium* (cf., e.g., Livy 1.33.2, 2.7.10; Val. Max. 3.2.7; Tacitus, *Ann.* 11.23) is probably simply tautological, the Capitolium and arx being inseparable. If the northeastern height ever had a name, no one tells us what this might have been. It may well have been called Auguraculum (see Auguraculum [1]), from the station where Numa was consecrated king of Rome (Livy 1.18.6–10) and the augurs took monthly auspices for the new month, because that is the earliest shrine we hear of there and seems to have been kept deliberately in its primitive state until a late period. In the early settlement of Rome after the war with Titus Tatius, the Capitoline was believed to have been given to the Sabines, and Titus Tatius is said to have had his house on the northeastern height, on the spot later occupied by the Temple of Iuno Moneta (Solinus 1.21). This may explain the persistence of the term *collis* for the Capitoline (Livy 1.12.1; Martial 12.21.6; Arnobius, *Adv. Nat.* 4.3; Augustine, *De civ. D.* 2.22, 3.8, 3.12, 4.23), in accordance with the pattern of the Quirinal and Viminal, despite its usual designation as mons.

The slopes of both heights were steep and possibly improved for defense by scarping in various sectors. The only road from the direction of the Forum Romanum up the hill was the Clivus Capitolinus (q.v.), which began at the Temple of Saturn and climbed steeply along the slope to the southwest before turning and making directly for the entrance to the Area Capitolina. A stair, the Gradus Monetae (q.v.), later replaced by the Scalae Gemoniae (q.v.), led from the end of the Sacra Via directly up the northeastern height (E. Platner et al., *Beschreibung der Stadt Rom* 3.2 [Stuttgart and Tübingen 1838], 16; cf. *AJA* 82 [1978]: 241 [L. Richardson]). A second stair led from the lower slopes, the level of the Temple of Concordia, through the Tabularium to the saddle between crests. A third stair, the Centum Gradus (q.v.), led from the Forum Holitorium to the top of the Saxum Tarpeium. Ancient streets have been found under Piazza del Campidoglio that ran to both heights and connected with the Clivus Capitolinus behind the Porticus Deorum Consentium (q.v.), as well as one that probably ran down along the line of the Cordonata to the Campus Martius, but it has not been possible to follow this far enough to be sure where it led. The lower slopes of the hill seem to have been covered with shops and housing from a very early period, building that came right up to the walls by the early imperial period (see, e.g., Tacitus, *Hist.* 3.71).

The Capitoline was not included in the city of the Regiones Quattuor (q.v.), and it did not have any shrine of the Argei, so far as we know, which suggests that it was regarded as special and possibly outside the pomerium. However, the presence of the Porta Stercoraria (q.v.) along the Clivus Capitolinus can be taken to indicate that it was regarded as a sort of no man's land, an idea that the presence of the Asylum (q.v.) and Saxum Tarpeium could also be used to support. Because this was the very heart and head of the official religion of the Roman state, it was above the limitations and characterization of other places in the city.

Jordan 1.2.1–154; Lugli 1946, 1–53.

Capitolium Vetus (Fig. 72): a sacellum on the Quirinal dedicated to Jupiter, Juno, and Minerva, believed to be older than the Capitoline temple (Varro, *Ling.* 5.158). It was still a landmark in the time of Martial (5.22.4, 7.73.4) and is listed in the regionary catalogues. It may have been the source of a group of inscriptions belonging to dedications

(*CIL* 1².726–28 = 6.30925–27 = *ILS* 32–34 = *ILLRP* 175–77, but see Degrassi's note on nos. 174–81). It stood at one end of the Clivus Proximus a Flora susus versus Capitolium Vetus, a clivus probably beginning at Porta Quirinalis and ending at Alta Semita, possibly the street that became Ad Malum Punicum beyond Alta Semita.

Caprae Palus (**Capreae**, Ovid, *Fast.* 2.491): a place in the Campus Martius mentioned only in connection with the disappearance of Romulus, who was holding a *contio*, or a review of the army, there when there was a sudden local squall and darkness of brief duration, in the midst of which Romulus disappeared (Livy 1.16.1; Florus 1.1.16; Solinus 1.20; etc.). It is widely assumed that this would have been in the basin of the Pantheon, the lowest part of the Campus Martius, and this likelihood is strengthened by the proximity of the Saepta here, which replaced the Ovile, a natural place for a contio. But there is no proof. If it was in the basin of the Pantheon, Agrippa must have drained it in preparation for the construction of his complex of buildings here.

Capralia: according to Paulus *ex Fest.* (57L), the correct name for the district commonly called *ad caprae paludes*. Because in the Augustan period the Caprae Palus must have disappeared under Agrippa's Saepta and Thermae, one wonders about the persistence of the designation.

Capraria, Aedicula: see **Aedicula Capraria.**

Caput Africae (Fig. 16): listed by the regionary catalogues in Regio II and known from inscriptions to have been the site of a *paedagogium* for slaves in the imperial house (*CIL* 5.1039 = *ILS* 1826, *CIL* 6.1052, 8982–87 [8983 = *ILS* 1832]), one of whom was to be a *vestitor*. A base bearing a dedication to Caracalla of A.D. 198 lists twenty-four *paedagogi*, all freedmen, six of them *vernae*. They describe themselves as *a capite Africae*, but usually *caput* is not declined. Presumably the name came from an allegorical head of Africa wearing the spoils of the elephant; because this survived as late as the Einsiedeln itinerary of the eighth century, it must have been sculpted, and it might be the standard of a street fountain or similar landmark.

This gave its name to a vicus, convincingly identified by G. Gatti (*AdI* 54 [1882]: 191–220) with the ancient street under Via della Navicella. He also demonstrated that Caput Africae lay southwest of the vicus, toward the Temple of Divus Claudius. Probably it stood at or near the juncture of the Vicus Capitis Africae and a nameless street perpendicular to it leading in the direction of SS. Quattro Coronati, and the paedagogium was behind it.

Caput Gorgonis: mentioned only in the regionary catalogues, listed in Regio XIV. Granted the enormous popularity of the motif used decoratively in every medium and at every scale, one feels this ought to have been in some way remarkable, perhaps in the round or of exceptional material, but nothing further is known about it.

Caput Tauri: see **Forum Tauri.**

Carcer (Figs. 19, 20): the only public jail of Rome, at the foot of the Capitoline between the Temple of Concordia and the Curia, and with a façade on the Clivus Argentarius. It was not a place for long imprisonment, simply a place of detention, and especially the place where non-citizens condemned of capital crimes were executed, usually by strangulation. These were especially the kings who had fought against Rome, such as Jugurtha and Vercingetorix, who would be taken to the Carcer immediately after having been exhibited in the triumphal procession. The Catilinarian conspirators were also executed there (Sallust, *Cat.* 55.1–6). See Livy 1.33.8; Vell. Pat. 2.7.2; Val. Max. 9.12.6; Pliny, *HN* 7.212; Festus 325L.

It is described by Sallust (*Cat.* 55.1–6) and still consists of two parts, as he says. The underground part was called the Tullianum, a name derived, according to our ancient sources (Varro, *Ling.* 5.151; Festus 490L), from its having been built by Servius Tullius, but more likely deriving from a spring (*tullius*) that still rises in its floor. This existed in antiquity (cf. Propertius 4.4.3–14 and the nearby Porta Fontinalis), as shown by an ancient drain that conveyed its water to the southeast, evidently to empty into the Cloaca. In antiquity this lower chamber was accessible only by a shaft in the center of the roof. This chamber was originally round, almost 7 m in diameter, built of large blocks of peperino. The walls are three courses high, only about 2 m, with a strong batter, while Sallust says it was 12 feet high, so higher parts may have been lost when the present flat-arched roof was installed. Frank dates the construction of the chamber to the third century B.C., and the roof to sometime after 100 B.C., after the upper chamber was constructed. This roof was extensively repaired at a later date. Before the upper chamber was built, the ring was cut by a straight wall of Grotta Oscura tufa across its front on the Comitium, presumably during work of regularization in connection with the Comitium.

The upper chamber is a trapezoid vaulted north and south. Its east wall follows the line of the Com-

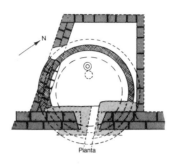

Figure 20
Carcer, Plan of Both
Storeys
and Section

itium; its south wall, that of the Temple of Concordia. It is constructed largely of Monteverde tufa and is dated 120–80 B.C. by Frank. The façade, in blocks of travertine, is the work of the consuls Vibius Rufinus and Cocceius Nerva, as the inscription informs us, between A.D. 39 and 42 (*CIL* 6.1539, 31674); it has the grim forbidding strength one associates with prisons.

One is a bit surprised that the Romans should have chosen a place with a spring for their jail. It may be that originally criminals were condemned to death by starvation, and the spring functioned as the jug of water deposited with Vestal Virgins condemned for unchastity. Or it may be that the Carcer began its existence as a springhouse and was converted to use as a jail when the spring failed to produce an adequate supply. It was still in use in the fourth century (Amm. Marc. 28.1.57). The epithet Mamertinus is post-classical.

Frank 39–47; Lugli 1946, 107–11; Nash 1.206–8; *Roma sotterranea* (show catalogue, Rome 1984), 112–16 (R. Luciani); Coarelli 1985, 64–76.

Carinae: probably the whole brow of the western end of the Oppius from the vicinity of the church of S. Pietro in Vincoli around to the Thermae Titi (see, e.g., Livy 26.10.1; Varro, *Ling.* 5.47–48; Horace, *Epist.* 1.7.48; Dion. Hal. 1.68.1, 3.22.8), probably deriving its name from a fancied resemblance between the natural shape of the edge and a row of upturned boats (but see Servius *ad Aen.* 8.361). It was a fashionable place to live, especially in the late republic; Pompey's Domus Rostrata was there (Cicero, *Har. Resp.* 49; Suetonius, *Gramm.* 15; Florus

2.18.4), and Augustus was brought up there (Servius *ad Aen.* 8.361). Its most conspicuous monument was the Temple of Tellus (see Tellus, Aedes). Toward the east it was bounded by the Murus Terreus (q.v.), which was probably a terrace wall of crude brick (Varro, *Ling.* 5.48), certainly not an agger, as many commentators have supposed.

Eranos 85 (1987): 122–30 (Å. Fridh).

Carmentis, Fanum (Sacellum, Ara, Arae): the shrine of Carmentis (or Carmenta), a goddess of prophecy widely supposed to be the Arcadian mother of Evander, a divinity who also helped women in childbirth, probably originally a water nymph. The Carmentalia was celebrated on 11 and 15 January (Degrassi 394–95, 398). The shrine was at the foot of the Capitoline at the Porta Carmentalis of the Servian Walls, which took its name from her (Solinus 1.13; Servius *ad Aen.* 8.337). It is variously called a fanum (Solinus 1.13; A. Gellius 18.7.2), a sacellum (Ovid, *Fast.* 1.629), an ara (Vergil, *Aen.* 8.337), and arae (Varro, *ap. Gell.* 16.16.4). The last is probably most accurate. Varro says that to avert the danger of having a child born feet first, altars were set up in Rome to the two Carmentes, one surnamed Postverta, the other surnamed Prorsa (or Porrima). Ovid (*Fast.* 1.633–36) explains these two Carmentes as sisters or companions of the Arcadian goddess, deriving their names from their ability to look into both the past and the future. It may be that originally there was a single altar and subsequently others were added in its proximity.

In the recent excavations of the Area Sacra di S. Omobono, despite careful research, no trace of either the Porta Carmentalis or the shrine of Carmentis has been identified. These must have been very close to this area, the Porta Carmentalis opening in the Servian Walls where they crossed the Vicus Iugarius and the shrine just inside it (*iuxta portam*, not *extra portam*, Servius *ad Aen.* 8.337).

Casa dei Grifi: the modern name given remains of a building of the late republican period found by Boni in 1912 under the "lararium" of the Domus Augustiana (q.v.) that preserved important decorations in the early Second Style, now for the most part removed to the Antiquario Palatino. The general plan of the building is impossible to read given the state of our knowledge. It is clear that there were two storeys, but these may not have been in communication with each other, and the lower storey seems to have been abandoned and buried while the upper was still in use, to which circumstance we owe the excellent preservation of the painting. The lower storey has walls faced with opus incertum, with later modifications in walls faced with opus reticulatum,

and was clearly largely subterranean, the only windows being in the crowns of the vaulted ceilings. There are remains of four rooms, all originally vaulted, but for only one of these is the plan complete. It is small and trapezoidal, one wall running at a distinct angle, with a rather deep vestibule and an alcove, probably for a piece of furniture, adjacent to the entrance. The other rooms seem to have been regularly rectangular and may have given on a courtyard or peristyle to the northeast. The use of all of them is obscure. The pavements are fine mosaic.

The decorations are highly architectonic, reproducing the schemes of Pompeian First Style decorations, but with the addition of illusionistic columns raised on a continuous plinth in one room and on individual plinths in another. These appeared to carry the vaults. Opus sectile of trompe l'oeil effect is reproduced in some panels, and throughout there is meticulous attention to detail and the rendering of the mottling of certain stones shown. Much of the painting is close to being a translation of First Style decoration into painted illusion. The only stucco relief is in the vaults and the lunettes, one of which shows a pair of gryphons in heraldic symmetry flanking an elaborate scrolled vine springing from a clump of acanthus. This has given the building its name.

G. E. Rizzo, *Le pitture della "Casa dei Grifi"* (*Monumenti della pittura antica scoperti in Italia*, sec. 3, Roma fasc. 1 [Rome 1936]).

Casa dei Paesaggi dell'Odissea: a large late-republican house on the northwest slope of the Cispian above Via Cavour at the corner between Via Sforza and Via dei Quattro Cantoni, evidently developed in terraces, the lowest being a portico or cryptoporticus of at least two wings decorated in the late Second Pompeian Style. High on the continuous wall was a landscape frieze, 1.16 m high, originally continuous, but broken into panels by pairs of pillars of the architectural frame. This showed in bird's-eye perspective the adventures of Odysseus, the nine panels recovered whole or in part representing events from the landing in the land of the Laestrygonians to the encounter with the sirens, but these are neither the beginning nor the end of the sequence. They are unique, very fine work; important figures are identified by name in the Greek alphabet. The paintings were discovered in 1848 and are now, except for one fragment, in the Biblioteca Vaticana.

RömMitt 70 (1963): 100–146 (P. H. von Blanckenhagen); A. Gallina, *Le pitture con paesaggi dell' Odissea dall'Esquilino* (StMisc 6 [1964]).

Casa della Farnesina: a splendid house with superb decorations on the right bank of the Tiber just above the Cellae Vinariae Nova et Arruntiana discovered in the garden of Villa Farnesina during work on the new Tiber embankment in 1879 and then partially excavated. It seems to have been, in effect, a portico villa set facing northeast across the river, probably of symmetrical plan, although the ruinous condition of the northern half did not permit certainty on this point. The main features recovered were part of a hemicyclical corridor jutting out toward the river, a suite of painted rooms behind this in highly organized symmetry facing a lateral garden area of its own, and a long, straight cryptoporticus divided in half by a line of pillars on the landward side. This was the entrance side, and the cryptoporticus was here backed against a long line of small service rooms. The river front was evidently terraced and gardened, probably in more than one level. The decorations are in early Third Pompeian Style and are still highly architectonic and employ cinnabar but include a wealth of figures and narrative and genre panels. A date of 20–10 B.C. is proposed; the ownership of the house has been much discussed, and it is frequently assigned to Agrippa, but there is no evidence. The vaults of three of the smaller rooms were decorated with fine stucco reliefs, including landscapes and scenes of mythology and religious ritual. Much of the subject matter of the decorations is enigmatic and has provoked lively debate, but the excellence of the workmanship and the brilliance of the decorative effect are beyond question. What could be salvaged from the decorations is now in the Museo Nazionale Romano delle Terme.

I. Bragantini and M. de Vos, *Le decorazioni della villa romana della Farnesina (Museo Nazionale Romano, Le Pitture, 2.1,* Rome 1982), with bibliography.

Casa di Augusto: see Domus, Augustus.

Casa di Livia (Fig. 63.3): the modern name given to a building discovered by P. Rosa in 1869 on the Palatine behind the Domus Tiberiana, between the Temple of the Magna Mater and the Domus Augustiana. Although the southwest corner of the "triclinium" had been breached in Farnese excavations of 1722–1724 and part of that decoration removed at the time, the building was evidently not further explored. It shows a very complicated history of construction, and large parts of it are of scant architectural interest, but it preserves wall decorations of the greatest importance. The name is assigned it on the basis of a lead pipe found in the excavations bearing the name of Iulia Augusta (*CIL* 15.7264), but this is now believed to be of questionable date and value. The decorations belong to a phase intermediate between the Second and Third Pompeian Styles and are to be dated to the Augustan period. The house eventually must have belonged to some member of the imperial family, but whether it did at the time of this decoration is doubtful.

The decorated part consists of a large lobby, its roof originally supported by a pair of stout pillars, onto which open three deep halls parallel to one another and together filling one long side of the lobby. The central hall is somewhat wider than those flanking it and has been called the "tablinum," while its companions are called "alae," but the identification is groundless. Another room opening at the southwest corner of the lobby has been called the "triclinium." These names are often retained for convenience. All these rooms were largely subterranean and windowless, unless there were lights opened in the missing ceilings. They were approached by a stair and a ramped corridor leading to the exterior, which has been thought to be a posticum, but it is handsome and more commodious than the connection with the rest of the house, which is by a narrow stair leading up to a corridor at a higher level. Off this corridor to the southwest lies a series of service rooms, while behind the "tablinum" and "alae" was a courtyard flanked or surrounded by porticoes supported on stout square pillars. This part of the house was later rebuilt as a series of rather cramped and ill-planned rooms that seem not to have been living quarters. And off the southwest side of the house, at some uncertain period, was added another squarish courtyard with pillars of tufa at the corners and columns along the sides that seems to have been surrounded with rooms on three sides. All this part of the house has come down in poor condition, especially the second courtyard.

The decorated suite is very fine, both in architectural concept and in the quality of the painting, but there is no indication of how these rooms functioned, and sometime in antiquity they were butchered by the cutting of doors and addition of new walls that were left undecorated. Presumably by that time they had been relegated to use as a cellar. The lobby had a rather severe late Second Style decoration proper to an atrium or similar apartment, its main feature an arcuated cornice supported on figured (?) brackets. The "tablinum" had an elaborate early *scaenae frons* decoration, including large central subject pictures of Io watched by Argus and Polyphemus and Galataea. The right "ala" is famous for its continuous frieze in yellow monochrome of exotic landscapes and the rich garlands swung between fancifully embellished columns. The left "ala" has a frieze of heraldically posed winged figures on delicate scrolled brackets. And the "triclinium" has large central landscapes of sacro-idyllic character. There are scant remains of fine mosaic pavements throughout.

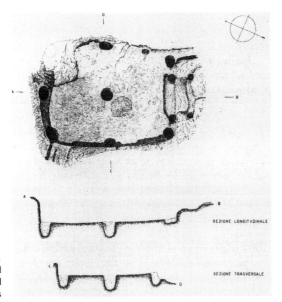

Figure 21
Casa Romuli, Plan and
Sections of Floor and
Post Holes

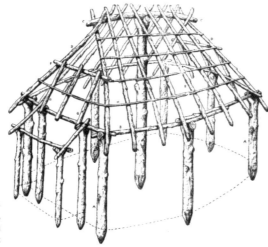

Figure 22
Casa Romuli,
Reconstruction
of Framework

The building is in every way a puzzle. When the decorations were removed to protect them from the humidity, it was discovered that the somewhat irregular reticulate-faced walls showed older doors had been closed with masonry before the plaster was laid, so the building must be dated some years before the painting. Perhaps the building is mid-first century B.C. and the decorations ca. 25–20 B.C.

G. E. Rizzo, *Le pitture della "Casa di Livia"* (*Monumenti della pittura antica scoperti in Italia*, ser. 3, Roma fasc. 3 [Rome 1936]).

Casa Romuli (Figs. 21, 22): the hut of Romulus on the Cermalus slope of the Palatine beside the Scalae Caci (q.v.). It is best described by Dionysius: a prim-

itive hut built of wattle and daub, roofed with thatch, which was preserved and repaired whenever damaged in a form as close as possible to the original (Dion. Hal. 1.79.11; Plutarch, *Rom.* 20.4). Damage to it was regarded as an evil omen (Cass. Dio 48.43.4, 54.29.8). It was evidently the same as the Tugurium Faustuli (Solinus 1.18), although the discovery of cuttings and post holes for several huts near the top of the Scalae Caci may possibly indicate that more than one was known to have existed. It was preserved at least until the fourth century, for it is listed in the regionary catalogues in Regio X. An Aedis Romuli on the Palatine is listed as the location of one of the shrines of the Argei (Varro, *Ling.* 5.54: *apud aedem Romuli*); it is probably the same as the Casa.

A second Casa Romuli, a duplicate of the first, was maintained in the Area Capitolina (q.v.) (Vitruvius 2.1.5; Seneca, *Contr.* 2.1.5; Conon, *Dieg.* [*FGrH* 1 p. 210]). We know nothing about this after A.D. 78.

Lugli 1946, 34, 455; *MonAnt* 41 (1951): 1–146 (S. M. Puglisi, P. Romanelli, A. Davico, and G. de Angelis d'Ossat); Coarelli 1974, 138–39; *REL* 62 (1984): 57–80 (A. Balland).

Castor, Aedes (Figs. 23, 63): the Temple of Castor (or of the Castors) at the southeast corner of the Forum Romanum flanked by the Vicus Tuscus and fountain of Juturna (Cicero, *Nat. D.* 3.13; Plutarch, *Coriolan.* 3.4; Dion. Hal. 6.13.4; Martial 1.70.3; also shown on the Marble Plan [*FUR* pl. 21.18; Rodriguez pl. 13]). According to tradition it was vowed at the battle of Lake Regillus in 493 B.C. by the dictator Postumius, first in the heat of battle and then after the Dioscuri were seen watering their horses at the spring of Juturna following the victory, and dedicated in 484 by the son of Postumius (Livy 2.20.12, 2.42.5). The day of dedication is given as 27 January by everyone but Livy (2.42.5), who gives 15 July, the day of the Transvectio Equitum, which may be the date of the dedication of the first temple (Degrassi 403–4).

Its correct name was Aedes Castoris (Suetonius, *Caes.* 10.1; Cass. Dio 37.8.2), and so it regularly appears, but we also find Aedes Castorum (e.g., Pliny, *HN* 10.121; *Not.* Regio VIII; Chron. 146), and even Aedes Castoris et Pollucis (e.g., Asconius *in Cic. Scaur.* 46 [Stangl 28]; Suetonius, *Tib.* 20).

The foundations of the oldest temple show a plan like that of Temple A at Pyrgi and suggest reconstruction with three rows of four columns preceding the cella and a cella flanked by lateral features. The Danish excavators believe there were three cellas, but lateral colonnades or alae seem more likely, and alae preferable.

The temple was rebuilt by L. Caecilius Metellus in

117 B.C. (Cicero, *Scaur.* 46 [Stangl 28], with Asconius *in Cic. Scaur.* 46; *Verr.* 2.1.154; Plutarch, *Pomp.* 2.4). The concrete of the podium associated with this rebuilding is the earliest dated concrete known (Frank 78–79). Verres made some repairs to it (Cicero, *Verr.* 2.1.129–54), and it was completely rebuilt by Tiberius and dedicated in A.D. 6 in his name and that of his brother Drusus (Suetonius, *Tib.* 20; Cass. Dio 55.27.4; Ovid, *Fast.* 1.707–8). Caligula in some way incorporated the temple in his palace, making an approach to the palace between the two statues, so the Dioscuri became his gatekeepers (Suetonius, *Calig.* 22.2; Cass. Dio 59.28.5). Claudius abolished this modification. A restoration is ascribed to Domitian (Chron. 146), and here the temple is called Templum Castoris et Minervae, a name also found in the regionary catalogues. But scholars are agreed that the existing remains are essentially Augustan and that any subsequent restoration must have been limited. It is also one of the finest of all ancient Roman buildings.

It served frequently as a meeting place for the Roman senate (e.g., Cicero, *Verr.* 2.1.129). Its stair was arranged to form a rostra with small stairs leading off from either end of a platform running the width of the temple at midstair (cf. Nash 1: figs. 239, 241). This must be one of the Rostra III of the regionary catalogues, although there is no indication that it was ever decorated with beaks. In the temple were kept the standards for weights and measures (cf. *CIL* 5.8119.4, 11.6726.2 = *ILS* 8638, *CIL* 13.10030.13–14), and a series of chambers in the podium in the intercolumniations closed by metal doors served as repositories for the imperial fiscus (*CIL* 6.8688–89) and for the wealth of private individuals (Juvenal 14.260–62).

As rebuilt in the Augustan period, the temple was octastyle, Corinthian, peripteral, with eleven columns on each long side and almost certainly a double row to either side of the relatively shallow pronaos. The podium is very high, the floor standing about 7 m above the Sacra Via. The pronaos is 9.90 m deep and 15.80 m wide, the cella is 19.70 m deep and 16 m wide, and the whole building is some 50 m long and 20 m wide. The podium is concrete, enclosing remains of earlier phases encased in tufa walls from which spur walls project to make the *loculi* for safekeeping of valuables. Under the columns, footings of travertine replace the tufa. From the pronaos a flight of eleven steps leads down to the rostra in front, 3.66 m above the street level. The rostra was provided with a railing and could accommodate a fairly large number of persons. From references in literature (Plutarch, *Sulla* 33.4; Cicero, *Phil.* 3.27), it is clear that there were similar arrangements in Metellus's temple. Of the superstructure,

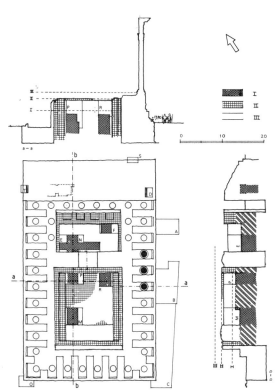

Figure 23
Temple of Castor in the Forum Romanum, Plan Showing Three Building Periods, Together with Sections

the three surviving columns on the east side were all that was standing in the fifteenth century, for the area near them was called Tre Colonne. These are of white marble, 12.50 m high, and carry an entablature with a plain frieze and a richly worked modillion cornice. The design of the capitals is especially admirable.

The temple was standing in the fourth century and was included in the regionary catalogues, but virtually nothing is known of its history in the imperial and medieval periods. Its identity was early lost, and in the early nineteenth century it was often wrongly identified, most frequently as the Temple of Iuppiter Stator.

Frank 78–79; *MAAR* 5 (1925): 79–102 (T. Frank); Lugli 1946, 179–83; Nash 1.210–13; *ActaArch* 56 (1985): 1–29 (I. Nielsen, J. Zahle, et al.), 59 (1988): 1–14 (I. Nielsen).

Castor et Pollux, Aedes (Fig. 24): a temple *in Circo Flaminio*, its day of dedication 13 August (Degrassi 494, 496). It is cited by Vitruvius (4.8.4) as a temple of unusual plan, and from a fragment of a detailed plan of its immediate area on a marble plate it is now known to have been a temple with a transverse cella, like those of Concordia and Vediovis on the Capitoline. It is shown as hexastyle with a pronaos three columns deep, approached by a stair of

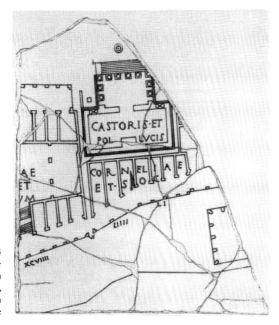

Figure 24
Temple of Castor
and Pollux in
Circus Flaminius,
Representation
on Marble

curi nel Circo Flaminio (Rome 1984); *StRom* 33 (1985): 205–11 (F. Castagnoli); *BullCom* 91.1 (1986): 91–96 (M. Conticello de'Spagnolis); *JRA* 1 (1988): 120–31 (E. Rodriguez Almeida).

Castra: The earliest castra we hear of in Rome are the Castra Praetoria, built by Tiberius some distance beyond the Servian Walls but on high ground, commanding the important approaches to the city from the north, northeast, and east. These must have been preceded, however, by the *stationes* of the Cohortes Vigilum, the seven barracks of the police and fire brigades created by Augustus in his reorganization of the city into fourteen regiones beginning in 7 B.C. Each cohort served two of the Augustan regiones, and the statio was strategically located to cover the territory best. There were also fourteen *excubitoria,* smaller stations, presumably one in each regio, but the location of only one of these, in the Transtiberim, is known, and it was not original, but installed about the beginning of the third century after Christ in a building already nearly a century old. The three stationes that are known, those of cohorts II, IV, and V, are known principally from finds of inscriptions, not excavations, traces of the actual building being known only for that of V on the Caelian, west of the church of S. Stefano Rotondo, and these not sufficient for us to infer from them the building's plan. Because it is known, however, that in the early third century the cohort had at one time 930 men and 113 officers, and a little later 1,013 men and 109 officers (*CIL* 6.1057, 1058 = *ILS* 2157), we can calculate that the cohorts at that time numbered about seven thousand men, with an officer for every nine or ten men, and were organized on military lines with prefects and centurions. It follows that from the beginning they would have been housed in barracks of castrum plan and with the regular features of such. Indeed the room in which the statue bases of *CIL* 6.1057 and 1058 were found was believed to be the praetorium of the camp, and sockets in the mosaic pavement were thought to be intended for standards of military type.

The Castra Praetoria were built on the standard plan of all Roman army camps, a rectangle somewhat longer than wide with rounded corners, divided into four parts by streets, the cardo and decumanus, that ran their length and width and ran to gates at their ends. These did not divide the camp into exact quarters, the cardo being displaced toward the west. Camp headquarters was at their crossing, where an open square was left in front of the praetorium. The camp was fortified from an early period, probably from the beginning, but the fortification was not a formidable one. Not much is known about the arrangements in the interior, but

eight steps, with what must be a pair of windows flanking the pronaos. A round feature in front of the temple is interpreted as its altar. Because the scale of the plan, 1:240, is the same as that of the Marble Plan and a curiously represented building behind the temple on what appears to be the bank of the Tiber agrees perfectly with a building shown on a fragment of the Marble Plan preserving other features (*FUR* pl. 56.614; Rodriguez pl. 24), it becomes possible to locate the temple very precisely just west of Via della Cinque Scole, occupying most of the area of Piazza delle Cinque Scole behind the southern end of Piazza Cenci. Because an open area is shown in front of the temple, we must presume that this is Circus Flaminius, which means that Circus Flaminius was extended beyond the line of the Petronia Amnis and was at least 200 m long. From the near neighborhood of the temple come the two colossal marble statues of the Dioscuri with their horses that adorn the balustrade of Piazza del Campidoglio (Helbig⁴ 2.1164), but they were evidently an addition of the second century after Christ, presumably set up in front of the temple, possibly flanking the stair of approach.

The temple is dated by its order in the *fasti* after the temples of Fortuna Equestris and Hercules *ad Portam Trigeminam* of 173 B.C. and by its appearance in the Fasti Allifani and Fasti Amiternini before 46 B.C. A date close to 100 B.C., when the transverse cella plan was most popular, may be indicated, because the plan shows that it was not dictated wholly by the exigencies of the space available.

M. Conticello de'Spagnolis, *Il Tempio dei Dios-*

enough to see that it followed the usual pattern of long, thin units of uniform cells set back-to-back with passages between. We can presume that the Castra Misenatium and Ravennatium for the detachments from the fleet kept in Rome to rig and manipulate the awnings that regularly protected the spectators in the theaters and amphitheater and occasionally elsewhere were similar, but smaller, but we have no information about these, except that the former were near the Amphitheatrum Flavium (Colosseum) and the latter in the Transtiberim. Probably both detachments were used in the naumachiae, as well as for the awnings, and it was prudent to keep them distant from each other.

The Castra Equitum Singularium and Castra Peregrina on the Caelian are the urban castra best known to us, part of the former discovered in 1934–1938 under the basilica of S. Giovanni in Laterano, part of the latter in 1905 under the convent of the Little Company of Mary nearby. The former was a very extensive complex, in fact two castra, the Castra Priora and the Castra Nova Severiana of the Equites, the remains under the basilica belonging to the latter. Only a small part of these could be excavated, but soundings could be made at various points, and what was excavated included a good part of the praetorium with the Schola Collegii Equitum Singularium with an altar made of a column drum topped with an inverted Ionic capital carrying an interesting inscription identifying the schola and proving that the castra were built in A.D. 193–197. The whole complex was very large, extending under the Palazzo del Laterano and cloisters of the basilica as far as the Aurelian Walls. These Equites were an elite corps of cavalry organized as a special bodyguard for the princeps about the end of the first century after Christ. Under Septimius Severus the Praetorian Guard was disgraced and replaced by the Equites, their number being doubled to enable them to perform the service, hence the construction of the new castra. The Castra Peregrina, headquarters of soldiers who performed special services in Rome, housed especially the Frumentarii, a detachment at first responsible for the provisioning of the army, the *annona militaris,* who later became first couriers and then, under Hadrian, a secret police. Their barracks, of which only bits, not enough to permit reconstruction of even a general outline, were found, seem to have been built in the early second century, under Trajan or Hadrian.

All these were professional army men, and we should expect them to accord with the patterns of the Roman army elsewhere, even when they were assigned to duty in Rome itself. But many other branches of the imperial household and bureaucracy were also organized on the same lines and housed in what were known as castra. Thus we hear of the Castra Lecticariorum, Castra Silicariorum, Castra Tabellariorum, and Castra Victimariorum. Only the last is surprising; one would not have expected the demands of the state religion to have been heavy enough to call for military organization.

Castra Equitum Singularium (Fig. 16): the barracks of the Equites Singulares, an elite cavalry corps that was a bodyguard for the princeps. Remains of these were found in 1885 in Via Tasso north of the Scala Santa, especially the wall of a large rectangular court. This wall is broken by niches, and in front of it were inscribed pedestals, dedications of veterans at the completion of their service (*BullCom* 13 [1885]: 137–56 [R. Lanciani]). The earliest of these that is dated is early Hadrianic, the latest mid-third century. Sepulchral inscriptions of Equites Singulares mention Castra Priora (e.g., *CIL* 6.3183, 3191 = *ILS* 2205, 3196) and Castra Nova (e.g., *CIL* 6.3198 = *ILS* 2207, 3207, 3254), and a diploma speaks of Castra Nova Severiana (*CIL* 16.144, dated A.D. 230). One manuscript of the *Notitia*, the Laurentiana, also speaks of Castra Equitum Singularium II (Jordan 2.573). There therefore must have been two barracks, the second built by Septimius Severus. That in Via Tasso would be the earlier. The other was discovered in 1934, when it became possible to lift the pavement of S. Giovanni in Laterano and explore under it. There was found a complex of barrackslike rooms and also an apsidal room with an altar in front of the apse carrying a long inscription of two officials of the Equites Singulares, in honor of Septimius Severus and Caracalla. This then was the barracks built when Septimius Severus doubled the number of the Equites Singulares following the abolition of the Praetorian guard. It was destroyed a century later when Constantine abolished the Equites Singulares.

Lugli 1938, 518–22; Lugli 1970, 540–41; Nash 1.214–18; R. Krautheimer, S. Corbett, and A. K. Frazer, *Corpus Basilicarum Christianarum Romae* 2, fasc. 5 (Rome 1976), 25–30.

Castra Lecticariorum: listed by the regionary catalogues in Regio XIV and in the *Breviarium*. It must have been the barracks of litter-bearers who were assigned to the service of public officials. These must have been organized along military lines, probably around the time of Augustus, for they had not only *castra* but also *decuriones lecticariorum.*

Castra Misenatium: headquarters of the contingent of sailors from the base of the Tyrrhenian fleet at Misenum kept in Rome to maneuver the awnings of the amphitheaters and theaters. The *castra* are listed in Regio III in the regionary catalogues and presumably would be close to the Colosseum. In 313 a couple speaks of living in a *castra para tas Titianas* (*IG* 14.956b.15 = *IGUR* 246), and an inscription found just south of the hemicycle of the Baths of Trajan speaks of an enlargement of the camp under the Gordians (*CIL* 6.1091). A lost fragment of the Marble Plan (*FUR* pl. 10; Rodriguez pl. 4) showed parts of buildings labeled]LICAL[ ]MENTARIA and CA]STRAMISE[NA]TIUM. Rodriguez (70 and fig. 19) assigns this fragment to a place beyond the Ludus Magnus with the inscription of the Castra Misenatium cut on the street running between the Ludus Magnus and Ludus Dacicus, placing these on the north side of the street just below the Baths of Trajan, a place already assigned the castra by Lanciani (LFUR sheet 30), but he admits that it could be moved along the street in either direction.

Castra Peregrina

(Fig. 16): the camp on the Caelian for soldiers detached from the provincial armies for special service in Rome. The regular officers of the camp were a princeps, a subprinceps, and probably a single optio. The soldiers were especially the *frumentarii* and *speculatores*, although occasionally there seem to have been others. The frumentarii, originally concerned with the commissariat and supply service, were mounted and gradually came to be used first as couriers and escorts for prisoners being sent to Rome for trial, a little later (as early as the time of Hadrian; cf. S.H.A. *Hadr.* 11.4) as secret police, a spy service, and executioners. The speculatores were orderlies sent by various army commands to the headquarters in Rome.

The camp was found in digging for the foundations of the convent and hospital of the Little Company of Mary in 1904–1909 and partially excavated. The remains consisted principally of five parallel rows of cells fronting on continuous porticoes with three alleys between and at least four apses introduced seemingly at random, but where they would not interfere with traffic, probably for the cults of the camp. A great many inscriptions were recovered, including dedications to the Genius Castrorum and Iuppiter Redux (*CIL* 6.428 = *ILS* 2219). The stone ships found here, one of which was the original ornament of the fountain of Piazza della Navicella, also attest to the travels of those quartered in the castra. There is also mention of a bath (*CIL* 6.354 = *ILS* 2218).

From the masonry it appears that the camp was founded by Augustus and almost completely rebuilt in the second century. Mention in Ammianus Marcellinus (16.12.66) shows that it was still in use in the fourth century.

JRS 13 (1923): 152–89 (J. B. Baillie Reynolds); *MemPontAcc* 7 (1944): 240–45 (A. M. Colini).

Castra Praetoria (Castra Praetorium, *CIL*

15.7239b, c) (Fig. 72): the barracks of the Praetorian guard built by Tiberius in A.D. 21–23, when these forces were given permanent quarters in the city (Suetonius, *Tib.* 37.1; Tacitus, *Ann.* 4.2; Cass. Dio 57.19.6). These were in the extreme northeast corner of Rome beyond the inhabited areas, about 500 m east of the Agger (Pliny, *HN* 3.67; Suetonius, *Nero* 48.2) on a site that was one of the highest points in Rome (59–60 meters above sea level), with a commanding view of the city and the roads of approach from the north and northeast. The design was that usual for camps, a broad rectangle with rounded corners, 440 m long and 380 m wide. The cross of main streets through the camp was regular on the long axis, the via praetoria, with the porta praetoria and porta decumana at its ends, but displaced to the northwest on the short axis by some 30 m, the via principalis, with the portae principalis dextra and sinistra at its ends.

The camp walls of Tiberius are of brick-faced concrete, 4.73 m high, where preserved, with battlements and towered gates (Tacitus, *Hist.* 3.84). On the inside of the wall were lines of vaulted chambers 3 m high, the masonry faced with opus reticulatum and veneered with stucco; these carried the wall walk. As might be expected from its historical importance, the camp is repeatedly mentioned in the events of the Roman empire and figures in many inscriptions, especially of merchants who did business there. A group of inscriptions of special interest are those on lead pipes that supplied water to the camp (*CIL* 15.7237–44; *ILS* 8697–99) that show constant attention to the provisioning of the barracks.

A series of coins of the early part of the reign of Claudius shows the praetorian camp schematically as a reverse type (*B. M. Coins, Rom. Emp.* 1 Claudius, nos. 5, 20, 21, 23–25, 37, 38). It appears as a low curving fortification wall in which there are two arched entrances crowned by five battlements, above which appears a divinity enthroned (Jupiter?) with an aquila to his right, under a pediment supported by columns or pillars. A continuation of the front wall is shown as passing behind this group.

Aurelian incorporated the Castra Praetoria in his fortifications. These joined the castra at the northwest corner and near the middle of the south side. The height of the wall was then raised by an addition of 2.50–3 m, while the foot was cut away for a depth of about the same amount and refaced with brick. The old battlements can be seen encased in the wall at points, and new battlements were added along the new wall top. At some time the gates to the exterior were walled up. In 312 Constantine disbanded the last vestige of the Praetorians and apparently dismantled their camp by destroying the west wall, though part of this is reported to have been still standing in the sixteenth century (Zosimus 2.17.2; Aur. Vict., *Caes.* 40.25; cf. LS 2.243).

The interior arrangements of the camp are very poorly understood. There was a shrine of the standards, as one would expect (Herodian 4.4.5, 5.8.5–7), a shrine of Mars (*CIL* 6.2256 = *ILS* 2090), an altar of Fortuna Restitutrix (*NSc* 1888, 391 [G. Gatti]; *CIL* 6.30876), an armamentarium (Tacitus, *Hist.* 1.38, 80; *CIL* 6.999 = *ILS* 333, 2725 = *ILS* 2034), and a tribunal (Tacitus, *Hist.* 1.36).

Renaissance antiquarians speak of an Arcus Gordiani near the Porta Chiusa (cf. HJ 390n.45). No very reliable account of this arch has come down to us, and no remains that can be identified as belonging to it are known. While it seems very probable that triumphal arches to emperors might have been erected in conjunction with the Castra Praetoria, none has been positively identified, and there is no sign of rebuilding of any of the gates in monumental form.

PBSR 10 (1927): 12–22 (I. A. Richmond); Nash 1.221–24; *CAR* 3-D, 125 pp. 103–5.

Castra Ravennatium: mentioned in the addenda to the regionary catalogues (Jordan 2.574) and in the *Mirabilia* (Jordan 2.617; VZ 3.26), where it is said to be *in Transtiberim templum Ravennatium effundens oleum, ubi est S. Maria.* This must have been the barracks for a detachment of the imperial fleet based at Ravenna, detached for special duty in the capital, probably especially in the naumachiae and for the manipulation of awnings in the theaters and amphitheaters that protected spectators from the sun (cf. Castra Misenatium). The location of the Castra Ravennatium in the Transtiberim would seem most likely due to the presence of the Naumachia Augusti (q.v.) there. It was opened in 2 B.C. This would also put the camp closer to the theaters of Rome than the Castra Misenatium. So it may be that this was the contingent of the navy first assigned to urban duty. Hülsen (HCh 483) sees the name of the medieval church of St. Stephanus Rapignani as allusive to the name of the camp and so places it just west of the church of S. Crisogono.

HJ 647–48.

Castra Silicariorum, Castra Tabellariorum, Castra Victimariorum: listed only in the addenda to the regionary catalogues (Jordan 2.574). Their location is unknown, but their names reveal their char-

acter as the seats of corps of public servants organized along military lines (cf. Castra Lecticariorum). Probably all date to a time in the late third century.

Castra (Urbana): a camp built by Aurelian *in Campo Agrippae*, placed by the regionary catalogues in Regio VII, Via Lata, and linked with Aurelian's Templum Solis (cf. also Chron. 148). A certain amount of good evidence indicates that this was for the Cohortes Urbanae, at first stationed in the Castra Praetoria (q.v.), but later in their own camp (cf., e.g., Symmachus, *Epist.* 9.57[54]; *Dig.* 48.5.16[15].3). This must have housed all four urban cohorts (cf. *CIL* 6.1156 = *ILS* 722; *NSc* 1909, 430–31), as well as their equipment and offices, so it must have been a complex of some size, but nothing that can be identified as belonging to it has yet come to light. Because troops bivouacked in the Porticus Vipsania (q.v.) as early as A.D. 69 (Tacitus, *Hist.* 1.31; cf. 1.6), there may have been advantages and conveniences there that dictated the choice of the Campus Agrippae for the new camp. Certainly there was unencumbered space here and a good supply of water from the Aqua Virgo and Aqua Marcia.

Catabulum: the headquarters of the Cursus Publicus, the public post and transport, essentially a great stables. From the life of Saint Marcellus (LPD 1.164; VZ 2.228–29), we learn that Maxentius condemned him to serve in these stables. Marcellus was rescued by friends and then created a church in the house of the matrona Lucina at her request, after which he was arrested a second time by Maxentius, and his church was profaned by use as a stall for animals *(catabulum publicum),* to which Marcellus was obliged to minister until his death. The church of S. Marcello, which is extremely old, may be confidently identified as the site of his martyrdom, but what the relation of Lucina's house to the original catabulum may have been is doubtful. Still, it is tempting to locate this headquarters on Via Lata at the head of Via Flaminia. The name suggests that it may also have served as a customs office.

HJ 462; *MonAnt* 1.469–75 (R. Lanciani).

Cati Fons: a spring on the western slope of the Quirinal, the source of the Petronia Amnis (q.v.), named for the man on whose land it was found (Paulus *ex Fest.* 39L). It is beyond reasonable doubt that this is the same as the Acqua di S. Felice, which rises today in the courtyard of the Palazzo del Quirinale.

HJ 403; LA 24 (236).

Catialis Collis: known only from Placidus (*CGL* [Goetz] 5.15.36; 5.53.5), where it is identified as the location of a *lacus*. The explanation of the name is corrupt, but it probably derived from an owner's name. It is apparently a name for the northwest lobe or slope of the Quirinal. See Cati Fons.

Cella Civiciana: a warehouse in the Transtiberim located on the river in Via del Porto di Ripagrande opposite the Aventine, known from an inscription (*BullCom* 62 [1934]: 177 [E. Gatti]; *AE* 1937: 61).

Cella Groesiana: a warehouse of unknown location, known from a single inscription (*CIL* 6.706).

Cella Lucceiana: a warehouse known from an inscription found in the neighborhood of the Theater of Marcellus (*AE* 1971: 29). This is dated A.D. 161–162 (*RendPontAcc* 43 [1970–71]: 110–17 [S. Panciera]).

Cella Nigriana: a warehouse of some sort known only from the inscription on a fragment of a marble aedicula found in the garden of Palazzo Antonelli in Via Tre Canelle on the west slope of the Quirinal (*CIL* 6.31065). There seem to have been numerous rather fine warehouses in this neighborhood, some of which were buried in the substructures of the Thermae Constantinianae (q.v.).

HJ 418–20; *BullCom* 4 (1876): 102–6 (V. Vespignani).

Cella Saeniana: a warehouse in the Transtiberim known from an inscription found in the Lungotevere Portuense opposite Monte Testaccio (*AE* 1971: 30).

Cella Vinaria Massae: a warehouse known only from an inscription (*CIL* 6.32033), a bronze plate found "in Caeliolo."

Cellae Vinariae Nova et Arruntiana: warehouses for wine on the right bank of the Tiber excavated when the new Tiber embankment was created. It was a vast complex and lay in the garden of Villa Farnesina, just north of the line of the Aurelian Walls. What was found consisted of two parts. One was a warehouse built on the plan of horrea with a lower storey entirely of vaulted cellars and an upper storey in which rooms of uniform size were arranged in rows around colonnaded courts, the columns being of travertine finished with stucco. The other was a vast edifice on a different orientation closed on the east (river) side by a long double colonnade with a broad gutter along the west and a line of *dolia* outside the gutter, an arrangement strongly resembling that of the fermentation yards of *villae rusticae*. Excavation, however, revealed traces of horreumlike buildings further to the west on the same orientation,

so if wine was also manufactured here, it was only on a limited scale. An inscription (*CIL* 6.8826 = *ILS* 7276) dated A.D. 102 was found in the first building, and quantities of sherds of amphoras and dolia are reported to have been encountered in the excavation. The whole complex seems to have been destroyed at the time of the construction of the Aurelian Walls and was then built over with houses and gardens.

NSc 1880, 127–28, 140–41 and pl. 4 (G. Fiorelli); Nash 1.225–26.

Centum Gradus (Fig. 19): a stair leading up to the Area Capitolina (q.v.) near the Tarpeian Rock at the southwest corner of the hill (Tacitus, *Hist.* 3.71). The figure of one hundred may be only approximate. It may well be shown on a fragment of the Marble Plan (*FUR* pl. 29 fr. 31abc; Rodriguez pl. 23); if so, it seems to have been in two flights, one turning back on the other, with an arch midway along the upper flight.

Ceres, Liber Liberaque, Aedes: a temple on the lower slope of the Aventine near the northwest end of the Circus Maximus, just above the carceres (Dion. Hal. 6.94.3), vowed by the dictator A. Postumius Albus following a consultation of the Sibylline Books during a famine in 499 or 496 B.C. (Tacitus, *Ann.* 2.49; Dion. Hal. 6.17.2–4). It was dedicated by the consul Sp. Cassius in 493 (Dion. Hal. 6.94.3). It was in the Italo-Tuscan fashion, araeostyle, with a heavy roof and deep eaves, the roof surmounted by statues of terracotta (Vitruvius 3.3.5). It resembled the Capitoline temple at a smaller scale and may have had three cellas for its three divinities. The walls were decorated with paintings and reliefs by the Greek artists Gorgasus and Damophilus, and there was an inscription in Greek there stating that Gorgasus had done the left half, Damophilus the right (Pliny, *HN* 35.154). When the temple was rebuilt, the decorations were cut from the walls and encased in frames. It was a rich temple (Cicero, *Verr.* 2.4.108) containing many works of art, including golden pateras and statues paid for by the fines levied by plebeian magistrates (Livy 10.23.13, 27.6.19, 33.25.3, 36.9). It contained a bronze statue of Ceres supposed to be the oldest bronze statue made in Rome, paid for from the proceeds from the sale of the confiscated property of Sp. Cassius (Livy 2.41.10; Pliny, *HN* 34.15), and also a famous painting of Dionysus by Aristides, which Mummius had brought from Corinth (Pliny, *HN* 35.24 and 99; Strabo 8.6.23 [381]).

It was twice struck by lightning, in 206 and 84 B.C. (Livy 28.11.4; Appian, *BellCiv* 1.78). In 182 B.C. a windstorm tore one of the doors from the Temple of Luna and hurled it against the back wall of the Temple of Ceres. In 31 B.C. it burned, together with a great part of the circus (Cass. Dio 50.10.3), but it was rebuilt by Augustus and dedicated in A.D. 17 by Tiberius (Tacitus, *Ann.* 2.49). It was still standing in the fourth century and is listed by the regionary catalogues in Regio XI. No remains of it are known.

The temple was a plebeian stronghold and possessed the right of asylum, as did the neighboring Temple of Diana (Varro *ap. Non.* 63L). It was also a center of distribution of food to the poor. The plebeian aediles had their headquarters here and kept their archives here. Here also was the treasury in which were kept the proceeds of auctions of property confiscated from those who assaulted the plebeian magistrates (Dion. Hal. 6.89.3, 10.42.4; Livy 3.55.7). After 449 B.C. copies of all senatus consulta were delivered to the plebeian aediles and kept on display here (Livy 3.55.13). Its close association with the Statio Annonae (q.v.) must date from its very conception; it was built above the warehouses in the Forum Boarium where grain was unloaded and stored. Its relation to the Circus Maximus seems to have been entirely casual, although it is frequently alluded to.

The temple is regularly called *aedes;* Pliny (*HN* 35.24) once calls it a *delubrum.* Ordinarily its full name was abbreviated to Aedes Cereris. The priestesses of the temple were always brought from southern Italy, usually from Naples and Velia, and the worship here was entirely Greek, and even the prayers were in Greek (Cicero, *Balb.* 55). But the Cerialia, the festival of Ceres, which at first was votive and held only on extraordinary occasions, became in time annual, in the charge of the plebeian aediles, a spring festival celebrated 12–19 April with *ludi circenses.* On the last day of the games foxes, to the backs of which lighted torches had been tied, were let loose in the circus, a very curious custom (Ovid, *Fast.* 4.679–712).

Ceres Mater et Ops Augusta, Ara: an altar consecrated on 10 August in A.D. 7 *in Vico Iugario,* probably in consequence of a famine that year (Cass. Dio 55.31.3–4), possibly with associated honor to Livia (Degrassi 493).

Cermalus (Fig. 75): the slope of the western side of the Palatine above the Velabrum and at least part of the Circus Maximus, evidently not, as formerly thought, the northwest lobe of the Palatine.

ArchCl 16 (1964): 173–77 (F. Castagnoli); *RivFil* 105 (1977): 15–19 (F. Castagnoli).

Ceroliensis (or **Ceroniensis**): an area listed in the distribution of the shrines of the Argei (q.v.), including a shrine near the Minervium, *qua in Caelium montem itur* (Varro, *Ling.* 5.47). The indications are that it was near the base of one of the approaches to the Caelian, but it is entirely uncertain which approach (cf. Ovid, *Fast.* 3.835–38). Varro derives the name from Carinae, to which he says the Ceroliensis is joined. PA would therefore see it as the basin of the Colosseum.

Eranos 85 (1987): 130–33 (Å Fridh).

Chalcidicum: a generic word, not properly a name, for the porch or portico forming the approach to a more important building but having its own program of decoration (hence, perhaps, the derivation of the word). It is used by Augustus for the porch preceding the Curia Iulia in the form in which he rebuilt it (Augustus, *RG* 19; cf. Cass. Dio 51.22). This porch is shown on coins as a high platform with Ionic columns set far apart running across the front, extending to either side, and probably continuing at least partway down the sides of the building. The approach must also have been arranged by ramps or stairs along the sides (*B. M. Coins, Rom. Emp.* 1 Augustus, nos. 631–32 and pl. 15.12–13).

RendLinc, ser. 8.26 (1971): 237–51 (F. Zevi); *RömMitt* 85 (1978): 359–62 (L. Richardson).

Cicinenses: inhabitants of a district in Rome mentioned only in a late inscription (*CIL* 6.9103 =31895), as were others equally mysterious and impossible to identify. Attempts to connect this designation with Sicininum (q.v.) seem mistaken; it would be at least equally logical to try to connect it with the Ciconiae (q.v.).

Ciconiae: listed in the regionary catalogues in Regio IX and known from a late inscription (*CIL* 6.1785 =31931) to have been a point from which *falancarii* transported casks of the *vina fiscalia* to a temple. The temple in question must be Aurelian's Temple of Sol, because we know that the vina fiscalia were stored there. The Ciconiae must therefore be presumed to be a point on the Tiber where the wine was unloaded from river boats. If Aurelian's Temple of Sol is that discovered at the end of the eighteenth century east of Via del Corso just north of Via Condotti, as seems likely, then a point just downstream from Ponte Cavour in the area of Lungotevere Marzio would offer the shortest route from the river to the temple. The Ciconiae were probably a sculpture or relief of no special importance, by which the quay or square where the unloading took place could be identified.

The juxtaposition of Ciconiae and Nixae in the regionary catalogues produced a hypothetical Ciconiae Nixae that has long exercised topographers, but from the inscriptions it is quite clear now that these were separate places.

E. LaRocca, *La riva a mezzaluna* (Rome 1984), 60–65; *CEFR* 98 (1987): 191–210 (J.-M. Flambard); *TAPS* 80, fasc. 2, pt. 2 (1990): 52–55 (R. E. A. Palmer).

Cimbrum: see **Nymphaeum Alexandri.**

Cincia: a place designation, in earlier times called Statuae Cinciae, because the tomb of that family was located there, *ubi ex epistylio defluit aqua,* the Arcus Stillans (q.v.) of the Forum Boarium (Paulus *ex Fest.* 49L, Festus 318L). The tomb must have been a very ancient one, fourth or third century B.C., if Festus is right in his identification, and it must have lain outside the line of the Servian Walls on the riverbank.

Circus, Trigarium, Stadium, Ludus: A circus was a course for chariot racing carefully leveled and designed to give equal opportunity to all the teams competing, and provided with seats for spectators. The contestants raced around a long, narrow island in the middle, the *spina,* which terminated at either end in groups of three elongated tapering cones, the *metae,* often described as goal posts, but actually not functioning as such. The spina was decorated with various dedications and shrines and was considered the best place from which to view the circus games, although the presiding official and his company sat in a box above the starting gates and in the Piazza Armerina circus mosaic the rounded end, or *sphendone,* is shown occupied by a richly dressed company including women and children. The front rows of the spectators' seats were reserved for senators and equites, as in the theater, a tradition supposedly going back to the time of Tarquinius Priscus. But in the circus, unlike the theater, men and women spectators freely mingled (Ovid, *Ars Am.* 1.135–42). In Rome there was only one circus, the Circus Maximus between the Palatine and Aventine, down to the time of Caligula, who built the Circus Gaii et Neronis, which Nero finished. This was in the Transtiberim, in the valley between the Vatican and Janiculan hills. Although it was very splendid, this seems to have been in use for only a short time, the area of the seating being invaded by tombs already in the second century. It may be that the collapse of the Pons Neronianus, which is undated but probably occurred before the compilation of the regionary catalogues, for they omit it, made it difficult to get large crowds of people to this circus, and that was responsible for its decline. Furthermore, in the early third century Elagabalus (A.D. 218–222) built a new circus, now called the Circus Varianus, as part of the imperial villa Ad Spem Veterem, near Porta Maggiore, access

to which would be easy from anywhere in Rome. This circus was destroyed when Aurelian built his fortifications of Rome later in the century; the wall cuts across the circus about a quarter of its length from the starting gates. So this circus was in use for only half a century. It was in some sense replaced by the circus of Maxentius (A.D. 306–312), built as part of his sumptuous villa on the Via Appia, but the distance from the city made that, too, difficult of access. Throughout history the Circus Maximus was always uppermost among Roman circuses. The Circus Flaminius was, of course, not a circus at all, and no one seems to have known how it got that name.

Although the Circus Maximus was designed only for chariot racing, spectacles of every sort were offered there. *Ludi circenses* might include different sorts of races, gladiatorial combats, venationes, athletic events, and any sort of novelty the donors of these games might invent. The circus was especially the site of the Ludi Romani, 4–19 September, and Ludi Plebei, 4–17 November, but new ludi were repeatedly decreed and included in the calendar, such as the Ludi Victoriae Sullanae, celebrating the victory at the Colline Gate, 26 October–1 November, and the Ludi Victoriae Caesaris, also known as the Ludi Veneris Genetricis, 20–30 July. Any dedication of a building could call for several days of ludi circenses, and every triumph had to be celebrated. Consequently the Romans could and did spend much of their time in the circus. It was also especially important for the ceremony of the triumph itself, as well as the games that followed it. The route of the triumph lay through the circus, and although the spoils seem to have been regularly put on show in the Circus Flaminius for some days before the triumph itself, the Romans crowded the circus for the actual parade, when the various *fercula* representing the towns and rivers that had figured in the campaign appeared and the proper sequence unfolded in all its splendor. The parade marched the length of the circus and may even have circled the spina, for it could then have wound back by the street outside the circus at the foot of the Palatine. But the temples dedicated by victorious generals all seem to have found their place on the Aventine above that side of the circus, and the triumphal arch awarded to Titus and Vespasian for the capture of Jerusalem seems to have been inserted at the sphendone end of the axis of the circus opposite the Porta Pompae.

A trigarium was a place for exercising horses by racing them. We do not know how it got its name, for the Romans regularly raced in teams of an even number. We know nothing about the architectural form of the trigarium in Rome, if it had one, and we are unable to place it more precisely than somewhere in the Campus Martius. We presume that like the

Ludus Magnus it would have offered spectators some sort of accommodation, but on this point we have no information.

A stadium was a place for athletic events, and because foot races of various sorts figured large in these, it took the general form of a circus but was shorter and without a spina. Although some form of stadium probably became a regular feature of the great imperial baths after Nero's combining of a gymnasium with his baths, and one can see a stadium form at the back of the peribolus of the Baths of Caracalla, the only fully developed stadium in Rome was that of Domitian, which has become Piazza Navona. This was an exceptionally handsome building faced with travertine and with a system of exits and entrances patterned on that of the Colosseum and capable of handling large numbers of spectators in minimum time. It was regarded as one of the greatest buildings in Rome and excited the admiration of Constantius on his state visit to Rome in the middle of the fourth century, 250 years after its construction.

A ludus was a training school for gladiators of various sorts, where they lived under strict discipline and exercised, probably almost daily. There were private ludi from an early period, but those we know most about are four public ones that Domitian built in connection with the Amphitheatrum Flavium (Colosseum) and close in its shadow. The Ludus Magnus, next to the Colosseum and connected to it by an underground tunnel, has come to light in excavation and been carefully explored. Others, the Ludi Dacicus, Gallicus, and Matutinus, are known from literature and fragments of the Marble Plan and were similar. The central feature was apparently always an oval arena with a bank of seats for spectators around it, so the Romans could go and watch their favorites train or decide where best to place their bets. Around this was then a rectangular bank of rooms in several storeys, the living quarters of the gladiators and their trainers. There does not seem to have been a bath suite included.

Circus Flaminius: a public square built by C. Flaminius as censor in 221 B.C. (Livy, *Epit.* 20; Paulus *ex Fest.* 79L) in the Prata Flaminia (Livy 3.54.15) in the southern Campus Martius that gave its "name" to the ninth regio of Rome in the regionary catalogues. It is shown on a fragment of the Marble Plan, now positively placed by a sure join, just south of the Porticus Octaviae and Porticus Philippi, the square on which these faced (*Capitolium* 35.7 [1960]: 3–12 [G. Gatti]). On the east it was bounded by the Theatrum Marcelli, on the northeast by the porticoes just mentioned, and on the northwest by the Temple of Hercules Custos (see Hercules Custos, Aedes; cf. Ovid,

Fast. 6.205–12). Another line of temples probably filled or nearly filled the southwest side. One of these, that of Castor and Pollux (see Castor et Pollux, Aedes), is now known from a fragment of a new marble plan of the area. Evidently the course of the Petronia Amnis (q.v.) crossed the circus, and this must have been bridged at strategic points. It was probably not culverted before the Cloaca was, which seems to have been shortly before 179 B.C., and may have remained open in much of its course until the time of Agrippa's systematization of the water and sewer systems of Rome beginning in 33 B.C. The lower part of the culvert below Piazza Mattei, which is in large blocks of Gabine stone, appears to be Agrippan work.

The square was unlike a proper circus in every way, and the derivation of its designation as such perplexed Varro (*Ling.* 5.154). It had no banks of seats for spectators, and the only games known to have been held there were the seldom celebrated Ludi Taurii, in which there were horse races around *metae* (Varro, *Ling.* 5.154). *Contiones* (public assemblies) were regularly held here (Cicero, *Att.* 1.14.1, *Sest.* 33, *Red. Sen.* 13, 17; Livy 27.21.1; Plutarch, *Marcel.* 27.3), and it was evidently regularly the site of a market (Cicero, *Att.* 1.14.1; Martial 12.74.2). It was the staging ground for triumphs, where the spoils were displayed on the days preceding the actual ceremony, and probably all great pompae passed through the circus as part of their route (Livy 39.5.17; Val. Max. 1.7.4; Plutarch, *Lucul.* 37.2). Augustus delivered the *laudatio* for Drusus here (Cass. Dio 55.10.8), and in 2 B.C. water was brought in and thirty-six crocodiles killed here as part of the ceremony of dedication of the Forum Augustum (Cass. Dio 55.10.8). It was chosen as the site for an arch honoring Germanicus after his death (see Arcus Germanici). So far as the evidence goes, the circus had no architectural form. On the Marble Plan (Rodriguez pl. 23) a single line bounds it on the northeast, which might be marking off a street along it or a margin raising this part a step above the surrounding area. At the east corner was an arch, presumably triumphal, because the triumphal processions regularly passed through the circus, and there were probably others. But probably the central area was left entirely unencumbered.

PBSR 42 (1974): 3–26 (T. P. Wiseman), 44 (1976): 44–47 (T. P. Wiseman); Humphrey 540–45; *CEFR* 98 (1987): 347–72 (E. La Rocca).

Circus Gaii et Neronis (also called **Circus Vaticanus**) (Fig. 25): a circus laid out by Caligula but built largely by Nero on the right bank of the Tiber in the valley between the Janiculan hill and the Mons Vaticanus (Pliny, *HN* 16.201, 36.74; Sueton-

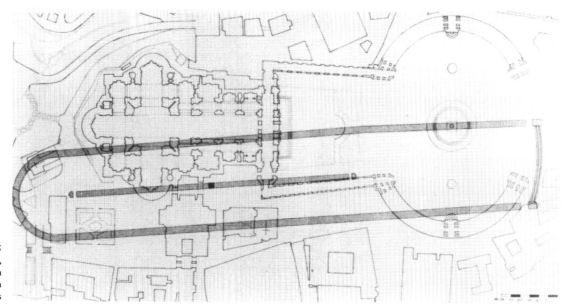

ius, *Claud.* 21.2). The axis lay east and west at a slight angle to that of the basilica of S. Pietro, which is built over the northern half of the circus. If the Neronian curved wall reported by Gatti (*FA* 4 [1949]: 3771) under the Via del Sant'Uffizio is a wall of the carceres, as it is believed to be, then the circus must have stretched the full length of the basilica and the colonnades of Bernini. The only significant remnant of it was the obelisk that Caligula brought from Heliopolis and erected on the spina. This stood in place until 1586, when it was removed to its present place in the middle of Piazza S. Pietro on orders of Pope Sixtus V. The ancient footing in Piazza dei Protomartiri was excavated, examined, and measured in 1957–1958 (*RendPontAcc* 32 [1959]: 97–121 [F. Castagnoli]). The circus seems not to have been long in use; the arena was invaded by tombs as early as the second century, and in the time of Caracalla the great mausoleum known from its later dedication as the Rotonda di Sant'Andrea was constructed there.

RendPontAcc 45 (1972–73): 37–72 (F. Magi); Humphrey 545–52.

Circus Hadriani: see **Naumachia Traiani.**

Circus Maximus: the oldest and largest of the theaters for games in Rome, traditionally founded by Romulus in the Vallis Murcia (the valley between the Palatine and Aventine), with horse races on the Consualia. The Consualia were in honor of Consus (see Consus, Ara), regarded as the Roman equivalent of Poseidon Hippios. This became the occasion of the rape of the Sabines (Varro, *Ling.* 6.20; Plutarch, *Rom.* 14). Down the middle of the valley, which is unusually straight, ran a brook, which must have been channeled and bridged from a very early date. A number of temples and shrines (see, e.g., Sol et Luna, Aedes; Mater Deum, Aedes; Iuventas, Aedes) that came to have places within the limits of the circus may originally have been victory monuments put up by successful competitors. This was the theater for all ludi circenses and especially the Ludi Romani in September. Tarquinius Priscus (Livy 1.35.8; Dion. Hal. 3.68.1) is credited with granting the individual senators and equites rights to build places on stepped wooden platforms or stands *(fori)* from which to view the games. Subsequently, more stands were built under Tarquinius Superbus by forced labor of the plebs (Livy 1.56.2; Dion. Hal. 4.44.1). The first starting gates (carceres) were erected in 329 B.C. (Livy 8.20.1); they must have been of wood, for they were brightly painted (Ennius *ap. Cic., Div.* 1.108). The spina must originally have been simply the channeled brook; the statues mounted on columns of which we hear (Livy 40.2.2) and that of Pollentia (Livy 39.7.8) must have stood along the margin of this, where perhaps the Arch of Stertinius (see Fornices Stertinii) also stood. Later the spina took the form of a euripus bridged at points and provided with islands on which a great variety of pavilions and aediculae, as well as statuary, was erected; it seems never to have been covered over completely.

In 174 B.C. the censors Q. Fulvius Flaccus and A. Postumius Albinus seem to have overhauled the whole complex (Livy 41.27.6). They rebuilt the carceres and set up the ova, sets of seven large wooden eggs by movement of which the number of laps run is believed to have been indicated to the spectators. This arrangement became permanent (Varro, *Rust.* 1.2.11; Cassiodorus, *Var.* 3.51). In the games at the dedication of Pompey's Temple of Venus Victrix in 55 B.C., the elephants exhibited in a battle in the circus broke down the iron railing intended to serve as a protection for the spectators (Pliny, *HN* 8.20–21), and in 46 B.C. this was replaced by a second euripus (Pliny, *HN* 8.20–21; Suetonius, *Iul.* 39), which Nero later removed. In 33 B.C. Agrippa added a set of seven dolphins to match the ova (Cass. Dio 49. 43.2).

Pliny (*HN* 36.102) credits Caesar with enlarging the circus to the size we know, three and one-half stades (621 m) long and four plethra (118 m) wide, surrounding it, except at the starting end, with a euripus 2.97 m wide and 2.97 m deep, and providing it with seating for 150,000 spectators. After a fire in 31 B.C. (Cass. Dio 50.10.3) Augustus constructed the Pulvinar ad Circum Maximum (Augustus, *RG* 19; cf. Cassiodorus, *Var.* 3.51), a box on the Palatine side, perhaps about halfway along the length, where the regalia and exuviae (symbols) of the gods were set on thrones during the games after having been brought in procession (Festus 500L). He also set up on the spina, probably on the axis of the Temple of Sol et Luna, the obelisk of Ramesses II brought from Heliopolis (Pliny, *HN* 36.71; Amm. Marc. 17.4.12) now in Piazza del Popolo (see Obeliscus Augusti in Circo Maximo).

Dionysius (3.68) describes the circus as it was in 7 B.C. The seats rose in three tiers, the lowest being of stone, the others of wood. The twelve carceres were vaulted and closed by barriers of double gates, which could be opened simultaneously. Between each pair stood a herm. Around the outside of the building was a single-storeyed arcade containing shops with living quarters above and passages through which one reached the seats by corridors and stairs in a repeating pattern similar to that of the Colosseum (see Amphitheatrum Flavium), but less complicated, so entrance and exit were made very easy. The shops constituted a great bazaar; Tacitus (*Ann.* 15.38) says it was the inflammable goods in these that particularly fed the fire of Nero at its beginning. We hear especially of the unsavory characters it drew, cookshop keepers (Cicero, *Milon.* 65), astrologers and fortunetellers (Cicero, *Div.* 1.132; Juvenal 6.588; Horace, *Sat.* 1.6.113–14), and prostitutes

(Juvenal 3.65; *Priapea* 27; *Anth. Lat.* 1.190; S.H.A. *Heliogab.* 26, cf. 32; Cyprian, *De Spect.* 5), but there is also the tombstone of a fruit vendor (*CIL* 6.9822 = *ILS* 7496).

Augustus watched the games from the houses of his friends and freedmen (on the surrounding hills?) and occasionally from the Pulvinar (Suetonius, *Aug.* 45.1), but the Pulvinar made those there unpleasantly conspicuous (Suetonius, *Claud.* 4.3). He is said to have assigned places to the senators and equites, but evidently not in fixed order (Cass. Dio 55.22.4); Claudius assigned special seats to the senators (Suetonius, *Claud.* 21.3; Cass. Dio 60.7.3–4), Nero to the equites, to obtain adequate space for which he had to fill in the euripus on the margin (Pliny, *HN* 8.21; Suetonius, *Nero* 11.1; Tacitus, *Ann.* 15.32).

In November A.D. 36 the part of the circus toward the Aventine burned (Tacitus, *Ann.* 6.45; Cass. Dio 58.26.5; *BullCom* 44 [1916]: 211–12 [R. Paribeni]) but seems to have been repaired at once, for Caligula gave ludi circenses notable for their innovations, enhancing the sand with minium and green pigment (Suetonius, *Calig.* 18.3) or with flecks of mica (Pliny, *HN* 36.162). Claudius built carceres of marble and new metal that was gilded (Suetonius, *Claud.* 21.3). At some time the dolphins of Agrippa were piped and turned into a fountain playing into the euripus (Tertullian, *De Spect.* 8; cf. the Barcelona and Lyons circus mosaics [Humphrey figs. 36, 119]), at which time they must no longer have served to keep a record of the laps. The great fire of Nero broke out in the circus near the northeast end in the tabernae on the Palatine side and swept up that side driven by the wind (Tacitus, *Ann.* 15.38). Probably the circus was nearly a total loss (see Arae Incendii Neronis), but it was soon rebuilt, for Nero used it in 68 on his return from Greece (Suetonius, *Nero* 25.2; Cass. Dio, *Epit.* 62[63].20.4, 21.1). In the time of Domitian it burned again and was repaired by Trajan, who used stone from the naumachia of Domitian for the purpose (Suetonius, *Dom.* 5). At the same time Trajan added two stadia to the length of the seating, probably on the Palatine side, by roofing the street behind the circus and carrying the tiers of seats up the slope of the Palatine, where foundations suitable for these have been found. Under Trajan the circus apparently reached its greatest splendor.Under Antoninus Pius there was a disastrous collapse of a part of the circus with great loss of life (S.H.A. *Ant. Pius* 9; cf. Chron. 146) and another under Diocletian (Chron. 148). Caracalla is recorded as having enlarged the *ianuae circi* (Chron. 147), probably the central entrance in the middle of the carceres, but possibly the whole of this end. It was magnificently restored by Constantine (Aur. Vict., *Caes.* 40.27), who proposed to bring the great obelisk of Thutmose III from Heliopolis to adorn the spina. This was actually accomplished by Constantius in A.D. 357 (Amm. Marc. 17.4.12–16; see Obeliscus Constantii). There are frequent mentions of the circus in the literature of the fourth and fifth centuries, but nothing that adds substantially to our knowledge. The last is the letter of Cassiodorus already cited (*Var.* 3.51), which explores the subject fully and informs us that the spina carried reliefs showing Roman generals in triumphal procession marching over the bodies of the vanquished.

Aside from the information we glean from literature, our knowledge of the circus depends on numerous representations of it in art, a group of fragments of the Marble Plan (*FUR* pl. 17; Rodriguez pls. 5, 14) and especially a number of mosaics, reliefs on sarcophagi, and coins commemorating improvements and restorations. For a catalogue of these, cf. *EAA* 2.647–55. Modern excavations, especially explorations in 1936, have brought to light only a few uninformative foundations of the seating around the sphendone. These are in concrete, in part faced with brick and in part unfaced (cf. Nash 1.236–40). Excavation has also produced the line of the paved street bounding the circus, enough to give its precise position, orientation, and main dimensions in its final form. The circus was 600 m long, 150 m wide, and with an arena 550 m long and 80 m wide. The average depth of the cavea was 35 m, but it was greatly increased by additions built over the streets and up the slopes of the Palatine, where it has been estimated that it reached a depth of 80 m.

The exterior rose in three storeys with arches and an engaged order in the base storey, like the Colosseum and Theater of Marcellus, and with similar arrangements of entrances and stairs. The cavea was divided into three zones, probably corresponding to the three storeys and separated by baltei. Only the lowest zone was of stone. The Pulvinar was evidently a handsome building on the Palatine side, but we really know nothing about its architectural form (cf. *BullCom* 72 [1946–48]: 27–32 [P. Mingazzini]). It must have been impressive to warrant special mention in the *Res Gestae* of Augustus. At the northwest end the twelve carceres were disposed on a curve, canted to give all contenders an equal distance to cover from the starting gate to the *linea alba* marking the beginning of the first lap (Cassiodorus, *Var.* 3.51.7). There were six carceres to either side of a central monumental entrance from the Forum Boarium. The gates themselves seem to have been of ornamental grillwork, and over them was the box adorned with statues of athletes from which the presiding magistrate and his company watched the

games. At either end of the carceres was a tower with battlements, and this end of the circus was given the nickname *oppidum* (Varro, *Ling.* 5.153; Festus 201L). The southwest side of the circus was slightly irregular, a jog being introduced just before the *linea alba* at the end of the spina to ensure fair starting positions. This is a regular feature in circuses. Further along this side, near the beginning of the sphendone, the cavea is interrupted by the Temple of Sol et Luna (see Sol et Luna, Templum), which probably did not project into the arena but was built with its bottom step flush with the margin of the arena. There may have been other shrines elsewhere in the cavea, included in it as the circus and its seating were enlarged in the course of time. The sphendone is shown on the Piazza Armerina mosaic as a choice position for spectators and filled with a richly dressed company, including women and children. At its center was an arched entrance, probably the passage used by triumphal processions on their way to the forum. This was rebuilt in A.D. 80–81 by the senate as a triumphal arch of three passages commemorating the conquest of Palestine by Vespasian and Titus (*CIL* 6.944 = *ILS* 264). It appears on the Marble Plan, and remains of it were discovered in 1934 and 1982 (*BullCom* 91.2 [1986]: 544 [P. Ciancio Rossetto]; *QArchEtr* 19 [1990]: 68–71 [P. Brandizzi Virrucci]).

The spina down the middle of the arena was apparently not a euripus before the middle of the second century after Christ; eventually it was raised above the level of the arena, its basin faced with marble, and bridged at regular intervals. At the ends of the bridges were sculptures of animals and athletes, and the Piazza Armerina mosaic shows a Victoria mounted on a column. In the euripus were islands that carried two-storeyed pavilions, the syzygia on which the ova and dolphins were mounted at either end, and toward the southeast end the obelisk of Augustus, a statue of the Magna Mater mounted on a rampant lion, a palm tree, which in the third century grows to great size, and a mysterious cubical building, like an altar with a door in one side, probably the shrine of Murcia, because at this shrine a space for a curule chair was granted the dictator M. Valerius Maximus and his descendants in perpetuity, from which to watch the games. At either end of the spina, set off from it, was a high semicircular base carrying the metae, groups of three elongated cones tapering to a rounded end and decorated at intervals with bands. The base of the metae at the carceres end, at least, seems to have been covered with reliefs at large scale.

The capacity of the circus is given variously in our sources and probably varied through the period of the empire almost as much as it did in that of the republic. Dionysius (3.68) gives the capacity in 7 B.C. as 150,000; Pliny (*HN* 36.102) gives the capacity as 250,000; and the *Notitia* gives the capacity in the fourth century as 385,000 loca, probably the number of running feet of seating, or places for about 250,000 spectators. These figures have all been questioned.The games presented in the circus were especially chariot races of quadrigas, but other sorts of races were also popular, and ludi circenses included battles and hunts of several different sorts through the republic. Later such shows were probably always removed to the Amphitheater of Statilius Taurus and the Colosseum, where spectacular effects and surprises could be introduced. The most important games in the Circus Maximus were the Ludi Romani, 4–19 September, and Ludi Plebei, 4–17 (Fast. Maff.) or 12–16 (Filocalus) November, but probably all the great games had at least a day or two of ludi circenses, as did victory celebrations and games given for the dedication of buildings.

Nash 1.236–40; *Roma, archeologia nel centro* (1985), 1.213–23 (P. Ciancio Rossetto); J. H. Humphrey, *Roman Circuses: Arenas for Chariot Racing* (London 1986), 56–294.

Circus Varianus (Figs. 16, 78): a circus in the imperial enclave Ad Spem Veterem for which the only literary testimony is in the life of Elagabalus (S.H.A. *Heliogab.* 13.5, 14.5) but which has come to light in excavations at various points, most recently in 1959, when its western end (the starting end) was found inside the Aurelian Walls, east of the Sessorium and the church of S. Croce in Gerusalemme. The last stretch of the bridge of the Acqua Felice is based on the north wall of the circus, and its sphendone end reached nearly to modern Via Alcamo. It was then about 565 m long and 125 m wide, slightly smaller than the Circus Maximus, but larger than the Circus of Maxentius (about 520 m long and 92 m wide). The name Varianus is modern, formed from the gentilicial name of Elagabalus. See also Obeliscus Antinoi.

RömMitt 64 (1957): 250–54 (E. Nash); Nash 1.241–42; Humphrey 552–57.

Circus Vaticanus: see Circus Gaii et Neronis.

Cispius Mons (Fig. 75): the northern lobe of the Esquiline Hill, separated from the Oppius by the valley up which ran the Clivus Suburanus and from the Viminal by the valley up which ran the Vicus Patricius (Varro, *Ling.* 5.50). It figured in the Septimontium (Festus 459L, 476L) and in the ceremonies of the Argei (Varro, *Ling.* 5.50). It is supposed to have got its name from Laevus Cispius of Anagnia, who in the time of Tullus Hostilius encamped there with

a military force and guarded the area (Festus 476L). It is the name of a plebeian family. Its most conspicuous monument seems to have been the Temple of Mefitis (see Mefitis, Aedes, Lucus), although that of Iuno Lucina (see Iuno Lucina, Aedes) was certainly equally, if not more, important. Today its summit is crowned by the church of S. Maria Maggiore.

Claudius, Divus, Templum (Figs. 3, 16): a temple to the deified Claudius on the Caelian in Regio II, which was begun by Agrippina, almost entirely destroyed by Nero after the fire of 64, and completed by Vespasian (Suetonius, *Vesp.* 9; Aur. Vict., *Caes.* 9.7, *Epit.* 9.8). Its platform is identified by the fact that Frontinus (*Aq.* 2.76) tells us Nero extended the arches of the Aqua Claudia as far as this temple, and fragments of the Marble Plan (*FUR* pl. 16; Rodriguez pl. 2) identifiable as this platform carry the inscription TEM]PLVM DI[VI] CLA[VDI. Martial (*De Spect.* 2.9–10) tells us that Nero extended the Domus Aurea: *Claudia diffusas ubi porticus explicit umbras;* he may possibly be referring to the arcaded and porticoed substructures. Part of these Nero converted to use as a series of fountains and nymphaea, from which the water mantled the slope of the Caelian with cascades and supplied the stagnum in the valley below; it was really only the temple itself that Nero destroyed.

The temple faced the Palatine, and there was a grandiose stair of approach on its main axis. It was hexastyle with a pronaos three bays deep and a frontal stair. The cella was without interior columns. Around the temple, covering most of its platform, the Marble Plan shows narrow bands, those toward the front of the platform symmetrical banks of seven straight bands to either side, those toward the back symmetrical banks of four, which turn at right angles. The interpretation of these is difficult; they seem neither substructures, as Jordan thought, nor hedges (*RömMitt* 18 [1903]: 20n.1 [C. Hülsen]). Because we are told by Pliny (*HN* 14.11) that a single vine stock covered all the walks in the open area of the Porticus Liviae (q.v.), these might be wooden arbors of the sort familiar from Pompeian paintings of gardens. This area in turn seems to have been surrounded by a colonnade on all sides, but through negligence the cutter of this part of the Marble Plan omitted to indicate the columns and cut only the margin.

The terrace on which the temple stood measures 180 m deep and 200 m wide and stands to a height of nearly 50 meters above sea level, one of the highest positions in Rome. It is framed on all sides by substructures. On the south these reach a height of more than 15 m. The east (rear) front is well preserved, ornamented with niches alternately semicircular and rectangular, symmetrically disposed to either side of a larger central exedra. Between each pair of these niches are three or four semicircular niches at much smaller scale. Vaulted corridors and well-like chambers appear behind this façade in a complicated and irregular pattern, but they show no sign of having been used as reservoirs or for aquatic effects. In front of these niches ran a portico, either arcuated or columnar, and in its vaulted roof appear remains of a water channel. Apparently here water fell behind an architectural façade in nymphaea and was then channeled out through this to the north.

The west front of the terrace was faced with arcades in two storeys built of massive blocks of travertine, heavily rusticated. The lower storey carried flat arches, and the upper carried rounded ones. Even the frieze is rusticated, and the only finish is a Doric pilaster capital between each pair of arches in the upper storey and the architrave and cornice this carries. The vaulted substructures behind these arches were completed as rooms in brick-faced concrete masonry and probably used as shops. A street ran along the base of this front. The stair of approach was axial and evidently spanned this street on a bridge.

The north front, where the fall of the hill was greatest, was supported by a series of vaulted chambers making a plain face along this front. In a number of these chambers the walls show incrustations of lime, evidence that there were water pipes here, and there are traces of building and terracing lower on the slope. We must imagine that in the time of Nero this whole slope was a garden enlivened with architecture, stairs, and fountains. One fountain piece, a ship's prow decorated with sea monsters and a boar's head, survives, and others have been found in the past (Flaminio Vacca, *Memorie di varie antichità trovate in diversi luoghi della città di Roma,* in F. Nardini, *Roma antica* [Rome 1704], 22). This general scheme, somewhat modified and with reduction of the amount of water used, seems to have survived under the Flavians.

The south front, where the temple terrace was lifted only a little above the neighboring terrain, shows vaulted chambers only at the extremities; the rest was evidently supported only by retaining walls. Off this front opened a number of subsidiary annexes of uncertain use. The most important of these was a large rectangular room with an axial apse containing a statue base, flanked by a pair of smaller rooms apparently designed to be symmetrical.

Despite its size and the importance of its position, the temple is mentioned only rarely in literature. It is mentioned in only a single inscription (*CIL* 6.10251a = *ILS* 7348), and there is no record at all of its history.

Nash 1.243–48.

Clementia, Ara: an altar decreed by the senate in A.D. 28, as was another of Amicitia, both to be embellished with statues of Tiberius and Sejanus (Tacitus, *Ann.* 4.74). If these were ever built, they must have been dismantled soon after the fall of Sejanus.

Clementia Caesaris, Aedes: a temple decreed by the senate in 44 B.C., in which the personifications of Clementia and Caesar were portrayed clasping hands (Cass. Dio 44.6.4; Appian, *BellCiv* 2.106; Plutarch, *Caes.* 57.3). Antony was appointed priest of the cult. It is shown on a coin of Sepullius Macer as tetrastyle, with closed doors and a globe in the tympanum (*B. M. Coins, Rom. Rep.* 1 p. 549 nos. 4176–77; Crawford 480/21). The site is entirely unknown.

Clitellae: Paulus *ex Fest.* (52L) tells us that there was a place in Rome so called from its likeness to a saddle (*clitellae dicuntur locus Romae propter similitudinem*) and that there were places on the Via Flaminia so called from their ups and downs. There is no point on the Via Flaminia nearer than the sixteenth milestone which could be described as a series of ups and downs, and there are so many saddles in the hilly parts of Rome that one wonders whether Festus is not defining a common use of the word rather than explaining a toponym.

Clivus: see **Via, Vicus, Clivus.**

Clivus Argentarius (Fig. 19): the street connecting the Forum Romanum and the Campus Martius at the head of Via Lata (Via Flaminia). It began at the Area Volcani (see Volcanal) and ran in front of the Carcer over the northeast shoulder of the Capitoline. Somewhere along it in this area stood the Porta Fontinalis of the Servian Walls, and as it emerged in the campus it ran west of the Sepulcrum Bibuli in the pomerial reserve. The name is found only in medieval documents (Jordan 2.634; VZ 2.326, 3.53, 219, 220, 4.140), but it was probably in use in antiquity and derived from the tabernae of the *argentarii* there (cf. Basilica Argentaria [q.v.]). PA suggests that the republican name was Lautumiae (q.v.), but that seems unlikely.

Nash 1.249.

Clivus Bassilli: known only from *CIL* 6.36364 = *ILS* 8218, a road branching from the Via Tiburtina in the neighborhood of the Campo Verano cemetery.

Clivus Capitolinus (Fig. 19): the principal approach to the Capitoline Hill, the only road that could be negotiated by vehicles from the forum side. It began at the Area Volcani (see Volcanal), climbed steeply to the southwest along the Temple of Saturn (Servius *ad Aen.* 2.116, 8.319), and bent sharply back at the corner of the Porticus Deorum Consentium, part of the back wall of which serves as terracing for the clivus. Its upper course is very uncertain and was probably changed and extended by branches several times. Originally this must have been simply a path and led to the saddle, Inter Duos Lucos, from which other paths led to the crests of the hill. After the construction of the Capitoline temple, it was made a processional way and suitable for vehicles. It was paved by the censors of 174 B.C., Q. Fulvius Flaccus and A. Postumius Albinus (Livy 41.27.7). In 190 B.C. Scipio erected an elaborate arch somewhere along it, *adversus viam,* but probably not a gateway to the Area Capitolina, as otherwise this would be specified (Livy 37.3.7). It may have been considered part of the Sacra Via, but was no longer so in Varro's day (Varro, *Ling.* 547; Festus 372L).

Because it commanded the Forum Romanum, it was a convenient place for a show of strength (Livy 3.18.7, 19.7; Cicero, *Att.* 2.1.7). Along some part of it there were private houses (Cicero, *Milon.* 64). And about halfway up was the Porta Stercoraria (Festus 466L), leading to an *angiportus.* Portions of the pavement still exist in the lower reaches, but nothing in the upper parts.

Nash 1.250–51.

Clivus Capsarius: a street known from a fragment of the Acta Fratrum Arvalium of A.D. 240 (*NSc* 1914, 466, 473 [G. Mancini and O. Marucchi] = *ILS* 9522): *in Clivo Capsar. in Aventino Maiore. Capsarii* seem to have been those who looked after the clothes of people in the public baths (*CIL* 6.9232 = *ILS* 7621), as well as those who made *capsae,* but a clivus is hardly likely to have taken its name from the concentration there of dwellings of bath attendants. We must incline to seeing this as the center of the manufacture of capsae. Its location is quite uncertain, except as it was a clivus rather than a vicus.

Clivus Cosconius: a street known only from Varro (*Ling.* 5.158), who says that it was built by a *viocurus* of the same name. Its location is quite unknown.

Clivus Delphini: a street listed by the regionary catalogues in Regio XII after the Temple of the Bona Dea Subsaxana. PA and Lugli and Gismondi take it to be the street north of the Thermae Antoninianae that connected the Via Nova (possibly extending be-

yond it to Porta Capena) with Via Laurentina/Ardeatina just outside Porta Naevia. This seems to have been a natural track, and the identification is likely enough, although there is no proof. Nor is there any indication of why this street should have been singled out for inclusion in the catalogues, a distinction otherwise reserved for streets such as the Sacra Via and Vicus Iugarius. Perhaps the dolphin was a prominent landmark; it might have been a fountain figure.

Clivus Mamuri: a street mentioned in medieval documents (cf. *BullCom* 42 [1914]: 373 [M. Marchetti]) that took its name from the Statua Mamuri (q.v.) listed in the regionary catalogues in Regio VI. This was presumably the statue of Mamurius Veturius, the legendary bronze smith who made the eleven *ancilia* of the Salii in imitation of the one that had fallen from heaven (Paulus *ex Fest.* 117L; Ovid, *Fast.* 3.379–92; Plutarch, *Numa* 13.3) and was therefore probably near the Curia Saliorum Collinorum (q.v.). The humanist Pomponio Leto (VZ 4.429) says the Vicus Mamuri and statue were at the church of S. Susanna on the Quirinal, but the regionary catalogues put it close to the Capitolium Vetus and Temple of Quirinus. We seem to have a choice between the street (vicus) leading southeast from Piazza S. Bernardo and the slope (clivus) leading down from the crossing of Quattro Fontane to Vicus Longus in the valley between Quirinal and Viminal. The latter seems slightly preferable.

Clivus Martis: the slope of the Via Appia leading up to the Temple of Mars (see Mars, Aedes) between the first and second milestones outside Porta Capena (*CIL* 6.10234 = *ILS* 7213). This was provided with a walk paved with squared stone in 295 B.C. (Livy 10.23.12) and the road cobbled in 189 B.C. (Livy 38.28.3). At some unknown time before Ovid it became known as Via Tecta (Ovid, *Fast.* 6.191–92); this may have been in reference to the *ambulatio* of Crassipes mentioned by Cicero (*QFr.* 3.7.1). At another time the road was graded, evidently considered a major public undertaking (*CIL* 6.1270 = *ILS* 5386). Cf. Degrassi 463; *NSc* 1921, 97 (G. Mancini).

Clivus Orbius (Urbius): a street leading from the top of Vicus Cuprius (*summus Vicus Cuprius*) up to the top of the Oppius. Because of the abominable desecration of her father's corpse by Tullia when her carriage turned right into this street and she forced the driver to drive over the body, at least a stretch of this street became known as the Vicus (not Clivus) Sceleratus. Livy (1.48.6–7) gives a very detailed account of this incident, from which it appears that the Vicus Cuprius must be the street leading from the north corner of the Basilica Constantini to Piazza di S. Pietro in Vincoli following the line of Via di S. Pietro in Vincoli (what is called Clivus Orbius on the Lugli and Gismondi map), and the Clivus Orbius must be a street crossing this, either that running from the Subura to the Colosseum, the Vicus Sandaliarius of Lugli and Gismondi, or a street running northwest/southeast in the neighborhood of Piazza S. Pietro in Vincoli. The former is clearly more likely, because it mounts and descends fairly steep slopes. The Vicus Sceleratus would have been the stretch from the intersection with Vicus Cuprius across the Oppius, a relatively level stretch, while the stretch climbing the slope could still have been called Clivus Orbius.

Solinus 1.25; Dion. Hal. 4.39.3; Ovid, *Fast.* 6.601–10.

Clivus Palatinus (Fig. 63): the modern name for the paved roadway to the Palatine from the Summa Sacra Via (see Sacra Via) at the Arcus Titi (q.v.). Its ancient name is unknown. Considerable remains of ancient pavement of various periods survive in the vicinity. It was a broad processional way and ran in a straight line, probably as far as the Domus Augustiana, but all trace of it disappears at the top of the slope.

Nash 1.152–53.

Clivus Patrici: see **Vicus Patricius.**

Clivus Primoris: possibly a name by which the stretch of the Sacra Via from the Fornix Fabianus to Summa Sacra Via was commonly known (Varro, *Ling.* 5.47).

Clivus Publicius (Fig. 14): the main approach to the Aventine in antiquity, constructed by the plebeian aediles, L. and M. Publicius Malleolus, in 241–238 B.C. (Broughton, *MRR* 1.219–20). It began at Porta Trigemina near the head of the Pons Sublicius (Frontinus, *Aq.* 1.5) and mounted the slope behind the Circus Maximus, running northwest/southeast, probably descending the opposite slope to join Vicus Piscinae Publicae. It was always in heavy use, served the great series of temples crowning the brow of the Aventine above the Circus Maximus, and must have been densely built up from an early period. Livy (30.26.5) speaks of its having burned to the ground in 203 B.C.

Varro, *Ling.* 5.158; Ovid, *Fast.* 5.277–94; Festus 276L; Livy 26.10.6, 27.37.15, 30.26.5.

Clivus Pullius: a street leading to the top of the Esquiline near the Fagutal (Solinus 1.26). It can with confidence be put on the north side of the Esquiline near the church of S. Pietro in Vincoli and must have led up from the Subura (Maior). Lanciani shows street pavement found in three places near here running in the right direction. It might be any of these but is not likely to be the continuation of the Clivus Orbius of Lugli and Gismondi. Varro says it received its name from its viocurus, or builder. The name persisted late, and the fourth-century edict of Tarracius Bassus mentions Clivumpullenses (*CIL* 6.31893c). The medieval church of S. Ioannis in Clivo Plumbi or in Carapullo, which existed on the slope north of S. Pietro until the end of the sixteenth century, shows a corrupted form of the name (HJ 257; HCh 271).

Clivus Rutarius: known from a single inscription (*CIL* 6.7803 = *ILS* 7899); it seems to have been a branch from the Via Aurelia running south from this, not far from the Porta Aurelia (Porta S. Pancrazio), but is otherwise unknown.

Clivus Sacer: see **Sacra Via.**

Clivus Salutis: a street mentioned only by Symmachus (*Epist.* 5.54[52].2) and the *Liber Pontificalis* (LPD 1.221, [Innocentius, 402–17]; VZ 2.235) but probably that part of the Vicus Salutis (q.v.) that climbed from the Campus Martius to Porta Salutaris (roughly equivalent to the modern Via della Dataria). It took its name from the Collis Salutaris and, ultimately, from the Temple of Salus (q.v.).

Clivus Scauri (Fig. 16): a street that ascended east from the valley between Palatine and Caelian, running through a natural cleft, to the top of the Caelian and Porta Querquetulana (or Querquetularia), the Arcus Dolabellae et Silani (q.v.), in general coinciding with modern Via di SS. Giovanni e Paolo. The name is found only in postclassical documents (Jordan 2.594–95; HCh 256–57), but it is almost certainly ancient (cf. *CIL* 6.9940 = *ILS* 7619: Vicus Scauri).

Nash 1.254–55.

Clivus Suburanus: the continuation of the Argiletum where it ascended between the Cispian and Oppius to Porta Esquilina (Arcus Gallieni [q.v.]). Remains of ancient paving show that it followed in general the course of Vie S. Lucia in Selci, di S. Martino, and di S. Vito. Cf. Martial 5.22.5, 10.20[19].5.

Nash 1.256.

Clivus Triarius: a street known only from a single inscription (*CIL* 15.7178 = *ILS* 8728) but probably part of the Vicus Triari of the Capitoline Base (*CIL* 6.975 = *ILS* 6073) listed in Regio XII. It might be the unnamed continuation of the Clivus Publicius of Lugli and Gismondi southeast of Vicus Piscinae Publicae.

Clivus Victoriae (Fig. 63): the ascent to the Palatine along the northwest side of the hill beginning at the Velabrum. It took its name from the Temple of Victoria (see Victoria, Aedes). Its original start must have been the Porta Romana of the Romulean pomerium (Festus 318L). At present its course runs more or less straight, rising steadily to the north corner of the hill. Here it probably originally turned back on itself and ran higher on the slope to the precinct of the Magna Mater and Victoria at the west corner of the hill. Now it turns abruptly east and follows a somewhat irregular path through the substructures of the Domus Tiberiana, ending at a clivus parallel to the Clivus Palatinus and separated from that by a line of tabernae fronting on a deep portico. Once it probably ran to the Clivus Palatinus. Its line was probably changed in the first century after Christ; various distinguished men, including Cicero and Metellus Celer, are known to have had houses there (see Domus: M. Cicero, Caecilius Metellus Celer), but all trace of these has disappeared in the reorganization of the Palatine under Tiberius and Caligula. What had once been an important thoroughfare had become little more than a service alley for the imperial palace.

Nash 1.257.

Cloaca Maxima: the stream that drains all the valleys between the Quirinal and Esquiline hills, running through the middle of the Forum Romanum on a northeast/southwest course and emptying into the Tiber a little below the east end of the island. It became one of the main drains of Rome, and Pliny (*HN* 36.105) says it gathered into its course seven tributaries. There is no reason to doubt this, and all may have been more or less permanent waters. Livy (1.38.6, 56.2) says the work of making the brook a sewer was carried out under Tarquinius Priscus and Tarquinius Superbus, the latter using forced labor of the plebs, but he must mean the channeling of the course, because in the time of Plautus (*Curc.* 476) there was still an open channel in the middle of the Forum Romanum.

It follows a very irregular course, reflecting the Romans' reluctance to interfere with a potentially hostile and dangerous power. Within the excavations in

the vicinity of the forum, it can be followed the length of the Forum Nervae and clearly continued beyond, culverted under the Argiletum (Fig. 39). At the lower end of the Forum Nervae it divides; one channel, the Braccio Morto, runs beneath the Basilica Paulli, the other, probably an artificial modification, runs around the end of the basilica to rejoin the Braccio Morto at the little sacellum of Cloacina. On the south side of the Forum Romanum, it runs under the Basilica Iulia parallel to the Vicus Tuscus, presumably having run in an open channel earlier, and zigzags through the Velabrum, running under the Ianus Quadrifrons and between the round and rectangular temples ("Vesta" and "Fortuna Virilis") of the Forum Boarium. Its mouth on the Tiber, framed in three concentric arches of Gabine stone, is a conspicuous landmark kept visible in the modern Tiber embankment.

Except for the Braccio Morto, the walls of part of which are of cappellaccio, the lower course has walls of squared blocks of Gabine stone, a floor of selce paving, and a vaulted roof of concrete and brick-faced concrete. The Gabine stone walls must be due to the general rehandling of the water and sewer systems of Rome by Agrippa beginning in his aedileship in 33 B.C. (Cass. Dio 49.43); Gabine stone was relatively expensive and used extensively only from the time of Julius Caesar through that of Nero (Blake 1947, 38–39), and Narducci describes the construction as very similar to that of the lower course of the Petronia Amnis (q.v.) from Piazza Mattei to the Tiber (Narducci 36–37, 40–42). The rest of the course is presumably of later date, reworked as new building made demands for more capacious branch lines. Ultimately, it received the wastes from the Thermae Diocletianae.

The Cloaca Maxima was an object of great admiration to Pliny for its size, so great that men could traverse it in boats, and so strong that the walls could resist the most violent storms, and even floods when the water backed up in its channel, and the roofs stood up under the passage of great blocks of stone in the streets overhead and the collapse of burning buildings (Pliny, *HN* 36.104–8). It continues to function today, but connected with the main sewer of Rome to prevent the backwash from flooding the Forum. Ficoroni (*Le vestigia e rarità di Roma antica* [Rome 1744], 1.74) reports that the lower course was all cleared in 1742, the conduit being found 10 m below the ground level and built of blocks of travertine. Narducci (4) gives the dimensions at the Tiber mouth as 4.50 m wide and 3.30 m high, while at the corner of Via di S. Teodoro and Via dei Foraggi it is 2.12 m wide and 2.72 m high.

PA gives the dimensions in the stretch from the northwest corner of the Forum Augustum to Via Alessandrina as 3.20 m wide and 4.20 m high. Despite the variation, it was clearly capacious through the area of the Subura (cf. Strabo 5.3.8 [235]).

Nash 1.258–61; *Roma sotterranea*, 170–72 (C. Mocchegiani Carpano).

Cloacina, Sacrum (Fig. 39): a small sacellum to the divinity of the brook running across the Forum Romanum. It stood near the Tabernae Novae (Livy 3.48.5), and Plautus (*Curc.* 471) places it between the Comitium and an unnamed basilica. It is shown on coins (*B. M. Coins, Rom. Rep.* 1.577–78 nos. 4242–54) as a low circular platform crowned by an open balustrade holding two draped statues, each with the right hand lowered to a small support (thymiaterion?), one with the left hand raised and holding an indistinct object usually identified as a flower. Other additions to either side of the platform are also unclear. These are presumably the *signa Veneris Cloacinae* of Pliny (*HN* 15.119). It is identified beyond question by a round marble base molding found in 1899–1901 in front of the Basilica Paulli encroaching on the Sacra Via, where the Braccio Morto of the Cloaca under the basilica joins the main channel. It is 2.40 m in diameter, with a rectangular projection to the northwest, presumably for a small stair of approach. This molding rests on a base of travertine blocks, below which are eight courses of various sorts of stone, showing that the shrine was very old and had to be raised as the ground level around it rose. It is not known when or why Cloaca was assimilated to Venus, or why there should have been two statues in the sacellum.

Nash 1.262–63.

Codeta (also evidently called **Codeta Maior** and **Campus Codetanus** or **Caudetanus**): listed in the regionary catalogues in Regio XIV, called *ager* by Paulus (Paulus *ex Fest.* 34L and 50L), who adds that a plant resembling horsetails grew there. This seems to have been an equisetum, probably the common arvense or maximum, known in Italy today as code di cavallo and code equine, called horsetails and scouring rushes in English. These are marsh plants, and therefore we should look for a swamp or depression in the Transtiberim. One was identified under Via Morosini just west of the Viale di Trastevere in 1888 (LFUR sheet 33), and we can presume this extended for some distance to the northeast. The land is rising to the south and west. This is part of the Nemus Caesarum and probably that part in which Augustus constructed his naumachia. A boundary stone of the late republic found in the Tiber near Ponte Principe Amedeo inscribed FINEIS[. . .]AVDETA[. . .] (*CIL* 6.30422.3) indicates a location upstream of this point, but might equally well refer to the Codeta Minor.

Codeta Minor: a swampy place in the Campus Martius where Julius Caesar excavated his naumachia (Suetonius, *Iul.* 39.4; Cass. Dio 43.23.4). From the discovery of a boundary stone in the Tiber near Ponte Principe Amedeo inscribed FINEIS[. . .] AVDETA[. . .] (*CIL* 6.30422.3), we can presume one Codeta lay upstream of that point. A place in the loop of the river somewhere across from the Mausoleum Hadriani seems indicated.

Cohortes Vigilum, Stationes: the seven barracks of the seven cohorts of city watchmen established by Augustus following his reorganization of the city into fourteen regiones, each cohors being responsible for two regiones and its statio located strategically to control these. There were also fourteen smaller posts, *excubitoria,* which seem to have been the stations from which closer watch was kept night and day (see P. K. Baillie Reynolds, *The Vigiles of Imperial Rome* [Oxford 1926], especially 43–63). The following is known about the individual stationes:

I (Fig. 18): This was the barracks of the cohors responsible for Regiones VII and IX. For a long time it was believed that it was shown on a fragment of the Marble Plan, placed just east of Via Lata. This was shown conclusively by G. Gatti (*BullCom* 62 [1934]: 123–49, especially 148–49) to be part of the Horrea Galbana and to belong near Monte Testaccio, in quite a different part of the city. We then have no notion of the architectural form of this barracks and no real indication of its precise location, though its place, second in the list for Regio VII in the regionary catalogues, tends to indicate a location toward the southern end of Regio VII, where it would be central to the densely built up and thickly inhabited portions of Regiones VII and IX, and this is confirmed by the discovery of several inscriptions pertaining to the cohort in the vicinity of Piazza SS. Apostoli, especially toward the northern end of the piazza (cf. *CIL* 6.233, 1092, 1157, 1226). Remains discovered in the area do not permit reconstruction of even a tentative plan (cf. *NSc* 1912, 337–42 [G. Mancini]).

II: in Regio V *(Not., Cur.),* a barracks on the Esquiline for the cohors responsible for Regiones V and III, at the south end of Piazza Vittorio Emanuele (cf. *CIL* 6.414, 1059, 2962–68, 32752; *ILS* 8382).

III: in Regio VI *(Not.),* but the epigraphical evidence will not permit precise identification of the site (cf. *CIL* 6.2969–71, 3761 = 31320, 32753–56; *ILS*

2165, 2167). It may have been just inside the Porta Viminalis, near the east corner of the Thermae Diocletianae, where Lugli and Gismondi put it. This cohors must have been responsible for Regiones IV and VI of Augustan Rome.

IIII: listed by the regionary catalogues in Regio XII and traditionally associated with the church of S. Saba, under which have been found walls of concrete faced with reticulate (NSc 1902, 270–73, 465–66 [M. E. Cannizzaro and L. C. Gavini], 357 [G. Gatti]) and near which was discovered a Mithraeum (NSc 1925, 382–87 [R. Paribeni]). Several inscriptions have been found that help to confirm this identification (CIL 6.219, 220, 643, 1055, 2972–76; ILS 2162, 2163; AdI 1858, 285–89 [G. B. De Rossi]). No plan of any substantial part of the complex has been recovered, and its location suggests that this cohort was responsible for Regiones XII and XIII, but not, as has sometimes been suggested, XI, which must have been under Cohors VII.

V (Fig. 16): in Regio II (Not., Cur.), on the Caelian southeast of S. Maria in Domnica and southwest of S. Stefano Rotondo. Parts of this statio were found in 1931 when the Via della Navicella was widened. Earlier, in 1920, an inscribed base with a dedication by the fifth cohort to Caracalla was discovered in situ at the entrance to Villa Celimontana. Other inscriptions belonging to it are CIL 6.221, 222, 1057, 1058, 2977–83; ILS 2157, 2160, 2161, 2173. The remains are of brick-faced concrete, but it is not possible to reconstruct the plan more than hypothetically. This cohort must have been responsible for Regiones I and II.

Nash 1.264–65.

VI: listed in Regio VIII by the Notitia. The inscriptions pertaining to it (CIL 6.2984–92, 32757) are without topographical value. Logically this cohort must have been responsible for Regiones VIII and X, a section small in area but very important and densely built up. To be central to its area, the statio would have had to lie in the immediate vicinity of the Forum Romanum.

VII: listed by the regionary catalogues in Regio XIV and argued by Baillie Reynolds to have been responsible for Regiones XIV and XI. No trace of the statio has come to light, but remains of one of the excubitoria were found in 1866 at Monte di Fiore, east of the church of S. Crisogono. The building, of which only a small part has been excavated, seems originally to have been a private bath complex of the second century (CIL 6.579 = ILS 3520), which was then modified and possibly enlarged at the end of that century. The excavated part consists of a large hall or court with a black-and-white mosaic pavement of marine subjects and a hexagonal fountain of brick covered with signinum toward the center, off which open other rooms, including a large lararium to the Genius Cohortis and a bath. There are numerous inscriptions and graffiti (CIL 6.2993–3091, 32751; ILS 2172, 2174–77) dated A.D. 215–245. Most of these are associated with the lararium and express thanks of some common soldier of the cohors on completion of his month of sebaciaria, a service the nature of which is not precisely known, but which seems to have been tedious and somewhat dangerous, as a number of the inscriptions contain the words omnia tuta and/or salvis commanipulis. It may have been some sort of night watch; the first element of sebaciaria seems to be the root of the word for "tallow." But it also seems to have been done singly.

Nash 1.266–67; PBSR 54 (1986): 147–69 (J. S. Rainbird).

Collis Hortulorum: see **Pincius Mons.**

Colosseum: see **Amphitheatrum Flavium.**

Colossus: see **Statua, Signum, Equus, Colossus.**

Colossus Solis (Neronis): a bronze portrait statue of Nero, nude, the work of Zenodorus, that originally stood in the entrance court (vestibulum) of the Domus Aurea on the Velia (Suetonius, Nero 31; Pliny, HN 34.45). Its height is given variously as 102½ Roman feet (Not., Cur.) to 120 Roman feet (Suetonius, Nero 31). After Nero's death it was modified by Vespasian and became a statue of Sol with the addition of a radiate crown, each of the seven rays being 23½ Roman feet long (Suetonius, Vesp. 18; Pliny, HN 34.45). It was moved by Hadrian, probably in A.D. 128, to a position just northwest of the Colosseum, where a square in the pavement of the street still marks the place of the base (S.H.A. Hadr. 19.12–13) (Figs. 3, 16, 90). The base was 7 m square, of brick-faced concrete, and originally veneered with marble. For the transference, which was carried out to make place for Hadrian's Temple of Venus et Roma, Hadrian employed the services of the architect Decrianus, who is said to have moved the statue upright (suspensum) and to have required the use of twenty-four elephants. Later Commodus removed the head, substituting for it a portrait of himself, and added the attributes of Hercules (S.H.A. Commod. 17.9–10; Cass. Dio 73.22.3; Herodian 1.15.9), but these were removed after his death and the statue restored as Sol. An annual festival on 6 June in which the colossus was crowned and covered with garlands persisted into Christian times (Degrassi 466). It was still standing in the fourth century and is listed by the regionary catalogues in Regio IV, but it is not mentioned in the Einsiedeln itinerary of the late eighth–early ninth century.

The adage quoted by Bede (*Opera Paraenetica* 2, *Excerptiones Patrum, Collectanea* 543B [Migne 94]), *quamdiu stabit colossus, stabit et Roma; quando cadet, cadet et Roma; quando cadet Roma, cadet et mundus,* should refer not to the amphitheater but to the statue, as should early medieval mention of an *insula, regio* and *rota colisei.* The name Colosseum seems not to have been applied to the amphitheater until about A.D. 1000. Cf. Jordan 2.119, 319, 510.

Nash 1.268–69.

Columna Antonini Pii: a column raised to the memory of Faustina and Antoninus by his adoptive sons and heirs, M. Aurelius and Lucius Verus. It stood in the Campus Martius just west of Montecitorio, oriented with the nearby commemorative altars of the Antonines and the Column of Marcus Aurelius. The shaft was of red granite, unfluted, and 14.75 m high; after serious damage by fire in the eighteenth century and the use of undamaged parts to repair the obelisk in Piazza di Montecitorio, only a slab of the foot of the column was preserved. This gives the masons' inscription with the date of its quarrying, A.D. 106 (*IG* 14.2421.1). The column is shown on coins surmounted by a Corinthian capital and a statue, presumably of bronze, and set off by an openwork balustrade, which the accounts of the excavation of the base report to have been of marble (cf., e.g., *B. M. Coins, Rom. Emp.* 4.528 no. 893).

The unusually large base of white marble carried a short dedicatory inscription on its principal (northwest) face (*CIL* 6.1004 = *ILS* 347) and had reliefs on the other three. This was excavated in 1703, together with the column, of which only 6 m projected above ground at that time. The base was then removed to Piazza di Montecitorio, where it was restored. In 1789 it was moved to the Cortile (Giardino) della Pigna in the Vatican, where it fared badly, exposed to the weather. After a second restoration concluded in 1846, it was installed in the large apse at the north end of the garden (Helbig⁴ 1.480); more recently, it was moved to the Cortile delle Corazze in the Museo del Vaticano.

The relief opposite the dedicatory inscription shows the imperial couple borne aloft on the wings of a genius figure, sometimes identified as Aion, and flanked by eagles. At the lower corners are the goddess Roma, who lifts her hand in salutation, and an allegorical figure of the Campus Martius, a genius reclining on the ground and holding an obelisk. The

reliefs on the sides, intended to be identical, show the *decursio equitum* performed at the funeral before the pyre was lit. Riders of several sorts, including senators, move in a ring around a group of foot soldiers representing the praetorian guard.

Helbig⁴ 1.378 no. 480; *CAR* 2-G, 152 pp. 181–82; Nash 1.270–75; L. Vogel, *The Column of Antoninus Pius* (Cambridge, Mass. 1973); *RendPontAcc* 51–52 (1978–80): 389–400 (D. E. E. Kleiner and F. S. Kleiner); *BullCom* 88 (1982–83): 73–75 (B. Frischer); *PBSR* 57 (1989): 90–105 (R. Hannah).

Columna Antoniniana: see **Columna Marci Aurelii Antonini.**

Columna Bellica: a diminutive column *(columella)* that stood in a plot, probably marked off by cippi, in front of *(ante)* the Temple of Bellona in the Campus Martius. A soldier of Pyrrhus had been made to buy this plot so that it might permanently represent foreign territory. In declaring war, the fetial threw a spear over the column into the enemy territory, a rite that persisted as late as the time of Marcus Aurelius (Cass. Dio 72.33.3).

Ovid, *Fast.* 6.205–9; Servius *ad Aen.* 9.52; Festus 30L; Lindsay, *Gloss. Lat.* 4.55 (pseudo-Placidus).

Columna Lactaria: a column in the Forum Holitorium mentioned by Paulus (Paulus *ex Fest.* 105L), who says infants were taken there to be given milk. Presumably he means the children of the poor, and this was a charitable institution. It has been associated with the Temple of Pietas (see Pietas, Aedes), one of the few buildings known to have been in the Forum Holitorium, and also with the story of Cimon and Pero (Caritas Romana), the latter without good reason.

Columna Maenia: a column erected in 338 B.C. in honor of C. Maenius, victor over the Latins in the naval battle of Antium (Pliny, *HN* 34.20). It stood west of the Curia Hostilia, because the *accensus consulum* announced the final hour of the day when from the Curia he saw the sun pass the Columna Maenia moving toward the Carcer (Pliny, *HN* 7.212: *a Columna Maenia ad Carcerem inclinato*). This indicates that the column was located near the northeast end of the Arch of Septimius Severus. The column was used in the time of Cicero for public posting of the names of delinquent debtors by their creditors (Cicero, *Div. Caec.* 50, *Sest.* 18 and *Schol. Bob. ad loc.* [Stangl 128]).

A second explanation of the column was that when Cato was purchasing land for the Basilica Porcia (q.v.), Maenius, whose house Cato needed to complete the parcel, stipulated that one column should be salvaged from his house to provide a vantage point from which he and his descendants could watch the games given in the forum, and that on this column he constructed a wooden platform. Such a column would have had to be some distance from the house in question in order to provide a good spectator's vantage point, and houses of such size as would include a column suitable for supporting such a platform would have been extremely rare at so early a date. Other improbabilities involved are also apparent. We can therefore reject this tradition as an invention (cf. [Ascon.,] *Div. Caec.* 50 [Stangl 128]; Porphyrion *ad Hor. Sat.* 1.3.21). But it probably means that there was no inscription on the column and no statue crowning it from a relatively early date. Because the column was still standing in the fourth century (Symmachus, *Epist.* 5.54.3), the story was probably made up after the destruction of the Basilica Porcia and after its location was forgotten.

Coarelli 1985, 38–53.

Columna Marci Aurelii Antonini (Columna Antoniniana) (Fig. 18):

a large column, like that of Trajan in his forum, raised by the senate and the Roman people to Marcus Aurelius in honor of his victories over the Marcomanni and Sarmatians in A.D. 172–175 (Aur. Vict., *Caes.* 16, *Epit.* 16). It stands on the west side of Via Lata, aligned with it and isolated in a piazza, probably with a view to the construction of a temple to M. Aurelius similar to that to Divus Traianus. An inscription dated A.D. 193 found nearby (*CIL* 6.1585 = *ILS* 5920) speaks of a procurator of the column and a shelter for him. The column is variously called Columna Divorum Marci et Faustinae, Columna Divi Marci, Columna Centenaria, and Columna Centenaria Divi Marci. In the regionary catalogues, listed in Regio IX, it is called Columna Cochlis, probably in reference to the spiral band of relief on the exterior rather than to the spiral stair in the interior.

Through the ages it has received better care than most monuments of antiquity. In the tenth century it was given, together with the church of S. Andrea de Columna, which stood on its north side, to the Benedictines of S. Silvestro in Capite (HCh 182–83). At an unknown date its upper half was displaced a little by an earthquake; the displacement is most apparent in the figure of Victoria inscribing a shield. In 1589–1590, under Pope Sixtus V, extensive repairs were carried out by Domenico Fontana. A statue of Saint Paul was set atop the column, the ruined reliefs of the base were chiseled away, and a new plain marble casing was added. The height of the base was considerably reduced by raising the pavement, and the reliefs of the shaft were restored. The dedicatory inscription, if any trace of it survived, must have gone at this time; there is no record of it. But in recent years the fumes of the heavy automotive traffic in the vicinity have eroded many parts of the high relief beyond recognition; it has in this respect suffered perhaps more than any other monument.

The column is in many ways a close copy of that of Trajan. Shaft, torus base, and capital together measure 100 Roman feet (29.77 m). The base was originally considerably higher than that of the Column of Trajan, and the shaft tapers less, while the relief is much deeper, with extensive undercutting. The shaft is composed of twenty-six drums of Luna marble with a spiral stair of 200 steps carved out of the core. This is lit by fifty-six small rectangular windows. The specifications given in the regionary catalogues are slightly inaccurate; there it is said to be 175½ Roman feet high, with a stair of 203 steps. The torus at the base is carved with a wreath of oak leaves; the capital is essentially Doric, with the echinus carved with an egg molding. The shaft is wound with a spiral band of relief of twenty-one turns, on which are shown scenes from the two campaigns of Marcus, separated by a figure of Victoria inscribing a shield. Most scenes are designed in two clearly distinct planes, one above the other, with sometimes a third between. There is a strong feeling of a drive forward to the composition, with occasional pauses to emphasize the introduction of the princeps. Incidental elements of landscape and setting are reduced to a minimum and often schematic or treated symbolically. Violence and pathos are abundantly in evidence, and the drama of the war is emphasized, as it is not on the Column of Trajan.

The base of the column is shown in numerous sixteenth-century drawings, which together probably give us fairly accurate views of it from all sides. The earliest of these is by Enea Vico, ca. 1540, and shows the east face; others are by Francisco d'Hollanda, Dosio, and Étienne Du Pérac. By Vico's time the base of the column had been buried up to the middle of the third course of the great travertine blocks forming the core of the base, and the marble revetment had been stripped away, except for the band of reliefs facing the fourth course. These showed on the principal face the ultimate submission of the barbarians to Marcus Aurelius, and on each of the other three faces garlands swung in deep loops from the shoulders of four draped Victorias, who hold up wreaths of victory in their outstretched hands. Above this band are three more courses of rough travertine blocks and then a well-finished plinth under the torus of the base of the column. It is easy to imagine that the base of the column was surrounded by steps on all sides, leading on the east front to the door of access, above which the dedicatory inscription would have filled the space between the lintel and the zone of relief, but it is difficult to imagine that the revetment was plain, except for the inscription, as we must to explain why these slabs would have been robbed out and the relief left. Perhaps the decoration was in such low relief as that of the base of the Column of Trajan, and the plunderers saw that it could easily be chiseled away. Enea Vico's drawing shows, lying in the foreground, a slab of frieze decorated with a garland of leaves wound with ribbon and a block of deep cornice of which the most conspicuous feature is a line of deep dentils. Coins of Trajan (e.g., *B. M. Coins, Rom. Emp.* 3 pls. 38.3, 39.4 and 5, 40.2, 41.6) show a column with a base in two storeys, the upper storey recessive above the lower and surmounted by freestanding eagles at the corners, which carry garlands swung between them in their beaks. It seems highly likely that this was the design of the base of the Column of Marcus, that the cornice should be installed immediately above the zone of reliefs and a recessive storey rise plain above this to be crowned by freestanding eagles, which might have been of either marble or bronze.

It is likely that the Temple of Divus Marcus (see Marcus, Divus, Templum) stood west of the column and that a square framing both was bordered with colonnades, at least in part, but remains of all these are entirely unknown.

C. Caprino, A. M. Colini, G. Gatti, M. Pallottino, and P. Romanelli, *La colonna di Marco Aurelio* (Rome 1955); G. Becatti, *Colonna di Marco Aurelio* (Milan 1957); Nash 1.276–79; *CAR* 2-G, 219 p. 198.

Columna Minucia: a column erected in honor of L. Minucius Augurinus, praefectus annonae in 439 B.C., by decree of the people and paid for by popular subscription (Pliny, *HN* 18.15, 34.21). Pliny believed it might be the first such honor awarded by the people; it seems also to have been the first statue raised on a lofty column in Rome. It stood just outside the Porta Trigemina (cf. Porta Minucia), near the Statio Annonae (q.v.), and is shown on denarii of the late second century B.C. (*B. M. Coins, Rom. Rep.* 1.135–36 nos. 952–54, 148 nos. 1005–6; Crawford 242/1; 243/1). The interpretation of the coins is difficult. The column is composed of drums with convex exterior faces, possibly representing rustication. It stands on a rectangular plinth and has an Aeolic capital from which dangle bells. The statue atop it is shown as diminutive, togate, with a long staff. At the base are two lions' heads or forequarters, each surmounted by a large grain ear (?). The column is flanked by two togate figures, the one on the right an augur with a lituus, the other a praefec-

tus annonae (?). Whether these are to be interpreted as other statues is not clear, but the probability seems strong.

The gilded bull reported by Livy (4.16.2) to have been presented to Minucius *extra Portam Trigeminam* probably results from confusion of the column with a sacrificial bull also presented to Minucius (see R. M. Oglivie, *A Commentary on Livy, Books I-V* [Oxford 1965], ad loc.). We know that a bronze bull in the Forum Boarium (q.v.) marked the beginning of the pomerium of Romulus (Tacitus, *Ann.* 12.24). This was an Aeginetan bronze, spoils of the conquest of Greece (Pliny, *HN* 34.10) and therefore not installed before the second century B.C. It may be that Livy was unaware of the discrepancy and that the column and bronze bull stood close enough to each other that they might be thought to belong together (cf. Ovid, *Fast.* 6.477–78), for it is most unlikely that there were two statues of bulls here. This will also give a better beginning for the pomerium.

Columna Phocae (Figs. 40, 41): a column erected in A.D. 608 by Smaragdus, exarch of Italy, to Phocas, emperor of the East (*CIL* 6.1200 = *ILS* 837, 31259a). It stands in the Forum Romanum between the Rostra and the Lacus Curtius, on a high plinth atop a pyramid of steps faced with white marble. The column itself is of white marble and fluted, with an Attic base and Corinthian capital of good workmanship, clearly robbed from an early imperial monument. The statue that crowned it was gilded. There seems to be work of several periods here, Smaragdus having made use of an old foundation and a still older column. The steps of the pyramidal base on the north and east sides were removed in 1903.

Nash 1.280–81; GV 174–77.

Columna Rostrata (M. Aemilii Paulli): a column ornamented with the beaks of captured ships of war erected on the Capitoline in honor of M. Aemilius Paullus, cos. 255 B.C. It was completely destroyed by lightning in 172 B.C. (Livy 42.20.1).

Columna Rostrata (Augusti): a column erected in the Forum Romanum in 36 B.C. to celebrate the victory of Octavian over Sextus Pompey (Appian, *BellCiv* 5.130). The column was decorated along the shaft with beaks and anchors and surmounted by a gilded statue of Octavian, supposedly wearing the dress he wore when he returned to Rome. The column is shown on coins issued between 35 and 28 B.C. (*B. M. Coins, Rom. Emp.* 1 Augustus nos. 633–36), where Octavian's statue is nude, except for a cloak floating behind it, and holds a long spear in the right hand.

Columnae Rostratae Augusti et Agrippae: After the conquest of Egypt, Augustus is said to have had four columns cast from the bronze of the beaks of captured warships, which were later removed by Domitian to the Capitoline and to be seen there in Servius's day (Servius *ad Georg.* 3.29). Evidently Servius did not know about the earlier single column (see Columna Rostrata Augusti). Where the four columns were originally erected is unknown, but it seems likely that it was in the precinct of Apollo Palatinus, because the passage in Vergil where such columns are mentioned clearly takes that temple as its model.

Columna Rostrata C. Duilii (1): a column erected by C. Duilius in celebration of his naval victory over the Carthaginians in 260 B.C., which stood *ante circum a parte ianuarum* (Servius *ad Georg.* 3.29). The *ianuae* of the Circus Maximus are also mentioned in Chron. 147, where they are said to have been enlarged by Caracalla. Probably the exterior of the carceres with the axial ceremonial entrance is meant, although only the latter ought properly to qualify as a *ianua*.

Columna Rostrata C. Duilii (2): a second column erected by Duilius on the Rostra to celebrate the same victory as (1), later moved to the Forum Romanum (Servius *ad Georg.* 3.29; Pliny, *HN* 34.20; Quintilian 1.7.12). The long archaic dedicatory inscription seems to have been restored repeatedly, perhaps last under Claudius; part of it was discovered in 1565 (*CIL* 6.1300 = 31591 = *ILS* 65; A. E. Gordon, *Illustrated Introduction to Latin Epigraphy* [Berkeley 1983], 124–27 no. 48) and is preserved in the Museo Nuovo Capitolino.

Nash 1.282.

Columna Traiani: see **Forum Traiani.**

Comitium: the earliest place of public assembly of the Romans and throughout history the meeting place of the Comitia Curiata, an inaugurated templum in front of the Curia Hostilia, between this and the Forum Romanum. In shape it was a broad rectangle, slightly longer than wide, oriented to the cardinal points of the compass. It was essentially open, though awnings were sometimes employed to protect those assembled there from the sun (Livy 27.36.8; Pliny, *HN* 19.23). Troops could march into it (Livy 5.55.1), and prodigies, such as a rain of blood, could be observed in it (Livy 34.45.6). It was throughout republican history closely connected with the Curia Hostilia, which stood on axis with it at the middle of its north side. Livy calls it the *vesti-*

bulum curiae (45.24.12). A speakers' platform in front of the curia was the traditional location of the tribunal of the praetor urbanus (Varro, *Ling.* 5.155; Macrobius, *Sat.* 3.16.15; cf. Livy 27.50.9), probably at one extremity of the platform, while in time the praetor in charge of the Quaestio de Repetundis came to occupy the other. This platform was later ornamented with the beaks of captured warships and called Rostra (q.v.).

The center of the Comitium became in time, certainly by the beginning of the third century B.C., a circular amphitheater of steps rising on all sides, on which the citizens stood in their assemblies, while in front of the curia these steps formed a stair of approach to the speakers' platform and senate house. This cavea must have been interrupted by throats of entry leading in from the Forum and the Clivus Argentarius, and perhaps from the Argiletum. For various monuments set up in the Comitium in early times, see Ficus Navia, Puteal in Comitio, Statua Atti Navii, Statua Hermodori, and Statua Horatii Coclitis.

Until the second century B.C., the Comitium was the place where the Romans regularly assembled by tribes to pass laws. C. Licinius Crassus, as tribunus plebis in 145 B.C., was the first to lead the people from the Comitium to the Forum for the hearing of laws (Varro, *Rust.* 1.2.9; Cicero, *Amic.* 25.96). Plutarch (*C. Gracch.* 5) must be wrong in ascribing this change to Gaius Gracchus.

Stratigraphic excavations in the Comitium by G. Boni at the turn of the century revealed twenty-seven strata in a depth of 3.5 m, some of the strata barely 1 cm thick. In the middle of the century E. Gjerstad made a new stratigraphic exploration of the area and discovered the same twenty-seven strata. The dating and significance of these is much disputed, as is their association with various scanty remains of construction in the area of the "Rostra Vetera" southeast of the Niger Lapis (q.v.). Most of the reconstructions suggested for the successive phases of the "Rostra Vetera" are unacceptable as architecture; only the last phase at 11.80 meters above sea level, a segment of the stepped cavea of the Comitium, can be accepted as a viable building. At various points in the Comitium are twenty-one shallow pits lined with tufa slabs set vertically and covered with stone plates. Most of these seem to have been deliberately filled with debris toward the end of the republic, and their abandonment is probably to be associated with the rehandling of parts of the complex by Sulla, Faustus Sulla, Julius Caesar, and Augustus in close succession. Some of the pits were probably connected with the rigging of awnings, others with monuments set up here. The irregular shape of some of them is puzzling, but they are not likely to have had a religious function.

By the time Julius Caesar paved this area, and perhaps from the time Faustus Sulla rebuilt the Curia Hostilia (q.v.), the Comitium had lost most of its importance, and the cavea of steps was destroyed, though it had been kept in repair and rebuilt when necessary, at least in front of the Rostra, until sometime after August 59 B.C. (cf. Gradus Aurelii; Cicero, *Flacc.* 66). Caesar's (?) clearing of the area and paving of it with flags of Luna marble at 13.50 meters above sea level marks a new departure. Numerous old monuments had been assembled under the Niger Lapis (q.v.) and floored over with special stone. The area was then fenced off to prevent the unwary from walking over it. If the Comitium now had definition, it was only by its marble pavement and perhaps a light fence that could be run up, and it seems to have been much reduced in size, because its public assemblies had now almost entirely been moved to the Saepta Iulia (q.v.). However, its existence continued to be recognized, especially in the formal phrase *in curia in Comitio,* at least until the time of Hadrian.

In the fourth century a new pavement of roughly laid travertine flags was installed about 20 cm above the marble pavement, the last repair of antiquity. The Comitium was now in effect a small entrance court in front of the curia. In this were erected a number of monuments, notably a very large circular fountain with an octagonal foot in front of the door of the curia of Diocletian and a square monument on a base faced with blocks of marble with a fence around it that has been taken as for a bronze quadriga, but is more likely for the Ianus Geminus (q.v.) of the late imperial period.

NSc 1900, 295–340 (G. Boni); *Archaeology* 10 (1957): 49–55 (L. Richardson); *ActaInstSueciae* 17, pt. 3 (1960): 217–59 (E. Gjerstad); Nash 1:287–89; *RömMitt* 80 (1973): 219–33 (L. Richardson), 85 (1978): 359–69 (L. Richardson), 83 (1976): 31–69 (C. Krause); Coarelli 1983, 119–60; Coarelli 1985, 11–123, especially 11–27.

Compitum: see **Forum, Area, Compitum.**

Compitum Acili (Fig. 90): a street crossing with a compital shrine on the northern spur of the Velia, the juncture at an oblique angle of a street leading up from the Vicus Cuprius and a street leading up to the Carinae following the course of the modern Via della Polveriera. It is mentioned as having the Tigillum Sororium (q.v.) in its near vicinity (Degrassi 515 [Oct. 1]) and as the site of a taberna purchased at public expense in 229 B.C. for Archagathus, the first Greek physician to establish himself in Rome (Pliny, *HN* 29.12). In the cutting of the Via dei Fori Imperiali in

1932, the compital shrine with an inscribed architrave and a consular date of 5 B.C. came to light. This consisted of a low platform approached by a flight of four steps, together with fragments of unfluted columns and a very richly carved entablature with a modillion cornice. The decorative detail is finely carved, and the lettering of the inscription is elegant. The explanation of the name is elusive.

Nash 1.290–91; *CEFR* 98 (1987): 87–109 (M. Dondin-Payre).

Compitum Aliarium: a street crossing known from four inscriptions (*CIL* 6.4476, 9971, 33157; *ILS* 7569, 7809; *BullCom* 41 [1913]: 81 [G. Gatti]) and presumably a point of some importance, but otherwise unknown. The name seems to derive from *alium* (garlic), and a place in the Subura in the vicinity of the Macellum (q.v.) may therefore be not unlikely. The inscriptions indicate that it was a center for clothiers.

Compitum Fabricium: probably the intersection of the Vicus Fabrici of Regio I (*CIL* 6.975 = *ILS* 6073) and another street where there was also a lacus. It was next to the Curiae Novae (Festus 180L), therefore presumably on the Caelian. Lugli and Gismondi suggests the vicus was the street along the main front of the Temple of Divus Claudius, which would allow identification of the compitum as the important juncture of streets at the northwest corner of the temple precinct (Figs. 3, 16), but the Curiae Novae were probably not so far from the Curiae Veteres. It is reported to have got its name from a house given to a Fabricius *ob captivos recuperatos de hostibus* (*CGL* 4.62–63 [Placidus]). This would presumably have been C. Fabricius, the ambassador sent to Pyrrhus in 278 B.C. (Cicero, *Brut.* 55).

Concordia, Aedes (1): a temple to Concordia vowed by L. Manlius when praetor in Gaul in 218 B.C. (Livy 22.33.7) and begun in 217 by the duovirs C. Pupius and K. Quinctius Flamininus. It was *in arce* and dedicated the following year by the duovirs M. and C. Atilius (Livy 23.21.7). The day of dedication was 5 February (Degrassi 406–7). If our sources are correct, this must have been somewhere on the crest of the Capitoline Hill, presumably on the northeastern height. It is located *in arce* in the Fasti Praenestini and *in Capit(olio)* in the Fasti Antiates Maiores.

Concordia, Aedes (2) (also **Templum**) (Fig. 19): the temple at the foot of the northeastern lobe of the Capitoline Hill overlooking the Forum Romanum at the end of the Sacra Via. It was traditionally vowed by Camillus in 367 B.C. during the troubles connected with the passage of the Licinian laws (Plutarch, *Cam.* 42.3). Camillus was released from his vow on the following day when the people, having obtained their goal, voted to build the temple for him (Plutarch, *Cam.* 42.4; Ovid, *Fast.* 1.641–44). But this temple seems never to have been built, though Plutarch specifies that the place for it, where the present temple stands, was designated. This was the Area Concordiae (Livy 39.56.6, 40.19.2; Obsequens 4), between the Volcanal and the base of the Capitoline, and beside the Gradus ad Monetam (Ovid, *Fast.* 1.637–38). The first monument here seems to have been the Aedicula Concordiae (see Concordia, Aedicula) of Cn. Flavius, built in 304, which was replaced by the temple of Opimius of 121.

In 121 B.C., following the death of C. Gracchus, the senate ordered the construction of this temple by L. Opimius (Appian, *BellCiv* 1.3.26; Plutarch, *C. Gracch.* 17.6). The day of dedication was probably 22 July (Degrassi 486). Thereafter, the temple was very frequently used for meetings of the senate, especially when there was a question of civic discord or disturbance to be discussed (cf., e.g., Cicero, *Cat.* 3.21, *Sest.* 26, *Dom.* 11, *Phil.* 2.19; Cass. Dio 58.11.4). It was also used occasionally as a meeting place by the Arval Brethren (Henzen, p. iv). See also Basilica Opimia.

In 7 B.C., as part of his triumph, Tiberius undertook to restore the temple, using the spoils of his German campaigns for the purpose (Cass. Dio 55.8.2). This rebuilding was carried out on a lavish scale, and the finished temple was dedicated in the names of Tiberius and his dead brother Drusus on 16 January (Ovid, *Fast.* 1.637–38; Degrassi 398–400) A.D. 10 (Cass. Dio 56.25.1) or A.D. 12 (Suetonius, *Tib.* 20). The latter is more likely to be correct.

Tiberius's temple was of unusual plan, thanks to the restrictions imposed on it by the site. The cella has a transverse axis, being 45 m wide and 24 m deep, while the hexastyle pronaos is only 34 m wide and 14 m deep. The back wall comes tight against the base of the Tabularium. The approach was by a wide stair running the full width of the pronaos. Exploration in the interior of the podium indicates that Opimius's temple was of similar size and proportions. In the cella a row of white marble columns raised on a continuous plinth projecting from the wall divided the walls into eleven bays, each containing a niche. The axial niche on the northwest wall must have been for the cult figure of Concordia, shown as enthroned, carrying a patera and a cornucopia. The Corinthian columns of the interior order are of great elegance; pairs of leaping rams replace the corner volutes. Pilasters of the same design responded to them along the walls (E. von Mercklin, *Antike Figuralkapitelle* [Berlin 1962], 201–4 no.

494). The modillion cornice of the exterior, of which a large fragment is preserved in the open gallery of the Tabularium, is widely regarded as the finest architectural fragment surviving from the Augustan period, a model of classical decorative motifs combined with harmony and restraint. Of the decoration of the temple, only the threshold of the cella in two blocks of Porta Santa marble and some bits of the pavement survive on the site. The exterior of the temple was covered entirely with marble, and it carried an extraordinarily elaborate program of statuary on the roof, though the pediment was evidently left blank. This is shown on coins of Tiberius (*B. M. Coins, Rom. Emp.* 1.137, 139 nos. 116, 132–34). The statues on the roof are identified as the Capitoline triad in the center, flanked by Ceres and Diana, with Victorias at the corners of the pronaos and cella roofs. The stair of approach is flanked by statues of Hercules and Mercury.

Tiberius enriched his temple with works of art, and it seems to have become a museum. He obtained a statue of Vesta from Paros (Cass. Dio 55.9.6), and Pliny mentions an Apollo and a Juno by Baton (*HN* 34.73), a Latona with her twin children by Euphranor (34.77), an Aesculapius and a Hygeia by Niceratus (34.80), a Mars and a Mercury by Piston (34.89), and a Ceres, a Jupiter, and a Minerva by Sthennis (34.90). There were also paintings: a bound Marsyas by Zeuxis (35.66), a Liber Pater by Nicias (35.131), and a Cassandra by Theodorus (35.144). There were also four elephants of obsidian, a gift of Augustus (36.196), and a sardonyx that had belonged to Polycrates of Samos and was a gift of Livia (37.4). Dedicatory inscriptions were found in the ruins (*CIL* 6.90–94, 30856–57; *ILS* 153, 3782–83), and others mention an *aedituus* of the temple (*CIL* 6.2204–5, 8703; *ILS* 4998).

The temple is shown on coins of Orbiana, the wife of Alexander Severus (*B. M. Coins, Rom. Emp.* 6.144 no. 307), and an inscription preserved only in the Einsiedeln sylloge (*CIL* 6.89 = *ILS* 3781) records a restoration after it had become dilapidated. It was still standing in the fourth century and was listed in the regionary catalogues in Regio VIII, but seems to have collapsed in the time of Pope Hadrian I (A.D. 772–95, LPD 1.512, 522).

MAAR 5 (1925): 53–77 (H. F. Rebert and H. Marceau); *CQ* 36 (1942): 111–20 (A. Momigliano); *RendPontAcc* 34 (1961–62): 93–110 (M. Guarducci); Nash 1.292–94; *PP* 33 (1978): 260–72 (L. Richardson).

Concordia, Aedes (3): a temple built by Livia to Concordia, according to Ovid (*Fast.* 6.637–38), where a description of the Porticus Liviae (q.v.) immediately follows (639–48). Evidently the porticus and aedes were substantially identical. The Aedificium Eumachiae at Pompeii, dedicated to Concordia Augusta and Pietas, seems to have been built in imitation of this.

PP 33 (1978): 260–72 (L. Richardson); *Historia* 33 (1984): 309–30 (M. B. Flory).

Concordia, Aedicula: a bronze shrine of Concordia set up by the curule aedile Cn. Flavius in 304 B.C. *in Graecostasi* (Pliny, *HN* 33.19) and *in Area Volcani* (Livy 9.46.6), therefore approximately where the later Temple of Concordia stood. If it was not incorporated into the temple when it was built, it must have been destroyed. Pliny tells us that Flavius vowed the temple if he should reconcile the orders of the people after he had alienated the nobility by publishing the calendar of days for legal proceedings. Because public money for a temple was not granted him, he built the shrine from the fines of usurers, and Cornelius (Scipio) Barbatus, pontifex maximus, was then forced by agreement of the people to dictate the proper formula of dedication, although he maintained that only a consul or a general could dedicate a temple.

Concordia Augusta, Ara: A travertine altar, restored as inscribed to Concordia Augusta and standing in front of a travertine statue base, was discovered in Piazza Bocca della Verità at the juncture of Via Teatro di Marcello at a depth of a little over 2 m below present ground level and has been reset in roughly the correct location across from the rectangular temple called Fortuna Virilis. This seems to be remains of a compital sacellum.

RendPontAcc 43 (1970–71): 55–70 (A. M. Colini).

Concordia Nova: a temple decreed by the senate in 44 B.C. in honor of Julius Caesar on the eve of his assassination (Cass. Dio 44.4.5). There is no evidence that this was ever even begun.

S. Weinstock, *Divus Julius* (Oxford 1971), 260–66.

Consentes Dei (Porticus): see **Porticus Deorum Consentium.**

Consus, Ara: an altar of a god, considered the equivalent of Poseidon Hippios, of great antiquity in Rome. It was in his honor that games including horse and chariot races were first held in the Vallis Murcia, where the Circus Maximus came to be. This became the occasion of the rape of the Sabine women (Livy 1.9.6–16; Plutarch, *Rom.* 14.2–7). His altar stood at the *primae metae* of the circus, at the southeast (sphendone) end of the spina, and was kept underground (Dion. Hal. 2.31.2–3; Tertullian, *De Spect.* 5.8). It was exposed on 7 July and 21 August (Tertullian, *De Spect.* 5.8; Degrassi 481, 499–500), at which times burnt sacrifice was offered on it, in July by the sacerdotes publici and in August by the Flamen Quirinalis, attended by the Vestal Virgins. It must also have been exposed for the Consualia on 15 December (Degrassi 538), but about the ceremonies in connection with this last festival we have no information. It is unlikely to have been exposed on 1 January, as Mancini has proposed (Degrassi 388).

Dionysius (2.31.2) thought Consus the Roman equivalent of Poseidon Seischthon, the "earthshaker"; Servius (*ad Aen.* 8.636) thought him Neptunus Equestris. There is now a widespread belief that Consus was a primitive god of agriculture. Whereas in antiquity it was common to connect his name with *consilium,* in modern times it is fashionable to connect it with *condere* and to associate him with the harvest. And other divinities of agriculture are known to have been worshiped in the Circus Maximus (Sessia, Messia, Tutilina [see Tutilinae, Ara, Columna]). But his festivals do not occur at, or even near, dates of real significance in the harvests of Italy and the agricultural year. What we know about him suggests that he was originally, like Terminus, a god of boundaries and associated with the underworld. His altar was at the primae metae of the circus and was one of the turning points of the pomerium of the city of Romulus (Tacitus, *Ann.* 12.24), and the omphalos form of the metae, the ova of the circus, and the interpretation of the omphalos at Delphi as at once the tomb and the egg of the Pytho—in addition to the common use of that form for boundary stones—strengthen the case. Terminus had to receive sacrifice under the open sky, and an opening had to be left in the roof of the Capitoline temple on this account. Might it be that Consus was a sort of antithesis of Terminus and, like the Mundus (see Mundus [2]), had to be covered and concealed, except on special occasions, a guardian spirit of the pomerium in the earth?

Coriaria Septimiana: listed in the regionary catalogues in Regio XIV. Tanneries were regularly relegated to the outskirts of cities because of the stench they produced, and they required water in plentiful supply (cf. Juvenal 14.200–204). So one might expect to find them both up and down river on the outskirts of the Transtiberim. From the evidence of *CIL* 6.1682 = *ILS* 1220, one may presume that Septimius Severus and Caracalla undertook to build extensive tanning works under official control and supervision, and, from the name Septimianum given to the stretch of the right bank of the Tiber from the Aurelian Walls to Porta S. Spirito in the Middle Ages, one might suggest that these were located somewhere here. However, inscriptions (*CIL* 6.1117–18) found near the church of S. Crisogono that mention a *corpus coriariorum magnariorum* suggest that they might have lain farther downstream, and in 1899 a small tannery was found in excavations under the church of S. Cecilia in Trastevere (Nash 1.295–96).

Corneta: The location given by Varro (*Ling.* 5.146) for the Forum Cuppedinis is *ad Corneta*. Paulus (Paulus *ex Fest.* 42L) has it that Forum Cuppedinis was another name for the Macellum (q.v.), which also seems to be the sense of Donatus's note on Terence, *Eun.* 256, although it may be that the Forum Cuppedinis was only part of the larger complex. A gloss (Lindsay, *Gloss. Lat.* 4.56 [pseudo-Placidus]) has been corrected to read: *corneta, locus quem nunc ex parte magna Templum Pacis* (cf. HJ 1n.2). The remains of the Corneta is therefore probably to be identified as the short street between the Basilica Paulli and the Temple of Divus Antoninus et Faustina (Fig. 48).

Corniscae, Divae: a place, perhaps a grove, on the right bank of the Tiber, consecrated to the crows believed to be under the protection of Juno (Paulus *ex Fest.* 56L). A travertine boundary cippus of the republican period from the temenos (*CIL* 6.96 and 30691 = *ILS* 2986 = *ILLRP* 69; cf. also *CIL* 6.30858 = *ILS* 2987) was found between the foot of the Janiculum and the church of S. Francesco a Ripa. Nothing more is known about this cult, and Paulus speaks of it in the past tense.

Crypta Balbi (Fig. 80): mentioned only in the regionary catalogues in Regio IX, but always presumed to have been an adjunct of the Theatrum Balbi (q.v.) and built at the same time. With the recent relocation of the theater in the area previously thought to have been the Circus Flaminius, the crypta are now thought to occupy the area east of the theater. On the evidence of modern investigations and some fragments of the Marble Plan (see Rodriguez pl. 22), this is now believed to have been a three-sided theater portico directly attached to the theater, with windowed bays giving to an interior garden or court and a semicircular exedral niche opening on axis out of its east side. This niche had an interior line of columns that was presumably a small semicircular colonnade around a separate garden, but its purpose is not clear. The treatment of the rectangular court is also obscure.

An important building long thought to be the Crypta Balbi, known from several Renaissance drawings and from the remains of one bay still surviving in Via S. Maria de'Calderari, is now nameless. If Peruzzi's plan of the whole edifice (Wurm 2: pl. 477; cf. Nash 1.298–99) is anywhere near correct, this was a double arcade, five bays by thirteen, around a core of baroque planning with semicircular niches ending alternate bays and a series of five round chambers down the middle. The storey above this had blind arcades, double the number of those in the lower storey, lit by square and rectangular windows. There is no indication of what purpose the building served. The architecture suggests a Severan date or later (Nash 1.297–300).

D. Manacorda, *Archeologia urbana a Roma: Il progetto della Crypta Balbi* (Florence 1982); *Roma, archeologia nel centro* (1985), 2.546–53 (D. Manacorda), 554–56 (S. Tortorella), 557–64 (A. Gabucci); *CEFR* 98 (1987): 597–610 (D. Manacorda).

Curia: see **Aedes, Aedicula,** etc.

Curia Acculeia: mentioned only by Varro (*Ling.* 6.23) as the place where on the Angeronalia a sacrifice to Angerona was offered. Macrobius (*Sat.* 1.10.7) says that on the feast of Angerona, 21 December, the pontifices performed a rite in the sacellum of Volupia, because an image of Angerona with her mouth bound and sealed stood on the altar of Volupia. In the fasti (Praen., Maff.) this day is labeled Divalia (Degrassi 541–42). Pliny (*HN* 3.65) explains the bound mouth as exemplifying the silence to be maintained with respect to the sacred name of Rome, and that may also be the intention of Verrius Flaccus in a much-mutilated note in the Fasti Praenestini (Degrassi 139). Because 21 December is the winter solstice, one would expect the celebrations on that day to focus on the new year.

Macrobius (*Sat.* 1.10.7) says Verrius Flaccus derived the name of Angerona from her dispelling *angores ac sollicitudines animorum*. He adds that Masurius explains her presence on the altar of Volupia: *quod qui suos dolores anxietatesque dissimulant perveniant patientiae beneficio ad maximam voluptatem.* Such explanations can be dismissed as fanciful, as can another from *angina* (Paulus *ex Fest.* 16L). The Curia Acculeia was probably simply an unroofed enclosure, like the Curia Calabra, possibly an augural station for observation of celestial signs attendant on the solstice.

Varro suggests a connection between the Curia Acculeia and Acca Larentia, whose feast came on 23 December, two days after the Divalia, and whose tomb was in the Velabrum near the Porta Romana (Varro, *Ling.* 6.24). If the Sacellum Volupiae and the Curia Acculeia were not identical, the three places must have been contiguous, or nearly so, clustered together at the foot of the Palatine, a bit to the east of S. Giorgio in Velabro. None needs to have been very large.

It appears that Divalia and Curia Acculeia were names devised to conceal the name of Angerona, if indeed that was her true name. If her bound mouth had to do with the secret name of Rome and the location of her shrine just outside the Porta Romana is significant, we may see her as a protectress of the gate.

(For a very different view that would put the Curia Acculeia in the vicinity of the Lacus Iuturnae, see Coarelli 1983, 227–82.)

Curia Athletarum: collegial headquarters of the organized athletes of Rome who styled themselves Herculanei, at a place granted them by Antoninus Pius in A.D. 143 (*IG* 14.1055). Numerous dedicatory inscriptions in Greek (*IG* 14.1054–55, 1102–10 = *IGUR* 235–45, 251) found between S. Pietro in Vincoli and S. Martino ai Monti attest to its presence somewhere here in close proximity to the Thermae Traiani and its continued existence until the fourth century. In the one Latin inscription mentioning it (*CIL* 6.10154 = *ILS* 5164), it is called Acletarum Curia; the inscription has numerous other touches that show it is the work of someone whose Latin was very imperfect. The curia cannot be identified with any existing remains. Because the inscriptions mention such sports as boxing and the pancratium, these athletes must have been those who performed in the public games, especially in the amphitheater and circus. Their entitlement to a curia raises imponderable questions; one might have expected rather an atrium or a basilica.

Curia Calabra: Servius (*ad Aen.* 8.654) equates this with the Casa Romuli in Capitolio (q.v.). Macrobius (*Sat.* 1.15.10) says it was next to the Casa Romuli. Because Macrobius says that on the Kalends the pontifex minor performed a *res divina* to Juno in the Curia Calabra (*Sat.* 1.15.19) and that the people attending were summoned only *iuxta Curiam Calabram* (*Sat.* 1.15.10), we should think of it probably as an enclosure or precinct in front of an augural hut *in Area Capitolina*, like that of the Auguraculum (which Vitruvius [2.1.5] says was similar), that was then given the name Casa Romuli because of its similarity to the Casa Romuli on the Palatine and because Romulus was believed to have built it. Festus (180–82L) supports the idea that its use was purely religious, so an elaborate structure would have been superfluous.

It seems to have been originally a station, or templum, occupied by the pontifex minor for observation of the new moon. On the Kalends of the month, after a sacrifice by the Rex Sacrificulus and the pontifex minor, the people were summoned *in comitia calata* and announcement was made of when the Nones and Ides of the month would fall and of the holidays and celebrations proper to that month. Varro (*Ling.* 6.27) and Macrobius (*Sat.* 1.15.10–19) believed that the name Calabra was derived from *calare*, "to summon." The etymology is probably correct, but the sense of the word is rather "proclaim" than "call together." Jordan (1.497) thought the curia should be on the east side of the Area Capitolina, but the new moon is first observed in the west as it sets, and the view of it would have to be unimpeded. A place beside the southwest flank of the Capitoline temple might best suit the requirements.

Curia Hostilia: the original senate house of Rome standing on the north side of the Comitium on axis with it, so the steps of the Comitium formed a stair of access to the curia and the Comitium was a forecourt, or vestibulum, to it (Livy 45.24.12). The construction was assigned to Tullus Hostilius (Varro, *Ling.* 5.155), and it was regarded as very venerable, though it must have been rebuilt after the fire of the Gauls, if not more frequently. Throughout history it was, like the Comitium, an inaugurated templum (Varro *ap.* A. *Gellium* 14.7.7).

On the exterior of its west wall was displayed the Tabula Valeria (q.v.), a painting showing the victory of M'. Valerius Messalla over Hiero and the Carthaginians in 263 B.C. (Pliny, *HN* 35.22); according to Pliny this was the first such picture in Rome. This was later incorporated in the Basilica Porcia, in which the builders either used this wall as a party wall in its construction or transferred the picture from its original location, where the new building would have hidden it, to a new parallel wall. The latter is more likely right (cf. Basilica Porcia), but cf. Asconius *in Milon.* 29 (Stangl 32): *Porcia Basilica quae erat ei (sc. curiae) iuncta ambusta est.*

Sulla restored and enlarged the curia in 80 B.C., at which time the statues of Pythagoras and Alcibiades that had stood at the corners *(cornua)* of the Comitium were removed (Pliny, *HN* 34.26). In 52 B.C. the mob of his henchmen and supporters built Clodius's pyre of the furniture of the curia, and in the conflagration it and the Basilica Porcia burned (Cicero, *Milon.* 90; Asconius *in Milon.* 29 [Stangl 32]; Cass. Dio 40.49.2–3). It was then rebuilt by Sulla's son Faustus and again enlarged (Cicero, *Fin.* 5.2). For reasons that are not entirely clear, the new curia met with little favor, and in 44 B.C. it was decided to rebuild it (Cass. Dio 44.5.2). Dio's explanation that the senate wished to erase the name of Sulla from the curia seems improbable. The other explanation put forward, that a temple of Felicitas (see Felicitas [2]) was to be built on the site of the old curia, which

Lepidus eventually built, is almost equally perplexing, all trace of any such temple having completely disappeared, as well as all notice apart from Dio's casual remark. The rebuilding of the curia was eventually carried out by Augustus, the Curia Iulia.

The indications are that the Comitium was oriented to the cardinal points of the compass; the line of the façade of the Carcer seems to confirm this. Until the First Punic War, at midday the *accensus consulis,* standing in the curia, looked south between a rostra and a graecostasis and announced noon when he saw the sun there (Pliny, *HN* 7.212). What the landmarks were and where they lay are matters of some dispute; at so early a period they might have been quite different from their later equivalents.

Curia Iulia: the curia begun by Julius Caesar in 44 B.C. to replace the Curia Hostilia as rebuilt by Faustus Sulla (Cass. Dio 44.5.2, 45.17.8) and completed by Augustus in 29 (*RG* 19; Cass. Dio 51.22.1). As completed, it was preceded by a Chalcidicum; this is shown on coins (*B. M. Coins, Rom. Rep.* 2.16 nos. 4358–59; *B. M. Coins, Rom. Emp.* 1.103 nos. 631–32) as a porch with wide-spaced Ionic columns raised on a high podium. It extends beyond the façade of the curia to either side, and, because there is no stair in front, it must be presumed that stairs or ramps led up to it from behind. A very light architrave joins the columns, and if there was a roof, it does not appear. On the coins the gable of the roof of the curia is shown surmounted by large acroteria; a Victoria is mounted on a globe at the peak, and warrior figures are at the corners. In the pediment is a single figure of uncertain character. In the interior of the curia Augustus put a statue of Victoria from Tarentum (Cass. Dio 51.22.1) and two paintings, an encaustic Nemea by Nicias and a double portrait by Philocares (Pliny, *HN* 35.27–28).

This curia was *in Comitio* (Pliny, *HN* 35.27) and probably had the same orientation as the curia of Diocletian, aligned with the tabernae of the Forum Iulium, but it may have stood somewhat to the northwest of Diocletian's to allow a place for the Chalcidicum's lateral colonnade and the Ianus Geminus (but see Morselli and Tortorici, 22–27). Domitian rebuilt the curia, evidently in connection with his work on the Forum Transitorium (Hieron. *a. Abr.* 2106). Because at that time he built a new Ianus Quadrifrons (see Ianus Quadrifrons [2]), it is probable that he destroyed the Ianus Geminus and relocated the curia in its present position. At the same time he must have eliminated or redesigned the Chalcidicum. The curia burned down in the fire of Carinus of A.D. 283, and Diocletian restored it (Chron. 148). It is Diocletian's building that we see today (Fig. 39).

It is a large plain hall of brick-faced concrete, a broad rectangle 25.20 m deep and 17.61 m wide with a very lofty roof, which necessitated the addition of a great rectangular buttress at each corner. It was approached by a stair that ran across most of the façade, returning to the façade at the ends. The lower part of the façade was veneered with plates of marble, and the parts above were finished with stucco. There is a single axial door, above which are three large rectangular windows with slightly bowed lintels. The low pediment is framed by travertine consoles supporting a brick cornice. There is a single window high in each side wall of the building and another in back, where there are also doors to either side leading to the main hall, the precise function of which is unknown.

The interior has been restored according to the evidence found in the dismantling of the church of S. Adriano, into which it had been converted. To either side are three broad low steps to accommodate the curule chairs of the more important senators, the top one broader than the others for those who stood. At the far end, between the doors mentioned above, is a low dais of two steps for the presiding magistrate. The central floor is paved with panels of opus sectile, in which porphyry and serpentine figure large. Along each side wall is a marble wainscoting finished with a molding, above which are three widely spaced niches, the center one with an arched head, the others flat-headed. These seem to have had rich architectural frames. Nothing remains of the decoration of the upper walls.

The curia was converted to use as the church of S. Adriano under Pope Honorius I (A.D. 625–638). The bronze doors were removed in the seventeenth century by Borromini, restored and relocated to serve the baptistery of S. Giovanni in Laterano. At that time several coins were found between the plates, including one of Domitian. In 1935–1938 the church was deconsecrated, and the curia was restored to its ancient form. It is now used for the mounting of archaeological exhibitions of a temporary nature.

To the northwest of the curia other buildings were added between the time of Augustus and the rebuilding of Diocletian. The plan of these is shown in a drawing by Antonio da Sangallo il Giovane (Lugli 1946, 133 fig. 27). These buildings seem not to have been in close sequence with the curia, but aligned with it. They are commonly identified as the Secretarium Senatus and Atrium Minervae and ascribed to Domitian. Nash proved this identification mistaken. That to the northwest, of which remains were built into the northeast and southeast walls of the church of SS. Luca e Martina, is in all probability the Athenaeum of Hadrian (Aur. Vict., *Caes.* 14.3), known also as the Atrium Minervae, an auditorium for rhetorical and poetical performances. Sangallo's drawing shows that next to it was a long narrow hall with a row of pillars down the middle, the walls broken into a series of rectangular bays, which might well have held cupboards in which to keep books. This then would be the library known to have been attached to the Athenaeum (Sid. Apoll., *Epist.* 2.9.4). The area between this and the curia was probably an open court.

A. Bartoli, *Curia senatus* (Rome 1963); Nash 1.301–3; *RömMitt* 85 (1978): 359–69 (L. Richardson); C. Morselli and E. Tortorici, *Curia, Forum Iulium, Forum Transitorium* (Rome 1989), especially 1–263.

Curiae Novae: built at an uncertain date to replace the Curiae Veteres of Romulus, which had become too small to accommodate the population of a curia at the ceremonies performed there. The Curiae Novae were next to the Compitum Fabricium (Festus 180–82L), which was very probably adjacent to the Vicus Fabrici listed last for the vici in Regio I (*CIL* 6.975 = *ILS* 6073). There is no adequate reason for believing this was the street in the valley dividing the Palatine from the Caelian (the modern Via di S. Gregorio), as that would involve giving Regio I a strangely gerrymandered shape. More likely it was one of the streets in the neighborhood of S. Gregorio Magno, perhaps one of the Septem Viae (q.v.) running into the square southeast of the Circus Maximus. The curiae were probably only a precinct, perhaps with an enclosing wall, but, because this had to be fairly large, we should probably look for it away from, rather than toward, the heart of the city. Here twenty-six of the thirty curiae met for religious observances.

Curia Octaviae: mentioned only by Pliny (*HN* 36.28) in connection with a statue of Cupid holding a thunderbolt, the authorship of which was assigned to both Scopas and Praxiteles, while the model was agreed to have been Alcibiades. Whether Octavia would have wished to add a curia to the other buildings in her Porticus (q.v.) is doubtful, because the Temple of Bellona was nearby, and the lack of any mention of a senate meeting here adds to the mystery. Moreover, the portico is well represented on the Marble Plan, and there does not seem much free space available for the insertion of a curia. The senate might better have met in one of the temples here. It has therefore been suggested that the curia was identical with the *schola* or, better, *scholae* that appear behind the temples on the plan and are mentioned by Pliny (*HN* 35.114, 36.22) as the location of a famous Cupid by Praxiteles, as well as other works of art. However, scholae do not seem suitable

places for meetings, except of a small informal sort. In these circumstances it seems best to reserve judgment; the curia may, of course, have been for some special purpose; it does not have to have been for meetings of the senate.

Curia in Palatio: mentioned only once by Tacitus (*Ann.* 2.37.3) for the year A.D. 16. The word *curia* is almost certainly used casually, and the Bibliotheca Apollinis Palatini (q.v.) meant. The senate met here frequently during the old age of Augustus, and the mention of a portrait of the orator Hortensius *inter oratores* seems' to clinch the matter (cf. Suetonius, *Aug.* 29.3).

Curia Pompeii: a meeting place for the senate, an annex of the Porticus Pompeii (q.v.), where Julius Caesar was assassinated (Cicero, *Div.* 2.23; Plutarch, *Caes.* 66.1–2, *Brut.* 14.1–2). Augustus later removed the statue of Pompey that stood in the curia, and the curia was walled up (Suetonius, *Iul.* 88, *Aug.* 31.5); later it was converted into a latrine (Cass. Dio 47.19.1). It seems likely that the enormous base of blocks of tufa on a platform of concrete behind Temple B in the Area Sacra di Largo Argentina (q.v.) is part of the fill that destroyed the curia and the latrine south of this the one meant by Dio.

G. Marchetti Longhi, *L'area sacra del Largo Argentina* (Rome 1960), 76–78; Nash 1.148.

Curia Pompiliana: a meeting place of the senate mentioned only in two passages in the Historia Augusta (S.H.A. *Aurel.* 41.3, *Tacit.* 3.2). It is generally presumed to be an alternate name for the Curia Iulia invented to suggest the return of an era of peace and innocence, but there is no confirmation of this explanation (cf. Amm. Marc. 14.6.6). The Curia Iulia is regularly called simply Curia in our sources, or even Senatus (cf., e.g., the regionary catalogues), although Aulus Gellius 14.7.7 may be taken to indicate that even after Domitian's rebuilding it still formally carried the name Iulia.

Curia Saliorum Collinorum: a sacrarium (cf. Val. Max. 1.8.11) on the Quirinal where the Salii Collini kept their sacred implements (Dion. Hal. 2.70). These were a priesthood of twelve young men founded by Tullus Hostilius on the pattern of the Salii Palatini; they danced in military regalia *(paludati)* and carried, or were accompanied by, ancilia (bronze shields), one of which was supposed to have descended from heaven in the time of Numa. Their dancing began 1 March and continued through the month at different places. Because the Salii were closely connected with the worship of Mars, one might expect their sacrarium to have been in the precinct of Quirinus, but by tradition they antedated that precinct and most other things on the hill.

Curia Saliorum Palatinorum: a sacrarium (Val. Max. 1.8.11) on the Palatine in which was kept the lituus of Romulus (Cicero, *Div.* 1.30; Val. Max. 1.8.11; Plutarch, *Cam.* 32), presumably together with other sacred implements and the archives of the priesthood. However, the ancilia, their special attribute, the bronze shields made on the pattern of one that was supposed to have descended from heaven, were kept in the Regia. The Palatine curia was probably a very small building, but an independent one.

Curia Tifata: see **Tifata Curia.**

Curiae Veteres: Varro (*Ling.* 5.155) says that curiae were of two sorts, one being a place such as the Curiae Veteres, where priests attended to matters of religion, the other a place where the senate attended to human affairs. Festus (180–82L) adds the interesting information that Romulus created the Curiae Veteres and divided the people and religious observances *(sacra)* into thirty parts. Subsequently, the Curiae Veteres became too small, and the Curiae Novae were built, but a ceremony of evocation, or exauguration, was required for each curia before moving to the new place, and the observances of four curiae could not be disturbed, there being religious obstacles. So the four, the Foriensis, Rapta, Veliensis, and Velitia, continued to perform their rites in the Curiae Veteres. Furthermore, the Curiae Veteres were one of the points by which the line of the pomerium of the Romulean city was defined (Tacitus, *Ann.* 12.24), between the Ara Consi at the southeast end of the spina of the Circus Maximus and the Sacellum Larum, so it must have been in the neighborhood of the Meta Sudans toward the Palatine, for the points Tacitus lists are all turning points and inside the pomerium.

It is striking that a belt of very ancient altars, buildings, and places of religious importance surrounded the foot of the Palatine within the pomerium. Comparatively few of these were temples; only that of Vesta springs to mind, and it was clearly of very special character because it had to shelter the sacred fire. More were simply places—the spring of Juturna, the tomb of Acca Larentia, the Lupercal—of high veneration but no architectural embellishment until a comparatively late period, if then. They seem by and large to go back to a time when the Romans did not have images of their gods and worshiped in the open air, in sacred groves, at springs, and on heights and mountaintops. If the Curiae Veteres were indeed Romulean, they ought to have been

an enclosure, a templum rather than a building, and that is what Varro suggests. It was especially for the priests, but they performed on behalf of the people, curia by curia, and, if in time it became too small, the members of each curia must have attended.

Each curia had two priests, a curio and a flamen, elected for life by the membership and chosen for their suitability for the office. A priest could not be physically deformed or maimed, or of insufficient means. His wife had to perform whatever rites there were from which men were excluded, or for which women were required. And both were to be assisted by their children. If they were childless, they were to have chosen the most beautiful boy and girl of the curia to be their attendants. To each curia were assigned gods and genii to worship, and most of the worship was very simple, offerings of barley cakes, spelt, first fruits, and the like. And for each curia a banqueting hall was built where all the members feasted in common on their holidays (Dion. Hal. 2.21.2–23.6).

These banqueting halls cannot be the Curiae Veteres. A complex of thirty banqueting halls is unthinkable. It is also impossible that the great gods of Rome were assigned to the curiae, for these had their own flamens and were worshiped by the Roman people as a whole. The gods of the curiae must have been minor divinities, perhaps gods whose province had been largely forgotten, but whose names were remembered. But all of these were important to the well-being of Rome.

The curiae were, at least originally, geographical, as some of their names show: Foriensis, Veliensis, Tifata. Some of them, like the tribes, carry old family names and must refer to areas in which these families dominated: Titia, Faucia. Possibly these were, or seemed, a distinct majority, and hence the explanation of the derivation of their names from those of the Sabine women carried off in the rape (Livy 1.13.6; Plutarch, *Rom.* 14.6). The proposition that each of the three original tribes of Rome was divided into ten curiae seems logical but cannot be proved. If the tribes, as their names—Ramnes, Tities, Luceres—suggest, represented the ethnic divisions of the city after union with the Sabines, one might look for a Latin quarter in the area of the Palatine/Velia/Oppius, a Sabine quarter on the Quirinal and Viminal, and an Etruscan quarter in the area of the Caelian and Subura Minor (the basin of the Colosseum), the localities traditionally associated with these peoples. In that case it looks as though a balance among these peoples was being deliberately maintained.

The tradition seems to be that the banqueting halls that fostered brotherhood among the members of the individual curiae were scattered about the city, each at the center of, or in an important position in, its district. But to emphasize the unity of the city on important holidays of the curiae they gathered at a common templum to perform certain rites and then returned to their own banqueting halls for the holiday feast that followed. The most important of these festivals was the Fornacalia in February, *feriae conceptivae*, a movable feast, the last day of which was the Quirinalia (17 February). In the course of the Fornacalia occurred the Lupercalia (15 February) and probably the Parentalia (beginning 13 February). Apparently just before the beginning of the Fornacalia the priests of the curiae assembled under the guidance of the curio maximus and determined the order in which the curiae would perform their rites, except for the last day, reserved for those who missed, or who did not know, their proper curia, the *feriae stultorum*. Probably the order was determined by lot and changed every year, with resulting confusion (Ovid, *Fast.* 2.527–32). But the point of the sequence seems to be that a major part of the rite had to take place in the Curiae Veteres (and later Novae), and the members of the curia, as well as the priests, were expected to attend.

The Fornacalia seems to have been a double celebration, private and public. Privately sacrifices were made *ad fornacem*, at the bakery one frequented (Paulus *ex Fest.* 82L). These were made *farris torrendi gratia* (Paulus *ex Fest.* 82L; cf. also Pliny, *HN* 18.8); that is, to ensure proper preparation of the grain for consumption and sacrifice for the year to come. Pliny adds that the Fornacalia was also a festival dedicated to the boundary stones *(terminis agrorum)*, so it seems likely that part of the ceremony consisted in beating the bounds of both private property and the curiae. With the waning of winter and the beginning of work in the fields, a check on the boundary stones is a logical ritual. In the public part of the festival there may have been a beating of the bounds of the Curiae Veteres, because no one suggests that there was an oven there. Otherwise we may imagine a sacrifice in a templum shared by all Romans to the gods of each curia individually.

The other great holiday of the curiae was the Fordicidia on 15 April, a very primitive ritual in which a pregnant cow was sacrificed on the Capitoline and one for each of the thirty curiae of the city. These were sacrificed to Tellus. The attendants of the Virgo Vestalis Maxima then tore the fetus from the womb of the mother, and this was burned and the ashes kept by the Vestal Virgins for use as a *suffimen* on the Parilia a few days later (cf. Ovid, *Fast.* 4.633–40). Because Ovid is specific in saying that one was sacrificed on the Capitoline but then reverts to the singular: "pars cadit arce Iovis. ter denas curia vaccas / accipit, et largo sparsa cruore madet . . ." he must mean that the thirty of the curiae were all sacrificed in the Curiae Veteres and Curiae Novae. These then would have good reason to be awash with blood, but this would simplify the task of the ministri of the Vestalis Maxima and the transportation of the ashes to the Temple of Vesta, where they were kept. The carcasses of the sacrificial victims were presumably subsequently taken to the banqueting halls of the individual curiae for roasting and eating. Because the Parilia, as the birthday of Rome, was a festival ascribed to Romulus (Plutarch, *Rom.* 12) and connected with the Fordicidia, we must ask whether it also, as an urban and public ritual, was not celebrated in the Curiae Veteres. Propertius (4.4.73–78) suggests by *pagana . . . fercula* that the holiday feast was held at various centers throughout the city. But Ovid seems clear (*Fast.* 4.721–34) that the ceremony of lustration took place early in the morning with materials fetched from the Temple of Vesta and was very solemn, the drunken leaping over bonfires characteristic of the day being a repetition in parody of the lustration ritual late in the afternoon. It seems likely that the morning lustration ceremony originally took place in the Curiae Veteres, and this also might explain the difficulties the restricted size gave rise to. Because the institution of both the Fordicidia (Ovid, *Fast.* 4.641–72) and the Fornacalia (Pliny, *HN* 18.8) is explicitly ascribed to Numa, while among those festivals said to have been established by Romulus (Plutarch, *Rom.* 21: the Parilia, Matronalia, Carmentalia, and Lupercalia) only the Parilia seems appropriate to the Curiae Veteres, the case for locating it there is somewhat stronger.

RendLinc, ser. 8.34 (1979): 345–47 (F. Castagnoli).

Cybele, Tholus: see **Magna Mater.**

Dea Carna, Sacrum: a shrine on the Caelian dedicated on the Kalends of June (Degrassi 464) by M. Iunius Brutus in fulfillment of a vow following the expulsion of the Tarquins (Macrobius, *Sat.* 1.12.31–33). This divinity presided over the human vital organs and received sacrifice of bean porridge and bacon fat. Tertullian (*Ad Nat.* 2.9.7) says that the altars of imported *(adventiciorum)* divinities were erected *ad fanum Carnae,* whereas those of native *(publicorum)* ones were set up on the Palatine, and that this could be seen in his day. Carna must have been a very ancient divinity, but seems unknown outside Rome. Her shrine was probably no more than an enclosure.

Dea Nenia, Sacellum: a shrine outside the Porta Viminalis, mentioned by Festus (156–57L), of the goddess of lamentations sung at funerals (Augustine, *De civ. D.* 6.9). The area is almost entirely devoid of ancient monuments, and the shrine is otherwise unknown.

Dea Roma: see **Roma, Dea.**

Dea Satriana, Lucus: known only from an inscription known in the sixteenth century and now lost (*CIL* 6.114 = 30695 = *ILS* 3989), supposed to have been found near S. Pietro. The divinity is presumed to be a family goddess of the Gens Satria, but nothing further is known about her.

CAR 1-H, 87 p. 90.

Dea Suria, Templum: known only by conjecture, as a correction of *templum Iasurae,* an entry in Chron. 147 for the reign of Alexander Severus (*Hermes* [1872], 314–22 [H. Jordan]). The goddess in question would be Atargatis, the counterpart of Hadad (Iuppiter Heliopolitanus), together with whom she seems regularly to have been worshiped in Rome. See Lucus Furrinae and Iuppiter Heliopoli-tanus. For the most part the worship of the Syrian gods seems to have been centered outside the city, especially along Via Portuensis.

PAPS 125.5 (1981): 372–81 (R. E. A. Palmer).

Dea Viriplaca, Sacellum: a shrine on the Palatine to which, according to Valerius Maximus (2.1.6), husbands and wives who quarreled were accustomed to resort and, having pled their cases in turn, to return home in harmony. Although Valerius Maximus uses the present tense for the shrine, he uses the imperfect for the custom and lists it among the *instituta antiqua.* The identity of the goddess is perhaps deliberately mysterious.

Decem Tabernae: listed in the regionary catalogues in Regio VI after the Cohors III Vigilum *(Cur.)* and the Castra Praetoria *(Not.)* and before the Gallinae Albae (q.v.) in both, therefore presumed to be toward the western end of the Viminal or in the valley between the Viminal and the Quirinal. It is supposed to have been mentioned in an inscription known at the end of the fifteenth century but now lost (Jordan 2.121–22). It is quite uncertain whether it was a street or a building complex.

Decenniae: a name appearing in medieval documents for the valley of the Aqua Marrana southwest of the Lateran, just outside the Aurelian Walls east of the Porta Metrovia. The inhabitants of the area are called Decennenses in the decree of Tarracius Bassus of ca. A.D. 370 (*CIL* 6.31893 = *ILS* 6072). Cf. Jordan 2.318; HJ 220. It has been conjectured that the ancient form of the name was Decennium, but for this there is no evidence, the origin of the name being quite unknown.

Dei Consentes: see **Porticus Deorum Consentium.**

Delubrum: see **Aedes, Aedicula,** etc.

Diaetae Mammaeae: apartments created in the Palatine palace by Alexander Severus, named in honor of his mother, Iulia Mammaea, but popularly known as *ad Mammam* (S.H.A. *Alex. Sev.* 26.9). It is uncertain where they were, but they should be conspicuous rooms enjoying a view, perhaps in a tower or towers overlooking the Circus Maximus.

Diana (1): a temple on the Vicus Patricius, the only temple of Diana in Rome from which men were excluded (Plutarch, *Quaest. Rom.* 3). Nothing else is known about it.

Diana (2): a tetrastyle temple shown on a coin of Augustus of 29–27 B.C. (*B. M. Coins, Rom. Emp.* 1 Augustus no. 643 pl. 15.14). In the center stands a trophy on a prow, while *aplustra* are used as acroteria. In the pediment is a triskelion. Whether this was actually a temple of Diana, despite a bust of her on the obverse, and whether, if so, it was in Rome, is doubtful.

Diana, Aedes (1) (Fig. 14): usually called Diana Aventina (Propertius 4.8.29; Martial 6.64.13) or Aventinensis (Festus 164L; Val. Max. 7.3.1), the oldest temple on the Aventine and the earliest temple to this goddess in Rome. Martial (7.73.1; 12.18.3) called the hill Collis Dianae. The temple was traditionally founded by Servius Tullius and paid for by a league of Latin towns to be a Latin equivalent of the temple of Diana of the Ephesians, at which it was believed all the Ionian cities worshiped individually and collectively (Varro, *Ling.* 5.43; Livy 1.45.2–6; Dion. Hal. 4.26; [Aur. Vict.,] *De Vir. Ill.* 7.9). It was near the Baths of Sura (Martial 6.64.13) and was rebuilt in the time of Augustus by L. Cornificius (Suetonius, *Aug.* 29.5), after which it was also known as Diana Cornificiana (*CIL* 6.4305 = *ILS* 1732). It is almost certainly represented on a fragment of the Marble Plan (*FUR* pl. 23; Rodriguez pl. 15), although of the name only CORNIFICIA[survives. It is shown as octastyle, peripteral (possibly sine postico), with a pronaos five bays deep and an extra file of columns added on the line of each lateral cella wall. There is a broad stair of approach across the whole temple front and an ample precinct with a double colonnade or lines of small trees along at least one side and probably both, and perhaps a single line, wider spaced, close to the precinct wall at the façade end. The fragment can be placed with great precision, thanks to a finished edge, and we see that the temple must have stood on the plateau of the Aventine, away from the brow, and faced east.

It was called by a variety of names, besides aedes (templum, fanum, etc.), and the whole complex seems to have been commonly known as the Dianium (Orosius 5.12.6; *CIL* 6.33922 = *ILS* 7570). The day of dedication was 13 August, the Ides of August, shared with a number of other celebrations (Degrassi 494–96). The holiday was especially celebrated by slaves throughout Italy (Festus 460L).

The similarities and differences between this Diana and the Diana Nemorensis of Aricia on the Lago di Nemi are striking. Diana Nemorensis was worshiped in the depths of a crater on a shelf of land beside a lake, in contrast to Iuppiter Latiaris, worshiped in the grove crowning the Alban Mount, the highest point in the Alban Hills. Both groves were the cult centers of leagues of Latin towns, but while the festival of the Alban Mount seems to have been broadly inclusive (Dionysius, 4.49.2, says that in the time of Tarquinius Superbus there were forty-seven member peoples, whereas Pliny, *HN* 3.69–71, implies that there were even more), the league of Diana Nemorensis was small and exclusive. Cato (*ap. Priscian.* 4.21; Keil, *Gramm. Lat.* 2.129), apparently quoting from the dedication formula, lists only eight members, and neither Rome nor Alba Longa is among them. It looks as though, after Rome had taken over control of the Feriae Latinae, a small group of the stronger Latin towns had banded together to form a new league that Rome could not control or be a member of. If Servius Tullius's sanctuary on the Aventine was founded in response to this and welcomed all the towns of the Latins, it can be seen as a shrewd political move with interesting religious implications.

At the annual festival on the Ides of August, the representatives of the member towns met there and settled any dispute between towns that might have arisen in the course of the year by arbitration of the other members (Dion. Hal. 4.26.3–5). If the sanctuary was as old as tradition has it, it was probably originally a grove on the highest part of the Aventine. A substantial temple would not have been built before the construction of the Temple of Iuppiter Capitolinus. The rules governing the precinct and its rites were especially elaborate and inscribed in full detail in the archaic Greek alphabet on a bronze stele set up in the precinct; Dionysius (4.26) examined this. It was known as the Lex Arae Dianae (further evidence that there was originally no temple building) and served as a model for similar constitutions (*CIL* 3.1933 = *ILS* 4907; *CIL* 11.361, 12.4333 = *ILS* 112). On this law, see R. E. A. Palmer, *Roman Religion and the Roman Empire: Five Essays* (Philadelphia 1974), 57–78.

The worship of Diana at Nemi must have been very old and, though it was immensely popular, had a dark and bloody side, as well as many rituals whose explanation was neither easy nor obvious. The worship of Diana on the Aventine was worked out in great detail and inscribed on bronze; it seems to have been untainted by violence or mystery. Instead, it emphasized community, asylum, and arbitration, the brotherhood of the Latins. The Romans claimed to have modeled it on a pan-Ionian temple of Ephesus and also claimed that the cult statue traced its descent from a xoanon in the Ephesian temple by way of Massilia (Strabo 4.1.4–5 [179–80]). The Massiliote model is evidently shown on coins of L. Hostilius Saserna (Crawford 448/3, pl. 53), an archaic figure with heavy hair falling on the shoulders and a spiked crown, armed with a spear with a curiously beaded shaft, and accompanied by a diminutive stag. This is not at all the Diana of the Ephesians, nor yet the triple Diana of Aricia. It has the frontality of the archaic, and the drapery covering the legs is done in archaic fashion, with a strong center fold falling straight between the legs and looped folds falling away from this around the legs to either side, but the trailing sleeves hanging from the elbows look archaistic, as does the crown. If Saserna's die cutters were following the cult statue in Massilia, it may have been a replacement made comparatively late. If they were working from the Diana of the Aventine, as one would think natural and probable, they may have made incorrect sketches in accordance with their notions of archaic drapery, for Strabo seems explicit in his account of this statue, as though he had examined its history closely.

The connection with Ephesus was, then, a fancied one in constitution, rather than cult, and in the Ephesian temple's right of asylum (Strabo 14.1.23 [641]), which was famous. The Massiliote statue may have been an afterthought. The Hekate of Menestratos from Ephesus, a marble statue of great brilliance, was set behind the temple proper (Pliny, *HN* 36.32).

Besides the stele of bronze on which was engraved the agreement of Rome and the Latin cities, probably the same as that known as the Lex Arae Dianae, there was another with the Lex Icilia de Aventino Publicando of 456 B.C. (Dion. Hal. 10.32) and probably a good many ancient documents of the same sort. Censorinus (*D. N.* 23.6) says one of the oldest sundials in Rome was here. There were also the horns of a cow of enormous size, to which a curious legend was attached (Livy 1.45.4–5; Val. Max. 7.3.1; [Aur. Vict.,] *De Vir. Ill.* 7). The temple was still standing in the fourth century and is listed in the regionary catalogues, but no trace of it has been found in modern times.

The origins of this cult were the subject of an extended debate between A. Alföldi and A. Momigliano. The positions of these two great scholars are perhaps best set forth in A. Alföldi, *Early Rome and the Latins* (Ann Arbor, Mich. 1965), 85–100, and *RendLinc*, ser. 8.17 (1962): 387–96 (A. Momigliano).

Roma, archeologia nel centro (1985), 2.442–51 (A. Cassatella and L. Vendittelli); *REA* 89 (1987): 47–61 (M. Gras); *CEFR* 98 (1987): 713–45 (L. Quilici).

Diana, Aedes (2): a temple vowed by M. Aemilius Lepidus in 187 B.C. (Livy 39.2.8) and dedicated in 179 (Livy 40.52.1) *in Circo Flaminio*, 23 December (Degrassi 544–45). It is linked with the Temple of Iuno Regina in Circo Flaminio, also built by Lepidus and dedicated on the same day, though with slightly different games for the dedication of each, Diana receiving only two days of *ludi scaenici* to Juno's three. The location of the temple is a puzzle; it might have stood opposite the Temple of Juno on the opposite side of the circus. It does not figure in history later.

For a possible reconstruction of this temple by Octavian to celebrate his naval victory at Naulochus, see *DialArch* 2 (1968): 191–209 (F. Coarelli).

Diana, Sacellum: a shrine on the Caeliolus described by Cicero (*Har. Resp.* 32) as *maximum et sanctissimum*, removed by L. Calpurnius Piso not long before 58 B.C. Cicero says many people living in the vicinity were accustomed to perform *sacrificia gentilicia* there, which suggests that it was not a major monument, possibly even a compital shrine. A more precise location for it is impossible.

Diana Planciana, Aedes: a temple known from inscriptions and discovery of material, notably part of a statue, in 1932 under the cellars of the Angelicum at the corner of the Salita del Grillo and Via Panisperna, therefore on Vicus Longus. It was probably built by Cn. Plancius, curule aedile in 55 or 54 B.C., who put Diana and her attributes on his coins.

RendPontAcc 43 (1970–71): 125–34 (S. Panciera); *CEFR* 98 (1987): 80–84 (S. Panciera).

Dianium: a shrine at the juncture of the Vicus Cuprius and Clivus Orbius (or Urbius) on the Oppius (Livy 1.48.6). By Livy's day it had disappeared, but only recently; he cites it as still a landmark. Dianium seems also to have been used as a common designation for the Temple of Diana on the Aventine (see Diana, Aedes [1]).

Diribitorium (Fig. 26): an elongated rectangular building at the south end of the Saepta Iulia (q.v.), coterminal with the Saepta on the west and extending a little beyond it on the east, where the votes cast in the Saepta were counted by the election officials

Figure 26
Diribitorium, Divorum,
Minerva Chalcidica, and
Serapaeum,
Representation on the
Marble Plan

(*diribitores*). It is shown on fragments of the Marble Plan (*FUR* pl. 31; Rodriguez pl. 26). Cozza calculates the short side to have been about 43 m wide. The south wall seems to have been discovered in 1884 under the line of the Corso Vittorio Emanuele (*BullCom* 21 [1893]: 190 [G. B. De Rossi and G. Gatti]; *NSc* 1884, 103–4 [G. Fiorelli]), and the north wall was under the church of the Stimmate. From the Marble Plan it appears that the principal entrance was from the west, where large doors opened between broad piers into a lobby with corresponding doors opposite. An aisle marked off on the north side seems to have run the length of the building, but the architecture and purpose of this is not clear. A deep space is reserved at the east end of the building, in front of which are shown at least a few niches or small chambers, with others projecting inward from the side aisle, and both sets have columns in front of them. The purpose and extent of these features are uncertain.

The Diribitorium was begun by Agrippa in connection with the Saepta, but finished by Augustus and opened in 7 B.C. (Cass. Dio 55.8.3). It was the largest building under a single roof in Rome until Dio's time, its roof carried on beams of larch. One that was not used was 100 feet long and 1.5 feet thick, kept in the Saepta as a curiosity (Cass. Dio 55.8.4; Pliny, *HN* 16.201, 36.102). Caligula had the

Diribitorium furnished with tiers of benches and used it instead of a theater when the sun was especially hot. During the fire that destroyed the Aemiliana, Claudius made it his headquarters for directing fire-fighting operations through two nights (Suetonius, *Claud.* 18.1).

It burned in the great fire of Titus, A.D. 80, and thereafter remained unroofed, because it was impossible to find beams to replace those that had been lost (Cass. Dio 55.8.4; 66.24.2). What changes this may have entailed in the architecture of the building is not clear, nor how it was then used. It is not listed in the regionary catalogues.

Dis Pater, Aedes: a temple in Regio XI listed in the *Notitia* (not the *Curiosum*) after the Temple of Mercury and before that of Ceres. It has therefore been supposed that the Temple of Summanus (see Summanus, Aedes) is meant, because the name of Summanus was explained as deriving from Summus Manium, and he was equated with Dis Pater in the third and fourth centuries (Martianus Capella 2.161; Roscher 4.1601 [R. Peter]).

Dis Pater et Proserpina, Ara: an altar inscribed to Dis and Proserpina kept underground at a depth of 20 feet, supposed to have been miraculously discovered by the servants of the Sabine Valesius digging to lay foundations following instructions given in dreams of Valesius's children (Val. Max. 2.4.5; Festus 440L, 479L). This was at a place called Tarentum (q.v.) or Terentum, *in extremo Martio campo*, along the Tiber. On this altar sacrifices were offered in the Ludi Saeculares (Livy, *Epit.* 49; Censorinus, *N. D.* 17.8–9; Phlegon, *Peri Macrob.* 5.4 [*FGrH* 2.2 p. 1189]; Zosimus 2.4). The discovery of fragments of inscriptions with records of the Ludi Saeculares celebrated under Augustus in 17 B.C. near the head of Ponte Vittorio Emanuele gives the approximate location of the Tarentum (*CIL* 6.32323 = *ILS* 5050; cf. Nash 1.58–59). F. Coarelli (*QITA* 5 [1968]: 33–37) has shown that coins of Domitian showing the sacrifices of the Ludi Saeculares of A.D. 88 show the altar as round. His further attempt to identify the buildings in the background as twin temples of Dis and Proserpina has been refuted by S. Quilici Gigli (*AnalRom*, suppl. 10 [1983]: 47–57). It seems possible that what is represented is a *scaenae frons*.

Dius Fidius: see **Semo Sancus.**

Divorum, Aedes: see **Augustus, Divus, Sacrarium.**

Divorum, Templum (Figs. 18, 26): a large complex in the Campus Martius east of the Saepta Iulia and west of the great porticus along Via Lata (Porticus Minucia Frumentaria?). It is shown on the Marble Plan (*FUR* pl. 31; Rodriguez pl. 26). It was built by Domitian after the fire of Titus, evidently to honor his deified father and brother, and consisted of a long rectangle framed by colonnades entered at the north through an elaborate triple arch, just inside which a pair of small temples faced each other. These are shown as tetrastyle prostyle. Two other buildings of megaron plan flank the arch, but it is not clear what purpose these served. The open area is shown covered by regularly spaced dots, probably representing files of large trees, and on axis near the south end is a square structure with steps at the front and back and columns at the corners, probably an altar. There seems to have been an axial entrance at the south end with a columnar porch in front of it, but the architecture of this is difficult to read, and one cannot see where it led. This building seems to have replaced the Villa Publica (q.v.), and the "altar" is therefore probably the altar of Mars (see Mars, Ara).

This complex is commonly called simply Divorum until late, although the earliest mentions of it, in the Fasti Ostienses for the time of Hadrian (Degrassi, *Inscriptiones Italiae* 13.1.203, 233) and *CIL* 10234 = *ILS* 7213 of A.D. 153, call it Templum Divorum. The common modern designation Porticus

Divorum seems to have no justification.

L. Bonfante and H. von Heintze, eds., *In Memoriam Otto J. Brendel* (Mainz 1976), 159–63 (L. Richardson, jr, "The Villa Publica and the Divorum").

Doliola: a place alongside the Cloaca Maxima in the Forum Boarium where it was not permitted to spit. There were believed to be earthenware storage jars, dolia, buried underground here, about which there were several traditions: that they contained bones of the dead (Varro, *Ling.* 5.157), that they contained sacred objects that had belonged to Numa Pompilius (Varro, *Ling.* 5.157), and that during the invasion of the Senonian Gauls the Vestal Virgins had deposited there ritual objects that they were unable to carry with them in their flight (Livy 5.40.8; Paulus *ex Fest.* 60L). Livy's account puts the place on the road from the Temple of Vesta to the Pons Sublicius, and he adds that it was a sacellum next to the house of the Flamen Quirinalis, so already in existence and consecrated at that time. The area must have been marked off, but is not said to have been a locus saeptus, like the Niger Lapis in the Comitium. It is sometimes confused with the Busta Gallica (q.v.) in the Forum Boarium, but without reason. The Doliola should be fairly near the Temple of Vesta, but outside the pomerium, if it was believed to be an ancient graveyard. The suggestion is that the Vestal Virgins were going along the Vicus Tuscus when they found their burdens too heavy to carry and then took advantage of the nearest sacred ground.

Dolochenum: see **Iuppiter Dolichenus.**

Domus, Insula, Atrium, Horti, Villa: A *domus* was a private house not more than two storeys high and usually for the most part one. It might be broken into a number of individual units, but these interconnected. Along the front there were shops, if the street was a busy one; these might be run by freedmen of the family or let out. In the republican period the principal unit was probably always an atrium complex, a ring of rooms around a central lobby, lit by a central opening in the roof. At the far end were a tablinum, or reception room, flanked by a pair of dining rooms, one for winter and one for summer use. The rooms along the front and sides were much smaller, principally bedrooms and storerooms. To this after the middle of the second century B.C. might be added one or more peristyles, colonnaded pleasure gardens with rooms opening off the colonnades, especially dining rooms and rooms for special purposes. Here there might also be a dining pavilion arranged in a second storey and a small bath suite. A service quarter accessible by a corridor might contain kitchen, latrine, storage spaces, and work spaces, but effort was made to separate these from the rest of the house. If a hospitium was included, it consisted of a small atrium complex and might have a small peristyle as well. Large houses might have more than one hospitium. A domus might occupy the whole of a city block, but usually occupied only a fraction of one.

An *insula* might be a single apartment for a family unit, or a building of multiple such apartments in many storeys. The single apartment usually consisted of a large central lobby, the *medianum*, flanked by one large reception room and one smaller one, the exedras, and with a few small windowless rooms opening behind the medianum. The plan could be varied, but once established had to be repeated on every floor. The ground floor in the center of the city was usually given over to shops and workshops around a central courtyard that was paved and might contain a fountain. The dwellings were in the storeys above. Cooking was done on balconies, and a common latrine on the ground floor led off the stairwell. An insula might occupy the whole of a city block but usually occupied only a fraction of one. Under the empire this was the commonest form of habitation for those of the middle range, the domus being reserved for the very rich, while the laboring class lived in their workshops and no consideration was taken of the slaves.

An atrium, as a building, was for the classical period always an atrium complex, as described above, but sometimes the name was a survival from an earlier period and the building had with time acquired an entirely different form. This would have been the case with the Atrium Libertatis, which began as the office of the censors and seems to have wound up as the hemicycles at either end of the Basilica Ulpia. The Atrium Vestae that we know shows no sign of an atrium plan in any of its phases. Thus by the late republic atrium as a term seems to have become used for any large hall or complex, essentially independent of other buildings, devoted to public or semi-public use.

Horti is a term used for a house of villa form within, or in the immediate neighborhood of the city. The first horti in Rome are said to be those created by Lucullus on the Pincian, which became known as the Collis Hortulorum. Within a few years thereafter we find Cicero speaking of horti in the Transtiberim and on the way to Ostia and gather that they ringed the city. The Horti Maecenatis on the Esquiline were famous, and the Horti Sallustiani regarded as one of the showplaces of Rome. Julius Caesar gave his horti in the Transtiberim to the Roman people to be a pub-

lic park, and Agrippa did the same with his in the Campus Martius. It is impossible to say how far out from Rome the belt of horti extended; probably it was not more than two or three kilometers. One hears little about the houses included in horti, although the surviving pavilion in the Horti Sallustiani shows that they could be magnificent. Emphasis was put rather on the fountains and fishponds, the plantations of trees, and the development of terraces. Buildings were not clustered together, but scattered through the landscape to provide great variety of experience and vista. One gathers that both the Domus Transitoria and Domus Aurea were essentially horti in character but were not so called only because of the tradition of calling imperial houses in Rome domus.

A villa, on the other hand, in the time of the empire had to be a certain distance from the urban center, clearly a country place. Down to the time of Augustus villas seem always to have kept the character of working farms, although the houses might be extravagant in size and appointments. This is shown in the opening of the third book of Varro's *De Re Rustica*. The Romans prided themselves on their abilities as farmers and spent lavishly of both money and effort to make their villas productive and showplaces. Beginning with Augustus one begins to find the villa that served only for pleasure, especially in the seaside villas perched on rocky promontories and island retreats. In the vicinity of Rome villas probably once began immediately beyond the pomerium, and examples surviving from the earlier period were scattered among the horti throughout antiquity. The Villa Coponiana mentioned by Cicero (*Att.* 12.31.2) seems to have been one of these. The Villa Publica of Rome, built in 435 B.C., was so designated in all seriousness. But the fact that while mentions of horti are extremely common, mentions of villas near Rome are extremely rare is testimony to the revolution that took place in such residences immediately following Lucullus's lead, and the speed with which it operated.

Domus (identified by the owner with the name in the nominative, when no commoner name is available).

M. Acilius Glabrio Faustus: see Domus Palmata.

Aebutii: At least two houses of this family on the Aventine are known from Livy's account of the scandal of the Bacchanalia in 186 B.C. In one Publius Aebutius, son of an eques Romanus, lived with his mother, Duronia, and his stepfather, T. Sempronius Rutilus (Livy 39.9.2 and 6; 39.12.1). In the other lived an elderly aunt (Livy 39.11.2–3).

Aelia Athenais: on the Esquiline inside the Porta Esquilina (Arcus Gallieni) and to the south of it, known only from a lead pipe of the third century found in Via del Statuto running to Piazza Vittorio Emanuele at its west corner (*CIL* 15.7377).

Aelii: a house just off the Forum Romanum along the Sacra Via on land later occupied by the Mariana Monumenta; i.e., the Temple of Honos et Virtus and adjacencies (Val. Max. 4.4.8). Valerius Maximus expresses surprise that so small a house *(domuncula)* could have accommodated sixteen Aelii at once. Plutarch *(Aemil. Paul.* 5.4) says one of these was Q. Aelius Tubero, son-in-law of L. Aemilius Paullus, which would give a date ca. 175 B.C.

Aelius Maximus Augustorum Libertus: a house somewhere near the Thermae Antoninianae, the location given by an inscription on a lead pipe (*CIL* 15.7374).

T. Aelius Naevius Antonius Severus (*PIR²* N 5): a house on the Quirinal at the corner of Via Nazionale and Via Milano. The owner was a man of consular rank in the time of Decius (?).
   CIL 6.1332 = 31632, 1469 = 31663, 1470, 9147; *IG* 14.1071.

P. Aelius Romulus Augg. lib.: see **Domus Q. Blaesius Iustus.**

Aemilia Paulina Asiatica (*PIR²* A 424): a house on the Quirinal found in 1887 in Via Milano during the construction of Via Nazionale. It was oriented to the Vicus Longus but considerably to the northwest of it (*RömMitt* 4 [1889]: 276 [C. Hülsen]).

M. Aemilius Aemilianus: a house within the bounds of the Thermae Diocletianae off Via XX Settembre, known from inscribed lead pipes, one piece found in the Campo Verano, another in work for the Ministero delle Finanze (*CIL* 15.7378 = *ILS* 528). The inscriptions carried the name of the maker of the pipe, Marcia Caenis, as well as that of the house owner. The owner is not likely to have been the Aemilianus who became emperor in A.D. 253 (cf. *PIR²* A 330).

L. Aemilius Iuncus: on the Esquiline, known from a lead pipe (*CIL* 15.7379). He may be the suffect consul of A.D. 127 (*PIR²* A 355), to whom the Figulinae Iuncianae are believed to have belonged (*CIL* 15.257 of A.D. 123). Cf. also *IG* 3.622 and 5.485.

M. Agrippa: see **Domus, M. Antonius.**

Albinovanus Pedo: see **Domus, C. Plinius Secundus.**

Alfenius Ceionius Iulianus Kamenius (*PLRE* 1.177): on the Quirinal southeast of Palazzo Barberini, where its ruins were discovered (*CIL* 6.1675 = 31902, 31940). Kamenius, a man of senatorial rank, was accused in A.D. 368 of dabbling in poison to further the success of the charioteer Auchenius, but acquitted (Amm. Marc. 28.1.27). Presumably his grandfather was the praefectus urbi in 333 (*MGH, Chron. Min.* 1.68), and his brother, Tarracius Bassus, also accused in the Auchenius affair, became praefectus urbi (Amm. Marc. 28.1.27).

Amethystus Drusi Caesaris: below the Pincian, known only from the inscription on a lead pipe (*CIL* 15.7383).

Ampelius: on the slope of the Collis Salutaris, belonging to P. Ampelius of Antioch, praefectus urbi in A.D. 371–372 (*PLRE* 1.56; Symmachus, *Epist.* 5.54[52].2). It is more likely to have been on the southeast side of the hill, where there were numerous houses, than on the northwest one.

Ancus Marcius: *in summa Sacra Via,* where the Temple of the Lares (see Lares, Aedes) later stood (Solinus 1.23). Varro *(ap. Non.* 852L) puts it *in Palatio ad portam Mugionis secundum viam,* that is, presumably, inside the gate to the northwest of the road leading to it, or roughly opposite the Temple of Iuppiter Stator (see Iuppiter Stator, Aedes [1]).

Anicii (1): see **Domus, Gregorius Magnus.**

Anicii (2): believed to have stood in Via delle Botteghe Oscure, where an inscription was found recording the restoration of some public building by Anicius Acilius Glabrio Faustus (*PLRE* 2.452–54), praefectus urbi between 421 and 423 in the time of Honorius and Theodosius (*CIL* 6.1676; HJ 549). The location of the church of S. Lucia dei Ginnasi, which seems to be the same as Sanctae Luciae in Xenodochio Aniciorum (HCh 300, 306), would put this in the area of the Porticus Minucia Vetus (q.v.), which was still identifiable at the time the regionary catalogues were compiled but may have been invaded by building shortly thereafter.

Anniana: see **Domus, Milo Papianus, T. Annius.**

A. Annius Plocamus (*PIR*² A 676): on the upper Quirinal northeast of the east corner of the Thermae Diocletianae, known from an inscription on a lead pipe (*CIL* 15.7391) said to have been found at the corner of Via Volturno and Via Goito (a mistake for Via Gaeta?). This may be the man who contracted for the revenues from the Red Sea under Claudius (Pliny, *HN* 6.84; Solinus 53.8).

Annius Verus: on the Caelian near the Lateran, the family house in which Marcus Aurelius was brought up (S.H.A. *M. Aurel. Antonin.* 1.1–8). M. Annius Verus (*PIR*² A 695), his grandfather, was consul three times, first under Domitian, then in A.D. 121 and 126, and praefectus urbi. His father died while praetor. The *Historia Augusta* makes it clear that there were actually two properties, a horti in which Marcus was born and a paternal domus adjacent to the Lateran. The horti belonged properly to his mother, Domitia Lucilla (see Horti Domitiae Calvillae). The Lugli and Gismondi location of the Domus L. Veri near the northwest corner of the Praedia Lateranorum and the Horti Domitiae Lucillae adjacent to this to the west is arbitrary; the horti may have been anywhere on the Caelian.

RendPontAcc 41 (1968–69): 167–89 (V. Santa Maria Scrinari); *MEFRA* 100 (1988): 891–915 (P. Liverani).

Antonia Caenis (*PIR*² A 888): known from lead pipes found in the area of Villa Patrizi on the south side of Via Nomentana in the area of the present Ministero dei Trasporti. This was the freedwoman of Antonia, the mother of Claudius and the concubine of Vespasian. In this location it might more properly be called horti than domus. It must have become imperial property after her death, for a Balineum Caenidianum (q.v.) that was part of it became a public institution.

RendPontAcc 50 (1977–78): 145–52 (R. Friggeri).

M. Antonius (cos. 44, 34 B.C.): on the Palatine, presumably inherited. This was subsequently given to Agrippa and Messalla jointly (Cass. Dio 53.27.5). Because both were very rich men, this division of a house is difficult to understand and may imply that the house was a very large one composed of more than one building unit. Because Antony himself had taken possession of the Domus Rostrata of Pompey (see Domus, Cn. Pompeius Magnus [1]) on the Ca-

rinae in preference to his Palatine house, it may have been old-fashioned and inconvenient. It burned down in 25 B.C. during the joint ownership. See also Domus, Caesetius Rufus.

L. Appuleius Saturninus: destroyed and left a vacant plot following the assassination of Saturninus on the grounds that he was seditious. He was tribunus plebis in 103 and 100 B.C. and was stoned to death in the Curia Hostilia, 10 December 100 B.C. The location of the house is unknown but was presumably in a conspicuous place (Val. Max. 6.3.1c).

C. Aquillius Gallus: on the Viminal, generally considered the most beautiful house of the mid-first century B.C. in Rome, outshining even the house of Catulus on the Palatine (Pliny, *HN* 17.2). The owner was an eques Romanus and a celebrated jurist; he was praetor in 66 B.C., together with Cicero.

Arippi et Ulpii Vibii: a house discovered in 1930 in laying foundations for the Collegium Russicum on Via Napoleone III, southeast of the Basilica Iunii Bassi (q.v.). The names of the owners are known from an inscription in a mosaic pavement of geometric pattern in a small apsidal room of the third or fourth century built into another complex with walls faced with reticulate judged Augustan in date. An adjacent room had remains of a black and white figural mosaic of Bacchic subject, interesting for the representation of Bacchus discovering Ariadne in this sort of mosaic. The plan of the house cannot be made out, and the owners are otherwise unknown.

Nash 1.307–8.

L. Arruntius Stella (*PIR*² A 1150): in the *prima Subura*, the house of the suffect consul of A.D. 101 or 102 (Martial 12.2[3].9–12), described as *alta atria*. Presumably the west end of the Subura close to the imperial fora is meant.

L. Asinius Rufus: on the Aventine (?), known from an inscription on a lead pipe (*CIL* 15.7396), perhaps the intimate and admired friend of Pliny (*Epist.* 4.15.1–2) and Tacitus (*PIR*² A 1248).

Aufidia Cornelia Valentilla (*PIR*² A 1396): south of Porta Maggiore, a house or urban villa of the second half of the second century (*NSc* 1887, 70, 108 [G. Fiorelli]; 1888, 225 [G. Gatti]; *BullCom* 15 [1887]: 100 [G. Gatti]; 53 [1925]: 276–78 [E. Gatti]; *CIL* 15.755, 7398).

Augustiana (*CIL* 6.8640, 8647–49; 15.1860; *ILS* 1630, 1775), also called **Domus Augustana** (*CIL* 6.2271, 8651; 15.7246; *ILS* 4270, 8694) (Figs. 27,

28, 63.6 and 7): The names DOMUS FLAVIA and DOMUS SEVERIANA are modern names for parts of the whole complex assigned to different periods. The whole is also called DOMUS PALATINA and PALATIUM. Parts of the imperial compound on the Palatine that were apparently always distinguished from the Domus Augustiana are the Domus Tiberiana, Domus Germanici, Domus Transitoria, and Domus Aurea.

The imperial palace we see today is almost entirely the work of Domitian and his architect Rabirius. Although modifications and masonry of other periods can be distinguished, these are work of repair and redecoration rather than remodeling and rebuilding. The only significant additions of a later period seem to be those of Septimius Severus (see no. 4 below). Domitian's palace, work on which may possibly have begun under Vespasian, but more likely at the beginning of Domitian's own reign (cf. *CIL* 6.31496a), entailed enormous works of terracing to create a platform of sufficient size for the deploying of the main state apartments, and the whole was only completed about A.D. 92 (Martial 7.56). Martial (8.36) describes it as a work outdoing the pyramids and towering into heaven. For buildings found buried in the terracing for the foundations, see Casa dei Grifi, Aula Isiaca, and Domus Transitoria.

The main floor is composed of four principal blocks. (1) That to the northwest includes the main reception rooms and was preceded by a colonnade on the north and at least part of the west front. The north front commanded an open space, probably the Area Palatina (q.v.), and here the line of the colonnade is broken by projecting platforms that probably served as balconies for public appearances. Later the west colonnade was reinforced by spur walls running back from the columns to the wall behind, and underground chambers were constructed against the façade. Immediately behind this colonnade are three important halls, that to the northwest basilical in architectural form, with lateral Corinthian colonnades leading to a large semicircular apse set off by a marble balustrade. The vaulted (?) roofing evidently overtaxed the supporting walls, and massive piers had to be added in the forward corners, and the apse had to be thickened to carry it. In the center was the largest and grandest hall, the so-called Aula Regia, nearly square, the walls broken into shallow niches separated by fluted columns of pavonazzetto. The niches contained colossal statues of divinities in greenish Egyptian basonite (grovacca), two of which, a Bacchus and a Hercules, are now in Parma. The third room, the so-called Lararium, is smallest, a rectangle with a broad entrance, three rectangular niches in each side wall, and a plain rear wall with a small door at either end leading back to more private

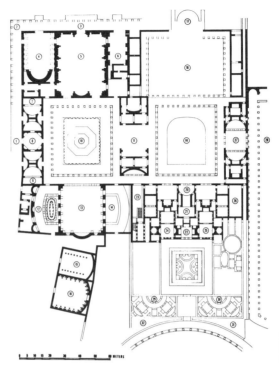

Figure 27
Domus Augustiana,
Upper Level, Plan

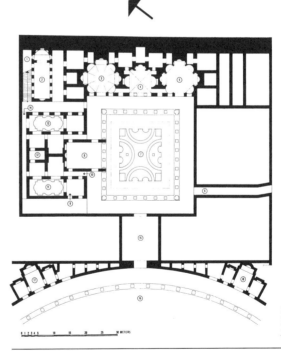

Figure 28
Domus Augustiana,
Lower Level, Plan

apartments. Here there was a stair leading up to rooms and probably balconies in an upper storey. Behind this bank of rooms was a peristyle with columns of Porta Santa containing at its center an octagonal maze around a central pool. The whole may have been a very elaborate fountain. To the west of this peristyle is a series of small rooms of highly baroque plan, symmetrically arranged to either side of a central axis, the purpose of which is unclear, while to the east is a block of rectangular rooms through which one passed to a second peristyle. At the southwest end of the first block was the great banquet hall, balancing the "Aula Regia," a broad rectangle with a shallow axial apse and five windows in each side wall, through which one glimpsed an elaborate fountain of oval plan framed on three sides by colonnades. The conception of these fountains may owe something to the Meta Sudans (q.v.). The pavement of the banquet hall was in opus sectile; this was raised on suspensurae, so the hall could be heated. This must be the banquet hall celebrated by Martial (8.39) and Statius (*Silv.* 4.2), the Cenatio Iovis.

(2) The block immediately to the southeast of this is arranged around two adjacent and conjoined peristyles. The outer one of these to the northeast was probably a ceremonial entrance court, very large and broad, preceded by a semicircular projection, a vestibule of unusual plan or an imperial box. The open area appears to have been divided into three strips of approximately equal width to make a promenade leading back from this vestibule to another peristyle beyond. This second peristyle is nearly square and has in its center a large shallow pool, the walls scalloped into niches, the forward corners rounded. Slightly off the axis of this pool is an island joined to the northeast side by a bridge of seven arches, which holds the remains of a small temple, tetrastyle prostyle with a nearly square cella. This last is a very late addition, assigned to the time of Maxentius. The rooms northwest of this peristyle have already been mentioned in connection with the first block. Those to the southeast are again symmetrical, the central one an interesting colonnaded square with rounded apses opening beyond to either side and a view commanding the hippodrome garden to the southeast.

The main residential rooms are the complex to the southwest of this peristyle and the rooms in a lower storey below this. In the upper storey strict symmetry is observed, and we must posit the existence of light wells. Large rooms are regularly provided with niches, rounded or rectangular, which suggest the display of statuary; columns are conspicuously absent; and only a few rooms seem designed to accommodate more than a small company. Rooms do not develop in enfilades or sequences, frequent short corridors providing most connections and important rooms tending to turn their backs to one another rather than connect.

On the lower level, some 11 m below the upper and connected with it by a long straight stair in the northeast corner, so the two storeys functioned independently of each other, the rooms are grouped around a square court. This was colonnaded or arcaded on all sides, and the open area was taken up by a large shallow pool in which four peltate islands made bases for statuary and potted greenery. On the northeast side a central exedra of square plan is flanked by large octagonal rooms, all having their walls carved into deep niches of various shapes. These rooms were probably all vaulted with sectional vaults following the lines of the architecture, although there is some doubt about the roofing of the central exedra. A bank of small rooms behind these is of uncertain purpose. On the northwest side of the peristyle is a suite of eight closely interconnected rooms of rectilinear plan, again in symmetry, which may have been the private imperial suite. They were provided with light and air by the introduction of light wells enclosing large nymphaea of baroque form to either side. On the southeast side of the court opposite this suite the evidence is confused, but clearly the plan here was different, and rooms of elaborately curved form appeared. A stair on this side led directly to the hippodrome garden.

On the southwest side of the sunken court, the palace fronted on the Circus Maximus, and this front was treated as a continuous gentle curve, with focus on a monumental axial entrance from the palace. All along this front was a colonnade, and behind the axial door was a large plain room. But whether the princeps made his entrance for the circus games through this is not clear. Because this front of the palace faces southwest, it would have made a good promenade on winter afternoons and may have been especially designed for that, because ancient Romans were fond of promenading. Behind the walk to either side open a few small rooms fitted into the roughly triangular spaces between the curve of the walk and the straight lines of the rest of the palace. The block of rooms behind the walk has almost entirely disappeared, but part of it on the upper level is known from its appearance on a lost, but copied, fragment of the Marble Plan (*FUR* pls. 3 and 22; Rodriguez pl. 14). It seems to have been very bold in concept, with a pair of elongated wings or, perhaps better, pavilions of curious form radiating from a semicircular light well framed by a colonnade. The purpose of these rooms is mysterious, but it appears that the design was repeated in the wing opposite.

(3) The third block of the palace is a sunken garden in the form of a hippodrome, 160 m long by 50 m wide. This has a gently curved southwest end, straight sides, and a straight northeast end, where a series of rooms gives the effect of starting gates. The other sides are arcaded with an engaged Tuscan order faced with Porta Santa applied to the piers.

Above the arcades ran a colonnade of composite order. At either end of the garden area is a semicircular pool, and across it just northeast of the imperial exedra ran a colonnaded walk of late date. Also of late date is an oval enclosure that fills much of the open area toward the southwest end, for which various explanations, but none entirely satisfactory, have been advanced. At the middle of the southeast side rises a vast semicircular exedra. On the ground floor this was divided into three parallel vaulted chambers, which supported an upper storey in which a series of niches, alternately curved and rectangular, was framed by a Corinthian colonnade and the whole covered by a half-dome. This is commonly called the imperial box (*podium, pulvinar*), and it is presumed that the imperial party assembled here to watch spectacles given in the arena below. It is perhaps more likely that it served simply as a garden pavilion. Behind it runs a curved corridor with a coffered ceiling apparently supported on a similar corridor below. Suites of rooms extend the hippodrome block at either end. Those at the curved end are not of great interest, a double bank except for a single large central room. Those at the northeast end are much more extensive and seem to have centered around a nymphaeum of semicircular plan with a long throat leading out of it on axis, something like the Serapaeum of Villa Adriana but much more modest in scale. How this was integrated with the hippodrome, if in fact it was, is not clear. But all this part appears to be Domitianic, as is also the aqueduct bridge that brought the Aqua Claudia across the valley between the Caelian and the Palatine on two or three storeys of arches and supplied the palace abundantly with water.

(4) Septimius Severus added a wing to the Domus Augustiana extending from the hippodrome southeast to the Septizodium (q.v.). In part this seems to have been a rebuilding based on constructions of Domitian, but in effect it amounted to a whole new complex, almost a new palace. Above the Via dei Cerchi along the Circus Maximus, it was carried on lofty substructures of brick-faced concrete, two storeys of arcades with a grid of piers at regular intervals. Although denuded and stark, these are one of the most impressive sights of the Palatine today. The apartments they carried must have been pleasantly secluded and have commanded dramatic views, and here we can put the Diaetae Mammaeae (q.v.). Presumably this part of the palace extended down to the Via dei Cerchi, but most of it would have been built in levels that stepped back along the slope, and the plan of the superstructure is entirely lost. The most spectacular remains are those south of the pulvinar of the hippodrome, which are not Severan but Maxentian and belong to a large bath complex with

rooms exploiting use of apses and windows. Because these require sunlight and are carefully oriented to the southwest, the superstructures of the palace southwest of them should not be so high as to darken them. However, the report that Septimius Severus wished to make the principal approach to the palace one from the Via Appia and that he was followed in this by Alexander Severus is probably to be taken seriously, and the Severan additions to the Domus Augustiana must have been appropriately splendid (S.H.A. *Sept. Sev.* 24.4–5).

While the large platform of S. Sebastiano and S. Bonaventura is to be excluded from the Domus Augustiana, because it is now known to belong to a temple, a structure halfway down the slope of the Palatine below the northwest end of the lower storey probably belongs to it. This is a row of parallel rooms with a central semicircular exedra, in front of which is a row of columns. Numerous inscriptions scratched on the walls suggest that it was the headquarters of the keepers of imperial vestments. Other inscriptions suggest it was called the Paedagogium, and that name has now become attached to it. A famous graffito caricaturing the crucifixion (Lugli 1946, 522 fig. 165) comes from it.

The whole complex has been repeatedly ransacked for treasure, intensively from the late eighteenth century, and quantities of material of every sort have gone to enrich buildings and collections. It is no longer possible to identify any substantial part of these, and even study of the remains of the hippodrome and Severan additions is still woefully inadequate.

Lugli 1946, 486–523; *AnalRom*, suppl. 2 (1962) (H. Finsen); MacDonald 1.47–74; Nash 1.316–38; *AnalRom*, suppl. 5 (1969) (H. Finsen); *NSc* 1971, 300–318 (G. Carettoni); *ArchCl* 24 (1972): 96–104 (G. Carettoni); *RömMitt* 83 (1976): 403–24 (J. J. Herrmann); *Rivista di Archeologia* 3 (1979): 106–16 (L. Ungero); *Roma, archeologia nel centro* (1985), 1.176–78 (L. D'Elia and S. Le Pera Buranelli); *BullCom* 91.2 (1986): 481–98, 526–34, 540–42 (M. G. Borghi et al.).

Augustus (1) *ad Capita Bubula*: see **Domus, C. Octavius.**

Augustus (2) *iuxta Romanum forum supra scalas anularias*: see **Domus, C. Licinius Calvus.**

Augustus (3) (Figs. 29, 63.3): the house of Augustus on the Palatine, which earlier belonged to the orator Hortensius (q.v.), an unpretentious house in which the porticoes had columns of peperino and the reception rooms were without marble revetment or fine pavements (Suetonius, *Aug.* 72.1). It was adja-

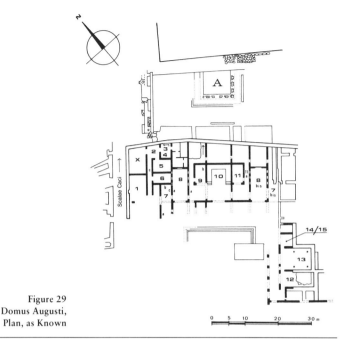

Figure 29
Domus Augusti,
Plan, as Known

scure and the reading of the whole difficult, it is clear that this was an elegant but not sumptuous house of its time. The rooms are relatively small, but not cramped. The house seems not to have had an atrium and combines elements of a peristyle complex with others of a portico villa plan.

The principal rooms are arranged on a large peristyle with peperino pillars, while others lie in a second bank behind them on at least the northeast and northwest sides. The lighting and functioning of these parts are obscure. Along the northeast side of the peristyle the rooms form an elaborate symmetry of seven members behind a row of shallow antechambers. Those at either end are identified as libraries, because of the presence of a series of three large rectangular niches in each side wall; the room in the center is called the "tablinum" because of its size (10.50 m x 6.70 m). A podium (0.80 m high and 1.20 m wide) runs around three sides of the room; it and the floor were paved with opus sectile. All these rooms seem to have been very fine and intended as reception rooms. The rooms on the southeast side of the peristyle include an oecus with four columns raised on plinths, which supported an arched ceiling dropped over the back part of the room, where dining couches must have been arranged. This communicates with a small ladies' dining room beside it, decorated similarly but not *en suite*. In a room just southwest of this pair, the back wall has been broken out, and a ramp has been constructed that leads to the platform in front of the Temple of Apollo. This intimate connection of house and temple strengthens the case for identification of the temple.

Carettoni believes that the house was abandoned after the death of Augustus and that at sometime during the first century modifications were undertaken with a view to creating a new monumental entrance for the temple. This was never completed, perhaps interrupted by the fire of Nero in A.D. 64. Thereafter, Domitian filled in the whole lower Augustan part and raised the level to that of the temple terrace, thus preserving much of the decoration of the house. The decorations are of excellent Second Style, which include small pinakes with genre scenes and large panel paintings, both landscape and narrative with figures, though the subjects of the narrative panels cannot be identified. They seem to represent a stage nearly contemporary with the decorations of the Casa di Livia, possibly slightly older. The one early Third Style room must have been painted a decade or so later.

NSc 1967, 287–319 (G. Carettoni); *RömMitt* 87 (1980): 131–36 (G. Carettoni); *RömMitt* 90 (1983): 373–419 (G. Carettoni); G. Carettoni, *Das Haus des Augustus auf den Palatin* (Mainz 1983); CEFR 98 (1987): 393–413 (T. P. Wiseman).

cent to the Temple of Apollo Palatinus (Suetonius, *Aug.* 29.3), and the house of Q. Lutatius Catulus was annexed and incorporated in it (Suetonius, *Gramm.* 17).

The Temple of Apollo was built on part of the house plot struck by lightning and announced by the haruspices to be demanded for sacred use, and, in consequence of this, the people voted that a new house for Augustus should be erected at public expense (Cass. Dio 49.15.5). On 13 January 27 B.C. the senate voted that an oak crown should be mounted over the door and a laurel tree planted to either side (Augustus, *RG* 34.2; Cass. Dio 53.16.4). Somewhere in the house was a tower room that served as a private study that Augustus called his Syracuse and *technyphion* (Suetonius, *Aug.* 72.2). It also contained an aedicula and an altar of Vesta (see Vesta, Ara).

The house burned, perhaps in A.D. 3, but was then rebuilt (Suetonius, *Aug.* 57.2; Cass. Dio 55.12.4–5) and, according to Dio, at that time made state property. Suetonius speaks of it in the past tense, so it may be presumed that it was destroyed in the fire of Nero.

It has recently been identified as a house northwest of the Temple of Apollo, between this and the Scalae Caci. This was a fine house with rooms in at least two storeys stepping down the slope of the Cermalus. The rooms are decorated with fine painting in the late Second Pompeian Style, and while the loss of large parts along the southwest front and rebuilding over much of the area have made many points ob-

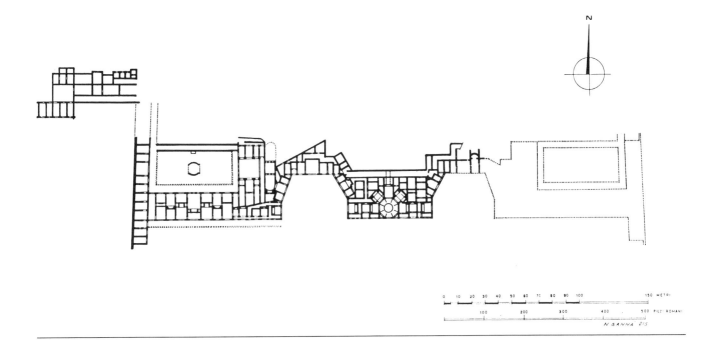

Aurea (Figs. 30, 31, 62): the great imperial residence built by Nero to replace the Domus Transitoria that burned in the fire of A.D. 64. The architects and engineers were Severus and Celer, famous for their ability to conquer natural obstacles. It is calculated that its grounds covered the whole of the Palatine, Velia, and Oppius, extending on the Esquiline as far as the Horti Maecenatis (see Horti Maecenatiani), which was an annex not incorporated into the Domus. The end of the Caelian with the substructures of the Templum Divi Claudii was included, and the basin framed by the Oppius, Caelian, and Palatine, where the Colosseum now stands. The main approach, from the direction of the Forum Romanum, began at, or just beyond, the Atrium Vestae.

The Domus Aurea was especially notable for its landscaping. Fields and vineyards, meadows and woods were populated with every sort of animal, wild and domesticated (Tacitus, *Ann.* 15.42.1). The centerpiece was an ornamental water, where the Colosseum now stands, like a sea surrounded by buildings in the appearance of cities (Suetonius, *Nero* 31.1). This was fed by cascades down the slope of the Caelian, one front of the terracing for the Templum Divi Claudii being converted into a vast nymphaeum supplied by the Neronian branch of the Aqua Claudia.

The main approach was dominated by a colossal statue of the princeps, over a hundred Roman feet high (see Colossus Solis [Neronis]), that stood in an entrance court (*vestibulum*) so spacious that its triple porticoes measured a mile long (Suetonius, *Nero*

31.1). The colossus crowned the Velia, but Hadrian moved it to a position beside the Amphitheatrum Flavium to make way for his Templum Veneris et Romae. Van Deman and Clay have reconstructed the portico as arcaded and extending from the Regia along a straightened Sacra Via to the line of the Clivus Palatinus, along which it branched at right angles to its original direction and ran to the Nova Via and up the Palatine to the Area Palatina (?). Behind the arcades along the street were large buildings composed of forests of piers, like hypostyle halls, which could be subdivided and used for many different purposes. The court of honor around the colossus would have begun at the Clivus Palatinus and run east from this. This reconstruction has been questioned and in some areas rests on very slight evidence, but seems right in its general concept and use of space. If the Domus Aurea did not come down so close to the Forum Romanum, the placing of the colossus and sweep of approach must be essentially correct.

The treatment of the Palatine and the Domus Tiberiana in the Domus Aurea are enigmas. Although they were included in the compound, they seem not to have been important elements and seem likely to have been relegated to the status of offices and guesthouses. But large concrete foundations, including one on a curve, under the triclinium of the Domus Augustiana, which cut through remains of the Domus Transitoria, must belong to it.

The main residence was on the Oppius, a park in which pavilions and pleasances were scattered, many

119

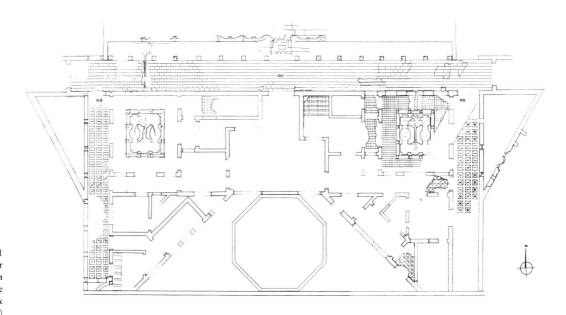

Figure 31
Domus Aurea, Upper
Storey of Remains on
the Oppius over the
Octagon Complex
(1cm = 5.55m)

independent of one another. A block incorporated and buried in the substructures of the Thermae Traiani has been known since the fifteenth century and has been much studied and discussed, but it is now clear that this was not the principal wing of the palace, as had sometimes been thought, but essentially a work of terracing along the brow of the hill on which to set more important constructions above. It is built over the remains of a large complex of horrea and incorporates several parts of these in its fabric. These are in brick-faced concrete with travertine blocks at points of stress and extensive use of flat arches. They must date from almost immediately before the fire of 64. The Neronian structure originally consisted of at least three main blocks separated by two deep trapezoidal courts. One hundred and fifty rooms are known at least in some part. The western block was arranged between a colonnaded façade and a rectangular interior peristyle with rooms in a double bank along the south and a single bank along the west. Along the north there is simply a crypto-porticus. In the southern bank the rooms are planned in a symmetry and interconnected very freely. Although once handsomely finished, they are not architecturally impressive. At the east side of the interior peristyle opens a magnificent nymphaeum, a large square vestibule with a line of four columns in front and four in back giving to a smaller fountain room embellished with rustication and mosaic.

Around the western trapezoidal court the large axial hall, the Sala della Volta Dorata, preserves ruins of a superb decoration, but the other rooms are un-

remarkable, although the painted decorations in some of them clearly anticipate the Fourth Pompeian Style and are executed with admirable fluency and assurance.

In the central block, the axial room is octagonal in plan, surrounded by radiating rooms of different shapes, which all give to it and take their focus from it. It is roofed with a dome of concrete with a very large oculus, perhaps the earliest true dome known, although the dome of the Tempio di Mercurio at Baiae and one in the Domus Transitoria may have preceded it. Over the slope of the dome, light pours through large transom windows into the rooms around it. The room on axis to the north was a nymphaeum, a cascade fed by an aqueduct brought in just under the roof. How the suite may have been used is not entirely clear, but there is a strong suggestion that it was for summer dining. Because it is now known that additional apartments to the south have been lost, it is not possible to reconstruct the whole effect accurately.

The eastern trapezoidal court seems to have had essentially the same design, even to the rooms around it, as the western one, and it is to be presumed that the eastern block beyond this mirrored the western block with its peristyle, but at the edge of the Thermae Traiani the evidence gives out and certainty is impossible. However, there is ample space available for the development of an eastern wing symmetrical with the western one.

Recent exploration of the roofs over the area of the octagon room and its adjacencies has revealed remains of an upper storey surprisingly freely planned in relation to the lower one. Here two symmetrical peristyles, each of four columns on a side, were surrounded by small elegant rooms of loggia-like architecture. Behind them is a long colonnade along a splendid euripus, with walls scalloped into niches (*AnalRom,* supp. 10 [1983]: 169–85 [L. Fabbrini]). A long rectangular room with an apse at either end incorporated into the northeast wing of the peribolus of the Thermae Traiani has the same orientation and may once have belonged to the Domus.

Suetonius singles out for comment dining pavilions with coffering of movable ivory panels so arranged that flowers and perfumes could be showered on the guests, a rotunda that revolved continuously day and night, and baths supplied with both sea and sulfur water (Suetonius, *Nero* 31.2). Of all these, nothing seems to remain today.

At the time of Nero's death the Domus Aurea was still incomplete, and Otho is known to have assigned a vast sum for its completion (Suetonius, *Otho* 7.1). But it seems to have continued in use as an imperial residence until the fire of Trajan in 104. After Domitian created his own palace in the Domus Augustiana, it must have been relegated to an inferior role, but earlier it had probably been the main residence of Vespasian and Titus.

The destruction of the Domus Aurea began with Vespasian, who drained the stagnum of Nero and on its site built the Amphitheatrum Flavium (Martial, *De Spect.* 2.5–6). He also destroyed the nymphaeum Nero had created out of the platform of the Templum Divi Claudii and completed the temple Agrippina had begun (Suetonius, *Vesp.* 9.1). Under Titus an area west of the Oppius complex was used for the Thermae Titi (q.v.), and a monumental approach to these led down to the square surrounding the Amphitheatrum Flavium. After a fire in A.D. 104 (Hieron. *a. Abr.* 2120; Orosius 7.12.4), Trajan used much of what was left of the Oppius complex in the creation of a platform on which to build his Thermae and by so doing preserved extensive remains of the lower storey, because to build his platform he ran a series of heavy parallel walls through the western peristyle and out in front of the façade and filled the interior with earth. Finally in about 121 Hadrian, to make space for his Templum Veneris et Romae (see Venus et Roma, Templum), moved the Colossus Neronis to a place beside the Amphitheatrum Flavium and destroyed the entrance court of the Domus. Large parts of the approaches seem already to have given way to the Horrea Piperataria (q.v.); perhaps they were sacrificed a little at a time to more important public needs.

The Domus Aurea was noted for decorations by the painter Famulus (or Amulius or Fabullus), who painted only a few hours a day and while wearing his toga, even when mounted on scaffolding (Pliny, *HN* 35.120). It is presumed he was responsible for the creation of the Fourth Pompeian Style of decoration, of which the existing wall paintings are an early example. However, the quality of what survives leaves much to be desired, because it is hastily executed and decoration in a manner and scale ill-suited to the vast and lofty apartments of the palace. One room, the Sala della Volta Dorata, is vastly superior to the rest, but here, too, little attention is paid to the scale of the whole. These paintings were discovered in the early Renaissance, and many of the rooms were explored and examined by the foremost artists of the time. They provided much of the basis for the development of the "grotesque" style of the early sixteenth century. The collection of art with which Nero filled the palace was early dispersed, much going to adorn Vespasian's Templum Pacis (Pliny, *HN* 34.84). Later Trajan's workmen stripped the rooms to be buried in the platform of his Thermae of their revetments and pavements of colored marble before filling them it. It is impossible today to identify any of these with certainty.

In the Renaissance the remains were known as the Palazzo di Tito, thanks to the misidentification of the Thermae Traiani as the Thermae Titi.

A. Boethius, *The Golden House of Nero* (Ann Arbor, Mich. 1960), 94–128; MacDonald 1.20–46; Nash 1.339–48; *MEFRA* 82 (1970): 673–722 (H. Lavagne); *PP* 26 (1971): 153–66 (G. Maddoli); *RömMitt* 81 (1974): 323–43 (H. Prückner and S. Storz); *MEFRA* 88 (1976): 719–57 (D. Bizzari Vivarelli); *JSAH* 40 (1981): 271–78 (P. G. Warden); *MEFRA* 94 (1982): 843–91 (G. Perrin); *MemPontAcc* 14 (1982): 5–24 (L. Fabbrini); *AnalRom,* supp. 10 (1983): 169–85 (L. Fabbrini), with bibliography; *RendPontAcc* 58 (1985–86): 129–79 (L. Fabbrini); *CEFR* 98 (1987): 509–41 (J.-L. Volsin); *Palladio,* n.s. 1 (1988): 121–34 (G. Rocco); *Athenaeum* 78 (1990): 186–91 (D. Campanile).

Aurelia Severa (*PIR*[2] A 1667 ?): on the site of the Thermae Diocletianae, or to the east of this, known from a lead pipe (*CIL* 15.7415).

M. Aurelius Solanus: on the Esquiline east of the Horti Maecenatis, and probably west of Via Merulana, known from a lead pipe (*CIL* 15.7409).

Avianus Vindicianus (*PLRE* 1.968): on the Quirinal (?) (*CIL* 6.31005); he also had property along the Tiber, perhaps southwest of the Mausoleum Augusti, known from inscriptions on a lead pipe (*CIL* 15.7399). He was Consularis Campaniae and Vicarius Urbis Romae in A.D. 378.

T. Avidius Quietus (1): on the Esquiline just outside the Porta Esquilina (*BullCom* 5 [1877]: 66–75 [C. L. Visconti]).

T. Avidius Quietus (2) (*PIR*[2] A 1410): on the Quirinal, where a nymphaeum with pipes bearing his name was found (*CIL* 15.7400). This man was governor of Thrace in A.D. 82, and two other pipes bearing his name are recorded, but without clear provenience.

Balbinus: on the Carinae (S.H.A. *Balbinus* 16.1), said to be large and impressive.

Baronia Iusta: on the Esquiline, known from a lead pipe (*CIL* 15.7416).

L. Bellienus: a house that was burned in the funeral of Julius Caesar (Cicero, *Phil.* 2.91), presumably near the southeast end of the Forum Romanum, perhaps in the area later occupied by the Temple of Antoninus and Faustina. The owner is otherwise unknown.

Betitius Perpetuus Arzygius (*PLRE* 1.689): under the Palazzo delle Esposizioni on the Quirinal, the house of the Corrector Siciliae under Constantine (A.D. 315–330).
  NSc 1888, 493–96 (C. Hülsen).

Q. Blaesius Iustus: on the Esquiline (?), known from a lead pipe (*CIL* 15.7418) bearing his name and that of P. Aelius Romulus Augg. lib. It belongs to the end of the second century.

Bruttius Praesens (*PIR*[2] B 164): in Regio III *(Cur., Not.)* listed after the Ludi (Magnus, Matutinus) and before the Summum Choragium, so presumably in the immediate vicinity of the Colosseum. This Bruttius may have been the consul of A.D. 180 or a descendant of his.

Caecilii: According to the story of her martyrdom under M. Aurelius, Saint Caecilia was tortured for three days in an overheated bathroom in her family house. Excavation under the church of the saint in the Trastevere (1899–1900) brought to light substantial remains of the second century mingled with earlier walls, as well as some later masonry and coarse mosaic pavements of the third or fourth century. These seem in part to have been a tannery with seven cylindrical vats, in part residential. One room

is provided with a hypocaust system; it lies to the right of the present church.
  NSc 1900, 12–14, 230 (G. Gatti); Nash 1.349–51.

Caecilius Capito: known from a lead pipe (*CIL* 15.7419) found west of Via Lata in the vicinity of the Hadrianeum.

Q. Caecilius Metellus Celer: on the Palatine (Cicero, *Cael.* 18). This was the house of the consul of 60 B.C., the husband of Clodia and friend and neighbor of Cicero. It was next-door to the house of Catulus (Cicero, *Cael.* 59) on the Clivus Victoriae.

Q. Caecilius Metellus Numidicus: on the Palatine (Cicero, *De Or.* 2.263). This was the house of the consul of 109 B.C.

Caecina Decius Albinus (*PLRE* 1.35–36): on the southwest side of the Aventine near the church of S. Alessio, known from inscriptions of the fourth century, one of which was on a lead pipe (*CIL* 6.1192 = *ILS* 796; *CIL* 15.7420). He was praefectus urbi in A.D. 402.

Caecina Largus: see **Domus: L. Crassus, M. Scaurus.**

Caelia Galla: see **Domus, Maecius Blandus.**

M. Caelius Rufus (praetor 48 B.C.): on the Palatine, not far from the houses of Cicero and Crassus (Cicero, *Cael.* 18). In fact, the insula belonged to P. Clodius (see Domus, P. Clodius), and Caelius rented only a part of it (Cicero, *Cael.* 17).

C. Caelius Saturninus (*PLRE* 1.866), **C. Caelius Urbanus** (*PLRE* 1.983): a house of the fourth century located east of Via Lata just north of Piazza della Pilotta, known from inscriptions (*CIL* 6.1704, 1705 = *ILS* 1214, 1215). Urbanus was the son of Saturninus.

C. Iulius Caesar: Caesar's first house, a modest one, in the Subura (Suetonius, *Iul.* 46). Cicero (*Att.* 12.45) in May 45 B.C. called Caesar a neighbor of Atticus, Quirinus, and Salus, which suggests that he had moved from the Domus Publica (q.v.), to which he was entitled as pontifex maximus, and returned to his former house, or perhaps a new one on the Quirinal. We may incline to the latter.

Caesetius Rufus: a handsome house near that of Fulvia, the wife of Mark Antony, who coveted it and procured the proscription of its owner to obtain it

(Appian, *BellCiv* 4.29; Val. Max. 9.5.4). It may well be that the house of Fulvia in question was that of Antony on the Palatine. This was later given to Agrippa and Messalla Corvinus jointly and burned in 25 B.C. (Cass. Dio 53.27.5). Had it been enlarged by the addition of this second house, this joint ownership would be more understandable. However, see Vicus Caeseti.

Calistus (Calixtus, Callixtus): the house of the second century pope (A.D. 217–222) and martyr in the Transtiberim in the vicinity of the Castra Ravennatium, according to the *Liber Pontificalis* (VZ 2.224). Because Calistus was the founder of the church of S. Maria in Trastevere, the nearby church of S. Callisto, which is very ancient, is believed to mark the site of his house (HCh 234).
MEFRA 96 (1984): 1039–83 (G. N. Verrando).

Q. Canusius Praenestinus (*PIR²* C 402): on the Esquiline near S. Maria Maggiore, known from a lead pipe (*CIL* 15.7423). He was consul suffectus ca. A.D. 157 and is mentioned in several inscriptions.

Carminia Liviana Diotima (*PIR²* C 442): Her name occurs in conjunction with several others on a large lead pipe of the late second or early third century, found just under the Aurelian Walls between Porta Tiburtina and Porta Labicana (*CIL* 15.7424a). There is then no way of telling more precisely where her house may have been.

Spurius Cassius (cos. 502, 493, 486 B.C.): on the Carinae, the precinct of the Temple of Tellus. After Cassius was put to death for treason in 485 B.C., his house was pulled down and the temple erected on part of the site (Livy 2.41.11; Cicero, *Dom.* 101; Dion. Hal. 8.79; Val. Max. 6.3.1b). The suggestion is that Cassius's had been an impressive mansion.

Cassius Argillus: probably fictional, supposed to have been a house pulled down by order of the senate after its owner advised making peace with Hannibal following the Battle of Cannae (Servius *ad Aen.* 8.345). The story was used to explain the name of the Argiletum.

L. Sergius Catilina (praetor 68 B.C.): probably the *Catulina domus* mentioned by Suetonius (*Gramm.* 17) on the Palatine, to which Verrius Flaccus moved his school when he was appointed tutor to the grandsons of Augustus. It was described as *pars Palatii*, which must mean it had become part of the imperial enclave and can be located with some confi-

dence in the southwest quadrant of the hill. This house is often identified as the house of Catulus, but the adjective then should be *Catuliana*.

Q. Lutatius Catulus (cos. 78 B.C., cens. 65 B.C.): an unusually fine house, one of the greatest of its period (Pliny, *HN* 17.2), on the Palatine between the house of Caecilius Metellus Celer (Cicero, *Cael.* 59) and the Porticus Catuli (q.v.). It must have stood on the Clivus Victoriae.

Ceionius Rufius Volusianus: see **Domus, Lampadius.**

Censorinus: see **Domus, M. Cicero.**

Censorinus Tyrannus (*PIR²* C 656): on the Quirinal south of Alta Semita, an especially beautiful house next to the Templum Gentis Flaviae. It probably fronted on the street represented by Via delle Quattro Fontane (S.H.A. *Tyr. Trig.* 33.6).

M. Tullius Cicero: on the northwest side of the Palatine, on the Clivus Victoriae overlooking the Forum Romanum, *in conspectu prope totius urbis* (Cicero, *Dom.* 100). It was between the Porticus Catuli (q.v.) and the house of Q. Seius Postumus (Cicero, *Dom.* 103, 114–16). Cicero bought it in 62 B.C. for 3.5 million sesterces from M. Crassus, presumably the triumvir (Cicero, *Fam.* 5.6.2); to pay for it he borrowed 2 million sesterces from P. Sulla (A. Gellius 12.12). The site had previously been occupied by the house of M. Livius Drusus, and Cicero's house was later occupied by L. Marcius Censorinus, cos. 39 B.C., and Statilius Sisenna, cos. A.D. 16 (Vell. Pat. 2.14.3). After Cicero went into exile Clodius burned his house and used parts of the site to enlarge the Porticus Catuli and build a monument to Libertas (Cicero, *Dom.* 116). After Cicero's recall he undertook legal proceedings and recovered the site and damages that covered the rebuilding at least in part (Cicero, *Att.* 4.2.5; Cass. Dio 39.11).

Q. Tullius Cicero (1): on the Carinae, a house that had belonged to Cicero's father. It was near, possibly adjacent to, the Temple of Tellus (Cicero, *QFr.* 2.3.7, *Har. Resp.* 31).

Q. Tullius Cicero (2): a Domus Luciniana (or Liciniana) rented for Quintus in 56 B.C. while his own house was occupied by tenants (Cicero, *QFr.* 2.3.7).

Q. Tullius Cicero (3): a house near that of his brother Marcus on the Palatine, which adherents of Clodius set on fire in 57 (Cicero, *Att.* 4.3.2, *QFr.* 2.4.2, 2.5.3). It may have been adjacent to the house of Marcus at the back, because Cicero says that the two brothers would be *contubernales* when it was finished, and we know that Marcus's house was flanked by other buildings to either side.

L. Fabius Cilo (*PIR*[2] F 27): listed by the regionary catalogues in Regio XII and the name inscribed on a lead pipe found near the church of S. Balbina on the Aventinus Minor (*CIL* 15.7447). It was a present from Septimius Severus to his friend and praefectus urbi in A.D. 204 (Aur. Vict., *Epit.* 20.6). It is believed that remains of several periods, but especially Hadrianic, in the vicinity of the church are all parts of an extensive and opulent residence, but these are too fragmentary for any certainty. Cf. also the Marble Plan (*FUR* frag. 677, p. 157 and pl. 59; Rodriguez pl. 1).

Nash 1.352.

Claudii: on the Quirinal near the Thermae Constantinianae and the modern crossing of Via Nazionale and Via Mazzarino, where lead pipes have been found inscribed with the names of T. Flavius Claudius Claudianus (*PIR*[2] F 238) and Claudia Vera (*PIR*[2] C 1131) (*CIL* 15.7450, 7434). They belong to the period II–III after Christ. Cf. also Balineum Claudianum.

Appius Claudius: mentioned by Livy (3.49.5), in reporting the events of 449 B.C., as being close to the Forum Romanum.

Appius Claudius Martialis (*PIR*[2] C 931): known from a lead pipe found in the sixteenth century in an area corresponding to the western part of the Palazzo del Quirinale (*CIL* 15.7427). The owner was propraetor of Thrace in A.D. 161–169.

Ti. Claudius Centumalus: a house on the Caelian that Claudius Centumalus was ordered to demolish because its height interfered with the sight lines of the augurs taking observations from the arx. He then sold it to P. Calpurnius Lanarius but was condemned for fraud (Cicero, *Off.* 3.66; Val. Max. 8.2.1). The house seems to have stood in the area of the precinct of the Templum Divi Claudii.

Clemens: The church of S. Clemente is built over the remains of the saint's house. It is mentioned already on a slave's collar of the Constantinian period (*CIL* 15.7192). Presbyters of the titulus church took part in the synods of 499 and 595. Excavations under the lower church have brought to light two buildings: under the nave was a horreum with barrel-vaulted rooms opening on three sides of a large rectangular court, and under the apse was a large private house of insula character. The horreum antedates the fire of Nero in A.D. 64, whereas the house dates from the end of the first century. In the third century a Mithraeum was built into one room of the house (see Mithraeum Domus Clementis). Both buildings are of excellent architecture, and the house had fine decorations.

Nash 1.353–56 with plan.

P. Clodius Pulcher: a house on the Palatine on the Clivus Victoriae, near that of Cicero. Part of it was a house that originally belonged to Q. Seius Postumus, an eques Romanus; this must have stood between Clodius's original house and Cicero's. When Cicero went into exile, Clodius offered to buy Seius's house but was refused, after which Clodius threatened to block off Seius's light, presumably by construction of a wall (Cicero, *Dom.* 115–16). Cicero accuses him of then having poisoned Seius and bought his house at auction at an exorbitant price in order to construct there and on additional land taken from Cicero's a magnificent portico 300 feet long.

M. Cocceius Nerva (*PIR*[2] C 1225): A lead pipe bearing his name was found on the Esquiline (*CIL* 15.7437), but, because the grandfather of the emperor was curator aquarum in A.D. 24–33 (Frontinus, *Aq.* 2.102), this might have been pipe laid in connection with his office, rather than a supply line for his house.

Commodiana: A Domus Palatina Commodiana is mentioned once, for 22 October A.D. 180 (S.H.A. *Commodus* 12.7). This was apparently simply a flattering renaming of the Domus Augustiana, because it came at the beginning of his reign, and no work of importance in the imperial residence can be ascribed to him.

Cornelia Tauri f. T. Axi (**uxor**) (*PIR*[2] C 1477): on the Quirinal, known from a lead pipe (*CIL* 15.7440) found in building Via Nazionale, just east of Via dei Serpenti. This woman was evidently the adoptive daughter of a Statilius Taurus, perhaps T. Statilius Sisenna Taurus, cos. A.D. 16. Her husband is unknown. The family had a brilliant record in the early Julio-Claudian period but disappears after the mid-first century.

Cornelia L. f. Volusi Saturnini (**uxor**) (*PIR*[2] C 1476): known from a lead pipe found south of the great exedra of the Thermae Diocletiani (*CIL* 15.7441). The family of her husband had a brilliant record beginning under Augustus and running to the end of the first century.

Cornelii Fronto et Quadratus: Lead pipes inscribed with these names come from the vicinity of the Auditorium Maecenatis on the Esquiline (*CIL* 15.7438). Fronto may be the tutor of Marcus Aurelius and Lucius Verus (*PIR*² C 1364, 1426).

L. Cornelius Pusio (*PIR*² C 1425): probably where an inscription (*CIL* 6.31706) and fragments of a bronze portrait statue were found on the Quirinal near the Banca d'Italia toward the southwest end of Via Nazionale. This man was commander of the sixteenth legion in the time of Claudius.

Sex. Cornelius Repentinus (*PIR*² C 1428): known from a lead pipe (*CIL* 15.7439) found on the Aventine near the church of S. Alessio and identified as praefectus praetorio, an office he held at the end of the reign of Antoninus Pius.

Cornificia: listed in the regionary catalogues in Regio XII after the Cohors IV Vigilum and before the Privata Hadriani, and known also from a lead pipe of unknown provenience (*CIL* 15.7442). The house was probably between the barracks of the vigiles (see Cohortes Vigilum, Stationes, IIII) and the Vicus Portae Raudusculanae. The Cornificia in question may have been Annia Cornificia (*PIR*² A 708), the younger sister of Marcus Aurelius, who married M. Ummidius Quadratus, cos. A.D. 167 (*PIR*¹ V 601), but on her tiles she is called Annia Faustina (*CIL* 15.731). It might also be his daughter (*PIR*² C 1505).

BullCom 19 (1891): 210–16 (R. Lanciani); *RömMitt* 7 (1892): 296 (C. Hülsen).

Cosmus Aug. lib. a rationibus (*PIR*² C 1535): known from a lead pipe (*CIL* 15.7443 = *ILS* 1476) found in remains of a building of the early second century near S. Sabina on the Aventine.

L. Crassus (cos. 95 B.C., cens. 92 B.C.): the house on the Palatine of the distinguished orator of the years 118–91 B.C., famous for its elegance and luxury. It was the first house in Rome to have marble columns. Six of Hymettus marble, originally used to ornament a stage during Crassus's aedileship, were employed in the atrium. It also boasted six exceptional lotus trees of broad spreading branches that survived until the great fire of Nero in A.D. 64, at

which time they were more than 180 years old (Pliny, *HN* 17.3–6). Whether the fishponds where he kept his famous lampreys (Aelian, *NA* 8.4.1) were part of this house, or rather a villa, is unknown. Because of the marble columns M. Iunius Brutus called Crassus "the Palatine Venus" (Pliny, *HN* 36.7). The house came to Crassus by inheritance, probably from his father; it later was the property of Caecina Largus, cos. A.D. 42.

M. Licinius Crassus Dives (cos. 70 B.C., cens. 65 B.C.) (1): a house on the Palatine not far from the house that M. Caelius Rufus rented from P. Clodius Pulcher (Cicero, *Cael.* 9, 18).

M. Licinius Crassus Dives (2): the house bought by Cicero in 62 B.C. on the Clivus Victoriae, on the northwest side of the Palatine. Crassus had vast dealings in real estate and built for himself only the house in which he lived. The rest were built simply for sale in the market (Plutarch, *Crassus* 2.4–5).

M. Curius Dentatus (cos. 290, 275, 274 B.C.): given to him by the people (together with five hundred iugera of land outside the city) after his triumph over the Samnites in 290 B.C. It was *apud tifatam* (Paulus *ex Fest.* 43L; [Aur. Vict.,] *De Vir. Ill.* 33.10), and according to Festus (503L) a *tifata* was a grove of ilex or holm oak, the word probably dialect and of pre-Roman origin. This is supposed to have given rise to the name Tifata Curia, although the adjective from Curius ought to be Curiana. It seems at least possible that the story of Curius's house was an invention to explain the name Tifata Curia, which was a sacred precinct of some sort that included holm oaks. Its location is unknown.

Daphnis: a house *primae . . . in limine Tectae,* in A.D. 88 the residence of Julius Martialis (Martial 3.5.5–6), but formerly the house of an otherwise unidentified Daphnis (*PIR*² D 8). One Via Tecta seems to have led from the neighborhood of the Tarentum across the Campus Martius toward the Forum Romanum (Seneca, *Apocol.* 13), possibly the same street that later became the Porticus Maximae. A second may have been a colonnade along part of the Via Appia in the vicinity of the Temple of Mars, or a colonnade leading from the Via Appia to the Temple of Mars. Possibly it was also known as the Ambulatio Crassipedis (Cicero, *QFr.* 3.7.8). The former Via Tecta is more likely to be meant here, but it is impossible to determine where it began. The end near the city would be indicated, possibly just beyond the Petronia Amnis.

Diadumenus Aug. l. a libellis (*PIR²* D 65): known from a lead pipe (*CIL* 15.7444) of the mid-first century found on the Caelian near the Ospedale Militare del Celio. It is impossible to identify him or his house more precisely.

Dio: listed in the *Notitia* in Regio X after the Aedes Iovis and before the Curia Vetus. It may have been situated on the northwest slope of the Palatine, but there is no way of identifying Dio.

Domitiana: the house of Cn. Domitius Ahenobarbus (*PIR²* D 127), the father of Nero, on the Sacra Via, in front of which the Fratres Arvales offered sacrifices to his memory during the principate of Nero (*CIL* 6.32352, 2041.25, 2042d; *ILS* 229, 230). The house must have stood on the slope of the Velia leading up from the Forum, near, perhaps opposite, the Temple of the Penates (see Penates, Aedes) mentioned in *CIL* 6.2042d = *ILS* 230. Possibly he had inherited the house from his father (cf. Seneca, *Controv.* 9.4.18).

Cn. Domitius Calvinus (*PIR²* D 139): a house on the Velia to which baths were added in the principate of Augustus. For space for these baths *(balneatio)*, an ancient shrine *(sacellum)* of Mutunus Tutunus had to be removed (Festus 142L). The baths may be those built during the owner's consulship mentioned in a sally of Vallius Syriacus (Seneca, *Controv.* 9.4.18).

Elpidius: on the Caelian, known from a slave's collar (*CIL* 15.7190).

Ennius: The house of the great republican poet was on the Aventine and was said to have been very simple, with the services of a single maidservant (Hieron. *a. Abr.* 1777). Varro (*Ling.* 5.163), in listing the names of the gates of the Servian Walls, quotes Porcius Licinus as saying Ennius lived in *Tutilinae loca.* Because Tutilina was one of the gods worshiped on the spina in the Circus Maximus (Tertullian, *De Spect.* 8), we can with confidence place Ennius's house on the northeast slope of the Aventinus Minor toward the Porta Capena.

Equitius: on the Esquiline, a titulus church founded by Pope Silvester I (314–335), originally called S. Silvestri, enlarged by Pope Symmachus (498–514) with the addition of a church of S. Martino, which in time became S. Martino ai Monti. The name of S. Silvestro falls into disuse only after the tenth century (HCh 382–83).

Sex. Erucius Clarus (*PIR²* E 96): known from a lead pipe found in the Campus Viminalis *sub aggere* (*CIL* 15.7445), therefore beyond the Servian Walls. A man of this name mentioned by Aulus Gellius (13.18.2) was twice consul and praefectus urbi, consul for the second time in A.D. 146. He is said to have been an earnest student of ancient literature and old customs.

Faberius *(scriba)*: on the Aventine (Vitruvius 7.9.2), famous because the walls of the peristyle, painted with cinnabar, turned black.

Fabia Paulina: see **Domus, Vettius Agorius Praetextatus.**

Fabius Fortunatus (*PIR²* F 34): a house on the Clivus Capsarius (q.v.) *in Aventino Maiore*, mentioned in a fragment of the Acta Arvalia for A.D. 240, when Fabius was promagister (*NSc* 1914, 473–74 [G. Mancini and O. Marucchi] = *ILS* 9522).

L. Fabius Gallus (*PIR²* F 35): a name found inscribed on five lead pipes found in Via degli Annibaldi, the continuation of Via dei Serpenti, between Via Cavour and the Colosseum, and on two found under the Ministero delle Finanze in Via XX Settembre on the Quirinal (*CIL* 15.7449). Probably his house was on the Carinae, but he may have been curator aquarum.

C. Fabricius: see **Compitum Fabricium.**

Faecenia Hispala: A libertina, neighbor of P. Aebutius (see Domus, Aebutii), her house was evidently on the Aventine (Livy 39.9.5–6; 11.3; 14.3).

Fausta (*PLRE* 1.325–26): mentioned once in A.D. 313 (Optatus Milevitanus, *De Schismate Donatistorum* 1.23 [Migne 11.931]); it seems to have been an apartment in the Domus Lateranorum.
   RendPontAcc 43 (1970–71): 207–22 (V. Santa Maria Scrinari); *ArchCl* 24 (1972): 386–92 (M. Guarducci).

Flamen Quirinalis: At the time of the sack of Rome by the Gauls, the house of the Flamen Quirinalis was in the Velabrum by the Doliola (q.v.), but it is not clear whether this was an official residence. It seems an odd place for any official residence and very odd for the Flamen Quirinalis (cf. Livy 5.40.8).

Flaminia or **Aedes Flaminiae:** the house of the Flamen Dialis (Paulus *ex Fest.* 79L; A. Gellius

10.15.7; Servius *ad Aen.* 2.57 and 8.363). It was on the Palatine (Cass. Dio 54.24.2) but cannot be more precisely located.

Flavius Eugenius Asellus (*PLRE* 2.164): on the Capitoline. He was comes sacrorum largitionum in A.D. 469 (Sid. Apoll., *Epist.* 1.7.4) and later praefectus urbi (*CIL* 6.1668).

T. Flavius Claudius Claudianus: see **Domus, Claudii.**

T. Flavius Sabinus (*PIR²* F 352): the house of the brother of Vespasian on the Quirinal between Alta Semita and Vicus Longus. It is vaguely located by the discovery of a cippus in Villa Sadoleti near the church of S. Susanna and by a lead pipe found near the juncture of Via XX Settembre and Via Firenze (Tacitus, *Hist.* 3.69; *CIL* 6.29788 = *ILS* 5988 and *CIL* 15.7451). Its proximity to the Templum Gentis Flaviae (see Gens Flavia, Templum) is probably especially significant. M. Torelli has proposed that a splendid wall mosaic in the Fourth Pompeian Style, probably remains of a sumptuous nymphaeum, found under the barracks of the Corazzieri in attendance on the president of Italy north of the juncture of Via XX Settembre and Via di S. Nicola Tolentino, originally belonged to the house of Flavius Sabinus. This seems not unlikely.
   Roma sepolta (show catalogue, Rome 1984), 146–55 (F. Coarelli).

T. Flavius Salinator: known from a lead pipe (*CIL* 15.7452) found to the east of the house of T. Flavius Sabinus on the Quirinal.

T. Flavius Tiberianus: known from a lead pipe of the second century (*CIL* 15.7453) found on the Esquiline near Piazza Vittorio Emanuele at the corner of Via Cattaneo (formerly Via Mazzini) and Via Napoleone III. The house appears later to have belonged to M. Tuticius Capito.

Flavius Vedius Antoninus (*PIR²* F 392): known from a lead pipe of the second or third century (*CIL* 15.7456) found on the Quirinal near the Ministero delle Finanze.

Fronto: see **Domus, Cornelii Fronto et Quadratus, Domus Horatiana, Horti Maecenatiani.**

Fulvia: see **Domus, Caesetius Rufus** and **Domus, M. Antonius.**

M. Fulvius Flaccus: on the Clivus Victoriae on the northwest side of the Palatine, destroyed after the murder of Fulvius Flaccus in 121 B.C. The Porticus Catuli (q.v.) was then erected on the site (Cicero, *Dom.* 102, 114; Val. Max. 6.3.1c).

C. Fulvius Plautianus (*PIR²* F 554): on the northwest slope of the Quirinal north of the Giardini del Quirinale, known from two water pipes (*NSc* 1902, 132–33 [G. Gatti]; 1903, 20 [G. Gatti]). This was the close friend and fellow townsman of Septimius Severus, the father-in-law of Caracalla.

Gaiana: see **Domus Tiberiana.**

Galeria Fundana (*PIR²* G 33): the house of the wife of Vitellius, somewhere on the Aventine (Tacitus, *Hist.* 3.70). This is probably the same as the house of Vitellius's father, which Suetonius (*Vit.* 16) also places on the Aventine.

Gelotiana: a house on the Palatine overlooking the Circus Maximus, from which Caligula inspected preparations in the circus (Suetonius, *Calig.* 18; *CIL* 6.8663). The origin of the name is uncertain, and it is not clear whether this was incorporated in the Domus Augustiana.

Geminia Bassa (*PIR²* G 157): known from a lead pipe of the beginning of the third century (*CIL* 15.7463) found just inside the Porta Viminalis.

Genucius Marinianus (*PIR²* G 166): known from a lead pipe of the mid-third century (*CIL* 15.7464) found probably southeast of the church of S. Maria Maggiore on the Mons Cispius.

G . . . Ar . . . T . . . Germanianus (*PLRE* 1.392): known from a lead pipe of the fourth or fifth century (*CIL* 15.7462) found on the Quirinal at the southeast corner of the Thermae Constantinianae near the Banca d'Italia.

Germanicus (*PIR²* I 221): the house of the father of Caligula, on the Palatine, mentioned by Josephus (*AntIud* 19.1.15 [117]). It was part of the imperial compound and contiguous to the Domus Gaiana. It may have been part of the northeast wing of the palace overlooking Nova Via, but certainty is impossible.

Gregorius Magnus: on the end of the Caelian opposite the Domus, Iohannes et Paulus (q.v.) on the Clivus Scauri. This was the family home of the Anicii

Petronii (cf. *PLRE* 1.732–33) to which Gregory belonged, and in it he founded a church of Saint Andrew and a monastery, ca. A.D. 580. By the tenth century the monastery is called Monasterium Sanctorum Andreae et Gregorii, and after 1000 the church becomes that of S. Gregorio. There are numerous remains of antiquity in the vicinity of the present church of S. Gregorio Magno. Among those closest to the Clivus Scauri is an apsidal building of masonry faced with brick that Lugli (Lugli 1946, 386–87) suggests may be the Bibliotheca Agapeti founded by Pope Agapetus I (535–536), the dedicatory inscription for which survives. This was to collect and preserve the history and literature of early Christianity in Rome. Near the church there is also a source of excellent water, which is almost certainly the Fons Camenarum (see Camenae).

(H)aterius Latronianus (*PIR*² H 28): known from a lead pipe of the middle or late second century (*CIL* 15.7467) found at the north (?) corner of the Ministero delle Finanze on Via XX Settembre (Quirinal). The tomb of Q. Haterius was found nearby in the foundations of the Porta Nomentana (Porta Pia) of the Aurelian Walls (see Sepulcrum Q. Haterii).

L. Hermonius Iustus: see **Stabula IIII Factionum.**

Homullus: mentioned once in S.H.A. (*Ant. Pius* 11.8) and notable for its porphyry columns, probably the house of M. Valerius Homullus, cos. A.D. 152 (*PIR*¹ V 61).

Horatiana: mentioned by the scholiast on Juvenal 1.12 (*Frontonis plantani convolsaque marmora clamant): in Horatiana domo, in qua poetae recitabant.* No Horatius Fronto is known, nor is a Fronto of Juvenal's day who would have lived in a house that had once belonged to the poet Horace. The house Juvenal describes is sumptuous. Some people have supposed that the Fronto meant by Juvenal was Catius Fronto, a noted orator of the time of Vespasian (Pliny, *Epist.* 4.9.15; 6.13.3), but there is no indication that he might have lived in Horace's house.

A. Hortensius Licinianus: Lead pipes with his name belonging to the late second or early third century (*CIL* 15.7469) were found on the right bank of the Tiber, upstream from the Mausoleum Hadriani.

Q. Hortensius Hortalus (cos. 69 B.C.): the great orator and rival of Cicero. His house on the Palatine was purchased by Octavian (Suetonius, *Aug.* 72) and is said to have been conspicuous for neither size nor luxury. It was without marbles or splendid pavements, and the porticoes were of peperino. Its identification with the Casa di Augusto at the top of the Scalae Caci, between this and the Aedes Apollinis Palatini, is very attractive and widely accepted today, although positive proof is lacking. See Domus, Augustus (3).

G. Carettoni, *Das Haus des Augustus auf dem Palatin* (Mainz 1983).

Iohannes et Paulus (Fig. 32): the house in which two army officers, Saints John and Paul, were martyred under Julian, situated on the slope of the Caelian just southwest of the precinct of the Templum Divi Claudii on the Clivus Scauri. The site is now marked by the church of SS. Giovanni e Paolo. Excavations under the church have brought to light a good-sized private house of insula type of the second century, enlarged by the addition of parts of at least two others and remodeled in the third and fourth centuries. In this was established the Titulus Byzantis, probably in the second half of the third century, and the senator Pammuchius is responsible for founding the basilica in 410. Upward of thirty rooms have been discovered. They include an entrance court with a nymphaeum (A), large vaulted rooms of irregular shape with painted decorations, baths, storerooms, and stairs. The main part of the house once had at least three storeys, which can be traced on the south façade (Nash 1.358, fig. 434), the lower storey being arcaded on the façade (originally with shops behind), the others windowed. The painted decorations are of the highest interest and include pagan subjects (Proserpina and other divinities) and vaguely Christian ones (orant, philosopher). The sequence of constructions here is complicated, and the use and reuse of the various apartments is impossible to sort out completely.

Nash 1.357–61.

Iulia Vitalis: known from an inscribed lead pipe (*CIL* 15.7480) found on the Esquiline at the corner of Viale Principe Amedeo (formerly Viale Principessa Margherita) and Via Cattaneo (formerly Via Mazzini).

Iulii Cefalii (*PIR*² I 1254): known from an inscribed lead pipe (*CIL* 15.7472) found a little north of the Aqua Antoniniana, about halfway between the Porta Ardeatina and Porta Appia.

C. Iulius Avitus: known from a lead pipe (*CIL* 15.7471) found on the Viminal under the Teatro Costanzi. He may have been the husband of Iulia Maesa (*PIR*² I 190).

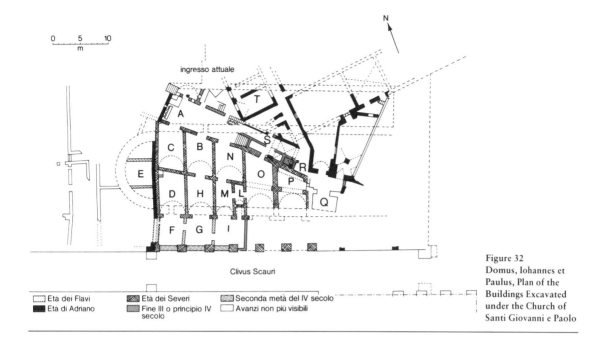

0 5 10
m

ingresso attuale

N

Clivus Scauri

Figure 32
Domus, Iohannes et
Paulus, Plan of the
Buildings Excavated
under the Church of
Santi Giovanni e Paolo

☐ Età dei Flavi   ▨ Età dei Severi   ▦ Seconda metà del IV secolo
■ Età di Adriano   ▧ Fine III o principio IV secolo   ☐ Avanzi non più visibili

---

Iulius Martialis (*PIR*² I 411): at the head of Via Tecta (Martial 3.5.5), probably the street in the Campus Martius, rather than that associated with the Aedes Martis on Via Appia, and probably near the Circus Flaminius end, rather than the Tarentum (cf. Seneca, *Apocol.* 13.1).

Iulius Pompeius Rusonianus (*PIR*² I 476): known from three inscribed lead pipes (*CIL* 15.7475) found under the Teatro Nazionale on the southwest slope of the Quirinal. He is probably the quindecimvir of the Severan period (*CIL* 6 p. 3261).

Iulius Proculus (*PIR*² I 500): low on the Palatine, evidently on the east side of the so-called Clivus Palatinus, near the north corner of the present Vigna Barberini, said by Martial (1.70) to be an imposing house of splendid architecture.

Iunia Procula: known from a lead pipe (*CIL* 15.7482) found in a fountain southeast of the great fountain of the Aqua Iulia in Piazza Vittorio Emanuele. The pyramidal form of the fountain suggests that it belonged to a private house.

Iunius (*PIR*² I 722): the house of a senator situated on the Caelian (Tacitus, *Ann.* 4.64.3), otherwise unknown. It was remarkable because a likeness of Tiberius in the house survived unscathed when the hill burned in A.D. 27.

Iunius Bassus: see **Basilica Iunii Bassi.**

Laeca: see **Domus, M. Porcius Laeca.**

M. Laelius Fulvius Maximus (*PIR*² L 53): known from an inscribed lead pipe (*CIL* 15.7483) found at the north corner of the Ministero delle Finanze on the Quirinal. He may be the consul of A.D. 227.

Lamiae: see **Horti Lamiani.**

C. Ceionius Rufius Volusianus Lampadius (*PLRE* 1.978–80): near the Thermae Constantinianae on the Quirinal (Collis Salutaris) (Amm. Marc. 27.3.8). Lampadius was praefectus urbi in A.D. 366.

Laterani: a house lying in part under the baptistery of S. Giovanni in Laterano. This was presented to T. Sextius Lateranus (*PIR*¹ S 469), cos. A.D. 197, by Septimius Severus and is identified by an inscribed lead pipe (Aur. Vict., *Epit.* 20; *CIL* 15.7536). It is probable that it was on the site of the sumptuous house of Plautius Lateranus, cos. des. A.D. 65, who was executed for complicity in the Pisonian conspiracy (Tacitus, *Ann.* 15.60; Juvenal 10.17). Later the house evidently returned to imperial ownership, for Constantine presented it to Pope Miltiades in A.D. 313, after which it became the official residence of the popes and remained such until 1305 and the Babylonian captivity at Avignon.

Careful excavations begun in 1962 and continuing to 1968 in connection with the restoration of the baptistery of S. Giovanni in Laterano, although limited in area, revealed a building sequence that goes far to illuminate the history of this property. In the lowest level were found walls faced with opus reticulatum characteristic of the first half of the first century after Christ, which were oriented in conformance with other buildings in the area, and parts of a long pillared walk that seem to be related to the scant remains of a villa suburbana found under the Castra Equitum Singularium Severiana (q.v.) beneath the basilica of S. Giovanni. Later in the same century there was a radical transformation of the area through the construction of large rooms with very thick walls on a slightly different orientation. This remodeling has been thought to reflect the passage of the estate into the imperial properties following the Pisonian conspiracy. Little of this period remains; it has been thought that the building may have been destroyed in the earthquakes of A.D. 85 and 94. Beginning perhaps under Hadrian, certainly brought to completion under Antoninus Pius, a bath complex was built on the site, which collapsed toward the end of the second century and was reconstructed under Septimius Severus. Under the same emperor, the whole area seems to have undergone division into two distinct parcels, with a broad street running between them. This may reflect the donation of the western parcel to T. Sextius Lateranus, while the eastern parcel continued to function as a fairly luxurious bath of medium size, very likely in conjunction with the Castra Equitum Singularium that Septimius constructed. At some point later in the third century, this bath complex was converted to use as a residence by closing down doorways and running partition walls across the great public spaces of the bath rooms. But the scale remained very large, and much of the heating system seems to have remained in use. This remodeling is dated roughly to the time of Aurelian. Then at the beginning of the fourth century there came a complete rebuilding, with the eradication of all remaining traces of its origin as a bath complex; this we can see as following the abolition of the Equites Singulares by Constantine and his presentation of the Domus Lateranorum and its adjacencies to Pope Miltiades. A large circular room in the Aurelian house with a central basin built over the basin of the frigidarium of the Severan baths appears to have been a nymphaeum. It was now rebuilt as octagonal and became the baptistery, but still an apartment intimately connected with the papal residence rather than a part of a church; hence its isolated position with respect to the basilica today. Around it clustered the other rooms of the residence, large in size but comparatively few in number and formal in character.

MemPontAcc, ser. 3.12, fasc. 1 (1973) "Le nuove scoperte sulle origini del battistero Lateranense" (G. Pelliccioni); *MEFRA* 100 (1988): 891–915 (P. Liverani).

Lenaeus (*PIR*[1] P 467): A freedman of Pompey, devoted to his memory, maintained a school on the Carinae in the neighborhood of the Temple of Tellus, where the house of Pompey (Domus Rostrata) had stood. This was after the death of Pompey and his sons (Suetonius, *Gramm.* 15).

Liciniana: see **Domus, Luciniana.**

C. Licinius Calvus: the house of the orator and poet, who was a friend of Catullus, near the Forum Romanum. This was the first house Octavian had in Rome, before he moved to the Palatine. It stood *supra scalas anularias* (Suetonius, *Aug.* 72), the location of which is unknown. Probably the house was on the slope of the Palatine, and probably toward the north corner of the hill.

Licinius Sura (*PIR*[2] L 253) (1): a house on the Aventine close to the Temple of Diana and overlooking the Circus Maximus (Martial 6.64.12–13).

Licinius Sura (2): possibly a house on the Caelian near the Lateran, where the base of a statue with a dedicatory inscription, probably to be assigned to Sura, was found in the sixteenth century (*CIL* 6.1444 = *ILS* 1022).

M. Livius Drusus: on the Palatine on the Clivus Victoriae in the place where later the house of Cicero stood. It is notable for having been the work of an architect who was concerned for the privacy of his client (Vell. Pat. 2.14.3).

Lucina: in Via Lata where a titulus church was established by Pope Marcellus I (A.D. 309). It was near the Catabulum (HCh 308).

Luciniana (usually corrected to Liciniana, but there is no certainty): a house rented by Cicero for the use of his brother Quintus, *ad lacum Pisonis,* while his house on the Carinae was occupied by tenants (Cicero, *QFr.* 2.3.7). It was probably on the Palatine (see Domus, Q. Tullius Cicero [2]).

L. Lusius Petellinus: known from the inscription on a lead pipe belonging to the middle or end of the first century after Christ found on the site of S. Giovanni in Laterano (*CIL* 15.7488). The owner is otherwise unknown.

Q. Maecius Blandus (*PIR*[2] M 48): known from lead pipes bearing his name and that of Caelia Galla found on the Capitoline under the monastery of Ara-coeli (*CIL* 15.7489).

Mamurra: on the Caelian, the house of Julius Caesar's praefectus fabrum in Gaul, noted for its extravagance. All the walls were revetted with marble; it was the first such house in Rome (Pliny, *HN* 36.48).

Mancinus: see **Tifata Mancina.**

M'. Manilius: a small house *(aediculae)* on the Carinae (Cicero, *Paradoxa* 6.50). This Manilius was consul in 149 B.C.

M. Manlius Capitolinus (cos. 392 B.C.): on the Capitoline where the Temple of Iuno Moneta was built, consequently where the house of Titus Tatius had stood. It was razed to the ground by order of the senate in 384 B.C. after its owner was condemned to death for aspiring to monarchy (Livy 6.20.13; 7.28.5; Ovid, *Fast.* 6.183–90). After Capitolinus's disgrace patricians were forever forbidden to live on the arx and Capitoline.

Marcella: on the Aventine, mentioned by Jerome (*Epist.* 47[a].3 [Migne 22.493]).
BullCom 87 (1980–81): 7–36 (G. Giannelli).

Publia Marcia Sergia Fusca: known from a lead pipe found on the slope of the Quirinal in Villa Aldobrandini in a group of tabernae or horrea (*CIL* 15.7493; cf. *BullCom* 9 [1881]: 17 [R. Lanciani]). It was found close to a pipe of L. Naevius Clemens.

C. Marius (cos. VII 86 B.C.): adjacent to the Forum Romanum (Plutarch, *Marius* 32), probably close to the Temple of Honos et Virtus (see Honos et Virtus, Aedes [2]) and included in the Monumenta Mariana of Valerius Maximus (2.5.6; 4.4.8). The area is probably that now occupied by the Temple of Antoninus and Faustina.

M. Valerius Martialis (*PIR*[1] V 77): on the Quirinal near the Temple of Quirinus (Martial 10.58.10), on the street leading from the Capitolium Vetus to the Temple of Flora (Martial 5.22.3–4). Because the latter was a clivus (Varro, *Ling.* 5.158), the temple is more likely to have stood on the northwest slope of the Quirinal than the gentle southeast slope *ad Malum Punicum,* and on an ancient street that roughly followed the line of Via delle Quattro Fontane in this sector.

L. Marius Maximus Perpetuus Aurelianus (*PIR*[2] M 308): known from inscriptions found in Villa Fonseca on the Caelian in 1553 (*CIL* 6.1450–

53; *ILS* 2935–36). This Marius Maximus was consul in 198 or 199 and wrote biographies of the Caesars from Trajan to Elagabalus.

C. Marius Pudens Cornelianus (*PIR*[2] M 317): known from a bronze tablet of A.D. 222 found on the Aventine near the church of S. Prisca (*CIL* 6.1454 = *ILS* 6109). He was legate of the seventh legion.

P. Martius Philippus (*PIR*[2] M 345): known from an inscribed lead pipe found on the right bank of the Tiber opposite the island (*CIL* 15.7492; cf. *CIL* 14.169 = *ILS* 6172).

Merulana: known from a letter of Pope Gregory the Great (*Epist.* 3.19 [*MGH Epist.* 1.177]) of A.D. 593, but probably dating at least from the early empire. It was near the ancient church of S. Matteo in Merulana (HCh 386–87). The ancient street that came to be known as Via Merulana ran from a point in Piazza Vittorio Emanuele west of the nymphaeum of the Aqua Iulia almost due south to the Neronian branch of the Aqua Claudia. The house must have been on the Esquiline toward the north end of this street, near the church (near Piazza Dante).

M. Valerius Messalla Corvinus (*PIR*[1] V 90) (1): on the Palatine, earlier the house of Mark Antony, presented to Messalla Corvinus and Agrippa by Augustus (Cass. Dio 53.27.5). See also Domus, Caesetius Rufus.

M. Valerius Messalla Corvinus (2): on the Pincian known from inscriptions found in the gardens of Villa Medici (*CIL* 6.29789 = *ILS* 5990). The house was probably not a domus but a horti. It appears that Messalla bought the Horti Luculliani (q.v.).

T. Annius Milo Papinianus (1): on the Clivus Capitolinus (Cicero, *Milon.* 64), possibly only a house alleged to have been hired by Milo for nefarious purposes. Because the Clivus Capitolinus was steep and ran in a switchback, such a house would almost certainly have had to have lain in the narrow area between the Vicus Iugarius and the clivus, behind the Temple of Saturn.

T. Annius Milo Papinianus (2): an ancestral house known as Domus Anniana, on the Cermalus, the slope of the Palatine toward the Circus Maximus (Cicero, *Att.* 4.3.3). This house apparently passed into the possession of Q. Lucretius Vespillo, the husband of Turia, the republican wife praised for her enterprise and loyalty in the inscription known as the Laudatio Turiae (*CIL* 6.1527 = 31670 = *ILS* 8393). She had to defend it against an attempt by Milo's supporters to recover it by force (fr. 2.8–10).

Mucianus: known from a lead pipe (*CIL* 15.7496) apparently found within the area of the Thermae Constantinianae.

Q. Munatius Celsus: known only from an inscribed lead pipe found just inside the Porta Viminalis (*CIL* 15.7497). This man was probably procurator of Mauretania under Caracalla.

Naeratius Cerialis: see **Balnea Naeratii Cerealis.**

L. Naevius Clemens (*PIR*² N 11): known from two inscribed lead pipes, one found inside the Porta Viminalis, the other in Villa Aldobrandini on the Quirinal (*CIL* 15.7499). The first was found near the distribution center of the aqueducts in this region, and the other was found probably closer to the site of Clemens's house.

Narcissus (probably Claudii lib. [*PIR*² N 23]): known from inscribed lead pipes (*CIL* 15.7500 = *ILS* 1666) found near the Teatro Nazionale on the west slope of the Quirinal.

Numa Pompilius: at first on the Quirinal; later he is supposed to have moved to the Regia near the Temple of Vesta (Solinus 1.21).

Cn. Numicius Picus Caesianus (*PIR*² N 203): on the Viminal at the corner of Via Viminalis and Via Principe Amedeo, near the Teatro dell'Opera (*CIL* 6.31742, 31743 = *ILS* 911). He was propraetor of Asia, possibly under Augustus (see Varro, *Rust.* 3.2.2).

Nummii: on the Quirinal, just east of the Ministero della Difesa, where inscriptions show that several members of the Gens Nummia lived in the third and fourth centuries (*CIL* 6.1748, 31378, 32024–26; *ILS* 643, 1238).

C. Octavius (praetor 61 B.C.): *ad Capita Bubula* on the Palatine, probably its eastern slope, where Augustus was born (Suetonius, *Aug.* 5). Later a sacrarium was created there, and later still a temple.

Cn. Octavius: on the Palatine, built by the consul of 165 B.C. Its splendor was supposed to have promoted Octavius's election to the consulship. Aemilius Scaurus later bought and demolished it in order to build an addition to his own house (Cicero, *Off.* 1.138), which must have stood next to it.

L. Octavius: on, or very close to, Sacra Via (Sallust, *Hist.* fr. 2.45); here in 75 B.C. the consuls, Octavius and C. Aurelius Cotta, took refuge when attacked by a mob on Sacra Via (cf. Broughton, *MRR* 2.96).

L. Octavius Felix (*PIR*² O 31): on the Viminal, known from the discovery of an inscribed lead pipe in its atrium at the southwest corner of the Stazione Termini (*CIL* 15.7503).

M. Opellius Macrinus and **M. Opellius Diadumenianus** (*PIR*² O 108, 107): on the Caelian, known from an inscribed lead pipe found under the Lateran (*CIL* 15.7505 = *ILS* 461). The former was the man responsible for the assassination of Caracalla; he became emperor in 217 and was defeated by Elagabalus and killed in 218.

Pactumeia Lucilia: on the west slope of the Aventine under the church of S. Anselmo, where remains of an ancient house with mosaics showing an Orpheus and a centauromachy and an inscribed lead pipe (*CIL* 15.7507) were found.

HJ 169; *BullCom* 88 (1982–83): 213–23 (D. Cavallo).

Palmata: next to the Porticus Curva (see Forum Traiani) according to Cassiodorus (*Var.* 4.30), perhaps the same as the Domus ad Palmam of L. Acilius Glabrio Faustus (*PLRE* 2.452–54), cos. A.D. 438, in which the Theodosian Code is said to have been promulgated.

Parthorum (Aedes ?): listed in the regionary catalogues in Regio XII and said by Aurelius Victor (*Epit.* 20) to be among the most notable of the houses Septimius Severus presented to his friends. Because the regionary catalogues list these immediately after the Thermae Antoninianae, they have been identified with ruins northwest of the baths, but there is no supporting evidence for this identification.

Pescenniana: the house of Pescennius Niger (*PIR*¹ P 185) in the Campus Iovis (S.H.A. *Pescennius* 12.4). The whereabouts of this is unknown, but it was probably outside the line of the Servian Walls. The only suitable shrine of Jupiter known is one of Iuppiter Dolichenus in the neighborhood of Piazza Vittorio Emanuele (see Iuppiter Dolichenus [2]), the Transtiberim being very unlikely to have been the location of Pescennius's house. The discovery of lead pipes bearing the names of two members of the family probably southeast of Porta S. Lorenzo (*CIL* 15.7509) and of fragmentary inscriptions that may be attributed to them (*CIL* 6.31745) has led to the identification of a house there as possibly the one in question.

Petronius Maximus (*PLRE* 2.749–50): on the Oppius north of S. Clemente, identified by ruins and inscriptions (*CIL* 6.1197, 1198 = *ILS* 807–8). He was consul in 433 and 443 and became emperor briefly in 455.

Philippus: listed by the regionary catalogues in Regio II, possibly the house of Iulius Philippus (Philippus Arabs), emperor 244–249 (*PIR*² I 461).

Pinciana: on the Pincian, a house of the fourth century that later passed into the imperial properties. It is mentioned as a domus by Cassiodorus (*Var.* 3.10), and as a *palatium* in the *Liber Pontificalis* (60.6.8 = LPD 1.291; VZ 2.248). It was apparently served by its own branch aqueduct (see Aqua Pinciana). Earlier the property had been the Horti Aciliorum (q.v.). Theodoric took some of the marbles of the house to Ravenna. See also HCh 252, Sancti Felicis in Pincis. Later this house seems to have been called a Palation (Procopius, *BellGoth* 2.9.1–11).

L. Piso: known from an inscribed pipe found in Via della Ferratella near Porta Metrovia (*CIL* 15.7513). This may have been the house of the consul of A.D. 57 (*PIR*² C 294).

Plautius Lateranus: see **Domus, Laterani.**

C. Plinius Secundus (*PIR*¹ P 370): in Esquiliae near the Lacus Orphei (Martial 10.19.5–9; Pliny, *Epist.* 3.21.5). The house had earlier belonged to Albinovanus Pedo, the epic poet and friend of Ovid (Martial 10.19.10).

Cn. Pompeius Magnus (cos. III 52 B.C.)(1): on the Carinae near the Temple of Tellus (Suetonius, *Gramm.* 15.1; Vell. Pat. 2.77; Cicero, *Har. Resp.* 49). The vestibulum was embellished with rostra from pirate ships, from which it was called Domus Rostrata (Cicero, *Phil.* 2.68; S.H.A. *Gordian.* 3). After Pompey's death Mark Antony acquired it (Cass. Dio 48.38; Florus 2.18.4; [Aur. Vict.,] *De Vir. Ill.* 84.3), and later it passed into the imperial properties. Tiberius lived there for a time before his accession (Suetonius, *Tib.* 15), and later it is said to have been the house of the Gordians (S.H.A. *Gordian.* 2, 3, 6, 17).

Cn. Pompeius Magnus (cos. III 52 B.C.) (2): Plutarch says that during the construction of his theater Pompey built a house for himself close to it and that this was a finer one than he had previously had (Plutarch, *Pomp.* 40.5); this was like a tender towed behind a large ship, indication that the house lay west of the theater.

Pomponii: on the Quirinal, neighbor to the Temple of Salus and the Temple of Quirinus, so presumably between these, but closer to the former. It originally belonged to a Tampilus or Tamphilus and then to T. Pomponius Atticus, who inherited it from his uncle, presumably Caecilius (Cicero, *Att.* 4.1.4, 12.45.3; *Leg.* 1.1.3; Nepos, *Att.* 13.2 and cf. 5.1). According to Nepos, the house was old-fashioned but charming, and Atticus changed nothing, except as age forced repairs. Its particular attraction was its trees (*silva*). The house continued in the possession of the family, and an inscription found at the southeast corner of the crossing of Alta Semita and Clivus Salutis in 1558 indicates that T. Pomponius Bassus, curator alimentorum under Trajan, lived here in A.D. 101 (*CIL* 6.1492 = *ILS* 6106).

M. Porcius Laeca: *inter falcarios* (Cicero, *Cat.* 1.8, *Sulla* 52); we have no further indication of where this might be.

Postumii: on the western slope of the Quirinal, where inscriptions have been found recording M. Postumius Festus (*PIR*¹ P 660) (*CIL* 15.7517), T. Flavius Postumius Varus (*PLRE* 1.946–47), praefectus urbi in A.D. 271 (*CIL* 6.1417 = *ILS* 2940), and T. Flavius Postumius Titianus (*PLRE* 1.919–20), praefectus urbi in A.D. 305 (*CIL* 6.1418 = *ILS* 2941).

Potitus: on the Aventine near the Thermae Decianae, known from an inscription on a slave's collar (*CIL* 15.7181). A Potitus was vicarius urbis in A.D. 379–381 (*PLRE* 1.721), but the name was borne by a great many members of the Gens Valeria in late antiquity.

Sex. Propertius: in Esquiliae (Propertius 3.23. 24, 4.8.1), perhaps near the nymphaeum of the Aqua Iulia in Piazza Vittorio Emanuele and the Lacus Orphei, because the poet describes the area as *aquosa*.

Publica (see also **Regia** and **Atrium Vestae**): a house on Sacra Via in the precinct of Vesta where the pontifex maximus lived until the time of Augustus (Suetonius, *Iul.* 46; Cass. Dio 54.24.2). After Augustus's election as pontifex maximus in 13 B.C., the residence was moved to the Palatine and the Domus Publica was given to the Vestal Virgins, because it was separated from the Atrium Vestae only by a wall (Cass. Dio 54.27.3). Excavations have revealed remains of an atrium house contiguous to the republican Atrium Vestae, but entirely separate, stepped up with respect to the Atrium Vestae and different in concept, which has been identified as the Domus Publica. It lay on Sacra Via across from the so-called Templum Romuli.

Nash 1.362–64; *RendPontAcc* 51–52 (1978–80): 346–55 (G. Carettoni).

Pulverata: known from the inscription on a slave's collar (*CIL* 15.7179), possibly to be located in the southern Campus Martius along the river, where the name Pulverone still survives (*AnalRom,* suppl. 10 [1983]: 70, 81n.64 [L. Quilici]).

Rex Sacrorum: on the Velia at Summa Sacra Via, where the Sacra Via turned from its course from the Forum Romanum to run to the Sacellum Streniae on the Carinae (Festus 372L; Varro, *Ling.* 5.47).

Roius Hilario: known from an inscribed lead pipe of the time of Augustus or earlier found under the margin of the ancient street between the Circus Maximus and the Palatine (*CIL* 15.7522). This pipe ran toward the Palatine and probably supplied a house here (LA 447).

L. Roscius Aelianus Paculus (*PIR*[1] R 64): on the Caelian, known from an inscribed lead pipe found at the entrance to Villa Wolkonsky (*CIL* 15.7523). Roscius was consul in A.D. 187.

Rostrata: see **Domus, Cn. Pompeius Magnus** (1).

Rubellia Bassa (*PIR*[1] R 86): known from an inscribed lead pipe found with that of Roius Hilario (see Domus, Roius Hilario), but running at right angles to it (*CIL* 15.7524), so probably belonging to a house in the neighborhood (LA 447). Rubellia Bassa was probably the grandniece of Tiberius.

C. Sallustius Crispus: see **Horti Sallustiani.**

M. Sallustius Rufus Titilianus (*PIR*[1] S 67): known from a lead pipe found in the Campus Viminalis sub aggere (*CIL* 15.7526).

M. Aemilius Scaurus: a house next to that of Cn. Octavius (cos. 165 B.C.) on the Palatine. Scaurus

bought Octavius's house and demolished it, although it was considered very fine, in order to build an addition to his own (Cicero, *Off.* 1.138). Scaurus's house was further notable for four columns of Hymettus marble brought to Rome for the decoration of his theater, which was built during his aedileship in 58 B.C. (Pliny, *HN* 17.5–6, 36.6). These columns were later removed to the Theater of Marcellus. Scaurus's house was the same as, or came to include, that of L. Crassus the orator (see Domus, L. Crassus), and the enlarged whole became the house of Caecina Largus in the first century after Christ. There is some confusion over the marble columns; in one place Pliny (*HN* 17.6) says there were six columns of Hymettus marble imported by Crassus during his aedileship for the stage of his theater, the first marble columns to be used in a public building; in another place (*HN* 36.6) he says there were four columns and they were brought to Rome for the decoration of Scaurus's theater. The first is probably correct.

P. Scipio Africanus (cos. II 194 B.C., cens. 199 B.C.): behind the Tabernae Veteres (see Tabernae Circum Forum) adjacent to the Forum Romanum, probably fronting on the Vicus Tuscus *(ad Vortumni signum).* Tiberius Sempronius Gracchus, censor in 169 B.C., bought this house and the adjacent shops and built the Basilica Sempronia here (Livy 44.16.10–11).

Scipio Nasica: on Sacra Via, presented to Nasica by the state, *quo facilius consuli posset* (*Dig.* 1.2.37). This is probably the consul of 191 B.C.

Q. Seius Postumus: on the Palatine on the Clivus Victoriae, between the house of P. Clodius Pulcher and the house of Cicero. Clodius bought it after Seius's death, which Cicero alleges to have been procured by poisoning (Cicero, *Dom.* 115–16).

L. Sempronius Rufus (*PIR*[1] S 275): known from a lead pipe found on the right bank of the Tiber opposite the Pons Agrippae, outside the line of the Aurelian Walls (*CIL* 15.7530).

Septem Domus: listed in the regionary catalogues in Regio XII after Parthorum, but otherwise unknown.

M. Servilius Fabianus Maximus (*PIR*[1] S 415): on the Esquiline south of the Clivus Suburanus and east of the Porticus Liviae, known from an inscription (*CIL* 6.1517 = *ILS* 1080). Servilius was suffect consul in A.D. 158.

Servius Tullius: on the Oppius *supra Clivum Urbium* (Solinus 1.25), in the neighborhood of S. Pietro in Vincoli.

C. Sestius: in the Subura, known from an inscription of the republican period (*CIL* 6.29790 = *ILS* 5993 = *ILLRP* 493) and remains discovered near the church of S. Maria dei Monti.

Sextia Cethegilla (*PIR*¹ S 484): known from an inscribed lead pipe, found perhaps on the Esquiline in Piazza Vittorio Emanuele (*CIL* 15.7537). She was the daughter of the emperor Pupienus.

T. Sextius Africanus (*PIR*¹ R 464): believed to have been at the corner of Via del Babuino and Via di Gesù e Maria (*CIL* 6.31684). The inscription is fragmentary, and its provenience is somewhat uncertain. This man was suffect consul in A.D. 59. It seems an unlikely location for an important town house at this period.

Silverius: A lead pipe inscribed with this name was found near the Lateran (*CIL* 15.7538) (*PLRE* 2.1012).

App. Silvius Iunius Silvinus (*PIR*¹ S 524): on the Quirinal, known from an inscribed lead pipe found in the vineyard of the Cardinal d'Este (the western part of the Quirinal palace) in the sixteenth century (*CIL* 15.7539).

D. Simonius Proculus Iulianus (*PIR*¹ S 529): known from an inscribed lead pipe bearing his name found southwest of the Casino dell'Aurora in Villa Ludovisi (*CIL* 15.7528). He was praefectus urbi sometime before A.D. 254.

Spurius Maximus (*PIR*¹ S 583): on the Quirinal under Palazzo Barberini, known from an inscribed lead pipe (*CIL* 15.7540) and the ruins of a private house, including a nymphaeum with well-preserved paintings. The owner was perhaps L. Spurius Maximus, tribunus vigilum under Septimius Severus.

Statilius Sisenna (cos. A.D. 16): see **Domus, M. Cicero.**

C. Stertinius Xenophon (*PIR*¹ S 666): on the Caelian, known from an inscribed lead pipe (*CIL* 15.7544). This was the physician of Claudius, alleged to have procured his death by poisoning (*CIL* 6.8905 = *ILS* 1841; Pliny, *HN* 29.7; Tacitus, *Ann.* 12.67).

C. Suetrius Sabinus (*PIR*¹ S 696): perhaps on the Aventine, but the evidence is inadequate (*CIL* 6.1476, 15.7546). This man is probably the consul of A.D. 214, C. Octavius Appius Suetrius Sabinus.

P. Sulla: on or near the Cermalus (Cicero, *Att.* 4.3.3). Publius Clodius took it as headquarters for his assault on the house of Milo in 57 B.C.

Sulpicia Pacata: known from an inscribed lead pipe of the second century found between the church of S. Crisogono and the Excubitorium of the seventh cohort of the vigiles in the Transtiberim (*CIL* 15.7548).

Sulpicia C. f. Triaria (*PIR*¹ S 745): known from an inscribed lead pipe found north of the Temple of Isis et Serapis in Regio III (*CIL* 15.7550).

Sura: see **Domus, Licinius Sura.**

L. Aurelius Symmachus (*PLRE* 1.863–65): a house of the father of the following on the right bank of the Tiber (Symmachus, *Epist.* 1.44.1; Amm. Marc. 27.3.4). This was burned by a mob in A.D. 367.

Q. Aurelius Symmachus (*PLRE* 1.865–70): on the Caelian (Symmachus, *Epist.* 3.12.2, 7.18.1) near Villa Casali, where inscriptions have been found (*CIL* 6.1699, 1782, 31903; *ILS* 2946, 2947).

Tampiliana: see **Domus, Pomponii.**

Tarquinius Priscus: *ad Portam Mugoniam supra summam Novam Viam* (Solinus 1.24) and *ad Iovis Statoris* (Livy 1.41.4), therefore on the Palatine slope above the temple.

Tarquinius Superbus: on the Oppius *supra Clivum Pullium ad Fagutalem Lacum* (Solinus 1.26). Pliny's statement (*HN* 34.29) that his house was opposite Iuppiter Stator seems to have been due to a confusion of Tarquinius Superbus and Tarquinius Priscus.

T. Tatius: on the Capitoline on the site later occupied by the Temple of Iuno Moneta (Solinus 1.21; Plutarch, *Rom.* 20.4). See also Domus, Manlius Capitolinus.

Terentius Culleo (*PIR*¹ T 54): known from an inscribed lead pipe (*CIL* 15.7551) found at the corner of modern Via Merulana and Via dello Statuto, inside and a little southwest of Porta Esquilina in the

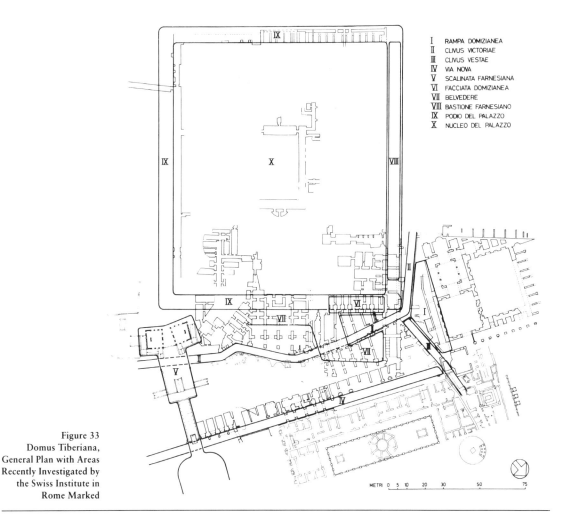

I   RAMPA DOMIZIANEA
II   CLIVUS VICTORIAE
III CLIVUS VESTAE
IV VIA NOVA
V   SCALINATA FARNESIANA
VI FACCIATA DOMIZIANEA
VII BELVEDERE
VIII BASTIONE FARNESIANO
IX PODIO DEL PALAZZO
X   NUCLEO DEL PALAZZO

METRI 0 5 10 20   30   50   75

Figure 33
Domus Tiberiana,
General Plan with Areas
Recently Investigated by
the Swiss Institute in
Rome Marked

area known as Forum Esquilinum. He was suffect consul in A.D. 40.

Tetrici: on the Caelian *inter duos lucos,* opposite a temple of Isis (S.H.A. *Tyr. Trig.* 25), so probably close to the division between Regiones II and III. It was probably near the church of SS. Quattro Coronati and is described as *pulcherrima.* It belonged to C. Pius Esuvius Tetricus (*PLRE* 1.885), defeated by Aurelian in A.D. 274.

Tettius Damio: on, or very near, the Sacra Via in 57 B.C. (Cicero, *Att.* 4.3.3).

Tiberiana (Figs. 33, 34, 63.5): the house built by Tiberius and modified and enlarged by subsequent principes at the north corner of the Palatine overlooking the Forum Romanum. It eventually covered the area between the Temple of the Magna Mater and the Nova Via and from the Clivus Victoriae to the Domus Augustiana. No one describes the palace

that Tiberius built; our sources agree that he did little work in Rome, his only significant public contributions being the Temple of Divus Augustus and the restoration of the Theater of Pompey (Suetonius, *Tib.* 47). However, the name Domus Tiberiana appears repeatedly in history, and its location in a position overlooking the Forum and Capitoline is confirmed by Suetonius (*Vit.* 15.3), Tacitus (*Hist.* 1.27), and Plutarch (*Galb.* 24.3). Moreover, the name persisted in regular use until the time of the regionary catalogues and appears in numerous inscriptions.

From the beginning it must have been an impressive pile, intended to draw together the public and private lives of the princeps. Much of the central block has never been excavated, and much that has been excavated is reburied under the handsome sixteenth-century Orti Farnesiani, which make the Palatine so pleasant a place today. In the center was a large rectangular courtyard surrounded on all sides by arcades, off which on the northwest opened a series of rooms of uniform depth, while to the southwest was a separate complex of cubicles in two lines opening off a broad central aisle. Other parts probably belonging to the original construction are an oval tank for fish, the interior arranged in steps, and a long series of rooms behind a pillared portico on the southwest front, where graffiti indicate the praetorian guards were quartered. The last was remodeled under Nero.

The most interesting parts of the house are on the northeast front and around the north corner. These were repeatedly remodeled, especially after the fires of Nero and Titus. At first the palace of Tiberius ran only to the Clivus Victoriae, to which one descended from the top of the hill by a long, broad staircase in two flights. Off the stair to the northeast was a suite of large rooms facing out to the clivus. Other constructions seem to have been chiefly substructures.

On the far side of the Clivus Victoriae was originally the palace of Caligula, which after the fire of Nero was absorbed into the Domus Tiberiana. The palace of Caligula extended the imperial properties to the edge of the Forum and made the Temple of Castor and the Atrium Vestae gateways into the palace. Caligula was fond of placing himself between the twin brothers in the Temple of Castor to be worshiped (Suetonius, *Calig.* 22.2). A large and handsome vestibule complex behind the Temple of Castor has been almost entirely obliterated by rebuilding, but traces of a large rectangular pool (9 m x 26 m) in a large court and bits of masonry here and there can be discovered. No trace remains of the famous bridge by which Caligula was able to cross from the Palatine to the Temple of Jupiter on the Capitoline (Suetonius, *Calig.* 22.4); presumably it was entirely of wood and destroyed immediately following Caligula's death.

Following the fire of Nero, there seem to have been many alterations in the palace. Those most notable today are the rehandling of the southwest front of the palace and a cryptoporticus along the southwest flank, which seems to have been part of a network that joined a series of existing and originally separate buildings with the complex of the Domus Aurea. This is lit by a series of windows in the shoulder of the vault and was decorated with fine stuccoes. Stairs connected it with the palace of Tiberius, and branches led off from it at either end. Probably the whole palace was thoroughly remodeled at this time, because our sources agree that in the fire the Palatine was almost totally destroyed.

How much the palace may have suffered in the fire of Titus remains a moot point, because little in the Forum Romanum was damaged at this time. However, Domitian constructed a new façade with a long loggia with a marble parapet supported on consoles of travertine along the Clivus Victoriae and rebuilt

the vestibule complex behind the Temple of Castor with a completely different orientation, producing the great building we now know as the church of S. Maria Antiqua. If we may take this as indication, it must have been both extensive and innovative. Numerous fragments of architecture of Domitianic date are scattered about the site today.

Under Trajan there was only limited work here, but under Hadrian a vast and ambitious building program carried the façade of the palace to the Nova Via, creating a unified architectural backdrop in multiple storeys, which joined the Temple of Venus et Roma with the Forum Romanum. In the present state of our knowledge, it is very difficult to see more than the broadest outline of what Hadrian had in mind, but it seems to have been intended to be at once grand and yet without strong axial focus in the way that more recent royal palaces have made familiar.

The Domus Tiberiana continued in use as an imperial residence at least under the Antonines (S.H.A. *Ant. Pius* 10.4, *M. Aurel.* 6.3, *L. Verus* 2.4, 6.4). Its library is spoken of as an important public institution by Fronto (*ad M. Caesar* 4.5.2) and Aulus Gellius (13.20.1).

More or less systematic excavations have been carried out in the complex since 1728, when much architectural material was unearthed on the summit of the hill (*RömMitt* 3 [1895]: 266–68 [C. Hülsen]). The most extensive work seems to have been that of 1860 and the years following, but about the discoveries made at that time our information is lamentably meager.

Nash 1.365–74; *RendPontAcc* 48 (1975–76): 309–13 (E. Monaco); R. Locher and B. Sigel, eds., *Domus Tiberiana: Nuove ricerche, studi di restauro* (Rome and Zürich 1985); *Roma, archeologia nel centro* (1985), 1.158–69 (C. Krause), 170–75 (E. Monaco); *RivIstArch*, ser. 3.8–9 (1985–86): 111–17 (E. Rodriguez Almeida); *BullCom* 91, pt. 2 (1986): 438–70 (A. F. Caiola, C. Krause, et al.); *CEFR* 98 (1987): 781–98 (C. Krause).

Titus Flavius Vespasianus: on the Quirinal south of Alta Semita, *ad Malum Punicum*, the modern Via delle Quattro Fontane. It was probably identical with the Domus Vespasiani and inherited by Titus after his father became princeps. Later it was rebuilt by Domitian as the Templum Gentis Flaviae (S.H.A. *Tyr. Trig.* 33.6). Pliny puts the Laocoon group *in Titi imperatoris domo* (*HN* 36.37) and Polycleitos's group of Astragalizontes, two nude youths playing with the *tali, in Titi imperatoris atrio* (*HN* 34.55). Because the Laocoon was found on the Oppius in 1506 in the area of the Domus Aurea, it has been presumed that a part of the Domus Aurea was made

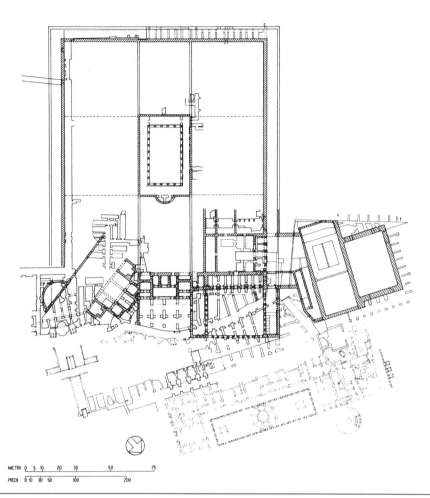

Figure 34
Domus Tiberiana,
General Plan with
Conjectural Restoration
of the Ground Storey

METRI 0 5 10 20 30 50 75
PIEDI 0 10 30 50 100 200

into a residence for Titus, probably the part nearest the Thermae Titi, but there is no real basis for this. More likely the statues were in the Quirinal house, and later Trajan brought the Laocoon to the Oppius to adorn his baths.

Transitoria: the first palace built by Nero, designed to connect the Domus Tiberiana and the other imperial properties on the Palatine with the Horti Maecenatis and imperial possessions on the Esquiline (Tacitus, *Ann.* 15.39.1; Suetonius, *Nero* 31.1). This was destroyed in the great fire of A.D. 64 and then rebuilt as the Domus Aurea. Its extent and geography are not known. All that survives of it are two fragmentary complexes, one on the Palatine buried beneath the state apartments of the Domus Augustiana, and the other on the Velia buried in the platform of Hadrian's Temple of Venus et Roma.

The first is a deeply sunken garden focused on a long nymphaeum in front of a gently curving wall broken by niches. The water ran down steps and from fountains into a high basin, from which it spilled over a front embellished with an elaborate

miniature architecture of columns and cornices in bronze and colored marble and was collected in a shallow trough, possibly containing more fountains. On axis opposite this was a dining pavilion, an open-air triclinium under an arbor supported on columns, and to either side were small suites of rooms with high ceilings and exquisite decorations. One of these preserves small scenes from the Homeric cycle very delicately executed within a rich framework. The fragments of the polychrome marble pavements and wall coats that escaped plundering in the Farnese excavations of 1721 show that these were especially fine. This complex is cut by a series of heavy foundations that must belong to the Domus Aurea, but it is impossible to reconstruct anything of its plan from them.

Adjacent to this, at a slightly higher level, are two rooms to the northeast with finely decorated ceilings known as the "Baths of Livia" and a very large latrine that continued in use until the time of Domitian. The former were accessible before the beginning of excavations by Boni.

From the nymphaeum symmetrical marble stairs

led up to an upper storey some feet below the floor of Domitian's state banquet hall. Here the bedding of pavement, as well as some plates of white marble, can be seen, while under Domitian's nymphaeum to the northwest of the banquet hall are remains of a fine pavement of opus sectile still visible today. Of the architecture, one can make out only that there was a portico supported on pillars combined with columns, with fountains in the intercolumniations.

The principal campaigns of excavation here are those of 1721–1729 for Francesco I, Duke of Parma, directed by Marchese Ignazio De Santi and Conte Suzzani but published by Francesco Bianchini in 1738, and those of 1910–1913 directed by Giacomo Boni.

Under the platform of Hadrian's Temple of Venus et Roma on the Velia, Antonio Nibby found in 1828 a rotunda from which four barrel-vaulted arms branch at right angles to one another. Two of these were closed a short distance beyond the rotunda by screens of columns, and in the space beyond in that to the northwest is a shallow pool resembling an impluvium. The rotunda is usually reconstructed as roofed with a dome, but too little survives to be sure. The roof might have been of wood, or the area might even have been essentially unroofed. The problems of lighting here have not been addressed by those who have discussed the complex. It was on a small scale and so recalls the sunken garden and nymphaeum of the Palatine, and the fragments of pavement that survive show it to have been richly decorated. But there is no way of telling how this rotunda functioned in a larger architectural whole, and excavation has not been carried far enough to suggest any use for these apartments. At this point it remains a tantalizing possibility that we see here remains of the earliest true dome in the city of Rome. (On the basis of building technique, Friedrich Rakob, after carefully weighing the evidence and various objections raised, has concluded that the Tempio di Mercurio at Baiae is Augustan [*RömMitt* 95 (1988): 257–301] and points out that the Baths of Agrippa may well have included a domed rotunda.) But if this was a true dome, it would not have rivaled in engineering the dome of the octagon of the Domus Aurea on the Oppius. Other remains of the Domus Transitoria are insignificant. There are some near the juncture of the Nova Via and the Clivus Palatinus.

The identification of both of the major fragments as belonging to the Domus Transitoria has been disputed. The Palatine nymphaeum has been ascribed to Claudius on the basis of a fragment of a cornice block bearing his name found loose there. And the rotunda on the Velia has been thought to be as early as the late republic. But on balance the evidence weighs heavily for the identification, because both

are cut by foundations of the Domus Aurea, and both show sophistication of design with an affinity of style that it would be difficult to put earlier.

MacDonald 1.21–25; Nash 1.375–79; *NSc* 1971, 321–23 (G. Carettoni).

Tullus Hostilius (1): high on the Velia, on the site later occupied by the Temple of the Penates (Cicero, *Rep.* 2.53; Varro *ap. Non.* 852L; Solinus 1.22).

Tullus Hostilius (2): Late in his reign, after the Caelian was added to the area of the city, Tullus built himself a house there. This was struck by lightning and burned, and Tullus himself was killed at the same time (Livy 1.30.1, 1.31.8; Dion. Hal. 3.1.5).

Turcii (1): south of S. Marco, between this and the foot of the Capitoline, in the area known as the Aemiliana, where inscriptions and remains have been found (*CIL* 6.1772, 1773; *ILS* 1230). L. Turcius Secundus was corrector Flamineae et Piceni between A.D. 340 and 350 (*PLRE* 1.817–18).

Turcii (2): a house on the Esquiline from which came a silver treasure now in the British Museum (O. Dalton, *Catalogue of Early Christian Antiquities in the British Museum,* nos. 304–45) inscribed with the names of Turcius Secundus (*PLRE* 1.817) and Proiecta Turci. This is marked with Christian symbols and dated in the fourth century.

Turia (*PIR*[1] T 290): see **Domus, Milo Papinianus, T. Annius** (2).

M. Tuticius Capito: see **Domus, T. Flavius Tiberianus.**

L. Vagellius: known from an inscribed lead pipe found on the Caelian near the Ospedale Militare del Celio (*CIL* 15.7555). Vagellius was suffect consul in A.D. 44–46 and a friend of Seneca.

Publia Valeria Comasa (*PIR*[1] V 156): known from an inscribed lead pipe found on the Esquiline and another found on the Aventine (*CIL* 15.7559). She seems to have been the daughter of the consul of A.D. 220 (*PIR*[1] V 42). The actual location of the house, or houses, cannot be determined.

Valeria Eunoea: known from inscribed lead pipes found in 1776 in the garden of the Barberini nuns, southwest of the southwest exedra of the Thermae Diocletianae (*CIL* 15.7560).

Valerii: on the Caelian on the site now occupied by the Ospedale dell'Addolorata, where extensive remains have been found, with eleven inscriptions pertaining to family members of the fourth century (*CIL* 6.1684–94; *ILS* 1240–42, 6111). The house was offered for sale in A.D. 404 but found no buyer, because of its magnificence, whereas after the sack of Alaric it was sold for very little. It seems to have been made a hospital, the Xenodochium Valeriorum, or a Valeriis.

A little north of this in what was Villa Casali were found other remains and an inscribed base of L. Valerius Poplicola Maximus, cos. A.D. 252 or 253 (*CIL* 6.1532 = *ILS* 1191; cf. *CIL* 6.1531 = *ILS* 1190).

M. Valerius Bradua Mauricus (*PIR*[1] V 31):
known from an inscribed lead pipe found on the Aventine near S. Alessio (*CIL* 15.7556). He was consul in A.D. 191 and curator aquarum.

P. Valerius Publicola:
a house begun *in summa Velia* by P. Valerius Publicola, cos. 509 B.C., which he was forced to pull down because it seemed an impregnable fortress (Livy 2.7.6 and 11–12; Cicero, *Rep.* 2.53; Plutarch, *Poplic.* 10.2–4; Dion. Hal. 5.19.1–2; Val. Max. 4.1.1). It was then reconstructed on a more modest scale *infra Veliam . . . in infimo clivo,* where the Temple of Vica Pota later stood (Livy 2.7.6 and 11–12); that is, on the forum side of the Velia, perhaps not far from the Regia. According to another tradition, a place for his house *sub Veliis* was given to Publicola as a public honor (Asconius *in Cic. Pis.* 52 [Stangl 19]; Pliny, *HN* 36.112). Cicero (*Har. Resp.* 16) says the house itself was a public gift, but he must be wrong in this, and he also locates it erroneously *in Velia.*

Q. Valerius Vegetus (*PIR*[1] V 150):
known from an inscribed lead pipe found on the Quirinal between Alta Semita and Vicus Longus, near the Ministero della Difesa (*CIL* 15.7558), together with some other remains. He was suffect consul in A.D. 91.

M. Valerius Volusius Maximus:
a house on the Palatine presented to Valerius Maximus, dictator in 494 B.C., at public expense in honor of his victory over the Sabines. It had the further distinction of having the house door open out, rather than in (Valerius Antias *ap. Ascon. in Cic. Pis.* 52 [Stangl 18–19]; Pliny, *HN* 36.112).

M. Varenius Liberalis:
known from an inscribed lead pipe found on the Esquiline (*CIL* 15.7562).

Vectiliana:
listed in the regionary catalogues in Regio II, on the Caelian (S.H.A. *Commodus* 16.3). Commodus was killed here (S.H.A. *Pertinax* 5.7; Orosius 7.16.4; Chron. 147).

Vedius Pollio (*PIR*[1] V 213):
on the Clivus Suburanus on the site later occupied by the Porticus Liviae. In 15 B.C. Vedius willed his magnificent house to Augustus, who had it razed, and the site was left vacant until the construction of the Porticus Liviae, dedicated in 7 B.C. It seems to have been here that Vedius had his famous fish tanks stocked with lampreys, to which he fed slaves condemned to death (Ovid, *Fast.* 6.637–48; Cass. Dio 54.23.1–6). For a possible trace of this house, see *CEFR* 98 (1987): 624 (C. Panella).

P. Vergilius Maro:
in Esquiliae, adjacent to the Horti Maecenatis (Donatus, *Vita Verg.* 13).

Annius Verus:
see **Domus, Annius Verus.**

Vespasianus:
on the Quirinal, south of Alta Semita, *ad Malum Punicum,* later converted into the Templum Gentis Flaviae (see Gens Flavia, Templum). It is probably the same as the Domus Titi (see Domus, Titus Flavius Vespasianus).

Vettius Agorius Praetextatus (*PLRE* 1.722–24) et Fabia Paulina (uxor):
northeast of Porta Esquilina in the block surrounded by the Vie Rattazzi, Filiberto Turati, Cappellini, and Principe Amedeo, where inscribed lead pipes (*CIL* 15.7563) and considerable remains of building have been found. The property seems to have been extensive enough to classify as horti. Vettius was praefectus urbi in A.D. 367.

BullCom 2 (1874): 58 (R. Lanciani).

Virius Lupus Iulianus (*PIR*[1] V 481):
on the eastern slope of that part of the Quirinal known as the Collis Mucialis, where remains and inscriptions have been found in Via dei Serpenti near the Banca d'Italia (*CIL* 6.31774, 37078; *NSc* 1910, 420; 1911, 316 [G. Mancini]). Virius was legate of Lycia and Pamphylia in the second century.

L. Vitellius:
The father of the princeps had a house on the Aventine (Suetonius, *Vit.* 16).

L. Vitellius (*PIR*[1] V 501):
The brother of the princeps had a house conspicuous from the Forum Romanum, evidently on the Palatine (Tacitus, *Hist.* 3.68, 70).

M. Vitruvius Vaccus:
on the Palatine, destroyed in 330 B.C. when its owner was put to death for treason; the site was made public and then called the Prata Vacci (Livy 8.19.4, 20.8; Cicero, *Dom.* 101). The prata survived as a place designation until the time of Cicero and possibly as late as that of Livy.

L. Volumnius: on the Quirinal near Vicus Longus (Livy 10.23.6). He was consul in 296 B.C. His wife, Verginia, dedicated part of the house as a sacellum of Pudicitia Plebeia (see Pudicitia Plebeia, Sacellum).

Vulcacius Rufinus (*PLRE* 1.782–83): on the Quirinal near Vicus Longus. Ruins and an inscribed base (*CIL* 6.32051 = *ILS* 1237) were found under the Ministero della Difesa. Vulcacius was consul in A.D. 347, praefectus urbi in 349, and an uncle of the emperor Julian.

Duas Domos, Ad: the location given for the church of S. Susanna on the Quirinal in the *Liber Pontificalis* in documents of the seventh and eighth centuries (HCh 486–87). A house of the third century has been found under the church.

Duo Aedes: listed in the *Notitia* in Regio IX after the stabula of the racing teams and before the Porticus Philippi, which might place it in the southwestern part of the Campus Martius. PA suggests it was probably a street, but, because the Porticus Octaviae is not listed, this might more probably have been an alternate name for that complex (q.v.).

Duodecim Portae: listed by the regionary catalogues in Regio XI, mentioned by Obsequens (70) and Pliny (*HN* 3.66), who suggests it was, or might be taken for, one of the thirty-seven *portae* of Rome. The figure thirty-seven is too high to be only the gates of the Servian Walls. PA suggests the Duodecim Portae should be a square at the west end of the Circus Maximus deriving its name from the twelve carceres of the circus (Cassiodorus, *Var. Epist.* 3.51), but one must ask whether the number of carceres was so many in the early empire (Humphrey 132–38). In representations of races in the circus, never more than eight chariots are shown. Moreover, the walls of Rome seem never to have passed close enough to the circus for there to have been a confusion of the name with a gate in the walls. More likely this was a name given to the arches on which the Aqua Appia crossed the valley between the Caelian and Aventine just inside the Porta Capena (Frontinus, *Aq.* 1.5). Once the walls in this sector had been dismantled, the identification of the aqueduct bridge with the gate would have been almost inevitable. If this is correct, Regio XI extended farther to the southeast than had previously been thought.

Duos Amantes: a locality mentioned in the *Liber Pontificalis* in the life of S. Silvestro (LPD 1.171; VZ 2.230), the name probably going back to antiquity. If the church of S. Salvatore *ad duos amantes* is the same as S. Salvatore de Camiliano (HCh 433–34, 601–2), it would lie in the vicinity of Piazza del Collegio Romano.

E

Elagabalus, Templum (1) (Fig. 63.8): a temple of the Syrian sun god, officially called Sol Invictus Elagabalus, his sacred stone having been brought to Rome and established on the Palatine near the imperial palace by the emperor Varius Elagabalus Antoninus Bassianus (S.H.A. *Heliogab.* 3.4). The site is also said to have been earlier occupied by a temple of Orcus (see Oreus, Aedes), by which the Mundus (see Mundus [2]) may be meant (S.H.A. *Heliogab.* 1.6). To this new temple the emperor intended to transfer all the holiest objects and principal cults of Rome, including the fire of Vesta and the Palladium (S.H.A. *Heliogab.* 3.4). Herodian (5.5.8) says that the temple was very large and magnificent, surrounded by numerous altars. It was known as the Elagaballium and was dedicated in 221 (Chron. 147; Hieron. *a. Abr.* 2236). It survived Elagabalus's assassination and was known to the author of the biography of Elagabalus in the *Historia Augusta,* but burned (Passio S. Philippi, 9 October 545), presumably before the compilation of the regionary catalogues, from which it is omitted. It is believed to be shown on a coin of Elagabalus, and other coins show the sacred stone of the god (*RömMitt* 9 [1901]: 273–82 [F. Studniczka], 10 [1902]: 67 [C. Hülsen]).

The location of the temple is fraught with difficulties, because space on the Palatine was by this time exceedingly scarce. Because the supremacy of the god led to his identification with Jupiter (S.H.A. *Heliogab.* 17.8), some have wished to identify Alexander Severus's Temple of Iuppiter Ultor (see Iuppiter Ultor) with that of Elagabalus, but there is no proof that Alexander's temple was even in Rome. Given these conditions and difficulties, it seems likely that Elagabalus rebuilt and enlarged the Temple of Iuppiter Victor (see Iuppiter Victor, Aedes), which originally had been built by Q. Fabius Maximus Rullianus, and dedicated it to his patron divinity and

that this is the temple of Vigna Barberini. The evidence of Elagabalus's coin could be used to support this identification. After Elagabalus's death, Alexander Severus would naturally have returned the temple to its original dedicant, but he may have used the epithet Ultor in commemorating this action on his coins (see also Iuppiter Victor).

RendLinc, ser. 8.34 (1979): 331–47 (F. Castagnoli); *CEFR* 98 (1987): 429–42 (F. Coarelli).

Elagabalus, Templum (2): A second temple to the Syrian god was built by the emperor Elagabalus on the fringes of the city, and to this the god was brought ceremonially each year at midsummer in a sumptuous chariot drawn by six white horses (Herodian 5.6.6–10). Because circus games and theatrical spectacles are mentioned in connection with the transfer, we can with confidence locate the temple near the Amphitheatrum Castrense and Circus Varianus (qq.v.), in the general area known as ad Spem Veterem (see S.H.A. *Heliogab.* 13.5, 14.5). Herodian (5.6.6–10) says the temple was very large and magnificent. It is impossible to identify it positively with any of the existing remains, but the hall converted by Constantine into the church of S. Croce in Gerusalemme must be regarded as a possibility (see Sessorium).

For a proposal that this temple was in the Transtiberim at the foot of the Janiculan hill midway between the Temple of Iuppiter Heliopolitanus and Hercules Cubans, see *PAPS* 125.5 (1981): 377–80 (R. E. A. Palmer).

Elephas Herbarius: listed by the regionary catalogues in Regio VIII and in medieval documents as simply Elephas (*Mirabilia:* Jordan 2.641, VZ 3.6; Einsiedeln itinerary 9); preserved in the name of the church of Sanctorum Abbacyri et Archangeli ad Ale-

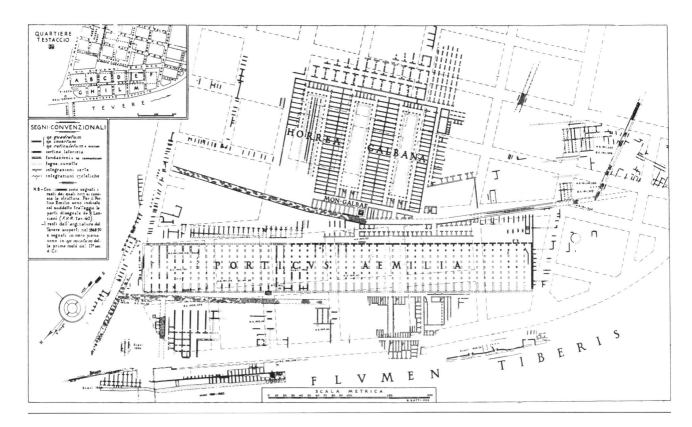

QUARTIERE TESTACCIO

TEVERE

SEGNI·CONVENZIONALI

HORREA GALBANA

MON·GALBAE

PORTICVS · AEMILIA

FLVMEN

TIBERIS

SCALA METRICA

Figure 35
Emporium, Horrea
Galbae, and
"Porticus Aemilia"

fantum (HCh 162–63). It was near the Tiber and the Forum Holitorium and was overlooked by the Temple of Iuppiter Optimus Maximus Capitolinus (HCh 338; cf. Jordan 2.667). Everything points to a location along the Vicus Iugarius more toward the river than toward the Forum Romanum, and it is very tempting to see this as one of the elephants that drew the triumphal cars with which Domitian crowned the Porta Triumphalis (see Porta Carmentalis). These elephants are presumed to have been of gilded bronze. They are shown on coins and on an adventus relief from an arch of Marcus Aurelius reused on the Arch of Constantine (see Arcus Constantini). They are shown advancing with lowered heads and might be interpreted as cropping the grass. That seems preferable to more fanciful explanations. But the origin of the epithet is doubtful. The fact that there is no mention of the Elephas earlier than the fourth century and that it continued to be a landmark as late as the twelfth suggests that it was large and well protected and might be taken as evidence that it was stone rather than metal.

Emporium (Fig. 35): the wholesale market of Rome, where merchandise brought up the Tiber by barge was landed, stored, and sold. It was probably extended downstream gradually through the course

of the republican period. In 193 B.C. the curule aediles M. Aemilius Lepidus and L. Aemilius Paullus are recorded to have built a *porticus extra Portam Trigeminam emporio ad Tiberim adiecto* (Livy 35.10.12). This was probably a relatively simple arrangement of a single-wing portico for use in hot or otherwise inclement weather along an open quay, artificially leveled, lying along the river. It was apparently not cobbled, fenced off, or provided with stairs down to the river until 174, when the censors let contracts for a general overhaul of the complex (Livy 41.27.8). It probably began immediately outside the Porta Trigemina and south of the road from this to the Pons Sublicius. Eventually it stretched for well over a kilometer along the river, and the quarter southwest of the Aventine bounded by the Tiber, Via Ostiensis, and Aurelian Walls seems to have been almost entirely taken up with warehouses. The narrow stretch of riverfront immediately under the lee of the Aventine came probably to be less used relatively early, as space was lacking here for handling goods in volume. A vast warehouse in the southwest quarter built of concrete faced with opus incertum (commonly, but probably erroneously, called Porticus Aemilia) is probably early first century B.C. in date. North and south of Ponte Aventino, wharves and warehouses fronting on the river have come to light

143

at various times since 1868 during work on the Tiber embankment. These run true to type. The wharves are of concrete faced with opus reticulatum punctuated with bands of brick, paved with travertine, and with heavy travertine mooring rings. Ramps of access in symmetrical pairs flanked one set of mooring rings set low on the river face. Behind these wharves a line of stoutly built barrel-vaulted chambers shows similar construction but greater use of brick facing. These are of uniform size and plan, with doors framed in large blocks of travertine and façades of brick that shows no sign of stuccoing. Most of this work is probably late first and second century after Christ. The Emporium continued in use until at least the time of the construction of the walls of Aurelian, which use the lower stretches as a footing. After the construction of the great horrea of Rome, the upper stretch of the Emporium was used more and more for the landing and storage of marble, and the bank along the Aventine is still called the Marmorata (q.v.). In excavations here numerous large blocks of marble in various states of working have been discovered.

Nash 1.380–86; *RendPontAcc* 43 (1970–71): 109–21 (S. Panciera); *BullCom* 90 (1985): 86–88 (C. Mocchegiani Carpano); *Roma, archeologia nel centro* (1985), 2.433–41. (R. Meneghini); *CEFR* 98 (1987): 235–49 (R. Étienne).

Epictetinses: a name found in one inscription, the fourth-century edict of Tarracius Bassus (*CIL* 6.31893 = *ILS* 6072), evidently designating those who lived in the Vicus Epicteti, probably in Regio XIV (HJ 669n.124).

Equus Caesaris: a statue of Julius Caesar's favorite horse, whose forefeet were almost human in shape, set up in the middle of the court of the Forum Iulium on axis with the Temple of Venus Genetrix (Pliny, *HN* 8.155; Suetonius, *Iul.* 61). Statius (*Silv.* 1.1.84–90) asserts that this was a statue originally made by Lysippus for Alexander and that the likeness of Julius Caesar was added (or substituted). Neither Pliny nor Suetonius mentions the rider, both emphasizing the singularity of the horse and that the statue in Forum Iulium was its portrait. Because it is now known that Domitian very extensively rebuilt the Forum Iulium and it is presumed that this may have been in consequence of the fire of Titus, we may be justified in believing that in the Forum Iulium as originally built the horse was riderless and a portrait, that this was destroyed in the fire, and that when Domitian rebuilt the forum he substituted a horse alleged to be by Lysippus and surmounted it with a portrait of Julius Caesar. Pliny's mention of a cuirass statue of Julius Caesar in his forum (*HN* 34.18) is not pertinent to the problem, because he distinguishes this from equestrian portraits, which he takes up a little later.

Equus Cloeliae: see **Statua Cloeliae.**

Equus Constantii: an equestrian statue of Constantius erected in the Comitium just in front of the northeast end of the Arch of Septimius Severus. The marble pedestal survives with a dedicatory inscription (*CIL* 6.1158 = *ILS* 731), which proclaims it the work of Naeratius Cerealis, praefectus urbi in A.D. 352–353.

Nash 1.387.

Equus Constantini (Fig. 40): an equestrian statue of Constantine dedicated by Anicius Paulinus, consul ordinarius et praefectus urbi in A.D. 334 (*CIL* 6.1141 = *ILS* 698). The inscription is included in the Einsiedeln sylloge, which locates it in the middle of the forum. The statue is listed by the *Notitia* in Regio VIII and in the Einsiedeln itinerary (1.7, 7.8). A low pedestal in the open square of the Forum Romanum, just west of the Cloaca and east of Boni's Equus Domitiani, has been suggested to be the remains of its base. It is certainly late work, a rough core of secondhand material, and stands directly on the Augustan travertine pavement, but there is no proof. More recently, P. Verduchi has proposed that remains of another pedestal just east of the "Rostra Vandalica" might make a better candidate for this.

Nash 1.388; GV 69–73.

Equus Domitiani (Fig. 40): a colossal (?) bronze equestrian statue of Domitian erected in the Forum Romanum in A.D. 91 in honor of the princeps' campaigns in Germany. Statius devotes a poem to its description (*Silv.* 1.1), and it appears on coins (Nash 1.389 fig. 476). It was believed by Boni to have stood on a concrete base, 11.80 m long by 5.90 m wide, discovered in 1902 during work in the cuniculi under the forum and exposed the next year after lifting a section of the pavement of travertine blocks. The deep mass of concrete cuts into the main cuniculus and a cross passage of the network of passages of late republican date under the forum but is now considered itself of early Augustan date at the latest. Into the top surface are let three large square blocks of travertine with square mortises, 0.044 m on a side and 0.15 m deep, in positions that suggest the placing of the feet of a striding horse, while the coins show the right forefoot rested on an allegorical head of the Rhine. In the east end of the base was found a hollowed-out block of travertine provided with a lid containing material from a prehistoric burial, including five impasto vessels, a quartz crystal, and a bit of gold. Hülsen proposed the explanation that, in digging out the place for the concrete base, the workmen had encountered a burial of the type of the nearby Sepulcretum (q.v.) and Regia and, not understanding their discovery, had piously enclosed what could be recovered in the base.

With the redating of this base to the Augustan period, it has had to be abandoned as belonging to the Equus Domitiani, but next to it, slightly overlapping on its area, is a well-marked rectangle of blocks in the travertine pavement, 7.80 m wide by 12.20 m long. This covers a mass of concrete that respects the network of cuniculi and seems likely to have been the foundation for the statue of Domitian.

The statue faced east and showed the heavily muscled horse striding forward. The princeps was in military dress, with paludamentum and sword. On his left hand was poised a figure of Minerva, evidently facing forward and lifting the aegis (Statius, *Silv.* 1.1.37–40); with his extended right hand the princeps made a gesture of peace. The statue stood on a massive base to which Statius calls special attention (*Silv.* 1.1.56–60). The statue must have been destroyed following the damnatio memoriae decreed by the senate after Domitian's death, and the pedestal must have been leveled.

Nash 1.389–90; *BullCom* 88 (1982–83): 95–98 (E. Rodriguez Almeida); GV 118–22, 133–39.

Equus Marci Aurelii: a bronze equestrian statue of Marcus Aurelius that stood in front of S. Giovanni in Laterano. Whether its location there was original has been doubted; it is not mentioned earlier than the tenth century, when it is known by the name Caballus Constantini. However, early drawings show it on a rectangular pedestal of classical design and proportions, and, because Marcus is known to have been raised in his grandfather's house, the Domus Annii Veri (see Domus, Annius Verus), adjacent to the Lateran, it seems likely to have been in its original location. The couchant lions mounted on low columns in front of it, which appear in a van Heemskerck drawing (vol. 1 folio 71), are clearly a later addition. The statue was taken to the Capitoline in 1538, mounted on a new base, and made the centerpiece of Michelangelo's magnificent Piazza del Campidoglio. It was removed for restoration in 1980 and probably will not be returned, because the deterioration of the fabric was then found to be far advanced.

It shows the princeps in military dress, but unarmed, mounted on a spirited horse, his right hand lifted a little in a gesture of peace. The calm impassivity of the rider is in contrast to the nervous energy of his mount. It has been thought that there would have been a suppliant barbarian to respond to the

gesture of the princeps or an allegorical figure to support the lifted hoof of his horse; there was one for the Equus Domitiani, and the composition appears on coins. But this does not seem necessary. The scale is heroic, slightly larger than life. It was originally gilded, and traces of the gilding survive in protected areas. It is the only bronze equestrian statue to come down from antiquity complete and may well be the finest surviving bronze portrait.

Nash 1.391–92; *RendPontAcc* 41 (1968–69): 167–89 (V. Santa Maria Scrinari); *Xenia* 7 (1984): 67–76 (A. Giuliano); *Marco Aurelio, mostra di cantiere* (show catalogue, Ministero per i Beni Culturali e Ambientali, Istituto Centrale per il Restauro, Comune di Roma 1984); *BdA* 72 (1987): 103–27 (G. Basile, M. Bottoni, et al.); *RömMitt* 97 (1990): 276–89 (E. R. Knauer); *BdA* 74 (1990): fasc. 61.1–52, 75 (1990): fasc. 62–63.1–56 (L. de Lachenal).

Equus Severi: a large bronze equestrian statue of Septimius Severus erected in the middle of the Forum Romanum to commemorate an ominous dream that he had had. It was still standing in Herodian's day (2.9.6). It may be shown on certain coins of Septimius (*B. M. Coins, Rom. Emp.* 5.194 no. 208 pl. 32.3). No certain trace of it has ever been found.

Equus Sullae: see **Statua Sullae.**

Equus Tiridatis Regis Armeniorum: listed in the regionary catalogues in Regio VII, after the Porticus Gypsiani et Constantini in the *Curiosum* (where the reading is *equos*), after templa duo nova Spei et Fortunae in the *Notitia* (where the reading is *equum*), and before the Forum Suarium in both. If the position in the lists has any topographical value, we should look for the statue in the vicinity of Galleria Colonna, possibly a bit south of it. Because the three Armenian kings who bore the name Tiridates reach from the mid-first century to the early fourth and all had dealings with Rome, it is impossible to determine which is meant. Tiridates I made a famous visit to Rome in the time of Nero and was received with great pomp and splendor (Suetonius, *Nero* 13, 30.2), but no mention is made of a statue, nor does one seem appropriate.

Equus Traiani: see **Forum Traiani.**

Equus Tremuli: an equestrian statue of Q. Marcius Tremulus, cos. 306 B.C., erected in front of the Temple of Castor to commemorate his victory over the Hernicans (Livy 9.43.22). It was still standing in the time of Cicero (*Phil.* 6.13), but had disappeared before the time of Pliny (*HN* 34.23). It showed the general togate and must have appeared old-fashioned. If it survived the refurbishing of the forum by Julius Caesar and Augustus because of its venerable age, it may have been lost in the fire of Nero. Pliny's knowledge of the statue suggests that he had seen it. No trace of it survives today, nor should we expect any; the so-called Tribunal Praetoris would have obliterated any.

Esquiliae (1): according to Varro (*Ling.* 5.50) the general name given to the Mons Oppius and Mons Cispius, the two significant masses projecting from the tableland behind known as Mons Esquilinus, but Varro's citation of the order of the sacra of the Argei to show this tends rather to show that the Oppius and part of the Cispian were not included until the creation of the city of the Regiones Quattuor (q.v.), and originally Esquiliae was actually a small part of the Cispian (if we reject the questionable emendation: *princeps Esquiliis uls lacum* [or *lucum*] *Facutalem*). This would also suit Cicero's location of the altar of Mala Fortuna as simply Esquiliis (*Nat. D.* 3.63, *Leg.* 2.28) and Ovid's of the Temple of Iuno Lucina (*Fast.* 3.245–48). Because there was a Lucus Esquilinus on the Oppius from an early period (Varro, *Ling.* 5.50), it seems natural to see Esquiliae as the throat between Cispian and Oppius and the juncture of the two hills where the Porta Esquilina and Forum Esquilinum were situated. Ancient attempts at etymology have doubtless clouded the issue (cf. Varro, *Ling.* 5.49; Ovid, *Fast.* 3.245–48), but it is curious that no one wishes to derive the name from *aesculus*. Modern scholars favor a derivation from *ex* + *colo* (Walde-Hofmann 1.247), meaning an external settlement, but we may doubt this, in view of the Lucus or Lacus Esquilinus of the Argei and the fact that the Esquiline village was, so far as we know, confined to the Oppius. It seems best to leave the derivation of the name, like that of the names of most of the hills, in doubt.

If Esquiliae was originally the throat up which passed all the traffic bound to and from the northeast and east (Via Tiburtina, Via Praenestina, Via Labicana), it would have been of immense importance from a very early period, and it is easy to understand how it would have given its name to the gate to which it led and the market that found a place just inside that gate. With the division of the city into four quarters and four tribes, the Esquiliae became the most conspicuous feature of the one that embraced Cispian and Oppius, and it was natural to give them the name Esquiliae, as it was natural to give that of the Caelian and the Subura the name Suburana, and thereafter the name became general for everything in this sector.

OpRom 15 (1985): 63–65 (H. Erkell).

Esquiliae (2): the name that was given to the fifth Regio of Augustan Rome, lying entirely outside the line of the Servian Walls. In the fourth century it was bounded by the line of the Aurelian Walls from the Porta Chiusa on the southeast side of the Castra Praetoria to the posterula west of Porta Asinaria through which the Via Tusculana entered the city, except between the Amphitheatrum Castrense and Aqua Claudia, where it bent out to include the Circus Varianus. On the north it was bounded by the road from Porta Viminalis to Porta Chiusa, on the south by Via Tusculana, and on the west by the Servian Walls and Agger from Porta Viminalis to Porta Esquilina, and south of that point, after a jog, by a street running almost due north and south from the fork of Via Tiburtina and Via Labicana to Via Tusculana. It makes a very large regio and geographically a somewhat awkward one, but it is defined especially by the lines of the major aqueducts that entered the city in a cluster ad Spem Veterem (Porta Maggiore) and fanned out over the high ground of the Esquiline and Caelian hills. Originally the regio was probably somewhat smaller, especially toward the north, but always largely defined by the aqueducts; Propertius gives it the epithet aquosae (4.8.1), and it had already been given the name Esquiliae in his day. It had been the site of the potter's field of Rome (see Horace, *Sat.* 1.8), but, with its organization as a part of the city, improvements were made that made it a popular place to live. It fell victim to the Augustan craze for horti, and large sections were divided among such urban pleasure villas, especially in the neighborhood of ad Spem Veterem and along the main aqueduct lines, where it was easy to tap these for a water supply, in the outer reaches of the regio.

Euripus: an artificial watercourse, especially one used as a feature in a garden. It is distinguished from a piscina by having running water, usually fed by a fountain. The term is probably generic, although Seneca may use it meaning only the Euripus Virginis (q.v.). It is taken from the name of the narrow channel between Boeotia and Euboea at Chalcis, where the water flows alternately in opposite directions, a natural phenomenon of great interest.

Euripus (also called **Euripus Thermarum Agrippae**): the modern name given to the canal that drained the Stagnum Agrippae (q.v.), possibly following, at least in part, the course of a brook that had drained the Caprae Palus (q.v.). It has been located at a number of points in excavations between 1885 and 1938 and can be followed for most of its course, its intake from the Stagnum still remaining obscure and its outlet falling between Ponte Vittorio Emanuele and Ponte Sant'Angelo. It follows roughly the line of Corso Vittorio Emanuele and is about 800 m long. Its easternmost known section is near the church of S. Andrea della Valle, and its westernmost is in Via Paola. A small stretch under the Palazzo della Cancelleria is still visible. It is entirely artificial, its bed semicircular, of concrete faced with signinum, its width 3.35 m, and its depth a maximum of 1.70 m. The margins are of travertine, and along each side ran a paved walk. Along the south side two walls parallel to the course have been found at various points, the inner one faced with reticulate and probably originally veneered with marble, although only fragments of the socle survive. The outer wall is of blocks of tufa. Where streets crossed the euripus, it was provided with little bridges, ingeniously designed, raised three steps above the margin.

CAR 1-H, 116 p. 96; Nash 1.393–94; *MEFRA* 89 (1977): 830–37 (F. Coarelli).

Euripus in Circo Maximo: a channel Julius Caesar had dug around the edge of the arena of the Circus Maximus, probably in 46 B.C., to protect spectators from the wild beasts exhibited in the venationes. It was 10 feet broad and 10 feet deep and ran down both long sides and around the sphendone (Dion. Hal. 3.68.2; Pliny, *HN* 8.21; Suetonius, *Iul.* 39.2). This was filled in by Nero to make space for seating for the equites (Pliny, *HN* 8.21). Probably the water to fill this channel was chiefly that of the circus brook (see Murcia), but Frontinus (*Aq.* 2.97) speaks of the use of aqueduct water in the circus on days of ludi circenses, when the permission of the aediles or censors was required. This may have been either a supplement to the supply of the brook or drinking water for the spectators. After the filling in of the euripus around the arena, probably as part of Nero's remodeling of the circus and certainly at least as early as the reign of Trajan, the spina was converted into a broad euripus interrupted by islands supporting pavilions and crossed at intervals by bridges. The margins were embellished with statuary. This seems to have taken the place of the earlier euripus and probably drew its water from the same source. This

then became a standard arrangement in circuses elsewhere.

Humphrey 36–42, 74, 76, 275–77.

Euripus Virginis: a channel that took 460 quinariae, just about one-fifth of the total volume of water delivered to the city by the Aqua Virgo (Frontinus, *Aq.* 2.84). Strabo (13.1.19 [590]) says that Agrippa dedicated the fallen lion of Lysippus in a grove between a euripus and a lake, by which he means either the Stagnum Agrippae (q.v.) or the piscina of *CIL* 6.39087. This fragmentary inscription discovered near the Ponte Sisto (*NSc* 1908, 327–28 [D. Vaglieri]) indicates that the euripus was close to the Tiber, a landmark, and in clear relation to a piscina. This may have been a reservoir of the Aqua Virgo on the left bank of the Tiber near the Pons Agrippae, on which the aqueduct must have been carried across the river for distribution in the Transtiberim (Frontinus, *Aq.* 2.84). Seneca (*Epist.* 83.5) speaks of diving into the euripus on the Kalends of January as characteristic of those who were addicted to cold baths, and Ovid (*Ex Pont.* 1.8.37–38) speaks of the euripi (plural) as one of the beauties of the Campus Martius. Lloyd has made a case for locating the Euripus Virginis in a course that winds from the neighborhood of the church of S. Maria in Monterone (Stagnum Agrippae) around the Theater of Pompey and reaches the river at the Pons Agrippae, the euripus and aqueduct line running more or less parallel to each other. Because the only use we know for the euripus is swimming, we might prefer to see it as a long swimming pool like the natatio in the Palaestra of Herculaneum, but larger, laid out as part of a sports complex along the Tiber northwest of the Pons Agrippae. Here there would have been space for the playing fields that were traditionally characteristic of the Campus Martius, and Agrippa's aqueduct made new facilities for aquatic sports possible.

AJA 83 (1979): 193–204 (R. B. Lloyd).

Evander, Ara: an altar to the Arcadian founder of Rome on the slope of the Aventine near Porta Trigemina that survived until at least the time of Augustus (Dion. Hal. 1.32.2), presumably on the Clivus Publicius. Sacrifices were offered there annually.

F

Fagutal (Figs. 74, 75): one of the places where sacrifice was offered in the festival of the Septimontium. In Festus's list (Festus 459L, 476L) it appears between the Velia and the Subura and is distinguished from the Oppius, which is another of the seven places. But in Varro's list of the Argei (*Ling.* 5.50), the Lacus or Lucus Fagutalis is listed as part of the Oppius. The only landmarks there seem to have been a Sacellum Iovis Fagutalis (Varro, *Ling.* 5.152; Pliny, *HN* 16.37; Paulus *ex Fest.* 77L), with a Vicus Iovis Fagutalis (q.v.) and a Lacus Fagutalis (Varro, *Ling.* 5.50; Solinus 1.26). Our sources disagree as to the origins of the name; Pliny ascribes it to a beech grove that had once existed, and Festus ascribes it to a single beech tree. No one suggests that it might have been from a beechwood xoanon, so that must be ruled out. It must have been an area large enough to have borne at least a small beech grove, but there seems no reason to assume it was geographically marked off in any way. Solinus locates it for us at the top of the Clivus Pullius (q.v.). It was probably in the neighborhood of the church of S. Pietro in Vincoli.

RendPontAcc 36 (1963–64): 75–91 (C. Buzzetti and A. M. Colini); *Eranos* 85 (1981): 123–30 (Å. Fridh).

Fanum: see **Aedes, Aedicula, Templum,** etc.

Faunus, Aedes: the only known temple of this god in Rome, at the upstream end of the Tiber island, vowed by the plebeian aediles Cn. Domitius Ahenobarbus and C. Scribonius Libo in 196 B.C. (Livy 33.42.10) and built out of the fines of three *pecuarii* convicted of fraud, probably in the number of their flocks using public pasture. Two years later it was dedicated by Domitius as praetor urbanus (Livy 34.53.4); the day of dedication was the Ides of February (Ovid, *Fast.* 2.193–94; Degrassi 409), two days before the Lupercalia, the great festival of Faunus. The temple was tetrastyle prostyle (Vitruvius 3.2.3), and Vitruvius says Jupiter and Faunus were worshiped together there. He is alone in this assertion. Because Faunus was a very ancient Latin god, protector of the flocks, and Vergil makes him father of Latinus, son of Picus, and grandson of Saturnus (*Aen.* 7.45–49), it is difficult to see why he should have been relegated to the island. His statue stood in the Lupercal, and his sinister quality as the prophetic voice in the forest was certainly no more menacing than that of many others.

Fausta Felicitas: a shrine, probably only an altar, in Capitolio, where in association with the Genius Publicus and Venus Victrix this divinity was worshiped on 9 October (Degrassi 518). Because this was also the day of dedication of the Temple of Apollo Palatinus, it is tempting to see these three divinities of good fortune as some sort of attendant spirits, but they do not form a triad, and the Genius Populi Romani (q.v.) is known to have had a shrine near the Temple of Concordia, which would probably count as in Capitolio. Moreover, Felicitas was worshiped alone in Capitolio on the Kalends of July (Degrassi 475). One should therefore think of three separate altars or aediculae, but these may have stood in a row.

Faustina, Aedicula: a small arch of concrete faced with brick built against the base of the Tabularium, on which it has left the print of its vault between the Temple of Concordia and that of Divus Vespasianus, the temple podium projecting to support it. It measures 4.10 m wide and 2.50 m deep. Its purpose is uncertain, and its name is due to the discovery of a marble base dedicated to Diva Pia Faustina (the wife of Marcus Aurelius) by the *viatores quaestorii ab aerario Saturni* (*CIL* 6.1019 = *ILS* 382).

Nash 1.395–96.

Diva Faustina Maior, Ara: the monument commonly called Ustrinum Antoninorum, a name given it by the antiquarian architect F. Bianchini when it was discovered in 1703 during construction of the Casa della Missione, just west of Palazzo di Montecitorio. It consisted of a concentric series of three square enclosures on an area paved with travertine. The outermost, 100 Roman feet on a side, was a line of square travertine pillars with molded bases on a footing of peperino. Between these were panels of iron grillwork or fences of iron rods. The next enclosure was a wall of marble on a footing of travertine trimmed with a base molding and a crown with dentils, 23 m on a side. This was broken by a door in the middle of the north side surmounted by a triangular pediment supported on consoles. To either side of the door was a round-headed niche crowned with a triangular pediment. Within this was a second wall of marble on a footing of travertine similarly finished at base and crown, 13 m on a side, but without any opening. Bianchini was able to establish that the building had the same orientation as the Antonine Column and Column of Marcus Aurelius and stood at the same level; moreover, it was in axial relation to the Antonine Column.

It is obviously unsuited to be an ustrinum, as the use of marble shows, but it might well be the base of a monumental altar and accords in design with the altar discovered in the course of work on Corso Vittorio Emanuele commonly known as the Ara Ditis et Proserpinae (see Sabina, Diva, Ara), where a large fragment of the *pulvinus* finishing the altar at one end was recovered (see Nash 1.57, 59). Such altars, as shown on coins, were popular for deified members of the imperial house for only a limited time, the principates of Antoninus Pius and Marcus Aurelius. The sculptured base of the Columna Antonini Pii (q.v.) shows the apotheosis of Antoninus and Faustina with an allegorical figure representing the Campus Martius, and the altar may well have been raised on the site of the pyre. Because Faustina predeceased Antoninus and by the time of his death there was already a temple on Sacra Via waiting to receive him, the altar was probably originally erected to her memory and on the place where her pyre had stood, whereas the column was erected where his pyre had stood and the temple then rededicated to the imperial couple. For representation of the altar to Faus-

tina on coins, see *B. M. Coins, Rom. Emp.* 4.236 nos. 1464–67; for that of Antoninus, see *B. M. Coins, Rom. Emp.* 4.394–95 nos. 67–77 and 526–28 nos. 880–90.

CAR 2-G, 168 p. 186; Nash 2.487–88.

Diva Faustina Minor, Ara: Beginning in 1907, in excavations for the parliament building extending Palazzo di Montecitorio to the north, were discovered parts of a large monument consisting of a series of three concentric square enclosures on an area paved with travertine. These were duly reported (*NSc* 1907, 525–28, 681 [D. Vaglieri]; 1909, 10–11 [A. Pasqui]; 1915, 322–24 [F. Fornari]; *BullCom* 35 [1907]: 326–27; 36 [1908]: 86; 37 [1909]: 113; 38 [1910]: 245 [G. Gatti]), and at the conclusion of work Mancini (*StRom* 1 [1913]: 3–15) offered an attempt at synthesis. Later it was possible to recover and reconstruct two magnificent acroteria, probably from a set of four (*BdA* 4 [1910]: 314–15 [R. Paribeni]). The outermost of the enclosures was a fence of iron between pillars of travertine, six on a side, framing a square of 100 Roman feet on a side. This was aligned with the Ustrinum Antoninorum and Columna Marci Aurelii, but not on axis with either, and the single entrance was in the middle of the south side. Inside this, the second enclosure was also a fence of iron between pillars of travertine. Inside this a third wall was of marble, square, and 10.50 m on a side. Although much ruined, it could be determined that this had base and crown moldings and at least one pedimented door, possibly a false one. At the upper corners were elaborate floral acroteria, shaped like the horns of horned altars and sarcophagi. The base has now been reconstructed in the Museo Nazionale Romano delle Terme (Helbig⁴ 3.2159; Nash 2.487–89).

The strong similarity of this monument to the Ustrinum Antoninorum and its close proximity indicate that this is another of the altars erected to commemorate deified members of the Antonine family. Faustina Minor, the wife of Marcus Aurelius who died in A.D. 176, seems the obvious choice. Coins commemorating her deification show just such an altar (*B. M. Coins, Rom. Emp.* 4.491 nos. 725–27, 654 nos. 1579–83, 854 no. 725bis), and no other candidate has equal claim. Evidently Lucius Verus, although deified, was not given an altar.

CAR 2-G, 153 pp. 182–83; *BullCom* 89 (1984): 27–28 (C. Buzzetti); *L'urbe* 47 (1984): 143–46 (A. Danti).

Febris, Templum: Valerius Maximus (2.5.6) says that there were three *templa* to Febris in Rome, one still in existence in his day on the Palatine, a second *in area Marianorum monumentorum,* and a third in the highest part of Vicus Longus. In these amulets *(remedia)* worn by the sick were dedicated.

1. The Palatine shrine is called a *templum* by Valerius and Augustine *(De civ. D.* 3.25), a *fanum* by Cicero *(Nat. D.* 3.63), Seneca *(Apocol.* 6), and Pliny *(HN* 2.16), a building and altar by Aelian *(V. H.* 12.11), and an *aedes* by Priscian (3 p. 250 Rose). Cicero speaks explicitly of an *ara vetusta in Palatio Febris (Leg.* 2.28). It appears to have been an ancient altar to which a sacellum of some sort was added. It cannot now be more precisely located.

2. The *templum in area Marianorum monumentorum* would have been along the Sacra Via as it led out of the Forum Romanum up the slope of the Velia, just beyond the Fornix Fabianus. This is where the Domus Marii (see Domus, Marius) and his Temple of Honos et Virtus (see Honos et Virtus, Aedes [2]) were built. The area of the so-called Temple of Romulus is indicated, or a little east of that. This shrine of Febris was apparently destroyed to make room for Marius's buildings.

3. The *templum in summa parte Vici Longi* still extant in Valerius's day must have been on the Quirinal, somewhere near the west corner of the Thermae Diocletianae (the church of S. Bernardo). If, as seems likely, the Vicus Longus originally continued to the northeast and joined Alta Semita near the west corner of the modern Ministero delle Finanze, it may have been anywhere along the stretch of relatively flat plateau here, but again it seems to have been only a minor monument.

Fecunditas, Templum: a temple voted by the senate in A.D. 63 on the occasion of the birth of the daughter of Nero and Poppaea (Tacitus, *Ann.* 15.23; cf. *CIL* 6.2043.2.9 *cum notis*). The child died within four months, and it is unlikely that the temple was ever built.

Felicitas (1): see **Theatrum Pompeii, Fausta Felicitas,** and **Genius Populi Romani.**

Felicitas (2): a temple projected by Julius Caesar in 44 B.C., just before his assassination, and then built by M. Aemilius Lepidus on the site of the Curia Hostilia (q.v.) of Faustus Sulla, which was demolished for this purpose (Cass. Dio 44.5.2). If the curia as rebuilt by Sulla stood in its traditional location, which there is no reason to doubt, the temple was on ground now occupied by the church of SS. Luca e Martina, but the real reason for the demolition of Sulla's curia must have been to permit rebuilding it as an adjunct of the Forum Iulium (q.v.). The allegation that the motive of the senate in ordering the

rebuilding of the curia was to remove the name of Sulla from it (Cass. Dio 44.5.2) is unlikely, because it was never called by his name, though it may have been inscribed with it. Because the new curia must have been a building of more or less the same size that we see, space for the Temple of Felicitas was limited, and it is not mentioned later. It seems certainly abolished by the time of Hadrian, who seems to have built the Athenaeum there.

Felicitas, Aedes: a temple in the Velabrum (Suetonius, *Iul.* 37.2) that L. Licinius Lucullus built using booty from his campaign in Spain in 151–150 B.C. (Strabo 8.6.23 [381]). It was in front of this temple that the axle of Caesar's chariot broke during his Gallic triumph in 46 B.C. (Suetonius, *Iul.* 37.2; Cass. Dio 43.21.1), so it stood on the route of the triumph, and we can with confidence locate it on the Vicus Tuscus. For its adornment Lucullus obtained from Mummius a number of statues that the latter had from the spoils of Greece, including the Muses of Praxiteles from Thespiae, called the Thespiades, which stood in front of the temple, and a Venus by Praxiteles (Cicero, *Verr.* 2.4.2.4; Pliny, *HN* 34.69, 36.39). The temple burned in the principate of Claudius, and the Venus was destroyed, but the Muses were evidently rescued (Pliny, *HN* 34.69). Apparently the temple was not then rebuilt.

Felicitas in Capitolio: mentioned in the Fasti Antiates (Degrassi 208 for 1 July and 475) and generally considered the same as Fausta Felicitas (q.v.). Cf. Genius Populi Romani.

Ficus Navia: a fig tree in the Comitium named for Attus Navius, near whose statue in front of the Curia Hostilia it stood (Festus 168–70L; Dion. Hal. 3.71.5). Pliny *(HN* 15.77) says it grew from a spot struck by lightning *(fulguribus ibi conditis)* and was regarded as sacred, but was also revered because of the memory of the Ficus Ruminalis (q.v.) and the she-wolf, "a miracle proclaimed in bronze nearby, as though she had crossed the Comitium while Attus Navius was taking the omens." The text is difficult and has been emended to say that Attus Navius had miraculously transported the Ficus Ruminalis to the Comitium by augury, but that seems a patent absurdity. Rather, it appears that what Pliny means is that the statue of Attus Navius showed him with raised lituus, as though taking omens, and near enough the fig and the statue to permit association with them was a bronze she-wolf in an attitude not unlike that of the Capitoline Wolf. The Capitoline Wolf stood for centuries in Piazza S. Giovanni in Laterano, but mounted on a lofty column in the manner popular in the Middle Ages and certainly not its original base. It is therefore possible that this is the wolf intended, though the Capitoline Wolf seems more likely to be the wolf mentioned by Cicero (*Cat.* 3.19, *Div.* 1.20, 2.47) as having been in Capitolio and struck by lightning in 65 B.C., because there are traces of such damage (*EAA,* s.v. "Lupa Capitolina").

The Ficus Navia was regarded as important to the well-being of Rome. Whenever it died this was taken as an omen, and the priests planted a replacement (Pliny, *HN* 15.77). It died in A.D. 58 but then revived, and put forth new shoots (Tacitus, *Ann.* 13.58). Tacitus calls it the Arbor Ruminalis, perhaps in the belief that it was a descendant of, or surrogate for, the Ficus Ruminalis, which by this time had disappeared.

Ficus, Olea, Vitis (Fig. 40)**:** a fig tree, an olive tree, and a grapevine that grew *in medio foro* at the Lacus Curtius (q.v.). Pliny (*HN* 15.78) says that the fig was self-sown, as was also the grape, whereas the olive was planted for the sake of shade, and an altar there was removed at the time of the gladiatorial games for Divus Iulius. On the Plutei Traiani (Nash 2: figs. 902, 905) a fig is shown beside the Statua Marsyae (q.v.), but it is very likely artificial, perhaps of bronze, and has nothing to do with these. A square unpaved area between the pavement inscription of Naevius Surdinus and the bases on which the Plutei were discovered mounted has been taken to be the garden plot of these, but Pliny seems to indicate that they grew on the Lacus itself. This is paved today, but need not have been completely paved in Pliny's day.

Nash 1.397, and cf. 542–43; GV 95–102.

Ficus Ruminalis: the fig tree, close to the Lupercal at the foot of the Cermalus, under which the twins Romulus and Remus were believed to have been washed ashore and where Faustulus found them suckled by the she-wolf (Varro, *Ling.* 5.54; Pliny, *HN* 15.77; Plutarch, *Rom.* 4.1; Servius *ad Aen.* 8.90; Festus 332–33L). Some Romans believed the name was derived from *rumis, ruma,* "breast," but others and modern linguists are inclined to think it is from the same root as the names Roma and Romulus, perhaps *rumon,* either "river" or an ancient name for the Tiber. Livy (1.4.5) says the Ficus Ruminalis survived in his day. Ovid (*Fast.* 2.411) says *remanent vestigia,* by which he seems to mean a stump, for he goes on to say *quaeque vocatur Rumina nunc ficus, Romuli ficus erat.*

Livy (10.23.12) says that in 296 B.C. the curule aediles Cn. and Q. Ogulnius put images of the babes Romulus and Remus under the dugs of the she-wolf by the Ficus Ruminalis. This is confirmed by Diony-

sius (1.79.8), and the group may be shown on coins (*B. M. Coins, Rom. Rep.* 1.131–32 nos. 926–27; Crawford 39/3, 235/1).

Fides, Aedes: the Temple of Fides, also called Fides Publica and Fides Publica Populi Romani, on the Capitoline. A sacrarium to the divinity is ascribed to Numa (Livy 1.21.3–4; Dion. Hal. 2.75.3; Plutarch, *Numa* 16.1). A temple to Fides was dedicated by A. Atilius Calatinus (cos. 258, dictator 249 B.C.) and restored by M. Aemilius Scaurus, perhaps as curule aedile in 58 B.C. (Cicero, *Nat. D.* 2.61). The day of dedication was the Kalends of October (Degrassi 515). The temple was in Capitolio and *vicina Iouis Optimi Maximi* (Pliny, *HN* 35.100; Cato *ap. Cic. Off.* 3.104). It is believed to have been within the Area Capitolina, along with several other temples, and probably stood on the southwest part of the hill west of the square in front of the Temple of Iuppiter Capitolinus.

It was occasionally used for meetings of the senate (Val. Max. 3.2.17; Appian, *BellCiv* 1.16), and around it were displayed bronze tablets containing laws and treaties, a number of which were dislodged by a storm in 44 or 43 B.C. (Cass. Dio 45.17.3; Obsequens 68). Diplomata of honorably discharged soldiers were also very commonly fastened up here in the first century after Christ (*CIL* 16.1, 2, 26, 32). The temple contained a painting by Aristides of Thebes of an old man instructing a boy to play the lyre (Pliny, *HN* 35.100). Nothing is known of its architecture or later history.

Fides, Templum: a temple of Fides on the Palatine supposed to have been dedicated by Rhome, the daughter of Ascanius and granddaughter of Aeneas, at the arrival of the Trojans and occupation of the site of Rome (Festus 328L, following Agathocles, a chronicler of Cyzicene history). The story is one of the more improbable foundation legends invented to explain the name of Rome, and the temple is never mentioned elsewhere.

Figlinae: a potters' quarter on the Oppius (Varro, *Ling.* 5.50; cf. Festus 468L). Because there was no good water source that we know of on the Oppius, this is not apt to have existed before the bringing in of aqueduct water, and, because it is mentioned only in the catalogue of the Argei, it may well have been a limited and short-lived concentration. It was probably only a descriptive term, not a place designation.

Flora, Aedes: a temple built by the aediles L. and M. Publicius Malleolus in 241 B.C. (Vell. Pat. 1.14.8) or 238 (Pliny, *HN* 18.286) *ex oraculis Sibyllae.* The day of consecration is given as 28 April (Degrassi

452), and the Floralia extended from that day to 3 May. A restoration of the temple was begun by Augustus and completed by Tiberius in A.D. 17 (Tacitus, *Ann.* 2.49). The celebration to Flora on 13 August (Degrassi 496) is believed to refer to that rededication. It is located *iuxta Circum Maximum* and *ad Circum Maximum,* and, because these aediles built the Clivus Publicius leading up to the Aventine at the northwest end of the circus, we should probably look for the temple between clivus and circus. It was probably restored in the fourth century by the younger Symmachus as consul (*Anth. Lat.* 1.1. [Shackleton Bailey] p. 22.112–14), although it is not listed in the regionary catalogues. At that time it seems to have been the focus of a gathering of barbers (cf. *ad tonsores*).

The repeated association of this temple with that of Ceres, Liber, and Libera (see Ceres, Liber Liberaque, Aedes) nearby (cf., e.g., Tacitus, *Ann.* 2.49) suggests that this was another plebeian stronghold, but nothing is known about its architectural form.

Flora, Templum: a temple of Flora on the northwest slope of the Quirinal below the Capitolium Vetus and connected to it by a clivus, possibly the Clivus Cosconius (Martial 5.22.4; Varro, *Ling.* 5.158). It was almost certainly on the site of an altar believed to have been dedicated by Titus Tatius to the Sabine Flora (Varro, *Ling.* 5.74). It was also near the Temple of Quirinus, and between them were workshops where cinnabar (minium) was prepared (Vitruvius 7.9.4). We do not know the date of the construction of the temple, but it is listed in the regionary catalogues in Regio VI. As a foundation of Titus Tatius, it is unlikely to have been outside the line of the Servian Walls, so one inclines to put it near the point where Via delle Quattro Fontane crosses that line, just up from Palazzo Barberini.

Flora was an ancient divinity with her own flamen and the Floralia, an elaborate festival including both ludi scaenici and ludi circenses. Part of the celebration was nocturnal, and the ceremonies included some odd ancient customs (Scullard 110–11).

Fons, Lacus, Nymphaeum: A *fons* is a spring and, so far as we know, nothing else. There were numerous springs in Rome and especially on the Quirinal and in the Campus Martius. Across the river the Janiculan hill was, and is, also rich in water. Many of the springs of Rome were good water and highly esteemed. A *lacus* is a street fountain with a watering trough adjacent, the usual arrangement. These varied in size. They seem to have been named from the device depicted on the standard holding the feed pipe, from some peculiarity, or for their builder and

were used as place designators. Hence we find a Vicus Laci Fundani and a Vicus Laci Tecti. The spring-fed pool of Juturna was also called a lacus. These were usually quite simple but could be elaborate, as was, for example, the Lacus Orphei, which was, in effect, more a nymphaeum than a lacus.

A nymphaeum was any sort of ornamental fountain. Ideally it should be in the form of a grotto, and originally, in the late republic, it must usually have taken that shape, but with the passage of time the forms became more and more architectural, so that by the time of Trajan purely architectural forms dominated. A favorite form was the water wall, essentially a *scaenae frons,* the façade of a stage building in two or three storeys adorned with columns, cornices, and statuary, with water piped into as many openings as possible, so one saw the architecture through a veil of falling water. Of these the charming nymphaeum surviving from the Domus Transitoria is an excellent example. Another was the stadium, or water theater, in which a cavea-like flight of steps had water pour down in a cascade from openings and fountain figures arranged above. This was usually set at the end of an enclosed garden or vista. Of these the so-called Auditorium Maecenatis and Lacus Orphei are Roman examples. A third popular form was the water pavilion, in which one was in a room more or less surrounded by water, which might be either outside the room or inside; the banquet hall of the Domus Augustiana and the triconch pavilion of Hadrian's villa at Tivoli are examples of this. But architects liked to exercise their ingenuity and, called upon to design a fountain, did their best to produce something novel and arresting. It would involve sculpture and columnar architecture, but otherwise it would be as inventive as they could manage.

Fons (or **Fontus**), **Ara:** an altar not far from the tomb of Numa (Cicero, *Leg.* 2.56), which was *sub Ianiculo* (Solinus 1.21). Because there were and are numerous springs in the Janiculan hill on the right bank of the Tiber, any one of these might be meant. But the designation Ianiculum probably originally referred only to the ridge leading out to the west from Porta Aurelia (Porta S. Pancrazio) on which the road ran, and it seems likely that the king's tomb would have been built somewhere along this major artery (while Via Campana/Portuensis ran in the flat of the flood plain, keeping away from the hill). An abundant spring at the juncture of Via Garibaldi and Via di Porta S. Pancrazio is as likely as any to have been the one honored, but there is no proof. Another shrine of Fons was found in the area of the courtyard of the Ministero della Pubblica Istruzione on Viale di Trastevere (*NSc* 1914, 362–63 [G. Mancini]), a modest affair of A.D. 70.

Fons, Delubrum: a shrine of Fons dedicated by C. Papirius Maso in 231 B.C., from the spoils of Corsica (Cicero, *Nat. D.* 3.52). The day of dedication seems to have been the feast of the Fontinalia on the Ides of October (Degrassi 215, 520), and the temple seems to have been located *extra Portam Fontinalem.* However, the gate probably did not take its name from the temple, but rather from the Tullianum spring a little inside the gate (but cf. Paulus *ex Fest.* 75L). It may be that the inspiration for the dedication of the temple came from the name of the gate, for there is no spring known in this part of the Campus Martius.

Fons Apollinis: mentioned by Frontinus (*Aq.* 1.4), and listed with the Fons Camenarum and Lacus Iuturnae as an especially salubrious water, but its site is not further indicated, and it is otherwise unknown. The name is odd in view of the rarity of temples of Apollo in early Rome, and the usual association of springs with divinities of their own.

Fons Camenarum: see **Camenae.**

Fons Cati: see **Cati Fons.**

Fons Lollianus: known from a single inscription (*CIL* 6.162) found together with a number of others in the general area known as Piscina Publica in the valley between the Aventine and Caelian. The inscriptions were found around 1558, and those dated span a period from A.D. 69 to A.D. 166, ours falling in 160. They mention *magistri* and *ministri fontis* and suggest that these were officials overseeing Piscina Publica (q.v.). The inscription in question seems to have been found below the western end of the Caelian (LA 235).

See also L. Avetta, ed., *Roma: Via Imperiale* (Rome 1985), 27–28.

Fons Muscosus: a spring beside which stood the Temple of Fortuna Virgo known to Plutarch (*De fort. Rom.* 10). The foundation of this temple is ascribed to Servius Tullius (Plutarch, *Quaest. Rom.* 74), and it has been supposed to be that of the Forum Boarium. But that is unlikely, because there was no spring here, and other important features would invite notice. More likely the temple belongs on the fringes of the city.

Fons Pal . . . : known only from inscriptions (*CIL* 6.157–60) found in the area of Piscina Publica, so

probably not to be completed as Palatinus. Cf. Fons Lollianus, Fons Scaurianus.

Fons Scaurianus: a spring known from inscriptions found in the area of Piscina Publica (*CIL* 6.164–65; *ILS* 3889); the most complete lists four magistri and four ministri of a sacred college, the former freedmen, the latter slaves (LA 235).

Fornices Stertinii: three arches erected by L. Stertinius in 196 B.C., one in the Circus Maximus and two in the Forum Boarium in front of the temples of Mater Matuta and Fortuna (Livy 33.27.4). These celebrated his victories in Farther Spain and were adorned with gilded statues. Because these were the earliest "triumphal" arches of which we have any knowledge and they were quickly followed by the Arch of Scipio on the Capitoline, it seems likely that we should credit Stertinius with the creation of the architectural form that was to become so important. The arches in front of the twin temples of Forum Boarium are apt to have been axial entranceways, but that in the Circus Maximus may have been located almost anywhere. None of these is mentioned subsequently, so they may have been short-lived.

Fornix Augusti: known from an inscription found in the fourteenth century, together with remains of an arch (*CIL* 6.878). The inscription merely records a restoration made by Augustus as pontifex maximus, therefore sometime after 12 B.C. The arch is described as *arcus marmoreus in platea pontis S. Mariae,* so it was probably not a triumphal arch, but simply an arch marking the bridgehead of the Pons Aemilius, like the Arch of Augustus at Rimini, a common architectural feature. Other inscriptions (*CIL* 6.897–98 = *ILS* 131–32) to Gaius and Lucius Caesar that were found near the temple called Fortuna Virilis have been thought to have belonged to the arch, but without sufficient reason.

The theory that this might be the Arcus Stillans (q.v.) and part of the aqueduct carrying the Aqua Claudia to the Transtiberim (Frontinus, *Aq.* 1.20) has little to recommend it. Such aqueducts were regularly carried in the parapets of the Tiber bridges, and the lack of any other arches of an aqueduct bridge in the vicinity speaks conclusively against its existence.

Fornix Calpurnianus: mentioned only once by Orosius (5.9.2) in his account of the death of Tiberius Gracchus. Gracchus was at an assembly of the people on the Capitoline at the Temple of Iuppiter Optimus Maximus Capitolinus (Appian, *BellCiv* 1.15). The senate at the same time assembled in the

153

nearby temple of Fides (Val. Max. 3.2.17; Appian, *BellCiv* 1.16). At the end of the meeting of the senate Scipio Nasica, the pontifex maximus, led an attack on Gracchus and his supporters, who gave way before him. When Gracchus turned to flee and ran around the temple, his toga was torn off him, and, as he ran down the steps *qui sunt super Calpurnianum Fornicem* (also described as being the gateway beside the statues of the kings), he was struck by a club and felled, and when he tried to rise he was struck a second mortal blow. It seems clear that this must have been one of the subsidiary approaches to the Area Capitolina (q.v.), but because the statues of the kings must have been given prominence, presumably set on a continuous high base, like that of the eponymous heroes in the agora of Athens, facing toward the Temple of Jupiter but visible from below, it is impossible to tell from which direction this may have been. On the Marble Plan a stair in two switchback flights is shown approaching the Capitoline from the southwest, the general direction of the Theatrum Marcelli (*FUR* pl. 29; Rodriguez pl. 23). This may be the Centum Gradus of Tacitus (*Hist.* 3.71). Midway along the upper flight is an arch that might be the Fornix Calpurnianus.

The only Calpurnius known to have triumphed before 133 B.C. was C. Calpurnius Piso (Livy 39.42.2–3), but no one says that the Fornix Calpurnianus was triumphal, nor in this location would it seem likely to have been. For a different view, see *Helikon* 1 (1961): 264–82 (B. Bilinski).

Fornix Fabianus (or **Fabiorum**) (Fig. 48): an arch on the Sacra Via at the east end of the Forum Romanum, regarded as one of the boundaries of the forum, as in the phrase *a rostris usque ad arcum Fabianum* (Seneca, *Dial.* 2.1.3). It is variously described as *iuxta Regiam in Sacra Via* (Cicero, *Schol. in Act. I in Verrem* [Stangl 211]), *prope Vestam* (Cicero, *Schol. in Act. I in Verrem* [Stangl 336]), *Sacram ingredientibus Viam post templum Castoris* (Cicero, *Schol. in Act. I in Verrem* [Stangl 350]), and *ad puteal Scribonii Libonis quod est in porticu Iulia* (Persius, *Schol. ad* 4.49). Q. Fabius Maximus Allobrogicus built it in 121 B.C. to celebrate his victories over the Allobroges. It was decorated with statues of a number of members of his family, possibly part of a restoration, and was the first triumphal arch in or near the forum. It was restored by his grandson of the same name, as curule aedile in 57 B.C. (*CIL* 6.1303, 1304, 31593; *ILS* 43); the inscriptions, which were discovered in 1540 and 1543, have since been lost. In 1953 it was identified with the foundations of a single-fornix arch over the "southern branch" of Sacra Via just after this forks from the

northern branch at the east end of the Regia (q.v.). Coarelli, with greater logic, places it over the "northern branch" of Sacra Via at the western end of the Regia. Because the area has been repeatedly ransacked, it is impossible to assign any fragments of elements of a superstructure to it, but presumably this will have been of tufa faced with travertine and adorned with statuary and other ornaments in gilded bronze.

Nash 1.398–400; Coarelli 1985, 171–73.

Fornix Scipionis: an arch that Scipio Africanus erected in 190 in Capitolio. It stood *adversus viam*, which suggests that it flanked rather than spanned the roadway, and was adorned with seven gilded statues and two horses. In front of it were set two marble basins (Livy 37.3.7), presumably fountains, but because Q. Marcius Rex's bringing of the Aqua Marcia to the Capitoline was regarded as a feat worthy of record (Livy, *Epit.* 54) and the Anio Vetus ran at a much lower level than the Marcia, the basins may originally have been purely ornamental. It seems to have been a single-fornix arch and does not seem to have served as an entrance to the Area Capitolina.

Fors Fortuna, Fanum: a temple on the right bank of the Tiber, supposed to have been founded by Servius Tullius (Varro, *Ling.* 6.17; Dion. Hal. 4.27.7). It was outside the city, beside the Tiber, and its dedication day was 24 June (Degrassi 473). As we learn from the fasti, there were actually two temples, one at the first and one at the sixth milestone of the Via Portuensis, with the same festival day. The dedicator of the second temple is unknown. Dionysius (4.27.7) misunderstood the name of the goddess and interpreted it as Fortis Fortuna, and he was followed in this by Plutarch (*De fort. Rom.* 5), who ascribes the foundation of the temple to Ancus Marcius. But one is not apt to confuse Servius Tullius with Ancus Marcius, especially not someone as versed in Roman antiquities as Plutarch, so it may be that the second temple is the one in question and a foundation of Ancus Marcius.

In 293 B.C. Sp. Carvilius let a contract for another temple to Fors Fortuna near the temple of Servius Tullius (*prope aedem,* Livy 10.46.14), and in A.D. 17 Tiberius dedicated yet another temple close to the river in the gardens that Julius Caesar had willed to the people of Rome (Tacitus, *Ann.* 2.41.1).

Four temples to the same divinity, all on the right bank of the Tiber, are a puzzling phenomenon. In 209 B.C. there was a minor prodigy: a bust that adorned the crown of one of the cult statues fell spontaneously into the statue's hand. Other mentions of the temples are rare and uninformative, except for the appearance of one in the regionary catalogues of the fourth century. But the temples of Servius, Carvilius, and Tiberius were all close to the river (cf. Ovid, *Fast.* 6.773–86) and may all have stood in a group, because the first milestone of Via Campana/Portuensis is apt to have fallen within the area of the Horti Caesaris (2)(q.v.). The temple at the sixth milestone was close to the headquarters of the Fratres Arvales. No positive identification of remains of any of these temples has been made.

Fortuna: a temple that Trajan dedicated to the universal Fortuna, at which offerings were to be made on 1 January (Lydus, *Mens.* 4.7). The idea seems to have been to gather all the multiple aspects of Fortuna into a single cult, and the offerings at the opening of the new year go with related ceremonies of the augurs (see Strenia, Sacellum) and magistrates (Scullard 52–54). We have no idea where this temple may have stood.

Fortuna, Aedes (1) (Figs. 9, 37.10): a temple in the Forum Boarium believed to have been founded by Servius Tullius (Dion. Hal. 4.27.7), twin to a Temple of Mater Matuta, with which it shared a dedication day, 11 June (Degrassi 468–69). It burned in the fire of 213 B.C. (Livy 24.47.15) and a special commission restored it the next year (Livy 25.7.6). It contained an archaic statue of gilded wood that survived the fire unscathed (Ovid, *Fast.* 6.625–26; Val. Max. 1.8.11; Dion. Hal. 4.40.7). This statue was draped in two togas described as *praetextae* (Pliny, *HN* 8.197) and *undulatae* or *regiae undulatae* (Varro *ap. Non.* 278L; Pliny, *HN* 8.194). It was so thoroughly concealed by these that the identity of the subject was in dispute, some believing it to be a statue of Servius Tullius (Ovid, *Fast.* 6.569–72, 613–24; Varro *ap. Non.* 278L; Pliny, *HN* 8.197; Dion. Hal. 4.40.7; Val. Max. 1.8.11), others a statue of the goddess (Cass. Dio 58.7.2). According to Dio, Sejanus removed this statue to his own house.

In the zone known as the Area Sacra di Sant' Omobono, the temple has come to light. With its twin, it stood inside the Porta Carmentalis, its back to the Vicus Iugarius, from which an entrance passage led between the two temples. Their architectural form was odd, the deep pronaos being enclosed by lateral walls, distyle in antis, but with a second line of two columns midway between façade and cella, the cella small, with alae to either side. In front of each temple on axis is an archaic U-shaped altar turned ninety degrees to face east.

The whole area is enormously complicated by building and rebuilding. Excavation was begun in 1937 and soon laid bare a welter of walls and pavements, the complete publication of which is still awaited. In 1974 the first deep stratigraphic excavations were carried out at selected points, and these have continued intermittently ever since. The material of every sort is of the highest interest and attests to the early occupation and continued intense use of the area.

Nash 1.415–17; *PP* 32 (1977): 1–128 (various authors); Coarelli 1988, 205–437, especially 205–44; *La grande Roma dei Tarquini*, 111–30 (G. Pisani Sartorio, A. Sommella Mura, et al.).

Fortuna, Aedes (2): see **Lacus Aretis.**

Fortuna, Templum Novum: listed by the *Notitia* in Regio VII: *templa duo nova Spei et Fortunae*, so the adjective is probably not an epithet. The temple is otherwise unknown.

Fortuna Apotropaios: a shrine that Plutarch (*Quaest. Rom.* 74) ascribed to Servius Tullius, but otherwise unknown. The Latin translation of *Apotropaios* has been suggested to be *Averrunca*, but this does nothing to advance our knowledge. Plutarch ascribes numerous *hiera* to Fortuna to Servius, but only two temples are usually mentioned; the others may have been altars.

Fortuna Augusta Stata: see **Fortuna Stata.**

Fortuna Brevis: a *hieron* ascribed to Servius Tullius by Plutarch (*Quaest. Rom.* 74).

Fortuna Dubia: see **Vicus Fortunae Dubiae.**

Fortuna Equestris, Aedes: a temple of Fortuna of the equites vowed by Q. Fulvius Flaccus in 180 B.C. during his campaign in Spain (Livy 40.40.10 and 44.9) and dedicated in 173 (Livy 42.10.5) on 13 August (Degrassi 494–95). For this temple Flaccus took some of the marble tiles of the Temple of Iuno Lacinia near Croton, but the senate ordered him to restore them (Livy 42.3.1–11; Val. Max. 1.1.20). It is referred to in 92 B.C. (Obsequens 53) and possibly 156 (Obsequens 16). It was near the Theatrum Pompeii and an example of systyle column spacing, the intercolumniations being equal to twice the diameter of the columns (Vitruvius 3.3.2). It is said that Flaccus strove to make his temple so magnificent that there should be none larger or more splendid in Rome, but by A.D. 22 it had apparently disappeared (Tacitus, *Ann.* 3.71.1). It seems unlikely that a large temple familiar to Vitruvius could have been forgotten in so short an interval, so probably it was destroyed in the fire of A.D. 21 that burned the scaena of the Theater of Pompey (Tacitus, *Ann.* 3.72.4, 6.45.2; Hieron. *a. Abr.* 2037).

Fortuna Euelpis (Bonae Spei): one of the shrines Plutarch credits Servius Tullius with having established to Fortuna. He calls it a *hieron* (*Quaest. Rom.* 74) and a *bomos* (*De fort. Rom.* 10). It was in Vicus Longus on the Quirinal and seems to have been to the combination of Fortuna and Spes known from coins (Roscher 1.1537–39 [R. Peter]). The Latin epithet is not attested in our sources, and the history and more precise location of the shrine are entirely unknown.

Fortuna Huiusce Diei: A shrine of some sort to the goddess in this aspect on the Palatine is indicated by the existence there of a Vicus Huiusce Diei (q.v.). It is otherwise unknown. However, the omission of the name of Fortuna in the name of the vicus is surprising, and it may mean that we are dealing with something quite different.

Fortuna Huiusce Diei, Aedes (Fig. 8): a temple vowed by Q. Lutatius Catulus at the Battle of Vercellae, 30 July 101 B.C. (Plutarch, *Marius* 26.2) and dedicated on an anniversary of the battle (Degrassi 488). The fasti put it *in campo (Martio)*, and it has been identified with great probability as Temple B of the Area Sacra di Largo Argentina. Varro's description (*Rust.* 3.5.12) of Catulus's building as a tholus with a colonnade and the fact that it is pointed out as an example in a conversation set in the nearby Villa Publica seem nearly conclusive. The temple is raised on a low podium, with a broad stair of approach projecting toward the east. The peripteros was of eighteen Corinthian columns, the shafts of tufa, and the bases and capitals of travertine. The walls are of concrete faced with opus incertum, and the podium is faced with tufa plates and moldings. At a later period the walls of the cella were dismantled, walls were run between the columns of the peripteros to make a new cella, and an enormous statue base was installed to carry a colossal cult statue.

Pliny (*HN* 34.60) tells us that seven nude statues and one of an elderly man, all by Pythagoras of Samos, a contemporary of Myron, stood *ad aedem Fortunae Huiusce Diei* and were much admired. It is more likely to be this temple that is meant than the one on the Palatine, but certainty is impossible. Procopius (*BellGoth* 1.15.11) says that in the sixth century a stone replica of the Palladium that Diomedes brought from Troy to Italy existed in the Temple of Fortuna; this is commonly thought to be the temple that is meant, but without adequate reason.

Because it is hardly thinkable that Catulus would have dedicated statues in someone else's temple, were he intending to build one of his own, we must suppose that the three statues that Pliny ascribed to Phidias (*HN* 34.54) and located *ad aedem Fortunae Huiusce Diei* belonged here. Two of these were *palliata* (draped figures), and the third was a colossal nude. Moreover, Aemilius Paullus is said to have dedicated an Athene, also by Phidias, in the same temple. If the hero of Pydna is meant, then we must assume that the statue was originally dedicated elsewhere, presumably in the shrine to that goddess on the Palatine, and subsequently transferred to Catulus's temple, which is certainly not impossible. But it is also possible that an Aemilius Paullus of the time of the revival of the name in the Lepidus branch of the family dedicated the statue.

Fortuna Mala, Ara: an altar located (Cicero, *Nat. D.* 3.63, *Leg.* 2.28; Pliny, *HN* 2.16) simply *Esquiliis* (see Esquiliae [1]). It seems likely that it was at the top of the Clivus Suburanus, inside the Porta Esquilina.

Fortuna Mammosa: a shrine or altar listed by the regionary catalogues in Regio XII and to be connected with the Vicus Fortunae Mammosae of the Capitoline Base (*CIL* 6.975 = *ILS* 6073). In the regionary catalogues it appears after Via Nova and before Isis Ahenodoria, for which reason PA suggests it should be located between Porta Capena and the Baths of Caracalla. But we know very little about the topography of this region, especially of the Aventinus Minor.

Fortuna Obsequens: a shrine ascribed to Servius Tullius by Plutarch (*De fort. Rom.* 10, *Quaest. Rom.* 74) and located by the Vicus Fortunae Obsequentis of the Capitoline Base in Regio I (*CIL* 675 = *ILS* 6073). It should therefore be inside Porta Capena, possibly on the western slope of the Caelian. Cf. Venus Obsequens, Aedes.

Fortuna Primigenia, Hieron: a temple of the Fortuna of Praeneste supposed to have been founded by Servius Tullius on the Capitoline (Plutarch, *De fort. Rom.* 10, *Quaest. Rom.* 74); the day of dedication seems to have been the Ides of November (Degrassi 530). In *CIL* 14.2852 = *ILS* 3696 Fortuna is described as *Tarpeio . . . vicina Tonanti*, so the temple must be presumed to have been in the Area Capitolina (q.v.). Cf. also Fortunae (Tres), Aedes.

Fortuna Privata, Hieron: a temple of Fortuna as patroness of the individual, in contrast to Fortuna Publica (see Fortunae [Tres], Aedes). It was on the Palatine, and its foundation was ascribed to Servius

Tullius (Plutarch, *De fort. Rom.* 10, *Quaest. Rom.* 74). It was extant in Plutarch's day, but no one else mentions it.

Fortuna Redux, Ara: an altar that the senate erected in 19 B.C., probably in the precinct (*iuxta*) of the Temple of Honos et Virtus near Porta Capena, to celebrate the return of Augustus from the East (Augustus, *RG* 11). A festival was established in his honor on the anniversary of his reentry into the city, 12 October, the Augustalia (Degrassi 519–20), but the altar itself was dedicated on 15 December (Degrassi 538). The altar is shown on coins (e.g., *B. M. Coins, Rom. Rep.* 3 pl. 63 nos. 2–5; *B. M. Coins, Rom. Emp.* 1 pl. 7 nos. 10–13) and seems to have been relatively modest.

Fortuna Redux, Templum: a temple that Domitian built after his triumphal return to Rome following campaigns in Germany in A.D. 93 (Martial 8.65). The temple overlooked the Porta Triumphalis, which Domitian rebuilt and crowned with triumphal cars drawn by elephants, and is certainly that shown in an adventus panel on the attic of the Arch of Constantine, a panel taken from an arch of Marcus Aurelius (Nash 1.111 fig. 115). The temple is shown as tetrastyle, prostyle, of the Corinthian order, and with symbols of Fortuna in the pediment. The Porta Triumphalis was probably the fornix of Porta Carmentalis that the Fabii were believed not to have used on their way to Veii, that on the right as one approached the gate from the exterior (Livy 2.49.8), and the Temple of Fortuna Redux must have stood on the slopes of the Capitoline. It is at least conceivable that it is the tetrastyle temple shown on a fragment of the Marble Plan at the head of the Centum Gradus (?) (*FUR* pl. 29; Rodriguez pl. 23). From coins bearing this legend and *Fortuna Augusti*, one gathers that the cult statue showed the goddess standing, with her usual attributes of steering oar and cornucopia (*B. M. Coins, Rom. Emp.* 2 passim).

Fortuna Respiciens: a shrine of unknown sort on the Palatine responsible for the name of the Vicus Fortunae Respicientis recorded on the Capitoline Base (*CIL* 6.975 = *ILS* 6073). It is also listed in the regionary catalogues after the Curiae Veteres and before the Septizodium, which encourages us to locate it on the east slope of the hill, perhaps about midway along it.

Fortuna Respiciens, Hieron: a temple of Fortuna on the Esquiline which Plutarch ascribed to Servius Tullius (*De fort. Rom.* 10, *Quaest. Rom.* 74). This is presumably the temple meant by Dio (42.26.4) in recounting a prodigy of 48 B.C., when a stream of

blood issued from a bakery and flowed to a temple of Fortuna. If the emendation of Plutarch (*en Aiskuliais*) is correct, the temple probably stood along the Clivus Suburanus not far from the Porta Esquilina.

Fortuna Restitutrix, Ara: see **Castra Praetoria.**

Fortuna Seiani, Aedes: Pliny (*HN* 36.163) says that in the time of Nero a stone was discovered in Cappadocia of the hardness of marble, white, and translucent even where tawny veins occurred, probably an alabaster or onyx. Of this stone Nero built a temple for the Fortuna "of Sejanus," which had been originally dedicated by Servius Tullius, and included it in the Domus Aurea. The quality of the stone was such that by day with the doors closed it was as bright as daylight within. Pliny uses the past tense of the temple, as though it no longer existed, thus suggesting that it was in the parts of the Domus Aurea destroyed under Vespasian, especially the Stagnum, where the Colosseum was built, and the area surrounding this.

The Fortuna Seiani can only be the statue draped with two togas that stood in the Temple of Fortuna in the Forum Boarium and was removed by Sejanus to his own house (Cass. Dio 58.7.2). Why it was not restored to its proper place after Sejanus's death is not clear, nor yet what may have become of it after the dismantling of Nero's temple.

Fortuna Augusta Stata: a shrine known only from an inscription (*CIL* 6.761 = *ILS* 3308) recording its dedication on the Kalends of January A.D. 12 by the vicomagistri of the Vicus Sandaliarius (q.v.) of Regio IV. It was consequently on the western end of the Oppius near the Temple of Tellus, probably a small compital shrine.

Fortuna Augusta is known from Pompeii, where she had an important temple and her worship was in the charge of a college of four Ministri Fortunae Augustae whose inscriptions range in date from A.D. 3 to A.D. 56. It is surprising that the cult of Fortuna Augusta or Augusti was not more widespread and publicized in the early years of the principate. She does not seem to have appeared on coins until the time of Galba (*B. M. Coins, Rom. Emp.* 1.352 no. 241). Perhaps it is because she was worshiped as a compital divinity and her worship was always in the charge of Augustales. A base to Fortuna Augusta was dedicated on 28 January A.D. 119 by the officers of the mint of gold and silver near S. Clemente (see Moneta), eighteen freedmen and nine slaves (*CIL* 6.43 = *ILS* 1634).

Stata Mater, a divinity credited with the ability to stop fires, had an image (*simulacrum*) in the Forum

Romanum and was widely worshiped in the compital shrines of the vici (Festus 416L). She is also known from a Vicus Statae Matris (q.v.) on the Caelian and a Vicus Statae Siccianae in the Transtiberim (*CIL* 6.975 = *ILS* 6073). Numerous dedications to her by vicomagistri attest to her popularity as a compital god (cf. *ILS* 3306–9).

Fortuna Tulliana: known from a single inscription found near Porta Flaminia (Porta del Popolo), the sepulchral inscription of a freedman aedituus of the temple (*CIL* 6.8706 = *ILS* 3717). Almost certainly one of the numerous shrines supposed to have been dedicated by Servius Tullius is meant. PA thinks Fors Fortuna most likely, but the Temple of Fortuna in the Forum Boarium was certainly at least as well known and venerable.

Fortuna Virgo (Hieron): a shrine that Plutarch (*De fort. Rom.* 10, *Quaest. Rom.* 74) said was dedicated by Servius Tullius. Plutarch locates it near the Fons Muscosus (q.v.). This makes it unlikely to have been the Fortuna of Forum Boarium, and one would like to locate it on the edge of the city, but there is no other evidence.

Fortuna Virilis (Hieron, Hedos): a temple ascribed by Plutarch (*De fort. Rom.* 10, *Quaest. Rom.* 74) to Servius Tullius. The goddess was worshiped on 1 April, on the same day as Venus Verticordia (Degrassi 433–34), and was credited with concealing the blemishes of women's bodies from men. Consequently, she was worshiped especially in baths and bathing places (Ovid, *Fast.* 4.145–50), but the association of Fortuna Virilis with Venus Verticordia suggests that she, too, might have had her temple in Vallis Murcia. There is no mention of a temple, except by Plutarch. The temple in Forum Boarium commonly ascribed to Fortuna Virilis is certainly not hers, but is probably the Temple of Portunus (see Portunium).

Fortuna Viscata (Hieron): a temple ascribed by Plutarch (*De fort. Rom.* 10, *Quaest. Rom.* 74) by implication to Servius Tullius, but without explicit attribution. The epithet was explained as meaning that Fortuna, like a fowler, catches her prey at a distance and holds it tenaciously. The explanation seems unlikely, unless the divinity was shown with a fowler's reed as attribute. There is no indication of the temple's location.

Fortunae (Tres), Aedes: three temples of Fortuna on the Quirinal just inside the Porta Collina; the name *ad tres Fortunas* seems to have been given to a small district there (cf. Vitruvius 3.2.2).

The principal temple was that of Fortuna Primigenia, the great goddess of Praeneste, to whom in the fasti are also given the names Fortuna Publica Populi Romani Quiritium and Fortuna in Colle (Quirinali), whereas Lydus (*Mens.* 4.7) styles her Populi Fortuna Potentis Publica. The consul P. Sempronius Tuditanus vowed the temple in 204 B.C. at the outset of his battle with Hannibal at Croton (Livy 29.36.8), and Q. Marcius Ralla dedicated it in 194 (Livy 34.53.5). The day of dedication was 25 May (Degrassi 461). It was probably in this temple that prodigies were observed in 169 B.C. (Livy 43.13.5).

The second temple is called the Temple of Fortuna Publica Citerior (in Colle), i.e., that nearest to the center of the city. Its day of dedication was 5 April (Degrassi 437). Ovid (*Fast.* 4.375–76) mentions it, but nothing is known of its form or history.

The third temple seems to have been insignificant and may have escaped certain mention in any of our ancient sources (cf. Degrassi for 13 November).

In recounting the prodigies of 48 B.C., Dio (42.26.3–4) says that the Temple of Fortuna Publica was struck by lightning and the doors of the temple opened of their own accord. This was probably the most important of the three. Vitruvius (3.2.2) says that the temple nearest the gate was an example of a temple distyle in antis. In recounting the dedication of the temple of Sempronius Tuditanus, Livy (34.53.6) confuses him with Sempronius Sophus (cos. 268), saying that Sophus vowed the temple as consul and let the contract for it as censor. This is so wildly wrong chronologically that it may be that Livy got hold of records for more than one temple of Fortuna and confused them because the men who vowed them belonged to the same gens, and whereas the Temple of Fortuna Primigenia belonged to Tuditanus, one of the others belonged to Sophus, in which case it is probably Fortuna Publica Citerior.

The picture that emerges is of three temples in a row or arc just inside the Porta Collina, all belonging to Fortuna Publica, the largest in the center to Fortuna Publica Primigenia, that nearest the city to Fortuna Publica without further epithet and consequently probably the oldest of the three, and that nearest the gate the least important of the three architecturally and historically.

Discoveries in excavations in the neighborhood have produced material that is suggestive but inconclusive. Cf. Lugli 1938, 338 and literature cited there; Lanciani, *LFUR* sheet 10.

Fortunium: see **Portunium.**

Forum, Area, Compitum: Originally the forum was simply the open space in the center of the city around which public buildings, temples, offices, and shops clustered. Its location was determined by convenience; because the salt route on which Rome heavily depended descended the Quirinal by Alta Semita and took the Vicus Iugarius to reach the ferry at the mouth of the Cloaca, a market to sell provisions to those using that route must have sprung up on the lower slopes of the Capitoline very early, and as Rome grew, it expanded into the area below. Romulus and Titus Tatius are supposed to have struck their treaty of peace on the Sacra Via, and statues of them stood there to prove it, Romulus on the Palatine side, Titus Tatius toward the Rostra (Festus 372L; Servius ad Aen. 8.641). Presumably these were near the foot of the Velia. The Comitium, so far as we know, was never in any other than its traditional location, midway between the Quirinal and the Palatine, and the Curia Hostilia was believed to have been built by Tullus Hostilius. Dionysius (2.50.1–2) ascribes the creation of the forum to Romulus and Titus Tatius, saying they cut down the wood growing at the foot of the Capitoline to fill most of the lake in the forum basin, but then he goes on to say that they conducted their business and assemblies at the Volcanal. The real work of channeling the Cloaca is always ascribed to the Tarquins; this permitted expansion of forum activity to cover the whole of the basin. The butchers were expelled from the forum by 310 B.C. and replaced by money-changers and bankers (Varro ap. Non. 853L), but a market in items of feminine adornment still continued to thrive there in Plautus's day (Curc. 472–73). We hear of tabernae there in the time of Cicero (Cicero, De Or. 2.266; Varro, Ling. 6.59), but probably these were by this time largely government offices. The conversion of the forum into a purely civic center was probably no earlier than the time of Augustus, although work on the project was initiated by Julius Caesar, and one sees attempts in this direction under Sulla. The earliest temple on the forum was that of Saturn of the early fifth century, but sanctuaries such as the Volcanal and Lacus Curtius dated from time immemorial.

With the growth of Rome other areas took on forum character and were called by that name. The open area behind the port on the river just below the island became the Forum Boarium, and its extension toward the Campus Martius became the Forum Holitorium. The markets into which the provisioners moved after expulsion from the main forum were the Forum Piscarium (or Piscatorium) and Forum Cuppedinis, and we know of a Forum Esquilinum, where the forces of Marius and Sulla fought a pitched battle in 88 B.C. (Appian, BellCiv 1.58). Probably this use of the term was natural and instinctive. The Forum Piscarium and Forum Cuppedinis were adjacent to the original forum and in some sense simply exten-

sions of it. The Forum Boarium existed as early as 218 B.C., when a portent was observed there (Livy 21.62.3); and in 212 B.C. the first gladiatorial games offered in Rome were held there as part of a funeral, but it is not perfectly clear whether the Forum Boarium was inside or outside the Servian Walls, which were standing in this area through the Second Punic War, although they seem to have been dismantled almost immediately after its successful conclusion. From Livy's account of the fire of 213 B.C. (Livy 24.47.15) one gathers that it was outside the walls, but the Temple of Portunus is described as in portu Tiberino (Varro, Ling. 6.19), not in foro Boario. In 216 B.C. the Romans, on instruction of the Sibylline Books, performed an extraordinary sacrifice by burying alive four people, a Gaulish man and woman and a Greek man and woman; this was done in foro Boario (Livy 22.57.6). It seems more likely that this would have been done outside the pomerium than inside, but the exact location is unknown. However, Varro (ap. Macrob. Sat. 3.6.10) carefully distinguished a temple of Hercules ad portam Trigeminam from one in foro Boario. On balance, then, the evidence weighs that the Forum Boarium was originally outside the Servian Walls, probably extending only as far as the Cloaca, defined by this, the Circus brook, the Servian Walls, and the river. Later it extended to the Velabrum and the Porta Carmentalis and included the Portus Tiberinus, being probably then bounded by streets. The Forum Holitorium seems to have been similarly loosely bounded but, unlike the Forum Boarium, seems to have shrunk with time, rather than expanded.

With the gradual remodeling of the main forum into a unified public square especially for public business and ceremony, other fora took this character, although the fora of provincial towns never lost their heterogeneous character and continued to provide place for the market in provisions. But the Forum Iulium, the first of the imperial fora and essentially a temple in a square framed by colonnades with offices (tabernae) behind, is never called anything else, and forum begins to be the official designation for such a square, provided there is official business conducted there. The distinction of the Templum Pacis of Vespasian, which is not called Forum Pacis until after the time of Constantine, although architecturally it is indistinguishable from its neighbors, may be that at the beginning it was not connected with government business or official ceremony.

In a late period the term forum is extended to include a great range of insignificant squares that were probably small market squares. Their names appear in our catalogues of the fourth and fifth centuries, but they have disappeared without leaving a trace, and it is impossible to say whether they showed a common character and, if so, what it might have been.

Until late antiquity *area* seems to have been the term used for a square, or open space, of moderate size or special dedication. When such space is sacred, it is usually the possession of a single divinity and equivalent to a templum or delubrum, as the Area Concordiae and Area Saturni. The Area Capitolina, however, was the whole terraced top of its hill and included within its boundaries a number of temples to a variety of divinities. A secular area is simply an open space, as the Area Palatina or Area Radicaria. It is surprising that there are not more spaces so designated than in fact we find in our sources.

A *compitum* is a crossing of streets, technically any crossing of streets, but usually one where there was a shrine to the Lares Compitales, and under the empire one where the vicomagistri assembled and performed their rites, so usually a distinct widening, or emphasis, in the street. One compital shrine has been discovered, the Compitum Acili on the Velia at the crossing of Vicus Cuprius and the extension of Sacra Via leading to the Carinae, a very elegant little aedicula of marble. It is not known how the compitum got its name; most seem to have been named for one of the streets involved, but only a few names have come down to us, although there must have been compita all over the city.

Forum: see **Forum Romanum** or **Magnum.**

Forum Ahenobarbi: listed only in the first appendix to the regionary catalogues and otherwise completely unknown. We must doubt that it ever existed, but the source of the name is puzzling.

Forum Aproniani: mentioned in the *Codex Theodosianus* (13.5.29) with the date A.D. 400 and possibly by Polemius Silvius in his list of fora (*Apurani*). If it is to be associated with one of the two L. Turcii Aproniani who were praefectus urbi in 339 and 363, as seems likely, it may well have been an alternate name given to the more familiar Forum Pacis (Templum Pacis), where the praefectus urbi had part of his headquarters, or some part thereof where there was a statue or monument to identify it (Jordan 2.212–14).
TAPS 80.2 (1990): 45–50 (R. E. A. Palmer).

Forum Augustum or **Augusti** (often called **Forum Martis**) (Fig. 36): Augustus's greatest architectural achievement, a magnificent colonnaded square containing the great Temple of Mars Ultor. Octavian vowed a temple to Mars Ultor on the eve of the Battle of Philippi (Suetonius, *Aug.* 29.2; Ovid, *Fast.* 5.569–78) and, following the return of the standards of Crassus by the Parthians, may have dedicated a small one on the Capitoline, 12 May 20 B.C., in which the standards were placed. But Octavian must from the beginning have intended building a complex to rival the Forum Iulium with its Temple of Venus Genetrix, adjacent, or in close relation, to it. The site was purchased with the proceeds of the spoils of war (Augustus, *RG* 21), but we are told that the princeps was unable to acquire all the land he wished and that the plan had to be modified (Suetonius, *Aug.* 56.2). Suetonius says that the land he was unable to obtain was occupied by houses and that Augustus was reluctant to dispossess their owners. If this is correct, these must have lain northwest of the forum as built, between it and the Atrium Libertatis, and the original intention had been to lay out the forum parallel to the Forum Iulium. But one may question whether this story was not an apocryphal invention to explain the broad squarish proportions of the forum and the irregularity of its rear wall, because the general area of the imperial fora was largely, if not entirely, occupied by a series of markets, and subsequent builders seem not to have encountered any such difficulties. Macrobius (*Sat.* 2.4.9) says work on the forum was much delayed by the architect, but no one says when it was begun. Because it was built *ex manubiis* and the Temple of Apollo Palatinus (see Apollo Palatinus, Aedes) served as a victory monument for the conquest of Egypt, we may think of the spoils of the Spanish and German wars as the major sources of funds and think of work as beginning in earnest about 25 or 24 B.C. According to Suetonius (*Aug.* 29.1), work on the forum at the end was hurried, and the dedication was made with the Temple of Mars Ultor still unfinished. The date of the dedication was 12 May 2 B.C. (Cass. Dio 55.10.1–8, 60.5.3; Vell. Pat. 2.100.2; Degrassi 490; *JRS* 67 [1977]: 91–94 [C. J. Simpson]). Suetonius (*Aug.* 29.1) says the purpose of the forum was to provide space for law courts, because with the increase in population the two existing fora were no longer adequate, but Dio's (55.10.1–5) detailed list of activities decreed to take place there omits any mention of courts and makes it quite clear that the main purpose of the forum was as a foreign office, the center from which the provinces were administered (see Anderson 88–97). There is no other evidence that the forum was ever regularly used for courts, although the princeps might sit in judgment there (see below).

The forum was a broad rectangle about 125 m long and 90 m wide. In some way that is not known, its main entrance must have been on axis from the

Forum Iulium, to which it was perpendicular, or from a street separating it from the Forum Iulium. It was flanked by deep colonnades, and the Temple of Mars Ultor nearly filled the far end of the open square. Behind the colonnades along the temple flanks opened great hemicycles lined with niches, like the colonnades. The roofing of these has been much debated, but their chief purpose must have been to bring abundant light down behind the colonnades in order to illuminate and enhance the flanks of the temple, which would otherwise lie in a deeply shaded canyon, and to suggest spacious expansions of the square opening out beyond it to either side. The southeast colonnade ends abruptly on a straight line; the northwest one ends in a squarish hall screened from the colonnade by a pair of columns. In the space at this end between colonnade and temple to either side a broad stair leads up through an archway, angled to increase the focus on the temple, to a broad street at the back; the arch to the southeast is known as the Arco dei Pantani. From this street behind the forum, one had access to some unimportant chambers tucked into unused and irregular spaces and to a courtyard surrounded by vaulted arcades at the north corner, which must have been of some importance but had no direct communication with the forum.

The forum colonnades were lifted three steps above the square and paved with rectangular flags of colored marble. The columns were of cipollino and other colored marbles, 9.50 m high, the Corinthian capitals and entablature of white marble, surmounted by a deep attic, implying a vaulted ceiling behind it, on the façade of which caryatids, replicas of those of the Erechtheum in Athens reduced in size, alternated with large and richly carved shields bearing the heads of divinities (Iuppiter Ammon survives) as bosses, a decorative version of imagines clipeatae. The caryatids stand forward from the face of the wall, so the architrave breaks forward to be carried by them, and a line of coffers is introduced between each pair. The back wall of the colonnade is broken by rectangular niches framed by an engaged order responding to the colonnade. The engaged order continues on a line of piers across the opening to each hemicycle and also frames the line of niches along each curved wall, while a larger aedicular niche breaks the line at the center of the curve, and a second line of niches is added above. It is presumed that the lower niches were for the bronze statues of the Iulii and the Summi Viri of Rome, who, we know, were honored here, each with an inscription recording his offices and accomplishments (Suetonius, *Aug.* 31.5; Cass. Dio 55.10.3; Pliny, *HN* 22.13; A. Gellius 9.11.10; S.H.A. *Alex. Sev.* 28.6, where the

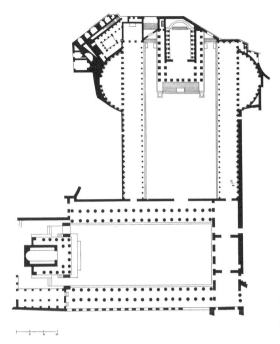

Figure 36
Forum Augustum
and Forum Iulium,
Restored Plan

statues are said to be of marble; for the inscriptions, of which a considerable number are known, see A. Degrassi, *Inscriptiones Italiae* 13.3.1–36. Only a few fragments of some of the statues in white marble survive, but enough to show that some were togate and others loricate and that some were portraits and others idealized. At the centers of the hemicycles were a group of Aeneas carrying Anchises on his shoulder and leading Ascanius by the hand in flight from Troy and Romulus carrying a trophy of the *spolia opima* of Acron, king of the Caeninenses. The niches in the upper zone in the hemicycles are shorter than those in the lower zone. It is not known what may have been placed here; it is often conjectured that there were trophies, but there is no evidence. Later other statues were added to the collection (Tacitus, *Ann.* 4.15 and 13.8).

The Temple of Mars Ultor is octastyle, peripteral sine postico, raised on a high platform and backed against the precinct wall. An extra pair of columns on either side in line with the cella wall closes down the pronaos. The order is Corinthian, all of white Luna marble, with a ceiling richly coffered around elaborate rosettes. All the moldings and ornaments follow classical models, and the Corinthian columns are considered among the finest in Rome, rivaling those of the temples of Castor and Concordia.

The pediment of the temple is shown on one of the reliefs from an arch of Claudius in Villa Medici, commonly known as the Ara Pietatis reliefs (P. Zanker, *Forum Augustum* [Tübingen 1968], figs. 45,

46). It shows Mars in the center flanked by Venus and Fortuna, then seated figures of Romulus and Roma, and in the gable corners recumbent place divinities identified as Palatinus Mons and Tiberinus Pater.

The interior of the temple was a surprise in the Augustan manner, in strong contrast to the classical exterior and with revetments and architecture of Greek marble. The vaulted nave was comparatively short and broad, leading back to a curved apse of the full breadth of the nave filled with a statue base. The side walls were lined with a colonnade on a very high continuous plinth with a pilaster behind each column, the order Corinthian in which winged Pegasus protomes replaced the volutes, a very elegant invention. The apse was approached by a flight of five steps running in effect its full width, and the cult figures seem to have been a triad of Mars Ultor in full armor, Venus with Cupid to his right, and Divus Iulius to his left.

The wall of the forum along the street behind has been justly admired. It is of large blocks of Gabine stone (sperone) and peperino, elegantly rusticated on the exposed face, with massive frames around all openings. The courses are alternately all stretchers and all headers, and the wall is broken into three equal bands and finished at the top by projecting stringcourses of travertine blocks slightly larger than the others. The belief in the resistance of these stones to fire may be responsible in part for their choice, but it is also a very handsome wall. On the interior of the circuit wall travertine is used more freely, wherever there would be stress, to cap niches with flat arches, and to frame doorways.

In A.D. 19 Tiberius added two arches, one to either side of the temple at the foot of the stairs in from the back to celebrate the victories of Germanicus and Drusus in Germany (Tacitus, Ann. 2.64; CIL 6.911). Tiberius may also have been responsible for the redecoration of the square hall at the end of the northwest colonnade. The Corinthian columns at its entrance are of pavonazzetto, and the hall was completely revetted with panels of colored marble (giallo antico and africano) and bands of pavonazzetto, into which were let metal reliefs or pictures. The focus of the room is on a colossal statue at the far end, perhaps Augustus himself, about 12 m high. The low base with a footprint of the statue survives. Pliny (HN 36.102) considered the forum, the Basilica Paulli (Aemilia), and Templum Pacis the three most beautiful buildings in Rome and relates (HN 16.192) that the timber for the forum's construction was cut in the Rhaetian Alps during the dog days to assure its excellence. In the sixteenth century, wooden dowels used in its construction were found so well preserved that they could be used again

(Flaminio Vacca, Memorie di varie antichità trovate in diversi luoghi della città di Roma [in F. Nardini, Roma antica [Rome 1704], 89; MemLinc 3.13 [1884]: 402 [L. Borsari]). It was restored by Hadrian (S.H.A. Hadr. 19) and is listed in the regionary catalogues in Regio VIII.

Many works of art were collected and dedicated in the forum and the temple. The most notable were a quadriga that the senate dedicated to Augustus (Augustus, RG 35), two pictures by Apelles—one of War and Alexander in triumph, the other of Castor and Pollux with Victory (Pliny, HN 35.27 and 93–94)—and an ivory Apollo (Pliny, HN 7.183). Cf. also Pliny, HN 34.48 and 141; Servius ad Aen. 1.294; Pausanias 8.46.4–5; Suetonius, Calig. 24.3; Tacitus, Ann. 13.8.

Dio (55.10.2–5) gives a list of activities appointed to take place in the forum: boys were to assume the toga virilis in it. Governors being sent to their provinces should make it their starting point. The senate should deliberate on war and the award of triumphs there, and triumphators dedicate their crowns and scepters to Mars. Military standards recovered from an enemy should be housed in the temple. The Seviri Equitum should celebrate an annual festival beside the steps. Censors at the close of their office should drive a nail there to signify this (cf. also Suetonius, Aug. 29.2, Calig. 44.2). It became the scene of feasts of the Salii (Suetonius, Claud. 33.1; CIL 6.2158 = ILS 4944), and the Arval Brethren sacrificed here (CIL 6.2042.29 = 32354, 2051.88 = 32359; ILS 230.29–30, 241.91). Claudius and Trajan sat in judgment here (Suetonius, Claud. 33.1; Cass. Dio 68.10.2). But clearly its most important function was always as Rome's foreign office.

Nash 1.401–10; P. Zanker, Forum Augustum (Tübingen 1968); DialArch, n.s., 3 (1981): 69–84 (S. Rinaldi Tufi); RömMitt 90 (1983): 421–48 (V. Kockel); Anderson 65–100; JdI 99 (1984): 161–85 (B. Wesenberg); RömMitt 92 (1985): 201–19 (J. Ganzert); BullCom 90 (1985): 341–61 (I. Gismondi's architectural drawings, made for the excavations); Roma, archeologia nel centro (1985), 1.241–44 (V. Kockel); Athenaeum 64 (1987): 505–8 (G. Camodeca); CEFR 98 (1987): 251–78 (M. Bonnefond), 763–70 (H. Bauer).

Forum Boarium (or **Bovarium**) (Fig. 37): the area along the Tiber from the base of the Aventine to the base of the Capitoline, more precisely from the Velabrum (q.v.) and Porta Trigemina (q.v.) to Vicus Iugarius (q.v.). It was probably once bounded on the east by the line of the Servian Walls, but after the dismantling of these ran from the crest of the ridge separating it from the Forum Romanum to the Tiber. There is no evidence that it was ever the cattle market of Rome, as is often asserted. That would have required open space of easy access and abundant fresh water, and the Campus Martius would always have been better suited for it. Its origin as the cattle market was maintained by Varro (*Ling.* 5.146) and Festus (Paulus *ex Fest.* 27L); Propertius derived its name rather facetiously from the story of Cacus and the cattle of Geryon (4.9.19–20); other Romans derived it, probably correctly, from the Aeginetan bronze statue of an ox believed to mark the beginning of the pomerium (q.v.) of Romulus there (Ovid, *Fast.* 6.477–78; cf. Pliny, *HN* 34.10; Tacitus, *Ann.* 12.24). No one tells us when the bronze ox was installed, but presumably it was not before the conquest of Macedonia.

As the end of the Vicus Iugarius and the point from which in early times the ferry departed to take those seeking salt across the Tiber (Holland 141–78), the Forum Boarium must always have been an important hub of traffic. Three gates in the Servian Walls were located here, the Porta Carmentalis, Porta Flumentana, and Porta Trigemina. It was the bridgehead of the Pons Sublicius and Pons Aemilius, the two earliest of Rome's bridges, and the site of certain important early cults, notably the Ara Maxima Herculis (see Herculis Invicti Ara Maxima). The Emporium (q.v.) was located just below it on the river, and it perhaps came to be the location of the Statio Annonae (q.v.), presumably because of granaries nearby.

It was crisscrossed by thoroughfares. The Vicus Iugarius at the northern end divided just inside the Porta Carmentalis, the northern branch leading through the Porta Scelerata and around the foot of the Capitoline to the Campus Martius, the southern branch running through the Porta Triumphalis (?) originally down to the mouth of the Cloaca brook. The Vicus Tuscus, joined by the Nova Via and Scalae Caci, led through the Porta Flumentana, probably following the southern bank of the Cloaca. And an unnamed road led from the Porta Trigemina to the Pons Sublicius, probably following the brook of the Circus Maximus (perhaps called Murcia). Presumably the open pomerial zone outside the Servian Walls became in the course of time a road connecting and crossing these, as may have also a wall street inside that line.

The division of the forum among the regiones of Augustan Rome is not entirely clear. The Theatrum Marcelli was in Regio IX, the Elephas Herbarius was in Regio VIII, and the Velabrum, Porta Trigemina, Temple of Hercules Olivarius, and Portunium (?) were in Regio XI. The road leading from the Porta Flumentana to the Pons Aemilius may have divided Regio VIII from Regio XI, and the continuation of Vicus Iugarius alongside the southernmost of the

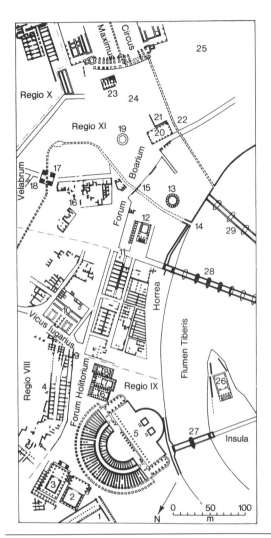

Figure 37
Forum Boarium and
Forum Holitorium, Plan
of the Ancient Remains,
as Known

temples of S. Nicola in Carcere may have divided Regio VIII from Regio IX, but there is great uncertainty here.

In the course of time the area became heavily built up with horrea and insulae, although the low elevation made the whole zone very prone to flooding. It was also frequently devastated by fire, most disastrously in 213 B.C. (Livy 24.47.15–16). Cippi probably of Tiberius (*CIL* 6.31574 = *ILS* 5941) and Claudius (*CIL* 6.919 = *ILS* 211) show that encroachment by private citizens on public land in the area was a continuing abuse and indicate by their location a boundary in line with the west front of the "Statio Annonae" (q.v.).

Around the Ara Maxima Herculis clustered temples and dedications to Hercules. Just inside the Porta Carmentalis, Servius Tullius was believed to have built the twin temples of Fortuna and Mater Matuta, while the altars of Carmenta herself were nearby. The ancient Temple of Portunus (see Portunium), probably the rectangular temple still standing that is commonly called Fortuna Virilis, became the center of the flower business in Rome. And certain mysterious monuments such as the Doliola (q.v.) and possibly the Busta Gallica (q.v.) were here. Where in the Forum Boarium the Greek and Gaulish couples were buried alive in 216 B.C. following consultation of the Sibylline Books (Livy 22.57.6; Pliny, *HN* 28.12; Plutarch, *Marcel.* 3.4; Orosius 4.13.3) we are not told, but it was a *locus saxo consaeptus* earlier used for the same purpose. One presumes it was like the Campus Sceleratus (q.v.) but outside the pomerium. The subterranean chambers discovered in 1901 near the Ianus Quadrifrons (1)(q.v.) of the Velabrum (*NSc* 1901, 354–55 [G. Gatti], 481–83 [G. Tomassetti]; *BullCom* 29 [1901]: 141–45 [G. Gatti]) sometimes suggested to have been the place are too numerous to have served and were most likely simply horrea. That the Forum Boarium was the setting of the first gladiatorial games offered in Rome, funeral games held in 264 B.C. for D. Iunius Scaeva (Val. Max. 2.4.7; Livy, *Epit.* 16), may have been of little significance, because the Forum Boarium was on the way from the Forum Romanum to the Campus Martius and Transtiberim.

There must always have been an open square of some sort here, the forum proper, probably originally of considerable size, but by the time of the late republic confined to the area between the Portunium (?) and the Navale Inferius, extending eastward perhaps no farther than the cippi of Tiberius and Claudius in line with the west façade of the "Statio Annonae."

Nash 1.411–17; *BullCom* 89 (1984): 249–96 (G. Cressedi); *QArchEtr* 11 (1985): 157–97 (C. Buzzetti, G. Pisani Sartorio, and A. M. Colini); Coarelli 1988.

Forum Caesaris: see **Forum Iulium.**

Forum Coquinum: possibly a facetious name given to that part of the Forum Romanum where cooks sat when waiting to be hired (Plautus, *Pseud.* 790–91), but, because in Plautus's catalogue of the kinds of men one could find in the forum (*Curc.* 467–85) cooks do not figure, this may be simply a translation of something in the Greek original of Plautus's play. It would have been included to permit the wordplay that follows: *furinum est forum.*

Forum Cupidinis: a punning name or mistake for Forum Cuppedinis (Varro, *Ling.* 5.146).

Forum Cuppedinis: an alternate name for the Macellum (q.v.) derived, according to Varro (*ap. Donatum in Ter. Eun.* 256), from the name of N. Equitius

Cuppes, a notorious brigand and companion of another, M'. Macellus. After their exile, the sale of their property, and the destruction of their house, the site of the house, where food came to be sold, was called Macellum from one and Forum Cuppedinis from the other. But Varro elsewhere (*Ling.* 5.146) puts the Forum Cuppedinis ad Corneta, the Corneta being between the Sacra Via and Macellum *editum* (Varro, *Ling.* 5.152), so perhaps we should think of it as a particular part of the Macellum. Varro's derivation of the name is, of course, nonsense, but probably there was never a separate Forum Cuppedinis.

Forum Esquilinum: apparently mentioned only by Appian (*BellCiv* 1.58), who calls it an agora, otherwise known only from sepulchral inscriptions (*CIL* 6.2223, 9179, 9180; *ILS* 6071a, 7503). Appian makes it the scene of a battle between the forces of Marius and Sulla in 88 B.C., the first battle ever fought within the city in full military fashion, so the forum must have been rather large.

On entering Rome by the Porta Esquilina, Sulla took possession of this and the Porta Collina and sent a detachment to "the wooden bridge," by which the Pons Sublicius would ordinarily be meant, but the point of this maneuver is obscure. In the course of the battle Sulla sent a force around by the Clivus Suburanus to attack the Marians from the rear. From these indicia we can place the Forum Esquilinum just inside the Porta Esquilina, either south of it, toward the Auditorium Maecenatis (as the Lugli and Gismondi map locates it, following HJ and PA), or north of it on the Cispian between S. Maria Maggiore and the wall. The location of the Macellum Liviae (q.v.) just outside the line of the walls here and the recent discovery of an important market building under S. Maria Maggiore suggest the latter location is correct. In view of the amount of traffic that must have flowed through the Porta Esquilina, it is not surprising that a large market should have been located just inside it.

This may be the forum recorded in inscriptions (*CIL* 6.1662, 31888; *ILS* 5357) as having been restored by Fl. Eurycles Epitychianus, praefectus urbi in A.D. 450.

Forum Gallorum: mentioned only in the appendix of the regionary catalogues, and otherwise completely unknown.

Forum Holitorium (Figs. 37, 38): said by Varro (*Ling.* 5.146) to have been the original macellum of Rome and to have got its name from the abundance of edible vegetables sold there, but the name is not formed like those of other fora and seems to mean "of vegetable sellers" rather than "of vegetables." It

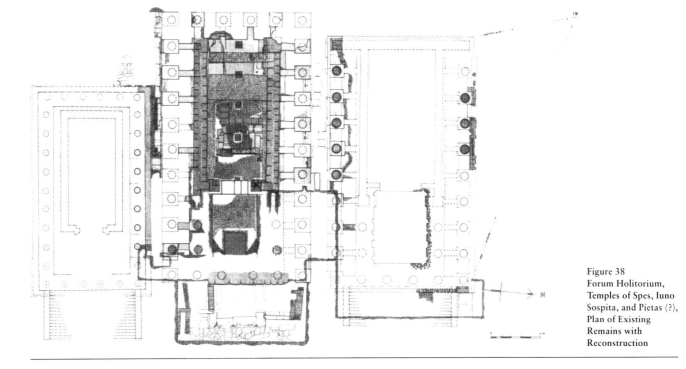

Figure 38
Forum Holitorium,
Temples of Spes, Iuno
Sospita, and Pietas (?),
Plan of Existing
Remains with
Reconstruction

is also rather oddly located for a fruit and vegetable market, being outside the Porta Carmentalis in the Campus Martius.

In the period for which we have evidence it was very small, cramped between the Forum Boarium on one side and buildings described as in Circo Flaminio on the other. The Theatrum Marcelli (q.v.) is described as in Circo Flaminio (*CIL* 6.32323.157–58 = *ILS* 5050.157–58), but never with respect to the Forum Holitorium. The Temple of Bellona (see Bellona, Aedes) is also put in Circo Flaminio (Fast. Ven. *ad III Non. Iun.*), never in Foro Holitorio. The Temple of Apollo Medicus is once located *inter Forum Holitorium et Circum Flaminium* (Asconius, *Orat. in tog. cand.* [Stangl 70]), but Livy (3.63.7) puts it *in Pratis Flaminiis*. On the east the forum was bounded by the base of the Capitoline Hill.

We know of four temples located there, the oldest being a temple of Janus built by C. Duilius after his naval victory over the Carthaginians at Mylae in 260 B.C. (Tacitus, *Ann.* 2.49). This was soon followed by a temple of Spes built by A. Atilius Calatinus (cos. 258, 254, dict. 249) during the same war (Cicero, *Leg.* 2.28; Tacitus, *Ann.* 2.49). A half-century or so later these were joined by a temple of Iuno Sospita (see Iuno Sospita, Aedes), vowed in 197 and dedicated in 194, and a temple of Pietas (see Pietas, Aedes), vowed in 191 and dedicated ten years later. Julius Caesar removed the last in 44 B.C. to make space for the theater that became the Theatrum Mar-

celli (Pliny, *HN* 7.121), but it may have been rebuilt nearby, because it continued to appear in the fasti. Three of these four temples are believed to be those incorporated in the fabric of the church of S. Nicola in Carcere. Across a trapezoidal square from the church, the ancient square paved with travertine flags, are remains of a vast portico built of rusticated travertine blocks and brickwork, a complex of shops and/or offices opening behind an arcaded walk in front and to either side of a central corridor behind. This is of imperial date and adjoins at its southern end a short portico of peperino in two storeys, with arcading framed in an engaged Tuscan order below and Corinthian colonnading above. This appears to be work of the first century B.C., perhaps about the middle. It was only one bay deep and ran for only a short distance, perhaps four bays in all. Behind the Temple of Spes the censor of 179 B.C., M. Fulvius Nobilior, built a portico that probably framed the forum on the other side (Livy 40.51.6). If this was still standing in the first century B.C., it must have been demolished by Julius Caesar to make way for his theater, but probably it had long since disappeared.

Nash 1.418–23.

Forum Iulium (often called **Forum Caesaris**)

(Fig. 36): the first of the series of imperial fora, conceived at least as early as 54 B.C., when Caesar commissioned Oppius and Cicero to buy the land he would need (Cicero, *Att.* 4.16.8). This was very costly, as it had to be purchased from individual owners in a zone of intense commercial exploitation. In the end the final cost of the land alone is said to have been a hundred million sesterces, an enormous sum (Pliny, *HN* 36.103; Suetonius, *Iul.* 26.2). Caesar's object was to expand the Forum Romanum as far as the Atrium Libertatis (q.v.) by building an annex for the transaction of public business, more specifically the activities of the Roman senate (Appian, *BellCiv* 2.102; Anderson 39–63).

The scheme was basically a temple in a colonnaded square and the descendant of such Hellenistic complexes as the Temple of Artemis Leucophryene at Magnesia on the Maeander, but the temple was set at the far end of the court and raised on a high podium, and the principal entrance may have been arranged off axis. Caesar dedicated the forum and the Temple of Venus Genetrix on the last day of his triumph, 26 September 46 B.C. (Cass. Dio 43.22.2; Degrassi 514), although at that time the forum was not complete and had to be finished later by Octavian (Augustus, *RG* 20; Cass. Dio 45.6.4). The Curia Iulia (q.v.), an essential part of the design, had perhaps not even been begun, as Augustus (*RG* 19) takes full credit for it.

The temple was rebuilt by Domitian and rededicated by Trajan, 12 May A.D. 113 (Degrassi 457). Trajan probably added the Basilica Argentaria, which presumably served to link the Forum Iulium and Forum Traiani, but his work on the Temple of Venus Genetrix may have been very little, no more than final touches to Domitian's rebuilding. The failure to rededicate the temple earlier is probably due to developments in the scheme of the Forum Traiani. Domitian's rebuilding seems to have been part of an architectural scheme preliminary to the Forum Traiani that he was then unable to complete and may have included something like the Basilica Argentaria (Aur. Vict., *Caes.* 13.5). It has been conjectured to have been in consequence of the fire of Titus that destroyed the Capitolium, but without reason. The forum burned in A.D. 283, and was restored by Diocletian (Chron. 148). The granite columns mounted on individual plinths of the lateral colonnades are not uniform and seem to belong to a still later restoration.

The forum lies along the base of the northeast flank of the Capitoline Hill, filling the space between the Clivus Argentarius and the fora of Augustus and Trajan, space earlier covered by the adjacencies of the Macellum of Rome. It was approached from the Forum Romanum along the flanks of the Curia Iulia, which fronted on the Sacra Via. It was accessible also from the Argiletum through a colonnade continuing

the lateral colonnades at right angles to these and with a colonnaded front added by Augustus in which an extra column was inserted in the middle of each intercolumniation to screen the forum from the street. The square in front of the temple was proportionately long and narrow, more than twice as long as wide, with a deep double colonnade down either side and across the forward end and the temple at the far end. The base of the Capitoline Hill had to be cut away to level the area, and between the colonnade and the Clivus Argentarius a series of tabernae, some very deep, others shallow, was inserted. These had uniform doors, almost square, responding to the intercolumniations, and were originally flat-ceilinged and multistoreyed, but eventually roofed with heavy barrel vaults in the ground storey, permitting the development of an upper storey accessible from the Clivus Argentarius. The places of two of the tabernae are taken by broad stairs down from the clivus. These tabernae served as the archives and committee rooms of the senate; one of them became the Secretarium Senatus (q.v.). Out in the square in front of the temple stood the Equus Caesaris (q.v.), a portrait statue of Caesar's favorite horse with forefeet approaching human feet in shape (Pliny, *HN* 8.155; Suetonius, *Iul.* 61), probably later replaced by an equestrian statue attributed to Lysippus (Statius, *Silv.* 1.1.84–85).

The Temple of Venus Genetrix stood at the far end of the forum, its base originally partly embedded in the slope. Caesar had vowed a temple to Venus Victrix on the eve of the Battle of Pharsalus (Appian, *BellCiv* 2.68) but chose instead to build one to Venus Genetrix, the ancestress of the Gens Iulia. The temple stood on a very high podium approached by a pair of narrow lateral stairs along the pronaos that led to a slightly lower platform in front of the columns of the façade that held the altar and may have served as a rostra. In front of the temple in the time of Hadrian, and perhaps earlier, were three fountain basins set at either end of the façade and on the main axis with a low wall run between them, possibly intended to carry statuary. The base of a statue of Sabina came to be set against this. The temple was octastyle, pycnostyle, the intercolumniations being unusually narrow, only one and one-half diameters (Vitruvius 3.3.2), and in effect peripteral sine postico, the colonnades running down the flanks to closed alae, but the cella projecting considerably beyond the back wall of the alae. The temple was of marble (Ovid, *Ars Am.* 1.81), the cella a nave flanked with colonnades of giallo antico on a continuous plinth ending in a curved apse. Presumably the ceiling was vaulted. An interesting frieze of erotes engaged in various activities was part of the architectural decoration of the interior. The cult statue was created by Arcesilas for the temple (Pliny, *HN* 35.156).

Caesar himself dedicated numerous works of art in the temple, including pictures by Timomachus of Ajax and Medea (Pliny, *HN* 7.126, 35.26 and 136), a golden statue of Cleopatra (Cass. Dio 51.22.3; Appian, *BellCiv* 2.102), six collections of engraved gems, or *dactyliothecae* (Pliny, *HN* 37.11), and a corselet made of British pearls (Pliny, *HN* 9.116). Somewhere in the forum Caesar permitted the dedication of a loricate statue of himself (Pliny, *HN* 34.18). The bronze statue showing Divus Iulius with a star above his head that Dio (45.7.1) says Augustus set up in the temple of Venus may actually have been in the Temple of Divus Iulius (cf. Pliny, *HN* 2.93–94). Later, in A.D. 30, a colossus of Tiberius was erected near the temple by fourteen cities of Asia Minor that had received earthquake relief in A.D. 17, 23, and 29 (Tacitus, *Ann.* 2.47 and 4.13; Phlegon, *De arab.* 18; *CIL* 10.1624 = *ILS* 156).

The Basilica Argentaria is so identified on the basis of the appearance of this in the regionary catalogues, listed in Regio VIII, and its proximity to the Clivus Argentarius. It is essentially a portico, rather than a basilica, but has certain basilical qualities. For its construction the slope of the Capitoline Hill was excavated further, and a broad passage was cleared around the temple. Then in continuation of the southwest colonnade of the forum square, but at a level nine steps higher, great pillars of bossed and rusticated blocks of travertine and peperino in the outer row, faced with brick on the inner, carried a system of concrete vaults and projecting balconies. These followed first the lines of the Temple of Venus Genetrix and then the curve of the southwest hemicycle of the Forum Traiani. It is not clear how the building would have terminated. The use of the few tabernae that open behind it is unknown.

The use of Gabine stone combined with travertine at points of stress in the façade of the tabernae of the lower square indicates that this is part of the Caesarean complex and that subsequent modifications did not change the orientation of the forum. A diagonal wall faced with reticulate embedded in the northwest corner of the podium of the temple has been taken to be a fragment of the original rear face of this podium. The surviving fragments of the superstructure seem remarkably harmonious in style and clearly Domitianic; even the characteristic rings between dentils appear. The Basilica Argentaria is Trajanic, and the granite colonnade belongs to late antiquity, fourth or fifth century.

Part of the forum, including the whole of the Temple of Venus Genetrix and about one-half of the southwest colonnade, together with a portion of the Basilica Argentaria, was excavated in 1930 to 1933 under the direction of Corrado Ricci.

Lugli 1946, 245–58; *AnalRom* 2 (1962): 45–61 (T. Hastrup); *RendPontAcc* 37 (1964–65): 105–26 (N. Lamboglia); *QITA* 5 (1968): 91–103 (G. Fiorani); Nash 1.424–32; *Cuadernos de trabajos de la Escuela Española de historia y arqueologia en Roma* 14 (1980): 123–34 (N. Lamboglia); Anderson 39–63; *RömMitt* 93 (1986): 405–23 (R. B. Ulrich); C. Morselli and E. Tortorici, *Curia, Forum Iulium, Forum Transitorium* (Rome 1989), especially 1–263.

Forum Nervae (also called **Forum Transitorium**) (Fig. 39): the fourth of the imperial fora, built by Domitian but dedicated by Nerva at the beginning of A.D. 97 (Martial 10.28; Suetonius, *Dom.* 5; Statius, *Silv.* 4.3.9–10; Eutropius 7.23.5; Aur. Vict., *Caes.* 12.2; *CIL* 6.953, 31213). It occupied the space between the Forum Augustum and Templum Pacis, what had been the Argiletum and a strip of land to either side of this from the Basilica Paulli (Aemilia) to the center of the southeast hemicycle of the Forum Augustum. With the annex of the Porticus Absidata (q.v.), it made the northeast line of the Forum Augustum and Templum Pacis continuous. To build it Domitian must have taken space from the Templum Pacis and moved the northwest wall of this to stand just behind the colonnade on this side, making in effect an addorsed colonnade. In the space thus obtained he lined the lateral walls with addorsed colonnades, the entablature and attic broken out over each column to give greater plasticity, pushed the Temple of Minerva to the northeast end of the central axis so that its rear left corner abuts on the hemicycle of the Forum Augustum, and concealed the irregularities of the plot at this end by screen walls just behind the temple's pronaos. He took attention from the entrance's being off axis at the west corner of the complex by the introduction of a splendid Ianus Quadrifrons on axis in front of it. The scheme is a triumph of ingenuity and imagination.

In devising the plan, the architects had to cope with the heavy traffic of the Argiletum/Subura artery and the course of the Cloaca brook. The brook had probably been buried under the road for a long time, perhaps since the mid-second century B.C., but it was now carried in a culvert of massive construction under the podium of the Temple of Minerva and continuing the length of the forum to the Argiletum entrance, presumably passing directly under the Ianus. Wheeled traffic has left deep ruts along the southeast flank of the temple, where it was funneled through a throat from the Porticus Absidata, but probably these are chiefly, or entirely, the effects of

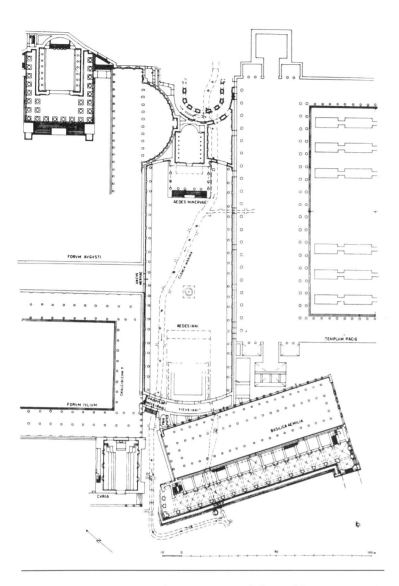

the figured frieze shows a continuous sequence of the arts and crafts over which Minerva presided: Minerva in the company of the Muses and women spinning and weaving, together with the myth of Arachne, in what is left. In the center of the remaining section of the high attic is a large figure of Minerva, 2.65 m tall, in high relief. While it would have been difficult, if not impossible, to read the frieze from floor level, the attic relief carries easily. The temple was prostyle, hexastyle, and on a high podium with a frontal stair of approach. The order was Corinthian, and the pronaos was three bays deep in the Roman manner. Much of the temple was still standing until Pope Paul V had it pulled down in 1606 to provide material for the Acqua Paola fountain on the Janiculum. Now only the core of the podium remains, but the temple appears on a fragment of the Marble Plan (*FUR* pl. 20 fr. 16; Rodriguez pl. 12), and there is enough to show that the interior was a nave flanked by colonnades with an apse at the far end. The gently curving walls that attached the front of the cella to the lateral walls of the forum are, according to P. H. von Blanckenhagen, a modification of an originally rectilinear project introduced with the intention of making the scheme more graceful. At the same time the façade of the temple was moved back and the cella made shallower. The curved wall to the east of the temple was broken by a large arch known in the Middle Ages as Arcus Aureus or Aurae, and the entrance arch at the opposite end, which was still standing in the time of Du Pérac, was called Arcus Nerviae.

No positively identified remains of the ianus at the opposite end have come to light. The statue of the divinity was four-faced and said to look out on four fora (Martial 10.28.5–6). The image is also said to have been brought to Rome from Falerii in 241 B.C. (Macrobius, *Sat.* 1.9.13; Servius *ad Aen.* 7.607), but there is no indication of where it had been kept prior to the building of Domitian's forum. Servius adds that its establishment in the Forum Nervae was as a replacement for the Ianus Geminus of Numa. It is presumed that because Martial says the god could now look out on four fora, the shrine must have been a four-sided arch, like that of the Velabrum, but Martial speaks of *limina*, and Servius (*ad Aen.* 7.607) of *quattuor portarum unum templum*, so a four-sided version of the ianus enclosure shown on coins of Nero (Nash 1.503 fig. 619) seems more likely and more appropriate. It would then have been a comparatively light structure and less likely to leave substantial traces, but this part of the forum is still largely buried underground.

The long sides of the forum were apparently broken by a number of doors giving to the Templum Pacis on one side and the Forum Augustum and

wear in late antiquity and the Middle Ages. During the high imperial period wheeled traffic must have been excluded from the forum, as the design of the Porticus Absidata makes clear. The pavement that Domitian installed was of travertine, and over this at a later date was laid a pavement of irregular flags of marble.

The front wall of the forum, of which only the foundation remains, was gently curved, responding to a similar curve at the opposite end. The long straight side walls of squared blocks of peperino were completely revetted with marble, of which little but the clamp holes remains. A single pair of the addorsed columns with their entablature and attic survives, about 11 m of the northeast end of the southeast side. This was known in the Middle Ages as Arca Noe, and later until the excavations of 1932–1933 as Le Colonnacce. The order is Corinthian, and

Forum Iulium on the other. This and the fact that for people coming from the Forum Romanum and Subura the Forum Nervae would have acted as a vestibule to the other imperial fora may be responsible for the name Forum Transitorium, which is given it regularly after the middle of the third century (e.g., S.H.A. *Alex. Sev.* 28.6, 36.2; Servius *ad Aen.* 7.607; Eutropius 7.23.5). In the regionary catalogues it is listed in Regio IV as Forum Transitorium and in Regio VIII and the appendix as Forum Nervae, evidently because the line dividing the two regiones ran along the Argiletum. But Martial (10.28.3) describes the old Ianus Geminus as *pervius* and entreats the god to keep his doors in the new forum forever closed, and Aurelius Victor (*Caes.* 12.2) calls it Forum Pervium, so the name may have begun as a grim witticism with allusion to more than one feature. During the time it was under construction, Martial calls it Forum Palladium (1.2.8) and Forum Caesaris (1.117.10).

Although the small space would have allowed for little further embellishment, Alexander Severus is said to have erected colossal statues of the deified emperors here, some standing nudes, others equestrian, together with bronze columns recording their accomplishments in the pattern of the Forum Augustum (S.H.A. *Alex. Sev.* 28.6).

Excavations undertaken in 1932–1933 under the direction of Corrado Ricci have laid bare the northeast end of the forum with the foundations of the Temple of Minerva and Porticus Absidata. Unfortunately, not enough of the forum was exposed to show the quality of its architecture or to clarify the problems connected with it. It is not at all clear, for example, how the interval between the forum and the Porticus Absidata was treated.

P. H. von Blanckenhagen, *Flavische Architektur und ihre Dekoration untersucht am Nervaforum* (Berlin 1940); Lugli 1946, 273–76; Nash 1.433–38; *RendPontAcc* 49 (1976–77): 117–50 (H. Bauer); *RömMitt* 84 (1977): 301–29 (H. Bauer); *RömMitt* 90 (1983): 111–84 (H. Bauer); Anderson 119–39; *BullCom* 91.2 (1986): 380–88 (C. Morselli and E. Tortorici); C. Morselli and E. Tortorici, *Curia, Forum Iulium, Forum Transitorium* (Rome 1989), especially 1–263.

Forum Palladium: see **Forum Nervae.**

Forum Pervium: see **Forum Nervae.**

Forum Petronii Maximi: Petronius Maximus, consul and praefectus urbi under Valentinian III (between A.D. 420 and 443) and emperor briefly in 455, in a dedication to Valentinian (*CIL* 6.1197, 1198 = *ILS* 807/8) describes himself as *fori conditor.*

It has therefore been presumed that this forum was somewhere in the neighborhood of the find spot, a little northeast of the church of S. Clemente. There was always an important thoroughfare running up the valley between Oppius and Caelian, and somewhere along this a small market square that had only a brief life might well have been created.

TAPS 80.2 (1990): 45–50 (R. E. A. Palmer).

Forum Piscarium (or **Piscatorium**): an alternate, perhaps older, name for the Macellum or part of the Macellum, the great food market northeast of the Forum Romanum (Plautus, *Curc.* 474, who lists it after the unnamed basilica and before *in foro infumo,* which would put its entrance in the vicinity of the Temple of Antoninus and Faustina and agree with other evidence). It burned in 210 B.C. in a fire that destroyed buildings in a wide swath from the Atrium Regium (Regia) to the Lautumiae, but apparently spared the Comitium and Curia Hostilia (Livy 26.27.2–4). Contracts were let for rebuilding these the following year, at which time it is called Macellum (Livy 27.11.16). In 179 B.C. M. Fulvius Nobilior let contracts for rebuilding the Forum Piscatorium and sold the shops around it to private individuals (Livy 40.51.5). The persistence of the name Forum Piscatorium is probably due to the prominence of a central tholus that was, indeed, the fish market (cf. Varro *ap. Non.* 719L), and the complex as a whole consisted of a large open square around this, surrounded in turn by a deep portico with shops behind it.

But elsewhere Varro says that the Forum Piscarium is by the Tiber and, if Jordan's correction of the text is accepted, *ad Portunium* (Varro, *Ling.* 5.146), and cites Plautus (presumably the passage in the *Curculio*) in support of this. There may have been a second market or place where fishmongers gathered by the Tiber below the Portunium, but as a market it would not be very conveniently located, and no one else mentions it.

Forum Pistorum: mentioned only in the regionary catalogues, listed in Regio XIII. Presumably it was a square around which millers congregated, and it has been therefore supposed to be near the great complexes of horrea at the southern end of the Aventine. But most milling was done in the individual bakeries (cf. the reliefs of the Sepulcrum Eurysacis) or where there was water power available (see Molinae), so this seems apt to have been a square connected with a *collegium pistorum* and may then have been almost anywhere. Milling and bread-making seem to have been organized and state-supervised beginning in the second century after Christ; see, for example, *CEFR* 98 (1987): 445–56 (F. Coarelli).

Forum (**Romanum** or **Magnum**) (Figs. 40, 41):
originally the marketplace of Rome, which in time
evolved into the business center of the republican
city, and throughout antiquity was regarded as the
city's heart. Its designation is usually simply *forum*,
a word of uncertain origin. After the construction of
the Forum Iulium, it was sometimes called Forum
Magnum (Cass. Dio 43.22.2), and in the *Notitia*
Regio VIII is named Forum Romanum vel (et) Magnum. The adjective *Romanum* does not appear before Vergil (*Aen.* 8.361) and is never common.

In its earliest phase the market was probably a
simple affair of barrows set up along the track that
became the Vicus Iugarius, where the farmers and
herdsmen of the Palatine city sold provisions to those
who came down from the uplands and mountains
seeking salt from the works at the mouth of the Tiber. This impromptu market, like the track that governed its existence, must have kept to the high
ground along the shoulder of the Capitoline, because
the basin over which it was to spread later, framed
by the Capitoline, Velia, and Palatine, was threaded
by watercourses and marshy during much of the
year. The Cloaca brook, draining the valleys among
the Quirinal, Viminal, Cispian, and Oppius, crossed
the forum basin from northeast to southwest and
was augmented by an important tributary from the
Velia now buried under the Sacra Via and lesser tributaries from the lower Palatine (marked by the
"southern branch" of the Sacra Via) and the Tullianum spring under the Carcer. Only in the driest
seasons can the floor of the forum have been usable.
Burials discovered in its eastern reaches, not only the
Sepulcretum (q.v.) beyond the Temple of Antoninus
and Faustina, but under the Regia and "Equus Domitiani," show that these parts were not exploited in
any other way before the seventh century. The Romans remembered the original condition of the
forum (Ovid, *Fast.* 6.401–6) and had floods to remind them should they forget. The forum was always among the first places inundated (Horace,
Carm. 1.2.13–16).

Human activity of some sort in the area has been
found as low as 3.60 meters above sea level, and
skeletons have been found at 6 and 7 meters above
sea level (*NSc* 1906, 46–54 [A. Mosso]). Real use of
the basin seems to have begun with the channeling
and control of the Cloaca brook. For a long time it
was believed that the Tarquins culverted the Cloaca,
but it is clear from Plautus (*Curc.* 476) that in his
day it ran in an open canal across the middle of the
forum, while the existing vaulting of the lowest
stretch and the mouth on the Tiber, with its familiar
aperture framed in a triple arch of voussoirs of Gabine stone, are the work of Agrippa in his monumental rebuilding and modernization of the water and

sewer systems beginning in 33 B.C. The work of the
Tarquins (Livy 1.38.6, 1.56.2) must have consisted
in dredging out the bed of the stream and its tributaries and building walls to contain them, possibly
combined with flagging of the floors. As a network
of canals only slightly straightened from their natural courses, they were to exert influence on the
growth of the forum for several centuries. Tarquinius
Priscus is credited with having divided the land
around the forum into building plots for individual
private owners and having constructed porticoes and
tabernae, covered walks with shops behind them
(Livy 1.35.10; Dion. Hal. 3.67.4).

With the forum dry and safe, monumental building crept down from the Vicus Iugarius. The temples
of Saturn and Castor were dedicated in the early
years of the republic, and the lines of shops—the Tabernae Veteres (see Tabernae Cirum Forum) stretching between the two temples and facing away from
the sun, and the Tabernae Argentariae and Septem
on the opposite side, the two northern lines, probably divided by the Cloaca—must have taken definite form at the same time. These, so far as we know,
were without porticoes in front of them and were
first occupied by provisioners, especially butchers,
tabernae lanienae (Varro *ap. Non.* 853L), but by the
end of the fourth century the provisioners had been
relegated to the area north of the forum, and the
shops on the forum were occupied by bankers and
called argentariae (Livy 9.40.16). By then the forum
was given over entirely to business, politics, and ceremony.

The Comitium (q.v.) had always bordered on the
forum on the northeast without being part of it. An
inaugurated templum consecrated to public assemblies, elections, and legislation, it occupied the slope
up to the north from the forum and Cloaca, between
it and the course of the Tullianum rivulet. At first it
may have been without architectural form. Later it
was a circular amphitheater of steps, on which the
Romans stood in their assemblies, leading up to the
curia of the senate on the north side. It may have
taken this form about the time that the forum shops
were reserved for business and banking, and we may
see these as separate parts of a master plan that came
into existence in consequence of the Battle of Antium
and the final subjugation of the Latin League in 338
B.C. That that victory was commemorated by the
raising of a *suggestus* ornamented with the beaks of
the captured vessels in medio foro makes this more
likely. And with the construction of this suggestus
politics and the administration of justice spilled over
from the Comitium to the forum.

The forum had also long been the scene of ceremonies and games. Romulus's dedication of the *spolia opima* in the Temple of Iuppiter Feretrius suggests

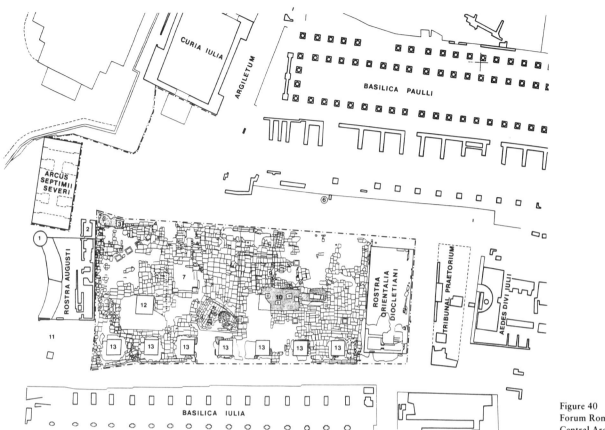

Figure 40
Forum Romanum,
Central Area, Plan

that a form of the triumphal procession had been imagined to exist even at that early date, and, with the construction of the Temple of Iuppiter Optimus Maximus on the Capitoline, the ceremonial parade of spoils and captives along the Sacra Via, through the forum, and up the Clivus Capitolinus became one of the greatest of all Roman celebrations. Similarly, funerals, especially those of prominent citizens, probably had been held there from a very early period, in part because the open square provided space for the funeral games that were traditionally part of the obsequies. Funerals at other locations are certainly known, and the first gladiatorial games were for a funeral held in the Forum Boarium (Val. Max. 2.4.7; cf. Livy, *Epit.* 16), but the forum proper was always the preferred location, and the Rostra the place for displaying the corpse and delivering the eulogy.

As the forum was remarkable for the convergence of watercourses there, so it was remarkable for the convergence of streets, roads that had originally followed the watercourses and others that had branched from these. Coming in from the northeast was the road later called the Clivus Argentarius that connected Alta Semita and Vicus Iugarius and that

probably also took traffic to and from the forum and the eastern Campus Martius. Below this along the Cloaca ran the Argiletum, which linked up with the Clivus Suburanus and Vicus Longus. Beyond the Basilica Paulli (Aemilia) was a throat leading back to the Macellum, the Corneta or an extension of this. From the east the Sacra Via brought the traffic from the Velia and Palatine to the forum; this forked at the Regia and then ran along both sides of the forum to frame it. Into the "southern branch" descends an important stair beside the Temple of Vesta, which leads up to the Nova Via and Clivus Victoriae, and further along its course are the two important connections with the Tiber bank, the Vicus Tuscus and Vicus Iugarius. Almost the only roads entering the forum that did not originally follow a watercourse of some sort seem to have been the Vicus Iugarius and the Clivus Capitolinus itself.

The orientation of buildings on the forum varied. As long as the Cloaca divided the forum there was little connection between the two halves. The Comitium and its dependencies seem to have been oriented to the cardinal points of the compass. So in general are the remains of early buildings under the Atrium Vestae and in its neighborhood. These are all technically outside the forum area and clearly do not influence planning within it. Planning within it seems to have been governed principally by the streets through it and entering around it. The forum square seems always to have been decidedly trapezoidal, and the buildings fronting on it conformed to this or to the available plot.

According to PA, the first indication of development of the forum as a public square is a few remains of paving in cappellaccio: a patch in front of the Basilica Paulli (Aemilia), one in front of the Temple of Divus Iulius, one under the Lacus Iuturnae, and one behind the republican Atrium Vestae, all at 10.60–10.90 meters above sea level. But one of the four scraps identified might be the floor of a basin of the Lacus Iuturnae, and the east side of the Cloaca is hardly likely to have been paved at a level uniform with the west before the burying of the Cloaca in a culvert and the unification of the area. In 210 B.C. the northwest side of the forum burned in a conflagration that destroyed everything from the Atrium Regium (Regia) by the Temple of Vesta to the Lautumiae; the Septem Tabernae and the Tabernae Argentariae were lost (Livy 26.27.1–4). In the following year most of the buildings destroyed were rebuilt, including the Septem Tabernae (Livy 27.11.16), but not the Tabernae Argentariae. However, the plebeian aediles M. Iunius Brutus and L. Oppius Salinator rebuilt these as the Tabernae Argentariae Novae in 193 B.C., and because when the Basilica Fulvia et Aemilia was built in 179 (Livy 40.51.5) it was located *post Argentarias Novas,* the forum stretch of the Cloaca had probably been housed in a culvert by 193, certainly by 179 at the latest. Probably the culverting of the Cloaca was undertaken in conjunction with a general repavement of the forum.

This pavement at about 11.80–11.90 meters above sea level was of Monteverde tufa in the parts that were not subject to heavy traffic, in selce for the roads framing the forum and leading into it, and possibly with some additional parts in brick. Extensive remains in distinctive Monteverde tufa around the shrine of Cloacina (see Cloacina, Sacrum) and Lacus Iuturnae (q.v.) indicate that the whole forum was refloored at this time, and monuments that lay so low that they might be obliterated had to be raised or remodeled, notably the Lacus Curtius and the Rostra of the forum. Probably to this period also belongs the series of low vaults that Boni called "Rostra Vetera" but that are in reality a little viaduct carrying the margin of the Vicus Iugarius up the foot of the Capitoline to meet the Clivus Capitolinus.

In the *Curculio* (470–81), Plautus gives us a good picture of what the forum was like in the early years of the second century, a very open but populous place. The law courts were clustered in the Comitium, investors interested in speculation and entrepreneurs before the tabernae in the vicinity of the shrine of Cloacina. A nameless basilica of modest scale stood on the eastern side of the Cloaca, in front of which was a busy market in feminine adornments. At the eastern end of the forum was a cluster of venerable shrines which Plautus does not mention, the Regia, the temples of Vesta and Castor, the spring of Iuturna, and against this backdrop *boni homines atque dites ambulant,* presumably intent on serious business. The banks of the Cloaca and Lacus Curtius were the haunts of loiterers and gossips, and the Tabernae Veteres was the gathering place of hardheaded businessmen, while behind the Temple of Castor one would find those one would do well not to trust too quickly. The impression of confusion and little in the way of monumental architecture is probably correct.

This picture was to change in the next quartercentury. The building in quick succession of three basilicas, the Basilica Porcia in 184, the Basilica Fulvia et Aemilia in 179, and the Basilica Sempronia in 170, effectively surrounded the forum with their masses, and much of the business that earlier had been transacted in the open now moved indoors. The Basilica Porcia was not immediately on the forum, but the other two, built behind the Tabernae Argentariae and Veteres, respectively, flanked the long sides of the square and, in conjunction with the Comitium and existing temples, almost completely enclosed it. Before the construction of the Basilica Fulvia et Aemilia it was necessary that a section of the Cloaca (the Braccio Morto) be buried, and we find a new course for it dug along the Argiletum and around the northwest end of the basilica. Exploration in the interior of the later Basilica Paulli has brought to light tufa foundations and column footings of two earlier basilicas, the older presumably of the Basilica Fulvia (*NSc* 1948, 111–28 [G. Carettoni]). It had the same orientation as its Augustan successor but lay farther to the northeast. The columns were 1.10 m in diameter and 4.93–4.95 m apart.

Another epoch in the history of the forum opened in 145 B.C., when the tribunus plebis C. Licinius Crassus took the people from the Comitium into the forum for legislation in the Comitia Tributa (Cicero, *Amic.* 96; Varro, *Rust.* 1.2.9). Thereafter, the forum became the main theater of Roman politics until the end of the republic.

In the time of Sulla, probably shortly after his death, the forum seems to have undergone a general repaving (ascribed to an Aurelius Cotta) at about 12.60 meters above sea level, though the only great building added in this period seems to have been the Tabularium (q.v.) on the Capitoline, a splendid series of arcades, probably in two storeys, atop a massive rusticated base, all in Gabine stone with accents of travertine. This acted as a backdrop at the northwest end of the forum, pulling together the various constructions covering the lower slopes of the hill. In preparation for Cotta's repavement, the elaborate system of subterranean passages usually called cuniculi seems to have been constructed. The main artery of these runs from the southeast end of the forum in front of the Temple of Divus Iulius to the Rostra Augusti, while branch passages at right angles to this run to either side at regular intervals. These are accessible by manholes framed with travertine, which must once have held travertine covers. The general pavement at this time lay at 12.60 meters above sea level and is of travertine flags with travertine insets to mark special features, such as the Lacus Curtius. The Niger Lapis (q.v.), a pavement of Taenarian black marble measuring about 4 m x 3 m covering a group of very ancient monuments between the Comitium and the forum, also belongs to this time (GV 60–61).

The next major work on the forum was that of Julius Caesar in connection with an elaborate scheme for rebuilding the whole of the Comitium/Curia complex and both the great basilicas on the long sides. And Caesar was the first to cover the forum with awnings to protect spectators from the sun during a gladiatorial show (Pliny, *HN* 19.23). Although Caesar was unable to do more than make a good start on his scheme for the renovation of the forum before his assassination, Augustus took up his work and carried it to a successful conclusion. The forum we see today is essentially the Augustan forum, preserved and rebuilt throughout antiquity with only a few additions. The temples of Divus Iulius, Castor, Saturn, and Concordia, the basilicas Iulia and Paulli, the Curia Iulia, and the Rostra Iulia and Augusti all took their final form during the triumvirate and principate of Augustus. The only significant additions to the forum thereafter until the time of Diocletian were the temples of Divus Vespasianus and Antoninus et Faustina, the Arch of Septimius Severus, and the portico of the Dei Consentes. The pavement of flags of white marble is dated by the inscription of the praetor peregrinus L. Naevius Surdinus (*CIL* 6.1468, 31662; Nash 1.397 fig. 485) and stands from 12.60 meters above sea level in front of the Temple of Divus Iulius to 14 meters above sea level in front of the Rostra Augusti. The most significant change in this period in the use of the forum was that it ceased to be the political heart of Rome, that honor passing in part to the Saepta Iulia in the Campus Martius, whereas the rostra of the forum served more often for ceremonial purposes.

Before the time of Diocletian changes in the central area of the forum were few. We can point only to the Equus Domitiani (q.v.), which briefly dominated everything else there, some scant traces of ephemeral installations of relatively small size and doubtful character, and a general repavement and the erection of the Equus and Arch of Septimius Severus in the time of Septimius Severus, ca. A.D. 203. But the fire of Carinus in A.D. 283 wrought widespread destruction in the forum, and Diocletian took the opportunity to alter it to conform with the new aesthetic of his time (Fig. 41). A line of five columns carrying honorary statues had probably adorned the Rostra Augusti at least since the time of Domitian. A new rostra with a corresponding line of columns seems now to have been built to balance this at the opposite end of the forum in front of the Temple of Divus Iulius, and a line of seven larger columns along the south side of the forum square in front of the Basilica Iulia joined the two. Nor was this all. To the airy frame of columns and statues one larger and higher than the rest was added, which was eventually reworked to become the Columna Phocae (q.v.); this we may presume must have honored Diocletian himself. The forum now became a ring of columns within a ring of buildings and remained such to the end of antiquity, the statues being changed and their bases reworked, possibly repeatedly, additions of various sorts being introduced from time to time that increased the clutter, but the overall aesthetic remaining the same. This is shown by a relief on the north side of the Arch of Constantine, where a rostra with a row of five columns surmounted by statues appears (Nash 1.198 fig. 223). And part of the sculptured base of a column celebrating the Decennalia of the Caesars (*CIL* 6.1203, 31261) found in 1547 at the northeast end of the Rostra Augusti, together with others, now lost, celebrating the Vicennalia (*CIL* 6.1204, 1205, 31262), give some notion of the sort of program such columns might follow. The facts that the seven columns of the south row all have bases with cores of opus quadratum encased in brick-faced concrete that includes stamps of the time of Constantine (*CIL* 15.1569, 1643) and that the steps surrounding the Columna Phocae are built of tufa blocks taken from other buildings show how extensive such revision of the program might be and at what close intervals it may have occurred (cf. Nash 1.198–201, 280–81; GV 184–87 and passim).

After the time of Diocletian additions to the forum were numerous, but usually ephemeral and inconsequential. The Basilica Paulli is believed to have been destroyed in the fires accompanying the sack of Alaric in A.D. 410. There was a violent earthquake in 442 (Paulus Diaconus, *Hist. Rom.* 13.16). Numer-

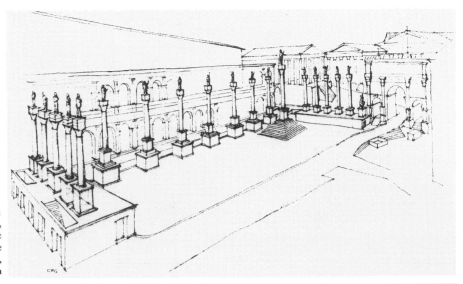

Figure 41
Forum Romanum,
Rehandling of the
Central Area in the
Time of Diocletian,
Reconstruction

ous brick-stamps of Theodoric (483–526) attest to repairs in his time (*CIL* 15.1665a, 1669). The first church recorded in the forum is that of SS. Cosma e Damiano (A.D. 526–530), whereas S. Maria Antiqua is probably older. The greatest destruction in the area was probably that caused by the earthquake of Pope Leo IV ca. 847 (*LPD* 2.108) and the fire of Robert Guiscard in 1084.

Interest in antiquity and the treasures of the forum was reawakened in the Renaissance, especially the sixteenth century, and much of the area was ransacked, but scientific excavation came only in the nineteenth century. In 1803 Fea began clearing the Arch of Septimius Severus, and his work was continued by the French, who isolated the temples of Saturn, Vespasian, Castor, and Concordia before 1836. Then in 1870 systematic work began with the object of clearing the whole forum, but only to the level of late antiquity (the fourth to fifth century). This was continued by G. Boni beginning in 1898, who also aimed at uncovering the deeper strata and the whole history of the forum. In this he was conspicuously successful, and many of the most important discoveries were his, notably the deep stratification in the Comitium, the archaic cemetery of the Sepulcretum (q.v.), and the complicated history of the Temple of Vesta and Lacus Iuturnae (*Atti del Congresso di Scienze Storiche* 5 [1904]: 493–584 [G. Boni]; *BullCom* 31 [1903]: 3–239 [D. Vaglieri]). More recently, deep stratigraphic excavations have been undertaken by G. Carettoni in the Basilica Paulli, E. Gjerstad in the Comitium, R. Gamberini-Mongenet in the area between the Temple of Divus Iulius and the Temple of Vesta, F. E. Brown and R. T. Scott in the Regia and Atrium Vestae, and E. M. Steinby at the Lacus Iuturnae.

For a general history of the forum and a study of all the problems involved, see F. Coarelli, *Il foro romano*, 1 (Rome 1983) and 2 (Rome 1985), though many of his theories cannot be accepted. A more conservative and rational approach is offered by Lugli 1946, 55–242, Lugli 1947, and Lugli 1975, 210–82. Also useful is P. Zanker, *Forum Romanum, die Neugestaltung durch Augustus* (Tübingen 1972).

Nash 1.446–49; C. F. Giuliani and P. Verduchi, *L'area centrale del foro romano* (Florence 1987); *AJA* 94 (1990): 627–45 (A. J. Ammerman).

Forum Rusticorum: mentioned only in the first appendix to the regionary catalogues, where it is the last item, following the Forum Gallorum. It is possible that this was a facetious name for one of the squares of Rome, but it is impossible to identify it more precisely.

Forum Suarium: placed by the regionary catalogues in Regio VII (Via Lata) and identified by inscriptions as a center of *actores* (*CIL* 6.3728, 31046) and a *mercator* (*CIL* 6.9631 = *ILS* 7516). In principle it was under the supervision of the praefectus urbi (*Dig.* 1.12.1.11), who was responsible for the control of the price of meat. Twice we find it under the jurisdiction of a tribune of the urban cohorts *et fori suari* (cf. *CIL* 6.1156a = *ILS* 722), a dependent of the praefectus urbi, who was probably regularly in charge of this. We may therefore see in it the central meat market of Rome, but it is not mentioned before the end of the second century after Christ and had great importance only in the fourth. Its character and the space it logically would require seem apt to relegate it to the edge of the city; HJ (452–53) would therefore like to put it beyond the *castra urbana* near the Collegio della Propaganda Fide, in which he is followed by the Lugli and Gismondi map. More likely it is the macellum-like building that filled the angle between the Via del Corso and Via Frattina, of which Palladio has left us a drawing (Zorzi fig. 68). This identification is supported by its connection with the Cohortes Urbanae. The castra of the Cohortes Urbanae were in Campo Agrippae (Chron. 148) and evidently near Aurelian's Templum Solis, which seems to have been close to the juncture of the Via del Corso and Via dei Condotti.

A. Chastagnol, *La Préfecture urbaine à Rome sous le bas-empire* (Paris 1960), 325–30; *Palladio,* n.s. 3, no. 6 (1990): 9–24 (A. Moneti).

Forum Tauri: mentioned only in medieval documents, but probably to be connected with Porta S. Lorenzo, which was called Porta Taurina in the twelfth century, and the Horti Tauriani (q.v.), probably belonging to some member of the family of M. Statilius Taurus (cos. A.D. 44), on the Esquiline, conjoined with the Horti Calyclani (q.v.). The Forum Tauri figures in the martyrdom of Santa Bibiana (*BullCom* 18 [1890]: 280–83 [G. B. De Rossi and G. Gatti]) and is linked with an area known as Caput Tauri, perhaps in reference to a decorative use of bulls' heads or skulls at the entrance or on the walls of the horti. In view of the proximity of the church of S. Bibiana, the forum was probably a market just inside Porta S. Lorenzo on the southeast side of Via Tiburtina Vetus (cf. Forum Esquilinum). How far Caput Tauri may have extended is unknown.

Forum Traiani (in later antiquity sometimes called **Forum Ulpium**): the last and largest of the imperial fora. Domitian began it (Aur. Vict., *Caes.* 13.5), but work was suspended, when still close to its beginning, at his death. However, Domitian's work on the Forum Iulium (q.v.) and the monumental apse built by Domitian north of the northwest hemicycle of the Forum Augustum and subsequently blocked off by Trajanic construction suggest that he had got as far as a well-developed plan that would integrate the new forum with its predecessors to the south and east but had not swung into full construction. Trajan enjoyed the services of the brilliant architect Apollodorus of Damascus (Cass. Dio 69.4.1) and dedicated at least some parts of the complex before his departure for the East in 113 (Cass. Dio 68.16.3).

The area covered included everything from the Forum Augustum to, and including, the Atrium Libertatis. Because the Servian Walls, which had once run just beyond the Atrium Libertatis, had probably long since been dismantled throughout the whole stretch from the Capitoline to the part of the Quirinal called Collis Mucialis, whether the forum ran

over their line is unclear, but probable. The area was probably largely one formerly occupied by shops and markets, pushed in this direction by the construction of the Forum Augustum and Templum Pacis, to which was added the site of the Atrium Libertatis (q.v.) and land at the base of the Quirinal hill, which was cut back on a massive scale to level the area. Some of the activities dispossessed to make room for it may have found new quarters in the complex known as the Mercati di Traiano (q.v.)

As completed, the forum consisted of two almost wholly discrete complexes arranged on a single axis parallel to that of the Forum Iulium, and at right angles to that of Forum Augustum. The first complex began with a monumental entrance arch and consisted of a vast square flanked by colonnades, behind which opened hemicycles, and closed at the far end by the mass of the Basilica Ulpia. The second complex, reached only through the Basilica Ulpia and after deviating from the dominant axis, consisted of the Columna Traiani, which was flanked by libraries, and the Temple of Divus Traianus, which Hadrian built after Trajan's death. The temple has unfortunately never been excavated and is represented by only a few fragments of architecture, and the way it was integrated with the other elements is entirely unknown. It seems possible that the second complex is wholly a creation of Hadrian and that the column originally stood in the northeast hemicycle of the main square, where, as the inscription on its base proclaims, it showed how great an excavation of the hill and area (*quantae altitudinis mons et locus*) had been necessary (*CIL* 6.13 = 960 = *ILS* 294). The length of the whole forum was about 310 m, and the width of the widest part was about 185 m. Interpretations of the inscription on the base have abounded. At first it was presumed that there had been a high ridge connecting the Quirinal and Capitoline that had been cut away. But geology militated against this, and excavation around the base of the column brought to light at a lower level a paved street and remains of a portico in front of a line of shops of the early empire (*NSc* 1907, 389–410, 414–27 [G. Boni]; Amici 58–61). Despite the ingenuity of some of the theories advanced, it seems clear that the excavation of the slope of the Quirinal is what is meant.

Between the Forum Augustum and Forum Traiani was an intermediate area that is very little understood. It does appear that the Forum Traiani turned mainly inward toward the square, and there may have been nothing truly monumental about the approach. The front wall is gently curved with an addorsed colonnade broken in the middle by a triumphal arch of five bays but only a single central fornix. This is shown on coins (*B. M. Coins, Rom. Emp.* 3

pls. 18.3, 21.15). The bays are separated by single columns, and there is a very deep attic broken out over the columns. Each side bay contained an aedicular niche capped by a triangular pediment framing a statue, while a series of five medallions (imagines clipeatae?) above these and the central arch made a second zone. The attic was crowned by an elaborate program of statuary, a central chariot with six horses and driver led on by soldiers to either side, flanked in turn by a Victoria dedicating a trophy. The central block of the attic over the fornix seems designed to carry a lengthy inscription. The senate erected or remodeled this in 117 to commemorate Trajan's victories in the East (Cass. Dio 68.29.3). At either extremity of the front wall of the forum, secondary entrances to the flanking colonnades led in from the Forum Iulium and Mercati di Traiano.

The center of the square was adorned with a splendid equestrian statue of Trajan (Amm. Marc. 16.10.15). This may be shown on coins (e.g., *B. M. Coins, Rom. Emp.* 3 pl. 16.18), where the indication is that it was an offering by the senate to Trajan. The square was 118 m long by 89 m wide, paved with blocks of white marble. Along the sides ran two porticoes 12 m deep with fluted columns of pavonazzetto and responding pilasters of the same stone behind. These were raised above the square by three steps of giallo antico and paved with flags of colored marble. The attic, like that of the Forum Augustum, was very deep, implying a vaulted ceiling behind, adorned with figures of Dacian captives alternating with shields and windows. On the roofs of the colonnades were gilded horses and military trophies provided ex manubiis (A. Gellius 13.25.1). Behind the midpoint of each lateral colonnade opened a hemicycle with a central aedicular niche in clear imitation of the hemicycles of the Forum Augustum, but providing a minor axis of greater importance. The central focus of these hemicycles is unknown. In the porticoes and square Trajan and his successors set up a great number of statues of generals and other distinguished men (S.H.A. *M. Aurelius* 22.7; *Alex. Sev.* 26.4; *Tacitus* 9.2; Sid. Apoll., *Carm.* 8.8, 9.301). A great many inscriptions belonging to these statues have been found, some of which are explicit about their having been erected *in Foro Traiani* or *in Foro Ulpio* (CIL 6. 1377=31640, 1599, 1710, 1721, 1724, 1727, 1749; ILS 809, 1098, 1244, 1275, 1326, 2949, 2950).

The end of the forum opposite the entrance was filled by the façade of the Basilica Ulpia turned broadside to the axis of the forum. The principal entrance to the basilica took the form of a triumphal arch and is shown on coins (*B. M. Coins, Rom. Emp.* 3 pl. 17.15) as having three bays, each consisting of a pair of columns mounted on a stepped platform

carrying a deep attic surmounted by statuary. Over the central bay is a quadriga led on by a pair of soldiers or Victorias. Over each side bay is a biga flanked by trophies or standards. In the background the architecture of the basilica itself appears, showing columns in both storeys and large antefixes or vases along the edge of the roof. Excavation has shown that the central door was triple, preceded by a porch of four columns, while symmetrical secondary entrances to either side had porches of two columns. The coins may show a project that was never carried out, or a telescoped version of the whole façade.

In the interior the basilica consisted of a large central nave surrounded on all sides by a double aisle with a hemicycle opening at either end. The columns were all Corinthian, with slight differences; those around the nave were of gray granite, and those of the aisles were of giallo antico, cipollino, and pavonazzetto. Capitals and plinths were of white marble, the walls revetted with white Luna marble, the beams of Pentelic, and the roof covered with gilt-bronze tiles (Pausanias 5.12.6, 10.5.11). Fragments of a frieze of Victorias sacrificing bulls and decking candelabra with garlands are of especially fine workmanship.

The hemicycles at either end were lined with an addorsed colonnade and had a central aedicular niche as focus. A substantial part of the basilica is shown on the Marble Plan (*FUR* pl. 28; Rodriguez pl. 21), where the northeast hemicycle is labeled LIBERTATIS. Because we are here in the area formerly occupied by the Atrium Libertatis, it seems likely that the other hemicycle was labeled ATRIUM and that these were the Bibliotheca Ulpia, libraries that replaced those of Asinius Pollio's rebuilding of the Atrium Libertatis (q.v.). The architecture, with an addorsed colonnade dividing the wall into shallow bays suitable for the installation of shelved cases to hold the books, further suggests this, as does the pavement of colored marble, which must have been under a roof. The upper parts and roofing of the whole building present a series of difficult problems in the use of columns, windows, and clerestoreys which has yet to be resolved to complete satisfaction. Certainly as it appears today, it was essentially a single-storey building.

From the Basilica Ulpia two inconspicuous doors led back to a small colonnaded court beyond, 24 m wide and 16 m deep, in the center of which stood the Columna Traiani. This is a column, essentially Tuscan in form, measuring with base and capital 100 Roman feet (29.78 m) in height, set on a high rectangular block (5.37 m high and 5.48 m on a side) covered with military trophies of enemy arms in low relief. The diameter of the column is 3.83 m at the base and 3.66 m at the summit. The column is composed of seventeen drums of Luna marble, and there is perceptible entasis in the shaft. It is carved with a spiral band of relatively low relief, 0.89 m high at the base, gradually deepening to 1.25 m at the summit, while the figures increase from about 0.60 m at the base to 0.90 m at the summit. In a continuous sequence it shows the campaigns of Trajan in Dacia between A.D. 101 and 106, and at the same time a compendium of the life, organization, and activities of the Roman army. The composition of scenes and the narrative clarity are exceptionally fine; Trajan appears with great frequency, always clearly portrayed and slightly larger than those around him; and the artist's knowledge of the Roman army, the Dacians, and the story of the campaigns is impressive. Whether the reliefs were colored and how legible they were to those viewing them from the ground are debated questions.

The column is entered by a doorway in the southeast face of the base. From a little vestibule, a corridor leads back to the left to a small chamber in the base, where Trajan's ashes were deposited in an urn of gold (Cass. Dio 69.2.3; Eutropius 8.5.2; Aur. Vict., *Epit.* 13.11). This was lit by a tiny window. At a later time it was walled off by a thick brick wall. From the vestibule to the right, a staircase of 185 steps ascends in rectilinear flights inside the base, then in a spiral cut from the heart of the drums, leading to the top. It is lit by forty-three narrow slit windows, framed but inconspicuous in the relief band, thanks to there being more than twenty-five hundred figures represented in the relief.

Originally the column seems to have been designed to be surmounted by an eagle (see *B. M. Coins, Rom. Emp.* 3 pl. 41.7), but then a statue of the princeps himself was substituted. From the representations on coins (see *B. M. Coins, Rom. Emp.* 3 pls. 16.19 and 20, 17.1 and 2, 19.11 and 12, 21.15, 39.4 and 5, 40.1, 2 and 11, 41.6, 42.3), the column was slow in taking shape, and eagles that had in a second design been intended to flank the base were ultimately omitted. We have no authoritative representation of the statue of Trajan on the summit. The inscription on the base (*CIL* 6.960 = *ILS* 294) makes it clear that the column was a present to Trajan from the senate and the Roman people. It was dedicated 18 May A.D. 113 (*NSc* 1932, 201 [G. Calza]; A. Degrassi, *Inscriptiones Italiae* 13.1 p. 203). The theory that the relief spiral had its origin as a book roll, a theory first propounded by Birt and endorsed repeatedly by others, ignores the excellence of the overall design, in which patterns are worked out vertically, as well as in sequence. And such continuous narrative is at least as old as the Odyssey Landscapes from the Esquiline, which seem hardly likely to have been derived from

a book roll. The precision of the carving and the lack of damage at joints are such that many authorities have asserted that the reliefs could only have been carved once the column was in place, but this also is an assertion that will not bear scrutiny. The suggestion that the column was originally intended to stand in the northeast hemicycle of the forum square, and if the dedication in 113 is correct must once have stood there, could be proved by excavation under the floor of that hemicycle. If true, there must be a concrete footing of the dimensions of that under the column in its present location hidden beneath the pavement.

The tiny church of S. Nicola de Columna at the base of the column is recorded as early as 1029–1032 (HCh 394–96) and was deconsecrated sometime between 1560 and 1570. It has left the outline of a roof over the door to the column's interior, somewhat defacing the reliefs. In 1588 Pope Sixtus V had the present bronze statue of Saint Peter by Giacomo della Porta erected in place of that of Trajan, long lost.

To either side of the column is a library (Bibliotheca Divi Traiani), a small rectangular building, one for Greek authors, one for Latin, in the usual fashion. The libraries were originally handsome buildings with extraordinarily fine brickwork facing the concrete core. Down the sides and across the end, the walls were broken into bays by Corinthian columns set opposite responsive pilasters that framed large rectangular niches, in which the cabinets for books must have been housed. One mounted three steps between columns to reach a continuous walk in front of the niches, and the proportions of surviving fragments of architecture suggest that there was a slightly lower second storey above this, but access to this is a problem. Stairs behind the libraries in the corners between library and basilica do not appear to have been for public use. A larger semicircular niche in the center of the end wall seems to have been for the statue of a tutelary divinity, and statues of celebrated authors also embellished the interiors (Sid. Apoll., *Epist.* 9.16.25–28). The notion that a gallery over the colonnades in front of the libraries and connecting them provided a vantage point from which to examine more of the reliefs of the column than could be seen from the ground does not strongly recommend itself, because the advantage would be only slight. Everything suggests that once the column had been installed in this location the narrative value of the reliefs was considered unimportant.

The Temple of Divus Traianus, and later perhaps Plotina (*CIL* 6.966 = 31215 = *ILS* 306), was added by Hadrian (S.H.A. *Hadr.* 19.9), to whom we should perhaps ascribe everything northwest of the Basilica

Ulpia, because his brick-stamps were found in great quantity in the area (Bloch 57–61). A likely candidate for the temple is shown on coins as octastyle with a stair of approach across the whole of the principal façade and a massive altar in front of this. Fragments of gray granite columns 2 m in diameter and others 1.80 m in diameter have been found, together with corresponding Corinthian capitals of white marble. On coins the temple is shown flanked by colonnades, and the design of these and connection of them with the complex of libraries and column is a great problem. The great size of the temple elements and sumptuousness of material suggest that it was designed to complement the column, and the play with scale between this and the libraries may well have been extended to the subsidiary colonnades.

The purpose of this enormous complex was especially to provide a suitable place for the much-expanded business of the courts of Rome. State archives, such as the Libri Lintei recording the acts of the emperors (S.H.A. *Aurelian.* 1.7, *Tacitus* 8.1–2) and the edicts of the praetors (A. Gellius 11.17.1), were kept here. Here the consuls held court (A. Gellius 13.25.2), and Hadrian burned the records of delinquent debtors to the government (S.H.A. *Hadr.* 7.6). Here Marcus Aurelius auctioned off the treasures of the imperial palace to pay for the Marcomannic War (S.H.A. *M. Aurel.* 17.4–5, 21.9; Eutropius 8.13.2; Aur. Vict., *Epit.* 16.9). Here Aurelian burned public records (S.H.A. *Aurelian.* 39.3), and here laws inscribed on bronze were frequently displayed (cf. *Cod. Theodos.* 14.2.1; *Leges Novellae Divi Valentiniani* passim). The last may be in continuance of the functions of the Atrium Libertatis (q.v.), as may also be the continued manumission of slaves here (Sid. Apoll., *Carm.* 2.544–45).

From unspecified parts of the Forum Traiani come a number of decorative panels and figures, including reliefs now in the Vatican, Villa Medici, the Louvre, and elsewhere (*PBSR* 4 [1907]: 229–57 [A. J. B. Wace]; *MonPiot* 18 [1909–10]: 206–12 [E. Michon]); the colossal protomes of horses, rhinoceroses, elephants, and other animals in the cloister of the Museo Nazionale Romano delle Terme; the familiar relief of an eagle with spread wings mounted in a wreath now in the church of SS. Apostoli; and possibly four large relief panels, once part of a single frieze, now employed in the decoration of the Arch of Constantine.

The destruction of the forum began in the fourth century, when parts of its decoration were taken to embellish the Arch of Constantine. It was still one of the most impressive buildings in Rome, and Ammianus Marcellinus (16.10.15) records the astonishment of Emperor Constantius before it when he visited Rome in A.D. 356. Throughout the Middle Ages it was plundered for building material and decorations for the churches and palaces of Rome. The column and central third of the Basilica Ulpia were first excavated by the French in 1812–1814, with some additions, hardly more than soundings, in 1824 and 1866–1867. The hemicycle on the northeast side of the forum square was partially excavated in the early part of this century (*NSc* 1907, 414–27 [G. Boni]). A major clearance was undertaken in connection with the construction of the Via dei Fori Imperiali in 1928–1934, and this completed what is known today: the northeast colonnade of the forum square with its hemicycle, the central part of the Basilica Ulpia with the Columna Traiani behind and the southwest library flanking the column, and the southwest hemicycle of the Basilica Ulpia, the last two parts now largely hidden in a crypt under the modern street. The excavations have all been only summarily published, but the column and parts of the architecture have been objects of special studies in recent years.

Lugli 1946, 278–99; Nash 1.283–86, 450–56; *BdA* 53 (1968): 63–71 (G. Gullini); *AA* 1970, 499–544 (P. Zanker); L. Rossi, *Trajan's Column and the Dacian Wars* (London 1971); C. H. Leon, *Die Bauornamentik des Trajansforums und ihre Stellung in der früh- und mittelkaiserzeitlichen Architekturdekoration Roms* (Vienna, Cologne, and Graz 1971); *RömMitt* 83 (1976): 165–74 (A. Malissard); *ArchN* 6.4 (1977): 101–7 (L. Richardson); W. Gauer, *Untersuchungen zur Trajansäule, 1 Teil: Darstellungsprogramm und kunstlericher Entwurf* (Berlin 1977); *RömMitt* 87 (1981): 301–6 (G. Koeppel); *Prospettiva* 26 (1981): 2–9 (V. Farinella); C. M. Amici, *Foro di Traiano: Basilica Ulpia e biblioteche* (Rome 1982); I. A. Richmond, *Trajan's Army on Trajan's Column* (London 1982); Anderson 141–77; R. Brilliant, *Visual Narratives: Story-telling in Etruscan and Roman Art* (Ithaca, N.Y. 1984), 90–123; *AJA* 89 (1985): 641–53 (M. Waelkens); Boatwright 74–94; S. Settis, A. La Regina, G. Agosti, and V. Farinella, *La colonna traiana* (Turin 1988); L. Lepper and S. Frere, *Trajan's Column, A New Edition of the Cichorius Plates* (Gloucester 1988); *ArchCl* 41 (1989): 27–286 (P. Pensabene et al.), 237–92 (S. Stucchi); *JRA* 3 (1990): 290–309 (J. C. N. Coulston); J. Packer, *Basilica Ulpia* (forthcoming).

Forum Transitorium: see **Forum Nervae.**

Forum Ulpium: see **Forum Traiani.**

Forum Vespasiani: see **Pax, Templum.**

Forum Vinarium: known only from inscriptions that mention *argentarii* and a *coactor vinarius de*

Foro Vinario (*CIL* 6.9181, 9182 = *ILS* 7502), but probably to be connected with the Portus Vinarius (q.v.). The Ciconiae (q.v.) on the Tiber was a landing place for wine, or near one, and the Portus Vinarius may have been adjacent to this. The forum would presumably have been a small square in the vicinity.

Fossae Quiritium: a popular name attested in the *Liber de viris illustribus* of pseudo-Victor for the Cloaca Maxima (q.v.), because in its construction Tarquinius Superbus employed the whole work force of Rome. But the name is used by no one else.

Fregellae: said by Festus (Paulus *ex Fest.* 80L) to be a place in the city where visitors from the city of Fregellae lived, perhaps following its destruction by Opimius in 124 B.C. Because Fregellae was on the Via Latina near the southern end of the Hernican valley, we might expect such a settlement to be on the eastern reaches of the Esquiline, but there is no evidence.

Frigianum: see **Phrygianum.**

Furca: a place designation found in one inscription: *Casarus a furca* (*CIL* 6.9238). Because *furca* might be either "throat" (as in the Furcae, or Furculae, Caudinae) or "gallows," the possibilities seem many, but none is especially attractive.

Furrina: see **Lucus Furrinae.**

G

Gaia: In the Fasti Antiates Maiores for 8 December is the note *Tiberino/Gaiae,* whereas the Fasti Amiternini give *Tiberino in insula* (Degrassi 534–35). According to the ancient sources, there were two Gaiae: (1) Gaia Taracia, also known as Fufetia, a Vestal Virgin who presented the Roman people with the Campus Tiberinus (q.v.), another name for the Campus Martius, or part thereof, in return for which she was accorded special privileges and honors, including a statue (Pliny, *HN* 34.25; A. Gellius 7.7.1–4; Plutarch, *Public.* 8.4); and (2) the admirable wife of Tarquinius Priscus, Gaia Caecilia, earlier called Tanaquil, whose distaff and spindle were preserved in the Temple of Semo Sancus, and a toga of whose making that had belonged to Servius Tullius was kept in the Temple of Fortuna. Brides called upon her name for a good omen at their wedding (Pliny, *HN* 8.194; Paulus *ex Fest.* 85L; Plutarch, *Quaest. Rom.* 30). These two are understandably confused, and Taracia is suspected of being a corruption of the name Tanaquil. The points of contact are too many to be accidental, and the threads are too intertwined to disentangle. However, we may conclude that Gaia was worshiped, probably in conjunction with Tiberinus at a small shrine of unknown location on the Tiber island, and that she was regarded as a patroness of the Roman people who had also perhaps had a hand in the formation of the Tiber island.

Gaianum: an area in the Transtiberim, listed in the regionary catalogues in Regio XIV, where Caligula was fond of holding chariot races (Cass. Dio 59.14.6–7). It lay south of the Naumachia Traiani (q.v.) and east of Via Triumphalis (*BullCom* 24 [1896]: 248–49 [R. Lanciani]). Inscriptions sometimes supposed to come from its area (*CIL* 6.10052–10054, 10057, 10058, 10067, 33937, 33953; *ILS* 5289, 5296, 5298) that have been taken to indicate that it was extensively adorned with statues of victors seem to have belonged to statues originally in the Circus Gaii et Neronis (q.v.) that were reused, and nothing can be argued from them. The Gaianum was probably simply a track and is not to be confused with the circus. In the regionary catalogues it is linked with the Frigianum (Phrygianum, q.v.), a shrine of the Magna Mater *in Vaticano,* but this is probably fortuitous. A note in Filocalus for 28 March, *Initium Caiani,* has been taken to mean the beginning of a festival in honor of the Magna Mater (cf. Degrassi 432–33; the Ludi Megalenses ran traditionally 4–10 April) or else to a race meeting in the Gaianum. But chariot racing had no special season and seems to have continued throughout the year. Because 28 March was the day on which Caligula entered Rome in A.D. 37 and was acclaimed princeps (*CIL* 6. 2028e; Suetonius, *Calig.* 14.1), there may well be allusion to this.

CAR 1-E, 2 p. 20.

Gallinae Albae: a place designation in Regio VI listed in the regionary catalogues and in the fourth ecclesiastical region, which seems to have been much the same as the fourth Augustan region (Gregor. Mag., *Epist.* 3.17 [*MGH Epist.* 1.175]; Jordan 2.122, 319), on the southeast slope of the Viminal near its western end, between the churches of S. Lorenzo in Panisperna and S. Lorenzo in Fontana, where the name is preserved in the church of S. Sixtus in Gallina Alba (Jordan 2.122, 319; HCh 471). It was more likely a crossroads than a street; Gregory describes it as a *locus.* This is not to be confused with the part of the Villa of Livia at Prima Porta also known as Ad Gallinas (Albas).

Ad Gemellos: a place designation cited twice by Frontinus (*Aq.* 1.5, 65), located *infra Spem Veterem*

180

(see Spes Vetus), where there was a juncture of the Aqua Appia with a branch of the Aqua Augusta, added by Augustus to supplement the Appia. Parker proposed that the "twins" were two great reservoirs just outside the boundary wall of the Sessorium (q.v.) close to the line of the Aqua Appia, but in that case Frontinus would probably have been more specific. If *infra* means "just below," then it should be somewhere on the Esquiline, where the Aqua Appia runs at approximately right angles to the other aqueducts entering ad Spem Veterem. Features that appear in pairs are so common that any attempt to pin these down seems futile.

Gemoniae: see **Scalae Gemoniae.**

Genius Castrorum, Sacellum: a shrine of the Castra Peregrina (q.v.) on the Caelian, known from inscriptions of the time of Alexander Severus (*CIL* 6.230–31 = *ILS* 2215–16).

Genius Populi Romani: (1) a shrine near the Temple of Concordia mentioned by Dio in connection with a prodigy of vultures in 43 B.C. and a prodigy of an owl in 32 B.C. (Cass. Dio 47.2.3, 50.8.2) and recorded in a late inscription (*CIL* 6.248 = *ILS* 3678) found between the Basilica Iulia and Clivus Capitolinus. Aurelian is said to have dedicated a gold image of the genius on the Rostra (Chron. 148), and the regionary catalogues list the genius immediately after *rostra III* and before the Equus Constantini and senatus (Curia). One would be inclined to think of this as a sacellum that was destroyed to make way for the Temple of Divus Vespasianus, possibly even rebuilt as the so-called Aedicula Faustinae (see Faustina, Aedicula). Granted the Romans' fondness for dedicating statues on the rostra, there is no difficulty with Aurelian's gesture, except for its isolation and the existence of a proper temple of this divinity nearby. But Aurelian might have wished to give fresh prominence to a neglected divinity and resorted to this expedient.

RömMitt 97 (1990): 134–36 (F. S. Kleiner).

(2) On 9 October, according to the fasti, sacrifices were offered to the Genius Populi Romani, Fausta Felicitas, and Venus Victrix on the Capitoline (Degrassi 518). This is a puzzling triad, and it has been supposed that either a single altar or a triad of altars is all that is meant. But Servius (*ad Aen.* 2.351) tells of a shield dedicated on the Capitoline inscribed: *Genio urbis Romae sive mas sive femina,* and, because the idea of a Genius urbis is paradoxical (the Urbs as feminine should have a Iuno), one might see this triad as mysterious agents of victory, and their association is too close to be fortuitous. See also Venus Victrix.

Gens Flavia, Templum (also **Templa** in Martial 9.3.12; S.H.A. *Tyr. Trig.* 33.6; *Claudius Gothicus* 3.6; Statius, *Silv.* 4.3.19–20, 5.1.240–41): a shrine that Domitian established on the site of the house where he was born (Suetonius, *Dom.* 1.1; Chron. 146). Martial speaks as though the house were leveled to make space for the temple (9.20.1–2) and repeatedly lauds its size and splendor (9.1.8–9; 9.3.12; 9.34). It was struck by lightning in A.D. 96 (Suetonius, *Dom.* 15.2), but was still standing in the fourth century and is listed in the *Notitia* in Regio VI. It was at least in part intended as a mausoleum, and we know that Julia's ashes were deposited there, as were Domitian's (Suetonius, *Dom.* 17.3). Probably Vespasian's and Titus's ashes had also been transferred to it.

There is a strong suggestion that the temple was round and domed, the ceiling decorated to represent the heavens (Martial 9.3.18–19, 9.34; Statius, *Silv.* 4.3.19, 5.1.240–41), and it was regarded as a symbol of Rome's eternity (Martial 9.1.8; Statius, *Silv.* 4.3.18–19). It stood on the Quirinal on the street called Ad Malum Punicum, presumably on the south side of Alta Semita and not far from it in the vicinity of Via delle Quattro Fontane, but no identifiable element of it has ever come to light (*BullCom* 17 [1889]: 383–89 [R. Lanciani]). The Templum Minervae described by Pirro Ligorio and Vacca (ibid., 383–84) seems too small to have been the Templum Gentis Flaviae. Perhaps it was, as Ligorio describes it, simply an elaborate house shrine.

Gens Iulia, Ara: an altar in the Area Capitolina near the statue of Numa Pompilius (*JRS* 16 [1926]: 95–101 [A. H. Smith]). The statues of the kings of Rome stood at a secondary entrance to the Area Capitolina via a stair above the Fornix Calpurnianus (Appian, *BellCiv* 1.16–17; Orosius 5.9.2), very likely the Centum Gradus (q.v.), perhaps a stair on the southwest flank of the hill and, if so, near the Temple of Fides. This would explain why it was regarded as an appropriate place for the posting of diplomata of honorably discharged soldiers in the years A.D. 68–71 (cf. *CIL* 16.7–17).

Gnomon: see **Obeliscus Augusti.**

Gradus Aurelii: mentioned only by Cicero, once in connection with the trial of C. Iunius in 74 B.C. (*Clu.* 93) and once in 59 B.C., again with reference to a trial (*Flac.* 66). In 74 the steps were new, presumably the work of M. Aurelius Cotta, who was consul in that year, or his brother Gaius, consul in the preceding year. The trial of Iunius was for misconduct of a *quaestio* over which he had presided, and the tribune Quinctius brought the charge before the praetor urbanus, whose court regularly sat in the Comitium. Cicero says the Gradus Aurelii were thronged by a *contio* of supporters of the accusation, so they seemed a theater built for the trial. Flaccus was brought to trial on a charge of *repetundae* in the oldest of the *quaestiones perpetuae,* probably also held in the Comitium. So the Gradus Aurelii were probably a sector of the stepping of the Comitium restored by Aurelius, hence Cicero's description of them *quasi pro theatro.*

RömMitt 80 (1973): 225 (L. Richardson).

Gradus Gemiturii: see Scalae Gemoniae.

Gradus Heliogabali: mentioned in medieval documents, described as *in introitu Palatii* (*Mirabilia:* Jordan 2.616; VZ 3.24). They figured in the Acta S. Sebastiani (20 January, p. 642), where the martyr, whose passion is set in the Circus Maximus, addressed the emperor: *stans super Gradus Heliogabali.* They are also linked to the Septizodium (HCh 305, 595). The combined evidence indicates that they were a monumental stair, perhaps leading from the Templum Elagabali (see Elagabalus, Templum [1]) on the east side of the Palatine near the south corner down in the direction of the Circus Maximus.

Gradus Monetae: a stair mentioned by Ovid (*Fast.* 1.638) as leading from the Temple of Concordia, so an approach from the Forum Romanum to the Temple of Iuno Moneta on the northwest crest of the Capitoline. Under the northeast end of the cella of Tiberius's Temple of Concordia was found part of a stair in continuation of the line of the Sacra Via, but this was interrupted by Tiberius's enlargement of the temple, which was dedicated 16 January A.D. 10. The stair was then moved to the northeast side of the temple, between it and the Carcer, and became the Scalae Gemoniae (q.v.). While Ovid may be remembering the earlier stair and using the name by which it was known, he is probably thinking of the new stair now splendidly rebuilt. The earliest use of the name Scalae Gemoniae comes in the time of Tiberius (Val. Max. 6.3.3 and 9.13).

Gradus Sanctae Sabinae: mentioned only by Pope Gregory the Great (*Epist.* 2.10 [*MGH Epist.* 1 p. 109]) and presumably short-lived, a stair leading from the church of S. Sabina to the Tiber down the northwest side of the Aventine. On Bufalini's map of Rome of 1551, a stair is shown leading down the slope of the Aventine just north of the church of S. Maria in Aventino (S. Maria del Priorato) labeled *Scalae Gemonie.* PA takes this to be the Gradus Sanctae Sabinae, but it is more likely simply an invention of Bufalini.

Graecostadium: listed in the regionary catalogues in Regio VIII, between the Vicus Iugarius et Unguentarius and Porticus Margaritarius in the *Notitia,* and between the Vicus Iugarius and Basilica Iulia in the *Curiosum.* It was apparently shown in part on a lost fragment of the Marble Plan (*FUR* pl. 21e, labeled]RECOST[; Rodriguez pl. 13). The fragment was small, and it is not clear that the drawing and inscription belong to the same building; very likely they do not. The drawing shows a temple front with a broad stair of approach and an octastyle or larger façade, but the pronaos, if such it be, was shallow, only two bays deep.

The Graecostadium was restored by Antoninus Pius after a fire (S.H.A. *Ant. Pius* 8.2) and burned again in the fire of Carinus in 283 (Chron. 148). It otherwise figures in history only perhaps as Plutarch's Agora of the Greeks (*De Soll. An.* 10). The indications then are that it was located close to the Basilica Iulia and Temple of Saturn, just southwest of one or the other, more likely the former, if the fragment of the Marble Plan is correctly identified. But the Graecostadium cannot have been a temple; rather than anything else, one expects it to be a racecourse or exercise field, laid out in Greek fashion and consequently unlikely to have been anywhere near the forum. To resolve the implicit contradictions, topographers have supposed that it was an open square surrounded by combustible buildings. The large temple shown in conjunction with it might be the Temple of Divus Augustus (see Augustus, Divus, Templum) and the Graecostadium might be its temenos (see Plutarch, *De Soll. An.* 10), but why this name should have been given it is puzzling, unless it be in reference to its dimensions. This is perhaps the best one can say at present.

On 24 August, according to the Fasti Pinciani of the early imperial period, sacrifice was offered *in Graecost.* (Degrassi 502), but no other source mentions this. This might be either the Graecostasis or the Graecostadium, more likely the latter. See also Graecostasis.

Graecostasis: the shoulder of the Capitoline Hill from the Lautumiae to the Area Concordiae, traditionally the place assigned for embassies from foreign states to station themselves in order to show their strength and numbers to the Romans in the Comitium and to the senate and to await being summoned to address the senate (Varro, *Ling.* 5.155). Varro says it was a *locus substructus* to the right of the Rostra Comitii, which implies terracing, but of this there is no trace. Pliny (*HN* 33.19) implies that it had ceased to exist in his day, and, with the dismantling of the Comitium and building of the Curia Iulia, the relation of things had changed so much that the Graecostasis could no longer serve its original purpose. In 304 B.C. C. Flavius erected a bronze aedicula to Concordia *in Graecostasi* (Pliny, *HN* 33.19); Livy then located this *in Area Volcani* (Livy 9.46.6). This was a forerunner of the Temple of Concordia of later times.

A further statement of Pliny's complicates matters, namely, that until the time of the First Punic War the accensus consulum announced noon when from the Curia he sighted the sun between the Rostra and the Graecostasis (*HN* 7.212). Because at such time he should have been looking due south, and would himself have been standing behind the midpoint of the Rostra Comitii, it is impossible to make this square with our other information. However, if we take the rostra in question to be the Rostra Antiana in the middle of the forum, then we must look for a Graecostasis south of the Curia (cf. *RömMitt* 80 [1973]: 223 [L. Richardson]). This might be either a forerunner of the Graecostadium or a Graecostasis connected with the Rostra Antiana, but not only is evidence for such a platform lacking but also even the rationale for it. As long as the Comitium and Curia kept their original form and place, the Graecostasis at the base of the Capitoline was adequate, however much its original area may have been reduced by the encroachment of other buildings. Once the Comitium was demolished there was no reason to preserve the Graecostasis, and it seems to have disappeared. So unless Pliny, who can have seen neither of the original monuments in question, is mistaken, or the text corrupt, this Graecostasis must be a forerunner of the Graecostadium south of the Tabernae Veteres and toward the east end of these.

The Graecostasis at the base of the Capitoline was several times the site of prodigies, a flow of blood in 137 B.C. (Obsequens 24), and rains of milk in 130 (Obsequens 28) and 124 (Obsequens 31).

Gymnasium Neronis (Fig. 87): part of the Thermae Neronianae (q.v.), together with which it is said to have been dedicated in A.D. 60 (Suetonius, *Nero* 12.3; Cass. Dio 62.21.1) or 62 (Tacitus, *Ann.* 14.47.3). The former is more likely to be correct, as in 62 the gymnasium burned after being struck by lightning, and the statue of Nero there melted (Tacitus, *Ann.* 15.22), after which it must have been rededicated. Along with the dedication went the establishment of the Neronia, quinquennial games with contests in music, gymnastics, and horse-racing, and for the dedication there was a distribution of oil to the senators and equites. Philostratus (*Vit. Apol.* 4.42) considered it the most wonderful building of its type in Rome.

The passage in Philostratus makes it clear that baths and gymnasium were parts of a single complex. Nero, so far as we know, was the first Roman builder to combine the two harmoniously. Cassius Dio (53.27.1, 54.29.4) calls the Baths of Agrippa *balaneion* and *laconicon*, while those of Nero, Trajan, and Sura he calls *gymnasion* (68.15, 69.4.1). Vitruvius (5.10) gives specifications for baths separate from those for palaestrae (5.11) and says palaestrae are not *italicae consuetudinis*. His specifications for palaestrae include baths, but these are described only very briefly. So Nero's complex as a public institution was probably innovative. Palladio's plan of these baths (Zorzi fig. 96) shows a complex in which the genesis of later bath complexes is very plain. Although this was rebuilt by Alexander Severus and probably much changed and modernized at that time, the central core is probably Neronian. Bathing seems to have been confined to the central block on the south front and the rest given over to other activities, as in the palaestra Vitruvius describes.

183

H

Divus Hadrianus, Templum

(also **Hadrianeum**): a temple to the deified Hadrian, built by Antoninus Pius and dedicated in A.D. 145 (S.H.A. *Ant. Pius* 8.2, *L. Verus* 3.1). It is listed in the *Notitia* in Regio IX between the Column of Marcus Aurelius and the Baths of Alexander Severus and Agrippa. It is now universally recognized to be the temple converted into the stock exchange of Rome, of which substantial remains are visible in Piazza di Pietra and to which reliefs in a number of museums belong. This was formerly erroneously called the Basilica of Neptune (see Basilica Neptuni).

Eleven fluted columns of white Proconnesian marble with Corinthian bases and capitals belonging to the north flank are still standing. These carried a richly carved entablature with a frieze of convex profile and deeply projecting cornice carried on modillions. At present the entablature is much repaired in stucco, and the cornice is so badly restored that three versions appear, of which only the central one resembles the original. The columns are 1.44 m in diameter and 15 m high, and the capitals seem large and deep. The cella wall behind the colonnade is of blocks of peperino left rough, which must have been covered with marble revetment. The traces of clamps suggest that pilasters responded to the colonnade. The existing ceiling is an ancient concrete vault that shows clearly the settings for a lining in plates of marble, presumably richly coffered. The temple is presumed to have been octastyle, peripteral, with fifteen columns on the long sides. It stood on a podium and probably had a stair of approach covering the whole eastern end and a deep pronaos of three bays.

The interior of the squarish cella was barrel-vaulted over a vaulted cellar. The vaulting was of concrete with deep coffering, presumably finished with stucco. An anonymous drawing, in conjunction with a few fragments preserved on the site, shows that the wall crown under the vault was like the entablature of the exterior but was more richly decorated, the architrave being worked with garlands hung in swags and the convex frieze with a serpentine design of acanthus candelabra between reversing S-spirals. Indeed, almost every available surface seems to have been decorated. Presumably there was an engaged order or pilasters mounted on a continuous podium around the interior of the cella.

The face of the temple podium (?) was broken into panels, vertical plinths under the columns bearing allegorical figures of the provinces of the empire in high relief and framed panels under the intercolumniations with simple trophies of armor and weapons at larger scale. Twenty-one of the figures of provinces and nine trophy panels are known; twenty-three survive whole or in part. Sixteen that are well preserved are divided among five collections in Rome and Naples; those most familiar are in the courtyard of the Palazzo dei Conservatori. Identification of the provinces is in some cases disputed; it is conjectured that originally there were twenty-five of these, corresponding to the number of such personifications appearing on the coinage of Antoninus Pius, to which one turns for identification of the attributes and iconography. They are identified especially by costume and weapons; ethnic traits do not appear.

The temple stood in a generous precinct surrounded by a colonnade, parts of which Lanciani discovered in his excavations. The columns were fluted, at least some of them of giallo antico, the order Corinthian, with an entablature related to that of the exterior of the temple. Whether there was a monumental entrance is unknown but seems likely. If the Temple of Matidia (see Matidia, Templum) stood just west of the Temple of Divus Hadrianus, then one might expect monumental entrances at both ends.

J. M. C. Toynbee, *The Hadrianic School* (Cambridge 1934), 152–59; *PBSR* 21 (1953): 123–26 (D. Strong); Nash 1.457–61; A. M. Pais, *Il "podium" del tempio del Divo Adriano a piazza di Pietra in Roma* (Rome 1979); L. Cozza, *Tempio di Adriano* (Rome 1982).

Hecatostylon: a portico of one hundred columns linked by Martial (2.14.9–10) with the Theatrum Pompeii and shown on the Marble Plan (*FUR* pl. 32; Rodriguez pls. 31–32) to lie along the north side of the Porticus Pompeii and Area Sacra di Largo Argentina. It appears to have been a double colonnade facing north, the inner aisle raised a step above the outer and with more numerous columns, but not twice as many. In the outer aisle the columns seem to have stood in the middle of the aisle, with a cantilevered roof projecting beyond them. Along the back wall opened occasional large semicircular exedras with lines of columns separating them from the portico. Although conjoined with the Porticus Pompeii, it did not function together with these and was probably entirely separate (as Martial implies). If anything, it belonged rather with the Thermae Agrippae (q.v.), but the relationship is not clear. It burned in A.D. 247 (Hieron. *a. Abr.* 2263).

Hülsen's (HJ 532–33) likening of this to the so-called Pecile of Villa Adriana at Tivoli is mistaken, because were the central line a wall rather than a step, the southern half would become a cryptoporticus, and the colonnade on this side would cease to have any function.

Martial (3.19.1–2) associated the Hecatostylon with a plantation of plane trees in which bronze animals, including a bear, were displayed. This might be the Porticus Pompeii, where we know there were plane trees (Propertius 2.32.11–13), but the implication is rather that it was a park north of the Hecatostylon, a *nemus* surrounding the Stagnum Agrippae (q.v.).

BullCom 82 (1970–71): 7–9 (G. Marchetti Longhi).

Hercules (Signum): a statue on the Capitoline, near the Temple of Isis and Serapis (see Isis et Serapis in Capitolio). See Cass. Dio 42.26.2.

Hercules, Templum (1): a temple of Hercules outside the Porta Collina, the farthest point to which Hannibal advanced in his march on Rome in 211 (Livy 26.10.3). Two inscriptions (*CIL* 6.284 = *ILS* 11, 30899 = *ILS* 3423), one found near Via Tiburtina, the other from an uncertain place on the Esquiline, have been associated with this temple, but without sufficient reason. Because Hannibal had made camp by the Anio 3 miles from the city, the Temple of Hercules must have been relatively close to the gate, but nothing further is known about it.

Hercules, Templum (2): found on the site later occupied by Teatro Apollo on the left bank of the Tiber near Ponte Sant'Angelo (Pons Aelius), remains of a small round columnar building with two capitals in the form of an animal's skin (*BullCom* 20 [1892]: 175–78 [F. Azzurri]; A. Giuliani, *Museo Nazionale Romano: Le sculture,* 1.1 [Rome 1979], nos. 197, 198), while a third capital is in the Musei del Vaticano (Galleria dei Candelabri no. 100). With these was found a base beautifully decorated with bucrania and plane-tree branches, fine work of the Augustan period (A. Giuliani, *Museo Nazionale Romano: Le sculture,* 1.1 [Rome 1979], no. 162). The identification of this as a temple of Hercules is doubtful, and some authorities have preferred to ascribe it to Liber.

E. La Rocca, *La riva a mezzaluna* (Rome 1984), 63–64.

Hercules Cubans: listed by the regionary catalogues in Regio XIV. The *Curiosum* adds the unusual note in an interpolation: *Herculem sub terram medium cubantem sub quem plurimum auri positum est.* In 1889 just east of the Viale di Trastevere, a little more than halfway from the line of the Aurelian Walls to the Stazione di Trastevere, was found the ruin of a sanctuary of Hercules arranged in a gallery of an ancient quarry, the roof of which had collapsed. The focus of the shrine was a niche surmounted by a pediment hewn in the tufa. The tympanum was decorated with a club between skyphoi, and in the niche were parts of at least two statuettes of Hercules, one a rough tufa carving showing him reclining on a couch with a tripod table in front of him, on which he rests a cup. This has been generally accepted as showing Hercules Cubans. Before the niche was a table of brick, its front decorated with reliefs in stucco, perhaps representing dancers. Before this were two small altars, one of tufa and one of travertine. The lintel of the niche and the altars bore inscriptions showing that L. Domitius Permissus had dedicated them (*CIL* 6.30891, 30892). A quantity of material belonging to the sanctuary was recovered, notably seven fine marble busts of charioteers mounted on herms.

NSc 1889, 243–47 (R. Lanciani); Nash 1.462–70

and earlier literature cited there. The material from the sanctuary is preserved in the Museo Nazionale Romano (Museo Nazionale delle Terme).

Hercules (Magnus) Custos, Aedes: a temple at or near the west end of the Circus Flaminius built in accordance with instruction from the Sibylline Books and dedicated on 4 June (Ovid, *Fast.* 6.209–12; Degrassi 465). Filocalus and Polemius Silvius add that on this day there were *Ludi in Minucia*. Because the Porticus Minucia Vetus (q.v.) is now known to lie at some distance from the Circus Flaminius, between the Corso Vittorio Emanuele and Via delle Botteghe Oscure, this is puzzling. Ovid ascribes the temple to Sulla; this is often held to be mistaken and that Sulla's work on it must have been only a restoration. In 218 B.C. a *supplicatio* was decreed *ad aedem Herculis* (Livy 21.62.9), and in 189 a statue of the god was installed in his temple by decree of the decemvirs (Livy 38.35.4), and these are thought to have been in this temple. But the association of Hercules with the Ara Maxima (see Herculis Invicti Ara Maxima) is so strong that it is difficult to imagine that there was no temple in its vicinity older than this one *in Circo Flaminio*. The Forum Boarium was always the chief seat of his worship. See also Hercules Musarum.

Although most buildings on the Circus Flaminius seem to have been first built in the second century, Domitius Ahenobarbus was able to add the Temple of Neptune (see Neptunus, Aedes) in the time of the triumvirate, and there is nothing inherently improbable in the notion that Sulla might have built a temple of Hercules (see Hercules Sullanus), but that it should have been built following consultation of the Sibylline Books and with the epithet Custos implies that it was built in response to a crisis, and about such an occasion we have no information. If Coarelli's identification of the Temple of Bellona (see Bellona, Aedes) as that just east of the Temple of Apollo Medicus is correct, as seems almost certain, we must look for that of Hercules Custos at *altera pars Circi* under Monte de'Cenci. About the architectural form of the temple and the cult nothing is known.

Hercules Fundan(i)us, Templum: a temple the location of which in Rome rests on a single inscription (*CIL* 6.311 = *ILS* 3449) of uncertain provenience. The inscription is on the base of a small bronze dedication. In the literary record we have a note of Porphyrion on Horace, *Epist.* 1.1.4, mentioning a gladiator's dedication of his weapons to Hercules Fundanus and occurrence in the life of Emperor Tacitus (S.H.A. *Tacitus* 17.2) of a miraculous change of the color of wine in a libation *in templo Herculis Fundani*. These combined seem good evidence for

the existence of at least a modest temple, but the meaning of the epithet is obscure. We know of no important cult of Hercules at the Auruncan town of Fundi in southern Latium (cf. Roscher 1.3007 [R. Peter]), and there was a Lacus Fundani (q.v.) in Rome.

Herculis Invicti Ara Maxima: an altar in the Forum Boarium, the oldest and most venerable cult center of Hercules in Rome. It was supposed to have been built following the hero's victory over Cacus and is in one version ascribed to Evander in recognition of the divinity of Hercules (Servius *ad Aen.* 8.269; Macrobius, *Sat.* 3.11.7, 12.4; Tacitus, *Ann.* 15.41; Strabo 5.3.3. [230]), in a second to Hercules himself (Livy 1.7.10–11; Ovid, *Fast.* 1.581; Propertius 4.9.67–68; Solinus 1.10), and in yet a third to companions of Hercules left behind in Italy (Macrobius, *Sat.* 3.6.17). Its site is given most precisely by Servius *ad Aen.* 8.269: *post ianuas Circi Maximi* (behind the carceres). It was within the pomerium of Romulus and was one of the turning points for that (Tacitus, *Ann.* 12.24), from which the line ran to the altar of Consus. Despite our precise knowledge, no remains of it have been certainly identified, and our sources stress that the epithet Maxima alluded to its importance rather than to its size. If a picture in Pompeii (VI xvi 15; *NSc* 1908, 78 fig. 8 [A. Sogliano]) is correctly identified as showing Hercules taking leave of Evander and depicts the altar at all accurately, it was rather small, and Tacitus's inclusion of it (*Ann.* 15.41) in the list of monuments utterly destroyed in the fire of Nero is probably correct. It must have stood between the Temple of Hercules Victor (see Hercules Victor, Aedes [1]) and the carceres of the circus, but nearer the latter.

After the fire of Nero it was restored, for Festus (270L) and Servius (*ad Aen.* 8.271) speak of it as existing in their time. A series of inscriptions on altars to Hercules Invictus offered by praetores urbani in the second to fourth centuries (*CIL* 6.312–19 = *ILS* 3402–9) was discovered near the round temple identified as that of Hercules Victor when it was excavated and destroyed during the pontificate of Pope Sixtus IV. These may have belonged to either the temple or the altar, or even to one of several other shrines of Hercules nearby (cf. Varro, *Ling.* 6.54). Strabo (5.3.3. [230]) speaks of a *temenos*, Solinus (1.10) of a *consaeptum sacellum*, and Plutarch (*Quaest. Rom.* 90) of *periboloi*, so an area around the altar was marked off in some way. A statue of Hercules Triumphalis in the Forum Boarium ascribed to Evander (Pliny, *HN* 34.33) probably stood in the open air, but not within the precinct of the altar.

Remains of a large platform of large blocks of

Anio tufa under the rear half of the church of S. Maria in Cosmedin and extending for a considerable distance beyond the church have repeatedly been associated with the Ara Maxima, most recently by Coarelli. These show no architectural form, but reached the considerable height of 3.28–4.17 m. The overall measurements of the platform exceeded 21.70 m in length and 31.50 m in width. It is clearly not temple foundations but a solid mass. But attractive as the notion that this is the base of the Ara Maxima may be, it is poorly located to be a turning point in the pomerium of Romulus; that seems to call for a location toward the middle of Piazza Bocca della Verità. And the construction in large blocks of Anio tufa seems to suit neither the original construction nor a rebuilding in the second half of the first century after Christ.

R. Krautheimer, W. Frankl, and S. Corbett, *Corpus Basilicarum Christianarum Romae*, 2.2 (Rome 1962), 288–89; Coarelli 1988, 61–77.

Hercules Invictus (H)esychianus, Aedes: known from an inscription and dedicated by Hierus and Asylus, slaves of Ti. Claudius Livianus, praefectus praetorio under Trajan (*RendPontAcc* 1 [1921–23]: 89–94 [O. Marucchi]; *NSc* 1924, 67–69 [O. Marucchi]). The epithet may be explained by another inscription, a dedication to Hercules by M. Claudius Hesychus, possibly a freedman of Livianus. It was probably a small affair, and its location is entirely unknown.

Hercules Musarum, Aedes: a temple listed in the *Notitia* in Regio IX and located precisely by fragments of the Marble Plan (*FUR* pl. 29; Rodriguez pl. 23). It fronted southwest on the Circus Flaminius and lay just northwest of the Porticus Octaviae. M. Fulvius Nobilior created it after his campaigns in Ambracia in 189 B.C. and probably after his triumph in 187. He is said to have made the choice of the divinity after learning in Greece of Hercules Musagetes, the hero as companion and leader of the Muses (*Panegyrici Latini* 9[4].7–8 = Eumenius, *Pro Instaur. Scholis* 7–8). Cicero (*Arch.* 27) says Fulvius Nobilior devoted his *manubiae* to the construction, but Eumenius says it was built *ex pecunia censoria*. In the temple were statues of the nine Muses from Ambracia by an unknown artist and one of Hercules playing the lyre (Pliny, *HN* 35.66; Ovid, *Fast.* 6.797–812). These are believed to have been the models for the Muses and Hercules that Q. Pomponius Musa put on his coins (*B. M. Coins, Rom. Rep.* pl. 45.13–23; Crawford 410/1–10). An inscription found in the vicinity (*CIL* 6.1307 = *ILS* 16) may have come from the pedestal of one of the statues: *M. Fulvius M. f. Ser. n. Nobilior cos. Ambracia cepit.*

In the temple Fulvius Nobilior also put a small bronze shrine of the Muses supposed to have dated from the time of Numa, which had been housed in the Temple of Honos et Virtus after having been struck by lightning (Servius *ad Aen.* 1.8), and set up a copy of the fasti with explanatory commentary (Macrobius, *Sat.* 1.12.16; cf. Varro, *Ling.* 6.33).

The temple was restored by L. Marcius Philippus, the stepfather of Octavian, in 29 B.C. and enclosed in the Porticus Philippi (Suetonius, *Aug.* 29.5). The day of dedication was 30 June (Ovid, *Fast.* 6.797–812; Degrassi 475). The temple is regularly called Herculis Musarum Aedes, but Servius (*ad Aen.* 1.8) has Aedes Herculis et Musarum. Servius also says that the temple first existed as a temple of Hercules and only became the Temple of Hercules Musarum after Fulvius transferred Numa's bronze aedicula to it, in which case it might be the temple of Hercules of Livy 21.62.9 and 38.35.4. However, it is certainly not the same as the Temple of Hercules Custos (see Hercules Custos, Aedes).

The temple appears to have been round, like many temples of Hercules, raised on a podium with frontal approach and projecting pronaos. Other particulars of the architecture are not clear.

Nash 1.471; *AJA* 81 (1977): 355–61 (L. Richardson); *BdA* 66 (1981): 1–58 (M. T. Marabini Moevs); *AnalRom*, suppl. 10 (1983): 93–104 (F. Castagnoli); *Roma, archeologia nel centro* (1985), 2.376–84 (R. A. Gianfrotta).

Hercules Olivarius: a mysterious monument listed by the regionary catalogues in Regio XI. An inscription found in 1895 on a base that seems designed for a recumbent figure reads:]o Olivarius opus Scopae Minoris (*CIL* 6.33936 = *ILS* 5483). This was discovered near the round temple in the Forum Boarium. The epithet Olivarius is not easy to explain; oil dealers would more naturally look to Minerva as their patron divinity. The evidence is insufficient to make the connection that Coarelli would like: Hercules Victor (called Olivarius) ad Portam Trigeminam, which he would then identify as the round temple by the Tiber (Coarelli 1988, 92–103). See also Roscher 1.2960 (R. Peter).

Hercules Pompeianus, Aedes: a temple of Hercules in archaic style, araeostyle with a spreading wooden roof decorated with terracotta or bronze sculptures (Vitruvius 3.3.5). It stood *ad Circum Maximum* and contained a statue of Hercules by Myron (Pliny, *HN* 34.57). The temple was built, or restored, by Pompey the Great, and his name was then attached to it. The dedication day has been supposed to be 12 August, but the notice in the fasti is for Hercules Invictus ad Circum Maximum without any additional epithet, so it must be rather a celebration at the Ara Maxima that is meant (Degrassi 493–94). In view of the multiplication of temples of Hercules in this vicinity, one would like to be able to combine this with another, but the evidence is against it.

No remains of this temple have been identified. It has been supposed that remains of a temple of the republican period that survived in ruined state under the eastern part of the church of S. Maria in Cosmedin but were completely destroyed in the time of Hadrian I, when he rebuilt and enlarged the church (HCh 327–28 with bibliography), might belong to this temple, but this is very uncertain. It is natural to suppose that the temple was near the Ara Maxima, but it could have stood anywhere in the vicinity of the circus.

Coarelli 1988, 77–84.

Hercules Primigenius: a place designation in two sepulchral inscriptions (*CIL* 6.7655 = *ILS* 7707 and *CIL* 6.9645) and a cippus found in situ in Piazza Fiume (*CIL* 6.30907 = *ILS* 3433) evidently a compital shrine (*CAR* 3-A, 22–23 p. 23). The epithet is proper to the Fortuna of Praeneste, and its application to Hercules is curious (cf. Roscher 1.2968–69 [R. Peter]). The epitaph of an ivory worker from the same locale is especially interesting (S. Panciera, *La collezione epigrafica dei Musei Capitolini* [Rome 1987], no. 32). It is probably a compital shrine that is in question, but one cannot go further.

Hercules Sullanus: listed by the regionary catalogues in Regio V, after the second cohort of the Vigiles and before the Horti Pallantiani in the *Notitia*, therefore possibly on the ancient Via Labicana. Because the Forum Esquilinum (q.v.) was the scene of a major battle between Sulla and the Marians in 88 B.C., Sulla may have erected some sort of memorial of that occasion, stopping short of a victory monument (cf. Hercules Custos), but as there is no other record of this, its nature is uncertain, and it may have been no more than a statue. However, because the Rivus Herculaneus of the Aqua Marcia (q.v.) branches from the main conduit southeast of Porta Tiburtina *(post Hortos Pallantianos)* and then runs across the plateau of the Esquiline, first southwest and then south, there may be a connection between that and Hercules Sullanus. The name has no other obvious explanation. Cf. Roscher 1.2921–22 (R. Peter).

Hercules Triumphalis: a statue of the divinity in the Forum Boarium, ascribed by tradition to Evander (Pliny, *HN* 34.33), which on the occasion of a triumph was dressed in triumphal costume. One presumes the figure was primitive and essentially nude, because it seems incongruous to drape an archaic Hercules wearing a tunic and a lion's skin in a toga. We do not know where the statue stood, but it must have been somewhere along the route of the triumph.

Hercules Victor, Aedes (1): a temple of Hercules in the Forum Boarium distinguished from another temple of Hercules Victor ad Portam Trigeminam (Macrobius, *Sat.* 3.6.10). It is therefore believed to be the same as the round temple of Hercules in the Forum Boarium (Livy 10.23.3). In Festus (282L) we find the corrupt note: *Pudicitiae signum in Foro Bovario est, ubi familiana aedisset Herculis,* for which Scaliger proposed the correction: *ubi Aemiliana aedis est Herculis,* and Mommsen: *ubi familia edisset* (i.e., *sedisset*) *Herculis,* and now Palmer: *ubi Flaminini aedis est Herculis.* This has been presumed to be a rebuilding of the temple that Masurius Sabinus (*ap. Macrob. Sat.* 3.6.11) reported was founded by the merchant Octavius Hersennus following a dream (cf. Servius *ad Aen.* 8.363; *Panegyrici Latini* 10.13.5). In this temple was a painting by the poet Pacuvius (Pliny, *HN* 35.19), and neither flies nor dogs would enter it (Pliny, *HN* 10.79; Solinus 1.10–11; cf. Plutarch, *Quaest. Rom.* 90). Solinus gives the explanation that it was because of the lingering scent of the hero's club, which he left in the entrance when preparing to make an offering. This would, of course, not suit the temple of Hersennus but would be appropriate to the Temple of Hercules Victor ad Portam Trigeminam. However, it is clearly a fantastic invention and told of the temple *in Foro Boario.*

Because there were two temples of Hercules Victor in Rome, one ad Portam Trigeminam, the other ad Forum Boarium, they must have been repeatedly confused. Because the temple ad Portam Trigeminam had claim to a place in the state religion, however tenuous, that ad Forum Boarium is more likely that which the merchant M. Octavius Hersennus built.

It was probably in this temple that the cult image appeared *capite operto;* that is, with the mask of the lion's skin pulled over his head in a cap, giving rise to the explanation that Hercules was worshiped in the Greek fashion with the head uncovered because no one should copy the god's dress (Servius *ad Aen.* 3.407 and 8.288; Macrobius, *Sat.* 3.6.17). Because this custom was of great antiquity, we can presume that this was a late archaic statue and Hercules was shown wearing the lion's skin belted at the waist with the paws along the thighs like a tail coat, as in the group of Hercules and Minerva from the Area Sacra di Sant'Omobono.

Under Pope Sixtus IV (1471–1484), a round temple near the church of S. Maria in Cosmedin, between Piazza Bocca della Verità and Via dell'Ara Massima, was excavated and dismantled, but later (1503–1513) Baldassare Peruzzi made a reconstruction drawing of it (Nash 1.473). This shows a tholus with a peripteral colonnade of Tuscan order and cella of ashlar masonry with a tall door with heavy lintel flanked by a small window with similar lintel. It stands on a platform of two steps running all around and is roofed with a low dome in part stepped like the lower portion of the dome of the Pantheon. The roofing can be presumed to be invented. At the same time a gilded bronze statue of Hercules, nude, with the apples of the Hesperides, was found. This is now dated to the second century after Christ and displayed in the Palazzo dei Conservatori (Helbig⁴ 2.1804). And together with this were found the inscriptions of the praetors on dedications to Hercules Invictus (CIL 3.312–19 = ILS 3402–9). Although technically this temple stood well within the Forum Boarium, it might also be described as in Circo Maximo but not, given two temples and a choice, ad Portam Trigeminam; it does not fit clearly any one of the place designations we are given. However, if the medallion of Antoninus Pius shown in Roscher 1.2289 (= Banti II–3, 79 no. 94) is the temple ad Portam Trigeminam, it is certainly not that temple, nor is it the araeostyle Hercules Pompeianus. This leaves only the temple in Foro Boario as a possibility. If it were the only round temple available, we could accept it, although perhaps with reservations. But the existence of the round marble temple by the Tiber complicates the question, because it is a temple near which was found a dedication almost certainly to Hercules. These factors combine to make it the more attractive choice for the temple in question.

On the problems surrounding the worship of Hercules in the Forum Boarium and ad Circum Maximum, see Roscher 1.2901–20 (R. Peter); Jordan 1.2.477–83; Lugli 1946, 574–89; Nash 1.472–74; F. Rakob and W. D. Heilmeyer, *Der Rundtempel am Tiber in Rom* (Mainz 1973); Coarelli 1988, 60–103; *JRA* 3 (1990): 234–40 (R. E. A. Palmer).

Hercules Victor (also called **Invictus**), **Aedes** (2): a temple of Hercules ad Portam Trigeminam (Macrobius, *Sat.* 3.6.10; Servius *ad Aen.* 8.363). The epithet is Invictus in the Fasti Allifani, but Victor in the Fasti Antiates Maiores and our other sources. The day of dedication was 13 August, the day after celebrations to Hercules Invictus, presumably at the Ara Maxima, because it is specified ad Circum Maximum (cf. Degrassi 493–96). Probably the temple was associated with the altar of Iuppiter Inventor (see Iuppiter Inventor, Ara), also located ad Portam Trigeminam and supposed to have been consecrated by Hercules on his recovery of the cattle of Geryon

stolen by Cacus. What the physical relationship may have been we are not told. A medallion of Antoninus Pius (Roscher 1.2289 = Banti II–3, 79 no. 94) seems to show Hercules sacrificing on the altar of Iuppiter Inventor in front of a tetrastyle temple façade that might be the temple in question.

Hercules Victor, Aedes (3): according to an inscription in Saturnians, a temple vowed by L. Mummius in 145 B.C. and dedicated in 142 following his triumph over the Achaeans (CIL 6.331 = ILS 20). The inscription was found on the Caelian used as building material in a wall behind the Lateran hospital (S. Salvatore), and another found near SS. Quattro Coronati (CIL 6.30888 = ILS 6081) may refer to the same temple, which would seem to have been in this vicinity. Nothing further is known about it, but it seems to have been the most important of Mummius's monuments.

Phoenix 42 (1988): 309–33 (A. Ziolkowski).

Hermaeum: the name given to a *diaeta* to which Claudius withdrew in the confusion attending the assassination of Caligula, and from which he made his way to a balcony next-door (*solarium:* Suetonius, *Claud.* 10.1). It is mentioned only on this one occasion and possibly in two inscriptions (CIL 6.8663, 9949). A *diaeta* in this period seems to have been especially a room or building for use in summer (cf. Pliny, *Epist.* 2.17.15). This one might have received its name from the use of herms in its decoration. It was somewhere in the Domus Tiberiana, at this time much enlarged by additions, but greater precision is impossible.

Hippodromus Palatii: see **Domus Augustiana.**

Holovitreum, Templum: known only from the *Mirabilia* (Jordan 2.642; VZ 3.63), the palatium (palace) of Chromatius, probably Agrestius Chromatius, praefectus urbi ca. A.D. 248, *ad Sanctum Stephanum in Piscina*, remains of which, especially some columns of verde antico, were found in 1741 when that church was rebuilt (Armellini 393; HCh 482). It was destroyed shortly before 1870. It was on Via dei Banchi Vecchi, almost opposite S. Lucia del Gonfalone, and appears on Nolli's map of Rome, no. 660. According to the *Mirabilia*, it got its name from mosaics of glass and gold in which there was an "astronomy" with all the constellations of the heavens depicted.

Honos, Aedes: probably the oldest temple of Honos in Rome, *extra Portam Collinam*. Cicero (*Leg.* 2.58) relates that there was a tradition that there was an altar there and when, near this, a metal plate was discovered on which was written DOMINA HONORIS, on that account a temple was built on the site. Because there were many burials in the vicinity, these were removed on the grounds that a *locus publicus* could not be bound by *religio privata*. An archaic inscription with a dedication to Honos (*CIL* 6.3692 = 30913 = *ILS* 3794 = *ILLRP* 157) was found under the east wing of the Ministero delle Finanze, evidently in its original location, and another to Virtus may have belonged with it (*CIL* 6.3735 = 31061).

Honos et Virtus, Aedes (1): a double temple said by Cicero (*Nat. D.* 2.61) to have been founded by Q. Maximus during the Ligurian War as a single temple dedicated to Honos; the dedication day was 17 July (Degrassi 483–84). The builder seems to have been Q. Fabius Maximus Verrucosus, afterward Cunctator, and the date 234 B.C. But Cicero also says that it was built many years before M. Claudius Marcellus attempted to rededicate the temple in 208. So perhaps Cicero is mistaken about the Ligurian War, and the Fabius meant is Q. Fabius Maximus Rullianus (or Rullus), great-grandfather of Verrucosus, who triumphed twice over the Samnites and once over the Etruscans in 322–296 B.C. (cf. [Aur. Vict.,] *De Vir. Ill.* 32, who records that when Rullianus inaugurated the Transvectio Equitum he made it start from this temple). In 222 B.C., after the Battle of Clastidium, M. Claudius Marcellus vowed a temple to Honos et Virtus and renewed his vow after the capture of Syracuse. He then attempted to fulfill this by refurbishing Maximus's temple and rededicating it to Honos et Virtus in 208, but the pontifices forbade this on the grounds that the two could not occupy the same cella. Marcellus then restored the Temple of Honos and added a new cella for Virtus, making it a double shrine, which his son dedicated in 205 (Livy 25.40.1–3, 27.25.7–9, 29.11.13; Val. Max. 1.1.8; Plutarch, *Marcel.* 28.1). It stood in Regio I *ad Portam Capenam,* just inside the gate (Livy 26.32.4: *in vestibulo urbis*), and originally contained many works of art dedicated by Marcellus out of the spoils of Syracuse (Cicero, *Rep.* 1.21, *Verr.* 2.4.121; Livy 26.32.4; Asconius *ad Cic. Pis.* 44 [Stangl 18]), many of which had disappeared by Livy's day (25.40.3). It also for a time sheltered the bronze aedicula of the Muses, supposed to date from the time of Numa, after this was struck by lightning (Servius *ad Aen.* 1.8). This had earlier probably stood above the spring of the Camenae. In ca. 187 B.C. M. Fulvius Nobilior removed it to the Temple of Hercules Musarum (see Hercules Musarum, Aedes).

According to Asconius (*ad Cic. Pis.* 44 [Stangl

18]), M. Claudius Marcellus (cos. 166, 155 and 152) erected statues of himself, his father (cos. 194), and his grandfather (cos. 222, 215, 214, 210, 208) inscribed III MARCELLI NOVIES COSS in the precinct of the temple. In 19 B.C. an altar of Fortuna Redux commemorating Augustus's return from the East was dedicated near the temple, probably in the precinct (Augustus, *RG* 29). Vespasian restored the temple, perhaps after damage or destruction in the fire of Nero, and at that time the artists Cornelius Pinus and Attius Priscus decorated it (Pliny, *HN* 35.120). It is last mentioned in the regionary catalogues of the fourth century.

AJA 82 (1978): 240–46 (L. Richardson).

Honos et Virtus (**Mariana**, Vitruvius and Val. Max.), **Aedes** (2): a temple that C. Marius built from the spoils of the Cimbri and Teutones. The architect was C. Mucius (Scaevola?, the father of Marius's daughter-in-law), whose work Vitruvius (7 *praef.* 17) praises for the refinements of its design, while he deplores that it was not of marble. It was peripteral sine postico (Vitruvius 3.2.5) and *submissior aliis* (Festus 466–68L) lest it interfere in the taking of public auspices and the augurs oblige Marius to demolish it. It stood on the lower slopes of the Velia near the house of Marius on the Sacra Via (cf. Plutarch, *Marius* 32.1); together these were known as the Monumenta Mariana (Val. Max. 1.7.5).

AJA 82 (1978): 240–46 (L. Richardson).

Hora Quirini: the consort of Quirinus, to whom special honor was paid on 23 August (Degrassi 500–502), presumably in the precinct of Quirinus (see Quirinus, Aedes).

Horologium Solare Augusti (Fig. 42): a large sundial of double-axe design laid out in the Campus Martius west of Via Flaminia.

This covered an area about 160 m wide by 75 m deep in a zone bounded by Piazza del Parlamento and Via dei Prefetti on the south, Via del Giardino Theodoli on the east, Piazza S. Lorenzo in Lucina on the north, and Via della Lupa on the west. It was thus loosely connected with the Mausoleum Augusti and the park surrounding this, and more closely connected with the Ara Pacis Augustae, which was almost immediately adjacent to it on the east. For its gnomon a red granite obelisk of Psammetichus II of the sixth century B.C. was brought from Heliopolis in 10 B.C., the first obelisk brought to Rome (see Obeliscus Augusti). It was surmounted by a gilded bronze sphere, presumably, like others, crowned with a short spire. The inscription on the base (*CIL*

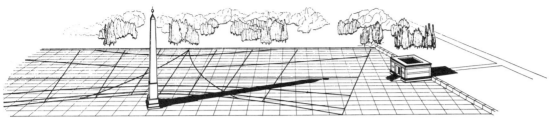

Figure 42
Horologium Augusti,
Bird's-eye View,
Showing Relation to
Ara Pacis Augustae and
Via Lata (Flaminia)

6.702 = *ILS* 91) describes it as a dedication to Sol. Pliny (*HN* 36.72–73) says that the design of the sundial was the work of the mathematician Novius Facundus, so worked out that the length of the shadow at noon on the winter solstice corresponded exactly to the width of the pavement. Pliny also says that for thirty years before he wrote the readings had been inaccurate, due either to a shift of the obelisk in an earthquake or flood, or a settling of the base, although the footing was supposed to be as deep as the obelisk was high.

Soundings at strategic points in 1979–1981 brought to light under the building at Via del Campo Marzio no. 48 a portion of the western half of the meridian strip of the dial, preserving the Greek inscriptions *parth*[*enos*] and [*kri*]*os*, [*le*]*on* and *taur*[*os*], and the notations *etesioi pauontai* before *parth*[*enos*] and *therous arche* in the middle of *taur*[*os*]. On the other side of a central channel may have been inscribed *September* and *Aprilis*, *Augustus* and *Maius*, *etesiae cessant* and *aestatis initium*. The letters are of bronze, large and handsome, with serifs and a broken-barred A, inlaid in blocks of travertine about 0.40 m thick. They lie on either side of a line marked by crossbars to show the lengthening and shortening of the shadow on individual days. This was discovered at a height of 1.60 m above the level of the Augustan pavement, known from the Ara Pacis Augustae and confirmed by soundings that found its *rudus* at various points in the area. They must belong to a "Domitianic" remodeling of the dial to restore it to accuracy, but the letters appear to have been reused from the original Augustan installation. Later, perhaps not before the beginning of the third century, a basin or euripus lined with excellent opus signinum was installed over the meridian strip of the "Domitianic" dial, using it as a foundation and so preserving it. This is mysterious and requires further investigation.

RömMitt 83 (1976): 319–65 (E. Buchner), 87 (1981): 355–73 (E. Buchner); *RendPontAcc* 51–52 (1978–80): 195–212 (E. Rodriquez Almeida), 53–54 (1980–82): 331–45 (E. Buchner); E. Buchner, *Die Sonnenuhr des Augustus* (Mainz 1982); *CEFR* 98 (1987): 687–712 (F. Rakob).

Horreum, Cella, Portus: A *horreum* was a storeroom in a warehouse, originally and always especially for grain, but increasingly used for any sort of goods, and the complexes of horrea in Rome served as great bazaars (cf, e.g., *CIL* 6.9972, 10026, 14.3958). The earliest of them that we hear of are the Horrea Sulpicia (Horace, *Car.* 4.12.18), which belonged to Galba's family and were rebuilt by him as the vast Horrea Galbae close to the Emporium; presumably they were first constructed soon after the Emporium moved to this stretch of the riverbank about the beginning of the first century B.C. In their present form they are entirely imperial and show the characteristics of this type of building. They are arranged in long narrow rectangles around large arcaded or colonnaded courtyards, banks of uniform barrel-vaulted chambers opening only on the portico, although sometimes there are banks back-to-back that open in opposite directions. There is often a single entrance to the courtyard, although there may be more, and there are usually several storeys that repeat the same plan exactly. An earlier version of a horrea complex is probably offered by the so-called Porticus Aemilia between the Horrea Galbae and the river. Horrea tend to be plastered, but not painted, and the architecture of the courtyards, while often pleasantly finished, emphasizes strength, security, and utility. There were horrea in every part of the city; the regionary catalogues provide a count of them for each regio, but the small numbers, usually about twenty, are not informative.

Cellae seem to have been warehouses much like horrea complexes, but they are not listed in the regionary catalogues. We hear of seven of these in Rome, all only from inscriptions, three of them in the Transtiberim. Like horrea they are known by the name of their builder or owner and do not inform us about what was dealt in, except in the case of the Cellae Vinariae Nova et Arruntiana and the Cella Vinaria Massae. Here the use of the singular for a complex as large as a horrea complex, plus the fact that for the Cella Nigriana the inscription is for a dispensator who puts a dolium to either side of his inscription (*CIL* 6.31065), while for the Cella Saeniana the inscription is for a dedication to Liber Pater (*AE* 1971.38), suggests that cellae were all warehouses exclusively for wine. The architecture of the one that has come to light seems to have been very much like that of horrea; it was in the Transtiberim on the bank of the Tiber in the gardens of Villa Farnesina, a long rectangular courtyard with Doric colonnades of travertine surrounded by barrel-vaulted chambers. A schola of the negotiantes here was adjacent.

A *portus* was an unroofed yard, simply an enclosed place to which goods were brought and from which they were taken (Ulpian, *Dig.* 50.16.59), the term being related to *angiportus*. Consequently most of those we hear about were brickyards, but we do hear of a portus vinarius, also called portus vinarius lagonaris (*CIL* 6.9189, 9090, 37807), which also had negotiantes, and presumably such goods as marble and lumber were sold from portus rather than anything else. The term must be very old, and it is surprising that one does not hear more about these.

G. Rickman, *Roman Granaries and Store Buildings* (Cambridge 1971); *CEFR* 98 (1987) 235–49 (R. Etienne).

Horrea Agrippiana: listed in Regio VIII by the regionary catalogues and discovered under the northwest slope of the Palatine between the Clivus Victoriae and Vicus Tuscus, a trapezoidal complex narrowing as the streets flanking it approached one another, with a series of shoplike chambers around the periphery opening inward toward a courtyard. It lay immediately behind Domitian's vestibule complex of the Domus Tiberiana (sometimes called "Templum Novum Divi Augusti"). The identification is assured by the discovery in the center of the courtyard of a sacellum with an altar with an inscription recording the erection of a statue of the Genius Horreorum Agrippianorum. In front of this was a fountain. The original Agrippan construction was in opus quadratum of tufa with pavements in flags of travertine. Above this a Domitianic rebuilding was faced with brick and opus mixtum vittatum. The courtyard seems to have combined columns and arcading with an engaged order, the order being simplified Corinthian in travertine. Presumably the

building was multistoreyed from the beginning. At a later date the courtyard was surrounded by small shops of lighter construction than the outer ring, which also faced inward. The sacellum of the Genius is second century, and other construction is still later. Inscriptions of *vestiarii de Horreis Agrippianis* (*CIL* 6.9972, 10026, 14.3958; *ILS* 7571, 7572) give a clue to the sort of goods sold here.

For many years it was believed that the Horrea Agrippiana were shown on fragment no. 42 of the Marble Plan (*FUR* pl. 33; Rodriguez pl. 33), despite discrepancies between the building shown and the actual remains. This was chiefly because a street labeled Clivus Victoriae also appears in roughly correct relationship to the horrea. G. Gatti (*FUR* 1.110) first expressed doubts about the assignment, and Rodriguez was able to relocate the fragment correctly on the Caelian between the Temple of Divus Claudius and Porta Capena (Rodriguez 1.65–69); he has now renumbered it 5A.

Nash 1.475–80; G. Rickman, *Roman Granaries and Store Buildings* (Cambridge 1971), 89–97; *ArchCl* 30 (1978): 132–46 (F. Astolfi, F. Guidaboldi, et al.).

Horrea Agrippiniana: known only from an inscription of a *vestiarius* found at Nomentum (*CIL* 14.3958 = *ILS* 7572) and very likely a mistake for the Horrea Agrippiana (q.v.), but possibly a complex of unknown location built by one of the two Agrippinas.

Horrea Aniciana *(Not.)* **Anicetiana** *(Cur.)*: listed in the regionary catalogues in Regio XIII along with the Horrea Galbes (*BullCom* 85 [1976–77]: 159 [R. E. A. Palmer]).

Horrea Caesaris: known only from *CIL* 6.33747 = *ILS* 5914 and *Dig.* 20.4.21.1, so probably another name for the Horrea Galbae.

Horrea Candelaria: known only from a fragment of the Marble Plan (*FUR* pl. 33; Rodriguez pl. 34), which is very uninformative about the architecture of the complex, showing a large rectangular building or enclosure, otherwise featureless. The name suggests wax tapers, and tallow candles may have been sold there, but it does not seem especially suited for this.

G. Rickman, *Roman Granaries and Store Buildings* (Cambridge 1971), 119–20.

Horrea Chartaria: listed by the *Notitia* in Regio IV after Templum Telluris, which was *in Carinis,* and evidently a center of the trade in paper.

Horrea Cornificia: known from a single sepulchral inscription of a *negotiator* (*AE* 1946.230) and of unknown location.

Horrea Faeniana: known from one inscription, *CIL* 6.37796; possibly named for L. Faenius Rufus, praefectus annonae in A.D. 55.

Horrea Galbae (Figs. 35, 43): extensive warehouses in the district known as Praedia Galbana (*CIL* 6.30983 = *ILS* 3840), between the southwest slope of the Aventine and Monte Testaccio, possibly extending as far east as Porta Ostiensis and as far west as the so-called Porticus Aemilia. This was probably part of a suburban villa that had belonged to the family of the Sulpicii Galbae from at least the early first century B.C., when the tomb of Ser. Sulpicius Galba, more likely the consul of 108 B.C. than his father of the same name (cos. 144 B.C.), was erected beside the road in front of the area covered by the complex. These warehouses were probably originally known as Horrea Sulpicia (Horace, *Carm.* 4.12.18; cf. Porphyrion ad loc.) but seem to have got the name Galbae, or a variant of this, after the accession of the princeps (cf. *CIL* 6.30855 = *ILS* 1621). Many variations on the name are known from inscriptions: Galbae (*CIL* 6.9801 = *ILS* 7500), Galbana (*CIL* 6.30983 = *ILS* 3840), Galbiana (*CIL* 6.30855 = *ILS* 1621, *CIL* 6.33906 = *ILS* 7584), Galbes (*CIL* 6.33886 = *ILS* 7539), Galbeses (*CIL* 6.30901 = *ILS* 1622), Galbienses (*CIL* 6.710 = 30817 = *ILS* 4337). Evidently the princeps Galba sacrificed what was left of the property to enlarge the warehouses (Chron. 146) and may also have restored them. There is no date given for their foundation; presumably it will have been well after the building of the tomb, which lies close to the middle of the front of the complex along the road, as it was later developed.

What has come to light in the area and what was shown on the Marble Plan (*FUR* pl. 24; Rodriguez pls. 16–17) indicates that there were three parallel courtyards, long rectangles, each entered by a single principal entrance on axis at a short end, and each surrounded by a bank of uniform chambers, again long rectangles, opening on a travertine colonnade. The courtyard of the northeast unit has a series of other divisions down the middle, which are difficult to read, but Rodriguez suggests a great *lavacrum*. Later the colonnade seems to have been replaced with arcading, if the discrepancy is not simply carelessness on the part of the cutters of the Marble Plan. Another single bank of tabernae tapering at the western end filled the space between the main building and the road and was separated from the main build-

ing by an ample passageway. There may also have been other units. Inscriptions indicate that the personnel of the horrea were organized in three cohortes (Ruggiero, *Diz. Epigr.* 3.979).

These horrea came under imperial control after the principate of Galba. They provided storage for not only the *annona publica* (public grain supply) but also oil and wine and a great variety of foodstuffs, clothing, even marble (*CIL* 6.33886 = *ILS* 7539). The remains that have come to light are walls faced with reticulate and brickwork with sills and similar members of travertine. This work can hardly be older than the middle of the first century after Christ, and large lead pipes bearing inscriptions of Hadrian have also been found.

Nash 1.481–84; G. Rickman, *Roman Granaries and Store Buildings* (Cambridge 1971), 97–104; *RendPontAcc* 50 (1977–78): 9–26 (E. Rodriguez Almeida); Rodriguez 1.102–5.

Horrea Germaniciana: listed by the *Notitia* in Regio VIII, together with the Horrea Agrippiana (q.v.), but omitted by the *Curiosum*. If they were a separate complex, as seems likely, their whereabouts is unknown, but presumably they lay between the Forum Romanum and the Tiber.

Horrea Graminaria: known from a recomposed fragment of the Marble Plan (*FUR* pls. 49, 50, frags. 432, 481; Rodriguez pl. 34). The fragment cannot be located in the city, and too little is shown to give any real indication of the architecture, which may have been very simple. Presumably these were warehouses for fodder for animals, but they cannot have been the only such complex in Rome, although the scale of the inscription suggests they were as large as the Horrea Candelaria (q.v.).

Horrea Leoniana: known from a single inscription (*CIL* 6.237 = *ILS* 3664) and of entirely uncertain location.

Horrea Lolliana: known from a large fragment of the Marble Plan (*FUR* pl. 25; Rodriguez pl. 18). The precise location of this is determined by a large blank area and what appear to be quays along one side of the fragment, which must be the riverfront, and by parts of three finished edges of the plate on which it appears. The complex lay near the lower margin of the map, downstream from the Horrea Galbae and just upstream from modern Ponte Testaccio in an area now covered by the old slaughterhouses. Downstream of it in antiquity were buildings that seem to have been relatively small horrea and a bath complex laid out together with it in an orderly grid, but this

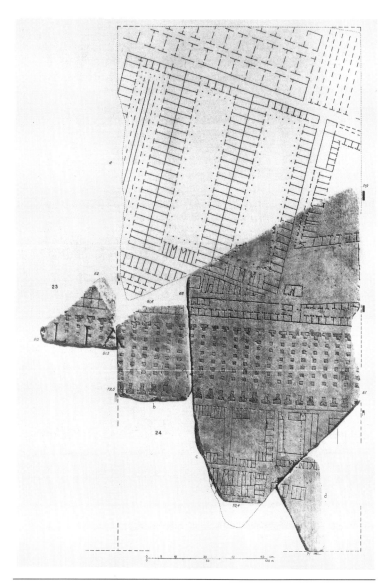

Figure 43
Horrea Galbae and
"Porticus Aemilia,"
Representation on the
Marble Plan

is not shown completely on what survives but seems to have been provided with larger chambers than its companion, those on the front opening both in to the peristyle and out to the exterior, and to have had an extra bank opening to the street behind the horrea. As preserved, there is a single entrance passage from the front to one corner of the peristyle and a stair to an upper storey off another corner. No stair appears connected with the larger peristyle.

The horrea are mentioned in inscriptions: *CIL* 6.4226, 4226a, 4239, 9467; *ILS* 1620). From these it appears that they were imperial property in the time of Claudius.

G. Rickman, *Roman Granaries and Store Buildings* (Cambridge 1971), 109–12.

Horrea Nervae: known from a single sepulchral inscription (*CIL* 6.8681 = 33744 = *ILS* 1627); perhaps the same as the Horrea Caesaris (q.v.) of the lex horreorum found inside the Porta Salaria, not in situ (*CIL* 6.33747 = *ILS* 5914).

Horrea Peduceiana: a hypothetical building proposed for reconstruction of a fragmentary inscription (*CIL* 6.33745) by Henzen and Dessau *(ILS 1626)*. An Ager Peduceianus is mentioned in *CIL* 10.6706 = *ILS* 8217, which seems to have lain outside the city but not far from it, near, if not on, the Via Latina. Cf. Horti Peduceiani.

Horrea Petroniana: known only from two sepulchral inscriptions, one of a slave of Nero (*CIL* 6.3971 = *ILS* 1625), the other of M. Aurelius Xenonianus Aquila, a Bithynian who had a *statio* in these horrea and describes himself as "foremost of the stone merchants" (*IGUR* 2.413). He must have been a dealer in marble, probably especially Proconnesian marble. The horrea in question must therefore be presumed to be in the neighborhood of the Emporium or Marmorata (qq.v.).

Horrea Piperataria: a market that Domitian built in the porticoes north of the Neronian Sacra Via that formed part of the grand approach to the Domus Aurea (Chron. 146). These had been built over an area earlier occupied by rows of shops and a travertine portico, so Domitian may only have been restoring it to its earlier function. Domitian's complex burned in the fire of Commodus, A.D. 191, and after restoration burned again in the fire of Carinus, A.D. 284, after which Maxentius built the Basilica Nova (Basilica Constantini), completed by Constantine after 313, over its ruins. In 1899 the Sacra Via along the Basilica Constantini was excavated to pre-Neronian levels, and the sequence of construction was uncovered. In 1935 excavations under the nave

grid did not mesh with those in the neighborhood of the Horrea Galbae. It seems to have been determined by a major artery running roughly parallel to the river but laid out in straight segments.

The Horrea Lolliana consisted of two large peristyles, the one nearer the river being twice the size of the other. Each is surrounded by banks of chambers, which seem to have varied in size from bank to bank, and a single broad passage connected the two peristyles. The larger peristyle had entrances at the four corners, two to the front and two to the rear, and an extra bank of small chambers opening away from the peristyle onto a passage along the front of the complex. Along the side of this half is a very broad quay with two relatively small stairs down to the river, which does not seem to have communicated directly with the interior. The inner, smaller peristyle of the Basilica Constantini laid bare more of the Horrea Piperataria.

The complex seems to have followed the typical plan of such markets, with parallel courts, or naves, flanked by banks of chambers of uniform size and plan opening to them. It follows the general orientation of the Templum Pacis and, from the evidence of the Marble Plan, seems to have extended as far as its eastern flank (*FUR* pl. 20; Rodriguez pl. 12). In reporting the fire of Commodus, Dio (72.24.1–2 = *Epit.* 73) calls it "the storehouse of Egyptian and Arabian goods"; others have called it "the spice market." But the Sacra Via was traditionally a center of traffic in luxuries of every sort, and we should probably think of it as offering a very wide range of such merchandise.

Nash 1.485–87; G. Rickman, *Roman Granaries and Store Buildings* (Cambridge 1971), 104–6.

Horrea Postumiana: known from the inscriptions on two bricks (*CIL* 15.4 = *ILS* 8667a), one of which was found at Ostia, so it is even uncertain that these horrea were in Rome.

Horrea Seiana: known from inscriptions (*CIL* 6.238 = *ILS* 3665, 9471, 36778, 36786) that show these to have been prominent and extensive. They are not the complex long so identified (see, e.g., PA 263), because the join of another fragment of the Marble Plan now shows the name of that building to have ended]LIA (*FUR* pl. 24; Rodriguez pl. 16). However, they are almost certainly somewhere in the neighborhood of the Emporium.

Horrea Sempronia: mentioned by Festus (370L) as a place where by Gracchan legislation there were storehouses for keeping the public grain supply. These must have been among the oldest such complexes in Rome, older than the Horrea Galbae and probably located somewhere along the river.

Horrea Severiana (?): horrea (?) found under the Ministero della Difesa on the Quirinal, where an amphora with an address painted on the neck seems to have read: *usibus cellari Severi* (*CIL* 15.4807).

Horrea Sulpicia: see **Horrea Galbae.**

Horrea Q. Tinei Sacerdotis: known from an inscription from the church of S. Martino ai Monti on the Esquiline (Oppius) northwest of the Porticus Liviae. Tineus was consul in A.D. 158.

Horrea Umm(idiana): known from an inscription (*CIL* 6.37795) found in excavations at the church of S. Saba on the Aventinus Minor.

Horrea Vespasiani: mentioned by the Chronographer of 354 (Chron. 146) as among the buildings of Domitian, but otherwise unknown.

Hor(rea) Volusiana: mentioned in one inscription (*CIL* 6.9973 = *ILS* 7573), the gravestone of a *vestiarius de hor Volusianis,* so the reference might be to either horrea or horti, but cf. *CIL* 6.7289.

Horta, Naos: a temple of a divinity mentioned by Plutarch (*Quaest. Rom.* 46) as in earlier times having been always kept open. Because this divinity is otherwise unknown and Plutarch admits to there being some doubt and confusion as to whether the name was Horta or Hora, it seems likely that Hora Quirini (q.v.) is meant and the temple in question was a sacellum in the precinct of Quirinus on the Quirinal.

Horti: see **Domus, Insula, Atrium,** etc.

Horti Aciliorum: a villa on the Pincian, the successor to the Horti Luculliani, extending from the vicinity of the church of S. Trinità de'Monti possibly as far as S. Maria del Popolo and back over the crown of the hill into Villa Borghese. To the east it may have extended to Porta Pinciana. The boundaries are in many places uncertain and perhaps varied with time. The Acilii Glabriones bought the villa during the second century after Christ (an Acilius Glabrio was consul in A.D. 91). In the fourth century it belonged to Anicia Faltonia Proba and her husband, Petronius Probus (*CIL* 6.1751, 1754; *ILS* 1265, 1269), and in the fifth it passed to the Gens Pincia. Thereafter, it became imperial property, known as the Domus Pinciana (q.v.). It was unquestionably one of the finest estates in Rome in every way. On the north, west, and east it was bounded by massive works of terracing along the slope of the hill, the line to the east and north being incorporated by Aurelian as part of his defenses of the city and then in part rebuilt. The original structure is faced with opus reticulatum, a series of buttresses connected by arches in two storeys, the piers massive and the whole work admirable for its engineering and construction. The famous Muro Torto is a lower buttress at the north corner faced with opus reticulatum with quoins of tufa blocks (*CAR* 2-A, 16 p. 13). Within the gardens were various buildings and amenities. Just north of S. Trinità de'Monti was a gently curving terrace flanked by straight arcades with large chambers behind them at the top of a series of terraces connected by monumental stairs descending to the plain below. Pirro Ligorio has left a plan of this suggesting that it owed much to the design of the Temple of Fortuna Primigenia at Praeneste and, like it, was crowned by a small round temple (*CAR* 2-E, 24–25 p. 107; Nash

1.488 fig. 599). Excavation has shown this to be largely his invention. A pair of unusual capitals from this complex adorn the stairs to S. Trinità de'Monti. Beneath the modern Casina Valadier was a fishpond divided into two sections and connected with a reservoir created by carving an elaborate series of tunnels in the rock some 80 m long. The belvedere of Villa Medici is built over the ruins of an octagonal pavilion or nymphaeum (called Parnassus). Other remains are scattered along the brow of the hill from the church of the Trinità to S. Maria del Popolo.

Nash 1.488–90; Lugli 1975, 478–79; *CEFR* 98 (1987): 747–61 (H. Broise and V. Jolivet).

Horti Agrippae: a villa in the Campus Martius that Agrippa left in his will to the people of Rome, together with the Thermae Agrippae (q.v.), and provided for their maintenance by giving Augustus certain real estate (Cass. Dio 54.29.4). This tantalizing information requires further explanation. A substantial part of the baths appears to have been built at the same time as the Pantheon, which was finished in 25 B.C. (Cass. Dio 53.27.1); they followed completion of the Saepta Iulia (q.v.), begun twenty years earlier by Julius Caesar, and lay along the Saepta, just to the west of it. Both must have been intended for the use of the public from the beginning. But the Aqua Virgo (q.v.), which was built to supply the Campus Martius and the baths with water, was not completed until 19 B.C., so the baths must have functioned on only a limited scale, perhaps almost entirely as a dry sweat bath, as Dio implies, until that time, and Agrippa may have gone on adding to their refinement and beautification for a number of years (cf. Pliny, *HN* 34.62, 35.26), during which time they remained in his possession and were maintained at his expense. The Stagnum Agrippae and Euripus would have been such embellishments, while between these was a park in which was displayed the famous lion of Lysippus, which Agrippa brought from Lampsacus (Strabo 13.1.19 [590]). Strabo's word, *alsos*, is usually translated as *nemus*, the word used by Tacitus (*Ann.* 15.37) in describing the revels of Nero at the Stagnum (*quantum iuxta nemoris*), but might equally well be rendered *horti*. The area available is bounded by the baths and Pantheon on the east, Hecatostylon on the south, and Thermae Neronianae on the north. On the west the Stadium Domitiani eventually provided a boundary, and probably the nemus never extended into its area. The Hecatostylon (q.v.) was probably another work of Agrippa's and gives the measurement of this side of the complex, while the *platanon* of Martial (3.19.2) adorned with statuary of animals may be the same as the *nemus*.

The word *horti* is, however, usually reserved for a private residence with extensive gardens within the confines of a city, although not necessarily within the pomerium, and the Nemus Thermarum would not suit that definition, because there was, so far as we know, no residence and certainly not likely to have been any. In this case we should look for the Horti Agrippae along the Tiber, where an inscription (*CIL* 6.39087) puts the Euripus and a *piscina* between the Pons Agrippae and the Trigarium. With this location one should probably associate *CIL* 6.29781 = *ILS* 6003: M. AGRIPPAE PRIVAT. ITER, found in the Tiber near Ponte Garibaldi. See also Euripus Virginis.

MEFRA 89 (1977): 807–46, especially 815–20 (F. Coarelli).

Horti Agrippinae: the estate of Agrippina the Elder on the right bank of the Tiber, subsequently inherited by Caligula and then presumably by Nero. Seneca (*Ira* 3.18) records that it came down to the Tiber and was separated from the river by a portico behind which lay a xystus, or tree-lined promenade. Long Christian tradition has it that the martyrs who suffered under Nero for presumed responsibility for the fire of Rome of A.D. 64 were put to death where the basilica of S. Pietro rose over the ruins of the Circus Gaii et Neronis, and this would accord with Tacitus's comment that for their punishment Nero offered his horti and a *circense ludicrum* of singular cruelty (*Ann.* 15.44; cf. 39). Because the Circus Maximus and Domus Transitoria were destroyed in the fire, the Circus Gaii et Neronis and Horti Agrippinae must be intended. It therefore appears that these were very extensive horti, but it is difficult to bound them. The Via Cornelia giving access to the circus may be presumed to have been the northern border and the Tiber and Via Triumphalis the eastern. The others are impossible to fix, and conceivably the whole minor eminence at the northern end of the Janiculan hill as far as the church of S. Onofrio was included.

Horti Alli Faletiani: known only from mention in a single inscription, *CIL* 6.9240.

Horti Anniani: known only from a fifteenth-century copy of an inscription, *CIL* 6.8666.

Horti Antoniani: neighboring, probably contiguous with, the Horti Caesaris on the right bank of the Tiber and bordering on the river (Cass. Dio 47.40.2). *CIL* 6.9991 = *ILS* 7374 (cf. *CIL* 6.9990a) may refer to this property. It is uncertain precisely where these horti were located.

Horti Antonii: see **Horti Pompeiani** (1) and **Horti Scipionis.**

Horti Aquilii Reguli: the estate of the notorious delator, elder contemporary of Pliny the Younger, who describes it (*Epist.* 4.2.5) as being in the Transtiberim, of a very broad extent with vast porticoes and adorned with statues of Regulus himself along the riverbank. Its location is unknown.

Horti Aroniani: in the Transtiberim (*NSc* 1901, 356; cf. *CIL* 6.671 = *ILS* 3543 of the time of Caracalla, *CIL* 6.30808).

Horti Asiatici: see **Horti Luculliani.**

Horti Asiniani: gardens mentioned by Frontinus (*Aq.* 1.21) as being at the end of the Specus Octavianus, the branch of the Anio Vetus constructed by Augustus, which arrived *in regionem Viae Novae.* The Specus Octavianus branched to the south from the main line and can be traced as far as Porta Latina. It is impossible that Frontinus, writing in the time of Trajan, should mean the Via Nova constructed by Caracalla to serve his baths, although clearly he must mean a street in the same general neighborhood. No solution to the confusion suggests itself.

Horti Atticiani: known from a single inscription, *CIL* 6.8667 = *ILS* 1618. The location of these is unknown.

Horti Caesaris (1): an estate of Julius Caesar *ad Portam Collinam,* mentioned by Obsequens (71) in recounting prodigies of 17 B.C., and possibly the property meant by Dio (42.26.3) in recounting prodigies of 47 B.C. It seems very probable that these horti were absorbed into the great Horti Sallustiani (q.v.), but pseudo-Cicero (*in Sall. Crisp. orat.* 19) cannot be adduced as evidence for this. That the property is designated ad Portam Collinam suggests that it was inside the line of the Servian Walls, but, because these were by this time obsolete and in many places dismantled, it may well have run over the line of the wall. In either case it would have lain on the northwest side of Alta Semita.

Horti Caesaris (2): a villa on the right bank of the Tiber along the river (Suetonius, *Iul.* 83.2; Cass. Dio 44.35.3) that Caesar left by will, together with its appointments and statuary, to the Roman people (Cicero, *Phil.* 2.109; Appian, *BellCiv* 2.143). It was a considerable distance from the city (Horace, *Sat.* 1.9.18), and the Temple of Fors Fortuna (see Fors Fortuna, Fanum), at the first milestone on the Via Campana/Portuensis, appeared to be within its limits (Tacitus, *Ann.* 2.41). Apparently there was no connection between this and the Nemus Caesarum (see Naumachia Augusti). It was here that Julius Caesar entertained Cleopatra in 44 B.C. (Cicero, *Att.* 15.15.2). It is impossible to bound the property precisely, but it must have lain between the Via Campana/Portuensis and the river from the vicinity of the Porta Portuensis for a kilometer or more downstream of it. It was probably adjacent to the Horti Antoniani (q.v.), which may have lain upstream of it.

Horti Calyclani: gardens on the Esquiline, known from inscriptions on two boundary stones found in 1874 beyond the line of the Servian Agger (*CIL* 6.29771 = *ILS* 5998) that separated the Horti Calyclani from the Horti Tauriani. These were in situ near the church of S. Eusebio, but there is no indication of which gardens lay to which side of the boundary. In view of the association of the Forum Tauri (q.v.) with the church of S. Bibiana, it seems likely that the Horti Tauriani lay to the east, the Horti Calyclani to the west. The origin of the name of the latter is completely mysterious.

Horti Cassiani: mentioned only by Cicero (*Att.* 12.21.2), third in a series with the Horti Drusi and Horti Lamiani, on the right bank of the Tiber (cf. Cicero, *Att.* 12.19.1, 22.3, 23.3).

Horti Ceioniae Fabiae: identified on fragments of the Marble Plan of uncertain location (*FUR* pl. 34 frag. 45; Rodriguez pl. 34). Shown are what appear to be two spacious parterres connected by a broad stair, together with a portion of a building of generous scale but obscure plan. The owner was presumably the sister of Lucius Verus. The reading of the manuscript drawing of the fragment (*FUR* pl. 9.1) HORTI CELONIAE FABIA[was first corrected by Klebs in 1897.

Horti Clodiae: a property *ad Tiberim* (Cicero, *Cael.* 36) on the right bank of the Tiber, evidently approximately opposite that part of the Campus Martius laid out in sports fields. Cicero repeatedly mentioned these horti when he was trying to find a place for the projected temple to Tullia (Cicero, *Att.* 12.38.4, 41.3, 43.2, 47.1, 52.2).

Horti Commodiani: a property in which *in porticu curva* was a mosaic decoration showing a procession in honor of Isis in which, among the closest friends of Commodus, Pescennius Niger appeared carrying ritual objects (S.H.A. *Pescennius* 6.8). Its location is unknown.

Horti Coponiani: a property probably on the Via Ostiensis (Cicero, *Att.* 12.31.2; cf. 12.23.3 and

27.1). Cicero describes it as *villam et veterem ⟨et⟩ non magnam . . . silvam nobilem.* It is almost certainly the same as the Horti Siliani (q.v.), because Velleius Paterculus (2.83.3), in relating the events leading to Actium, mentions a remark of a Coponius, whom he identifies as father-in-law to P. Silius (cf. Cicero [ed. Shackleton Bailey], *Att.* 5.408–9). The Silius in question is probably P. Silius Nerva (cos. 20 B.C.), who may have acquired the property as part of his wife's dowry.

Horti Cottae: on the Via Ostiensis, beyond the Horti Siliani (Cicero, *Att.* 12.23.3, 27.1). Cicero describes the property as *villula sordida et valde pusilla, nil agri,* but in a very prominent location. Cicero never uses the term *horti* of it, so it may have been too far from Rome to be properly so called. Shackleton Bailey (Cicero, *Att.* 5.407) wishes to identify the owner as L. Aurelius Cotta (cos. 65 B.C.), but that seems questionable, because Aurelius Cotta seems to have been a man of wealth and taste.

Horti Crassipedis: a property belonging to Furius Crassipes, the second husband of Cicero's daughter Tullia. They were married in 56 B.C. and divorced sometime before her marriage to Dolabella in 50. The property was beyond the city limits, near, or on, Via Appia, not far from the Temple of Mars (Cicero, *Att.* 4.12, *QFr.* 3.7.1, *Fam.* 1.9.20).

Horti Cusinii: a property that had belonged to a Publicius, but at the time Cicero was writing in 45 B.C. had passed into the possession of a certain Trebonius and Cusinius (Cicero, *Att.* 12.38.4, 41.3). From the context, it is likely that it was on the right bank of the Tiber.

Horti Damasippi: a property on the Tiber, presumably on the right bank, subdivided into parcels with an eye to a profitable sale at the time Cicero was looking for such a place in 45 B.C. (Cicero, *Att.* 12.29.2, 33.1).

Horti Demetriou: gardens in the suburbium of Rome belonging to the freedman of Pompey (Plutarch, *Pomp.* 40.5), proverbial for their beauty and costliness, but of entirely unknown location.

Horti Dolabellae: a property of Cn. Dolabella, near which the cohort of German soldiers who were the imperial bodyguard were encamped in A.D. 69 (Suetonius, *Galba* 12.2). This must be the Dolabella relegated by Otho to Aquinum and ordered killed by Vitellius (Tacitus, *Hist.* 1.88, 2.63), and his horti were probably on the outskirts of the city, because

the troops in the city were *sine castris* (Suetonius, *Aug.* 49.1), but one cannot be more specific.

Horti Domitiae: a villa on the right bank of the Tiber listed in Regio XIV by the regionary catalogues, perhaps originally belonging to Domitia Longina, the daughter of Corbulo and wife of Domitian (*CIL* 6.16983), in which Hadrian constructed his mausoleum (S.H.A. *Ant. Pius* 5.1). It continued to exist into the fourth century and is said to have been a favorite residence of Aurelian when he was in Rome (S.H.A. *Aurelian.* 49.1). It probably lay largely to the east of the Mausoleum Hadriani and along the river, because the Campus Neronis seems to have begun not far west of the mausoleum.

Horti Domitiae Calvillae: the property of the mother of Marcus Aurelius on the Caelian, inherited from her father, P. Calvisius Tullius Ruso (S.H.A. *M. Aurel.* 1.3 and 5; *CIL* 15 p. 267), where Marcus was born and raised. Her name is given as both Domitia Calvilla and Domitia Lucilla; the former seems correct.

RendPontAcc 41 (1968–69): 167–89 (V. Santa Maria Scrinari).

Horti Domitiorum: see **Sepulcrum Domitiorum.**

Horti Drusi: a property on the right bank of the Tiber that was for sale when Cicero was considering buying a suburban place in 45 B.C. It figures repeatedly in his correspondence with Atticus, but Drusus wanted too high a price, and there were various defects and drawbacks about the place. Consequently Cicero did not buy it. Shackleton Bailey (Cicero, *Att.* 5.407) identifies Drusus as M. Livius Drusus Claudianus, the father of Livia Augusta. See Cicero, *Att.* 12.21.2, 22.3, 23.3, 25.2, 31.2, 33.1, 37.2, 38.4, 41.3, 44.2.

Horti Epaphroditiani: a property in the vicinity of which the Aqua Tepula received a supplement of 163 quinariae from the Anio Novus (Frontinus, *Aq.* 2.68). PA would put this just beyond the terminal castellum of the Anio Novus and Claudia, southwest of the building called Minerva Medica, where the distance between the two lines is about 100 m. However, in that case it does not seem likely that Frontinus would have specified that the Anio Novus alone was the source of the supplement. Because the two lines run more or less parallel and close to each other for a considerable distance, it seems more likely that the connector lay farther to the southeast, somewhere outside Porta Maggiore. Among those known who bore the name Epaphroditus, it seems impossible to determine which might have been likeliest to have been the owner of these horti.

Horti Frontonis: a property of Fronto, the teacher of Marcus Aurelius, that he calls *Maecenatianos hortos* (Fronto 1.8.5), with the implication that they belonged to Maecenas, but whether they were part of the famous Horti Maecenatis on the Esquiline (see Horti Maecenatiani) or an entirely different property is unknown.

Horti Galbae: on the Via Aurelia not far from Rome, where the body of Galba was buried by his servants after his murder in the Forum Romanum (Suetonius, *Galba* 20.2; Eutropius 7.16.3).

Horti Getae: a villa mentioned only in the regionary catalogues, listed in Regio XIV. In the Middle Ages the area along the river between the Aurelian Walls and the Porta S. Spirito bore the name Septimianum, but, because this could be accounted for by the Coriaria Septimiana and other works of Septimius Severus in the neighborhood, there is no reason to locate the Horti Getae in this vicinity.

Horti Lamiani (1): gardens near those of Maecenas on the Esquiline just outside the city limits of Rome (Philo, *Leg.* 2.597). L. Aelius Lamia (cos. A.D. 3) may have created them and left them to Tiberius, for they became imperial property (*CIL* 6.8668), and the place where Caligula's body was partially cremated and buried (Suetonius, *Calig.* 59). They were probably adjacent to the Horti Maiani, because at one time the same man was *procurator* of both (*CIL* 6.8668). The Horti Maiani were evidently more famous (*CIL* 6.6152, 8669 = *ILS* 1617); Pliny (*HN* 35.51) tells of a portrait of Nero on canvas 120 Roman feet long that he had painted there, which was destroyed, together with the better part of the horti, in a fire started by lightning. That the painting was of the same dimension as the Colossus Neronis (see Colossus Solis [Neronis]) must be significant, but it is not clear how these were related. The origin of the name of these horti is obscure.

Most topographers put both properties on the Esquiline south of Piazza Vittorio Emanuele in an area including Piazza Dante, where a number of interesting structures and notable sculptures, including the Esquiline Venus and the thirteen Niobids of the Uffizi in Florence, have been discovered (HJ 354n.31). The identification is attractive, but not certain. The structures discovered in the area include a large cryptoporticus with apsidal ends, from the ends of which annexes of very complex plan develop and in which

the finds of sculpture and colored marble were especially rich, a large hemicycle with radiating vaulted chambers behind, a broad portico running through Piazza Dante, and numerous smaller features, including baths, nymphaea, and cisterns, thickly scattered in close proximity to one another. These date from the first half of the first century after Christ to the middle of the third century. The sculptures found here in the later part of the nineteenth century are kept together and displayed in the Galleria degli Orti Lamiani of the Palazzo dei Conservatori (Helbig[4] 2.300–309); they include the so-called Esquiline Venus and the famous bust of Commodus with the attributes of Hercules.

M. Cima and E. La Rocca, *Le tranquille dimore degli dei: La residenze imperiale degli horti Lamiani* (Venice 1986).

Horti Lamiani (2): gardens on the right bank of the Tiber that Cicero contemplated buying when he was looking for such a place in 45 B.C. (Cicero, *Att.* 12.21.2, 22.3; cf. 19.1). Presumably they belonged to Cicero's friend and supporter L. Aelius Lamia, a rich eques Romanus.

Horti Largiani: listed only in the *Notitia,* in Regio VII, the only horti listed there and otherwise completely unknown.

Horti Liciniani: a property of Emperor Licinius Egnatius Gallienus (S.H.A. *Gallien.* 17.8), but the location is not given. By their association with a colossus projected to be larger than that of Nero and to stand *in summo Esquiliarum monte* (S.H.A. *Gallien.* 18.3) and with the Arcus Gallieni (q.v.) at the Porta Esquilina, it has been conjectured that these horti were on the eastern Esquiline, not far from ad Spem Veterem (see Spes Vetus). The building known as the Tempio di Minerva Medica is often alleged to belong to these horti, but there is no proof. There seems no adequate reason to try to connect these horti with the Horti Volusiani (q.v.) that belonged to Ferox Licinianus. There is better reason to believe that the medieval Palatium Licinianum (q.v.) near the church of S. Bibiana preserved a memory of them, in which case they belong near the Porta Tiburtina, roughly where the Lugli and Gismondi map puts the Horti Pallantiani.

Lugli 1938, 478–80.

Horti Lolliani: a property on the Esquiline on the boundary between Augustan Regiones IV and VI, as is shown by a boundary stone found at the corner of Via Principe Amedeo and Piazza dei Cinquecento (*CIL* 6.31284). M. Lollius was consul in 21 B.C. and his granddaughter Lollia Paulina was a contender with Agrippina for marriage with Claudius.

Horti Luculliani: the first great horti of Rome that then continued to be famous throughout the Julio-Claudian period, second only in glory and magnificence to the Horti Sallustiani (q.v.). They were the creation of the great shaper of style L. Licinius Lucullus, who retired from public life after his triumph in 63 B.C. and devoted himself to the cultivation of art and literature and to gratifying his taste for luxury of every sort. His horti were on the Pincian covering the summit of the hill and descending the slopes to the Campus Martius. The arches of the Aqua Virgo began *sub Hortis Lucullianis* (Frontinus, *Aq.* 1.22). Plutarch (*Lucul.* 39.2) has left only a general estimate of their splendor, and unfortunately excavation has brought to light only stretches of terracing and fragments of building, from which it is impossible to form any satisfactory notion of what the whole was like. But Plutarch (*Lucul.* 41.5–6) also tells us that each of the dining rooms was named and had a fixed budget for the dinner to be served there, one of the more costly being named Apollo. And Lucullus's libraries, which were exceptional for the number and quality of the books, were opened for public use (Plutarch, *Lucul.* 42.1–4).

In A.D. 46 the horti had passed into the hands of Valerius Asiaticus and seem then sometimes to have been called Horti Asiatici (Cass. Dio 60 [61].31.5). Messallina coveted them and forced Asiaticus to suicide to obtain them (Tacitus, *Ann.* 11.1) and later was herself killed there (Tacitus, *Ann.* 11.32, 37). Thereafter, they seem to have been an imperial property (Plutarch, *Lucul.* 39.2). They were evidently put up for sale and sold to the Acilii Glabriones in the course of the second century (see Horti Aciliorum).

In 1913 and 1969–1970 were found under Palazzo Zuccari and the building next door to it, Via Sistina no. 60, important remains of garden architecture belonging to these horti. They consist of parts of a series of semicircular niches, believed originally to have been fifteen in number, crowned with half-domes. At first they seem to have been simply a terrace wall; with the introduction of the Aqua Virgo they were piped for water and turned into a cascade, every niche and every pillar between niches showing piping. Still in the Augustan period the niches were partially filled with masonry and revetted with marble as frames for fountain figures that were now added in alternate niches. And finally, perhaps toward the middle of the first century after Christ, all but three niches were completely walled up, and the whole wall was covered with a decoration in glass mosaic, shells, and rustication that included architec-

ture and figures at large scale. Behind this façade appears to have been a cryptoporticus. These are the most substantial remains of the Horti Luculliani known, although some topographers would like to include the great hemicycle of the Horti Aciliorum (q.v.) to the north.

G. Kaster, *Die Garten des Lucullus* (Munich 1973); *CEFR* 98 (1987): 747–61 (H. Broise and V. Jolivet); *RömMitt* 95 (1988): 159–86 (K. Parlasca); *QITA* 10 (1988): 45–57 (C. Fiorini).

Horti Maecenatiani: on the Esquiline, covering much of the cemetery of the poor that lay beyond the ancient Agger south of the Porta Esquilina (Horace, *Sat.* 1.8.7, with the scholia of Acron and Porphyrion). The scholia locate the horti entirely in the area of the cemetery but are unreliable. Horace (*Sat.* 1.8.14–16) says that the Agger itself was at least in part, perhaps only north of the Porta Esquilina, made into a promenade for the public. The Agger adjacent to the horti seems to have been absorbed into them. Their attractions and amenities are barely sketched in our sources, but Maecenas was said to be the first to have a swimming pool of heated water in the city (Cass. Dio 55.7.6), which was almost certainly part of the horti, and they included a lofty tower of some sort from which Nero is supposed to have watched the progress of the great fire of 64 (Horace, *Carm.* 3.29.10 [?]; Suetonius, *Nero* 38.2). After Maecenas's death they became an imperial property, and Tiberius lived there after his return to Rome from Rhodes in A.D. 2 (Suetonius, *Tib.* 15.1). Eventually Nero built the Domus Transitoria (q.v.) with the express purpose of connecting the Horti Maecenatis to the Palatine, but without including the horti in the domus. Probably the Horti Maecenatiani of Fronto (1.8.5) included at least some part of the original complex, but they are not included in the regionary catalogues (cf., however, LPD 1.182 [Silvester (314–35) 25]).

The extent of the horti in the time of Maecenas was probably not enormous; they were remarkable chiefly for their luxury and refinements. The so-called Auditorium Maecenatis (q.v.), a sunken nymphaeum and dining pavilion built across the line of the Servian Walls, almost certainly belonged to them, and we can otherwise bound them by the Porta Esquilina and the line of the Via Tiburtina Vetus on the north and a street running due south from the juncture of Via Tiburtina and Via Labicana on the east. It seems impossible to bound them on the west or south.

Of the works of art discovered in the area, the most remarkable is the painting known as the Aldobrandini Wedding (discovered under Pope Clement VIII, 1592–1605), which is now in the Biblioteca Vaticana (Helbig[4] 1.360–66 no. 466). It is of the Third Pompeian Style and may come from a tomb.

Lugli 1938, 456–60; *RendLinc*, ser. 8.34 (1979): 239–50 (A. M. Colini); *Roma capitale 1870–1911, l'archeologia in Roma capitale tra sterro e scavo* (show catalogue, Venice 1983), 204–22 (C. Häuber).

Horti Maiani: see **Horti Lamiani** (1).

Horti Marsiani: known from an inscribed boundary stone separating them from the Horti Volusiani (q.v.) now in the American Academy in Rome (no. 169). At the time the stone was set up (ca. A.D. 80–120) the Horti Marsiani belonged to Aithalis Aug. lib. (cf. *AJP* 48 [1927]: 27–28 [A. W. Van Buren]).

Horti Messallae Corvini: known from an inscription found in Villa Medici (*CIL* 6.29789 = *ILS* 5990). He is believed to have been briefly the owner of the Horti Luculliani.

Horti Neronis: see **Horti Agrippinae.**

Horti Othonis: see **Horti Scapulani.**

Horti Pallantiani: gardens on the Esquiline mentioned three times by Frontinus (*Aq.* 1.19,20, 2.69) and listed in the regionary catalogues in Regio V, supposed to have been laid out by Pallas, the powerful freedman of Claudius. According to Frontinus, the Rivus Herculaneus branched from the Aqua Marcia post Hortos Pallantianos, and the terminal castellum of the Anio Novus and Claudia was post Hortos Pallantianos. This suggests that they were large, if not enormous, because the Rivus Herculaneus branches from the Marcia about 175 m southeast of Porta Tiburtina, while the castellum is about 250 m northwest of Porta Praenestina. The presumed existence of the Horti Liciniani in this area complicates matters. Although these might not have been in existence in Frontinus's day, their name shows that they were in the possession of the family of the princeps Gallienus before his accession to the purple and may have been long in the family. The evidence suggests that the Horti Pallantiani belong in the neighborhood of the building known as the Tempio di Minerva Medica (see Nymphaeum), where many topographers have located the Horti Liciniani, although without adequate reason.

Horti C. Passieni Crispi: known only from a lead pipe bearing his name found under the Palazzo di Giustizia on the right bank of the Tiber (*CIL* 15.7508). Passienus was the husband of Agrippina,

stepfather of Nero, and consul for the second time in A.D. 44. He had been adopted by C. Sallustius Crispus, grandnephew of the historian and creator of the Horti Sallustiani, which he may have inherited, along with enormous wealth. After Passienus's murder, ca. A.D. 48, his property passed to Agrippina.

Horti Peduceiani: gardens known only from an inscription (*CIL* 6.276; cf. 6.33745 = *ILS* 1626). *CIL* 10.6706 (= *ILS* 8217) mentions an Ager Peduceianus on, or near, Via Latina that may have been connected with the horti, but no more precise location is possible. They may have belonged to M. Peducaeus Priscinus, cos. A.D. 110, or his son M. Peducaeus Stloga Priscinus, cos. A.D. 141.

Horti Pompeiani (1): gardens apparently connected with the Domus Rostrata (see Domus, Cn. Pompeius Magnus [1]) on the Carinae, because after Pompey's death Caesar gave them to Antony (Appian, *BellCiv* 3.14; Cicero, *Phil.* 2.109). These were sometimes called *superiores* to distinguish them from his residence adjacent to his theater, which also seems to have been provided with handsome grounds (Asconius *ad Cic. Milon.* 32; cf. 29 and 45 [Stangl 32, 34, 43]).

MEFRA 95 (1983): 115–35 (V. Jolivet).

Horti Pompeiani (2): in the Campus Martius, evidently connected with Pompey's house adjacent to his theater, though known only by implication, the gardens of the Domus Rostrata on the Carinae being described as *superiores*. Because Plutarch is explicit (*Pomp.* 40.5) that Pompey lived very modestly in Rome, having only one house down to the time of his third triumph, by which the Domus Rostrata must be meant, it is clear that the terms *domus* and *horti* were often interchangeable. The sepulchral inscription of Eros *insularius ex Hortis Pompeia⟨nis⟩* (*CIL* 6.6299 = *ILS* 7442c) of the early empire is puzzling. He must belong to the horti in the Campus Martius, because the Domus Rostrata passed into the imperial properties, but whether we should think that Horti Pompeiani in the Campus Martius had become simply a place designation, or whether the house of Pompey was so large that after passing into public ownership it could be described as an insula (one presumes the superintendents of the theater complex lived there) cannot be decided.

Horti P. Pomponii Secundi: gardens of unknown location belonging to the consul of A.D. 44 (Tacitus, *Ann.* 5.8 [6.3]).

Horti Reguli: see **Horti Aquilii Reguli.**

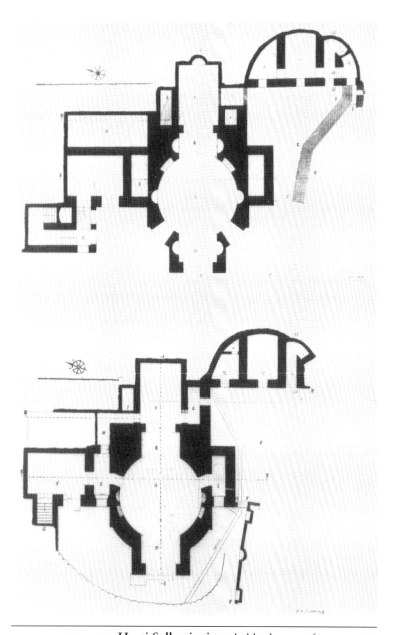

may ask whether these gardens did not enter the imperial possessions through her after Passienus's murder and her inheritance of his wealth. Thereafter, they were a favorite residence of the imperial house. Vespasian seems to have preferred them to the Domus Aurea (Cass. Dio 65.10.4); Nerva died there (Chron. 146); and Aurelian embellished them with a mile-long portico (S.H.A. *Aurelian.* 49.2). They were still an important residence in the fourth century (*Panegyrici Latini* 12[IX].14.4) and were sacked in 410 by the Goths and left in ruins by them (Procopius, *BellVand* 1.2.24).

The features of this vast property included a *conditorium*, or sepulchral vault, in which were preserved the bodies of two giants, Pusio and Secundilla, 10 feet, 3 inches tall, who lived in the time of Augustus (Pliny, *HN* 7.75); a Temple of Venus Hortorum Sallustianorum (*CIL* 6.122 = *ILS* 3184, *CIL* 6.32451, 32468), possibly the same as the Temple of Venus Erucina *extra Portam Collinam* (see Venus Erucina, Aedes [2]); and a *porticus miliarensis* built by Aurelian (S.H.A. *Aurelian.* 49.2) in which he daily exercised his horses. Such a portico should be a mile long, and it is difficult to see where in the horti it can have been located. The difficulty has led to the supposition that this is an invention, but without adequate grounds. In the Acta Martyrorum are references to *thermae, palatium, forum, tribunal,* and *pyramis Sallusti* (Jordan 2.124–25). The *palatium* will have been the main residence, the *forum* a court in front of it, and the baths an annex *(iuxta).* The *tribunal* is located only *extra portam quae nuncupatur Salaria* and might well be on the so-called forum for ceremonial occasions. The *pyramis* is the obelisk (Amm. Marc. 17.4.16) brought to Rome sometime later than Augustus (cf. Obeliscus Hortorum Sallustianorum). These can have been only the central core of the complex, while other pavilions and pleasances were scattered through the park.

The boundaries of the horti can be set at the Via Salaria on the east and the Aurelian Walls on the north (cf. Tacitus, *Hist.* 3.82). On the south the boundary may have followed the line of the Servian Walls along the brow of the Quirinal, possibly crossing it in places (cf. Fortunae Tres and *Anth. Pal.* 16.40). The boundary on the west is hardest to set; the horti would probably not have extended beyond Piazza Barberini and very likely not beyond Via Bissolati.

Within this area have been found many works of art and recognizable remains of a number of buildings, notably a hippodrome, probably a garden one, along the north side of the valley between the Quirinal and Pincian hills, a nymphaeum near the northeast angle of the Servian Walls, and three *piscinae.* The only remains visible today are a complex at the

Figure 44
Horti Sallustiani, Pavilion ("Palazzo di Sallustio"), Plans of Ground Level and Upper Level

Horti Sallustiani: probably the most famous estate of its kind in Rome. The gardens were originally created by the historian, possibly using at the beginning the gardens of Caesar ad Portam Collinam (see Horti Caesaris [1]) ([Cicero,] *Resp. in Sall.* 19; cf. *Anth. Pal.* 16.40). Sallust spent much of the wealth he had amassed in Numidia in embellishing his property, and the work was continued by his grandnephew and heir of the same name (*Anth. Pal.* 16.40 by Crinagoras). A sepulchral inscription (*CIL* 6.9005 = *ILS* 1795) indicates that they had become imperial property before A.D. 43, but because it is unique and Agrippina, the mother of Nero, married C. Passienus Crispus, the heir of the younger Sallust, in 44, one

end of Via Sallustiana including a structure of four storeys built into the hillside (Figs. 44, 45). This has a very interesting domed room, the dome segmental with sections alternately flat and bowed. On Via Lucullo are remains of a massive terrace wall scalloped into curved niches, and at right angles to this along Via Friuli is part of a vaulted cryptoporticus with remains of painting (now in the garage of the United States embassy).

The brook that ran down the valley between Quirinal and Pincian must always have been an important feature of the horti, but we do not know what it was called. The name Aqua Sallustiana has been given it in modern times for convenience; possibly it was the Spino or Nodinus of Cicero (*Nat. D.* 3.52). Its importance seems to have been enhanced by elaborate terracing, probably with monumental stairs to connect the various levels after the pattern of the Horti Luculliani and Horti Aciliorum. The surviving pavilion is set so as to look obliquely down the valley to the brook and consists of a domed rotunda preceded by a deep vestibule and opening to a lobby symmetrical with the vestibule between the rotunda and a lofty vaulted oecus. All these rooms are provided with large niches, some rectangular, others semicircular, presumably for statuary. North of the rotunda is a group of spacious rooms in two storeys, essentially a separate apartment, while to the south a honeycomb of rooms built into the hillside was surmounted by yet further structures opening on a cantilevered balcony. The function of this balcony and the architectural development behind and above it are not clear. The date of the building is not earlier than mid-second century.

Among the works of art found in the area of the horti should be mentioned the Ludovisi Throne (Helbig[4] 3.2340) and its counterpart now in the Museum of Fine Arts, Boston, the Ludovisi Gaul (Helbig[4] 3.2337); the falling Niobid (Helbig[4] 3.2279), believed by many to be a Greek original, now in the Museo Nazionale Romano delle Terme; and the Silenus holding the infant Bacchus, now in the Louvre. For the obelisk, see Obeliscus Hortorum Sallustianorum. The disposition of these and the extent to which they may be regarded as parts of a distinguished collection are uncertain.

Lugli 1938, 320–37; Nash 1.491–99; *CAR* 2-F, 50 pp. 128–29; I. Manotti, ed., *C. Sallusti Crispi Opera* (Rome 1972), Appendix (F. Castagnoli); G. Cipriani, *Horti Sallustiani*[2] (Rome 1982), 13–67; *BdA* 49 (1988): 53–62 (M. Castelli).

Horti Scapulani: a property on the right bank of the Tiber that Cicero was eager to buy when he was looking for such a place in 45 B.C. The heirs of Scapula proposed to divide his property into four shares

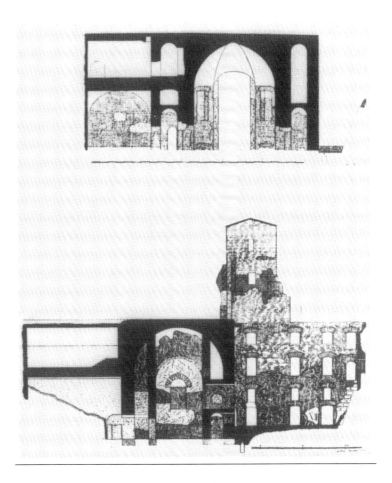

and to bid among themselves for the horti (Cicero, *Att.* 12.28.4). Otho, who was one of the heirs and a rich man, was eager to acquire the property for himself (Cicero, *Att.* 12.43.2). From the sequence of Cicero's letters, we gather that the question of whether the horti would come up for public auction was still open in early July 45 (*Att.* 13.33.4) when Cicero learned of Caesar's scheme to divert the Tiber into a new channel, which would either have ruined the property or have gravely reduced its value. Thereafter, Cicero does not bring up the subject again (cf. also *Att.* 12.37.2, 40.4, 41.3, 52.2, 13.12.4). Whether Otho ever came into possession of the property is not clear.

Horti Scatoniani: known only from a single sepulchral inscription (*CIL* 6.6281 = *ILS* 7442a) from the tomb of the Statilii (see Sep. Staliliorum).

Horti Scipionis: a property presumably of P. Cornelius Scipio Africanus, the elder son of the great Africanus, because it is first recorded in 163 B.C. (Broughton, *MRR* 1.440–42). It was in the Campus Martius outside the pomerium (Cicero, *Nat. D.* 2.4.11), probably west of the Ovile, but at any rate

Figure 45
Horti Sallustiani,
Pavilion ("Palazzo
di Sallustio"),
Cross Sections,
Front and Rear

near it. Cicero (*Phil.* 2.109) indicates that this had passed into the possession of Mark Antony by 44 B.C. but was still known as Horti Scipionis.

Horti Senecae: a property of the philosopher, evidently of great luxury, presented to him by Nero (Tacitus, *Ann.* 14.52–55). Its location is entirely unknown, but Juvenal (10.16) ranks it with the house of the Laterani (q.v.).

Horti Serviliani: an imperial property in the last years of Nero's reign (Tacitus, *Ann.* 15.55; Suetonius, *Nero* 47.1), possibly having earlier belonged to M. Servilius Nonianus, cos. A.D. 35, one of the most celebrated orators and historians of his day (cf. Tacitus, *Ann.* 14.19). Pliny lists among its embellishments the Ceres of Praxiteles, the boxers of Dercylides, and the portrait of the historian Callimachus by Amphistratus (*HN* 36.23, 25, 36). Pliny ranks the house with the Atrium Libertatis, Temple of Apollo Sosianus, and Porticus Octaviae as a repository of art. It is also mentioned in two inscriptions (*CIL* 6.8673, 8674) and probably in a papyrus (*PBerol* 511). It is often placed in the southwest quarter of the city, but for this there is no real evidence.

Horti Siliani: one of the properties Cicero was interested in when he was looking for a suitable location for the temple to Tullia. It was on the Via Ostiensis (Cicero, *Att.* 12.27.1; cf. 12.23.3). During his attempt to purchase this property, Cicero mentions it frequently in his letters to Atticus dated from March to May 45 B.C. (*Att.* 12.22–52), but ultimately judged it inadequate (*Att.* 12.44.2: *non satis oikodespotika*).

Horti Spei Veteris: mentioned only once as a retreat to which Elagabalus retired (S.H.A. *Heliogab.* 13.5), therefore probably the site of the Circus Varianus (q.v.), Elagabalus's family name being Varius, and the Temple of Elagabalus to which the god was ceremonially taken at midsummer (see Elagabalus). These cannot be the same as the Horti Variani mentioned in S.H.A. *Aurelian.* 1.2. See also Sessorium.

Horti Tauriani: a property of M. Statilius Taurus, cos. A.D. 44, whose suicide Agrippina procured in 53 in her machinations to get possession of it (Tacitus, *Ann.* 12.59). These gardens were on the Esquiline adjacent to the Horti Calyclani (*CIL* 6.29771 = *ILS* 5998) and probably also the Forum Tauri and Caput Tauri (see Forum Tauri).

Horti Terentii: a property of the comic poet of twenty iugera in extent on the Via Appia near the Temple of Mars (Suetonius, *Terent.* 5). Suetonius calls it *hortuli*.

Horti Thraseae Paeti: mentioned only once (Tacitus, *Ann.* 16.34.1) and of unknown location.

Horti Torquatiani: mentioned only once (Frontinus, *Aq.* 1.5), where the juncture of the Aqua Appia and the Aqua Augusta is said to fall on the boundary between these and other horti of uncertain name in the general area Ad Spem Veterem. The place was also called Ad Gemellos (q.v.) and was infra Spem Veterem. These gardens were therefore west of Spes Vetus and south of the Via Labicana.

Horti Trebonii: mentioned by Cicero during his prolonged search for suitable horti in 45 B.C., described as *locus Publicianus* (*Att.* 12.38.4) and spoken of disparagingly as a mere threshing floor. The property had earlier belonged to a Rebilus and was being offered for sale by Trebonius and Cusinius (Cicero, *Att.* 12.41.3). If Publicianus means that it was on an extension of the Clivus Publicius, it was on or beyond the Aventine.

Horti Variani: mentioned only once (S.H.A. *Aurelian.* 1.2). A journey by carriage from the Palatine to the Horti Variani took one past Aurelian's Temple of Sol (see Sol, Templum) in Regio VII, probably on the Via Flaminia. Because by this time the Pincian Hill had been entirely taken up by such well-known estates as the Horti Aciliorum, the Horti Variani should lie either in the northern Campus Martius or farther out Via Flaminia. They were probably not created by Elagabalus, whose family name was Varius, because he had a very extensive estate ad Spem Veterem (see Sessorium).

Horti Vettiani: see **Domus, Vettius Agorius Praetextatus.**

Horti Volusiani: known only from an inscribed boundary stone now in the American Academy in Rome (no. 169) from the line between this property and the Horti Marsiani (q.v.). The Horti Volusiani belonged to Ferox Licianus, who is probably C. Pompeius Ferox Licianus, a courtier of Domitian (Juvenal 4.109–10), which would tend to date the inscription A.D. 80–100. Cf. *CIL* 6.9973 and Horrea Volusiana. The location of the horti is unknown, unless through inheritance these became the Horti Liciniani on the Esquiline.

Archeologia, materiali e problemi 6: I Volusii Saturnini (Bari 1982), 37–38 (F. Coarelli).

Ianiculum: the name now given to the whole ridge on the right bank of the Tiber from just south of the Vatican City on the north to the Stazione di Trastevere on the south, divided from the plateau beyond by the Vallis Fornacum, down which ran the Via Posterula and now runs the Vatican railway line. In antiquity the Ianiculum proper was probably much more restricted, because Numa is said to have been buried simply *ad Ianiculum* or *sub Ianiculo.* The suffix *-iculus, -icula* is regularly diminutive in Latin, but the Janiculum is the highest of the hills of modern Rome and from much of the city the most conspicuous. Here during the holding of the Comitia Centuriata in the Campus Martius a red flag was raised and a detachment of the army was stationed to guard the approach to Rome against possible enemy attacks during the proceedings (Cass. Dio 37.27.3–28.1). The area of this guard post can only have been the point where the later Via Aurelia crested the hill and ran out along a narrow ridge to the west into Etruscan territory. This was a vulnerable point, the natural approach to Rome from the west, from which an enemy force could survey the situation of the city and move to seize the Pons Sublicius before the body of the Roman army could mount an adequate defense of this bridge. But the guard would have required a station of some sort, a watchtower or small fort, to avoid a surprise assault of disastrous consequences, such as occurred in the attack of Lars Porsenna (Livy 2.10.3). This outpost might have been named Ianiculum in consideration of its general geographical character, but probably it stood athwart the road, and its architectural character was akin to that of the Ianus Geminus (q.v.), as this is shown on coins of Nero (Nash 1.503). A Vicus Ianuclensis (Ianiculensis) is listed on the Capitoline Base (CIL 6.975 = *ILS* 6073), and there was a Pagus Ianiculensis (q.v.), further indication that it was limited in area.

Ianus: a passageway, probably well down into imperial times, always allowing for closure at either end, and originally a bridge or crossing of the pomerium, a permanently inaugurated templum. Cicero is explicit (*Nat. D.* 2.67): *transitiones perviae iani . . . nominantur.* Later the word came to be applied to gateways, but perhaps always those that had closings at either end. Thus Livy (2.49.8), in describing the departure of the Fabii for Veii, speaks of their leaving: *dextro iano Portae Carmentalis,* the gate that thereafter was called the Porta Scelerata. Such gateways must have been relatively common in Rome, not only as gates in fortifications but also as entrances to sacred precincts and even houses, which would account for Ovid's *cum tot sint iani cur stas sacratus in uno* (*Fast.* 1.257). Whether all iani were regarded as in some sense sacred is not known.

Of the important iani in Rome, one was known as the Ianus Primus (*CIL* 6.12816); its site is unknown and, because it is known only from this inscription, might have been anywhere. Another was the Ianus Medius, which was where bankers and investors congregated (Cicero, *Off.* 2.87; Horace, *Sat.* 2.3.18; cf. Ovid, *Rem. Am.* 561–62). The scholia on the passage in Horace are clearly largely guesswork and contradictory. Porphyrion would explain it as a ianus in a basilica; Acron would have it that there were three statues of Ianus, the middle one mounted on the Rostra, or else have the Ianus Medius that by the Basilica Paulli, i.e., the Ianus Geminus. This has confused the issue. No one would be apt to call the familiar Ianus Geminus by the name Ianus Medius, unless it were clearly in a middle position, like the Rostra. Probably the scholia preserve a remnant of real information in that comment, and the Ianus Medius was actually in front of the Rostra, the middle of the Forum Romanum, where we should have expected bankers and share-sellers to have congregated from a very early period. In Plautus's catalogue of the types of men in the forum, it is these he means by *in medio propter canalem, ibi ostentatores meri* (*Curc.* 476). There would have been a bridge there, and, after the Cloaca was culverted, the place designation, possibly even still marked out in some way, would have continued in use.

The Ianus Geminus, *ad infimum Argiletum* (Livy 1.19.2) or *circa imum Argiletum* (Servius *ad Aen.* 7.607), leaves little room for question about its location, although no trace of it has ever been found, doubtless because, as Servius tells us, after the construction of the Forum Transitorium the worship was removed to a new position in that forum, where it would still have been in a position spanning the Cloaca. There might well have been another ianus here earlier, and probably the Ianus Geminus of Livy was not in the location established for it by Numa Pompilius, because the Cloaca and Argiletum seem to have been diverted to a course around the northwest end of the Basilica Fulvia et Aemilia at the time of the construction of that basilica in 179 B.C., but it was always intended to carry the Sacra Via across the Cloaca to the Comitium. As the name suggests, this ianus was almost certainly double in the days when it still functioned as a bridge, so that one-half could continue to be used when the other had to be closed for religious reasons. As shown on coins of Nero, however, it is single (Nash 1.503).

Another passage in Horace (*Epist.* 1.1.53–54) has produced further confusion: "*o cives cives quaerenda pecunia primum est; virtus post nummos*": *haec ianus summus ab imo* seems clearly a catch phrase, meaning something like "the forum from end to end," or "the whole length of the Cloaca." The latter is particularly attractive, but the suggestion that has been advanced that there must have been three iani in the Forum Romanum, if one was the Ianus Medius, an argument bolstered by reference to Livy 41.27.12, where mention is made of the construction of three iani, possibly in connection with the laying out of a forum, rests on poor foundations. Probably there were iani at frequent intervals along the Cloaca from its mouth on the Tiber in the Forum Boarium to high on its course along the Clivus Suburanus, and business of one sort and another was brisk all along its length, while the position of the Ianus Medius in the middle of the Forum Romanum explains that name adequately.

The scholia on yet a third passage in Horace (*Epist.* 1.20.1) roused Porphyrion to further flights of the imagination and the invention of a Vicus Ianus that derived its name from the Ianus Geminus. Whether Porphyrion thought of this as a stretch of the Sacra Via or as the end of the Argiletum does not

matter in the absence of any other evidence for its existence.

When it became first permissible and then regular to substitute arches for post-and-lintel doors at the ends of a ianus, no one tells us, nor when one was first vaulted. On Nero's coins the Ianus Geminus still has the traditional architectural form, although the lintel shown is arched, and an ash urn from Chiusi shows a ianus with arched doors at either end under a gable roof, which may have been added simply to make a cover. Probably as soon as the defensive advantages of arched fortification gates were appreciated in the early third century, that variation began to be accepted, but vaulting with its introduction of a perilous barrier between the sacred passage and the open heaven did not appear before the invention of the *ianus quadrifrons*, perhaps not before the time of Domitian.

L. A. Holland, *Janus and the Bridge* (Rome 1961).

Ianus, Templum: a temple in the Forum Boarium built by C. Duilius after the naval victory at Mylae in 260 B.C. (Tacitus, *Ann.* 2.49). The dedication day was the Portunalia, 17 August (Degrassi 497), and the temple stood *ad Theatrum Marcelli* (Fast. Vall. and Allif.) or *extra Portam Carmentalem* (Festus 358L). The evidence of Festus is suspect, because he says the ill-fated Fabii were instructed to proceed to Veii by a senatus consultum voted in the Aedes Iani here, not only a patent anachronism but also a gross error in assigning an aedes to a god who never received one. Augustus began restoration of this ianus, and Tiberius completed it in A.D. 17, when the dedication day was 18 October (Degrassi 523). According to Pliny (*HN* 36.28), Augustus put in this temple (or just possibly in the Ianus Geminus) a Ianus Pater brought from Egypt, the work of either Scopas or Praxiteles, which in the course of time was gilded. Presumably this was a herm. The area around the Theater of Marcellus has been extensively explored without revealing any remains that we can identify as this temple.

Attempts to identify the Temple of Janus with one of the three temples of the Forum Holitorium incorporated in the church of S. Nicola in Carcere are unconvincing, and better attributions for these are available. For many years the presence of four quadrifrontal herms of marble, the posts of a low square, or rectangular, enclosure, gave the name Contrada Quattro Capi to the area at the head of the Pons Fabricius on the left bank; two of these were mounted in the parapet of the bridge in 1849 and are there today. These herms are ancient, and two of the heads that crown them, although much battered, are clearly bearded, while two are beardless. Because the set of four herms was still complete as late as 1697, beside the church of S. Gregorio at the bridgehead, they are not apt to have strayed far from their original location, and they may well be the remains of an imperial restoration of this templum. Remains of a temple platform just northeast of the Temple of Apollo Medicus and earlier frequently identified as Duilius's Temple of Janus are now recognized to be probably the Temple of Bellona (see Bellona, Aedes).

Duilius's choice of Janus to honor with a temple after the victory at Mylae can be explained by the close association of the god with water, as well as beginnings. Why Augustus's restoration of the templum should have taken several years to complete is less clear.

Holland 200–223.

Ianus, Concordia, Salus, Pax, Statuae: According to Ovid (*Fast.* 3.881–82), on 30 March these four divinities were worshiped, but he does not elaborate on this. Cassius Dio (54.35.2) says that in 11 B.C. Augustus set up statues to Salus Publica, Concordia, and Pax, but says nothing of Janus, who would in any case sort ill with the others, and does not say where the statues were located. It has been supposed that there were only three statues and they stood in or on a ianus, but Ovid speaks explicitly of an altar for Pax, which could hardly have been set up in a ianus. Unless one should think of two entirely separate ceremonies (despite Ovid's *cumque hoc*), the conjunction is obscure (cf. Degrassi 433).

Ianus Curiatius, Ara: one of two altars at the ends of the Tigillum Sororium (q.v.), the other being to Iuno Sororia (Festus 380L; Dion. Hal. 3.22.7; *Schol. Bob. in Cic. Milon.* 7 [Stangl 113]). As the story came to be told, these were to the Juno of the sister killed by the Horatius who emerged victorious from the contest of the Horatii and Curiatii and to the Ianus (Genius) of the Curiatius to whom she was betrothed. The story seems to have been invented to account for the Tigillum. The association of Janus and Juno in public worship on the Kalends of each month is well known, and a Janus who received sacrifice from the *curiae,* which supposedly got their names from the Sabine women carried off by the men of Romulus, might well have been balanced by a Iuno Sororia, a counterpart perhaps not very different from the Iuno Curitis of the Sabines (cf. Ianus Geminus).

Holland 77–91; R. Altheim-Stickel and M. Rosenbach, eds., *Beiträge zur altitalischen Geistesge-*

schichte: Festschrift Gerhard Radke (Aschendorff Münster 1986), 257–68 (E. Simon).

Ianus Geminus: the most important shrine of Janus in Rome, usually called Ianus Geminus or Ianus Quirinus, but described variously as a sacellum (Ovid, *Fast.* 1.275), a sacrarium (Servius *ad Aen.* 7.607), and a twin-doored shrine (Plutarch, *Numa* 20.1). It was also described by a number of poetical equivalents; e.g., *geminae belli portae* (Vergil, *Aen.* 7.607). It stood between two fora, the Forum Romanum and Forum Iulium (Ovid, *Fast.* 1.257–58), *ad infimum Argiletum* (Livy 1.19.2), or *circa imum Argiletum* (Servius *ad Aen.* 7.607), close to the point where the Argiletum (q.v.) entered the Forum Romanum, until Domitian moved it to the Forum Transitorium (Servius *ad Aen.* 7.607).

There are various accounts of its foundation. By one tradition the Sabines under Titus Tatius were checked in a successful attack on the Romans by floods of hot water issuing from an Aedes Iani and pouring through a gate *sub radicibus Collis Viminalis,* a gate that was thereafter called Porta Ianualis (Macrobius, *Sat.* 1.9.17–18). But the Porta Ianualis was one of the three gates of the Romulean settlement on the Palatine and, as such, can have been nowhere near the Viminal, and Janus, so far as we know, did not have an aedes, let alone one at so early a date. A variant of this tradition would make the Ianus Geminus a monument to the god's intercession and have the hot water issue from that point (Ovid, *Fast.* 1.263–76; Servius *ad Aen.* 1.291, 8.361). Yet another would have the ianus a monument built by Romulus and Titus Tatius jointly to show the union of the two communities (Servius *ad Aen.* 1.291). However, most people seem to have thought of it as a foundation of Numa Pompilius, *index pacis bellique* (Livy 1.19.2; Pliny, *HN* 34.33); Rome was at war when the gates were open and at peace when they were closed. The gates were closed throughout the reign of Numa, but not again until after the First Punic War. They were closed in 235 B.C. (Varro, *Ling.* 5.165), in 30 B.C. after Actium (Livy 1.19.2), and ordered shut by the senate twice more in the time of Augustus (*RG* 42–45; Suetonius, *Aug.* 22). Thereafter through the imperial period, they were closed at more frequent intervals.

Although there is no mention of any rebuilding of this temple, it must have been moved at the time of the construction of the Basilica Fulvia et Aemilia in 179 B.C., when the Argiletum and the Cloaca, which ran in a channel beside it, were diverted and moved west to make room for the basilica. The ianus had always been a permanently inaugurated bridge carrying the Sacra Via over the Cloaca to the Comitium and, to judge from its name, a double bridge, so, when the doors had to be closed for religious reasons, the bridge could continue to function. If the forum stretch of the Cloaca was culverted at the time of the move, as seems likely, because the so-called Braccio Morto under the basilica must have been culverted then, the ianus as rebuilt may well have appeared single. It is so shown on coins of Nero (Nash 1.503) but in a form that can hardly be older than the late republic, because the door is arched and the palmette and serpentine vine motifs in the decoration of the attic become common only after the Second Punic War. It appears to have been a small rectangular structure of two long walls of ashlar masonry under a long window covered by grating set relatively high, and with a deep, richly decorated attic above. At one end are shown double doors framed by engaged (?) columns and an arched head rising into the attic. Presumably there were similar doors at the opposite end. There is no indication of a roof, and one presumes there was none. When Domitian moved the ianus to the Forum Transitorium, he rebuilt the Curia Iulia and repaved the Argiletum, covering the place of the old Ianus Geminus. Later a new temple of Janus was built in front of the Curia, a small square shrine entirely of bronze. It is this that Procopius describes in some detail (*BellGoth* 1.25.18–23). He does not tell us when it was built, but from Cassius Dio (74.14) it is clear this was before A.D. 193. Traces of a small square enclosure surviving on the pavement in front of the Curia, sometimes identified as the place of the quadriga of Arcadius and Honorius (cf. Nash 2.272, where it appears to the right of center), may be traces of it.

The ancient bronze statue of the god believed to have been dedicated by Numa showed him as a man, but with two identical faces facing in opposite directions (*biceps* in Ovid, *Fast.* 1.65, *biformis* in *Fast.* 1.89, and *bifrons* in Vergil, *Aen.* 12.198). He was bearded (Ovid, *Fast.* 1.259) and held a staff in his right hand and a key in his left (*Fast.* 1.99). Pliny (*HN* 34.33) says his fingers were so arranged as to indicate the 355 days of the year. Whether this was the same as the image that Procopius (*BellGoth* 1.25.18–23) says was five cubits high may be doubted.

Holland 108–37; Nash 1.502–3; *RömMitt* 85 (1978): 359–69 (L. Richardson); *ArchCl* 37 (1985): 283–89 (R. Staccioli); R. Altheim-Stickel and M. Rosenbach, eds., *Beiträge zur altitalischen Geistesgeschichte: Festschrift Gerhard Radke* (Aschendorff Münster 1986), 257–68 (E. Simon); *BullCom* 92 (1987–88): 11–16 (F. Castagnoli).

Ianus Germanici: see **Arcus Germanici (1).**

Ianus Quadrifrons (1) (Fig. 37.17): the name commonly given to a four-sided arch in the Forum Boarium so placed that two of the four piers of the arch are on the right bank of the Cloaca, the other two on the left. It is entirely sheathed in white marble, and above a high socle each pier is adorned on each exterior face with six rounded and round-headed niches, the half-domes decorated with fluted shells, in two zones of three each, forty-eight in all. These have been presumed to be for statues, but their small size in proportion to the arch as a whole makes this doubtful. Sixteen of the niches on the two minor faces are undeveloped, simply decorative panels, only the central ones being developed as full niches. The piers are connected by quadripartite vaulting, the interior being relatively plain but continuing the lines of articulation of the exterior. The arches are 10.60 m high, 5.70 m wide, and had sculptured keystones, Minerva on the north and Roma on the east being still discernible. The block of the arch as a whole is 12 m square and 16 high, but the attic is missing. Parts removed in 1830 as medieval may actually have belonged to the attic, but there is no convincing evidence for the pyramid with which Hülsen would finish it (see Töbelmann, *Römische Gebälke* 1.131–35).

The monument is of relatively late date, storage jars being used to lighten the mass of the masonry, and is commonly identified as the Arcus Divi Constantini listed by the *Notitia* in Regio XI. It does not appear to have been a triumphal arch. Because it spans the Cloaca, it can be taken as a rebuilding of an older ianus, perhaps the Ianus Primus of *CIL* 6.12816, on monumental scale. There is no clear place for a cult statue here, but the original function of a ianus would have been to carry the road from the Clivus Victoriae and Nova Via, united just above this point, across the Cloaca. There may be an allusion to a precursor of this ianus in Horace, *Epist.* 1.20.1: *Vortumnum Ianumque, liber spectare videris.*

Nash 1.504–5; Lugli 1975, 315–17.

Ianus Quadrifrons (2): a quadrifrontal ianus that Domitian erected in the Forum Transitorium to replace the Ianus Geminus (Martial 10.28; Servius *ad Aen.* 7.607). In it he put an image of Janus with four faces, said to have been brought to Rome from Falerii in 241 B.C. (Servius *ad Aen.* 7.607; Macrobius, *Sat.* 1.9.13). The god was said to look out on four fora (Martial 10.28), presumably the Fora Romanum, Iulium, Augustum, and Transitorium, although Templum Pacis may be substituted for Forum

Augustum or Forum Transitorium. It is not known where the statue may have stood earlier, or what its relation to the Roman Janus might have been, if any. According to Lydus (*Mens.* 4.1), it was still standing in the sixth century, but this seems very doubtful. The ianus must have stood toward the southwest end of the Forum Transitorium, presumably spanning the Cloaca, and may well have replaced an earlier ianus there. No substantial trace of it has ever been identified. That it was a quadrifrontal arch, as has sometimes been suggested, is unwarranted by the evidence (see Servius *ad Aen.* 7.607: *quattuor portarum unum templum*).

Holland 92–107.

Ianus Quirinus: see **Ianus Geminus.**

Ilicium: see **Iuppiter Elicius, Ara.**

Indulgentia (?): a shrine of Euergesia on the Capitoline built by Marcus Aurelius in A.D. 180 (Cass. Dio 72.34.3). A statue type with the legend *Indulgentia Augusti* appears on coins of Antoninus Pius and Lucius Verus, and a shrine at Cirta in Africa was dedicated to this divinity (*B. M. Coins, Rom. Emp.* 4.320–29, 378, 609; *CIL* 8.7095 = *ILS* 2933). Presumably this was no more than an aedicula.

Insula: a building containing a number of apartments used as dwellings, together with shops and workshops of various sorts and sizes. From the Insula Arriana Polliana in Pompeii (Regio VI, vi), we gather that an insula need not be more than one or two storeys high, but in Rome and Ostia insulae regularly ran to multiple storeys. And whereas the same insula in Pompeii occupies a whole city block, an insula might occupy only a small fraction of a block. Blocks of a half-dozen insulae are quite regular in Ostia. The regionary catalogues of the fourth century regularly list the number of insulae in each regio, as well as the number of domus, horrea, and balinea. The very high numbers of insulae (in all, 44,300) suggest that all but very few Romans lived in such dwellings, but shops are not counted, and some insulae are listed separately by name as landmarks. No norm of size, either for the insula or for the individual apartment, seems possible, and it is impossible to guess how many people might have been housed in one. See also Domus, Insula, Atrium, Horti, Villa.

Insula Aesculapii: see **Insula Tiberina.**

Insula Bolani: a building in Regio XIV west of Pons Aemilius and north of the church of S. Cecilia,

known from an inscription (*CIL* 6.67 = *ILS* 3501a), where mention is made of a statue of Bona Dea. In conjunction with *CIL* 6.65 = *ILS* 3500, we learn that this insula was the property of M. Vettius Bolanus, consul under Nero.

Insula Q. Critoni: known from the sepulchral inscription of a *popa* (*CIL* 6.9824); the owner was a freedman.

Insula Cuminiana: a building on the Caelian, mentioned in the Acta S. Pancratii, 12 May, p. 21 (Jordan 2.120).

Insula Eucarpiana: known from a single inscription (*CIL* 6.10250), in the suburbium on the right bank of the Tiber, to the right (west) of Via Campana.

Insula Eutychetis: on the Quirinal, known from an inscription from the slope below the Fortezza dei Caetani toward the Salita del Grillo, an identifying signboard (*NSc* 1933, 510 no. 237 [R. Paribeni]).

Insula Felicles: a building listed in the regionary catalogues in Regio IX, famous for its height (Tertullian, *Adv. Valent.* 7). There is no reliable indication of its location.

Insula Saeni: known from an inscription from Via Marmorata now in the Galleria Lapidaria Capitolina (*AE* 1971.45 = *RendPontAcc* 43 [1970–71]: 119–20 [S. Panciera]).

Insula Serpentis Epidauri: see **Insula Tiberina.**

Insula Sertoriana: known only from an inscription (*CIL* 6.29791 = *ILS* 6034), a dipinto on plaster found in the Forum Boarium.

Insula Tiberina: the only island in the Tiber in the neighborhood of Rome, opposite the Forum Holitorium and Circus Flaminius, but separated from them by a narrow zone of buildings on the left bank, as well as by the river. It is an old geological ridge, approximating the pointed shape of a ship, and divides the Tiber stream into almost equal channels. But the diversion of the left-hand channel in an arc to the north slows the flow of the river and creates a quiet stretch below the island, where a ferry must have been established in early times to take across those using the riverbank as a highway and coming down from the Sabine hills and ultimately the Apennines to get salt at the river mouth. Evidence of this traffic is the Via Salaria and its continuation through Rome as Alta Semita and the Vicus Iugarius and the ancient salt works on the right bank of the river at its mouth. The ferry must have departed from the mouth of the Cloaca on the left bank and put in at a similar mouth on the opposite side downstream from this.

There seems to have been no regular bridge to the island before the construction of the Pons Fabricius in 62 B.C. Presumably the Pons Cestius, connecting the island to the right bank, was built at the same time or soon thereafter. Prior to that time the island was accessible only by boat, and it may have been regarded as suspect, if not a place of ill omen. It was put in Regio XIV of Augustan Rome, lumped with the whole of the Transtiberim, and never had a real name. On the Marble Plan (*FUR* pl. 30; Rodriguez pl. 24) and in most of our other sources it is called Inter Duos Pontes (Plutarch, *Poplic.* 8.3; Chron. 145). Vitruvius (3.2.3) and Acron (*ad Hor. Sat.* 2.3.36) call it Insula Tiberina, and Festus (Paulus *ex Fest.* 98L) calls it Insula. Other designations seem to be either fanciful or poetic.

At present the island is 269 m long and 67 m wide at its greatest width. There was a tradition that it was formed after the expulsion of the Tarquins when the people of Rome threw the grain from the fields of the Tarquins in the Campus Martius into the Tiber (Livy 2.5.3–4; Dion. Hal. 5.13.3–4). This story might have been invented to explain the suspicion with which the island was viewed. In 291 B.C. the snake of Aesculapius, which was being brought to Rome from Epidaurus with the statue of the god, left the ship while it was in the river and swam ashore to the island, which was then consecrated to Aesculapius, whose temple was built there (see Aesculapius, Aedes). Later other divinities also found places here: Iuppiter Iurarius, Faunus, Semo Sancus, Tiberinus, Vediovis (1)(qq.v.). The temenos at the southeastern end of the island was made to resemble the stern of a ship by the addition to the embankment below the temple of a travertine revetment, on the north side of which was carved the snake-wound staff of Aesculapius and a bust. Some of this with the carving still remains. Below this, the end of the island seems to have been treated as an almost featureless platform. A small obelisk, two fragments of which are preserved in the Museo Nazionale Archeologico in Naples and another in Munich, stood in front of the church of S. Bartolomeo, near the waist of the island, until the sixteenth century. The notion that this represented the mast of the ship seems unwarranted in view of the lack of indication that the whole island was treated similarly. The relative locations of the Pons Fabricius and Pons Cestius indicate that there was a thoroughfare across the island after their construction. This may have been the Vicus Censorius mentioned in two inscriptions found near here (*CIL*

6.451 = *ILS* 3619 and *CIL* 6.821) and listed on the Capitoline Base (*CIL* 6.975 = *ILS* 6073). We have almost no information about other streets on the island and its organization and appearance.

Nash 1.508–9; Lugli 1975, 87–91; *RendLinc*, ser. 8.26 (1971): 267–81 (M. Guarducci); *La nave di pietra: Storia, architettura e archeologia dell'isola tiberina* (show catalogue, 22 October–27 November 1983, Ente Provinciale per il Turismo di Roma), 12–27; *BullCom* 92 (1987–88): 372–76 (M. Conticello De' Spagnolis).

Insula Vitaliana: a building on the Esquiline in Via delle Sette Sale known only from an inscription (*CIL* 6.33893 = *ILS* 3679), a dipinto on one of its walls (NSc 1895, 80 [G. Gatti]).

Insula Volusiana: known from a cippus found in the excavations of the Area Sacra di Sant'Omobono of A.D. 48 confirming possession of a property granted to a Volusius by Augustus in 27 B.C. The insula in question lay south of the temples of Fortuna and Mater Matuta in a busy commercial area on the Forum Boarium.

Archeologia, materiali e problemi 6: I Volusii Saturnini (Bari 1982), 90–95 (S. Panciera).

Insula . . . alatiana: known from a single inscription (*CIL* 6.10248) giving the terms of a will and without indication of location.

Inter Duos Lucos (1): probably not a place designation but rather a description of the situation of the Domus Tetricorum (see Domus, Tetrici) on the Caelian (S.H.A. *Tyr. Trig.* 25.4), in which case the groves were probably not sacred.

Inter Duos Lucos (2) (Fig. 19): the part of the Capitoline Hill toward the Forum Romanum where now stands the Palazzo del Senatore. It was a locus saeptus in Livy's day, where Romulus had established and consecrated an asylum (Livy 1.8.5). By Dionysius's time the groves had disappeared, but he thought of them as adjacent to the asylum, not crowning the heights to either side (Dion. Hal. 2.15.4). A Temple of Vediovis (see Vediovis, Aedes [2]), in which the cella was broader than the pronaos, was also built there (Vitruvius 4.8.4), but it is not clear whether this encroached on the asylum or why it should have had its unusual plan. It was older than the Tabularium (q.v.), the plan of which accommodates it. Whether the Tabularium should also be described as *inter duos lucos* is not known. Excavations under Piazza del Campidoglio have revealed streets and shops of the early empire and show that the asylum, if it still existed as a locus saeptus, must by then have

ISIS, AEDES

been a rather small area occupying the southern corner of the piazza between the Palazzo del Senatore and Palazzo dei Conservatori (Lugli 1946, 38–39).

If Dionysius is right about the groves in question, they were not separate sacred groves, let alone groves crowning the heights, and this seems confirmed by occasional references to the asylum as having itself been established in a grove (Florus 1.1.9; *Schol. ad Iuvenal.* 8.273).

Inter Duos Pontes: a designation of the Insula Tiberina (q.v.) or, more particularly, the square in the middle of the island between the Pons Fabricius and Pons Cestius.

Inter Falcarios: a location mentioned twice in Cicero (*Cat.* 1.8, *Sull.* 52), where M. Porcius Laeca had his house and the members of the Catilinarian conspiracy met. It is not known where the scythe-makers congregated, but presumably it was in the heart of the city.

Inter Vitores: evidently a street on the Aventine side of the Circus Maximus (q.v.) where basket-makers and wicker-workers must once have had their workshops (*CIL* 14.4535; cf. Tacitus, *Ann.* 6.45).

Iovis Coenatio: on the Palatine, one of the more public apartments of the Domus Augustiana (S.H.A. *Pertinax* 11.6), probably the same as the Sicilia (q.v.).

Isis, Aedes (1) (Figs. 46, 47): always the chief temple of Isis in Rome, in the Campus Martius, adjacent to the Temple of Serapis and in a single precinct with it. It is often called Isis Campensis (cf. Apuleius, *Met.* 11.26) and, with the Temple of Serapis, Iseum et Serapeum (Eutropius 7.23.5; S.H.A. *Alex. Sev.* 26.8; Chron. 146; *Not.; Cur.*). It stood next to the Saepta Iulia (Juvenal 6.528–29) and is shown on fragments of the Marble Plan (*FUR* pl. 31; Rodriguez pl. 27) east of the Saepta, between it and the Temple of Minerva Chalcidica.

As early as the time of Catullus (10.26), we find mention of a temple of Serapis as a haunt of libertines and *meretrices,* and Cassius Dio (47.15.4) says that in 43 B.C. the triumvirs voted a temple to Isis and Serapis, but repressive measures against the worship of the Egyptian gods were repeatedly introduced, by Augustus (Cass. Dio 53.2.4), Agrippa (Cass. Dio 54.6.6), and especially Tiberius in A.D. 19 (Tacitus, *Ann.* 2.85; Suetonius, *Tib.* 36.1). Tiberius is said to have destroyed the Temple of Isis and thrown the cult image in the Tiber (Josephus, *AntIud* 18.3.4 [79]), but the story seems embroidered. By

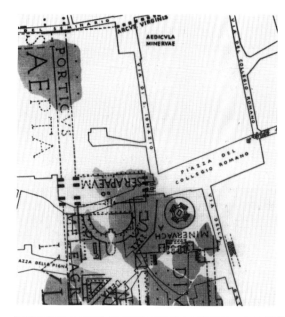

Figure 46
Iseum Campense and Serapaeum, Area as Represented on the Marble Plan

the time of Lucan (8.831) the cult of Isis had been officially accepted, very likely under Caligula, and if the temple had not been already standing for a century, it must have been built then. It burned in the great fire of Titus in A.D. 80 (Cass. Dio 66.24.2) and was rebuilt by Domitian (Eutropius 7.23.5; Chron. 146) and handsomely embellished by Alexander Severus, especially with statuary (S.H.A. *Alex. Sev.* 26.8). It is shown on coins of Vespasian commemorating the fact that Vespasian and Titus spent the night before their triumph there (Josephus, *BellIud* 7.5.4 [123]; *B. M. Coins, Rom. Emp.* 2.189 no. 780). As shown, it was frontal, approached by a flight of steps, with a façade of four Corinthian columns surmounted by a deep lunate pediment containing a statue of Isis Sothis seated on a dog running right. This statue is said to have turned its face inward in A.D. 219–220 (Cass. Dio 80.10.1). The cult statue was a standing figure and is shown before the doors to the inner shrine, which may have been a separate building.

As shown on the Marble Plan, the complex was architecturally very exotic. The Serapeum lay south of the Iseum and communicated with it by a broad doorway divided into bays by three columns. Little of the Iseum appears on what survives, but enough to show a colonnade addorsed to the wall at the south end and very widely spaced columns or, better, trees, along the sides. The temple proper probably stood toward the north end. Whether there were other entrances from the north and east is not clear, but there seems to have been none from the west.

The Serapeum was a separate building, a rectangular open square running east and west, probably

211

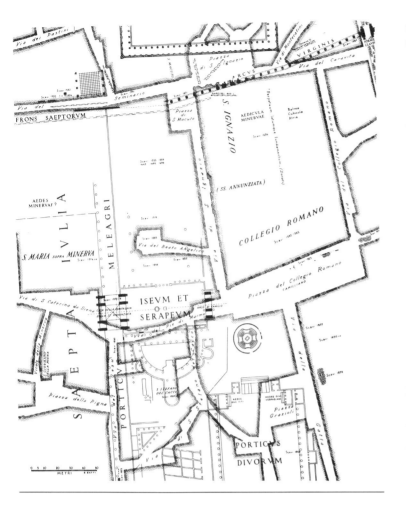

Figure 47
Iseum Campense and
Adjacencies, Plan,
as Known

tions. In the throat leading in from the Arco di Camigliano, four foundations suggest a tetrapylon but
are more likely aediculae. In the center of the south
side of the square, a broad door led to a colonnade
shaped like the letter *D*, off the curved arm of which
opens a series of four apsidal exedras with columns
in the openings. These seem to have been chapels.
The temple proper is probably the feature on axis
shown projecting into the middle of the *D*. South of
this colonnade, in the irregular area behind it, are
numerous annexes, including a colonnade along the
west, but with no clear pattern, that may best be read
as sacristies and housing for the priests of the cult. A
fancied resemblance of the plan of the Serapeum to
the "Canopus" of Hadrian's villa at Tibur will not
stand up under scrutiny.

Numerous works of art, especially Egyptian sculptures, columns, and obelisks, have been found in the
neighborhood. Among these should be mentioned
the obelisks of Piazza della Minerva, Piazza della Rotonda, and Viale delle Terme Diocletiane (see Obelisci Isei Campensis), the statues of the Nile (Vatican), Tiber (Louvre) and Oceanus (Naples), the
lifesize basalt baboon of the church of S. Stefano del
Cacco, and the colossal marble foot of an acrolith
known as the Pie' di Marmo. For a partial list of the
finds, see Lanciani (LRE 502–4) and the references
given by Roullet (34–35). The architectural oddity
of the complex has given rise to speculation about
the possible introduction of avenues of sphinxes, entrance pylons, and the like, but for these there is no
evidence.

Nash 1.510–11; A. Roullet, *The Egyptian and
Egyptianizing Monuments of Imperial Rome* (Leiden
1972), 23–35; M. Malaise, *Inventaire préliminaire
du documents égyptiens découverts en Italie* (Leiden
1972), 187–214; Lugli 1975, 435–36.

Isis, Aedes (2): The third region of Augustan Rome
is given the name Isis et Serapis in the regionary catalogues, and in the Historia Augusta (S.H.A. *Tyr.
Trig.* 25.4) we find mention of an Isium Metellinum
opposite the Domus Tetricorum on the Caelian. An
inscription found in Via Labicana near the Baths of
Trajan (*CIL* 6.30915) mentions dedication of an
Anubis, an altar, and doors to Isidi Lydiae educa-
trici, and material that might have been associated
with a cult of the Egyptian gods has been found at
scattered points from Via Labicana to Via Machiavelli. Ruins of a sacellum decorated in the Egyptian
style were discovered near the western end of the
church of SS. Pietro e Marcellino in 1653, and this is
the best candidate for the temple we are seeking (HJ
304–5n.49).

with monumental entrances from both the Saepta
and the square to the east containing the Temple of
Minerva Chalcidica, the latter later known as the
Arco di Camigliano. On the relief of the Haterii in
the Lateran collection (Nash 1.119 fig. 123) is shown
a triple arch inscribed *Arcus ad Isis* (q.v.), with an
armed figure of Minerva shown in the central fornix
and figures of Serapis and Isis (?) in the side arches.
F. Castagnoli (*BullCom* 69 [1941]: 65–66) has argued that this is a representation of the Arco di Camigliano as built, or rebuilt, by Domitian. It seems
rather to be a triumphal arch of uncertain location
(*RömMitt* 97 [1990]: 131–34 [F. S. Kleiner]). Only
a single footing of the north central pier of the Arco
di Camigliano is known to survive (*BullCom* 90
[1985]: 77 [E. Gatti and F. Scoppola]; *Roma, archeologia nel centro* [1985], 2.400–403 [M. C. Lau-
renti]).

Around the square there seem to have been scattered a number of small buildings or large dedica-

This would put the temple just inside the southern and eastern boundaries of Regio III. Nothing definite is known of the history of the shrine or why it should have given its name to the regio, but it may have been one of those destroyed in 48 B.C. and adjacent to the shrine of Bellona Rufilia (cf. Cass. Dio 42.26.2; *CIL* 6.2234 = ILS 4181a).

Malaise 171–77.

Isis Athenodoria: mentioned only in the regionary catalogues, listed in Regio XII, possibly a statue by the Rhodian sculptor Athenodorus, son of Hagesandros, and, if so, of the mid-first century B.C.

Malaise 222–24; Helbig⁴ 2.1523; L. Avetta, *Roma, Via Imperiale* (Rome 1985), 32–33.

Isis Patricia: mentioned only in the regionary catalogues, listed in Regio V. It is inconceivable that the Vicus Patricius continued beyond the line of the Servian Walls, so another explanation must be sought for the epithet. It is unknown what sort of monument is intended.

Malaise 178.

Isis Pelagia: a shrine of Isis known from a single inscription (*CIL* 6.8707 = ILS 4421), the funerary inscription of an aedituus of the shrine. Because Isis was very widely worshiped as a patroness of sea traffic, it may be that one of the better-known temples is meant.

Ab Isis et Serapis: known from inscriptions (*CIL* 6.2234 = ILS 4181a; *CIL* 6.32462 = ILS 4280; cf. Rostovtzeff, *Sylloge* no. 494). It is linked in one inscription with the shrine of Bellona Rufilia (see Bellona Rufilia, Aedes), and in another with that of Dea Suria (see Dea Suria, Templum). This makes it more likely that Isis, Aedes (2) in Regio III is meant, rather than Isis, Aedes (1) in Regio IX. However, one of the inscriptions is the funerary inscription of a man described as *fanaticus*, and, in view of the proclivity of Oriental and orgiastic cults to find acceptance on the right bank of the river, we may well be dealing with a third temple, either in Regio XIV or in the suburbium along Via Campana/Portuensis.

Isis et Serapis in Campo: see **Isis, Aedes** (1).

Isis et Serapis in Capitolio: shrines on the Capitoline, near the statue of Hercules, ordered razed by the soothsayers following an omen of a swarm of bees in 48 B.C. (Cass. Dio 42.26.2). Presumably these were rebuilt shortly thereafter, for there was a temple of Isis on the Capitoline in A.D. 69 (Suetonius, *Dom.*

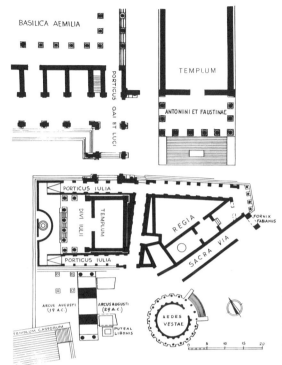

Figure 48
Temple of Divus Iulius, Arcus Augusti, Temple of Vesta, Regia, and Adjacencies, Restored Plan, after R. Gamberini-Mongenet

1.2; cf. *CIL* 6.2247 = ILS 4405, 2248). See also Obeliscus Capitolinus.

Isium Metellinum: see **Isis, Aedes** (2).

Iulius, Divus, Aedes (Figs. 48, 49): the Temple of the Deified Julius Caesar, begun by the triumvirs in 42 B.C. (Cass. Dio 47.18.4) in the place where the corpse had been cremated by the people, and completed by Octavian and dedicated on 18 August 29 B.C. (Cass. Dio 51.22.2; Augustus, *RG* 19; Degrassi 497). Where the body was burned, at the east end of the Forum Romanum in front of the Regia, an altar and a column of giallo antico marble inscribed Parenti Patriae were erected shortly after the event (Suetonius, *Iul.* 85; Appian, *BellCiv* 2.148), but then Dolabella removed them and obliterated all trace of them (Cicero, *Att.* 14.15.1; *Phil.* 1.5). The dedication of the temple was celebrated with great games (Cass. Dio 51.22.4–9); it had the right of asylum (Cass. Dio 47.19.2); and the Arval Brethren met there (*CIL* 6.2051.55). Later it was repaired by Hadrian, a fact attested by coins, but with no change of the architectural style.

The available space dictated to some extent the architectural form. A high platform in front, 3.50 m high, served as a rostra and was decorated with the beaks of the ships taken at Actium (Cass. Dio

213

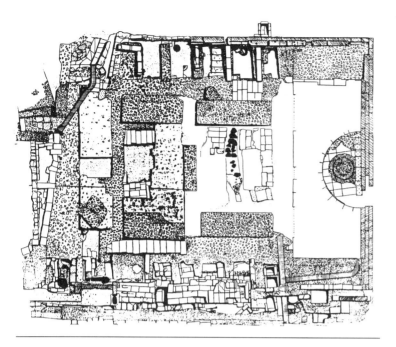

Figure 49
Temple of Divus Iulius,
Plan of
Existing Remains

aesthetic of the Forum Iulium and the Temple of Venus Genetrix. From the fragments we learn that the order was Corinthian (?), the frieze decorated with floral scrollwork and archaizing winged figures.

In the cella was a colossal statue of Julius Caesar, possibly with a star mounted on the head (Suetonius, *Iul.* 83; Pliny, *HN* 2.93–94; but cf. Cass. Dio 45.7.1). On coins of Augustus (Crawford 540/1; Lugli 1946, 201 and fig. 45) the cult statue is shown *capite velato*, holding a lituus, with a star in the pediment of the temple. Because Caesar is known to have been an augur (as well as Pontifex Maximus), this is probably correct. Here Augustus (*RG* 21) dedicated offerings from the spoils of war, among which may have been the paintings of Apelles of the Dioscuri with Victoria and Venus Anadyomene mentioned by Pliny (*HN* 35.27, 91, 93). When the latter deteriorated and could not be restored, Nero substituted for it another by Dorotheus.

Lugli 1946, 198–201; Nash 1.512–14; S. Weinstock, *Divus Iulius* (Oxford 1971), 385–401; *MonAnt* 48 (1973): 257–83 (M. Montagna Pasquinucci); *Athenaeum* 52 (1974): 144–55 (M. Montagna Pasquinucci); *Roma, archeologia nel centro* [1985], 1.67–72 [M. G. Cecchini]; *Arctos* 21 (1967): 147–56 (E. M. Steinby).

Iuno Curitis: a shrine in the Campus Martius, of which the dedication day was 7 October (Degrassi 518). This is probably the same as Iuno Curritis (or Quiritis) of Falerii (*CIL* 11.3100, 3125, 3126; *ILS* 3111, 5374), and the cult may have been brought to Rome by evocation at the destruction of Falerii in 241 B.C. Temples A and C of the Area Sacra di Largo Argentina have been suggested to be the shrine in question, but there is no proof. Cf. Paulus *ex Fest.* 55L, where there is the strong implication that Iuno Curitis was originally a Sabine divinity.

Iuno Iuga: an altar in the Vicus Iugarius (q.v.) from which Festus (Paulus *ex Fest.* 92L) believed the vicus derived its name. This Juno was supposed to *matrimonia iungere*. Because the Vicus Iugarius was certainly very old and probably derived its name quite differently, the altar is apt to have received its name from the vicus, rather than vice versa, a punning invention from Juno's role as patroness of marriage, but the form Iuga is puzzling. There is no telling exactly where it was situated, but presumably it was adjacent to neither the Forum Romanum nor the Porta Carmentalis.

Iuno Lucina, Aedes: a temple built in 375 B.C. (Pliny, *HN* 16.235) in a precinct *(lucus)* consecrated

51.19.2); it was known as the Rostra Aedis Divi Iuli, or Rostra Iulia (Frontinus, *Aq.* 2.129; Cass. Dio 56.34.4). Tiberius delivered the eulogy of Augustus from it (Suetonius, *Aug.* 100.3), and the emperors frequently used it for public addresses. It was approached from behind by a lateral ramp on either side, and in the center of the front a deep semicircular niche walled off across the front contains the concrete core of a small circular structure in three steps, which has been interpreted as a restoration of the altar first installed on the site of the pyre, but is more likely the Puteal Libonis (q.v.). At ground level the ramps of approach are extended along the sides of the platform as arcades, being connected behind the temple by an oblique cryptoporticus and continued along the northeast side of the Regia. These covered walks have been identified as the Porticus Iulia (q.v.).

The temple proper thus was surrounded by single-storey annexes on all sides and rose on a second platform 2.36 m high, which was approached from the front by a short stair passing between the columns of the façade. It was hexastyle, prostyle, with both pronaos and cella broad shallow rectangles of equal depth. Little remains of the columns or superstructure, except for a few fragments of the entablature, pilasters that decorated the interior, and marble beams of the roof, but Vitruvius (3.3.2) tells us that the temple was pycnostyle, with columns spaced at close intervals of one and one-half diameters, which must have emphasized the verticality of the whole building and repeated with significant emphasis the

to this divinity from very early times. Varro (*Ling.* 5.49, 74) assigns the introduction of the cult to Titus Tatius. Servius Tullius is said to have ordered a coin for the birth of each child to be paid into the treasury of Iuno Lucina (Dion. Hal. 4.15.5), so there must have been some sort of building here from an early date. It was on the Cispian, and the sixth shrine of the second regio of the Argei was in, or adjacent to, the precinct. It lay probably near the end of the Cispian above the Clivus Suburanus, perhaps extending down to it. Here inscriptions relating to the cult have been found (*CIL* 6.357–61, 3694, 3695; *ILS* 366, 3101–4; *ILLRP* 160–64). Here the feast of the Matronalia, an occasion for widespread offering of presents to women, was celebrated on 1 March, the dedication day of the temple (Ovid, *Fast.* 3.247–58; Festus 131L; Degrassi 418–19).

In the precinct were two lotus trees of great age, believed to antedate the temple (Pliny, *HN* 16.235). In 190 B.C. the temple was struck by lightning, and the roof and doors were damaged (Livy 37.3.2). In 41 B.C. Q. Pedius, a quaestor, contracted for building a very expensive wall, presumably around the precinct (*CIL* 6.358 = *ILS* 3102 = *ILLRP* 160). The temple continued to be frequented under the empire but is not mentioned in the regionary catalogues.

Iuno Lucina, Lucus: see **Iuno Lucina, Aedes.**

Iuno Matuta: see **Iuno Sospita, Aedes.**

Iuno Moneta (in *CIL* 6.362: Iuno Moneta Regina), **Aedes** (Fig. 19): a temple vowed by M. Furius Camillus as dictator during a war with the Aurunci in 345 B.C., built by duovirs appointed by the senate after Camillus resigned his dictatorship, and dedicated the following year (Livy 7.28.4–6). It was built on the site of the house of M. Manlius Capitolinus (see Domus, M. Manlius Capitolinus), which had been razed in 384 (Livy 6.20.13), which was also the site of the house of Titus Tatius (Plutarch, *Romulus* 20.4; Solinus 1.21). The day of dedication was 1 June (Degrassi 463); another celebration at the temple on 10 October probably commemorated a restoration of it (Degrassi 519). In it were kept the Libri Lintei (Livy 4.7.12 and 20.8), annalistic records of magistrates and significant events kept by the priests of the temple. The temple is mentioned among the prodigies of 196 B.C.; the points of two spears *ad Monetam* burst into flames (Livy 33.26.8), which suggests that the goddess had a warrior aspect.

The origin of the epithet Moneta is obscure. The ancients tended to associate it with warnings (*mo-nere*) (cf. Cicero, *Div.* 1.101; Suidas s.v.), but more likely it came with the establishment of the mint there in 273 B.C. (Suidas s.v.). It continued to be there in the time of Augustus (Cicero, *Att.* 8.7.3; Livy 6.20.13) and was probably not moved to a place in Regio III before the Flavian period or the end of the first century (cf. Moneta). Thereafter, there is no mention of the Temple of Iuno Moneta, and no trace of it has turned up in any of the work on the Capitoline. It is presumed to lie under the church of Aracoeli.

This is very strange. It was a major temple occupying one of the most magnificent sites in Rome. In it was kept one of the principal sets of public records. And somewhere in the precinct all the silver coined in Rome for nearly four hundred years was minted. Yet not a single vestige of this venerable shrine has been positively identified. It has been presumed that it represented one of the two groves of the designation Inter Duos Lucos (2) (q.v.), the other being the Area Capitolina, but there could hardly have been much open space left around a site occupied from earliest time by houses, let alone anything that could claim to be a grove. It is also unlikely on other grounds. It continues to be one of the great enigmas in the topography of ancient Rome.

Nash 1.515–17; *BullCom* 87 (1980–81): 7–36 (G. Giannelli).

Iuno Regina, Aedes (1): see **Iuppiter Optimus Maximus (Capitolinus), Aedes.**

Iuno Regina, Aedes (2): The Temple of Iuno Regina on the Aventine is reported to have been built by M. Furius Camillus immediately after the destruction of Veii in 396 B.C. The temple of this goddess at Veii had played a central role in the story of the taking of this city, and according to tradition she had been the object of an *evocatio* by the dictator on the eve of the final assault (Livy 5.21.1–3). After the sack of Veii was over, the goddess's image was brought to Rome with elaborate care and solemn ritual and installed on the Aventine (Livy 5.22.3–7). And here in 392 was dedicated the temple Camillus had vowed (Livy 5.22.7, 31.3). In the meantime the statue was presumably housed in one of the neighboring temples ascribed to Servius Tullius, either that of Diana or that of Luna, probably the former. Camillus, who was a deeply religious man, seems to have felt a special devotion to Juno, and almost fifty years later, in 345, his son is said to have dedicated the temple of Iuno Moneta (Regina) on the Capitoline (see Iuno Moneta, Aedes). Thus Juno came to claim a place on three of the commanding heights of Rome and as Iuno Lucina had a grove on the Cispian from a very early period.

The cult of Iuno Lucina seems to have been a birth cult and the concern of women. Iuno Curitis and Iuno Sospes, or Sospita, were warrior goddesses, protectresses of cities, and perhaps closely related. Iuno Regina, the consort of Iuppiter Rex and a member of the Capitoline triad, stands very close to the heart of Roman religion. She wore the diadem and veil of a queen and carried a long scepter and a patera; her bird was the peacock. She could command the lightning bolt (Servius *ad Aen.* 1.42, 8.430). Her sacrificial animal was the *aurata iuvenca*.

In the cult on the Aventine Dionysius (13.3) describes the cult image brought from Veii as a xoanon, an ancient wooden figure, and in the expiation offered in 207 B.C. two images of the goddess made of cypress wood, as well as a golden vessel, were dedicated in this temple. We should therefore probably reckon the image as archaic, but may be surprised that it was not of terracotta. Iuno Regina is not shown in full figure alone on coins, so far as we know, though she does appear as a member of the Capitoline triad, at which time she stands left of Jupiter in long drapery, carrying a scepter. The head, in the few cases where it appears on coins, shows no sign of archaism.

The offerings known to have been made in the temple on the Aventine are made by women, a bronze statue in 218 B.C. (Livy 21.62.8), and a golden basin *(pelvis)* in 207 (Livy 27.37.10). The temple was struck by lightning in 207 (Livy 27.37.7), and this was taken as a leading from heaven, because at the time the Romans were in the process of preparing an elaborate procession and sacrifice to expiate the birth of a monstrous hermaphroditic child. Thereafter, all such expiations seem to have followed a pattern and ended at this temple (Livy 31.12.9; Obsequens 46, 48), and Iuno Regina took over the offerings that had formerly been made to many gods (cf. Livy 22.1.17–18).

There must always have been some association of Juno and Diana. Probably Diana was hostess to the xoanon of Veii when it was first brought to Rome, and the precincts of the two goddesses were adjacent. Both are described as at the top of the Clivus Publicius (q.v.). Both represented the gathering into the Roman community of neighboring people who had a special veneration for a particular goddess, neither one alien to Rome, but each given an emphasis not previously found at Rome, Diana as a goddess of asylum, Iuno Regina as a savior and protectress.

Augustus (*RG* 19) restored the temple, but, despite its ancient importance, it is not mentioned thereafter or listed in the regionary catalogues. Its general location is given by two dedicatory inscriptions found near the church of S. Sabina (*CIL* 6.364, 365 = *ILS* 4321a). The dedication day was 1 September, which Degrassi (505) thinks must also have been the dedication day of the original building.

Iuno Regina, Aedes (3) (Figs. 70, 71): After Iuppiter Stator received a second temple built on the Circus Flaminius sometime after the laying out of that square in 221 B.C., the vowing of a temple to Iuno Regina in 187 B.C. by M. Aemilius Lepidus during the Ligurian wars (Livy 39.2.11) may be seen as completion of an imperfect offering. Iuppiter Stator had been associated with Iuno Regina for a century; it was there that Livius Andronicus was training his chorus of girls when the Temple of Iuno Regina on the Aventine was struck by lightning in 207, and presumably whenever expiatory processions had to be trained the temple was used for this purpose. Iuppiter Stator was unthinkable without Iuno Regina; it was the most natural thing in the world for the pontifices to have postulated, or suggested, that the next temple vowed ought to be, all things being equal, to Iuno Regina, or for the consul to have thought of it on his own initiative.

That was not quite the way things happened. In the first regular battle of his campaign, Aemilius Lepidus vowed a temple to Diana instead, perhaps because he was fighting in mountainous country against a tough and fiercely independent people. Thus he skipped the next temple in the natural sequence in favor of one that was closely related but more appropriate to his circumstances. Then he rectified his omission a few months later, and in his final battle against the Ligurians he vowed a temple to Iuno Regina. The space for this had probably already been set aside flanking Iuppiter Stator, for the Temple of the Muses vowed by M. Fulvius Nobilior in 189 and built soon after his triumph in 187 lay west of both Iuppiter Stator and Iuno Regina and farther from the Porta Carmentalis, but probably not on the axis of the circus square. Where the Temple of Diana may lie is an interesting question.

The temple of Iuno Regina was dedicated by Lepidus as censor in 179 (Livy 40.52.1). Its dedication day is given in the republican Fasti Antiates Maiores as 23 December (Degrassi 544–45), which is probably the original dedication. A portico between this temple and that of Fortuna was struck by lightning and several buildings severely damaged in 156 B.C. (Obsequens 16); the Temple of Fortuna has been thought to be that of Fortuna Equestris (see Fortuna Equestris, Aedes), which may have stood northwest of the Temple of Iuno Regina. Because it had disappeared by A.D. 22 (Tacitus, *Ann.* 3.71), its precinct may have been divided between the Porticus Octaviae and the Porticus Philippi.

Q. Caecilius Metellus Macedonicus may have rebuilt the Temple of Iuno Regina when he built the Porticus Metelli (q.v.) after 146 B.C. (Vell. Pat. 1.11.3–5), but it seems very unlikely in view of there still being a Ligurian shield on the temple when it was struck by lightning in 134 B.C. (Obsequens 27). Octavia certainly rebuilt it as part of her rebuilding of the Porticus Metelli to make a splendid new complex commemorating her son, Marcellus. It will have been at this time that the story of the architects Saurus and Batrachus and the mistake of the workmen in installing the cult statues of Iuppiter Stator and Iuno Regina in each other's temples (Pliny, *HN* 36.42–43) got started. The cult statue of Juno was by Dionysius (Pliny, *HN* 36.35). This temple burned in the fire of Titus in A.D. 80 (Cass. Dio 66.24), and Domitian presumably rebuilt it. It burned again in 203, and Septimius Severus and Caracalla (*CIL* 6.1034) restored it. It is of this rebuilding that considerable remains, including three marble columns with composite capitals and enough of the plan to permit an almost complete reconstruction, survives embedded in existing buildings. The temple was prostyle, hexastyle, with a deep pronaos and an ample cella, its floor raised four steps above the pronaos, in which Piranesi, our best source for the building, shows an extra aedicula for the cult statue. It is also so shown on the Marble Plan (*FUR* pl. 29; Rodriguez pl. 23), where it appears almost complete.

Nash 2.254–58; Lugli 1970, 298–303; *QITA* 5 (1968): 77–88 (A. M. Palchetti and L. Quilici).

Iuno Sororia, Ara: see **Ianus Curiatius, Ara.**

Iuno Sospita, Aedes (Figs. 37.6, 38): a temple vowed in 197 B.C. by the consul C. Cornelius Cethegus during the Insubrian War (Livy 32.30.10) and dedicated by him as censor in 194 (Livy 34.53.3). It was in the Forum Holitorium, and the dedication day was 1 February (Degrassi 405–6). The consul L. Iulius Caesar restored it in 90 B.C. following a dream of Caecilia Metella, daughter of Q. Caecilius Metellus Balearicus (Cicero, *Div.* 1.99; Obsequens 55). The temple had fallen into such neglect that when it was cleaned a bitch was found to have made her lair and had a litter there. In all probability, it is the northernmost of the three temples built into the church of S. Nicola in Carcere, a single-cella temple, peripteral sine postico, with six columns on the façade and originally eight, plus a terminal anta, down each long side. It is usually shown with nine columns on the sides, but this is an error; the footings of the first two are cut in a single block of travertine for greater strength and stability and make this clearly the termination. Later the Temple of Spes, next to it

on the south, was rebuilt and its façade advanced in front of that of Iuno Sospita by the depth of a column and intercolumniation. The façade of Iuno Sospita seems subsequently to have been advanced to match this.

The temple was frontal and stood on a relatively low podium faced with travertine and finished with base and crown moldings; it was approached from the front by a stair the width of the façade. Under a continuous crown molding along the long sides, loculi for the deposit of valuables open in the intercolumniations. These are brick-faced, low-ceilinged chambers, at least some of which were given concrete vaults. A Severan date is suggested for the construction. They must have been finished on the exterior with bronze frames and doors. Above Attic bases of travertine, the columns and entablature are of peperino and were finished with stucco. The order is Ionic of rather classical design, and the volutes lie flat, in a plane with the architrave. The frieze must have been deeply plastic; two, and in places three, undulant lines of closely, but irregularly, spaced holes show where metal spikes of the armature were fixed, but unfortunately the design cannot be deduced from the location of these. The ceiling of the peripteros was coffered. The pronaos was originally relatively shallow, the depth of two intercolumniations, later apparently enlarged to three, which made it disproportionate. The single cella was long and narrow.

Seven columns and the terminal anta of the south side still remain in place with the entablature above them, while parts of three columns of the north side have been restored to position. The podium is in excellent condition on the south side, heavily restored on the north, and ruinous on the façade. Only the footings of the cella walls remain, except for the terminal anta mentioned above. The existing architecture is clearly of the first century B.C.; Crozzoli Aite thinks it Augustan.

A very small portion of the north flank of the temple is shown on a fragment of the Marble Plan, and part of the south flank and stair of approach are depicted on another (*FUR* pl. 29 frag. 69 g and h; Rodriguez pl. 23). The latter indicates that the stair was divided, a flight the width of two columns and the space between rising to either side, presumably flanking the altar. Existing remains neither confirm nor contradict this.

Ovid (*Fast.* 2.55–58) seems to have believed there was once a Temple of Iuno Sospita on the Palatine adjacent to the Temple of the Magna Mater, a temple that had disappeared before his time. Such a temple is otherwise unattested and unlikely to have actually existed. Because he gives it the same foundation day as the temple in the Forum Holitorium, it seems possible that Ovid or his source had confused Magna

Mater with Mater Matuta, whose temple might somewhat inaccurately be described as coterminous with that of Iuno Sospita. One might also note that Livy (34.53.3) has Iunonis Matutae where he clearly means Iunonis Sospitae.

Nash 1.418–21; L. Crozzoli Aite, *I tre templi del Foro Olitorio* (*MemPontAcc,* ser. 3.13 [1981]): especially 87–106.

Iuppiter, Iuno, Minerva, Sacellum: see Capitolium Vetus.

Iuppiter Africus:

a statue in the Area Capitolina known from two military diplomata of A.D. 76 and 85 (*CIL* 16.21, 31). It has been conjectured that a statue of Ammon is meant.

Iuppiter Arborator:

mentioned only in the *Notitia,* listed in Regio XI. The reading is curious: *aedem Matris Deum et Iovis Arboratoris,* with the suggestion that it was in the Circus Maximus, along the spina. In the fourth century the statue of Cybele on the spina is sometimes shown with a tree or trees close by, and unidentified sacella are also shown. It may be one of these that is meant.

Humphrey 275.

Iuppiter Conservator, Sacellum:

a shrine that Domitian built during the reign of Vespasian in the Area Capitolina on the site of the lodge of the *aedituus* (sacristan) who had sheltered him when the Vitellians stormed the Capitoline in A.D. 69 (Tacitus, *Hist.* 3.74). The marble altar bore reliefs showing the rescue. Later, after he became princeps, Domitian built a full-scale Temple of Iuppiter Custos, perhaps on the site of the sacellum, in which the cult statue showed the princeps in the arms of the god (Tacitus, *Hist.* 3.74; Suetonius, *Dom.* 5). A large square concrete platform through which the Via del Tempio di Giove, formerly Via di Monte Tarpeio, was cut in 1896 has been rather improbably identified as remains of this temple (see Iuppiter Tonans), and it has been believed to be shown on an attic relief of the Arch of Trajan at Benevento (F. J. Hassel, *Der Trajansbogen in Benevent* [Mainz 1966], pls. 15, 17.4), but in too schematic a form to be really useful.

Nash 1.518–20.

Iuppiter Custos: see Iuppiter Conservator.

Iuppiter Depulsor (Alexikakos):

an altar reported by Phlegon (*Mirac.* 6 [*FGrH* 2.2 p. 1179]) to have been set up by Claudius on the Capitoline, otherwise unknown. The equivalence of the Latin epithet is not entirely certain.

Iuppiter Dolichenus, Templum (1):

a temple of Syrian Ba'al listed in the regionary catalogues in Regio XIII (where it is called simply Dolocenum) and discovered in 1935 under the Via di S. Domenico in front of houses numbered 18–22, between Via di S. Alessio and Via Raimondo da Capua. After excavation it was filled in again. The finds of sculpture and inscriptions are in the Museo Capitolino, Room Three of the Culti Orientali (Helbig⁴ 2.1190).

What of the sanctuary could be explored consisted of three rooms, a vestibule room ending in an apse containing a series of round-headed niches above a masonry counter with some remains of marble veneer; a long narrow cella with an axial altar trimmed with colonnettes at the corners at one end and remains of a long platform, probably for dedications, although this is not quite clear, along one long wall; and a squarish room not directly communicating with the others but containing a cipollino column at its center. Evidently there were other chambers to the southeast, but their character remains unknown. The two principal rooms were floored with black-and-white mosaic of rather coarse workmanship but bold patterns of squares and bands. The long cella was found full of a collection of dedications, including statuary, reliefs, and altars. These show that three couples, Iuppiter Dolichenus and Iuno Regina, Isis and Serapis, and Sol and Luna, were worshiped together here and evidently considered equivalents. A number of other gods seem to have been worshiped here as well.

The foundation of the shrine seems to be Antonine. The cult flourished for a century, then gradually declined but continued to exist. Coins of the Ostrogothic period were found among the ruins.

BullCom 83 (1935): 145–59 (A. M. Colini); *Epigraphica* 1 (1939): 119–41 (A. M. Colini); *Atti del quarto congresso nazionale di studi romani,* 1.126–35 (A. M. Colini); C. Pietrangeli, *Musei Capitolini: Monumenti dei culti orientali* (Rome 1951), 34–46; Helbig⁴ 2.36–39; Nash 1.521–24.; *CEFR* 98 (1987): 545–62 (M. Le Glay).

Iuppiter Dolichenus (2):

a shrine on the Esquiline known from four inscriptions found in the neighborhood of Piazza Vittorio Emanuele (*CIL* 6.414, 30942, 30946; *ILS* 4307, 4308, 4315). These indicate that it was dedicated, after enlargement and redecoration, on 31 July A.D. 191.

Iuppiter Dolichenus (3):

a shrine in the Transtiberim, known only from two inscriptions (*CIL* 6.415, 418).

Iuppiter Elicius, Ara:

an altar said to have been erected by Numa on the Aventine for the purpose of consulting the god by augury to discover what prodigies by lightning or other manifestations should be considered (Livy 1.20.7 and 31.8; Varro, *Ling.* 6.94; Ovid, *Fast.* 3.327–30; Plutarch, *Numa* 15.6; Pliny, *HN* 2.140). Many authorities on Roman religion believe that the epithet had originally rather to do with the invocation of rain (cf. *aquaelicium*). However, there seems no real reason to associate this with the Remoria (q.v.).

Iuppiter Fagutalis: see **Fagutal** and **Vicus Iovis Fagutalis.**

Iuppiter Feretrius, Aedes: according to Livy (1.10.4–7), originally simply a templum high on the Capitoline Hill that Romulus bounded and dedicated to receive the spolia opima that he had taken from Acron, king of Caenina (see also Livy 4.20.3; Plutarch, *Rom.* 16.4–7; Dion. Hal. 2.34.4; Val. Max. 3.2.3–6; Servius *ad Aen.* 6.859). The site was chosen because an oak tree there had come to be regarded as sacred. But Dionysius makes it a temple building from the beginning, and Plutarch has Romulus cut down an oak to make a suitable trophy of the spoils. Following Romulus's example, the spolia opima were dedicated twice afterward in the same temple, by A. Cornelius Cossus in 428 B.C. after he had killed Lar Tolumnius, king of Veii, and by M. Claudius Marcellus in 222 B.C. after he had killed Viridomarus (or Britomarus), king of the Insubrian Gauls (see also Plutarch, *Marcellus* 8.1–3).

The temple was probably within the Area Capitolina and always a small building, although Livy (1.33.9) says it was enlarged by Ancus Marcius, speaking of it then as an aedes. According to Dionysius (2.34), the long sides measured less than 15 feet. It is represented on a coin of P. Cornelius Lentulus Marcellinus of ca. 50 B.C. as tetrastyle, the columns in pairs crowded to either side of a broad central opening of enigmatic character (*B. M. Coins, Rom. Rep.* 1.567 no. 4206; Crawford 439/1). The columns have bases as well as capitals and seem to have been Tuscan; the triangular pediment is high but empty. In Augustus's day it was sadly dilapidated and had lost much of its roof, and he restored it at Atticus's suggestion (Nepos, *Att.* 20.3; Livy 4.20.7; Augustus, *RG* 19). At the time of the restoration Augustus is said to have entered the temple and read the dedicatory inscription on the linen corselet dedicated by Cossus, which shows that the *adyton* of the temple was not regularly accessible. The statement of Dionysius (2.34) that in his day a trace of the ancient plan could still be seen suggests that the rebuilding preserved the dimensions of the original, or had them marked on it.

There seems never to have been a cult statue, and

none is shown on the coins cited above. Apart from the dedications made here, the temple was used as a repository for the ritual implements of the Fetiales, the scepter by which they swore and the flint knife with which the ritual pig was sacrificed (Paulus *ex Fest.* 81L). Presumably their deposit there was one of the religious ordinances of Numa, the founder of the college of Fetiales (Dion. Hal. 2.72).

Various derivations for the epithet Feretrius were offered in antiquity, from *ferre, feretrum,* and *ferire,* none of which is thoroughly satisfactory, although most authorities today incline toward *ferire* and the ritual stroke implicit in the phrase *foedus ferire* and connect this with the solemn oath by Iuppiter Lapis (Cicero, *Fam.* 7.12.2; A. Gellius 1.21.4). But the relationship is tenuous.

No trace of the temple has ever been identified, which is hardly surprising, considering its small size and the vagueness with which it is located in our sources.

Iuppiter Fulgur: a hypaethral temple somewhere in the Campus Martius (Vitruvius 1.2.5); the day of dedication was 7 October, the same as that of Iuno Curitis in Campo (Degrassi 518). According to Festus (254L) this Jupiter was god of the lightning by day (cf. Summanus). It seems at least possible that Temple D in the Area Sacra di Largo Argentina (Fig. 8) is the one in question, because there is no sign of columns or roofing. It is a large building raised on a very high and massive platform of concrete finished with base and crown moldings. It is approached by a broad stair of travertine on the east, within which have been found remains of an older stair. The deep pronaos has remains of marble flagging. The cella, with walls of brick-faced concrete, has a low step of tufa blocks along its walls and good remains of a marble sill in its enormous door. It is also paved with marble. Three building periods have been distinguished within what remains, the latest probably Domitianic, but the plan and dating of its predecessors is very uncertain, as it has not been possible to empty the platform.

Marchetti Longhi 44–46; Nash 1.146.

Iuppiter Heliopolitanus (Fig. 50): a sanctuary of the Syrian gods that was discovered on the eastern slope of the Janiculum in 1906 and excavated in 1908–1909. It lies on the fringes of Villa Sciarra/ Wurts, within what was probably the Lucus Furrinae (q.v.), a temenos surrounding a sacred spring. An inscription shows that the dedication was to Iuppiter Optimus Maximus Heliopolitanus, chief god of the Syrian triad (*CIL* 6.422, 30765 and p. 3756; *ILS* 4292). There seem to have been three major building periods. Of the first all that survives is parts of the

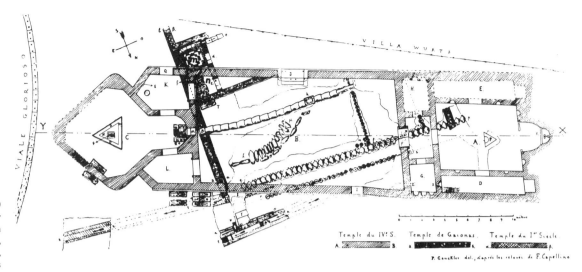

Figure 50
Temple of Iuppiter
Heliopolitanus in
the Lucus Furrinae,
Plan of Remains,
All Periods

perimeter wall, enough to show that the sanctuary was oriented east/west. The date suggested is mid-first century after Christ. Between A.D. 176 and 181 M. Antonius Gaionas rebuilt it with the same orientation. This reconstruction is dated by inscriptions (*CIL* 6.420, 30764, 36793, 14.24; *ILS* 398 and add.). After the destruction of the second temple, a third was built in the middle of the fourth century under Julian. This had a decidedly different orientation from its predecessors and consisted of three parts: (1) at the end a small basilica-plan temple with three naves, the larger central one ending in an apse and the whole preceded by a narthex divided into three chambers; (2) a rectangular central court entered by an axial door from the south; and (3) a curiously shaped sanctuary consisting of a lozenge-shaped inner sanctuary with a triangular altar at the center entered through an apse-ended extension of the western apex of the lozenge, which is flanked by small vestibules of irregular pentagonal shape.

Buried in the triangular altar was found a small idol of gilded bronze representing a youthful Hadad wrapped in enshrouding drapery, which rises in a flaring collar to frame the face; the body is then wound round by a large snake. Around this had been placed seven hen eggs. In the apse at the west end of the sanctuary was evidently an Egyptian statue of a pharaoh in basalt at slightly under life size, work of the third century B.C., found broken to pieces. In the south pentagonal vestibule was a Bacchus pouring wine from a jug, again at slightly under life size. The face and jug of this statue had been gilded. And in the north pentagonal vestibule was a fragment of a triangular marble candelabrum decorated with three figures of dancing Horae at the corners, evidently broken by iconoclasts. Numerous other fragments of

sculpture found in the vicinity suggest that the program was very rich and that the very numerous niches, concentrated especially in the western part, were all for sculpture.

Of the second temple, one can only say that it was rectangular, evidently bounded at least in part by lines of jars set vertically or horizontally and aligned with strict regularity and buried. Off the temple was a small room with a mosaic pavement to which water was piped, which has been thought to be a baptistery or hall of initiation. This temple was destroyed by fire, probably about A.D. 341.

The association of the temple with water, the great abundance of votive offerings found here, and the deliberate eclecticism with which it drew on the traditions of Egypt and the Graeco-Roman world, as well those of as Syria, suggest that this was a popular cult that attracted devotees especially from the foreign population in Rome and the laboring classes. The architecture bears this out; it is exotic and eclectic, full of small secrets and surprises, windowless rooms and unexpected apses, but without columns, vistas, or classical proportions. Numerous simple graves were found within the temple and in the temenos; it has been proposed that these were of victims who had been sacrificed.

P. Gauckler, *Le Sanctuaire syrien du Janicule* (Paris 1912); Nash 1.525–29; N. Goodhue, *The Lucus Furrinae and the Syrian Sanctuary on the Janiculum* (Amsterdam 1975); M. Mele, ed., *L'area del "Santuario siriaco del Gianicolo"* (Rome 1982); *CEFR* 98 (1987): 545–62 (M. Le Glay).

Iuppiter Inventor, Ara: an altar at the foot of the Aventine near the Porta Trigemina, supposed to have been set up by Hercules after recovering the cattle of

Geryon stolen by Cacus (Ovid, *Fast.* 1.579–82; Solinus 1.7; Dion. Hal. 1.39.4). There is some doubt about the epithet and about the survival of this altar into classical times. There is a strong suggestion that this is simply an alternate name for the Ara Maxima (see Herculis Invicti Ara Maxima) or an invention by rationalizers of the story of the Ara Maxima.

Iuppiter Invictus: see **Iuppiter Victor, Aedes.**

Iuppiter Iurarius: a shrine of some sort known only from a dedicatory inscription picked out in white tesserae on a signinum pavement found in 1854 under the cloister of S. Giovanni Calabita in the northern part of the Tiber island (*CIL* 12.990 = 6.379 = *ILS* 3038 = *ILLRP* 186). Whether this was an independent temple or only part of a sacred complex is uncertain.

Iuppiter Lapis: the divinity invoked in an especially solemn oath (Cicero, *Fam.* 7.12.1; A. Gellius 1.21.4), sometimes supposed to be the same as Iuppiter Feretrius (q.v.), but without real reason. There is no evidence for a temple of any sort to Iuppiter Lapis.

Iuppiter Libertas, Aedes: a temple on the Aventine, originally dedicated on 13 April (Degrassi 440); it was restored by Augustus (*RG* 19) and rededicated on 1 September (Degrassi 504). It was evidently not the same as the Temple of Libertas on the Aventine (see Libertas [1]), but an older shrine. In the fasti of the Fratres Arvales for the Kalends of September the name appears as Iuppiter Liber (*CIL* 6.2295 = 32482 [Kal. Sept.]), but apparently this is a mistake.

Iuppiter Metelli (or Metellina), Aedes: Pliny (*HN* 36.40) records that Pasiteles, the contemporary and favorite sculptor of Pompey, made an ivory Jupiter *in Metelli aede qua campus petitur.* This is generally identified as the Temple of Iuppiter Stator in the Porticus Octaviae, which replaced the Porticus Metelli, but without adequate reason. Pliny was very familiar with the Porticus Octaviae and the wealth of art displayed there. He identifies the cult statue of Iuppiter Stator there as the work of Polycles and Dionysius, sons of Timarchides, and at the same time lists other remarkable sculptures in the same temple without mentioning this one (Pliny, *HN* 36.35). And whereas the Temple of Iuppiter Stator that Pliny knew was almost certainly the work of Octavia, the temple she rebuilt is never said to have been the work of Metellus, nor is it likely to have been; Metellus built the portico enclosing the two temples, not the temples themselves. Moreover, *qua campus petitur* seems a very strange way to describe the location of the

Temple of Iuppiter Stator, which would normally be described as *in Circo Flaminio* (Macrobius, *Sat.* 3.4.2) or *in Porticu Octaviae* (*CIL* 6.8708).

It therefore seems likely that Metellus built a temple of Jupiter (Festus 496L) distinct from his portico, *qua campus petitur,* but near enough the portico for Velleius to locate it *in iis ipsis monumentis,* and this was the temple celebrated for being the first one entirely of marble in Rome (Vell. Pat. 1.11.5). The only problem is to determine what route Pliny, or his source, thought one would naturally take to go to the Campus Martius. In Metellus Macedonicus's day there were probably only a few places where one could conveniently cross the Petronia Amnis: (1) wherever the road from the Porta Fontinalis that magistrates took on their way to the Villa Publica and the Ovile crossed it, probably the point where Via Lata (Via Flaminia) crossed it; (2) somewhere in the neighborhood of the Area Sacra di Largo Argentina; and (3) at Circus Flaminius, where the circus spread on both sides of the Amnis. Of these, only the second is really apt to have been described so vaguely. And it is certainly possible that there were more temples south of the Argentina row, one of which might have belonged to Metellus.

In Pliny's day, however, the southern Campus Martius had been so heavily built up that it was probably impossible to find open space that one might describe as campus east of the Nemus Agrippae (see Nemus Thermarum) or south or west of the so-called Euripus Agrippae (see Euripus). And the Petronia Amnis had by that time certainly been culverted along its entire length through the Campus, so there would be no clearly defined routes to take to reach the Campus. On balance the evidence seems to weigh in favor of a location for Metellus's temple between Via Florida and Piazza Costaguti, in which case it was probably destroyed in the fire of Titus of A.D. 80, its being of marble making it especially vulnerable, and might then not have been rebuilt.

Besides the ivory Jupiter of Pasiteles, which may or may not have been the cult image, the temple seems to have contained a statue of Tarpeia, or a statue popularly known as Tarpeia (Festus 496L). Because Festus speaks of this in the present tense, it might be presumed that the temple had been rebuilt, but he may be quoting Verrius Flaccus.

Iuppiter Optimus Maximus (Capitolinus), Aedes (Fig. 19): the great temple on the lower crest of the Capitoline Hill, dedicated to Jupiter with his consort, Iuno Regina, and his daughter Minerva, the Capitoline triad. Tarquinius Priscus vowed the temple during his war with the Sabines, leveled and terraced the site for it, and may have laid some of the foundations, but most of the construction is assigned

221

to Tarquinius Superbus, who is said to have brought it to completion. Parts at least of the area taken by Tarquinius Priscus for his temple had already been dedicated to a variety of other divinities, all of whom permitted exauguration and relocation elsewhere, except Terminus (q.v.) and Iuventas (see Iuventas, Aedicula). These sanctuaries were therefore incorporated in the new temple. Terminus's refusal to move was regarded as a good omen for the city of Rome (Cicero, *Rep.* 2.36; Livy 1.38.7, 55.1–56.1; Pliny, *HN* 3.70; Dion. Hal. 3.69 and 4.59–61; Tacitus, *Hist.* 3.72; Plutarch, *Poplic.* 13–14). The temple was dedicated on 13 September in the first year of the republic, the honor of dedication having fallen by lot to the consul Horatius Pulvillus (Livy 2.8.6–8, 7.3.8; Polybius 3.22.1; Tacitus, *Hist.* 3.72; Plutarch, *Poplic.* 14; cf. Pliny, *HN* 33.19).

The original temple was probably built of mud brick faced with stucco on foundations of cappellaccio, the poor tufa that covers the hills of Rome, quarried at least in large part as part of the scarping and leveling of the area intended to receive the temple. During this work a human head whose features were miraculously well preserved was found (Livy 1.55.5; Varro, *Ling.* 5.41). The Etruscan haruspex asked to interpret this pronounced it an omen of the domination of Rome over Italy (Servius *ad Aen.* 8.345; Arnobius, *Adv. Nat.* 6.7; Isidore 15.2.31; Cass. Dio 2 frag. 11.8 [Zonaras 7.11]).

The temple was Tuscanic in character, but with three cellas side by side, that in the middle dedicated to Iuppiter Optimus, that to the left dedicated to Iuno Regina, and that to the right dedicated to Minerva. The cult image of Jupiter was of terracotta, said to be the work of the master coroplast Vulca of Veii (Pliny, *HN* 35.157). It showed the god standing, brandishing the thunderbolt (Ovid, *Fast.* 1.201–2), and on feast days the face was painted with minium (Pliny, *HN* 33.111–12, 35.157). The general character of the image is shown by the life-size terracotta statues from the roof of the Portonaccio Temple at Veii, which are close to it in date and have therefore sometimes been ascribed to Vulca. The deity wore the *tunica palmata,* a tunic originally so called from the width of the stripe but later embellished with palms (Festus 228L), and the *toga picta,* which was originally simply dyed red and called *purpurea* but later embroidered with gold (Festus 228L). These garments became the costume of Roman generals celebrating a triumph (Livy 10.7.10; 30.15.11–12; Juvenal 10.38–40; S.H.A. *Alex. Sev.* 40.8, *Gordian.* 4.4, *Probus* 7.4–5; Servius *ad Aen.* 11.334). The statue types of Juno and Minerva are not known, but each divinity had a separate hearth-altar (Varro *ap. Serv. ad Aen.* 3.134). The pronaos was especially deep, there being three rows of widely spaced

columns, rather than the usual two, and a row down either flank made this, in effect, a peripteral temple sine postico. It may have been unique in form.

The roof was entirely of wood, probably extensively sheathed in decorative terracotta revetments. Of these only a very few fragments have been discovered, but they include a splendid antefix of a silen's head. At the peak of the façade was a terracotta group of Jupiter mounted in a four-horse chariot, also the work of Vulca, which was supposed to have expanded miraculously while being fired, so the kiln had to be dismantled in order to remove it (Pliny, *HN* 28.16, 35.157; Festus 340–42L; Plutarch, *Poplic.* 13). This was replaced by another group in 296 B.C., the new one probably of bronze, because brazen thresholds and other luxuries were installed in the temple at this time. The pediment and rooftree were decorated with terracotta figures, among them a statue of Summanus, the head of which was broken off by lightning in 275 B.C. (Cicero, *Div.* 1.16; Livy, *Epit.* 14). In 193 B.C. the aediles M. Aemilius Lepidus and L. Aemilius Paullus put gilded shields on the gable, perhaps on the architrave in imitation of the Parthenon.

We hear of various repairs and improvements. In 179 B.C. the walls and columns were restuccoed (Livy 40.51.3), and a tablet bearing a copy of L. Aemilius Regillus's dedication of the Temple of the Lares Permarini (see Lares Permarini, Aedes) was installed over the door (Livy 40.52.7). After the Third Punic War a mosaic pavement was laid in the cella (Pliny, *HN* 36.185), and in 142 B.C. the coffering of the ceiling was gilded (Pliny, *HN* 33.57).

The temple stood in the Area Capitolina (q.v.) and was preceded by the altar of Jupiter, an important landmark (Suetonius, *Aug.* 94.8; Zonaras 8.1). The temple became a repository of treasures offered by victorious generals, dedications, and trophies of victory. The earliest dedication recorded was a golden crown that the Latins presented in 495 (Livy 2.22.6). The clutter of gifts became so great that in 179 B.C. numerous statues and shields attached to the columns were removed (Livy 40.51.3).

The temple of Tarquin burned on 6 July 83 B.C. (Plutarch, *Sulla* 27.6; Cicero, *Cat.* 3.9; Sallust, *Cat.* 47.2; Tacitus, *Hist.* 3.72; Appian, *BellCiv* 1.83, 86; Obsequens 57); the loss was complete, including the cult statue (Plutarch, *De Is. et Os.* 71) and the Sibylline Books kept in a stone chest underground (Dion. Hal. 4.62.5–6). However, the temple treasure seems to have been taken to safety to Praeneste by the younger Marius (Pliny, *HN* 33.16). The rebuilding was undertaken by Sulla (Val. Max. 9.3.8; Tacitus, *Hist.* 3.72), who is said to have brought marble columns from the Olympieion in Athens to Rome for this purpose. But the temple continued to be shown on coins with Doric columns, whereas the rebuilding of the Olympieion begun in 174 B.C. by Antiochus Epiphanes and designed by the Roman architect Cossutius was of the Corinthian order and disproportionately high (Vitruvius 7 *praef.* 15 and 17). It therefore seems likely that what Sulla had brought from Athens was columns of the late archaic Peisistratid temple, which was Doric but of poros. It may be that stuccoing disguised the nature of the material. Q. Lutatius Catulus did most of the rebuilding, which the senate assigned to him (Cicero, *Verr.* 2.4.69; Varro *ap. A. Gell.* 2.10; Lactantius, *De Ira Dei* 22.6; Suetonius, *Iul.* 15), and he dedicated the finished building (Livy, *Epit.* 98; Plutarch, *Poplic.* 15; Pliny, *HN* 19.23; Suetonius, *Aug.* 94.8). The architect was L. Cornelius, who had earlier been his praefectus fabrum (*RendLinc,* ser. 8.26 [1971]: 41–49 [G. Molisani]). The name of Catulus was inscribed over the entrance and remained there until the destruction of the temple in A.D. 69 (Tacitus, *Hist.* 3.72), so the vote of the senate, in connection with Caesar's triumph in 46 B.C., to inscribe Caesar's name there was not carried out (Cass. Dio 43.14).

This temple was built on the foundations of the original building and to the original plan, differing in nothing but the costliness of the materials, according to Dionysius (4.61.4). Varro remembered that Catulus had wished to lower the level of the Area Capitolina in order to lift the temple and make its podium better proportioned to its roof, probably meaning more in accord with the taste of his day, but he was prevented by the favissae of the temple (A. Gellius 2.10). These favissae were underground chambers, like cisterns, in which consecrated material that was old, broken, or no longer useful was stored (Paulus *ex Fest.* 78L; A. Gellius 2.10). The roof was supported in some way on eagles of wood, perhaps carved brackets (Tacitus, *Hist.* 3.71), and the tiles covering the roof were of gilded bronze (Pliny, *HN* 33.57; Seneca, *Controv.* 1.6.4, 2.1.1). The pediment is shown variously on coins, and it is not possible to be definite about the program of its sculptures (cf. *B. M. Coins, Rom. Rep.* 1.571–72 nos. 4217–25; Crawford 487/1, 2), but the gable is always surmounted by statues and crockets, probably with a quadriga driven by Jupiter at the summit. The cult statue was replaced by a seated image (Josephus, *AntIud* 19.1.2 [11]), perhaps in imitation of the Zeus of Olympia. He carried a scepter and thunderbolt (Suetonius, *Aug.* 94.6) and may have held an image of Roma in one hand (Suetonius, *Aug.* 94.6; Cass. Dio 45.2.3). Catulus also dedicated a statue of Minerva by Euphranor *infra Capitolium* (Pliny, *HN* 34.77).

In its elevated location, this temple was exposed to frequent damage by lightning (Cicero, *Cat.* 3.19, *Div.* 1.19, 2.45; Cass. Dio 41.14.3, 42.26.3, 55.1.1; Tacitus, *Ann.* 13.24), but evidently was never set on fire. Augustus restored it at great expense, but without the addition of his name (Augustus, *RG* 20).

In A.D. 69 the second temple was burned during the storming of the Capitol by the Vitellians (Tacitus, *Hist.* 3.71; Suetonius, *Vitel.* 15.3; Cass. Dio 64.17.3; Statius, *Silv.* 5.3.195–98; Aur. Vict., *Caes.* 8.5) and was then restored by Vespasian, again on the foundations and to the plan of its predecessors (Tacitus, *Hist.* 4.53; Suetonius, *Vesp.* 8.5; Cass. Dio 65.10.2; Plutarch, *Poplic.* 15.2; Aur. Vict., *Caes.* 9.7, *Epit.* 9.8). Now, however, greater height was given to the building, and the evidence of coins shows that the order was Corinthian (Cohen 1, Vesp. 486–93, Titus 242–45; *B. M. Coins, Rom. Emp.* 2, Vesp. 614, 647, 721, 722, 850, 877). These also show that an elaborate program of statuary crowning the roof, as well as pedimental sculpture, was included. Parts of the former were a quadriga at the apex of the roof and bigae driven by Victorias as lateral acroteria. Variations in the representations of these sculptures may be due to changes in the decoration in the course of time.

This temple burned in the great fire of Titus in A.D. 80 (Cass. Dio 66.24) and was restored by Domitian following a beginning by Titus (Suetonius, *Dom.* 5; Plutarch, *Poplic.* 15.3; Eutropius 7.23.5; Chron. 146). The new temple surpassed its predecessors in magnificence, the columns being of Pentelic marble (Plutarch, *Poplic.* 15.4), the doors plated with gold (Zosimus 5.38.5), and the tiles of the roof of gilded bronze (Procopius, *BellVand* 1.5.4). Domitian is reported to have spent twelve thousand talents on the gilding of the temple alone. On the evidence of a coin, the dedication of the temple has been put in 82 (*B. M. Coins, Rom. Emp.* 2, Dom. 251), but Jerome puts it in 89 (*a. Abr.* 2105), giving a likelier interval for the accomplishment of so great an undertaking. For the sculptures of the pediment and roof, we depend on the coin and on representations on reliefs, especially one from the Forum Traiani in the Louvre that now lacks the part showing the pediment but kept some of it long enough for this to appear in a Renaissance drawing. It shows a quadriga at the apex and a biga as the right lateral acroterion, with single figures of Mars and Venus between. In the pediment are the Capitoline triad enthroned above an eagle with spread wings, flanked by bigae of the sun and moon and other less distinct figures toward the corners (*PBSR* 4 [1907]: 230, 240–44 [A. J. B. Wace]). It is presumably to this temple that we should assign the chryselephantine statue of Jupiter created by a Greek sculptor named Apollonius

(Chalcidius, *schol. in Platon. Timaeum* 337 [361]); he is not more precisely identified.

This temple was considered by Ammianus (22.16.12) as the finest in Rome, and Ausonius (*Ord. Nob. Urb.* 19.17) speaks of the *aurea Capitoli culmina*. Its destruction began when Stilicho carried off the gold plates of the doors in the fifth century (Zosimus 5.38) and continued when Genseric took away half the gilded tiles of the roof (Procopius, *BellVand* 1.5.4). Cassiodorus (*Var.* 7.6.1) could still consider it one of the most magnificent of all buildings in the sixth century. But Narses pulled down much, if not all, of the statuary ca. 571 (*MGH, Chron. Min.* 1.336: *de Neapolim egressus Narsis ingressus Romam et deposuit palatii eius statuam et Capitolium*). The story of its destruction is little known until the time of the construction of Palazzo Caffarelli on its ruins in the sixteenth century (LS 2.94–96).

Excavations, together with the information provided by Vitruvius (3.3.5) and Dionysius (4.61), show the general layout of the temple, which was unchanged from the time of its foundation. The plan was almost square, slightly longer than wide, and faced southeast, looking toward the Velabrum and the northwest end of the Circus Maximus. The platform was not solid, but consisted of a grid of walls following the lines of the walls and columns. Those of the perimeter vary in width from about 5 m to about 8 m; those in the interior are about 4.15 m wide. The walls were built of blocks of cappellaccio laid dry and dug deep into the ground so that their total height was between 4 and 5 m; parts of them are visible in the Museo Nuovo Capitolino and its garden. Three corners of the platform have been located, one in the garden of the museum, toward the Via delle Tre Pile, one in Via di Monte Tarpeio on the east side of the museum, and one in the little Piazza di Monte Tarpeio. From these it is possible to project the overall dimensions of the platform as having been 53.50 m x 62.25 m, equal to 180 x 210 Roman feet. Gjerstad deduces the lower diameter of the columns, the measurement Vitruvius uses as a modulus, to have been 8 Roman feet. The proportion of length to width was 7:6 and the widths of the cellas were in the proportion 4:5:4. The lateral colonnades were of the same width as the side cellas, and the whole was araeostyle, with widely spaced columns, which required wooden architraves (Vitruvius 3.3.5). A very few fragments of the marble architecture of the temple of the last period survive, kept in the Palazzo dei Conservatori and its vicinity; the most important of these are a fragment of a column shaft, 2.10 m in diameter, and a fragment of an Attic base, 2.22 m in diameter. Lugli has calculated the column height as 21.58 m, which seems excessive. The columns of the Olympieion in Athens are only 16 m high, with a base diameter of 2.42 m. Fragments of marble cornices may come from the interior.

The temple was always hexastyle, with rows of columns aligned with the cella walls. Thus the central intercolumniation, axis to axis, would have measured 15.84 m (40 Roman feet), and those to either side of it 9.47 m (32 Roman feet). The central cella was ideally 40 Roman feet wide, 96 Roman feet long on the axis of its walls, large enough to accommodate meetings of the senate, which were not infrequently held there. This was the center of the state religion of Rome and always of great political, as well as religious, importance. Here the consuls offered sacrifice on entering office. Here triumphing generals ended their solemn procession through the city and offered their crowns and a share of the spoils to Jupiter. To the Romans it was the touchstone of Roman sovereignty and immortality.

E. Gjerstad, *Early Rome*, 3 (*Acta Instituti Romani Regni Sueciae* 17.3, 1960), 168–90; Nash 1.530–32; *RömMitt* 76 (1969): 110–21 (H. Riemann); Lugli 1975, 127–32; Coarelli 1974, 44–45; *MEFRA* 98 (1986): 217–53 (J.-C. Grenier and F. Coarelli); *Historia* 36 (1987): 243–48 (G. B. Townsend).

Iuppiter Pistor, Ara: a small altar on the top of the Capitoline, probably within the Area Capitolina (Ovid, *Fast.* 6.349–50), *candida*, therefore perhaps of marble, supposed originally to have been set up to commemorate the ruse of throwing bread upon the Gauls during their siege of the Capitoline to deceive them about the supplies of food available to the defenders (Ovid, *Fast.* 6.349–94; Lactantius, *Div. Inst.* 1.20.33). This is clearly a rationalizing story, and Wissowa (*RK* 122) thought the epithet indicated a thunder god. One gathers from Ovid that the Vestalia (9 June) was regarded as its anniversary.

Iuppiter Propugnator, Aedes: a temple on the Palatine known only from inscriptions of A.D. 180–238 (*CIL* 6.2004–9; *ILS* 466) fragments of the fasti of an unidentified college of priests whose regular meeting place it was. This has been conjectured to be the Sodales Flaviales Titiales, the college in charge of the worship of Divus Vespasianus and Divus Titus, but the evidence is scant, and the location of the temple is entirely unknown.

Iuppiter Redux: see **Castra Peregrina.**

Iuppiter Salutaris, Aedes: a temple mentioned in one inscription (*CIL* 6.425) and probably another (*CIL* 6.82). Its location is entirely unknown.

Iuppiter Soter: a suggested emendation for Iuppiter Sutor (q.v.) mentioned by Servius (*ad Aen.* 8.652), but this seems unnecessary.

Iuppiter Stator, Aedes (1): a temple supposed to have been vowed by Romulus at a critical moment in the battle between the Romans and the Sabines, when the Romans had been driven from the forum to the Porta Mugonia (Livy 1.13.3–6; Ovid, *Fast.* 6.793–94; Dion. Hal. 2.50.3; Florus 1.1.1.13; [Aur. Vict.,], *De Vir. Ill.* 2.8). The epithet seems to mean "stayer," for the Romans stood and rallied there. Romulus's temple was never built as an aedes, but in 294 B.C. the consul M. Atilius Regulus made a similar vow at a critical point in a battle with the Samnites, and an aedes was then built (Livy 10.36.11, 37.15–16) where Romulus had laid out his templum. It is listed by the regionary catalogues in Regio IV, and its site is variously described as being at or near the Porta Mugonia (Livy 1.13.3–6; Dion. Hal. 2.50.3; Ovid, *Trist.* 3.1.31–32), at the foot of the Palatine (pseudo-Cicero, *Orat. priusquam in exsilium iret* 24), and at the beginning of the Sacra Via going up to the Palatine (Plutarch, *Cic.* 16.3; cf. Livy 1.41.4; Pliny, *HN* 34.29; Appian, *BellCiv* 2.11). Ovid (*Fast.* 6.793–94) gives the day of dedication as 27 June (Degrassi 474).

Just east of the Arch of Titus on the south side of Sacra Via fronting on the Clivus Palatinus, the concrete core of a large rectangular temple including some very large blocks of peperino and travertine came to light with the dismantling of the medieval Turris Cartularia in 1829 (Lugli 1957, pl. 97.4). Nothing of the superstructure survives. The foundations suggest that the temple was prostyle, hexastyle, with a deep pronaos and a squarish cella.

In 207 B.C., while a chorus of twenty-seven maidens was rehearsing a hymn by Livius Andronicus in this temple, the Temple of Iuno Regina on the Aventine was struck by lightning (Livy 27.37.7). The connection of these events in the tradition suggests that the hymn, which was to be sung in a lustral procession, was especially in honor of Iuno Regina. On 8 November 63 B.C. Cicero as consul convened the senate here to denounce to them Catiline's attempt to murder him on the previous day (Cicero, *Cat.* 1. 11, 33). The meeting was an extraordinary one, and we know of no other occasion when the senate met there. Perhaps it was convenient to Cicero's house. Although we cannot be sure where Cicero was living at this time, it may very well have been in the house where he grew up on the Carinae. But the implication of the epithet Stator may also have played a part in the choice.

Lugli 1946, 240–42; Nash 1.534.

Iuppiter Stator, Aedes (2) (Figs. 70, 71): a temple on the Circus Flaminius (Macrobius, *Sat.* 3.4.2), ascribed in the manuscripts of Vitruvius to Hermodius, a name that is usually corrected to Hermodorus (so first by Turnebus), although the arguments against this are very strong and the temple should in all logic antedate that of Iuno Regina (see Iuno Regina, Aedes [3]) that stood just west of it, and can hardly be other than the Temple of Iuno Regina that M. Aemilius Lepidus built and dedicated in 187 B.C. The Temple of Iuppiter Stator, as Vitruvius describes it, was peripteral, hexastyle, with eleven columns on the flanks, the intercolumniations equal to the breadth of the pteron (Vitruvius 3.2.5). The cult statue was by Polycles and Dionysius, sons of Timarchides (Pliny, *HN* 36.35).

After his triumph in 146 B.C., Q. Metellus Macedonicus surrounded both temples with a portico (see Porticus Metelli), very probably the first portico in Rome of more than one wing. His chief object in this seems to have been to provide a setting for a group of thirty-four equestrian statues by Lysippus commissioned by Alexander to commemorate those of his men who had fallen in the Battle of the Granicus, which Metellus brought as part of the spoils of Macedon (Vell. Pat. 1.11.3–4). These statues faced the temples. Other works of art in the Temple of Iuppiter Stator were a group of Olympus struggling with Pan by Heliodorus, a Venus bathing by Doidalsas, and a standing Venus by Polycharmus (Pliny, *HN* 36.35).

After the death of Marcellus, the nephew and son-in-law of Augustus, his mother, Octavia, undertook to rebuild the Porticus Metelli and the temples it enclosed in his honor (Ovid, *Ars Am.* 1.69) and to these added a curia, libraries, and many works of art (see Porticus Octaviae). Apparently about this time the legend related by Pliny must have originated, that the temples were the work of the Spartan artists Saurus and Batrachus, who hoped to be honored by an inscription and, when they were disappointed in this, signed their work by carving figures of a lizard and a frog *in spiris columnarum* (Pliny, *HN* 36.42–43). Furthermore, the decoration of the Temple of Iuppiter Stator was feminine in character and intended for Iuno Regina, the porters having made a mistake and installed the wrong divinity in the wrong temple. The first legend was created because there was no inscription on the temples (Vell. Pat. 1.11.3); the second is mysterious.

Octavia's temple burned in the fire of Titus, and Domitian must have restored it. Because Septimius Severus restored the Porticus Octaviae and Temple of Iuno Regina, it seems likely that he restored the Temple of Iuppiter Stator as well. It appears on the Marble Plan (*FUR* pl. 29; Rodriguez pl. 23) as peripteral sine postico, with six columns in front and nine down the flanks, and with a stair only in front, clearly not the building of Vitruvius and perhaps best ascribed to Octavia's rebuilding. The ruins of the building are concealed under the church of S. Maria in Campitelli.

The Temple of Iuppiter Stator seems to have figured in the fasti on both 5 September (Degrassi 508) and 23 September (Degrassi 512). The first may have been the original dedication day, the second the dedication of the rebuilding of Octavia. It is listed in Regio IX in the *Notitia* but thereafter disappears from history, and the story of its destruction is completely unknown.

PBSR 21 (1953): 152–59 (M. J. Boyd); *AJA* 80 (1976): 57–64 (L. Richardson).

Iuppiter Sutor, Ara: mentioned once by Servius (*ad Aen.* 8.652) as an altar on the Capitoline where hides and old shoes were offered and burned. The reading is often corrected to Soter or Tutor, but without adequate reason.

Iuppiter Tonans, Aedes: a temple on the Capitoline Hill vowed by Augustus after he narrowly escaped being struck by lightning during a journey by night on his Cantabrian campaign in 26 B.C. (*RG* 19; Suetonius, *Aug.* 29.3; Cass. Dio 54.4.2). It was dedicated on 1 September 22 B.C. (Degrassi 504) and seems also to have been especially honored on the Kalends of February (Ovid, *Fast.* 2.69). It was very splendid and had walls of solid marble (Pliny, *HN* 36.50) and a cult statue by Leochares (Pliny, *HN* 34.79), which may account for the epithet, a translation of Zeus Bronton, found transliterated in two inscriptions (*CIL* 6.432 = *ILS* 3046 and *CIL* 6.2241). In front of it stood a group of Castor and Pollux by Hegias. Augustus frequented it, and it became very popular, so much so that Augustus reported a dream in which Iuppiter Capitolinus protested that the new temple was withdrawing worshipers from his temple, to which Augustus answered that Iuppiter Tonans was only the gatekeeper of Iuppiter Capitolinus. In token of this he hung bells from the eaves of the new temple (Suetonius, *Aug.* 91.2). These must have disappeared by Dio's day, for he tells the story somewhat differently and hangs a bell on the hand of the cult statue (Cass. Dio 54.4.3–4). There is naturally confusion of Iuppiter Tonans and Iuppiter Capitolinus in the literary sources, so it is impossible to tell which is meant sometimes (see, e.g., Martial 7.60.1–2).

The story of Augustus's dream shows that the temple stood near the entrance to the Area Capitolina, therefore on the southeastern brow of the hill

overlooking the Forum Romanum. It is shown on a coin of Augustus (*B. M. Coins, Rom. Rep.* 2.28–29 nos. 4412–15) as hexastyle, Corinthian, the cult statue nude, the uplifted left hand steadying a long scepter, and the right down, advanced, and holding a thunderbolt. A temple shown on the relief of the Haterii has been identified as that of Iuppiter Tonans as rebuilt by Domitian (Nash 1.536 fig. 662). If this is correct, it remained hexastyle, but the order was composite. The frieze is decorated with sacrificial implements and eagles, and the pediment with a large wreath. The cult statue is shown frontal, emerging at the knees from a rock or pile of rocks. It probably had a scepter in the left hand (it is hidden) and cradles a thunderbolt in the right. Above the temple a curious attic storey or *cenaculum* is added, the purpose of which is very obscure. It has short unfluted pillars with Ionic capitals and a flat roof, evidently strongly projecting, and the parapet is decorated with large thunderbolts. As a loggia it might be a place from which to view Rome, given the vantage point of the temple's location, but this must remain very uncertain.

A large square mass of concrete, evidently the core of a temple podium, about 20 m southeast of the Temple of Iuppiter Capitolinus, came to light in 1896 during the construction of Via di Monte Tarpeio (Via del Tempio di Giove) and was cut through for the street. This is commonly identified as the remains of the Temple of Iuppiter Custos (or Conservator, see Iuppiter Conservator, Sacellum), Domitian's temple built on the site of the lodge of the aedituus of the Temple of Iuppiter Capitolinus, but in this location it is likelier to have been the Temple of Iuppiter Tonans. The lodge of the aedituus should be in an inconspicuous location, and, because the principal assault of the Vitellians was up the Clivus Capitolinus, this temple would have been directly in the line of fire, not a good place for Domitian to have sought refuge. But between the Temple of Iuppiter Capitolinus and the Clivus, it might very well be described as the gatekeeper's lodge for the great temple. The flank of this building has been thought to be shown on a panel from an arch of Marcus Aurelius now on the stair of the Palazzo dei Conservatori (Helbig⁴ 2.1444C; Ryberg 1967, pls. 15, 17, 20). It offers a façade of ashlar masonry punctuated by five plain pillars, or pilasters, surmounted by three groups of a man fighting an animal in a *venatio*, and the building is incomplete, arbitrarily broken at the edge of the panel. This could hardly be a temple, because there is no pronaos and the roof was either flat or only slightly sloping. More likely, as Ryberg suggests, it is part of the porticoes with which we know the Area Capitolina was framed and has been introduced arbitrarily into this scene beside the Temple of Iuppiter Capitolinus mainly to help identify the locale by readily recognizable features.

Nash 1.535–36; cf. 518–20.

Iuppiter Tragoedus, Statua: mentioned by Suetonius (*Aug.* 57), along with Apollo Sandaliarius (q.v.), as one of the prized images of divinities that Augustus dedicated *vicatim,* presumably meaning in conjunction with the compital shrines. Because no part of the city is known to have been associated with tragedians and an image of Jupiter as a tragic actor is unthinkable, everything about this statue is mysterious, and one wonders whether the reading in Suetonius is correct.

Iuppiter Tutor: a suggested emendation for Iuppiter Sutor (q.v.) mentioned by Servius (*ad Aen.* 8.652), but this seems unnecessary.

Iuppiter Ultor: a hypothetical temple of the time of Alexander Severus for which there is no evidence other than some coins (Cohen 4 pp. 411–12, nos. 101–4; *B. M. Coins, Rom. Emp.* 6.134, nos. 207–9; *RIC* 4.2: 64–65 and 104 nos. 412–13). The temple shown strongly resembles that of Iuppiter Capitolinus, and it is unlikely that so close a duplicate would have been built in Rome. A similarity that has been observed between this building and one shown on a small bronze of Elagabalus (Gnecchi 3.41 and pl. 152.11; Nash 1.537 fig. 663), which has been presumed to be the temple built by that emperor on the Palatine to Sol Invictus Elagabalus, goes only as far as the general layout. Discrepancies in individual features abound, and Elagabalus's coin offers nothing to identify this temple. Until we have a complete excavation of the Vigna Barberini on the Palatine, it would be rash to assign either of these temples to that location, although it certainly conceals a large temple in a temenos surrounded by a portico. In the late fourth century Avienus (*Descr. Orb. Terr.* 1090) describes the Temple of Elagabalus at Emesa as towering and splendid.

Iuppiter Victor, Aedes: a temple originally vowed by Q. Fabius Maximus Rullianus at the Battle of Sentinum in 295 B.C. He burned the spoils of the Samnite enemy to this divinity after the battle (Livy 10.29.14 and 18). In 293 L. Papirius at the Battle of Aquilonia vowed a cup of wine to Iuppiter Victor, but this does not necessarily mean that Fabius's temple had yet been built. It was dedicated on 13 April (Ovid, *Fast.* 4.621; Degrassi 440). Josephus (*AntIud* 19.4.3. [248]) says that after the assassination of Caligula the consuls convened the senate in

the Temple of Iuppiter Victor (Nicephorus), and in the *Notitia* of the fourth century it is listed in Regio X.

In 42 B.C. the altar of Iuppiter Victor was struck by lightning (Cass. Dio 47.40.2), and in A.D. 54 the temple door opened spontaneously, which was taken to presage the death of Claudius (Cass. Dio 60[61].35.1). It is mentioned repeatedly in the acta of the Arval Brethren (*CIL* 6.2051.1.87, 2074.40, 2086.2.27). In the regionary catalogues it is listed toward the end of its regio, after the Auguratorium and before the Curiae Veteres, Fortuna Respiciens, and Septizodium. This seems to place it toward the east corner of the Palatine, and probably it is the temple in Vigna Barberini, where it would have overlooked the route of triumphal processions (see Fig. 63: the church of S. Sebastiano). It seems likely that in the time of Elagabalus it was rebuilt in magnificent style and size as the temple to his sun god (who was identified with Jupiter). After Elagabalus's death, Alexander Severus would then have returned it to the original dedicant.

The question of whether Iuppiter Victor is the same as Iuppiter Invictus cannot be settled, because both, especially the latter, might be epithets applied to the divinity casually. Ovid (*Fast.* 6.650) says that on the Ides of June *invicto sunt data templa Iovi,* but in the fasti his name appears without any epithet (Degrassi 470), and, of course, all the Ides were sacred to Jupiter. In these circumstances it seems likely that there was no real cult of Iuppiter Invictus in Rome and that Iuppiter Victor was not also called Invictus (but cf. Hercules Victor and Hercules Invictus).

A republican inscription (possibly on an altar) found on the Quirinal in the seventeenth century, but now lost (*CIL* 1².802 = 6.438 = 30767a = *ILS* 2994 = *ILLRP* 187), commemorated a restoration for Iuppiter Victor by T. Mefu[a tresvir, presumably appointed for the restoration of temples and monuments. This has been taken as evidence for a shrine to Iuppiter Victor on the Quirinal.

For explorations in Vigna Barberini, see *MEFRA* 97 (1985): 531–32 (M. Royo), 98 (1986): 217–53 (J.-C. Grenier and F. Coarelli), 387–97 (P. Gros, M. Lenoir, et al.), 707–66 (M. Royo); *BullCom* 91.2 (1986): 507–14 (M. Lenoir et al.); *MEFRA* 99 (1987): 481–98 (M. Lenoir et al.), 100 (1988): 507–25 (P. Pergola et al.), 101 (1989): 489–513 (various authors).

Iuppiter Viminus, Ara: an ancient altar on the Viminal from which Varro (*Ling.* 5.51) believed the hill took its name, whereas Festus (516L) held that the altar and hill took their names from a stand of willows there. The form of the epithet is unusual; one expects *Viminalis* or *Vimineus,* or better still *Salicta-rius;* and the Viminal does not seem a likely place for a stand of willows. So Varro may be correct and the origin of the epithet obscure. The discovery in 1977, in Piazza dei Cinquecento, of a statue of Jupiter, nude except for the aegis, a dedication of the late fourth century after Christ, may give us the location of this shrine and a representation of the divinity (*BdA* 65 [1980]: 15–24 [I. Jacopi]).

Iuturna, Lacus: see **Lacus Iuturnae.**

Iuturna, Templum: the first temple of Juturna in Rome, built by Lutatius Catulus in the Campus Martius (Servius *ad Aen.* 12.139); this is probably C. Catulus, the victor of the First Punic War, cos. 242, who triumphed in 241, rather than the Sullan builder of the Tabularium. The temple stood somewhere near the Aqua Virgo: *hic ubi Virginea Campus obitur aqua* (Ovid, *Fast.* 1.463–64). Its day of dedication was the same as the Carmentalia, 11 January, also apparently sometimes called the Iuturnalia (Degrassi 395). All that is known about the temple is that C. Aelius Staienus, a figure in the trial of Cluentius in 66 B.C., set up gilded statues there with inscriptions identifying them as kings whom he had restored to favor with Rome (Cicero, *Clu.* 101). The suggestion is that the temple stood on or near the west side of Via Lata, between this and the Temple of Divus Hadrianus. The temple has nothing to do with the Temple of the Nymphs in the Campus Martius, al-though a connection has repeatedly been proposed and the two stood not far from each other.

Iuventas, Aedes: a temple vowed by the consul M. Livius Salinator on the day of the Battle of the Metaurus, 207 B.C., begun by him as censor in 204, and dedicated by C. Licinius Lucullus in 191. It burned to the ground in 16 B.C. (Cass. Dio 54.19.7), and Augustus restored it (*RG* 19). The temple was *in Circo Maximo* near that of Summanus (Pliny, *HN* 29.57), therefore presumably on the Aventine side of the circus, but still within Regio XI. No remains of it are known.

The notion that after the construction of this temple Roman boys who had come of age made a traditional offering of a coin here, rather than at the shrine of Iuventas on the Capitoline, seems to have nothing to support it (cf. Dion. Hal. 4.15.5).

Iuventas, Aedicula: a small shrine in the cella Minervae of the temple of Iuppiter Optimus Maximus Capitolinus (Pliny, *HN* 35.108), Iuventas, along with Terminus, having been a divinity who refused exauguration at the time of the building of the Capitoline temple (Livy 5.54.7; Dion. Hal. 3.69.5; Florus 1.1.7.8; Augustine, *De civ. Dei* 4.23). On coming of age and receiving the toga virilis, a Roman boy offered a coin at this shrine, a custom supposed to have been instituted by Servius Tullius as a means of keeping an annual census of the population of Rome (Dion. Hal. 4.15.5).

Lacus: see **Fons, Lacus, Nymphaeum.**

Lacus Aretis: mentioned in a sepulchral inscription that associates it with a temple of Fortuna (*CIL* 6.9664 = *ILS* 7536). Because Fortuna is given no epithet and the lacus is *sub aede,* and because the subject of the inscription describes himself as a *negotiator aerarius et ferrarius,* it is natural to think of Servius's Temple of Fortuna in the Forum Boarium rather than any other temple, but there is no proof. The meaning of the name is also obscure.

For a different view, see *RivStorAnt* 4 (1974): 144–46 (R. E. A. Palmer).

Lacus Cunicli: a watering place in Regio IX known only from an inscription of A.D. 375 (*BullArchCr* 2.2 [1871]: 75–76 [De Rossi]). Presumably the standard of the feed pipe of the lacus was carved with the figure of a rabbit. One may compare such a standard in Pompeii (Overbeck-Mau 241).

Lacus Curtius (Fig. 40): a monument in the Forum Romanum supposed to mark the place of a miraculous event of which three versions were given in the classical period: (1) A certain Procillus, possibly the tribunus plebis of 56 B.C., reported that in 362 B.C. a chasm opened here, which the soothsayers announced could only be closed by offering that *quo plurimum populus Romanus posset.* Thereupon a young patrician, M. Curtius, armed and mounted, rode his horse into the pit, which forthwith closed (Varro, *Ling.* 5.148; Livy 7.6.1–6; Dion. Hal. 14.11.3–4; Val. Max. 5.6.2; Pliny, *HN* 15.78; Cass. Dio fr. 30.1–2; Paulus *ex Fest.* 42L; Zonaras 7.25; Orosius 3.5). This was the commonest explanation. (2) Calpurnius Piso, the annalist and consul of 133 B.C., wrote that during the war between Romulus and Titus Tatius the Sabine leader Mettius Curtius, being hard-pressed by the Romans, rode his horse

into a swamp in this place and so escaped (Varro, *Ling.* 5.149; Livy 1.12.9–10 and 13.5; Dion. Hal. 2.42.5–6; Plutarch, *Rom.* 18.4, who tells the story rather differently). This is the story commemorated by a relief found in 1553 between the Column of Phocas and the Temple of Castor and preserved in the Museo Capitolino Nuovo. It bears on its back an inscription of the praetor peregrinus L. Naevius Surdinus (*CIL* 6.1468 = 31662) of the early empire, but it is probably a copy of a late republican original. (3) An unidentified Cornelius and Q. Lutatius Catulus, the consul of 102 B.C., wrote that the lacus was a spot that had been struck by lightning in 445 B.C. and was then fenced off and marked with a puteal by the consul C. Curtius (Varro, *Ling.* 5.150).

In the time of Augustus there was no sign of a lacus there (Ovid, *Fast.* 6.403–4), but Suetonius (*Aug.* 57.1) says that it was the custom for all Romans annually to throw a small coin in the lacus to discharge vows for the princeps' health and well-being. Thus it continued to have the associations with the underworld implicit in the first explanation of its origin, and there was an altar or altars there (Ovid, *Fast.* 6.403–4; Pliny, *HN* 15.78).

The remains today consist of an irregular polygonal area, roughly 10.15 m x 8.95 m, which was enclosed in antiquity by a fence or balustrade of marble. Within this are parts of three layers of pavement, the lowest of slabs of cappellaccio, the middle of slabs of Monteverde tufa, and the topmost and poorest preserved of travertine. In the western part are cuttings for four rectangular bases, very likely Ovid's *siccas . . . aras.* The most conspicuous feature is a twelve-sided plinth of tufa, which had at its center a setting suitable for a puteal. One was often installed over a place struck by lightning and would make a convenient place for the Romans to deposit their coins.

Because there is no sign of any natural source of

water in the vicinity nearer than the Cloaca, and all three explanations of the origin of the lacus plainly appear rationalizing inventions of one sort or another, we must conclude that it was a very ancient monument with strong associations with the cult of the dead, because, had it been simply a watering place, there would have been no hindrance to its removal.

J. Poucet, *Recherches sur la legende Sabine des origines de Rome* (Kinshasa, Zaire 1967); Nash 1.542–44; GV 104–16.

Lacus Esc[. . .]: found only on a lead tessera (Rostovtzeff, *Sylloge* no. 499). The supplement *Esculinum* is supported by Varro, *Ling.* 5.50, which suggests that it was a very ancient watering place.

Lacus Fabricius: see **Compitum Fabricium.**

Lacus Fagutalis (see also **Fagutal**): a watering place on the Fagutal behind which the first station of the Argei in Regio II Esquiliae was located. The correction of *lacus* to *lucus*, advocated by many, does not recommend itself in view of the vagueness of topography that results. Moreover, the association of watering places with compital shrines is well known. It may have been at the top of the northwest slope of the Esquiline (cf. Solinus 1.26), but is more likely to have been on the western tip.

Lacus Fundani: a watering place that gave its name to a vicus (*CIL* 1².721 = 6.1297 = *ILS* 872 = *ILLRP* 352). According to Tacitus (*Hist.* 3.69), during the crisis in Rome on Vitellius's abdication of the principate, Flavius Sabinus and his supporters were descending from his house, almost certainly one of those later rebuilt by Domitian as the Templum Gentis Flaviae (see Gens Flavia, Templum) or very close by, presumably in the direction of the Forum Romanum, when they encountered supporters of Vitellius *circa lacum Fundani*. After a skirmish there Sabinus and his followers seized the arx of the Capitoline. This would put the Lacus Fundani in the saddle between Quirinal and Capitoline, perhaps closer to the Quirinal in the section called Collis Latiaris. But the street to which it gave its name was a vicus rather than a clivus, so it must have been relatively flat. We may incline to put it not far from the street discovered at the base of the Columna Traiani (see Forum Traiani).

Lacus Gallines: known only from a single inscription of unknown provenience (*CIL* 6.33835).

Lacus Ganymedis: a watering place, the first monument listed by the regionary catalogues in Regio VII. Ligorio claimed to have seen its remains, a ten-sided basin of marble, 15 feet in diameter, with a rock in the middle from which the figure that gave it its name rose. This was in the cellars of the monks of SS. Apostoli, toward the piazza called Dell'ulmo de Colonnesi (LS 3.202). The statue of Ganymede was subsequently supposed to have been presented to the bishop of Pavia, governatore di Roma, but the fountain, as described, is so unlike any other ancient fountain known that we must doubt Ligorio's testimony here.

Lacus Iuturnae (Fig. 51): the spring-fed pool of Juturna at the south corner of the Forum Romanum between the Temple of Castor and the Atrium Vestae, where Castor and Pollux were seen watering their horses after the Battle of Lake Regillus in 496 B.C. Thereafter, the Temple of Castor was built just west of the lacus (Ovid, *Fast.* 1.705–8; Dion. Hal. 6.13.4). This epiphany was believed to have been repeated after the Battle of Pydna in 168 B.C. (Florus 1.28.15; Val. Max. 1.8.1). The twins are shown watering their horses on coins of the Gens Postumia, to which the victor of Lake Regillus belonged, of about 96–90 B.C. (*B. M. Coins, Rom. Rep.* 2.310 nos. 718–23; Crawford 335 no. 10); the lacus is there shown as a low trough or puteal. Servius (*ad Aen.* 12.139) says that Iuturna was properly the name of a spring near the River Numicus, given this name because of its salubrious water *(iuvare)*. From this spring in ancient times water was said to have been brought to Rome for all sacrifices. A temple to Juturna was first built in the Campus Martius (see Iuturna, Templum). When the forum spring was assigned to her is not known, but its water was always regarded as especially fine and healthful (see also Varro, *Ling.* 5.71; Frontinus, *Aq.* 4). PA suggests that the name might also be derived from Diuturna (its being a perpetual spring).

The area was explored only in 1900. What came to light was a basin 2.12 m deep, measuring at the bottom 5.13 m x 5.04 m. In the middle of this is a rectangular base about 3 m long, 2 m wide, and 1.78 m high. This presumably held a marble group of the Dioscuri and their horses, fine work of the early classical period, which was found smashed to fragments in the basin and is now partially reassembled and on display in the Forum Antiquarium (Helbig⁴ 2.2067). Nash, however, thinks this base is too small and would therefore like to locate the group on a pair of little squares marked on the Marble Plan on the north side of the basin (*ArchCl* 11 [1959]: 227–31). The basin was entirely lined with marble, and the springs emerged in the northeast and northwest corners. The walls behind the revetment are faced with reticulate, and the whole appears to be an early imperial refurbishing of a late republican treatment. Under the floor of the basin have been found extensive remains of a pavement in blocks of tufa laid on a different orientation (that of the precinct of Vesta).

At the top of the basin is a ledge, about 1.50 m wide, framed in a heavy wall of rubble masonry 1.23 m high, capped by a travertine coping with traces of the setting of a metal fence. At the top the whole measures about 10 m square. In the fourth century the east side of the basin was rebuilt in different form, apparently to create a place for the Statio Aquarum. A marble altar that was found in the basin has been set up on the intermediate ledge; on its four faces it shows the Dioscuri, Helen (as Selene), Leda, and Jupiter.

About 4 m south of the lacus, facing it at an angle, is the Aedicula Iuturnae, a pretty little shrine on a high base without a stair of approach. This must have held a statue of the divinity in the apsidal cella. Its shallow porch is framed by two slender Corinthian columns and a neat triangular pediment. In front of it, over a well, is a large marble puteal, unfluted, with an inscription commemorating a restoration by M. Barbatius Pollio, believed to be the adherent of Mark Antony (CIL 6.36807 = ILS 9261). Just in front of this and obscuring it has now been set a marble altar of Severan date commonly believed to represent Juturna taking leave of Turnus. However, the gesture is ambiguous, and it might equally well represent Mars and Venus. It is not properly in place here; it was found used as a step in a medieval stair. The aedicula is identified by an inscription on the epistyle: IVTVRNA(i) s(acrum) (NSc 1901, 74 [G. Boni]). It all but abuts on an apsidal room in which the brickwork is considered Hadrianic.

East of the lacus, between it and the Atrium Vestae, a ramp mounts to the Nova Via, and the triangular space between was filled with later construction, some of which encroached on the lacus itself, a large brick-faced vault carrying it over the basin. Inscriptions found here show that it became the headquarters of the water department of Rome, the Statio Aquarum. One, a base of a statue to Constantine, erected 1 March 328, commemorates a restoration at the time by Fl. Maesius Egnatius Lollianus, curator aquarum (NSc 1901, 129). It therefore appears that the statio had already been located here for some time. Statues of Aesculapius and Apollo found in the vicinity have been taken as evidence that it had also become the center of a healing cult, perhaps as early as the second century. Finds of pottery show that the spring continued in use as late as the eighth century, and even at present it produces water pronounced excellent by the experts.

NSc 1901, 41–144 (G. Boni), the most detailed ac-

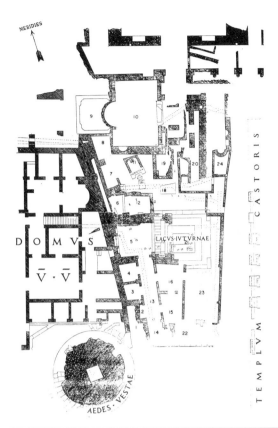

Figure 51
Lacus Iuturnae, Statio Aquarum, and Adjacencies, Plan

count of the excavation and finds; BdA 40 (1955): 346–47 (A. Davico), the account of the restoration of the Aedicula Iuturnae; Nash 2.9–17, 395–97; Roma, archeologia nel centro (1985), 1.73–92 (E. M. Steinby); E. M. Steinby, Lacus Iuturnae I (Rome 1989).

Lacus Longus: known only from the edict of Tarracius Bassus of the fourth century (CIL 6.31893 b9 = ILS 6072). It is listed following the Decennenses (see Decenniae) and Monetarii (q.v.) and therefore probably in Regio III.

Lacus Miliarius: see **Vicus Laci Miliari.**

Lacus Orphei: on the Esquiline, listed by the regionary catalogues in Regio V. Martial (10.19.4–9) described it as at the head of the Clivus Suburanus, a theater dominated at its summit by Orpheus drenched in water and surrounded by wild animals charmed by his music. The residents of the neighborhood seem to have been known as Orfienses (CIL 6.31893 d12) in the fourth century, and the name persisted into the medieval period to designate the churches of S. Lucia in Orfea and S. Martino iuxta Orfeam (HCh 306, 382).

CEFR 98 (1987): 415–28 (E. Rodriguez Almeida).

Lacus Pastorum: listed by the regionary catalogues in Regio III and usually explained by citation of a passage in the "Acta S. Eusebii Presbyteri": *ad petram sceleratam iuxta amphitheatrum ad lacum pastoris* (Jordan 2.119–20; HJ 318–19). It would put the lacus east of the Colosseum, between it and the church of S. Clemente, a likely enough location.

Lacus Philippi: a reservoir that Philippus Arabs built in the Transtiberim to relieve a shortage of water there (Aur. Vict., *Caes.* 28.1), often mistaken for a naumachia.

Lacus Pisonis: mentioned by Cicero (*QFr.* 2.3.7) in 56 B.C. to locate a house rented for Quintus's temporary use. The manuscript reading is *ad lucum Pisonis* but can hardly be right, because luci at this time belong to divinities. Its location is unknown.

Lacus Poetelius: a public watering place on the Cispian listed as one of the landmarks in the ceremonies of the Argei (Varro, *Ling.* 5.50). The reading is usually corrected to Lucus Poetilius, but without real warrant.

Lacus Promethei: a watering place listed by the regionary catalogues in Regio I after the Camenae (q.v.). It almost certainly showed Prometheus crucified, and the water may have issued from his wound.

Lacus Restituti: in Regio XIV; see **Vicus Laci Restituti**.

Lacus Servilius: a watering place in the Forum Romanum at the end of the Vicus Iugarius adjacent to the Basilica Iulia, probably at the northwest corner of the basilica (Festus 370–72L: *continens*). The heads of senators killed in the proscriptions of Sulla were displayed here (Cicero, *Rosc. Am.* 89; Seneca, *Prov.* 3.7.8; Firm. Mat. 1.7.34). Agrippa embellished it with a figure of the Hydra, probably a fountain figure similar to that discovered in the *natatio* of the Palaestra of Herculaneum (*BdA* 39 [1954]: 193–99 [A. Maiuri]), which may be a copy of it. Festus speaks of it in the past tense, and there is nothing to prove it outlived the Augustan period. It probably was damaged in the fire that destroyed the Basilica Iulia late in Augustus's life and was swallowed up in the enlargement of the basilica in its rebuilding (Augustus, *RG* 20).
Nash 2.18–20.

Lacus Tectus: in Regio XII: see **Vicus Laci Tecti**.

Lapis Manalis: see **Manalis Lapis**.

Lapis Niger: see **Niger Lapis**.

Lapis Pertusus: listed in the regionary catalogues in Regio VII, so probably in the northern reaches of the regio. It ought to be a tunnel of some sort, but identification as the mouth where the Aqua Virgo emerged from the slope of the Pincian seems farfetched. Nordh (*Prolegomena* 1936, 72–75) wished to identify it as the Muro Torto (see Horti Aciliorum), a broken stretch of the Aurelian Walls between Porta Flaminia and Porta Pinciana. In support of this he cited the wording of Procopius, *BellGoth* 1.23.3–4. This, too, seems unlikely to be correct.

Lares, Aedes: a temple *in summa Sacra Via* (Solinus 1.23), first mentioned in connection with prodigies in 106 B.C. (Obsequens 41) and by Cicero (*Nat.D.* 3.63) and Pliny (*HN* 2.16) to locate the shrine of Orbona (q.v.). It was one of the temples that Augustus restored (*RG* 19), probably in 4 B.C. (*CIL* 6.456 = *ILS* 99). The day of dedication was 27 June (Ovid, *Fast.* 6.791–92; Degrassi 474). Because it shared its dedication day with Iuppiter Stator, also *in summa Sacra Via*, and is used to locate the Fanum Orbonae, we should look for its remains near the Arch of Titus. Although the entrance portico of the Domus Aurea of Nero and the platform of Hadrian's Temple of Venus et Roma have overrun most of the area in question, Solinus (1.23) mentions the temple as still in existence in his day (ca. A.D. 200).

In describing the line of the pomerium of the city of Romulus, Tacitus (*Ann.* 12.24) apparently gives points where the course changed direction. It began at the bronze bull in the Forum Boarium, ran to the Magna Herculis Ara, then to the Ara Consi, Curiae Veteres, Sacellum Larum, and Forum Romanum. If the Curiae Veteres were at the northeast corner of the Palatine, the likeliest location for them, then the Sacellum Larum might conceivably be connected with the Aedes Larum and mentioned because of the change in level, rather than any great change in direction. Because Tacitus speaks of it as though it would be familiar to his reader, this is preferable to imagining an otherwise unattested sacellum at the northeast corner of the Palatine.

The discovery of *CIL* 6.456 = *ILS* 99 near the entrance to the Farnese gardens on the Palatine about 1555 tends to confirm a location northwest of Iuppiter Stator for the Sacellum Larum.

Lares Alites: see **Vicus Larum Alitum**.

Lares Augustorum et Genii Caesarum, Ara: an altar on Sacra Via opposite the mouth of Vicus Statuae Verris first erected under the Flavians and restored in A.D. 161. The Vicus Statuae Verris (q.v.) is identified as the street along the northwest side of the Basilica Constantini, but this is not certain.

RendPontAcc 51–52 (1978–79): 111–36 (R. E. A. Palmer).

Lares Curiales: see Vicus Larum Iu(ga)lium.

Lares Permarini, Aedes: a temple vowed by the praetor L. Aemilius Regillus during a naval battle with Antiochus the Great in 190 B.C., dedicated by M. Aemilius Lepidus on 22 December 179 (Livy 40.52.4; Macrobius, *Sat.* 1.10.10). Livy and Macrobius locate it in the Campus Martius, while the Fasti Praenestini *(ad Kal. Ian.)* locate it *in porticu Minucia.* It has therefore been identified as the temple of which part of the south flank was discovered in 1938 during the widening of Via delle Botteghe Oscure near the corner of Via Celsa and at first identified as the Temple of Bellona. It is now known from the Marble Plan to have stood off axis to the southeast within a square surrounded by a portico labeled MINI[. . .], presumably the Minucia Vetus (see Porticus Minucia Vetus), between the Diribitorium on the north and the Theatrum and Crypta Balbi on the south.

The temple is an imposing one, peripteral, octastyle, with apparently twelve columns on the flanks, raised on a moderately high podium finished with deep moldings at base and crown. It is frontal in the Roman manner, with a stair of approach on the west, a pronaos almost as deep as the cella given an extra file of columns in continuation of each lateral wall of the cella, and with lateral colonnades of six columns on either side inside the cella. The remains show a mixture of materials, column shafts of peperino with bases and Corinthian capitals of travertine, a podium revetment of marble, and a marble entablature including a modillion cornice.

It was apparently always a very splendid building, commensurate with Aemilius Regillus's victory. What we see must be a late republican or Augustan rebuilding of the original with extensive Domitianic repairs after the fire of Titus. Over the doors of the temple was a long dedicatory inscription in Saturnians preserved by Livy (40.52.4), a second copy of which was put over the doors of a temple of Jupiter *in Capitolio,* presumably the Temple of Iuppiter Optimus Maximus, further testimony to the greatness of Aemilius Regillus's victory.

QITA 5 (1968): 9–18 (L. Cozza).

Lares Praestites: known only from Ovid (*Fast.* 5.129–30), where the Kalends of May are recorded as the festival of these Lares, to whom an altar was set up and *parva simulacra.* This might be the same as the altar supposed to have been erected by Titus Tatius (Varro, *Ling.* 5.74); if so, we might expect to find it in the Colline district of Quirinal and Viminal. These Lares were shown wearing the skins of dogs and accompanied by dogs (Plutarch, *Quaest. Rom.* 5.74), quite unlike all other Lares we know. They are shown on denarii of L. Caesius of about 90 B.C., two seated youths, each with a spear, and with a dog seated between them, nude except for what must be presumed to be a dog skin over the right leg (*B. M. Coins Rom. Rep.* 2.290 nos. 585–89; Crawford 298). Their resemblance to the Dioscuri and consequently to the Penates, as they are described, is very striking.

Lares Querquetulani, Sacellum: a shrine on the Esquiline (Varro, *Ling.* 5.49), therefore not to be associated with the Querquetulanus Mons, which is said to have been an old name for the Caelian, or the Porta Querquetulana on the Caelian. The epithet suggests more than a single tree, but Varro clearly implies that there was no sign of an oak wood or grove there in his day. At the same time he indicates that he regarded this as a very ancient shrine.

Latiaris Collis: see Quirinalis Collis.

Lauretum: see Loretum.

Lautolae: a place designation explained by Varro (*Ling.* 5.156) as from washing: *quod ibi ad Ianum Geminum aquae caldae fuerunt.* He goes on to say that this water created the Velabrum Minus. Macrobius (*Sat.* 1.9.17–18) relates that during the war with Titus Tatius, when the Romans were hard-pressed, through the Porta Ianualis, *quae sub radicibus collis Viminalis erat,* a great force of very hot water originating from the Temple of Janus had repelled the enemy, and this was the origin of the custom of opening the doors of Janus in time of war (cf. also Servius *ad Aen.* 8.361). Macrobius is wrong about the location of the Porta Ianualis, but if Velabrum is an ancient name for a subsidiary channel, there may well once have been one in the basin of the Subura, and if there were a *ianus* crossing the Cloaca stream there, Varro or his source might at a later date have mistaken the Ianus Geminus for this. However, the similarity of the words *Lautolae* and *Lautumiae* (might the first be a contraction of *Lautumiolae?*), the known location of the Ianus Geminus *ad infimum Argiletum,* and the existence of a spring (not a hot spring, but Varro uses the past tense) in the Tullianum make it likely that the real location of the Lautolae was at the base of the Capitoline on the northeast and the Velabrum Minus (see Velabrum Maius and Ianus Geminus) was at the foot of the slope down from the Tullianum to the Forum Romanum.

Lautumiae: stone quarries on the northeast slope of the Capitoline that were also used as prisons (Livy 32.26.17 and 37.3.8; Seneca Rhetor, *Controv.* 9.4[27].21). The word is supposed to have been borrowed from the Syracusans, who also used their quarries (latomiae) for that purpose (Varro, *Ling.* 5.151; Paulus *ex Fest.* 104L). Cato built the Basilica Porcia *in lautumiis* (Livy 39.44.7), so they were probably in use only from sometime after the fall of Syracuse in 212 to about 180. Thereafter, the Carcer (q.v.) was the only prison in Rome.

Lavacrum: see **Thermae, Balineum, Lavacrum.**

Lavacrum Agrippinae: baths built by one of the Agrippinas, known from inscriptions on lead pipes found on the Viminal near the church of S. Lorenzo in Panisperna, toward S. Vitale. With the area are associated finds of statuary as well (*CIL* 15.7147; see also 6.29765). One inscription also recorded a restoration of this bath by Hadrian, so in S.H.A. *Hadr.* 19.10 *Lavacrum Agrippae* should probably be corrected to *Lavacrum Agrippinae.*

Lavacrum Plautini: mentioned only once (S.H.A. *Heliogab.* 8.6) as a bath that had been private, or exclusive, which Elagabalus threw open to the use of the people. Presumably it was on the Palatine, and one may ask whether the reading might be a corruption of *Palatini.*

Laverna, Area, Lucus: see **Porta Lavernalis.**

Liber (? or Bacchus?): a shrine "of Dionysos" mentioned by Pausanias (8.46.5) as in some unknown imperial gardens where the one remaining tusk of the Calydonian boar was preserved. Because Octavian was supposed to have taken it from Tegea after the defeat of Mark Antony (Pausanias 8.46.1), the Horti Caesaris at the Porta Collina may be meant.

Liber Pater: see **Lyaeus.**

Liber Pater, Signum: a statue on the Capitoline, presumably in the Area Capitolina, mentioned in two military diplomata of A.D. 70 (*CIL* 16.10, 11).

Libertas (1): a temple on the Aventine that T. Sempronius Gracchus (cos. 238 B.C.) built, in which his son of the same name had painted the feast following the Battle of Beneventum in 214 (Livy 24.16.19;

Paulus *ex Fest.* 108L). Its precise location is unknown, but it should not be confused with Iuppiter Libertas on the Aventine (see Degrassi 440).

Libertas (2): a small shrine that Clodius erected on part of the site of Cicero's house on the Palatine, which he razed to the ground after Cicero went into exile. On Cicero's return he was able, despite Clodius's opposition, to regain possession of his property and to have the shrine removed (Cicero, *Dom.* 116; Plutarch, *Cic.* 33.1; Cass. Dio 38.17.6, 39.11.1, 39.20.3). Cicero (*Dom.* 111) asserts that the cult statue of Clodius's shrine was originally the funerary monument of a courtesan of Tanagra.
　REL 43 (1965): 229–37 (G.-C. Picard).

Libertas (3): a temple voted by the senate in 46 B.C. in honor of Caesar, in connection with the title of Liberator awarded him (Cass. Dio 43.44.1). It is very unlikely that it was built.

Libertas (4): see **Iuppiter Libertas, Aedes.**

Libertas, Atrium: see **Forum Traiani** and **Atrium Libertatis.**

Libitina: see **Lucus Libitinae.**

Ligures: a monument on the Capitoline named in the location of a military diploma of A.D. 80 (*CIL* 16.158). Presumably this was a victory monument, a trophy of some sort.

Litus Etruscum: see **Ripa Veientana** and **Vaticanus Ager.**

Loretum (also **Lauretum**): a place on the Aventine where there had been a stand of laurels, but this had disappeared by the time of Varro (*Ling.* 5.152; see also Dion. Hal. 3.43.1 and Pliny, *HN* 15.138). It was here that Titus Tatius was supposed to have been buried (Varro, *Ling.* 5.152; Festus 496L). According to Servius (*ad Aen.* 8.276), Varro also reported that laurels cut in this stand were used in the ceremonies of the Ara Maxima Herculis, although the poplar was Hercules's appointed tree.
　There were two Loreta, or perhaps better two parts of the Loretum, for a Vicus Loreti Minoris and a Vicus Loreti Maioris are listed in Regio XIII on the Capitoline Base (*CIL* 6.975 = *ILS* 6073), and in the Fasti Vallenses for 13 August we find *Vortumno in Loreto Maiore* (Degrassi 494–95). It was apparently adjacent to, but distinct from, the Armilustrium (Plutarch, *Rom.* 23.2). The Vicus Armilustri follows the Vicus Loreti Minoris on the Capitoline Base, but precedes the Vicus Loreti Maioris, with three vici inter-

vening. Thus we can place the Loretum Minus on the northwestern part of the hill but are in some doubt about the Loretum Maius.

Loricata: *ad Loricatam* and *a Loricata* are designations given agents of the imperial fiscus (*CIL* 6.8688–92), sometimes in conjunction with *ad Castorem* (see Castor, Aedes). This suggests an office identified by a loricate statue (of the reigning princeps?), but this cannot be identified.

Lucus: see **Aedes, Aedicula, Templum,** etc.

Lucus Albionarum: see **Albionarum Lucus.**

Lucus Asyli: see **Inter Duos Lucos** (2).

Lucus Bellonae: see **Bellona Pulvinensis, Aedes.**

Lucus Camenarum: see **Camenae.**

Lucus Esquilinus: a conjectural emendation of Lacus Esquilinus in the text of Varro (*Ling.* 5.50), for which there is inadequate warrant.

Lucus Fagutalis: see **Fagutal.**

Lucus Furrinae (or **Furinae**): the sanctuary of an ancient goddess, a grove on the right bank of the Tiber well up on the slope of the Janiculan hill, where Gaius Gracchus met his death in 121 B.C. (Plutarch, *C. Gracch.* 17.2; [Aur. Vict.,] *De Vir. Ill.* 65.5–6). From inscriptions found in the vicinity, this appears to have covered part of the middle slope of the Janiculan with the present lower reaches of Villa Sciarra/ Wurts (*CIL* 6.422, 423, 30765; *ILS* 4287, 4292). Its extent is not known. The goddess in early times had a flamen (Varro, *Ling.* 5.84) and a festival, the Furrinalia or Fornalia, on 25 July (Degrassi 487), but Varro says that in his time she had been almost forgotten (*Ling.* 6.19), and her character is disputed. Plutarch believed she was a nymph, whereas Cicero (*Nat. D.* 3.46) and Martianus Capella (2.164) believed she was a divinity of the underworld. The latter identification may rest on no more than the similarity of Furrina to Furiae, but there was another shrine of Furrina not far from Arpinum (Cicero, *QFr.* 3.1.4), so she was not simply a local nymph. Later we find mention of Nymphae Furrinae (*CIL* 6.36802) and a Genius Forinarum (*CIL* 6.422 = *ILS* 4292), but these may have been associated with springs or other features in the grove, rather than with Furrina herself.

The character of the Furrinalia is unknown, but in later times the grove was evidently considered a suitable place for a temple of Iuppiter Heliopolitanus (q.v.) and other divinities associated with him. Because this sanctuary has numerous suggestions of a death and underworld cult and the Lucus Furrinae lay close to the edge of the city, there is reason to think Cicero and Martianus may not have been entirely wrong, but the flamen and festival would be difficult to account for in a death cult. Her name suggests an Etruscan origin.

P. Gauckler, *Le Sanctuaire syrien du Janicule* (Paris 1912), 1–137; N. Goodhue, *The Lucus Furrinae and the Syrian Sanctuary on the Janiculum* (Amsterdam 1975), 1–24, 71–76; M. Mele, ed., *L'area del santuario siriaco del Gianicolo* (Rome 1982).

Lucus Iunonis Lucinae: see **Iuno Lucina, Aedes.**

Lucus Libitinae: a grove containing a temple of Venus Libitina (or Libentina or Lubentina), identified by the Romans with Libitina (Plutarch, *Numa* 12.1), originally the headquarters of the funeral undertakers of Rome, the libitinarii. Here lists of the dead were kept and a coin was deposited for each, a custom supposed to have been initiated by Servius Tullius as part of a system for keeping the census of the city (Dion. Hal. 4.15.5). Here all the equipment necessary for a funeral could be bought (Plutarch, *Quaest. Rom.* 23), and here the mob of Clodius's adherents found firewood that they carried to the houses of the consuls and Pompey in their rioting after his murder (Asconius *in Milon.* 29 [Stangl 32]). Funerary inscriptions speak of a *vestiarius* and a *lanius ab luco Libitinae* (*CIL* 6.9974 = *ILS* 7574, 33870 = *ILS* 7471). Festus (322L) says that the day of dedication of the Temple of Venus was 19 August, but the Fasti Antiates Maiores and Vallenses omit it (Degrassi 498). Obsequens (12) tells of a bronze equestrian statue there from which water ran in 166 B.C. No one locates the grove for us, but because the Domus Rostrata of Pompey was on the Carinae (see Domus, Cn. Pompeius Magnus [1]), while those of the consuls Hypsaeus and Scipio are unlocated, it is possible that the Lucus Libitinae was not far from the Esquiline cemetery outside the Porta Esquilina, but within the Servian pomerium rather than beyond it.

Lucus Martis: according to the scholia on Juvenal 1.7, a grove on the Via Appia where poets were accustomed to read their works. But this is so patently an invention based on a misreading of the passage in Juvenal and knowledge of the important Temple of Mars on the Via Appia that it must be regarded with great skepticism.

Lucus Mefitis: see **Mefitis Aedes, Lucus.**

Lucus Petelinus: a grove outside the Porta Flumentana from which the Capitoline could not be seen, in which the comitia were assembled to try M. Manlius Capitolinus in 381 B.C. (Livy 6.20.11; Plutarch, *Cam.* 36.6) and in which in 342 B.C. the people were again assembled for a plebiscite with respect to a mutinous army. Because there was very little space between the Porta Flumentana and the river, we must put the lucus immediately outside the pomerium here, where the height of the walls would cut off the view of the Capitoline. The origin of the name is obscure and is not explained in our sources.

Lucus Pisonis, Ad: the reading of all the manuscripts in Cicero's location of a house he has rented for his brother (*QFr.* 2.3.7), but a lucus that is not assigned to a divinity and is instead the grove of a well-known historical figure would be an anomaly (surely it would be described as horti). Therefore, the emendation to lacus is to be preferred. See Lacus Pisonis.

Lucus Poetilius: an unwarranted correction of *Lacus Poetilius,* a landmark on the Cispian mentioned in connection with the ceremonies of the Argei (Varro, *Ling.* 5.50).

Lucus Stimulae: a grove sacred to Stimula, a divinity confused with Semele (Ovid, *Fast.* 6.503; *CIL* 6.9897 = *ILS* 7551), where the scandalous and criminal Bacchic orgies of the senatus consultum of 186 B.C. took place. It was both near the Aventine (Ovid, *Fast.* 6.518) and near the Tiber (Livy 39.13.12), so presumably in the area southwest of the Aventine. Although obscure, the goddess Stimula seems to have continued to be recognized until the time of Augustine (*De civ. D.* 4.11).
 MEFRA 95 (1983): 55–113 (O. de Cazanove).

Lucus Streniae: see **Strenia, Sacellum.**

Lucus Vestae: see **Atrium Vestae.**

Ludus: see **Circus, Trigarium, Stadium, Ludus.**

Ludus Aemilius: mentioned by Horace (*Ars P.* 32). Acron tells us that an Aemilius had a gladiatorial training school adjacent to which was the workshop of a sculptor in bronze. Porphyrion makes this Aemilius Lepidus and adds that by his day in the fourth century it had been converted into the Balneum Polycleti, a private bath (q.v.). A private training school might have been established by either Aemilius Lepidus the triumvir or his father. This might have been in the Campus Martius, where most such activities

congregated and the Amphitheater of Statilius Taurus (see Amphitheatrum Statilii Tauri) was also built.

Ludus Dacicus: one of the four training schools for gladiators that Domitian founded (Chron. 146). It is listed in Regio II by the *Curiosum* and in Regio III by the *Notitia.* It was presumably not far from the Colosseum, and logic seems to demand that it lie somewhere in the valley between the Oppius and the Caelian, along with the other dependencies of the Colosseum. Rodriguez Almeida (Rodriguez 72–73; cf. *BullCom* 82 [1970–71]: 115–18) identifies fragments 142 and 161 of the Marble Plan as showing this ludus and locates it on two adjacent slabs of the plan. The case is very convincing. It cannot be the ludus parts of which were found in excavations in 1938 and which has been identified as the Ludus Matutinus, for there are discrepancies in the design and there would not be sufficient space and accuracy in location with respect to other fragments. However, Rodriguez believes the fragments belong to the slabs of the Ludus Magnus and the Colosseum. The only place it seems possible to insert this ludus would then be between the hemicycle of the Thermae Traiani and the Ludus Magnus, but this places it so firmly in Regio III that it is difficult to account for the error in the *Curiosum.* A similar error with respect to the Ludus Matutinus (q.v.) suggests that these ludi might have been confused with one another.

Ludus Gallicus: mentioned only by the *Notitia,* which lists it in Regio II, and an inscription of uncertain reading, *CIL* 6.9470. Presumably this was one of the four training schools for gladiators that Domitian founded (Chron. 146) and ought to be close to the Colosseum. Perhaps a place for it can be found southwest of the square of the Colosseum below the Temple of Divus Claudius.

Ludus Magnus (Figs. 3, 52): the largest of four training schools for gladiators that Domitian created in the vicinity of the Amphitheatrum Flavium (Colosseum) (Chron. 146). It appears on a fragment of the Marble Plan that originally preserved about one-half of its plan (Vat. Lat. 3439 f. 13 r; *FUR* pls. 1, 17; Rodriguez pls. 4, 11) but has been broken and eroded. The ludus was discovered in 1937 between the Via Labicana and Via di S. Giovanni in Laterano, just east of the Colosseum square. The area excavated amounts to a little less than one-half the complete building. Further explorations were carried out in 1960–1961 in connection with excavations for the foundations of the Nuova Esattoria Comunale just east of the Ludus Magnus in 1958–1960. With the

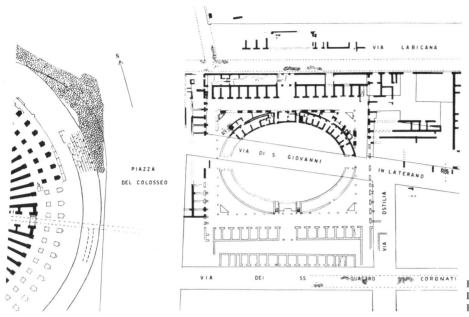

Figure 52
Ludus Magnus,
Restored Plan

help of the Marble Plan and a strong presumption that the complex was symmetrical, an almost complete understanding and reconstruction are possible.

It is not on the axis of the Colosseum, but to the north of this, and lay along the square of the Colosseum between the ancient Via Labicana and the ancient street found under SS. Quattro Coronati. It consisted of a large arena with axes of 210 and 140 Roman feet (62.15 m x 41.45 m) surrounded by a cavea, which the excavators calculate as of nine gradus, supported on concrete vaults over brick-faced concrete walls, the chambers underneath probably used for storage. One reached the cavea by small external stairs. The arena had ceremonial entrances on the long axis and what appear to be ample boxes on the short one. The base of the cavea was raised 2.75 m above the arena and provided with a metal balustrade. Around the cavea ran a rectangular portico with columns in two storeys, the orders being of travertine and unfluted, Tuscan in the lower storey and presumably Ionic above, but no capital survives. The Ionic column elements to be seen in the area today belong to a late repair. In the open triangles between cavea and portico were small triangular fountain basins. On the portico on all sides opened a series of small rectangular chambers of roughly similar dimensions. These served as lodgings for the gladiators and their various needs, and here were stairs to the upper storey. Behind this on the north and south sides facing out to the street there was then a second row of small rooms, presumably let out as shops. The second storey must have reproduced the plan of the first in its general lines; the third would have been the same, but is believed to have had an open gallery replacing the portico. The plan of the rooms on the east, where the Via Ostilia and modern buildings interfered with exploration, is uncertain; there may well have been important annexes here of which we are ignorant. Soundings indicate that there was a large axial hall surrounded on three sides by colonnades and with five entrances, possibly a sacrarium or armamentarium.

An imposing entrance, probably the main one, led in from the Via Labicana on the short axis of the arena. Originally one descended a broad flight of steps to the level of the floor of the arena, well below street level, but Trajan found the building incomplete at his accession, raised the pavements of the buildings behind the portico itself by 1.40 m, and rebuilt the whole at this level, which is the building we know. Hadrian introduced refinements. Devastated by a fire in the late second century, it was immediately repaired. Other work seems to have been carried out under Caracalla, and there are numerous undated repairs and modifications. A subterranean corridor connected the Ludus Magnus with the substructures of the Colosseum; there may well have been another connecting passage above ground. In excavations under the floors of the ludus were found remains of houses, at least one of which had a fine Pompeian Third Style pavement.

The same men may have been procurators of both the mint and the Ludus Magnus (*CIL* 6.1647 = 10.1710; see also Moneta).

237

A. M. Colini and L. Cozza, *Il Ludus Magnus* (Rome 1962); Nash 2.24–26.

Ludus Matutinus: presumably one of the four training schools for gladiators that Domitian founded (Chron. 146). It is put in Regio II by both the *Notitia* and the *Curiosum*, in Regio III a second time by the *Notitia*. Finds of inscriptions are not helpful (*CIL* 6.352, 10172 = *ILS* 5152, 10173; 14.2922 = *ILS* 1420; *IG* 14.1330; *IGUR* 2.282). If it lay on, or athwart, the boundary between Regio II and Regio III, as the *Notitia* suggests, it should lie south of the Ludus Magnus and in similar relationship to the square of the Colosseum. Here in investigations in 1938 were found bits of a building with a plan suggestively like that of the Ludus Magnus, but on a smaller scale (*MemPontAcc*, ser. 3.7 [1944]: 287 [A. M. Colini]). Its name suggests that it was the training school for hunters for the venationes, which took place in the morning (Ovid, *Met.* 11.26; Martial 8.67, 13.95; Suetonius, *Claud.* 34).

Luna, Aedes: The location of the Temple of Luna is provided by the story of the death of C. Gracchus (Orosius 5.12.3–10; [Aur. Vict.,] *De Vir. Ill.* 65). He had occupied the Temple of Diana on the summit of the Aventine with a body of armed men a few days after a riot on the Capitoline had ended in the death of a *praeco* of the consul Opimius. Here his party intended to mass the slaves, promising them freedom, and to make a stand against the oppressive government of Opimius. Opimius and his faction seem to have been too strong and decisive for the Gracchans. D. Brutus took a force up the Clivus Publicius and attacked Gracchus, who was unable to withstand the fury of the onslaught. He fell back with his men, first to the Temple of Minerva, then to the Temple of Luna. He was making his way toward the north end of the Aventine, and the precinct of Luna was terraced, for the Gracchans had to jump down from this to try to make their way toward the Porta Trigemina. In the jump Gracchus injured his ankle and was so crippled that he had great difficulty in making his way as far as the Pons Sublicius. They must have been working their way along the Aventine parallel to the Clivus Publicius from the Temple of Diana at the top of the Clivus Publicius to the Temple of Luna at the northern point. The jump for the two Flacci, father and son, took them into a private house, where they barricaded themselves. Presumably the Clivus Publicius, the only road up the hill in this sector, was in the hands of Brutus's men, and the Gracchans could not hope to escape that way. Some of the temples must have been set at least in part along the brow of the hill, with private buildings coming up against their precinct walls from below, and by jumping onto the roofs of these they could elude their pursuers at least temporarily.

Thus, though the Temple of Luna was ascribed to Servius Tullius, it seems to have been set on dramatic terracing (cf. Iuppiter Optimus Maximus Capitolinus). Tacitus (*Ann.* 15.41) believed it was Servius's temple that was destroyed in the fire of Nero, but if so, it must have been restored in the course of time. The duplication of Servian temples in close proximity but clearly separate, Luna at the top of the slope and Diana at the crest, is in itself perplexing.

The temple is first mentioned in connection with a great windstorm in 182 B.C. that tore off its doors and blew them down into the back wall of the Temple of Ceres (see Ceres, Liber, Liberaque, Aedes) on the slope below it (Livy 40.2.2). In 84 B.C., at the time of Cinna's death, it was struck by lightning (Appian, *BellCiv* 1.78). The day of dedication was 31 March (Ovid, *Fast.* 3.883–84; Degrassi 433).

Luna Noctiluca, Templum: a temple on the Palatine that shone by night (Varro, *Ling.* 5.68). Whether this was because of the material of which it was constructed or because of artificial illumination, the epithet must originally have belonged to Luna, and the temple must have been whitened or illuminated in her honor. Nothing further is known about this shrine.

Lupanarii: listed by the regionary catalogues in Regio II Caelimontium, usually presumed to be a zone where brothels were numerous and notorious. Because Nero built the Macellum Magnum here, we can presume that the district was populous and there would be a demand for prostitutes, but from other sources we learn that they were especially to be found in the center of Rome, on the Sacra Via (Propertius 2.23.13–16) and Subura (Persius 5.32–33; Martial 2.17, 6.66.1–2, 11.61.3, 11.78.11). But the word *Lupanarii* is masculine, not neuter, in the catalogues. Because prostitutes had to register with the aediles (Tacitus, *Ann.* 2.85) and were taxed from the time of Caligula (Suetonius, *Calig.* 40), this might have been the office of those in charge of the official governance of the trade (cf. *PW* 15 [1931]: 1021–27 [K. Schneider]).

Lupercal: the cave at the foot of the Palatine in front of which Faustulus discovered the she-wolf nursing the twins Romulus and Remus and in which she took refuge when driven off by him or his comrades (Dion. Hal. 1.79.8; Ovid, *Fast.* 2.381–424; Livy 1.5.1–2). It contained a spring, was believed originally to have been preceded by a grove, which had disappeared except for the Ficus Ruminalis (q.v.) by the time of our sources, and was supposed to have been dedicated to Pan Lycaeus from the time of Evander (Dion. Hal. 1.32.3–5; Servius *ad Aen.* 8.90 and 343).

It is listed by the regionary catalogues in Regio X, but is located *in circo* (Servius *ad Aen.* 8.90), and far enough away from the Palatine to have permitted construction of a permanent theater, though perhaps not a large one, between it and the Palatine (Vell. Pat. 1.15.3). Excavations of the whole west corner of the Palatine as far as the Scalae Caci (q.v.) failed to produce any trace of it (Lugli 1946, 420–23), and it is almost certainly to be sought nearer to the Circus Maximus.

In time it was given monumentality. It contained a bronze group of the she-wolf suckling the twins (Dion. Hal. 1.79.8) and was restored by Augustus (*RG* 19). It was evidently considered a suitable place for the erection of an equestrian statue in honor of Drusus (*CIL* 6.912 = 31200). It was the cult center for the priestly college of the Luperci and the celebration of the Lupercalia on 15 February. Its exact form and appointments continue to be matters for speculation.

Latomus 44 (1985): 609–14 (A. W. J. Holleman).

Lyaeus (=**Liber** or **Bacchus**), **Tecta:** a temple known only from a casual reference in Martial (1.70.9–10). It stood *in summa Sacra Via,* together with a tholus of the Magna Mater (see Magna Mater, Tholus), where the way to the Palatine branched from the Sacra Via; i.e., in the vicinity of the Arch of Titus. Because we know of the existence here already of temples of the Lares and Iuppiter Stator, and the Arch of Titus had been constructed by the time Martial wrote (1.70.6: *plurima qua summi fulget imago ducis*), we must look for these two additional temples within a very crowded neighborhood northeast of the arch in a zone now covered by the platform of Hadrian's Temple of Venus et Roma. Both were evidently very small. In 1899 in front of the Basilica Constantini was found a large fragment of the marble entablature of a small round structure, about 3.90 m in diameter. This bears the figure of a Maenad and an inscription recording a restoration by Antoninus Pius (*RömMitt* 17 [1902]: 95–96 [C. Hülsen]). A medallion of the same princeps shows a circular building containing a statue of Bacchus (Cohen 2: no. 1187; Gnecchi 2.22–23 Antoninus Pius no. 118). These have been associated with this temple, but the case is anything but strong.

M

Macellenses: a designation found in a single, poor fragment believed to be part of the edict of Tarracius Bassus of the late fourth century (*CIL* 6.31897). It may refer to those living in the neighborhood of the Macellum Liviae (q.v.) in Regio V or those living in the neighborhood of the Macellum Magnum (q.v.) in Regio II, but the context is lost.

Macellum: This term for an organized market is supposed to be of Punic origin and was used by the Greeks as well as the Romans. Earlier the Romans had simply used the term *forum,* but after the Forum Piscarium burned in 210 B.C. and was rebuilt the following year (Livy 26.27.2) it apparently seemed inadequate to the Romans, and in the great building year 179 it was rebuilt by M. Fulvius Nobilior and at that time took the form of a macellum (Livy 40.51.5; Varro, *Ling.* 5.146–47).

The identifying characteristics of a macellum are a central tholus and a ring of shops around this. The tholus is for the sale of fish and is provided with water and drains. The shops are of the same size and are let out to individual provisioners. There may be a portico in front of the shops, and there may be space here for barrows to be set up. There may also be shops in a double bank, facing out to a street, as well as in toward the tholus. If accommodations for meat are provided, the butchers are gathered to one area provided with marble counters and drains. Such markets may be very handsome and given a range of embellishments; they seem to have regularly been public benefactions. They vary very much in size, depending on the size of the community to be served and the number of provisioners to be accommodated. Some had no shops at all; small ones might have no tholus. There is often a shrine or a shrine-like room on the main axis at the far end, possibly the schola of the collegium of provisioners. The earliest known is that of Rome of 179 B.C., the latest

that of Ostia of A.D. 418–420. They occur all over the Roman world, but are especially common in central Italy, Africa Proconsularis, and Numidia.

In Rome besides the macellum of 179, which continued in operation down to the time it was sacrificed to create the Forum Augustum and Forum Traiani, we know of a Macellum Liviae, somewhere on the Esquiline in Regio V and a Macellum Magnum built by Nero on the Caelian and put on coins that he issued. In this both the portico and the tholus were two-storeyed and the tholus contained a nude male statue with a long scepter or trident, so not Mercury, the Genius Macelli, or Fortuna, the divinities one would expect to find in a macellum. Part of it may be represented on Fragment 157 of the Marble Plan.

C. De Ruyt, *Macellum, marché alimentaire des romains* (Louvain-La-Neuve 1983).

Macellum: the great food market of republican Rome. Festus (Paulus *ex Fest.* 112L) ascribes its creation to the censors M. Aemilius Lepidus and M. Fulvius Nobilior in 179 B.C., whereas Varro (*Ling.* 5.145–47) says that this brought together a number of more specialized markets, the Forum Boarium, the Forum Holitorium (which he says was the old macellum of Rome), the Forum Piscarium, and the Forum Cuppedinis (qq.v.). Livy, (40.51.5) in his account of the censorship of Aemilius and Fulvius, says only that M. Fulvius Nobilior rebuilt the Forum Piscarium and sold the tabernae with which it was surrounded to individuals. This had burned in 210 B.C. (Livy 26.27.3), along with many other buildings on and around the northeast side of the Forum Romanum, and though it must have been rebuilt very soon thereafter, that rebuilding was probably only in very temporary form. So Fulvius's reconstruction, which Livy links with the building of the Basilica Fulvia et Aemilia behind the Argentariae Novae on the Sacra Via, was probably a major undertaking.

Festus (Paulus *ex Fest.* 42L) says that Forum Cuppedinis was simply another name for the Macellum, and it is hardly likely that the individual more specialized markets would ever have been widely scattered, as Varro's explanation would seem to require, so while we may incline to think that there were always distinct areas within the organization, Varro is probably wrong about this.

Varro (*ap. Non.* 719L) mentioned a tholus Macelli, so it probably had the form familiar elsewhere in the Roman world of a colonnaded square surrounded by banks of shops, possibly in places a double bank opening both in and out, with a round building for the sale of fish at the center. There was evidently a main entrance, the *fauces Macelli* (Cicero, *Verr.* 2.3.145, *Quinct.* 25), probably leading in from the Argiletum, and another from the Corneta, the short street between the Basilica Paulli and Temple of Antoninus and Faustina, leading to the part known especially as Forum Cuppedinis, which lay at a higher level than the rest (Varro, *Ling.* 5.146 and 152). There must have been other entrances as well. The Macellum must have been largely or entirely destroyed in order to build the Forum Augustum, by which time the growth of Rome had made a central market inconvenient, and its area had become entirely inadequate. Whether it continued to exist even in much reduced form is doubtful. Local markets such as the Macellum Liviae (q.v.) would have replaced it for most consumers, and a wholesale market may have been created in the neighborhood of the Emporium (q.v.).

The word *macellum* is supposed to be Semitic in origin and was borrowed by the Greeks (Varro, *Ling.* 5.146) as well as the Romans. However, the Romans had a story of two brigands, Numerius Equitius Cuppes and Manius Macellus, whose houses were razed and the land on which they stood then converted to this public use (Varro, *Ling.* 5.147; Donatus *ad Ter. Eun.* 256). In Latin the word seems always to have been used to designate a building of a particular architectural form.

C. De Ruyt, *Macellum, marché alimentaire des romains* (Louvain-la-Neuve 1983), especially 225–52.

Macellum Liviae: known only from the regionary catalogues, where it is called Macellum Liviani and listed in Regio V, and from a marble beam (*CIL* 6.1178 = *ILS* 5592) that records a restoration of the complex by Valentinian, Valens, and Gratian (A.D. 364–378). In the *Liber Pontificalis* Liberius is said to have built the church of S. Maria Maggiore *iuxta macellum Libiae* (LPD 1.209 and cf. 232 [Xystus III]; VZ 2.233 and cf. 237; HCh 342). The church of S. Vito is described as *in macello* (HCh 499). And in the chronicle of Benedict of Soracte for the year

921 the church of S. Eusebio is described as *iuxta macellum parvum* (*MGH Script.* 3.715). The picture is further complicated by a slave collar (*AE* 1946.211), probably of the late fourth century, that locates the Macellum Liviae in Region III. Finally, in the *Ordo Benedicti* one finds *intrans sub arcum* (the Arch of Gallienus) *ubi dicitur macellum Livianum* (Jordan 2.665).

In the late nineteenth century just outside the line of the Servian Walls, somewhat north of the Arch of Gallienus (Porta Esquilina), was found a large market complex consisting of a very large court, 80 m x 25 m, surrounded on three sides by brick-faced piers making an arcaded portico 6.25 m deep. Opening on this were shops, and there were more shops behind these opening in the opposite direction. A street ran along the east side of the complex, but the court was not aligned with this. In the middle of the court, toward its northern end, was a large fountain, and a complicated system of drains and sewers underlay it. By the third century the southern end of the complex had been invaded and occupied by private dwellings. The construction showed work of many periods, including concrete faced with reticulate, but was chiefly concrete faced with brick. This was immediately identified as the Macellum Liviae (*BullCom* 2 [1874]: 36 and 212–19 [R. Lanciani]; 42 [1914]: 363 [M. Marchetti]). However, Lanciani demurred, thinking the building too ordinary and utilitarian to be an imperial construction (*MonAnt* 1.531–32), and wished to locate the Macellum Liviae just to the south of the Porta Esquilina, outside the walls, so as to fall within Regio V, in an as yet unexplored area.

From 1966 to 1971 excavations under the Basilica of S. Maria Maggiore brought to light parts of a large colonnaded court, almost square but slightly trapezoidal. On the northwest side seems to have opened a series of rooms that might be shops, but the long northeast and southwest walls were unbroken, except for a pretty little apsidal exedra near the north corner. The lower parts of the side walls were revetted in colored marble, and the upper parts were decorated with a painted calendar in which narrow panels with lists of the days of the months and festivals alternated with large panoramas of the months' activities. Magi wished to identify this as the Macellum Liviae, but this has not found approval. Although there is construction of many periods, including concrete faced with quasi-reticulate, the majority, like the decoration, is clearly fourth century, and the location well within the walls argues against the location in Regio V. We are still uncertain where to put the Macellum Liviae and what it was, but, because it figures in the historical record only peripherally, it was probably not a major monument.

MemPontAcc, ser. 3.11.1 (1972) (F. Magi).

Macellum Magnum: listed by the regionary catalogues in Regio II after the Temple of Divus Claudius, so presumably on the height of the Caelian, built by Nero and dedicated in A.D. 59 (Cass. Dio 62 [61].18.3) and represented on coins (*B. M. Coins Rom. Emp.* 1, Nero, 236–37 nos. 191–97, and 266 nos. 335–37). What is shown is a columnar tholus of two storeys raised on a high podium and roofed with what is clearly sometimes a dome and sometimes a truncated cone, which apparently had a large oculus at its center (domed roof: Gnecchi 3.7, Nero no. 42; *B. M. Coins Rom. Emp.* 1, Nero 236 no. 191; Mazzini, Nero 143 no. 129; *RIC* 1: Nero 173 no. 374; truncated cone roof: Cohen 1, Nero 288 no. 126; *B. M. Coins, Rom. Emp.* 1, Nero 237 no. 196; Mazzini, Nero 143 no. 130 and 159 no. 359; *RIC* 1: Nero 159 no. 110). Because it is impossible to imagine that anyone would have shown a dome unless it existed, we must presume that this is the earliest dome for which we have a fixed date and that the coins showing a truncated cone show the line of the exterior of the dome, which concealed it, or are reminiscent of such circular structures as the frigidaria of republican baths. The former is clearly preferable. It is approached by a flight of steps with balustrades in the form of dolphins, and at the center of the lower storey is a standing male figure, nude, carrying a scepter or trident. Behind the tholus is shown what must be a specimen section of the porticoes of the surrounding court, again columnar and in two storeys, but with occasional arcuation of the entablature of the lower storey and with garlands swung between the columns in the upper storey.

The belief that this macellum was transformed into the church of S. Stefano Rotondo by Pope Simplicius (468–482) has now been abandoned. It was based on a misreading of the Neronian coins and inadequate study of the fabric and architectural antecedents of the church. Except for the introduction of a second storey and the doming of the roof of the tholus, Nero's macellum must have followed the traditional architectural form of such complexes, a large court with a tholus at the center, surrounded by porticoes behind which opened banks of more or less uniform shops.

PBSR 39 (1971): 40–45 (J. S. Rainbird and F. B. Sear), 45–46 (J. Sampson).

Magna Mater, Aedes (Figs. 53, 63.2): the temple on the Palatine built to hold the black stone that represented the goddess brought from Pessinus in Phrygia in 204 B.C. The contract for the temple was let by the censors in that year (Livy 29.37.2), and the temple was thirteen years in building, being dedicated in 191 by the praetor M. Iunius Brutus (Livy 36.36.4–5). During that time the black stone was given to Scipio Nasica for safekeeping ([Aur. Vict.,] *De Vir. Ill.* 46.1–3). At the dedication on 11 April the Ludi Megalenses were instituted and celebrated in front of the temple (Cicero, *Har. Resp.* 24; Livy 36.36.4–5). The temple burned in 111 B.C. and was restored by a Metellus, probably Numidicus, who was consul in 110 (Ovid, *Fast.* 4.347–48; Val. Max. 1.8.11; Obsequens 39). In 39 B.C. it figured in the expiation of prodigies, and four palm trees sprang up around it (Cass. Dio 48.43.4–6). It burned again and was restored by Augustus in A.D. 3 (Val. Max. 1.8.11; Ovid, *Fast.* 4.347–48; Augustus, *RG* 19). It continues to figure in history occasionally (cf. Juvenal 9.23; S.H.A. *Claud.* 4.2). Elagabalus proposed to transfer the image of the Magna Mater to the Temple of Elagabalus (S.H.A. *Heliogab.* 3), but, if he did so, it was soon restored to its own temple. The temple was still standing in the fourth century and is listed in Regio X by the regionary catalogues. Christian authors tell us that the black stone was a small affair set into a silver image of the Magna Mater in place of a face (Prudentius, *Peristeph.* 10.156–60; Arnobius, *Adv. Nat.* 7.49).

The temple has been discovered near the west corner of the Palatine above the Scalae Caci (q.v.), together with inscriptions relating to the cult (*CIL* 6.496, 1040, 3702 = 30967) and a headless marble statue of an enthroned goddess originally flanked by lions. The temple faced southwest and had a massive concrete podium with unusually thick walls divided into pronaos and cella. The podium was faced with blocks of peperino, except at the back, where the concrete was simply stuccoed. The stair of approach extended across the façade, and the temple was prostyle, hexastyle, with Corinthian columns of stuccoed peperino. An interior colonnade in marble, possibly in more than one storey, ran around three sides of the cella. The total length of the temple is calculated as 33.18 m, the width as 17.10 m. The façade of the temple with a pediment in which a central throne holding a mural crown is flanked by reclining figures holding *tympana* under their arms, flanked in turn by felines filling the corners of the triangle, is shown on a Claudian relief in Villa Medici (Nash 2.31), and Hülsen (*RömMitt* 10 [1895]: 3–28) offers a full description of the remains and careful reconstruction.

The temple fronted on a precinct with arrangements apparently designed to accommodate the Ludi Megalenses. Steps on which spectators might have disposed themselves, in continuation of the stair of the temple, led down to an area paved with slabs of Monteverde tufa on which temporary stages might have been erected. This precinct was bounded on the southwest by a street that in a later period was covered by a series of vaults to permit the extension of the precinct over it, at that time raised to cover the lower steps, and extend as far as the brow of the hill. Remains of two smaller buildings, both probably temples, to the southwest of the temple, one close to the temple and having much the same orientation, the other at the head of the Scalae Caci and of entirely different orientation, are not positively identified; the latter is thought to be the Temple of Victoria.

Lugli 1946, 431–34; *MonAnt* 46 (1963): 201–330 (P. Romanelli); Nash 2.27–31; *Roma, archeologia nel centro* (1985), 1.179–212 (P. Pensabene); *QArchEtr* 16 (1988): 54–67 (P. Pensabene).

Magna Mater, Templum: the place on the course of the River Almo, between the crossing of it by Via Appia and its mouth on the Tiber, where the black stone of Pessinus was taken annually on 27 March and bathed in the river. It seems to have been closer to the Via Appia than to the Tiber. It seems never to have had any significant development as a shrine. The discovery of a small basin (3.05 m x 3.65 m, 1.70 m deep) lined with blocks of Grotta Oscura tufa and framed by the steps in front of the Temple of the Magna Mater on the Palatine leads to the supposition that the ritual bathing originally took place in the Palatine precinct and was moved to the Almo only in the time of Augustus (*MonAnt* 46 [1963]: 303 [P. Romanelli]; *QArchEtr* 4 [1980]: 69 [P. Pensabene]). The ritual bathing in the Almo is mentioned by a great many sources (Ovid, *Fast.* 4.337–40; Lucan 1.600; Martial 3.47.2; Statius, *Silv.* 5.1.222–24; Silius Italicus 8.363; Amm. Marc. 23.3.7; Vibius Sequester, *Flumina* 21; *CIL* 6.10098 = 33961 = *ILS* 5172; Prudentius, *Peristeph.* 10.156–60; Degrassi 432).

Magna Mater, Tholus: a small temple *in summa Sacra Via* where the Clivus Palatinus branches from the Sacra Via (Martial 1.70.9–10), possibly balancing a tholus of Lyaeus (see Lyaeus, Tecta). It has been proposed that a contorniate of Diva Faustina showing a temple of the Mater Deum and part of the relief of the Haterii showing a statue of the Magna Mater with an altar in front of it seen through a four-sided (?) triumphal arch may represent this little shrine (see Nash 2.34–35), but the first is clearly not a tholus, and the second, because the statue appears at the top of a long flight of thirteen steps, is more apt to represent the great Palatine temple than this little shrine. A portent of 43 B.C. involving the turning of a statue of the Magna Mater that Dio (46.33.3) records is generally supposed to refer to this temple.

Magna Mater (in Circo Maximo): Tertullian (*De Spect.* 8) says the Magna Mater *praesidet euripo (in*

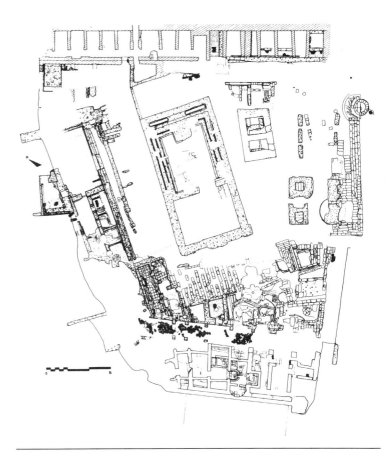

Figure 53
Temple of the Magna Mater, Temple of Victoria, and Adjacencies, Plan of Existing Remains

Circo Maximo), and a large statue of the Magna Mater wearing the mural crown and riding sidesaddle on a rearing or bounding lion appears on coins, reliefs, and mosaics showing the circus. This stands on the spina, just southeast of the central obelisk, facing the Aventine. It appears as early as coins of Trajan, and in the fourth-century representations the lion is shown with water issuing from its mouth. In some representations one or two palm trees appear behind the group. A large cube with a door in its northwest wall and sometimes a fire on its flat roof, which appears just southeast of the group, might conceivably be the Aedes Matris Deum.

Nash 2.32–33; Humphrey 273–77

Magna Mater in Vaticano: see **Phrygianum.**

Ad Malum Punicum: a place designation, perhaps better a square or crossroads than a street, on the Quirinal in Regio VI, where the house in which Domitian was born stood (Suetonius, *Dom.* 1.1; *Notitia, om. Cur.*). It was later converted into the magnificent Temple of the Gens Flavia (see Gens Flavia, Templum). Lanciani (LFUR sheet 16) identifies Ad Malum Punicum as a street nearly coincident with modern Via delle Quattro Fontane and puts the temple just south of its crossing with Alta Semita. No trace of either street or temple is known.

Ad Mammam: see **Diaetae Mammaeae.**

Manalis Lapis: a stone kept at the Temple of Mars outside the Porta Capena that the pontifices carried through the streets of the city in periods of excessive drought in a rite called *manale sacrum* (Varro *ap. Non.* 877L; Paulus *ex Fest.* 115L). Rain was believed to follow immediately. But by Festus's day this was a thing of the past, and he prefaces his explanation with a second one, that this was an entrance to the underworld through which ghosts *(manes)* could make their way *(manare)* up to the world above. This also was only antiquarian knowledge by his day, and he does not locate it. Attempts to associate the Lapis Manalis with the Mundus (2) (q.v.) seem clearly mistaken, because Festus was interested in the Mundus and makes no mention of it in this connection. More likely the Lapis Manalis was a vent, possibly any volcanic vent, like the Tarentum (q.v.).

Mancina Tifata: see **Tifata Mancina.**

Mansiones Saliorum Palatinorum: shrines in various parts of the city where the ancilia were deposited during the nightly stops of the Salii in the course of their processional dance through the city at the beginning of March, known only from a single inscription (*CIL* 6.2158 = *ILS* 4944) on the marble blocks facing the exterior of the Temple of Mars Ultor in the Forum Augustum recording a restoration of these places after A.D. 382. Mention in Suetonius (*Claud.* 33.1) of a feast of the Salii prepared in the Temple of Mars Ultor shows that this was one of their regular stops, but exactly what the *mansiones* were is not clear.

Mansuetae: a locality listed in the regionary catalogues toward the end of Regio VII, so presumably toward the northern limit of the regio. Its name and character are completely obscure.

Mappa Aurea: a locality listed in the regionary catalogues in Regio XIII and occurring again on a late-antique slave collar (*CIL* 15.7182). There seems to be no warrant for associating this with the *mappa* used by the presiding magistrate to start circus games.

Divus Marcus, Templum: a temple decreed for M. Aurelius by the senate and the people after his death (S.H.A. *M. Aurel.* 18.8; Aur. Vict., *Caes.* 16.15 and *Epit.* 16.14). In the regionary catalogues it is linked with his column in Regio IX. It is presumed to have

stood west of the column (see Columna Marci Aurelii Antonini) in much the same relationship that the Temple of Divus Traianus had to his column, but it might equally well have stood north of it. No trace of it has ever been identified.

L'urbe 49 (1986): 74–79 (A. Danti); cf. *OpRom* 15 (1985): 67–78 (H. Kampmann).

Marmorata: a name appearing on a bull of A.D. 926 for a locality on the Tiber adjacent to the Ripa Greca (HCh 253–54, S. Geminiani), i.e., the left bank of the river under the Aventine between the Schola Greca and Horrea, upstream of the district called Marmorata today, but still so called down to the beginning of this century. Many blocks of marble awaiting use could be seen there until relatively recently (Jordan 1.1.434). The area called Marmorata today was part of the medieval district called Horrea; in antiquity it formed part of the Emporium (q.v.).

Mars: Augustine (*De civ. D.* 4.23) adds Mars to Iuventas and Terminus as a divinity who refused exauguration at the time of the laying out of the Temple of Iuppiter Optimus Maximus on the Capitoline, but he is alone in this. Cassius Dio (41.14.3) says that in 49 B.C. a helmet and shield of Mars, votive dedications on the Capitoline, were damaged by lightning, but this need not mean that he had a separate shrine there. If Augustine knew of dedications to Mars in the Area Capitolina, he might have misinterpreted these, for it is most unlikely that had Mars refused evocation, our other sources would have passed over that fact in silence.

Mars, Aedes: the main temple of Mars in Rome, especially in his aspect as a warrior god (Vitruvius 1.7.1; Servius *ad Aen.* 1.292), vowed during the invasion of the Gauls and dedicated in 388 B.C. by T. Quinctius (Livy 6.5.7). It lay outside the city, between the first and second milestones from Porta Capena, on the northeast side of the Via Appia (*CIL* 6.10234 = *ILS* 7213; Appian, *BellCiv* 3.41; Servius *ad Aen.* 1.292). There is a distinct rise in the road approaching it, the Clivus Martis (q.v.), and the site lies just outside Porta S. Sebastiano (Porta Appia) of the Aurelian Walls. The day of dedication was 1 June (Ovid, *Fast.* 6.191–92; Degrassi 463).

The temple is mentioned frequently in history and in inscriptions (*CIL* 6.473, 474 = 30774, 478; *ILS* 3139, 3144), and the area around it as far as the River Almo was known as *ad Martis* (Cicero, *QFr.* 3.7.1; Suetonius, *Ter.* 5). Its pediment, but more likely that of the Temple of Quirinus (see Quirinus, Aedes), may be shown on a relief previously thought to show the pediment of Hadrian's Temple of Venus et Roma (*AJA* 91 [1987]: 441–58 [F. C. Albertson]). As early as 295 B.C. a way *(semita)* was paved leading from Porta Capena to the temple, and three years later the Via Appia was paved from the temple to Bovillae, so it must already have been paved from the Porta Capena to the temple. In 189 B.C. the road was repaved from Porta Capena to the temple (Livy 10.23.12, 38.28.3). The army assembled there before setting out on campaign (Livy 7.23.3), and the Transvectio Equitum, the parade of the equites on the Ides of July, started from it (Dion. Hal. 6.13.4). In it were a statue of Mars and probably images of wolves (Livy 22.1.12). The Lapis Manalis (see Manalis Lapis) was kept in it or nearby. There is no reliable evidence for a grove in connection with it, although this is often asserted. After the Via Appia was paved from the Porta Capena to the Aedes Martis, it became known as the Via Tecta (2)(q.v.). It is commonly believed that this refers to a portico along it, but that is unlikely; it is more likely that originally it referred simply to its being paved, an unusual improvement at this early date.

Mars, Aedes in Circo Flaminio: a temple built *ex manubiis* for D. Iunius Brutus Callaicus by the architect Hermodorus of Salamis (Nepos *ap. Priscian.* 8.18), presumably after his triumph, ca. 133 B.C. In the approach to the temple were inscribed lines by the poet Accius in Saturnians (Val. Max. 8.14.2; *Schol. Bob. in Cic. pro Arch.* 27 [Stangl 179]). It contained a colossal seated Mars by Scopas and a nude Venus also by Scopas, which Pliny (*HN* 36.26) says excelled that of Praxiteles. Its exact location is unknown, but presumably it was somewhere along the southwest side of the square, between it and the Tiber. Degrassi (512) thinks the sacrifice to Mars known for 23 September was made at this temple and that this indicates a restoration by Augustus, because it was his birthday.

QITA 10 (1988): 59–75 (E. Tortorici).

Mars, Ara: the earliest cult center of Mars in Rome, perhaps responsible for the name of the Campus Martius. Its earliest citation seems to be in what purports to be a law of Numa (Festus 204L: *Pompili regis legem . . . secunda spolia, in Martis ara in campo solitaurilia utra caedito*). In 193 B.C. the aediles M. Aemilius Lepidus and L. Aemilius Paullus built a portico from the Porta Fontinalis to the Altar of Mars so that one could walk under shelter to the Campus Martius (Livy 35.10.12). This was of particular benefit to the censors, because it connected their office and archives in the Atrium Libertatis (q.v.) with the place where they conducted the census. After their election it was customary for the new censors to set their curule chairs by the altar (Livy

40.45.8), and at the conclusion of the census one of the censors chosen by lot performed a solemn purification of the assembled citizens with a suovetaurilia sacrificed on the Altar of Mars (Livy 1.44.1–2). The altar stood in the Villa Publica (q.v.); after the fire of Titus in A.D. 80 what survived of the Villa Publica was probably replaced by the Divorum, and the new Altar of Mars is perhaps the small square feature shown on the Marble Plan in the open area toward its southern end (*FUR* pl. 31; Rodriguez pl. 26). Degrassi (417–18) thinks it was especially honored on the Feriae Martis of 1 March.

There was never a temple of Mars in conjunction with this altar, and probably never a temple of Mars in the Campus Martius proper. The three passages that have been adduced to prove the existence of such a temple are Ovid, *Fast.* 2.859–60, where it is clearly the god himself and not a statue that the poet has in mind; *Consolatio ad Liviam* 231, where the god is described as *accola campi,* which would indicate rather the temple *in Circo Flaminio;* and Cassius Dio 56.24.3, where the location of the temple struck by lightning is general enough to suit the temple *in Circo Flaminio.* Although the whole Campus Martius was regarded as the demesne of Mars (cf. Ovid, *Fast.* 2.859–60), additional temples seem to have been regarded as inappropriate.

Mars, Sacrarium: see **Regia.**

Mars Invictus: known only from the Fasti Venusini for a celebration on 14 May (see Degrassi 457). A fourth-century base in the Forum Romanum also carries a dedication to Mars Invictus (*CIL* 6.33856 = *ILS* 8935). Because in the *Feriale Duranum* the Mars of 1 March is called Mars Pater Victor, it seems possible that the Ara Martis (see Mars, Ara) in the Campus Martius is meant (cf. Degrassi 417–18).

Mars Ultor, Aedes: see **Forum Augustum.**

Mars Ultor, Templum: A temple supposed by Mommsen to have been built by Augustus on the Capitoline to hold the standards that had been recovered from the Parthians immediately after their recovery in 20 B.C. (Cass. Dio 54.8.3) is now generally believed to be imaginary. The standards were in all probability deposited in the Temple of Iuppiter Capitolinus between their recovery and the building of the Temple of Mars Ultor in the Forum Augustum (Horace, *Carm.* 4.15.6–8), and the tholus shown on coins minted in Spain and Ephesus (*B. M. Coins, Rom. Emp.* 1.58 no. 315, 65–66 nos. 366–75, 114 no. 704) inscribed Martis Ultoris, or an abbreviation of this, refer only to the decision to build the temple, or to a Temple of Rome and Augustus built in these provincial cities.

Eos 64 (1976): 59–82 (L. Morawiecki); *JRS* 67 (1977): 91–94 (C. J. Simpson).

Marsyas: see **Statua Marsyae.**

Mater Deum, Aedes: listed in the regionary catalogues in Regio XI, but otherwise unknown. It may be that the statue of the Magna Mater on the spina of the Circus Maximus stood in front of a shrine dedicated to her. See Magna Mater (in Circo Maximo).

Mater Matuta, Aedes (Figs. 9, 10, 11, 37.10): a temple on the Forum Boarium just inside the Porta Carmentalis ascribed to Servius Tullius, the twin of his Temple of Fortuna, which stood beside it (Ovid, *Fast.* 6.477–80; Livy 25.7.6). Camillus restored and rededicated it following the siege of Veii (Livy 5.19.6 and 23.7; Plutarch, *Cam.* 5.1). In 213 it burned in the great fire that destroyed the area from the Salinae (q.v.) to the Porta Carmentalis (Livy 24.47.15–16), and it was rebuilt in the following year (Livy 25.7.6). In 196 B.C. L. Stertinius erected two arches *de manubiis* in the Forum Boarium in front of the temples of Fortuna and Mater Matuta and adorned them with gilded statues, the first arches in Rome that might be called triumphal (Livy 33.27.4). In 174 Ti. Sempronius Gracchus dedicated there a bronze tablet showing a map of Sardinia and representations of the major battles in his conquest of the island (Livy 41.28.8–10). The day of dedication was 11 June, the same as that of Fortuna, but known as the Matralia (Degrassi 468–69).

The temple was discovered in excavations begun in 1937 under the church of Sant'Omobono, the cella built into the fabric of its nave, while the twin temple, of Fortuna, could be completely excavated and exposed. The remains present a small cella on an ample platform, and the temple has been reconstructed as having an odd plan, a variation of a plan *in antis*, with four columns in two rows of two each on the lines of the cella walls in the deep pronaos and alae flanking the cella. It was araeostyle, facing south, its blank back wall bordering the Vicus Iugarius. In front of the temple is a large precinct with an archaic U-shaped altar on axis with it but facing east. The chief remains are considered to belong to the rebuilding of 212 B.C. and are in Monteverde tufa, while a travertine pavement at a higher level is believed to be Domitianic. The arches of Stertinius have not yet been discovered, nor the Porta Carmentalis. Excavations, especially soundings in depth, have been, and continue to be, carried out here and have brought to light rich deposits going back to the early Iron Age. Seven major periods are distinguished, as follows:

1. An early phase where there were traces of life of the early Iron Age but not of religious use of the area.

2. A period when the sanctuary was delimited and contained an altar facing east but no temple, VII to early VI B.C.

3. The archaic temple, first period, second quarter VI B.C., a small podium temple of nearly square plan divided between a pronaos and a small cella flanked by alae one-half the width of the cella. The pronaos was flanked by antae and had two columns in continuation of each of the lateral walls of the cella. It was preceded by a narrow stair and a precinct containing an altar oriented to the east and not squared with the temple. This temple was completely redecorated in the second half of the century, ca. 530 B.C. This is regarded as the Servian temple.

4. A raising of the level in the area by some 6 m. This fill is particularly rich and contains material from the Bronze Age, as well as fragments of imported Greek pottery. The area was then paved with slabs of cappellaccio, and the twin temples were built in their first phase. This phase is associated with Camillus's rebuilding of the temples after the siege of Veii in 396 B.C.

5. A repaving of the sanctuary in blocks of Monteverde and Anio tufa with the rebuilding of the temples and their altars. A dedication here by M. Fulvius Flaccus from the spoils of Volsinii gives the date 264 B.C.

6. A rebuilding in consequence of a fire on a new pavement of Monteverde tufa, 212 B.C.

7. A repavement of the area in travertine, probably in the time of Domitian.

BullCom 77 (1959–60): 3–143 (A. M. Colini et al.); *BullCom* 79 (1963–64): 3–90 (A. M. Colini et al.); *PP* 32 (1977): 9–128 (A. M. Colini et al.); *La grande Roma dei Tarquini* (1990), 111–30 (G. Pisani Sartorio, A. Sommella Mura, et al.).

Matidia, Ara: an altar to the deified mother-in-law of Hadrian, known from a single fragment of the edict of Tarracius Bassus (*CIL* 6.31893 b10 = *ILS* 6072).

Matidia, Templum: a temple to the deified mother-in-law of Hadrian, known from an inscription on a lead pipe found in the seventeenth century in Via del Seminario between the façade of the church of S. Ignazio and the old Seminario Romano (later Collegio Germanico Ungarico), just northwest of the church (see LFUR sheet 15). A rare medallion of Hadrian inscribed DIVAE MATIDIAE SOCRUI (Gnecchi 2.5 no. 25; A. Banti, *I grandi bronzi imperiali* 2.2 [Florence 1984], p. 129 no. 250) shows an aedicula flanked by porticoes that stand on a high base continuous with that of the aedicula. The aedicula is distyle with a triangular pediment and contains an enthroned image. There are sculptures in the pediment, and large acroterial figures are at the summit and corners of the roof. To either side of the aedicula is a small statue on a high base under a flat lintel. The flanking colonnades have a high lower storey with a much lower attic above, probably not colonnaded and possibly vaulted. The oddness of this representation is matched by the inability of everyone who has tackled the problem to come up with a plausible reconstruction of the complex. The best that can be said is that it was a shrine in a colonnaded court, probably with colonnades on all four sides. The statues flanking the cult image might have been in side chapels.

On opposite sides of the Vicolo della Spada d'Orlando are the remains of an ancient wall faced with brickwork (west) and the stump of a column of cipollino, 1.70 m in diameter (east), while two other columns of cipollino are said to be built into the building on the west side of the vicolo. Piranesi (*Le antichità romane* [Rome 1756], 1 pl. 14 fig. 1; *Il Campo Marzio* [1762], pl. 34) shows seven unfluted columns with five Corinthian capitals in a somewhat confused arrangement, possibly five of the columns in a line running east and west, in approximately this location. This is labeled Tempio di Giuturna. As this temple is without other certain assignment, it might be the Temple of Matidia and is so identified by Lanciani (LFUR sheet 16). The proximity of the Hadrianeum (see Hadrianus, Templum) increases that likelihood.

The recent identification by Rodriguez Almeida (Rodriguez 1.127–29) of a previously unassigned fragment of the Marble Plan as very probably representing part of this temple and its enclosure gives us some more elements. It would have been peripteral, pycnostyle, eight columns by thirteen, in a colonnade with deep porticoes covering an area of at least 100 m x 65 m. It would thus be of the same size as, and very similar in plan to, the Temple of Divus Hadrianus, to which it was adjacent.

Nash 2.36–37; *NSc* 1972, 398–403 (E. Lissi Caronna).

Mausolea Augustorum: see Sepulcrum Mariae.

Mausoleum Augusti (Figs. 54, 55):

the first Augustan building in the Campus Martius, dated by Suetonius to 28 B.C., but evidently not finished by 23, in the northern reaches of the campus between the Via Flaminia and the Tiber and perhaps technically not within the limits of the campus, but adjacent to it. From the beginning Augustus designed the surrounding area as a public park with plantations

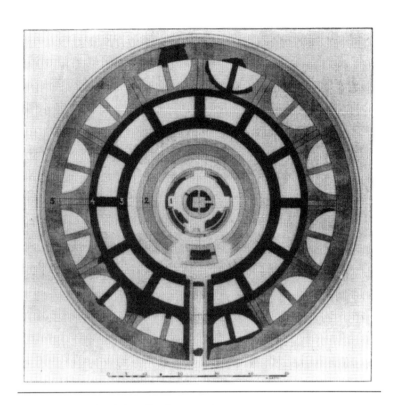

Figure 54
Mausoleum
Augusti, Plan

of trees and splendid walks for popular enjoyment (Suetonius, *Aug.* 100.4; Strabo 5.3.8 [236]). The sources agree about the appearance of the mausoleum proper, that it was essentially a mound, or tumulus, with a base of white stone, covered above with evergreen trees up to the summit, where there was a bronze statue of Augustus. The trees are usually restored as cypresses, but, because these would in time have grown to great size and have threatened the fabric of the monument and hidden the crowning statue, it is better to think of them as something more like low-spreading junipers. Strabo is particular in noting that the trees in the nearby *ustrinum* were poplars.

The monument has always been known, and has been put to many uses in the course of time, as a fortress of the Colonna family, as an amphitheater and bullring, as a garden, and, most recently, as a concert hall. In the building and rebuilding of these and in the plundering of ancient ruins for construction material, the mausoleum has been reduced to a naked skeleton. During construction of the concert hall in 1907, excavations were undertaken to analyze the nature of the complex. These were resumed in 1926 and continued to 1930. In 1934 work on removal of surrounding buildings and isolation of the mausoleum began, followed in 1936 by dismantling of the concert hall and final excavation and restoration of the remains, completed in 1938.

The Mausoleum Augusti consists essentially of a

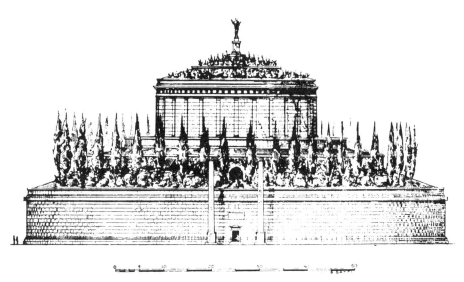

Figure 55
Mausoleum Augusti,
Restored Elevation by
G. Gatti

series of concentric rings of concrete faced with reticulate, except where there was further dressing with
blocks of travertine or marble veneer. The entrance
faces south, a vaulted tunnel piercing the outer rings
and leading to an annular passage; over the entrance
was a vaulted chamber of uncertain purpose, perhaps only to lighten the pressure on the vault below.
Behind the very heavy outer ring wall was a series of
semicircular chambers divided by radial walls to
make quarter-circles, which were without access.
Within this ring a second one of long, roughly trapezoidal chambers, also without access and here
vaulted, continued the pattern. The inner wall of this
ring, which is the outer wall of the annular passage,
is especially heavy, 5.70 m thick, and has been
thought to have risen to carry a colonnade high on
the exterior, but this would be at variance with Strabo's description and the traditions of tumulus architecture in Etruria. It seems better to take Strabo's description at face value and to think that above the
base drum the green slope was unbroken, the complicated interior arrangements serving only to support the weight of the earth mantle.

Arriving at the annular passage, the visitor was
stopped by a wall and had to detour left or right to
one of two symmetrical doors through this that are
set off axis. There may also have been the intention
of allowing the cortège to make a ritual circuit of the
burial chamber before depositing the ashes of the
dead. From a second annular passage, one then had
access to the circular burial chamber, with a great
concrete pier in the center containing a square chamber, probably intended for the ashes of Augustus
himself. The outer burial chamber has three large
niches, one opposite the entrance and two on the
cross-axis, to receive other urns containing ashes.

Little remains of the superstructure, but, given the

complicated system of compartments and rings that
makes up the base storey, it has been presumed that
the same arrangements would be repeated above,
stepping back progressively in four storeys. The
overall diameter has been calculated as 87–89 m, the
height without the statue as 44 m.

The mausoleum stood isolated in a rectangular
area marked off by cippi and paved. Before the door
stood a pair of red granite obelisks that are first mentioned by Ammianus Marcellinus (17.4.16), being
omitted in Pliny's discussion of the obelisks of Rome
(*HN* 36.69–74); they have therefore been supposed
to be a later addition, perhaps of Domitian or Hadrian. These are uninscribed and have therefore been
presumed to be of the Roman period. They have now
been reerected behind S. Maria Maggiore and in Piazza del Quirinale (Montecavallo). The location and
form of the two bronze tablets or *pilae* on which by
his instructions Augustus's *Res Gestae* were inscribed (Suetonius, *Aug.* 101.4; Augustus, *RG
praef.*) is also uncertain, although one may compare
the marble tablets in front of the tomb of the Plautii
near Tivoli, a tomb that was probably a deliberate
imitation of the Mausoleum Augusti (see Crema 253
fig. 276).

The first to be deposited in the mausoleum was
Marcellus, Augustus's nephew and son-in-law, in 23
B.C. (Cass. Dio 53.30.5). The marble tombstone inscribed with his name and that of his mother, Octavia, was discovered in 1927. Then followed most of
the Julio-Claudian family who died while still in favor. The Flavians had their own family tomb, but as
a special honor Nerva's ashes were deposited here
(Aur. Vict., *Epit.* 12.12). The belief that finally, more
than a century later, the mausoleum was reopened
to receive the body of Julia Domna, the wife of
Septimius Severus, for a short time seems to be mis-

taken. She was probably entombed in a cenotaph of Gaius and Lucius Caesar (see Sep. C. et L. Caesarum).

The complete lack of decorative elements here has been attributed to the plundering of the monument in the Middle Ages, but it is more likely to be deliberate and aesthetic. The tumulus form had a long tradition in both Etruria and the East, and it relied chiefly on the size of the mound to impress people. It was a tomb form already employed in the Campus Martius for the tombs of Sulla and Julia (where Julius Caesar himself was buried). The Campus Martius had been chosen as a site not only because so many of the great had been buried there, but because it was flat, and Augustus chose to build it in its farthest reaches, where the size would show to best advantage, and carefully surrounded it with a park and walks.

BullCom 54 (1926): 191–234 (A. M. Colini and G. Q. Giglioli); *PBSR* 10 (1927): 23–35 (R. A. Cordingly and I. A. Richmond); *Capitolium* 6 (1930): 532–67 (G. Q. Giglioli); *L'urbe* 3.8 (1938): 1–17 (G. Gatti); *CAR* 2-D, 88 pp. 90–98; *Historia* 16 (1967): 189–206 (K. Kraft); Nash 2.38–43; *RömMitt* 86 (1979): 319–24 (M. Eisner).

Mausoleum Hadriani (Fig. 56): the modern Castel Sant'Angelo on the right bank of the Tiber at the head of, and on axis with, the Pons Aelius (q.v.), the modern Ponte Sant'Angelo. The site, *in Hortis Domitiae* (q.v.), seems to have been carefully chosen to avoid appearing competitive with the Mausoleum Augusti (q.v.) and to command the view across the more or less open stretches of the Campus Martius. Its date is uncertain, and it was apparently completed by Antoninus Pius in 139, the year after Hadrian's death. It was intended to receive the ashes of Hadrian and his successors, but the bridge leading to it suggests that it was also meant to encourage building, especially residential building, in the area now known as Prati di Castello. Inscriptions (*CIL* 6.984–95; *ILS* 322, 329, 346, 349–52, 369, 383–85, 401) from the mausoleum testify to the entombment there of Hadrian and his wife, Sabina, of Antoninus Pius and his wife, Faustina the Elder, and three of their children, of L. Aelius Caesar, of L. Verus Commodus, and of three other children of Marcus Aurelius. From Herodian (4.1.4) we learn that Marcus Aurelius himself was placed here, and Cassius Dio records that Septimius Severus, Julia Domna, Geta, and Caracalla were laid to rest here (Cass. Dio 76[77].15.4; 78[79].9.1 and 24.3).

The tomb always stood very close to the river, and by the time of Procopius it had been included in the fortifications of the city and transformed into a fortress guarding the head of the bridge. It figured im-

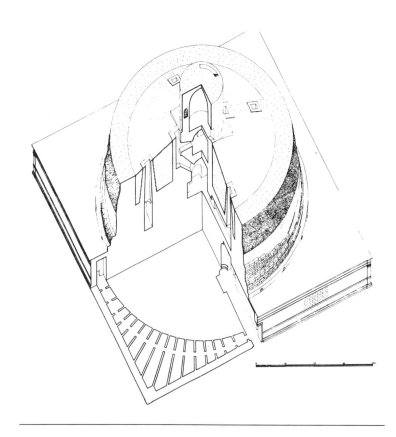

portantly in a battle with the Goths under Vittigis in A.D. 537 (Procopius, *BellGoth* 1.22.12–25). In the eighth century, John Malalas (Antiochenus) describes a colossal quadriga crowning the tomb (cf. HJ 665n.113), though by his time the little church of S. Angelo de Castro S. Angeli, also called Inter Nubes, had been built there to commemorate the vision of Pope Gregory the Great in 590 of Saint Michael sheathing his sword (HCh 58). In the *Mirabilia* of the twelfth century (Jordan 2.627–28; VZ 3.46–47) is a description of bronze fences that surrounded it surmounted by the peacocks of gilded bronze later removed to the entrance courtyard of the basilica of S. Pietro and then to the Cortile della Pigna of the Vatican (Helbig⁴ 1.377–78 no. 479), a bronze bull, four gilt bronze horses, bronze doors on each side, and also bronze doors below (i.e., in the square base of the tomb). Already earlier, perhaps in the tenth century, the Crescenzi family had taken possession of the site and constructed a tower on the summit, converting the monument into a fortress, and in 1277 Pope Nicholas V built the elevated walk connecting the Castel Sant'Angelo with the Vatican palace. From that time on it was a papal stronghold, and its history became a very different story until archaeological investigations were undertaken in modern times, beginning first with regard to the Pons Aelius

Figure 56
Mausoleum Hadriani, Plan and Axonometric Section of the Ancient Remains

in 1892. However, reconstructions, most of them more or less fantastic, are at least as old as Filarete in the first half of the fifteenth century, who put one on the doors of S. Pietro in Vaticano.

The whole complex was enclosed by a low wall of peperino broken by an entrance opposite the bridge, where there were four travertine pillars that held the bronze peacocks, the pillars connected by grillwork, while a fence surmounted the wall. An outwork around the drum, making in effect a base for it, is square, about 87 m on a side and 10 m high. Originally it was entirely faced with Parian marble, according to Procopius. Over the entrance was the dedicatory inscription (CIL 6.984 = ILS 322), while those of the others deposited in the mausoleum would have been arranged to the sides of this. Behind the marble was a wall at least in part of blocks of travertine, and behind this a wall faced with brick. In the center of the square is the drum of the tomb proper, and from it radiate walls faced with brick that divide the space between into seventy-three chambers that were roofed with vaults. These communicate with one another by a ring of doors just outside the drum. At each corner the exterior wall is thickened to make a base for the colossal marble statues of men and horses that crowned the external wall, many of which Procopius says were broken up and thrown down on the Goths in their siege of the fortress. Some fragments of colossal statues have been recovered and are displayed in the Castello, but these probably come from figures that crowned the drum.

The entrance was always on the axis of the Ponte Sant'Angelo, a broad passage lined and vaulted with blocks of travertine, the walls originally revetted with marble, leading directly to a square chamber with an apsidal niche in the back wall, generally believed designed to hold a statue of Hadrian, and a rectangular niche in the left wall. From the balancing niche in the right wall opens a ramped passage that makes one full spiral turn around through the mass of the drum and arrives back over the entrance; along the way it rises about 10 m and is lit by four light wells. From the end of the spiral a corridor ran straight back to the burial chamber at the center of the drum, 8 m square, but made a Greek cross in plan by three arched niches to hold the funerary urns. This, too, was once revetted with marble and lit by oblique windows cut through the vault.

The drum is 64 m in diameter, probably originally about 21 m high, and perhaps in two distinct storeys above the square base, rising to the height of the top of the ancient chamber above the tomb chamber. It is constructed of concrete faced with a wall of travertine, which was originally revetted with marble. It is thought that the spiral corridor must have contin-

ued, perhaps as a stair, to give access to the chamber above the tomb chamber; this seems otherwise to have been reached only by a corridor cutting through the drum, indicated by a deep setback of the ancient concrete wall at the top of the main drum. The chamber over the tomb chamber was similar to it in dimensions and vaulting, but lower and without niches. Over this was planting, as a deep level of earth over a sloping roof of concrete proves, but the nature of this planting is, of course, very uncertain. At its center was a third chamber of circular plan, but very high, divided into two storeys by the insertion of a floor, and in the thickness of the wall around this wound an ancient staircase, whose purpose seems clearly to take visitors to an observation platform. Above this circular chamber nothing ancient is preserved, but the size of it suggests that it must have carried a smaller superstructure on which the terminal group of Hadrian mounted in a triumphal quadriga would have stood. This would then have stood somewhat higher than the present figure of Saint Michael, but over the center of the tomb. Pierce, in studying the sight lines and the size of the enclosure, decided that the total height from the entrance to the platform on which the quadriga stood ought to be about 180 feet (55 m).

The place of the statues of which fragments survive is much discussed. Pierce decided to put the statues midway on the drum, above the level of the tomb chamber but below that of the chamber above it, set on a balustrade with an open gallery behind them. The evidence for this is a setback in the concrete core at this level. But here the statues would show poorly against the massive drum rising behind them, and a position at the top of the drum, where they would stand out against the sky and the garden behind them, is surely to be preferred.

It can be seen that the Mausoleum Hadriani, as reconstructed, had little in common with the Mausoleum Augusti, except in its circular plan. The Mausoleum Augusti was splendidly simple, impressive in its mass and its setting. The Mausoleum Hadriani was novel and playful in its assembly of forms and architectural spaces and experiences. From the time one first set foot on the Pons Aelius until one emerged at the base of the colossal quadriga, one was treated to a continuous series of visual shocks and excitements, the elegance of the approach with its bronze peacocks, the rich mystery of the spiral tunnel and tomb chamber, the exhilaration of the funerary garden hanging far above the rest of Rome, the sudden revelation of the size of the colossal quadriga seen close at hand. The mausoleum has no clear antecedents, though it may owe something to the design of funeral pyres; in its general masses and tholus form one might compare it to a number of earlier monuments, perhaps best the Augustan Trophée des Alpes at La Turbie on the Riviera, but in its development of space and architectural experience it is unique.

JRS 15 (1925): 75–103 (S. R. Pierce); M. Borgatti, *Castel Sant'Angelo in Roma* (Rome 1931); *CAR* 1-H, 24 pp. 73–75; Nash 2.44–48; C. D'Onofrio, *Castel S. Angelo* (Rome 1971); *BdA* 61 (1976): 62–68 (M. de'Spagnolis); C. D'Onofrio, *Castel S. Angelo e Borgo tra Roma e Papato* (Rome 1978); *RömMitt* 86 (1979): 319–24 (M. Eisner); Boatwright 161–75.

Mefitis, Aedes, Lucus: in late republican times evidently the most conspicuous building on the Cispian cusp of the Esquiline (Varro, *Ling.* 5.49; Festus 476L). Its grove, much reduced in size by Varro's day, was possibly adjacent to that of Iuno Lucina (q.v.). It must have stood southwest of S. Maria Maggiore. It seems to be mentioned in an inscription of the time of Septimius Severus (*CIL* 6.461 = *ILS* 3361; cf. *Eranos* 1924, 82–85); if so, by that time it had been abandoned and the name corrupted to Memphi. Because Mephitis was the divinity of evil-smelling water, especially volcanic springs, and her chief shrine in southern Italy was the dying volcano of Ampsanctus in the Hirpine country, it seems strange to find her on the Cispian, where nothing of the sort is known. Attempts to associate her with the Esquiline cemetery are mistaken, because all place indications separate her grove from the cemetery by a considerable distance.

Memphis: a toponym found in a single inscription of the time of Septimius Severus (*CIL* 6.461 = *ILS* 3361). If this is not the same as the Lucus Mefitis (see Mefitis, Aedes, Lucus), it may be a place of Egyptian association, such as an Iseum, or an Egyptianizing garden.

ANRW 2.16.2: 1088–92 (R. E. A. Palmer).

Mens, Aedes: a temple on the Capitoline vowed by the praetor T. Otacilius Crassus, together with another vowed by Fabius Maximus to Venus Erucina (1) (q.v.), after consultation of the Sibylline Books in 217 B.C. following the disaster of Lake Trasimene (Livy 22.9.10 and 10.10). It was built and dedicated in 215, again by T. Otacilius Crassus, appointed duovir for the purpose, together with Fabius Maximus, who dedicated the Temple of Venus Erucina (Livy 23.31.9 and 32.20). The two temples were separated only by a gutter or drain *(canalis)* and may well have been twins. The Temple of Mens was evidently restored by M. Aemilius Scaurus (cos. 115 B.C.), probably after his campaign against the Cimbri in 107 (Cicero, *Nat. D.* 2.61; Plutarch, *De fort.*

Rom. 5). The day of dedication was 8 June (Ovid, *Fast.* 6.241–48; Degrassi 467). It is presumed that these temples were somewhere in the Area Capitolina, but no one gives further topographical details. Because they are not mentioned after the time of Galba, it is presumed that they were destroyed either in the fire of A.D. 69 that destroyed the Capitoline temple, or in that of 80.

Mercati di Traiano (Fig. 57): the modern name given to the complex of buildings of at least six storeys and more than 170 rooms in a succession of terraces covering the slope of the Quirinal (Collis Latiaris and Collis Mucialis) northeast of the Forum Traiani. These were clearly built as part of the forum project, although there seems to have been no close communication between the two complexes in antiquity, the separation emphasized by the high northeast wall of the forum, which acted as a fire wall, with a street running along it to increase its effectiveness. The Mercati seem to have been begun by Domitian, the project then radically altered after his death, and completed in the first decade of the second century, somewhat in advance of the Forum (Bloch 49–57). The Mercati are divided into numerous large blocks that make different groupings of rooms at several different levels and consist of corridors, some of them in effect streets, lined on one or both sides with shoplike units, almost always a single room with a large squarish door framed in travertine with an ample transom window over the door. Some of these preserve pavements in mosaic or signinum, but few traces of other decoration survive. The blocks are connected by stairs, but these are generally not designed for heavy use; they are often narrow and sometimes apparently deliberately hidden. The most important communication was by two streets, one just behind the forum, skirting this and terminating in a broad stair opposite the southeast corner of the great square that led up to yet another block behind the Forum Augustum, the second, known by the medieval name Via Biberatica, halfway up the slope, two storeys above the lower street, following roughly the same line. At their ends one could get from one street to the other, but traffic between them was in no way facilitated. Among the blocks of shoplike units were scattered large and lofty halls, notably three domed ones of semicircular plan at the lowest level, of spectacular architecture and mysterious purpose. The experimentation with fenestration and structural concrete is apparent and impressive throughout. The most dramatic complex that survives is a basilical hall, known as the Aula Traiana (Basilica Traiani?; cf. S.H.A. *Commod.* 2.1), the main space roofed with a succession of groin vaults carried on piers. This roof hangs above flank-

derson 161–67), one may ask whether such a complex would have been necessary for the increase in court business, but that is unlikely. The lack of communication between the Mercati and the forum may be taken as indication that the two parts functioned independently of each other. Lugli (Lugli 1946, 306–9) wished to see this as the headquarters of the *arcarii*, the cashiers of the fiscus, and those responsible for the basic provisioning of the city of Rome, especially the supplies of grain, wine, and oil, and for the distribution of these, but the evidence does not really support such a notion. Brokering of the provisioning may have gone on here, but the distribution would have been elsewhere, in places such as the Porticus Minucia Frumentaria (q.v.).

Lugli 1946, 299–309; Nash 2.49–58; MacDonald 1.75–93; Boethius-Ward-Perkins 239–43; *Quaderni dell'Instituto Nazionale per Storia dell'Architettura*, n.s., 1–10 (1983–87): 25–28 (C. F. Giuliani).

Mercurius, Aedes: a temple dedicated to Mercury, apparently in company with his mother, Maia (Martial 7.74.5; Macrobius, *Sat.* 1.12.19; Lydus, *Mens.* 4.80), in 495 B.C. by the centurion *primi pili* M. Laetorius, to whom the people voted this honor (Livy 2.21.7 and 27.5–6; Val. Max. 9.3.6). It was on the slope of the Aventine overlooking the Circus Maximus, but listed in the regionary catalogues in Regio XI and described as *retro metas Murtias* (i.e., *Murcias* or *Murciae*) at the southeast end (Apuleius, *Met.* 6.8). The dedication day was the Ides of May (Livy 2.21.7; Ovid, *Fast.* 5.669–70; Paulus *ex Fest.* 135L; Degrassi 458–59); it was celebrated especially by tradesmen and merchants. Although no record of rebuilding or restoration has come down to us, coins of Marcus Aurelius inscribed RELIG AVG and showing a temple of Mercury may refer to this temple. If so, it had by that time taken on a very exotic appearance. The temple is shown with four herms in front, instead of columns, supporting a lunate pediment in which are the animals of Mercury (tortoise, cock, and ram) and his symbols. The statue in the middle shows the god nude, or with a short cloak, on a high base. There is no indication of walls, but the temple is not circular (*B. M. Coins, Rom. Emp.* 4.628–29 nos. 1441–48; Mazzini 2, Marcus Aurelius nos. 534–35). This was the only full-scale temple to Mercury in Rome of which we know. No certain trace of it has ever been discovered, but cf. HJ 128n.27.

Mercurius Sobrius: see **Vicus Sobrius.**

Meta Romuli: the name given in the Middle Ages to an ancient sepulchral pyramid on the right bank of the Tiber west of the Mausoleum Hadriani at the

ing rows of shoplike units and in front of a sky-lighted gallery behind which open other shops, arched buttresses for the central vault spanning the gallery. The intricacy and ingenuity of the design are without known parallel. The construction throughout the Mercati is of brick-faced concrete, presumably to be finished with stucco, with travertine corbels and simple travertine decorative accents and door frames. The curved façade of the upper storey behind the forum hemicycle is enlivened with a series of brick pilasters and shallow pediments, triangular, lunate, and broken, over a line of arched windows that is especially successful. The roofing above the concrete vaults is a complicated problem, despite the evidence of drains at a number of points.

These are clearly essentially office buildings, not markets, and served to house parts of the bureaucracy that managed the Roman empire. Because the Forum Traiani seems to have been created especially to house the enlarged courts of justice of Rome (An-

intersection of Via Cornelia and Via Triumphalis, east of the latter. It is said to have been larger than the Pyramid of Cestius (see Sepulcrum C. Cestii) and very beautiful, sheathed in marble that was used in the tenth century to pave the paradise of S. Pietro in Vaticano and the steps of the basilica (*Mirabilia:* Jordan 2.626–27, VZ 3.45; see also Jordan 2.405–6, VZ 4.134; Urlichs 161 [Anonymous Magliabechianus]). Its destruction began in 1499 under Pope Alexander VI, when its southern angle was demolished to cut the Via Alessandrina (Borgo Nuovo; see LS 1.126); the rest stood only a little longer, and there is no record of it after 1551, when it is shown on Bufalini's map of Rome inaccurately and with the name Sepulcrum Scipionis, so he probably never saw it (LS 1.161, 186–89). It is frequently called simply Meta, sometimes Sepulcrum Romuli, and in the early Renaissance also Sepulcrum Scipionis. It owes its common name to the designation of the Pyramid of Cestius as Meta Remi, the origin of which is completely obscure; there is no record of for whom it was built. It appears a number of times in medieval and early Renaissance views of Rome, looking much like the Pyramid of Cestius. Its foundations were discovered in 1948 at the northeast corner of Via della Conciliazione at Piazza Pia.

FA 4 (1949): 3771 (G. Gatti); *CAR* 1-H, 34 p. 37; Nash 2.59–60.

Meta Sudans (Fig. 3): a large fountain that Domitian built (Chron. 146) southwest of the Colosseum at the end of the street leading down to the Colosseum from the Arch of Titus, but not precisely on its axis. It takes its name from a general similarity to one of the turning posts of a circus and seems to have been a well-known fountain form, for Seneca (*Epist.* 56.4) mentions one, possibly somewhere on the Bay of Naples, certainly earlier than Domitian's, and another is known at Djemila (Cuicul) in Algeria. The Meta Sudans is represented on coins of Titus and Domitian (*B. M. Coins, Rom. Emp.* 2.262 nos. 190–91, 356 after no. 270) showing the Colosseum, and also on coins of Alexander Severus (*B. M. Coins, Rom. Emp.* 6.128–29 nos. 156–58; Mazzini 3, Alexander Severus no. 468), but at so reduced a scale as to be uninformative. It is listed in the regionary catalogues in Regio IV. The notion that it served to mark the extraordinary convergence of five of the Augustan regiones of the city, I, II, III, IV, and X, may be correct, but other convergences do not seem to have been marked.

The concrete core stood until 1936, when it was removed, but the place marked in the pavement of the street. It was first excavated and studied in 1743 and thoroughly explored in 1933 before its removal. It was reexcavated and studied in 1983–1984. It

consisted of an elongated cone with bowed sides, 5 m in diameter at the base and probably about three times as high. The base seems to have been surrounded by arched niches, probably for statuary; whether these were also fountains is in doubt. Above this the base stepped back sharply to the principal element. The form of the terminal finial is also in doubt; it appears on the coins as a sort of stylized flower, but the central element might be a pine cone. How the water issued is also unknown, because the name suggests that it welled out of the top to run down the sides, while the form suggests rather a play of jets from the summit. The original basin had a diameter of 13.60 m and was surrounded by an open drain that caught the overflow. Later, probably in the time of Constantine, a wall 0.90 m thick was built beyond this. It does not seem to have been an enlargement of the basin, but rather a retaining wall to isolate the fountain, part of a regrading and repaving of the area around it.

RendPontAcc 13 (1937): 15–39 (A. M. Colini); Nash 2.61–63; *Roma, archeologia nel centro* (1985), 1.113–21 (E. Leone et al.).

Metae Mercuriae: evidently a mistake for Metae Murciae; see Murcia.

Mica Aurea: a building listed in the regionary catalogues in Regio II and defined by Martial (2.59) as a *cenatio parva*, a dining pavilion from which one could see the *Tholus Caesareus*. The poem concludes *ipse iubet mortis te meminisse deus*. This has led PA to conclude that the Tholus Caesareus must be the Mausoleum Augusti. Domitian constructed the Mica Aurea in A.D. 90 (Hieron. *a. Abr.* 2106; Cassiodorus in *MGH Chron. Min.* 2.140), and Martial's epigram seems appropriate for inscription on a building. But the Mausoleum Augusti could hardly be conspicuous from the Caelian and does not lend itself to description as a tholus. It seems quite possible that the Templum Gentis Flaviae might be meant, for it was a round building, a new one, and evidently a towering one (Martial 9.3.12; 9.34.2) on the Quirinal. The conceit of being able to see one tower from another seems to be involved here.

BullCom 88 (1982–83): 92–93 (E. Rodriguez Almeida), 92 (1987–88): 296–98 (E. Rodriguez Almeida).

Mica Aurea in Ianiculo: a place on the Janiculan hill mentioned in the Einsiedeln itinerary (6.2 = Jordan 2.653) between the Molinae (q.v.) and S. Maria in Trastevere and repeated in the names of two medieval churches, SS. Cosma e Damiano in Mica Aurea (= S. Cosimato) and S. Iohannes in Mica Aurea (HCh 240, 273). A sepulchral inscription from S. Cosimato, possibly of the sixth century, may also preserve the designation (*BullCom* 17 [1889]: 392–99 [G. Gatti]). Gatti presumes that the allusion is to the yellow sand of the Janiculum (Mons Aureus, Montorio), but the Einsiedeln itinerary seems to fix the Mica Aurea as a definite locality. Because it is not attested before late antiquity and may be entirely medieval, it need not concern us greatly, but a dining pavilion of the sort Martial describes seems very unlikely in this location, while a belvedere from which to view Rome would be highly appropriate. It also seems possible that *Aurea* is a corruption of *Aurelia*, the Via Aurelia running through this part of Rome.

Milliarium Aureum: erected by Augustus as superintendent of the road system, a charge he assumed in 20 B.C., and conceived as a point where all the roads converging on Rome met (Cass. Dio 54.8.4; Plutarch, *Galba* 24.4). It stood *sub Saturni aede in capite Romani fori* (Pliny, *HN* 3.66; Tacitus, *Hist.* 1.27; Suetonius, *Otho* 6.2). It was almost certainly a monument in the form of a Roman milestone made of, or sheathed in, gilded bronze, but there seems to be no support in our ancient sources for the notion that it was inscribed with the names of the major cities of the empire (or Italy) and the distances of these from Rome; this seems a modern inference based on the example of other ancient milestones. From the way Dio relates the erection of the Milliarium, it seems much more likely that inscribed on it were the names of the roads out of Rome and the men of praetorian rank Augustus had made Curatores Viarum to see to the upkeep of them. Still less credible is that the carved stone members labeled Milliarium Aureum at the northwest end of the Forum Romanum today actually belonged to the base of that monument. The frieze decorated with an anthemion belongs relatively high on a building, and both elements are of a diameter equal to that of the Umbilicus Romae (q.v.), too large for a milestone, unless it were of colossal scale.

During the excavation of the five-column monument of the Tetrarchs behind the Rostra Augusti in 1959, Kähler found a circular concrete base at the southeast corner of the Hemicyclium of the Rostra that might well from size and location be the remains of the Milliarium Aureum (H. Kähler, *Das Funfsäulendenkmal für die Tetrarchen auf dem Forum Romanum* [Cologne 1964], 23, 58–59).

Nash 2.64–65.

Minerva, Aedes (1) (Fig. 14): a temple on the Aventine shown on a fragment of the Marble Plan labeled MINERBAE (*FUR* pl. 23; Rodriguez pl. 15). It was adjacent to, but not aligned with, the Temple of Diana; the reason for the difference in orientation is not clear. Its precinct seems to have been deep in front and back and very shallow on the sides. In front the area is irregular, but there is no sign of an altar. The temple stands on a podium, approached from the front, but is peripteral, with a deep pronaos. Although it is very carelessly drawn, one can see that it was Hellenistic in character. Six columns are shown in front, eight in back, and thirteen along either side. PA estimates the dimensions as about 22 m wide by 45 m long.

The age of the temple is not known, but it is older than the Second Punic War, because in that war it was by vote of the people assigned to the *scribae* and *histriones* as a meeting place and a place for their dedications (Festus 446–48L). It was at this time that poetry, and especially dramatic poetry, was beginning to assume importance, and Livius Andronicus had written a hymn to be performed by a chorus of twenty-seven young women. Livy (27.37.7) says the hymn was ordered by the pontifices in expiation of a portent in 207 B.C., and similar expiations are known (cf. Livy 31.12.9–10), but Festus says the hymn was written *quia prosperius res publica populi Romani geri coepta est*, which can only refer to the Battle of the Metaurus. Because Livius Andronicus had been the slave of Livius Salinator, either the consul who was the victor of the Metaurus or his father (in which case he was the teacher of the consul), it looks very much as though the hymn had been undertaken for Salinator as a victory ode and then converted to other purpose on the occurrence of the portent. Earlier such portents had not been so expiated (cf. Livy 27.11.4–6). In the performance of this hymn the chorus marched in solemn procession from the Temple of Apollo through the Forum Romanum and Forum Boarium, up the Clivus Publicius, and so to the Temple of Iuno Regina. We must presume that thereafter Livius Andronicus wished to dedicate a copy of his hymn (Livy seems clearly to have studied it) or some part of the reward he received on this occasion, but that the Temple of Iuno Regina did not seem a suitable place for such a dedication (it seems to have belonged especially to the women of Rome). The Temple of Minerva was nearby, as chance would have it, and eminently suitable, and because Livius Andronicus was a playwright and actor, as well as a poet, the people at this time designated the Temple of Minerva as the meeting place of all those engaged in such activities, and especially, presumably, the *collegium poetarum*, of which we get hints in the prologues of Terence. During this period one might suppose the temple would have become almost the exclusive interest of such people, a repository of their records and a clubhouse they frequented at least in part in the hope of finding commissions.

The rest of the history of the temple is obscure. Minerva's chief festivals were the Quinquatrus of 19 March and a celebration on 19 June. The former came to be a five-day festival, thanks to a misunderstanding of the name, which really meant only the fifth day after the Ides. Ovid (*Fast.* 3.809–14) tells us that the first day was considered the birthday of the goddess, while the remaining four were given over to ludi circenses. He lists her worshipers as all those engaged in any art or craft, especially the makers of cloth and clothing, and those involved with poetry and the fine arts. The temple he associates with this is that of Minerva Capta on the slope of the Caelian near its base (q.v.), while he gives 19 June as the foundation date for the Aventine temple (*Fast.* 6.725–28). But Festus (306L) and the Fasti Praenestini both associate the Quinquatrus with the Aventine temple, so probably it was celebrated at both, perhaps by the artisans especially at Minerva Capta and by the artists at the Aventine temple. In the *Res Gestae* (19) Augustus records a restoration of this temple, but we know nothing further about this.

Degrassi 426–28, 472; *RdA* 2 suppl. (1985): 9, 63–69 (W. Schürmann).

Minerva, Aedes (2): a temple listed by the *Notitia* in Regio I (*om. Cur.*) about which nothing is known. It is linked with the temples of Mars and Tempestates (see Mars, Aedes and Tempestates, Aedes).

Minerva, Delubrum: a shrine said to have been dedicated by Pompey the Great after his successful return from the East. Pliny (*HN* 7.97) preserves the dedicatory inscription, but nothing further is known about it.

See *TAPS* 80.2 (1990): 2–10 (R. E. A. Palmer), where the suggestion is made that it lay in the northeastern part of the Campus Martius.

Minerva, Templum: among the buildings ascribed to Domitian by the Chronographer of 354 (Chron. 146), a Templum Castorum et Minervae, and listed by the *Curiosum* in Regio VIII. This seems to indicate a Domitianic restoration and rededication of the Aedes Castoris in the Forum Romanum, for which there is no other evidence, or the creation of a new shrine in an already cluttered part of the city. The Dioscuri are not usually associated with Minerva, so it has been presumed that Domitian might have carried out minor repairs to the Temple of Castor and added a sacellum for his patron divinity in the little rooms behind the Lacus Iuturnae or in the vestibule building of the Domus Tiberiana, but this seems to contradict what little evidence we have. It would be better to suppose that in connection with his repair

of the Temple of Castor Domitian dedicated a statue of Minerva in it.

Martial, however, speaks of *penetralia nostrae Pallados* (4.53.1–2), and in the *tabulae honestae missionis* after A.D. 89 the formula for location is regularly *in muro post templum divi Augusti ad Minervam* (*CIL* 16.36–156, 160–89), which seem to indicate that the rededication must have included a sacellum of Minerva built against the back wall of the Temple of Castor in much the same way that a sacellum of Bacchus was built against the back wall of the Temple of Isis in Pompeii (cf. Overbeck-Mau 106–7). Because the base of the Temple of Castor was extraordinarily high, with loculi for the deposit of valuables built between the column footings (see Castor, Aedes), one of these would have lent itself to remodeling as a sacellum, and Martial might then be thinking of the whole bank of strong chambers along the back as the penetralia nostrae Pallados. This is perhaps the best solution to the problem.

A fragment of a statue, possibly of Minerva, was found near the Lacus Iuturnae (*NSc* 1901, 114 fig. 73), but not enough is preserved to identify the type.

RivIstArch, ser. 3.8–9 (1985–86): 111–17 (E. Rodriguez Almeida).

Minerva Capta (**Minervium**): a small temple (delubrum) near the foot of the Caelian, a point emphasized by Ovid (*Fast.* 3.835–38) and the list of the shrines of the Argei (Varro, *Ling.* 5.47). It was in a place between the Caelian and the Carinae, on a street leading to the former. Two streets leading to the Caelian are known in this area, one commonly called Vicus Capitis Africae leading toward the Arch of Dolabella and Silanus and one running up the valley and along the shoulder of the hill past SS. Quattro Coronati. Because the former is more distinctly a clivus and more clearly opposite the Carinae, it is to be preferred, but the Temple of Divus Claudius may have confused the picture. A handsome Minerva, slightly under life size, in Oriental alabaster, found in Via Celimontana and now in the Museo Nazionale delle Terme, might have belonged to it (*NSc* 1926, 58–61 [G. Bendinelli]; Helbig⁴ 3.2368). An inscription from the Orto Teofili (*CIL* 6.524) seems likely to pertain.

The epithet is puzzling. Ovid offers various explanations, the most plausible being that the cult statue came as part of the spoils of Falerii in 241 B.C., and he says this is supported by an ancient inscription (Ovid, *Fast.* 3.843–44). But if so, why does he offer other explanations? The day of dedication was 19 March, the Quinquatrus, the great festival of Minerva especially celebrated by artisans (Degrassi 426–28).

RdA 2 suppl. (1985): 63–69 (W. Schürmann).

Minerva Chalcidica: a tholus listed in the *Curiosum* in Regio IX and shown on a fragment of the Marble Plan (*FUR* pl. 31; Rodriguez pl. 26) labeled MI[. . .]RVACH, just north of the Divorum and east of the Serapeum. It is listed among the buildings of Domitian (Chron. 146; Hieron. *a. Abr.* 2105) and is mentioned in the Einsiedeln itinerary (7.7, Jordan 2.654) as Minervium (see also *Mirabilia:* Jordan 2.631, VZ 3.50). It is responsible for the name of the church of S. Maria sopra Minerva (earlier De Minerva). On the Marble Plan no columns are indicated, simply a ring wall with at its center an arrangement of four radial flights of steps narrowing inward, rather like certain Pompeian fountains with water stairs, leading to a circular platform with a rectangular feature at its center. One thinks of an elaborate base for a colossal statue, perhaps one employing water, because the Aqua Virgo is here close to its terminus north of the Saepta Iulia, but if the rectangle represents the statue, it faced northwest or southeast, which seems illogical in view of the proximity of the Divorum. The epithet is usually taken to mean simply that the statue came from Chalkis in Euboea. The notion that the temple might be regarded as the type of building called chalcidicum seems highly improbable.

A drawing by Onofrio Panvinio in the Vatican Library (Cod. Vat. Lat. 3439 fol. 25 r; Nash 2.68 fig. 755) shows the northern half of a round temple with interior and exterior colonnades, the exterior colonnade of twenty-four unfluted columns, and the interior colonnade of sixteen fluted columns. There are apparently four doors at the cardinal points of the compass, but no special feature in the interior. The temple is said to be *prope arcum camilianum in angulo plateae T(empli) Minervae,* and there are numerous notes of measurements. The diameter (?) is given as 56 palmi, about 14 m. The temple is identified as a temple of Isis and Serapis, or Sol Serapis, or Sol, and other notes in the margins are casual additions. Panvinio is known to have relied on Pirro Ligorio for much of his material, but the precision of the measurements encourages belief in the authenticity of this, and the location makes it certain that it must be the Temple of Minerva Chalcidica.

It cannot be the temple shown on the Marble Plan, however, nor yet in all likelihood the temple shown on a rare coin of Domitian (*B. M. Coins, Rom. Emp.* 2.346 no. 241 and pl. 67.7), where we see a round temple with Corinthian columns on a podium of three steps and with an epistyle of three fasciae surmounted by a flat roof ornamented with large palmettes and globes along the edge. No wall is shown, and the statue is a helmeted Minerva in swift movement who carries a shield and spear in her left hand and raises her right hand as though to urge on fol-

lowers. While the representation on the Marble Plan might be interpreted as intended for this temple, that in Panvinio's drawing is clearly a more elaborate building. Either we must presume a rebuilding of the Temple of Minerva Chalcidica after the time of Septimius Severus and the Marble Plan, or we must conclude that Panvinio (Ligorio?), finding remains of a round building, completed it on evidence from another source. Certainly the four doors are very odd.

FUR 97–102 (L. Cozza); *ArchCl* 12 (1960): 91–95 (F. Castagnoli); Nash 2.66–68; *RdA* 2 suppl. (1985): 13–15, 77–88 (W. Schürmann).

Minerva Medica: a temple listed by the regionary catalogues in Regio V (Esquiliae), dating from the republic (Cicero, *Div.* 2.123; CIL 6.10133 = ILS 5229, 30980 = ILS 3125 = ILLRP 235). In 1887 *favissae* containing several hundred votive objects, including one inscribed with the name of Minerva, were discovered in Via Carlo Botta (Via Curva), between Via Buonarotti and Via Machiavelli. These almost certainly belonged to the temple in question, but no remains of the architecture were recovered. The votive objects show that the shrine was hospitable to Apollo and other divinities, as well as Minerva, but they show also that it was a relatively humble place. Only one bronze figure was found. For the building commonly called Minerva Medica, see Nymphaeum.

L. Gatti Lo Guzzo, *Il deposito votivo dell' Esquilino detto di Minerva Medica* (Florence 1978).

Minutus Minucius, Ara, Sacellum: see **Porticus Minucia.**

Mithraeum:

1. Mithraeum Prope Carceres Circi Maximi: In 1931, during conversion of a factory into storage space for the Rome opera, were found remains of an enigmatic building of the second century northwest of the *carceres* of the Circus Maximus and separated from them only by a narrow street. This building was of brick-faced concrete and consisted of at least four parallel chambers of the same dimensions, all probably originally roofed with barrel vaults and connected by doorways in series with arches or lintels finished with flat arches. They provided support for a monumental stair, which at one time probably ran the length of the four and led up opposite the carceres of the circus to some important edifice above. One thinks of a temple, but the stair was early broken by modifications, rooms and an approach to the substructures being built into and carved out of it and heavy buttressing added in places, probably as a result of lesions caused by the circus brook. Even in a mutilated state the stair must have been impressive and intended for use by large numbers of people. Because it rose so close to the circus, it must have been a public building.

A Mithraeum was built into three of the substructure chambers in the second half of the third century. One entered from the circus side through a small vestibule and then down a narrow corridor, turning at right angles to enter the *spelaeum*. The outer part of this is paved with bipedal tiles; the chamber in front of the niche intended for the relief of Mithras Tauroctonos is paved with colored marble, all secondhand; and the lower parts of the walls and numerous bases were all revetted with marble, also secondhand. Benches for the diners were constructed in the two inner chambers, one of them a triclinium in form, and niches for statues of the attendants of Mithras were carved out of the thickness of the walls in the doorways between. These must once have been finished with marble and framed with colonnettes, consoles for which are still in place. The terminal niche, sunk deep under an arch and preceded by a welter of altars and offerings, was finished with rustication as a cave. Originally it probably held a large relief of the god, but later this seems to have been moved to the outer room and something smaller substituted.

BullCom 68 (1940): 143–73 (C. Pietrangeli); Vermaseren, *Corpus* 1.181–87; Nash 2.69–71.

2. Mithraeum Domus Barberinorum: In 1936, during building operations in the garden behind Palazzo Barberini, three rooms of a house of the first century were found, the narrow westernmost one converted into a simple Mithraeum. There is a narrow central aisle flanked by raised side benches for the diners, each with a ledge in front of it, and each with a hollow for a basin in the middle. The left bench supports four brick piers, which support the segmentally vaulted roof. The cult niche against the end wall preserves remains of rustication and a large painting of Mithras Tauroctonos under an arch with the signs of the zodiac.

BullCom 71 (1943–45): 97–108 (G. Gatti and G. Annibaldi); Vermaseren, *Corpus* 1.168–70; Nash 2.72–74.

3. Mithraeum Domus Clementis: Excavations under the church of S. Clemente begun in 1857 led to the discovery in 1869 of a Mithraeum of the early third century built into a house of the first century (see Domus, Clemens). This had been later deliberately destroyed, filled with earth and the door walled up. Because of the level of the ground water at that time, excavation became possible only in 1914, after a drain, the Emissarium Clementinum, was built 14 m below street level. The Mithraeum consists of a

rectangular room with a low segmental vault divided between a central aisle and side benches provided with broad ledges along the aisle, which are interrupted by niches, three to the right and two to the left. Three meters in front of the cult niche is a rather deep hole in front of each side bench. The ceiling is rusticated and pierced by eleven apertures once framed in mosaic, four rectangular and seven round; the latter are believed to be connected with the worship of the planets. Mosaic lunettes at the ends had been deliberately destroyed.

An altar of Parian marble found partly in the sanctuary and partly in the room opposite the spelaeum is carved with mithraic reliefs, the front with Mithras Tauroctonos, and surmounted by heads of Sol and Luna. The cult niche was stripped at the time of the destruction of the Mithraeum in the fourth century. The rooms preceding the Mithraeum on this level are of uncertain character. It has been argued that they functioned in conjunction with the Mithraeum, but because some of them were originally parts of a private bath, this is doubtful.

E. Junyent, *Il titolo di San Clemente in Roma* (Rome 1932), 66–81; Vermaseren, *Corpus* 1.156–59; Nash 2.75–78.

4. Mithraeum Domus Sanctae Priscae: In 1934, during building operations, the monks of S. Prisca on the Aventine discovered a Mithraeum, the entrance end of which underlies the apse of the church. Over the next four years they conducted excavations here, but World War II interrupted the work. It was renewed in 1953 by the Netherlands Historical Institute in Rome and essentially completed in 1958. Parts of two houses of late first–early second century date were discovered, into a room of one of which a small Mithraeum was built in the late second century. It consisted of a central aisle flanked by side benches, into the forward ends of which were built niches for statues of Cautes and Cautopates. The whole spelaeum was painted, and on the side walls were processions of the *mystae* with verses added above them. The large cult niche contained a stucco group of Mithras Tauroctonos.

This Mithraeum was then rebuilt and enlarged ca. A.D. 220. Benches were added in what had earlier been the vestibule. The old benches were refurbished, and a throne was added to that on the right. Large parts of the sanctuary were repainted, and new frescoes of the mystae were installed. The whole of the cult niche was stuccoed and rusticated. In the center was the stucco group of Mithras Tauroctonos, reworked and repainted; this was subsequently broken up and scattered over the whole room by early Christians. Filling the whole front of the cult niche was a reclining figure of a full-bearded divinity that the excavators identify as Caelus-Oceanus. Three other rooms that served for rites of initiation were also added to the Mithraeum at this time.

Vermaseren, *Corpus* 1.193–201; Nash 2.79–84; M. J. Vermaseren and C. C. Van Essen, *The Excavations in the Mithraeum of the Church of Santa Prisca in Rome* (Leyden 1965).

5. Mithraeum Thermarum Antoninianarum:

Excavations of the subterranean service corridors running under the Baths of Caracalla were begun in 1908 and led in 1912 to the discovery in those to the northwest of the main building of the largest Mithraeum known in Rome. It is a nave 23 m long floored with black-and-white mosaic, flanked by relatively low side benches with a broad ledge along their front broken into four sections by large brick-faced concrete piers that carried the roof as a series of cross vaults. In the front of the side benches are shallow niches, two on each side, and down the center of the nave are a dolium sunk in the floor so its mouth is flush with the pavement, a shallow impluvium-like basin, and two square breaks from which some feature has been removed. The cult niche was sunk in the back wall, preceded by the usual assemblage of altar and bases for dedications. Only small fragments of the relief of Mithras Tauroctonos were found.

NSc 1912, 319–25 (E. Ghislanzoni); Vermaseren, *Corpus* 1.187–90; Nash 2.85.

6. Mithraeum in Campo Martio (in the area of

the Palazzo della Cancelleria Apostolica): Discovery of a Mithraeum under the Palazzo della Cancelleria was made in the first months of 1938. It lay near the main entrance to the palace, to the right of this, oriented north and south. There were scanty remains of the architecture, but enough to recognize the typical plan of such shrines. The impressive finds included a round altar, a long commemorative inscription, and a fragment of the relief of Mithras Tauroctonos in an unusual textured style. The remains date from the middle of the third century, and the shrine is believed to have had a relatively short life.

Hommages à Joseph Bidez et à Franz Cumont (*Collection Latomus* [Brussels 1949]), 2.229–44 (B. Nogara and F. Magi); Vermaseren, *Corpus* 1.178–79.

Mithraeum: Other Mithraea are known to have been found in Rome:

1. In Piazza S. Silvestro, built by Tamesius Argentius Olympus, nephew of Nonius Victor, in 357–362 and probably destroyed in 391–392.

CIL 6.754 = *ILS* 4269; Vermaseren, *Corpus* 1.173.

2. See Domus, Nummii.

3. Found in 1883 on the Esquiline east of S. Martino ai Monti (Via S. Giovanni Lanza 128) in a house of the time of Constantine or a little earlier. A lararium with statues of Isis-Fortuna and Serapis, as well as the Olympians, stood in a room above a Mithraeum, accessible by a stair from the lararium. This was a small vaulted room with a marble Mithraic relief supported on brackets, in front of which was a rude altar. Several small niches appear in the walls, and niches on the stair landing were probably for statues of Cautes and Cautopates.

Vermaseren, *Corpus* 1.160–61.

4. Found in the sixteenth century in the Vigna Muti opposite the church of S. Vitale, notable for a statue and a relief of Aion.

Vermaseren, *Corpus* 1.166.

5. A small Mithraeum on the Quirinal in Via Mazzarino (*CIL* 6.31039).

Vermaseren, *Corpus* 1.165.

6. A Mithraeum was known on the Capitoline as early as the time of Cyriacus of Ancona and was visited by Smetius as late as 1550, but destroyed between then and 1594, when Montfaucon arrived in Rome. It was evidently a large sanctuary between the stair of the church of S. Maria in Aracoeli and the Museo Capitolino.

Vermaseren, *Corpus* 1.176–77.

7. A small cave found in 1872 near the Salita delle Tre Pile on the Capitoline with a relief of Mithras Tauroctonos.

Vermaseren, *Corpus* 1.177.

Molinae: public mills on the Janiculan hill inside the Porta Aurelia driven by the water of the Aqua Traiana. These served for grinding grain. No one tells us how early they were functioning, but they appear in the regionary catalogues and were in regular use until the Goths cut the aqueduct in the siege of Rome in 537. Belisarius then invented floating mills powered by the Tiber (Procopius, *BellGoth* 1.19.19–22). The molinae are mentioned again in the seventh and eighth centuries (LPD 1.324 [Honorius, 625–33] an interpolation = VZ 2.252–53; LPD 1.504 [Hadrianus, 772–95] = VZ 2.280–81; Einsiedeln itinerary 6.2 = Jordan 2.653; Einsiedeln sylloge 47 = *CIL* 6.1711). Parts of the reservoirs and sluice gates for use in keeping the mills in operation when the aqueduct had to be shut off and millstones were found under Via Giacomo Medici 25 m southwest of its juncture with Via Angelo Masina in 1880 (*MAAR* 1 [1917]: 59–61 [A. W. Van Buren]) and again in May 1990. Most of the mills would have stood farther down the slope, where the grade is steeper. No one says how extensive these mills were, but from *CIL* 6.1711 one gathers that they were important. See also Lanciani, LFUR sheet 27, where the complex is misplaced about 20 m north of its actual location.

OpRom 11 (1979): 13–36 (Ö. Wikander); CEFR 98 (1987): 442–56 (F. Coarelli); BullCom 92 (1987): 167–69 (L. Cozza).

Moneta (or **Moneta Caesaris**): the imperial mint of Rome, the first monument listed by the regionary catalogues for Regio III, lying east of S. Clemente, where inscriptions recording dedications by officials of the mint have come to light. These are to Apollo (CIL 6.42), Fortuna (CIL 6.43 = ILS 1634), Hercules (CIL 6.44 = ILS 1635), Victoria (CIL 6.791), and the Genius Familiae Monetalis (CIL 6.239 = ILS 1633). Cf. also CIL 6.298, 1145, 1146, 1636, 1647 = 10.1710, 33726 = 15.7140. The earliest is dated A.D. 115, but the mint was probably established here considerably earlier. Whether this area was included in the grounds of the Domus Aurea of Nero, which may have run to the line of the Servian Walls, makes no difference, because the mint, as an imperial bureau, may have been absorbed into the imperial enclave. It would not have been highly visible from the main blocks of the Domus Aurea. One official seems to have styled himself *procurator monetae et eodem tempore proc. ludi* (CIL 6.1647 = 10.1710), which suggests one of the four training schools for gladiators. But because these seem to have clustered close to the Colosseum, a short distance away, it is impossible to say which it might have been.

Monetarii: the name given workers in the imperial mint, apparently also applied to the district around the mint in Regio III, but known only from the edict of Tarracius Bassus of the late fourth century (CIL 6.31893 b8 = ILS 6072).

Mons Romuleus: see **Statua Salonini Gallieni.**

Montani Mons Oppius: see **Oppius Mons.**

Monumentum: see **Sepulcrum, Sepulcretum, Bustum,** etc.

Monumentum Argentariorum: see **Arcus Septimii Severi (in Foro Boario).**

Monumentum Arruntiorum: see **Sepulcrum Arruntiorum.**

Monumentum Aureliorum: see **Sepulcrum Aureliorum.**

Monumentum Cinciorum: see **Cincia.**

Monumentum Domitiorum: see **Sepulcrum Domitiorum.**

Monumentum Iuliorum: see **Tumulus Iuliae.**

Monumenta Mariana (Monumenta Marii): see **Honos et Virtus (Mariana), Aedes.**

Monumenta Marii (in Capitolio): see **Tropaea Marii.**

Monumenta Statiliorum: see **Sepulcrum Statiliorum.**

Mucialis Collis: see **Quirinalis Collis.**

Mundus (1): according to Plutarch (Rom. 11) a circular trench dug around the Comitium in which, together with specimen fruits of all that was useful and necessary for a city, each of the founders of the city deposited a handful of earth from his native place. With this circle then as center, the city was laid out in a ring around it, and the trench of the pomerium furrowed to bound it. Plutarch seems to have here a genuinely ancient foundation ritual, but must be mistaken in associating this mundus with the Comitium of republican Rome. Such a comitium would have had to lie near the center of the Palatine, while we have no record of public assemblies of comitial character on that hill in the regal period, or under the republic. There must have been civil assemblies of the men of the Palatine village, and presumably these were held within the pomerium, but we do not know where. Probably Plutarch's source has concocted a Romulean origin for a foundation ceremony that was used for early Latin colonies. For example, at Cosa in Etruria, founded in 273 B.C., the comitium is the oldest building on the forum, at the middle of one long side, and although the forum is not at the geographical center of the city, it is the heart of the city plan. Here a trench such as Plutarch describes might well have been dug around the area for the comitium as the first of the foundation ceremonies (but cf., e.g., F. E. Brown, *Cosa: The Making of a Roman Town* [Ann Arbor, Mich. 1980], 16–17). Ovid (Fast. 4.819–36) gives a similar account of the foundation rituals of Rome but does not specify where the *fossa* for the handfuls of earth and first offerings was dug, or what its shape was. He adds the detail that after the trench was filled, an altar was set up over it. See also Roma Quadrata.

Mundus (2): a sacrarium connected with the gods of the underworld. Cf. Varro (*ap. Macrob. Sat.* 1.16.18): *mundus cum patet, deorum tristium atque* *inferum quasi ianua patet;* Servius (*ad Aen.* 3.134): *quidam aras superorum deorum volunt esse, medioximorum id est marinorum focos, inferorum vero mundos;* Festus (126L): *Cereris qui mundus appellatur, qui ter in anno solet patere: VIIII Kal. Sept. (postridie Volkanalia) et III Non. Octobr. et VI Id. Novembr. Qui vel †enim† dictus est quod terra movetur.*

Festus (144L) relies on the description of Cato in his *commentarius iuris civilis,* who says the mundus got its name from the mundus above us, having the same form, *ut ex is qui intravere cognoscere potui.* In its base, *veluti consecratam Dis Manibus,* was an *inferior pars* kept closed at all times, except for the three prescribed days. The days when it was open were regarded as unlucky, and no public business was conducted on them, except the most necessary, although they were not *nefasti.* The association with Ceres may mean no more than that the need was felt to find an association less dread than the real one for the monument, and Ceres, who as the mother of Proserpina could pass back and forth between Olympus and the underworld, could serve here. No one gives any indication of where the Mundus was located or why the Tarentum with its smoking vent and Ara Ditis et Proserpinae is never called a mundus.

It must have been a domed, or beehive-domed, chamber at least big enough for a man to enter, but rather difficult of access; very likely it was largely, or entirely, underground. How the opening and closing of its aperture were effected no one says, but one thinks of a well head and a stone lid.

Discovery by Boni in 1914 of a pair of beehive-domed chambers with connecting corridors under the Domus Augustiana stirred hopes that the solution to the difficulties of the Mundus might be found here; there was even a well shaft opening in the middle of the floor of one of them. But these were entirely covered over in the construction of the Domus Augustiana, whereas the Mundus was still accessible until late antiquity. They have since been convincingly identified as archaic cisterns or granaries. However, it seems entirely possible from the description we have of the Mundus that it was originally a granary of the same archaic type that was discovered after having been long forgotten and then interpreted as a shrine to the gods of the underworld, and thereafter it became a cult center. In this case it is perhaps more likely to have been on the Palatine than anywhere else.

DialArch 9–10 (1976–77): 346–77 (F. Coarelli); R. Altheim-Stiehl and M. Rosenbach, eds., *Beiträge zur altitalischen Geistesgeschichte: Festschrift Gerhard Radke* (Aschendorff Münster 1986), 32–36 (F. Castagnoli).

Murcia: an ancient Roman divinity worshiped in the valley of the Circus Maximus, between the Palatine and the Aventine, which was called Vallis Murcia in late antiquity (Servius *ad Aen.* 8.636; Symmachus, *Relat.* 9.6; Claudian, *De Cons. Stilich.* 2.404; Cassiodorus, *Var.* 3.51.4), a name that has been revived in modern times. Specific reference was to a shrine within the circus toward the southeast end of the spina, where the turning posts were called Metae Murciae (Apuleius, *Met.* 6.8; Tertullian, *De Spect.* 8). As Varro (*Ling.* 5.154) says: *Intumus circus ad Murciae vocatur* (cf. Livy 1.33.5; Paulus *ex Fest.* 135L; A. Degrassi, *Inscriptiones Italiae* 13.3.78). There is every indication that the actual shrine, which is called an *ara vetus* (Pliny, *HN* 15.121), *sacellum* (Varro, *Ling.* 5.154; Paulus *ex Fest.* 135L), and *fanum* (Servius *ad Aen.* 8.636) was on the spina. The ancients themselves did not know the meaning of the name but equated the divinity with Venus and attempted to derive the name from Venus Myrtea (Varro, *Ling.* 5.154; Pliny, *HN* 15.121; Plutarch, *Quaest. Rom.* 20) on the theory that there had once been a stand of myrtle there. This is highly unlikely, but the circus brook is without a name, and Cloacina also was eventually equated with Venus, so it seems not impossible that originally Murcia was the divinity of the brook. The earliest evidence for the euripus of the Circus Maximus is close to A.D. 200, and the first mention of it in literature is by Tertullian (Humphrey 276). Earlier the circus brook must have been culverted, and during those centuries the nature of Murcia might well have been lost to memory, while her altar survived.

Muri Aureliani: the city fortifications begun by Aurelian between the war with the Marcomanni and that with Zenobia in A.D. 271–272 (S.H.A. *Aurel.* 21.9 and 39.2; Aur. Vict., *Caes.* 35.7; Chron. 148; Eutropius 9.15.1; Orosius 7.23.5; Hieron. *a. Abr.* 2290) and finished by Probus about ten years later (Zosimus 1.49.2). They were extensively restored and improved in the early fourth century, almost certainly by Maxentius in anticipation of the attack of Constantine (Chron. 148), and again by Arcadius and Honorius in 402–403, as is attested by inscriptions on the Portae Portuensis, Praenestina, and Tiburtina (*CIL* 6.1188, 1189 = *ILS* 797, 1190) and by Claudian (*De Sext. Cons. Hon.* 531). The description of the walls appended to the Einsiedeln itinerary is believed to have been made in preparation for this repair (Jordan 2.155–78). Repairs by Theodoric are attested by brick-stamps (*CIL* 15.1665 b27 = *ILS* 828) and by the historical chronicle (Cassiodorus, *Var.* 2.34; *MGH Chron. Min.* 2.108 for A.D. 547). Popes Hadrian I (772–795) and Leo IV (847–855) were especially noteworthy for their work on the walls; Pope Leo brought the Vatican, the Civitas Leonina, within the circuit (LPD 1.501, 513 and 2.115, 123–24; VZ 2.278–79, 289–90, 321–22). The senate of Rome voted a restoration of the walls at the Porta Metrovia in 1157, as an inscription attests. The popes of the Renaissance repeatedly repaired the walls and the gates, as their arms and inscriptions show. Today the circuit is preserved along its ancient course, except for (1) the stretches along the left bank of the river, that from Pons Aurelius to the takeoff to the Porta Flaminia having disappeared in the Middle Ages, that from the point where the wall reaches the river west of Porta Ostiensis north to the crossing of the river to the Porta Portuensis having been largely destroyed in the early part of this century; (2) the Bastione di Sangallo built by Antonio da Sangallo the Younger for Pope Paul III (1534–1549), from a point about a half-kilometer west of the Porta Appia to the Porta Ardeatina; and (3) the wall on the right bank of the river, the wall here having been replaced under Pope Urban VIII (1623–1644) by a fortification that runs from the Leonine City, which had received new fortifications under Pope Paul III and Pope Pius IV, along the spine of the Janiculan hill to the Porta Aurelia and from the Porta Aurelia to the river along a line that brought the Porta Portese, replacing the Porta Portuensis, a half-kilometer further upstream. The remains of the walls have repeatedly come to light in the Trastevere, especially remains of the stretch from Porta Aurelia to Pons Aurelius, and the Porta Settimiana still stands to mark an important exit.

The line chosen by Aurelian for the wall was at least in part an already existing boundary for purposes of collecting municipal customs, established in the time of Marcus Aurelius and Commodus and marked by a series of cippi (*CIL* 1016a-c, 8594, 31227; *ILS* 375). The wall was built hastily and incorporated everything that could be made use of occurring in its path, including houses and tombs, the Amphitheatrum Castrense, stretches of aqueduct bridge from Porta Tiburtina to Porta Maior (Porta Praenestina), the terrace walls of the Horti Aciliorum, and the walls of the Castra Praetoria. It is estimated that about one-sixth of the circuit is based on already existing structures.

The wall is made of concrete faced with brick inside and out, and the curtain, 4 m thick and 6.50 m high, is provided with roughly square towers at intervals averaging 100 Roman feet (29.60 m), which project beyond the wall only on the exterior. These towers have bases of solid masonry to the height of the wall walk and rose above it with a barrel-vaulted chamber in which a stair led to a flat roof provided with battlements. Windows in the tower chamber allowed the emplacement of two ballistae, which could swivel ninety degrees. In places the wall is provided with an interior gallery roofed with a barrel vault on which the battlemented wall walk is supported. The floor of the gallery is raised a storey above ground level on the interior and is arcaded behind, the vault being supported on brick-faced piers. Loopholes in the shape of vertical slits with reveals splayed on the interior occur, nine to a bay, between towers. In those sectors the gallery runs through the backs of the towers, and stairs lead from it up to the tower chambers. In very exceptional instances a tower with a semicircular front is introduced.

In the rebuilding of the second period (Maxentian), the wall was raised to double its height by the addition of a gallery at the height of the original wall walk, or by a simple heightening wall about one-half as thick as the original curtain with a narrow battlemented wall walk above. Variations in these two types of addition also appear. The new wall would have been impregnable against any sort of siege machinery then known, including scaling ladders, and communication along the circuit was on the whole efficient, although not for the transport of heavy equipment. The towers at this time had another storey added above, sometimes with walling up of the old windows. The new storey regularly had a hipped roof and round-headed windows for ballista emplacements.

The gates are of four distinct types. Porta Appia and Porta Ostiensis East represent the four first-class gates. They had semicircular towers with one covered chamber reached by a stair from behind; the chamber had a flat crenellated roof, and the curtain connecting the towers was faced with stone. It is presumed that there were two arched openings and a single chamber with five window openings above these crowned by a crenellated roof. The eight second-class gates had curtains faced with brick and single arched openings framed in travertine flanked by semicircular towers. They were otherwise like the first-class gates in design, but with a smaller chamber over the gate. The seven third-class gates were simple archways set in ordinary curtains. The fourth-class gates were posterns with travertine jambs capped with flat arches, of which nine are known.

In the Maxentian rebuilding the towers flanking the Porta Appia were much enlarged and made to project a full diameter in front of it, becoming in effect attached circles, while two storeys were added to the superstructure. An interior court was created by attaching the ornamental Arco di Druso of the Aqua Antoniniana to the Porta Appia by lateral wings, which probably included guard rooms and

261

tax-collection offices. Other gates were less elaborately rebuilt, but the minor Porta Asinaria was given flanking towers and an interior court, and others were strengthened. Numerous minor gates and posterns were walled up.

Under Arcadius and Honorius, the wall and towers were restored in great haste over a period of sixteen months. The gates received new stone curtains in one or two storeys. The double gates were reduced to gates of a single arch, and all gates were fitted with portcullisses. Most of the gate towers were made rectangular in their lower parts and faced with stone taken from other structures, travertine for the most part, but marble in the case of the Portae Flaminia and Appia.

Work on the walls between this period and the Renaissance is of minor importance and consists of repair rather than redesign. In 536 Belisarius is said to have introduced a new sort of merlon that protected the defenders on the wall more effectively. And he dug a ditch in front of the wall, a project that Maxentius had undertaken but left incomplete. But the greatest work of Belisarius was tactical, the strategic deploying of machinery. And after his time work on the walls was extremely shoddy and inept.

I. A. Richmond, *The City Wall of Imperial Rome* (Oxford 1930); Lugli 1934, 139–261; Bloch 313; *BullCom* 80 (1965–67): 149–83 (P. Romeo); Nash 2.86–103; M. Todd, *The Walls of Rome* (London 1978); *BullCom* 91.1 (1986): 103–30 (L. Cozza); *AnalRom* 16 (1987): 25–52 (L. Cozza); *BullCom* 92 (1987–88): 137–74 (L. Cozza); *PBSR* 57 (1989): 1–6 (L. Cozza).

Murus Mustellinus: Festus (142L) says there was a shrine of Mutinus Titinus (see Mutunus Tutunus, Sacellum) on the Velia: *adversum murum mustellinum in angiportu,* and that this was destroyed to make a private bath for Cn. Domitius Calvinus, although it had existed from the founding of the city until the time of Augustus. Mutinus was a Priapic divinity of great antiquity. *Murum* is Scaliger's conjecture for *mutum* in the manuscript. The epithet has never been explained, nor the shrine located, but Domitius's rebuilding of the Regia is commonly adduced as supporting evidence for a location near that building.

Murus Servii Tullii (Fig. 58): the great republican walls of Rome, assigned by tradition to Servius Tullius (Livy 1.44.3; Dion. Hal. 4.13.5), the sixth king of Rome and last recognized to have enlarged the city, which he did by the addition of the Esquiline and Viminal hills. Ascriptions of fortifications to earlier kings ([Aur. Vict.,] *De Vir. Ill.* 5.2; Florus 1.1.13; Livy 1.36.1; Strabo 5.3.7 [234]) have always been

regarded as referring only to work of very limited extent. But the Servian Walls are now seen as in reality a fortification of the second quarter of the fourth century, following the sack and burning of the city by the Gauls, for the stone used is predominantly the grayish yellow tufa of the Grotta Oscura quarries of Veii, which would have become available to the Romans only after the destruction of Veii, and the failure of the Romans to put up any defense of the city against the Gauls is understandable only if the city was essentially without fortifications. Other stone included in the system, especially the poor granular cappellaccio that is the surface stone of Rome, may be due to existing works of terracing for either defense or building, or to scarping as part of the work of construction. Probably there was an agger and fossa fortification on the tableland from the Quirinal to the Esquiline from a very early period, as there seem to have been separate walls defending the Palatine and Capitoline, but the first comprehensive wall system including all seven of the hills of Rome is that of the fourth century, and this is also recorded in fragmentary fashion in Livy (6.32.1 for 377 B.C.; 7.20.9 for 353 B.C.), where the emphasis on cut stone may be significant.

The circuit was about 11 kilometers in length and ran from the north side of the Capitoline across the saddle between it and the Quirinal and along the northwest brow of the Quirinal almost to the head of the valley between the Quirinal and Pincian. Along this stretch were five gates, from the Porta Fontinalis on the shoulder of the Capitoline to the Porta Collina by which the Via Salaria entered Rome. The wall then turned sharply south and ran along the plateau behind Quirinal, Viminal, and Esquiline. Here it kept the character of an agger and fossa fortification and in the Esquiline sector continued to be known as the Agger until the time of Juvenal (8.43). Dionysius (9.68.3–4) describes it as an earthwork 50 feet wide and preceded by a fossa 100 feet wide and 30 feet deep. In the building of the Servian Walls, the agger was revetted with stone inside and out and came to be provided with towers (Varro *ap. Censorin.* 17.8). In this section, because of its vulnerability, there were only two gates, the Porta Viminalis and Porta Esquilina.

The line from Esquiline to Aventine is very uncertain, except for the Porta Capena in the throat between the Caelian and the Aventinus Minor. It would make the best sense to have the line run beyond the church of SS. Quattro Coronati, where a gully separating the Oppius from the tableland of the Esquiline would have given a certain natural advantage in that stretch, cross the Caelian immediately, and run along the southern brow of the Caelian back toward the narrows where the Porta Capena was situated. The wall embraced both lobes of the Aventine and crossed the Forum Boarium on a line roughly parallel to the river to link up again with the Capitoline. On the Caelian were two gates, the Porta Querquetulana and Porta Caelimontana, on the Aventine three, the Portae Naevia, Raudusculana, and Lavernalis, and in the Forum Boarium three, the Portae Trigemina, Flumentana, and Carmentalis.

The walls are built of large rectangular blocks, regularly 2 Roman feet (0.59–0.60 m) high but of variable length, laid dry in alternate courses of headers and stretchers with occasional irregularities for small stretches. One fragment of it still stands as high as 10 m, and the others have a regular thickness of about 4 m. No example of either tower or gate survives to give us some notion of these elements, though there are vestiges of towers in places. The quarry marks, which are very numerous, have excited great interest but are apparently of no special significance.

The walls had repeatedly to be repaired. The principal restorations of which we have notice are those in 217 B.C., during the Second Punic War (Livy 22.8.7), in 212 after a fire (Livy 25.7.5), and in 87 during the Social War (Appian, *BellCiv* 1.66). But these must be simply a random sample, because the walls continued to be serviceable and impressive for at least two and a half centuries (Pliny, *HN* 36.104). In the course of time improvements, such as arched ballista emplacements, were introduced, and lithoid tufas were employed in repairs to the facing and concrete in the core.

The best remains of the Servian Walls are a stretch in Piazza dei Cinquecento on the Viminal and stretches along the south side of the Aventine, especially at Viale Aventino in the gap between the Aventinus Maior and Aventinus Minor. The former, a considerable stretch in the vicinity of Porta Viminalis on both sides of the gate, shows its character as an agger with stone revetment. The latter shows the improvements introduced in the first century B.C., the use of concrete and a well-preserved ballista emplacement. Other bits of the fortification can be picked up all along the northwest brow of the Quirinal, especially in Piazza Magnanapoli and Via Antonio Salandra, or on the Esquiline at the Auditorium Maecenatis, which stands athwart the wall, and elsewhere, but these are difficult to read and less impressive.

The agger, as it appeared in final form, was not only an impressive achievement but its summit was the highest eminence in Rome. For Horace (*Sat.* 1.8.15) it was sunny and a place to stroll; for Juvenal (8.43) it was windy. It was used to denote a part of the city (*pomario de agger a proseucha, CIL* 6.9821 = *ILS* 7495), and we find both *super aggerem*

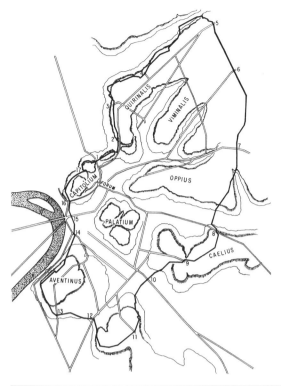

Figure 58
Murus Servii Tullii and
Principal Roads
Entering Rome,
with the Gates in the
Walls Numbered

(S.H.A. *Heliogab.* 30.4) and *subager (Not., Cur.: Campum Viminalem subager).*

G. Säflund, *Le mura di Roma repubblicane* (Uppsala 1932); Lugli 1934, 112–38; Nash 2.104–16; *RömMitt* 76 (1969): 103–10 (H. Riemann); M. G. Picozzi and P. Sommella, eds., *Roma medio repubblicana* (Rome 1973), 7–31; *CAR* 3-D, 160 pp. 112–13, 3-G, 167–68 pp. 252–57; *NSc* 1979, 297–327 (E. Lissi Caronna); R. Thomsen, *King Servius Tullius* (Copenhagen 1980), 218–35; *BullCom* 89 (1984): 67–68 (R. Egidi), 78–79 (R. Quinto); Coarelli 1988, 35–59.

Murus Terreus: known only from a passage in Varro (*Ling.* 5.48): *eidem regioni adtributa subura quod sub muro terreo Carinarum.* The Carinae are known to have been the southwestern part of the Oppius, and it has been widely supposed that the Murus Terreus was an agger, or earthwork, that provided defense for a village there. But the Subura in question is not the familiar Subura in the valley between the Oppius and Viminal, but a Subura between the Oppius and the Caelian, for Varro is explicitly discussing the Regio Suburana, the Caelian and its adjacencies. Moreover, the Romans were familiar with earthwork fortifications and seem always to have called these aggeres. Here we must be dealing with a massive terrace wall of the unaccustomed material sun-dried brick, which served to retain the brow of the hill and distinguish the summit, the Carinae, from what lay below, the Subura.

Mutatorium Caesaris: listed in the regionary catalogues in Regio I and shown on the Marble Plan (*FUR* pl. 15; Rodriguez pl. 1) inscribed MUTATORIUM, an open area a block and a half northeast of the Via Appia, opposite the Baths of Caracalla. The open area is surrounded by insulae with rows of shops on one or more fronts, except for a single building, a rhombic hall divided into aisles by three rows of four columns each, roughly equally spaced, with an annex along the southeast side and perhaps a row of small rooms along the southwest. An inscription (Forcellini, s.v.) informs us that this might have been either a place where members of the imperial administration changed from the litter used in the city to a traveling carriage (so Hülsen) or a covered bazaar.

Mutunus Tutunus (or **Titinus**), **Sacellum:** a shrine of an ancient Italic fertility god of Priapic character in an angiportus on the Velia. In the time of Augustus, Cn. Domitius Calvinus destroyed it to make room for the baths of his house, and it has therefore been supposed to be not far from the Regia, which he rebuilt, but there is no proof. On this god, see Roscher 2.204–7 (R. Peter) and R. E. A. Palmer, *Roman Religion and Roman Empire* (Philadelphia 1974), 187–206.

Naevia, Nemora (or **Silva**): a wood on the Aventine outside the Porta Naevia (q.v.) of the Servian Walls that had allegedly belonged to a certain Naevius (Festus 171L), but by Varro's day this had become merely a place-name (Varro, *Ling.* 5.163). A mutilated passage in Festus (170L) suggests that it got an evil reputation from those who frequented it.

Naumachia: see **Piscina, Stagnum, Naumachia.**

Naumachiae V: listed in the regionary catalogues in Regio XIV without further description. Sidonius (*Epist.* 1.5.9) implies that in his day the naumachiae were an impressive sight, but it seems impossible that there could have been five in existence at the same time, and so scholars have suggested the obvious correction of V to II.

Naumachia Augusti: the basin that Augustus created in 2 B.C. on the right bank of the Tiber, where a magnificent show of naval warfare was staged in connection with the dedication of the Temple of Mars Ultor (Vell. Pat. 2.100.1; Augustus, *RG* 23; Suetonius, *Aug.* 43.1; Cass. Dio 66.25.3; Hieron. *a. Abr.* 2013). It was 1,800 feet long and 1,200 feet wide (Augustus, *RG* 23), and to supply it Augustus brought in a new aqueduct of water of inferior quality, the Aqua Alsietina (q.v.; Frontinus, *Aq.* 1.11, 22). From the beginning it seems to have had a park (nemus) connected with it, and perhaps gardens as well (Tacitus, *Ann.* 14.15; Suetonius, *Tib.* 72.1), but by the time of Suetonius only the name, Nemus Caesarum, was still preserved (Suetonius, *Aug.* 43.1). There was some sort of *pons naumachiarius,* probably a lofty bridge leading to an island in the center, clearly an exceptional feat of engineering (Pliny, *HN* 16.190, 200; Cass. Dio 66.25), which Tiberius restored after a fire.

Nero (Cass. Dio 62.20.5) and Titus (Cass. Dio 66.25; Suetonius, *Titus* 7.3) used the naumachia, and Statius (*Silv.* 4.4.6–7) mentions it, but by the time of Alexander Severus only fragments remained (Cass. Dio 55.10.7). It is believed that the naumachia lay in the vicinity of the church of S. Cosimato and that the Nemus Caesarum was probably adjacent to, but not originally part of, the Horti Caesaris (2)(q.v.). The location is further confirmed by reports of the discovery of large blocks of travertine cut to a curve during excavations for the store named Standa on the northwest side of the Viale di Trastevere.

Naumachia Caesaris: a basin constructed by Julius Caesar in the Codeta Minor (q.v.) bordering on the Campus Martius for the naval show mounted in connection with his triumph in 46 B.C. (Suetonius, *Iul.* 39.4; Cass. Dio 43.23.4; Appian, *BellCiv* 2.102). This was soon filled in, Suetonius (*Iul.* 44.1) says because Caesar projected building a magnificent temple of Mars on the site. Cassius Dio (45.17.8) gives the more plausible explanation that it was by vote of the senate in 43 B.C. because of an epidemic. It is not clear whether this was a measure of hygiene or a gesture of atonement.

Naumachia Caligulae: see **Saepta Iulia.**

Naumachia Domitiani: a basin that Domitian constructed *iuxta Tiberim* (Suetonius, *Dom.* 4.2) for naval spectacles. It is said to have been in a new place (Cass. Dio 67.8), so most topographers conjecture that it was on the right bank of the river, but all Domitian's other building for shows was in the Campus Martius. Before Suetonius's time stone from it was used to repair the Circus Maximus after a fire (Suetonius, *Dom.* 5); this is usually seen as Trajan's work on the circus (Pausanias 5.12.6; Cass. Dio 68.7.2). This would be the more understandable if

Trajan built a naumachia of his own (see Naumachia Traiani).

Naumachia Philippi: see **Lacus Philippi.**

Naumachia Traiani: possibly the large building of which remains were discovered just northwest of the Castel Sant'Angelo. The remains consist of the end of a rectangle, two parallel vaulted corridors with heavy walls joined by a corridor perpendicular to these, the corners being slightly bowed. Remains of four rows of seating were found at points over the vault, and spur walls indicate that this was carried higher on radial vaults with stairs of access, shops, and services arranged underneath, as commonly in theaters and amphitheaters. The construction in concrete faced with reticulate and brick is typical for Trajan, and the facing of the corridor with fine signinum and arrangements for drainage make it highly likely that this, which is certainly not a circus, was for water spectacles. It will then be one of the naumachiae of the regionary catalogues. It has been thought to be a replacement for the naumachia of Domitian, destroyed by Trajan for material to repair the Circus Maximus (Suetonius, *Dom.* 5; Cass. Dio 68.7.2). It was possibly the building whose ruins Procopius (*BellGoth* 2.1.5) took to be of a stadium for gladiatorial combats.

It gave its name to S. Pellegrino in Naumachia, a church of the eighth century, and in the sixth to the eleventh centuries the designation Naumachiae came to be applied to a very large area stretching from the Vatican Hill to the Castel Sant'Angelo and as far south as the Via Cornelia.

CAR 1-E, 2 pp. 20–22; *QITA* 5 (1968): 105–11 (C. Buzzetti).

Naumachia Vaticana: see **Naumachia Traiani.**

Navale Inferius: see **Navalia.**

Navalia: the ship sheds of the war fleet along the left bank of the Tiber. The original set is known to have been in the lower Campus Martius opposite the Prata Quinctia (q.v.). Livy (3.26.8) gives a very circumstantial account of the process of making Cincinnatus dictator, clear enough to be sure that the stretch from a little above the end of the island upstream perhaps as far as Palazzo Farnese is where the Navalia lay.

The earliest certain mention of the Navalia, for 179 B.C. (Livy 40.51.6), speaks of building a *porticus post navalia*. The passage is mutilated, and the purpose and extent of the portico seem not to have been given. This was a time when the portico as an architectural form had just come into popularity,

and some were built for utility, others for ornament. Too little is known about the topography of this part of the Campus Martius to permit conjecture as to what this portico might have been. But after 167, when the royal flagship of Perseus of Macedon was brought to Rome, it could not be housed in the existing navalia, and a special shed had to be constructed for it (Livy 45.35.3 and 42.12, with Polybius 36.5[3].9). It seems, therefore, natural to suppose that the navalia were extended from time to time as need arose. In 338 B.C., after the great Roman naval victory at Antium, the ships of the Latins were in part destroyed, but in part *in navalia Romae subductae* (Livy 8.14.12), and there is every reason to believe the navalia meant are those in question. The fact that they are outside the protection of the Servian Walls has been introduced as evidence against this, but we now know that no stretch of the riverbank was included within the fortifications, and presumably in time of war the fleet would not be kept in its sheds.

The account of the return of Cato the Younger bringing the treasure of Cyprus further confirms this location for the navalia in his day, for, although the people of Rome lined the riverbank to receive him, he took his ships past them without stopping and continued upstream to the ships' proper berths, then unloaded the treasure and paraded it through the Forum Romanum to deposit it in the Temple of Saturn and on the Capitol (Plutarch, *Cato Min.* 39.1–3; Vell. Pat. 2.45.5). However, the ship of Aeneas of which Procopius (*BellGoth* 4.22.7–8) gives an account, saying that it was preserved in his day in navalia in the middle of the city, must remain suspect. Not only does no other source mention this, but it runs counter to what is explicitly written in the *Aeneid*. If Procopius was not the victim of a hoax, he must be confused about the identity of the ship in question. However, it might well have been displayed in the navalia.

Other mentions of the navalia show that they were architecturally important enough to have engaged the labors of Hermodorus of Salamis (Cicero, *De Or.* 1.62) and that they were used as a place of confinement for hostages (Polybius 36.5 [3].9) and animals intended for use in circus games (Pliny, *HN* 36.40). Festus's mention (187L) of a Porta Navalis is puzzling, because no gate of the Servian Walls could be thought of as leading very directly to the navalia. This is either a mistake or a monument otherwise unknown.

On a fragment of the Marble Plan (*FUR* pls. 8, 15) appeared the inscription NAVALEMFER, apparently complete. This has been interpreted as Navale Inferius and the slab assigned with great probability to the upper-right-hand corner of the plan, beyond

Monte Testaccio and the Mattatoio in an area between the Via Ostiensis and the river. While there is no reason to exclude the possibility of such a navale, it is unsupported by other evidence, and the inscription is far from satisfactory. The buildings indicated on the fragment are also puzzling and do not suggest ship sheds, and they are evidently some distance from the river itself. Medallions of Antoninus Pius (Cohen 2.271–72 nos. 17–19; Gnecchi 2.9 nos. 1–3 and pl. 43.1–2; Banti 2.3: 35–36 nos. 5–7) showing the approach of the snake of Aesculapius to the island have been thought to show a section of the navalia with the prow of a trireme emerging, but the arched opening and the flat roof above make it clearly a bridge. Navalia are always shown with individual peaked roofs over each ship.

QITA 5 (1968): 27–33 (F. Coarelli).

Nemus Caesarum: see Naumachia Augusti.

Nemus Thermarum: a park adjacent to the Stagnum Agrippae (q.v.), lying west of the Thermae Agrippae, mentioned only by Tacitus (Ann. 15.37) in connection with the orgiastic revels of Nero just before the account of the great fire of A.D. 64. It has therefore been supposed to have extended from the Stagnum Agrippae to the Thermae Neronianae over an area otherwise devoid of known remains of buildings.

Neptunus, Aedes: Evidently as early as 206 B.C. there was a temple of Neptune in Circo Flaminio, for Cassius Dio (17 fr. 57.60) records among the portents of that year that both the doors and altar of this sweated profusely (and cf. CIL 6.8423), although Livy (28.11.4) mentions only the altar. Pliny (HN 36.26) says that in the temple of Domitius in Circo Flaminio was a group of Neptunus (ipse), Thetis, Achilles, Nereids riding on dolphins, cetuses, and hippocamps, Tritons, and the chorus of Phorcus with fishes and many other marine creatures. This was considered the masterpiece of Scopas (Minor?) and would have been a magnificent achievement had it been his whole life's work. A coin of Cn. Domitius Ahenobarbus of 42–38 B.C. (Crawford 527 no. 519, dated 41 B.C.) shows a tetrastyle temple and carries the inscription NEPT.CN.DOMITIUS.L.F.IMP (B. M. Coins, Rom. Rep. 2.487 no. 93). The temple is shown raised on a podium but without a stair of approach, prostyle or amphiprostyle, and on the obverse is the head of a heavyset, clean-shaven man inscribed AHENOBARB. The suggestion is that Ahenobarbus vowed the temple on the eve of his naval battle with Cn. Domitius Calvinus, for after his victory in that battle he was saluted as imperator. In 40 B.C. he was made governor of Bithynia, and he re-

mained there for some years, but became consul in 32. It seems possible that he brought the group by Scopas back from his governorship, having acquired it in Bithynia or elsewhere in the Greek world, and rebuilt the old Temple of Neptune when he was consul, for he died before Actium.

A large frieze decorated in part with a magnificent marine thiasos and in part with a lustration of a Roman army was for many years in Palazzo Santacroce and is now divided between the Louvre in Paris (lustration) and the Glyptothek in Munich (marine thiasos). Costume and style date it clearly in the last half of the first century B.C. It must have decorated an altar or a large base, and it has been suggested that this was the base for Scopas's group. That is possible, but there is no proof one way or the other, and the thiasos would amount to an inappropriate duplication of the subject.

The Temple of Neptune has been generally supposed to be the temple (pycnostyle, hexastyle, and peripteral) built into the church of S. Salvatore in Campo, which seems rather remote from the Circus Flaminius. Now that we know that the Temple of Castor and Pollux (see Castor et Pollux, Aedes) stood on the southwest side of the circus, the Temple of Neptune might better be similarly located.

Nash 2.120–22; DialArch 2 (1968): 302–68 (F. Coarelli); MEFRA 85.1 (1973): 148–54 (P. Gros); S. Lattimore, The Marine Thiasos in Greek Art (Los Angeles 1974), 13–27; QITA 10 (1988): 59–75 (E. Tortorici).

Neptunus, Ara: see Neptunus, Aedes.

Neptunus, Templum: see Basilica Neptuni and Hadrianus, Divus, Templum.

Niger Lapis: In a mutilated passage that can be restored with considerable probability, Festus (184L) says the Niger Lapis is a locus funestus in the Comitium intended to mark the place of the death, or burial, of Romulus, but actually used for the burial of Faustulus, Romulus's foster father, or of Hostus Hostilius, the grandfather of Tullus Hostilius. The scholia on Horace, Epod. 16.13–14, state that Romulus was buried either pro Rostris or post Rostra, the tomb marked by funerary lions. Dionysius (1.87.2) says a lion stood over the burial place of Faustulus by the Rostra, but then later (3.1.2) he says that the grandfather of Tullus Hostilius was buried there with a stele attesting to his valor.

These various stories do not need to concern us overmuch. In fact, in 1899 was found an irregular four-sided area in front of the Curia Iulia, about 4 m x 3 m, paved with slabs of black marble (marmor Taenarium) that had been marked off so no one would walk on it inadvertently with a pluteus of plates of white marble about 1 m high set in a base of travertine. Under this were found the base of a U-shaped altar, part of a tapering cippus or stele of Grotta Oscura tufa inscribed on all four faces with a boustrephedon inscription at large scale in an archaic alphabet, which not only took all the space available but also required the slicing of one corner to make an extra face so that it could be completed (*ILLRP* 3), and a plain truncated cone of tufa. Together with these things were archaic votive bronzes and terracotta revetments, pottery, and the remains of a sacrifice of the fourth century. It appears that the cippi and other archaic material had been set about the altar base almost haphazardly, all viewed as sacred material but at the time no longer understood, a sacrifice of expiation performed, and the area isolated. The present pavement of black marble is at the level of the Caesarean pavement of the Comitium, but must replace an earlier one.

The material under the Niger Lapis is all of the highest interest and importance. It is easy to see that the altar, once it had lost its upper parts and was associated with burial, would have been interpreted as the base for a pair of funerary lions, though such altars cannot have been unfamiliar. The truncated cone might have been either a boundary stone or a statue base. The inscribed stele, the reading, completion, and interpretation of which has occupied nearly every student of Roman antiquity, continues to be a bone of contention. In view of its unusual material, obviously foreign and unsuitable for inscribing, it is more likely to be a boundary stone than anything else, and the inscription on it is then likely to be a curse on anyone who moved it. The appearance of the name of Jupiter and words such as *sakros* and *iouxmenta* also supports this notion. The alphabet is close to the version of the Greek alphabet in use in southern Etruria and the Faliscan territory in the late seventh and sixth centuries, with certain additions. The only area in the neighborhood likely to have been so religiously bounded is the Comitium, but the votive material found together with the cippus seems unlikely to have been dedicated in the Comitium.

Exploration under this area has ascertained that there is no burial here. The Comitium having always been an inaugurated templum, that is what we should have expected.

Lugli 1946, 121–26; R. E. A. Palmer, *The King and the Comitium* (Wiesbaden 1969); *BullCom* 88 (1982–83): 61–64 (B. Frischer); Coarelli 1983, 161–99; *MonAnt* 52 (ser. misc. 3.1 [1984]): 1–37 (P. Romanelli); *PP* 39 (1984): 56–61 (F. Castagnoli); *BullCom* 89 (1984): 245–48 (F. Ammannato).

Nixae: a place designation listed in the regionary catalogues in Regio IX. For the Ides of October the Fasti Filocali of A.D. 354 (Degrassi 257) carry the annotation *equus ad nixas fit.* This must be the sacrifice of the October horse, rather than the race, but, because the sacrifice was performed with a spear, it might have been performed somewhere near the racetrack, rather than at the Altar of Mars, though the entrails must have been offered on the altar. At this time the only part of the Campus Martius that was not built up was probably that north of the east/west street leading to the Pons Neronianus, now buried under Via dei Coronari. According to Festus (182L), the *nixi di* were three statues brought from abroad as spoils and dedicated in the Capitoline temple in front of the cella of Minerva. They were kneeling and seem to have been telamon figures like those popular in theaters in Italy in the second and first centuries B.C. The Nixae then might be caryatid figures used architecturally or simply decoratively, but the regionary catalogues list them and the Trigarium (q.v.) separately. Others have wished to see these as figures of women in parturition or goddesses who protected women in parturition. They are not mentioned in sources earlier than the fourth century.

La Rocca 1984, 57–65; *CEFR* 98 (1987): 191–210 (J.-M. Flambard); *TAPS* 80 (1990): 33–35 (R. E. A. Palmer).

Nodinus: a brook of Rome mentioned only by Cicero (*Nat.D.* 3.52), without indication of its location. It was included in the augural prayer along with Tiberinus, Spino, and Almo, so it should be in the immediate vicinity of the city and not culverted in Cicero's day.

Noenses de Ara Matidiae: known from a single fragment of the edict of Tarracius Bassus (*CIL* 6.31893 b10–11 = *ILS* 6072) of the late fourth century. The reading is not entirely certain. See Matidia, Ara and Matidia, Templum.

Nova Via (Fig. 63): so called to distinguish it from Sacra Via, the only other street within Rome known to have been called a via in the republican period. It was very old (Varro, *Ling.* 6.59). It started at Porta Mugonia on the Clivus Palatinus and in front of the Temple of Iuppiter Stator, where it was called *summa Nova Via* (Livy 1.41.4; Solinus 1.24), and ran along the base of the north side of the hill in a straight line to its northwest corner, passing along the way between the Lucus Vestae and the Aedes Vestae (Cicero, *Div.* 1.101). At the northwest corner of the hill it originally turned sharply, almost at a right angle, and ran to the Velabrum, where it apparently merged with the Clivus Victoriae. Its end in the Velabrum was originally called *infima Nova Via* (Varro, *Ling.* 5.43). In the late republican or Augustan period, for reasons unknown, this stretch was abolished and the street terminated at the point where it had turned, at the stair leading from the Temple of Vesta to the Clivus Victoriae. Its termination here then became known as infima Nova Via (Livy 5.32.6, 50.5, and 52.11; A. Gellius 16.17.2). In Ovid's day it already had a direct connection with the Forum Romanum (Ovid, *Fast.* 6.396), probably by the stair mentioned earlier, and because Ovid speaks of this as an innovation, he may give a date for the destruction of the west leg of the street.

It was originally a street of great importance, running from Porta Mugonia to Porta Romana or Romanula (Varro, *Ling.* 5.164) and very likely passing Porta Ianualis at the northwest corner of the Palatine along the way, in which case it must have followed the original pomerium of the Palatine settlement. As the Atrium Vestae and Domus Tiberiana were enlarged, the importance of the Nova Via diminished, until it became little more than a service corridor. Verrius Flaccus (Festus 372L) objected that the common people ran the two words of the name into one in his day, whereas they should be distinguished.

Nash 2.123–24.

Novum Templum: see Augustus, Divus, Templum.

Ad Nucem: a locality outside the pomerium of Rome given as the burial place in a funerary inscription (*CIL* 6.28644). This was a cemetery about 300 m beyond Porta Salaria. It is found again on a lead tessera (Rostovtzeff, *Sylloge* 498). The name is too plain to be informative.

C. Numitorii, Aedificia (?): recorded in an inscription listing public works on the streets of Rome in 100–80 B.C. (*CIL* 1².809 = *ILLRP* 464). The word *aedificia* is a supplement of]ICIA on the stone, and identification is impossible.

Ad Numfium: known from a single fragment of the edict of Tarracius Bassus of the late fourth century against fraudulent merchants and shopkeepers (*CIL* 6.31898 11). The reading is not entirely certain. This might be the same as Ad Nymphas (q.v.).

Nymphae, Aedes: a temple in the Campus Martius where records pertaining to the census were kept,

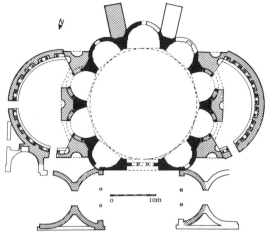

Figure 59
Nymphaeum ("Tempio di Minerva Medica"), Plan, Showing Two Building Periods

presumably temporarily, and that Cicero claims Clodius set on fire to destroy these records (Cicero, *Cael.* 78, *Milon.* 73, *Paradoxa* 4.31, *Har. Resp.* 57). Because the census was taken in the Villa Publica, the temple must have been nearby. It probably stood somewhere along the Porticus Aemilia (q.v.) connecting the Porta Fontinalis and the Ara Martis, where the censors set their curule chairs, and probably not far from the altar. It is not likely to have been in the Villa Publica itself. The day of dedication was 23 August, the same as the Volcanalia (Degrassi 501).

Ad Nymphas: a location in the Subura (Maior), evidently at the foot of the Cispian cusp of the Esquiline (*CIL* 6.461 = *ILS* 3361, 9526 = *ILS* 7565).

Nymphaea Tria: listed in the regionary catalogues in Regio XIII (Aventinus), possibly the same as the *nymfia tria* said to have been built by Diocletian (Chron. 148). Because nymphaea were relatively common, this must have been one in which three were united in some special way.

Nymphaeum: see **Fons, Lacus, Nymphaeum.**

Nymphaeum (Fig. 59): on the Esquiline on Via Giovanni Giolitti between Via Labicana and the Aurelian Walls, a large structure of concrete faced with brick commonly called Tempio di Minerva Medica because of the mistaken belief that the Athena Giustiniani was found here. This is now believed to be the remains of a spectacular nymphaeum of the second half of the third century. The main hall is decagonal, about 24 m in diameter and 33 m in height, roofed with a dome built on a skeleton of brick ribs,

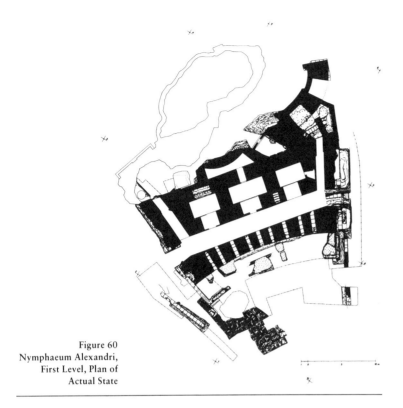

Figure 60
Nymphaeum Alexandri,
First Level, Plan of
Actual State

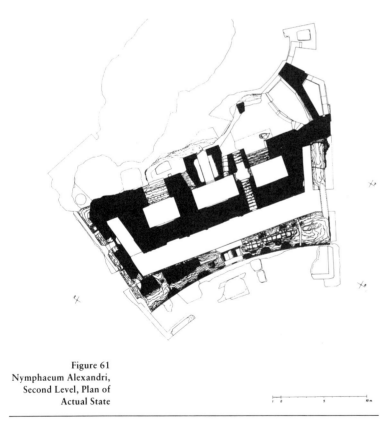

Figure 61
Nymphaeum Alexandri,
Second Level, Plan of
Actual State

but still stepped at the base on the exterior. At ground level the walls of the main room open out into apsidal niches with half-domes, one on each side of the decagon, except for the entrance side, four of them, those to either side, open, their domes supported on columns, five closed. Opposite the entrance two large exterior buttresses took some of the thrust of the main dome. In the upper wall in each wall of the decagon is a large arched window. The engineering of the dome is of the greatest interest and has been repeatedly studied. The building was faced with marble outside as well as inside. It has been presumed that it was fed by the Aqua Anio Vetus (see Anio Vetus), the line of which runs close by, but this is not known, and the use of water in the building is a matter of speculation. It might better be a dining pavilion. Later a monumental entrance with two large lateral exedras of curved plan was added, as were two huge curved rooms behind the cross axis of the main hall that look like nymphaea in their own right, along with other minor constructions that confuse the reading of the architecture. This complex is often assigned to the Horti Liciniani, but again without proof. In the fifteenth century it acquired the name Le Galluzze, of uncertain meaning and origin.

Lugli 1938, 480–83; Nash 2.127–29.

Nymphaeum Alexandri (Figs. 60, 61): a magnificent fountain, the terminus of the Aqua Iulia, in the fork of the Via Tiburtina Vetus and Via Labicana, in what is now Piazza Vittorio Emanuele. The existing remains are of brick-faced concrete in two main storeys. The upper storey is a large apsidal niche flanked by open arches, the whole to be restored with Corinthian columns and entablature, of which fragments exist, and finished above with an attic. The side arches held the marble trophies that Pope Sixtus V removed in 1590 and set on the balustrade of Piazza del Campidoglio; these are generally recognized as Domitianic work and were probably not made for this setting. The group of the central niche is entirely unknown. Below the upper storey water poured from severely architectural niches in a half-storey forming a podium for the upper storey into a broad channel invisible to those viewing it from ground level. From this it passed to the lower storey. The lower storey is much ruined, but it seems to have consisted of a relatively solid block thrust forward and relieved by the addition of a columnar architecture framing numerous niches from which water poured into a large, probably semicircular basin. The niches were probably furnished with fountain statuary.

This appears to be the Nymphaeum Alexandri listed by the regionary catalogues in Regio V (cf. *CIL* 6.31893 d5). On a medallion of Alexander Severus

270

struck in A.D. 226 (Cohen 4.449 no. 479; Gnecchi 2.82.20 and pl. 99 no. 8; Banti 4.2: 138 nos. 137–38) is a monument that is strikingly like this. It consists of two storeys, the upper storey containing three niches framed by columns, the central niche with a two-figure group, the side niches with trophies. The roof of this storey is crowned by a quadriga, possibly flanked by trophies. The lower storey is a relatively solid block decorated with columns and niches that continue down the sides, which seem to splay, and in front is a triangular basin. On other coins of the same year showing the same monument, the basin is clearly semicircular, and the half-storey is dominated by a recumbent water divinity in the center, while other figures, possibly trumpeting Victorias, crown the forward corners. The groups flanking the quadriga on the attic here seem to be clearly Victorias with trophies (*B. M. Coins, Rom. Emp.* 6 pl. 11 nos. 323–25).

The monument is clearly triumphal in character, and it has been conjectured that it was created out of a triumphal arch, but that seems unwarranted. In the Middle Ages, as early as 1176, it was connected with Marius and his victory over the Cimbri (Jordan 2.517). This legend then grew and was embroidered, probably because of the story of Caesar's restoration of the trophies of Marius that Sulla had dismantled (Vell. Pat. 2.43.4; Suetonius, *Iul.* 11). It persists as the popular name of the ruin today: Trofei di Mario.

Nash 2.125–26; G. Tedeschi Grisanti, *"I trofei di Mario," il ninfeo dell'Acqua Giulia sull'Esquilino* (Rome 1977); *RendPontAcc* 50 (1977–78): 165–77 (G. Tedeschi Grisanti); *BullCom* 91.2 (1986): 343–50 (D. Cattalini and G. Tedeschi Grisanti).

Nymphaeum Flavi Philippi: known from a fifth-century inscription recording a restoration by this praefectus urbi (*CIL* 6.1728). There were originally three copies of this inscription known, two of which have been lost, so it must have been a monument of some importance. The existing inscription was found in Via Cavour near the church of S. Francesco di Paolo, and ruins beneath the church have been thought to belong to the nymphaeum.

Nymphaeum Iovis: listed by the regionary catalogues in Regio VII, probably in the southern part of the regio and supplied by the Aqua Virgo.

Obeliscus: A large unidentified obelisk is said to lie buried in the Campus Martius between the Salita dei Crescenzi and Piazza S. Luigi dei Francesi, mainly under Palazzo Giustiniani and Palazzo Patrizi. It has been supposed that this belonged to the Stadium of Domitian (see Stadium Domitiani), but that stadium had no spina, and no obelisk in it would have fallen here. The location is within the southern reaches of the Thermae Neronianae, of which considerable remains not only existed in the seventeenth century and were drawn by Alò Giovannoli in just this area, but also still exist today, built into buildings of later date. An obelisk is an unlikely ornament for a bath complex, and we must doubt that whatever gave rise to this tradition has been properly identified.

Il Buonarotti, ser. 3.1 (1882): 41–59 (C. Maes); *Roma, rivista di studi e di vita romana* 2 (1924): 505–9 (W. von Winterfeld).

Obeliscus Antinoi: the obelisk now standing on the Pincian Hill in Viale dell'Obelisco, found outside Porta Maggiore between the Via Labicana and the line of the Aqua Claudia. It was almost certainly the central ornament of the spina of the Circus Varianus (q.v.), brought there probably by Elagabalus. It was made in the time of Hadrian and probably originally stood before the Temple of Divus Antinous in the city of Antinoopolis in Egypt, as the hieroglyphic inscription in clumsy and difficult language declares. The notion that it ornamented a tomb or cenotaph in the Villa Adriana at Tivoli, more specifically along the "Canopus," is not convincing, because the inscription is in hieroglyphs and the rites it mentions would be inappropriate there. It is about 9 m high.

It was found in pieces by the Saccoccia brothers in their vineyard in the sixteenth century and reerected in 1570 at a point marked by an inscription affixed to one of the piers of the Acqua Felice footed on the north side of the Circus Varianus. In 1633 it was taken to the courtyard of Palazzo Barberini. Princess Cornelia Barberini presented it to Pope Clement XIV (1769–1774), and it was moved to the Giardino della Pigna in the Vatican palace. Pope Pius VII arranged to have it set up on the Pincian, which Marini accomplished in 1822.

D'Onofrio 1965, 295–97; Iversen 1.161–73; Nash 2.130–33; *AnalRom* 11 (1982): 69–108 (N. Hannestad); *MEFRA* 98 (1986): 217–53 (J.-C. Grenier and F. Coarelli); Boatwright 239–60.

Obeliscus Augusti (Gnomon) (Fig. 42): an obelisk of red granite, 21.79 m high, originally erected in Heliopolis in the early sixth century B.C. by Psammetichus II, and brought to Rome by Augustus in 10 B.C. and set up as a monument to the conquest of Egypt and a dedication to the sun (*CIL* 6.702 = *ILS* 91; Amm. Marc. 17.4.12; Strabo 17.1.27 [805]; Pliny, *HN* 36.71). It was made the gnomon of a colossal sundial laid out on a pavement extending from a little north of Piazza del Parlamento to Piazza della Torretta and from a little east of S. Lorenzo in Lucina to a point south of the axis of the south façade of Palazzo Borghese (see Horologium Solare Augusti). Thus it was part of the Augustan complex that included the Ara Pacis and the Mausoleum Augusti. The obelisk was presumably fitted with a gilded sphere surmounted by a short spire at its apex and probably mounted on a stepped base. Into the pavement was sunk a network of bronze markers to show the length of the shadow throughout the year and inscriptions indicating the seasons and signs of the zodiac and various meteorological phenomena (Pliny, *HN* 36.72). Pliny observed that by his day the readings had been inaccurate for thirty years, apparently due to settling of the obelisk in the soft soil of the Campus Martius (Pliny, *HN* 36.73).

In 1979–1980 a series of borings and small excavations was carried out to try to rediscover parts of the sundial, some of which had come to light in the fifteenth and sixteenth centuries (LS 1.83, 136, 169). A section inscribed with *krios* and *parthenos* and noting the cessation of the etesian winds between Leo and Virgo was found; this permitted a general reconstruction of the whole. It was discovered that in or about the time of Domitian the sundial had been raised about 1.60 m and corrected, with a calendar in Greek to west of the central axis, and presumably one in Latin to east. Probably it was similar in its original layout and the inscriptions were salvaged and reused.

The obelisk was still standing in the eighth century (Einsiedeln itinerary 2.5 and 4.3, Jordan 2.648–49), but was thrown down and broken subsequently and not rediscovered until 1512. It was excavated in 1748 and, after several attempts, reerected in 1790–1792 in Piazza di Montecitorio, at which time it was repaired with material from the Columna Antonini Pii (q.v.; LS 4.151; *BullCom* 42 [1914]: 380–81 [M. Marchetti]; *PBSR* 2 [1904]: 3 [T. Ashby]). See also Horologium Solare Augusti.

D'Onofrio 1965, 280–91; Iversen 1.142–60; Nash 2.134–36; E. Buchner, *Die Sonnenuhr des Augustus* (Mainz 1982).

Obeliscus Augusti in Circo Maximo: an obelisk originally erected by Sethos I with further hieroglyphs by his son Ramesses II (1304–1237 B.C.), which Augustus brought from Heliopolis in 10 B.C. at the same time as the Gnomon (see Obeliscus Augusti [Gnomon]) and set up on the spina of the Circus Maximus as a monument to the conquest of Egypt and a dedication to the sun (*CIL* 6.701 = *ILS* 91), this inscription identical with that of the Gnomon (Strabo 17.1.27 [805]; Amm. Marc. 17.4.12; Pliny, *HN* 36.71; Chron. 145). It is 23.70 m high. After the fourth century it is not mentioned.

Fragments of the base and inscription were found during the reign of Pope Gregory XIII (1572–1585), and the obelisk itself, broken in three pieces, was discovered in 1587. It was then taken and reerected in Piazza del Popolo, where it still stands (LS 4.148–51).

D'Onofrio 1965, 52, 173–77; Iversen 1.73–75; Nash 2.137–38.

Obeliscus Capitolinus: an obelisk originally erected by Ramesses II at Heliopolis that stood on the Capitoline near a palm tree on the slope east of the stair that in the sixteenth century led south from the east end of S. Maria in Aracoeli down to the saddle between crests (Piazza del Campidoglio). It is shown in a number of drawings by van Heemskerck. In 1542 it was dismounted. Its history in antiquity is entirely unknown, and its association with a temple

of Isis et Serapis in Capitolio is entirely hypothetical. After it was dismounted, it was given in 1582 to Ciriaco Mattei by the Conservatori. It was transported to Villa Celimontana and set as the central ornament of a large hippodrome garden arranged on the left flank of the casino. It stood there until 1817, when it was moved to the end of an avenue, where it stands today. In its location on the Capitoline it was supported on four couchant lion protomes at the angles atop a high square plinth and carried a spiked globe at its summit. The shaft consisted of two distinct pieces, the lower and larger uninscribed and flaring at the base, the upper covered with Ramesses's hieroglyphs on all four faces. Clearly this was a pastiche, and the lion protome supports indicate that as a whole it is not ancient Roman work.

It has recently been argued that this obelisk was an invention of Cola di Rienzo, erected in 1347 to stand together with an already existing palm tree as a symbol of Libertas and Roma Caput Mundi. Certainly the iconography is supportive of such an interpretation. It stood until Pope Paul III's construction of a new entrance portico to the monastery of Aracoeli, when it was moved to the cemetery of Aracoeli, a short distance away, for safekeeping. There it remained until it was given to Ciriaco Mattei.

Where the small Egyptian obelisk extended by the new shaft originally stood in Rome, and where the granite for the new shaft came from, is not known. So small an obelisk might have been even a private donation to a temple of the Egyptian gods and is not likely to have got into the historical record.

D'Onofrio 1965, 204–16; Iversen 1.106–14; Nash 2.139–41.

Obeliscus Constantii: the largest obelisk in Rome, brought by Constantius and set up in A.D. 357 on the spina of the Circus Maximus (Amm. Marc. 16.10.17, 17.4.18; Cassiodorus, *Var.* 3.51.8). It was originally cut for Tuthmosis III in the fifteenth century B.C. and erected by his grandson Tuthmosis IV before the Temple of Ammon in Thebes. Augustus is said to have contemplated bringing it to Rome; Constantine brought it down the Nile to Alexandria. Its transportation to Rome by a special ship and its reerection in the circus are described in detail by Ammianus (17.4.13–16) and were recorded in the inscription on the base (*CIL* 6.1163, 31249 = *ILS* 736). Ammianus tells us that it was originally surmounted by a gilded bronze sphere, like many Roman obelisks, but, after this was early struck by lightning, it was replaced by a gilded bronze torch. It is of red granite, 32.50 m high, the largest in the world, and covered with hieroglyphs. It is also the oldest obelisk in Rome and the last to be brought there.

It is mentioned in the past tense in the twelfth century (*Mirabilia*: Jordan 2.639, VZ 3.58). It was encountered in an excavation in 1410–1417 (Anonymous Magliabechianus 17 = VZ 4.131; LS 1.45). In 1587 it was discovered broken in three pieces and buried at a depth of about 7 m. It was excavated by Pope Sixtus V and reerected as part of his scheme of streets and obelisks in Piazza S. Giovanni in Laterano to the right (west) of the principal façade of the Lateran palace at the fork of Via di S. Giovanni and Via Merulana (LS 4.148–51).

D'Onofrio 1965, 160–72; Iversen 1.57–64; Nash 2.142–43.

Obeliscus Domitiani: see Obelisci Isei Campensis.

Obeliscus Hortorum Sallustianorum: an obelisk 13 m high brought to Rome at some uncertain time, but after the time of Augustus (Amm. Marc. 17.4.16), and carved, evidently at Rome, with hieroglyphs copying those of the obelisk of Augustus in the Circus Maximus, but so ineptly that some signs are reversed. It stood in the northern reaches of the Horti Sallustiani (q.v.); its foundation was found in 1912 in the block bounded by the Vie Sicilia, Sardegna, Toscana, and Abruzzi. It was still standing in the eighth century and is mentioned in the Einsiedeln itinerary (2.7; Jordan 2.649). Apparently it was never completely buried; the Anonymous Magliabechianus mentions it as lying broken by its base in 1410–1415 (VZ 4.130), and there are a number of Renaissance drawings of it. In 1733 Princess Ludovisi gave it to Pope Clement XII, and in 1736 it was taken to Piazza S. Giovanni in Laterano but left lying on the ground there. Following the erection of the Quirinal obelisk in Montecavallo in 1786, Pope Pius VI decided to take the Sallustian obelisk to Trinità de'Monti and erect it in a balancing position to the Quirinal obelisk at the juncture of Via Sistina/Via delle Quattro Fontane and Via dei Condotti. This was accomplished in 1789. The base, a large block of red granite, was covered over after the removal of the obelisk in 1734 but rediscovered in 1843. In 1926 it was transported to the Capitoline and made into a monument to the martyrs of the Fascist movement, a monument that was dismantled following the collapse of fascism.

D'Onofrio 1965, 268–79; Nash 2.144–47.

Obeliscus Insulanus: see Insula Tiberina.

Obelisci Isei Campensis: several small obelisks have been found at various times in the vicinity of the Temple of Isis Campensis (see Isis, Aedes [1]). These were probably brought to Rome during the first and second centuries after Christ and set up (in pairs?) before the entrance to the temple. The following are known:

1. The obelisk standing as the central ornament of the fountain in Piazza della Rotonda, of the time of Ramesses II, originally erected in front of the Temple of Ra at Heliopolis. It is 6 m high and covered with hieroglyphs. Because in the fifteenth century it was in front of S. Macuto just west of S. Ignazio, it is often called the Obelisco di S. Macuto, and it was erected in the piazzetta there, probably toward the end of the fourteenth century. There is no record of its discovery, but it was known to the Anonymous Magliabechianus (VZ 4.130). At that time its base was poorly proportioned and awkward. In 1711 Pope Clement XI had it moved to stand in the center of Della Porta's fountain basin in Piazza della Rotonda. The architect was F. Barigioni, and the sculptors of the new base were F. Pincellotti and V. Felici.

D'Onofrio 1965, 250–55; Iversen 1.101–5; Nash 2.150–51.

2. The obelisk mounted on the back of an elephant in Piazza della Minerva, found in 1665 in the garden of the convent of the Dominicans attached to the church of S. Maria Sopra Minerva to the northeast. It is of rose granite and 5.47 m high. Originally Pharaoh Apries (589–570 B.C.) had erected it at Sais. A single line of hieroglyphs ornaments each face. The designer of the new base was G. L. Bernini, and the sculptor was E. Ferrata.

D'Onofrio 1965, 230–37; Iversen 1.93–100; Nash 2.152.

3. The obelisk standing in Viale delle Terme Diocletiane, found in 1883 intact under the apse of S. Maria Sopra Minerva, originally erected by Ramesses II at Heliopolis. It is about 6 m high and has hieroglyphs on all four faces. In 1887 it was decided to use it as part of a monument to the soldiers who fell at Dogali in the African War. This was erected in front of the main railroad station in Rome. In 1924 the whole monument was moved a short distance to a small public garden between Viale delle Terme and Via delle Terme Diocletiane. This is probably the counterpart of (1) above, being the same size and dedicated by the same pharaoh.

D'Onofrio 1965, 303–8; Iversen 1.174–77; Nash 2.148–49.

4–6. Ligorio mentions three obelisks, one of which was discovered in an excavation in front of S. Maria Sopra Minerva. This is probably that which came into the possession of the Medici, was used to ornament their villa on the Pincian until 1787 (LS 3.114, 121), and then was taken to Florence and erected in the Boboli Gardens. Its inscriptions are almost identical with those of (1) above. The fragmentary remains of the other two had the same measurements and the same hieroglyphs. These were given to Cardinal Alessandro Albani, who gave them to the city of Urbino in 1737. They have been made up into a single obelisk with the addition of an uninscribed fragment and stand in front of the church of S. Domenico in Urbino. The inscription is of the time of Apries (589–570 B.C.), like (2) above.

Nash 2.153–54, 157–58.

7. A portion of a small obelisk of red granite that may have come from the Iseum was once in Palazzo Cavalieri Maffei in Piazza Cairoli, passed then to Villa Albani, where Cavaceppi restored it, and appears to have been sent to Paris under unknown circumstances. It is now in the Glyptothek in Munich. Only the middle portion, 3.20 m long, is ancient. The inscription in hieroglyphs of Roman date and content is mutilated but shows that one T. Sextius Africanus erected it. G. Zoega (*De Origine et Usu Obeliscorum* [Rome 1797], 63–84, 192) says this was probably the counterpart of an obelisk of which a fragment was found in the Temple of Fortuna Primigenia at Praeneste in 1792 that eventually passed to the Museo Nazionale Archeologico in Naples. Another fragment found in Praeneste in 1872 belongs to yet another counterpart. It is still in Palestrina. From these fragments, we learn that the obelisks were erected in the time of Claudius. A T. Sextius Africanus, presumably our man, was consul in A.D. 59 and an Arval Brother.

BullCom 32 (1906): 252–57 (O. Marucchi); A. Fürtwängler and P. Wolters, *Beschreibung der Glyptothek zu München*[2] (Munich 1910), no. 22; A. Ruesch, *Guida illustrata del Museo Nazionale di Napoli* (Naples 1908), no. 335; Iversen 1.180–81.

Obelisci Mausolei Augusti (Fig. 55): a pair of obelisks of red granite a little over 14 m high that stood in front of the Mausoleum Augusti (q.v.) in the Campus Martius, first mentioned by Ammianus Marcellinus (17.4.16) and listed in the regionary catalogues. As they are not mentioned by either Strabo in his description of the mausoleum (5.3.8 [236]) or Pliny (*HN* 36.69–74), it is presumed that they were placed there only late, but there is no telling when. Their relationship to the bronze tablets inscribed with the *Res Gestae Divi Augusti* is a further problem. Because they are uninscribed, it is likely that they were made expressly for this location. One was excavated in 1519 during work on the Via di Ripetta (LS 1.192) and for sixty-odd years lay in four pieces along the west side of the mausoleum behind the church of S. Rocco, where it was a considerable obstacle to traffic in the Via di Ripetta. Finally, in 1586 it was removed and in 1587 erected in Piazza Esquilina behind the apse of S. Maria Maggiore. The other seems to have been discovered at the same time, but

it was not excavated until 1556 (LS 2.15). It was then reburied for unknown reasons. It was rediscovered in August 1781, during work connected with the hospital of S. Rocco, and brought to light in three pieces, together with its base, split in two. It was immediately decided to reerect this as part of a monumental resystematization of the Dioscuri of Montecavallo. This was carried out by the architect Antinori.

D'Onofrio 1965, 154–59, 256–67; Iversen 1.47–54, 115–27; Nash 2.155–56.

Obeliscus Mediceus: see **Obelisci Isei Campensis** (4–6).

Obeliscus Pamphilius: the obelisk that has been reerected as part of Bernini's fountain of the four rivers in Piazza Navona. This ornamented the middle of the spina of the Circus of Maxentius out on Via Appia, where in the seventeenth century it lay broken in five pieces. Here Pope Innocent X saw it in 1647 and had it brought to Rome with the intention of using it as part of a fountain in Piazza Navona. The competition for the design of the fountain was won by Bernini with the design we see today. The hieroglyphs carved on the shaft include the names of Domitian and Divus Vespasianus and Titus and allude to restoration of that which was destroyed. It has therefore been concluded that the obelisk was made by order of Domitian to be erected in the Temple of Isis Campensis, which burned in the fire of Titus in A.D. 80, Domitian being known to have been favorably disposed to the cult of the Egyptian gods. This is possible, but, because the Iseum was still a place of worship in the fourth century, the removal of an obelisk from it to ornament a circus seems unlikely, and one must prefer to look for a more secular building that it might have ornamented. The dedication is not to Isis, but to Harmachis (see Roscher 1.1828–30 [W. Drexler]), the newly risen sun, which seems to make this one with the obelisks of Augustus and suggests that it might have been similarly used, perhaps in the Circus Gaii et Neronis (q.v.).

BullCom 36 (1908): 254–74 (G. Farina); D'Onofrio 1965, 222–29; Iversen 1.76–92; Nash 2.159–60; *MEFRA* 99.2 (1987): 937–61 (J.-C. Grenier).

Obeliscus Vaticanus (Fig. 25): the obelisk now in the center of Piazza S. Pietro, brought from Heliopolis in the time of Caligula and set up on the spina of the Circus Gaii et Neronis (q.v.). It is a monolith of red granite without hieroglyphs, but with dedications to Divus Augustus and Tiberius overlying partially erased inscriptions of Cornelius Gallus on opposite faces at the base of the shaft (A. E. Gordon,

Illustrated Introduction to Latin Epigraphy [Berkeley 1983], no. 35). It is 25.36 m high and required a specially built ship to transport it from Egypt (Pliny, *HN* 16.201–2, 36.74; Suetonius, *Claud.* 20.3). Later the ship was sunk to make the foundation of one of the breakwaters of the Claudian port at Portus Augusti and a lighthouse built on it. It is the only obelisk known not to have fallen at some time and is shown standing on the south side of the basilica of S. Pietro in several Renaissance drawings, especially those of van Heemskerck. In 1586 it was moved from its original position to the center of the piazza by Domenico Fontana at the behest of Pope Sixtus V. It was originally surmounted by a spiked globe of gilded bronze; in the Middle Ages a legend developed that the ashes of Julius Caesar were contained in this. At the time it was moved a cross was substituted for the globe, which was given to the Comune Capitolino. It is now in the Palazzo dei Conservatori (Helbig[4] 2.1581).

D'Onofrio 1965, 13–103; Iversen 1.29–46; *Capitolium* 38 (1963): 489–94 (F. Magi); Nash 2.161–62.

Odeum: a building for musical performances and contests that Domitian erected in the Campus Martius (Suetonius, *Dom.* 5; Chron. 146; Hieron. *a. Abr.* 2105), probably in conjunction with his Stadium (see Stadium Domitiani). Dio (69.4.1) says it was built by Apollodorus of Damascus; this is usually regarded as referring to a restoration under Trajan, but without warrant. Apollodorus is credited with the Forum Traiani, now recognized to have been conceived and begun under Domitian, and Rabirius is credited only with the Domus Augustiana and Capitolium (Martial 7.56), works of the earlier years of Domitian's reign. The Odeum was much admired by Ammianus (16.10.14), and Polemius Silvius (545) considered it one of the seven wonders of Rome. In the *Curiosum* it is said to have had 10,600 loca, which would mean that it could accommodate about 7,000 spectators. It has never been located. The curved façade of Palazzo Massimo alle Colonne on Corso Vittorio Emanuele has often been thought to reflect the curve of the cavea used as a foundation, and its proximity to the Stadium of Domitian is used to support this identification. It has also been thought to lie under the low hill of Monte Giordano, but that seems rather remote and therefore unlikely.

Officinae Minii: workshops for the production of the red pigment minium (cinnabar) from mercury ore brought to Rome from mines in Spain (Vitruvius 7.9.4). These workshops in Vitruvius's day were on the slope of the Quirinal between the Temple of Quirinus (see Quirinus, Aedes) and the Temple of Flora (see Flora, Templum). The fact that Vitruvius locates them for his reader suggests that they were rather obscure.

Oppius Mons (Figs. 62, 75): the southwestern lobe of the Esquiline Hill, separated from the Cispian to the north by the valley up which ran the Clivus Suburanus, from the Caelian to the south by the basin of the Colosseum and the valley up which run Via di S. Giovanni and the modern Via Labicana, from the Velia to the west by a shallow depression formerly represented by Via del Colosseo and then a steeper rise to the height of the Oppius, and from the tableland of the Esquiline on the east by the valley up which runs Via Merulana. It is joined to the tableland on the northeast by a waist running from the church of S. Martino ai Monti to a point a little south of the Auditorium Maecenatis. In the festival of the Septimontium (q.v.) the Oppius is distinguished from the Fagutal, as well as the Cispian (Festus 458–59L, 476L), which is probably not significant for configuration, because the Cermalus is distinguished from the Palatium. In the ceremony of the Argei, Varro (*Ling.* 5.50) describes the second division of the city as made up of two *montes*, the Oppius and the Cispian, and locates the Fagutal on the Oppius. According to Varro (*ap. Fest.* 476L), it got its name from Opiter Oppius, a Tusculan sent to Rome with a force to guard the city while Tullus Hostilius was besieging Veii. It is a plebeian gentilicial name of uncertain origin.

In *CIL* 1[2].1003 = 6.32455 = *ILS* 5428 = *ILLRP* 698, an inscription of late republican date found near the reservoir called Sette Sale, mention is made of magistri and *flamines* of the Montani of Mons Oppius, as well as a sacellum and money belonging to these for public works. To have such officers this must have been more than a compital organization, but this is the latest appearance of the name Oppius (see Pagus Montanus).

The cemeteries of the Esquiline from just east of the church of S. Martino ai Monti to the vicinity of Piazza Vittorio Emanuele, extending on both sides of the agger of the Servian Walls, may belong to the settlement of Titus Tatius and the Sabines on the Quirinal, Viminal, and Capitoline, or may be evidence that the Oppius was the site of one of the earliest villages of Rome. They go back to the Early Iron Age of the eighth century, possibly even earlier. As the evidence of such sites as Acqua Rossa and Veii shows, this does not mean that there were rival villages on Palatine, Oppius, Quirinal, and so on, but rather that clusters of habitations belonging to a single polity were scattered over the site adjacent to the fields farmed by their inhabitants. Some of the graves in the Esquiline cemetery are as old as any in the Sepulcretum (q.v.) of the Forum Romanum (*MonAnt* 15 [1905] [G. Pinza]; Ryberg, *Archeological Record,* 1–50).

Ops, Aedes, Templum (Fig. 19): a temple on the Capitoline, almost certainly within the Area Capitolina, first mentioned when struck by lightning in 186 B.C. (Livy 39.22.4). A L. Metellus, pontifex (Mommsen believed this to be L. Caecilius Metellus Diadumatus, cos. 117 B.C., while PA and Degrassi would make him L. Caecilius Metellus Dalmaticus, cos. 119 B.C.), at sometime dedicated a temple to Ops Opifera (Pliny, *HN* 11.174), which might be a restoration of this temple or an entirely new one, in which case we have no other notice of it, except in the fasti. There were two holidays in honor of Ops, one to Ops Opifera on 23 August, which was certainly an anniversary (Degrassi 501–2), and one on 19 December, the Opalia (Degrassi 540–41), also recorded in the calendar with the added note in the Fasti Amiternini: *Ops ad forum.* Because nothing is known of a temple of Ops ad forum, it has been presumed that this celebration was held at the Temple of Saturn, generally conceived to be Ops's consort (Macrobius, *Sat.* 1.10.19–20), or at the shrine of Ops Consiva in the Regia (q.v.). But after A.D. 7 there was an altar of Ceres Mater et Ops Augusta (see Ceres Mater et Ops Augusta, Ara) on the Vicus Iugarius, and that might be meant. Granted the extension of the festival of the Saturnalia beginning on 17 December to three days (and unofficially to as many as seven), the link of the Saturnalia and Opalia seems deliberate.

The Capitoline Temple of Ops became known in history as the place where Julius Caesar deposited a treasure of 700 million sesterces that Antony subsequently appropriated (Cicero, *Att.* 14.14.5, 16.14.4; *Phil.* 1.17, 2.35 and 93, 8.26; Vell. Pat. 2.60.4). It also figured in the evil omens of 44 B.C., when a gale broke open the doors (Obsequens 68). It is mentioned casually by Cicero (*Att.* 6.1.17; cf. also *Schol. Veron. ad Verg. Aen.* 2.714), then as the place of assembly for women at one point during a celebration of the Ludi Saeculares (*CIL* 6.32323.75 = *ILS* 5050), and as a place where priests gathered in A.D. 80 to vow the restoration of the Temple of Jupiter Capitolinus after it burned (*CIL* 6.2059.11). It was a suitable place for the display of military diplomata (*CIL* 16.3, 29). It may well have been the place where an official set of weights and measures was kept (see *ILS* 8637).

In the Fasti Vallenses we find for 25 August: OPIC, the festival of Ops Consiva, known also from other sources, which took place at the sacellum of this divinity in the Regia, followed by OPII IN CAPITOLIO, the only certain date in connection with the temple

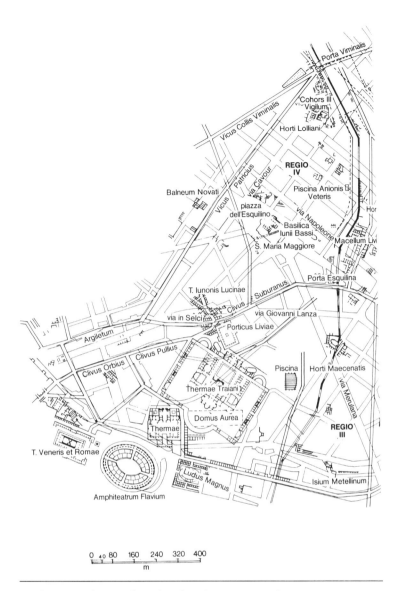

on the Capitoline. It has therefore been presumed that the temple was dedicated on this day (Degrassi 502–3), but the further inference that Ops *in Capitolio* is identical with Ops Consiva is unwarranted. The addition of the epithet Augusta on bronze weights (*ILS* 8637) is a bit puzzling; despite the early dedication of the altar of Ceres Mater et Ops Augusta, Ops Augusta does not appear on coins before the time of Antoninus Pius (*B. M. Coins, Rom. Emp.* 4.34 no. 221 and 202–3 nos. 1258–62), and there is no record of an imperial rebuilding of the Temple of Ops on the Capitoline.

Ops Consiva: see **Regia.**

Orbona, Fanum: the shrine, perhaps no more than an altar, of a divinity of sinister character associated

Figure 62
Mons Oppius and
Mons Cispius,
General Plan Showing
Known Remains of
Antiquity in Relation to
Modern Streets

with Febris and Mala Fortuna by Pliny (*HN* 2.16, a passage probably copied from Cicero, *Nat. D.* 3.63, where the text is mutilated). It is located by Pliny near the Aedes Larum (q.v.) on the Velia in summa Sacra Via, but no one else mentions it. For a discussion of the divinity and her character, see Roscher 2.209 (R. Peter) and the literature cited there.

Orcus, Aedes: a temple on the Palatine near the imperial palace that Elagabalus destroyed to make space for his Temple to Elagabalus (S.H.A. *Heliogab.* 1.6). The passage is corrupt, and *Orcus* is a conjecture for *orti* or *horti* in the manuscripts. Because this temple is otherwise unattested, some prefer correction to *Horta* (q.v.). The difficulties with every aspect of the question are enormous.

Orfienses: see **Lacus Orphei.**

Ovile (Ovilia): the enclosure forming part of the Villa Publica where the Romans assembled in the comitia centuriata to vote, to take the census, to hold military levies, and the like. The name was joking, from its forming part of the Villa Publica and some-

what resembling a sheep pen during assemblies. It was also called Saepta (Cicero, *Milon.* 41; cf. Servius *ad Ecl.* 1.33), but the name Ovile or Ovilia persisted even after it had been magnificently rebuilt as the Saepta Iulia (Livy 26.22.11; Lucan 2.197; Juvenal 6.529; Ausonius, *Gratiarum Actio* 3). It was an inaugurated templum throughout history (Cicero, *Rab. Perd.* 11).

Originally it was probably somewhat smaller than the Saepta Iulia, because Cicero was enormously impressed by the extent of the building Julius Caesar projected (*Att.* 4.16.8). But it was probably always proportionately long and narrow, permitting division into corridors corresponding in number in some way to the voting units of the assemblies, down which the voters passed to cross the *pontes* and cast their votes. The actual process of voting is shown on a coin of P. Nerva, dated by Crawford 113–112 B.C. (Crawford 292.1; *B. M. Coins, Rom. Rep.* 2.274 no. 526 and pl. 93.15). There is no reason to believe the Saepta Iulia did not occupy the site of the Ovile.

L. R. Taylor, *Roman Voting Assemblies* (Ann Arbor, Mich. 1966), 47–58, 78–113.

Pacati F(undus): mentioned in one inscription, *CIL* 6.9103 = 31895, a fragment of the edict of Tarracius Bassus of the late fourth century against fraudulent merchants and shopkeepers.

Paedagogium: see **Domus Augustiana.**

Paedagogium Puerorum a Capite Africae: see **Caput Africae.**

Pagus: see **Regio, Vicus, Pagus.**

Pagus Aventinensis: known from an inscription of the Augustan period found at Lanuvium (*CIL* 14.2105 = *ILS* 2676), in which among his titles a certain Castricius has listed Paganor(um) Aventin(ensium) XXVIvir. Evidently, at least for religious purposes, this pagus persisted as an organization into the imperial period. After the inclusion of the Aventine within the pomerium in the time of Claudius, it may have been dissolved.

Pagus Ianiculensis: known from two inscriptions found in laying the foundations for the tobacco works on Piazza Mastai, both of the republican period, one worked in a pavement of opus signinum (*CIL* 1².1000, 1001 = 6.2219 = ILS 6079, 2220 = *ILLRP* 699, 700). This indicates that the Transtiberim was divided into more than one pagus, because the name applied to it as a whole was Vaticanus Ager (q.v.).

Pagus Montanus: found in an inscription on a travertine cippus found in situ behind the tribune of the church of S. Vito on the Esquiline, northwest of Piazza Vittorio Emanuele (*CIL* 1².591 = 6.3823 = 31577 = *ILS* 6082). This is a senatus consultum of the second century B.C. with respect to abuse of public land belonging to the pagus and shows that the

districts beyond the Servian Walls continued to keep their organization as pagi relatively late. The boundaries of the Pagus Montanus cannot be set definitely. The tableland beyond the Servian Walls is unified from Porta Collina to Porta Esquilina, but the Quirinal and Viminal were always called *colles,* not *montes,* so Montanus has usually been interpreted as equivalent to Esquilinus, and the location of the cippus supports this.

Pagus Succusanus: according to Verrius Flaccus a *praesidium stativum,* the purpose of which was to come to the aid of the Esquiliae when the Gabines threatened that part of the city (Festus 402L). It was in, or at the head of, the valley between the Esquiline and the Caelian and gave the name Subura (q.v.) to this by the change of the third letter from *C* to *B.* Varro (*Ling.* 5.48) gives substantially the same information, but adds that M. Iunius Gracchanus of the second century B.C. explained the name *Subura* as deriving from *sub urbe.* All this appears to be learned speculation or invention. Gabii and Rome were on friendly terms from a very early period and, except for a brief period of hostilities in the time of Tarquinius Superbus, ending with the Battle of Lake Regillus in 493 B.C., almost always allies. It is hard to think that a permanent garrison would ever have been established against the Gabines. Because the abbreviation for the Tribus Suburana was SUC, this suggested an original form *Sucurana* and a derivation from *succurrere,* hence the Pagus Succusanus, an invention that was then used to explain *Subura* by a circular argument.

Palatinus, Mons (Figs. 58, 63): the central mesa-like hill of Rome toward which the others all seem to converge in an arc. It dominated the old Tiber crossing, by both ferry and bridge, and the traffic along the riverbank. It is an irregular quadrilateral in

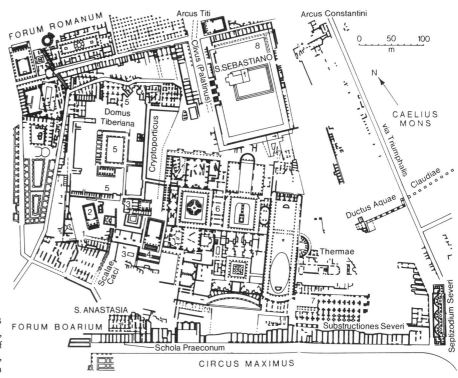

**Figure 63
Mons Palatinus,
General Plan of
Remains of Antiquity,
as Known**

shape and about 2 kilometers in circuit, with an area of about twenty-five acres. It was believed to be the site of the oldest settlement in Rome, and Tacitus (*Ann.* 12.24) gives an account of the pomerium of Romulus that would confirm this. The only natural approach to its summit is the throat up which the so-called Clivus Palatinus runs. It is also almost completely surrounded by water, on the north and northwest by the Cloaca and a small tributary of the Cloaca running from the slope of the Velia along the line of Nova Via and later culverted under Nova Via, and on the southeast and southwest by the Circus Maximus brook and its tributary running from the basin of the Colosseum between the Palatine and Caelian. Only the short stretch from Summa Sacra Via (see Sacra Via) to the Meta Sudans (q.v.) seems to have been undefended by running water.

The hill had two distinct crests, but the old distinction of these by the names Palatium and Cermalus has been disproved by Castagnoli, who has shown that the Cermalus was not a crest, but the southwest slope of the hill. The slopes were probably scarped, at least in places, and the hill was a natural stronghold improved by defense works along its brow. There was probably always a descent to the Forum Boarium for the convenience of those in charge of the Tiber ferry, if nothing else, and this may be represented by the Scalae Caci (q.v.).

The name Palatium, the usual form, differs from

the names of all the other hills of Rome, except Capitolium, in being a substantive. From it the odd early adjective Palatualis was formed (Ennius *ap. Varron. Ling.* 7.45) and shortened to Palatuar (Festus 476L). The first vowel varied in length, being usually short, but long in Martial (1.70.5, 9.101.13). Various derivations of the name were offered, all more or less fanciful; as in the case of many old place-names, the true derivation cannot be traced, and speculation is fruitless.

The fortifications of the Palatine are a very complicated problem (Säflund 3–17). In most places they have disappeared, thanks to later building, but around the west corner of the hill as far as the Scalae Caci there are remains of a wall of blocks of Fidenae and Grotta Oscura tufa in courses 0.58–0.62 m high that strongly resemble the Servian Walls and must be roughly contemporary with them, perhaps a little earlier than them in date. This must have been a separate system making an arx within the larger circuit. Just at the west corner inside the wall of blocks of Fidenae tufa are poor remains that may have belonged to an earlier fortification in smaller blocks of cappellaccio. These have been assigned a date in the sixth century, but the character of this system and its date are very uncertain. Since the discovery that the Servian Walls (see Murus Servii Tullii) were a closed circuit running through the Forum Boarium, the nature and importance of the walls of the Palatine have been called into question. The gates of the Palatine mentioned by Varro (*Ling.* 5.164–65; cf. Pliny, *HN* 3.66) were not gates in the fortifications, but gates in the pomerium, all lying at the base of the hill. The Porta Mugonia was the entrance to the Clivus Palatinus; the Porta Romana, or Romanula, was in the Velabrum at the foot of the Clivus Victoriae and just beyond its juncture with Nova Via, the river gate; and the Porta Ianualis was probably at the north corner of the hill where the stair now goes up from the Aedes Vestae, the approach to the Ianus Geminus. The names are interesting and puzzling. Those who give the Palatine a fourth gate (Pliny, *HN* 3.66) probably put it at the foot of the Scalae Caci, but we do not know its name. The only gate of real importance seems to have been the Porta Mugonia, and it was without architectural form, simply a place designation. Recent excavations by the University of Pisa under the direction of A. Carandini have brought to light remains of an archaic wall at the base of the hill along the line of Via Nova, but it is by no means clear that this was a fortification (*Archeo* 48 [February 1989]: 57–59 [A. M. Steiner and N. Terrenato]).

Among early remains on the Palatine are an archaic cistern or granary excavated in the rock and given a revetment of small blocks of cappellaccio with a layer of clay between this and the rock for insulation, plastered on the interior. It has a beehive roof with corbeled dome, and beside it was a well or entrance shaft. The cistern is 5.80 m deep and 2.80 m in diameter. Near it is a second open cistern, circular, similarly built of cappellaccio with a layer of clay between the wall and the rock, in which were found fragments of archaic pottery. These are on the edge of an *area sacra* at the west corner of the hill in which the most conspicuous monument is the Temple of the Magna Mater. Despite the increasing expansion of imperial palaces over the surface of the hill, and the enormous substructures that eventually carried them over the Clivus Victoriae and out toward the Circus Maximus, this area sacra was always respected. Many of the constructions are puzzling, and there certainly is not room here for all the early public buildings and sanctuaries we hear of on the Palatine, but most important are the cuttings for a group of primitive huts near the top of the Scalae Caci. These consist of oval floors that approach a rectangle with rounded corners in plan dug into the rock, in which post holes have been dug along the edge and in the center, sometimes with additional smaller holes for a porch at one end. The construction must have been wattle-and-daub over a framework of poles of varying dimensions with deeply overhanging thatched roofs, the drainage from which was carried off in apposite gutters carved in the rock. The ceramic material recovered in the excavation included some belonging to the Early Iron Age. This was traditionally the site of the hut of Faustulus and the Casa Romuli, and the importance of the area is confirmed by its relation to the Scalae Caci, which gave access to the Forum Boarium and the river. Of the shrines known to have existed on the Palatine, only those of the imperial period are likely to be found, because the hill was repeatedly swept by fire and in the great fire of Nero must have been among the worst devastated. Even so, except for the Temple of the Magna Mater, there is no agreement among scholars as to the identity of those we have, although Lugli's identification of that just northwest of the banquet hall of the Domus Augustiana as the Temple of Apollo Palatinus has now won wide acceptance. The great temple complex at the east corner of the hill around the little church of S. Sebastiano is especially puzzling, because it remains largely unexcavated, although its essential character is quite clear.

Although we hear of early residences on most of the hills of Rome, including the Capitoline, which was excluded from the city of the four regions, no king after Romulus is supposed to have lived on the Palatine. By the last century of the republic it had become the most fashionable place in Rome to have a house, although Rome was not a great follower of fashion in house locations. But the earliest republican house there of which we have record is that of Vitruvius Vaccus (see Domus, Vitruvius Vaccus) destroyed in 330 B.C. Except along the slopes of the hill, the republican planning and street system have been obliterated by later building, but Cicero's troubles in the recovery of his house after it had been burned by Clodius and a part dedicated as a shrine to Libertas have provided us with important evidence as to how tightly packed housing here was and also with the names of several owners. Q. Lutatius Catulus built a portico on the site of the house of M. Fulvius Flaccus (cos. 125 B.C.) and a house for himself. Cicero's house was next to this, with Metellus Celer's on the other side. Nearby were houses of M. Livius Drusus, P. Clodius Pulcher (let to M. Caelius Rufus), P. Sulla, Q. Cicero, and M. Licinius Calvus. The house of Hortensius later bought by Augustus has recently been identified on the southwest brow of the hill between the Scalae Caci and Lugli's Temple of Apollo. There is much to recommend this identification, but it lacks positive proof. This makes the identification of the so-called Casa di Livia difficult; it was certainly part of the imperial compound, and the decorations can be dated 30–20 B.C., but no likely occupant suggests himself, unless this is the rebuilding of part of the house of Mark Antony on the Palatine that Augustus gave to Agrippa and Messalla and that burned (Cass. Dio 53.27.5).

Tiberius seems to have covered most of the northwest lobe of the hill with his Domus Tiberiana (q.v.), and Caligula then extended this in the direction of Nova Via and the Forum Romanum. Nero seems to have built at least part of the Domus Transitoria on the southeast lobe, and Domitian and his successors, especially Septimius Severus, expanded the imperial possessions until the whole hill became in effect an imperial enclave. It continued to be the chief residence of the emperors in Rome until the time of Constantine, and one hears occasionally of additions, paintings illustrating games by Carinus (S.H.A. *Carin.* 19.1), and baths by Maxentius (Chron. 148), the latter recently identified.

At the time of the composition of the regionary catalogues in the fourth century, however, a considerable part of the slopes of the hill was apparently still occupied by vici (20), insulae (2644 or 2742), domus (88 or 89), and baths (36 or 44). After the removal of power to Constantinople the Palatine palace continued to be an imperial residence, and Constantius was received there on his state visit to Rome (Amm. Marc. 16.10.13). In the fifth century the emperors again took up residence there: Honorius (Claudian, *Sext. Cons. Hon.* 35), Valentinian III (*MGH Chron. Min.* 1.303, 2.27, 79, 86, 157), Lucius Severus (*MGH Chron. Min.* 2.158), Odoacer and Theodoric (*MGH Chron. Min.* 1.324; Cassiodorus, *Var.* 7.5.5). Narses died there (*MGH Chron. Min.* 1.336). Later functionaries of the bureaucracy used various parts of it; one hears especially of the *cartularius,* the head of the military archives in the seventh and eighth centuries, who lived near the Arch of Titus and who seems to have been succeeded by the head of the papal archives, for they were kept here, and the region became known as Palladium (eleventh to thirteenth centuries). There are a number of early churches around the foot of the hill (S. Anastasia, S. Teodoro, S. Maria Antiqua), but few on top (S. Maria in Pallara, S. Cesareo).

The hill was strangely abandoned in the later Middle Ages and is practically ignored in such documents as the Einsiedeln itinerary and the *Mirabilia.* It was rediscovered only in the sixteenth century, at which time it was covered with gardens and vineyards through which numerous ruins jutted. Between 1540 and 1550 the northern half, the Domus Tiberiana, came into the possession of Cardinal Alessandro Farnese, who converted it into magnificent gardens, still one of the showplaces of Rome. Excavations were carried out in the eighteenth century in the Domus Augustiana, and Boni conducted intensive work there in the first two decades of this century. Much of the slope around the west angle toward the Velabrum, from S. Teodoro to S. Anastasia,

was stripped away in 1934–1936 under Bartoli in a search for the Lupercal, which was without positive result. However, work here was not in general carried below the early imperial level. Large areas remain virtually untouched today, especially the Vigna Barberini at the east corner and the Domus Tiberiana. And deep excavations, while they have produced some fascinating discoveries under the Domus Augustiana, have been very limited in scope. There is a great deal yet to be done here. Most recently the area around the Temple of the Magna Mater (see Magna Mater, Aedes) has been the object of exhaustive work by the University of Rome under the direction of P. Pensabene (1977–1987). See also Pectuscum Palati.

HJ 29–111; Lugli 1946, 393–420; *ArchCl* 16 (1964): 173–99 (F. Castagnoli); Nash 2.163–69; *RFIC* 105 (1977): 15–19 (F. Castagnoli); *RendLinc,* ser. 8.34 (1979): 331–47 (F. Castagnoli); *AJA* 84 (1980): 93–96 (H. B. Evans); *REL* 65 (1987): 89–114 (M. Royo); *CEFR* 98 (1987): 771–79 (G. Carettoni).

Palatium Licinianum: the name given in several medieval documents to a complex on the Esquiline near the church of S. Bibiana, at the crossing of Via Giolitti and Via Cairoli (*Mirabilia:* Jordan 2.640 = VZ 3.60; LPD 1.249–50 [Simplicius, A.D. 468–483] = VZ 2.242). This has naturally led to association with the Horti Liciniani (q.v.), the emperor Licinius Gallienus's villa of uncertain location, and it has been conjectured that by the fourth century the whole area from Via Tiburtina to Via Labicana and from the Servian Walls to the Aurelian Walls had come into the possession of the emperors. This seems improbable, but the zone is very poorly known archaeologically.

HJ 359; Lugli 1938, 478–80.

Palatium Sessorianum: see **Sessorium.**

Pales, Templum: a temple that M. Atilius Regulus built after his victory over the Salentini in 267 B.C. (Florus 1.15.20; Schol. Veron. and Bern. *ad Verg. Georg.* 3.1). There is no indication of where this temple stood, and it is at least possible that it was not even in Rome. But the note in the Fasti Antiates Maiores for 7 July, PALIBUS II (*NSc* 1921, 101–2; Degrassi 479), probably gives us a date for the anniversary of the temple. The plural may be explained as an allusion to the nature of the divinity, Pales usually appearing as feminine, but occasionally as masculine (Roscher 3.277–78 [G. Wissowa]). A double temple is also possible, but less probable. Attempts to take the Parilia on 21 April away from Pales on the grounds that she is not mentioned in connection with that date in any of the fasti and that her festival is now established on an entirely different date are mistaken (see, e.g., Ovid, *Fast.* 4.721–806). Ironically enough, the general inclination to put this temple on the Palatine seems to derive from the association of the Parilia with the birthday of Rome. Because it was a victory monument and Atilius enjoyed a triumph, it is more likely to have stood somewhere along the route of the triumphal procession, in the Campus Martius perhaps, or on the Aventine above the Circus Maximus.

Pallacinae: a name that appears in classical literature only in Cicero (*Rosc. Am.* 18, 132) as the name of a vicus and baths before which (*ad balneas*) Sex. Roscius was killed on his way back from dinner. In early Christian sources the name appears several times (cf., e.g., HCh 291–92, 308, and the sources cited in HJ 556); these establish that a district near the church of S. Marco was known as Pallacinae. This is probably a name surviving from antiquity, but the fragments of the Marble Plan (Rodriguez pl. 22) suggest such a welter of streets and houses in this area that identification of a particular vicus is impossible.

Palma Aurea: see **Ad Palmam.**

Ad Palmam: a name that is found in late antiquity, beginning not before the fifth or sixth century, for the area between the Curia Senatus and the Arch of Septimius Severus, where the emperor made public appearances and addresses (*MGH Chron. Min.* 1.324 for A.D. 517 [Anon. Vales.]; Jordan 1.2.259 and citations). It was the area earlier known as Ad Tria Fata (q.v.) and a favorite place for the erection of imperial statues and monuments of appropriate dignity. Presumably some emperor had presented the city with a palm of gilded bronze as a symbol of the eternity and supremacy of Rome. It might have been regarded as an acceptable replacement for the Altar of Victoria (see Victoria, Ara) that Gratian removed definitively from the Curia in A.D. 382.

Palus Capreae: see **Caprae Palus.**

Pantheon (Fig. 64): a temple that Agrippa originally erected, together with his baths, the Basilica Neptuni, and the Saepta Iulia (qq.v.), in a group in the Campus Martius. The relationships among these buildings are not at all clear, and their functions seem to have been very different from one another, but all seem to have been major monuments. Because Julius Caesar is credited with having conceived the

plan of the Saepta Iulia, it may be that more of the original scheme belongs to him. The inscription on the façade (*CIL* 6.896 = 31196 = *ILS* 129: M.AGRIPPA.L.F.COS.TERTIUM.FECIT) dates the Pantheon to 27 B.C., but Dio (53.27.2) implies that it was finished in 25 and goes on to say that it might have been given the name Pantheon because of the many statues of gods it contained, but he believed it was due to the resemblance of the dome to the dome of the heavens, which shows that he did not know the history of the building. Dio also reports that Agrippa wished to include a statue of Augustus and call the building Augusteum and, when Augustus refused him permission, included a statue of Divus Iulius and put statues of Augustus and himself in the porch. From this it appears that the design of the building was in honor of Augustus's divine forebears, especially Mars and Venus, a forerunner of the Temple of Mars Ultor. To what extent Dio was relying on historical documents, and to what extent he was using his own firsthand knowledge of the building, is not clear. In the ears of the statue of Venus were earrings made of the halves of a pearl of Cleopatra (Pliny, *HN* 9.121; Macrobius, *Sat.* 3.17.17), and in the pediment were noteworthy sculptures, which Pliny (*HN* 36.38) says were not sufficiently appreciated because of the height at which they were displayed. They were the work of Diogenes of Athens, and his caryatids on the columns of the building were considered especially fine, while the capitals of the columns were of bronze (Pliny, *HN* 34.13). This information has given rise to much discussion of the architecture. The simplest solution of the problem is to see the pronaos as columnar with Corinthian (?) capitals of bronze supported by caryatid figures of marble.

The Pantheon of Agrippa burned in the fire of Titus in A.D. 80 (Cass. Dio 66.24.2) and was restored by Domitian (Chron. 146, Hieron. *a. Abr.* 2105). In the time of Trajan it was struck by lightning and burned again (Orosius 7.12.5; Hieron. *a. Abr.* 2127). The restoration then carried out by Hadrian (S.H.A. *Hadr.* 19.10) seems to have been an entirely new building, probably on an entirely new plan. It is dated by brick-stamps after A.D. 126, and even the foundations have produced clear evidence of being Hadrianic. Work by Antoninus Pius (S.H.A. *Ant. Pius* 8.2), if it was not a completion of Hadrian's building, must have been a minor repair. And evidence for the restoration of Septimius Severus and Caracalla recorded in an inscription on the architrave (*CIL* 6.896 = *ILS* 129) is elusive. On 12 January A.D. 59 the Arval Brethren met in the Pantheon (*CIL* 6.2041 = *ILS* 229). For Hadrian it was one of three favorite places in Rome where he held court

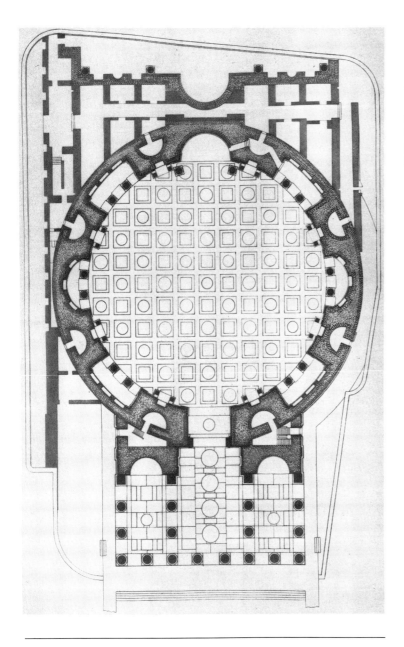

longs to this complex, an entrance arch. Access to the court was apparently always possible through lateral doors as far south as the pronaos.

The pronaos resembles that of a classical temple with a triangular pediment, except that the pediment is exceptionally high and shallow to help hide the dome behind it. One originally mounted to the pronaos by steps. The columns were of granite, eight gray ones in front, eight rose ones behind, with Corinthian capitals of white marble, finely carved. They are arranged to make three aisles, one leading to the main door and one to a large apsidal niche to either side of the door. A thick sprinkling of nail holes in the shallow pediment indicates that the decoration was in bronze, possibly a great wreath, while the ceiling of the pronaos was also bronze, hung from trusses of great bronze beams, arranged as three vaults over the three aisles. The great bronze doors of the main entrance, embellished with handsome bosses and given a deep transom filled with grillwork, were recast in the sixteenth century, but with fairly scrupulous attention to the original design.

Between the pronaos and the rotunda is a rectangular intermediate block that rises high above the pronaos. It carries some of the moldings of the pronaos in continuation, but it adds a deep attic storey decorated with a separate pediment echoing that of the pronaos. This effectively hides the view of the dome for anyone approaching from the forecourt but seems awkwardly separated from the pronaos. In it are arranged stairs of triangular plan by which the public could climb to the roof and chambers in the upper portion like those in the attic of a triumphal arch. It seems likely that the whole design of this element derives from the triumphal arch and that it was intended to carry an elaborate program of statuary that would further have helped to conceal the dome.

The rotunda is a great drum of brick-faced concrete, 6.20 m thick, into which from the interior open seven large niches and the entrance throat, the niches being alternately curved and as rectangular as fitting the curve of the drum admits, while between these are eight semicircular rooms that open to the exterior. So effectively the drum is a complicated serpentine wall. In the second storey are unfloored chambers above the interior niches provided with windows filled with grillwork through which light filtered down into the niches, changing with the movement of the sun. The niches in the ground storey are given pairs of columns to screen them from the central space, except for the entrance throat and the niche opposite this. In the latter the columns are moved to flank the niche, and the cornice is broken forward to emphasize the apse. Between each pair of niches is an aedicula, now converted into an altar, a

Figure 64
Pantheon, Floor Plan with Adjacencies (1 cm = 6.5m)

(Cass. Dio 69.7.1). For Ammianus (16.10.14) it was one of the wonders of Rome, and it is listed in the regionary catalogues in Regio IX.

The existing building faces due north and consists of a pronaos, an intermediate block, and a rotunda. It was preceded by a colonnaded forecourt, rather narrow in proportion to its length, but the length and the question of monumental access from the north are debatable. The arch that many topographers have wished to place in the center of this court, the Arcus Pietatis of the Anonymous Magliabechianus (Urlichs 155; VZ 4.122), should be, if it be-high base brought forward and carrying a pair of columns that support a pediment, either triangular or lunate. The marbles used are very rich and varied, almost the full range of the imperial repertory, except for Oriental alabaster. The pavement is of large discs and squares of colored marble, especially granite and porphyry, framed in contrasting squares. Of the revetment of the upper storey, only a portion in the southwest quadrant shows the original design, the whole having been removed and replaced with a new design in 1747. Originally this was much less plastic, but richly colored, a deep plain band surmounted by rather simple rectangular windows with four shallow pilasters between each pair of them, finished at the top with a simple cornice.

At this height on the interior the curve of the dome takes off, a perfect half-sphere equal to the height of the drum that supports it, the diameter 43.20 m (144 Roman feet). It is coffered with five rings of square coffers that gradually diminish in size and must originally have been colored and ornamented with bronze mounts or sheathing. At the top is a circular opening, 9 m in diameter, finished with a curious bronze ring with hooks for attachments. This opening, the oculus, is the only source of light but entirely adequate throughout the year.

On the exterior the drum rises another storey vertically through the height of one and one-half rows of coffers and contains a series of chambers with travertine-framed doors accessible by a wide cornice that once ran around the whole on the exterior and must have been a promenade from which to look over the Campus Martius. The chambers may even have been let out as shops. Above this the exterior of the dome rises in a series of seven steps, the thickness of the shell diminishing gradually. The fabric is of concrete in which the aggregate is of progressively lighter material, beginning with travertine, then tufas of different weight, terracotta, and, finally, pumice at the top. In the lowest part of the dome is a complicated series of relieving arches corresponding to the architecture below, but these do not continue higher, and no one knows how the dome was cast; it is in effect a dome of a single piece and has often been described as a teacup. The three divisions of the building—pronaos, intermediate block, and rotunda—stand structurally entirely free of one another, but there is every indication that this was only because the building was so daringly innovative, and that they were all designed together.

Although the brickwork of the drum is especially fine, it shows no trace of stucco finish and may never have had any; it was certainly not revetted with marble. The pronaos and the intermediate block were faced with marble and bronze, but the drum

was not intended to be seen. In back it was hidden by a series of parallel chambers with heavy brick-faced walls filling the space between it and the Basilica Neptuni, another Hadrianic building to the south. These must have acted as buttresses as well. Along the east side the wall of the Saepta Iulia came tangent to the drum. On the west we do not know what there may have been, perhaps the Nemus Thermarum of Agrippa. But it is quite clear that there was no planned exterior prospect of the Pantheon, except from the forecourt that preceded it.

In A.D. 609 Pope Boniface IV rededicated the Pantheon as the church of S. Maria ad Martyres (LPD 1.317; VZ 2.251). Constantius II removed the gilt bronze tiles of the roof in 663 (LPD 1.343; VZ 2.255); it was then apparently allowed to decay until Pope Gregory III (731–741) repaired the fabric and sheathed the roof with lead (LPD 1.419; VZ 2.264). By the twelfth century an interesting collection of antiquities had been gathered in the piazza in front of it (cf., e.g., the drawing of van Heemskerck reproduced in Nash 2.174). At some unknown time the two rear columns of the east front of the pronaos collapsed, and the northeast corner was then repaired with brickwork. In the seventeenth century Pope Urban VIII replaced the corner column with one of red granite, and Pope Alexander VII replaced the others using two columns of gray granite from the Thermae Alexandrinae. In 1270 a small Romanesque campanile was built at the apex of the pronaos; this survived into the sixteenth century. In the seventeenth century Pope Urban VIII took the bronze beams from the roof of the pronaos, and Bernini added the pair of bell towers known as "the asses' ears" to the intermediate block. These were not removed until the late nineteenth century. The building had a very rich and complicated history in the Renaissance and thereafter that lies outside the scope of this dictionary. It is still a church.

The podium of an earlier building, presumably Agrippa's Pantheon, has been found and mapped. It lies about 2.50 m under the pronaos of Hadrian's building, a rectangular edifice, 43.76 m wide and 19.82 m deep, facing south, so the front columns of Hadrian's Pantheon stand over its back wall, while the doorways almost coincide. The pronaos of Agrippa's building was only 21.26 m wide, so it had a T-shaped plan like that of the Temple of Concordia. A succession of marble pavements found beneath the floor of the rotunda without clear association with architecture has been taken to represent the vicissitudes of the Pantheon between Agrippa and Hadrian. But it is quite clear that whatever ideological connection there may have been between Agrippa's Pantheon and Hadrian's, there was no architec-

tural similarity whatsoever. The seven main niches have often been suggested to be for the seven planetary divinities of the week, which is an attractive notion, given the design of the building and the plan to honor Augustus, but there is simply no proof, and it does not help us to identify divinities to fill the numerous remaining spaces and subsidiary niches.

Nash 2.170–75; *BdA* 53 (1968): 73–76 (G. Gullini); K. de Fine Licht, *The Rotunda in Rome* (Copenhagen 1968); W. L. MacDonald, *The Pantheon: Design, Meaning, and Progeny* (London 1976); *Quaderni dell'Istituto di Storia dell'Architettura*, n.s. fasc. 13 (1981): 3–10 (G. Martinez), 10–18 (M. Pelletri); *AnalRom*, suppl. 10 (1983): 41–46 (F. Coarelli), 109–18 (L. Cozza); *BullCom* 89 (1984): 55–64 (M. E. Micheli); *ArtB* 68 (1986): 24–34 (P. Hutchinson and R. Mark); *Architectura* 18 (1988): 121–22 (H. Saalman); *JSAH* 49 (1990): 22–43 (W. C. Loercke).

Parianenses: inhabitants of a district known only from a single inscription (*CIL* 6.9103 = 31895), a fragment of the edict of Tarracius Bassus against fraudulent merchants and shopkeepers.

Parthorum: houses of great distinction with which Septimius Severus enriched some of his friends (Aur. Vict., *Epit.* 20.6). They are said to have been comparable to the house of Lateranus. They are listed in the regionary catalogues in Regio XII and may be presumed to have stood in a group, but there is no further evidence for their location. An attempt to identify them with ruins just northwest of the Baths of Caracalla (*BullCom* 44 [1916]: 204 [R. Lanciani]) seems to rest on very little evidence (G. Lugli, *La*

zona archeologica di Roma [Rome 1925], 278–79). The explanation of the name is unknown.

Pavor et Pallor, Fanum: a shrine said to have been vowed by Tullus Hostilius, together with a college of Salii (presumably the Salii Collini), at a crisis when the Albans deserted the Romans in a battle against the Fidenates and Veientes (Livy 1.27.7). This is then not mentioned again, but it seems likely that a shrine in the headquarters of the Salii Collini on the Quirinal is meant. The Curia Saliorum was probably in the vicinity of the Temple of Quirinus (Dion. Hal. 2.70.1), and the shrine of Pavor et Pallor may have been either the curia itself or an aedicula contained in it.

Pax, Templum (Figs. 65, 66): the great Temple of Peace, in effect the third in the sequence of imperial fora, begun by Vespasian after the capture of Jerusalem in A.D. 71 and dedicated in 75 (Suetonius, *Vesp.* 9.1; Josephus, *BellIud* 7.5.7 [158]; Cass. Dio 65.15.1; Aur. Vict, *Caes.* 9.7, *Epit.* 9.8). Statius ascribes the dedication of the cult statue to Domitian (*Silv.* 4.3.17), which may have been a replacement for the original one. In the time of Aulus Gellius (5.21.9; 16.8.2) the complex contained a well-known public library, the Bibliotheca Pacis. In the temple were placed many of the spoils of Jerusalem and works of famous Greek artists, including many that had been used to decorate the Domus Aurea of Nero (Josephus, *BellIud* 7.5.7 [158–61]; Pliny, *HN* 12.94, 34.84, 35.102–3 and 109, 36.27 and 58; Pausanias 6.9.3; Juvenal 9.23). Pliny considered it, the Basilica Paulli, and the Forum Augustum the three most beautiful buildings in Rome, equal to any in the world.

Just before the death of Commodus, presumably in 191, it burned (Cass. Dio 73.24.1; Herodian 1.14.2–3). It must have been immediately restored, for it continued to be one of the finest buildings in the city and a library (S.H.A. *Tyr. Trig.* 31.10; Amm. Marc. 16.10.14). It gave the name Templum Pacis to the fourth region of Augustan Rome. In 408 it was the site of uncanny rumbling of the earth for seven days (*MGH Chron. Min.* 2.69 [Marcell. Comit.]). For Procopius in the sixth century (*BellGoth* 4.21.11–12) it was a thing of the past, although fountains and statuary from it still survived.

The plan is known from fragments of the Marble Plan (*FUR* pl. 20; Rodriguez pl. 12), which show it as a colonnaded square, about 145 m long, the colonnade addorsed to the wall on the northwest (entrance) side, but the wall here is apt to have been moved at the time of the creation of Domitian's Forum Transitorium. In each of the lateral walls open two small rectangular exedras. One of these, built into the thirteenth-century Torre dei Conti, is still preserved. The important end of the complex was at the southeast, where a great axial hall, rectangular, but with an apse containing a base, possibly for a statue of Pax, is screened from the colonnade in front of it by only a row of columns. These columns and those in the colonnade responding to them are shown as different from the rest. Great rectangular rooms continue the line to either side. One or two of these must have been the library, and that south of the axial room carried on a later wall built across it to divide it the slabs of the Marble Plan (Forma Urbis Romae), fragments of which first came to light in May and June 1562. It is of the highest importance for the study of the topography of ancient Rome, but its purpose in antiquity and the meaning of its presence in this building have been much discussed, because, although it is on slabs of marble and when whole was clearly a showpiece, it is rather clumsily and inaccurately executed. It seems likely that by the time of the Severans and probably from the time of its construction, the Templum Pacis was in part used for the municipal administration under the praefectus urbi (Anderson 116–17).

In the open area of the colonnaded square appear mysterious chains of rectangles, usually interpreted as garden beds, sometimes as topiary trees or hedges. Neither explanation is satisfactory. Similar features appear in the court of the Temple of Divus Claudius (see Claudius, Divus, Templum) and the Adonaea (q.v.), somewhat different but probably related features in connection with the Temple of Hercules Musarum (see Hercules Musarum, Aedes). Access to the Templum Pacis is perhaps the most difficult problem connected with it. So far as we know, there was no monumental approach and no emphasis on the axis of the complex. It is presumed that there must have been an important approach from the Forum Romanum, and it used to be believed that this was through the hall now made into the church of SS. Cosma e Damiano. The approach is now believed more likely to have been through the throat between the Basilica Paulli and the Temple of Antoninus and Faustina, the Corneta, but there is no evidence. No substantial part of the complex has ever been excavated.

The complex was known as Templum Pacis until late antiquity, despite its clearly being another in the sequence of imperial fora. Perhaps this is because at first it was separated from the others by the Argiletum and was the creation of a member of a new dynasty. Pliny (*HN* 36.27) calls the whole complex *Pacis opera*. It is called Forum Pacis by Ammianus, Forum Vespasiani by Symmachus (*Epist.*

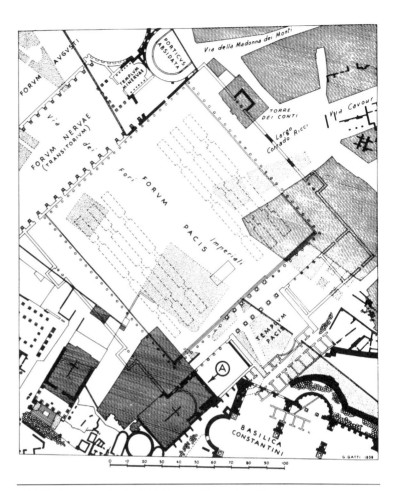

Figure 66
Templum Pacis, Plan, as Known

10.78 = Migne, *PL* 18.403), Forum Vespasiani Pacis by Polemius Silvius (VZ 1.309), and Forum Pacis by Marcellinus Comes (*MGH Chron. Min.* 2.69).

HJ 2–7; *FUR* 73; Rodriguez 1.95; *AJA* 86 (1982): 101–10 (J. C. Anderson); Anderson 101–18.

Pax Augusta, Ara (Fig. 42): an altar decreed by the senate *ad Campum Martium* on Augustus's return from Spain and Gaul, 4 July 13 B.C. (Degrassi 176), on which the magistrates, priests, and Vestal Virgins were to offer annual sacrifice (Augustus, *RG* 12). The altar was dedicated on 30 January 9 B.C. (Ovid, *Fast.* 1.709–22). Which ceremony, if either, is represented on the reliefs of the altar and altar screen is much disputed. The altar is shown on coins of Nero (*B. M. Coins, Rom. Emp.* 1.271–72 nos. 360–65) but is not mentioned elsewhere in literature or inscriptions.

The altar stood just west of Via Lata (Via Flaminia) near the Horologium Solare Augusti (q.v.) with which it may have been brought into relation (*RömMitt* 83 [1976]: 319–65 [E. Buchner]), but otherwise isolated, under Palazzo Fiano at the corner of Via del Corso and Via in Lucina. Fragments of the decorative and figurative sculptures began to come to light in quantity as early as 1568 and in the course of time were scattered among numerous collections as far away as Paris and Vienna. More were found in an extensive work of consolidation under the palazzo in 1859. Systematic excavations were carried out under the palazzo in 1903 and resulted in the recovery of more fragments and an accurate plan of the platform on which the altar stood, but had to be abandoned because of ground water and the precarious condition of the palazzo. In 1937–1938, thanks to a technique of freezing the waterlogged soil surrounding the area, it became possible to excavate the remains completely and to rebuild the foundations of the palazzo. Thus everything recoverable has now been recovered. The altar was then carefully studied and reconstructed, using casts when the original pieces could not be obtained, although not in its original location or orientation. Recently work of cleaning and restoration has produced more information about the technique and quality of the work.

The altar faced east on an almost square platform level with Via Lata, but because of the slope of the land had to be approached by a broad stair on the west. The platform was bounded by a high screen wall with broad axial doors with slightly tapering frames, and the screen was embellished with sculptures inside and out. The coins of Nero show acroteria at the corners that are missing today. The altar itself, which nearly fills the interior, stands on a base of four steps, U-shaped so the officiating priest was surrounded by the altar table. Only one of the remarkable flanks of this table has been found, an elegant scrolled gable above a narrow frieze carved with a procession and terminating in winged lions. One side of the relief shows a suovetaurilia sacrifice in procession, and the other shows the Vestal Virgins and pontifex maximus. Presumably when complete the altar frieze showed the annual sacrifice in idealized form. Only poor fragments of the rest survive, but there are also a few fragments of another figured frieze at larger scale believed to have decorated the base of the altar.

The altar screen is divided into two zones horizontally, inside and out, and divided into panels by Corinthian pilasters at the corners and doorways. On the exterior the lower zone is filled with rich scrolls of acanthus peopled with small animals and birds. Above this on the east and west ends are allegorical panels flanking the doorways. These are commonly identified as Italia or Pax (often called Terra Mater or Tellus) and Roma (with the Genius figures of the senate and the Roman people, or Honos and Virtus)

on the east, and Aeneas sacrificing the white sow to the Penates and Faustulus discovering the twins Romulus and Remus at the Lupercal on the west. About the western pair there is much doubt, because there are only very poor remains of the Lupercal panel, and the iconography of the Aeneas panel is very difficult.

The long sides showed processions, or a procession in two companies, converging toward the door on the west. That on the north is made up of men wearing the toga and wreathed for a sacrifice, some of them *capite velato,* accompanied by camilli with various sacrificial implements, followed by a group in which women and children are prominent. The first part of this procession has been thought to represent some of the major priesthoods of Rome, the Septemviri, Augurs, and Quindecimviri. On the opposite side is a similar procession. The first two slabs are extremely fragmentary. Then comes a group in which Augustus appears, wreathed and capite velato, surrounded by lictors, followed by the Flamens accompanied by camilli with sacrificial implements. There then follows a large company of men, women, and children, most of the members young, at least one man in military dress, and at least one child not togate and of a decidedly alien appearance.

The usual interpretation makes this procession the imperial family and household accompanied by the major priesthoods, those instructed by the senate to perform annual sacrifice here. This is also usually read as the immortalization of the ceremony performed on 4 July 13 B.C. Against this must be observed that only Augustus can be identified positively, while all others seem rather idealized figures with an emphasis on youth and beauty in the tradition of the Parthenon frieze, to which this is clearly heavily indebted.

On the interior the lower half of the screen is in narrow vertical rectangular panels, alternately raised and sunk with the effect of wooden paling, crowned with an anthemion. In the upper zone are rich garlands of fruit and leaves swung in loops between bucrania, to the horns of which they are attached by fluttering ribbons. The loops made by the garlands are filled with paterae, which float free.

In the time of Hadrian the ground level in this part of the Campus Martius was raised in an effort to make it more suitable for construction and brought up nearly level with the top of the lower frieze of the altar screen. Thereafter the altar stood in a well, the edge protected by a coping and a fence.

G. Moretti, *Ara Pacis Augustae,* 2 vols. (Rome 1948); *CAR* 2-G, 85 pp. 164–68; E. Simon, *Ara Pacis Augustae* (Tübingen 1967); Nash 1.63–73;

RömMitt 83 (1976): 319–65 (E. Buchner); E. La Rocca, *Ara Pacis Augustae, in occasione del restauro della fronte orientale* (Rome 1983); *RömMitt* 92 (1985): 221–34 (R. De Angelis Bertolotti); *Numen* 33 (1986): 3–32 (G. Freibergs, C. S. Littleton, and O. Stratynski); *QITA* 10 (1988): 10–14 (E. Tortorici).

Pectuscum Palati: mentioned once by Festus (232L) and defined as "the part of the city that Romulus *obversam posuit*, in that part in which lay the majority of the Ager Romanus, toward the sea, and where the city was most easily approached, whereas the Ager Etruscus was separated from the Ager Romanus by the Tiber, and the other neighboring cities *(civitates)* had hills for defense *(colles aliquot haberent oppositos)*." The text is perplexing, but if it is toward the sea, a gentle approach to the city (after its enlargement by inclusion of Titus Tatius and the Sabines?), and in some way related to the Palatine, we are probably dealing with the slope from Summa Sacra Via to the Meta Sudans, and everything hinges on our interpretation of the word *obversam*. It does not seem possible to make *obversam posuit* mean "fortified," and there is no trace of fortification. Perhaps it means "made a no man's land," "excluded from habitation." A derivation of *pectuscum* from *pectus* might support this.

Penates Dei, Aedes: on the Velia on the site formerly occupied by the house of Tullus Hostilius (Varro *ap. Non.* 852L; Solinus 1.22), not far from the Forum Romanum on a short street leading to the Carinae (Dion. Hal. 1.68.1). What is meant must be the stretch of Sacra Via leading from Summa Sacra Via to the Lucus Streniae, as it is the only street connecting the Velia and Carinae. According to Varro (Donatus *ad Ter., Eun.* 256), the stair of the Penates was built with money received from the sale of the property of Numerius Equitius Cuppes and Manius Macellus (see Macellum). Presumably an impressive stair led up to the temple, but one might also think of a stepped street leading from the temple to the Carinae. It is first mentioned in the list of sanctuaries of the Argei as the sixth station in the Palatine region (Varro, *Ling.* 5.54).

Dionysius (1.68.1) describes the temple in detail as a small shrine containing images of two seated youths in military dress with spears. An inscription identified these as the Penates (cf. Servius *ad Aen.* 3.12), and they were generally believed to be Trojan gods, though some said Samothracian. They seem to have been the Dioscuri in a different guise, and their names were secret. They are shown on coins (*B. M.*

Coins, Rom. Rep. 1.192–95 nos. 1204–30, 202–3 nos. 1314–26, 522 no. 4032; Crawford 307/1a and b, 312/1, 455/2a).

The temple was struck by lightning in 167 B.C. (Livy 45.16.5). Augustus restored it (*RG* 19). The location of the temple is much disputed. Because the enormous buildings of Nero's Domus Aurea, Domitian's Horrea Piperataria, Hadrian's Temple of Venus et Roma, and Maxentius's Basilica Nova (Basilica Constantini) quite changed the character of the Velia, requiring the destruction or removal of everything in their way, and the cutting of the Via dei Fori Imperiali completed the obliteration of the hill, we have no good fixed points by which to orient ourselves. Coarelli (Coarelli 1983, passim, but especially 49) would put the original location under the western apse of the Basilica Constantini and see the Templum Romuli as a Maxentian replacement for the Temple of the Penates, an identification Ashby had called "ridiculous." I prefer to put the temple on the highest part of the Velia, because of the strike by lightning, because the stair of approach seems to have been a conspicuous feature, and because a royal residence would probably have been in a prominent location. In which case the Temple of the Penates was probably destroyed in the fire of Nero and thereafter gave way to the Domus Aurea.

BullCom 92 (1987–88): 293–98 (E. Rodriguez Almeida).

Pentapylon: listed in the regionary catalogues in Regio X between the Temple of Apollo Ramnusius and the Domus Augustiana et Tiberiana. It has been thought to be a monumental entrance to the temple or the gateway to the temple precinct of Vigna Barberini, where one sees the ruin of a grand approach, but neither identification has other support or seems apt to be right.

Petra Scelerata: *iuxta amphitheatrum*, used frequently by the hagiographers, but by no one else (e.g., Acta SS. Eusebii, Marcelli, Hippolyti). It was next to the Colosseum in the direction of the Lacus Pastorum (q.v.), so probably in the direction of S. Clemente. It seems to have been simply a stone of no special character on which numerous Christian saints were believed to have been beheaded. Other stones claiming this distinction are shown preserved in at least two churches in Rome (see *Analect. Bolland.* 16 [1897]: 209–52 [Delehaye], especially 230–32).

Petronia Amnis: a brook that had its origin at the Fons Cati (see Cati Fons) on the west slope of the

Quirinal, now known as the Acqua S. Felice, in the courtyard of the Palazzo Quirinale close to the Porta Salutaris. It flowed west to Via Lata and is apparently represented by culverting under the southern stretch of Via Lata; it may have determined in a general way the location of that thoroughfare. Under Piazza Venezia the brook turned west again and is represented by culverting under Via di S. Marco and along the north side of the Theatrum Balbi, just beyond which it turned south again at almost a right angle and ran to join the ancient sewer known as the Chiavicone dell'Olmo, which shows construction analogous with that of the Cloaca Maxima, presumably part of the overhaul of Rome's water and sewer systems carried out by Agrippa. The brook emptied into the Tiber opposite the northwest end of the island. In its upper stretches it was still open in the time of Festus (296L), presumably running in an open trench alongside the street, and magistrates had to take the *auspicia peremnia* before crossing it to preside at assemblies in the Campus Martius. It was the boundary of the city auspices and probably originally the boundary distinguishing the Prata Flaminia from the Campus Martius, although it must have crossed the Circus Flaminius near its northwest end.

The brook is often said to be joined by the Aqua Sallustiana, which is certainly not the case. It is also said to be responsible for the Caprae Palus in the area of the Pantheon; that is at best highly unlikely.

P. Narducci, *Sulle fognature della città di Roma* (Rome 1889), 34–39.

Phrygianum: listed in the regionary catalogues in Regio XIV (spelled Frigianum) and identified by the discovery in 1609 in excavating for the foundations of the façade of the new basilica of S. Pietro of a group of marble altars dedicated to the Magna Mater and divinities associated with her (*CIL* 6.497–504 = 30779; *ILS* 4145, 4147–51, 4153), some of which had been deliberately smashed by iconoclasts. These carry consular dates running from A.D. 305 to A.D. 390 and mention completion of the taurobolium and criobolium by devotees. The temple must have stood nearby, and further finds indicate that it was near the southeast corner of the basilica, within the Circus Gaii et Neronis, suggestively close to the spina. An inscription on an altar to the Magna Mater found at Lyon in France (*CIL* 13.1751 = *ILS* 4131) of L. Aemilius Carpus, a dendrophorus, adds *vires excepit et a Vaticano transtulit*. It is dated A.D. 160. This indicates that the Vatican shrine was an important cult center already at that time, and we know that Antoninus Pius favored the cult (M. J. Vermaseren, *Cybele and Attis* [London 1977], 179–80). So far as we know, the ceremonies of taurobolium and criobolium were performed in Rome only at the Vat-

ican temple, never on the Palatine. It is interesting that the temple should have prospered as long as it did in close proximity to the tomb and later basilica of S. Pietro.

CAR 1-G, 62 pp. 63–64.

Pietas, Aedes (1): *in Circo Flaminio,* a temple that was struck by lightning in 94 B.C. (Obsequens 54; Cicero, *Div.* 1.98); its anniversary was the Kalends of December (Fasti Amiternini; Degrassi 533). This temple is almost certainly identical with the next one.

Pietas, Aedes (2): *in Foro Holitorio,* a temple vowed by M'. Acilius Glabrio on the eve of the Battle of Thermopylae in 191 B.C. and begun by him, but dedicated by his son of the same name, created duovir for the purpose, in 181 B.C. (Livy 40.34.4–6; Val. Max. 2.5.1); it contained a gilded equestrian statue of the elder Glabrio, the first such statue seen in Rome (Livy 40.34.4–6; Val. Max. 2.5.1). Julius Caesar destroyed it in 44 B.C. to make space for the theater that afterward became the Theatrum Marcelli (Pliny, *HN* 7.121; Cass. Dio 43.49.3). Because this temple is almost certainly the same as the preceding one and the anniversary of the Kalends of December is still observed according to the Fasti Amiternini dated after A.U.C. 775, it seems likely that Caesar simply moved the temple, in which case it is likely to be the little Doric temple in travertine of which six columns built into the south wall of the church of S. Nicola in Carcere survive (Fig. 38). On the basis of what survives and a number of drawings made by architects in the Renaissance, it can be reconstructed as peripteral, hexastyle, and with eleven columns on the flanks. It was frontal in the Roman manner, raised on a podium 2.52 m high, with a stair of approach only at the east end. The pronaos was four intercolumniations deep. The cella had walls of peperino and a doorframe of white marble. The travertine columns are at present unfluted but somewhat rough. The entablature is of travertine, and the frieze was Doric with single contraction at the corners.

With this temple came to be associated the Greek story of the daughter who nourished her imprisoned father (or mother) with the milk of her own breasts, sometimes called Caritas Romana (Val. Max. 5.4.7; Festus 228L). It has been plausibly suggested that the presence of the Columna Lactaria (q.v.) in the Forum Holitorium was responsible for the association. The column itself is enigmatic.

R. Delbrück, *Die drei Tempel am Forum Holitorium in Rom* (Rome 1903), 22–23, 44–49; Lugli 1946, 545–53; Nash 1.418–20; *MemPontAcc,* ser. 3.13 (1981): passim, especially 27, 58–61, 70–71, 103–4 (L. Crozzoli Aite).

Pietas Augusta, Ara: an altar (?) voted by the senate in A.D. 22 on the occasion of a serious illness of Livia, but not erected until 43, long after Livia's death in 29, and really known only from an inscription now lost (*CIL* 6.562 = *ILS* 202; cf. Tacitus, *Ann.* 3.64). Because we do not know any of the particulars of the inscription, it is conceivable that something other than an altar was in question. The reason for the delay in the fulfillment of the vow is puzzling. The theory that certain reliefs of religious ceremonies now in Villa Medici belonged to this altar and that it was similar in design to the Ara Pacis Augustae has now been disproved (*RömMitt* 89 [1982]: 435–55 [G. Koeppel]). The monument seems to have been a modest one.

ArchCl 37 (1985): 238–65 (L. Cordischi).

Pila Horatia: the place where the spoils of the Curiatii had been set up in the Forum Romanum (Livy 1.26.10; *Schol. Bob. in Cic. Milon.* [Stangl 113]). Dionysius (3.22.9) tries to be explicit, saying that in his day it had become the corner pillar of one of the basilicas in the forum. Because Horatius was supposed to have entered Rome on this occasion by the Porta Capena (Livy 1.26.2), he would presumably have entered the forum by the Sacra Via, and the southern corner of the Basilica Paulli is meant. And any other corner would have suggested different definition. The wordplay on *pila* (spears) and *pila* (pillar, column) suggests that the pillar was so named for other reasons and the story of the dedication of spoils here invented to explain it, although the forum would seem an inappropriate place for such a dedication. But why a pillar of the Basilica Paulli (and before it the Basilica Fulvia et Aemilia) should be called Horatia is mysterious.

Pila Tiburtina: Martial (5.22.3–4) describes his house in Rome as next to this pillar, "where rustic Flora looks at ancient Jupiter." Ancient Jupiter must be the Capitolium Vetus (q.v.), and Flora was on a clivus that led up to this (Varro, *Ling.* 5.158) from the direction of Piazza Barberini (see Flora, Templum). The Pila Tiburtina should be a conspicuous landmark of some sort, but boundary stones, milestones, columns, or even bollards of travertine were so common in the Rome of Martial's time that one could hardly have singled one out as *the* Pila Tiburtina. So perhaps Martial is using it as a common noun, not an identifying name, and what he means is simply one of the markers of the precinct of Flora on the side toward the Capitolium Vetus.

The difficulties induced Hülsen to conjecture that there might have been a Vicus Pilae Tiburtinae, but there no evidence for this and it hardly removes the difficulty.

Pincius Mons: the large hill divided from the Quirinal by the valley down which runs Via del Tritone. The brow of the hill runs generally west from Porta Salaria in the Aurelian Walls to a point about 300 m southwest of Porta Pinciana, and then turns rather abruptly to run northwest to Porta Flaminia. It was thus entirely within Regio VII. In the first century B.C. Lucullus set a fashion by creating the first of the great horti there (see Horti Luculliani), and it became known as Collis Hortorum or Hortulorum (Suetonius, *Nero* 50); what its name may have been earlier is not known. The postclassical name Mons Pincius comes from its owners in the fourth century, the Gens Pincia. See Domus Pinciana, Horti Aciliorum, Horti Luculliani. Terracing and scarping in the creation of the sumptuous horti that covered it have substantially changed the slopes and contours of this hill.

HJ 444–50.

Ad Pirum: a landmark or vicus name by which Martial once identifies the location of his house in Rome (1.117.6). A little earlier (1.108.3) he has provided the information that his apartment looks out over the laurels of the Porticus Vipsania (q.v.), so it must have been on the slope of the Quirinal. There is no reason to think that this is different from his house near the Temple of Flora, up the slope from Piazza Barberini.

Piscina, Stagnum, Naumachia: A *piscina* was a reservoir or a fishpond. It might be spring-fed, as apparently the Piscina Publica was, or aqueduct-fed. Every aqueduct was provided with a *piscina limaria* on the outskirts of the city to clarify the water, but this was for that special purpose only. Inside the city the only piscinae we know are either reservoirs connected with the great imperial bath complexes or the fishponds of private horti. The former are divided into multiple chambers, usually of about the same size, that interconnect and are roofed with vaults. The latter were usually single tanks.

A *stagnum* was an ornamental water, probably always of considerable size and usually the focus of a park. We hear of only two in Rome, one of Agrippa that probably drew water from the Aqua Virgo and was the central feature of his horti. Here Nero gave an extravagant and scandalous party, the banquet being served on a raft that was kept in motion by other vessels (Tacitus, *Ann.* 15.37). The other was the Stagnum Neronis on the site of the Colosseum, a lake fed by the Aqua Claudia brought in cascades down the slope of the Caelian. Suetonius (*Nero* 31.1) compares it to a sea with buildings like cities on its margins. It was one of the chief attractions of the Domus Aurea and the first to be destroyed, probably

291

especially in order to restore the water to the people of Rome.

A *naumachia* differed from a stagnum in being designed as a place to stage mock sea battles. These were relatively shallow tanks, but evidently usually of considerable size, and must have been provided with banks of seats for the spectators. They seem to have been regarded as unjustifiable waste of space, water, and money by the Romans, and those of Julius Caesar in the Codeta Minor and Domitian on the river in the Transtiberim (?) were destroyed shortly after they were built. Only that of Augustus, which depended on the poor Aqua Alsietina for its water, seems to have met with approval, and it was a fair distance out of the city. We know very little about it, except that there was an island in the middle and a bridge, presumably giving access to this, although it probably served other purposes as well. The so-called Naumachia Vaticana in the flat beyond the Mausoleum Hadriani is the only such building for which we have reasonably accurate information from excavation. It was apparently a long rectangle with bowed corners surrounded by a low bank of seats raised on vaulted substructures, very much like a circus in general design.

Piscina "Aquae Alexandrinae": a distributing reservoir of the Severan period, conjectured on the basis of its date to have been for the Aqua Alexandrina. It lies north of the Thermae Helenae (q.v.) and southwest of the Porta Labicana (Porta Maggiore). It consisted of twelve compartments in two rows of six, all lined with opus signinum and all intercommunicating. Only some rather uncertain remains of this still survive.

MemPontAcc, ser. 3.8 (1955): 141–42 (A. M. Colini).

Piscina Aquae Virginis: a distributing reservoir of the Aqua Virgo on the west slope of the Pincian Hill just north of the modern Spanish Steps, commonly called Il Bottino, not mentioned by Frontinus and therefore presumed to be of later date (LA 124–25 [336–37]; LFUR sheet 9).

Piscina in Capitolio: a reservoir in the Area Capitolina located in a military diploma (*CIL* 16.22) in front of the Tribunal Deorum (q.v.).

Piscina Publica: first mentioned in 215 B.C. as a point just inside Porta Capena to which the praetors moved their tribunals in the crucial days of the Second Punic War so that they might be near the senate and the road along which news from the south

would come (Livy 23.32.4). Festus (232L), presumably quoting Verrius Flaccus, says that it was a place to which people went to swim and exercise, but that it no longer existed in his day. We can put it between the Via Appia, the Vicus Piscinae Publicae, running from the south end of the Circus Maximus between the Aventinus Maior and Aventinus Minor (*CIL* 6.975 = *ILS* 6073; Amm. Marc. 17.4.14), and the Servian Walls. Its location and early date suggest that it was originally a great public reservoir that in this district, which abounds in springs and is crossed by the circus brook, would probably not have been aqueduct-fed. Once aqueduct water was available in sufficient supply, the reservoir might have been turned to use as a swimming pool and then eventually filled in. The persistence of the name and the fact that it gave its name to Regio XII of the Augustan city can perhaps be explained by the importance of the Vicus Piscinae Publicae. Regio XII was bounded by the Vicus Piscinae Publicae and Vicus Portae Raudusculanae on the northwest, the Via Appia on the northeast, the Vicus Sulpicius and a line probably drawn from the end of the Vicus Sulpicius to the Posterula Laurentina on the southeast, and the line of the Aurelian Walls on the south and southwest. Its chief features were the Aventinus Minor and Baths of Caracalla.

Near the Piscina Publica itself were the headquarters of the *Lanii Piscinenses* (*CIL* 6.167 = *ILS* 3682a), a college of butchers, but about this we known nothing further.

Piscina Thermarum Diocletianarum: see **Thermae Diocletiani.**

Platanonis: listed by the regionary catalogues in Regio XIII. The genitive must depend on a missing noun, perhaps Vicus or Platea. Plane trees are excellent shade trees, and there was a plantation of them in the Porticus Pompeii (Propertius 2.32.13), perhaps the same that Martial (3.19.2) alludes to near the Hecatostylon. This one is otherwise unknown.

Platea Traiani: a street mentioned only by Symmachus (*Epist.* 6.37 [38] = *MGH* 6.1.163) in A.D. 398, where he writes of the collapse of an insula. The name might have been due to proximity to the Forum Traiani or the Thermae Traiani, more likely the latter, which seem, at least in large part, to have been bordered by an isolating street.

Plutei Traiani (Anaglypha Traiani): two large reliefs, each composed of several blocks of white marble, sculptured on both faces, found in the excavations of the Forum Romanum in 1872, where they had been mounted on clearly makeshift bases in the open area just northeast of the unpaved area sometimes conjectured to be the place of the Statua Marsyae and the Ficus, Olea, Vitis (qq.v.). One is substantially complete; the other lacks one end and the top of the middle part. They are obviously a pair, but are finished at the preserved ends, so must have stood separately. Both show on one face the three animals for a suovetaurilia properly decked, the boar leading. On the other face is shown an historical event in which the statue of Marsyas appears beside a fig tree, which is probably artificial because it seems to have a base, although some have seen this as an enclosure. One relief shows the burning of documents, presumably tax records burned in one of the periodic remissions of tax debts. The other relief shows an address from a rostrate platform to a group of men who do not wear the toga gathered between this and another large platform with molded borders on which a woman in long drapery with two children seems to address an enthroned princeps of heroic size. This is almost universally interpreted as a statue commemorating the *institutio alimentaria,* Trajan's establishment of food relief for indigent children. In the background of each relief appear several buildings, some clearly temples, others arcaded like the Basilica Iulia. An arch is shown behind the rostra, and another on the other relief is seen in the distance between two temples. There has been great discussion of the identification of the buildings shown without reaching a consensus, and probably they are not intended to be read literally, as the repetition of the Marsyas and a temple with only five columns on the façade shows. However, there is fair agreement that the Plutei are of Hadrianic date. Where they stood originally is a very difficult question. The best suggestion seems to be that they stood on the ends of one of the rostra, but their size, especially their considerable height, accords poorly with such a location. In 1949 they were removed to the Curia Senatus for their protection.

Lugli 1946, 160–64; Nash 2.176–77; *Antike Plastik* 12 (1973): 161–74 (U. Rüdiger).

Pomerium (Fig. 67): Most Romans seem to have believed the word *pomerium* was derived from *post* and *murus* in some way, although the discrepancy between this and what the pomerium was seems to have been apparent to a good many. Varro (*Ling.* 5.143) gives a fair account of the founding of a city *Etrusco ritu,* which he says obtained in Latium. On an auspicious day a bull and a cow were harnessed to a plow, and this was driven about the site in such a way that the furrow lay outside the ridge of earth

thrown up by the plowshare. The furrow was the fossa, or trench of symbolic fortifications, and the earth was the *agger,* or earthwork. This ring was the *urbis principium,* the line at which the *auspicia urbana* ended; auspices would have to be taken within it before leaving it, which seems to mean the augur's *templum* would have to be laid out facing toward an area lying outside it toward which he was proceeding. The actual walls were then laid out behind this line, and the space between it and the walls was maintained free of building, burial, and planting. A second ring of open space was usually maintained free of building just inside the walls as long as the walls functioned as a defense work, and Livy (1.44.4–5) regarded the whole of this band, inside and out, as the pomerium and thought it should properly be called *circamoerium*. However, he is contradicted by Suetonius (frag. p. 313 Roth), who thought only the strip outside was so designated.

A mutilated passage in Festus (294–95L) gives the learned Antistius Labeo as authority for the word *posimirium* in pontifical use for pomerium, a place that the pontifex crosses only after taking the auspices, and we may ask whether this does not contain a germ of the truth, that the true elements of the word were *ponere* and *murus*. The boundary was of the greatest religious importance for every Roman magistrate and priest.

Tacitus (*Ann.* 12.24), possibly following Claudius, describes the original pomerium of Romulus. It began at the bronze bull in the Forum Boarium, ran to the Ara Maxima Herculis, which it included, turned and ran along the base of the Palatine to the Altar of Consus, thence to the Curiae Veteres, and thence to a Sacellum Larum and the Forum Romanum (where the manuscript reading is *deforumque*). The pomerium was marked by stones at regular intervals, presumably inscribed cippi. One leg of this pentagonal area has been left open, that from the Forum Romanum to the Forum Boarium. Presumably the line turned at the entrance to the Forum Romanum and ran along the Vicus Tuscus, with the Regia, the Temple of Vesta, and the Temple of Castor inside, but the relationship to the Cloaca is unclear. It is also not plain whether Tacitus is simply relying on a literary source for his information. His line is logical enough, and the points he mentions would make suitable turning points, while the line of the fortifications should lie along the brow of the Palatine, with terracing and scarping to make an easily defended, tightly organized area. All that is surprising is that the line of the pomerium is so far in front of the line of the wall, a line in the valley that the plowman would have found easy to drive. Of course, parts of the hill have been lost through erosion, and the line of the walls along the brow is nowhere absolutely certain.

The city is supposed to have been enlarged by Servius Tullius, who added to its territory the Quirinal and Viminal, and then the Esquiline. He then "fortified this with an agger-and-fossa system and so advanced the pomerium" (Livy 1.44.3), though ritual would require that these be done in reverse order. The Caelian is not mentioned, but the Suburana is the first regio in the list of sacraria of the Argei (see Argeorum Sacraria), and traditionally it was a very old center of habitation. It is included within the circuit of the Servian Walls and, except for the hills excluded for other reasons, the Capitoline and Aventine, is the only hill of republican Rome omitted from consideration. Its omission must be an oversight by Livy or his source.

This pomerium persisted in use until the time of Sulla. Because we now know the Servian Walls are work of the first half of the fourth century and that Rome was far too occupied with its enemies and empire to give thought to urban magnificence and enlargement until after the Second Punic War, the duration of this line will occasion less surprise, and through the second century the area within the walls may still have been sufficient. Suburban settlements must have grown up irregularly along the roads leading out of the city, in part dependent on the traffic along these, but not requiring annexation and organization. What prompted Sulla to action is not clear, for it is not certain in what his enlargement of the pomerium consisted. But three terminus cippi of the praetor L. Sentius (CIL 1².838–39 = 6.31615 = ILS 8208; NSc 1943, 26–28 [C. Caprino]; ILLRP 485) with slightly archaic forms and clearly of republican date, all discovered in the neighborhood of the main railroad station of Rome and southwest of the Castra Praetoria, are probably to be referred to this enlargement. They forbid the construction of *ustrina* and the disposal of waste between their line and the city. The boundary is made *de senatus sententia,* and Sentius is probably a moneyer known from denarii assigned by Crawford to 101 B.C. (Crawford 325; B. M. Coins, Rom. Rep. 1.227–28 nos. 1642–59). This enlargement thus appears to have aimed especially at taking the Campus Esquilinus into the city, what Horace (Sat. 1.8.14) calls *Esquiliae salubres.* This had been the great cemetery of the common people of the city, as well as many distinguished Romans, and its liberation from funeral monuments and its general organization as a quarter with orderly streets and sewers must have involved considerable effort. Probably the new line of the pomerium was drawn

from Porta Collina in a gradually widening arc, widest opposite the Porta Esquilina, that then drew in to the line of the Servian Walls again as it approached the Via Labicana valley.

Sulla's extension of the pomerium is attested by a number of sources, that of Julius Caesar by Cassius Dio (43.50.1, 44.49.2) and Aulus Gellius (13.14.4), that of Augustus by Tacitus (Ann. 12.23), who in effect denies Caesar's enlargement, Dio (55.6.6), the Historia Augusta (Aurel. 21.11), and possibly certain coins, the evidence of which is not unequivocal, because they might better refer to the foundation of colonies. Degrassi (Doxa 2 [1949]: 84–85) points out that the cippi of Augustus that have been found that refer to public land do not stand on a pomerial line or offer a pomerial formula and seem likely to date from Augustus's censorship in 8 B.C., when he may well have attended to the recovery and bounding of public land at various points on the periphery of Rome. This then (more likely than his reorganization of the city into fourteen regions) might have led historians to suppose he extended the pomerium, when in fact he did not. Julius Caesar's enlargement seems equally doubtful, for the two obvious areas for anyone to have added between the time of Sulla and that of Claudius, the Aventine and the Campus Martius, seem clearly not to have been included until Claudius redrew the pomerium. We have specific testimony to this effect for the Aventine (Seneca, De Brev. Vit. 13.8; A. Gellius 13.14.4–7), whereas the continuance of burial in the Campus Martius (e.g., Hirtius and Pansa in 43 B.C., the bustum of Hirtius having been found under the Palazzo della Cancelleria) is proof that it was not included until late. Except for Sulla's inclusion of the Campus Esquilinus, a real revision of the pomerium seems to have been put off to the time of Claudius.

Eight cippi belonging to the Claudian revision have so far come to light, four of them preserving numbers from a continuous sequence, as well as the inscription commemorating this revision and the word *pomerium* inscribed on the top. This revision is further attested in our literary sources by Tacitus (Ann. 12.24) and Aulus Gellius (13.14.7). It appears to have been very thorough and very much needed. The line seems to have run counterclockwise from the river at a point below the Aventine on a course a bit inside a line that was later to become that of the Aurelian Walls as far as Porta Pia, and then to have swept considerably to the north to a point 330 m north of Porta Flaminia. However, the Via Flaminia was almost certainly excluded in some way, together with the area west of this in which the ustrina of the Antonines (see, e.g., Faustina Maior, Diva, Ara) were built. A cippus of Hadrian found in the foundation of a wall near S. Stefano del Cacco seems to prove that the line ran following a roughly circular arc as far as Via Flaminia and then turned south along the east side of that street, at least as far as the Petronia Amnis under modern Piazza Venezia, then west past the Divorum, and returned north and west to include most of the rest of the Campus Martius, but to exclude the Mausoleum Augusti and Tarentum. Certain important rites had still to be performed outside the pomerium, and for these the northern reaches of the old Campus Martius seem to have been reserved. One Claudian cippus from the neighborhood of S. Lucia della Chiavica (or del Gonfalone) seems to give the boundary of this zone, and its evidence is supported by another cippus of Hadrian not far away. There is no way of telling whether Claudius included a section of the right bank of the Tiber within his pomerium, but it seems not unlikely, because he seems to have had some notion of drawing a circle around a central point, perhaps the Milliarium Aureum (q.v.), and then modifying this as necessity and utility might dictate.

Claudius's work on the pomerium was the most important since that of Servius Tullius and seems to have enlarged the city in every direction, except possibly to the east, where he may have maintained the line established by Sulla. The process must have entailed the neutralization of thousands of tombs, to say nothing of other difficulties, such as the inclusion of the Aventine, and was one of the major accomplishments of Claudius's reign. We would give much to know how the task was performed, but not only are our only sources very brief, Tacitus (*Ann.* 12.24) saying only that it was done *more prisco,* by which he seems to mean with a plow harnessed to a bull and a cow, but Claudius did not commemorate the work on his coinage, so we have no representation of it. Tacitus says that the right of Claudius to enlarge the pomerium came from his having enlarged the imperium of Rome by the conquest and annexation of Britain. This is confirmed by Seneca (*De Brev. Vit.* 13.8) and Aulus Gellius (13.14.3), both of whom say that such enlargement conferred this right, though few availed themselves of it. One suspects Claudius of looking for a pretext for a reform long overdue, rather than of a wish to make much of the conquest.

But Vespasian's enlargement of the pomerium, if it amounted to more than exercising his right to do so, must have been a very modest one. The power to do so was decreed him by law (*CIL* 6.930 = *ILS* 244), and three cippi belonging to his pomerium have come to light (*CIL* 6.31538a-c = *ILS* 248), none of

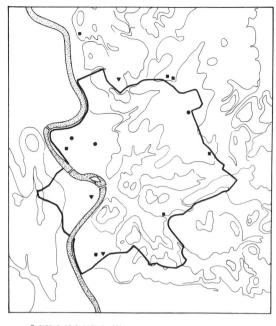

Figure 67
Pomerium of Imperial Rome with Location of Cippi Found in Situ, Showing Relation to the Aurelian Walls

■ CIPPUS OF CLAUDIUS (7)
▼ CIPPUS OF VESPASIAN (3)
● CIPPUS OF HADRIAN (3)

which can have marked a significant advance beyond the line we have suggested for Claudius, though the significance of their find spots has been doubted. We can dismiss Vespasian's pomerium as a token work at best, probably almost entirely a renewal of the pomerium of Claudius.

Hadrian is the next princeps we are sure was concerned with the pomerium, and his work was certainly simply restoration, as the inscriptions on his cippi attest. Four of these cippi have come to light, two of which show that the Divorum and the northern part of the Campus Martius at least were still maintained as areas *extra pomerium* (*CIL* 6.31539a-b = *ILS* 311). From the inscriptions on these cippi we learn that the actual work was done by the college of augurs, *ex senatus consulto, auctore imp. Caesare,* in A.D. 121, so Hadrian's part in the work was probably slight. Very likely Hadrian was off on his travels and no longer in Rome when it was carried out. The fact that it was the augurs, rather than the pontifices or a magistrate such as the praefectus urbi, who were charged with the task is not really surprising, because auspices must have had to be taken on every day of work and surveying the line after more than a half-century may have been a considerable undertaking. Unfortunately, no one tells us how long any of these resurveys of the pomerium took.

This pomerium remained in effect at least until the

time of Aurelian. He is reported (S.H.A. *Aurel.* 21.9–11) to have enlarged the circuit of Rome with the fortifications still standing today through most of their course on the left bank of the Tiber. These lie well outside the line known for any earlier pomerium in all but the north-northeast sector. However, at the time these were built, *adhibito consilio senatus,* he did not enlarge the pomerium, but waited until he had enlarged the imperium of Rome. Whether then he ran the pomerium a little distance in front of the wall is not stated, and no cippi belonging to it are known, but we may presume that was the case.

What then can we say about the others for whom it is claimed that they advanced the pomerium without further evidence for any advance: Julius Caesar, Augustus, Nero, and Trajan, the last two only on the dubious authority of the life of Aurelian? We already have dealt with Augustus; the assertion is probably the result of a confusion about his reorganization of the city. But the right to extend the pomerium was a high honor and is likely to have been eagerly pursued, even if it might have come to be expected as a sequel to any significant conquest. The life of Aurelian seems hardly to be trusted in view of silence elsewhere, and we can dismiss Nero's and Trajan's advances as unlikely. But Julius Caesar is likely to have wanted the power and to have contemplated using it. The date of his work on the pomerium is not given, but if Sulla did no more than include the Campus Esquilinus, Julius Caesar may have restored the line elsewhere around the circuit.

MEFR 54 (1937): 165–99 (M. Labrousse); *PW* 21 (1952): s.v. "Pomerium, 1867–76" (A. von Blumenthal); *RendPontAcc,* ser. 3.51–52 (1978–79): 195–212 (E. Rodriguez Almeida); Boatwright 64–66.

Pons Aelius: the modern Ponte Sant'Angelo, built by Hadrian in connection with the Mausoleum Hadriani (q.v.) but probably also with a view to opening the area adjacent on the right bank of the Tiber to development and habitation, finished in A.D. 134 (*CIL* 6.973; Cass. Dio 69.23.1; S.H.A. *Hadr.* 19.11). It is listed in the regionary catalogues (app.) and Polemius Silvius (VZ 1.308). It is also called Pons Hadriani a little later (Prudentius, *Peristeph.* 12.61; *Mirabilia,* Jordan 2.617, VZ 3.26; Pol. Silv., VZ 1.308) and eventually Pons S. Petri and Pons S. Angeli (Anon. Magliabech., VZ 4.128). It has three main arches, 18.39 m in diameter, with three smaller arches connecting it to the left bank, 3, 3.5, and 7.59 m in diameter, and two arches connecting it to the right bank, 7.59 and 3.75 m in diameter. From the central part over the main arches the bridge sloped down at an angle of fifteen degrees, and the ap-

proach to it from the left bank was by a long ramp. Its overall width was 10.95 m. The material is travertine with peperino on the interior. The inscription was probably on the parapet, which collapsed under the press of pilgrims in December 1450; it had been read as late as 1375. The bridge up to that time had stood apparently almost undamaged. In 1527 Pope Clement VII added the statues of saints Peter and Paul, and in 1669–1671 Pope Clement IX added the series of angels by Bernini. The approaches to the bridge were covered in time but remained until the building of the Tiber embankment in this sector in 1892, at which time they were uncovered and studied before they were destroyed. Now only the central part remains.

Jordan 1.1.416; *NSc* 1892, 231–33 (L. Borsari); *BullCom* 21 (1893): 14–26 (R. Lanciani); *JRS* 15 (1925): 95–98 (S. Rowland Pierce); *CAR* 1-H, 70 pp. 85–86; Nash 2.178–81; Gazzola 2: no. 179.

Pons Aemilius: According to Livy (40.51.4), M. Fulvius Nobilior, when censor in 179 B.C., let the contract for the construction of *pilas pontis in Tiberi.* In this most people believe he was associated with his colleague M. Aemilius Lepidus, but Livy seems to think that they acted independently in most of their works. In 142 B.C. P. Scipio Africanus and L. Mummius had arches *(fornices)* built on those piers. This was the first stone bridge in Rome. In 156 B.C. a great storm threw the *tectum* of a *pons maximus* into the Tiber (Obsequens 16), which almost certainly means this bridge and gives the name by which it was commonly known to distinguish it from the Pons Sublicius (and probably other wooden bridges and pontoon bridges that might have existed and explains why, when it was rebuilt, it should have received the name of its rebuilder. In all our other sources, which are all admittedly of relatively late date, it is almost never called anything but Pons Aemilius (Fast. Allif., Amit., Val. *ad XIII Kal. Sept.* = 17 August; Pol. Silv., VZ 1.308; regionary catalogues [app.]); the one exception is in the *Cosmographia* (Riese, *Geog. Lat. Min.* 83), in which we find: *per pontem Lepidi, qui nunc abusive Lapideus dicitur iuxta Forum Boarium.* Plutarch (*Numa* 9.3) seems to give the gist of the inscription of its rebuilder; he was an Aemilius Lepidus who was quaestor, but it is impossible to tell which of at least six men of this name in the period that interests us it might have been.

A marble arch *in platea pontis sanctae Mariae qui pons senatorum vocatur* (Anon. Magliabech., VZ 4.122) carried an inscription (*CIL* 6.878) recording a restoration by Augustus after 12 B.C. This was almost certainly a bridgehead arch, and his restoration was of the bridge itself. Besides Pons Senatorum, it seems also to have been called Pons Maior (Einsiedeln itinerary 6.4; Jordan 2.652–53). The identification of the Pons Aemilius with the present-day Ponte Rotto is regarded as certain. The Pons Sublicius (q.v.) led from the Forum Boarium to the southwest, carrying the traffic interested especially in the salt trade to the Via Portuensis and the saltworks near the mouth of the river. In contrast, the Pons Aemilius led almost due west, carrying the traffic bound for Caere and the cities of coastal Etruria. This difference explains why the earliest bridges in Rome should have stood so close together; they served very different purposes.

The ancient bridge stood almost intact until 1557, when a flood destroyed part of it. Pope Gregory XIII repaired it, but in 1598 the eastern half was swept away, and in 1887 two of the three arches still standing were removed, so a single arch still stands in midriver just above Ponte Palatino. Recent investigations show that the remains of an older bridge stood slightly to the north of this and crossed the river at a slightly different angle; this must be the bridge of Fulvius Nobilior. The later structure consisted of six main arches with a ramp of approach on the left bank carried on a lesser arch, the last main arch at either end also carrying a ramped roadway. The construction is of peperino faced with travertine; the cutwaters and flood lunettes between arches show great sophistication in engineering. An Augustan date is universally accepted.

Jordan 1.1.420–21; Delbrück, *Hellenistische Bauten,* 1.12–22; Nash 2.182–83; Gazzola 2: no. 28; Coarelli 1988, 139–47.

Pons Agrippae: a bridge 160 m upstream from Ponte Sisto, known from a cippus of the time of Claudius set up by the curatores riparum (*CIL* 6.31545 = *ILS* 5926; *NSc* 1887, 322–27 [L. Borsari]; *BullCom* 15 [1887]: 306–13 [G. Gatti]) and the discovery of the remains of four piers in the riverbed during work on the modern embankment. The purpose of this bridge is uncertain, because it seems to lack connection with known streets on either side of the river. It must have served to carry the Aqua Virgo across to the Transtiberim (Frontinus, *Aq.* 2.84), but that cannot have been its main purpose. We have record of its restoration and rededication by Antoninus Pius in A.D. 147 (A. Degrassi, *Inscriptiones Italiae*, 13.1, 207, 673).

BullCom 16 (1888) 92–98 (L. Borsari); Nash 2.184.

Pons Aurelius: mentioned in the fourth and fifth centuries (*Notitia* [app.]; Pol. Silv., VZ 1.308), but

certainly to be identified with the Pons Antoninus or Antonini in Arenula of the Middle Ages (*Mirabilia,* Jordan 2.617, VZ 3.26; *Graphia* 21, VZ 3.84; Anon. Magliabech., VZ 4.128). It is also called Ianicularis, Tremulus, Valentinianus, and, after its partial destruction, Ruptus and Fractus. This was partially destroyed in 791–792 and rebuilt in 1473–1475 by Pope Sixtus IV, from whom it received its modern name, Ponte Sisto. The spring of the first arch on the right bank and some of the foundations can still be seen and show that the original bridge was wider than the modern one. The original bridge must have been built by someone who carried both the names Aurelius and Antoninus, either Marcus Aurelius or Caracalla, but more likely the latter in view of the buildings of Septimius Severus in this part of the Transtiberim (S.H.A. *Sept. Sev.* 19.5).

In 1878 were found remains of the earlier bridge and also of a bridgehead arch, including inscriptions (*CIL* 6.31402–31412; *ILS* 766, 769) and substantial fragments of bronze statuary (*BullCom* 6 [1878]: 241–48 [R. Lanciani]; *RömMitt* 26 [1911]: 238–59 [G. Dehn]). An interesting fragment of a fluviometer was also found (*BullCom* 20 [1892]: 139–45 [D. Marchetti]). The inscriptions record a restoration of the bridge by Valentinian I in A.D. 365–366 and explain a reference in Ammianus Marcellinus (27.3.3). The name Pons Valentinianus may have been in use for at least a short time, for it appears in the *Mirabilia* (Jordan 2.617, VZ 3.26) but seems not to have been understood by the author. Certainly the name Pons Antoninus persisted.

Jordan 1.1.417–18; Nash 2.185–86.

Pons Caligulae: the wooden bridge by which Caligula was able to cross the valley between the Palatine and Capitoline so that he could go directly from the palace to the Capitoline temple (Suetonius, *Calig.* 22.4). The bridge went over the Temple of Divus Augustus, but it is not clear whether it used this as a support. Immediately after Caligula's death this must have been dismantled, for it has left no trace.

Pons Cestius: modern Ponte S. Bartolomeo, the stone bridge that connects the Tiber island with the Transtiberim. It is not mentioned before the regionary catalogues, but was probably originally a late republican work. Whether the name Pons Cestius refers to the original builder or to a restorer is unknown; in the late republican period the Cestii were an undistinguished family and first given prominence by the builder of the pyramid, C. Cestius Epulo (see Sepulcrum Cestii). It was restored by Antoninus Pius in A.D. 152 (A. Degrassi, *Inscriptiones*

Italiae, 13.1, 207, 673). In the fourth century the bridge was replaced by a new structure finished in 369 by the emperors Valentinian I, Valens, and Gratian and dedicated in 370 as the Pons Gratiani (Pol. Silv., VZ 1.308), the event being recorded on marble tablets mounted in the parapet of the bridge and on the bridge itself under the parapet (*CIL* 6.1175, 1176; *ILS* 771, 772). The bridge was 48 m long, 8.20 m wide, and composed of a single central arch 23.65 m in span and a smaller arch at either end 5.80 m in span. The materials are tufa and peperino with facings of travertine. Although the masonry shows signs of roughness, the design seems to have been elegant and to have followed the lines of its predecessor.

The bridge has been restored at various times since the twelfth century, but in 1880–1892, in the construction of the new embankment of the Tiber, it became necessary to dismantle the whole bridge and to replace it with one 80.40 m long with three arches all of the span of the central arch of the old bridge. Although some old material was used in its construction, at least two-thirds of this bridge is completely modern.

Jordan 1.1.418–20; Nash 2.187–88; Gazzola 2: no. 41.

Pons Fabricius: the stone bridge connecting the left bank of the Tiber with the island, named for its builder, L. Fabricius, curator viarum in 62 B.C. (Cass. Dio 37.45.3; Horace, *Sat.* 2.3.35–36 and Porphyrion ad loc.). A commemorative inscription appears in duplicate over the arches on each side, together with inscriptions commemorating a restoration after damage in the flood of 23 B.C. by the consuls Q. Lepidus and M. Lollius (*CIL* 1².751 = 6.1305 = 31594 = *ILS* 5892; Cass. Dio 53.33.5). In the Middle Ages it was known by its proper name (Pol. Silv., VZ 1.308; *Mirabilia*, Jordan 2.617, VZ 3.26) and as Pons Iudaeorum, because of its proximity to the ghetto. In *Graphia* 21 (VZ 3.84) we find *Fabricii in Ponte Iudaeorum*.

It is the best preserved bridge of Rome, built of tufa and peperino faced with travertine. It is composed of two semicircular arches with a large cutwater surmounted by a flood lunette between. It is 62 m long, with arches of 24.24 m and 24.50 m span. In 1679 Pope Innocent XI added the present parapet, and in 1849 were mounted in it two interesting four-headed herms in marble, which do not belong to the bridge but have given it its modern name of Ponte Quattro Capi (L. A. Holland, *Janus and the Bridge* [Rome 1961], 212–23).

Jordan 1.1.418–20; Nash 2.189–90; Gazzola 2: no. 40.

Pons Hadriani: see **Pons Aelius.**

Pons Ianiculensis: see **Pons Aurelius.**

Pons Lapideus: see **Pons Aemilius.**

Pons Lepidi: see **Pons Aemilius.**

Pons Maximus: see **Pons Aemilius.**

Pons Naumachiarius: see **Naumachia Augusti.**

Pons Neronianus: a bridge mentioned in the *Mirabilia* (Jordan 2.617; VZ 3.84), *pons Neronianus ad Sassiam,* and Anonymous Magliabechianus (VZ 4.128), *pons Neronis, id est pons ruptus ad Sanctum Spiritum in Sassia.* The latter therefore locates it very precisely for us and shows that it was in ruined condition in the fifteenth century. Because it is omitted from the regionary catalogues and does not figure in Procopius's account of the assault of the Goths on the bridgehead fortress of the Mausoleum Hadriani (*BellGoth* 1.22.12–24), we can presume it was already ruined in the fourth century. However, remains of the piers still exist deep in the riverbed and can be seen when the water is low. The bridge crossed the river running northwest just below Ponte Vittorio Emanuele, connecting the Campus Martius with the valley between the Janiculan hill and the Vatican, and in some sense with the whole of the northern part of the *ager Vaticanus*, although its main purpose at the time of construction may have been to provide access to the Circus Gaii et Neronis (q.v.). At the head of the bridge on the left bank was the Arcus Arcadii, Honorii, et Theodosii of A.D. 405 (q.v.), which may have been a bridgehead arch pressed into other service after the bridge had collapsed. Whether the name Pons Neronianus goes back to antiquity or was a medieval invention is unknown. The Via Triumphalis begins at its head on the right bank, so it got the name Pons Triumphalis in the sixteenth century, when Pope Julius II proposed to rebuild it in order to connect Via Giulia and Via Triumphalis.

Jordan 1.1.416–17; *CAR* 1-H, 102 p. 93; Nash 2.193–95.

Pons Probi: a bridge listed in the regionary catalogues and by Polemius Silvius (VZ 1.308), probably a new construction of the emperor Probus (A.D. 276–282) and lower on the Tiber than the other bridges, as it is listed last. This is now commonly identified with a still later bridge that spanned the Tiber just below the north corner of the Aventine, but Nolli shows "Muri Antichi" in the middle of the river just upstream from the western corner of the Aventine, so it may be that we really do have to do with two bridges here, in which case the Pons Probi is that farther upstream, and the Pons Theodosii was a replacement for it after its collapse. It is interesting that in that case the Pons Probi was a more durable ruin. In the Middle Ages we find mention of a Pons Marmoreus Theodosii (*Mirabilia*, Jordan 2.617; VZ 3.26) and Pons Theodosii in Riparmea (*Graphia* 21, VZ 3.84). The last is variously emended, by Jordan to *in ripa Romana*, by PA to *in ripa romea*, which is explained as allusion to the nearby Marmorata (q.v.). Because a marble bridge at this time would seem a strange extravagance, some allusion to the marble wharves seems not unlikely, but Jordan takes *marmoreus* as simply equivalent to *lapideus*.

From the papers of Symmachus (*MGH* 6: *Relationes* 25, 26; *Epist.* 4.70[71] and 5.76[74]), it appears that work had begun on the Bridge of Theodosius before 384 but had been fraught with difficulties of one sort and another, and the bridge was still unfinished in 387. It is described as a new bridge, and there is discussion of laying foundations for it, but, given its location and the lack of other evidence, it is generally believed to have been a rebuilding of the Pons Probi. It was partly destroyed in the eleventh century and almost entirely obliterated in 1484 by Pope Sixtus IV. The stumps of its piers, which showed that the arches and piers were faced with travertine, were removed in 1877–1878.

Jordan 1.1.421–22; Nash 2.196–97.

Pons Sublicius: the oldest and most famous of the bridges spanning the Tiber, originally built by Ancus Marcius (Livy 1.33.6; Plutarch, *Numa* 9.2–3; Dion. Hal. 3.45.2). According to these sources, its name came from *sublica* (pile), and it was constructed without the use of any metal (Dion. Hal. 3.45.2, 9.68.2; Pliny, *HN* 36.100; Servius *ad Aen.* 8.646). It was the direct concern of the college of pontifices, its construction and preservation being matters of religion. Its destruction by floods, which was not infrequent, was always regarded as a *prodigium* (Cass. Dio 37.58.3, 50.8.3, 53.33.5, 55.22.3), but it was always repaired and was still standing in the fourth century and listed in the regionary catalogues. Its final destruction is perhaps to be put in the fifth century. It is represented schematically on a medallion of Antoninus Pius showing Horatius swimming the river after his successful defense of the bridge (Gnecchi 2.9, Antoninus Pius no. 5; Banti 2.3.58 no. 52). The notion that it goes back to a time before the use of iron was known is mistaken; the use of metal of any sort was prohibited. Apparently religious scruples were at work here, rather than considerations of facility in dismantling the bridge when danger threatened, as the story of Horatius makes plain (Livy 2.10.2–11; Val. Max. 3.2.1; Dion. Hal. 5.23.2–24.3).

The location of the bridge is not entirely certain.

Its head lay in the Forum Boarium, and it is natural to think that the Porta Flumentana of the Servian Walls (which it antedated) led directly to it. But the story of the flight and death of Gaius Gracchus (Val. Max. 4.7.2; Plutarch, *C. Gracch.* 17.1; Appian, *BellCiv* 1.26; [Aur. Vict.,] *De Vir. Ill.* 65) suggests that its head was at a point between the Porta Flumentana and the Porta Trigemina, and between the mouth of the Cloaca and that of the Circus Maximus brook. Because its original purpose was to replace the ferry that had transported those in quest of salt to the right bank of the Tiber and the Via Portuensis, the opposite bridgehead must have lain downstream, but no trace of an ancient road connecting it with the Via Portuensis has been identified. The stories of Horatius and Gaius Gracchus show that the bridge was narrow and could be defended even by a single man, and the account of the flight of the Vestals to Caere before the approach of the Gauls (Livy 5.40.7–10; Val. Max. 1.1.10) shows that it was only a footbridge.

Jordan 1.1.399–407.

Pons Theodosii: see **Pons Probi.**

Pons Triumphalis: see **Pons Neronianus.**

Porta Agonensis: see **Porta Collina.**

Porta Appia: the modern Porta S. Sebastiano, a gate in the Aurelian Walls through which passed the Via Appia. All the gates in this wall seem to have been named for the roads they span, except the Porta Metrovia. The correct name survived as late as the twelfth century (Magister Gregorius, VZ 3.145).

The gate began as a broad twin-arched entrance with a two-storeyed facing of blocks of travertine, flanked by brick-faced towers of semicircular plan. The design was utilitarian; above the gate and in the second storey of the towers were chambers with loopholes for defenders, and there was a battlemented roof. In a second period, probably the time of Maxentius, when the gallery was added to the wall, a new structure engulfed the old wall and towers. The massive new towers were full circles in plan added in front of the wall and incorporated with it and rose four storeys in height. An inner court was constructed behind the gate, giving access to the towers by flights of stairs and probably providing guardrooms and offices. To create this, the ornamental arch of the Aqua Antoniniana known as the Arco di Druso was made a rear gate to this courtyard. In a third period, the time of Honorius, quadrangular bastions of marble and brick were built around the bases of the towers up to the height of the wall walk. The marble blocks of the lower storey were pillaged from other constructions, probably chiefly tombs in the vicinity, but redressed to the new work and given a finishing cornice. At the same time the gate itself was reduced to a single arch and given a new façade of marble and brick to make it conform to the tower bastions. This is essentially the gate we see today. Later there were changes made in the interior arrangements, and eventually another storey was added to the towers and curtain. The final height of the towers is about 28 m.

Richmond 121–42; Nash 2.198–99.

Porta Ardeatina (**Laurentina?**): assumed to be the name of the gate in the Aurelian Walls through which the Via Ardeatina (which may actually have been called Via Laurentina) passed, although this is not attested in our sources. The logical line of a road from Porta Naevia in the Servian Walls runs through the part of the Aurelian Walls destroyed to create the Bastione di Sangallo of 1537–1542, and one of Sangallo's drawings shows a small gate at this point of the sort used for third-class roads. It was early walled up and is not mentioned in the Einsiedeln list.

Richmond 217–19; Nash 2.200–203.

Porta Argiletana: mentioned only once (Servius *ad Aen.* 8.345) in a series of explanations of the name Argiletum; namely, that there was a gate of this name that a Cassius Argillus had built, or rebuilt. But no Cassius Argillus is known, and the cognomen is otherwise unattested. Where such a gate would have been and what its purpose might have been conceived to be are problems almost as great. While we can dismiss the explanation as a fabrication, we have not explained the difficulties.

Porta Asinaria (Fig. 16): the gate in the Aurelian Walls on the Caelian just southwest of the modern Porta S. Giovanni through which passed the Via Asinaria (q.v.). The road was comparatively unimportant, and the original gate was unimpressive. Its name is given correctly by Magister Gregorius in the twelfth century (VZ 3.145); in the *Mirabilia* (Jordan 2.607; VZ 3.18) it is called Porta Asinaria Lateranensis. It was closed in 1408 but apparently reopened within a few weeks and was not permanently closed until the construction of Porta S. Giovanni in 1574, at which time the Porta Asinaria was stripped of its travertine facing. In 1951–1955 it was reopened and restored and its vantage court excavated, so now it is one of the most informative of the gates in the Aurelian Walls.

The original gate was a simple arch between two of the usual square towers of Aurelian. In time, with the increase of importance of the road through it at the beginning of the fifth century, Honorius com-

pletely rebuilt the Porta Asinaria. It was then provided with two cylindrical towers addorsed to the wall just inside the older square ones, and the level of the archway was raised. The new towers were of three storeys, and the old square ones were used for stairs of access to these. The gate was faced with travertine and covered by two storeys corresponding to the lower storeys of the new towers with rows of arched windows on the façade for the defenders. In the interior was a vantage court with bowed sides and an inner gate.

Richmond 144–59; *Capitolium* 29 (1954): 97–104 (G. Gatti); Nash 2.204–5.

Porta Aurelia (1): modern Porta S. Pancrazio, the gate at the summit of the Janiculan hill through which the Via Aurelia (q.v.), the main road to the west and the coastal cities of Etruria, passed. The name occurs correctly in the Einsiedeln itinerary 6.1 (Jordan 2.652) and *Mirabilia* (Jordan 2.608; VZ 3.18) but is early altered to Pancratiana, in allusion to the nearby church of S. Pancratius, or Transtiberina (Procopius, *BellGoth* 1.18.35, 19.4, 28.19). In the rebuilding of the walls on the Janiculan hill by Urban VIII in 1644 this gate was completely rebuilt; it was then destroyed in the bombardment by the French in 1849 and reconstructed in its present form by Vespignani. Of the original form, one can only say that it was a gate of secondary importance, a single arch in the curtain between two square towers.

It is mentioned with the name Porta Aurea in Magister Gregorius (VZ 3.144) and the *Mirabilia* (Jordan 2.608; VZ 3.18; cf. LPD 1.152n.9).

Richmond 221–23; Nash 2.206–7; *BullCom* 91.1 (1986): 127–29 (L. Cozza).

Porta Aurelia (2): also known as Porta S. Petri (Procopius, *BellGoth* 1.19.4, 22.12–25; cf. 18.35) and usually so called in medieval documents (Einsiedeln itinerary 1.1, 2.1, 7.1, 9.1; DMH = Jordan 2.578–80). It seems clear from Procopius's narrative that it defended the Transtiberim end of the Pons Aelius and spanned the Via Cornelia and is identical with the Porta Cornelia. It seems likely that Via Cornelia linked up with Via Aurelia, and we know that it was under the supervision of the Curatores Viae Aureliae, so the confusion of the two might have been very easy. After the conversion of the Mausoleum Hadriani into an outpost of the defenses of Rome, the gate of the Aurelian Walls at the bridge on the left bank would have lost its importance.

For a different view, see *RendPontAcc* 61 (1988–89): 338–42 (N. Degrassi).

Porta Caelimontana (Figs. 16, 58.9): a gate in the Servian Walls on the Caelian (Cicero, *Pis.* 55, 61;

Livy 2.11.8, 35.9.2–3; Appian, *BellCiv* 1.58). There is some doubt about which of two gates believed to have been on the Caelian this would have been, but opinion is now in favor of that marked by the Arcus Dolabellae et Silani (q.v.), a rebuilding of the time of Augustus (A.D. 10) later used by Nero in his extension of the Aqua Claudia to carry the aqueduct across a road. This is on the crest of the Caelian, and toward it important arteries seem to have converged.
Säflund 201–2.

Porta Capena (Fig. 58.10): a gate in the Servian Walls in the valley between the Caelian and Aventinus Minor through which the Via Appia issued from the city, frequently described as *ad Camenas* (Livy 1.26.2, 3.22.4; Servius *ad Aen.* 7.697; Frontinus, *Aq.* 1.5 and 19; Ovid, *Fast.* 4.345, 5.673, 6.192; Dion. Hal. 8.4.1; Paulus *ex Fest.* 97L, 102L, Festus 470L). The derivation of the name is mysterious; there is no real reason to believe there is any connection with the Faliscan town of Capena, and attempts to derive it from Capua and Camenae are equally unsatisfactory. Domitian is said to have restored the Porta Capena (Chron. 146), but the point of so doing in his time is difficult to see, unless it was as a triumphal arch (see Suetonius, *Dom.* 13.2). This may well be a mistake for the Porta Carmentalis/Triumphalis, which Domitian did indeed rebuild. An aqueduct crossed the valley on, or very close to, the Porta Capena (Martial 3.47.1; Juvenal 3.11 and schol.), probably a branch of the Anio Vetus, which is said to have served Regio XII.
Säflund 199–201.

Porta Carmentalis (Fig. 58.16): the double gate in the Servian Walls through which the Vicus Iugarius passed, dividing into two branches just before reaching the gate, one branch curving to the right around the base of the Capitoline Hill and going through the Forum Holitorium, the other entering the Forum Boarium and probably originally running to the mouth of the Cloaca on the Tiber, but later diverted to run southeast parallel to the river. The gate took its name from the shrine of Carmenta (Vergil, *Aen.* 8.337–41; Dion. Hal. 1.32.3; Festus 450L; Solinus 1.13). The two arches were perhaps always at an angle to each other, and the shrine of Carmenta was by the right-hand gate as one left the city, the one that came to be called Porta Scelerata because the 306 Fabii were supposed to have left by it when they marched out on their disastrous campaign against Veii in 479/478 B.C. and all perished by the Cremera (Festus 450L, 358L; Ovid, *Fast.* 2.201–4; Cass. Dio frag. 20[21].3; [Aur. Vict.,] *De Vir. Ill.* 14.3–5). The other fornix must have been the Porta Triumphalis, the gate by which triumphators ceremonially entered

the city and by which as a special honor the cortege of Augustus departed (Cicero, *Pis.* 55; Josephus, *BellIud* 7.5.4.130–31; Tacitus, *Ann.* 1.8.4; Suetonius, *Aug.* 100.2; Cass. Dio 56.42.1). It was rebuilt by Domitian and surmounted by a triumphal car drawn by elephants (Martial 8.65.1–12), and it is shown on reliefs of the time of Marcus Aurelius (Ryberg, *Panel Reliefs* pls. 22, 23).

The exact location of the gate is elusive. During the excavations carried out in the vicinity of Sant'Omobono beginning in 1937, the whole of the area in which the Porta Carmentalis was believed to lie was uncovered without yielding any clear trace of either the gate or the shrine (but cf. *QArchEtr* 1 [1978]: 5–7 [P. Virgili]). It is therefore presumed that they must lie farther down toward the Forum Boarium.

Because the Servian Walls did not yet exist at the time when the disaster of the Cremera is supposed to have occurred, we must look for another explanation for the name Porta Scelerata and can find it in that this was the gate by which corpses were regularly carried out to pyres in the Campus Martius. Ovid (*Fast.* 2.201–4) and Festus (358L) say that it was regarded as unlucky to go out by this gate, so one must regularly have gone out by the adjacent Porta Triumphalis, unless one were part of a cortege. However, it seems to have been improper for any governor returning from a province to enter the city by the Porta Triumphalis, unless he were actually a triumphator (Cicero, *Pis.* 55), and this prohibition might have been extended to other people as ominous. One went out by the Porta Triumphalis and came in by the Porta Scelerata/Carmentalis, except in special circumstances. This explains the honor accorded Augustus.
Säflund 180–83, 194–95. On the Porta Triumphalis, see Coarelli 1988, 363–414 and the literature cited there.

Porta Catularia: Festus (Paulus *ex Fest.* 39L) tells us that this gate got its name from the fact that not far from it red dogs were sacrificed to appease the fury of the dog star and to ensure proper ripening of the grain. Ovid (*Fast.* 4.901–42) informs us that this was on the occasion of the Robigalia, 25 April, and the officiating priest was the Flamen Quirinalis. The grove of Robigo was at the fifth milestone of the Via Claudia/Clodia (Fast. Praen. *ad VII Kal. Mai.*), but Ovid is explicit that on this occasion he encountered the priest with a company of people solemnly dressed in white while on his way back from Nomentum to Rome, when he would naturally be on the Via Nomentana. The animals had already been slaughtered at that time, and the flamen was on his way to the grove. Because the Via Nomentana is a considerable distance from the Via Clodia, it seems logical to conclude that after the sacrifice of the animals the entrails were carried in solemn procession around the walls of the city in a lustration of the fields before they were taken to the grove and burned, though probably the procession did not make a complete circuit of the walls. This reconstruction of the ceremony might suggest that the Porta Catularia was a postern beyond Porta Collina, but we really have no indication of where it might have been. It does seem likely to have been a postern. Cf. Säflund 207–8, who derives Catularia from the name of Q. Lutatius Catulus, who he thinks remodeled the fortifications of the Capitoline in the time of Sulla. Säflund would put this gate at the top of the Cordonata of Michelangelo.

Porta Chiusa (Fig. 72): the modern name of an otherwise nameless gate in the Aurelian Walls just south of the Castra Praetoria in a direct line with the Porta Viminalis of the Servian Walls, the exit of an important road leading to Tibur and beyond. This was a comparatively unimportant gate in Aurelian's time, not much more than a postern, but in Honorius's time it was rebuilt entirely in travertine with a wide arch and a storey above this with six arched windows, the largest number known in such a storey. At that time it was clearly a gate of some importance, but it was walled up sometime late in antiquity, for it is omitted from the Einsiedeln list.

Richmond 181–84; Nash 2.208–9; *CAR* 3-H, 28–29 p. 317.

Porta Collatina: almost certainly a mistake in Festus (Paulus *ex Fest.* 33L) for Porta Collina, because the Via Collatina, an unimportant road leading to Collatia, branches to the right from the Via Tiburtina just outside the Porta Tiburtina.

Säflund 202–5.

Porta Collina (Figs. 58.5, 72): the gate in the Servian Walls at the north end of the Agger. Just beyond this gate the Via Salaria and Via Nomentana diverged, the Via Salaria running almost due north, the Via Nomentana northeast. The street from the gate within Rome is Alta Semita, which runs the length of the Quirinal and links up with Vicus Iugarius. This was a highway of the greatest economic importance from earliest times. The gate takes its name from the Regio Collina, one of the four regiones of republican Rome, made up of the Collis Quirinalis and Collis Viminalis, the only two major hills of Rome called colles. To complicate matters, Festus (Paulus *ex Fest.* 9L) says it seems to him possible that *montes* were

once called *agoni,* and the sacrifices made *in monte* were called *agonia,* and that it was from this that the Quirinal was once called Agonus (or Egonus) and the Porta Collina Porta Agonensis (or Egonensis). Varro (*Ling.* 6.14) confirms that the Salii of the Quirinal were called Salii Agonenses, and there seems to be no doubt that the words *agonus* and *agonium* indicated a sacred ritual of some sort. Because the Via Salaria offered the best approach to Rome from the north and northeast, the Porta Collina was the gate that the Romans had most often to defend, first against the combined armies of the Veientes and Fidenates (Livy 4.21.8). It was the gate through which the Gauls were supposed to have entered the city (Livy 5.41.4; Plutarch, *Cam.* 22.1) and the gate beyond which Hannibal pitched camp (Livy 26.10.1–2; Pliny, *HN* 15.76; Juvenal 6.287–91). It was also the gate outside which Sulla crushed the last of the Marian forces (Livy, *Epit.* 88; Vell. Pat. 2.27.1; Lucan 2.134–35 and schol.; Florus 2.9.23–24; [Aur. Vict.,] *De Vir. Ill.* 75.8; Eutropius 5.8.1; Ampelius 42.3; Orosius 5.20.9).

In 1872 some remains of the gate were discovered in Via XX Settembre under the north corner of the Ministero delle Finanze (*BullCom* 4 [1876]: 165–66 and pl. 19 [R. Lanciani]). These showed that in a second period two great square bastions with facings of peperino had been added to the fortifications just in front of the gate, which was otherwise a rather simple throat.

The Porta Collina of the Middle Ages has nothing to do with the Porta Collina of antiquity, but is rather a gate of the Leonine city.

Säflund 74–75, 206, 226–27.

Porta Cornelia: mentioned only once, in a document of about the seventh century (Jordan 2.580; VZ 2.141). It was on the right bank of the Tiber near the southwest corner of the Mausoleum Hadriani and spanned the Via Cornelia running west from the head of Pons Aelius. Its date is not known, but in Procopius's time (*BellGoth* 1.22.12–18) the mausoleum had been converted into a fortress defending the bridge and fortifications carried down to the river. Porta Cornelia must have been a gate in these fortifications. See also Porta Aurelia (2).

Porta Esquilina (Fig. 58.7): a gate in the Servian Walls on the Esquiline near the south end of the Agger. The Clivus Suburanus ends at this gate, and a little way outside it, at the Nymphaeum Alexandri (Nymphaeum Aquae Iuliae, Trofei di Mario) in Piazza Vittorio Emanuele, the road had a triple fork, the northern leg becoming Via Tiburtina, the center leg Via Labicana, and the southern leg Via Merulana. Strabo (5.3.9 [237]) says that the Via Labicana and Via Praenestina begin at this gate, but the Praenestina actually forks from the Labicana only at the place called Ad Spem Veterem (Piazza di Porta Maggiore).

This gate figures frequently in literature, but always incidentally. It seems never to have been the object of an attack, although it was an important link in the road system and must always have been in heavy use.

This gate is generally agreed to have been where the Arcus Gallieni (q.v.), sometimes called Arco di S. Vito, now stands. The existing arch is Augustan and was rededicated to Gallienus in A.D. 262.

Säflund 202.

Porta Fenestella: a mysterious monument probably on, or near, Summa Sacra Via, believed to have been originally part of the house of Tarquinius Priscus. It was a tiny doorlike window or loophole through which Fortuna was supposed to have descended to visit Servius Tullius, with whom she was in love (Ovid, *Fast.* 6.578; Plutarch, *Quaest. Rom.* 36, *De fort. Rom.* 10). It seems to have still existed in Plutarch's time, perhaps built into another structure.

Porta Flaminia: the gate in the Aurelian Walls by which Via Flaminia (q.v.), one of the principal arteries of Rome, issued. The gate has been repeatedly remodeled, and in 1877–1879 the last vestige of the ancient gate yielded to the needs of modern traffic, leaving only the central arch designed by Vignola and Bernini to remind us of its existence as a fortification. But descriptions of what was found when it was destroyed make reconstruction of its history fairly certain. Originally it was a gate of the first class, of twin arches flanked by semicircular towers. At some indefinite later time the western tower was refaced and strengthened, but the eastern one left as it was; this presumably would have been in the time of Maxentius. In the time of Honorius it took on a new appearance and a strong similarity to Porta Appia. The semicircular towers were encased in rectangular marble bastions, the marble pillaged from tombs along the road and preserving interesting inscriptions, but redressed and presenting the round bosses characteristic of Porta Appia. The double arch was now replaced by a single one set in a travertine curtain. But there were no rounded upper storeys to the bastions of Porta Flaminia like those of Porta Appia. Rather, there seems to have been simply a flat roof with battlements at the height of the fourth sto-

rey. It is now called Porta del Popolo from the adjacent church of S. Maria del Popolo.

Richmond 191–200; *CAR* 2-A, 34 pp. 17–18; Nash 2.210–12.

Porta Flumentana (Fig. 58.15): the river gate in the Servian Walls between the Porta Carmentalis and Porta Trigemina, probably to be located where the Vicus Tuscus, after its conjunction with Nova Via, crossed the line of the walls on the left bank of the Cloaca (see Cloaca Maxima). The wish to use the line of the Pons Aemilius to determine the location of this gate seems mistaken, because the present orientation of the bridge is Augustan, and, even at the time the bridge of the censors of 179 B.C. was built, the wall in this sector may have been largely dismantled, although the place of the Porta Flumentana was remembered as late as the time of Cicero (*Att.* 7.3.9 [9 December 50 B.C.]), though it seems clear that it no longer existed. The gate is seldom mentioned in literature, and nothing is known about its architecture.

Säflund 183–84, 195; Coarelli 1988, 20–25.

Porta Fontinalis (Fig. 58.1): a gate in the Servian Walls mentioned only twice in literature (Livy 35.10.11–12; Paulus *ex Fest.* 75L), but the passage in Livy, which tells of the aediles' construction of a portico from the Porta Fontinalis to the Altar of Mars in the Campus Martius in 193 B.C., makes its location fairly certain. The aediles were both Aemilii, M. Aemilius Lepidus and L. Aemilius Paullus, and the area through which their portico ran became known as the Aemiliana. The portico was designed as a covered walk for the censors, whose office, the Atrium Libertatis (q.v.), was just inside the walls, beyond the Forum Iulium, but who conducted the census in the Campus Martius, at or near the Altar of Mars, on which its completion was celebrated. Wherever the line of the walls crossed the road over the shoulder of the Capitoline Hill now known as the Clivus Argentarius, we must put the Porta Fontinalis. It presumably got its name from the Tullianum (see Carcer) spring under the Carcer (cf. Festus 482L), and because that spring flows in the direction of the Cloaca, which it joins, the closer we can put the line of the walls to this, the better it will suit the conditions.

Säflund 207.

Porta Ianualis: one of the pomerial gates of the Romulean city (Varro, *Ling.* 5.165), presumably that which led to the Ianus Geminus (q.v.), therefore located at the north corner of the Palatine where the

Nova Via turned and now a stair descends behind the Temple of Vesta. Macrobius (*Sat.* 1.9.17–18) seems to have mistaken the Porta Ianualis for the Ianus Geminus itself, but has badly mislocated it.

AJA 84 (1980): 93–96 (H. B. Evans).

Porta Labicana: see **Porta Praenestina.**

Porta Latina: a gate in the Aurelian Walls through which the Via Latina (q.v.) issued. It has a single arch, originally probably wider than what we see. There are three clear building periods: (1) the Aurelian original construction of an arch in a curtain between semicircular towers, of which only the western tower now remains; (2) a rebuilding in which the towers received a new and higher roof with a flat battlemented top that rose above the upper rampart walk; at this time a vantage court with an interior arched gate was added; and (3) a refacing of the arch with blocks of travertine and reconstruction of the gateway with a portcullis run in slots just behind the façade and a door of two leaves behind this. The portcullis chamber over the gate had five arched windows on the front and a flat roof decorated with tapered merlons. The stone arch is worked together with a relieving arch in an interesting way in order to carry the weight of the portcullis, and it was projected to build rectangular stone bastions around the bases of the towers, but for some obscure reason this project was not carried out, so the stone facing of the arch simply tails into the brickwork of the curtain to either side, and only the foundations for the bastions were laid. It is comparatively well preserved and an exceptionally interesting gate.

Richmond 100–109; Nash 2.213.

Porta Laurentina: see **Porta Ardeatina.**

Porta Lavernalis (Figs. 14, 58.13): a gate in the Servian Walls named for the grove of Laverna, which was probably not far outside the gate (Varro, *Ling.* 5.163–64; Paulus *ex Fest.* 104–5L), because thieves were supposed to hide their booty there and Laverna was supposed to be their patron divinity (Roscher 2.1917–18 [G. Wissowa]). The sequence of gates given by Varro is Porta Naevia, Porta Raudusculana, Porta Lavernalis, which suggests that it should be on the Aventine, where the site of a gate has been identified in a throat immediately to the east of the Bastione di Sangallo (Bastioni di Paolo III). This was on a road connecting Vicus Armilustri and Via Ostiensis, represented by the modern Via di Porta Lavernale. But as Säflund observes, the scholia on Horace (*Epist.* 1.16.60) state explicitly that the grove of La-

verna was on Via Salaria, so perhaps we should think of two groves.

Säflund 198.

Porta Maior: see **Porta Praenestina.**

Porta Metrovia (Metrobi, Metronia, Metrosi) (Fig. 16): First mentioned in the Einsiedeln *Descriptio Murorum Honoriana* (VZ 2.206) and the Einsiedeln itinerary, the name went through what one would think was every possible permutation in the course of the Middle Ages. It was originally only a postern in the Aurelian Walls, and the origin of the name is obscure. It was a simple arch in an ordinary curtain between towers, and its main purpose may have been to admit the Marana brook, which must have crossed the line of the wall in a culvert in antiquity. Later a guardhouse tower was added behind the archway, and the arch may have received a portcullis, but the former is regarded as not earlier than the fifth century. No road of any importance led to or from this gate.

Richmond 142–44; Nash 2.214–16.

Porta Minucia: known only from Festus (Paulus *ex Fest.* 109L; cf. 131L), who says it received its name from the Altar of Minucius. This suggests that what is meant is the Column of Minucius Augurinus (the Columna Minucia, q.v.), because it was very old (awarded in 439 B.C.) and odd, and showed Minucius with a long staff that might have been mistaken for the scepter of divinity. It is shown on coins (Crawford 242/1, 243/1). It stood just outside the Porta Trigemina and might well have given one of the fornices of that gate a second name.

Porta Mugonia (Mucionia, Mucionis): the best known of the pomerial gates of the Romulean city. Its place was just above Summa Sacra Via on the Clivus Palatinus (Ovid, *Trist.* 3.1.31–32; Dion. Hal. 2.50.3; Solinus 1.24). It was probably never more than a place-name. Attempts at explaining the name, although not uncommon, are all clearly fanciful, and what the name meant remains unknown.

AJA 84 (1980): 93–96 (H. B. Evans).

Porta Naevia (Figs. 14, 58.11): a gate in the Servian Walls known from the Capitoline Base to have been in Regio XII of the Augustan city (*CIL* 6.975 = *ILS* 6073) and given by Varro (*Ling.* 5.163) in the sequence: *Tutilinae loca, Porta Naevia, Raudusculana.* This makes it fairly certain that the gate in question is on the Aventinus Minor on the neck between the churches of S. Balbina and S. Saba connecting with the plateau beyond. It was not an important gate, and from it issued the Via Ardeatina/Laurentina. Festus (170L) tells us that it received its name from the Nemora Naevia that had once belonged to a certain Naevius and had in time got an evil reputation because vagabonds and profligates were accustomed to frequent it. One may wonder whether this reputation was not derived rather from the associations of the words *naevus* and *naevius*.

Säflund 199.

Porta Navalis: mentioned only by Festus (187L) as a gate in the vicinity of the Navalia (q.v.). If he is right, the Navalia in question must be the Navalia Inferiora on the Tiber somewhere below the Aventine, for which there seems to be no place at all near the Servian Walls. However, one might think of a postern at the end of the extension of Vicus Armilustri to the line of the walls. A road from this might then lead down behind the great warehouse now commonly called Porticus Aemilia in a straight line to the Navalia some 600 m away.

Säflund 208.

Porta Nomentana (Fig. 72): a gate in the Aurelian Walls from which issued the Via Nomentana, now replaced by Porta Pia. Although badly ruined, it is a reasonably clear example of a gate in the original fortifications of Aurelian and evidently was one of a standard pair with Porta Tiburtina. It consisted of a curtain with a single central archway flanked by semicircular towers of two storeys with a gate chamber between them, all faced with fine brickwork. Above the gate and towers was a flat roof with battlements. No extra storeys were ever added. The south tower was found to contain the altar tomb of Q. Haterius and was pulled down in the nineteenth century to recover this. Earlier, at the time of the creation of Porta Pia in 1564, the curtain was given a battered face of brick that completely masks the old curtain.

Richmond 93–100; Nash 2.217; *CAR* 3-D, 74 pp. 89–90.

Porta Ostiensis (East) (Fig. 14): a gate in the Aurelian Walls from which issued the Via Ostiensis (q.v.), the artery connecting Rome with its major suburb; Ammianus (17.4.14) confirms the name. The history of the gate in antiquity can be divided into three major periods, like that of most of the important gates in this fortification system. In the original construction of the time of Aurelian the gate was rather low, an affair of twin arches in a curtain be-

tween semicircular towers. In most ways the gate closely resembled the original Porta Appia. In a second period, when the gallery was added to the wall, the earlier towers were heightened, thickened on the outside, and provided with loopholes. New communication with the gallery of the wall was also arranged. A vantage court was added, but it seems to have been for tax collection rather than part of the defensive system. The walls curved, and the court was finished with twin arches to the city matching those on the exterior. The major change in external appearance was greater height. In the third period the twin arches of earlier time were removed and replaced by a single arch with a portcullis. The portcullis chamber over the arch had six round-headed windows. Each tower was given an extra storey, and the battlemented curtain between them was crowned by a pair of guardhouses. Finally, the base storey of the curtain and towers was sheathed in a wall of travertine blocks.

Richmond 109–21; Nash 2.218–19.

Porta Ostiensis (West) (Fig. 14): This gate, just west of the Pyramid of Cestius, was demolished in 1888, but Lanciani measured and drew it during the process. It was a small postern, 3.60 m wide, serving the traffic to the large quarter of warehouses on the adjacent Tiber bank. The gate was faced with travertine and trimmed on the jambs and lintel with moldings. It was bricked up in the time of Maxentius and never reopened. Because the road through it joined the Via Ostiensis only a little distance outside the walls, it was easy enough to build a short new road inside to link the two when the gate was abandoned.

Richmond 219–21.

Porta Pancratiana: see **Porta Aurelia** (1).

Porta Pandana: a gate in the fortifications of the Capitoline, supposed originally to have been called Porta Saturnia (Varro, *Ling.* 5.42; Solinus 1.13). According to Festus (246L, 496L), in the peace between Romulus and Titus Tatius it was stipulated that this gate, through which Tarpeia had admitted the Sabines, should always be open for them. Polyaenus (8.25.1) tells substantially the same story but makes the agreement with the Gauls, an obvious blunder. There must be a way around this, for a gate that always had to stand open would make any system of fortifications almost useless. We might see the answer in that it had to stand open only for the Sabines, but that seems hardly adequate. More likely it was a gate in a position of such strength that assault on it would be impossible. At the top of the Tarpeian Rock, where, if necessary, scarping could have made the cliff face sheer, the gate would be virtually impregnable. Of course it is also possible that the Romans got around the terms of the treaty by then building a wall inside or outside the Porta Pandana. It seems to have survived as late as the time of Varro, though perhaps only as a place-name, but Festus speaks of it in the past tense. Dionysius (10.14.1–2), in telling the story of Appius Herdonius, the Sabine who in 460 B.C. seized the Capitoline in an attempt at revolution, has him bring his forces into the Capitoline by this open gate, but calls it the Porta Carmentalis. If his mistake was simply in confusing the point at which they began their ascent of the Capitoline, *ad Carmentis* (cf., e.g., Livy 5.47.2 and the ascent of the Gauls), with the gate at the top of this cliff, then everything falls neatly into place. See also Centum Gradus.

Säflund 208.

Porta S. Petri: see **Porta Aurelia** (2).

Porta Piacularis: known only from Festus (235L) and said to be so named because of *piacula* performed there, which is less than helpful, because piacula must have been performed at every gate, at least every gate of any importance. Säflund sensibly ignores it.

Porta Pinciana: a gate in the Aurelian Walls that was originally a minor entrance serving "Via Salaria Vetus," a road running northwest from the valley of modern Via del Tritone following approximately the line of modern Via Francesco Crispi and Via di Porta Pinciana to link up with Via Salaria. Its ancient name is quite uncertain; it was probably not Pinciana, because that family does not seem to have occupied the Mons Pincius before the fourth century. It appears very complete, but has been much transformed in the course of time. It began as a gate in a curtain set at an angle to the road it spanned, flanked only on the east by a semicircular tower on a rectangular foundation. In a second period, when the gallery was added to the wall, it received a second tower on the west and was promoted from a third-class entrance to a second-class one. It was given a vantage court, which has now disappeared but was carefully shown on Nolli's map of 1748. At that time the gate became rather imposing. In a third period, by which time it can be presumed to have got the name Porta Pinciana, it was given a new travertine curtain, very close in measurements and effect to that of Porta Latina. The blocks of the curtain were robbed from

nearby tombs, and some preserve inscriptions. The gate was given a portcullis with a portcullis chamber over the gate, and probably at the same time an extra storey above this and above each of the towers.

The gate saw heavy fighting with the Goths in 536, and repairs were carried out in rough masonry of block and brick thereafter. At the time of the Einsiedeln list it was closed, but it seems to have been open in the eighth century. In 1808 it was again closed for a century and reopened in 1906.

Richmond 159–69; *CAR* 2-E, 4 p. 103; Nash 2.220–21.

Porta Pompae (Circensis, in Circo Maximo): the gate by which the circus procession entered the arena preparatory to circling the spina. This must have been at the carceres end of the arena, because all those who had any part in the ludi would be included, and among these were the *tensae* in which the images of the gods were transported and the racing chariots and charioteers. The triumphal arch of Titus at the apex of the sphendone end seems to have been mounted on steps that would have made negotiation by such vehicles awkward, if not impossible, unless temporary ramps were introduced, and the carceres end was traditionally the point at which everything started. An axial gate at this end is regularly shown as larger than the other gates of the carceres and without closure. It is therefore presumed that this was the Porta Pompae.

Humphrey 81.

Porta Portuensis: an important gate in the Aurelian Walls destroyed when Pope Urban VIII built the new fortifications of the Transtiberim. It originally was a gate of twin arches, and before its destruction carried an inscription of Honorius in four lines similar to that of Porta Tiburtina. It was flanked by semicircular towers and had a vantage court, and the lower storey of arch, curtain, and towers was faced with cut stone, presumably travertine. At some time the western arch was filled in, and the towers were given great battered reinforcement around their bases. There is much that is uncertain about this gate, but it was clearly a major entrance, as befitted the Via Portuensis, which carried the traffic between the capital and its port.

Richmond 200–205; Nash 2.222–24.

Porta Praenestina (Fig. 16): the present Porta Maggiore, a double arch of the Aqua Claudia and Anio Novus (qq.v.) that Claudius built to take the new aqueduct over the Via Praenestina (q.v.) and Via Labicana (q.v.) just beyond their point of divergence (the Labicana to the right, or southeast, the Praenestina to the left). The two arches are at a slight angle to each other and built entirely of blocks of travertine with heavy rustication. The whole is 32 m high and 24 m wide, and the principal arches are 14 m high, 6.35 m wide, and 6.20 m deep. In the central pier is a small arch, 5.10 m high and 1.80 m wide, now almost buried. Above this and to either side of the main arches are narrow arches framed with an engaged, but deeply projecting, Corinthian order and pedimented entablatures. The attic is divided by stringcourses into three fasciae, each of which bears an inscription relative to the building or repair of the aqueducts (CIL 1256–58; ILS 218). Just outside the arches, in the space between the two roads, was set the early Augustan Sepulcrum Eurysacis (q.v.).

Just in front of this aqueduct arch, with no space intervening, the Porta Praenestina/Labicana was built by Aurelian. The gate passages were walled down inside the aqueduct arches and carried forward as far as the tomb of Eurysaces, which was used as the foundation of a great tower with a semicircular front after the destruction of the tomb's front. Probably there were also semicircular towers to either side, but these have completely disappeared. In the time of Honorius stone curtains were added to the gates, and that of Porta Labicana was given a lengthy inscription (CIL 6.1189 = ILS 797) to record this. At this time each gate was equipped with a portcullis and a vaulted chamber over the gate for working this; a similar arrangement may have existed earlier. Each portcullis chamber was windowed, there being four round-headed windows over Porta Praenestina and five over Porta Labicana, and above each was a flat roof trimmed with merlons. The semicircular tower between the gates was given a stone facing, and a large quadrangular tower to either side, with a solid base faced with stone and no fewer than three chambered storeys under the flat merloned roof, completed the exterior. Stairs to the towers would have had to be arranged in front of the Claudian arches, which would have made this gate especially imposing. On the interior was a vantage court that is shown on Nolli's map of 1748 but has been completely destroyed without adequate record; this had a single gate to the city, because the two roads merged just inside the Claudian arches.

The Porta Labicana was blocked up sometime after its rebuilding, very likely during the siege of the Goths, certainly before 966, and thereafter only one gate was needed. Various works of patching and alteration on a small scale in the course of the centuries could be detected. The east tower, now that that gate was closed, was allowed to fall into disrepair. In 1838–1839, under Pope Gregory XVI, the gate was destroyed in order to reveal the tomb of Eurysaces and the Claudian arches.

Richmond 205–17; Nash 2.225–28.

Porta Querquetulana (Fig. 58.8): a gate, almost certainly in the Servian Walls, that derived its name from a grove or wood of oaks, said to have been inside the gate (Festus 314L, 315L; Pliny, HN 16.37). Tacitus (Ann. 4.65) preserves the interesting tradition that the Caelian was originally called Mons Querquetulanus and later received the name Caelian from the Etruscan condottiere Caele Vibenna. But because Caele Vibenna is supposed to have come to Rome under one or another of the kings, this would have been long before the building of the Servian Walls. It seems best then to accept Festus's explanation of the name of the gate and to suppose that there was still a remnant of the wood on the farther reaches of the hill. We can see this gate as that spanning the road that became Via Tusculana, ascending the hill obliquely in the vicinity of SS. Quattro Coronati. The notion that it was a gate in a very early fortification of the hill seems contradicted by the passage in Festus.

Säflund 168.

Porta Quirinalis (Figs. 58.4, 72): a gate in the Servian Walls taking its name from the Temple of Quirinus, which also gave its name to the hill on which it stood. The gate has been placed just north of the Temple of Quirinus, where an ancient street corresponding approximately to modern Via delle Quattro Fontane is known to have crossed the line of the walls. However it is odd that Paulus (Festus 302–3L), our only source, should attribute the name to a Quirini sacellum, if it were near the Temple of Quirinus (see Quirinus, Aedes), which, even before its rebuilding by Augustus, was one of the most impressive temples in Rome (Vitruvius 3.2.7). Because it is unthinkable that the Porta Quirinalis did not lead to the Quirinal, this is probably simply a blunder by Paulus.

Säflund 167, 206.

Porta Ratumena (**Ratumenna**) (Fig. 58.17): the name of a gate supposed to have been derived from that of an Etruscan charioteer who, having won a race at Veii, was carried away by his team and brought to Rome, thrown from his car, and killed at this gate. The horses then proceeded to the Area Capitolina and stopped in front of the terracotta quadriga of Jupiter on the roof of the Capitoline temple. This took place in the early days of the re-public (Festus 340–42L; Pliny *HN* 8.161; Solinus 45.15; Plutarch, *Poplic.* 13.3–4). It seems clear that this must be a gate in the defenses of the Capitoline. If what has been said about the Porta Pandana/Sa-turnia (q.v.) is correct, it is impossible to think that a chariot could have approached from that direction. In fact, the only approaches possible for a chariot must always have been by way of the Clivus Capi-tolinus and the north side of the hill by a switchback track like the Via delle Tre Pile and not far from it. For someone coming from Veii, this would seem the obvious route. We can put the Porta Ratumena at the top of Michelangelo's Cordonata, where Säflund puts the Porta Catularia. The name must be very old and suggests an Etruscan origin. It might well have been part of the works of the Etruscan kings on the Capitoline.

Säflund 167.

Porta Raudusculana (Figs. 14, 58.12): a gate in the Servian Walls mentioned by Varro (*Ling.* 5.163) in the sequence: Porta Naevia, Porta Raudusculana, Porta Lavernalis, and explained as meaning "bronze-sheathed," "bronze-bound," whereas Festus (338–39L) offers other explanations, deriving it from *rudis* or *raudus*. According to Valerius Maximus (5.6.3), the gate got its name from the praetor Genucius Ci-pus, from whose forehead sprouted horns as he was leaving on campaign in 239 B.C. When explanation of the prodigy was sought, he was told that if he re-turned to the city he would be king. To avoid this he went into voluntary exile, and in his honor a likeness of his head in bronze was affixed to the gate by which he had left, and it was from this bronze that it got its name. While the story has elements of the fan-tastic, apotropaic heads at gates are common in Italy at the period in question (cf., e.g., the Porta all'Arco at Volterra and Porta Marzia at Perugia), and an Achelous head is a common apotropaion. It seems clear that there must have been such an apotropaion at Porta Raudusculana at one time. Perhaps its sin-gularity was in its being bronze; stone carvings must have been commoner. However, it is difficult to imagine that any of the important gates of Rome was not provided with some sort of bronze reinforce-ments.

The place of Porta Raudusculana is established by the Capitoline Base as in Regio XII (*CIL* 6.975 = *ILS* 6073), where we find a Vicus Portae Raudusculanae. This is generally thought to have been a continuation of Vicus Piscinae Publicae (q.v.) and set in the depression between the Aventinus Maior and Aven-tinus Minor (modern Viale Aventino at Piazza Al-bania).

Säflund 175–76, 199.

Porta Romana (Romanula): one of the pomerial gates of the Romulean city at the juncture of Nova Via and Clivus Victoriae (Varro, *Ling.* 5.164; Festus 318L) in or near the Velabrum. It was not in form a gate, but simply a square platform with steps on all sides, perhaps only a couple of steps, evidently rather modest, which was the reason the people took to calling a nearby arch or fountain of architectural form (*ubi ex epistylio defluit aqua*) Porta Romana. Because it had never been more than a place desig-nation, it is understandable that nearby monuments might have been confused with it, especially in this part of Rome, where so many enigmatic bits of ear-lier ages still survived.

The name requires explanation, because gate names regularly allude to places to which they lead, not those from which they lead, and the Romans were aware of this difficulty, hence the substitution of the diminutive Romanula. Festus (318L) suggests that it got its name from the Sabines, for whom it was the closest approach to Rome, which is patent nonsense. The suggestion that Roma was originally the name of the Forum Boarium/Velabrum and later transferred to the Palatine creates more difficulties than it attempts to solve. The linguists' observation that the name of Rome should be connected with *ruma*, *rumen* (river, watercourse) and that this was the river gate is still far the most satisfactory, al-though it does not explain how that name got trans-ferred to the city.

Säflund 195–96; *AJA* 84 (1980): 94–95 (H. B. Ev-ans).

Porta Salaria (Fig. 72): the gate in the Aurelian Walls by which issued the Via Salaria (q.v.) running almost due north after branching from the Via No-mentana just outside the Porta Collina. The gate was so severely damaged in the bombardment of Rome in 1870 that it was demolished and replaced in 1873 by a new one designed by Vespignani. This gate was then demolished in 1921, and there is nothing there today. We depend on drawings and descriptions for our knowledge of the ancient gate.

It was a single-arch gate flanked by great semicir-cular towers with a blind lower storey and three large windows at wide intervals in the storey above. The gate also had a chamber above it with three large windows. These were probably all covered with concrete vaults and battlemented flat roofs. All of this is familiar and can be assigned to the time of Aurelian. Later the towers were heightened by the addition of an extra storey, the lower part of the cur-tain between was faced with blocks of travertine, and a portcullis was installed, perhaps a replacement for one already there. These changes can be assigned to the time of Honorius. Extensive refacing in block and brick is of a type associated with the repairs to the fortifications that Belisarius carried out in the time of the Gothic War, and before the end of antiquity a large central part of the face of the travertine arch collapsed and was replaced by a new brick facing.

Richmond 185–90; Nash 2.229–30; *CAR* 3-A, 26 pp. 26–28.

Porta Salutaris (Figs. 58.3, 72): a gate in the Servian Walls that derived its name from the Temple of Salus (see Salus, Aedes) and Collis Salutaris, presumably approached by the Clivus Salutaris (Festus 436–37L). Because in his account of the Argei (*Ling.* 5.52) Varro seems to list the sites on the Quirinal in an order descending from northeast to southwest, there is every reason to put this on the height just below the Quirinal proper and to see the Clivus Salutaris as the street found in conjunction with the Sepulcrum Semproniorum south of the east end of Via della Dataria, and the gate would have stood at the top of that slope in Piazza del Quirinale (Montecavallo). It seems to have been a minor gate, and the approach to it would have been difficult.

Säflund 206.

Porta Sanqualis (Figs. 58.2, 72): a gate in the Servian Walls named from the Temple of Semo Sancus (Festus 465L), listed by Varro (*Ling.* 5.52, where the divinity is called Dius Fidius) on the Collis Mucialis and following the Collis Salutaris. It must be the interior court gate identified by Säflund in Piazza Magnanapoli, for which the later arch still preserved in Palazzo Antonelli was a ballista emplacement covering its approach.

Säflund 88–98, 206; G. Brands, *Republikanische Stadttore in Italien* (BAR 458, Oxford 1988), 196–97.

Porta Saturnia: see **Porta Pandana.**

Porta Scelerata: see **Porta Carmentalis.**

Porta Septimiana: the modern gate on the right bank of the Tiber that Alexander VI built in 1498 to replace one that was in ruinous condition but, according to reports, carried an inscription of Septimius Severus. There are no views or accounts of the older gate, but it is in a location where one might expect there to have been a gate and seems to have been mentioned in the Historia Augusta (S.H.A. *Sept. Sev.* 19.5). The passage is corrupt, but Zangemeister has interpreted it with some likelihood of correctness as meaning that the Thermae Septimianae in this area, as well as other Severan works, were put out of commission by the construction of the Aurelian Walls, which had to cut through them. In compensation for this loss, this gate in the wall was named for Septimius, either by Aurelian or as a result of popular sympathy. The gate opened to a road along the river corresponding to the modern Via della Lungara and brought the complex of ancient buildings between the Circus Gaii et Neronis and the Mausoleum Hadriani into communication with the walled Transtiberim.

Richmond 223–27; Nash 2.231; *MAAR* 36 (1980): 223–24 (R. E. A. Palmer).

Porta Stercoraria: an alleyway on the Capitoline about midway on the ascent of the Clivus Capitolinus to which the refuse from the Temple of Vesta was carried and deposited on 15 June (Festus 466L; Varro, *Ling.* 6.32). Festus says it was closed by a door, but this detail seems to be added as an afterthought to explain the name. Varro implies that the sweepings were taken instead to a particular place, and Ovid (*Fast.* 6.713) says explicitly that they were thrown in the Tiber. Perhaps these conflicting accounts can be reconciled by supposing that the sweepings were ceremonially conveyed to an elevated place on the Capitoline, where they were deposited (*quando stercus* [or *stercum*] *delatum fas*) and the wind was allowed to blow them in the direction of the Tiber, for the river is too far from the Capitoline for the Vestal Virgins to have thrown such matter into it from the Capitoline, and the sources seem to emphasize their having deposited it. There may have been a gate closing the angiportus to the public, but there seems to be no question of a gate in any system of fortifications.

Porta Taurina: see **Forum Tauri** and **Porta Tiburtina.**

Porta Tiburtina: the gate in the Aurelian Walls through which issues the Via Tiburtina. It is built in front of, but tight against, an inscribed (*CIL* 6.1244 = *ILS* 98) Augustan arch that carried the Aqua Marcia/Tepula/Iulia over the Via Tiburtina and consequently presents certain oddities of planning and construction. The gate originally consisted of a single arch in a short curtain between semicircular towers of brick-faced concrete, and the southern tower was fitted onto a skewed wall but conforming as well as possible to standard measurements. At some time after the first construction a vantage court was added that made use of the Augustan aqueduct as one side. It had a new arch of stone blocks aligned with the road, which bent after passing under the aqueduct arch. The court was filled with a complex of medieval buildings and was destroyed in 1869.

In a rebuilding under Honorius (*CIL* 6.1190), the curtain was faced entirely in stone and flanked by quadrangular towers whose lower storeys were also faced with stone, probably all robbed from nearby tombs. There was a portcullis chamber over the gate lit by five round-headed windows in the façade, beneath which ran the commemorative inscription, and surmounted by a flat roof with ornamental merlons, between which may have stood the statues mentioned in the inscription. In this period the gate was a twin to the Porta Chiusa (q.v.) nearby to the north, and it may be the work of the same builder.

There is much medieval and later work encumbering the walls in the vicinity of the gate, but not in the gate itself. However, its study is complicated by the Acqua Felice of Pope Sixtus V, which used the city wall for support and was here taken over the gate. In the Middle Ages it was called Porta S. Lorenzo and Porta Taurina (from the bulls' heads on the keystone of the aqueduct arch).

Richmond 170–81; Nash 2.232–33.

Porta Trigemina

Porta Trigemina (Fig. 58.14): an important gate in the Servian Walls near the southern end of the Forum Boarium to which the Clivus Publicius leading down from the Aventine seems to have descended (Frontinus, *Aq.* 1.5). It is probably not necessary to posit a meeting of three streets here to account for the name. More likely it had a central passage for wheeled traffic flanked by side passages for pedestrians. Given the volume of traffic known to have passed through this part of Rome (cf. Plautus, *Capt.* 90), such an arrangement would have been practical, and the story of the death of Gaius Gracchus shows that the gate could be defended by a single man (Val. Max. 4.7.2; [Aur. Vict.,] *De Vir. Ill.* 65.5).

In the early second century B.C. the Emporium (q.v.) of Rome found its place outside Porta Trigemina, probably along the Aventine just beyond the limits of the Forum Boarium (Livy 41.27.8–9), and in connection with this numerous porticoes were erected (Livy 35.10.11–12, 35.41.10, 40.51.4–6, 41.27.8–9). These were probably all more or less temporary constructions and demolished as the Emporium moved farther down the river in the course of time. None is mentioned after 174 B.C. But we have sepulchral inscriptions for a *lagunaria* (*CIL* 6.9488) and a *mellarius* (*CIL* 6.9618 = *ILS* 7497) from the Porta Trigemina, and a *librarius* (*CIL* 6.9515 = *ILS* 7751) from *extra Porta Trigemina*.

Although the location of the gate cannot be determined precisely, now that we know that the Servian Walls were a closed circuit we can put it in its proper surroundings. From it one ascended the Aventine in one direction and reached the Pons Sublicius in the other. The Emporium was for a time just outside it.

The Circus Maximus brook must have crossed the line of the walls at this gate; though bridged at points, this cannot have been culverted before the second century B.C. So we can put the Porta Trigemina with great confidence in the immediate neighborhood of S. Maria in Cosmedin. See also Porta Minucia.

Säflund 176–79, 184–85, 197–98; *BullCom* 80 (1965–67): 5–36 (G. Sartorio and H. Lyngby); *RömMitt* 87 (1980): 327–34 (M. Pfanner); G. Brands, *Republikanische Stadttore in Italien* (BAR 458, Oxford 1988), 197–98; Coarelli 1988, 25–50.

Porta Triumphalis: see **Porta Carmentalis.**

Porta Vetus Palatii: see **Porta Mugonia.**

Porta Viminalis (Figs. 58.6, 72): a gate in the middle of the ancient Agger on the Viminal (Festus 156–57L, 516L; Strabo 5.3.7 [234]; Frontinus, *Aq.* 1.19). Remains that can be seen in the tract just north of the Stazione Termini are sufficient to present a hypothetical reconstruction (cf. Säflund 63–67). It was a simple, narrow, paved throat through the Agger, a little more than 3 m wide, running from a piazza of undetermined extent inside the Agger, and with an aqueduct line (Marcia/Tepula/Iulia) alongside it to the northwest. The closures and their location are not clear. This was evidently never an important gate, and the road issuing from it in a straight line led to the Porta Chiusa (q.v.) in the Aurelian Walls. This was possibly the old line of the Via Tiburtina.

Säflund 63–67, 205, 248–49; *CAR* 3-G, 167–68 pp. 252–57.

Porticus: the Roman version of the Greek stoa, consisting of a covered colonnade, usually with an essentially closed back wall and one or more parallel rows of columns, but occasionally entirely columnar. The earliest porticus in Rome do not antedate the Second Punic War. The earliest recorded are two built by the aediles of 193 B.C. and are probably a consequence of the Romans' encounter with Greek architecture in Sicily (see Porticus Aemilia). The earliest seem all to have been of a single wing; the first enclosing an area is the Porticus Metelli of ca. 146 B.C., and it seems to have been experimental. Earlier the porticus was used to border part of a temple precinct, to make a roofed walk between two points, or to provide shelter in which markets could operate. Although a porticus might be attached to a building, it seems usually to have had an essentially independent function. The Greek stoa built as a unit with shops is not found in Rome. Once the porticus enclosing a square is invented, one seldom finds recurrence to single-wing examples, except as additions to temple precincts. Together with the enclosed square comes the invention of the peristyle as an important addition to the private house and the peristyle garden for refreshment and pleasure. Something of the same sort probably happened with public porticus, and, from providing shelter and seclusion from the noise and traffic outside, they came in a short time to be embellished with works of art and to frame parks and gardens designed for enjoyment. It is interesting that whereas the colonnade as a connecting walk appears early in Rome, the colonnaded street, which soon becomes ubiquitous in the East, was never used more than sparingly in Rome itself.

The exploitation of the porticus as an architectural form comes in two bursts of activity, an early one when the porticus are especially for utilitarian purposes, the first half of the second century B.C., and one in the second half of the first century B.C., when they become luxurious and monumental complexes for public use and edification, which foreshadow the great bath complexes of the next century. As examples of these one might single out the Porticus Pompeii and the Saepta Iulia. A porticus regularly took its name from its builder, its purpose, or some striking feature or work of art that it contained (Porticus Corinthia, Porticus Argonautarum), but as late as the time of Pliny, if a porticus had more than one wing, it was regularly referred to in the plural.

The Campus Martius lent itself to the development of porticus because it was kept largely open and aqueductless until the time of Augustus. By the second century the whole lower Campus Martius was covered with them, and, together with the imperial fora, one could say that Rome had become a city of porticus. One could walk almost from one end of the city to the other going from colonnade to colonnade, and Vitruvius (5.9) waxes eloquent in praising their advantages and usefulness.

Porticus Absidata (Fig. 39): mentioned only in the regionary catalogues, where it is listed in Regio IV, and in the twelfth century Ordo Benedicti (Jordan 2.664; VZ 3.214), which indicates that it lay just outside the imperial fora, beyond an arch variously known as Aureus, of Aurea, and of Aura. Probably there is confusion here of the area known as Aura behind the Basilica Constantini and an Arcus Aureus in the Forum Nervae (cf. the churches of S. Andrea and S. Maria de Arcu Aurae, HCh 177, 312). The arch in question is that just southeast of the Temple of Minerva. The Porticus Absidata, as its name indicates, was a portico developed in an arc. Remains of this have been discovered behind the Temple of Minerva, a wall of complicated curvature behind a line of footings for an arcade. This made an entrance

court for the forum, a transition between Subura and forum. It is shown on a fragment of the Marble Plan (*FUR* pl. 20; Rodriguez pl. 12). It is a particularly clever piece of planning, because it fills the irregular space behind the southeast hemicycle of the Forum Augustum and the Temple of Minerva very handsomely and disguises the awkwardness of the approach to the Forum Nervae, which lies off the axis of the forum.

The Porticus Absidata was excavated in 1935–1940, and A. M. Colini published a very brief account of the excavation (*BullCom* 68 [1940]: 226–27). Recently it was reexcavated and studied exhaustively by H. Bauer, who has provided detailed drawings of almost every aspect. According to Bauer, it should be reconstructed as an arcade in two storeys, the lower storey vaulted and revetted entirely in white marble, the upper a marble arcade standing free in front of a wall of rusticated blocks of peperino. The evidence for most of the architectural features is very good. On less reliable evidence Bauer would roof the interior with a dome behind an open pediment under a high attic. This is difficult to accept; an open court seems more suitable.

RömMitt 90 (1983): 111–84 (H. Bauer).

Porticus Aemilia (1): extra Portam Trigeminam, built by the aediles M. Aemilius Lepidus and L. Aemilius Paullus in 193 B.C. (Livy 35.10.12). This was a utilitarian portico, for Livy adds that they added an Emporium (q.v.) along the Tiber. It required restoration by the censors Q. Fulvius Flaccus and A. Postumius Albinus in 174 (Livy 41.27.8). In the same passage Livy speaks of work on the Emporium and of another portico, either mounting the Aventine or, more likely, lying tight against its flank (the text is corrupt), which they paved with cobbles. Five years earlier, in 179 B.C., the censor M. Fulvius Nobilior had built yet another portico outside the Porta Trigemina (Livy 40.51.6). All these porticoes were probably wooden market buildings, not intended to be permanent and subjected to intensive use. They were also probably particularly prone to damage in floods of the Tiber.

Porticus Aemilia (2): a Porta Fontinali ad Martis aram (Livy 35.10.12), built by the same aediles and at the same time as Porticus Aemilia (1). If, as seems probable, the Porta Fontinalis was the gate on the Clivus Argentarius going over the northeast shoulder of the Capitoline Hill, it was in the immediate neighborhood of the Atrium Libertatis (q.v.), the office of the censors. The Altar of Mars in the Campus Martius was probably where they held the census and certainly where they closed the lustrum, and it is very likely the square feature shown near the south end of the Divorum on the Marble Plan (*FUR* pl. 31; Rodriguez pl. 26) and was always in more or less this location. The Porticus Aemilia was, then, a covered walk especially for the convenience of the censors, but also for anyone going from the neighborhood of the Forum Romanum to the Campus Martius, as the consuls must have when holding centuriate assemblies for any purpose. It was therefore a ceremonial walk and would have been suitably monumental. It seems to have given the name Aemiliana (q.v.) to this part of the Campus Martius.

Porticus Agrippiana: see **Porticus Argonautarum.**

Porticus Apollinis: see **Apollo Palatinus, Aedes.**

Porticus Argonautarum: the west colonnade of the Saepta Iulia (q.v.), built by Agrippa in 25 B.C. (Cass. Dio 53.27.1). It derived its name from paintings depicting the story of the Argonauts and was the counterpart of the Porticus Meleagri. The Saepta burned in the fire of Titus of A.D. 80 (Cass. Dio 66.24.2), but the Porticus Argonautarum must have been restored almost immediately, for it continued to be the scene of a great market in luxuries and one of the most frequented places in Rome (Martial 2.14.16, 3.20.11, 11.1.12). It and the Porticus Meleagri are both listed in the regionary catalogues in Regio IX. The idea that it might also at least sometimes have been called Porticus Agrippiana (schol. *ad Iuv.* 6.154) is probably wrong, for there would have been no way of telling which of Agrippa's porticoes the speaker meant.

Porticus in Aventinum: see **Porticus Aemilia** (1).

Porticus Boni Eventus: an exceptionally large portico (*porticum . . . ingentem lavacro Agrippae contiguam*) built by Claudius, praefectus urbi in A.D. 374 (Amm. Marc. 29.6.19). It must have been west of the baths, perhaps in the Horti or Nemus Agrippae. Five Corinthian capitals of white marble of extraordinary size, 1.70 m high, were brought to light between 1860 and 1891 in this area (*BullCom* 19 [1891]: 224–27 [R. Lanciani], 42 [1914]: 387–88 [M. Marchetti]); the line they give indicates that the portico to which they would have belonged ran diagonally, northeast/southwest. Its purpose is difficult to decide. The portico took its name from a Templum Boni Eventus (see Bonus Eventus, Templum) in the vicinity. Whether the Horti Agrippae survived at the time that this portico was built is not clear.

Porticus in Capitolio: see **Area Capitolina.**

Porticus Catuli: a portico that Q. Lutatius Catulus built from the spoils of the Cimbri adjacent to his house on the Palatine. It was apparently next-door to Cicero's house, and when Clodius destroyed Cicero's house after Cicero went into exile, he added a portion of the land to Catulus's portico. It was later restored to its original dimensions by decree of the senate. Presumably Catulus's portico was a public building and had plantations of trees (Cicero, *Dom.* 62), but it does not seem to have been known by a distinctive name (Cicero, *Dom.* 62, 102, 114, 116, 137, *Har. Resp.* 58, *Att.* 4.2.5, 4.3.2; Val. Max. 6.3.1).

Porticus in Clivo Capitolino: see **Clivus Capitolinus.**

Porticus Constantini: mentioned only in the regionary catalogues, listed in Regio VII together with the Porticus Vipsania, often presumed to have been a dependency of the Thermae Constantinianae, although this seems hardly likely in view of the situation of the baths on the Collis Salutaris toward the east, well inside Regio VI. Others connect the portico with the church of SS. Apostoli, a church of Constantinian date, but this originally faced east and was known as the Basilica Iulia, after Pope Julius I (A.D. 337–352), its builder, so the case is tenuous at best. Along both sides of Via Lata were porticoes, evidently in series, fronting buildings of multiple arcades. That under the Galleria Colonna, cleared in part in 1820, had piers faced with brick, which might conceivably be the portico in question (*BullCom* 15 [1887]: 144–45 [L. Borsari]).

Porticus Corinthia: see **Porticus Octavia** (1).

Porticus Crep(ereia?): a completion suggested for one inscription (*CIL* 6.675 = 30810 = *ILS* 3533), but very doubtful.

Porticus Curva: see **Forum Traiani** and **Domus Palmata.**

Porticus Decii: a portico conjectured by Lanciani (LFUR sheet 21: *porticus ingens*) based on an extremely fragmentary inscription (*CIL* 6.1099) reported to have been found in the area where the Porticus Aemilia (2) may have run, across from a building between the church of S. Venanzio dei Camerinesi and the Macellum Corvorum, which would put it in the near neighborhood of Palazzo Astalli

(Muti Bussi) in Piazza Aracoeli. But the evidence is too slight to trust.

Porticus Deorum Consentium: a poorly understood building across the Clivus Capitolinus to the northwest of the Temple of Saturn, in its present form Flavian, but that is due to the insertion of the Temple of Divus Vespasianus next to the Temple of Concordia. An older portico, built in 174 B.C., ran from the Temple of Saturn to the Senaculum (Livy 41.27.7) and made a dramatic backdrop for this end of the Forum Romanum. While this may have lost much of its importance after Opimius's reconstruction of the Temple of Concordia and creation of the Basilica Opimia in 121 B.C., it could still have served to unify this end of the forum visually. Even after Tiberius's enlargement of the Temple of Concordia, dedicated in A.D. 10 or 12, a portico adjacent to it could have been a handsome complement. But the Temple of Divus Vespasianus reduced the plot to an awkward trapezoid, and the portico erected there is an ungainly makeshift. It consists of a trapezoidal platform paved with marble, framed on two sides meeting at an obtuse angle with Corinthian colonnades, behind which open seven nearly square chambers built of brick-faced concrete. The two wings of the colonnade are different, one being of fluted columns, the other of unfluted columns of cipollino. The chambers are windowless and dark. At a lower level in the side of the platform along the Temple of Divus Vespasianus is another series of seven similar chambers that seem to have been offices, like the tabernae of the Forum Iulium.

An inscription (*CIL* 6.102 = *ILS* 4003) on the epistyle records a restoration of the *simulacra* of the Dei Consentes by the praefectus urbi Vettius Praetextatus in A.D. 367. It is generally presumed that the images stood in the intercolumniations and that the chambers behind were originally twelve, one for each of the divinities in Varro's list of them in pairs: Jupiter and Tellus, Sol and Luna, Ceres and Liber, Robigus and Flora, Minerva and Venus, Lympha and Bonus Eventus (Varro, *Rust.* 1.1.4). This is very unsatisfactory; there are today thirteen intercolumniations and only seven chambers. Varro says only that gilded statues of the twelve stood *ad forum,* so one would be inclined to see the statues displayed in the court well in front of the colonnade and the chambers as having nothing to do with any cult of the Dei Consentes, but rather as utilitarian space. Even so, it is not an aesthetically pleasing building.

Excavations were carried out here in 1834, and the colonnade and chambers were reconstructed in 1858 using ancient material. This may account in

part for the ruin's unsatisfactory quality. But clearly the builders were aiming at contrast with the Tabularium, which seems rather unfortunate.

Lugli 1946, 114–15; Nash 2.241–43; *Roma, archeologia nel centro* (1985), 1.24–28 (G. Nieddu); *BdA* 71 (1986): 37–52 (G. Nieddu).

Porticus Divorum: see **Divorum, Templum.**

Porticus Europae: a portico somewhere in the Campus Martius, mentioned only by Martial, so presumably a relatively late creation, but mentioned by him several times (2.14.3, 5 and 15, 3.20.12, 7.32.11, 11.1.11). It was distinguished by plantations of box (Martial 2.14.15), and it was especially used by runners (Martial 2.14.3–4, 7.32.11–12). We can therefore presume that it was adjacent to, or part of, a bath complex. That this was not the Baths of Agrippa seems adequately demonstrated by Martial 7.32.11–12, where the implication is that the running track of these baths lay along the Euripus Thermarum Agrippae (see Euripus). That leaves only the Thermae Neronianae. Because no part of that complex, as far as it is known, seems to have been designed for use as a running track, especially not one with plantations of box, we may see the Porticus Europae as a separate feature in the Nemus Thermarum (Tacitus, *Ann.* 15.37) adjacent to the baths.

Porticus Fabaria: listed by the regionary catalogues in Regio XIII, presumably headquarters of the dealers in beans and located among the warehouses below the Aventine.

Porticus Gaii et Lucii (Fig. 48): a monument known from literary sources (Suetonius, *Aug.* 29; cf. Cass. Dio 56.27.5) and identified by a large inscription (*CIL* 6.36908) in honor of Lucius Caesar found in 1898 near the southwest corner of the Basilica Paulli (Aemilia), broken, but clearly not far from the building from which it had fallen. Excavations in 1954 brought to light the remains of a monumental entrance to the forum between the Temple of Divus Iulius and the Basilica Paulli serving also as an entrance to the basilica. It consisted of a double arch, the half toward the basilica with its floor on the same level as that of the basilica, the other sunk four steps to the level of the Sacra Via. This was decorated with an engaged order and presumably served as the base for a program of statuary honoring Augustus's grandsons. The fact that it was balanced on the opposite side of the Temple of Divus Iulius by the Arcus Augusti should not be overlooked. The portico was, in effect, a triumphal arch for a triumph never won, hence its name. See also Basilica Paulli.

Lugli 1946, 96–99; Nash 1.93, 2.244–47; Coarelli 1985, 171–76.

Porticus Gallieni: a portico that Gallienus is said to have planned, extending along the Via Flaminia as far as the Pons Mulvius. It was to have four rows of columns and a row of pedestals carrying statues (S.H.A. *Gallien.* 18.5). So far as is known, it was never begun.

Porticus Gordiani: a grandiose scheme credited to Gordian III for the Campus Martius (S.H.A. *Gord.* 32.5–6). There was to be a portico 1,000 feet long, *sub colle (Pinciano? Quirinali?)* and a second of the same length parallel to this 500 feet away. Down the middle was to be a paved promenade lined with columns and small statuary, and the rest was to be planted. At the end was to be a basilica 500 feet long joining the two porticoes. One sees the influence of Forum Traiani in the design, but it is difficult to imagine that Gordian ever seriously entertained undertaking such a project.

Porticus Gypsiani: see **Porticus Vipsania.**

Porticus Herculea: see **Porticus Pompeii.**

Porticus Ilicii: a portico that the presbyter Ilicius built in the fifth century along the Vicus Patricius from the Memoria Sancti Martyris Hippolyti (S. Lorenzo in Ponte) to the church of S. Pudenziana, a distance of 400 m. Remains of it still exist (LR 391; LFUR sheets 17, 23; HJ 340–41; *BullArchCr* 5 [1867]: 51–60, especially 53–54 [De Rossi]).

Porticus Iovia: see **Porticus Pompeii.**

Porticus Iulia (Fig. 48): a poorly attested building (schol. *ad Pers.* 4.49; cf. Cass. Dio 56.27.5 and corrections; Jordan 1.2.386n.96, 391) identified by Gamberini-Mongenet as the arcuated porches along the flanks of the Temple of Divus Iulius. This seems apt to be correct, if the topographical indications given by the scholiast on Persius can be trusted.

Nash 1.93, 2.248–51.

Porticus Inter Lignarios: built in 192 B.C. extra Portam Trigeminam (Livy 35.41.10), evidently a utilitarian building connected with the Emporium (q.v.) of the period.

Porticus Liviae (Figs. 62, 68): a large portico on the Oppius in Regio III adjacent to the Thermae Traiani, which was built by Livia, the wife of Augustus, and

dedicated in 7 B.C. as part of the triumph of Tiberius. It was dedicated to Concordia, probably Concordia Augusta (Cass. Dio 54.23.6, 55.8.2; Suetonius, *Aug.* 29; Ovid, *Fast.* 6.637–48). The portico occupied the site of the house of Vedius Pollio (see Domus, Vedius Pollio) and was immediately accessible from the Clivus Suburanus over a broad stair in two flights. Although no part of it is visible today, it appears on fragments of the Marble Plan (*FUR* pl. 18; Rodriguez pls. 7–9), and, on the assumption that its plan was symmetrical, it can be reconstructed in its entirety. It was a rectangle surrounded by a double colonnade, behind which opened colonnaded niches, some small, both rectangular and semicircular, others larger, only rectangular. All shops adjacent to it seem to have opened away from it toward streets around it. In the open space was a large central feature, probably a fountain, and small features at the corners, also probably fountains. In overall dimensions the portico was about 115 m long and 75 m wide. It was a very popular resort and much admired (Ovid, *Ars Am.* 1.71–72; Pliny, *HN* 14.11; Pliny, *Epist.* 1.5.9; Strabo 5.3.8 [236]). Pliny tells us that a single prodigious vine stock covered all the walks of the open area, so it must have been gardened. It survived at least until the fourth century, but we know nothing of its later history.

PP 33 (1978): 265–72 (L. Richardson); *Historia* 33 (1984): 309–33 (M. Boudreau Flory); *CEFR* 98 (1987): 611–51 (C. Panella).

Porticus Margaritaria: known only from the regionary catalogues, where it is listed in Regio VIII between the Graecostadium (*Notitia*, Atrium Caci: *Curiosum*) and Elephas Herbarius. Because in the last two centuries of the republic the Sacra Via is known to have been a center of the trade in feminine luxuries, especially jewelry, it has been presumed that the Porticus Margaritaria should be located there. But after the time of Nero there is really no place where one might conveniently locate it, and we know that already in the early empire markets in articles for feminine adornment had sprung up in various places, such as the Saepta Iulia (q.v.). While it seems likely that the jewelers would have moved away from the forum by the time of Nero, it is difficult to guess where they might have moved to, or whether they had a center at all any longer. On the basis of the sequence in which the Porticus Margaritaria appears in the regionary catalogues, Jordan suggested (1.2.476) that the large portico at the base of the Capitoline Hill between the Forum Boarium and Forum Holitorium (Fig. 37.4) might be the Porticus Margaritaria. It is at least as good a suggestion as any made so far. The notion that after Domitian rebuilt the northern wing of Nero's monumental ap-

proach to the Domus Aurea as the Horrea Piperataria (q.v.) the southern wing was also converted
to commercial use is unlikely to be correct. The
architectural changes there suggest offices for the
bureaucracy of the empire rather than a covered
bazaar.

Lugli 1946, 531–33; Nash 2.252–53.

Porticus Maximae: built about A.D. 380, evidently
along the street leading from Circus Flaminius to
Pons Aelius (*CIL* 6.1184 = *ILS* 781). The arch at the
bridgehead commemorated the work, but remains of
architecture, especially granite columns and marble
capitals, have been found chiefly in the Via dei Giubbonari between Piazza Cairoli and the Theater of
Pompey. The reason for the use of the plural is somewhat puzzling at this late date.

Lugli 1938, 94–95; Lugli 1975, 470.

Porticus Meleagri: the east portico of the Saepta
Iulia balancing the Porticus Argonautarum, evidently deriving its name from a representation of the
Calydonian boar hunt and possibly other stories in
which Meleager figured. It appears on a fragment of
the Marble Plan (*FUR* pl. 31; Rodriguez pl. 27). It is
listed with the Porticus Argonautarum in the regionary catalogues, but without indication that both belong to the Saepta.

Porticus Metelli: built by Q. Caecilius Metellus
Macedonicus sometime after his triumph in 146 B.C.,
to enclose the temples of Iuppiter Stator (see Iuppiter
Stator, Aedes [2]) and Iuno Regina (see Iuno Regina,
Aedes [3]). These were probably both already standing, the Temple of Iuno having been dedicated in 179
B.C., the Temple of Iuppiter of uncertain date but
probably still older (*PBSR* 21 [1953]: 152–59 [M. J.
Boyd]). Metellus's portico seems from remains still
on the site to have been of peperino and to have included an Ionic order. It appears to have been closed
on the southeast front toward the Circus Flaminius
and to have been essentially a Hellenistic precinct enclosure. It seems also to have been the first portico in
Rome of more than a single wing and is always referred to in the plural. It was embellished with numerous works of art, notably the twenty-five equestrian statues of the Companions of Alexander by
Lysippus (Vell. Pat., 1.11.3–7, 2.1.2). The Porticus
Octaviae (q.v.) replaced it.

BullCom 87 (1980–81): 37–46 (H. Lauter).

Porticus Miliarensis: see Horti Sallustiani.

Porticus Miliariae: one of the features of Nero's
Domus Aurea (Suetonius, *Nero* 31.1). Suetonius's
language is ambiguous and can be taken to mean

Porticus Liviae,
Representation on the
Marble Plan

that either there was a triple portico a mile long, or
there were three porticoes each a mile long. Because
Suetonius is impressed by the spaciousness *(laxitas)*
of the Domus Aurea, the latter seems more probable.

Porticus Minucia Frumentaria: attested by the regionary catalogues and listed in Regio IX. It is called
Frumentaria to distinguish it from the Porticus Minucia Vetus. At least from the time of Claudius, distribution of grain regularly took place in the Porticus
Minucia (*CIL* 6.10223 = *ILS* 6071), and it continued
there to the time of Apuleius (*De Mundo* 35). It had
at least forty-five *ostia* (Chron. 144) and at each definite groups received their dole on a particular day
of the month (*CIL* 6.10224–25 = *ILS* 6069–70). Beginning in the time of Septimius Severus, the portico
appears in inscriptions of officials of the water department (*CIL* 5.7783 = *ILS* 1128: *curator aquarum
et Minuciae;* 6.1532 = *ILS* 1191: *cur. aquar. et Minuciae;* 10.4752 = *ILS* 1223: *consulari aquarum et
Minuciae;* 14.3902 = *ILS* 1186: *curator aquarum et
Minuciae;* NSc 1901, 129–31 [G. Boni]). It seems
clear from the inscriptions and the other high offices
held by these men that the dole and the water supply
were then united under a single curator.

The enormous rectangular building west of Via
Lata formerly identified as the Saepta Iulia and left
nameless after the proper identification of the Saepta
seems apt to have been the Porticus Minucia Frumentaria (Fig. 18). It extends from the Via del Cara-

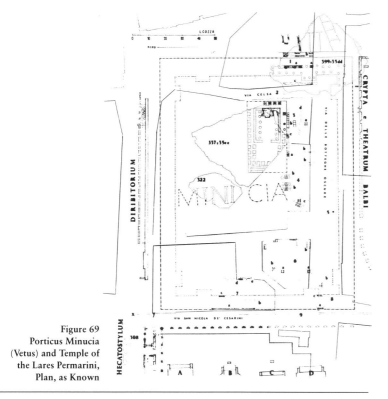

HJ 560–64; *NSc* 1911, 36 (A. Pasqui); *AnalRom*, suppl. 10 (1983): 105–8 (G. Rickman).

Porticus Minucia Vetus (Fig. 69): a postive join of fragments of the Marble Plan by L. Cozza has identified and located the Porticus Minucia (Minicia) as a rectangular complex lying just south of the Diribitorium and just north of the Theatrum and Crypta Balbi, just east of the portico framing the Area Sacra di Largo Argentina along its east side. There seems to have been a double colonnade on all four sides facing inward, the front line broken forward in bays of three columns toward the corners and perhaps elsewhere. This enclosed the Temple of the Lares Permarini (see Lares Permarini, Aedes) of L. Aemilius Regulus, dedicated in 179 B.C., which stood off-center to the southeast, probably because it antedated the portico, which was built by the consul of 110 B.C., M. Minucius Rufus, as a monument to his triumph over the Scordisci (Vell. Pat. 2.8.3). Here Mark Antony set up his tribunal as governor of Rome in 47 B.C. (Cicero, *Phil.* 2.63, 84), perhaps out of deference to Julius Caesar, the absent dictator, for although Velleius described the porticoes as *celebres*, we do not hear of any other magistrates' making use of them. The portico had some association with Hercules, for a statue of Hercules there sweated in the days before Commodus's assassination (S.H.A. *Commod.* 16.5), and games here are recorded for 4 June (Philocalus), which was consecrated to Hercules Custos. But why the games were not held in the Circus Flaminius, where the Temple of Hercules Custos stood at the northwest end, is not clear. The portico must have burned in the fire of Titus in A.D. 80, for although it is not listed among the losses, it is flanked by buildings that burned, and we have record of a restoration by Domitian (Chron. 146).

QITA 5 (1968): 9–20 (L. Cozza).

Porticus Ad Nationes: built by Augustus and given this name because of a gallery of statues representing all nations (Servius *ad Aen.* 8.721). Before its entrance stood a statue of the Punic Hercules, Melqart (Pliny, *HN* 36.39). These are the only references to this portico, and we have no idea how large it was, where it might have been located, or what the program of statues might have been like. It quite clearly should be distinct from the fourteen statues by Coponius representing the nations over which Pompey triumphed (Pliny, *HN* 36.41); those stood around the exterior of the cavea of the Theater of Pompey (cf. Suetonius, *Nero* 46.1). However, the story about Nero's nightmares makes the existence of a larger collection of statues representing nations suspect, and one may ask whether Servius's information is reliable. If we accept a Porticus ad Nationes without

vita on the north, just south of the point at which the Aqua Virgo crossed Via Lata, to Palazzetto Venezia and Via di S. Marco on the south, more than 400 m, a forest of rusticated travertine piers carrying vaults, seven bays, or 60 m, deep, and according to calculation at least seventy bays long. Good remains have been found under Palazzo Simonetti, S. Maria in Via Lata, Palazzo Doria-Pamphili, Palazzo Bonaparte, Palazzo Venezia, S. Marco, and Palazzetto Venezia. Piranesi made an etching of the parts under S. Maria in Via Lata and Palazzo Pamphili (*Campus Martius* pl. 25) that shows the piers heavily rusticated in the Claudian fashion known from the substructures of the Temple of Divus Claudius and Porta Maggiore with brick-faced vaulting above. The piers of the fourth and fifth rows under Palazzo Pamphili as measured by Hülsen are 1.70 m square, 4 m apart in the north/south direction, and 6.20 m apart east/west. Other piers further west show different measurements, and remains under Palazzo Simonetti are in Hadrianic brickwork, so there must have been either restorations or extensions of the original building, very likely both. The first row of piers along Via Lata had a balustrade run between them. One can imagine that the grain was delivered along the west side of the building, stored and moved about as needed in the interior, and distributed along Via Lata. The openness of the plan permitted maximum freedom in the arrangement of offices and storage.

the program of statuary, we might be able to identify it as the Hecatostylon, which Martial (2.14.9) separates from the *Pompei dona* and which is nameless, except for fragmentary identification on the Marble Plan.

HJ 525; *JRS* 78 (1988): 70–77 (R. R. R. Smith).

Porticus Post Navalia: built in 179 B.C. by M. Fulvius Nobilior as censor (Livy 40.51.6), one of a series of porticoes, all apparently essentially utilitarian in purpose. This was presumably behind the Navalia (q.v.) in the southern Campus Martius in the area above the modern Ponte Garibaldi.

Porticus Octavia (1): built by Cn. Octavius in 168 B.C. *ad Circum Flaminium* as a monument to his naval victory over Perseus of Macedon. According to Pliny (*HN* 34.13), this was double and had capitals of bronze, from which it took the name Corinthia. This must be the one Velleius (2.1.2) calls the most splendid of all the early porticoes and most sumptuous. In this Octavian put the standards of Gabinius recovered from the Illyrians (Appian, *BellIll* 28), and this he rebuilt as a monument to the final conquest of Dalmatia in 33 B.C., apparently his first gift to the Roman people that was not completion of a work that Julius Caesar had undertaken. At this time, Octavian says in his *Res Gestae* (19), he let the name of the original builder stand. This, Dio says (49.43.8), was rebuilt as the Porticus Octaviae, a statement about which most topographers seem skeptical.

Porticus Octavia (2): Festus (188L) says there were two porticoes of this name, one near the Theater of Marcellus, which will be that ad Circum Flaminium, and another near the Theater of Pompey. There is no reason to doubt this, nor is there a dearth of porticoes requiring names. The portico flanking the Area Sacra di Largo Argentina might be meant, or the edifice of which a fragment still survives in Via S. Maria dei Calderari, although the latter might better have been described as *in Circo Flaminio*. There are also areas around the Theater of Pompey where our ignorance is almost complete.

Porticus Octaviae (Figs. 70, 71): built by Octavia, the sister of Augustus, to complete work undertaken by her son, Marcellus (Ovid, *Ars Am.* 1.69–70), presumably as aedile, and then made a memorial to him (Livy, *Epit.* 140; Festus 188L, where there may be some confusion). Suetonius (*Aug.* 29.4) says the real builder was Augustus, and he is supported by Dio (49.43.8), but this is doubtful. According to Velleius (1.11.3), this portico replaced the Porticus Metelli (q.v.) but did not apparently substantially change its lines and form. At the same time the temples it en-

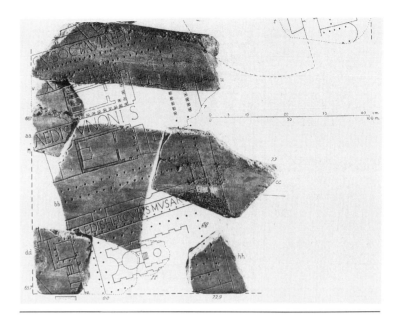

Figure 70
Porticus Octaviae and
Porticus Philippi,
Representation
on the Marble Plan

closed were rebuilt, allegedly by two Lacedaemonian architects named Saura and Batrachos (Pliny, *HN* 36.42). It burned in A.D. 80 (Cass. Dio 66.24.2) and must have been restored, presumably by Domitian. It burned again, and Septimius Severus and Caracalla restored it in 203 (*CIL* 6.1034).

Besides the two temples it enclosed, there were included in the complex a library (see Bibliotheca Porticus Octaviae) dedicated to Marcellus (Plutarch, *Marc.* 30.6), a curia (Pliny, *HN* 36.28), and scholae (Pliny, *HN* 35.114, 36.22). The senate is recorded as having met in the curia (Josephus, *BellIud* 7.5.4 [124]; Cass. Dio 55.8.1). Pliny repeatedly calls the whole complex *Octaviae opera* (*HN* 34.31, 35.139, 36.15), and it was enriched with an enormous collection of famous works of art (Pliny, *HN* 34.31, 35.114, 139, 36.15, 22, 24, 34, 35).

The portico itself was 119 m wide on the façade and about 132 m in depth. In the center of the façade on the Circus Flaminius was a propylaeum projecting in as well as out, now composed of four fluted columns on each face between antae. The columns are Corinthian and carry deep tympana. The side walls are broken by arches leading to the portico, which is raised above the surrounding ground, a high promenade. But on the Marble Plan (*FUR* pl. 29; Rodriguez pl. 23) the portico is shown as very open on the façade, the propylaeum of six columns on each front without side walls, and apparently not projecting on the interior. The unfluted columns of granite with white marble capitals and bases of the rest of the portico are late, Domitianic or Severan in date, and there is no sign of what they may have replaced. There were eight columns to either side of the propylaeum on the façade, and, although in Octa-

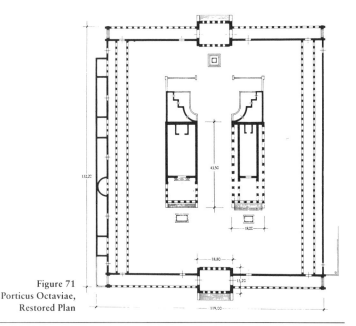

Figure 71
Porticus Octaviae,
Restored Plan

via's building the façade had been closed, later apparently one looked through the double line of columns from the circus to see the temples and the various embellishments beyond. On the sides, however, the double colonnades were still closed by exterior walls, and there is no indication of how the colonnade was treated behind the temples.

Lugli 1946, 562–67; *PBSR* 21, n.s. 8 (1953): 152–59 (M. J. Boyd); *BCSSA* 16 (1960): 37–56 (M. Petrignani); Nash 2.254–58; B. Olinder, *Porticus Octavia in Circo Flaminio* (Stockholm 1974); *AJA* 80 (1976): 57–64 (L. Richardson); *BullCom* 87 (1980–81): 37–55 (H. Lauter).

Porticus Pallantiana: known from a single inscription (*CIL* 6.9719 = *ILS* 7492) of a dealer in oil who claimed to be *Venetianorum* and possibly *Parmulariorum* (the latter is less certain). Because the stabula (q.v.) of the circus factions were all in the Campus Martius, so should the locations of their provisioners have been, unless this was one of the great warehouses in the district southwest of the Aventine.

For a location near the Circus Maximus, see *BullCom* 85 (1976–77): 157 (R. E. A. Palmer).

Porticus Palmata: evidently an alternate name for the atrium (forecourt) preceding the Constantinian basilica of S. Pietro, to the south of which Pope Honorius I (625–638) built the basilica of S. Apollinaris (LPD 1.323; VZ 2.252; HCh 201; cf. Frutaz 2: pl. 75b [tav. 147]), thereafter called S. Apollinaris ad Palmatam. This is shown on Alfaroni's plan of

1589–1590 (T. Alfaroni, *De Basilicae Vaticanae antiquissima et nova structura,* ed. D. M. Cerrati [Biblioteca Vaticana studi e testi 26, Rome 1914]) off the southeast corner of the atrium, so the Porticus Palmata, or ad Palmata, can hardly be anything else, although the source of the name remains mysterious.

Porticus Philippi (Fig. 70): listed in the regionary catalogues in Regio IX. This must be the portico surrounding Marcius Philippus's rebuilding of the Temple of Hercules Musarum (see Hercules Musarum, Aedes; cf. Martial 5.49.12–13), shown on the Marble Plan (*FUR* pl. 29; Rodriguez pl. 23), but the plan is odd and difficult to read. It seems to have been a single colonnade closed behind on the sides and front, but double and open (?) behind. And there seems to have been a line of trees running around inside this. It contained a number of noteworthy pictures (Pliny, *HN* 35.66, 114, 144). Behind, in the triangular space between the portico and the Theater of Balbus, was a market in hair goods (Ovid, *Ars Am.* 3.165–68).

AnalRom, suppl. 10 (1983): 93–104 (F. Castagnoli).

Porticus Pollae: see **Porticus Vipsania.**

Porticus Pompeii (Fig. 82): built by Pompey together with his theater (see Theatrum Pompeii), dedicated in 52 B.C., behind the scaena and adjoining it, so there would be shelter for the spectators in the event of a sudden shower and so there would be space for developing stage machinery (Vitruvius 5.9.1), but especially as a park with pleasant walks. It contained a collection of pictures, many of them famous (Pliny, *HN* 35.59, 114, 126, 132). In the open area were plantations of plane trees pollarded to a uniform height and fountains with sculptures (Propertius 2.32.11–16). Adjacent to it was a curia for the senate (see Curia Pompeii). It became immediately one of the most popular places in Rome to stroll (Cicero, *De Fato* 8; Catullus 55.6) and continued to be so in the time of Augustus (Propertius 4.8.75; Ovid, *Ars Am.* 1.67–68, 3.387–88) and even in the time of Martial (2.14.10, 11.1.11, 11.47.3).

The portico is shown on fragments of the Marble Plan (*FUR* 32; Rodriguez pls. 28, 32) as a single colonnade surrounding a large rectangular area with exedras, both rectangular and semicircular, screened off by columns, along the long sides and the far end, and columnar bays that break forward from the line of the colonnade at the scaena end. In the open area are four files of dotted squares, which probably represent the pollarded plane trees, shown along the margins of what may be two large rectangular basins of water. Along the south side, just outside the portico proper, there may have been a line of shops. How the fountains and statuary were arranged is, of course, not clear.

The porticus evidently burned in the fire of Carinus (cf. S.H.A. *Carin.* 19), for it was restored in the time of Diocletian by the praefectus urbi Aelius Helvius Dionysius, at which time one part was called Porticus Iovia and another Porticus Herculea in honor of the emperors Diocletian and Maximian (*CIL* 6.255–256 = *ILS* 621–622; Chron. 148: *porticus II*). It may have been destroyed in the earthquake of 442/443 (Consularia Italica, *MGH Chron. Min.* 1.301; *BullCom* 45 [1917]: 11–13 [R. Lanciani]). There is little to be seen there today; a large latrine was built into the northeast corner of the complex and another, somewhat smaller, a little south of center off the east colonnade. These are shown, somewhat schematically and inaccurately drawn, on the Marble Plan and are mentioned by Dio (47.19.1). They were in part uncovered in the excavations of the Area Sacra di Largo Argentina (G. Marchetti-Longhi, *L'area sacra di Largo Argentina* [Rome 1960], 74–79; Nash 1.147). These give some notion of the crowds that frequented the Porticus Pompeii, but nothing of its splendors.

Porticus Extra Portam Fontinalem: see **Porticus Aemilia** (2).

Porticus Extra Portam Trigeminam: see **Porticus Aemilia** (1).

Porticus Purpuretica: see **Forum Traiani**.

Porticus Saeptorum: see **Saepta Iulia**.

Porticus Severi: mentioned only in the Historia Augusta (S.H.A. *Sept. Sev.* 21.12; *Carac.* 9.6) and said to have been built in Severus's honor by Caracalla and to have encompassed his deeds, his triumphs, and his wars. It is otherwise unknown, but one might well imagine it as part of the Thermae Antoninianae (q.v.).

Porticus Post Spem: listed by Livy (40.51.6) as one of the works of M. Fulvius Nobilior as censor in 179 B.C. It is described as *post Spei ad Tiberim,* and one can imagine it as a handsome background for the temple or a utilitarian building serving river traffic at the Forum Boarium. The latter is certainly more likely at this period and in this location. It was probably not intended to be permanent and disappeared within a generation or so.

Porticus Thermarum Traianarum: mentioned only in a single inscription from Thrace (*CIL* 3.12336) as a place where a document is posted in A.D. 238. The proximity to the headquarters of the Praefectura Urbana (q.v.) has led to the supposition that this might be connected with it, but the evidence is too slight to warrant anything further.

Porticus Triumphi: known from a single inscription (*CIL* 6.29776 = *ILS* 5559) found outside the walls between Via Asinaria and Via Latina, near Porta Metrovia. The brief inscription states that by going back and forth along this portico one completed a mile. Presumably it is from a portico in a private villa. There is no other evidence for a public Porticus Triumphi in Rome.

Porticus Vipsania: a portico begun by Vipsania Polla, the sister of Agrippa, *in Campo Agrippae* (Cass. Dio 55.8.3–4). Martial (1.108.1–4) says that his house overlooked it. His house was on the Quirinal, on a street leading from the Temple of Flora to the Capitolium Vetus (5.22.3–4, 6.27.1–2). The location of the Temple of Flora is not precisely known, but the Capitolium Vetus and Martial's house were high on the hill, near the Temple of Quirinus (10.58.9–10, 11.1.9). Near the portico was a gate that carried a water channel, probably an aqueduct (Martial 4.18.1–4), and because the portico was in Campo Agrippae, it must have lain outside the Servian Walls. If it lay along the base, or the lower slopes, of the Quirinal, as our sources indicate, the gate in question may have been either the Porta Quirinalis or the Porta Salutaris, but Martial would surely remark on the irony in the name in 4.18, if it were the Porta Salutaris. The building must have been important, because it was still unfinished when Augustus dedicated the Campus Agrippae in 7 B.C. (Cass. Dio 55.8.3–4). It contained a famous map of the world in great detail, based on a collection of data begun by Agrippa and finished by Augustus (Pliny, *HN* 3.17) and had plantations of laurels (Martial 1.108.1–4). In it troops camped during the upheavals of A.D. 68–69 (Tacitus, *Hist.* 1.31; Plutarch, *Galba* 25), and it continued to be used until the time of the regionary catalogues, although by then its name had been corrupted to Porticus Gypsiani. Probably it lay along the southeast side of the Campus Agrippae, framing and bounding it. Because it is always referred to in the singular, it was probably a single wing. So little is known of the antiquities in this part of Rome that nothing can be identified, even tentatively, as belonging to it.

Attempts to identify the Porticus Vipsania with remains of an extensive building with arcades of travertine lying along the east side of Via Flaminia south of Via S. Claudio are certainly mistaken, because the building to which these arcades belong is of a type not known earlier than the time of Nero.

Portunium: The name is uncertain, but very probable, being found inserted in the margin of Fronto (*Epist.* 1.7), where it means the precinct or neighborhood of the Temple of Portunus, the center of the trade in flowers and garlands. It is then restored by conjecture in Varro (*Ling.* 5.146), where the manuscripts have *ad iunium,* and in the *Notitia* under Regio XI, where the manuscripts have *Fortunium.*

The Temple *(aedes)* of Portunus is mentioned by Varro (*Ling.* 6.19), where it is said to be *in portu Tiberino,* presumably the bank of the river along the Forum Boarium, where remains of warehouses have been discovered and where the earliest bridges were built. Here *portu* certainly cannot mean "warehouse." In the fasti (Allif. Amit. Vall.; Degrassi 496–97) the temple is *Portuno ad Pontem Aemilium,* and the dedication day, the Portunalia, is 17 August. Portunus is shown on one of the reliefs of the Arch of Trajan at Benevento (F. J. Hassel, *Der Trajansbogen in Benevent* [Mainz 1966], pls. 7.2 and 11.1) as youthful with long hair and the attributes of anchor and serpent. He was equated with the Greek Palaemon and was probably originally the god of the ferry crossing of the Tiber (L. A. Holland, *Janus and the Bridge* [Rome 1961], 141–78 and passim), later thought of as the god of the port.

On the north side of Piazza della Bocca della Verità is a small temple, well preserved, thanks to its having been converted to use as a church of S. Maria Egiziaca in 872, which may well be the Temple of Portunus, although its date is probably mid-first century B.C. It is tetrastyle, prostyle, set on a high (2.30 m) podium, 26 m long and 12 m wide. The order is Ionic in the classical manner and is carried around the cella as an engaged order. The pronaos is two bays deep. The material of the cella is Anio tufa, except at the corners; the podium, the corners of the cella, the pronaos columns, and the architrave are travertine; and the frieze and cornice are tufa. The frieze was worked in stucco with garlands looped between putti, candelabra, and bucrania, much of which has disappeared. The style is distinctly classicizing, with a low and shallow pediment. It was cleared of later accretions toward the beginning of this century, but the walls yielded no new information. It has been commonly called the Temple of Fortuna Virilis, but without adequate reason. Its position, parallel to the Tiber, facing toward the street leading to the Pons Aemilius, probably in the middle of a considerable precinct, makes the identification as the Temple of Portunus attractive. E. Fiechter provided a meticulous description of the temple (*RömMitt* 21 [1906]: 220–79); further details were added during a restoration of the temple in 1966 (*NSc* 1977, 299–341 [E. Lissi Caronna and S. Priuli]).

Lugli 1946, 582–84; Nash 1.411–12; *NSc* 1977, 299–325 (E. Lissi Caronna); *BullCom* 91.1 (1986): 7–34 (A. M. Colini, C. Buzzetti, P. Gros, and J. P. Adam).

Portus: see **Horreum, Cella, Portus.**

Portus Cor(neli): a yard (cf. *Dig.* 50.16.59 [Ulpian]) for the storage of bricks, known from brickstamps of A.D. 123 (*NSc* 1892, 347 [L. Borsari]; *RömMitt* 8 [1893]: 260 [C. Hülsen]). Its location is completely unknown.

Portus Licini: a yard for the storage of bricks mentioned in numerous brick-stamps of the time of Septimius Severus and Caracalla (*CIL* 15.408 and pp. 37–38, 121–24) and later (Cassiodorus, *Var.* 1.25.2). There is no indication of its location.

Portus Neapolitanus: mentioned only in a graffito made on a tile before it was fired that was found in the catacombs of S. Sebastiano (*CIL* 15.6123; *RömMitt* 1 [1886]: 188–89 [H. Marucchi]). The suggested date is fourth century.

Portus Parrae: a brickyard known from brickstamps of about the time of Hadrian (*CIL* 15.409–11).

Portus Tiberinus: probably before the time of Augustus a real river port of the Forum Boarium (Varro, *Ling.* 6.19). Earlier the word *portus* may have referred to a ferry across the Tiber (L. A. Holland, *Janus and the Bridge* [Rome 1961], 148–57). Beginning under Augustus the phrase *ad Pontem Aemilium* replaces the phrase *in portu Tiberino* (Fast. Allif., Amit., Vall. *ad XVI Kal. Sept.* = 17 August).

Portus Vinarius: a wine depot mentioned in three sepulchral inscriptions (*CIL* 6.9189 = *ILS* 7929, 9190, 37807 = *ILS* 9429) without further topographical indication.

Portus Xysti: mentioned only in the *Codex Theodosianus* (13.3.8) in connection with the appointment of *archiatri,* the chief physicians of areas of the city. Everything else about this is uncertain.

Poseidonion: see **Neptunus, Aedes.**

Posterulae in Muro Aureliano: see **Muri Aureliani.**

Praedia Galbana: known from a single large inscription (*CIL* 6.30983 = *ILS* 3840), of a funerary collegium of the second century after Christ, in which three men are described as *vilici Praediorum Galbanorum*. This is taken to include the Horrea Galbae (q.v.), and the case is reinforced by the finding of the inscription near Monte Testaccio. Apparently these warehouses remained imperial possessions, although assigned to the use of the urban cohorts (*BullCom* 13 [1885]: 51–53 [W. Henzen]).

Praefectura Urbana: In the fourth century the offices of the praefectus urbi were on the Oppius in the zone southwest of the church of S. Pietro in Vincoli (*BullCom* 20 [1892]: 19–37 [R. Lanciani]). They were probably fairly extensive. An inscription records the restoration of a part by the prefect Bellicius: *porticum cum scriniis tellurensis secretarii tribunalibus adherentem* (*CIL* 6.31959 = *ILS* 5523). The *scrinia* were the archives (S.H.A. *Aurel.* 9.1) and, because they were extensive, may have been kept in more than one place. The *secretarium* was a courtroom in which the proceedings were secret, the public being excluded by a *velum* and possibly a barrier across the door. The trials required the presence only of the praefectus urbi, the accused, and such persons as the praefectus urbi might deem necessary to the investigation, so it need not have been a large building. The fact that it was provided with *tribunalia* in the plural may be only to emphasize the dignity of the court, for because it is also called *tellurense*, clearly an allusion to the proximity of the Temple of Tellus, the secretarium in question must be singular. The portico that Bellicius restored may have been a very modest edifice. But the finds of inscriptions in the zone framed by the Vie di S. Pietro in Vincoli, della Polveriera, and degli Annibaldi suggest that it extended over the whole of this area. See also Porticus Thermarum Traianarum. None of the material found in connection with this complex is earlier than the fourth century; before that time the praefectus urbi may have had his headquarters in the Templum Pacis (q.v.).

L. Bonfante and H. von Heintze, eds., *In Memoriam Otto J. Brendel* (Mainz 1976), 191–204 (E. Nash, "Secretarium Senatus").

Praenestius Mons (or **Collis**): Lydus (*De Mens.* 4.155) gives the following list of the hills of Rome: (Pa)lation, Esquilion, Tarpeion, Aventinon, Tib(urtion), Praen(es)tion, Viminalion. He then gives the more familiar list: Aven(t)inus, Caelius, (Esq)ui-

lius, Capitolinus, Velinesius, Qu(irina)lius, Pala(tinus). Despite the discrepancies and lack of clear order, it seems evident that Tiburtius is another name for the Quirinal and that Praenestius or Praenestinus is another name for the Caelian. The Porta Praenestina was at the end of the Caelian, but unless, after the closing of Porta Chiusa, it became regular for those going to Tibur to leave by the Porta Nomentana, it is difficult to account for the other. The Porta Tiburtina is on the Esquiline. Hülsen (HJ 229n.27) writes Lydus's names off as the pure invention of an antiquarian.

Prata: see **Ager, Campus, Prata.**

Prata Flaminia: according to Livy (3.54.15 and 63.7), an earlier name for the area later called Circus Flaminius (q.v.) in the southern Campus Martius near the Tiber. Although the only building he places there is the Temple of Apollo (see Apollo, Aedes), we may be correct in bounding the Prata, but not the Circus, on the west by the Petronia Amnis (q.v.). How far north the Prata and Circus extended is more doubtful.

Prata Neronis: see **Campus Neronis.**

Prata Quinctia: a plot of four iugera (about one-half hectare or one and one-third acres) on the right bank of the Tiber opposite the Navalia (q.v.) that belonged to L. Quinctius Cincinnatus and where he was found engaged in farm work when he was to be made dictator (Livy 3.13.10 and 26.8; Festus 307L; Pliny, *HN* 18.20). This name for the district was still in use in the early empire (see also Vicus Raciliani).

Prata Vacci: see **Domus, Vitruvius Vaccus.**

Privata Hadriani: the house where Hadrian lived before becoming princeps and where Marcus Aurelius lived after Antoninus Pius adopted him (S.H.A. *Marc. Aurel.* 5.3). It is located by the regionary catalogues in Regio XII, last of all, after the Statio Cohortis Vigilum IIII, so a location southwest of S. Saba may be indicated.

Privata Traiani: a house in which Trajan lived before becoming princeps. It was on the Aventine in Regio XIII *(Not. om. Cur.)*, probably the southern part, where remains of sumptuous private dwellings have been found. The discovery of the Temple of Iuppiter Dolichenus in Via di S. Domenico in 1935 makes the suggestion that the extensive complex found under the Benedictine monastery of S. Anselmo in the middle of the nineteenth century (LFUR sheet 40) may be the Privata Traiani attractive, despite the find of a lead pipe stamped with the name of Pactumeia Lucilla. The building is very extensive, though fragmentary, and Pactumeia Lucilla may have been an earlier or later occupant.

Providentia Augusta, Ara: an altar of unknown location known from the Acta Arvalium for A.D. 38 (*CIL* 6.2028 d15) and 39 (*CIL* 6.2033.5 = 32346), and from coins. A lighted altar inscribed PROVIDENT appears on the coins of Tiberius (*B. M. Coins, Rom. Emp.* 1.141 nos. 146–50) and then in the years that follow, but then we have to wait for Titus to find PROVIDENT AVGVST (*B. M. Coins, Rom. Emp.* 2.259 nos. 178–81). See also Roscher 3.3187–89 (R. Peter).

Pudicitia, Ara: an altar to Pudicitia, erected by Plotina, the wife of Trajan, which appears on coins (*B. M. Coins, Rom. Emp.* 3.107 no. 529). According to Wissowa's interpretation of this gesture, Plotina then became honored as the personification of Pudicitia (*CIL* 8.993 = *ILS* 4433; see Roscher 3.3276–77 [R. Peter]).

Pudicitia Patricia, Sacellum (Templum, Signum): a shrine in the Forum Boarium, usually called a sacellum, but certainly having a statue, so perhaps a statue and an altar, and described as *ubi Aemiliana* (MS: *tamiliana*) *aedes est Herculis* (Festus 282L) and *ad aedem rotundam Herculis* (Livy 10.23.3–5). We know nothing of an Aemilian temple to Hercules, and the only round temple of Hercules in the Forum Boarium positively identified is that of Hercules Victor (see Hercules Victor [1]). If that is the temple in question, we can place the shrine of Pudicitia fairly precisely. Livy's account has been questioned as an aetiological invention to explain Pudicitia Plebeia, but without sufficient reason. Only a woman who had married only once was permitted to worship here. See Roscher 3.3273–75 (R. Peter).

   RivStorAnt 4 (1974): 113–59 (R. E. A. Palmer), especially 121–23.

Pudicitia Plebeia, Sacellum: a shrine created in 296 B.C. by a Virginia, a patrician, who married L. Volumnius, a plebeian who became consul. When she was excluded from the worship of Pudicitia Patricia (see Pudicitia Patricia, Sacellum), because of her marriage, she is said to have dedicated part of her house on Vicus Longus to Pudicitia Plebeia (Livy 10.23.6–10). Livy says that the cult was disgraced by its being taken up by women of every sort and then eventually fell into oblivion, but Festus (270L; cf. 271L) speaks of it as still existing in his day. Vicus

Longus (q.v.), in the valley between the Quirinal and the Viminal, was evidently primarily residential and well suited to such a shrine.

   RivStorAnt 4 (1974): 113–59 (R. E. A. Palmer), especially 123–25.

Pulvinar ad Circum Maximum: see **Circus Maximus.**

Pulvinar Solis (Indigitis): mentioned by Quintilian (1.7.12) as *Solis qui colitur iuxta aedem Quirini* on the Quirinal and listed in the Fasti Allifani and Amiternini on 9 August (Degrassi 493). A *pulvinar* should be a banquet couch, or place with couches, on which to display images of divinities or their symbols, so they are imagined as taking part in a celebration. It seems hardly likely that Quintilian would mention the Temple of Quirinus if Sol had a temple of his own on the Quirinal. Therefore, it seems likely that this is an independent structure, but a minor one, almost an adjunct to the great Temple of Quirinus. Permanent *pulvinaria* are rare in Rome; so far as we know, that of the Circus Maximus was a creation of Augustus (*RG* 19), and while those in temples must have been commoner, simply masonry bases on which mattresses and coverlets were spread when they were needed (cf. the arrangements in the temple of S. Abbondio near Pompeii), a *pulvinar Solis* described as adjacent to the precinct of Quirinus seems to require further explanation. Quintilian speaks of it in connection with the orthography of an inscription that mentions Vesperugo, the evening star; the fasti treat it as a separate place of worship with its own dedication day. Surely, then, this must be the Sol to whom Varro (*Ling.* 5.74) says Titus Tatius vowed an altar, and the altar must have stood adjacent. Because reclining at meals was a Greek custom taken over by the Romans, the pulvinar form is unlikely to be older than the Second Punic War, although the altar itself might be very ancient.

Puteal in Comitio: a stone wellhead in the Comitium set over the place where the whetstone and razor of Attus Navius were supposed to be buried (Cicero, *Div.* 1.33; Dion. Hal. 3.71.5; Livy 1.36.5). Pliny (*HN* 15.77) seems to have believed this was really a place that lightning had struck, and he is followed by Jordan (1.2.357) and PA (435), but because *bidentales* as markers of lightning strikes were perfectly familiar to the Romans (cf., e.g., Horace, *Ars P.* 471 and schol.), it seems better to accept the unusual explanation for this one.

Puteal Libonis (or Scribonianum): a stone wellhead set over a place in the Forum Romanum where lightning had struck (Festus 448–50L), set up by

Scribonius Libo on a charge from the senate. It was near the tribunal of the praetor urbanus in the late republic and early empire and repeatedly referred to as the scourge of debtors and the haunt of usurers, presumably suing to recover losses (Cicero, *Sest.* 18; Horace, *Sat.* 2.6.35, *Epist.* 1.19.8 and schol.; Ovid, *Rem. Am.* 561–62; Persius 4.49 and schol.). The wellhead was also near the Fornix Fabianus (q.v.; schol. *ad Pers.* 4.49) and the Porticus Iulia (q.v.). It is shown on coins of the Scribonii and Aemilii of the end of the first century B.C. and identified (Crawford 416/1, 417/1). It was apparently rather large for a puteal and handsome, almost an altar, decorated in relief with citharas between which swing garlands of laurel. An altar from Veii dedicated to Pietas, now in the collection of the Lateran, may reproduce it, at least in its general lines (Helbig[4] 1.1126). At some point someone tried to bury or conceal it and was prevented, for it had to stand permanently open to heaven (Festus 450L).

It seems not unlikely that this is the feature in the front of the podium of the Temple of Divus Iulius usually identified as the altar of Julius Caesar, but walled off in the Augustan period so it could not have functioned as an altar, and set in a special semicircular well to preserve it.

Lugli 1947, 46–52; Nash 2.259–61 (following Gamberini-Mongenet); *RömMitt* 80 (1973): 229–31 (L. Richardson); Coarelli 1985, 166–76.

Puticuli: a very old form of burial, spoken of only in the past tense by Varro (*Ling.* 5.25) and Festus (241L), evidently entirely unfamiliar to both of them, because they could not decide whether the word was derived from *puteus* or *putere*. But Varro assigned these burials a place *ultra Esquilias* in a locus publicus, evidently confusing them with the place of public execution *extra Portam Esquilinam* (Tacitus, *Ann.* 2.32; Suetonius, *Claud.* 25.3) and perhaps with some memory of the old Esquiline cemetery where inhumation tombs, sometimes of high antiquity, must have come to light from time to time. As the finds show and Pinza emphasizes, these are the burials of people of substance, often given rich grave goods, and not to be confused with Horace's potter's field (*Sat.* 1.8.8–16). Horace's potter's field on the Esquiline, 1,000 feet in frontage and 300 feet in depth, figures that are perhaps not to be taken literally, was a place where cheap burial could be arranged in common graves or cremation on public ustrina. Why both funeral practices should have been observed is not clear, but Horace speaks both of an *arca* (coffin) and of the remains of pyres, *albis informem . . . ossibus agrum*. The note of the Commentator Cruquianus on this passage in Horace, *a puteis fossis ad sepelienda cadavera pauperum locus dictus est puticuli*, is probably simply an invention, for the common graves were trenches and the *puticuli* seem always to have been individual burials (LR 411–12).

BullCom 2 (1874): 42–53 (R. Lanciani), 3 (1875): 41–56 (R. Lanciani), 40 (1912): 65, 82 (R. Pinza).

Q

Quadriga Arcadii et Honorii: a victory monument voted by the senate to commemorate the victory over Gildo and the army of Africa in A.D. 398, known from a large inscribed base (*CIL* 6.1187 = 31256, 36888 = *ILS* 794) composed of six blocks found and copied in 1549 and 1563 in front of the Arch of Septimius Severus. These have since been lost, except for three pieces that are now in the forum near where they were found. These show that the base was originally about 5 m long and 3.70 m high, appropriate for a quadriga, although the exact form is conjectural (cf. Claudian, *De Sext. Cons. Hon.* 369–80). Hülsen believed that the original location was a mass of concrete edged with two steps of marble, 8.30 m long and 3.60 m wide, on which the base of the decennalian monument of Diocletian's tetrarchy has now been mounted, but this is very doubtful.

Lugli 1946, 170–71; Nash 2.262–63; GV 69–70.

Quadrigae Pisonis: a monument that the senate erected after his death to an unknown Piso Frugi, included as one of the thirty tyrants of A.D. 268. It is supposed to have stood in the area now occupied by the Thermae Diocletiani and to have been removed when these were built. But the site is hardly appropriate, and A. von Domaszewski (*SBHeid* 1916, 7.A, 9; 1918, 13.A, 41–46) is probably right to doubt the reliability of this report.

Quattuor Scari: In the *Notitia* we find in Regio VIII: *aquam cernentem IIII scaros sub aede (Curiosum: sub eadem)*. This is listed between the Horrea Agrippiana and the Atrium Caci. A marble funerary altar in the Lateran collection carries the inscription of C. Clodius Euphemus, who styles himself *negotiator penoris et vinorum de Velabro a IIII scaris* (*CIL* 6.9617; Helbig⁴ 1.1029). Because the Velabrum is listed in the regionary catalogues in Regio XI, we must look for a place for the IIII Scari not far from the Ianus Quadrifrons toward the north or east. The name is an odd one, and it has been interpreted as indicating a fountain in which water ran down a slope in a course among four fish, possibly augmented by other water issuing from their mouths. Fountains designed around marine life are very common in antiquity.

Querquetulanus Mons: according to Tacitus (*Ann.* 4.65), the earliest name of the Caelian, derived from the oak woods with which the hill was covered. But the name Caelius Mons (q.v.) itself must be very old, and it sounds rather as though this were an antiquarian's invention to explain the name of the Porta Querquetulana toward the east end of the hill. There were also a vanished Latin polity, the Querquetulani (Pliny, *HN* 3.69) and Lares Querquetulani (q.v.).

Quies, Aedes: according to Augustine (*De civ. D.* 4.16), a temple *extra Portam Collinam*, but probably the same as the shrine on Via Labicana mentioned in passing by Livy (4.41.8; cf. Wissowa, *RK* 333).

Quinque Tabernae: see **Tabernae Circum Forum.**

Quirinalis Collis (Fig. 72): the only hill in Rome, except for its subdivision, the Collis Salutaris, taking its name from the divinity worshiped there, and the most northerly of the hills within the Servian Walls, that down which ran the salt route, connecting the Via Salaria entering Rome through the Porta Collina with the ferry at the mouth of the Cloaca by way of the Vicus Iugarius. The route ran along the ridge of the Quirinal, and on this carried the name Alta Semita, which it gave to Regio VI of Augustan Rome. The road ran nearly straight until the end of the hill

324

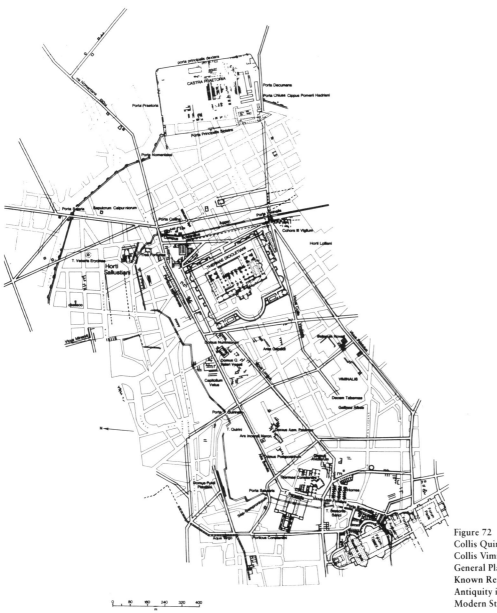

Figure 72
Collis Quirinalis and
Collis Viminalis,
General Plan Showing
Known Remains of
Antiquity in Relation to
Modern Streets

began to fall away in a series of lower eminences curving around to the south, and these the road followed, eventually probably crossing a low saddle to the shoulder of the Capitoline. By Augustan times the saddle had disappeared and the two hills were quite distinct, and this distinction was emphasized by the scarping of the Quirinal to create the forum and markets of Trajan.

The Quirinal and its nearest neighbor, the Viminal, were the only major hills called colles rather than montes, and together they made up the regio called Collina in the city of the four regiones. The list of the Argei given by Varro (*Ling.* 5.51–52) shows that the Quirinal was divided among four distinct lobes: Collis Quirinalis, from the Porta Collina to modern Piazza del Quirinale (Montecavallo); Collis Salutaris, from Piazza del Quirinale to Palazzo Rospigliosi; Collis Mucialis, from Palazzo Rospigliosi to Piazza Magnanapoli; and Collis Latiaris, from Piazza Magnanapoli to the southern tip. The last three will be seen to be minor divisions, and the names of the last two are of unknown derivation. Festus (Paulus *ex Fest.* 9L, 304L) says that the Quirinal was once called Agonus and the gate Porta Agonalis, *agonus* being either a generic word for *mons,* or *agonius* an adjective to describe a day on which a sacrificial victim was offered on a mons. PA dismisses this as an antiquarian invention, but the

325

Salii of the Quirinal were certainly called Agonenses (Varro, *Ling.* 6.14; Dion. Hal. 2.70.1), and the Agonalia (or Agonia) of 9 January (to Ianus), 17 March (to Mars?), 21 May (to Vediovis?), and 11 December (to Sol Indiges) were certainly very old festivals, and the last was at least closely associated with the Quirinal.

According to tradition, the Sabines settled here after the conclusion of peace between Romulus and Titus Tatius, and, although Titus Tatius himself lived on the Capitoline on the site later occupied by the Temple of Iuno Moneta (Solinus 1.21), the altars to Sabine divinities that he is credited with having established—to Ops, Flora, Vediovis and Saturn, Sol, Luna, Vulcan and Summanus, Larunda, Terminus, Quirinus, Vortumnus, the Lares, Diana, and Lucina (Varro, *Ling.* 5.74)—are scattered thickly about the Capitoline and Quirinal and give support to the notion that the Quirinal and Capitoline were regarded as in some way different from the rest of Rome (but see J. Poucet, *Les Origines de Rome* [Brussels 1985]). They were excluded from the Septimontium and had their own festivals. Archaic material has been found on the Quirinal and in graves associated with it (*MonAnt* 15 [1905]: 248–64, 776–81 [G. Pinza]), but unfortunately nothing like a cemetery. Perhaps the most interesting single object is the famous vessel with the Duenos inscription, a votive offering (*CIL* 1².4 = *ILS* 8743 = *ILLRP* 2).

The hill is a long, irregular tongue of land oriented northeast/southwest, stretching from a junction with the plateau with which the Viminal, Esquiline, and Caelian are also connected. It is separated from the Viminal by a gradually deepening valley carved by the natural drainage running off toward the Cloaca, up which now runs the modern Via Nazionale. The hill is separated from the Pincian Hill (Collis Hortulorum) to the northwest by a broad valley up which runs the modern Via del Tritone, under which lies culverted the watercourse commonly called Aqua Sallustiana from the Horti Sallustiani (q.v.) laid out there in the late republic. The overall length of the Quirinal is about 2 kilometers. The Servian Walls run along its northwest brow from the Collis Mucialis to Porta Collina, where the Agger began, running almost due south. The course of the link between the fortifications of the Capitoline and those of the Quirinal is a matter of dispute; most likely it ran more or less directly through the Forum Traiani. There were three approaches to the Quirinal along the fortified front corresponding to the modern Via Nazionale (Piazza Magnanapoli, Porta Sanqualis), Via della Dataria (Porta Salutaris), and Via delle Quattro Fontane (Porta Quirinalis); a fourth led to the hill near the tunnel under the gardens of the Palazzo del Quirinale (*BullCom* 54 [1926]: 145–75 [R.

Bonfiglietti]). In the late republic and early empire the Quirinal was covered with temples interspersed with fine houses. There were no secular buildings of importance until Diocletian built his great baths at the northeast end of the hill.

HJ 394–443; *MemPontAcc*, ser. 3.5.2 (1941): 77–217 (M. Santangelo); *BullCom* 91 (1986): 49–60 (E. Rodriguez Almeida); *QITA* 10 (1988): 17–29 (F. De Caprariis).

Quirinenses: mentioned only once (*CIL* 6.9103 = 31895, a fragment of the edict of Tarracius Bassus of the late fourth century against fraudulent merchants and shopkeepers; the sepulchral inscription of a *vestiarius a Quirinis*), but evidently those living in the neighborhood of the Temple of Quirinus or a Vicus Quirinensis near it.

Quirinus, Aedes (Templum, Delubrum) (Fig. 72): generally regarded as one of the most ancient temples in Rome (Pliny, *HN* 15.120), founded in response to an apparition of Romulus to Iulius Proculus, who was ordered to see to the foundation of a shrine to Romulus as the god Quirinus on this site. This was in the mid-sixth century B.C. (Cicero, *Rep.* 2.20, *Leg.* 1.3). The earliest temple building recorded is one that the consul L. Papirius Cursor dedicated in 293 B.C. following a vow made by his father as dictator (Livy 10.46.7), but there may have been one earlier, because we hear of a senate meeting there in 436/435 B.C. (Livy 4.21.9). There was probably an altar there from a very early period, and we learn that the Porta Quirinalis may have got its name from the proximity of a sacellum of Quirinus (Festus 302–3L). The existence of a Flamen Quirinalis is further proof of the high antiquity of the cult. The temple was struck by lightning in 206 B.C. (Livy 28.11.4) and burned in 49 (Cass. Dio 41.14.3). It was repaired or rebuilt (Cass. Dio 43.45.3) and ultimately completely rebuilt by Augustus, who dedicated it in 16 B.C. (*RG* 19; Cass. Dio 54.19.4). The original day of dedication, the Quirinalia, was 17 February (Ovid, *Fast.* 2.475–512; Fast. Ant. Mai., *NSc* 1921, 87 [G. Mancini]; Degrassi 411–12), and the day of rededication was 29 June (Ovid, *Fast.* 6.795–96; Fast. Venus.; Degrassi 475). There was also a festival on 23 August (Degrassi 500–502).

It was one of the largest temples in Rome, Doric, dipteral and octastyle, with seventy-six columns (Vitruvius 3.2.7; Cass. Dio 54.19.4). Vitruvius must have known Augustus's rebuilding of the temple. There was a portico, presumably on all sides of the precinct (Martial 11.1.9), and Ovid speaks of a shady grove (*Met.* 14.836–37). L. Papirius Cursor erected the first sundial in Rome in the precinct for its dedication (Pliny, *HN* 7.213). In front of it grew two myrtle trees, one known as patrician, the other as plebeian. The patrician was the stronger one until the Social War, when it withered, while the plebeian one burgeoned (Pliny, *HN* 15.120–21). In 45 B.C. the senate erected a statue of Julius Caesar in the temple (Cass. Dio 43.45.3). A fragment of a relief in the Museo Nazionale Romano delle Terme is generally believed to show its pediment with representations of Romulus and Remus's taking of the auspices for the foundation of Rome (*RömMitt* 19 [1904]: 23–37 [P. Hartwig]; Lugli 1938, 302 fig. 62; *AJA* 80 [1976]: 52–55 [R. E. A. Palmer], 91 [1987]: 441–58 [F. C. Albertson]).

The location of the temple is given by the discovery of an inscribed base in the gardens of the Palazzo del Quirinale (*CIL* 6.565 = *ILS* 3141). The temple stood on the northwest side of Alta Semita and can be identified as the eminence at the northeast end of the gardens leveled by Pope Urban VIII, identified by Lanciani (LFUR sheet 16) as the Capitolium Vetus, but far too large for that. It continued to stand at least until the fourth century and is listed in the regionary catalogues.

BdA 73 (1988): fasc. 52, 27–38 (R. Paris).

Quirinus, Sacellum: a shrine at the Porta Quirinalis, which gave it its name (Festus 303L), but one may doubt this, because the Temple of Quirinus must have been very close by and seems the obvious reference. However, small shrines at city gates were very common, and there might well have been one to Quirinus here.

R

Regia (Figs. 48, 73): the small building just outside the Forum Romanum between the Sacra Via and the Temple of Vesta that Numa built and either lived in (Solinus 1.21; Ovid, *Fast.* 6.263–64, *Trist.* 3.1.30; Servius *ad Aen.* 7.153, 8.363; Tacitus, *Ann.* 15.41) or used as his headquarters (Cass. Dio frag. 1.6.2; Plutarch, *Numa* 14.1). It is also said to have been the house of the pontifex maximus (Servius *ad Aen.* 8.363) and of the rex sacrorum (Servius *ad Aen.* 8.363; Cass. Dio 54.27.3; Festus 347L). However, the last is a mistake, a confusion of the rex and the rex sacrorum, for the latter's house was on the Velia and some distance away from the Regia (Festus 373L). In the historical period no one could have lived in the Regia, for it was a consecrated templum containing *sacraria* (Festus 346–48L; cf. 439L). The actual house of the pontifex maximus was probably the Domus Publica, connected with the Atrium Vestae, until Augustus moved the house of the pontifex maximus to the Palatine and gave the Domus Publica to the Vestal Virgins (Suetonius, *Iul.* 46; Cass. Dio 54.27.3). During the republic the Regia was the official headquarters of the pontifex maximus. The location is assured by the existing remains.

In the Regia was a Sacrarium Martis containing an image of the god, where the *ancilia* and the *hasta Martis* were kept (Servius *ad Aen.* 7.603; A. Gellius 4.6.1–2; Cass. Dio 44.17.2; cf. Obsequens 6, 44, 44a, 47, 50). There was also a Sacrarium Opis Consivae, into which none but the Vestal Virgins and public priests might enter (Varro, *Ling.* 6.21; Festus 202L, 292L; *Act. Arv. VIII Kal. Sept.* = *CIL* 6.32482; Degrassi 502–3). Certain sacrifices were regularly performed there (Varro, *Ling.* 6.12; Festus 439L; Macrobius, *Sat.* 1.15.19 and 16.30). The head of the October horse was nailed to the wall, if it had been won by the Sacravienses, and the blood of the tail was allowed to drip on the hearth (Festus 190L; Plutarch, *Quaest. Rom.* 97). The Annales Maximi

were probably kept there (A. Gellius 2.28.6), and the pontifices as a college were probably assembled there (Pliny, *Epist.* 4.11.6).

The Regia burned in 148 B.C. (Obsequens 19; Livy, *Epit. Oxyrh.* 50) and was immediately restored. It burned again in 36 B.C. and was restored by Cn. Domitius Calvinus, using the spoils from his conquests in Spain (Cass. Dio 48.42.1–6; Pliny, *HN* 34.48; *CIL* 6.1301 = *ILS* 42; *EE* 3.265–66). Most of the architectural remains usually assigned to it in the past and much admired have now been discovered to belong to the nearby Arch of Augustus, but a number of blocks of the cornice survive in the vicinity. Tacitus (*Ann.* 15.41) says that it was destroyed in the fire of Nero. It is not listed in the regionary catalogues, but it seems to be mentioned in an inscription of the late fourth century (*CIL* 6.511).

Deep stratigraphical excavations in 1964–1965 have revealed the history of the building. The first masonry edifice dates only to the last quarter of the seventh century; earlier there was a group of ten or a dozen huts that were deliberately destroyed to make a building plot, and their material buried in trenches. In quick succession the Regia went through five phases, often very different from one another, always in consequence of a fire, but certain elements persisted. There was always a large, irregular, but usually clearly pentagonal courtyard with a colonnade along one side, behind which opened a group of roofed spaces, fairly tightly organized. At the end of the sixth century the building received the form it was to preserve thereafter almost unchanged. There was a pentagonal courtyard with colonnades along two long sides and a group of three rooms in a block, the center one providing entrance from the street and the courtyard and giving access to a room on either side. One of these, a small trapezoid, is seen as the Sacrarium Opis Consivae, the other, preserving a large circular feature, 2.53 m in diameter, that might well be a hearth, is seen as the Sacrarium Martis. Under the courtyard is a large beehive-shaped cistern or silo for the storage of grain. There were two different decorations with architectural terracottas worked with Orientalizing friezes of animals and maenad antefixes along the eaves of the roof in the sixth-century building. After Calvinus's rebuilding, the courtyard was paved with marble.

In the Middle Ages, the seventh or eighth century, the Regia was transformed into a private house. Traces of this are visible everywhere, and for its adornment architectural elements were robbed from a variety of other buildings.

Nash 2.264–67; *Entretiens Hardt* 13 (1967): 47–60 (F. E. Brown); *PP* 26 (1971): 443–60 (C. Ampolo); *RendPontAcc* 47 (1974–75): 15–36 (F. E. Brown); L. Bonfante and H. von Heintze, eds., *In Memoriam Otto J. Brendel* (Mainz 1976), 5–12 (F. E. Brown, "Of Huts and Houses"); Coarelli 1983, 56–79.

Regio, Vicus, Pagus: The regiones of Rome were first the geographical units of the four urban tribes created by Servius Tullius: Suburana, Esquilina, Collina, and Palatina. They are not bounded for us, but they are fairly clear: the Suburana consisted of the Caelian and valley between Caelian and Oppius, the Esquilina of the Oppius and Cispian with the valley between, the Collina of the Viminal and Quirinal and the valley between, the Palatina of the Palatine and Velia. The Collina may have included the Capitoline, for a good many people lived there, or it may have been divided between the Collina and the Palatina. And the Palatina may have included most of the forum valley, or that may have been divided in three ways. These are matters of only small importance; the fact is that the city was divided into four roughly equal parts.

With the Augustan reorganization of the city and its municipal administration in 7 B.C. the city was divided into fourteen regiones. Its boundaries were now set well beyond the line of the Servian Walls, approximately along the line of the Aurelian Walls, although the precise line is not known. The regiones were numbered, beginning at the southeast with the area around Via Appia, and running counterclockwise as far as the twelfth, with XIII, the Aventine, and XIV, the Transtiberim, added as an afterthought. So far as we know, these regiones were known officially only by number.

These regiones were subdivided into *vici*, probably units of four blocks, 307 in all, the smallest number, seven, in Regio II, the Caelian, the highest number, seventy-eight, more than twice as many as the next highest, in XIV, the Transtiberim. Originally there were four *vicomagistri* for each vicus; later there

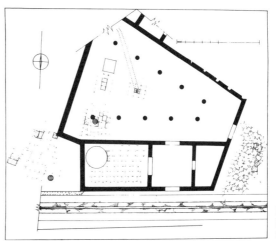

Figure 73
Regia, First Period,
Restored Plan

were forty-eight vicomagistri for each regio, regardless of the number of vici. When and why this change was made is not known. Over these was a *curator*, or sometimes two curatores, for each regio and a *denuntiator*. Later these were changed to two curatores. Their responsibilities are not clear. The vicomagistri were chiefly concerned with the religious life and ceremonies of their neighborhoods, compital worship and the like; how they related to the curiae is not told to us, but because, although originally the curiae had been geographical, by the late republic they had become entirely a matter of family and their sacra would have been of an entirely different character from those of the vici, we do not need to trouble ourselves very much about possible overlap.

Around the outskirts of the city the suburbium was divided into *pagi*. These presumably began at the pomerium, and an inscription of the Augustan period found at Lanuvium (*CIL* 14.2105) shows that the Pagus Aventinensis continued to exist down to the time it was included in the new pomerium by Claudius. We learn also of a Pagus Montanus on the Esquiline (*CIL* 6.3823 = 31577) and a Pagus Ianiculensis in the Transtiberim (*CIL* 6.2219, 2220). We might have expected these and several more as well, but there is no further record of any. We might presume that their purpose would be mainly religious, but *CIL* 6.2219 speaks of the building of a porticus, a cella, a culina and an ara (?) under the supervision of the magistri pagi, and *CIL* 14.2105 is of a XXVI-vir of the pagus who also held a number of high offices, so the officials of the pagus had broad administrative and judicial powers combining many of the competences of praetors and aediles. The administration of a pagus seems to have been a microcosm of the administration of Rome itself.

Reg(io) Mar(tis): known only from a poorly preserved lead tessera that is difficult to read showing

iina, the Viminal and Quirinal with the valley between them, and (4) Palatina, including the Cermalus and Velia. It should be observed that the Capitoline seems likely to have been excluded, although people are supposed to have lived there from the beginning, and that we know nothing about the forum valley and how it may have been divided among the four. It is generally believed that this represents a stage in urban development between the Palatine village and the city of the Servian Walls, which included the Aventine. It is now known that in the last two centuries of the republic at least, the Tribus Suburana and Esquilina were regarded as inferior to the Palatina and Collina, while all the urban tribes, being populous, were regarded as inferior to the suburban tribes, where the individual vote and voice had greater importance (*RendPontAcc* 27 [1952–54]: 225–38 [L. R. Taylor]). If this inferiority among the urban tribes can be laid to the same force at work as that distinguishing the urban from the suburban tribes, it may be that when the Aventine, which had been essentially public domain, was handed over to the plebs for settlement in 456 B.C. (Livy 3.31.1; Dion. Hal. 10.31.2–32.5) it was included in the Suburana, to which it was adjacent, while the Esquilina was always especially densely populated and may have included a large chunk of the forum valley. In any case, the division into four regiones seems to have been the geographical organization of the city still in force when Augustus undertook his reorganization, so it must have undergone modification from time to time.

The relation of the four regiones to the pomerium is not entirely clear. Presumably the regiones included all the territory within the pomerium, except possibly the Capitoline, at the time they were created. We cannot trace the expansion of the pomerium earlier than the time of Sulla, at which point it coincided with the line of the Servian Walls, except for the Aventine. In his account of the Argei (see Argeorum, Sacraria), Varro lists the sites of the shrines with relation to the individual regiones, and it is clear that although various of the landmarks he cites are no older than the third century, the ceremony as a whole must go back to a time before the plebs was settled on the Aventine and before the upper reaches of the Quirinal and Viminal had been included within the pomerium. One has then to presume that as the pomerium was enlarged, the new territory was added to the nearest, or geographically most logical, of the regiones, although on this point we have no information. But the distribution of the sacraria of the Argei among the regiones shows the importance of these in the state religion, as well as its political organization.

Regiones Quattuor and Sacraria of the Argei, as Known

Mars helmeted with shield and spear (Rostovtzeff, *Sylloge* 495 and pl. 4.20), which is believed to indicate the neighborhood of the Aedes Martis (see Mars, Aedes) outside Porta Capena, but is perhaps almost as likely to identify the neighborhood of the Ara Martis (see Mars, Ara) or that of the Temple of Mars Ultor (see Forum Augustum).

Regiones Quattuor (Fig. 74): the four regiones into which Servius Tullius is supposed to have divided the city of Rome. Each region corresponded to one of the four urban tribes, and at first those living in one were supposed to be forbidden to move to another or be enrolled in another (Livy 1.43.13; Dion. Hal. 4.14.1; Festus 506L; [Aurel. Vict.,] *De Vir. Ill.* 7.7). The four tribes persisted as a political organization well into the empire, but they must have lost their original geographical constraint fairly early, as those owning property in the more important suburban tribes got themselves enrolled in these. The four were given in various orders; Varro (*Ling.* 5.45–54), in his account of the Argei, lists them as (1) Suburana, the Caelian with the valley between the Caelian and Oppius, (2) Esquilina, the Oppius and Cispian with the valley between them, (3) Col-

R. Thomsen, *King Servius Tullius* (Copenhagen 1980), 212–18.

Regiones Quattuordecim: the fourteen regiones into which Augustus divided Rome when he reformed the municipal administration in 7 B.C. (Suetonius, *Aug.* 30.1; Cass. Dio 55.8.7). The regiones were divided into vici, and new magistrates were created, *magistri vicorum*, originally four for each vicus, elected annually by the inhabitants of the vicus, later forty-eight for each regio, regardless of the number of vici, plus two *curatores* for each regio chosen by lot among the eligible. The magistrates' responsibilities were chiefly religious and especially compital, the real administration residing higher (see J. Marquardt, *Römische Staatsverwaltung* [Leipzig 1885], 3.203–7; T. Mommsen, *Le droit public romain* [Paris 1889–1907], 5.333–36, 6.134–41; *BullCom* 34 [1906]: 198–208 [G. Gatti]; *CIL* 6.975 = *ILS* 6073). These regiones were at first known only by number (Tacitus, *Ann.* 15.40; Pliny, *HN* 3.66; Suetonius, *Dom.* 1.1; Frontinus, *Aq.* 2.79; S.H.A. *Heliogab.* 20.2), but the names by which they seem to appear in the regionary catalogues could be as old as the late first century after Christ. The fact that some of these names do not really describe the regiones to which they belong (Porta Capena, Isis et Serapis, Via Lata, Circus Flaminius) suggests that they had no official standing, and Elter's observation that they occur in no ancient author or inscription, not even a sepulchral inscription, suggests that he may well be right that they began as the first item under each regio in the original list from which the regionary catalogues derived and then got promoted into the prominence of names. Other names for regions of the city were known both earlier and later (Suetonius, *Iul.* 39.1, *Nero* 12.1; *De Gramm.* 2). This organization of the city lasted as late as the seventh century, when an ecclesiastical division into seven parishes was instituted and paved the way for a different organization in the Middle Ages. The parishes are supposed to have been the creation of Clement, fourth bishop of Rome, of the time of Domitian, and cannot be made to coincide with the Augustan regiones in any pattern.

From the regionary catalogues it is possible to draw up a picture of the fourteen regiones as they were in the fourth century, but the relation of this to the Augustan regiones, especially around the outer edge of the city, is uncertain. The pomerium (q.v.) had been extended under Claudius, Vespasian, and possibly Hadrian, but trying to draw the limits of the city from those cippi that marked the line and have survived is an exercise in ingenuity (see Fig. 67). Pliny's description (*HN* 3.66–67) of the size of the city

in his day is a bewildering set of statistics from which it is impossible to wrest more than a general meaning. The customs boundary of the city (the *octroi* boundary) marked by cippi of which five of the time of Commodus have been found (*CIL* 6.1016a–c = *ILS* 375, 8594, 31227) is too fragmentary to be much help. And the Capitoline Base of the vicomagistri inscribed in A.D. 136 (*CIL* 6.975 = *ILS* 6073) is an enormous help but includes information only for Regiones I, X, XII, XIII, and XIV. The Servian Walls were not used as a boundary, except where it was convenient, and the line of the Aurelian Walls generally seems to have followed the customs boundary, but with certain modifications.

The following is a short description of what is at present known of the boundaries of the individual regiones in the fourth century. The map of Lugli and Gismondi (Novara 1949) presents a convenient graphic representation of these, although arbitrary at some points.

I Porta Capena: named for the gate in the Servian Walls from which the Via Appia issued. An irregularly shaped region, possibly beginning at the Meta Sudans at the east corner of the Palatine and running down the valley between the Palatine and Caelian, turning southeast along the northeast side of Via Appia in the vicinity of the southeast end of the Circus Maximus, and then beyond the Baths of Caracalla running along both sides of Via Appia as far as the River Almo outside the Aurelian Walls. Beyond the Baths of Caracalla it widened to include a considerable area to the southwest of Via Appia. Regiones I, II, III, IV, and X may all have met at the Meta Sudans, but only if we accept a certain amount of gerrymandering for which there is no sound evidence. If the awkward northern point of Regio I running to the Meta Sudans should be subtracted from it, this might be included in either Regio II or Regio X.

II Caelimontium: essentially the Caelian, bounded on the southwest by Regio I, on the southeast by the line of the Aurelian Walls, and on the north by the straight street running from the Colosseum through Porta Querquetulana and continuing to a postern in the Aurelian Walls.

III Isis et Serapis: the valley between Caelian and Oppius and the Oppius, except for its western tip, running from the Colosseum to a straight street running north and south outside the Servian Walls (Via Merulana Vetus). It is bounded on the south by Regio II, on the east by Via Merulana Vetus, and on the northwest by the Clivus Suburanus. The western boundary is not entirely clear.

IV Templum Pacis: a much-gerrymandered regio including the Sacra Via and the buildings on its northeast side from the Basilica Paulli to Hadrian's

Temple of Venus et Roma, the southeast side of the Argiletum/Subura valley, including at least part of the Forum Transitorium, and the Cispian. In its eastern reaches it is bounded by the Vicus Patricius on the northwest, the Servian Walls on the east, and the Clivus Suburanus on the south.

V Esquiliae: an enormous region including everything between the Servian Walls and the Aurelian Walls from a line running from Porta Viminalis to Porta Chiusa on the north to the line between Porta Querquetulana and the postern of the Aurelian Walls bounding Regio II. But some authorities would assign a strip between Via Merulana Vetus and the Servian Walls to Regio III.

VI Alta Semita: the Quirinal and Viminal, the valley of the Horti Sallustiani and eastern half of the Pincian, and everything beyond these to the northeast as far as the Aurelian Walls. It is bounded on the west by the line of the Servian Walls and "Via Salaria Vetus" as far as Porta Pinciana, thereafter by the line of the Aurelian Walls as far as Porta Chiusa south of the Castra Praetoria, and on the southeast by the Vicus Patricius and its extension to Porta Chiusa.

VII Via Lata: the eastern Campus Martius and western half of the Pincian, everything from Alta Semita's western boundary to Via Flaminia and possibly just taking in Via Flaminia, from Porta Flaminia south to Forum Traiani.

VIII Forum Romanum vel Magnum: the Capitoline, the imperial fora to and including the Forum Nervae, the Forum Romanum, except for the buildings northeast of Sacra Via and southeast of the Argiletum, as far as Summa Sacra Via, the Vicus Iugarius but not the Velabrum, and probably the northwest half of the Forum Boarium. It is very difficult to bound this region with anything like a logical line.

IX Circus Flaminius: named for the square near its southern extremity. The western Campus Martius from Via Flaminia to the Tiber and from Porta Flaminia south to the Capitoline and Theater of Marcellus.

X Palatium: the Palatine, roughly within the boundaries given by Tacitus (*Ann.* 12.24) as the line of the pomerium of the Romulean city (the bronze statue of a bull in the Forum Boarium, Ara Maxima Herculis, Ara Consi, Curiae Veteres, Sacellum Larum, Forum Romanum), but somewhat diminished on the west and southwest.

XI Circus Maximus: an irregular regio embracing the circus, the slope of the Aventine above it, the Velabrum, and the southern half of the Forum Boarium, including the riverbank. Its limit on the southeast is doubtful, but is usually taken to be Vicus Piscinae Publicae, running between the Aventinus

Maior and Aventinus Minor. It is bounded by the Tiber and Regiones VIII, X, XII, and XIII.

XII Piscina Publica: named for an old tank that had probably originally been a public reservoir and later a public swimming pool. It included the Aventinus Minor, the area southwest of this as far as Porta Ostiensis, and the area southeast of it that was largely occupied by the Baths of Caracalla. It is bounded on the south by the irregular course of the Aurelian Walls, on the southeast and northeast by Regio I, and on the northwest by the Vicus Piscinae Publicae and its continuation as Vicus Portae Raudusculanae.

XIII Aventinus: the Aventinus Maior, except for its northeast slope, and the area southwest of it where the great warehouses and markets of Rome were located, as far as the line of the Aurelian Walls beyond Mons Testaceus.

XIV Trans Tiberim: everything on the right bank of the river and including the Tiber island. Its boundaries seem to have been almost unlimited; it embraced far more than the area included within the Aurelian Walls. It stretched at least from the Temple of Fors Fortuna (see Fors Fortuna, Fanum) on the south to the Gaianum (q.v.) and naumachia beyond the Mausoleum Hadriani on the north, and west to the Vatican Hill.

Jordan 1.1.296–339, 2.1–236.

Regium Atrium: see **Regia.**

Remora: the name Remus would have given to Rome had he received the right to found the city, according to Ennius, *Ann.* 1.77 (Skutsch, p. 76). This is probably simply a variant of Remoria (q.v.), *metri causa.*

Remoria (or **Remuria**): a place connected with the foundation story of Rome. According to one version it was a hill near the Tiber 8 kilometers (30 stades) south of the Palatine, where Remus wanted to build the city (Dion. Hal.1.85.6; [Aur. Vict.,] *Orig. Gent. Rom.* 23.1) and where he is buried (Dion. Hal. 1.87.3). Festus (345L) has a Remurinus Ager as the territory of Remus and his dwelling at Remona, which is a variant. This cannot now be located precisely. Uncertainty as to where the augural station of Remus was located also led to the identification of a place *in summo Aventino* as another Remoria (Festus 345L; Dion. Hal. 1.86.2). Finally, Plutarch (*Rom.* 9.4, 11.1) puts both the augural station and the burial place of Remus on the highest part of the Aventine with the name Remonion or Remonia, or "as it is now called" Rignarion. In historical times this was part of the Aventinus Minor, near S. Balbina, identified with the Saxum and commonly called by that name (Cicero, *Dom.* 136; Ovid, *Fast.* 5.149–52). See also Bona Dea Subsaxana, Aedes.

HJ 181–83.

Rignarion: see **Remoria.**

Ripa Veientana: the right bank of the Tiber, as opposed to the Ripa Romana. The name is found on the cippi of the curatores riparum under the empire (*CIL* 6.31547, 31548b, 31555; *ILS* 5928, 5929a, 5934), but it was probably a very old designation and included everything from the Cremera to the sea (Livy 1.33.9, and cf. Horace, *Car.* 1.2.14; Statius, *Silv.* 4.4.6–7; Dion. Hal. 3.45.1).

HJ 651–52.

Rivus Herculaneus: see **Aqua Marcia.**

Roma, Dea, Sacellum: a nymphaeum on the Vicus Iugarius, built against the slope of the Capitoline Hill opposite the church of S. Maria della Consolazione, that was converted to use as a shrine of Dea Roma in the second half of the fourth century after Christ. This was discovered in excavations in 1943.

RendPontAcc 53–54 (1980–82): 329–40 (A. M. Colini).

Roma Quadrata: a shrine on the Palatine *ante Templum Apollinis* (Festus 310–12L) in which were deposited those things used to found a city auspiciously. The augur's lituus and the sacrificial implements used in the foundation ceremonies might be meant, possibly including the plow used to drive the *sulcus primigenius* of the pomerium (q.v.), but more likely it is the *primitiae* of everything sanctioned by custom as good and by nature as necessary that Plutarch (*Rom.* 11.1–2) says were deposited in a trench dug around the comitium at the founding of a city (see Mundus [1]). The epithet quadrata seems to refer to the satisfying of religious, perhaps especially augural, requirements, but, because the sacrarium in which the offerings were deposited was of square shape (Festus 310–12L), it was early taken to refer to this. It is mentioned as a location in the acta of the Ludi Saeculares of Septimius Severus (*CIL* 6.32327.12).

Varro (*ap. Solin.* 1.17) may have confused the description of this: *dictaque primum est Roma quadrata quod ad aequilibrium foret posita,* with something quite different, if related. He continues: *ea incipit a silva quae est in area Apollinis et ad supercilium scalarum Caci habet terminum, ubi tugurium fuit Faustuli.* The latter seems to be describing the augural line that Romulus laid out for taking the

auspices for the new city in competition with Remus (Livy 1.6.4–7.1; Dion. Hal. 1.86.2–4 and cf. 2.5). If we take Lanciani's Aedes Iovis Propugnatoris to be the Temple of Apollo, as most authorities now do, the grove can hardly have been anywhere but in front of this to the southwest, and the augural line may have lain due north and south, but seems much too short for such a line. The head of the Scalae Caci or the Tugurium Faustuli also seems a poor landmark for someone laying out an augural line to have chosen, though perhaps originally it might have been a tree or similar vertical at the top of the Scalae that was chosen. Since Livy (1.18.6) is particular in specifying that in taking the auspices to determine whether Numa Pompilius should be king of Rome the augur seated him on a rock facing south, one wonders whether Varro may not have got things backward and Romulus actually took his station in front of the hut of Faustulus (cf. Auguraculum [1]) and looked south over the Circus Maximus. A fragmentary papyrus (*POxy* 2088) that mentions Roma Quadrata is unfortunately too mutilated to be helpful (see R. Thomsen, *King Servius Tullius* [Copenhagen 1980], 13–16).

Romuleius Mons: a name found once in the Historia Augusta (S.H.A. *Gallien.* 19.4) to describe the place of a statue between the temples of Faustina and Vesta, *ad Arcum Fabianum.* It is also *ante Sacram Viam.* This would seem clear enough, but it is also said to be *in pede Montis Romulei,* which is confusing. It may be that the Velia was briefly renamed Mons Romuleius, if the so-called Tempio del Divo Romolo actually was the construction of Maxentius to his deified son who died in A.D. 307, but more likely the Palatine is meant.

Romulus, Aedes: see **Casa Romuli.**

Romulus, Divus, Templum: a temple erected by Maxentius in honor of his young son, Romulus, who died and was deified in A.D. 307. The temple is shown on coins (Cohen 7.182–84, Romulus nos. 1–12; *RIC* 6.381–82 nos. 239–40, 243–57; Mazzini 5.32 and pl. 10) as round and domed, surmounted by an eagle, sometimes without columns, sometimes with four columns, and sometimes with six. So it is possible, if unlikely, that we are dealing with more than one building, the mausoleum on Via Appia and a temple elsewhere. The temple has often been thought to be the small circular brick structure on the east side of Sacra Via between the Temple of Antoninus and Faustina and the Basilica Constantini (Maxentii). On the fragmentary epistyle of the porch was an inscription still there in the sixteenth century with the name of Constantine (*CIL* 6.1147), and it has been presumed that after Maxentius's death Constantine took over and rededicated the building, as he did the basilica next to it. It has also been identified as a temple of Pax (see Penates Dei, Aedes) or of the Penates (q.v.), as the Fanum Urbis (see Venus et Roma, Templum), and, most recently, as the Temple of Iuppiter Stator flanked by sacella of the Penates, a replacement for the Temple of the Penates (Coarelli 1983, 29–31, 49).

It is a very curious building, a small rotunda behind a concave façade flanked by deep apsidal chambers with more imposing doors than the rotunda, emphasized by columns on high plinths and elaborate entablatures at the top of the stair of approach. The doors of the side chambers are missing, and one can get only a general impression of the effect from the condition of the ruin today. The door to the rotunda is comparatively small, but of fine bronze, tucked in a shallow niche behind a post-and-lintel frame of porphyry columns with plinths and Corinthian capitals of white marble. Because all three doorways are set at the same level, the flanking chambers are thrust forward and make the entrance to the rotunda almost secretive. The building was later converted into a vestibule for the church of SS. Cosma e Damiano, which was built into the south corner of the Templum Pacis under Pope Felix IV (526–530).

Lugli 1947, 184–90; Nash 2.268–71; Coarelli 1974, 94; A. K. Frazer, *Four Late Antique Rotundas* (Ann Arbor, Mich. 1978); *Quaderni dell'Istituto di Storia dell'Architettura* 26 (1980): fasc. 157–62 (Rome 1982), "Il 'tempio di Romolo' di Foro Romano" (various authors).

Rostra, Suggestus, Tribunal: *Rostra* is the term always used for the speakers' platform in the Comitium, although it was not decorated with the ships' beaks that gave it that name before sometime in the third century. But there must have been a speakers' platform there from the beginning, and the Curia was supposed to have been built by Tullus Hostilius. Earlier the kings are said to have used the Volcanal for that purpose. But after the Romans' great naval victory over the Latins at Antium in 338 B.C. some of the captured ships were added to the Roman fleet, and the rest were burned, and the beaks of those that were burned were used to decorate a *suggestus* erected *in medio foro* to celebrate that victory. Being in the forum, it was distinct from the speakers' platform in the Comitium, but before long that platform, too, received a contingent of beaks, probably after one of the great naval victories of the First Punic War. If the comitium/curia complex of Cosa can be taken as a fair copy of the Comitium and Curia of

Rome, then the original speakers' platform was simply a space at the top of the steps of the Comitium in front of the door of the Curia and extending the width of the Comitium. Here the magistrates wishing to address the people stood between the senate and the assembly, and here the praetor urbanus set up his *tribunal* to one side of the Curia door. The creation of a more imposing speakers' platform of the sort we see in the comitium of Paestum would have come in the middle of the third century, for the colonies of Cosa and Paestum were both deductions of 273 B.C., but Cosa was to an entirely new site, while Paestum was to an existing town. So it is reasonable to see the incentive to the creation of a second rostrate suggestus in Rome as one of the naval victories of the First Punic War. Because Comitium and Curia were both inaugurated templa, it follows that the speakers' platform was, too. The Antiate rostra must have been inaugurated separately, for it was a templum, but no one informs us on that detail.

The difference between a rostra and a suggestus may have been only in the beaks, though possibly it extended to size, for a suggestus could be quite small, while a rostra was always very large. Many Roman temples were preceded by suggestus, the stair of approach being broken at the middle by a platform that might hold an altar and also be used as a speakers' platform or magistrate's tribunal. Two of the temples of the Forum Holitorium show such an arrangement, and the Temple of Castor in the forum offered a refinement on it by having the platform approached by small stairs leading off left and right at either end, so the crowd could gather immediately in front of the platform and that front, too, could conceivably be decorated with beaks.

The need for speakers' platforms in every part of the city where people gathered or court was held was very great, and we hear of them in the Area Capitolina (the Tribunal Vespasiani, Titi, Domitiani) and Porticus Minucia (Cicero, *Phil.* 2.63 and 84). Temple platforms must always have provided the readiest opportunity, for they were elevated, already inaugurated, so suitable for holding court, and usually came with ample open space in front of them. This will also explain why there were few tribunalia in Rome, despite the ever increasing multiplication and demand for space for courts; a praetor needed only to mark out a place on a temple platform and install a small wooden dais ticketed with his name and office and sufficiently large to hold his curule chair to establish his court. And the simpler it was, the better.

Rostra: the platform from which orators addressed the people in assembly, both formal and informal. The original platform—if there was only one, which must remain doubtful, because the word itself was plural and the need for more than one *suggestus* must have been felt very early—must have been that in the Comitium, the traditional place of assembly, and was a platform in front of the Curia, on axis with it, possibly the whole breadth of the Comitium (Varro, *Ling.* 5.155; Asconius *ad Cic. in Milon. Arg.* 28–29 and 37 [12] [Stangl 31–32, 37]). Here the praetor urbanus traditionally had his tribunal and the laws of the Twelve Tables were put on display in 442 B.C. (Diod. Sic. 12.26.1).

This platform was augmented after the victory over the Latins at Antium in 338 B.C. by a suggestus (perhaps already in existence) *in foro* (not in the Comitium) that was decorated with the beaks of some of the captured ships (Livy 8.14.12; Pliny, *HN* 34.20). This was the first suggestus to be called rostra, and it was made a templum. It is located by its proximity to the stone lion marking the grave of Faustulus or Romulus (Dion. Hal. 1.87.2) and by the custom of having the accensus consulis announce noon when he saw the sun from the door of the Curia between the rostra and the Graecostasis (Pliny, *HN* 7.212), at which time he must have been looking due south. It almost certainly had the form of a segment of the Comitium, as the Rostra Augusti did later, with curved steps approaching it, but whether one spoke over the steps or, as seems more likely, from the front now decorated with beaks, no one tells us. This was the most conspicuous feature of the forum square, *quam oculatissimo loco, eaque est in rostris* (Pliny, *HN* 34.24), and statues of those who had met their death in public service or done deeds of singular valor were repeatedly erected there, as they had been earlier on the rostra of the Comitium (Cicero, *Phil.* 9.16; Livy 4.17.6; Vell. Pat. 2.61.3; Pliny, *HN* 34.23–25). This platform was then dismantled and rebuilt farther to the northwest sometime between 46 and 42 B.C. (see Rostra Augusti).

At some point, probably after one of the signal naval victories of the First Punic War, the rostra of the Comitium were rebuilt and decorated with the beaks of enemy ships. This complex will than have resembled the Comitium of Paestum (the so-called Teatro Circolare) with a suggestus cutting across the ring of the steps of the Comitium and accessible at the ends, rather than axially. This is implicit in the story of Cato's saving himself from the fury of the mob by hauling himself up to his feet by hanging onto the beaks themselves (Plutarch, *Cato Min.* 44.1–4).

Excavations in the Comitium adjacent to the Niger Lapis have brought to light remains of republican construction that have been interpreted as remains of the rostra. Five building periods are distinguished, the last three with some form of rostra. But the first two of these, as reconstructed, are architecturally bizarre and unworkable, buildings that can never have existed, and it is not until we get to the final phase, dated to the time of Sulla, that architectural logic emerges. What we see is the stepping of the Comitium rising to a broad platform behind it, although the latter might have been considerably narrower, because the number of steps is restored arbitrarily. But it is not the rostra, which should be on the opposite side of the Comitium in front of the Curia; this is part of the Comitium's stepped cavea. The fact that the group of monuments under the Niger Lapis is preserved at a level where it interrupts the stepping and includes remains of a monument interpreted as the tomb of Faustulus or Romulus shows that, as far as the remains go, the stepped plan need not be of high antiquity, but it is implicit in the story of how Tarquinius Superbus seized up the aged Servius Tullius bodily in the Curia and threw him down the steps into the Comitium (Livy 1.48.3; Dion. Hal. 4.38.5). If we cannot restore steps in stone, we must do so in wood.

The coins of Lollius Palicanus of 45 B.C. showing rostra with a curved front decorated with beaks may represent either the Antiate Rostra, at that time presumably dismantled, or a design for the new Rostra Augusti, which had, when dedicated in 42, a straight front, but the former is, of course, more likely.

OpRom 2 (1941): 97–158 (E. Gjerstad); Lugli 1946, 115–21; *RömMitt* 80 (1973): 219–33 (L. Richardson).

Rostra Aedis Divi Iulii: see Iulius, Divus, Aedes.

Rostra Augusti: the rostra of the imperial period at the northwest end of the forum square. Julius Caesar had decided on the removal of the old rostra (Cass. Dio 43.49.1), but their rebuilding does not seem to have taken place until after 42 B.C. Augustus certainly finished them (*Dig.* 1.2.9.43 [Pomponius]), and he appears seated on the rostra with Agrippa on a coin (Cohen 1, Aug. 529 = B. M. Coins, Rom. Emp. 1.23 no. 115 = Mazzini, Aug. 529). The rostra came to signify the northwest limit of the forum (Seneca, *Constant.* 1.3), and the funeral orations for Augustus were delivered presumably from these rostra, called *vetera*, by Drusus (Suetonius, *Aug.* 100.3; Cass. Dio 56.34.4), and from the Rostra Divi Iulii by Tiberius.

This was the site of two splendid spectacles described at length by Dio, Nero's reception of Tiridates of Armenia and Pertinax's funeral (Cass. Dio 62[63].4.3, 75.4.2). Didius Julianus's head was displayed there (Aur. Vict., *Epit.* 19). There were always statues on the rostra (cf. the seated statues shown on the panel of the Arcus Constantini showing the rostra [L'Orange and von Gerkan pls. 5a, 14b, 15a]; S.H.A. *Claud.* 3.5; *CIL* 6.1195, 1731 = *ILS* 1278). An archaic statue of Hercules wearing a tunic stood beside it (*iuxta:* Pliny, *NH* 34.93).

The existing remains are difficult to interpret but can be divided into four periods:

1. The Rostra Caesaris (?), a concrete core with curving front, over 13 m long, with five or six curving steps behind. This backs up against, and was probably built to encroach on, the line of low vaults supporting the Vicus Iugarius along the stair of the Temple of Saturn. It was 3.50 m high and revetted with marble; the façade shows plates of Porta Santa separated by slender pilasters of africano, probably remains of the original revetment. There are holes in the façade for the attachment of ornaments of some sort, but seemingly too small to have carried the great rostra of warships. This may be the rostra of the coin of Palicanus (see Rostra).

2. To this Augustus made an addition to make a larger and slightly higher core for the steps with an extension of the Caesarean steps on the west to reach the whole width of the construction, now with a front façade 23.80 m wide, and create a truly monumental flight. The formerly narrow Caesarean platform at the top now extended 10 m forward, with front and side walls of squared blocks of tufa faced with marble, to which were attached the bronze beaks in two rows. This has now been restored to full height. It evidently had a wooden floor supported on travertine beams that rested on the front and side walls and on three rows of travertine piers. Later brick pillars were added to strengthen or replace the travertine ones. A marble balustrade framed the sides and front, but a generous opening was left in the middle of the front, and to approach this a temporary frontal stair was erected on occasion.

3. The erection of the Arch of Septimius Severus necessitated removal of most of the northeast wall of the rostra and a small court, known as the "hemicycle," was created by cutting away the core of the Augustan platform down to the level of the forum pavement for a bit more than one-half its length. This exposed the facing of the Caesarean rostra in Porta Santa and africano with a plinth of Pentelic marble and a richly decorated crown molding and created a small triangular room that must have been roofed with a wooden floor. The purpose of this room is not clear, nor yet whether it communicated with the platform above. The room was paved with tile, some of which bears Severan stamps (*CIL* 15.405).

4. About A.D. 470 the forward rectangular block of the rostra was lengthened by the addition of a clumsy, slightly trapezoidal construction in brick at the northwest end in front of the pier of the Arch of Septimius Severus, the front of which was also decorated with beaks. An inscription recording a restoration by the praefectus urbi Iunius Valentinus in honor of the victory of Leo and Anthemius (?) over the Vandals has given this the name Rostra Vandalica (*CIL* 6.32005; *RömMitt* 10 [1895]: 59–63 [C. Hülsen]).

The two marble balustrades known as the Plutei, or Anaglypha, Traiani (see Plutei Traiani) found in the open area of the forum near the Columna Phocae are now commonly believed to have formed part of the Rostra Augusti and to have stood either flanking the approach or at the ends of the platform. They were found simply roughly mounted on blocks of travertine, clearly out of context. It is now fairly generally accepted that they date to the time of Hadrian. They show on one face of each a suovetaurilia procession, the victims decked out for sacrifice, at large scale, and on the other face at much smaller scale a historical event in its setting, on one the burning of bundles of tax records on the occasion of a remission of taxes (cf. *CIL* 6.967 = *ILS* 309), and on the other the princeps standing on a rostra addressing an assembly, while at the opposite end is a statue of Trajan receiving the thanks of a mother for the Institutio Alimentaria (*CIL* 9.1455 = *ILS* 6509 and *CIL* 11.1147 = *ILS* 6675). The topographical problems entailed in the correct reading of the backgrounds are difficult, and there is no agreement among scholars as to their solution, but it seems quite clear that both are intended to show the Forum Romanum and use the statue of Marsyas as a point of reference. However, because they are meant only to be read summarily, parts of the background are clearly arbitrary in the number of arches and columns and the angle of vision, and they do not help with the topography of the forum (see Plutei Traiani and Statua Marsyae).

Lugli 1946, 140–44; Nash 2.176–77; *RendPontAcc* 55–56 (1982–84): 329–40 (P. Verduchi); Coarelli 1985, 237–57; *Roma, archeologia nel centro* (1985), 1.29–33 (P. Verduchi).

Rostra Caesaris: the rostra that Julius Caesar built at the northwest end of the Forum Romanum to take the place of the Rostra Comitii, destroyed probably when the Curia was dismantled sometime before Caesar's assassination in March 44 B.C. Dio (43.49.1) puts the construction of the rostra early in 44 and makes this the occasion for the restoration of the equestrian statues of Sulla and Pompey destroyed by the plebs (Suetonius, *Iul.* 75.4; Cass. Dio 42.18.2). It would have been on the new rostra that Caesar sat to watch the celebration of the Lupercalia in February, when Antony publicly offered him a royal diadem, which he then refused (Vell. Pat.

2.56.4; Plutarch, *Caes.* 61.1–4; Cass. Dio 44.11.2–3). It must have been here that two statues of Caesar were erected, one representing him with the oak crown, or Corona Civica, as savior of the citizens, and one as deliverer of the city from siege, with the Corona Obsidionalis, considered the highest possible honor (Pliny, *HN* 22.6; Cass. Dio 44.4.5). One of these must have been the equestrian statue mentioned by Velleius (2.61.3). Here also must have stood the equestrian statue voted by the senate to Octavian in 43 (Vell. Pat. 2.56.4). All this argues that the Rostra Caesaris were of considerable size. They have been recognized in a concrete core, 3.50 m high and over 13 m long, built against and probably originally over the line of low vaults supporting the Vicus Iugarius along the stairs of the Temple of Saturn. This construction had a curving front facing the open square of the forum, a narrow platform at its summit, and a stair of probably seven steps behind,

which eventually became the stair up to the Rostra Augusti. The platform is clearly inadequate to accommodate the accumulation of monuments that must have found place there, and we have our choice of extending it on supports in the fashion of the Rostra Augusti, or of finding a place for the Rostra Caesaris elsewhere. The former is in every way easier, in view of the line of the Vicus Iugarius and Clivus Capitolinus, but it is not clear how the extension would have been engineered, or how it would have functioned architecturally.

Rostra Castoris: see **Castor, Aedes.**

Rostra Divi Iulii: see **Iulius, Divus, Aedes.**

Rostra Vetera: see **Rostra** and **Rostra Augusti.**

Rupes Tarpeia: see **Tarpeia Rupes.**

S

Sabina, Diva, Ara: an altar shown on coins of Hadrian of A.D. 138–139 (*B. M. Coins, Rom. Emp.* 3.363 nos. 960–63), following the deification of Sabina. The altar is of the form that later became standard for the commemoration of deified members of the Antonine family: rectangular, with base and crown moldings and acroteria of horned form at the upper corners, and with a door of four panels on axis in front.

This seems apt to be the altar of which parts were discovered during work on Corso Vittorio Emanuele just northwest of the Chiesa Nuova in 1886–1887, commonly known as the Ara Ditis et Proserpinae. It shows the general design of altars to deified members of the family found in the vicinity of the Columna Marci Aurelii Antonini, but with some variation. Its plan consists of three concentric rectangles equidistant from one another, probably with axial doors on the principal façade and matching doors in sequence in from either side, backed against a wall running parallel to the "Euripus Thermarum Agrippae." The large altar within the innermost enclosure stood on a base of three steps and had bolsters at the ends decorated with a scale pattern, a large fragment of one of which was recovered and is now in the courtyard of the Palazzo dei Conservatori. Because Sabina, who died only a short time before Hadrian, never received a temple, it seems likely that this was an altar erected where her pyre had stood, but there is no proof.

BullCom 15 (1887): 276–77 (G. Gatti); Nash 1.57, 59; *AJA* 89 (1985): 485–97 (M. T. Boatwright); Boatwright 218–30; *CEFR* 98 (1987): 191–210 (J.-M. Flambard).

Sacra Urbs, Templum: see **Venus et Roma, Templum.**

Sacra Via: the oldest and most famous street in Rome, it and the Nova Via (q.v.) being the only streets within the city called *viae* before the imperial period. The adjective almost always precedes, except in poetry (for exceptions, see Pliny, *HN* 19.23; Suetonius, *Vitel.* 17; Asconius *ad Cic. Milon.* 42 [Stangl 41]; *CIL* 6.9239, 9418, 9549; *ILS* 7700; regionary catalogues, Regio IV). There was even a common tendency to run the two words together into a single word in pronunciation (Festus 372L). Mentions of it are very frequent in all periods, but for the most part not informative. It is listed in Regio IV in the regionary catalogues.

The Sacra Via was commonly believed to extend from Summa Sacra Via, where were clustered the Temple of the Lares (Augustus, *RG* 19), the house of the rex sacrorum (Festus 372L), and the Temple of Iuppiter Stator (Plutarch, *Cic.* 16.3), to the Regia (Festus 372L) and Fornix Fabianus (Cicero, *Planc.* 17). Three times it is called Sacer Clivus (Horace, *Car.* 4.2.35; Martial 1.70.5, 4.78.7), but only in poetry, and to go from Summa Sacra Via to the forum was *Sacra Via descendere* (Cicero, *Att.* 4.3.3; Horace, *Epod.* 7.7). But Varro (*Ling.* 5.47) and Festus (372L) are explicit that the Sacra Via really began at the Sacellum Streniae on the Carinae and extended from the Regia *in arcem*. Varro explained this by saying sacra were carried from the sacellum to the arx every month, and the augurs setting out from the arx were accustomed to *inaugurare* by the Sacra Via. This must mean that in the late republic and early empire on the Ides, which were sacred to Jupiter, the priests bringing sacra from the Sacellum Streniae had to make a sharp turn at Summa Sacra Via (cf. the course of Nova Via) and probably had to ascend the Capitoline by the stair known as the Gradus Monetae (later replaced by the Scalae Gemoniae), for the only road up the Capitoline on this side was the Clivus Capitolinus. Unless the clivus was considered part of Sacra Via, which no one suggests (cf., e.g., Pliny, *HN* 19.23), the ascent must have been made by the stair. This really creates no difficulty, except as the Scalae Gemoniae came to be associated with disgrace and violence. But the sacra in question were the *idulia sacra* (Festus 372L) and involved a sheep, the *idulis ovis* (Paulus *ex Fest.* 93L; Macrobius, *Sat.* 1.15.16). This was a gelding, *alba . . . grandior agna* (Ovid, *Fast.* 1.55–56, 587–88), and it was sacrificed by the Flamen Dialis and the entrails offered at the Temple of Iuppiter Optimus Maximus (Ovid, *Fast.* 1.55–56, 587–88). One must ask why it should have been taken to the other peak of the Capitoline first. Perhaps it is because the worship of Jupiter was older on the higher peak.

The course and level of the Sacra Via varied considerably in antiquity, as can be seen dramatically at the Arch of Titus, where the footing of the arch stands well above the Augustan pavement that has now been exposed for most of the length of the street between the Regia and Summa Sacra Via. As it was always the principal route from the Palatine to the Forum Romanum (Plutarch, *Cic.* 22.1; Tacitus, *Hist.* 3.68; Cass. Dio 64.20.3, 78.4.3), in the republican period it probably followed a relatively straight course from Summa Sacra Via to the Regia. Under the empire ambitious building programs, such as those of Nero for the Domus Transitoria and Domus Aurea and that of Maxentius when a serious conflagration made a large area available for redevelopment, may well have forced it to deviate. After the construction of the Arch of Titus, this at Summa Sacra Via and the Fornix Fabianus at the Regia (no one ever uses the term *Ima Sacra Via*) must have seemed terminals. Herodian (2.9.5 and 7.6.9) has been taken to indicate that in his day a stretch was known as Media Sacra Via, but the case is weak.

Brown's excavations in and around the Regia led him to conclude that in the time of the kings and the early republic the Sacra Via "sloped downward on a long curve from the upper Palatium to its northeast, then between Vesta and the Regia along Castor and Pollux, whence it crossed the Forum beside the Doliola to the Comitium" (*Gnomon* 56 [1984]: 381–82 [F. E. Brown]), and that it was only after the pavement of the forum in 179 B.C. that the Sacra Via ran along the north side of the forum. It is difficult to follow Brown in this. The brook now buried under the Sacra Via on the Velia must always have determined the course of a thoroughfare, with first a path and then a road running along it bringing traffic into the forum. If it divided just above the Regia, the road will not have deviated to follow it to the northwest, but will have crossed it on a bridge. If another path developed along the branch to make a forked entrance to the forum, the more direct route will still have been the real Sacra Via, and it is difficult to see the Gradus Monetae as anything but an archaic approach to the northeast height of the Capitoline dictated by the necessities of religion and ritual, ascending the hill steeply in a straight line. Brown's new line will be only auxiliary. For Plautus (*Curc.* 470–75) proves that one could stroll along the northeast side of the forum from the Comitium to Forum Infimum while the Cloaca was still an open trench across the middle.

For the Sacra Via before the time of Augustus, our archaeological evidence is poor and fragmentary. In the late republican period it seems to have been lined with shops in front of houses from just beyond the Regia to Summa Sacra Via. The rebuilding of the Regia in 36 B.C. and the building of the Temple of Divus Iulius in the next few years did little to change it. Marius had already built his Temple of Honos et Virtus across from the Regia, but he also had a house there (see Domus, C. Marius), and Horace shows that in his day it was still the shopping street *par excellence* of Rome. The Augustan pavement has now been uncovered, 5 m wide, for most of the length of this sector; it rises from 12.60 meters above sea level at the northeast corner of the Temple of Divus Iulius to 28.30 meters above sea level at its crest east of the Arch of Titus. Some of its pavement has been found underlying the steps of Hadrian's Temple of Venus et Roma. How much change there was for the creation of the Domus Transitoria is not clear, but after the fire of A.D. 64 we see a considerable rise in level and the construction of handsome arcades on both sides of the street that fronted vast structures similar to the Porticus Minucia Frumentaria (q.v.), which must have served as offices for parts of the bureaucracy that ran the empire. These led to a grand colonnaded *cour d'honneur* at the top of the Velia, with the Colossus of Nero as its center and focus. Later Domitian converted at least some of the arcaded buildings flanking the Sacra Via into the Horrea Piperataria (q.v.), but without change in the Sacra Via. Change came with Hadrian's construction of the Temple of Venus et Roma (see Venus et Roma, Templum) to replace Nero's colonnaded court, after which time the Sacra Via became a broad avenue, flanked by porticoes and shops, those on the northeast side being eventually replaced by the Basilica Constantini (q.v.). Unfortunately, this avenue was removed in 1899 in the belief that it was medieval and the Augustan pavement uncovered. Consequently, all the imperial buildings now seem to float on their foundations. There is no evidence that the continuation of the Sacra Via beyond the Arch of Titus in the direction of the Meta Sudans was ever called, or thought of as part of, Sacra Via.

The Sacra Via and Velia was a residential quarter in republican times, probably always with a bank of shops fronting immediately on the street and the houses withdrawn behind these in the manner familiar from Pompeii. We hear of houses of the kings Numa Pompilius and Ancus Marcius here (Solinus 1.21–23), of Tullus Hostilius on the Velia (Solinus 1.22; Cicero, *Rep.* 2.53), of Publius Valerius (Cicero, *Rep.* 2.53; Livy 2.7.12), Cn. Domitius Calvinus (Festus 142L), P. Scipio Nasica, a public gift (*Dig.* 1.2.8.37 [Pomponius]), probably Marius (*AJA* 82 [1978]: 245 (L. Richardson]), Tettius Damio (Cicero, *Att.* 4.3.3), the Octavii (Sallust, *Hist.* frag. 2.45), and, in the early empire, Domitius Ahenobarbus (*CIL* 6.2041.25 = *ILS* 229, 2042d, 32352). The shops then seem to have dealt especially in luxuries (Ovid, *Ars Am.* 2.265–66, *Am.* 1.8.100; Propertius 2.24.13–14). There are numerous sepulchral inscriptions, especially of goldsmiths and jewelers from the Sacra Via (*CIL* 6.9207 = *ILS* 7685, 9221 = *ILS* 7694, 9239, 9418 = *ILS* 7700; 9419, 9545 = *ILS* 7602, 9546–49), but also of others (*CIL* 6.9283 = *ILS* 7617, 9795, 9935 = *ILS* 7645); Ovid (*Ars Am.* 2.265–66) speaks of buying fine fruit there.

On the Ides of October, after the sacrifice of the October horse at the Altar of Mars in the Campus Martius, the head of the horse was cut off and decorated with bread, and the Sacravienses and Suburanenses battled for the possession of it. If the Sacravienses were victorious, they nailed the head to a wall of the Regia. It is not clear exactly who made up these two factions or how they were marshaled. The struggle for possession of the head presumably took place in the Forum Romanum (Festus 190L, 246L; Plutarch, *Quaest. Rom.* 97).

As one ascends the Sacra Via from the forum, after passing the Basilica Paulli one has on the left the Temple of Antoninus and Faustina, the archaic Sepulcretum, remains of republican houses, the so-called Tempio di Divo Romolo, a medieval loggia, and the Basilica Constantini. On the right are the Regia, remains of houses and shops between the road and the Atrium Vestae, a medieval hemicycle facing the loggia, and the great forest of piers faced with brickwork commonly called the Porticus Margaritaria (q.v.). All these are, in effect, public buildings, or publicly controlled, and attest to the great importance that the Sacra Via apparently always had.

Jordan 1.2.274–86; Lugli 1946, 216–33; Nash 2.284–90; *AJA* 82 (1978): 240–41 (L. Richardson); Coarelli 1983, 11–118; *Roma, archeologia nel cen-*

tro (1985), 1.99–105 (A. Cassatella); *BullCom* 91.2 (1986): 241–62 (S. Buranelli Le Pera and L. D'Elia); *QITA* 10 (1988): 77–97 (D. Palombi), 99–114 (F. Castagnoli); *OpRom* 17 (1989): 229–35 (A. Ziolkowski).

Saepta Iulia: identified in 1934–1937 by Gatti's study of the evidence of fragments of the Marble Plan and the actual remains from antiquity (*FUR* pl. 31; Rodriguez pls. 26, 27, 31) as the great rectangular enclosure about 310 m long and 120 m wide just east of the Pantheon and Thermae Agrippae, and just west of the Temple of Isis Campensis and Serapeum. On the south it adjoined the Diribitorium, which, however, was always regarded as a separate entity. Along its two long sides were colonnades, that on the east the Porticus Meleagri and so inscribed on the Marble Plan, and that on the west the Porticus Argonautarum, which Martial (2.14.5–6) associated with the Saepta, while the two porticoes are listed separately in the regionary catalogues.

Julius Caesar projected the Saepta as early as 54 B.C. (Cicero, *Att.* 4.16.14) to replace the earlier Saepta, jokingly called the Ovile (q.v.), the voting place of the Romans in the *comitia centuriata* and *tributa* in the Campus Martius. It was to be of marble surrounded by a lofty portico a mile long. Whether work was actually begun in Caesar's lifetime has been doubted. Lepidus was in part responsible for the construction (Cass. Dio 53.23.2), and it was completed and dedicated in 26 B.C. by Agrippa, who adorned it with numerous pictures and reliefs. It was officially called Saepta Iulia, but ordinarily called simply Saepta, and once Saepta Agrippiana (S.H.A. *Alex. Sev.* 26.7). It also continued to be known as the Ovile (Ausonius, *Grat. act.* 3.13; cf. Servius *ad Ecl.* 1.33).

In the Saepta several of the Caesars, beginning with Augustus, staged gladiatorial shows (Suetonius, *Aug.* 43.1, *Calig.* 18.1, *Claud.* 21.4; Cass. Dio 55.8.5), and Nero put on a gymnastic exhibition there (Suetonius, *Nero* 12.4). In 17 B.C. the senate (?) was convened here during the Ludi Saeculares (*CIL* 6.32323.50), and Tiberius used it for an assembly of the people on his return from Illyria (Suetonius, *Tib.* 17.2; Cass. Dio 56.1.1). Pliny (*HN* 36.29) mentions statuary groups of Chiron and Achilles and Pan and Olympus here, supposed to be the work of either Scopas or Praxiteles but disputed as to which. And Seneca (*Ira* 2.8.1) characterizes it as one of the most frequented spots in Rome.

The Saepta burned in the great fire of Titus in A.D. 80 (Cass. Dio 66.24.2), but it must have been immediately restored, for Statius (*Silv.* 4.6.2) and Martial (2.14.5, 57.2, 9.59.1, 10.80.4) speak of it as the haunt of strollers and loungers and the site of a great market in luxury goods. Hadrian restored it again (S.H.A. *Hadr.* 19.10). The Porticoes of Meleager and the Argonauts are listed in the regionary catalogues, and the name Septa appears on a post-Constantinian slave collar (*CIL* 15.7195).

With the Saepta's proper identification we now know its form. The long porticoes to either side were essentially independent structures. At the south end a broad corridor without columns separated it from the Diribitorium. At the north end there seems to have been an ample lobby separated from the open area to the south by a wall in which there were at least eight doors, and outside the Saepta to the north was an open space left between the Saepta and the nearest building (the Templum Matidiae). At the opposite end of the open area of the interior, in front of the Diribitorium, was a feature of uncertain form and character. Lily Ross Taylor and Lucos Cozza have tried to reconstruct how the actual voting might have been organized (L. R. Taylor, *Roman Voting Assemblies* [Ann Arbor, Mich. 1966], 47–58). Entrances to the Saepta are a problem. There seem to have been none along the long sides and only minor entrances from the Diribitorium on the south. It is hardly thinkable that almost all Romans entered this important building from the north, the direction from which fewest, one would think, would naturally be coming, but that is what the evidence suggests.

Part of the west wall of the Porticus Argonautarum adjacent to the Pantheon has long been known (Fig. 64). It is built of brick-faced concrete, originally revetted with marble, of which only some stretches of the base molding survive, interrupted at regular intervals by large rectangular niches, presumably for the display of sculpture (cf. Pliny, *HN* 36.29). It is presumed that the name Porticus Argonautarum referred to a mural painting (Cass. Dio 53.23.2); certainly Jason was represented in some way (Martial 2.14.5–6), but there seems to be no suitable place for a large mural. Yet it continued to be known as the Porticus Argonautarum after repeated restorations. Perhaps we should imagine that an original painting was replaced by sculptures of the same subject in the course of time and that a gallery of the heroes known to have taken part in the expedition of the Argo filled the niches.

BullCom 62 (1934): 126–28 (G. Gatti); *L'urbe* 2, no. 9 (1937): 8–23 (G. Gatti); Lugli 1938, 96–107; Nash 2.291–93.

Salinae: a place at the foot of the Clivus Publicius just inside the Porta Trigemina where at one time there had been saltworks. By the time of our earliest mention, it was no more than a place-name (Livy 24.47.15; Frontinus, *Aq.* 1.5; Solinus 1.8). It is gen-

erally believed by topographers that this was the site of warehouses for salt brought up from the saltworks at the mouth of the Tiber, but that is not what the name suggests, and the location would not have been convenient for warehouses.

Salus, Aedes: a temple vowed by C. Iunius Bubulcus Brutus when he was consul and commander in the Second Samnite War, probably in 311 B.C. He let the contract for the temple as censor in 307 and dedicated the temple when dictator in 302 (Livy 9.43.25, 10.1.9). Its dedication day was the Nones of August (Fast. Vall. Amit. Ant., Philocalus; Cicero, *Att.* 4.1.4, *Sest.* 131; Degrassi 492). It stood on the part of the Quirinal known as the Collis Salutaris, so perhaps there was a very ancient altar or sacellum of Salus here. One of the gates of the Servian Walls was the Porta Salutaris (q.v.), and we know of a Clivus Salutaris and a Vicus Salutis (or Salutaris).

Despite the age and importance of the temple, we know little about it. Lightning struck it in 276 B.C. (Orosius 4.4.1), in 206 (Livy 28.11.4), and again in 166 (Obsequens 12), but evidently the damage was always limited, because paintings by C. Fabius, surnamed Pictor, executed when Brutus's temple was first built, survived until it burned in the time of Claudius (Pliny, *HN* 35.19). Fabius was proud enough of his work to have signed it (Val. Max. 8.14.6). The temple must have been restored after the fire, because it was still standing in the fourth century and was included in the regionary catalogues (its name corrupted to Templum Salusti in the *Curiosum*).

A statue of Cato Maior was set up in the temple in his honor (Plutarch, *Cato Mai.* 19.3). A swarm of bees settled in front of the temple in 104 B.C. (Obsequens 43). And Atticus's house was nearby, evidently between the Temple of Salus and the Temple of Quirinus (Cicero, *Att.* 4.1.4, 12.45.3). The temple must have been prominent to be repeatedly struck by lightning, and we may place it somewhere close to Piazza del Quirinale (Montecavallo).

Remains of a very large temple that faced east stood south of Montecavallo until the seventeenth century. Together with its stair, this extended from Piazza della Pilotta to the fountain of Montecavallo (Fig. 72). The rear corner of the temple, built of blocks of peperino and carrying the marble entablature and a corner of the pediment, against which was built a medieval defense tower, was known variously as Torre Mesa, Torre di Mecenate, and Frontispizio di Nerone. Remains of a great stair leading to the temple from the plain below still survive in the gardens of Palazzo Colonna and the Pontificia Università Gregoriana, and records of these have been left by artists, notably van Heemskerck, who gives a panorama of what was to be seen in the sixteenth century (2.81 v, 82 r). There are also a plan by Palladio (Zorzi pls. 153–55) and drawings of the entablature and corner of the pediment by Serlio and the Anonymous Destailleur (*RömMitt* 52 [1937]: 95 fig. 1). Fragments of the architecture, including an architrave block, parts of the frieze, and the corner block of the pediment, still lie in the gardens of Palazzo Colonna.

This complex was the subject of a famous debate toward the end of the nineteenth century between Hülsen, who wished to identify it as the Temple of Serapis (see Serapis, Aedes), built by Caracalla, and Lanciani, who held it to be the Temple of Sol (see Sol, Templum) built by Aurelian. Each advanced relays of argument for his identification, and since then topographers have generally held for one theory or the other. Most recently Nash (2.376–83) and Lugli (Lugli 1938, 304–7) have sided with Hülsen, whereas M. Santangelo (*MemPontAcc*, ser. 3.5 [1940–41]: 154–77) has sided with Lanciani. Only H. Kähler (*RömMitt* 52 [1937]: 94–105) has been bold enough to reject both identifications, yet he is unquestionably correct. The architectural ornament of the temple is unmistakably Hadrianic (cf. *PBSR*, n.s., 8, vol. 21 [1953]: 118–51 [D. Strong]). Moreover, the pronaos, as Palladio has drawn it, is a close congener of the pronaos of Hadrian's Pantheon, with its lines of columns leading back to important niches between pronaos and cella. It has been argued that the brickwork in the walls of the monumental stair approaching the temple is typically Severan (see Lugli 1938, 306–7), but there seems to have been no confirmation of this from the evidence of brickstamps. If it is Severan, it must be a later addition to a Hadrianic building.

Palladio shows the temple as peripteral, sine postico, pseudo-dipteral, with twelve columns on the façade and fourteen down the flanks. It is mounted on a platform with seven steps running around the three colonnaded sides. The pronaos is deep, with eight columns in pairs behind the third, fifth, eighth, and tenth columns of the façade. These flank niches in the cella wall, semicircular to either side, and rectangular for the door in the middle. The interior is believed to have been hypaethral, with colonnades down the sides in two storeys, Ionic below, Corinthian above. The total height of the main order has been calculated as 21.17 m (Alberti), the entablature as 4.83 m. It was a huge temple, on the order of the Temple of Venus et Roma, and set at the back of a large precinct finished, at least along the back, with a wall behind an addorsed colonnade, in the bays of which were niches, alternately rectangular and semicircular. At the front of the precinct were found the statues of the horse tamers that still adorn Montecavallo, although perhaps they belonged to the Thermae Constantinianae (*MemPontAcc*, ser. 3.5 [1940–41]: 158, 161 [M. Santangelo]).

The approach from the plain of the Campus Martius was complicated, and the drawings of it are difficult to read. It consisted of a double stair on each side of an open court, the inner stair on each side steeper than the outer. The stairs were roofed, so there was a subtle element of surprise introduced, but there were windows along the sides, so one could admire the view along the way. At the top one had to make a detour to enter the precinct, where the view of the flank of the temple would be enhanced. The stairs were carried on vaults, and a number of vaulted chambers filled the back of the court between them. It is not clear what the use of these rooms may have been. Lanciani (LS 1.38) believed that blocks of these stairs were robbed in 1348 to build the stair leading up to the church of S. Maria in Aracoeli.

The arguments in favor of identifying this as the Temple of Salus are simply that it is in approximately the right place with respect to the Porta Salutaris and would have a certain prominence, consonant with its having been repeatedly struck by lightning. We know of no Hadrianic rebuilding of the Temple of Salus, but coins bearing the image of Salus and the legend Salus Augusti are particularly numerous in Hadrian's principate (see, e.g., *B. M. Coins, Rom. Emp.* 3.cxlviii-clxix).

RömMitt 52 (1937): 94–105 (H. Kähler); Lugli 1938, 304–7; *MemPontAcc*, ser. 3.5 (1940–41): 154–77 (M. Santangelo); *PBSR*, n.s., 8, vol. 21 (1953): 118–51 (D. E. Strong); Nash 2.376–83; M. A. Marwood, *The Roman Cult of Salus* (*BAR*, Int. Ser. 465 [1988]): especially 2–15.

Salus, Ara: mentioned once, in connection with a prodigy of 113 B.C. (Obsequens 38), but possibly not the altar of the Aedes Salutis (see Salus, Aedes), nor necessarily in Rome.

Salutaris Collis: see **Quirinalis Collis.**

Samiarium: a place where weapons were polished and sharpened, mentioned only in the regionary catalogues, where the *Curiosum* has *saniarium*, but neither word is known elsewhere, and *samiarium* is the *lectio difficilior.* See Lydus, *Mag.* 1.46.5. It is listed in the catalogues in Regio II and was probably closely connected with the Armamentarium and Spoliarium (qq.v.).

Saturnius Mons: see **Capitolinus Mons.**

Saturnus, Aedes (Fig. 19): a temple about which there was much disagreement. Macrobius (*Sat.* 1.8.1) knew a tradition that ascribed a *fanum Saturni* and the establishment of the Saturnalia to Tullus Hostilius, but also knew that Varro thought that L. Tarquinius (Priscus?) had let the contract for the temple building and that Titus Larcius dedicated it as dictator, an office he may have held in connection with one of his consulships in 501 and 498, or shortly thereafter. This was the commonest belief (see Dion. Hal. 6.1.4). But there were those who assigned its dedication to other magistrates of the first years of the republic, Aulus Sempronius Atratinus and M. Minucius Mamercus, the consuls of 497 (Livy 2.21.1–2; Dion. Hal. 6.1.4), Postumus Cominius, consul in 501 and 493 (Dion. Hal. 6.1.4), the last tradition ascribed to a Gellius, probably Cn. Gellius, the annalist of the second century B.C. Almost everyone agrees that the temple belongs to the beginning of the republic and that it was the oldest temple whose building was recorded in the records of the pontifices. Its location was variously given as *in faucibus (Montis Capitolini)* (Varro, *Ling.* 5.42), *sub Clivo Capitolino* (Servius *ad Aen.* 8.319; [Aur. Vict.,] *Orig. Gent. Rom.* 3.6), *ante Clivum Capitolinum* (Servius *ad Aen.* 2.116; Hyginus, *Fab.* 261), *ad forum* (Macrobius, *Sat.* 1.8.1), and *in Foro Romano* (Livy 41.21.12).

In 174 B.C. a portico was built from the temple to the Senaculum, *ac super id Curiam*. This must have run along the shoulder of the Capitoline, but how it can have reached the Curia without passing through the Comitium is a hard question. The answer may be that a columnar porch similar to that of the Curia Iulia (q.v.) was added to the façade of the Curia Hostilia either at this time or earlier, and the new portico adjoined it at one end. The fact that such a porch was a feature of the third-century curia of Paestum may strengthen the argument. In any case, this portico must have been a relatively light structure that has disappeared without leaving any trace. In 42 B.C. L. Munatius Plancus rebuilt the temple (Suetonius, *Aug.* 29.5; *CIL* 6.1316 = *ILS* 41, *CIL* 10.6087 = *ILS* 886). It is mentioned casually in connection with the Arch of Tiberius of A.D. 16 (Tacitus, *Ann.* 2.41). It burned sometime in the later fourth century and was then restored by vote of the senate, as is recorded on the architrave (*CIL* 6.937 = *ILS* 3326). It is listed in the regionary catalogues in Regio VIII.

Throughout the republic, this temple contained the state treasury, the *Aerarium Populi Romani*, or *Aerarium Saturni* (Paulus *ex Fest.* 2L; Solinus 1.12; Macrobius, *Sat.* 1.8.3), administered by quaestors, for whom it became a sort of headquarters (Plutarch, *Ti. Gracch.* 10.6; Appian, *BellCiv* 1.31). In the

temple was kept a pair of scales in memory of a time when payment had been by weight (Varro, *Ling.* 5.183). Under the empire the Aerarium Populi Romani was distinguished from the *fiscus*, the privy purse of the emperor, and continued to reside in the temple, but seems now to have been administered by praefecti (Pliny, *Epist.* 10.3.1). For inscriptions mentioning the aerarium, see *DE* 1.300; for occurrences of the phrase Aerarium Populi Romani and Aerarium Saturni, see *TLL* 1.1055–58. Other public documents were affixed in numbers to the exterior (Varro, *Ling.* 5.42; Cass. Dio 45.17.3), perhaps because of the temple's association with the quaestors.

On the gable of the temple were acroteria of Tritons blowing trumpets (Macrobius, *Sat.* 1,8,4), and in the cella was a statue, probably with substantial parts of ivory, for it was filled with oil (Pliny, *HN* 15.32), whose feet were shackled with woolen bonds except on the Saturnalia (Macrobius, *Sat.* 1.8.5). It seems doubtful that this was the image carried in solemn processions and lectisternia (Dion. Hal. 7.72.13). The day of dedication was the Saturnalia, 17 December (Fast. Amit. *ad XVI Kal. Ian.*; Degrassi 538–40).

A very small part of the temple was shown on one fragment of the Marble Plan, now lost (*FUR* pl. 13.24 = 21.18d; Rodriguez pl. 13.18d), and another, also lost, has erroneously been thought to show the stair of approach (*FUR* pl. 3.3 = 21.19; Rodriguez pl. 13.19) but can be demonstrated not to belong to the temple at all.

A few blocks of the original structure survive, but most of what can be seen of the podium today belongs to the reconstruction of Plancus, a mass of concrete faced with walls of blocks of travertine and peperino that were revetted with marble. It is 22.50 m wide and about 40 m long; the back is at present in the process of being excavated for the first time. There is no evidence of any building period intermediate between the original construction and Plancus's reconstruction, unless Gellius's record of a dedication by the tribunus militum L. Furius of a building decreed by the senate (Macrobius, *Sat.* 1.8.1) refers to a rebuilding of the late fifth or fourth century B.C. In that case it might refer to a rebuilding after the fire of the Gauls.

The temple stands very high on its podium because of its situation on the slope of the Capitoline. The superstructure is that of the rebuilding after the fire in the fourth century. The columns are of granite, six on the façade of gray granite, the pairs behind them on either side of the pronaos of rose granite. The bases are of white marble and of three types, and the capitals are four-sided Ionic of very late type, almost proto-Byzantine. The entablature blocks are reused with sketchy patching of lacunas, of Proconnesian marble, perhaps of Severan date, whereas the cornice is considered Augustan, possibly part of Plancus's building but clumsily reassembled. The columns are 11 m high, but of unpleasing effect. The whole points to a reconstruction when the classical tradition of working stone had been lost, but a new aesthetic had not yet taken its place.

The steps of the temple have disappeared, but the Aerarium must have been arranged under them. In Pompeii the aerarium was in vaulted chambers under the Capitolium (Temple of Jupiter) at the end of the forum, accessible from a platform at midstair in the stair of approach across the façade. Here the stair divided into three parts, those on either side continuing up to the pronaos, and that in the middle descending to the aerarium (A. Maiuri, *Alla ricerca di Pompei preromana* [Naples 1973], 104–6). A similar arrangement in Rome would suit the information that during Milo's trial Pompey set his curule chair *pro aerario* (Asconius *in Cic. Milon. arg.* 36 [Stangl 36]). That there was a single door to the Aerarium seems shown by Tiberius Gracchus's sealing of this with his personal seal in 133 B.C. (Plutarch, *Ti. Gracch.* 10.6). The temple was well preserved until the fifteenth century, according to Poggio, and destroyed between 1402 and 1447 (VZ 4.235).

Lugli 1946, 149–51; *Collection Latomus* 58 (1962): 757–62 (E. Gjerstad); *AJA* 84 (1980): 51–62 (L. Richardson); R. Pensabene, *Tempio di Saturno, architettura e decorazione* (Rome 1984).

Saturnus, Ara: an ancient altar usually distinguished from, but sometimes confused with (e.g., Solinus 1.12), the Aedes Saturni, in front of which it stood. It was *in imo Clivo Capitolino* (Festus 430L) and was believed to date from before the time of the Trojan War, or even to have been established by Hercules (Dion. Hal. 1.34.4; Solinus 1.12). Macrobius puts it *ante senaculum*, which suggests that it lay too far east of the Temple of Saturn to be closely associated with it. Worship there was always in the Greek rite with the head uncovered, which was considered proof of its high antiquity. Coarelli has convincingly identified it as the ancient altar traditionally called the Volcanal behind the northeast end of the Rostra Augusti.

DialArch 9–10 (1976–77): 346–77 (F. Coarelli); Coarelli 1983, 202–10.

Saxum: see **Remoria** and **Bona Dea Subsaxana, Aedes.**

Saxum Tarpeium: see **Tarpeia Rupes.**

Scalae Anulariae: The location of the house of the orator and poet Licinius Macer Calvus in which Augustus lived during his early public life (Suetonius, *Aug.* 72.1) is given as *iuxta Romanum Forum, supra Scalas Anularias.* Cicero (*Acad.* 2.86) uses the word *anularius* to mean a worker of, or dealer in, seal stones, a jeweler, and in the republic and early empire there was always a concentration of jewelers along Sacra Via from the Regia to Summa Sacra Via, so we can with confidence put this stair somewhere on the Velia, but whether it was the same as the Scalae Deum Penatium (Varro *ap. Don. ad Ter. Eun.* 256) or an otherwise unknown stair between Sacra Via and Nova Via must remain uncertain.

Scalae Caci (Fig. 63): an ancient approach to the Palatine via the Cermalus in the form of a ramped stair cut in the tufa of the hill. At its *supercilium* (top) was the Casa Romuli (or Tugurium Faustuli; see Casa Romuli) and the termination of Roma Quadrata (Solinus 1.18; Plutarch, *Rom.* 20.4, where the text is corrupt; Diod. Sic. 4.21.2). At its lower end, which is not preserved, it must have emerged in the Forum Boarium in the area associated especially with the cult of Hercules. Its relation to the Atrium Caci (q.v.) is unknown. Its upper end was closed in the imperial period by a gate with travertine jambs and sill. Here it has been followed as far as it is preserved between the sacred precinct of the Magna Mater with the Casa Romuli and the Casa di Augusto. It was never more than a narrow alley, but one up which a mule or donkey could have been driven. Its association with Cacus is unknown.

Lugli 1946, 405–6; *MonAnt* 46 (1963): 202–6 (P. Romanelli); *NSc* 1965, suppl., 130–40 (G. Carettoni); Nash 2.299–300.

Scalae Cassii: a flight of steps in Regio XIII (*Notitia*), presumably built by Sp. Cassius and leading to the top of the Aventine from the neighborhood of the Temple of Ceres, Liber, and Libera, which he dedicated. Before the construction of the Clivus Publicius, about 238 B.C., this would have been the only approach to the Aventine in this vicinity, so it may be presumed to have been a ramped stair, like the Scalae Caci of the Palatine, capable of being negotiated by mules and donkeys. Such a stair is mentioned in the Einsiedeln itinerary of the eighth century (*MonAnt* 1 [1889]: 512 [R. Lanciani]) after a water, presumably the Aqua Appia, which ended at the foot of the Clivus Publicius near Porta Trigemina (Frontinus, *Aq.* 1.5).

Scalae Deum Penatium: see **Penates Dei, Aedes.**

Scalae Gemoniae: a flight of steps leading alongside the Carcer (q.v.) to the top of the Capitoline on which the bodies of executed criminals were thrown for public exposure and disgrace. The steps are called Scalae Gemoniae (Val. Max. 6.3.3, 9.13; Aur. Vict., *Caes.* 8.6, 33.31, *Epit.* 8.4; Orosius 7.8.8), simply Gemoniae (Suetonius, *Tib.* 53.2, 61.4, 75.2, *Vitel.* 17.2; Tacitus, *Ann.* 3.14, 5.9, 6.25, *Hist.* 3.74 and 85; Sid. Apoll., *Epist.* 1.7.12), *anabasmoi* (Cass. Dio 58.1.3, 5.6, 11.5, 64.21.2), Gradus Gemitorii (Pliny, *HN* 8.145), and Gradus Gemonii (Tertullian, *Adv. Val.* 36). Only two of our sources provide good topographical information; Valerius Maximus (6.9.13) says that the steps were in sight of the whole forum, and Dio (58.5.6) says that after sacrifice on the Capitoline, while Sejanus descended to the forum by the way leading to the Carcer, his lictors slipped and fell on the Scalae. This makes it highly probable that the Scalae followed fairly closely the course of the modern stair leading down from the top of Via S. Pietro in Carcere, just northeast of the Temple of Concordia. They are first mentioned only in the time of Tiberius, so it is likely that they were a replacement for the Gradus Monetae (q.v.; cf. Ovid, *Fast.* 1.638), destroyed when Tiberius rebuilt and enlarged the Temple of Concordia. However, the Gradus Monetae were not used for the exposure of the executed, so far as we know. In the popular mind Gemoniae was clearly derived from *gemere*, but it was a proper name, although we are unable to make a connection with a particular person (cf. *PW* 7.1 [1910]: 1115–16, s.v. "Gemoniae Scalae" [K. Ziegler]).

Scala Mediana: a stair known from a single inscription (*CIL* 6.9683 = *ILS* 7488), the sepulchral inscription of a *negotiatrix frumentaria et leguminaria ab scala mediana*. Obviously it could have been almost anywhere; it sounds like the designation of a stair up the Tiber bank in the area of the wholesale markets below the Aventine.

Scalae Tarquitiae: mentioned only once (Festus 496L). Verrius Flaccus said it was popularly thought that they were so called for the sake of obliterating the name of Tarquinius Superbus, who had built them. This must mean that they were very old and that Verrius himself did not accept this explanation. There is no indication of their location, and speculation seems futile.

Schola: *Schola* was a term used for two very different sorts of building. The older and simpler was simply a semicircular bench where a group of ten or twelve could gather and talk. It might be of stone or stuccoed masonry and variously embellished with a sundial or statuary. They seem to have been common features of sanctuaries, including rustic sanctuaries, and they were a popular tomb form, especially for tombs near the gates of a city.

Schola was also used as a term for the headquarters of a collegium of any sort, the usage clearly deriving from the preceding. Such a schola was usually exedral, but did not have to be. It could be an independent building. There was usually a shrine to the tutelary divinity of the collegium, and here were kept the collegial archives. In more elaborate form this could be adjacent to facilities for the preparation and consumption of meals that the collegium took in common, at which time the whole complex was called a schola.

(Schola) Calcariensium: an organization of the lime burners mentioned in two inscriptions (*CIL* 6.9223 = *ILS* 7289, 9224 = *ILS* 7289a; cf. *Cod. Theod.* 12.1.37), both found in the area just east of the Thermae Diocletiani. H. Armini (*Eranos* 22 [1924]: 85–88), arguing from inscriptions of *calcarienses* in Jewish catacombs, Juvenal 3.12–14, and the Vicus Pulverarius (q.v.) in Regio I would place the synagogue and headquarters of the calcarienses in Regio I. But there must have been a good many lime burners in Rome, and it is unlikely that they would all have been Jewish and all congregated in a single quarter. The evidence of the inscriptions in hand seems to indicate a collegial gathering place in or near the Thermae Diocletiani.

Schola Carrucariorum: see **Area Carruces.**

Schola Fabrum Soliarium Baxiarium: the collegial headquarters of a guild of shoemakers *sub Theatro Pompeiano*, presumably in the arcades supporting the cavea (*CIL* 6.9404 = *ILS* 7249).

Schola Fori Traiani: a room or rooms attached to the libraries of the Forum Traiani (q.v.). The only occurrence of the name is in a *subscriptio* of a manuscript (pseudo-Quintilian *in codd. Parisin.* 16230, *Sorbonian.* 629): *legi et emendavi ego Dracontius cum fratre Ierio incomparabili arrico urbis Rome, in scola fori Traiani feliciter* (see *RhM* 60 [1905]: 154–58 [G. Lehnert]). Despite the great variety of architectural forms that a schola might take, there seems always to have been a preference for the semicircular. So it is perhaps not too much to suppose that in late antiquity the hemicycles at the ends of the Basilica Ulpia, evidently labeled ATRIUM and LIBERTATIS on the Marble Plan and perhaps containing the Bibliotheca Ulpia (S.H.A. *Aurel.* 1.7, 8.1, 24.7), might have come to be called scholae. The manuscript subscriptio is believed to belong to the late fourth or fifth century.

Schola Kalatorum Pontificum: the name given in modern times to the headquarters of the *kalatores*, freedmen attending on the pontifices and flamines as assistants. It was in the forum near the Regia, known from an inscription found in two pieces, one in 1546, one in 1899, that together read *in honorem domus Augustae kalatores pontificum et flaminum*. The inscription is on a marble epistyle, probably the lintel of a door, 3.50 m wide overall. It is associated with other inscriptions of the kalatores on marble blocks from the forum area that suggest a rather pretentious edifice (*CIL* 6.32445; *NSc* 1899, 128 [G. Gatti]; *BullCom* 27 [1899]: 146 [G. Gatti]; *RömMitt* 16 [1901]: 10–12 [C. von Bildt], 17 [1902]: 65–66 [C. Hülsen], 29 [1914]: 7–11 [M. Bang]). It may be that one of the tabernae connected with the Atrium Vestae was used as the Schola Kalatorum, but it is impossible to identify which. The inscription seems to be of Severan date.

Lugli 1946, 99.

Schola Porticus Octaviae: see **Porticus Octaviae.**

Schola Praeconum (Fig. 63): collegial headquarters of the heralds of the Domus Augustiana (?), identified from wall paintings showing life-size figures in sleeved knee-length tunics in various activities as attendants against a setting of columnar architecture. The fragmentary building of the Severan period is separate from the Domus itself, lying low on the southwest slope of the Palatine close to Via dei Cerchi. What remains consists of an arcaded peristyle on which open three parallel vaulted chambers, almost exedras, a large central one flanked by symmetrical smaller ones, while other rooms seem to have extended to either side of the peristyle, but nothing clearly legible. This is sometimes mistakenly called the Domus Gelotiana (q.v.), sometimes Domus Praeconum. Its true character is uncertain, but the remains show that it was once a fine building. It has recently been the object of excavations by the British School at Rome using a wide range of new and sophisticated techniques.

Nash 1.336, 338; *PBSR* 50 (1982): 53–101, 347–84 (D. Whitehouse et al.), 53 (1985): 163–210 (D. Whitehouse et al.).

Schola Quaestorum et Caplatorum: listed by the regionary catalogues in Regio III. The name is almost certainly corrupt, because the quaestors who were magistrates of the government of Rome were elected and would have had no need of a schola, while *caplatores* (or *capulatores*) were those who refined and bottled olive oil and were organized in collegia in many parts of central and southern Italy (cf. *CIL* 9.665 = *ILS* 5784, 2336 = *ILS* 7298, 10.5917 = *ILS* 1909, 14.3677 = *ILS* 6244). They might well have had need for a headquarters building of some sort.

There seems no real reason to accept Hülsen's suggestion that the ancient church of S. Maria de Cambiatoribus may preserve a distorted memory of this schola in its name, because the church and the *trivium* from which it may have taken its name were in all probability in Regio IV rather than Regio III.

HJ 319; HCh 316–18.

Schola Quindecimvirorum Sacris Faciundis: In the creation of Corso Vittorio Emanuele in 1889, in the swath cut for the street just southeast of its junction with Vicolo dell'Arco della Fontanella, opposite the façade of S. Giovanni dei Fiorentini, were found remains of a building with a semicircular apse that Lanciani (LFUR sheet 14) has labeled SCHOLA XV VIR SAC FAC (cf. *MonAnt* 1 [1889]: 548 [R. Lanciani]). Nothing more seems to be known about this.

Schola Sodalium Serrensium: known from an inscription (*CIL* 6.839, cf. *ILS* 9419) found a little outside Porta Nomentana to the southeast, probably in the ruins of the schola itself, because two bronze measures of a *sextarius* and a *hemis* also inscribed *sodalium* were found in the same place. But no plan of the remains was made, and the nature of this *sodalicium* remains completely obscure.

Schola Tetrastyli: headquarters of a collegium of dealers in ivory and citrus wood, known from a single inscription, the lex collegii (*CIL* 6.33885) found in the Transtiberim near the church of S. Callisto, probably not far from its original location. It belongs to the time of Hadrian.

Schola Viatorum Triumvirum et Quattuorvirum: headquarters of the *viatores* (subalterns) of the tresviri capitales, tresviri monetales, and quattuorviri viarum curandarum on the Aventine in the neighborhood of the church of S. Alessio, known from *CIL* 6.1936 = *ILS* 1929 immured in the wall of the porch of the church and confirmed by finds of related inscriptions. However, there are no remains of buildings associated with these.

Epigraphica 8 (1946): 45–48 (F. Castagnoli).

Schola Xanthi: the headquarters of the *scribae, librarii*, and *praecones* of the curule aediles. Bebryx

Aug. lib. Drusianus and A. Fabius Xanthus rebuilt it in the time of Tiberius, and C. Avillius Licinius Trosius restored it in the early third century (*CIL* 6.103 = 30692 = *ILS* 1879, repeated with variations on both sides of the lintel of the doorway). It was a small building but elegantly appointed, as the inscriptions attest, and excavated in 1539 (LS 2.185–86) and destroyed for its building material. It was relocated in 1900–1902 and identified as a trapezoidal building just southeast of the little viaduct carrying the Vicus Iugarius into the forum along the stair to the Temple of Saturn. The principal entrance was on the southeast from the main square of the forum. It had a pavement of white marble and a marble bench around three walls, while in the middle of the northwest wall was a door from which a stair led up to the level of the Vicus Iugarius. The identification is generally accepted and all but positive.

Lugli 1946, 95–96, 152; Nash 2.301.

Secretarium Circi: mentioned only once (Symmachus, *Relat.* 23.9) and apparently a courtroom for secret, or secluded, hearings of the praefectus urbi. The only circus that could be meant seems to be the Circus Maximus, which was a long way from the other offices of the praefectus on the Oppius and in Templum Pacis. Perhaps a room in the Thermae Traiani with a circus mosaic decorating the pavement might have been meant (see Praefectura Urbana and Porticus Thermarum Traianarum).

Secretarium Senatus: one of the tabernae, the fifteenth counting from the north, of the Forum Iulium, used for criminal trials involving senators, established as a courtroom probably in A.D. 393/394, and restored in 412 and 414 by Flavius Annius Eucharinus Epifanius. It went out of use with, if not before, the construction of the church of S. Martina in the seventh century, because the church makes use of one of its walls as a foundation.

L. Bonfante and H. von Heintze, eds., *In Memoriam Otto J. Brendel* (Mainz 1976), 191–204 (E. Nash, "Secretarium Senatus").

Secretarium Tellurense: see **Praefectura Urbana.**

Secundenses: a name occurring in a very fragmentary inscription (*NSc* 1899, 335 [G. Gatti]; *Klio* 2 [1902]: 270 [C. Hülsen]) believed to be part of the edict of Tarracius Bassus against fraudulent merchants and shopkeepers dated shortly after A.D. 368 (*CIL* 6.31893–31901 = *ILS* 6072). The mention of *de Sicinino* two lines earlier might permit putting the Secundenses in a street in Regio IV on the Cispian,

not far from the church of S. Maria Maggiore (see Sicininum).

Semo Sancus Dius Fidius, Aedes (Sacellum, Livy 8.20.8, where perhaps he is referring to a small dedication within the precinct of the temple, because he specifies *in sacello Sangus adversus aedem Quirini*) (Fig. 72): a temple to a god originally Sabine (Ovid, *Fast.* 6.213–18; Varro, *Ling.* 5.66) but believed to have been built by Tarquinius Priscus. It was dedicated only much later, in 466 B.C. (Dion. Hal. 9.60.8), by Sp. Postumius, whose name was inscribed on the temple. The dedication day was the Nones of June (Ovid, *Fast.* 6.213–18; Fast. Ven.; Degrassi 465).

Probably there had been a templum with an altar here from very early times. The temple stood on the Collis Mucialis, the second rise of the Quirinal, but could evidently be related to the Temple of Quirinus on the crest of the hill. One of the gates of the Servian Walls was the Porta Sanqualis, so named because of its proximity to the temple (Paulus *ex Fest.* 464–65L). Almost certainly it was the gate of which remains have been found in Piazza Magnanapoli. We can locate the temple north of this, because an inscription to Semo Sancus was found near the church of S. Silvestro (*CIL* 6.568 = *ILS* 3473) and perhaps somewhat to the east, where a view of the Temple of Quirinus would have been possible from it.

The temple contained some curious dedications, the spindle and distaff of Tanaquil (Pliny, *HN* 8.194), a bronze statue of Gaia Caecilia, believed by some to be the same as Tanaquil, by others her daughter-in-law (Plutarch, *Quaest. Rom.* 30; Festus 276L), from the girdle of which filings were taken as an amulet against disease; a shield of wood covered with a sacrificial bull's hide on which were inscribed the terms of a treaty with Gabii dating from the time of Tarquinius Superbus (Dion. Hal. 4.58.4); and bronze *orbes* (rings, discs, or globes) made from the proceeds of the sale of the property of Vitruvius Vaccus (Livy 8.20.8).

The temple seems to have been in the charge of a *decuria sacerdotum bidentalium* that not only made dedications (*CIL* 6.568 = *ILS* 3473; cf. *CIL* 6.30994 = *ILS* 3472) but also inscribed its name on lead pipes leading from a water castle on the Quirinal (*BullCom* 15 [1887]: 8–9 [G. Gatti]).

Semo Sancus, Statua: a statue of Semo Sancus Dius Fidius on the Tiber island, known from the inscription on its base (*CIL* 6.567 = *ILS* 3474) found in 1574. The base is of the second century after Christ. Because of the similarity of names, Justin Martyr mistook it for a statue of Simon Magus, who he thought was worshiped as a divinity at Rome

(Justin Martyr, *Apol.* 1.26, 56). He was then followed in this error by a number of early Christian writers (Irenaeus, *Contra Haeres.* 1.16.3[1.23.1]; Tertullian, *Apol.* 13.9; Cyrill. Hierosol., *Catechesis* 6.14; Eusebius, *Hist. Eccles.* 2.13 and 14). There is no other evidence for the cult of Semo Sancus on the island, and it has been suggested that the statue stood in the precinct of Iuppiter Iurarius (q.v.), which is possible but hardly necessary. Both seem to have faced onto the little public square with an obelisk at its center that was the hub of planning for the island.

M. Besnier, *L'Ile tiberine dans l'antiquité* (Paris 1902), 286–89; Roscher 4.318–19 (G. Wissowa).

Senaculum: a place where the senators assembled on being summoned to a meeting until the magistrate convoking them considered there were enough to call the meeting to order. Consequently, there was a senaculum of some sort in the neighborhood of any building in which the senate met and a more or less formally established one near every building in which they met regularly. We hear of three, one near the Curia Hostilia, the most important, one near the Temple of Bellona, and one ad Portam Capenam, used only, so far as we know, during the year following the Battle of Cannae, 215 B.C.

The senaculum of the Curia Hostilia was on the shoulder of the Capitoline *supra Graecostasim ubi aedes Concordiae et Basilica Opimia* (Varro, *Ling.* 5.156; Val. Max. 2.2.6; Macrobius, *Sat.* 1.8.2; Festus 470L). These sources all make it clear that it was principally an area later occupied by Tiberius's Temple of Concordia. Valerius Maximus adds the interesting information that there was a tradition that in earlier days the senate had been accustomed to frequent the senaculum assiduously, so there would be no need of summoning them, and that they transacted their various businesses there and discussed matters of state with one another the rest of the time. Whenever a magistrate wished to call a meeting of the senate, a quorum was already on hand. The senaculum was never a building and never had architectural form or boundaries; it was simply a place where the senators gathered. However, the method of summoning the senate is implicit in Livy's account of Lucius Tarquinius's seizure of power (1.47.8), and it must reflect very old institutions. The magistrate summoning the meeting set his curule chair in front of the Curia and sent praecones throughout the city to announce the meeting. When he deemed that a sufficient number had assembled on the senaculum, he then moved his chair from the Curia door to the dais at the back of the Curia, and the senators filed in and took their places. The senaculum had to be in full view of the Curia door, but that is the only requirement. We may suppose that it was to some extent artificially leveled, but certainly nothing more.

Festus tells us on the authority of an otherwise unknown Nicostratus, probably a friend of Verrius Flaccus (*PW* 17.546, s.v. "Nikostratos 23" [W. Kroll]), that there was a second senaculum ad Portam Capenam and a third *citra aedem Bellonae* (see Bellona, Aedes). That ad Portam Capenam would have been necessary when the senate was constantly meeting there but must have fallen out of use as soon as it stopped; its existence would have been attested in the annals of Rome. That citra aedem Bellonae would have been in frequent use, because the senate met there to consider questions that had to be discussed outside the pomerium down to the time of the construction of the Curia Pompeii. It is odd that Verrius seems to have been unfamiliar with it. The Temple of Bellona was flanked closely on the west by the Temple of Apollo Medicus, but on the east and south, either of which might be considered *citra* with respect to the Porta Carmentalis, there was open space. A fourth senaculum proposed on the basis of Livy 41.27.7 derives from a misunderstanding of the passage. There were never more than three established senacula in Rome, and by Festus's time apparently there was none.

HJ 204, 553; *DialArch* 9–10 (1976–77): 346–77 (F. Coarelli).

Senaculum Mulierum: a hall of assembly on the Quirinal built by Elagabalus (S.H.A. *Heliogab.* 4.3) in a place where earlier there had been gatherings of women on certain festivals. At these gatherings special honors and rights seem to have been awarded in recognition of nobility and merit. The purpose of the hall seems to have degenerated into triviality, and it must have been soon destroyed, for Aurelian (S.H.A. *Aurel.* 49.6) is said to have wished to repeat the gesture and to assure women of recognition. There had long been *conventus matronarum* (assemblies of women), and recognition of exceptional womanly virtue (cf., e.g., Livy 27.37.9), but the institutionalizing of it was regarded as absurd.

The 1914 find of female statuary associated with reticulate-faced walls on the northwest side of Via XX Settembre, 39 m from its juncture with Via di Porta Salaria, is not likely to have any connection with the Senaculum Mulierum, although that was proposed at the time (*NSC* 1914, 141–46 [A. Pasqui]).

RendAccNap, n.s., 57 (1982): 91–107 (M. Elefante).

Septem Caesares: see **Caesares, Septem.**

Septem Domus: see **Domus: Septem Domus.**

Septem Tabernae: see **Tabernae Circum Forum.**

Septem Viae: probably the broad piazza around the exterior of the sphendone of the Circus Maximus, shown on fragments of the Marble Plan (*FUR* pl. 17; Rodriguez pl. 5). The streets debouching on this seem to have been three at the southwest extremity (the vicus along the southwest side of the circus, the Vicus Piscinae Publicae, and a vicus leading southwest toward the Aventinus Minor), three at the northeast extremity (one along the northeast side of the circus, the ancient street buried under Via di S. Gregorio, and one leading to Porta Capena), and one in the middle (the Via Nova leading southeast to the Thermae Antoninianae).

Septimianium: a name that does not occur in any ancient source (except perhaps S.H.A. *Sept. Sev.* 19.3, where it is a conjecture), but was probably given to the district on the right bank of the Tiber from the Aurelian Walls to the valley leading to the Vatican as a result of the numerous projects that Septimius Severus undertook here (see Porta Septimiana). The identification is inferred from its use in the Middle Ages in the designation of churches: S. Iacobi in Septimiano (HCh 268), S. Leonardo Sitignano (HCh 299), and S. Lucia de Septignano (HCh 305). See also Coriaria Septimiana.

Septimontium (1): according to Varro (*Ling.* 5.41), an ancient name for the place where Rome came to be, so called from the seven hills that were later enclosed by the Servian Walls. He then enumerates these, beginning with the Capitoline and Aventine. Varro takes the others from the city of the Quattuor Regiones (see Regiones Quattuor), evidently regarding each as a single hill. This, of course, leaves him with only six hills, as the Quirinal and Viminal are lumped together, and he does not elaborate on the difficulty. Festus (424L, 476L) preserves a fragment of the same tradition, evidently regarding Septimontium as the name of the site of Rome when Ligures and Siculi occupied it. Lydus (*Mens.* 4.155) supports this with two lists of the names of the hills, one with some antiquarian variations in which the seventh hill is the Viminal, and one in which it is the Velia. All this seems to be erudite rationalization that took its beginning from the name of the Septimontium festival.

Septimontium (2) (Fig. 75): a festival celebrated on 11 December by the Montani, whom Varro (*Ling.* 6.24) considers those living on the seven hills embraced by the Servian Walls. However, Festus (474–76L), following Antistius Labeo, has another tradition, that it belonged to these hills *(montibus)*:

Figure 75
Septimontium

Palatium, Velia, Fagutal, Subura, Cermalus, Oppius, Caelius, and Cispius. Some of these are not hills— namely, Fagutal, Subura, and Cermalus—and there are eight names in the list. Modern scholars have therefore been inclined to drop the Subura from the list, but without reason, because the places named are a tight group and coherent, and Festus must have been as well aware as we are that not all the places named were hills. Apparently, according to Antistius Labeo, at only two were there sacrifices made on this day, the Palatine, where the sacrifice had a special name, Palatuar, and the Velia. But in another passage Festus (458–59L) has sacrifices at all eight and provides the same list but calls them loci. The priest officiating at the Palatuar would have been the Flamen Palatualis (Varro, *Ling.* 7.45; Festus 284L) and the divinity would have been Pales (Roscher 3.1278 [G. Wissowa]), but it is not clear whether the sacrifices at other points were to place divinities (cf. Iuppiter Fagutalis, Iuppiter Viminus), or rather parts of a lustration of the flocks. Plutarch (*Quaest. Rom.* 69) adds the interesting information that on this day it was considered improper for anyone to make use of a horse-drawn vehicle. The Fasti Amiternini mark the day AG(ONALIA), which Festus (458L) confirms; this is the more interesting because the Quirinal, whose earlier name was Agonus (Festus 304L), is excluded. It seems to have been a very old festival of a time when the city was composed of the Palatine, Velia, Caelian, and Esquiline, and L. A. Holland is probably right that the name should be understood as deriving from *saepti montes,* rather than *septem montes.*

TAPA 84 (1953): 16–34 (L. A. Holland), 108 (1978): 147–54 (J. P. Poe).

Septizodium (Fig. 63): a building of Septimius Severus dedicated in A.D. 203 (*CIL* 6.1032 = 31229; Chron. 147; Hieron. *a. Abr.* 2216), which was at the southeast corner of the Palatine facing toward Porta Capena and the approach to Rome by the Via Appia. It was intended apparently simply as a magnificent façade, and it was almost the only monumental work for which Septimius was responsible in Rome (S.H.A. *Sept. Sev.* 19.5, 24.3–4, *Geta* 7.2). The story was told that Septimius had intended a splendid approach to the Palatine using the Septizodium as a façade and building behind it a royal reception hall *(regium atrium),* but that in his absence the praefectus urbi had prevented completion of the original program. This is a transparent fabrication to explain an otherwise enigmatic edifice. It was actually no more or less than what appears from the plans and drawings that survive, a *scaenae frons* intended as a frame for a program of statuary, probably portraits of the imperial family. There is no sign of water, and though the architectures of nymphaea and scaenae frontes were always closely related and crossed boundaries with each other, it seems unlikely that water was ever intended to be introduced. Rather, we should think of this as complete in itself. The program of statuary was never completed, or was edited by periodic removals that left gaps that could not be filled, but the figure of Septimius triumphantly dominated. The Septizodium survived and was recorded in the regionary catalogues of the fourth century, listed in Regio X, and enough remained in the sixteenth century to figure in drawings of Renaissance artists.

Its southwest end appears in part on a fragment of the Marble Plan (*FUR* pl. 17; Rodriguez pl. 5), two curved niches side by side with a line of columns in front of them interrupted by a statue base at the center of the inner niche and the line of columns then carried around a projecting wall, like an anta, at the southwest extremity. There is no building shown behind this façade, and if the building is to match the identifying inscription, what we see is less than one-third of the whole. There would have been at least seven niches of this size. The best Renaissance drawings, which show the ruins of the opposite end of the building, show an anta-like projection with columns running around three sides and a bit of straight wall, presumably just before the breaking back of a curved niche in symmetry with that at the opposite end. While a series of nothing but curved niches is very unlikely in Roman architecture, we might think

of pairs of curved niches at the ends flanking single rectangular niches with a large curved niche at the center. T. Dombart's reconstruction (*Das palatinische Septizonium zu Rom* [Mainz 1922]) suits neither the evidence nor the aesthetic of this sort of architecture.

The more correct form of the name is Septizodium, with reference to the seven planetary deities. This was evidently the form inscribed on the Marble Plan and is found in a nearly contemporary inscription (*CIL* 8.14372 = *ILS* 5076). The seven divisions must have been used in some way to honor these divinities. What was left in the sixteenth century was a building of three storeys, progressively diminishing in height like a scaenae frons, all three with Corinthian columns, some but not all of those in the lowest storey fluted, and possibly both fluted and unfluted in all three storeys. These carried rich entablatures, the frieze in the lowest storey embellished with a large inscription in a single line running the whole width of the façade, that of the second storey with a strongly convex frieze and dentils above, and that of the top storey with a second and deeper frieze above the usual one. There was evidently rich coffering in all three storeys, but the upper storeys can have been accessible only by ladders, and there is no sign of a building of any sort behind this façade.

The Septizodium had a long and lively history in the medieval period. Its name was corrupted into Septodia, Septem Viae, and Septem Solia. It was renamed Scuola di Vergilio in the belief that Septodia referred to the trivium and quadrivium of the liberal arts. Two churches are known to have been named from it, S. Lucia de Septem Soliis (HCh 305) and S. Leone de Septem Soliis (HCh 297–98). The Septizodium was also converted to use as a fortress of the Frangipani.

The east end was destroyed in 1588–1589 by order of Pope Sixtus V. The records of the demolition show that a variety of precious colored marbles had been used in the construction (LS 2.51–54).

C. Hülsen, *Das Septizonium des Severus* (*BWPr* 46, 1886); *BullCom* 18 (1888): 269–98 (E. Stevenson); *BdA* 3 (1909): 253–69 (A. Bartoli); Lugli 1946, 519–21; *MemLinc*, ser. 8.3 (1950–51): 178–99 (G. Spano); *MonPiot* 52.2 (1962): 77–93 (G. C. Picard); Nash 2.302–5; *BullCom* 91.2 (1986): 241–62 (P. Chini and D. Mancioli); *BullCom* 92 (1987–88): 346–53 (P. Chini and D. Mancioli).

Septizonium: mentioned once by Suetonius (*Tit.* 1) to locate the house where Titus was born. Because the Flavian family seems to have congregated high on the Quirinal, at Ad Malum Punicum (see Malum

Punicum), we should probably look for it there. H. Jordan (*FUR* [Berlin 1874]: 37) plausibly refers Ammianus Marcellinus 15.7.3 to this building, rather than the Septizodium of Septimius Severus, but that does not help with the topography. Presumably what is required is a building of seven storeys.

Sepulcretum: the modern name given to the small archaic necropolis that Boni discovered in 1902 just southeast of the stair leading up to the Temple of Antoninus and Faustina. It contained both cremation and inhumation burials, the latter principally of children, and pottery similar to that of the Early Iron Age cemeteries of the Alban Hills. In the cremation burials the ashes were deposited in an ossuary, commonly in the form of a hut, and placed in a well, sometimes within a large storage jar, with other grave furniture. In the inhumation burials the body was sometimes put in a coffin of stone or wood, and sometimes not. The pottery in the burials was of impasto decorated with sgraffito designs. The only jewelry is bronze fibulae, occasionally ornamented with beads of amber; there is no gold, and there is not much indication of any distinction in social class. The material runs from the ninth or eighth century to the end of the seventh. Sometimes the trench graves cut into well burials, but this seems accidental and not an indication of difference in epoch. The difference in rite is probably to be laid to Rome's being from the beginning an amalgam of Latins, Sabines, Faliscans, and Etruscans. The part called Sepulcretum is only a small part of the actual cemetery, which extended at least as far as the "Equus Domitiani" in the middle of the forum square, but it was entirely outside the pomerium of Romulus, according to Tacitus (*Ann.* 12.24), and at least for the most part, possibly all, on the far side of the brook, or brooks, that ran down from the Velia to join the Cloaca.

NSc 1902, 96–111, 1903, 123–70, 375–427, 1905, 145–93, 1906, 5–46, 253–94, 1911, 157–90 (G. Boni); *MonAnt* 15 (1905): 273–314 (G. Pinza); Lugli 1946, 221–24; Helbig⁴ 2.803–9 (T. Dohrn); Nash 2.306–7.

Sepulcrum, Sepulcretum, Bustum, Ustrinum, Monumentum, Mausoleum, Tumulus: *Sepulcrum* is the term used for any sort of burial place, without regard to the burial rite; it embraces everything from the simplest to the most elaborate and carries no suggestion of architecture. It is used in all periods very freely. *Sepulcretum* is a word used once by Catullus (59.2) for a cemetery, but apparently otherwise unknown. It has been revived in modern times to designate that part of the archaic cemetery

of the forum lying east of the stair of the Temple of Antoninus and Faustina and, as such, is convenient, but has no other justification.

Bustum designates an enclosure where the pyre was erected and the ashes of the dead buried after cremation. While the pyre might be elaborate, the bier being a couch richly embellished with ivory mounts and the corpse sumptuously dressed, the bustum was usually rather small, enclosed by a wall, and used repeatedly for members of the same family. After cremation the ashes were collected in an urn, which might be simple or elaborate, and buried within the bustum, a plate bearing the name of the deceased being let into the surrounding wall over, or near, the place of burial. A tube for libations might also be installed. A good example of a bustum is the grave of A. Hirtius found under the Palazzo della Cancelleria. This form of burial was that used regularly by families who cremated their dead throughout the republican period. More elaborate monuments were extremely rare before the time of Augustus. An *ustrinum* (or *ustrina*) is distinguished from a bustum by being the place where corpses were burned but buried elsewhere (Paulus *ex Fest.* 29L). Only a single ustrinum is known in Rome, that of the house of Augustus, which is described by Strabo (5.2.8 [236]).

Monumentum is the term used for any tomb of architectural form. Strictly speaking this should include construction above ground, but such construction need not be pretentious. During the Augustan period and the first half of the first century after Christ architects exercised their ingenuity in the design of tombs, producing extremely bizarre confections. While the altar tomb, the aedicula tomb, the rotunda, and the tumulus were always the most popular forms, every conceivable invention seems to have been tried, from the simple pyramid to the most baroque tower. Since the word *monumentum* embraces other buildings than tombs, it is generally eschewed in favor of a more particular term, but in common usage it always especially designated a tomb, as in the formula *hoc monumentum heredem non sequetur.*

Mausoleum was apparently coined to describe the tomb of Augustus (Strabo 5.3.8[236]), either by Augustus himself (Suetonius, *Aug.* 100) or, more likely, by some wit. It was the largest tomb in the neighborhood of Rome in its day, but hardly a rival of the greatest Etruscan tombs, let alone those of Asia Minor. Once coined the term was accepted and became standard. The use of the term for the tomb of Hadrian is modern. In antiquity it was called simply sepulcrum, or something equivalent, or else Antonineion (Cass. Dio 76 [77] 15.4, 77 [79] 9.1, 24.3). Its great difference from the Mausoleum Augusti in architectural form and almost everything but size did not encourage comparison between them. However, it has now become the term in general use.

Tumulus is specific for a tomb that is an artificial mound of earth, with or without architectural additions. This was the prevalent form of funerary monument among the Etruscans, although it usually stood over a tomb chamber that might be richly embellished and varied in its particulars from city to city. It is a very old form of tomb, used extensively in central Asia, South Russia, and Asia Minor. The Romans must have taken it from the Etruscans and used it only sparingly. The first to have such a tomb that we hear of is Sulla, but then it is used for Julia, the daughter of Julius Caesar, and Caesar himself was buried in the same tomb. Augustus's choice of the tumulus form with modifications must be allusive rather to Caesar than to the Etruscans, although there must also have been allusion to the tumuli of Asia Minor and the Trojan origin of the Gens Iulia. Thereafter he was much imitated, and tombs such as those of Munatius Plancus, Caecilia Metella, and Lucilius Paetus show how widespread this flattery became.

Sepulcrum Accae Larentiae: a place in the Velabrum near where it joined the Nova Via, but just outside the Porta Romana (or Romanula) of the Romulean pomerium (Varro, *Ling.* 6.23–24) where Acca Larentia, a legendary benefactress of the Roman people, was believed buried, and where the Flamen Quirinalis offered a solemn rite of *parentatio* on 23 December, the Larentalia (A. Gellius 7.7.7; Macrobius, *Sat.* 1.10.15). Cicero (*ad Brut.* 1.15.8) says the ceremony was conducted by the pontifices, who may also have been present. Presumably this was a very insignificant monument, according to Cicero (*ad Brut.* 1.15.8) an altar, and certainly not a *bustum*, for there was doubt in some people's minds that it actually was a tomb.

Degrassi 543–44; *BullCom* 88 (1982–83): 61–64 (B. Frischer); Coarelli 1983, 261–82 (who believes the tomb of Acca Larentia was near the north corner of the Palatine).

Sep. P. Aelii Guttae Calpurniani: an imposing monument to a very famous charioteer of the time of Hadrian and Antoninus Pius built during his own lifetime. The inscriptions (on three sides?) recounting his victories were copied in the Einsiedeln sylloge (*CIL* 6.10047 = *ILS* 5288) and recorded as coming from a tomb on the Via Flaminia. During the destruction of the rectangular bastions flanking the

Porta Flaminia in 1876–1877 numerous elements of tombs that had gone into their construction were recovered. Those from the eastern bastion included several large fragments of reliefs at two-thirds life size showing chariot races and the head of a horse in the round of similar style. These have been assigned to this tomb because of their subject and provenience. It is therefore believed that the tomb must have consisted of at least two storeys, a plain base, a storey covered with inscriptions, and a storey covered with reliefs, and the whole surmounted by a quadriga driven by Aelius Gutta Calpurnianus. But it is odd that the builders of the bastion of Porta Flaminia (q.v.), of the time of Honorius, should have taken the upper storeys of the tomb for building material and left the storey covered with inscribed slabs in situ. One would think these would have been much more useful to them. The reliefs are now on display in the garden of the Museo Nuovo Capitolino (Inv. nos. 2243–44; Helbig⁴ 2.1796).

BullCom 5 (1877): 186 (C. Visconti and V. Vespignani), 200–201 (V. Vespignani), 9 (1881): 176–79 (V. Vespignani), 39 (1911): 187–92 (G. Gatti); Nash 2.308.

Sep. Agrippae: the tomb of Agrippa that he is reported to have built for himself in the Campus Martius (Cass. Dio 54.28.5). His ashes were, in fact, deposited in the Mausoleum Augusti. We know nothing of the form, location, or further history of this tomb, and the imperial gesture of giving Agrippa a place in the mausoleum must seem an odd one, if he had already arranged his own tomb.

Sep. Antinoi: see **Obeliscus Antinoi.**

Sep. Arruntiorum: a complex of three columbaria in which were deposited the ashes of the dependents and descendants of L. Arruntius, cos. A.D. 6, found in the eighteenth century southwest of Via Giolitti between the Tempio di Minerva Medica and Porta Maggiore on the old Via Praenestina, a little more than 100 m inside the gate (*CIL* 6.5931–60). The vaults were decorated with elaborate stuccowork and painting, including figurative scenes said to be similar to the decoration of the "Underground Basilica of Porta Maggiore" (see Basilica Subterranea). By 1838 the complex was said to be so ruined as to be hardly recognizable.

MAAR 4 (1924): 36–37 (E. Wadsworth); Nash 2.309–10.

Sep. L. Aufidii Aprilis: a tomb found in 1965 east of Via Flaminia in the block opposite Via Filangieri and Via V. Gravina, where other tombs were found in 1932. It consisted of a handsome travertine base surmounted by an elaborately carved funerary altar. In the area was also buried one of his freedmen, described as *Corinthiarius de Theatro Balbi*.

NSc 1975, 199–232 (E. Lissi Caronna).

Sep. Aureliorum: the multichambered burial place of a Christian community of the first half of the third century, discovered in 1919 at the corner of Viale Manzoni and Via Luigi Luzzati, southwest of ancient Via Labicana. It takes its name from a family, four members of which are commemorated in the mosaic pavement of one chamber, while others are named on tombstones. One descended into the tomb by a stair to an upper chamber, now largely destroyed, from which a stair led down and branched to left and right. Here the wall paintings are well preserved. The slightly larger chamber to the northeast is the tomb of the Aurelii proper, with largely conventional decorations but also figures of the apostles. A later addition is a monumental doorway leading to a stair down to a catacomb. To the southwest a small vestibule precedes a burial chamber with arcosolia in three walls and paintings of more typically Christian character. Again a stair leads down from this to a catacomb. But neither catacomb is extensive, and after the construction of the Aurelian Walls (A.D. 270–282) the whole complex must have been abandoned, because it lay within the circuit of the walls.

NSc 1920, 123–41, 1921, 230–34 (G. Bendinelli); *MonAnt* 28 (1922): 289–520 (G. Bendinelli); *MemPontAcc.* ser. 3.1.2 (1924): 1–43 (G. Wilpert); Nash 2.311–18.

Sep. Bibuli: the tomb of C. Publicius Bibulus, plebeian aedile, built by decree of the senate at the base of the Capitoline Hill (*CIL* 1².834 = 6.1319 = *ILS* 862; *ILLRP* 357). The architecture shows an aedicula of travertine on a high plain base of tufa. There are Tuscanic pilasters and a frieze of garlands looped between bucrania, the loops filled with paterae. The tomb cannot be older than the period of Sulla, and the letter forms confirm this. But no Publicius Bibulus who attained the aedileship is known in the first century B.C. This is therefore seen as the rebuilding of the tomb of a famous man, possibly Broughton's aedile of 195 B.C. (cf. *PW* 23.1898–99: Publicius Bibulus 15 [F. Münzer]). It stands to the east of the Victor Emanuel Monument, outside the Porta Fontinalis to the right of Via Lata (Via Flaminia) as one left the city. Preserved are the principal façade, the southwest side, and the beginning of the southeast side. The base is 4.76 m high and 6.50 m wide. The architecture of the aedicula set above this is unusual,

a central doorway flanked by closed walls with small tablets for non-existent inscriptions. It must have been finished with a pediment, but of this no element survives. The inscription is cut on the base, only roughly centered, in large well-formed letters without serifs. The fact that the tomb was given at public expense, *honoris virtutisque caussa,* may indicate that C. Publicius Bibulus died in office.

NSc 1907, 410–14 (G. Boni); Delbrück, *Hellenistische Bauten,* 2.37–41; Nash 2.319–20; *BullCom* 88 (1982–83): 66–68 (B. Frischer).

Sep. Caecilii Statii: see **Sep. Statii Caecilii.**

Sep. Caesaris: see **Tumulus Iuliae.**

Sep. C. et L. Caesarum: a cenotaph or memorial to Gaius and Lucius Caesar in which the body of Julia Domna was deposited in 217 before entombment in the Mausoleum Hadriani (Cass. Dio 78[79].24.3). This is our only notice of this monument, and it has been generally assumed that the ashes of Augustus's grandsons would have been placed in the Mausoleum Augusti, but we have no reason to doubt Dio's explicit statement. Presumably it would have been somewhere in the Campus Martius with the other tombs of the family.

Sep. Caesoniorum: see **Sep. Quinctiorum et Aliorum.**

Sep. Calpurniorum: the tomb of the Calpurnii Pisones discovered in 1885 during the cutting of a new street on the east side of Via Salaria about 100 m outside Porta Salaria in Villa Bonaparte. It was a simple rectangle, probably a bustum, containing seven tombstones, all more or less handsomely carved (*CIL* 6.31721–27; *ILS* 240, 924, 954, 955), of the Calpurnii Pisones and their wives. These were members of the family of the first century after Christ, two of them consuls.

BullCom 13 (1885): 101–3 (R. Lanciani); *BdI* 1885, 9–13 (G. Henzen), 22–30 (E. Stevenson).

Sep. C. Cestii: the tomb of a man who may have been the praetor mentioned by Cicero (*Phil.* 3.26) but is otherwise unknown. He died before Agrippa, whom he made one of his heirs and who died in 12 B.C. (*CIL* 6.1375 = *ILS* 917a). The tomb is a pyramid set in the angle between Via Ostiensis and the street skirting the base of the Aventine, in what was to become the line of the Aurelian Walls close to Porta Ostiensis, so the wall abuts it on either side. It is a mass of brick-faced concrete on a foundation of travertine and is covered with slabs of white marble;

it is 27 m high, and about 21 m square at the base. The burial chamber in the interior is small, 5.95 m long, 4.10 m wide, and 4.80 m high, with painted decoration. The inscriptions stand about halfway up on the east and west sides, one on each side recording the name and titles of Cestius, and one below on the east side only recording the erection of the tomb in accordance with his will (*CIL* 6.1374 = *ILS* 917). On the west side in 1660 were found two large statue bases, one with a bronze foot still in place, with inscriptions recording their erection by the heirs of Cestius (*CIL* 1375 = *ILS* 917a). In the Middle Ages the monument was called Meta or Sepulcrum Remi; the origins of the name seem completely obscure. It was probably in response to this that the pyramid near the Mausoleum Hadriani got the name Meta Romuli (q.v.) rather than vice versa.

The decoration of the burial chamber in stucco and painting was already all but invisible a hundred years ago (Middleton 2.433). F. Wirth (*RömMitt* 42 [1927]: 66) classes it as Third Style, but without elaborating, and the date is questionable. P. Marconi (*La pittura dei romani* [Rome 1929], 111 and pl. 152) dates the decoration to the beginning of the third century. If G. B. Piranesi's (*Antichità romane* 3 pl. 44) and P. S. Bartoli's (T. Kraus, *Das römische Weltreich* [Propyläen Kunstgeschichte 2, Berlin 1967], 207 fig. 44) drawings are trustworthy, it was certainly not Third Style, but later. A date earlier than the second century seems quite impossible, so we must presume the tomb was redecorated and reused later.

Palladio 11 (1961): 165–70 (F. Sanguinetti); Nash 2.321–23; W. Ehrhardt, *Stilgeschichtliche Untersuchungen an römischen Wandmalerei* (Mainz 1987), 53–54 and pl. 25.

Sep. Cinciorum: According to Festus (318L), people commonly called a place where water ran off an epistyle the Porta Romana (or Romanula), but earlier people had called this the Statuae Cinciae, because in this place was the tomb of the Gens Cincia. Most topographers have plausibly taken this to mean that the Sepulcrum Cinciorum was not far from the Porta Romana and that the tomb was a ruin, but preserved a façade with an arch or door framed with columns and an epistyle, so it, having architectural form, had the name Porta Romana transferred to it from the true Porta Romana, which was merely a platform. That there were other tombs in this area follows from our knowledge of the Sepulcrum Accae Larentiae (q.v.). This all hangs together and places the Sepulcrum Cinciorum in the Velabrum. The statues had evidently disappeared by

the time of the change of name from Statuae Cinciae to Porta Romana and were merely a memory; nothing at all can be said about them. The question remains whether the epistyle from which water ran had anything to do with the medieval Arcus Stillans of Forum Boarium (*ecclesia S. Laurentii quae est iuxta arcum stillantem in regione Scholae Graecae*, HCh 287). Because the two must have been very close together, this seems highly likely, but whether the monument itself survived so late, or whether it was only a place-name, as seems more likely, there is no way of deciding. The source of the water that ran from the epistyle may have been one of the aqueducts in the area, because ancient conduits tended to leak and were commonly carried on arches over the streets, but the description in Festus makes it sound more like an architectural fountain. Perhaps the tomb façade had been rebuilt as a fountain.

Sep. Claudiorum: a tomb at the base of the Capitoline Hill on the west side of Via Lata (Via Flaminia) a little north of the Sepulcrum Bibuli (q.v.). For no real reason it was identified in the popular mind with Suetonius's *sepultura gentis Claudiae sub Capitolio* (*Tib.* 1.1). However, this was a large rectangular edifice of more than one storey built of blocks of tufa and at one time revetted with marble, while it is clear from what Suetonius says that the tomb of the Claudii was simply a bustum. It was destroyed to permit construction of the Victor Emanuel Monument.

Capitolium 2 (1926–27): 271–73 (L. Du Jardin).

Sep. Ti. Claudii Vitalis: a columbarium of the later first century after Christ discovered in 1866 in Villa Wolkonsky, southeast of an ancient road running parallel to the Neronian arches of the Aqua Claudia on the Caelian. It consisted of three storeys, the interior walls of the two lower ones covered with loculi of various sizes, for the most part arched but occasionally flat-headed, with an aedicula in the center of each wall. One entered the middle storey, descending then to an underground crypt or climbing to an upper storey that was probably of aedicular form. The crypt was barrel-vaulted, the upper storeys cross-vaulted. The whole is built of brick-faced concrete, the brick used decoratively to make friezes and cornices. There is no sign of stuccoing, and the only marble is the plate of the inscription recording that it was built for Ti. Claudius Vitalis by another man of the same name and for his family, all freedmen, two of them architects (*CIL* 6.9151; cf. *CIL* 6.9152).

MemPontAcc, ser. 3.7 (1944): 389–91 (A.M. Colini); *RendPontAcc* 36 (1963–64): 93–105 (S. Panciera); Nash 2.324–26.

Sep. C. Considii Galli: the tomb of a praetor peregrinus of the early empire (*CIL* 6.31705) found in 1883 just north of the Via Tiburtina Vetus at the intersection of the modern streets Via Mamiani and Via Principe Amedeo, northeast of Piazza Vittorio Emanuele. It was a small rectangular structure, 5.30 m x 4.10 m, with a façade revetted with marble and side walls of travertine. The inscription was on the frieze.

NSc 1883, 420 (R. Lanciani); *BullCom* 11 (1883): 223 (R. Lanciani).

Sep. Corneliae: known only from a fragmentary inscription found in 1871 under the north tower of Porta Salaria (*CIL* 6.1296) commemorating the daughter of a Scipio and wife of a Vatienus. This is associated with remains of a square travertine base supporting a circular drum faced with marble found at the same time. In 1950 the remains were reassembled to the west of their original position and now stand between Porta Salaria and Porta Pinciana.

Nash 2.327–28.

Sep. Corneliorum Scipionum: see **Sep. Scipionum.**

Sep. Domitiorum: known only from Suetonius's (*Nero* 50) account of the burial of Nero in the family tomb. It was on the summit of the Pincian in view of the Campus Martius. Interment was in a porphyry sarcophagus (*solium*) with an altar of Luna marble over it and a balustrade of Thasian stone around this. This presumes that inhumation was traditional in his family, and one remembers that Poppaea was embalmed and deposited in the Tumulus Iuliae (Tacitus, *Ann.* 16.6). One cannot say what the architectural form of the tomb may have been. In the Middle Ages it came to be believed that the tomb was in the vicinity of Piazza del Popolo, and to exorcise the malevolent ghost of Nero a small chapel was built there by Pope Paschal II in 1099, which in time became S. Maria del Popolo. But it is more likely that the tomb stood considerably farther south on the hill, perhaps in the vicinity of the Sepulcrum Octaviae.

Colloqui del Sodalizio tra Studosi dell'Arte, ser. 2.5 (1975–76): 35–40 (A. M. Colini).

Sep. Eurysacis: the tomb of M. Vergilius Eurysaces, a contract baker, in the fork of the Via Praenestina and Via Labicana just beyond the crossing of the Aqua Claudia (Porta Maggiore), given monumental form by Claudius and later built into the Porta Praenestina (q.v.) of Aurelian. The tomb was engulfed in the base of a central semicircular tower between the two roads, its front demolished and the rest englobed in concrete. However, the tomb was in some way accessible from the interior, for the inscriptions were known and in part read in the sixteenth century. The towers of the gate were dismantled in 1838 and the tomb was exposed, but its east side is almost completely gone.

The tomb was a trapezium in plan, measuring 8.75, 6.85, 5.80, and 4.05 m on its sides, built of concrete with a facing of travertine. The facing, framed by pilasters at the corners, is curious, in the form of vertical cylinders that support a block in which there are three zones of framed orifices of roughly the same diameters as the cylinders. These have sometimes been seen as grain measures crowned by oven mouths, in allusion to the source of Eurysaces's wealth. But there is really no good reason for this, and such an interpretation cannot be defended. It is more likely a pure experiment in geometrical forms. The inscription, repeated on all sides, is on a plain fascia separating the cylinders from the block above (*CIL* 1².1203–5 = 6.1958 = *ILS* 7460a-c = *ILLRP* 805). The inscription of Atistia, believed to be his wife, carved on a marble tablet, was also found (*CIL* 1².1206 = 6.1958 = *ILLRP* 805A). The alphabet is a fine late republican form approaching Augustan. Around the crown of the monument under a modillion cornice runs a continuous frieze in which at small scale various operations connected with the manufacture of bread are shown, from milling to baking, weighing, and delivery. In the center of the east front was a group of Eurysaces and Atistia in very high relief, almost freestanding, he wearing the toga *ad cohibendum bracchium*, she swathed in veils, but with her head uncovered. In the inscription commemorating her the tomb, or her urn, is called a *panarium* (bread basket). Relief and inscription were found used as fill in the tower. The roof of the tomb, of which no element survives, has been reconstructed as stepped, tiled, or a pyramid. Because the proportions of a pyramid of this ground plan would be apt to appear visually unpleasing, we may incline to a low tiled roof.

Nash 2.329–32; P. Ciancio Rossetto, *Il sepolcro del fornaio Marco Virgilio Eurisace* (Rome 1973).

Sep. Q. Fabii: a tomb in the Esquiline cemetery under the church of S. Eusebio, known from a fragment of the painted decoration found in 1885 in which parts of four relatively narrow bands, one above another, show historical scenes of battle and the siege and surrender of cities. Inscriptions name M. Fannius and Q. Fabius, and the scenes are generally believed to illustrate events of the Second Samnite War, but a consensus as to the events and individuals portrayed has not been reached. The painting is now in the Palazzo dei Conservatori (Helbig[4] 2.1600).

Sep. Familiae Marcellae et Aliorum: In the wedge between Via Latina and Via Appia, numerous columbaria of the early imperial period have come to light, some of them with hundreds of loculi for ash urns. Today only three are well preserved, known collectively as the Columbari di Vigna Cedini. They all served as burial places for the freedmen of the imperial house and its ramifications. The second to be excavated, in 1847, produced good numbers of inscriptions showing that it belonged especially to the households of the two Marcellas, nieces of Augustus, one of whom was the second wife of Agrippa. The first columbarium was excavated in 1840, the third in 1852. The architectural forms are simple, but many of the ash urns are handsome, and numerous portrait busts were added. For the inscriptions see *CIL* 6.4881–5178 (Columbarium I), 4414–4880 (Columbarium II), and 5179–5538 (Columbarium III).

Lugli 1930, 446–57; Nash 2.332–39.

Sep. Faustuli: see **Sep. Romuli** (1) and **Niger Lapis.**

Sep. Gaii et Lucii: see **Sep. C. et L. Caesarum.**

Sep. Galbae: the tomb of Ser. Sulpicius Galba, either the consul of 144 B.C. or, more probably, the consul of 108 B.C., in the district belonging to the family between the southwest flank of the Aventine and the Tiber, where the Horrea Galbae (q.v.) are located. The tomb was a small square structure of tufa faced with blocks of peperino and with a slab of travertine carrying the inscription (*CIL* 1².695 = 6.31617 = *ILS* 863 = *ILLRP* 339) on the façade between six fasces to either side. It was found in 1885. Presumably the Sulpicii Galbae had large land holdings here from an early date, and, with the development of the Emporium (q.v.) and the warehouses that grew up around it, they grew rich on the exploitation of their land. The survival of this tomb in such circumstances is especially interesting and shows that the family still kept a measure of control here.

Lugli 1938, 605–6; Nash 2.370; *BullCom* 88 (1982–83): 66 (B. Frischer).

Sep. Galloniorum: a tomb on the Via Flaminia of which a fragmentary inscription was found during the dismantling of the bastions outside Porta Flaminia in 1876–1877 (*CIL* 6.31714). This names the occupants as C. Gallonius and C. Gallonius Q. Marcius Turbo (*BullCom* 5 [1877]: 251–52 [C. Visconti and V. Vespignani], 8 [1880]: 176–78 and pl. 12–13 [C. Visconti and V. Vespignani]; cf. *PIR*² G-51). There must be a close relationship between these men and Q. Marcius Turbo, praefectus praetorio under Hadrian (S.H.A. *Hadr.* 9.4). A large circular tomb about 100 m north of Porta Flaminia on the west side of the road (marked on Bufalini's map of Rome of 1551) has been conjectured to have been the tomb in question.

Sep. Getae: see **Sep. Severi.**

Sep. Q. Haterii: a tomb on Via Nomentana covered by the south tower that Honorius built to flank Porta Nomentana, brought to light in 1826–1827. It consisted of a rectangular concrete core for a large funerary altar, of which fragments of the travertine facing and marble decoration were recovered. On the front was the somewhat incomplete inscription (*CIL* 6.1426), presumably of the celebrated orator who died in A.D. 26 (Tacitus, *Ann.* 4.61). This is not to be confused with the more famous tomb of the Haterii found in 1848 5 kilometers from Porta Maggiore on the south side of Via Labicana from which important reliefs come.

Nash 2.340; *CAR* 3-D, 74 pp. 89–90.

Sep. A. Hirtii: the bustum of the consul of 43 B.C., victim of the Battle of Modena, in the Campus Martius. It was found in 1938 under the northwest corner of Palazzo della Cancelleria, a simple enclosure of brick-faced concrete with a plain travertine coping and with travertine cippi, some of them inscribed with his name, at the corners (*ILLRP* 419). This is the more impressive because he was awarded a state funeral by vote of the senate (Livy, *Epit.* 119; Vell. Pat. 2.62.4).

Nash 2.341–43.

Sep. Horatiae: the tomb of Horatia, whom her brother, the hero of the combat of the Horatii and Curiatii, slew outside Porta Capena, known from Livy's statement (1.26.14) that her tomb was constructed in opus quadratum where she fell. Presumably it was a landmark in Livy's day.

Sep. Horatii: the tomb of the poet *in extremis Esquiliis,* next to the tumulus of Maecenas (Suetonius, *De Poet., Hor.* 20). Because Maecenas had a very extensive estate on the Esquiline, we should expect to find the tomb on the edge of this, but we cannot bound the Horti Maecenatiani (q.v.).

Sep. Iuliorum: see **Tumulus Iuliae.**

Sep. Lucilii Paeti: the tomb of M. Lucilius Paetus, tribunus militum, praefectus fabrum, praefectus equitum, in the time of Augustus, built for himself and his sister, Lucilia Polla, about the end of the first century B.C. (*CIL* 6.32932). It was found in 1885 on the west side of Via Salaria about 300 m from Porta Salaria, a round tomb with a ring wall of ashlar masonry of travertine surmounted by an earth mound. It was 34.90 m in diameter, with an estimated height of 16 m. At the back a corridor led to a small cross-vaulted burial chamber. The imitation of the Mausoleum Augusti is clear and intended to be complimentary. By the time of Trajan the base was concealed by earth washing down from the tumulus, but in the fourth century the tomb was reopened, and the walls of the entrance corridor were carved out in loculi, while a catacomb was dug into the tufa below the burial chamber beginning from the original entrance.

L'urbe 5, no. 11 (1940): 20–28 (C. Pietrangeli); *CAR* 2-C, 14 pp. 25–26; Nash 2.344–45.

Sep. Mariae: the circular mausoleum of Maria, the daughter of Stilicho and wife of Honorius, and also possibly of Honorius himself, also the tomb of Theodosius II and Valentinian III, built on the east end of the spina of the Circus Gaii et Neronis (q.v.) just south of the south transept of the Constantinian basilica of S. Pietro, together with a second circular mausoleum of similar size dedicated by Pope Symmachus to Saint Andrew (HCh 190). It was later known as S. Maria della Febbre and demolished only by Pope Pius VI for the construction of the present basilica of S. Pietro about 1520. The interior contained eight niches, one of which served as the entrance. In the eighth century the body of Saint Petronilla was deposited here, and it became known as the chapel of the Frankish kings. The sarcophagus containing the remains of Maria, together with much wealth, was found in 1544.

C. T. Rivoira, *Lombardic Architecture* (London 1910), 1.82–84; D. M. Cerrati, *De basilica Vaticana antiquissima et nova structura* (Studi e testi 26, Rome 1914), 132–45; HCh 190, 422–23; *CAR* 1-G, 45 p. 59.

Sep. Neronis: see **Sep. Domitiorum.**

Sep. L. Nonii Asprenatis: the tomb of either the consul of A.D. 6 or, more likely, his son, cos. A.D. 29 (*PIR*² N-118, 119). Some fragments of the frieze with an inscription (*CIL* 6.31689 = *ILS* 941) were found when the east bastion on the outer side of Porta Flaminia was demolished in 1876–1877. On the basis of the inscription and other fragments of decoration, the monument is believed to have been rectangular.

BullCom 5 (1877): 247 and pl. 20–21 (R. Lanciani).

Sep. Numae: the tomb of Numa Pompilius on the right bank of the Tiber sub Ianiculo (Festus 178–79L; Dion. Hal. 2.76.6; Pliny, *NH* 13.84–87; Solinus 1.21). This is generally taken to mean at the foot of the Janiculan hill, but, because farm workers discovered the tomb in the course of more or less customary activity, it is probably best to think of it as well up the slope, where erosion might have washed away the overburden. The Ianiculum proper was probably only a gatehouse on the site of the later Porta Aurelia, so the tomb might even have been near the crest of the slope. It was *in agro L. Petilii* (Livy 40.29.2) and near the Ara Fontis (Cicero, *Leg.* 2.56). There is an abundant spring on the slope of the Janiculan hill under Piazza S. Pietro in Montorio along the line of Via Aurelia, which might well have had an Ara Fontis connected with it, and we should expect the burial to have been along one of the principal roads. But there is no proof. In 181 B.C. the discovery of two stone chests, one supposed to contain the body of Numa but actually found empty, the other containing his writings on pontifical law and philosophy, caused a great alarm (Livy 40.29.2–14; Val. Max. 1.1.12; Plutarch, *Numa* 22.2).

Sep. Octaviae: the tomb of a daughter of Marcus and wife (?) of Appius found in 1616 at the corner of Via Sistina and Via di Porta Pinciana on the line of the ancient road that issued from Porta Pinciana and may have issued from the Servian Walls by Porta Salutaris. The tomb was of marble, and the inscription was on the frieze (*CIL* 6.23330). Because it was here in a zone that was built up with horti before the time of Augustus, one would like to date it as early as possible, but a marble tomb seems impossible before the middle of the first century B.C.

Sep. Orestis: Orestes is supposed to have died at Aricia and his bones to have been brought to Rome and buried in front of the Temple of Saturn in the Forum Romanum (Servius *ad Aen.* 2.116; Hyginus, *Fab.* 261; Scriptores Rerum Mythicarum Latini Tres [Mythogr. Vat.], ed. Bode, 2.202). The bones of Orestes were regarded as one of the guarantees of the greatness of Rome, so the grave itself must have been marked in some way, if only to prevent accidental sacrilege, but no one tells us how it was marked.

Sep. Pallantis: the tomb of Claudius's celebrated freedman on the Via Tiburtina *intra primum lapidem* (Pliny, *Epist.* 7.29.1–2, 8.6.1–2). It is worth noting that the cippus of one of Pallas's freedmen comes from the neighborhood of Porta Tiburtina (*CIL* 6.11965).

Sep. Pansae: the tomb of C. Pansa, cos. 43 B.C., who died of the wound that he received in the Battle of Modena and was awarded a public funeral and burial in the Campus Martius by decree of the senate (Livy, *Epit.* 119; Vell. Pat. 2.62.4). In 1899 a travertine tablet bearing Pansa's name was found at the corner of Corso Vittorio Emanuele and Vicolo Savelli, reused as building material (*CIL* 6.37077 = *ILS* 8890 = *ILLRP* 421). This unquestionably came from his funeral monument, and the discovery of the bustum of Hirtius (see Sep. Hirtii) under the northwest corner of Palazzo della Cancelleria makes it probable that if the tombs were not twins and side by side, at least they were similar and not far from each other. It is interesting that a little later a man who seems to have been the grandson of Pansa built a monumental tomb of circular form in the Campus Martius for his wife and brother-in-law (*CIL* 6.3542).

Sep. Passienorum: a tomb excavated in 1702–1705 in Vigna Moroni on the west side of Via Appia, not far inside Porta Appia, but greater precision is not possible. It was a large columbarium of two or three chambers of very irregular architectural form, the walls covered with loculi. Most of the burials were simple, with terracotta ossuaries, some sixty being found, but there was a wealth of inscriptions, estimated at one hundred, of which only twenty-five are known and recorded. These are of freedmen of the Passienus family and their families of the first two centuries after Christ (*CIL* 6.7257–80, 33248–49). The tomb is briefly described in *BullCom* 23 (1895): 170, 184–88 (R. Lanciani).

CIL 6 p. 3430; *PBSR* 7 (1914): 7–9 nos. 1–21 (T. Ashby).

Sep. Pomponii Hylae: a columbarium on Via Latina just inside Porta Latina, excavated in 1831, so named from a panel of glass mosaic prominently placed facing the visitor at the entrance with the funerary inscription of Pomponius Hylas and his wife, Pomponia Vitalis (*CIL* 6.5552), but the twenty-nine inscriptions found here show the greatest variety of names and show no family connection with Pomponius Hylas whatsoever. The tomb, of brick-faced concrete, was built in the time of Tiberius, and the latest inscription is of a freedman of Antoninus Pius.

PBSR 5 (1910): 463–71 and pls. 37–47 (F. G. Newton); Nash 2.346–48.

Sep. Publicii Bibuli: see **Sep. Bibuli.**

Sep. Quinctiorum et Aliorum: In the widening of Via S. Croce in Gerusalemme, 1916–1918, a row of four chamber tombs was discovered at its intersection with Via Statilia, facing toward the latter and originally in a band between the Neronian arches of the Aqua Claudia and a street running from the Arcus Dolabellae et Silani (q.v.) to Porta Maggiore. P. Quinctius built the tomb at the northeast end for himself, his wife, and his concubine Quinctia Agatea (*CIL* 1².2527a = *ILLRP* 795). The second was a double tomb of freedmen of the Gentes Clodia, Marcia, Annia, and Annaea (*CIL* 1².2527b = *ILLRP* 952). On the façade of this tomb are portrait busts carved in high relief. The third was not identified. The fourth was built for A. Caesonius. The tombs all date to the end of the republican period.

MemPontAcc., ser. 3.7 (1944): 393–96 (A. M. Colini); Nash 2.349–51.

Sep. Romuli (1): the traditional tomb of Romulus in the Comitium, commonly known as the Niger Lapis (Festus 184L), and located variously by writers after the destruction of the Comitium as an architectural entity *in rostris* or *post rostra* (schol. *ad Hor. Epod.* 16.13–14, where it is also stated that there had once been two lions there to mark the tomb). Because another tradition held that Romulus was translated bodily to heaven, Dionysius (1.l87.2) believed that this was actually the tomb of Faustulus, who threw himself between the factions of the quarreling brothers and was buried where he fell. He speaks of a single lion. In 3.1.2–3 he tells about the grandfather of Tullus Hostilius and says that he was buried in the principal part of the forum, his grave marked by a stele, but it is not entirely clear whether this was yet another explanation of the same monument, as it seems to be.

In 1899 was discovered some distance in front of the Curia Iulia and oriented with it a pavement of slabs of black Taenarian marble about 4 m long by 3 m wide, one side (southwest) irregularly bowed, surrounded by a pluteus of white marble about 1 m high set in a travertine base. Exploration under the pavement brought to light three monuments, which do not correspond to the area covered by the pavement, nor yet to its orientation, one of them a U-shaped base of Grotta Oscura tufa, the two broad wings symmetrical, with a deep cyma molding above a plain plinth, joined across the back by a narrower element. This has been interpreted as remains of the base for the pair of lions, sometimes with a shallow heroon added across the back. Others have seen it as the remains of an old altar misunderstood as the base for a pair of lions. In any case, it is seen as the tomb of Romulus proper.

See also Niger Lapis.

Sep Romuli (2): see **Meta Romuli.**

Sep. Rusticeliorum: a tomb discovered in 1686–1687 under the south side of Monte Testaccio completely covered by the dump and some 17 meters into its interior, a block of masonry, 10 meters on a side, with a profiled base and crown of peperino and the die of tufa in drafted ashlar blocks. The inscription was on a tablet of travertine (*CIL* 6.11534), and one of the travertine cippi marking the plot was also recovered (*CIL* 6.11535). The surviving part, as described and drawn, looks like the base for a more elaborate upper storey, possibly a tholus rather than anything else.

Sep. Scipionis: the name sometimes given in the early Renaissance to the pyramidal tomb between the Mausoleum Hadriani and the Vatican (cf., e.g., the map of Bufalini of 1551 = Frutaz 2: pl. 201), more commonly known as the Meta Romuli (q.v.). The ascription to Scipio is a learned one based on a scholion of Acron on Horace (*Epod.* 9.25) to the effect that in response to an oracle the ashes of Scipio Africanus the Elder were removed *de pyramide in Vaticano constituta* and reburied in a tomb at Portus. There seems to be no historical ground for this tradition.

Sep. Scipionum (Figs. 76, 77): the somewhat catacomb-like family tomb of the Cornelii Scipiones on Via Appia about a kilometer outside Porta Capena and 400 m beyond the point where Via Latina branched to the east, at the intersection of a crossroad that connected the two main roads, the main façade facing on the crossroad. It was one of the most famous tombs in Rome, in part because of the importance of the family, in part because of its situation and unusual form (cf. Cicero, *Tusc.* 1.13). Ennius was believed to be buried here and a marble statue of him erected by Scipio Africanus (Cicero, *Arch.* 22; Pliny, *HN* 7.114; Suetonius, *De Poet., Ennius* 8). The tombs and statues of P. Scipio Africanus the Elder and his brother Lucius were also shown here, although there were also others at Liternum (Livy 38.56.2–4).

As the Scipios regularly buried their dead in sar-

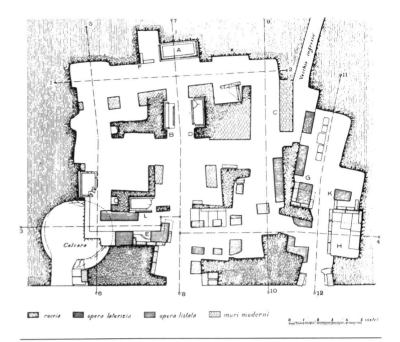

Figure 76
Sepulcrum Scipionum, Plan, Actual State

cophagi, rather than cremating them (Cicero, *Leg.* 2.57; Pliny, *HN* 7.187), the tomb became filled with sarcophagi arranged along the walls and in loculi cut in the rock. The tomb was rediscovered and opened in the early seventeenth century, and one sarcophagus, that of L. Scipio, cos. 259 B.C., was broken and its inscribed lid was removed. Final excavation of the tomb came in 1780 (F. Piranesi and E. Q. Visconti, *Monumenti degli Scipioni* [Rome 1785] = Visconti, *Opere varie* [Milan 1827], 1.1–70). Many of the sarcophagi were then damaged, but apparently much of the damage had already occurred in late antiquity, perhaps in the fourth century. One sarcophagus, that of L. Scipio Barbatus, cos. 298 B.C., and evidently the first of the family to be buried here, was removed and is preserved in the Vatican museums; this is the only one that was decorated, taking the form of an altar with a Doric frieze at small scale under a row of dentils just under the lid, and the lid given volute *pulvini*. It is believed not to be Barbatus's original sarcophagus, but a replacement, possibly even of the early first century B.C. Parts of several other sarcophagi with their inscriptions, those of eight members of the family, were also removed to the Vatican museums (*CIL* 1² pp. 373–82 nos. 6–16 = 6.1284–94 = *ILS* 1–10 = *ILLRP* 309–17); they run from Barbatus to Paulla Cornelia, wife of an Hispallus of unknown date, but probably the consul of 176 B.C. Some are written in Saturnian meter and are of great philological, as well as historical, interest.

The tomb is somewhat irregular, which has led to

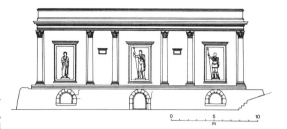

Figure 77
Sepulcrum Scipionum,
Façade, Restored

the supposition that it is an adaptation of an older stone quarry. There was a roughly cut central entrance leading to a main corridor running fairly directly back to the sarcophagus of Barbatus and flanked by other sarcophagi. To the right is a divergent corridor of larger dimensions, originally a separate and later burial place; as it is irregular, this has especially suggested that it is, in part, a reused quarry. Some eighteen places for sarcophagi in the main tomb are readily identifiable, and a good many more could be accommodated, perhaps twice as many.

Coarelli has recently and interestingly reconstructed the tomb façade of the second half of the second century B.C. (Fig. 77). Above a base of Grotta Oscura tufa in which opened three arched entrances, the central one to the principal tomb, are remains of a monumental façade articulated by engaged columns with Attic bases. Coarelli sees these as framing three niches with flat lintels over the arched entrances to contain the marble statues of P. Scipio Africanus the Elder, his brother Lucius, and the poet Ennius, about which we hear as ornaments of the tomb. This would make the tomb façade rather strongly resemble a *scaenae frons*. I should prefer to have the program of statuary crown the attic of the tomb, as it might a triumphal arch, and as the wording of the Latin in which we are told of these statues suggests (Cicero, *Arch.* 22; Val. Max. 8.14; Pliny, *HN* 7.114).

Lugli 1930, 4323–39; Nash 2.352–56; *DialArch* 6 (1972): 36–106 (F. Coarelli); *RömMitt* 89 (1982): 35–46 (H. Lauter Bufe).

Sep. Semproniorum: a well-preserved tomb of the very late republic under Palazzo S. Felice in Via della Dataria on the northern slope of the Quirinal. It faced southwest onto the clivus ascending to the southeast from the Campus Martius to the Porta Salutaris, presumably the Clivus Salutis (q.v.) The tomb is cut into the rock, the façade faced with travertine and with a deep arched niche that makes the tomb seem almost an arch. The crown is trimmed with a finely carved anthemion under a cornice with a line of dentils and an egg molding. The inscription over the niche (*CIL* 6.26152) records that it is for C. Sem-

pronius, his sister, and their mother, Larcia. The alphabet approaches that of fine Augustan inscriptions, but the owners cannot be identified. The tomb was excavated in 1863 (*BullCom* 4 [1876]: 126–27 and pl. 12 [R. Lanciani]).

Nash 2.357–58.

Sep. Severi: an alleged tomb of the family of the Septimii Severi, known only from one passage, which puts it on the Via Appia on the right to those approaching the gate (S.H.A. *Geta* 7.2) and compares it to the Septizodium. However, it is known from other sources that Geta, Severus, and Caracalla were all buried in the Mausoleum Hadriani (q.v.). It is not clear what has caused the confusion in the biographer's mind, or where he thought the tomb stood.

Sep. Statii Caecilii: the tomb of the comic poet along the Via Aurelia approaching, or along (*iuxta*), the Ianiculum (Suetonius, *De Poet., Statius Caecilius* 10). Clearly the location of the tomb depends on interpretation of both the words *Ianiculum* (q.v.) and *iuxta*, but the strong suggestion is that the tomb stood in the vicinity of Porta Aurelia.

Sep. Statiliorum: the columbarium of the slaves and freedmen of the Statilii, especially M. Statilius Taurus, cos. A.D. 44 and owner of the Horti Tauriani (q.v.) on the Esquiline. It stood on the north side of Via Praenestina-Labicana inside Porta Praenestina (Porta Maggiore) on the southwest side of Via G. Giolitti. Three chambers of the tomb were excavated in 1875–1877, and numerous inscriptions dating from Augustus to Claudius were recovered (*CIL* 6.6213–6640). A small adjacent tomb, 2.90 m × 1.95 m, was decorated with a very curious frieze of Augustan date showing subjects relating to Aeneas and the early history of Latium down to the time of Romulus. This is of special historical and iconographical interest and was removed to the Museo Nazionale Romano delle Terme (Helbig[4] 3.2489). The decorations of the upper half of the tomb and the vault are considered of early third century date and, after being photographed, were reburied. The whole program is much in need of study. See also *BullCom* 8 (1880): 51–75 (R. Lanciani); *CIL* 6.33083–33190.

Capitolium 34, no. 5 (1959): 3–10 (M. Borda); Nash 2.359–69.

Sep. Sullae: the tomb of the dictator L. Cornelius Sulla in the Campus Martius, erected by *senatus consultum* (Livy, *Epit.* 90; Appian, *BellCiv* 1.106; Plutarch, *Sulla* 38.4). Lucan (2.222) calls it a tumulus and describes its location as *medio campo*, which may well be correct, and Dio (77[78].13.7) says that Caracalla instituted a search for it and had it restored, which suggests that, as in the case of the tomb of Lucilius Paetus (see Sep. Lucilii Paeti), the earth of the tumulus had washed down in the course of time and hidden the base and the inscription identifying it.

Sep. Ser. Sulpicii Galbae: see **Sep. Galbae.**

Sep. Q. Sulpicii Maximi: a tomb found in the base of the east tower of Porta Salaria in 1871, which had been built over it. Q. Sulpicius Maximus died at the age of eleven, having won first prize in the competition in extemporaneous verse in Greek at the third celebration of the Ludi Capitolini in A.D. 94 (*CIL* 6.33976 = *ILS* 5177). The aedicular tomb was crowned by a massive stele in the form of an altar, in the front of which is a niche containing a togate figure of Sulpicius Maximus in high relief, the rest of the face of the stele being covered with his poetry. It is now in the Museo Nuovo Capitolino (Helbig⁴ 2.1734). The remains of the tomb stood in place from 1871 to 1921, when it became necessary to demolish Porta Salaria. The tomb was then reerected to the east of the new aperture.

BdI 1871, 98–114 (G. Henzen); Nash 2.371–73; *CAR* 3-A, 26 p. 27.

Sep. C. Sulpicii Platorini: the monumental tomb of a man who may have been the grandson of the triumvir monetalis of 18 B.C. (*PIR*¹ S 728, 729), on the right bank of the Tiber near the head of the Pons Agrippae (q.v.) just inside the Aurelian Walls, discovered during work on the Tiber embankment in 1880. It was a rectangular structure, 7.44 m x 7.12 m, with the entrance on the west. The base was travertine, the exterior of the walls was revetted with marble, the rest of fine brick-faced concrete finished with stucco, with marble ornaments and inscriptions. In the interior the pavement is of white mosaic. In niches alternately curved and rectangular framed by an engaged order at small scale were set cinerary urns with inscriptions. These date from the Augustan period to that of the Flavians (*CIL* 6.31761–68a; *ILS* 953). Two heroic statues and a fine bust of a young girl (Minatia Polla?) were also recovered. The tomb had been covered over in the construction of the Aurelian Walls and so preserved. In 1911 it was reconstructed in the Museo Nazionale Romano delle Terme (Helbig⁴ 3.2168).

BdA 5 (1911): 365–72 (R. Paribeni and A. Berretti); Lugli 1938, 654–57; Nash 2.374–75.

Sep. Titi Tatii: the tomb of the Sabine king in the Loretum (q.v.) on the Aventine near the Armilus-trium (Varro, *Ling.* 5.152; Plutarch, *Rom.* 23.3; Festus 496L). HJ (162) thinks Dionysius's comments on the Loretum (3.43) show that the grave of the king was a cult center, but it is difficult to accept the reasoning here.

Sep. Valeriorum: see **Domus, Valerii.**

Serapeum: see **Isis, Aedes** [1].

Serapis, Aedes (Templum, *Not.*): a temple in Regio VI, built, according to an inscription with letters about 30 centimeters high, by Caracalla (*CIL* 6.570; cf. *NSc* 1909, 80 [F. Barnabei]). This is supported by the Historia Augusta (S.H.A. *Caracalla* 9.10–11). No one tells us more precisely where the temple was located, nor for what it was remarkable, but finds of material and inscriptions related to the cult of Serapis indicate that it was on the southernmost part of the Quirinal, the Collis Latiaris (HJ 423; *BullCom* 42 [1914]: 374 [M. Marchetti]). It does not seem to have been of great importance.

Sessorium (Fig. 78): a vast palatial complex of villa character of unknown origins at the southeast extremity of Regio V adjacent to the Amphitheatrum Castrense and Circus Varianus (qq.v.). It antedated the Aurelian Walls, which cut through it, but it is not mentioned by name before then (unless we admit the conjecture Sessorion in Plutarch, *Galba* 28.3, which is not attractive). From the beginning of the sixth century it appears as Sessorium (*MGH Chron. Min.* 1.324 [*Excerpt. Valens.* 69]; Acron *ad Hor. Sat.* 1.8.14; pseudo-Acron *ad Hor. Epod.* 5.100). It probably became an imperial residence by the time of Elagabalus (cf. Circus Varianus and S.H.A. *Heliogab.* 13.5, 14.5–6), and at the beginning of the fourth century it was the residence of Helena, the mother of Constantine (LPD 1.179 [Silvester 22] and 196n.75; VZ 2.231). Hence it was called Palatium Sessorianum. By that time the parts of the complex beyond the Aurelian Walls had been razed, but a very extensive portion inside remained. The Thermae Helenae (q.v.), probably restored by Helena (*CIL* 6.1136), seem to have been a public bath, not part of the Sessorium.

Under Constantine or his sons, one of the large halls of the palace (the *atrium grande*) was converted into the basilica of S. Croce in Gerusalemme as a repository for the fragment of the cross that Helena brought from Jerusalem. This hall was 34.35 m long, 21.75 m wide, and 20 m high, with five open arches on piers on each side and rectangular windows in a second storey above. Constantine probably left the arches open, converted corridors along the sides into side aisles, and added an apse at the east end. Two

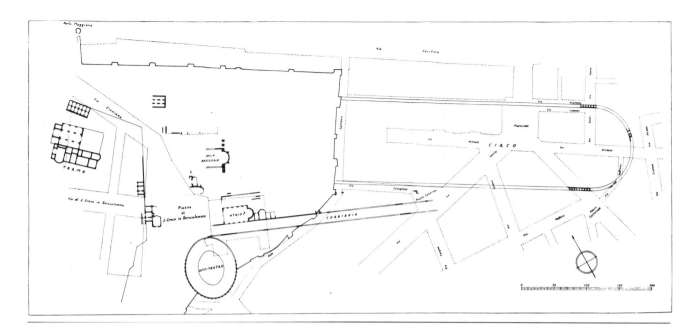

Figure 78
Sessorium,
Amphitheatrum
Castrense, Circus
Varianus,
and Thermae
Helenae, Plan

transverse screen walls with arches supported on paired columns divided the main nave crosswise into three sections, a curious architectural innovation. In the twelfth century the church underwent a radical transformation, being then divided into three naves by longitudinal walls with arches supported on columns in the more usual fashion. At this time the arches and windows along the sides were closed.

North of the church are remains of another hall of this palace, a vast apse, supported by big external buttresses added immediately after the construction, and the start of a nave, all in brick-faced concrete, probably of the time of Maxentius. This survived down to the sixteenth century and became known as the Templum Veneris et Cupidinis. In 1887 further remains of a building of about A.D. 100 were found in this location (*NSc* 1887, 70, 108 [G. Fiorelli]; *BullCom* 15 [1887]: 100 [G. Gatti]). The whole complex is much in need of careful study.

HJ 249–51; Lugli 1938, 486–90; R. Krautheimer, *Corpus Basilicarum Christianarum Romae* (Rome 1937), 1.171–77; *MemPontAcc*, ser. 3.8 (1955): 137–40, 154–68, 170–77 (A. M. Colini); Nash 2.384–86.

Sette Sale: see **Thermae Traiani.**

Sicilia: a place in, or part of, the Palatine palace (S.H.A. *Pert.* 11.6). Here soldiers, entering the palace through its porticoes, penetrated as far as the place called Sicilia and the Cenatio Iovis. The latter can hardly be anything but the great banquet hall at the

southwest corner of the Flavian part of the palace, and the unimpeded progress of the soldiers entering from the Area Palatina can be well understood, if this is correct. But the Sicilia remains a mystery, and there is nothing that by use or design suggests the name.

Sicininum: a place designation, perhaps for a site on the Cispian now occupied by the basilica of S. Maria Maggiore. It occurs in a single ancient inscription from the Forum Romanum (*CIL* 6.37111), a fragment of the edict of the praefectus urbi Tarracius Bassus against fraudulent merchants and shopkeepers issued shortly after A.D. 368. It then occurs in a number of Christian sources, beginning with the *Liber Pontificalis* (LPD 1.171 [Silvester 3] and 233 [Xystus III, 3]; VZ 2.230, 237). In Ammianus (27.3.13) we find an account of the contention of factions of Christians for power with mention of the deaths of 237 of them in the struggle *in Basilica Sicinini* in A.D. 367. Because there is now general agreement that Pope Liberius (A.D. 352–366) built the church of S. Maria Maggiore, this may be what is meant. Others maintain that it is the basilica of Bishop Julius (now S. Maria in Trastevere) that was the site of the struggle, and there is as yet no agreement. For the controversy over the location, see Ammianus Marcellinus, ed. A. -M. Morlé (Paris 1984) (Edition Budé), 5.241n.182.

R. Krautheimer et al., *Corpus Basilicarum Christianarum Romae* (Rome 1971), 3.1–60, especially 54–59.

Sigillaria: a district in Rome where luxuries such as would make suitable presents on the Sigillaria (the final days of the Saturnalia) were offered for sale (Suetonius, *Claud.* 16.4, *Nero* 28.2; *Dig.* 32.102.1). For Aulus Gellius it was especially a district of anti-quarian booksellers (2.3.5, 5.4.1). We do not know precisely where to locate it, but it might be a general term to describe the district around and including the Saepta Iulia, where most such markets seem to have been concentrated. There seems to be no ground for the popular notion that this was a district where small images were manufactured.

Signum: see **Statua, Signum, Equus, Colossus.**

Signum Aesculapii: see **Aesculapius, Aedes.**

Signum Vortumni: a statue of the Etruscan divinity that stood in the Vicus Tuscus behind the Temple of Castor on the border between the Forum Roma-num and the Velabrum and was regarded as very ancient (Varro, *Ling.* 5.46; Cicero, *Verr.* 2.1.154 and pseudo-Asconius ad loc. [Stangl 255]; Livy 44.16.10; Propertius 4.2.1–10; Horace, *Epist.* 1.20.1 and Porphyrion ad loc.). For the more precise location of this on the northwest corner of the cross-roads behind the Basilica Sempronia, see *AJA* 71 (1967): 177–79 (M. C. J. Putnam). Propertius gives the best description of this statue, which may have had an aedicula, but no more than that. Like the Ia-nus, it seems to have been much venerated. An in-scription on a base found in 1549 (*CIL* 6.804 = *ILS* 3588) may record a restoration of it in the time of Diocletian. Cf. also *CIL* 6.9393 = *ILS* 7696.

Silvanus, Sacella: shrines of the rustic divinity Sil-vanus erected by individuals and collegia under the empire and known from inscriptions. These are ex-tremely common and are for the most part very simple affairs, lararial in character, with altars and reliefs of the divinity. None seems to have been a public place of worship. Cf. *CIL* 6.575–698, 30999–31029. The following can be located with some confidence:

1. In Regio III in the Via Merulana (?) near the Auditorium Maecenatis (*CIL* 6.30930).
2. In Regio V near the Lateran (?) (*CIL* 6.580).
3. In Regio V near the Stazione Termini, found in the excavation of the Agger of the Servian Walls there (*CIL* 6.3716 = 31013 = *ILS* 3566; *CIL* 6.3697 = 30940).
4. In Regio VI near the southeast corner of the Thermae Constantinianae on the site of the Banca Nazionale (*CIL* 6.31020, 31022).

5. In Regio VI near the hemicycle of the Thermae Diocletiani (*CIL* 6.3714 = 31007).
6. In Regio VI in the Horti Sallustiani near Porta Pinciana in Via Ludovisi (*CIL* 6.310 = *ILS* 3467, 640 = *ILS* 3556, 30985 = *ILS* 5414, 31025).
7. In Regio IX on the site of the basilica di S. Marco (?) (*CIL* 6.626).
8. In Regio XII near the northwest side of the Thermae Antoninianae (*CIL* 6.543 = *ILS* 3544, 659).
9. In the Transtiberim near the church of S. Cosi-mato (*CIL* 6.692 = *ILS* 3542).
10. In the Transtiberim between Ponte Sisto and Villa Farnesina (*CIL* 6.31024).
11. In the Transtiberim in the vicinity of the Horti Caesaris (*CIL* 6.642, 31015).

A good many other inscriptions of uncertain prov-enience refer to aediculae, others to altars and stat-ues, and attest to the high popularity of the cult, but Silvanus never had a place in the state religion of Rome, no feast or flamen, and even the shrine near Porta Pinciana, the best attested in inscriptions, seems to have been a very modest affair. Cf. Roscher 4.854–59 (R. Peter).

PAPS 122 (1987): 22–47 (R. E. A. Palmer) gives a very full list of local shrines and possible shrines of this divinity.

Sol, Templum (Fanum, Aur. Vict., *Caes.* 35.7): a temple that Aurelian built after his triumph over the East in A.D. 273, famous for its magnificence (S. H. A. *Aurel.* 35.3; Aur. Vict., *Caes.* 35.7). It was in Regio VII according to the regionary catalogues, *in Campo Agrippae* (Chron. 148). Connected with it were porticoes in which was stored wine of the privy purse, *vina fiscalia* (S. H. A. *Aurel.* 48.4). R. E. A. Palmer (*MAAR* 36 [1980]: 217–33) has proposed the attractive theory that vina fiscalia were duty in kind. Because it would have been collected at every customs station around the periphery of the city, this would not help us to locate the temple, but might help with the location of the Ad Ciconias. Because Aurelian proposed to make public distributions of wine in addition to the distributions of oil, bread, and pork (S. H. A. *Aurel.* 35.2, 48.1), the temple may well have stood in close conjunction with Au-relian's Castra (Urbana) (q.v.) and the Forum Suar-ium (q.v.). A tribune of the urban cohorts was over-seer of the Forum Suarium.

No one remarks on the size or form of the temple. The Sol worshiped there seems to have been the Ba'al of Palmyra combined with other Oriental sun gods (Roscher 4.1147–48 [F. Richter]). The dedications that excited particular admiration were Oriental robes encrusted with jewels (S. H. A. *Aurel.* 28.5), a statue of Aurelian in silver, set up posthumously (S. H. A. *Tac.* 9.2), and a picture of Aurelian and a certain Ulpius Crinitus (S. H. A. *Aurel.* 10.2). Aurelian also proposed to make a throne for this temple from two magnificent elephant tusks, but for some unknown reason did not (S. H. A. *Firm.* 3.4). But the whole was remarkable for the Oriental richness of its appointments (S. H. A. *Aurel.* 39.6; Eutropius 9.15.1). The last mention of it in antiquity tells of the removal of eight of its porphyry columns, sent to Constantinople for the church of S. Sophia (T. Preger, ed., *Scriptores Originum Constantinopolitanarum* [Leipzig 1901], 1.76).

Discovery of an inscription (*CIL* 6.1785 = 31931) in a building "belonging to the convent of S. Silvestro in Capite" that alludes to the transportation of wine from the Ad Ciconias to a templum (sc. Solis) would be useful, if we could locate its provenience, even approximately, but the wording indicates that the building was only a dependency of the convent somewhere east of the church of S. Silvestro. Remains of a great complex extending from Piazza S. Claudio to Via Frattina, east of the Via del Corso, but west of S. Silvestro, were seen by Palladio, who has left a sketch plan of it and an elevation of one part (*BullCom* 22 [1894]: pl. 12–14 [R. Lanciani]; Zorzi fig. 68). This Hülsen proposed should be Aurelian's temple. It consisted of a long court with semicircular ends to the south, colonnaded, the columns being addorsed to the interior wall with deep rounded niches between them along the sides and rectangular niches in alternate bays in the rounded ends. Four great doors at the points where the rounded ends join the sides were emphasized with larger columns. The elevation seems to show the northwest entrance and shows that the sides at least were in two storeys, both with Corinthian orders, the lower order raised on a continuous plinth, with round-headed niches in the lower storey, square-headed ones in the upper, and the cornice broken out over the columns of the upper storey and surmounted by reversing broken pediments.

From this courtyard one passed to a small square intermediate court by a door in the center of the northern apse that seems strangely underemphasized. Whether there was a responding door at the southern end is not clear, because the drawing is cut and shows only the beginning of this apse. The intermediate court seems curiously plain.

The northern court was much larger than the southern one, but plainer, with three large exedras in each wall, except the entrance wall, and all but the central exedras in the side walls with pairs of columns in the openings. The entrance wall was enlivened with a series of twelve shallow niches, possibly for statues, and on its exterior were twelve rounded niches. In the center of this court was a tholus raised on a base of three steps with sixteen columns around a cella with doors to the north and south. In the interior of the cella were four shallow niches in the wall and something circular in the center.

Although they are connected, these two courts are very dissimilar in architectural approach, and one would suppose that they must have been built for very different purposes and at different times. The larger northern court is the older and has many of the characteristics of a macellum, and the tholus with its two axial doors and central circular feature like a fountain emplacement does not seem apt to have been a temple, but something more like a macellum tholus. Probably a portico should be restored on all four sides of the court. If the Forum Suarium was the central meat market of Rome, it may well have been this building.

The architecture of the southern court, to which this is connected, reminds one strongly of the Severan basilica at Leptis Magna in its play with double orders of Corinthian columns combined with single soaring columns, multiple niches, lateral approaches, and rounded ends. Column shafts of granite, cipollino, and africano have been found in the area (*BullCom* 22 [1894]: 299–300 [R. Lanciani]). Therefore, a date in the third century seems very likely. If the temple were at the center of the south apse, there might be room for it, although it could not have been a very large building. Otherwise it could have been driven through the south apse, so that only the façade projected into the court. But it is hard to think that this courtyard would ever have been described as a *porticus*. Possibly there were porticoes around it, or adjacent. The case for the identification is a very weak one.

If the southern court is rejected as unlikely to have been connected with Aurelian's temple, then perhaps it was the nameless temple discovered to the north of this complex in 1794. This was an Ionic temple, octastyle, with column shafts of red granite and bases and capitals of white marble. The walls were of brick veneered with colored marbles, and in the interior a Corinthian order at smaller scale was found (G. A. Guattani, *Memorie enciclopediche sulle antichità e belle arti a Roma* [Rome 1806], 1.4).

BullCom 22 (1894): 285–311 (R. Lanciani); *RendPontAcc,* ser. 3.51–52 (1978–79): 371–87 (F. Castagnoli); *QITA* 10 (1988): 15 (E. Tortorici).

Sol Elagabalus: see Elagabalus.

Sol et Luna, Aedes (Templum, *Not.*): an ancient Temple of Sol, probably dating to a time before the building of the cavea of the Circus Maximus, that

came to be included in the fabric of the cavea. It stood on the southwest side just before the beginning of the sphendone and is shown on coins of Trajan (*B. M. Coins, Rom. Emp.* 3.180 nos. 853–56 and pl. 32.2–4) and Caracalla (*B. M. Coins, Rom. Emp.* 5.477–78 nos. 251–53 and pl. 75.2–4) as tetrastyle, prostyle, with a very large central acroterion, which Tertullian (*De Spect.* 8) tells us represented the god himself, and smaller lateral acroteria. In other respects the architecture of the temple seems normal. It was approached in front by a flight of steps. It is usually called simply the Temple of Sol; the name of Luna is added only occasionally (Philocalus, *Notitia, Curiosum*). The day of dedication was 28 August (Degrassi 503). The obelisk of Ramesses II (see Obeliscus Augusti in Circo Maximo) brought to Rome from Heliopolis in 10 B.C. and erected on the spina of the circus may have stood on the axis of this temple, because it did not stand at the midpoint of the spina and was dedicated to Sol.

Sol Malachbelus (Belus): a shrine of the patron divinity of the city of Palmyra, established by the Palmyrene community in Rome before the introduction of the cult of Sol by Aurelian, and certainly before A.D. 102 (*CIL* 6.31034). The evidence is almost entirely epigraphical (*CIL* 6.50 = *ILS* 4334, 51, 52 = *ILS* 4335, 709 = *ILS* 4336, 710 = 30817 = *ILS* 4337, 31034, 31036 = *ILS* 4338; *IG* 14.971, 972; cf. Zosimus 1.61.1–2) and strongly indicates a location in the Transtiberim on Via Portuensis, near the limits of the city, if not beyond them.

HJ 645–46; Roscher 4.1147, 1150 (F. Richter); *PAPS* 125 (1981):372–81 (R. E. A. Palmer).

Spes, Aedes (Fig. 38): in the Forum Holitorium, built and dedicated by A. Atilius Calatinus in the First Punic War (Cicero, *Leg.* 2.28; Tacitus, *Ann.* 2.49). It was struck by lightning in 218 B.C. (Livy 21.62.4) and burned in the great fire of 213, but was restored the next year (Livy 24.47.15–16, 25.7.6). It burned again in 31 B.C., believed to be deliberate arson (Cass. Dio 50.10.3–6) and was apparently not restored until A.D. 17, although it seems strange that Tacitus (*Ann.* 2.49) should state that Augustus had undertaken the work of restoration. In 179 B.C. M. Fulvius Nobilior let the contract for a Porticus Post Spei ad Tiberim (see Porticus Post Spem). This was probably a relatively simple building, most likely utilitarian, and perhaps intended rather to serve commerce along the riverbank than as a frame for the temple. The day of dedication of the temple was 1 August (Degrassi 489).

It is almost certainly the middle temple of the three built into the fabric of the church of S. Nicola in Carcere, in large part belonging to the late republican period, a restoration intended to bring it into line with the restoration of the Temple of Iuno Sospita to the north of it undertaken by L. Iulius Caesar, cos. 90 B.C. The restoration of Spes is not recorded in our sources. It was Ionic, hexastyle, peripteral, with eleven columns along the flank and with a pronaos three bays deep. It was approached by a stair across the whole façade that divided on approaching the top of the platform to accommodate a platform for the altar. The material is travertine on the façade, peperino along the flanks. Much of the structure, including several of the fluted columns, is built into the church. Along the flanks and back of the temple podium were loculi arranged in the intercolumniations, small chambers that must have been closed by metal doors for the deposit of valuables.

R. Delbrück, *Die drei Tempel an Forum Holitorium in Rom* (Rome 1903); Lugli 1946, 545–53; Lugli 1975, 287–92; *MemPontAcc,* ser. 3.13 (1981): 7–136 (L. Crozzoli Aite).

Spes, Templum Novum: listed in Regio VII by the *Notitia (om. Cur.),* otherwise unknown.

Spes Vetus: a shrine of Spes, mentioned only to locate a battle of the consul Horatius against the Etruscans in 477–476 B.C. (Livy 2.51.2; Dion. Hal. 9.24.4), on the Esquiline, near Porta Praenestina (Porta Maggiore). The temple itself seems to have disappeared early, but it gave its name to a district that incidentally identified one of the imperial residences, the Horti ad Spem Veterem (or Horti Variani) of Elagabalus (S.H.A. *Heliogab.* 13.5), which must subsequently have become the Sessorium or Palatium Sessorianum (see Sessorium). Because this was the highest point on the east side of the city, most of the aqueducts of Rome entered here, and the location figures frequently in Frontinus (*Aq.* 1.5, 19, 20, 21, 65, 76, 87). However, the only mention of topographical value is the first, where the juncture of the Aqua Appia and Aqua Augusta *ad Spem Veterem* is said to be *in confinio Hortorum Torquatianorum et (Epaphroditia)norum* (the conjecture *Epaphroditianorum* is Lanciani's to fill a gap in the manuscript), but, because the Horti Torquatiani are otherwise completely unknown, it is of no real help. Cf. *CIL* 15.5929 = *ILS* 7543 of a *sutor* from Spes Vetus.

Spino: one of the watercourses of Rome, mentioned by Cicero (*Nat. D.* 3.52) and associated with the Tiber, the Almo, and the Nodinus. It was included in the augural prayer, and in such association it must have been of some importance, but it cannot be identified. It should be in the immediate vicinity of Rome and not culverted in Cicero's day. Cf. Nodinus.

Splenis, Ara: listed in the regionary catalogues in Regio I after the Area Apollinis and confirmed by a medieval legend in which robbers who were taking a miraculous picture of the Virgin from the ancient church of S. Sisto Vecchio on the Via Appia to the Lateran were stopped by supernatural manifestations *ad locum qui dicitur Spleni*. It is hardly conceivable that there would have been a shrine of any sort to Splen as a divinity, so there may be some reason for connecting the church of SS. Nereo ed Achille, *titulus fasciolae*, across the Via Appia from S. Sisto Vecchio, with *splenium* meaning "plaster" or "bandage." In that case the Area Splenis must be sought in the immediate environs of S. Sisto.

BullCom 54 (1926): 49–53 (C. Hülsen).

Spoliarium: the morgue for gladiators who were killed in the arena (S.H.A. *Commod.* 18.3, 5, 19.1, 3) and where the *coup de grace* was administered (Seneca, *Epist. ad Luc.* 93.12). To judge from the name, it was probably their dressing room as well. It is listed in the regionary catalogues in Regio II, and if there was, as it appears, one common dressing room for the amphitheater, it must have been situated on the Colosseum square, just inside the boundary of Regio II. Cf. Armamentarium and Samiarium.

Stabula Factionis Prasinae: see **Stabula IIII Factionum.**

Stabula IIII Factionum: the stables of the four companies that owned and trained the horses for the races in the circus (Tacitus, *Hist.* 2.94). The four were distinguished by their colors: Albata, Russea, Prasina, and Veneta. To these Domitian added two: Purpurea and Aurata. By the beginning of the fourth century, the Albata and Russea had merged with the Veneta and Prasina, so there were again four. In the *Notitia*, in Regio IX, we find *stabula numero IIII factionum VIII;* in the *Curiosum, stabula IIII factionum VI.* The *stabula* were all in the lower Campus Martius in the vicinity of the Trigarium (q.v.), where they probably could take advantage of exercise grounds and training tracks. They were probably all close to one another but carefully separated. In the inscriptions commemorating victories and those of various functionaries connected with chariot racing (*CIL* 6.10044–82; *ILS* 5281–5314), we find all four factions mentioned very frequently and learn that the charioteers passed from one faction to another, apparently with ease, but the Factio Prasina is the only one whose stabula can be located at all precisely. This became the most important company in the course of the first century after Christ and was favored by the emperors, especially Caligula (Suetonius, *Calig.* 55.2–3; Cass. Dio 59.14.6–7), who fre-

quently dined and slept there, and presented his favorite horse, Incitatus, with a marble stall and an ivory manger. It is located especially by the church of S. Lorenzo in Damaso connected with Palazzo della Cancelleria, on whose font is an ancient inscription saying that the church also went by the name of S. Laurentii in Prasino (HCh 284). An inscribed lead pipe, not in situ, was found not far away (*CIL* 15.7254).

MEFRA 89 (1977): 723–803 (H. Broise et al.), 96 (1984): 847–906, especially 899–902 (M. Royo).

Stabulum: one of the parts of the Palatine palace, mentioned only once (S.H.A. *Carinus* 19.1), as the location of paintings showing the extraordinary circus games given under Carinus; these were *circa porticum stabuli*. It cannot be located.

Stadium Augusti: a wooden stadium that Augustus erected in 28 B.C. somewhere in the Campus Martius, in which gymnastic contests were held as part of the first celebration of the Ludi Actiaci (Cass. Dio 53.1.5).

Stadium Caesaris: a temporary stadium in the Campus Martius that Julius Caesar erected and in which he exhibited athletic contests lasting three days as part of one of his entertainments (Suetonius, *Iul.* 39.3).

Stadium Domitiani (Fig. 79): the stadium that Domitian built in the Campus Martius for athletic contests (Suetonius, *Dom.* 5; Eutropius 7.23.5; Chron. 146; Hieron. *a. Abr.* 2105). It is listed in the regionary catalogues in Regio IX. After the Colosseum was severely damaged by fire in A.D. 217, the stadium was used for a number of years for gladiatorial shows (Cass. Dio 78[79].25.2–3). Like those of the Circus Maximus, its arcades came to accommodate numerous brothels (S.H.A. *Heliogab.* 26.3) and probably shops and workshops as well. Alexander Severus restored it (S.H.A. *Alex. Sev.* 24.3), and it was one of the buildings that most excited the admiration of Constantius during his visit to the city in the fourth century. According to the regionary catalogues, it had thirty thousand loca, or seating for about twenty thousand spectators. According to tradition, Saint Agnes found a martyr's death in the brothels here, and a church was built in her honor on the west side of the stadium, S. Agnese in Agone (HCh 168). Another church there is S. Nicolai in Agone (HCh 389).

It is now Piazza Navona, one of the largest piazze in Rome, and the arena preserves its original shape with remarkable fidelity, the surrounding buildings being constructed on the ruins of the cavea. The

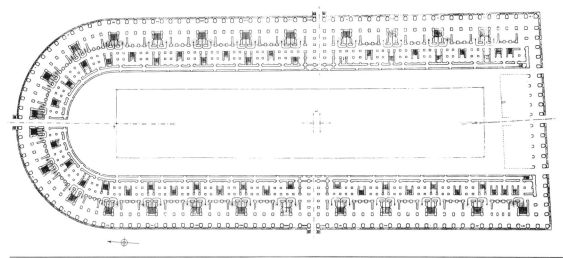

Figure 79
Stadium Domitiani,
Restored Plan
(1 cm = 18.4m)

arena is about 250 m long. Considerable remains of the cavea have been discovered at various points, especially under the church of S. Agnese and at the north end (sphendone), where it has been possible to preserve these in view, albeit under the encumbering mass of modern buildings. The construction is of brick-faced concrete with an exterior face of travertine throughout, construction strongly resembling that of the Colosseum. For the obelisk of Domitian erected as part of the fountain in the center of the piazza in 1651, see Obeliscus Pamphilius.

Lugli 1938, 218–23; *Capitolium* 16 (1941): 209–23 (A. M. Colini); A. M. Colini, *Stadium Domitiani* (Rome 1943); Nash 2.387–90; S. Bosticco et al., *Piazza Navona* (Rome 1970), 3–17 (A. M. Colini).

Stadium Palatinum: see Domus Augustiana.

Stagnum: see Piscina, Stagnum, Naumachia.

Stagnum Agrippae: an artificial water that Agrippa constructed, almost certainly in connection with his Thermae (q.v.). It was large enough to accommodate a raft on which Nero gave a banquet (Tacitus, *Ann.* 15.37). The raft was kept in motion by smaller vessels manned by oarsmen. The stagnum was set in a park, presumably the Horti or Nemus Agrippae, which Nero stocked with exotic birds and animals, while on the margins of the stagnum were constructed pavilions. A park of considerable size seems implied, which must have lain west of the Thermae, where the Marble Plan indicates open space. Strabo (13.1.19 [590]) says there was a grove between the stagnum and the Euripus, and, because no substantial construction has been found between the remains of the baths and the Via de'Sediari on the line of an ancient street, we may see the park as bounded by that street on the west and the Hecato-

stylon along the Theater of Pompey on the south. The northern limit is difficult to set, but after the construction of the Thermae Neronis, the southern façade of this complex, roughly on a line with the façade of the Pantheon, was as far as it could have run. The stagnum will presumably have lain in the western reaches of this park, for there was a grove of plane trees near the Hecatostylon (Martial 3.19.1–2), and at least five granite fountain basins have come to light in the neighborhood of Piazza S. Eustachio (LR 501), so it could not have lain near either end. Lugli (Lugli 1938, 158–59) reports that one side of the stagnum came to light in excavations for the new buildings of Corso del Rinascimento, a portico of large granite columns (diameter 1.50 m) on a platform of travertine with a walk 3 m wide in front of it, and along this a basin for water more than 60 m long. This Lugli identifies as a late imperial rebuilding of Agrippa's basin. He gives no documentation for these discoveries. The water supplying the stagnum was probably the overflow of the Aqua Virgo (cf. Ovid, *Ex P.* 1.8.37–38); it seems to have drained into an ornamental canal running through the Campus Martius following approximately the line of Corso Vittorio Emanuele and emptying into the Tiber just above the Pons Neronianus.

MEFRA 89 (1970): 826–30 (F. Coarelli).

Stagnum Neronis: the artificial lake in the basin where the Colosseum was later built (Martial, *De Spect.* 2.5–6), constructed by Nero as one of the chief features of the Domus Aurea (q.v.). Suetonius (*Nero* 31.1) compares it to a sea surrounded by buildings that seemed a city; but he could hardly have seen it himself, and his source was clearly exaggerating. It was fed by the Aqua Claudia, brought in a cascade down the slope of the Caelian, and probably by a stream already existing in the valley between the Oppius and the Caelian. It was apparently the first part of the Domus Aurea to be destroyed (Suetonius, *Vesp.* 9.1), perhaps especially to reclaim the water for public use and to permit circulation of traffic through that part of the city.

Stata Mater, Simulacrum: Festus (416L) says that after Cotta paved the Forum Romanum a simulacrum of Stata Mater was set up and worshiped in the hope of protecting the pavement from damage by fire. Stata Mater was a divinity credited with the power to prevent or stop fire; Peter included her among the Indigites (Roscher 2.223–34). Presumably this simulacrum was a statue, but we have no indication of where it might have stood (possibly on or near the Volcanal?), and Festus uses the past tense. After the cult was introduced in the Forum Romanum, it spread to the rest of the city, presumably as part of the compital worship. We have evidence for a Vicus Statae Matris in Regio II, Caelimontana, and a Vicus Statae Siccianae in Regio XIV, Transtiberim (qq.v.).

Statio Annonae (Fig. 37.20): the modern name, on the analogy of Statio Aquarum, for the headquarters of the praefectus annonae in charge of the food supply of the city. In the fourth century a large portico was built in the area now occupied by the front half of the church of S. Maria in Cosmedin and its adjuncts to the southwest. This was a hall with three colonnaded façades some 30 m long and 15 m wide, raised on a high platform approached by broad stairs on the three colonnaded fronts. There were piers at the corners, seven columns on the long front, and three on each of the short ones. The back wall was faced with brick, unbroken, and separated the hall from an important building behind, possibly the Temple of Ceres, Liber, and Libera (see Ceres, Liber Liberaque, Aedes), because it stands on the edge of what might well be the remains of a temple platform. The roof of the Statio must have been supported on timber trusses, but these were in turn supported by fluted columns with composite capitals that carried arches. The capitals show variations and are presumed to have been reused. The columns of the northeast and northwest fronts have been built into the fabric of the church. It must have been a towering building, but very open, resembling a Renaissance loggia.

The identification of this building depends on the discovery of inscriptions in honor of, or giving the names of, praefecti annonae (*CIL* 6.1151 = *ILS* 707, 31856 = *ILS* 1327) and lead seals from shipping (*CIL* 15.7940–51). The case is hardly a strong one. The distance of the Statio from the Porticus Minucia Frumentaria on Via Lata, if the identification of that

building is correct (and it was certainly in Regio IX), and from other centers for the distribution of food is puzzling, but, because the location is near the original Emporium of Rome, it may have been traditional. One may note the presence of the Columna Minucia (q.v.) in the immediate vicinity.

Into the Statio was built the Diaconia, founded before the sixth century. This was enlarged and enriched by Hadrian I in the eighth century and given to the Greek refugee community, hence the names De Schola Graeca, commonly used in the Middle Ages, and Cosmedin.

HCh 327–28; G. B. Giovenale, *La basilica di S. Maria in Cosmedin* (Rome 1927), especially 334–50; Lugli 1946, 585–87; Nash 2.391–94.

Statio Aquarum: see **Lacus Iuturnae.**

Stationes Municipiorum: mentioned only by Pliny (*HN* 16.236) in connection with the remarkable extent of the spread of the roots of a lotus tree, but evidently the headquarters of towns doing business with the Roman senate. They must be especially some of the *tabernae* along the southwest side of the Forum Iulium, probably both those opening on the forum itself and those above them opening on the Clivus Argentarius. Because we now know that the Forum Iulium was intended to accommodate the expanded business of the senate, these tabernae were probably intended for this purpose from the beginning, but whether they were assigned for extended periods or only on short term is not known. Suetonius (*Nero* 37.1) suggests that such space was very limited and its assignment, vigorously competed for and jealously guarded, was the prerogative of the central government. Later the *stationes* seem to have multiplied in number and to have been installed wherever adequate space could be found around the forum. These stationes were then more or less permanent, and inscriptions have been found identifying, among others, those of Claudiopolis (Tiberias) (*BullCom* 27 [1899]: 242–43 [L. Cantarelli], 28 [1900]: 124–34 [G. Gatti]; *RömMitt* 17 [1902]: 11 [C. Hülsen], 20 [1905]: 9–10 [C. Hülsen]; *IGUR* 82); Tarsus (*IG* 14.1064, 1066; *IGUR* 79), Sardis (*IG* 14.1008; *IGUR* 85–87), Sabratha (*AE* 1934.146); and Noricum (*CIL* 6.250 = *ILS* 3675). Whereas all of Noricum seems to have been able to make do with a single statio, Tarsus, which required a separate statio of its own, seems to have found space on the Sacra Via across from the Tempio del Divo Romolo and embellished its façade with a handsome marble lintel properly inscribed in the Greek alphabet.

Lugli 1946, 164; *Athenaeum* 36 (1958): 106–16 (L. Moretti); Nash 2.398; Anderson 52–54.

Stationes Vigilum: see **Cohortes Vigilum, Stationes.**

Statua, Signum, Equus, Colossus: The various terms for statuary overlap in usage and could be extended by the addition of others, such as *effigies* and *simulacrum. Statua,* however, is used by Pliny and our other sources especially for honorary statues erected to men and women either in their lifetime or after death. Here the Statua Marsyae and Statua Tiberis are exceptional. The Marsyas of Rome is simply called Marsyas in our earliest literary sources, but it is called statua by Acron (*ad Hor. Sat.* 1.6.120), and those in other cities are sometimes called statua in inscriptions (*CIL* 8.4219, 16417). That in Rome is only once called *signum* (Porphyrion *ad Hor. Sat.* 1.6.120); it is therefore called statua here. The statue of the Tiber is called simply Tiberis in the Einsiedeln itinerary and probably should be called signum, but here I have thought it best to follow tradition.

Signum is used for statuary generally, including equestrian, heroic, and colossal figures. It is used of pedimental sculpture and the effigies of divinities. Here, therefore, it is used of cult figures.

Equus is used for most equestrian statues, but the statue of Cloelia seems always to have been called *statua equestris;* I have therefore accepted this terminology.

A *colossus* is any statue of a human being of more than one and one-half times life size. These were very rare in antiquity. The Equus Domitiani is often described as a colossus, but seems to have been only heroic in scale. Had it been colossal, one would have seen little but the horse.

Statua Antonii Musae: a statue of the physician credited with curing Augustus of dangerous illness, erected by public subscription next to the statue of Aesculapius on the Tiber island (Suetonius, *Aug.* 59).

Statua Atti Navii: the statue of Attus Navius erected on the place in the Comitium where he had cut the whetstone with a razor to prove the validity of augury to Tarquinius Priscus (Livy 1.36.3–5; Dion. Hal. 3.71). This was to the left of the Curia on the steps of the Comitium near the Ficus Ruminalis. The razor and whetstone were believed to be buried under a puteal close by. The statue was of bronze, somewhat smaller than life size, and showed the augur capite velato. Dionysius says the statue was still standing in his time, but after the beginning of construction of the Curia Iulia (q.v.) in 44 B.C. the cavea of the Comitium must have been largely dismantled and the monuments of the Comitium removed for safekeeping. Livy speaks of the statue in the past tense, although he seems to have precise knowledge of it, and Pliny (*HN* 34.21) says that the base of the statue burned in the burning of the Curia at the funeral of P. Clodius, which seems not unlikely. Because Pliny mentions only the base, we may presume the statue had been removed earlier, perhaps in 80 B.C., when Sulla enlarged the Curia and removed the statues of Pythagoras and Alcibiades (Pliny, *HN* 34.26). These cannot have been wantonly destroyed, because they were sacred dedications in a templum, but we do not know what was done with them.

Statua L. Bruti: a statue of the liberator of Rome from monarchy and first consul that stood on the Capitoline in company with the statues of the seven kings (Pliny, *HN* 33.9; Cass. Dio 43.45.3–4). Later a statue of Julius Caesar was added to the line in 45 B.C. The date of the erection of this group is very uncertain, but is probably early; Pliny (*HN* 34.29) believed the kings themselves set up the statues. See Statuae Regum Romanorum.

Statua Cloeliae: an equestrian statue of Cloelia, the Roman hostage who escaped from the camp of Lars Porsenna by swimming the Tiber and who, when restored to Porsenna on his demanding it, was awarded singular honors for bravery, including a share of the other hostages (Livy 2.13.6–11; Servius *ad Aen.* 8.646). The statue is variously said to have been erected by the state (Livy, 2.13.6–11; Servius *ad Aen.* 8.646), by the hostages (Piso *ap. Plin. HN* 34.29), and by the parents of the hostages (Dion. Hal. 5.35.2). It stood *in summa Sacra Via* opposite the Temple of Iuppiter Stator *in vestibulo Superbi domus* (Pliny, *HN* 34.29); the last is probably a simple confusion of Tarquinius Superbus, whose house was on the Oppius, with Tarquinius Priscus, whose house was at Porta Mugonia (Livy 1.41.4; Solinus 1.24). This would place the statue on the northeast side of the Clivus Palatinus. According to Dionysius (5.35.2), the statue no longer existed in his time, being said to have been destroyed in a fire, but Seneca (*Marc.* 16.2) and Servius (*ad Aen.* 8.646) are explicit that the statue was still in existence in their day, so it must have been restored or replaced early in the first century. Pliny preserves the information that a certain Annius Fetialis, otherwise unknown, asserted that this statue was not of Cloelia, but of Valeria, the daughter of the consul Publicola, and that she was the only one of the hostages to escape.

The honor of an equestrian statue was extraordinary, and Servius explained it as the Romans' response to the request of Porsenna that she should be awarded something *virile* in recognition of her courage. The suggestion is that she was shown mounted astride, like an Amazon, rather than riding sidesaddle, like the Nereids, but our sources are not explicit on this point.

Statua Hermodori: a statue of Hermodorus of Ephesus in the Comitium, erected at public expense. He was credited with being the interpreter of the Laws of the Twelve Tables (Pliny, *HN* 34.21) or the assistant of the decemvirs in the framing of the Laws of the Twelve Tables, presumably as an authority on the laws of Greek cities on which these were modeled (*Dig.* 1.2.2.4 [Pomponius]). Because the law was posted on the rostra of the Comitium, and it was here that the praetor urbanus established his tribunal, the location was an appropriate one. Although our sources are not more precise about the location of the statue, the rostra would have accommodated such a statue most easily, as the Rostra Augusti did later.

Statua Horatii Coclitis: a statue of the hero of the defense of the Pons Sublicius against the army of Lars Porsenna, originally set up in the Comitium. After the statue was struck by lightning, Etruscan haruspices called in to advise on proper expiation of the prodigy duplicitously recommended that it be moved to a lower place where surrounding buildings would cut it off from ever being illuminated by the sun. When they were exposed and punished for their treachery, an opposite course was indicated, and the statue was moved to a higher position on the Area Volcani (A. Gellius 4.5). The probability is that the statue originally stood at the top of the cavea of the Comitium, either on the rostra or, more likely, in the space in the corners behind the ring of steps on the south side, where it would be most exposed, and that it was first moved to the floor of the Comitium on the south side, simply down from the top of the cavea to the bottom, kept within the templum where it had been dedicated. When it became known that the statue must be moved to a higher position, the Romans chose the nearest templum higher than its original location. According to Pliny (*HN* 34.22), the statue was still in existence in his day.

Statua (Loricata) Divi Iulii: a statue of Julius Caesar in the vicinity of which (conceivably to its base, but more likely to a nearby column) was ordered affixed a bronze tablet listing the honors that the senate voted to Pallas, the freedman of Claudius (Pliny, *Epist.* 8.6.13). This is almost certainly the statue that Caesar allowed to be dedicated to him in his forum during his lifetime (Pliny, *HN* 34.18), presumably somewhere in the open square. Because the Forum Iulium served especially the purposes of the senate, in many ways an extension of the curia, this would have been a fitting location.

Statua Mamuri: listed by the regionary catalogues in Regio VI, in the *Notitia* between the Capitolium Antiquum and Templum Dei Quirini, in the *Curiosum* between the Thermae Constantinianae and Templum Dei Quirini; both lists suggest that it stood somewhere along Alta Semita not far from the Temple of Quirinus, possibly in conjunction with the Curia Saliorum Collinorum. The location of this curia is unknown, but, because the Salii were priests of Mars, they might well be associated with Quirinus. A Clivus Mamuri (q.v.) mentioned in medieval documents almost certainly took its name from this statue, which is indication that it stood fairly independent of other buildings. Because Mamurius Veturius was a legendary bronze smith of the time of Numa, before the use of statuary of any sort in Rome, his statue must have been the dedication of someone, or some company like the Salii, especially devoted to him in later times. It is impossible to assign it a date, but it is probably late, possibly very late.

Statua Marci Aurelii: see **Equus Marci Aurelii.**

Statua Q. Marcii Regis: see **Basis Q. Marcii Regis.**

Statua Q. Marcii Tremuli: see **Equus Tremuli.**

Statua Marsyae: a statue of the Phrygian satyr that stood in close conjunction with the Rostra Caesaris (Horace, *Sat.* 1.6.120 and schol. ad loc.) and Rostra Augusti (Seneca, *Ben.* 6.32.1), possibly at one time even on the Rostra Caesaris (pseudo-Acron *ad Hor. Epod.* 5.100), and was intimately associated with the Tribunal Praetoris Urbani. It is shown on coins of L. Marcius Censorinus of ca. 82 B.C. (*B. M. Coins, Rom. Rep.* 1.338 nos. 2657–59 and pl. 40 nos. 3–4; Crawford 363) and on the Plutei Traiani (q.v.). It was a somewhat grotesque figure, a little smaller than life size, nude except for slippers, carrying a full wineskin on the left shoulder, the neck of which he squeezed with his left hand. The legs were slightly bent, the bearded head was thrown back, and the right arm and hand were lifted high in a gesture of uncertain import. On the coins he stands in front of a slender column that carries a draped figure variously thought to be Minerva or Victoria, possibly Libertas. On the Plutei he stands on a plinth in front of an artificial (bronze?) fig tree mounted on a plinth of its own. The location of these in the Forum Romanum depends on our reading of the other buildings shown on the Plutei, but it is clear that they are not in close association with any rostra; a place in, or near, the Lacus Curtius (q.v.) seems likeliest. The tree has generally been identified as the Ficus Ruminalis (q.v.) of the Comitium, or the fig of the Ficus, Olea, Vitis group (q.v.), but is unlikely to be either, because it is clearly artificial.

The statue of Marsyas came to be the symbol of *libertas,* and in the *civitates liberae* of the empire a statue of Marsyas was regularly set up in the forum in witness of this (Servius *ad Aen.* 3.20, 4.58; *CIL* 8.4219 = *ILS* 6849, 16417, 27771). Such a Marsyas has been found at Paestum, unfortunately out of context, a bronze figure about half life size, similar to, but probably not a close copy of, the Roman Marsyas. On the basis of this evidence, M. Torelli has persuasively argued that the Marsyas in Rome was originally set up by C. Marcius Rutilus Censorinus, the first plebeian to become pontifex and augur (300 B.C.), and, with his father or grandfather, one of the first plebeians to become censor (294 and 265 B.C.). Because C. and Q. Ogulnius, curule aediles of plebeian origin, had put a group of the she-wolf nursing Romulus and Remus under the Ficus Ruminalis in 296 B.C. (Livy 10.23.12), the first censorship of Censorinus seems an appropriate time for the dedication of the Marsyas, probably in the Comitium, along with other statues dedicated there, and close to the Tribunal Praetoris. Thereafter, the Marsyas moved with the tribunal from rostra to rostra until sometime late in the first century, when it found a place somewhere in the middle of the forum.

The Marsyas was apparently regularly garlanded with flowers. On one occasion a certain P. Munatius was jailed for stealing these to crown himself (Pliny, *HN* 21.8–9), so the statue must have been regarded as sacred, and Augustus publicly deplored that his daughter Julia crowned the satyr during her nocturnal revels, so the gesture must have had ulterior significance.

Nash 2.399–400; M. Torelli, *Typology and Structure of Roman Historical Reliefs* (Ann Arbor, Mich. 1982), 89–118, especially 98–106; F. Coarelli 1985, 91–119.

Statua Minucii: see **Columna Minucia.**

Statua Octaviani: an equestrian statue on the rostra voted to Octavian by the senate in 43 B.C. and still to be seen there in Velleius's day (2.61.3). This may be the same statue that Tacitus speaks of elliptically (*Ann.* 4.67) as *celeberrimo fori.*

Statua Planci: a statue mentioned in two inscriptions (*CIL* 6.9673 = *ILS* 7605, 10023), almost certainly in Vicus Longus. See Diana Planciana, Aedes.

Statua Pompeii (1): an equestrian statue of Pompey on the rostra smashed, together with that of Sulla, by the plebs in 49 B.C. and later restored by Julius Caesar (Suetonius, *Iul.* 75.4; Cass. Dio 42.18.2, 43.49.1).

Statua Pompeii (2): a statue of Pompey in the curia that was part of the complex of the Theatrum and Porticus Pompeii, at the foot of which Caesar was murdered (Plutarch, *Caes.* 66.7).

Statua Salonini Gallieni: a statue of the younger Gallienus that stood *in pede Montis Romulei, hoc est ante Sacram Viam inter Templum Faustinae †adventam† ad Arcum Fabianum* (S. H. A. *Gallien.* 19.4). For *adventam* Jordan suggested *ac Vestam,* but something else seems necessary. The description suggests that the Velia came for a time to be called Mons Romuleius from the Tempio del Divo Romolo (see Romulus, Divus, Templum) on its slope, but more likely it is the Palatine that is meant.

Statua Semonis Sanci: see **Semo Sancus, Statua.**

Statua Sullae: an equestrian statue of Sulla shown on coins of ca. 80 B.C. (*B. M. Coins, Rom. Rep.* 2.463 no. 16 = Crawford 381). It was gilded (Cicero, *Phil.* 9.13; Appian, *BellCiv* 1.97) and stood *in rostris* (Suetonius, *Iul. 75.4;* Cass. Dio 42.18.2, 43.49.1), although Appian puts it in front of the rostra. The plebs smashed the statue following the downfall of Pompey, of whom there was a counterpart statue, but Caesar later restored it when he moved the rostra to the northwest end of the forum (Suetonius, *Iul.* 75.4; Cass. Dio 42.18.2, 43.49.1). As shown on coins, the statue wore a laurel crown and *sagum* and lifted its right hand in a gesture of salutation. Another statue of Sulla with an inscription like the legend of the coins was erected in the Vicus Laci Fundani (*CIL* 1².721 = 6.1297 = *ILS* 872 = *ILLRP* 352).

Statua Taraciae Gaiae: a statue voted to a Vestal Virgin of Numa's day, to be erected in a place of her choosing, in return for her present of the Campus Tiberinus (q.v.) to the Roman people. We do not know where the statue stood; Pliny (*HN* 34.25), who is our only source for the statue, lists it after those on the rostra and among those in the Forum Romanum and Comitium, but it may even have been on the island, where the cult of Tiberinus (q.v.) had its center. See also Gaia.

Statua Tiberis: mentioned in the Einsiedeln itinerary (1.6, 7.9; Jordan 2.647, 655) between the Forum of Trajan and the Arch of Septimius Severus and generally believed to be the river god known as Marforio that stood near the church of S. Martina and is now in the Museo Capitolino (Helbig⁴ 2.1193).

Statua Valeriana: mentioned in the regionary cat-alogues, listed in Regio XIV. It gave its name to the Vicus Statuae Valerianae (*CIL* 6.975 = *ILS* 6073, 31893 = *ILS* 6072). Granted the great number of Valerii known in Rome (the original articles on the gens in *PW* run to 411), this is not likely to have been simply a portrait. A bronze equestrian statue that most people claimed represented Cloelia, but Annius Fetialis asserted to be Valeria, daughter of Valerius Poplicola, stood *in summa Sacra Via* near the Temple of Iuppiter Stator (Dion. Hal. 5.35.2; Livy 2.13.11; Pliny, *HN* 34.29; Plutarch, *Poplic.* 18.2–19.5, *De Mul. Vir.* 14). Dionysius says that this statue had been destroyed by a fire before his time, but it seems possible that the Statua Valeriana was a replacement for it erected by members of the Gens Valeria at the point in the Transtiberim from which Cloelia/Valeria was supposed to have begun her flight to freedom. If so, it was probably on the right bank of the Tiber a little below the island.

Statua Valerii Corvi: a statue of M. Valerius Cor-vus, one of the triumphators in the Forum Augus-tum, with the raven on his head (A. Gellius 9.11.10).

Statuae Cinciae: see **Sepulcrum Cinciorum.**

Statuae in Rostris: honorary statues erected in honor of those who had perished while on missions on behalf of the state. Pliny (*HN* 34.23–24) lists the following: Tullius Cloelius, L. Roscius, Sp. Nautius, and C. Fulcinius, the four ambassadors murdered by the Fidenates in 438 B.C.; P. Iunius and Ti. Corun-canius, killed by Teuta, queen of the Illyrians, in 230 B.C.; and Cn. Octavius, killed while on an embassy to Antiochus IV in 162 B.C. All these were three-foot, or half-life-size, statues, and Pliny speaks of them as still existing in his day. To these should be added the equestrian statues of Sulla, Pompey, Julius Caesar, and Octavian, voted by the senate for other reasons (Vell. Pat. 2.61.2–3), and that of Ser. Sulpicius Ru-fus, who died while on a mission to Antony in 43 B.C. (Cicero, *Phil.* 9.7; *Dig.* 1.2.2.43 [Pomponius]), the last still on view in the time of Hadrian.

Statuae Regum Romanorum: statues of the seven kings of Rome, including Titus Tatius and presum-ably excluding Tarquinius Superbus, plus an eighth of L. Brutus, the founder of the republic, and even-tually a ninth of Julius Caesar (Cass. Dio 43.45.3–4), set up in the Area Capitolina. The statues of Romulus and Titus Tatius showed them wearing the toga *sine tunica,* while the only ones wearing rings were those of Numa Pompilius and Servius Tullius (Asconius *in Cic. Scaur.* 25 [Stangl 29]; Pliny, *HN* 33.9–10 and 24, 34.22–23). These stood by one of

the entrances to the Area Capitolina (Appian, *BellCiv* 1.16), probably near the top of the Centum Gradus (q.v.) at the southwest corner of the hill. Pliny (*HN* 34.22) thought some of these might be older than the time of Tarquinius Priscus, but prob-ably they belonged at the earliest to the last years of the monarchy and first years of the republic, while Rome was still under Etruscan influence. They were probably all of the three-foot or half-life size Pliny says (*HN* 34.24) was used for early honorific statues, but they evidently stood on individual bases, because a military diploma (*CIL* 16.24) specifies that it is dis-played *in basi Pompil(i).*

Statuae Romuli et Titi Tatii: statues of Romulus and Titus Tatius performing the sacrifice of a pig to seal the treaty between them at the conclusion of the war over the Sabine women (Servius *ad Aen.* 8.641) that stood on the Sacra Via. Romulus was to the southeast (*a parte Palatii*), and Titus Tatius was to the northwest (*venientibus a rostris*). This suggests that they stood on the southwest side of the Sacra Via, somewhere between the Regia and the Basilica Constantini. This is to some extent confirmed by Dionysius (2.46.3), who says Romulus and Titus Ta-tius erected altars to confirm their treaty and oaths midway along the Sacra Via (and cf. Festus 372L), whereas Plutarch (*Rom.* 19.7) says the treaty was struck in the Comitium.

Statuae Stilichonis: Numerous statues were voted to this immensely brilliant and successful com-mander under Honorius, Arcadius, and Theodosius, including one on the Rostra Augusti. Parts of the bases of three of these have come to light in the Forum Romanum, beginning with one found in 1539 near the Arch of Septimius Severus, but only one still remains there today, a block of marble that was originally the base of an equestrian statue, but upended and recut with an inscription recording the honors awarded Stilicho, especially for his victory over the Goths in northern Italy in A.D. 403. His name was erased from the inscription after his dis-grace and murder in 408. See *CIL* 6.1730 = *ILS* 1277, 1731 = *ILS* 1278, 31988.

Lugli 1946, 171; Nash 2.401.

Statuae Trium Fatorum: see **Tria Fata.**

Stimula: see **Lucus Stimulae.**

Strenia, Sacellum: a shrine on the Carinae at the point where the Sacra Via originated (Varro, *Ling.* 5.47). From it sacra were carried every month on the Ides to the arx (Festus 372L), and Symmachus (*Ep-ist.* 10.15 [28, 35]) says that at the new year verbenae from an *arbor felix* were taken from the Lucus Streniae to the new consuls (earlier the king) as auspices for the new year. Lydus (*Mens.* 4.4) specifies that these were laurel. These were called *strenae*, a term that later came to mean a new year's present of any sort, but especially money (Suetonius, *Aug.* 57.1, *Tib.* 34.2, *Calig.* 42). Augustine (*De civ. D.* 4.16) says Strenia was a goddess who made one *strenuus*, but she must have had a more extensive province. Roscher (2.227 [R. Peter]) lists her among the Indigites. If the sacellum and the lucus were identical or adjacent, as seems probable, the shrine may still have been of very small physical extent.

Sub Novis: see **Tabernae Circum Forum.**

Sub Veteribus: see **Tabernae Circum Forum.**

Subager: see **Campus Viminalis.**

Subura (1): an area below the Murus Terreus (q.v.) of the Carinae (Varro, *Ling.* 5.48) and possibly the whole valley between the Oppius and the Caelian. It gave its name to one of the four urban tribes, the Suburana, so it must have been of some importance in the early city and relatively populous at that time. Antiquarians connected the name of the tribe with the Pagus Succusanus, but this was probably because the name of the tribe was abbreviated SVC. The abbreviation seems to have been simply a convention, like COS, because SVB would be apt to be mistaken for the preposition. The Pagus Succusanus (q.v.) seems to have been a village (or a military outpost) of uncertain location, but beyond the limits of the ancient city. Because it is said to have come to the aid of the residents on the Esquiline whenever the Gabines threatened (Verrius Flaccus *ap. Fest.* 402L), we are encouraged to put it in the neighborhood of the Amphitheatrum Castrense and Sessorium, but there is no proof. For the emendation of Subura to Suc(c)usa there are no grounds at all. This designation seems to have fallen into desuetude before the ascendancy of Subura (2).

TAPA 108 (1978): 147–54 (J. P. Poe); *OpRom* 15 (1985): 55–65 (H. Erkell); *Eranos* 85 (1987): 115–22 (Å. Fridh).

Subura (2): the valley between the southern end of the Viminal and the western slope of the Esquiline, and perhaps also, or especially, the artery through it connected to the Forum Romanum by the Argiletum, regarded as the heart of Rome (cf. Martial 12.21.5). Between the Oppius and the Cispian this artery ran east as the Clivus Suburanus to the Porta Esquilina (Arcus Gallieni). For Martial early in his career (1.2.7–8, 1.3.1, 1.117.8–11, 2.17), the Argiletum

still existed, despite the construction of the Forum Nervae (Transitorium), but he is the last to mention it. Presumably the part of it that was not absorbed into the Forum Nervae, perhaps the stretch west of its juncture with the Vicus Cuprius, was small and soon identified with the Subura. Ancient explanations of the name Subura are clearly fanciful, if not preposterous, and we have no knowledge of its true derivation.

This was one of the most populous and active districts of Rome, busy, noisy, dirty, and wet (Juvenal 11.51; Martial 5.22.5–9, 12.18.2). Every sort of provisioning and small artisan's workshop seems to have found a place here (Martial 7.31, 9.37, 10.94.5–6; Juvenal 11.141; *CIL* 6.1953, 9284 = *ILS* 7547, 9399, 9491 = *ILS* 7556, 9526 = *ILS* 7565, 33862). It was well provided with brothels (Persius 5.32; Martial 2.17, 6.66.1–2, 11.61.3, 11.78.11; *Priapea* 40.1). It was also the location of the houses of many important men, notably Julius Caesar (Suetonius, *Iul.* 46; cf. Martial 12.3.9–10, 12.21.5). There was also a synagogue here (*NSc* 1920, 147–51 [R. Paribeni]; *BullCom* 50 [1922]: 209–12 [B. Manna]).

For Martial (2.17.1) there were *primae fauces Suburae*, and in medieval times there was a *caput Suburae* (S. Lucia in Orfea, in Silice, was also *in capite Suburae;* see HCh 306, 595). The latter might refer to the head of the valley; the former might refer to the main street through the valley, which seems sometimes to have been divided into a Subura Maior (*CIL* 6.9526 = *ILS* 7565) and a Subura Minor. These might be the valley between the Oppius and Viminal (Maior) and the valley between the Oppius and Cispian (Minor). See Lanciani, LFUR sheet 22.

Suc(c)usa: see **Subura** (1) and **Pagus Succusanus.**

Suggestus: see **Rostra, Suggestus, Tribunal.**

Summanus, Aedes (**Templum,** Ovid): a temple *ad Circum Maximum* built during the war with Pyrrhus (Ovid, *Fast.* 6.731–32), possibly put on the Aventine slope beyond the pomerium because of the nature of the divinity, whose province was the night lightning (Vitruvius 1.7.1). It was very probably built because the terracotta statue of Summanus in the pediment of the Temple of Iuppiter Optimus Maximus Capitolinus was struck by lightning and its head thrown into the Tiber (Cicero, *Div.* 1.16; Livy, *Epit.* 14). The Temple of Summanus was also struck by lightning in 197 B.C. (Livy 32.29.1). The day of dedication was 20 June (Ovid, *Fast.* 6.731–32; Fast. Esquil., Venus., Amit.; Degrassi 472). It may have been still standing in the fourth century and by misunderstanding of the name have been listed in the regionary catalogues as a Temple of Dis Pater (see Dis Pater, Aedes). No remains of it are known.

Summum Choragium: the storehouse for machinery, costumes, and apparatus for public shows and spectacles (Paulus *ex Fest.* 45L: *choragium, instrumentum scaenarum;* cf. Plautus, *Capt.* 61). It is listed by the regionary catalogues in Regio III and, thanks to the find of an inscribed altar (*CIL* 6.776 = *ILS* 3727; cf. 30829), located between the Baths of Trajan and the church of S. Clemente. A fragment of the Marble Plan originally showed a VICUS] SUMMI CH[ORAGI, a street flanked on one side by a colonnaded courtyard surrounded by rooms turned inward and on the other by an arcade lined with rooms also turned away from the street (*FUR* pls. 10.1 and 15.3; Rodriguez pl. 1.3). Neither looks very appropriate for the Summum Choragium. This vicus was presumably a spur of the Via Labicana leading up toward the Oppius, but everything connected with the Summum Choragium is fraught with problems. It ought to have been an important building, because there are numerous inscriptions attesting to the importance of the operation and its administration, especially the procurator (*CIL* 6.297 = *ILS* 1767, 8950 = *ILS* 1771, 10083 = *ILS* 1768, 10084, 10085 = *ILS* 1770, 10086 = *ILS* 1769, 10087). These inscriptions show that imperial freedmen and slaves ran it. Apollodorus of Damascus is said to have criticized the plans for the Temple of Venus et Roma on the grounds that Hadrian should have set it in a higher position and lifted it up on vaults, so that its base might be used for the storage and construction of machines for the amphitheater, which having been built in secret could then be produced to the great astonishment of the crowd (Cass. Dio 69.4.4). It does not follow that the Summum Choragium did not exist before the time of Hadrian; it surely must have been necessary as soon as the Colosseum was dedicated, if not considerably earlier. So perhaps we may take Apollodorus's criticism as evidence that it stood farther from the Colosseum than the Temple of Venus et Roma did. A position north of Via Labicana under the lee of the Baths of Trajan is indicated.

Syracusae et Technyphion: a secluded place in an upper storey of the house of Augustus to which he was accustomed to withdraw when he had work that he wished to pursue in private or without interruption (Suetonius, *Aug.* 72.2). This he called *Syracusae et technyphion.* The second term means "little workshop," and the first probably refers to the isolation of the island of Ortygia, which made it easy to defend. This was a private joke, not a toponym.

Tabernae Argentariae: see **Tabernae Circum Forum.**

Tabernae Circum Forum: at first the shops built around the periphery of the open square of the Forum Romanum, when it became a marketplace, ascribed by tradition to Tarquinius Priscus. These were apparently thought of as built in rows of units of more or less uniform size fronting on porticoes that sheltered the shoppers (Livy 1.35.10; Dion. Hal. 3.67.4). They were on public ground and belonged to the state, but could be leased (*Dig.* 18.1.32 [Ulpian]). At first they housed merchants of any sort, apparently especially butchers, and came to be called *tabernae lanienae,* but before 310 B.C. the butchers had been confined to the southwest side and its vicinity, while the northeast side was taken over largely by bankers and brokers (Varro *ap. Non.* 853L; Livy 9.40.16). In 310 gilded shields were distributed among the *domini argentariorum* to ornament their shops during a triumph. In 210 the shops known as the Septem and the Argentariae burned (Livy 26.27.2). The next year the Septem were rebuilt as the Quinque (Livy 27.11.16). The Argentariae were eventually replaced by the Novae, which were apparently also occasionally called Plebeiae, having been built by the plebeian aediles M. Iunius Brutus and L. Oppius Salinator in 193 B.C. (Festus 258L; cf. Broughton, *MRR* 1.347). Usually they are called Argentariae Novae (Livy 40.51.5) or Novae (Livy 3.48.5). The earliest reference to Veteres is in Plautus (*Curc.* 480), and thereafter *Novae* or *sub Novis* (Varro, *Ling.* 6.59; Cicero, *De Or.* 2.266) came to be regularly used to designate the northeast side of the forum in front of the Basilica Fulvia et Aemilia (cf. Livy 3.48.5, 40.51.5), and *Veteres* or *sub Veteribus* to designate the southwest side between the Cloaca and the Vicus Iugarius (Livy 44.16.10; Cicero, *Acad.* 2.70; Pliny, *HN* 35.25 and 113). Although the con-struction of the Macellum antedates the fire of 210 (Livy 27.11.16), some of the shops on the southwest side of the forum were still called *lanienae* in 169. The Veteres survived as late as the time of Cicero (*Acad.* 2.70), but in the construction of the Basilica Iulia their removal to a place on the southwest side of that building effactually eliminated them as a separate entity. The Novae continued to exist in front of the Basilica Paulli, but so splendidly transformed by the portico in front of them as to be hardly recognizable.

The Tabernae Septem that burned in 210 and were rebuilt the following year as Tabernae Quinque are distinguished by Livy from the Tabernae Novae. What burned in the fire of 210 was the northeast side of the forum from the Lautumiae (q.v.) on the slope of the Capitoline to the Atrium Regium (= Regia?), the Temple of Vesta barely escaping (Livy 26.27.1–5), and the area to the northeast, including the Forum Piscarium. No mention is made of the Comitium and Curia, which clearly escaped. We can locate the Tabernae Septem on one of the streets leading into the forum, the Argiletum and Corneta, at the east end of the forum, or as a continuation of the Argentariae northwest of the Cloaca, but separated from them by it. Because they were the first to be rebuilt, they must have had considerable importance. Lugli (Lugli 1946, 74–75) would put them along the southeast side of the Argiletum along the flank of the Basilica Fulvia et Aemilia, but Carettoni's excavation of the basilica (*NSc* 1948, 111–28) shows insufficient room for them between the northwest columns of the basilica and the street, and they must have survived until late republican times. It seems more likely that they continued the line of the Argentariae.

Above the tabernae were cantilevered galleries from which spectators could view the ceremonies and games staged in the forum. These were called *maeniana* after a certain Maenius, who is credited

T

with having built the first one (Festus 120L). This is unlikely to be C. Maenius, the victorious consul of the Battle of Antium in 338 B.C., because such sophisticated engineering seems unlikely to have been understood in the fourth century, or indeed before the second. However, maeniana became a standard feature of Italian towns (Vitruvius 5.1.2; Isidore, *Orig.* 15.3.11) and were regarded as one of the amenities for those seeking shelter from the summer sun, as well as for spectators (Cicero, *Acad.* 2.70). Pliny (*HN* 35.113) quotes Varro about a painting by Serapio, an artist famous for his stage designs, that covered *omnia maeniana* on the southwest side of the Forum Romanum. We should probably think of this as a long panorama on the façade of the building behind the maeniana proper (a second storey of shops, perhaps?).

Tabernae Decem: see **Decem Tabernae.**

Tabernae Quinque, Septem: see **Tabernae Circum Forum.**

Tabula Sestia (Sextia): a place in, or near, the Forum Romanum where litigants and their supporters gathered to settle debts owing from the termination of partnerships (Cicero, *Quinct.* 25), therefore either the tribunal of the praetor urbanus in the Comitium or an office of the praetor urbanus where the preliminaries to a trial were handled. Because a large part of the Licinio-Sextian laws of the fourth century dealt with debt and its regulation, it may be that a *tabula* with their provisions was an important part of the Edictum Perpetuum of the praetor and regularly consulted, and that this is what is meant. However, it cannot be excluded that the tabula in question was a picture, because we know that there were pictures on display in the forum, in which case it is likely to have been displayed on the façade of the Curia behind the tribunal of the praetor urbanus and to have shown the exploits of a Sextius, possibly L. Sextius Calvinus, founder of Aquae Sextiae in 122 B.C. (so Pocock on Cicero, *In Vatin.* 180–82). But if a picture is meant, it must have hung on the Curia a comparatively short time, only in the years around 81, when Cicero delivered the *Pro Quinctio,* and it is impossible to find a suitable Sextius or Sestius with whom to connect it.

Tabula Valeria: a picture representing the battle in which M'. Valerius Maximus Messala defeated the Carthaginians and Hiero, which was hung on the flank of the Curia Hostilia in 264 B.C. (Pliny, *HN* 35.22). This was the first such picture to be displayed in Rome. It is twice mentioned in Cicero, once in a letter to Terentia during his exile in 58 (*Fam.* 14.2.2) in which he laments that she has been subjected to the humiliation of being escorted from the Temple of Vesta to the Tabula Valeria, and once in his attack on Vatinius (*In Vatin.* 21) when he uses it as a metaphor for the headquarters of the tribuni plebis. Plutarch (*Cato Min.* 5.1) tells us that the tribunes were accustomed to transact their business in the Basilica Porcia. Because the Basilica Porcia (q.v.) stood just west of the Curia Hostilia and was evidently a comparatively small building, we may presume either that when it was built the Tabula Valeria was moved into it, because otherwise it would have been to all intents and purposes hidden by the new building, or that Plutarch means that the tribunes had their headquarters adjacent to the basilica, in an ell, as it were, between the two buildings. Plutarch (*Cato Min.* 5.1) says that they wanted to move, or remove, one of the pillars of the basilica that they regarded as in the way of their seats and that Cato prevented them from doing this. This is not apt to have been one of the central supports of the nave, as those could not have been tampered with without jeopardizing the stability of the building, so it was probably one of the pillars of an outer aisle. One can imagine a tribunal fitted into a forward corner here, where the tribunes could enjoy access to both the Curia and the basilica, the two having their major axes perpendicular to each other.

Tabularium (Fig. 19): the record office in which were filed the official archives of Rome, built, as the inscription (*CIL* 1².736, 737 = 6.1313, 1314 = *ILS* 35, 35a; *ILLRP* 367, 368) informs us, by Q. Lutatius Catulus in his consulship in 78 B.C. The architect seems to have been an unknown Lucius Cornelius (*RendLinc.* ser. 8.26 [1971]: 41–49 [G. Molisani]). It was restored by Claudius in A.D. 46 (*CIL* 6.916 = 31201), and though it is not mentioned in our literary sources, to it were affixed military diplomata (*CIL* 16.35, 159; *AE* 1974.655). It consists of a number of distinct parts but served especially to provide a dramatic backdrop to the northwest end of the Forum Romanum, having a substructure of Gabine stone (*sperone*) that runs across the saddle between the two crests of the Capitoline from the Clivus Capitolinus to the Gradus Monetae and rises in a solid mass with perceptible batter, broken only by small windows, from the slope of the hill behind the Temple of Concordia to the floor of the saddle. Above this an arcade framed in a Doric engaged order connected the two heights of the Capitoline with a corridor 5 m wide and twice as high, which provided a place from which to view the activity of the forum. A second storey above this has been generally assumed, although very few fragments of its architecture survive, and those that exist seem to be Flavian in date. Some have even suggested a third storey, which would make it not unlike the earliest theaters with freestanding cavea. The façade on the opposite side has completely disappeared, while those of the short ends continued the architectural forms of the forum front. In plan it is essentially trapezoidal, with a piece taken out of the western corner to accommodate the Temple of Vediovis.

The interior is very complicated. A long narrow stair of sixty-six steps carried foot traffic from the forum to the Capitoline saddle directly, in a single flight, without communicating with any other part of the complex in its lower levels. In continuation of this a second flight beside it seems to have communicated with the second storey of arcading on the forum side. It is roofed with a barrel vault in a series of steps, rather than a ramp, a point of great architectural interest. The lowest storey of chambers is reached by a similarly narrow stair down from the northeast, but this is in part ramped and roofed with a ramped segmental vault. It leads to a long corridor parallel to the forum front and backed by the rock of the hill, off which open six small chambers, each lit by a single small window. These are presumed to have been the archives proper or, better, a small part thereof. Three larger chambers communicating with one another in sequence on the floor above along the northeast side seem to be other archives.

The arcaded walk is another completely independent part. It has a few small exedras opening behind it for the convenience of people who might like to loiter and converse, but it is especially simply a walk, divided into lofty bays. Behind it was abundant space for more archives, but of the development of this we know virtually nothing. Strangely enough, our literary sources do not mention the Tabularium.

The construction throughout is concrete faced with opus quadratum of Gabine stone on the exterior and Anio tufa on the interior. Travertine is introduced decoratively and at points needing extra strength. There is some rustication of the base. Segmental vaults and flat arches are used tentatively.

The building was used as a storehouse for salt, and as a result the inner walls have suffered severely from erosion. Under Pope Boniface IX, the existing tower and buttresses were added to the southwest side (ca. 1400); under Pope Martin V, the tower at the north corner (ca. 1427); and under Pope Nicholas V, the tower at the east corner (1453). In the middle of the sixteenth century Michelangelo destroyed the upper parts and built the present Palazzo del Senatore on the ancient foundations.

Jordan 1.2.135–54; Delbrück, *Hellenistische Bauten*, 1.23–46; Lugli 1946, 42–46; Nash 2.402–8.

Tarentum: a place in the Campus Martius (*in extremo Campo Martio*, Festus 440L) close to the Tiber, where a small volcanic fissure formerly emitted vapor. The story is told of a Sabine, Valesius, whose servants discovered here, 20 feet below the surface, an altar inscribed to Dis and Proserpina (Val. Max. 2.4.5; Festus 478–79L; cf. Ovid, *Fast.* 1.501). This led to the belief that it was a point of communication with the underworld. It is usually mentioned only in connection with the Ludi Saeculares, when sacrifices of dark victims were made to Dis and Proserpina (Censorinus 17.8; Livy, *Epit.* 49; Martial 4.1.8, 10.63.3; Statius, *Silv.* 1.4.18, 4.1.38; Ausonius 16.34).

Certain coins of Domitian that commemorate the celebration of the Ludi Saeculares (Mazzini pl. 88 nos. 91–92; *AnalRom.* suppl. 10 [1983]: 48 figs. 1–4) show a libation poured on an altar in front of a building of curious architecture, seeming to consist of twin colonnaded loggias surmounted by triangular pediments above an open, but featureless, lower storey. These are joined by an arch, possibly to be read as appearing at a greater distance, but it seems not unlikely that this represents a scaenae frons. A bearded recumbent figure in the left foreground probably represents the Tiber. Fragments of inscriptions recording celebrations of the Ludi Saeculares from the time of Augustus to that of Septimius Severus place the Tarentum in a paved square on the riverbank just northeast of Corso Vittorio Emanuele.

The usual form of the name is Tarentum, but Terentum also occurs, sometimes with a rationalizing etymology (Festus 479L; Servius *ad Aen.* 8.63). No satisfactory explanation of the name is known. Valerius Maximus (2.4.5) says that, after three days of games celebrated for the recovery of his children from a sickness, Valesius reburied the altar, and reburial is implicit in some of the explanations of the name offered (cf., e.g., Ursinus's supplements of Festus 478L).

QITA 5 (1968): 33–37 (F. Coarelli); La Rocca 1984, 3–55; *AnalRom.* suppl. 10 (1983): 47–57 (S. Quilici Gigli).

Tarpeia, Arx: a name found in Augustan poetry (Vergil, *Aen.* 8.652; Propertius 4.4.29) for the fortified summit of the Capitoline; cf. Tarpeius, Mons.

Tarpeia Rupes: From the precipitous cliffs of the Capitoline, criminals convicted of capital crimes were thrown to their death (A. Gellius 20.1.53; Seneca, *Controv.* 1.3 passim; Livy 6.20.12; Festus 458L;

Tacitus, *Ann.* 6.19; [Aur. Vict.,] *De Vir. Ill.* 24.6, 66.8). There has been a great deal of dispute as to precisely where this point, called the Tarpeia Rupes or Tarpeium Saxum, was, our sources being somewhat vague and contradictory, but Livy's story of Manlius Capitolinus and his execution by the tribunes on the very spot where he had won his greatest glory (Livy 6.20.12) makes it clear that he believed this was the cliff above the shrine of Carmenta (cf. Livy 5.47.1–5), which would put it at the southwest corner of the hill. The Saxum itself should then be a particular outcrop of rock and lie outside the Area Capitolina. However, the term *Rupes Tarpeia* (although Varro, *Ling.* 5.41, explains that the Tarpeium Saxum is, in fact, a *rupes*) is elsewhere reserved for the Area Capitolina, especially as the precinct of Iuppiter Optimus Maximus (Livy 6.17.4; Propertius 4.1.7; Lucan 3.154; Silius Italicus 3.623, 10.360; Tacitus, *Hist.* 3.71; Claudian, *Panegyr. de sext. cons. Hon.* 45; Firm. Mater. 1.10.14). Attempts to put the Saxum on the northeast crest of the hill, where it would be in full view of the Forum Romanum and in close conjunction with the Carcer and Scalae Gemoniae, seem mistaken. They are based on such evidence as Dion. Hal. 7.35.4 and 8.78.5, which are ambiguous, and the Gradus Monetae, the predecessors of the Scalae Gemoniae, are never mentioned in connection with the exposure of corpses, so they cannot be used as supporting evidence.

Tarpeius, Mons: the early name of the Capitoline, according to Varro (*Ling.* 5.41), named for the Vestal Virgin Tarpeia, who was killed by being crushed under the shields of the Sabine army and buried there (Propertius 4.4.93; Dion. Hal. 3.69.4; Plutarch, *Rom.* 18.1). It was commonly used as an alternate name for the whole hill, even after the name Capitolinus came into general use, perhaps because, strictly speaking, the Capitoline was only a part thereof (Livy 1.55.1; Dion. Hal. 4.60.3–61.1, 7.35.4; Suetonius, *Iul.* 44.1; Plutarch, *Numa* 7.2; Cass. Dio 2 [Zonaras 7.11.5]; [Aur. Vict.,] *De Vir. Ill.* 2.7; *Not.* addenda s.v. "Montes").

The tradition that the Capitoline was originally called Mons Tarpeius is probably correct, although the story of Tarpeia and her betrayal of the citadel seems a patent aetiological invention. Like so many of the hills of Rome, it took its name from a family, the Gens Tarpeia, some member or members of which must have had an important claim to it. The notion that the Capitoline height was originally called Saturnius Mons (see Capitolinus Mons) is not a contradiction of this, nor an obstacle, as the summit of the hill could, and evidently did, accommodate a number of sacred precincts by the time Tarquinius Priscus decided to build the Temple of

Iuppiter Optimus Maximus there. The name Mons Tarpeius persisted late, and in learned circles it was probably regarded as the correct designation of the hill as a whole (Propertius 4.4.93–94; *CIL* 6.37170 = *ILS* 4438; regionary catalogues, addenda s.v. "Montes"). The notion that it was used only of the southwestern crest is clearly wrong.

Lugli 1946, 18–19; Nash 2.409–10.

Tascogenses: those living in an area otherwise unknown listed in the edict of Tarracius Bassus of the late fourth century (*CIL* 6.31893 b5 = *ILS* 6072).

De Teglatu: an unknown locality listed in two inscriptions of the fourth century, one of them the edict of Tarracius Bassus (*CIL* 6.31893 b2 = *ILS* 6072; *CIL* 6.10099 = 31899), presumed to be a place where tiles were manufactured or sold.

Tellurenses: those living in the vicinity of the Temple of Tellus on the Carinae, listed in the late fourth century edict of Tarracius Bassus (*CIL* 6.31893 c11).

Tellus, Aedes: a temple vowed by P. Sempronius Sophus during a battle with the Picenes in 268 B.C., when there was an earthquake (Florus 1.14.2), and presumably built by him. But others (Val. Max. 6.3.1b; Dion. Hal. 8.79.3) say that the Roman people built it. It was on the Carinae (Suetonius, *De Gramm.* 15; Servius *ad Aen.* 8.361) on a part of the land of Sp. Cassius, who was condemned of aspiring to monarchy and put to death in 485 B.C., after which his house was pulled down (Cicero, *Dom.* 101; Livy 2.41.11; Dion. Hal. 8.79.3; Val. Max. 6.3.1b). It is hard to believe that a large plot in an excellent location would have been deliberately left vacant for more than two centuries, and therefore tempting to suppose that Sophus's work was rather a rebuilding of a temple that had already been in existence for some time. The temple was near the Domus Rostrata of Pompey, which Caesar gave to Antony after Pompey's death (Suetonius, *De Gramm.* 15; Appian, *BellCiv* 2.126), and near the house of Quintus Cicero, inherited from his father, where he and his brother Marcus had grown up (Plutarch, *Cic.* 8.3; Cicero, *QFr.* 2.3.7). The proximity of Cicero's house to the temple was such that Marcus Cicero was able to claim that there were Romans who asserted that he had responsibility for the safeguarding of it (*Har. Resp.* 31). The day of dedication was 13 December, at which time there was a lectisternium, the only annual one recorded in the fasti (Degrassi 537–38).

There were many interesting features to this temple. On its wall was a map, or allegorical representation, of Italy (Varro, *Rust.* 1.2.1). In it was a *magmentarium,* a reliquary of some sort regarded as both an object of great sanctity and possibly an *objet d'art.* This was removed and displayed in the house of Appius Claudius, perhaps as a lararium (Cicero, *Har. Resp.* 31, *Fam.* 8.12.3; cf. Varro, *Ling.* 5.112). On the day following the assassination of Julius Caesar, the senate was summoned to this temple by Antony, probably because of its proximity to his house and its distance from the conspirators encamped on the Capitoline, and held a meeting there (Cicero, *Phil.* 1.31, *Att.* 16.14.1; Appian, *BellCiv* 2.126; Plutarch, *Brut.* 19.1; Cass. Dio 44.22.3). So far as we know, this was the only occasion when the senate ever met there. In front of the temple was a statue of Ceres paid for from the property of Sp. Cassius (Pliny, *HN* 34.15) and another of Cassius himself that the censors ordered melted down (Pliny, *HN* 34.30). The contradictions and difficulties implicit in the latter statement lead one to suppose that the temple must have been very old. Later Cicero saw to the dedication of a statue on behalf of his brother Quintus there (Cicero, *QFr.* 3.1.14).

The site of the tribunalia and scrinia of the praefectus urbi was the Secretarium Tellurense, and several Christian sources speak of trials at a vicus in Tellude, or Tellure, and of a *forum ante templum.* The buildings of the praefecture must have bordered on the precinct of the Temple of Tellus, lying between it and the Baths of Trajan, but the temple itself was not absorbed into the complex (A. Chastagnol, *La Préfecture urbaine à Rome sous le bas-empire* [Paris 1960], 247–51).

QITA 10 (1988): 110–12 (F. Castagnoli).

Tempestates, Aedes: a temple vowed by L. Cornelius Scipio when caught in a storm off Corsica in 259 B.C. (*CIL* 1².9 = 6.12897 = *ILS* 3; *ILLRP* 310; Ovid, *Fast.* 6.193–94), listed in the *Notitia* in Regio I, perhaps not far from the tomb of the Scipios (see Sep. Scipionum). The day of dedication is given by Ovid as 1 June, but by the Fasti Antiates Maiores as 23 December. Because of the irregular order of the Fasti Antiates, Degrassi (463) accepts the former and thinks the latter refers to a restoration.

Tempio di Siepe: an octagonal building roofed with a dome, the northern half of which existed on the north side of Piazza Capranica in the Campus Martius down to the seventeenth century and was drawn by Alò Giovannoli. Its function is uncertain, as is its date of construction. The octagon had massive columns, monoliths of cipollino, at the corners, and between these opened arched niches, alternately deep and rounded and shallow and flat, except for that on the north, which was an elongated throat

terminating in an apse. The columns were surmounted by an exaggeratedly deep entablature broken out over them individually, above which rose the dome constructed in concave sections, springing from pendentive points over the columns between semicircular lunettes and rising to a collared oculus. As shown by Giovannoli, the dome was at least in part concealed under a gable roof supported on extensions of the octagon walls. However, bull's-eye windows in alternate sections of the dome must originally have been functional, so probably the gable was a later addition. The architecture is strongly reminiscent of that of the "Tempio di Minerva Medica" (see Nymphaeum) and the Tor de'Schiavi, and this suggests a date around the middle of the third century or later. It has been suggested that this might have been either a nymphaeum or a tomb, but neither seems very likely in this location at this date. The area is dominated by monuments of Hadrian and the Antonine emperors. It might have been a late annex to the Basilica of Matidia and Marciana (see Basilica Matidiae et Marcianae).

Lugli 1938, 231–33.

Templum: see **Aedes, Aedicula, Templum,** etc.

Tensarium: see **Aedes Tensarum.**

Terbentinum (or **Tiburtinum**) **Neronis:** mentioned only in the *Mirabilia* (Jordan 2.627; VZ 3.45–46) and located close to the Meta Romuli, mentioned after it and before the Mausoleum Hadriani. It was round, in two storeys, sheathed in splendid stone (marble?), and originally supposed to have been as high as the Mausoleum Hadriani. Evidently this was a tomb, but it seems to have disappeared completely. Its stone was used in the paving of the Paradise and steps of the basilica of S. Pietro. The origin of the name is mysterious; it has been suggested to be a corruption of Terebinthus, but that scarcely improves matters.

CAR 1-H, 20 p. 72.

Terminus, Fanum: a stone in the Cella Iovis of the Temple of Iuppiter Optimus Maximus Capitolinus near the cult statue, regarded as a shrine of Terminus, probably an ancient boundary stone (Dion. Hal. 3.69.4–5; Servius *ad Aen.* 9.446). Above it was an opening in the roof of the temple, a *foramen,* with the explanation that Terminus must be able to see the heavens, or must not be covered (Festus 505L; Ovid, *Fast.* 2.671–72; Servius *ad Aen.* 9.446). It was recounted that when the Capitoline temple came to be built, the augurs conducted ceremonies of exauguration for the various divinities already occupying the area, all of whom accepted the terms of resettlement, except Terminus, who could then not be dis-possessed. However, this was taken as a good omen, assuring the permanence of the cult and of Rome (Cato *ap. Fest.* 160L; Livy 1.55.3–4; Ovid, *Fast.* 2.667–76; Dion. Hal. 3.69.4–5). Later Iuventas was added as another divinity who refused exauguration (Livy 5.54.7; Dion. Hal. 3.69.4–5; Florus 1.1.7.8), and later still Mars (Augustine, *De civ. D.* 4.23). Probably Numa's curse on anyone who moved a boundary stone had something to do with the origi-nal decision to respect the location of Terminus (Fes-tus 505L), and a similar injunction against conceal-ing a boundary stone was responsible for the foramen.

Terra Mater: a shrine attested in three inscriptions (*CIL* 6.770–72; cf. 30828; *ILS* 1522). Two of these were found in the vineyards behind the church of S. Cesareo and indicate a location to the southeast of the Baths of Caracalla. Nothing further is known about the shrine.

Testaceus Mons (Fig. 14): Monte Testaccio, the modern name given to the irregularly pear-shaped mound of broken potsherds just inside the Aurelian Walls southwest of the Aventine and behind the Em-porium and the horrea along the river in Regio XIII. It is about 35 m high, 850 m in circumference, and composed entirely of sherds of the storage and ship-ping jars in which most products, especially food-stuffs, came to Rome. Many were stamped by the manufacturers on the handle or the neck; others are inscribed with scratched and painted inscriptions; and these provide a rich documentation of the sources from which Rome was supplied, the com-merce, and the quantities. Commodities tended to be shipped in jars of characteristic shapes (wine, oil, grain, fruit), often with local variations reflecting their origin. A corpus of the stamps has been com-piled (*CIL* 15 pp. 491–657) with supplements ap-pearing from time to time. The stamps date from A.D. 140 to 251, but dumping here is as early as Au-gustus, and at different periods particular zones were used. Under the east slope of the mound was found the Sepulcrum Rusticeliorum (q.v.).

Nash 2.411–13; E. Rodriguez Almeida, *Il Monte Testaccio* (Rome 1984).

Theatrum: A form of building for assemblies and the presentation of spectacles borrowed from the Greeks and then adapted and improved to meet the exigencies of Roman entertainments and the Roman terrain. At first plays were given on simple stages run up for the occasion, and the spectators stood in a crowd before these. This, one gathers, must have been the way the Etruscan dancers were presented when their art was first introduced in Rome (Livy 7.2.3–7) and the way Atellan farces were tradition-ally performed. But since all drama was a form of religious observance, it must soon have become customary to build the stage in front of the temple steps and use these to permit the spectators to get a better view of the proceedings. The steps in front of the Temple of the Magna Mater seem to have been designed with this in mind; the Megalensia included ludi scaenici from the time of their insti-tution.

With the increasing popularity of drama and the multiplication of occasions allowing for ludi scaeni-ci, those responsible for putting on plays built ever finer theaters, but at first these were always dis-mantled at the end of a set of games, and the senate was so alarmed when the censors of 151 B.C. under-took to build a permanent theater that on motion of P. Cornelius Nasica they decreed not only that the theater should be dismantled, but that the Roman people must watch their plays standing, lest they de-cline into Greek effeminacy (Livy, *Epit.* 48; Val. Max. 2.4.1–2; Tacitus, *Ann.* 14.20). This stricture cannot have lasted very long, however, for we begin hearing of the sumptuousness of theater construction by the time of L. Licinius Crassus, the orator, who as aedile, sometime before 100 B.C., brought col-umns of Hymettus marble to adorn the theater that he built, and by the time of Aemilius Scaurus's ae-dileship in 58 B.C. not only was his theater of extrav-agant luxury and rich adornment, but there was no question of dismantling it, and it stood for a number of years.

Once the prohibition on a permanent theater had been breached, the way was clear for Pompey to build his theater of 55–52 B.C., one of the greatest of all Roman buildings, said to have been patterned on the theater of Mitylene on Lesbos, although archae-ological excavation has been unable to find any real similarity, for Pompey's was a true Roman theater with a cavea of a perfect half-circle and built up from the plain of the Campus Martius in storeys, while the theater of Mitylene was cut into the slope of a hill with a cavea of more than a half-circle. But in some sense Pompey's theater set the pattern that all subse-quent Roman theaters followed. Pompey was fol-lowed by Julius Caesar, who began work on the the-ater that was to become the Theater of Marcellus, dedicated in 13 B.C. but used already for the Ludi Saeculares in 17. And Caesar was followed by Bal-bus, whose theater was also dedicated in 13. This rapid succession, after which no further theater was built until Domitian built the Odeum more than a century later, suggests that each was to serve for a different range of spectacles, but on this point our information is entirely inadequate.

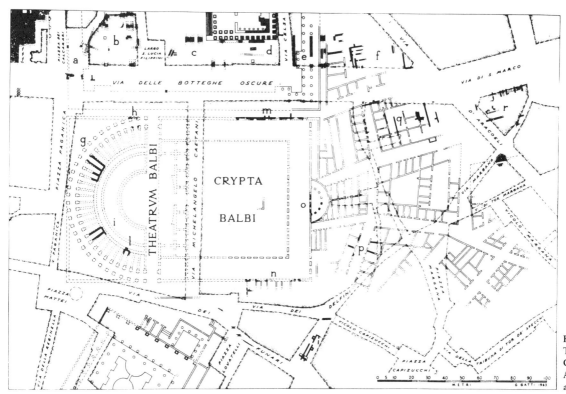

Theatra Curionis: two large theaters of wood built by C. Scribonius Curio, the tribune of 50 B.C., close together, each revolving on a pivot, so that in the morning they were turned back to back so that the plays performed should not produce confusion, and in the afternoon the caveae were wheeled about and brought together to make an amphitheater in which gladiatorial combats were exhibited. Pliny (*HN* 36.117–20) says that after a few days some of the spectators even remained seated while the caveae revolved, a nonchalance he regarded as foolhardy. On the final day of the games, when the pivots were worn and unreliable, Curio kept the caveae in amphitheatral position but had stages back to back across the middle of the arena on which there were athletic exhibitions. Then these stages were withdrawn to either side, and the gladiators victorious in the earlier combats were brought on (Pliny, *HN* 36.117–20). Because the original games were offered as funeral games for Curio's father in 53 B.C., the theaters were probably built in the Campus Martius, but one cannot be more precise. They were still standing in June 51 B.C. (Cicero, *Fam.* 8.2.1).

Theatrum Balbi (Fig. 80): the stone theater built by the Spanish-born L. Cornelius Balbus the Younger, following his triumph over the Garamantes when he was proconsul of Africa in 19 B.C. It was

dedicated in 13 (Suetonius, *Aug.* 29.5; Cass. Dio 54.25.2) with lavish games; four columns of onyx of only moderate size used in its decoration were regarded as especially sensational at the time (Pliny, *HN* 36.60). It was damaged in the fire of Titus in A.D. 80 (Cass. Dio 66.24) and restored, probably by Domitian. It is listed in the regionary catalogues in Regio IX, where it is said to have 11,510 loca, calculated to be space for about 7,700 spectators, the smallest of the three stone theaters of Rome.

Gatti's discovery of the true location of the Circus Flaminius between the Tiber and the Porticus Octaviae led to the identification of the remains beneath Palazzo Mattei di Paganica and nearby buildings along the Via delle Botteghe Oscure, long thought to belong to the seating in the sphendone of the Circus Flaminius, as belonging to the Theatrum Balbi. This was then confirmed by moving the fragments of the Marble Plan bearing the inscription THEATRUM BALBI to a new location in this vicinity and by the discovery that they fit perfectly with their surroundings. The theater lay just south of the Porticus Minucia (Minicia), between it and the Aedes Herculis Musarum, oriented east/west. It was built of concrete faced with reticulate, except on the exterior, where the construction is in large blocks of travertine, but the design is otherwise unknown. Immediately to the east of it was a large square with arcades,

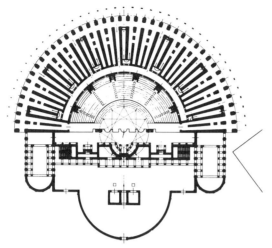

Figure 81
Theatrum Marcelli,
Restored Plan

or windowed walks, on three sides, presumed to be the Crypta Balbi mentioned separately in the regionary catalogues. At the center of its east side opens a curved exedra shown on the Marble Plan with a colonnade of six columns following the curve. The southern half of this still appears, used as the foundation of a garden front in a modern palazzo. Here the construction is of brick-faced concrete with arched and flat-arched windows, probably of Domitianic date. Soundings carried out in 1961–1962 confirmed the correctness of Gatti's identification and reasoning.

Nash 2.414–17; *MEFRA* 91 (1979): 1.237–313 (G. Gatti); D. Manacorda, *Il progetto della Crypta Balbi* (Florence 1982), 14–44; *JdI* 99 (1984): 215–55 (M. Fuchs); *CEFR* 98 (1987): 597–610 (D. Manacorda).

Theatrum Marcelli (Figs. 17, 81): a stone theater, the second to be built in Rome, coming almost immediately after the Theater of Pompey, begun by Julius Caesar, who cleared the area for its construction at the expense of the Temple of Pietas (see Pietas, Aedes), for which he was criticized, and numerous other shrines and buildings. It was believed he burned the statue of Pietas and appropriated large hoards of money which he had found in the demolition (Cass. Dio 43.49.3). Suetonius (*Iul.* 44) speaks of the project as calling for a theater of vast size, *Tarpeio Monti accubans,* but the theater as eventually built stood free and was only a little larger than the Theater of Pompey. The regionary catalogues give its capacity as 20,500 loca, estimated to be space for about 13,000 spectators, as opposed to 17,580 loca for the Theater of Pompey.

Caesar is credited with having laid the foundations for the theater, but Augustus (*RG* 21) implies that the area Caesar had obtained was insufficient and he

was obliged to buy up considerably more land from private owners. Augustus was certainly mainly responsible for the building, which was long in construction. Whether actual building was begun before the death of Marcellus in 23 seems doubtful; certainly at his death it was taken up as a memorial to him and never carried any other name (Cass. Dio 43.49.2–3, 53.30.5–6; Pliny, *HN* 7.121; Livy, *Epit.* 140; Suetonius, *Aug.* 29.4; Plutarch, *Marcel.* 30.6). By the time of the celebration of the Ludi Saeculares in 17 B.C., it was far enough advanced to have part of the ceremonies staged there (*CIL* 6.32323.157 = *ILS* 5050), but the dedication was delayed until 13 B.C. (Cass. Dio 54.26.1) or 11 (Pliny, *HN* 8.65). For the dedication Augustus offered splendid games, including the Lusus Troiae and a venatio in the circus (Cass. Dio 53.30.6, 54.26.1; Suetonius, *Aug.* 43.5). Four marble columns of remarkable size which Scaurus had used in the decoration of the theater that he built as aedile and then used to adorn the atrium of his house on the Palatine were used in the *regia* of the new theater (Asconius *in Cic. Scaur.* 45 [Stangl 28]). Whether they flanked the *porta regia,* the central entrance of the *scaena,* as seems most likely, or rather were in one of the dependencies, has been disputed. The common name was always Theatrum Marcelli, but we also find this called Theatrum Marcellianum (Suetonius, *Vesp.* 19.1; Martial 2.29.5; *CIL* 6.33838a = *ILS* 7505).

We know next to nothing about the shows that were put on there. Vespasian restored the theater (Suetonius, *Vesp.* 19.1), and Alexander Severus is reported to have intended to restore it again (S.H.A. *Alex. Sev.* 44.7). It was used for part of the celebration of the Ludi Saeculares under Septimius Severus (*CIL* 6.32328.33). It is frequently mentioned as a place designation (cf., e.g., Ianus ad Theatrum Marcelli).

Although Avianus Symmachus robbed some stone from the theater for the repair of the Pons Cestius in A.D. 370 (*NSc* 1886, 159), the theater continued in use, and Petronius Maximus, praefectus urbi, erected statues in it in 421 (*CIL* 6.1660). The compiler of the Einsiedeln itinerary visited its ruins in the eighth century. In the twelfth century it passed into the hands of the Fabii or Faffi, was transformed into a fortress, and became known as Monte Faffo (HCh 226). It then became a possession of the important Savelli family in 1368 and is still widely known as Monte Savello. In the early sixteenth century the Savelli had the great architect Baldassare Peruzzi build a magnificent palazzo upon the ruins as foundations. In 1712 this passed to the Orsini, who continued its embellishment. However, the lower arcades, a warren of squalid shops and dwellings going back to the Middle Ages, continued to house a con-

siderable population until 1926, when the Governo-
rato undertook the isolation and restoration of the
arcades of the cavea as part of the grandiose scheme
of the Via del Mare. At that time these arcades were
found to be buried under 4 m of debris, especially
mud and sand from repeated flooding of the Tiber.
At this time exploration of the interior could be only
very limited, and the scaena and parts beyond it were
scarcely touched.

Substantial parts of the cavea appear on fragments
of the Marble Plan (*FUR* pl. 29; Rodriguez pl. 23),
showing its location between the Forum Holitorium
and the Pons Fabricius, but these are more tantalizing than informative. The substructures of the cavea
follow a pattern of radial corridors and stairs to take
spectators to their seats efficiently, with an annular
corridor on the exterior on each of the two lowest
levels and responding annular corridors at mid-
storey just behind the seating and between the *baltei*.
The lowest level of the arcading is embellished with
an engaged order with Tuscan columns and a Doric
frieze under a cornice with dentils, and the level
above this with an unfluted Ionic order. Presumably
the next storey was blind with Corinthian columns
and square windows in alternate bays. Of this only
some Corinthian capitals remain, but a blind storey
is necessary to support the masts on which the awnings were rigged. The design of what survives is very
close to that of the Colosseum, and it is clear that the
architects of the Colosseum must have studied the
Theatrum Marcelli closely. The seating is reconstructed as divided into three principal zones, with
an extra zone of broader steps for the senators along
the orchestra and a colonnade containing seating for
the less privileged at the top.

The greatest uncertainty surrounds the design of
the scaena and its dependencies. As it appears on the
Marble Plan, the scaena consists of a narrow, featureless stage and a scene building of apparently the
same depth, but extending to either side, adorsed to
which runs a colonnade giving on a court between
symmetrical halls to either side shown as basilical in
concept, with three aisles separated by lines of columns, but opening wide into spacious lobbies off the
stage building and rounded at the opposite end.
These are very puzzling and difficult to roof satisfactorily. Equally puzzling is a pair of small square features, rather like sacella, in the courtyard flanking
the main axis of the complex, each with a smaller
square, like an altar, in front of it, apparently enclosed behind by a great hemicycle, which may be
simply a terrace overlooking the river. Because the
proximity of the Temple of Apollo Sosianus seems to
make any additional theater temple unnecessary, and
the Porticus Octaviae could serve admirably the
function of a theater portico, the interpretation of

this very extensive complex, nearly the size of the
cavea in its full extent, is especially difficult and important. Architects who have worked on the problem invariably have decided that the stage building
must have been more elaborate and have furnished it
with niches and columns like other stage buildings.
For these there is no evidence, while the scaena of
the Theatrum Pompeii is also shown on the Marble
Plan as very elaborate and with a wealth of detail.
We should probably ask rather what sorts of shows
were put on in the Theatrum Marcelli. We are told
that, on the death of Marcellus, Augustus gave orders that at the Ludi Romani a golden image of Marcellus and a crown of gold and curule chair should
be brought into the Theatrum Marcelli and set
among the magistrates in charge of the games (Cass.
Dio 53.30.6). And at the dedication of the finished
theater the special events included a performance of
the Lusus Troiae and a venatio with six hundred wild
animals imported from Africa. Whereas ludi scaenici
were from a very early period an established part of
the Ludi Romani, ludi circenses were the major interest and emphasis. Some of these, the various races
and shows, like the Lusus Troiae, could only be put
on in a circus or stadium, but others, such as venationes, could be staged in a variety of places and
probably to better advantage than in the circus. The
first amphitheater in Rome was built in 53 B.C.,
about the same time as the Theater of Pompey, and
was contrived by rotating two theaters to face each
other (Pliny, *HN* 36.116–20), a contrivance in which
the athletic events were performed on stages that
stood back to back. Then these were drawn away to
either side to make an arena for gladiatorial combats. We might well imagine that many of the events
of the Ludi Romani besides the plays not only might
well be given in a theater but also had traditionally
been given in a theater, and that for these a particular
sort of scaena was required, one in which the architecture was minimal and as simple as possible, a
frame for spectacles rather than plays.

The main axis of the complex lies north northeast/
south southwest, the scaena toward the river. It is
built entirely of travertine on the exterior, and of
large tufa blocks and concrete vaults on the interior,
with partitions faced with reticulate. In the parts immediately around the orchestra some walls are faced
with brick, evidently a precaution against the damp.
The recent work of restoration has also brought to
light some fine stuccowork in the vaults.

Lugli 1946, 568–72; Nash 2.418–22; P. Fiden-
zoni, *Il teatro di Marcello* (Rome 1970); *BullCom* 88
(1982–83): 7–49 (P. Ciancio Rossetto).

Theatrum Pompeii (Fig. 82): the first stone theater
in Rome, built by Pompey and, according to the

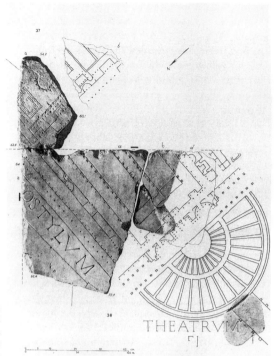

Figure 82
Theatrum Pompeii and
Porticus Pompeii,
Representation on
the Marble Plan

not crowning the cavea, but rather against the piers of the exterior arcade (Pliny, *HN* 36.41; Suetonius, *Nero* 46.1). At the top of the cavea was a series of four, or more likely five, temples or shrines, the most important, presumably on the main axis, to Venus Victrix, the others to Honos, Virtus, Felicitas, and V(ictoria?) (Fast. Amit., Allif., 13 August; Degrassi 493–94; cf. Suetonius, *Claud.* 21.1). For the dedication of the complex, Pompey invited the people of Rome to the dedication of the Temple of Venus Victrix, explaining the theater as simply a stair for shows subjoined to the temple (Tertullian, *De Spect.* 10). By so doing, Tertullian says, Pompey avoided censure for having built a theater, a form of building condemned by the stricter Romans. But by this time that was hardly necessary, and we should regard the invitation as at least half-joking. Gellius (10.1.7) says that when Pompey came to dedicate the temple he was uncertain whether to write *consul tertio* or *consul tertium*, and on the advice of Cicero he wrote simply *consul tert*. This would place the dedication of the temple three years after that of the theater, in 52 B.C. Gellius goes on to say that on the scaena, which had been restored, the inscription settled the question by using the numeral III, so it appears that theater, scaena, and temple were parts of a single project, the completion of the complex in all its component parts, and this is supported by Velleius Paterculus (2.48.2).

Augustus restored the building at great expense, but without the addition of his own name, in 32 B.C. (*RG* 20) and moved the statue of Pompey from the Curia Pompei (q.v.), where Caesar had been murdered at its feet, to a place opposite the regia of the theater, *marmoreo iano superposuit* (Suetonius, *Aug.* 31.5). This seems to mean that the statue now stood on a marble arch on the main axis of the complex. Because an arch in the theater proper would interfere intolerably with the sight lines of the audience, even if it were of modest size, we may see this as the arch shown on the Marble Plan in the Porticus Pompeii behind the porta regia of the scaena and on axis with it. The theater burned in A.D. 21 (Hieron. *a. Abr.* 2037), and Tiberius undertook its restoration (Vell. Pat. 2.130.1; Tacitus, *Ann.* 3.72). At this time the senate decreed that a bronze statue of Sejanus should be set up in the theater (Seneca, *Marc.* 224; Cass. Dio 57.21.3). Tiberius did not complete the restoration (Suetonius, *Tib.* 47); Caligula completed it (Suetonius, *Calig.* 21), and Claudius dedicated it (Suetonius, *Claud.* 21.1; Cass. Dio 60.6.8). Claudius inscribed his name and that of Tiberius on the scaena and restored the name of Pompey (Cass. Dio 60.6.8). Claudius also completed a marble arch to Tiberius near the theater that had been voted by the senate but left unfinished. This sounds like a countermea-

common version, dedicated in 55 B.C., the year of his second consulship (Asconius *in Cic. Pis.* 1 [Stangl 11]; Tacitus, *Ann.* 14.20; Cass. Dio 39.38.1–6). At the dedication lavish games were staged, including a venatio employing five hundred lions, an elephant fight, and other marvels (Cicero, *Pis.* 65; Plutarch, *Pomp.* 52.4). Besides Theatrum Pompeii, it was called Theatrum Pompeianum (see, e.g., Pliny, *HN* 36.115; Suetonius, *Tib.* 47), Theatrum Marmoreum (Fast. Amit. 12 August; see Degrassi 190–91), and occasionally simply Theatrum (Suetonius, *Nero* 13.2; cf. Pliny, *HN* 33.54). It was always the most important theater in Rome.

The design was supposed to have been copied from the theater of Mitylene but made larger and more splendid (Plutarch, *Pomp.* 42.4). Because the theater of Mitylene was built in traditional fashion on a hillside and would not have had a scaena in the style implied by Pliny's description of the Theater of Scaurus (see Theatrum Scauri), it is likely that this is mistaken. Either the project of Pompey proved unadaptable to the geographical conditions in Rome, or his architect persuaded him that a wholly new design would be preferable. As built, it was remarkable for the program of statuary, included in which were representations of marvels of history, such as a woman of Tralles who had borne thirty children (Pliny, *HN* 7.34). Another set of fourteen figures by Coponius represented the fourteen nations subdued by Pompey; these were set *circa Pompeium,* probably

sure to the statue of Sejanus, but there is no indication of where it was located, except that it was evidently not part of the theater proper. It may be the
arch shown in the Porticus Pompeii at the opposite
end from that behind the porta regia of the scaena.

In A.D. 66 when Tiridates, king of Armenia, paid
a state visit to Rome, Nero had the whole interior of
the theater gilded and purple awnings stretched over
it (Pliny, *HN* 33.54; Cass. Dio 62.6.1–2). In the great
fire of 80 the scaena burned (Cass. Dio 66.24.2), and
Domitian must have restored it. Under Septimius
Severus there was further restoration by Q. Acilius
Fuscus, procurator operis Theatri Pompeiani (*CIL*
8.1439 = *ILS* 1430, 14.154 = *ILS* 1431). In 247 the
theater burned again (Hieron. *a. Abr.* 2263). Other
restorations are recorded under Diocletian and Maximian (Chron. 148), Honorius and Arcadius (*CIL*
6.1191 = *ILS* 793; cf. 1193), and finally by Symmachus (Cassiodorus, *Var.* 4.51.3–4; cf. Symmachus,
Rel. 8.3). Throughout its history it was one of the
showplaces of Rome, as the Theatrum Marcelli was
not (Cass. Dio 39.38.1).

It was in the Campus Martius, listed by the regionary catalogues in Regio IX, almost isolated at the
time of its construction, the Porticus Pompeii that
served to shelter spectators in the event of rain and a
popular promenade at other times abutting on the
Area Sacra di Largo Argentina (q.v.) on the east, but
the other three sides free. It appears on fragments
of the Marble Plan (*FUR* pl. 32; Rodriguez pls. 28,
32) that show the ground plan in clear detail, especially that of the scaena, and an aerial photograph
shows that the buildings in the area bounded by Via
di Grotta Pinta, Via dei Giubbonari, Piazza Campo
de'Fiori, Piazza del Biscione, Piazza Paradiso, and
Via and Largo de'Chiavari are to a large extent built
on its ruins as foundations and show its outlines. The
cellars of buildings in this area preserve much of
the vaulted substructures in excellent condition, the
walls of concrete, about 1.50 m thick, faced with
quasi-reticulate and quoined with small blocks, on
bases of large blocks of tufa and peperino, the vaults
segmental and of unfaced concrete. The exterior was
arcaded, in forty-four arches of peperino. Columns
of red granite seem to have been added in front of
these in one of the restorations. The engineering of
the exits and entrances cannot be made out completely, but seems to have used a system of outer and
inner annular corridors in the substructures similar
to that of the Theatrum Marcelli. The diameter of
the cavea is estimated at 150–160 m, and the length
of the scaena at about 95 m. The capacity, given by
the regionary catalogues as 17,500 loca, is estimated
at about 11,000 people. The scaena is shown on the
Marble Plan as very deep, the back wall baroque in
its development, a series of three deep niches, the

outer pair semicircular, the broad central one with
the porta regia rectangular, with multiple colonnades in front of them, the lowest storey of an architecture that probably not only piled up colonnades
but also broke back to reveal statuary in the upper
tiers. It opened behind to the Porticus Pompeii without an intermediate space, taking the portico as its
backstage. On axis behind the cavea, a broad avenue
lined with trees led off at a slight angle to the south,
probably connecting it with the splendid house Pompey built in connection with his theater, said to be
like a tender towed behind a great ship.

Lugli 1938, 70–78; Nash 2.423–28; *Rend-
PontAcc* 44 (1971–72): 99–122 (F. Coarelli); *RdA* 3
(1979): 72–85 (A. M. Capoferro Cencetti); *AJA* 91
(1987): 123–26 (L. Richardson); *CEFR* 98 (1987):
457–73 (G. Sauron).

Theatrum Scauri: a theater erected by M. Aemilius
Scaurus as curule aedile in 58 B.C. It was exceptionally large; Pliny (*HN* 36.113–15) puts the capacity
at eighty thousand people, but then estimates the capacity of the Theatrum Pompeii as forty thousand,
so it is more likely to have been twenty thousand at
most. The scaena excited special admiration. It was
of marble, and the scaenae frons employed 360 columns in three storeys, the lowest of marble, the next
of glass (mosaic), and the topmost of gilded wood.
The columns of the lowest storey were 38 Roman
feet high. Three thousand bronze statues were used
in its decoration (Pliny, *HN* 34.36). No one tells us
where it was located, but we presume it was in the
Campus Martius.

Theatrum Traiani: a theater built by Trajan in the
Campus Martius that Hadrian destroyed, using the
excuse that this was done on Trajan's instructions
(S.H.A. *Hadr.* 9.1–2). Hadrian's real motive is difficult to fathom. The circular theater of Trajan mentioned by Pausanias (5.12.6) was more probably the
Naumachia Traiani (q.v.) than this theater.

The(n)sarium Vetus in Capitolio: see **Aedes
Tensarum.**

Thermae, Balineum, Lavacrum: The term *thermae*, which is always used for the big imperial bathing establishments from the time of Titus on, was
arrived at only slowly. Cicero, Sallust, and Livy never
use the word. Dio, writing about the Baths of
Agrippa, calls them first, when writing of their construction in 25 B.C., *laconicum* (53.27.1), which is
probably the term he found in his source, for the
Aqua Virgo was not completed until 19 B.C. When
writing about Agrippa's will and bequeathing of his
baths to the Roman people, he calls them a *bala-*

neion (54.29.4). The Baths of Nero were at first building called his *gymnasium* (Cass. Dio 61.21.1), although the complex seems to have consisted of both a sports complex and baths in fairly close conjunction (Tacitus, *Ann.* 15.22; Suetonius, *Nero* 12). The first to use the word *thermae* is Seneca Rhetor (*Controv.* 9.4.18), but since he uses it in a context in which the witticism he is reporting depends on being related in Greek, he is probably emphasizing the Greek character of the baths that are the object of the sally, and the use is not significant. Seneca the Younger uses the word *thermae* only twice, as against ten occurrences of *balineum* in his works. Thermae seems to have begun as a Neronian affectation, part of his fondness for Greek touches, and then, perhaps because of the splendor of his baths, it caught on. We hear of the Thermae Tigillini and at Pompeii of the Thermae Crassi Frugi (*CIL* 10.1063). In Rome the term seems to have been reserved for the big complexes that were imperial donations to the people until relatively late; even the sumptuous Baths of Claudius Etruscus admired by Martial (6.42) and Statius (*Silv.* 1.5) are called only *thermulae,* while the relatively modest baths of Septimius Severus, which have vanished without leaving a trace, and the baths that Maxentius added to the Domus Augustiana are called thermae. This distinction, which was never very strong or meaningful, breaks down after the time of Constantine.

Balineum (and a number of variants appear in the spelling of this loan word from Greek) is the word used for baths built or owned by a private individual. The regionary catalogues offer a count of the number of these for each regio of the city, the total amounting to the astonishing figure of 856. Most of these must have been very modest, but some, like that of Claudius Etruscus, seem to have rivaled the imperial complexes. Those known to us are all identified by a personal name, usually in the genitive but occasionally adjectival, except for the Balneum Diones, the Balineum Gratiarum, and the Balneum Mercurii, which undoubtedly took their names from the representation in a picture or statue. Most puzzling of all is the Balneum Caesaris known from a fragment of the Marble Plan (*FUR* pl. 33) that has been broken and part of it lost and in its complete form is known only from a drawing, but which appears to have been not a bath at all, but a large fountain in some part of the city where buildings of horreum or castrum plan appear next to large open spaces.

The high number of balinea in Rome is in contrast to Pompeii, where there were three large public bath complexes, thermae, but only four balinea, all rather luxurious. It is also in contrast to Ostia, where there are again three large complexes and so far fourteen balinea. The fee for admission was always modest

for balinea; a quadrans seems to have been standard in Cicero's day, but it probably varied somewhat with the range of amenities and the services offered. In the average balineum there was probably no palaestra, and probably very little exercise was possible. The sequence of bath rooms: frigidarium, tepidarium, and caldarium would be standard for a large balineum, with occasionally a laconicum provided as well. Dressing rooms and rooms for massage might fill out the complement of public rooms, while a furnace room behind the caldarium and storage for fuel would be all that was needed in annexes. The smaller bathing establishments could make do with only a couple of rooms, a cold plunge, if there was one, tucked into a corner of a lobby that also served as dressing room, and a single hot room. There must have been a good many that offered no more. Running a bath was a profession generally despised, hard, hot work, and the bath attendants shown in mosaics are an ill-favored lot.

Lavacrum is a term that seems to have been used very occasionally for a bath complex as an alternative for balineum, but because none survives in any form, we cannot say what, if anything, was their distinguishing characteristic.

Thermae Agrippae (Fig. 83): the first of the great bath complexes of Rome, probably begun in 25 B.C., when Cassius Dio (53.27.1) says Agrippa built a *laconicum* (dry sweat bath) in connection with the Pantheon. Because the Aqua Virgo, which supplied the baths with water, was not completed until 19 B.C. (Frontinus, *Aq.* 1.10), the full complex must belong later. Dio further says that Agrippa willed the baths to the Roman people for their free use at his death in 12 B.C. and endowed the gift by presenting real estate to support it to Augustus (Cass. Dio 54.29.4). The baths were adorned with works of art, the Apoxyomenos of Lysippus being set up before them (Pliny, *HN* 34.62), and pictures being let into the walls of even the hottest rooms (Pliny, *HN* 35.26). The terracotta parts were painted with encaustic, while the vaults and walls were decorated with stuccoes (Pliny, *HN* 36.189). These baths had to be restored shortly before Pliny wrote (*HN* 35.36) and burned in the fire of Titus in A.D. 80 (Cass. Dio 66.24.2). In Martial's day they were again in use (3.20.15, 36.6), and they were restored again by Hadrian (S.H.A. *Hadr.* 19.10) and possibly in 344–345 by Constantius and Constans (*CIL* 6.1165). They are listed in the regionary catalogues in Regio IX, mentioned by Sidonius (*Carm.* 23.496), and noted in the Einsiedeln itinerary, where they are called Thermae Commodianae. The *calcaria* of the lime burners were early established in the area, and the name *calcarium* came to be applied to the whole district (*Mirabilia:* Jordan 2.631; VZ 3.50); these continued in intermittent use through the sixteenth century (LS 1:25).

The location of the baths is provided by their listing in Regio IX in the regionary catalogues and the Agrippan buildings adjacent to them, and confirmed by a fragment of the Marble Plan labeled]ERMAE/]PAE (*FUR* pl. 32; Rodriguez pl. 31; *NSc* 1900, 633–34 [G. Gatti]; *BullCom* 29 [1901]: 3–19 [R. Lanciani]), which can be identified as showing the existing ruin known as the Ciambella (ring). The best account of what we know about these baths is that of C. Hülsen (*Die Thermen des Agrippa* [Rome 1910]). We are aided in a reconstruction of the plan by a drawing of B. Peruzzi (Uffizi Arch. 456 = Hülsen, *Die Thermen des Agrippa* pl. 1 and fig. 7), one by Palladio (Chatsworth port. 9 f. 14 = Hülsen, *Die Thermen des Agrippa* pl. 2; Zorzi figs. 136–40), and a rough sketch by S. Peruzzi (Uffizi Arch. 642 = Hülsen, *Die Thermen des Agrippa* fig. 6) made when more of the building survived. All of these confirm one another in showing the rotunda of which substantial parts remain, about 25 m in diameter, as the central element, with the main mass of the building lying north of it in only roughly symmetrical blocks, and the main axis probably east/west, with the main entrance on the east, toward the Saepta Iulia but not connecting with it. So the drawings show it, although the evidence of the Marble Plan is less clear on this point. It probably filled the space from the great hall (probably the Basilica Neptuni) south of the Pantheon to the southern limit of the Diribitorium, relatively long and narrow, from Largo Argentina nearly to Via della Palombella. West of it opened a great unencumbered space, where the inscription is inserted on the Marble Plan, presumably the place of the Horti and Stagnum Agrippae. The reading of the plan is uncertain on almost every point of importance, and the uses and roofing of all, except those shown as vaulted in the sixteenth-century drawing of Palladio, remain uncertain. The hot rooms probably lay to the west of the rotunda (Hülsen, *Die Thermen des Agrippa,* 20–24).

The existing ruins of the rotunda are of brick-faced concrete, and the dome was engineered with radial ribs of brick at regular intervals (Choisy 81–82 and pl. 10); it must date from the fourth-century rebuilding of the complex. But the lack of symmetry in the plan and the maintenance of axes in harmony with those of the other Agrippan buildings in the vicinity, rather than reorientation to the southwest exposure that came to be understood as optimum for baths, may indicate that Agrippa's plan was maintained largely unchanged.

Lugli 1938, 151–57; Nash 2.429–33; Lugli 1975, 445–46.

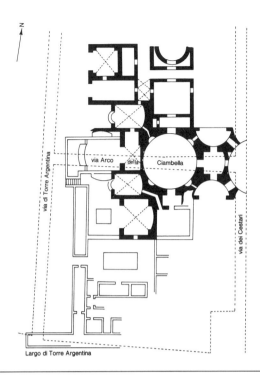

Figure 83
Thermae Agrippae,
Plan by C. Hülsen
based on a Plan by
A. Palladio and a
Fragment of the
Marble Plan

Thermae Alexandrinae: see **Thermae Neronianae.**

Thermae Antoninianae (Caracallae) (Fig. 84): more commonly called the Baths of Caracalla, located southwest of the Via Appia just outside Porta Capena in Regio XII. These were the first great public baths built in more than a hundred years, their immediate antecedent having been the Baths of Trajan. The date of their dedication is given by Jerome (Hieron. *a. Abr.* 2231; cf. Aur. Vict., *Caes.* 21) as A.D. 216, but they had presumably been many years in planning and building and may well have been a project of Septimius Severus, who took a special interest in this sector of Rome. The earliest brickstamps seem to be those of February 211–February 212, and the central block is entirely work of the years 212–216, whereas the rectangle of the peribolus is an addition of Elagabalus and Alexander Severus (Bloch 283–303). The work of Elagabalus and Alexander Severus is also attested in the Historia Augusta (S.H.A. *Heliogab.* 17.8, *Alex. Sev.* 25.6). For two very fragmentary papyri in Geneva that seem to preserve parts of lists of works of art on view in these baths, see J. Nicole, *Un Catalogue d'oeuvres d'art conservées à Rome à l'époque imperiale* (Geneva 1906), and G. Nicole in *Mélanges Holleaux* (Paris 1913), 145–52. Most, if not all, of these would have formed part of the original appointments.

The history of the building in antiquity is meager.

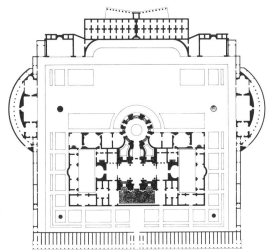

Figure 84
Thermae
Antoninianae, Plan
by A. Palladio

deep, is set well forward on a nearly square terrace to give maximum sun to the caldarium in winter. The plan is rigidly symmetrical in all its parts. The three big rooms on the central axis are: (1) an unroofed natatio with deep niches on the southwest side only, (2) a central hall adorned with eight granite columns that appeared to carry cross vaulting in three bays, off which open niches containing other niches, some separated from the main hall by screens of columns, others not, and (3) a circular caldarium about four-fifths the size of the Pantheon, domed and multi-windowed, with a small chamber in each pier between the windows, two of which are used to house stairs to the roof and two for passages to other rooms. The only column of the central hall remaining was taken to Florence by Cosimo I between 1561 and 1565 and now stands in Piazza della Trinità. To either side of the main axis, rooms are grouped around a court or palaestra. The apartments on the southwest, which face outward and are, for the most part, raised on *suspensurae,* were the bathrooms proper, symmetrical suites of large rooms, very different from one another, including a nearly oval room with a cross-vaulted roof. The rooms clustered about the palaestras seem to have been for dressing, exercise, massage, and so on; about half of them are vaulted. The palaestras are colonnaded around three sides, and the portico is raised a step above the open area. On the fourth side is a series of three rooms separated from the court and one another only by screens of columns. On axis opposite them is a great semicircular bay lined with a row of niches separated from the portico by a row of columns. This feature, copied from the Baths of Trajan and ultimately the Forum Augustum, is strongly emphasized; it was here that the famous mosaic pavements representing athletes were found in 1824. These are now in the Lateran collection in the Vatican and probably date only from the fourth century (Helbig[4] 1.1028).

Any discussion of the identity of the *cella solearis* mentioned in the Historia Augusta (S.H.A. *Carac.* 9.4–5) is probably futile. The word *solearis* should mean provided with basins for individual bathing (cf. *CIL* 8.897, 14700), but possibly it came to be applied, at first only jokingly, to the great central halls of imperial baths where there were fountains in the form of great tubs of colored marble. If there was a room with a roof such as the author describes, *nam ex aere vel cypro cancelli superpositi esse dicuntur, quibus cameratio tota concredita est,* it would have to have a false vault hung under another roof. Yet none of great size, such as he requires, could be found here. Probably he, or his source, misunderstood the function of tie rods used in the palaestra porticoes and concocted a myth about the roofing of

The praefectus urbi set up bases for statues of Valentinian and Valens toward the end of the fourth century (*CIL* 6.794, 1170–73). In the fifth century it is listed among the marvels of Rome (Polemius Silvius 545; Olympiodorus *ap. Photium* p. 63a [Bekker]). Brick-stamps attest to repairs in the time of Theodoric (*CIL* 15.1665.3, 4; 1669.7). The usefulness of the baths must have come to an end with the cutting of the aqueducts during the siege of Genseric in A.D. 537. The baths are mentioned in the Einsiedeln itinerary and kept their proper name, often somewhat distorted, through the Middle Ages. Beginning in the time of Pope Paul III, they were plundered for antiquities, the Farnese Bull, the Farnese Hercules, and the Farnese Flora (all now in the Museo Nazionale Archeologico in Naples) having come from them. So did the Belvedere Torso in the Vatican (Helbig[4] 1.265) and numerous other sculptures. Palladio made reasonably accurate plans of the complex, together with reconstructions of the elevations and sections, and drawings of cornices, moldings, and capitals (Zorzi figs. 110–24), as did a number of other architects of the sixteenth century. In the nineteenth century Ivanoff studied the parts above ground in great detail, 1847–1849, and made careful drawings and experiments in restoration of the decoration (S. A. Ivanoff and C. Hülsen, *Architektonische Studien,* vol. 3 [Berlin 1898]). Since then exploration of the underground parts, heating system, drainage, service corridors, and so forth has proved illuminating and rewarding. There have been numerous studies of the complex, but no comprehensive treatment of the whole.

The plan follows in general the lines laid down in the Baths of Trajan, but introduces many refinements and variations. The main block, 214 m wide 110 m

THERMAE ANTONINIANAE (CARACALLAE)

the great hall. The meticulous attention that the engineers gave to statics in their choice of materials, especially in their choice of caementa for the vaults and in their distributing weight and buttressing thrusts, may have promoted the invention of myths.

The terrace surrounding the central block is largely artificial, dug out to the southwest and built up on the northeast, where the approaches are found, especially that from the Via Nova. Along this front and around each end to about one-third of the depth of the sides was an arcade in two storeys, behind which opened a row of deep rooms, among which the stairs for taking one up to the upper level are arranged. These rooms served as shops, housing for the personnel of the baths, and service areas. At the back of the terrace was a stadium, evidently for athletic events, the seating carried only around the southwest half and helping to buttress the double row of cisterns in two storeys dug into the hill behind it, sixty-four in all. It was at this point, on the principal axis of the complex, that the aqueduct, a branch of the Aqua Marcia, entered. Flanking the stadium are two large rectangular halls, each with a large niche on the principal axis and rows of smaller niches; these have been identified as libraries, the niches being for wooden cases in which the scrinia were kept. The identification is very doubtful, because the library of Hadrian in Athens measures only about 23 m wide x 17.50 m deep overall, while each of these measures about 42 m x 25 m. Moreover, there are reservoirs for water behind the southwest wall of each; these would be deleterious to books, as Vitruvius (6.4.1) knew. On the sides of the complex, facing the greatest expanse of the gardens, are symmetrical bowed bays, each containing an octagonal nymphaeum roofed with a highly experimental dome offering the earliest example of windows in the drum of the dome, half-domed niches under these windows, and curved pendentives. There is also a large rectangular room open to the garden along one front through a screen of columns, and a somewhat smaller room with provision for heating. These we must think of as assembly rooms for use in summer and winter. Behind them runs a bowed portico, presumably for strollers. The planning of these bays is extremely ingenious and highly successful, but they are not imitated in subsequent baths.

The subterranean installations of the baths have been explored only in small part, but it is enough to show that great corridors, large enough for vehicular traffic, ran to all parts of the complex. Into these opened manholes, so that loading and unloading of fuel, linen, and various supplies could be brisk and efficient, and from them stairs led up inside the great

piers of the buildings that continued up to the roofs. Thus service could circulate with maximum freedom to all parts and without contact with the public except at the end. The roofs, perhaps even the plumbing, could be repaired while the baths continued in use, and at the end of the day much of the work of cleaning and supplying would already have been accomplished. Into one of these corridors along the northwest side of the complex was built a Mithraeum (see Mithraeum : 5. Mithraeum Thermarum Antoninianarum), the largest so far known in Rome, dating from the third century. This was accessible from a side street, rather than from the bath itself, and consisted of masonry bases for dining couches, four on each side, flanking a central nave. The nave is roofed with a barrel vault; the aisles in which the couches were recessed have vaults intersecting with this. There is a baptismal basin, a pit accessible from a chamber to one side for the sacrifice of the bull, and a triangular base for the cult image, behind which the relief of Mithras Tauroctonos was set into a niche. The nave is paved with black-and-white mosaic, and the impression one has is of a prosperous cult center. The rooms flanking the Mithraeum proper also belonged to the cult; one was a sacristy, and one was a stall for the bulls required for sacrifice. Close to this in the subterranean parts a mill was established at a late date (*OpRom* 14 [1983]: 47–64 [T. Scioler and O. Wikander]). No doubt a variety of small workshops remains to be discovered.

Below this level runs the level of the drains, an elaborate network. The main drain runs along the whole northeast side of the complex and empties out of the northwest side. The rationale of this is easy to see, because the Circus Maximus brook must have been used to take off the wastes to the Tiber.

Because we know nothing at all about the architecture, planting, or statuary of the gardens, little, except for the many sculptures known to have come from the baths, about the decoration and its program, and almost nothing about rooms and terraces in a second storey, we must admit that our knowledge of the Baths of Caracalla is woefully deficient, but we know this complex better than we know any other bath complex in Rome, and its sophistication and the subtlety of the planning are impressive even in its ruined state.

Nash 2.434–41; Lugli 1975, 567–75; H. Munderscheid, *Die Skulpturenausstattung der kaiserzeitlichen Thermenanlagen* (Berlin 1981), 73–76 (catalogue of sculptures found in these baths); *AJA* 87 (1983): 347–84 (M. Marvin); *Roma, archeologia nel centro* (1985), 2.578–622 (I. Iacopi et al.); *ArtB* 68 (1986): 379–97 (D. Kinney); *PBSR* 55 (1987): 147–56 (J. Delaine).

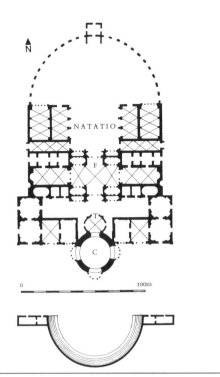

Figure 85
Thermae
Constantinianae,
Plan by A. Palladio

Thermae Cleandri: see **Thermae Commodianae.**

Thermae Commodianae: baths that Cleander, a favorite of Commodus, built in Regio I (*Not.*). They are recorded in our sources (S.H.A. *Commod.* 17.5; Chron. 147; Herodian 1.12.4) and dated by Jerome to A.D. 183 (Hieron. *a. Abr.* 2199). Herodian says that they were very large, but they seem to have disappeared without leaving a trace. The Thermae Commodianae of the Einsiedeln itinerary are really the Thermae Agrippae.

Thermae Constantinianae (Figs. 72, 85): the last great imperial baths, a comparatively small complex built by Constantine (Aur. Vict., *Caes.* 40.27.5) at an unknown date in Regio VI (*Not.*). They may have replaced the Balineum Claudianum (q.v.) and served a populous district in the heart of Rome earlier dependent on private baths. The baths suffered greatly in the course of the next century and were restored in A.D. 443 by Petronius Perpenna Magnus Quadratianus, praefectus urbi, who recorded his restoration in a colorful inscription (*CIL* 6.1750 = *ILS* 5703). They are referred to only by Ammianus (27.3.8) to locate a house, but figure in the Einsiedeln itinerary (1.10, 3.6, 6.11; Jordan 2:646, 648, 652). They were situated in an area between Alta Semita and Vicus Longus toward the south end of the Quirinal, the Collis Mucialis, where the ground was uneven and extensive terracing was necessary along the south

side. They seem to have been flanked by streets on both sides. So the north/south orientation they took was more or less forced upon the architect, who had also to work in a comparatively narrow area. Considerable remains of the main building survived at the beginning of the sixteenth century, and a number of Renaissance artists made plans and drawings; these, especially Palladio's, are our chief source of knowledge of the complex (S. Serlio, *De architectura*, 3.88 or 92; A. Palladio, *Le terme* pl. 14 = Zorzi figs. 84–88; E. Du Pérac, *Vestigi* pl. 32; A. van der Wyngaerde in *BullCom* 23 [1895]: pls. 6–13 [R. Lanciani]). The remains were almost totally destroyed in the building of Palazzo Rospigliosi, 1605–1621, but occasional bits of no great significance have been recovered from time to time (*NSc* 1876, 55, 99 [G. Fiorelli]; 1877, 204, 267 [G. Fiorelli]; 1878, 233, 340 [G. Fiorelli]).

Palladio's plan shows a large semicircular entrance court in the area now occupied by Palazzo della Consulta giving to a square court with addorsed columns along the sides between openings to two large vaulted loggias, an arrangement suggestive of a natatio, though none is shown. From this one passed into a cruciform central hall on which opened to either side a long exedra with apsidal end and four smaller rooms with niched walls and lateral apses, all with columnar doorways. This must have been the chief showplace of the complex. South of this were the bathing facilities proper, which opened off a long rectangular court. These were symmetrical wings with rooms with bathing tanks and niches to either side, a quadrilobate tepidarium, almost an oval in plan, and a very large round caldarium with three rounded apses for fenestration swelling out on the cross axes. Considerably south of this, on axis but evidently not connected with the rest, was a large hemicyclical stair, apparently descending the slope of the hill. The general impression one has is of a great conglomeration of curvilinear rooms and curved elements and forms at every scale, and the closest relation in architecture seems to be with the Imperial Baths of Trier, but there is nothing very revolutionary in the design nor any signal change from that of the Baths of Diocletian.

The area of the Thermae Constantinianae had earlier been covered with private houses and insulae with tabernae in the ground storey (*BullCom* 4 [1876]: 102–20 [V. Vespignani]), important parts of which were preserved in the terracing for the baths. These seem to have been buildings of the second to fourth centuries after Christ. See, e.g., Domus, T. Avidius Quietus (1).

Important works of sculpture were recovered from these baths. They include the bronze boxer (Borghese) and Hellenistic ruler now in the Museo

Nazionale Romano delle Terme (Helbig⁴ 3.2272, 2273), and two marble statues of Constantine, one now in the porch of S. Giovanni in Laterano, the other on the balustrade of Piazza del Campidoglio. There was also a marble statue of Constantine's son Constans (Helbig⁴ 2.1166, 1167). The horse tamers of Montecavallo may have come from these baths, if they did not belong in the precinct of the Temple of Salus.

LS 3.196–98; Nash 2.442–47.

Thermae Decianae: built by Emperor Decius in A.D. 252 on the Aventine (*MGH Chron. Min.* 2.147 [Cassiodorus]; Eutropius 9.4; Chron. 147 ["Commodianae"]; *CIL* 15.7181). A partial plan of the complex was made in rough form by Palladio (Zorzi fig. 145); he measured the extent of the southeast front as 32 *pertiche, 5 piedi* = 96.07 m.

Although the complex is similar to other imperial baths with an axial series of rooms and symmetrical wings to either side, it faced southeast, having a series of large rooms with large openings containing columns so oriented. The caldarium is omitted, but Lanciani (LFUR sheet 34) suggests that it may have been multilobate, something like that in the Thermae Constantinianae. The central hall seems unusually simple in its cruciform plan. No peribolus is shown, but the measurements of Palladio show that he considered the main building to stand on a prepared terrace, so presumably one originally existed.

The baths were located in the middle of the Aventine plateau, and walls still existing in the early part of this century could be identified as represented on Palladio's plan (PA 327). Numerous explorations have been conducted since the seventeenth century and have produced fragments of mosaic pavement, painted and stucco decoration, and marble statue bases erected by praefecti urbi in the fourth century (*CIL* 6.1159, 1160, 1167, 1192?; *ILS* 796, 1651?, 1672). The most famous pieces recovered from these baths are the infant Hercules in basalt and the relief of Endymion sleeping now in the Museo Capitolino (Helbig⁴ 2.1331, 1399).

QArchEtr 11 (1985): 139–44 (L. La Follette).

Thermae Diocletiani (Figs. 72, 86): the great bath complex that Diocletian built at the northeast end of the Viminal and Quirinal just inside the Agger of the Servian Walls. The dedicatory inscription (*CIL* 6.1130 = 31242 = *ILS* 646), known in at least four copies, puts the date of dedication between 1 May 305 and 25 July 306 and makes the baths especially the work of Maximianus after his return from Africa in 298, but dedicated by both the Augusti who had abdicated and the reigning tetrarchs. Maximianus takes special credit for the buying up of the land on

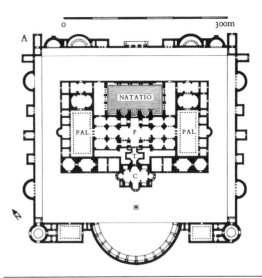

Figure 86
Thermae Diocletiani,
Plan by A. Palladio

which they were built. Jerome's date (Hieron. *a. Abr.* 2317 = A.D. 302) is incorrect. The bricks recovered from the fabric belong entirely to the period of Diocletian, no other material being employed, and the evidence strongly indicates that for the enormous project of the Thermae the brick industry was completely reorganized and concentrated in the hands of the emperor (Bloch 303–16). Among the buildings that were removed or destroyed to make a place for the baths, we can list only the Quadrigae Pisonis (S.H.A. *Tyr. Trig.* 21.6–7), a monument of the second century decorated with reliefs, including one probably showing the Temple of Quirinus (*RömMitt* 19 [1904]: 23–37 [P. Hartwig]), and the house of Cornelia L. f. Volusi Saturnini. Probably the area was largely residential, as its choice for this sort of complex also suggests. In laying it out a number of changes in the streets were necessary, a section of the Vicus Longus having to be suppressed and a new street run southwest of the baths to connect Alta Semita (Vicus Portae Collinae) and Vicus Portae Viminalis (see LFUR sheets 10, 17).

The statement in the life of Probus in the Historia Augusta (2.1) that the Bibliotheca Ulpia was in the fourth century housed in the Thermae Diocletiani has been challenged as an invention. However, because we hear of two sets of libraries in connection with the Forum Traiani, the Bibliotheca Templi Traiani (A. Gellius 11.17) and the Bibliotheca Ulpia, and because libraries seem to have been among the amenities offered those frequenting the baths (cf. Thermae Antoninianae, Thermae Traiani), it seems not unlikely that the Ulpian library might have been transferred here. Olympiodorus (*ap. Photium* 80 p. 63 Bekker) asserted that three thousand people could be accommodated here at once, almost double the number that could be accommodated in the Baths of

Caracalla, but this has been questioned. Although the bath building proper is significantly larger than that in the Baths of Caracalla, there is very little difference in the areas covered by the whole complexes. The baths were restored at some unspecified time (*CIL* 6.1131), and one does not know how extensively. The cutting of the aqueducts during the Gothic War in the sixth century put them out of commission, and there is no sign that they were ever in use thereafter. The church of S. Cyriacus in Thermis (HCh 245–46) seems to have been established there prior to A.D. 499 and continued to exist until the sixteenth century under that name, whereas in the *Mirabilia* of the twelfth century we find *in palatio Dioclitiani* (Jordan 2.640; VZ 3.60).

The baths followed the scheme initiated in the Baths of Trajan of a bath building proper set on axis in a spacious open area, off the periphery of which open numerous small dependencies. The main axis lies northeast/southwest, with the principal hot rooms along the southwest front to get the benefit of the afternoon sun, and with a large semicircular exedra in the middle of the southwest side to enhance this. The rectangular area measures about 356 m wide by 316 m deep, the block of the bath building 244 m wide by 144 m deep. Entrance to the bath building was on the three sides away from the southwest. In the middle of the northeast side was a huge swimming pool, its southwest side strongly resembling a scaenae frons, a baroque front built up in three storeys and adorned with columns and sculptures in niches. This was flanked by cross-vaulted porticoes leading back to the main hall, its central cruciform volume extended through broad colonnaded openings into a series of six squarish annexes to either side, the openness here a radical departure from tradition, as is also the free use of cross vaulting. In the sixteenth century Michelangelo converted the central space, which was exceptionally well preserved, into the church of S. Maria degli Angeli. To either side of the central hall opened a colonnaded court, probably a palaestra, with small dependencies along the far long side, probably for the adjuncts of exercise, and access at the southwest to a single cold room and a series of three rooms on suspensurae, presumably of increasing heat as one approached the central axis from either side, culminating in a vast caldarium thrust out from the rest to the southwest. This rivaled the great central hall in size and was furnished with four apses at the ends of the axes.

The parterre surrounding the bath building was undoubtedly laid out in part in walks and gardens and in part in playing fields, but it is unlikely that the great exedra on the southwest was ever used as a theater, as its shape has suggested. The absence of substructures for seating and the undesirability of interfering with the exposure of the southwest front of the bath block militate against it. It is more likely to have been a hemicyclical walk. The drawings of Dosio show the back wall as windowed, not treated with a series of aedicular niches. The niches seem to have been an invention based on Palladio's section (see Zorzi fig. 128), in which the windows were given aedicular frames, and these were then multiplied to make a scenographic effect for which there is no warrant at all. The peribolus wall survived up until relatively recently; when the Via Nazionale was created in 1867, it cut through the line of the exedra, and the modern Piazza dell'Esedra follows its curve. Elsewhere it has disappeared, except for portions of the dependencies that opened out of it that have been incorporated into modern structures. These seem to have been a collection of almost independent pavilions, of various sizes and plans, but for the most part not very large. These might have been libraries, clubrooms, or schools. Two large domed halls at the extremities of the southwest front are more important and must have served some special function, but there is no indication of what that was. One has been used since 1594 as the church of S. Bernardo, and the other is built into buildings on Via Viminale.

The brick facing was covered with stucco on the exterior, worked to simulate white marble in large drafted blocks. This had been done earlier in the Thermae Traiani and Thermae Antoninianae. The interior was revetted with marble; most of the columns seem to have been granite. The water for the baths was supplied by the Aqua Marcia, which Diocletian augmented for this purpose. The reservoir for the baths lay just outside the peribolus toward the east end of the southeast side in the angle between Vicus Collis Viminalis and the baths. The reservoir was of trapezoidal shape, nearly triangular, 91 m long and 31 m wide at the base, divided into aisles, increasing to five in number, by square pillars of brickwork supporting cross vaults.

At the time the central hall was remodeled as the church of S. Maria degli Angeli, Pope Pius IV assigned large portions of the rest of the complex to the Carthusian monks of S. Croce in Gerusalemme. The great cloister of one hundred columns that bears the date 1565 was constructed for the monks. As S. Maria degli Angeli was to be the monastery's church, Michelangelo made the principal axis southeast/northwest, with the entrance at the southeast end. In 1749 Cardinal Bichi, wishing to enlarge the church, engaged Vanvitelli for this project, and he then changed the axis and built a new choir and apse projecting into the great swimming pool of the baths. Michelangelo's church now became the transepts of Vanvitelli's. In 1575 Pope Gregory XIII took the northwestern parts for the construction of the Horrea Ecclesiae, the church granaries, and these were then enlarged successively by Pope Paul V in 1609 and Pope Clement XI in 1705. Pope Clement XIII added storehouses for oil in 1764, and they were not destroyed until 1936. In 1889 the Museo Nazionale Romano was established in the cloisters of the monastery and, after the main bath building was isolated in 1908–1911, extended to occupy the surviving parts of the baths back to the east corner.

A fine series of drawings by Dosio shows the baths in the middle of the sixteenth century, before the remodeling as a church and monastery (G. A. Dosio, *Roma antica e i disegni di architettura agli Uffizi* [Rome 1976], nos. 33, 60–62, 70, 73–75).

Lugli 1938, 359–71; *CAR* 2-I, 1–16 pp. 239–41; Nash 2.448–53; Lugli 1975, 490–93; *NSc* 1976, 246–47 (E. Lissi Caronna).

Thermae Domitii: baths built for Cn. Domitius Ahenobarbus, the natural father of Nero, on the Sacra Via (Seneca, *Controv.* 9.4.12), evidently private and in connection with his house there. See Domus Domitiana.

Thermae Etrusci: the Baths of Claudius Etruscus described in some detail by Martial (6.42) and Statius (*Silv.* 1.5), who marveled at their luxury. They especially admired the wealth of colored marbles employed and the variety of accommodations. Because the baths offered the water of both the Aqua Virgo and the Aqua Marcia, they must have been in the Campus Martius or the Transtiberim, these being the regiones that the Virgo supplied. The former is obviously more likely.

Thermae Gordiani: mentioned once (S.H.A. *Gord.* 32.7) as a project of Gordion III for the Campus Martius, a set of summer baths and one of winter baths in conjunction with his other projects. These were not even begun.

Thermae Helenae: baths that the dowager empress Helena restored in A.D. 323–326 after a fire (*CIL* 6.1136 = 31244). They are near the Sessorium and may have been part of the imperial villa (horti) Ad Spem Veterem, which we first hear of in the time of Elagabalus (see Circus Varianus and Sessorium), but stand somewhat apart and seem too large for the needs of the villa. They lie a little inside the Porta Praenestina (Porta Maggiore), southwest of the branching of the Aqua Claudia and Arcus Neronis. The plan is very asymmetrical, but the hot rooms were in a windowed bank facing southwest. Substantial remains survived up to the sixteenth century, and Palladio produced a plan (Zorzi fig. 144), but except for the reservoir the ruins have now disap-

peared under modern building. Palladio shows the plan as ell-shaped, the entrance wing consisting of a handsome vestibule, the side walls lined with niches, and a large hall cross-vaulted in three bays with columns addorsed to the walls to appear to support the vaulting. It copies the arrangements of the central halls of the great bath complexes on a reduced scale. Access to the bathing suite is not clear, but then one proceeded in series from a cold room at the south corner through a succession of three or four hot rooms. The furnaces seem to have been at the west corner, and there may have been a square palaestra at the east corner. There seems to have been free use of cross vaulting and colonnaded openings. The reservoir was separate and canted at an angle with respect to the rest of the complex, two rows of six uniform rectangular compartments communicating in both directions and roofed with cross vaults. It was supplied by the Aqua Alexandrina, built by Alexander Severus, which suggests the original date of the complex was Severan, like the rest of this villa.

Lugli 1938, 492–93; *MemPontAcc*, ser. 3.8 (1955): 140–47 (A. M. Colini); Nash 2.454–57.

Thermae Lateranenses: a modern name given to a bath complex southwest of the baptistery of S. Giovanni in Laterano at the point where Via Amba Aradam enters Piazza di S. Giovanni. Its northeast front lay along the ancient Via Tusculana. All that survives above ground is a large rectangular hall with a cross-vaulted roof, built of concrete faced with brick, 10 m x 12.50 m and 13.50 m high. In 1936 this was freed from other constructions, its arched doorways were reopened, and the area around it was explored, producing a complete plan of the baths. The existing hall seems to have been the central hall, northwest of which were two rows of rooms, those to the southwest being the hot rooms. The hall dates from the beginning of the third century, as brick-stamps prove. It seems too big for a private bath, and the situation on a street suggests also that it was public. But it was not a great bath, nor of very advanced design.

MemPontAcc, ser. 3.7 (1944): 334–39 (A. M. Colini); Nash 2.458–59.

Thermae Maxentii: baths Maxentius built as an addition to the Domus Augustiana (Chron. 148: *in Palatio*). See Domus Augustiana.

Thermae Neronianae (Fig. 87): the second of the great bath complexes of Rome, following that of Agrippa, built by Nero (Suetonius, *Nero* 12.3; Philostratus, *Vit. Apoll.* 4.42; Aur. Vict., *Epit.* 5.3; Eutropius 7.15.2). According to the chronicles, they were built in 64 (Hieron. *a. Abr.* 2079; *MGH Chron.*

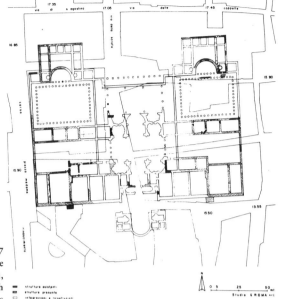

Figure 87
Thermae Neronianae
(Alexandrinae), Plan,
as Known, with
Restorations

Min. 2.138 [Cassiodorus]), but Suetonius has *dedi-catisque thermis et gymnasio,* and Tacitus (*Ann.* 14.47) says the gymnasium was dedicated in 62, whereas Dio (61.21.1) puts it in 60, together with the establishment of the Neronia, an association supported by Suetonius. The gymnasium was struck by lightning and burned in 62, and a bronze statue of Nero melted in the fire (Tacitus, *Ann.* 15.22). Given this evidence, it seems likely that the baths and gymnasium were parts of a single complex, perhaps the first time extensive athletic facilities were attached to a big bathing establishment, opened in 60 for the first celebration of the Neronia and finished in 62, that this was later in 62 struck by lightning and burned, and that it was rebuilt and rededicated in 64. Martial (2.48.8, 3.25.4, 7.34.4–5) admired these baths very much. They are mentioned incidentally on numerous occasions (cf., e.g., *CIL* 6.8676, 9797 = *ILS* 5173).

Beneath the courtyard of Palazzo Madama have been found brick-stamps of the time of Hadrian (*CIL* 15.481); on the site of S. Salvatore in Thermis (HCh 455–56) have been found brick-stamps of the time of Hadrian (*CIL* 15.364) and Septimius Severus (*CIL* 15.164, 371b, 404; see *NSc* 1907, 529 [D. Vaglieri]); and on the Salita dei Crescenzi have been found lead pipes of the time of Nero (*CIL* 15.7271).

Alexander Severus rebuilt and enlarged these baths in A.D. 227, and they were then called Thermae Alexandrinae (S.H.A. *Alex. Sev.* 25.3–4; Eutropius 7.15; Chron. 147; Hieron. *a. Abr.* 2243; *MGH Chron. Min.* 2.138, 146 [Cassiodorus]), although

the older name survived as well (cf., e.g., Sidonius Apollinaris, *Car.* 23.495). In later times they were sometimes misnamed Templum Alexandrini (HCh 200), but usually kept their true name with surprisingly little corruption (HCh 212, 326–27, 455–56). Alexander Severus is said to have added his baths to those of Nero, to have built an aqueduct, the Aqua Alexandrina (q.v.), to supply them, and to have added a park (nemus), which he created by pulling down buildings that he had purchased. He also instituted taxes for the maintenance of the public baths, assigned forests for their fuel, and supplied them with oil for illumination (S.H.A. *Alex. Sev.* 24.5–6).

These baths occupied an area extending from the northwest corner of the Pantheon to the Stadium of Domitian (Piazza Navona) and north to the straight street that Nero built connecting the Via Flaminia with the Pons Neronianus, a line now represented by Via dei Coronari and Via delle Cappelle; it measures about 190 m wide by 120 m deep. The baths faced north, with the principal hot rooms along the south front. Substantial portions were still visible in the sixteenth and seventeenth centuries, and Palladio studied them and provided a restored plan, elevations, and sections (Zorzi figs. 96–105). Alò Giovannoli made drawings of some of the more impressive ruins (Lugli 1938, 216–27; Nash 2.464), and large portions are built into later buildings, including Palazzo Madama and Palazzo Giustiniani, and can be recognized. They tend to confirm the accuracy of Palladio's plan. Two gray granite columns from the baths were used to repair the northeast corner of the porch of the Pantheon (q.v.) in the time of Alexander VII. Two others came to light in 1934 under Piazza S. Luigi dei Francesi and were reerected in Via di S. Eustachio in 1950, together with a chunk of cornice.

The plan seems to have been strictly symmetrical, with the main entrance from the north. A swimming pool flanked by arcaded and vaulted walks seems to have occupied the central position here and to have been given a theatrical south wall with deep semicircular niches, probably for fountains. To either side was a squarish colonnaded court, probably a palaestra, with a great semicircular exedra, which Palladio reconstructs with a massive half-dome. The great central hall is vaulted in three bays and flanked by a succession of niches. There is an extension of this to either side separated off by a screen of columns. A complex to either side consisting of a vaulted hall surrounded by smaller rooms, many of them vaulted, is probably to be associated with the palaestras. The bathing rooms seem to have been along the south front, beginning with a cold room at either end and progressing then through a series of three hot rooms to a central caldarium thrust out to the south from the rest. This was rectangular with a deep apse to the south flanked by blocks that may have contained small superheated chambers *(laconica)*.

The plan of these baths is so much more sophisticated than that of the Thermae Titi, and so much closer to that of the Baths of Caracalla, that it must be presumed that Alexander Severus and his architects completely transformed them. Yet the concrete, wherever in recent years it has been exposed, seems Neronian. Because this exposure has been especially in the northern parts, it is tempting to see the bathing rooms as a Severan addition, with extensive rehandling of the swimming pool and central hall, and to assign the palaestras and adjacencies to Nero. If Nero emphasized the gymnasium they included, the bathing facilities may have been subordinate.

Lugli 1938, 212–18; Nash 2.460–64; B. Tamm, *Nero's Gymnasium in Rome* (Stockholm 1970); *REA* 74 (1972): 94–106 (A. Vassileiou); *Roma, archeologia nel centro* (1985), 2.395–99 (G. Ghini).

Thermae Novati (or **Novatianae**): baths mentioned only in the Acta Sanctae Praxedis (*Acta Sanctorum Mai.* 4.297) *in Vico Patricii,* said to have been rededicated by Pope Pius I in the time of Antoninus Pius as the church of S. Pudenziana. The antiquity of this life is suspect; the information from it is inserted in the *Liber Pontificalis* only in the eleventh century (LPD 1.132 [Pius I]; VZ 2.223). Our earliest mention of the church otherwise is in an epitaph of 384 (HCh 424–25). Conversion of one of the halls of a bath to use as a church would not be surprising at a somewhat later date, but conversion of a whole bath complex, especially conversion described as *ex rogatu b. Praxedis,* must strike us as unlikely for this period, even if it were a small private bath. A fragment of epistyle in S. Pudenziana carries an inscription: *Maximus has olim thermas* (CIL 6.29769); this Maximus may be the same as the presbyter Maximus who in 390 restored the church in company with Ilicius and Leopardus.

Exploration under the church of S. Pudenziana begun in 1928–1933 and resumed again in 1961 brought to light much of the history of the site. The earliest identifiable building was a two-storey house of the Hadrianic period, dated by a brick-stamp of 123 extracted from its fabric (Bloch 244n.182). The principal façade of the house was on Vicus Patricius. It was destroyed toward the beginning of the reign of Antoninus Pius to build a bath complex, which was supported on a terrace in part retained by the house walls, but principally by a very extensive series of vaulted galleries running back to the slope of the Viminal and stretching far to either side of the church. Some of these are shown in sixteenth-century drawings, and they have been rediscovered in excavation. The church is built into a basilical hall of this bath in which a high central nave was surrounded by single-storey aisles, straight on the long sides but curved at the ends. The aisles were separated from the nave by columns of gray marble that supported arches of brickwork and an upper wall lit by a large clerestory window over each intercolumniation. The nave itself produced a series of tanks of curvilinear form sunk in its floor, one a large oval, another with straight sides and rounded annexes. These are very puzzling, and their purpose has never been explained. However, they were filled in while the building was still a bath and covered with a mosaic pavement of marine subjects.

This hall is all that is known of the Thermae Novatianae, and there is no clear evidence of just when it was converted to use as a church, although it was probably not before the fourth century. The design of the hall fits very well with Hadrianic architecture and the baths of Hadrian's villa at Tivoli and may be taken as representative of the form of the smaller baths of Rome in this period.

A. Pettignani, *La basilica di S. Pudenziana* (Rome 1934), 23–44; BullCom 63 (1935): 183–86 (A. M. Colini); R. Krautheimer et al., *Corpus Basilicarum Christianarum Romae* (Rome 1971), 3.289–96; Nash 2.465–66.

Thermae Septimianae: mentioned once in a damaged passage (S.H.A. *Sept. Sev.* 19.5), where Zangemeister conjectures *Septim]ianae.* This seems very probable, as a bath of some sort is clearly meant. These baths were in the Transtiberim in the vicinity of Porta Septimiana, an area where Septimius carried out a number of public works. The additional note that collapse of their aqueduct put these baths out of service almost immediately is puzzling, because the Aqua Traiana was not far distant and could furnish an abundant supply of water. Cf. Balneae Severi, another conjecture to emend this passage that would give substantially the same meaning. See also Thermae Timothei.

Thermae Severianae: baths built by Septimius Severus in Regio I that survived in the fourth century and are listed in the regionary catalogues. They are mentioned in various sources (S.H.A. *Sept. Sev.* 19.5; Chron. 147; Hieron. *a. Abr.* 2216 = A.D. 200) but not located more precisely. Presumably they were somewhere in the valley beyond Porta Capena, but no trace of them is known.

Thermae Surae (rarely **Suranae**): a bath complex on the Aventine, listed in the regionary catalogues in

Regio XIII, built by Licinius Sura (Cass. Dio 68.15.3), or by Trajan and dedicated in the name of his friend (Aur. Vict., *Caes.* 13.8, *Epit.* 13.6). It is shown on fragments of the Marble Plan labeled BAL SVRAE (*FUR* pl. 23; Rodriguez pl. 15) and can be located with great precision, thanks to the preservation of finished edges of the slabs of the plan. It stood just north of the church of S. Prisca, where some remains have been found, as well as an inscription (*CIL* 6.1703 = *ILS* 5715) recording a restoration of a *cella tepidaria* by Caecina Decius Acinatius Albinus, praefectus urbi in A.D. 414. An earlier restoration by Gordian III is attested by part of a marble block, probably a lintel (*NSc* 1920, 141–42 [R. Paribeni]; cf. S.H.A. *Gord.* 32.5). As shown on the Marble Plan, the baths are drawn back from the street behind a row of shops fronting on an arcade. The baths are not symmetrical, consisting of a large courtyard with colonnaded porticoes on three sides and a row of large rooms, evidently the bathing rooms, on the fourth side facing west on the courtyard, an arrangement similar to that found in the baths of Pompeii. There may have been more beyond what is preserved on the plan, but not a great deal.

Licinius Sura evidently had a house near the site of his baths (Martial 6.64.12–13), so it is conceivable that this was pulled down to make space for the baths. However, the modesty and utilitarian simplicity of the complex make it likely that this was the work of Sura rather than work in his honor.

Nash 2.467–68.

Thermae Timothei: mentioned in the Acta S. Iustinae 3[3] in conjunction with the church of S. Pudenziana, either the same as the Thermae Novati (q.v.) or an adjacent bath complex.

Thermae Titi (Titianae) (Figs. 62, 88): the third of the great public baths of Rome, following the Baths of Agrippa and the Baths of Nero. These were built on the Oppius in part of the area of the Domus Aurea, just west of the part later built over by the Baths of Trajan, and faced almost due south. They were in Regio III and were dedicated in A.D. 80, together with the Colosseum (Cass. Dio 66.25.1; Suetonius, *Tit.* 7.3; Hieron. *a. Abr.* 2095). The baths were connected with the square of the amphitheater by a stair, possibly the most magnificent one in Rome. Our knowledge of the plan is due largely to drawings of Palladio (Zorzi figs. 89–95), which show some very unusual and highly questionable features.

At the foot of the stair of approach, along the square of the Colosseum but 35 m from its façade, was a vaulted portico supported on brick-faced piers decorated with engaged columns echoing the architecture of the Colosseum. Palladio shows this as nine

bays wide. In 1895 remains of this portico were excavated, and they are visible today. But it was found that in late antiquity modifications had been introduced, walls run between piers, and new piers built out into the street bounding the Colosseum square, perhaps to make a row of shops behind an arcade. Some of this late work was then removed to free the space and make the original plan clearer.

The stair was in two flights, the lower divided by parapet walls into three equal parts corresponding to bays of the portico. At the landing was a second vaulted portico, also of nine bays, but with the three middle bays recessed the depth of the wings to either side. From this landing an unbroken stair led up between terrace walls to a platform in front of the bath building proper. This terraced platform is an extremely unusual feature, but then is echoed in the design of every subsequent bath. It is presumed to have been largely a garden.

Palladio shows the bath building as completely symmetrical with a large central hall, cruciform, the cross axis vaulted in three bays, with the north arm of the cross developed as an apse, and with four colonnaded exedras opening on the lateral arms. To either side of central hall is a court surrounded by vaulted arcades giving to a large vaulted room with a bowed rear wall and to a stair of uncertain purpose in the corner of the bath building.

On the principal axis going south from the central hall, one passed into a vaulted intermediate space on which opened large stairways to either side, then to a broad corridor by which one reached the pair of caldaria, great cruciform rooms, vaulted, apparently each with a small laconicum attached, thrusting forward from the rest of the building. A row of large rooms facing south behind the caldaria, all probably for bathing, completed the complex. Palladio shows, behind the bath building to the north, a complex of cisterns cut by the diagonal line of the wall of the peribolus of the Baths of Trajan.

The innovation that now becomes a standard feature of such complexes is the terraced open area behind which the baths proper are developed. The anomalies are the numerous stairs of mysterious purpose, the turning to the exterior of a number of small niches (possibly simply inventions of Palladio?), and the cramping of the bath facilities into two banks of rooms rather than three (as in the Baths of Nero, which were, however, rebuilt by Alexander Severus and may present many features that were not original). An unexplained apse to either side in the area that would have been used in a third bank of rooms suggests that Palladio may have misunderstood and misinterpreted the evidence and that actually there were three banks. The Baths of Titus were built in great haste, we are told (Martial, *Spect.* 2.7; Suetonius, *Tit.* 7.8). All that remains of them today is the apse of the central hall, which is decorated with niches alternately semicircular and rectangular, rather different from what Palladio shows.

Coarelli (Coarelli 1974, 203) has suggested that the Baths of Titus may be the baths of the Domus Aurea, rebuilt or adapted, but the relationship to the adjacent remains of the Domus Aurea is not persuasive; walls do not really line up, nor are plans and volumes similar.

Lugli 1946, 353–55; Nash 2.469–71; Lugli 1975, 406; Coarelli 1974, 203–4; *BullCom* 92 (1987–88): 317–23 (G. Caruso and A. Ceccherelli).

Thermae Traiani (Figs. 62, 89): the most important of the great imperial baths, built on the summit of the Oppius after the fire of A.D. 104 destroyed most of this section of the Domus Aurea (Hieron. *a. Abr.* 2120). The architect was Apollodorus of Damascus (Cass. Dio 69.4.1), and to obtain suitable space for his complex he filled the remains of the Domus Aurea with earth and threw out from the façade and through the big courtyard a series of parallel walls at equal distances, which were then connected with vaults. On this platform, a huge rectangle facing southwest, 250 m wide by 210 m deep, with various extensions, the most notable a huge semicircular apron in the middle of the southwest side, the baths stood as an independent, almost isolated building surrounded on three sides by gardens, in turn framed by a peribolus developed as a series of dependencies. The main entrance was in the middle of the northwest side, but there were several subsidiary entrances, including stairways at either end of the southwest front. In the bath building proper one came first to the natatio, a swimming pool surrounded by colonnades on all sides, giving to colonnaded exedras on the southwest side and rows of uniform rooms (shops?) northwest and southeast. Beyond these were more banks of similar rooms. Off the south and west corners of the natatio were large rotundas with niches filling the corners to make squares, possibly frigidaria.

Continuing along the principal axis from the natatio, one came to a magnificent central hall, cruciform in concept but baroque in its forms, vaulted in three bays, and provided with a series of exedras separated from the hall by screens of columns. Beyond this to either side was a rectangular courtyard surrounded by colonnades giving to a large hemicycle with a half-dome decorated with niches, probably not a library, although that has been suggested. A third bank of large rooms facing southwest was almost certainly the bathing facilities, and the caldarium, projecting beyond the mass of the main building at its center, was a series of three vaulted bays

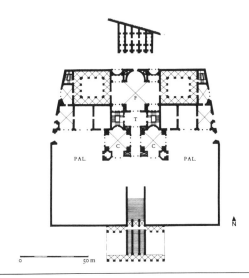

Figure 88
Thermae Titi, Plan
by A. Palladio

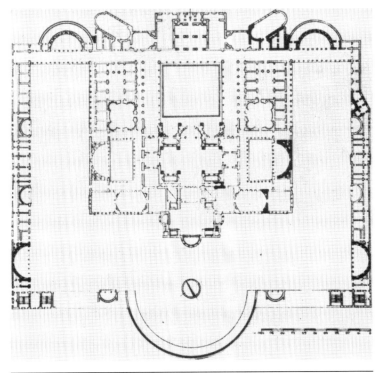

with niches and apses, both rectangular and semicircular.

Around the outer periphery of the complex we may note half-domed apsidal exedras provided with niches in two zones off the south and west corners, very likely libraries. The central semicircular exedra on the main axis provided with a bank of seats following the line of the curve was evidently an area for watching sporting events, and possibly plays as well. Hemicycles off the north and east corners on the northeast side were almost certainly nymphaea, and

Figure 89
Thermae Traiani, Plan
after A. Palladio

rows of symmetrical rooms down the short sides of the complex were probably clubrooms and meeting rooms. A rectangular room with an apse at either end off the northeast side does not follow the orientation of the rest of the baths, but rather that of the Domus Aurea and buildings outside the bath complex.

The masonry, where it survives, is of great beauty, concrete faced with brick of fine quality and precise disposition, the vaults carefully coffered and the brick facing set to give purchase to the stucco finish. Unfortunately only small parts survive, mostly apses, from both the main building and the enclosing peribolus. Discovery of a large inscribed lead pipe belonging to the water system shows that at least some of the water for the baths came from the Aqua Traiana (Nash 1.53–54). The reservoirs for the baths are the well-preserved complex of nine interconnecting chambers known as Sette Sale. These are raised on a foundation storey to ensure that the water would arrive under sufficient pressure, and they carried on their roof a building of two files of small rooms, probably originally housing for the personnel of the baths, although in late antiquity this was rebuilt into a sumptuous palace with a great basilical hall with an apsidal end, a multilobate hall, and a nymphaeum, all richly adorned with colored marble (*RendPontAcc,* ser. 3.47 [1974–75]: 79–101 [L. Cozza]; *AnalRom,* suppl. 10 [1983]: 186–201 [K. De Fine Licht]).

We are told that in the time of Trajan women used his baths (Chron. 146). Small presents, perhaps especially little clay images *(sigillaria),* were sold in the porticoes of the baths during the Saturnalia (schol. *ad Iuv.* 6.154). The baths appear to be mentioned in inscriptions (*CIL* 6.8677 = *ILS* 1628, 8678, 9797 = *ILS* 5173); and in late antiquity they were adorned with statues by Julius Felix Campanianus, praefectus urbi (*CIL* 1670 = *ILS* 5716). In early Christian writings they are regularly called Thermae Titianae. Lanciani is chiefly responsible for establishing their true identity.

Parts of the baths appear on a fragment of the Marble Plan (*FUR* pl. 18; Rodriguez pl. 8), and they are shown on several drawings of the Renaissance, notably some by Palladio (Zorzi figs. 106–9) and the Anonymous Destailleur (cf. HJ 313n.72); from these and what actual remains survive, it is possible to reconstruct a fairly accurate and complete plan of the complex.

Lugli 1946, 355–58, 369–74; Nash 2.472–77; *BdA* 53 (1968): 71–73 (G. Gullini); Coarelli 1974, 204–5; K. De Fine Licht, *Untersuchungen an den Trajansthermen zu Rom (AnalRom,* suppl. 7 [1974]); *BullCom* 84 (1974–75): 249–59 (P. Romeo); Lugli 1975, 402–6; *AJA* 89 (1985): 499–509 (J. C. Anderson).

Tiberinus: a shrine, perhaps only an altar, of the river god on the Tiber island. The anniversary celebration was on 8 December (Degrassi 534–35). No temple of Tiberinus is known. Other holidays in honor of the river were the Ludi Piscatorii on 7 June (Ovid, *Fast.* 6.235–40; Festus 274–75L; Degrassi 466) and the Volturnalia on 27 August (Varro, *Ling.* 6.21, 7.45; Festus 519L; Degrassi 503). Because there was a Flamen Volturnalis, it has been suggested that Volturnus was originally a god of all rivers, or that this was the original name of the Tiber, but neither seems actually to have been the case. The name Tiberis and its mutations Tibris, Tybris, and Thybris certainly seemed to need explanation for the Romans, as their explaining it as the name of a king of Alba who had drowned in the river shows (Varro, *Ling.* 5.29–30; Livy 1.3.8; Ovid, *Fast.* 2.389–90). But the river is seldom called Tiberinus, that name being usually reserved for the divinity. Probably in some sense the whole course of the river was sacred and the abode of the god, which would explain the absence of a temple, except possibly at its headwaters, and the lack of any history of a cult center. But there must have been at least an altar. The Vicus Tiberinus listed last in Regio XIV on the Capitoline Base (*CIL* 6.975 = *ILS* 6073) seems likely to have been on the right bank.

J. Le Gall, *Recherche sur le culte du Tibre* (Paris 1953), especially 40–45.

Tiberis: the river of Rome and the longest river in central Italy, running from headwaters in the Apennines between Umbria and Etruria close to the sources of the Arno and draining most of central Etruria, Umbria, and the Sabine territory, as well as Latium. Important tributaries are the Clanis, the Nar, and the Anio. Although it is not navigable by vessels of deep draft above Rome, its use as a highway for traffic to and from the interior, especially by those in the mountains coming down to the sea for salt, gave Rome its raison d'être (*MAAR* 36 [1980]: 35–42 [F. Castagnoli], 43–53 [A. M. Colini]). Below Rome the river swells to such volume that a crossing is difficult and dangerous, whereas the island at Rome broke the force of the current temporarily and created below it a slack water where a ferry could be maneuvered successfully. The Tiber is a treacherous river, having much of the character of a mountain torrent; it can rise with surprising rapidity and in winter is subject to flooding in the vicinity of Rome, its flood plain opening up below Prima Porta. Floods in Rome were frequent and often destructive (cf.

Horace, *Car.* 1.2.13–16; J. Le Gall, *Le Tibre, fleuve de Rome dans l'antiquité* [Paris 1953], 29–35, where a list of known floods is included). However, whether Julius Caesar's scheme to cut a new channel for the Tiber from Pons Mulvius *secundum Montis Vaticanos* (Cicero, *Att.* 13.33.4) was a scheme for better flood control—if indeed it was not simply a flight of fancy, as seems likely—may be doubted.

The origin of the name Tiberis is uncertain (Varro, *Ling.* 5.30; Servius *ad Aen.* 8.330), but it appears in the augural prayer (Cicero, *Nat. D.* 3.52), so it must be of considerable antiquity. Earlier the river is supposed to have been called Albula. Servius (*ad Aen.* 8.332) and Festus (Paulus *ex Fest.* 4L) believed this was from its color. It is more commonly characterized as *fulvus* (Horace, *Car.* 1.2.13, 2.3.18), and Vergil describes it as *caeruleus* (*Aen.* 8.64). The other adjectives should be understood as emphasizing its opacity. Because the city of Tibur clearly bears the same name and until quite recently the Anio, Tibur's river, was called the Teverone, the name Albula is probably to be connected with Albunea, the nymph of the sulfur springs of Tibur (Vergil, *Aen.* 7.83–84 and Servius ad loc. 8.332), which empty into the Anio and whiten its water. It may be that the tawny color of the Tiber at Rome was thought to be similarly produced.

The governance of the river was originally in the hands of the censors, like all similar public works. Embankment walls were constructed in the Forum Boarium as early as the second century B.C. and probably earlier. The earliest of which we have clear record is the work of P. Servilius Vatia Isauricus and M. Valerius Messalla Niger, censors in 55 B.C., who style themselves curatores riparum. They erected terminal cippi, of which nineteen are known, extending from Pons Mulvius to the mouth of the Almo (*CIL* 1².766 = 6.31540 = *ILS* 5922). They would have traced the boundary between public and private property and repaired and revetted embankments. They were followed in 8 B.C. by the consuls C. Asinius Gallus and C. Marcius Censorinus, twenty of whose cippi survive (*CIL* 6.31541 = *ILS* 5923), which were inscribed with the distance in feet to the next cippus. And these were followed in the next year by Augustus himself, twenty-two of whose cippi remain (*CIL* 6.31542 = *ILS* 5924). These also gave the distances between cippi, which turn out to be very variable, perhaps depending on the density of building in the area. It is not clear whether Augustus took up where the curatores riparum of the previous year had left off; he seems subsequently to have made the office of curator annual (Suetonius, *Aug.* 37).

In A.D. 15, after a great flood, Tiberius appointed five special curatores (Tacitus, *Ann.* 1.76; Cass. Dio 57.14.7–8). These replaced a number of cippi or added their inscription to those already existing. Their authority extended to Ostia (*NSc* 1921, 258–62 [G. Calza]). A little later there was a restoration of the bank near the Pons Cestius (*CIL* 6.31543) and elsewhere (*CIL* 6.31544 = *ILS* 5925). Under Claudius there was an interesting restoration *a Trigario ad Pontem Agrippae,* again by five curatores (*CIL* 6.31545 = *ILS* 5926).

Beginning with Vespasian, there is only a single curator named, and we have cippi for Vespasian, Trajan, Hadrian, Antoninus Pius, Marcus Aurelius, and Septimius Severus (*CIL* 6.31546–31555 = *ILS* 5927–5934). Thereafter, there is a gap until the time of Diocletian (*CIL* 6.31556 = *ILS* 5894), although Aurelian recorded his work on the river otherwise (S.H.A., *Aurel.* 47.3).

What the work of each successive team of curatores amounted to one cannot guess. Obviously special funds had to be allotted from time to time, and work along the wharves at the Emporium must have taken precedence over work along the Campus Martius. But both banks of the river came under their care, whether they were densely inhabited or not; the riverbed would have had to be dredged out regularly, almost constantly; and bridges and their approaches would have presented special problems. Since the building of the modern Tiber embankment in the nineteenth century, all trace of ancient work in the heart of the city has disappeared beneath and behind this, but some idea of the impressive scale of the work can be had from old prints and from the evidence of the Emporium (q.v.).

BullCom 17 (1889): 165–72 (L. Borsari), 21 (1893): 14–26 (R. Lanciani); Lugli 1934, 278–96; J. Le Gall, *Le Tibre, fleuve de Rome dans l'antiquité* (Paris 1953).

Tiburtinus Neronis: see **Terbentinum Neronis.**

Tiburtius Mons (or **Collis**): a name, possibly only an antiquarian invention, given the Quirinal by Lydus (*Mens.* 4.155) in his less familiar list of the hills of Rome. Cf. Praenestius Mons. It seems hardly likely that anyone going to Tibur would choose to leave by Porta Nomentana, and the Porta Tiburtina is on the Esquiline. It may be that Lydus or his source is confused about this. Hülsen (HJ 229n.27) dismisses it as a pure invention.

Tifata Curia: a grove of holly oaks *(iliceta)* named after M. Curius Dentatus after his victory over the Samnites. Because of his brilliant exploits and public works he was presented with a house *apud Tiphatam*

([Aur, Vict.,] *De Vir. Ill.* 33.10; Festus 503L). There is no indication of where this might have been. Cf. Tifata Mancina.

Tifata Mancina: a stand of holly oaks named for an unknown Mancinus whose house was made public property after his execution (Paulus *ex Fest.* 117L). Cf. Tifata Curia.

Tigillum Sororium: a beam that spanned the branch of the Sacra Via leading to the Oppius just above the Compitum Acilii (Degrassi 515, Oct. 1) listed in the regionary catalogues in Regio IV. Festus (380L) says that it was supported by two upright timbers, but for most people it simply spanned the street. Below it, to either side, was an altar, one to Iuno Sororia, the other to Ianus Curiatius. There was a common legend associating the Tigillum with the expiation of Horatius, the hero of the combat of the Horatii and Curiatii, for the murder of his sister (Livy 1.26.13; Festus, 380L; Dion. Hal. 3.22.7; [Aur. Vict.,] *De Vir. Ill.* 4.9), but it is told apologetically. Obviously this was a very ancient monument, and the gods of the altars are not known elsewhere. In view of the popularity of syzygia in rustic sanctuaries shown in Roman landscape painting, it seems unnecessary to seek a deep meaning for the Tigillum, although it is not clear why it should have spanned a street.

L. A. Holland, *Janus and the Bridge* (Rome 1961), 77–91.

Titus, Divus, Aedes: see **Vespasianus, Divus, Aedes,** and **Divorum, Templum.**

Ad To(n)sores: mentioned in an inscription on a slave collar (*CIL* 15.7172 = *ILS* 8727), a district near a temple of Flora. Another inscription locates a barber *ad circum* (*CIL* 6.31900). While we must suppose that there were barbers all over Rome, the existence of a temple of Flora on the slope of the Aventine at the west end of the Circus Maximus suggests a certain concentration of barbers there.

Traianenses: inhabitants of a district identified by one of Trajan's monuments, probably the Thermae Traiani, but perhaps the Platea Traiani or another, mentioned in a single inscription, the edict of Tarracius Bassus of the late fourth century respecting fraudulent merchants and shopkeepers (*CIL* 6.10099 = 31893.b1 = *ILS* 6072.1).

Traianus, Divus, Templum: see **Forum Traiani.**

Transtiberim: the name given Regio XIV in the regionary catalogues. It also occurs in a sepulchral in-

scription (*CIL* 6.9847). If the theory that the first items listed in the regionary catalogues for the regiones are not the names of these, but simply landmarks or buildings included in them, is correct, then this might be a square at the head of the Pons Sublicius, or possibly Pons Aemilius, although that does not seem very likely.

Ad Tres Fortunas: see **Fortunae (Tres), Aedes.**

Ad Tres Silanos: a place designation in an inscription found at Grotta Ferrata, but evidently referring to Rome and putting this in Regio VII (*CIL* 14.2496). Festus (482L) defines a *silanus* as a jet like the falls of the Anio at Tibur. Lucretius (6.1265) mentions such fountains, and one can easily imagine a nymphaeum with three cascades that might be known by this name, but it is impossible to locate it more precisely.

Tria Fata: statues of the three Fates or Sibyls supposed to have been set up by Tarquinius Priscus, believed by Pliny (*HN* 34.22) to be, with the statue of Attus Navius, the oldest statues in Rome, except for those of the kings in the Area Capitolina, so presumably about half life size. One was restored by Sex. Pacuvius Taurus and two by M. Messalla, presumably the men of these names of the early Augustan period. The statues stood near the Rostra Augusti toward the Curia Iulia (Pliny, *HN* 34.22; Procopius, *BellGoth* 1.25.19). The first occurrence of the name Tria Fata is in A.D. 250 (Cyprian, *Epist.* 21.13), where it means the area of the Forum Romanum in front of the Curia Iulia. By the fourth century it seems to have become a standard term. Later Tria Fata and In Tribus Fatis are alternate and equivalent to Ad Palmam (see Palmam), which then replaces them. No one describes the statues in detail, nor do they seem to be shown in any representation.

Jordan 1.2.258–59, 349.

Tribunal: see **Rostra, Suggestus, Tribunal.**

Tribunal Aurelium: mentioned four times by Cicero in connection with the enrollment of an army by Clodius, *nomine collegiorum*, early in 58 B.C. (Cicero, *Sest.* 34, *Pis.* 11, *Dom.* 54, *Red. Pop.* 13). Cicero implies that this army was composed of the worst elements of the city, including slaves, and organized for violence. In three of the passages he follows mention of this immediately with mention of Clodius's stocking of the Temple of Castor with weapons and turning it into a fortress and base of operations. Cicero also implies that the whole process was a parody of the formal levy (*dilectus*) held in the presence of the consuls, and he describes it in these terms. One might therefore associate the Tribunal Aurelium with the Ovile, where a dilectus would normally be held, and such a tribunal in the Ovile might have been rebuilt by L. Aurelius Cotta, censor in 64 B.C. However, one might think of a praetor's tribunal on the speakers' platform in front of the Temple of Castor belonging to an unknown Aurelius. The former seems more likely.

There is no real reason to associate the Tribunal Aurelium with the Gradus Aurelii (q.v.), as they are never mentioned together. The identification of older remains around the Temple of Divus Iulius as the Tribunal and Gradus Aurelii proposed by R. Gamberini Mongenet and accepted by Nash (2.478–81) cannot be correct. Whatever that building was, it was larger than the temple, while everything we know about *tribunalia* indicates that they were modest affairs.

Roma, archeologia nel centro (1985), 1.67–72 (M. G. Cecchini); *Arctos* 21 (1987): 144–47 (M. Steinby).

Tribunal Deorum:

Tribunal Deorum: a monument *in Capitolino post piscinam,* presumably in the Area Capitolina, known only from military diplomata that were displayed there (*CIL* 16.22; *AE* 1980, 788).

Tribunal Praetoris: the platform on which the curule chair of a praetor was set to indicate that he was ready to receive business or that court was in session. It was probably large enough to accommodate an *assessor* or two, should the praetor wish to invite one, but little more. The praetor's lictors did not stand on the tribunal. The tribunals of the praetors in charge of different courts seem to have had customary locations around the Forum Romanum, but these were not permanently fixed. The court of the praetor urbanus was originally held in the Comitium, that of the praetor peregrinus *in medio foro,* the *quaestio de ambitu* in the Comitium, and so on. The ends of the various speakers' platforms and altar platforms in front of temples were the usual locations. Here the tribunals themselves needed to be only a few inches high.

In the travertine pavement of the Forum Romanum southeast of the Columna Phocae are matrices for the bronze letters of an inscription of the praetor peregrinus L. Naevius Surdinus (*CIL* 6.37068; cf. 6.1460; Nash 1.397 fig. 485). This has sometimes been thought to show the location of his tribunal, but without adequate warrant.

Tribunal Praetorium: Lugli (Lugli 1947, 62–63) wished to identify remains in front of the Temple of Castor with the tribunal of the praetor urbanus after it was moved from the Comitium to the neighborhood of the Puteal Libonis. These remains consist of

four shallow steps leading up from the southwest and foundations of a platform that would fill the area in front of the Temple of Divus Iulius, together with some fragments of columns of verde antico and granite and fragments of a fine cornice in white marble. Lugli proposed that these last elements were used for a pavilion to cover the praetor's sella curulis, presumably set at the end of the platform so as not to interfere with the view of the façade of the temple. But the evidence for such a pavilion is nugatory, and the pavilion would run counter to Roman religious dictates. And the platform looks rather like an apron in front of the temple, working together with it, than a separate entity. In its present state it is not high enough to give the praetor the distinction his magistracy requires, and if it were built higher it would interfere with the view of the temple. It is better to think of this as the place for a court, or courts, whose presiding praetor(s) sat on the rostra of the Temple of Divus Iulius, a space marked off from the rest of the forum but not significantly elevated.

S. Stucchi, *I monumenti della parte meridionale del Foro Romano* (Rome 1958), 76–81; Nash 2.482–83.

Tribunal Divi Vespasiani, Titi, Domitiani: a tribunal erected in Capitolio, known only from a military diploma that was displayed affixed to it (*CIL* 16.28). This is generally presumed to have been a base for statues of the Flavian emperors (cf. Suetonius, *Dom.* 13.2).

Trigarium: see **Circus, Trigarium, Stadium,** etc.

Trigarium: listed by the regionary catalogues in Regio IX, a place along the Tiber (*CIL* 6.31545 = *ILS* 5926, found in situ on the river opposite the church of S. Biagio della Pagnotta) where horses were exercised (*CGL* [Goetz] 2.201 [Philoxenus]). Passages in Pliny (*HN* 28.238, 29.9, 37.202) show that this meant in racing competition. It is usually presumed that this course was for races in teams of three horses (so PA), but the Romans only occasionally raced teams of three, their chariot teams being almost always of even numbers, two, four, or six (Dion. Hal. 7.73.2; *CIL* 6.10047, 10048; *ILS* 5287, 5288). Because a *triga* is any set of three and the Equirria of 27 February and 14 March and the race of bigae on 15 October seem likely to have been celebrated here, there might have been three tracks here of different lengths or, because the word seems to have been used of racetracks generally (Pliny, *HN* 37.202), it might have meant a place where the three principal sorts of races were run. Cf. Friedländer, *Rom. Life* 2.453–72 and appendix 24.

Its location is in dispute. Scholarly opinion is

about equally divided between those who would put it southeast of S. Biagio della Pagnotta and those who would put it north of Via dei Coronari. The former would put it in proximity to the headquarters of the circus teams (see Stabula IIII Factionum), but in an area that was probably densely built up by the Severan period. Of course, by the time of the regionary catalogues it may have become no more than a place designation.

AnalRom, suppl. 10 (1983): 59–85 (L. Quilici); La Rocca 1984, 57–69; TAPS 80 (1990): 29–33 (R. E. A. Palmer).

Tropaea Germanici: attested only in inscriptions on the location of military diplomata (CIL 16.32, 33), which inform us that they stood on a base (tribunal) near the Temple of Fides (see Fides, Aedes) on the Capitoline.

Tropaea Marii: trophies that Marius erected to celebrate his victories that Sulla dismantled and Julius Caesar restored as aedile in 65 B.C. (Vell. Pat. 2.43.4; Suetonius, Iul. 11). Suetonius says that they were trophies for both his victory over Jugurtha and his victory over the Cimbri and Teutones. Plutarch (Caes. 6.1–2) gives the information that when Caesar restored the trophies they included portraits of Marius and Victorias bearing trophies and that they were exceptionally fine work and were gilded. They stood on the Capitoline (cf. also Propertius 3.11.45–46), and, because that was the traditional location for trophies, there is no warrant for supposing that the Cimbrian shield located by Cicero (De Or. 2.266) sub novis (i.e., the tabernae in front of the Basilica Fulvia et Aemilia) formed part of them (cf. also Pliny, HN 35.25; Quintilian 6.3.38). If anything, the shield is rather to be associated with Marius's Temple of Honos et Virtus. Nor should the trophies be confused with the marble trophies now mounted on the balustrade of the Piazza del Campidoglio that were brought here in 1590 from the nymphaeum known as the Trofei di Mario in Piazza Vittorio Emanuele. For these, see Nymphaeum Alexandri.

A second set of Marian trophies supposed by some to have been recorded by Valerius Maximus (6.9.14: cuius bina tropaea in urbe spectantur) seems to depend on a misunderstanding. As the context shows, what Valerius means are the two sets of trophies, one for the victory in Africa and one for the victory over the Cimbri and Teutones. See also Honos et Virtus (Mariana), Aedes (2).

Tropaea Neronis: trophies that Nero erected on the Capitoline, medio Capitolini Montis, to celebrate the victories over the Parthians of A.D. 62 (Tacitus, Ann. 15.18). Because Tacitus speaks of these together with the Arcus Neronis, it is probable that they were part of the program of sculpture crowning the arch, rather than a separate monument, but this is not borne out by the evidence of the coins showing the arch. See Arcus Neronis.

Tugurium Faustuli: see **Casa Romuli.**

Tullianum: see **Carcer.**

Tumulus: see **Sepulcrum, Sepulcretum,** etc.

Tumulus Iuliae: the tumulus in the Campus Martius in which Julia, the daughter of Caesar and wife of Pompey who died in childbirth in 54 B.C., was buried. Her body was not cremated, but buried by the people of Rome, despite the objections of the magistrates (Livy, Epit. 106; Plutarch, Pomp. 53.4, Caes. 23.4; Cass. Dio 39.64). Plutarch says that Pompey had made preparations for her burial at his villa at Albanum, so this burial must have been impromptu and the tumulus raised later. A pyre for Caesar himself was prepared in the vicinity of this tumulus (Suetonius, Iul. 84.1), and his ashes were apparently deposited in this tomb, which Dio (44.51.1) describes as the family tomb. If the body of Julia was buried in a sarcophagus, as seems probable, and the tomb later given monumental form, this is almost certainly the place where the embalmed body of Drusus was deposited after it was brought to Rome from Germany in 9 B.C. (Livy, Epit. 142) and the place where the body of Poppaea was placed (Tacitus, Ann. 16.6: tumuloque Iuliorum infertur). All indications are that it was an impressive and capacious monument and, as a tumulus, a forerunner of the Mausoleum Augusti. It has never been located.

Tumulus Maecenatis: known only from Suetonius's statement (Vit. Hor. 20) that Horace was buried on the boundary of the Esquiline: iuxta Maecenatis tumulum. Because Maecenas was of Etruscan origins and a minister of Augustus, whose mausoleum took the form of a tumulus, such a tomb would be fitting, but its location is unknown.

Tumulus Octaviorum: a tomb of the Octavii known from mention in Tacitus (Ann. 4.44) as the burial place of L. Antonius, the grandson of Octavia, in A.D. 25. Because Suetonius (Aug. 2–4) says Augustus's immediate forebears were quiet country aristocracy living at Velitrae in the Alban Hills until the time of Augustus's father, C. Octavius, the first of the family to become a Roman senator, it may be that this tomb was built for him and his family. Its location is unknown.

Turris Maecenatiana: a tower from which Suetonius (*Nero* 38.2) says that Nero watched the great fire that destroyed most of Rome in A.D. 64. He is also supposed to have recited an Iliupersis, dressed for the theater as he did so. Presumably it was part of the Horti Maecenatiani (q.v.) on the Esquiline. Horace (*Car.* 23.29.10) speaks of Maecenas's house in Rome as *molem propinquam nubibus arduis,* but that is probably in regard to the mass of the whole, rather than a particular tower.

Turris Mamilia: a tower in the *Suburae regio* on which the Suburanenses affixed the head of the October horse, if they were victorious in their annual battle with the Sacravienses for possession of it (Festus 190L). Elsewhere, Festus (Paulus *ex Fest.* 117L) says that the tower got its name from a certain Mamilius, a member of the leading *gens* of Tusculum. A C. Mamilius Turrinus was consul in 239 B.C., and a Q. Mamilius Turrinus was praetor peregrinus in 206. All this suggests that the *turris* was a familiar landmark and could be regarded as the heart of the Subura, but not necessarily a public building. The fact that the two factions contending for the head were clearly geographical, but not regiones of the city of Servius Tullius, nor any other familiar entity, suggests that the struggle for the possession of the head was not a religious ritual but an impromptu donnybrook. Plutarch (*Quaest. Rom.* 97) indicates that the battle took place in the Forum Romanum, after the tail of the horse had been taken to the Regia and blood from it allowed to drip on the hearth there. Then two gangs converged, one coming down from the Sacra Via, the other from the Subura, to contend for the head. Because most interested Romans must have attended the race and sacrifice of the horse in the Campus Martius, the formation of these factions poses a logistical problem. The head must have brought good luck, as well as glory, to the winning side. The Turris Mamilia was still standing in the early empire (*CIL* 6.33837 = *ILS* 7242) but is not listed in the regionary catalogues.

Tutilinae, Ara, Columna: on the spina of the Circus Maximus, mentioned by Tertullian (*De Spect.* 8) in conjunction with altars and columns of Sessia and Messia, other divinities of agriculture. The columns carried images. Tertullian says that people thought of them as Samothracian, but Roscher (cf. 2.204, 221–22, 228 [R. Peter]) lists them among the Indigites. The *Tutilinae loca* of which Varro speaks in a mutilated passage (*Ling.* 5.163) must be between Porta Capena and Porta Naevia, for Varro is speaking of gates and this is the sequence indicated. He says that Ennius lived here. Jerome (*Hieron. a. Abr.* 1777) says that Ennius lived modestly on the Aventine, but no contradiction is involved if we put the Tutilinae loca on the Aventinus Minor on the slope above Porta Capena near the church of S. Balbina.

U

V

Umbilicus Romae: probably to be identified with the Milliarium Aureum (q.v.), because it is unlikely that the city could have tolerated two supposedly precise centers of the city close to each other. The Umbilicus is first mentioned in the *Notitia,* after the Temple of Concordia and before the Temple of Saturn, then in the Einsiedeln itinerary (1.5, 6.7, 7.8; Jordan 2.647, 652, 655). It has been identified with a brick-faced cylinder rising in three stages, 4.60 m in diameter at the base and 3 m at the crown, at the north corner of the Rostra Augusti. This was once faced with marble. A small chamber in the interior is accessible, but the entrance is too narrow for access to have been regular. The construction is of the early fourth century, but later than the monument to the tetrarchy of A.D. 303. If this was finished as an omphalos in imitation of the omphaloi of Greek cities and carried the Milliarium on its summit, one can see how both names might have come into currency. The only source using both names, as though there were two monuments, is the *Notitia.* The transference of the Milliarium from one side of the Rostra to the other may be laid to a need to remove some of the clutter from the forum square; after the building of the Arch of Septimius Severus, the Milliarium would have been less in the way at the north corner of the Rostra. But it is just possible that it was always here.

An attempt by F. Coarelli to identify this monument with the Mundus (2) (q.v.) is not convincing (*DialArch* 9–10 [1976–77]: 346–77, especially 357–73); his identification of the Ara Saturni is of doubtful value for the topography of other monuments in the Forum Romanum.

Lugli 1946, 146–47; Nash 2.484–86; *DialArch* 9–10 (1976–77): 378–98 (M. Verzor); *RendPontAcc* 55–56 (1982–84): 329–40 (P. Verduchi).

Urbis Fanum: see **Venus et Roma, Templum.**

Ustrinum Antoninorum: a name given to a monument that the architect F. Bianchini discovered in 1703 under the Casa della Missione, just west of Palazzo di Montecitorio. See Faustina Maior, Diva, Ara.

Ustrinum Domus Augustae: the crematorium in conjunction with the Mausoleum Augusti in the northern Campus Martius; Strabo (5.3.8 [236]) describes it. It was surrounded by a circular iron fence within which was an enclosure wall of white stone, presumably travertine, around the actual crematorium. The space between was planted with black poplars. Excavations in 1777 at the corner of Via del Corso and Via degli Otto Cantoni just north of S. Carlo al Corso brought to light six large travertine cippi inscribed with the names of members of the family of Augustus, Germanicus's daughter and three sons, Drusus's son Tiberius, and a Vespasianus, nephew of the princeps (*CIL* 6.888–93; *ILS* 172, 181, 188); an alabaster urn was also found (Helbig⁴ 1.420). The first three cippi end with the formula *hic crematus est,* while the fourth and fifth end *hic situs (sita) est.* This makes it probable that the ustrinum lay east of the mausoleum, between it and the Via del Corso, and that, as the mausoleum began to become crowded, various members of the family were buried in and around the crematorium. The plan that Lanciani gives for this ustrinum (LFUR sheet 8) derives from the construction found under the Casa della Missione (see Faustina Maior, Diva, Ara), not from actual remains. Strabo (5.3.8 [236]; cf. also Suetonius, *Aug.* 100.4) says that the ustrinum and mausoleum were surrounded by a large park with splendid walks; these seem to have stretched from the Tiber to the Via Flaminia and from the mausoleum north, perhaps to the line of the Aurelian Walls.

HJ 620–21; Lugli 1938, 211–12; *CAR* 2-D, 97 p. 100; *QITA* 10 (1988): 7–15 (E. Tortorici).

Ustrinum Marci Aurelii (?): see **Faustina Minor, Diva, Ara.**

Vallis Egeriae: see **Camenae.**

Vallis Murcia: see **Murcia** and **Circus Maximus.**

Vallis Vaticana: a place designation occurring only once (Tacitus, *Ann.* 14.14), used to denote an area where Nero was at first allowed to exercise his passion for chariot racing in private *(clausum Valle Vaticana spatium)*. This can hardly be the Circus Gaii et Neronis, which already had architectural form, but no other area on the right bank of the Tiber suggests itself as a *vallis*. And were it the Gaianum (q.v.) that was meant, Tacitus would certainly have called it that. Because the whole right riverbank was regularly called Ager Vaticanus, one might even go as far north as Monte Mario to look for a suitable depression, but more likely a practice track in the vicinity of the Circus Gaii et Neronis is what is meant, and this is more likely to have been to the south of the circus than elsewhere. This probability is strengthened by the existence of the Horti Agrippinae (q.v.) here.

Vaticanus: 1. Vaticanus Ager: according to Pliny (*HN* 3.54; cf. Livy 10.26.15), the proper designation of the territory on the right bank of the Tiber below the point where it is joined by the Cremera, thus apparently an alternative for Veientanus (as in Ripa Veientana), except that Pliny uses Vaticanus Ager for the territory on the right bank also *above* the juncture with the Cremera. The term is more particularly used of the territory on the right bank in the neighborhood of Rome. This territory was farmed from early times, but generally regarded as rather poor land (Cicero, *Leg. Agr.* 2.96), and the quality of its wine disparaged, especially by Martial (1.18.2, 6.92.3, 10.45.5, 12.48.14). In the immediate neighborhood of Rome, it was largely divided into horti by the middle of the first century B.C., many of which were absorbed into the great imperial estates (see, e.g., Horti Caesaris (2), Horti Agrippinae, Horti Domitiae), but the hinterland continued to be farmland called Ager Vaticanus into late antiquity (Solinus 2.34; Symmachus, *Epist.* 6.58.1).

The origin of the name Vaticanus excited some interest, and Varro (*ap. A. Gell.* 16.17.1–2) asserted that there was a Deus Vaticanus, not only protector of the lands, but inspirer of prophetic powers and deriving his name from *vaticinium* and ultimately from the root of *vagire* (cf. Augustine, *De civ. D.* 4.8.12). The name actually appears to be adjectival, derived perhaps from the name of an Etruscan settlement (possibly Vatica or Vaticum) of which all trace is lost. The cognomen Vaticanus in the consular fasti for 455 and 451 B.C. is probably not testimony to this, because it appears as an additional name.

2. Vaticani Montes: used only once (Cicero, *Att.* 13.33.4) in connection with Julius Caesar's project to divert the Tiber into a new course running in a straight north/south direction beginning at Pons Mulvius and bringing the loop known as Prati di Castello into union with the old Campus Martius. The new course would run *secundum Montes Vaticanos,* and these would include Monte Mario, the modern Monte Vaticano, and the Janiculan hill, including Monteverde Vecchio.

3. Vaticanus Mons: used in the singular to mean the Janiculan ridge (Horace, *Car.* 1.20.7–8 and schol.; Juvenal 6.344). A variant on this is Festus's Vaticanus Collis (519L). As the noun Vaticanum came to be an alternate for the Circus Vaticanus (Circus Gaii et Neronis) and the martyrdom of Saint Peter there and his burial in an adjacent tomb focused Christian attention on that particular sector, Vaticanus Mons came to identify the modern Monte Vaticano. In the addenda to the regionary catalogues of the fourth century, we already find a distinction between Vaticanus Mons and Ianiculensis Mons.

4. Vaticana Vallis: see **Vallis Vaticana.**

5. Vaticanum: probably used at first to designate the level ground between the Vaticanus Mons and the Tiber, including Prati di Castello (Pliny, *HN* 8.37, 16.237, 18.20; Tacitus, *Hist.* 2.93). Cicero (*Att.* 13.33.4) once calls this Campus Vaticanus. At least part of it was regarded as unhealthy in summer, probably malarial (Tacitus, *Hist.* 2.93), and it was known for its indigent (Amm. Marc. 27.3.6). Tombs are mentioned near the Circus Vaticanus (S.H.A. *Verus* 6.4, *Heliogab.* 23.1, and cf. schol. *ad Hor. Epod.* 9.25, which is certainly unreliable).

The construction of the Circus Gaii et Neronis (q.v.) here brought increased interest and importance to its vicinity, and it began to be called simply Vaticanum (Suetonius, *Claud.* 21.2; Amm. Marc. 17.4.16); it is so called in the regionary catalogues. The inscriptions alluding to the Phrygianum and shrine of Virtus Bellona on the Vatican (*CIL* 13.1751 = *ILS* 4131, 7281 = *ILS* 3805) are not helpful, because the Phrygianum lay within the area of the circus and we cannot locate the shrine of Bellona.

RhM 46 (1891): 112–38 (A. Elter); HJ 623–25; *PAPS* 125 (1981): 367–97 (R. E. A. Palmer).

Vediovis, Aedes (1): a temple on the Tiber island attested in the Fasti Praenestini and Antiates Maiores, its anniversary the Kalends of January (Degrassi 388). This appears to be the temple that the praetor L. Furius Purpurio vowed in 200 B.C. at the Battle of Cremona (Livy 31.21.12, where the manuscripts read *deo Iovi* and editors correct to *Vediovi*) and dedicated in 194 by C. Servilius (Livy 34.53.7, where again the text must be emended). These emendations are relatively easy, and the fact that the same day was the anniversary for Aesculapius on the island strengthens the case. Vediovis was a divinity with a sinister side who might well have found a place on the island, and he would have been unfamiliar to most people in the Middle Ages. It is not so easy to explain Ovid's apparent confusion of Vediovis with Jupiter on this day (*Fast.* 1.293–94), unless we assume that all the divinities associated with the island were honored on this day and that Iuppiter Iurarius is meant (but cf. Faunus, whose proper anniversary was the Ides of February). Ovid's mention of Jupiter is so casual that it might be simply a misreading of the calendar.

Vediovis, Aedes (2) (Fig. 19): a temple *inter duos lucos* on the Capitoline in the saddle between the two crests of the hill, evidently the temple that L. Furius Purpurio vowed as consul in 198 B.C. and Q. Marcius Ralla dedicated in 192 B.C. (Livy 35.41.8). The dedication day was 7 March (Ovid, *Fast.* 3.429–30; Fast. Praen., Ant. Maior.; Degrassi 421).

The temple, which Vitruvius (4.8.4) described as being of unusual plan, was discovered in 1939 during work under the Palazzo del Senatore built over the Tabularium (q.v.). The temple occupies the southwest corner of the rectangle covered by the Tabularium, which had to be made irregular to accommodate it. It faces southwest and has a plan similar to that of the Temple of Concordia on the Forum Romanum, with a cella of transverse axis and a shallow pronaos of four unfluted columns. What we see appears to be a rebuilding of the time of the construction of the Tabularium, and the reason for the anomalous plan is not clear. The temple stood on a moderately high podium faced with travertine and trimmed with a crisp, tight molding. Soundings in the interior have located parts of the original building and of a rebuilding of the mid-second century.

The cult statue was also found, but lacking its extremities and attributes. It shows a youthful god with long, romantic hair and a powerful frame. Ovid (*Fast.* 3.437–44) describes him as a young Jupiter accompanied by a she-goat. Aulus Gellius (5.12.11–

12) adds that he holds arrows. Another statue of the god in the same temple was made of cypress wood and was believed by Pliny (*HN* 16.216) to be as old as the foundation of the temple in 192 B.C.

Jordan 1.2.115–18; *BullCom* 70 (1942): 5–56 (A. M. Colini); Lugli 1946, 39–42; Nash 2.490–95.

Velabrum Maius: the low saddle between the Forum Romanum and the Forum Boarium, especially the southeastern part of this where the Vicus Tuscus crossed it. The name is certainly very ancient and was of mysterious origin for Romans of the historical period. They also seem to have been unable to bound it. The inscription on the Arcus Argentariorum (see Arcus Septimii Severi in Foro Boario), which adjoins the church of S. Giorgio in Velabro, speaks of *negotiantes boari huius* (*CIL* 6.1035 = *ILS* 426). The wish to derive the name from *vehere* and/or *velum* may have influenced the Romans' own definition of the place. Varro (*Ling.* 5.43–44, 6.24) is explicit that it was the place where the ferry between the Aventine and the Forum Romanum and Palatine landed, and in memory of this there was a Sacellum Velabrum at the end of Nova Via. Propertius (4.9.5) and Tibullus (2.5.33) follow Varro in this explanation, but Ovid sees the area of the lower Forum Boarium as a canebrake (*Fast.* 6.405–7). Others derived the name from the awnings that covered the streets when games were given in the Circus Maximus (Plutarch, *Rom.* 5.5). None of the explanations offered for the name is, or was to the Romans, satisfactory.

From the time of Plautus (*Capt.* 489, *Curc.* 483) to the time of Martial (11.52.10, 13.32; cf. *CIL* 6.9184, 9259, 9993 = *ILS* 7485, 33933) the Velabrum was the site of a busy market, especially in foodstuffs, and Macrobius (*Sat.* 1.10.15) characterizes it as a *locus celeberrimus*. Because traffic between the Forum Romanum and Palatine and Forum Boarium must always have been intense and passed over it, this is not surprising, but the only monument mentioned as being in the Velabrum is the tomb of Acca Larentia (see Sepulcrum Accae Larentiae), although the Temple of Felicitas (see Felicitas, Aedes) may also have been there, so it must have been very restricted in area.

Varro (*Ling.* 5.156) distinguished a Velabrum Maius and a Velabrum Minus, and Propertius (4.9.5) and Ovid (*Fast.* 6.405–7) both use the plural Velabra. But for Ovid and Propertius these Velabra were together, whereas for Varro the Velabrum Minus was a swampy patch near the north corner of the Forum Romanum created by drainage from the Lautolae (q.v.). This swamp must early have been

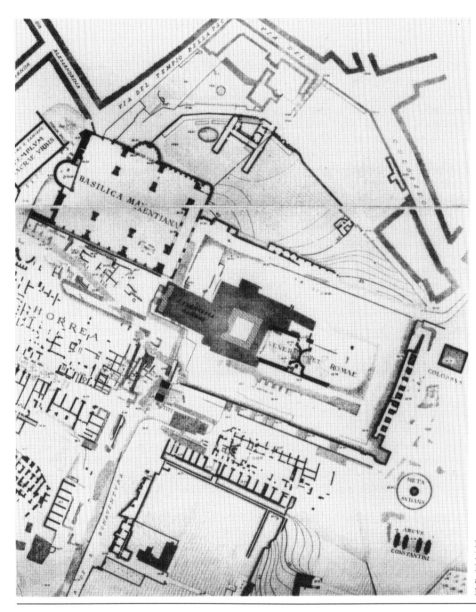

Figure 90
Mons Velia, Showing
Remains of Antiquity
and Important Modern
Features

channeled off into the Cloaca and forgotten, but the persistence of the distinction Maius may have led the poets to use the plural for that which remained.

BullCom 89 (1984): 249–96 (G. Cressedi).

Velabrum Minus: see **Velabrum Maius.**

Velia (Fig. 90): the hill between the Palatine and the Oppius, now completely eradicated by the cutting of the Via dei Fori Imperiali and always in the historical period of rather vague definition. In republican times the Velia seems to have been crowned by the Temple of the Penates (see Penates Dei, Aedes), and after the time of Hadrian dominated by his Temple of Venus et Roma (see Venus et Roma, Templum). Between these dates it must have undergone considerable modification in the building projects of Nero, the Domus Transitoria and Domus Aurea. The Velia may originally have been defined by two small watercourses, one beginning near Summa Sacra Via (marked by the Arch of Titus) and running along the base of the Palatine, and another beginning below the Carinae and running southwest to become the brook buried under Sacra Via in front of the Basilica Constantini. The Velia was originally high and always important, the site of one of the sacrifices of the Septimontium (Festus 459L) and one of the sacraria of the Argei (Varro, *Ling.* 5.54). One of the Curiae that could not have its rites moved to the Curiae Novae was the Veliensis (Festus 182L). The name is more commonly singular (e.g., Livy 2.7.6, 45.16.5), but not infrequently plural (Varro, *Ling.* 5.54; Festus 142L; Asconius *ad Cic. Pis.* 52 [Stangl 19]; Non. Marc. 852L). Dionysius (3.19.1) describes the Velia as high and steep, and the story of the Domus Valeriorum (see Domus, Valerii [3]) shows that the Romans always thought of it as commanding the Forum Romanum on the southeast in much the same way that the Capitoline did on the northwest. It was certainly a well-defined eminence in republican times, although it was the site of comparatively few monuments. Under the empire its outlines seem to have been blurred. The origin of the name is completely obscure and was so to the Romans (Varro, *Ling.* 5.54).

AnalRom, suppl. 10 (1983): 129–45 (A. M. Colini), 147–68 (G. Pisani Sartorio); *QITA* 10 (1988): 77–97 (D. Palombi).

Venus, Aedes: a temple that burned in 178 B.C. and was destroyed without leaving any vestige (Obsequens 8). It was somewhere in the vicinity of the Forum Romanum, but we know nothing more.

Venus Calva, Templum: a temple built by order of the senate to honor Roman matrons who had given their hair to make bowstrings or catapult cords during the siege of the Capitoline by the Gauls (S.H.A. *Maxim.* 33.2; Servius *ad Aen.* 1.720; Lactantius, *Inst.* 1.20.27). Servius mentions only a statue, and one can imagine a marble statue intended to be provided with bronze hair about which such a legend might have been invented. Servius goes on to tell another version of the story, in which the original dedication was a *piaculum,* a statue of the wife of Ancus Marcius set up after the women of Rome lost their hair in an epidemic, and that came to be worshiped as Venus when their hair was restored. The statue has the ring of authenticity, but we do not know where it was located.

Venus Cloacina: see **Cloacina, Sacrum.**

Venus Erucina, Aedes (1): a temple on the Capitoline, probably in the Area Capitolina, vowed by the dictator Q. Fabius Maximus after the disaster of Lake Trasimene in 217 B.C. and following consultation of the Sibylline Books (Livy 22.9.10, 10.10), and dedicated by Fabius in 215 (Livy 23.30.13–14, 31.9). It was one of a pair of temples, presumably twins, the other being to Mens (see Mens, Aedes),

vowed and dedicated at the same time. They were separated by only a drain. This is probably the temple later called Aedes Capitolina Veneris, where Livia dedicated a likeness of the young son of Germanicus in the guise of Cupid (Suetonius, *Calig.* 7) and Galba dedicated a necklace of pearls and precious stones (Suetonius, *Galba* 18.2) intended for his private Fortuna at Tusculum.

Venus Erucina, Aedes (2): a temple of the Venus of Mount Eryx in western Sicily vowed during the Ligurian wars by L. Porcius Licinius as consul in 184 and dedicated by him as duovir in 181 (Livy 40.34.4). It was supposed to be a reproduction of the Sicilian temple (but is called a templum by Ovid, Jerome, Strabo, and Appian) and stood in front of the Porta Collina, but apparently very close to it, and was remarkable for the colonnade enclosing it, which must have been a later addition (Strabo 6.2.6 [272]; Appian, *BellCiv* 1.93). Its festivals were the Vinalia on 23 April (Ovid, *Fast.* 4.863–76; Degrassi 446–47) and 24 October, the latter evidently the anniversary of its dedication after a restoration by Augustus (Degrassi 525). Ovid (*Fast.* 4.865–70) speaks of the temple as the haunt of unsavory characters, especially common prostitutes.

The location of the temple is in some doubt. Everyone agrees that it was very close to Porta Collina, and the fasti and Appian's account of the Battle of Porta Collina make it clear that it was outside the gate (although Livy 40.34.4 has *ad portam*). Its only mention after the Augustan period is in an inscription (*CIL* 6.2274) of a fortuneteller. This has led to the supposition that it is the same as the Venus Hortorum Sallustianorum (q.v.). No remains of it have ever been identified.

BdA 73 (1988): fasc. 49, 53–62 (M. Castelli).

Venus Felix, Aedes: attested by an inscription found in Villa Altieri, a dedication to Venus Felix (*CIL* 6.781; cf. 782 = *ILS* 3166, 8710). Villa Altieri lay in Regio V in the fork between Via Labicana and Via di S. Croce in Gerusalemme in the farther reaches of the Esquiline near Ad Spem Veterem. This was a district of horti and tombs and unlikely to be the site of a major temple. Nothing further is known about it.

Venus Genetrix: see **Forum Iulium.**

Venus Hortorum Sallustianorum, Aedes: a temple mentioned in three inscriptions (*CIL* 6.122 = *ILS* 3184, 32451, 32468), which show that the temple had *aeditui* and was a public building, therefore presumably on the periphery of the horti. This has led to identification of it with the Temple of Venus Erucina at Porta Collina, which is not mentioned after the Augustan period. In the sixteenth century Panvinio produced a plan of a temple *in capite fori Sallustii,* based on a drawing by Ligorio. This is shown as circular and peripteral, with columns of giallo antico and alabaster and adorned with niches in the interior (*Cod. Vat.* 3439 f. 28 = *BullCom* 16 [1888]: 3–11 [R. Lanciani]; *RömMitt* 4 [1889]: 270–74 [C. Hülsen]). It has been widely accepted (LFUR sheet 3; Lugli and Gismondi), but it is not known on what authority this rests. However, if this is the Temple of Venus Hortorum Sallustianorum, it cannot be identical with Venus Erucina extra Portam Collinam.

Lugli 1938, 333–36; *BdA* 73 (1988): fasc. 49, 53–62 (M. Castelli).

Venus in Palatio: see Aphrodision.

Venus Libitina (or Libentina), Templum:
a temple of Venus in the Lucus Libitinae (q.v.) on the Esquiline, Libitina having come to be identified with Venus (Plutarch, *Quaest. Rom.* 23). The day of dedication was 19 August, the Vinalia Rustica (Festus 322L; Degrassi 497–98). The foundation date is unknown, but, because Servius Tullius is credited with establishing the custom of paying a coin to the treasure of Libitina for each death (Dion. Hal. 4.15.5), it is presumed to be of high antiquity.

Venus Obsequens, Aedes:
the oldest known Temple of Venus in Rome, built from the fines levied against women convicted of adultery, begun by Q. Fabius Maximus Gurges in 295 B.C. and dedicated after the Third Samnite War (Livy 10.31.9, Servius *ad Aen.* 1.720). It was ad Circum Maximum (Fast. Vall.; Livy 10.31.9, 29.37.2; Festus 322L), and its dedication day was 19 August, the Vinalia Rustica, the same as that of Venus Libitina (Degrassi 497–98). One gathers from Livy 29.37.2 that the temple stood just behind the seating of the circus toward the southeast end, probably at the foot of the Aventine.

Lugli 1946, 557.

Venus et Roma, Templum (Figs. 90, 91, 92):
probably the largest and most splendid temple of Rome, a double temple on the slope of the Velia along the north side of the Sacra Via built by Hadrian beginning in A.D. 121 (Hieron. *a. Abr.* 2147; Bloch 252 and n.192) to Venus Felix and Roma Aeterna. It was also called Templum Urbis Romae (Servius *ad Aen.* 2.227), Templum Urbis (Amm. Marc. 16.10.14; S.H.A. *Hadr.* 19.12; *MGH Chron. Min.* 2.142 [Cassiodorus]), Urbis Venerisque Templa (Prudentius, *Contra Sym.* 1.221), and possibly Templum Veneris (S.H.A. *Tyr. Trig.* 32). The temple was

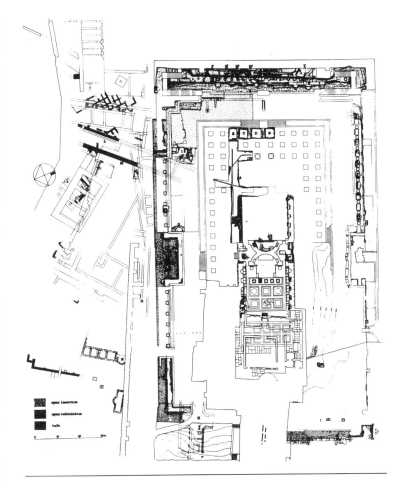

Figure 91
Temple of Venus et Roma, Plan of Existing Remains

probably dedicated in A.D. 135 (Cassiodorus *MGH Chron. Min.* 2.142), and the foundation day was apparently the Parilia, 21 April (Degrassi 445). The temple seems to have been incomplete at the time of Hadrian's death and to have been completed by Antoninus Pius (see *B. M. Coins, Rom. Emp.* 3.467 no. 1490, 4.205–6 nos. 1276–85, 215 nos. 345–46; Mazzini 2.150–51 nos. 1421–22, 205 nos. 699, 700).

To obtain space for the temple, Hadrian had to destroy the ceremonial entrance court of the Domus Aurea and move the Colossus Neronis (then Solis) (see Colossus Solis [Neronis]) to a place near the Colosseum. The design of the temple was Hadrian's own and is said to have been criticized by the architect Apollodorus of Damascus on the absurd ground that should the goddesses wish to rise and leave, they would be unable to do so (Cass. Dio 69.4.4). The two cellae stood back to back, that of Venus facing east, that of Roma west toward the Forum Romanum. Only the podium of the Hadrianic structure remains. In 307 the temple burned, and Maxentius then restored it (Chron. 148; Aur. Vict., *Caes.* 40.26). The cellae are apsidal and vaulted, but the

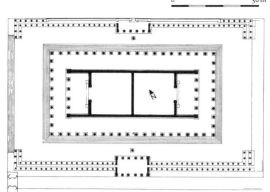

Figure 92
Temple of Venus
et Roma, Original
Plan, Restored

architectural form was disguised on the exterior by a continuous wall, so the temple appeared a classic peripteral temple. The interior we see today with porphyry columns, polychrome pavement, and deeply coved ceiling is in the taste of Maxentius rather than that of Hadrian. The original temple had no apses, and the ceiling was flat. This temple was among the buildings that Constantius most admired on his visit to Rome in 356 (Amm. Marc. 16.10.14). It is listed in the regionary catalogues in Regio IV and is mentioned by Prudentius (*Contra Sym.* 1.221). In 625, on a visit to Rome, Heraclius granted Pope Honorius I the right to use the bronze tiles of the temple to cover the basilica of S. Pietro. In 847–855 Pope Leo IV built the church of S. Maria Nova in its ruin; probably the earthquake earlier in his reign was chiefly responsible for the temple's destruction. The church was rebuilt in 1612 as S. Francesca Romana.

The temple was decastyle, Corinthian, dipteral at the ends, pseudo-dipteral along the sides, with a pronaos at each end tetrastyle in antis, and with twenty columns on the long sides. It stood on a high stylobate of seven steps flanked by colonnades along the sides. The construction is of brick-faced concrete, which was once covered with white marble; the order and entablature were also of white marble; and the tiles were gilded bronze. A stair arranged between the apses led to the roof. Two fragments of a relief now in the Lateran collection in the Vatican and in the Museo Nazionale Romano delle Terme (Helbig[4] 1.1013) once believed to show the west front of the temple with its pediment are now assigned to the time of Claudius and may show the Temple of Mars or the Temple of Quirinus (*AJA* 91 [1987]: 441–58 [F. C. Albertson]).

The temple and flanking colonnades stand on a vast platform of concrete 145 m long and 100 m wide faced with blocks of peperino between travertine footings for the columns. At the west end the platform is relatively low, but at the east, owing to the slope of the terrain, it stands about 9 m high and consists of parallel vaulted chambers in which machinery and apparatus for the amphitheater are sometimes said to have been stored, but there seems to be no real basis for this. At this end there are only two relatively small stairs at the corners leading down to an area paved with blocks of travertine in front of the platform, while at the west end there is a stair of eleven steps across almost the whole front. At the corners of the platform were small projecting porches. On the south side of the precinct the colonnade was double, and in the center of this side was an entrance five intercolumniations wide with a propylaeum, perhaps with columns of cipollino, projecting into the precinct. The order was Corinthian. The gray granite columns with white marble bases and capitals that survive from other parts of the colonnade are believed to be Hadrianic. On the north side of the precinct, a wall replaced the outer line of columns to block the view of the buildings higher on the Velia, and the central entrance was much more modest. The pavement of these colonnades, as of the peripteros of the temple, was in slabs of Proconnesian marble.

The statue types do not seem to have been decided on until late in Hadrian's reign, if then, although it was always understood that they would be enthroned. On Hadrian's coins both types appear, duly inscribed, but with a variety of attributes and changes in detail. It is not until after Hadrian's death that Roma Aeterna regularly appears as enthroned and helmeted, with the Palladium in her right hand and steadying a spear with her left, while her shield rests at her side. Venus Felix is similarly enthroned, carries a Victoria alighting on her right hand, and has a long scepter in her left.

There is space here for many hundreds of dedications, but all we know of were silver statues of Antoninus and Faustina, an altar on which newly married couples sacrificed (Cass. Dio 72.31.1), and a statue of Minerva (Servius *ad Aen.* 2.227). Because the temple had much in common with the imperial fora, and in many ways continued the tradition of these, there may have been a program for the use of its various parts but, if so, we are uninformed about this. The cella of Roma was clearly meant to dominate, as both the architecture and the common name Fanum Urbis indicate.

A. Muñoz, *La sistemazione del tempio di Venere e Roma* (Rome 1935); Lugli 1946, 234–40; Nash 2.496–99; *RömMitt* 80 (1973): 243–69 (A. Barottolo); *BullCom* 84 (1974–75): 133–48 (A. Barottolo); *RömMitt* 85 (1978): 397–410 (A. Barottolo); *Quaderni dell'Istituto di Storia dell'Architettura,* n.s.

1–10 (1983–87): 47–54 (M. Manieri Elia); *Roma, archeologia nel centro* (1985), 1.106–12 (S. Panella); *Athenaeum* 67 (1989): 551–65 (R. T. Ridley).

Venus Verticordia, Aedes: a temple built in 114 B.C., following consultation of the Sibylline Books, to atone for the conviction of three Vestal Virgins of inchastity (Obsequens 37; Orosius 5.15.21–22; Ovid, *Fast.* 4.157–60), the epithet alluding to the goddess' ability to change women's hearts from lust to chastity (Val. Max. 8.15.12).

The temple was in Vallis Murcia (Servius *ad Aen.* 8.636), so presumably on the slope of the Aventine behind the Circus Maximus, probably toward the southeast end. Servius says that the temple was surrounded by a plantation of myrtles and so gave its name to the circus valley, which suggests that he may have confused it with Venus Obsequens (see Venus Obsequens, Aedes). Ovid (*Fast.* 4.133–62) gives the anniversary of the temple as 1 April, the Veneralia (Degrassi 433–34). Because this was the great general festival of Venus, to whom all of April was in some sense dedicated, the temple must have been especially venerated. The cult statue is shown on coins of M'. Cordius Rufus of 46 B.C. (*B. M. Coins, Rom. Rep.* 1.523–24 nos. 4037–39; Crawford 463/1); the goddess stands draped, holding a balance in her lowered right hand, steadying a long scepter with her left, with Cupid appearing at her left shoulder.

According to Valerius Maximus (8.15.12; cf. Pliny, *HN* 7.120, Solinus 1.126), Sulpicia, the daughter of Servius Sulpicius Paterculus and wife of Q. Fulvius Flaccus, was chosen by the vote of ten drawn by lot from a pool of one hundred who had been chosen by the women of Rome as a body to dedicate a statue of Venus Verticordia. Sulpicia was deemed the chastest woman in Rome, and the method of selection was prescribed by the Sibylline Books. She must have been the wife of the great Fulvius Flaccus who was four times consul between 237 and 209 B.C. Because the statue antedates the temple by about a century, it must have been dedicated elsewhere, perhaps in the Temple of Venus Erucina on the Capitoline or the Temple of Venus Obsequens.

Venus Victrix: a shrine, probably an altar, on the Capitoline, mentioned in the fasti in conjunction with the Genius Populi Romani and Fausta Felicitas, to whom there was a sacrifice on 9 October (Degrassi 518). Degrassi thought this divinity ought to be Suetonius's Venus Capitolina (Suetonius, *Calig.* 7, *Galba* 18.2), although Venus Erucina seems likelier to be Venus Capitolina. The association of these three divinities as a triad is puzzling. However, Servius (*ad Aen.* 2.351) tells us that there was a shield on the Capitoline inscribed to the Genius Urbis Romae, *sive mas sive femina*, and we may be justified in seeing this as a triad of protective powers.

Venus Victrix, Aedes: a temple built into the top of the cavea of the Theater of Pompey that Pompey asserted was the main element in the complex by inviting the people of Rome to the dedication of the temple and pretending that the theater was a flight of steps leading to it that the people could then use as convenient seating for spectacles there (A. Gellius 10.1.7; Tertullian, *De Spect.* 10). This must be regarded as playful, because by this time there can have been no persistent prejudice against the corrupting influence of the theater, even among the most old-fashioned Romans. The temple was dedicated in Pompey's second consulship in 55 B.C., although the complex was not completed until 52, when the inscription was carved on the temple (A. Gellius 10.1.7); the day of dedication was 12 August (Degrassi 493–94). Although the Temple of Venus Victrix in connection with the Theater of Pompey seems to have been dominant, she was joined there by other divinities: Honos, Virtus, V[. . .], and Felicitas. These are a small pantheon of the political rallying cries of the Sullan period, and the missing one can probably be restored as Victoria. They had a series of shrines around the top of the cavea (Suetonius, *Claud.* 21.1), probably all of modest size and unpretentious architecture. The goddess, probably the cult statue, appears on coins of 45 B.C. She stands fully draped, holding an alighting Victoria on her outstretched right hand and steadying a long scepter with her left. Sometimes there is a shield by her side, and sometimes she is seated on a throne, but otherwise iconographically correct (*B. M. Coins, Rom. Rep.* 1.543–51 nos. 4137–86; Crawford 480/4–18). The temple seems mentioned in the scholia on Horace (*Sat.* 1.2.94), but as a reminiscence, so that one suspects that it was then no longer in existence. Cf. also *CIL* 6.785.

AJA 91 (1987): 123–26 (L. Richardson).

Verminus, Ara: an altar to the god of a cattle disease found in 1876 just north of Porta Viminalis in a tower of the inner wall of the agger of the Servian Walls. The duovir A. Postumius Albinus set it up in accordance with a Lex Plaetoria. It is now in the Museo Capitolino Nuovo (Helbig⁴ 2.1598; *ILLRP* 281). It is of peperino, square, and in archaistic hourglass shape, 0.89 m on a side at the base, and 1.15 m high. It resembles the altar of Aius Locutius from the Palatine.

Nash 2.500.

Vertumnus: see **Vortumnus, Aedes.**

Vespasianus, Divus, Templum (Fig. 19): a temple that Titus began and Domitian completed, called Templum Vespasiani et Titi (Chron. 146; regionary catalogues for Regio VIII), but only Vespasian's name appeared on the architrave (*CIL* 6.938 = *ILS* 255). Below Vespasian's name was added a second line commemorating a restoration by Septimius Severus and Caracalla. The inscription was complete in the eighth century and was copied in the Einsiedeln sylloge but is now reduced to the last few letters. The temple stands at the northwest end of the Forum Romanum against the base of the Tabularium, above the Clivus Capitolinus between the Temple of Concordia and the Porticus Deorum Consentium.

The temple was prostyle, hexastyle, 33 m deep by 22 m wide, and the order was Corinthian. The concrete core of the podium of the temple survives, which blocks the entrance to the stair that earlier led from the forum through the base of the Tabularium to the area Inter Duos Lucos on the Capitoline. The podium preserves some of its peperino lining and travertine facing. There are poor fragments of the cella wall in travertine and the base for the cult statues at the rear of the cella. Inside and out, the temple was revetted with marble. The glory of the temple is the three columns of the southeast corner of the pronaos that still stand and carry a part of the entablature, having been reinforced by Valadier in 1811, at which time a section of the whole entablature was restored, perhaps the finest example of the Flavian style of decoration in existence. The section is now kept in the Tabularium. The frieze of sacrificial implements and apparatus between bucrania and the resolution of classical moldings into floral ornament of various sorts are especially interesting. The columns are 1.57 m in diameter, 13.20 m high, and decidedly elongated. Because the space available was very limited, the cella was squarish, but broader than deep, and the stair of approach continued between the columns. It is believed that there were columns in the interior of the cella, but of these nothing remains.

Lugli 1946, 114; Nash 2.501–4; *RendPontAcc* 60 (1987–88): 53–69 (P. Rockwell), 71–90 (R. Nardi).

Vesta, Aedes (Figs. 12, 13, 63): the only temple of Vesta in Rome, at the southeast end of the Forum Romanum at the foot of the Palatine between the Regia and the Lacus Iuturnae (Dion. Hal. 6.13.2) and probably at the Porta Ianualis of the pomerium of the Romulean city. The temple was in an Area Vestae and surrounded by other buildings connected with the cult and the state religion, of which it was in some sense the very heart. Its foundation was ascribed by some to Romulus, but by most to Numa (Ovid, *Fast.* 6.257–60; Dion. Hal. 2.66.1; Festus 320L; Plutarch, *Numa* 11.1). The temple was round and supposed to have been originally a structure of wattles with a thatched roof, essentially a primitive Italic hut (Ovid, *Fast.* 6.261–66). It was not an inaugurated templum (A. Gellius 14.7.7.; Servius *ad Aen.* 7.153); the explanation offered for this, that it was so that the senate might not be convened where the Vestal Virgins were assembled, is clearly inadequate. The temple contained the sacred fire (Ovid, *Fast.* 6.297–98), the Palladium, believed to have been brought by Aeneas from Troy (Ovid, *Tr.* 3.1.29), and other sacred objects and implements kept in a place called the Penus Vestae, which was shielded from view by screens and might not be seen by anyone but the Vestal Virgins and pontifices (Dion. Hal. 2.66.3–6; Festus 152L, 296L; Servius *ad Aen.* 3.12). There was no image of the goddess (Ovid, *Fast.* 6.295–98).

The temple was presumably burned in the sack of Rome by the Gauls ca. 390 B.C., but not before the sacred objects had been removed to safety (Livy 5.40.7–10, 42.1–2; Plutarch, *Camil.* 21.1, 22.6; *CIL* 6.1272 = *ILS* 51 = A. Degrassi, *Inscriptiones Italiae* 13.3.11). It burned in 241 B.C., but Caecilius Metellus rescued the Palladium and the sacred implements at the cost of his sight (Livy, *Epit.* 19; Dion. Hal. 2.66.4; Val. Max. 1.4.5; Pliny, *HN* 7.141; Orosius 4.11.9). In 210 it was saved from a fire that ravaged the northeast side of the forum by the efforts of thirteen slaves, who were manumitted as a reward (Livy 26.27.4). In 48 B.C. it was threatened, and the sacred objects were removed (Cass. Dio 42.31.3). In 14 B.C. the temple burned again, but the sacred objects were rescued and taken to the Palatine (Cass. Dio 54.24.2). In the fire of Nero in 64 it burned again, but was apparently immediately restored by Nero (Tacitus, *Ann.* 15.41, *Hist.* 1.43), and it is shown on certain undated coins of Nero (*B. M. Coins, Rom. Emp.* 1.213 nos. 101–6). The temple appears to have been restored again at the time of the rebuilding of the Atrium Vestae under Trajan. After the fire of Commodus destroyed it again in 191, Julia Domna, the wife of Septimius Severus, restored it (Herodian 1.14.4: cf. Cass. Dio 72 [73].24). It is listed by the regionary catalogues in Regio VIII and was finally closed by Theodosius in 394.

The temple is represented on a number of coins, the earliest perhaps those of Q. Cassius of ca. 55 B.C. (*B. M. Coins, Rom. Rep.* 1.482 nos. 3871–75; Crawford 428), where it is shown with a curious parabolic roof surmounted by a figure holding scepter and patera and with large gryphon-head antefixes at the eaves, the latter evidently an identifying feature. Clearly at this time the temple preserved much of its character as a primitive hut. In its reconstruction in the imperial period, the temple appears to have been a more conventional tholus with a shallow dome, but it kept the figure surmounting its summit (*B. M. Coins, Rom. Emp.* 5.169–70 nos. 96–101). It is shown also on reliefs, notably one in the Uffizi in Florence (Nash 2.509) showing it as a tholus on a relatively high podium, the composite columns given individual plinths articulated on the podium, and the intercolumniations filled with grillwork, except for the double doors at the top of a narrow stair of approach. The roof is a flattened cone with a large finial at the summit, evidently the base for a small statue. This agrees with the evidence of the coins and what has been found in excavation.

Between 1883 and 1900, especially in 1899–1900, the podium and various parts of the architecture of the temple were brought to light, and a section of the exterior as it appeared after its rebuilding by Julia Domna has been restored in situ. The podium consists of four layers of concrete, the lowest being a circular foundation sunk in the ground, 15.05 m in diameter and 2.17 m thick. In approximately the center of the podium was a large trapezoidal cavity, 2.30–2.50 m long, which descended to the bottom of the foundation, a depth of 5 m. This has been conjectured to be the ash pit of the temple. Most of the podium is Augustan, but the highest stratum is believed to be Severan.

In its final rebuilding, the temple was of white marble, raised on a base of three steps, above which rose the podium. The peripteros was of twenty fluted columns with Corinthian capitals, 0.51 m in diameter and 4.45 m high, standing on plinths broken out from the drum of the podium. To these an engaged order along the cella wall responded, appearing also in the interior of the cella, while the intercolumniations were filled with grillwork. Earlier the order seems to have been Ionic, while the order in republican times cannot be distinguished on the coins. The entablature is unremarkable, the frieze decorated with sacrificial implements. Pliny (*HN* 34.13) says the roof was covered with bronze from an early date. The interior arrangements are all unclear.

Lugli 1946, 202–7; Nash 2.505–9; G. Fuchs, *Architekturdarstellungen auf römischen Münzen* (Berlin 1969), 51–57.

Vesta, Aedicula: see **Atrium Vestae.**

Vesta, Ara: a statue and altar that Augustus had installed on the Palatine after he was made pontifex maximus. It was erected by decree of the senate and dedicated 28 April 12 B.C. (Ovid, *Fast.* 4.949–54, *Met.* 15.864–65; Degrassi 452). From the way Ovid speaks in the *Metamorphoses,* it might appear that

the shrine of Vesta was at least as important as the Temple of Apollo Palatinus and occupied the end of the house of Augustus opposite to Apollo Palatinus, but the Fasti Praenestini and Caeretani seem explicit about its being only a statue and an altar. Because there was no statue of the goddess in her temple on the forum, we can presume that this statue took the place of the temple and that the pontifex maximus had to make a daily offering to Vesta.

Nash 2.511–13 (but the monuments he refers to this sanctuary seem to belong more properly to the Aedes Vestae on the Forum Romanum).

Vesta, Lucus: a grove that presumably was once part of the precinct of Vesta, although it stood above Nova Via: *a Palati radice in Novam Viam devexus est* (Cicero, *Div.* 1.101). Possibly it was only a possession of the Vestal Virgins. It had apparently disappeared before Cicero's time, probably under pressure of the demand for land in the vicinity. It figures in history only as the locale of the disembodied voice (Aius Locutius) that warned Rome of the coming of the Gauls (Livy 5.32.6).

Via, Vicus, Clivus: *Via* is the term used for the roads radiating from Rome, from their beginning at the gates of Rome to their arrival at their appointed destination. They may bear the name of their builder, as the Via Appia did, or the name of their destination, as the Via Tiburtina and Via Ostiensis did. Within Rome the only streets called via are the Sacra Via and Nova Via, both serving much the same area and in their stretches on the Velia running roughly parallel to each other. Other very ancient streets in Rome seem never to have been called either via or vicus, never anything but Argiletum and Alta Semita.

Within Rome a vicus was a relatively flat street, a clivus a street that climbed a slope. For the Romans a street that was continuous could change its name if it changed its character; Vicus X could become Clivus X or Clivus Y, and conversely a street could turn a relatively sharp corner without changing its name, as the Sacra Via and Nova Via did. The Romans seem to have been fairly strict in their observance of the difference between a vicus and a clivus throughout antiquity, but with the Augustan reorganization of Rome into regiones and vici, vicus came to have another meaning and to mean a neighborhood as well as a street, probably ideally a neighborhood of four blocks meeting at a compital shrine, for originally there were always four vicomagistri for a neighborhood vicus.

These neighborhood vici took their names from a principal, or central, street, but none took it from a known clivus. There are also some anomalies. On the Capitoline Base (*CIL* 6.975 = *ILS* 6073) three successive vici in Regio XII, Piscina Publica, are given as: Vico Compiti Pastoris, Vico Portae Rudusculanae, and Vico Porta Naevia. Did the Compitum Pastoris not take its name from a street, but rather give its name to a street? Or is this only the name for a neighborhood? And is the last in the nominative because the neighborhood was known as Porta Naevia, although there was no street of that name? Or is this merely a slip on the part of the compiler of these lists? So also in Regio XIV, Transtiberim, one finds Vico Ianuclensis and Vico Salutaris. What are the missing nouns? Pagi for the first? for we know there was a Pagus Ianiculensis, and Aedis for the second? but we know of no temple of Salus other than the temple on the Quirinal in Regio VI. There is much that is puzzling here and defies interpretation. In Regio X, Palatina, we find Vico Huiusce Diei, but the only temple known of Fortuna Huiusce Diei, who is the only divinity known to have carried this epithet, was in the Campus Martius, probably Temple B of the Area Sacra di Largo Argentina. To such questions no firm answer is possible at this point.

Via Appia: the oldest and most important of the great roads linking Rome with the farther parts of Italy, built in 312 B.C. by Appius Claudius Caecus as far as Capua, then extended to Venusia in 291, Tarentum in 281, and Brundisium in 264. Statius calls it *longarum regina viarum* (*Silv.* 2.2.12). It began at Porta Capena. The short stretch of road linking Porta Capena with the nexus of streets at the Septizodium, being older, must have had a different name, possibly Vicus Portae Capenae. The Via Appia issued from the Aurelian Walls by Porta Appia (Porta S. Sebastiano). Between the two gates it curves slightly and ascends a slope, the Clivus Martis. In its course near the city it was especially thickly lined with tombs on both sides. The first milestone lay just inside Porta Appia (*CIL* 10.6812–13 = *ILS* 5819), the Temple of Mars just outside.

The original surface was graveled (*glarea strata*). In 296 a paved walk was laid along it from the Porta Capena to the Temple of Mars (Livy 10.23.12). In 293 the whole road from the Temple of Mars to Bovillae was cobbled (Livy 10.47.4); and in 189 the first stretch was cobbled (Livy 38.28.3). This last must be a repaving. The first stretch got the name Via Tecta (Ovid, *Fast.* 6.191–92), probably from its being the first stretch of road beyond the walls to be paved, and this must have been part of the work of Appius Claudius. The earliest milestones from the road date to the end of the third century B.C. (*CIL* 1².21 = *ILS* 5801 = *ILLRP* 448).

Curatores for the Appia were first appointed by Claudius (Seneca, *Apocol.* 1.2). To the staff of the curator belonged *tabularii* (*CIL* 6.8466 = *ILS* 1606),

and we have record of at least one *manceps Viae Appiae* (*CIL* 6.8468 = *ILS* 1471).

L. Avetta, ed., *Roma: via imperiale* (Rome 1985), 21–45, 53–66.

Via Ardeatina: attested by an inscription of a *manceps Viarum Laurentinae et Ardeatinae* (*CIL* 6.8469 = *ILS* 1472). These must have issued as a single road from the Porta Naevia, to which the Vicus Portae Naeviae led after branching south off Vicus Piscinae Publicae. From Porta Naevia this ran along the ridge behind the Baths of Caracalla, where a large circular tomb stands southwest of it, and issued from the Aurelian Walls by the posterula destroyed when Antonio da Sangallo built his great bastion just west of it for Pope Paul III, but recorded in a drawing by Sangallo. In modern times it has been called Porta Ardeatina (q.v.) and Porta Laurentina. Pliny (*Epist.* 2.17.2) says one could reach his Laurentine villa by either the Via Ostiensis or the Via Laurentina, branching from the former at the eleventh milestone, and from the latter at the fourteenth. Carcopino has made a strong case for there being no town of Laurentum, the town of the Laurentes being Lavinium, the capital of Latinus. Then the Via Laurentina/Ardeatina will have followed pretty much the line of the modern Via Laurentina and branched only a short distance from Lavinium (Pratica di Mare) in the vicinity of the Solfatara sulfur springs, one branch going to Lavinium, the other to Ardea. Remains of tombs and traces of ancient work all along this course prove its antiquity. But this cannot be Pliny's Via Laurentina, for it keeps far from the coast until it reaches its termini. Pliny's must be an ancient road that branched off the Via Ostiensis at Vicus Alexandri and ran to Decimo and Capocotta; this is now commonly called Via Laurentina Nova by topographers and the other Via Laurentina Vetus.

This solution seems preferable to the other one offered for the difficulty, namely, to think of the Via Ardeatina as branching from Via Appia at the church of Domine Quo Vadis, where the modern Via Ardeatina branches, because modern Via Ardeatina does not go to Ardea at all and only at its beginning might be thought to be heading in that general direction.

Tomassetti 2.409–61; Ashby 1927, 207–13; L. Avetta, *Roma, via imperiale* (Rome 1985), 46–47, 67–93.

Via Asinaria: a road issuing from Porta Asinaria in the Aurelian Walls accessible from Via Latina, for Belisarius approaching Rome by the Via Latina diverged and entered by Porta Asinaria (Procopius, *BellGoth* 1.14.6 and 14). It is also mentioned by Festus (356L), who speaks of a water *supra Viam Ar-*

deatinam inter lapidem secundum et tertium by which estates were watered *infra Viam Ardeatinam et Asinariam usque ad Latinam.* If Via Asinaria followed roughly the line of the first part of Via Appia Nuova, as seems logical, the estates occupied a large wedge of land to the southeast of Rome, but the additional note, *usque ad Latinam,* implies a connecting road of this name some distance out from the city, and of this we are uninformed. The whole note in Festus is fraught with difficulty. Via Tusculana branched from Via Asinaria about 400 m beyond Porta Asinaria; it is odd, considering its importance, that it did not give its name to the gate.

Via Aurelia: the main road to the west from Rome that on reaching the coast ran northwest through coastal Etruria. It began at the Pons Aemilius on the right bank of the Tiber, crossed the low ground in a straight line, and climbed the slope of the Janiculan hill at an extremely steep gradient. It passed through the Aurelian Walls by Porta Aurelia (Porta S. Pancrazio) at the summit of the hill and ran out on a narrow ridge in an almost straight course. The difficulty of the grade on this, the Via Aurelia Vetus, seems to have led to the creation of the Via Aurelia Nova, which branched from Via Cornelia south of the Leonine city and joined the Aurelia Vetus at the Madonna del Riposo, a considerable distance from the city. The Aurelia ran through undulating terrain and reached the sea at Palo, 30 kilometers from Rome, beyond which it followed the coast closely, first to Vada Volaterrana. The periods of its construction are very uncertain; in some sense the line must have been used from very early times. In 109 B.C. it was extended by Aemilius Scaurus to Vada Sabata and Dertona (Tortona).

Some inscriptions of the curatores viarum speak of the Aurelia Vetus, Aurelia Nova, Cornelia, and Triumphalis as all united under a single administration (*CIL* 6.1512, 14.3610 = *ILS* 1071). Others mention only the Aurelia (*CIL* 2.1283, 2.1371, 6.1462, 9.973, 9.1126).

Tomassetti 2.463–547; Ashby 1927, 225–30; *RendPontAcc* 61 (1988–89): 309–42 (N. Degrassi).

Via Biberatica: see **Mercati di Traiano.**

Via Campana: the road leading from Rome to the mouth of the Tiber on its right bank; it may have received its name from the Campus Salinarum Romanarum, the salt pans north of the mouth, but the normal adjective from *campus* is *campestris* or *campensis,* and it was certainly one of the earliest of the roads of Rome, being the natural continuation of the Via Salaria and Vicus Iugarius, connected with these by a ferry. After the construction of the harbor of

Claudius at Portus its course was identical with that of the Via Portuensis for a short distance, but then the Via Portuensis diverged off to the right, running more directly toward its objective over the low hills, while the Via Campana kept to the flood plain and closely followed the river.

MEFRA 88 (1976): 639–67 (J. Scheid); *PAPS* 125 (1981): 368–97 (R. E. A. Palmer).

Via Collatina: the road to Collatia, diverging from the Via Tiburtina to the right just outside the Porta Tiburtina in the Aurelian Walls and of only minor importance, running to the village of Collatia, notable chiefly as the domain of Tarquinius Collatinus and the virtuous Lucretia and where Collatinus and Sextus Tarquin found her working with her women late at night. It was a place of vanished greatness by the time of Cicero. In later times the road served mainly as access to large quarries of Anio tufa and for the servicing of the Aqua Virgo and Aqua Appia. According to Ashby, he could trace it on a sinuous route crossing and recrossing the line of the Aqua Virgo, but it has been entirely obliterated by the building up of the periphery of Rome. Coarelli would have it branch to the left from the Via Praenestina at the Villa dei Gordiani (Tor de'Schiavi), but this is the modern Via Collatina. The original Via Collatina ought to be one of the oldest parts of the road system, tracks radiating out to the villages in the vicinity of Rome that depended on Rome as a metropolis.

Ashby 1927, 143–45.

Via Cornelia: the road leading to the west from Rome that ran along the north side of the Circus Gaii et Neronis from the head of the Pons Aelius and the late antique Porta Cornelia (q.v.) on the right bank of the Tiber. The existence of a number of tombs, including that of Saint Peter, along it argues that it existed from Nero's day, if not earlier, but at that time it must have been a spur road diverging from the Via Triumphalis (1) (q.v.) to serve the circus. Ashby (Ashby 1927, 226) believed it crossed the Via Aurelia Nova and ran on to the west to the south of it, but that stretch is very uncertain. It fell under the jurisdiction of the curatores of the Via Aurelia (q.v.).

RendPontAcc 61 (1988–89): 309–42 (N. Degrassi).

Via Flaminia: the main road north from Rome, running from the Porta Fontinalis of the Servian Walls on the northeast shoulder of the Capitoline through the Campus Martius, where it was called the Via Lata (modern Via del Corso), and issuing from the Aurelian Walls by Porta Flaminia (Porta del Popolo). From here it ran almost due north for 3 miles to the Pons Mulvius, by which it crossed the Tiber. At the bridgehead on the right bank the Via Cassia branched from it to the left and ran northwest through central Etruria to Clusium and Arretium, while the Flaminia ran nearly due north to Ariminum on the Adriatic coast. It was always of immense military and commercial importance, because it carried all the traffic to and from the Po Valley.

It was originally built by C. Flaminius as censor in 220 B.C. (Livy, *Epit.* 20; cf. Strabo 5.1.11 [217], where it is erroneously ascribed to C. Flaminius the Younger). Augustus restored it in 27 B.C. (Augustus, *RG* 20; Suetonius, *Aug.* 30.1; Cass. Dio 53.22.1). Its importance is measured by its having a special curator as early as 65 B.C. (Cicero, *Att.* 1.1.2), and it was thickly lined with tombs (see Sepulcrum P. Aelii Guttae Calpurniani, Bibuli, Claudiorum, Galloniorum; cf. Juvenal 1.171).

The care of the Via Flaminia was usually held alone (*CIL* 2.4126, 4510 [cf. 14.3599 = *ILS* 1061], 6.1333 = *ILS* 1077, 1529, 3836, 10.5061). It may once have been held together with that of the Via Tiburtina (*CIL* 14.2933), but the reading of the inscription is doubtful, and the logic of the combination is hard to understand. The care of the Via Cassia and Via Clodia, which diverged from the Via Flaminia just beyond the Pons Mulvius, and of the roads that branched from these seems always to have been held separately.

The Via Flaminia seems clearly to have been built in anticipation of the Second Punic War as a highway to facilitate the movement of troops and supplies to Spain by way of the Po as far as Turin and thence through the passes through the Cottian Alps or Alpes Maritimes. The Via Flaminia could not have been built before the pacification of Etruria (Falerii revolted in 241) and the crushing of the Gallic alliance in the Battle of Talamone in 225.

Ashby 1927, 247–51.

Via Fornicata: mentioned once by Livy (22.36.8) among the portents of 216 B.C. as being *ad campum* and a place where a number of people were killed by lightning. It was probably not a proper name, simply descriptive, and Livy uses the past tense, but at this time there were probably neither honorary arches nor arcuated buildings in the Campus Martius. Its location and character are entirely uncertain.

Via Gabina: the original name of the stretch of the Via Praenestina from Rome to Gabii, 12 miles away, this being part of the oldest road system connecting Rome with neighboring towns (Livy 2.11.7, 3.6.7, 5.49.6).

Ashby 1927, 128–36.

Via Labicana: an early road diverging from Via Praenestina just inside Porta Praenestina (Porta Maggiore) of the Aurelian Walls with the tomb of the baker Eurysaces (see Sepulcrum Eurysacis) filling the angle between the two roads just outside the gate (Livy 4.41.8; Frontinus, *Aq.* 1.21; S.H.A. *Didius Iulianus* 8.10). Strabo (5.3.9 [237]) says that the Via Labicana diverged from the Via Praenestina just outside Porta Esquilina, in which case one must imagine a course for the latter that originally crossed the line of the Aurelian Walls approximately midway between Porta Tiburtina and Porta Praenestina, but for this there is no other evidence. The fact that Porta Praenestina bears that name is proof that by that time the real importance of the gate was the Praenestine destination. Ashby thought the Via Labicana was the original road from Rome to Tusculum, but Labici (Labicum) lay a good way northeast of Tusculum and in the Hernican valley, and the design of the road must have looked much more to traffic in the valley than traffic with Tusculum. The road bypassed Labicum, leaving it on the right, and joined the Via Latina at Ad Pictas or Ad Bivium, 25 or 30 miles from Rome. It seems to have been under the same curator as the Via Latina (*BullCom* 19 [1891]: 112–21 [L. Cantarelli]). Within the city the modern Via Labicana, running from the Colosseum to a crossing with Via Merulana, though it follows the line of an ancient street, has scant claim to this name. The ancient name of this street is unknown.

Ashby 1927, 146–52.

Via Lata: the name given to the stretch of Via Flaminia from the Porta Fontinalis to Porta Flaminia (Porta del Popolo). It first occurs in the regionary catalogues, where it appears as the name of Regio VII, an anomaly, because Via Flaminia seems to bound the regio on the west, not lie within it. It then appears as a toponym on slave collars (*CIL* 15.7186, 7187), and the identification is assured by relatively frequent appearances of the name in the *Liber Pontificalis* and is brought down into modern times by the church of S. Maria in Via Lata, a church at least as old as the ninth century (HCh 376).

Via Latina: a road branching to the left from Via Appia 830 m beyond Porta Capena and issuing from the Aurelian Walls by Porta Latina. Like the Via Appia, it was thickly lined with tombs both inside and outside the Aurelian Walls (cf. Juvenal 1.170–71). The exact age of the Via Latina is unknown, but it runs in a line almost as straight as the Appia to Roboraria on the northwest edge of the Alban Hills, then circles the caldera on the south side of Algidus Mons to emerge through the pass at Algidus and join

Via Labicana at Ad Pictas or Ad Bivium. It has been considered a military road because of its straightness, and, because the pass at Algidus was secured only in 389 B.C., it cannot be older than that. But the course the Via Latina follows seems to indicate a wish to bring the settlements in the northern crescent of the Alban Hills into communication with one another and with Rome, rather than a wish to use the pass at Algidus, and it looks as though it might have been a very old Latin route that Rome then took over and improved, as its name also suggests. Livy (2.39.4) mentions the Via Latina in connection with Coriolanus in 488 B.C. The dispatch of a colony to Cales in 334 B.C. (Livy 8.16.13) is taken to prove that by that date it had been extended that far after linking up with Via Labicana. And at Casilinum, just below Cales on the Volturnus River, it joined Via Appia. Strabo (5.3.9 [237]) makes it clear that in his day the Via Latina was regarded as the principal road throughout its length, all others being byways or tributaries of the system.

At the beginning of the third century after Christ, the Via Latina Vetus and the Via Labicana were sometimes under a single curator (*CIL* 3.6154 = *ILS* 1174, 10.5394), whereas Via Latina sometimes had its own curator (*CIL* 2.1929, 3.1455, 6.1337, 1450 = *ILS* 2935, 10.3732 = *ILS* 1216, 11.2106 = *ILS* 1138, 14.2942, 3595), and sometimes there is a separate curator for the Via Latina Nova (*CIL* 10.5398 = *ILS* 1159). The Via Latina Nova might be the Via Tusculana, which joins Via Latina at the ninth milestone; its origin is much disputed, and there is no other record of it in antiquity, but the existence of the Porta Asinaria argues for development of this area of the *suburbium*. Even more mysterious is a fragment of a relief showing an allegorical figure of a road inscribed VIAE LATINAE GR (*CIL* 6.29811); the inscription is possibly incomplete (cf. Tomassetti 4.3: fig. 1).

Ashby 1927, 153–73.

Via Laurentina: see Via Ardeatina and Via Ostiensis.

Via Merulana: mentioned in the *Ordo Benedicti* (Jordan 2.665; VZ 3.217), where it is clearly the ancient street running from the Nymphaeum Alexandri (Trofei di Mario) in Piazza Vittorio Emanuele almost due south to the line of the Neronian arches of the Aqua Claudia on the Caelian near the Praedia Lateranorum (see Domus, Laterani). It appears in the names of three early churches: S. Bartholomaei de Merulana or in Capite Merulanae (HCh 207), S. Basilidis in Merulana (HCh 208), and S. Matthaei in Merulana (HCh 386–87). Although the modern Via

Merulana crosses the line of the ancient one toward its southern end, this follows a completely different course. See also Domus Merulana.

Via Nomentana: a road branching to the right from Via Salaria immediately outside Porta Collina in the Servian Walls and issuing from the Aurelian Walls by Porta Nomentana. It ran northeast from Rome, first to Ficulea, and this stretch was originally called Via Ficulensis (Livy 3.52.3). It was then extended to Nomentum, 14 miles from Rome, and in a further extension it rejoined Via Salaria at the twenty-sixth milestone. It was a road of only local significance. Its curatores were of equestrian rank (*CIL* 3.6098 = suppl. 7271, 14.3955 = *ILS* 2740). Along it there were brickyards (*CIL* 15.677–82) and quarries.

Ashby 1927, 82–92.

Via Nova (1): see **Nova Via.**

Via Nova (2): a street built by Caracalla parallel to Via Appia to serve the Thermae Antoninianae (q.v.), under the principal façade of which it ran (Aur. Vict., *Caes.* 21.4; S.H.A. *Caracalla* 9.9). It was considered one of the most beautiful streets in Rome. It may appear on a fragment of the Marble Plan (*FUR* pl. 15; Rodriguez pl. 1), in which case it appears that it was exceptionally wide, perhaps as much as 30 m, and replaced the Via Appia, engulfing it in its width, in this part of the city. It appears in the regionary catalogues, listed in Regio XII, and is mentioned in a single Christian inscription (*CIL* 6.9684).

Via Ostiensis: the road from Rome to Ostia on the left bank of the Tiber. Although there was always a road along the river under the lee of the Aventine, and in time a network of streets ran along the horrea behind the Emporium, the street that issued from the Porta Ostiensis (West) was probably never so important as an artery as that issuing from Porta Ostiensis (East), and we should think of Porta Raudusculana as the gate in the Servian Walls from which this road started. The Pyramid of Cestius is aligned with this road and carries an inscription on this face. The road from Porta Lavernalis fed into this artery as well, and doubtless there were several spur roads connecting it with the docks and the warehouses lying between it and the river, for it must have carried a fair share of the traffic from the Emporium into the heart of Rome, as well as the traffic to and from Ostia. It was always one of the four or five main roads of Rome. It ran due south to Ostia, keeping to the flood plain of the river for much of its course, a distance of 14 miles. From it at Vicus Alexandri, 4 miles south of

Rome, a road branched to the left that must be Pliny's Via Laurentina (Pliny, *Epist.* 2.17.2). For discussion of this, see Via Ardeatina. For an archaic milestone of the Via Ostiensis, see *CIL* 1².22 = 6.31585 = *ILLRP* 449.

For administrative purposes the Via Ostiensis and Via Campana, the roads in the flood plain of the Tiber south of Rome on either bank, were under a single curator of equestrian rank (*CIL* 6.1610, 10.1795 = *ILS* 1401).

Ashby 1927, 214–17; R. Meiggs, *Roman Ostia,* 2d ed. (Oxford 1973), 111–14.

Via Patinaria: listed in the addenda to the regionary catalogues and cited as the scene of the death of Nero (Chron. 146), therefore between Via Nomentana and Via Salaria near the fourth milestone (Suetonius, *Nero* 48.1).

Via Pinciana: see **Porta Pinciana.**

Via Portuensis: the road leading to Portus (or Portus Augusti), the harbor constructed by Claudius to the right of the Tiber mouth to replace Ostia as the main port of Rome. In some sense it started at the head of Pons Sublicius or Pons Aemilius on the right bank of the river, but in its first stretch it was identical with the Via Campana (q.v.), and the gate in the Aurelian Walls by which it issued was called Porta Portuensis. It diverged to the right from Via Campana about a mile beyond the gate to run through hilly country by a more direct route, but rejoined it at modern Ponte Galera (or Galeria) on the edge of the coastal plain, from which point the course is a straight line to the southwest.

With the growth in importance of Portus as a port, reflected in the harbor of Trajan and the buildings surrounding it, the volume of traffic on the road must have grown proportionally. The double gate of Porta Portuensis in the Aurelian Walls, one of only four such gates in this fortification system, shows how much Rome depended on it. It continued to grow until the time of the Gothic Wars in the sixth century. This is shown in Procopius's description of the towpath and the volume of barge traffic on the river in his day (*BellGoth* 1.26.9–13). However, Portus's eclipse of Ostia as a port did not mean Ostia's decline as a city.

Ashby 1927, 217–19.

Via Praenestina: a road beginning at Porta Esquilina in the Servian Walls and running southeast to Porta Praenestina (Porta Maggiore) in the Aurelian Walls, from which it emerged to run almost due east to Gabii and then southeast to Praeneste. Between the two fortification systems of Rome it is marked Via Labicana on the Lugli and Gismondi map, but this is certainly an error. In early times it was called Via Gabina (q.v.) as far as Gabii and was among the oldest of Rome's roads. Within the city the Via Praenestina continued as the Clivus Suburanus and Argiletum, one of the main approaches to the Forum Romanum. The extension to Praeneste, 25 miles from Rome, was probably part of the road from the earliest times, for this was the main link between Rome and the important highway running down the Hernican valley to connect with the valley of the Liris River and Campania, a trade route in heavy use from the Early Iron Age and probably earlier. Along its course in the vicinity of Rome certain roads branched from it, notably the Via Tiburtina, Via Merulana, and Via Labicana. Outside the suburbium of Rome, the Via Praenestina served as the main access to the outside world for the towns in the Hernican hills. Important tombs along it include the Casa Tonda in Piazza Vittorio Emanuele (HJ 356), the Monumentum (or Sepulcrum) Aureliorum (see Sep. Aureliorum), and the Tor de'Schiavi.

The Via Praenestina is mentioned by Frontinus (*Aq.* 1.5) in connection with the sources of the Aqua Appia and by Pliny in connection with the sources of the Aqua Virgo (*HN* 31.42). A single inscription mentions its curator (*CIL* 14.169 = *ILS* 6172). It is one of the best preserved of the Roman roads near Rome. For milestones from it, see *CIL* 1².833, 10.6886 = *ILS* 2930, 8306.

Ashby 1927, 128–42; L. Quilici, *La Via Praenestina, i suoi monumenti, i suoi paesaggi (Italia nostra),* 3rd ed. (Rome 1977).

Via Recta: see **Via Tecta** (1).

Via Sacra: see **Sacra Via.**

Via Salaria: the road leading almost due north from Rome, issuing at Porta Collina, just outside of which Via Nomentana diverges from it. After a short distance it turns northeast and, after crossing the Anio River, follows closely the edge of the flood plain of the Tiber along its east (left) bank as far as Eretum. It was always the main route into the Sabine country (Strabo 5.3.1 [228]) and the track followed by the Sabines coming down from the mountains to get salt at the Tiber mouth, hence its name (Festus 436–37L; Pliny, *HN* 31.89). As such it may have been prehistoric, although its usefulness depends on the maintenance of a ferry below the Tiber island, for the salt pans were always on the right bank of the river mouth. Along it near Rome lay Antemnae and Fidenae, with Crustumerium, Eretum, and Cures, the town of Titus Tatius and Numa Pompilius, farther along. These were all villages, the only Sabine town of importance served immediately by the road being Reate, but through Reate it was the gateway to the high valleys of the Apennines and commanded access to the Adriatic through Asculum.

We have inscriptions of five curatores (*CIL* 6.1507, 1509 = *ILS* 1123, 8.7033, 14.2405; *RA,* ser. 3.16 [1890]: 2.139 [R. Cagnat]), and there were brickyards situated along it (*CIL* 15.478–532, 683).

The Via Salaria Vetus mentioned in Christian sources (e.g., *MGH Chron. Min.* 1.72 [Depos. Mart. of A.D. 335–336]) is regarded by Ashby as the road forking to the left from Via Salaria a short distance outside Porta Collina that crossed the line of the Aurelian Walls between the second and third towers of the wall west of Porta Salaria, where there was later a postern opened for it. A number of tombs lined the first part of its course, and it can be traced as far as the Monti Parioli. However, the Lugli and Gismondi map shows the Salaria Vetus as the road from Porta Pinciana in the Aurelian Walls running northeast to join Via Salaria at the point where it veers to the northeast (modern Largo B. Marcello). The question of which is correct is an academic one and of small importance, because the name only appears late and neither candidate is at all likely to have been the line of the original Via Salaria.

RömMitt 24 (1909): 121–69 (N. Persichetti); Ashby 1927, 59–81.

Via Tecta (1): a street in the Campus Martius mentioned once by Seneca (*Apocol.* 13) and possibly twice by Martial (3.5.5, 8.75.1–2, but the latter is doubtful). Only the first is of help with the topography; it puts what must be the Tarentum *inter Tiberim et Viam Tectam.* If the Tarentum was near S. Giovanni dei Fiorentini, as seems almost certain, then Via Tecta can only have been part, or perhaps the whole, of the long street running from Circus Flaminius northwest to Pons Neronianus, which is represented in part by the modern Via de' Giubbonari, Via de'Cappellari, and Via dei Banchi Vecchi, where remains of pavement have been found. The discovery of numerous fragments of granite columns along this line has led to the Via Tecta's identification as the Porticus Maximae (*CIL* 6.1184 = *ILS* 781) of the fourth century (q.v.). If the work of the fourth century was an extension or a restoration, the name Via Tecta might simply allude to porticoes lining the street or some part of it.

Via Tecta (2): the name given by Ovid (*Fast.* 6.191–92) to a stretch of the Via Appia between the Porta Capena and the Temple of Mars, perhaps only a short section immediately in front of the temple, but more likely the whole of this stretch, and possibly given this name because it was the first stretch of

road outside the city to be paved, rather than graveled. The notion that there might have been a portico along the road from Porta Capena to the Temple of Mars strains credulity, while a colonnaded approach in front of the Aedes Martis (see Mars, Aedes) would be out of keeping with Roman custom.

Via Tiburtina: the road from Rome to Tibur, probably that diverging to the left from the Via Praenestina a little outside the Porta Esquilina of the Servian Walls and running to Porta Tiburtina (Porta S. Lorenzo) in the Aurelian Walls. Some topographers have proposed that the Via Tiburtina left the Servian Walls by Porta Viminalis and ran to the posterula called Porta Chiusa in the Aurelian Walls, just southeast of the Castra Praetoria, but there can be no doubt that by the time of the building of the Aurelian Walls the other line was in heavier use, and the fact that the Porta Tiburtina is built around a monumental arch by which Augustus took the three aqueducts, Marcia, Tepula, and Iulia, over the road argues that by his day this was also the more important road. The identity of the Porta Chiusa road remains uncertain; the name Via Tiburtina sometimes used for it has no ancient support.

The road ran east northeast to Tibur, 20 miles away, crossing the Anio River close to Rome and then running roughly parallel to it, but some distance away from it. The Via Tiburtina follows an irregular course through gently undulating country until it reaches the sharp rise of the Monti Tiburtini just below Tibur. Beyond Tibur it changes its name and becomes the Via Valeria as far as Cerfennia, northeast of the Lacus Fucinus in the country of the Marsi. Thereafter, it becomes the Via Claudia Valeria (*CIL* 9.5973). Claudius extended this road to the Adriatic at the mouth of the Aternus River, a noteworthy feat of engineering.

For Strabo (5.3.9 [236–37]) it was one of the best-known Roman roads, ranking with the Via Appia and Via Latina. A number of inscriptions commemorate its curatores (*CIL* 2.4126, 6.1517 = *ILS* 1080, 9.3667, 13.1803). These are all later than Claudius and seem generally to have been responsible for the whole system, but sometimes only the Tiburtina or the Valeria is mentioned.

Ashby 1927, 93–122.

Via Triumphalis (1): a road running northwest from the head of the Pons Neronianus on the right bank of the Tiber. It crosses the Prati di Castello, ascends the southern slope of Monte Mario, and eventually joins the Via Clodia 7 miles from Rome at the farm called La Giustiniana. Its name is mysterious; because it cannot have existed before the time of Nero, F. Coarelli (*MEFRA* 89 [1977]: 807–46, especially 819–23) has suggested that, following Claudius's extension of the pomerium to include much of the old Campus Martius, it became difficult to bring a victorious army to the outskirts of the city in preparation for a triumph and have it bivouac in the Campus Martius, as had long been the custom. To meet the new conditions a strip of the left riverbank was left outside the pomerium and armies could then approach Rome by the Via Triumphalis, bivouac in Prati di Castello, and march along the riverbank to enter the city by the Porta Triumphalis as they always had. Against this must be observed that the army of Vespasian and Titus on the occasion of their triumph bivouacked in the Campus Martius (Josephus, *BellIud* 7.5.4 [123]), and we are quite uncertain where the pomerium ran through the Campus. To solve such difficulties as Coarelli sees, it would have been easier and more logical to include the whole of the Campus Martius within the pomerium. Any army could then be kept on the right bank of the Tiber, and, if there were an extrapomerial strip reserved between the Pons Aemilius and the Porta Triumphalis, gerrymandering would be quite unnecessary.

The Via Triumphalis is linked with the network of roads of which the Via Aurelia is the chief member, having the same curators (*CIL* 6.1512, 8.946, 14.3610 = *ILS* 1071). Along the Via Triumphalis were brickyards (*CIL* 15.684). See also Apollo Argenteus and Bellona Pulvinensis. The evidence suggests that the Via Triumphalis was always relatively unimportant.

RendPontAcc 61 (1988–89): 309–42 (N. Degrassi).

Via Triumphalis (2): a name often given to the street between the Palatine and Caelian (modern Via S. Gregorio) from the Colosseum to the Septizodium, along which triumphal processions marched. There is no ancient authority for this name.

Vica Pota, Aedes: a shrine on the site of the Domus P. Valerii (see Domus, Valerii) at the foot of the slope of the Velia (Livy 2.7.12; Plutarch, *Poplic.* 10.4). Vica Pota was identified with Victoria (Asconius *in Cic. Pis.* 52 [Stangl 19]; cf. Cicero, *Leg.* 2.28), and an enigmatic passage in Seneca's *Apocolocyntosis* (9) makes her the mother of Jupiter (see also Arnobius 3.25, who derives her name from *victus* and *potus*). Her festival was 5 January (Degrassi 391).

The location of this shrine is difficult. It ought to be not far from the Regia, because the ground starts to rise perceptibly just beyond that, but no one locates it with relation to a familiar building. For that reason topographers tend to locate it on the Sacra

Via in front of the Basilica Constantini, but that will hardly suit the story of the removal of Valerius's house.

Victiliana: see **Domus Vectiliana.**

Victoria, Aedes (Fig. 53): a temple on the Palatine assigned by tradition to Evander (Dion. Hal. 1.32.5) but in its historical form the work of L. Postumius Megillus, built from the fines collected during his aedileship and on 1 August 294 B.C. dedicated by him as consul (Livy 10.33.9; Degrassi 489). When the black stone of the Magna Mater was first brought to Rome in 204 B.C., it was temporarily housed in the Temple of Victoria (Livy 29.14.14). Close to it, probably within the temenos, M. Porcius Cato dedicated an aedicula to Victoria Virgo in 193 B.C., also on 1 August (Livy 35.9.6). The temple must have been on the Clivus Victoriae and presumably not far from the Temple of the Magna Mater (see Magna Mater, Aedes). Dedicatory inscriptions found near the church of S. Teodoro (*CIL* 1².805 = 6.31059, 31060 = *ILLRP* 284) probably indicate the general area, but it would have stood high on the hill. The Victoria Germanica listed by the regionary catalogues in Regio X may be the same temple and record a restoration.

Remains of a large temple platform in blocks of tufa a little to the east of the Temple of the Magna Mater, but canted at an angle to it, have recently been identified as belonging to this temple (*QArchEtr* 16 [Rome 1988]: 54–67 [P. Pensabene]). The case is a very strong one. Fragments of architectural terracottas, as well as remains of the podium, attest to its republican phase and the excellence of its construction. In its final phase, which is ascribed to the Severan period, it was somewhat broader and shorter than the Temple of the Magna Mater, Corinthian, peripteral sine postico, with a frontal approach by a broad stair. This permits identification of the little "Auguratorium" set between the two temples as the Aedicula Victoriae Virginis of Cato. Unfortunately, absolute proof is as yet lacking.

Victoria, Ara: an altar in the Curia Iulia, presumably set up by Augustus in 29 B.C. at the same time that he installed a statue of Victoria there that had been brought from Tarentum (Cass. Dio 51.22.1; Suetonius, *Aug.* 100.2; Herodian 5.5.7). It was dedicated on 28 August (Degrassi 503). During the struggle between Christianity and paganism in the fourth century, this altar came to symbolize the strength of paganism. Constantius removed it in 357, but it seems soon to have been restored, presumably by Julian, and was finally abolished by Gratian in 382 (Symmachus, *Rel.* 3; Ambrosius, *Epist.* 1.17.4, 18.1, 7, 10, 32). Both statue and altar had a powerful hold on the imagination of Rome.

Victoria Virgo, Aedicula (Fig. 53): a shrine dedicated by M. Porcius Cato on 1 August 193 B.C., close to the Temple of Victoria, presumably within the temenos on the Palatine, it had the same dedication day (Livy 35.9.6; Degrassi 489). Livy cites an interval of two years between its being vowed and its being dedicated, which suggests that it was architecturally significant, but the occasion of its being vowed is unknown. This has recently been identified with some probability as the "Auguratorium" just east of the Temple of Magna Mater (*QArchEtr* 16 [Rome 1988]: 54–67 [P. Pensabene]). See Victoria, Aedes.

Vicus: see **Via, Vicus, Clivus** and **Regio, Vicus, Pagus.**

Vicus Aesculeti (or **Aescleti**): known from an inscription on an altar (*CIL* 6.30957 = *ILS* 3615) dedicated by the magistri Vici Aescleti to the Lares, found in situ in the construction of Via Arenula about 100 m north of the Tiber. It must take its name from the Aesculetum (q.v.). Ancient street pavement has been found under the nearby Via di S. Bartolomeo, but the vicus more probably lay on the other side of Via Arenula.
CEFR 98 (1987): 62–73 (S. Panciera).

Vicus Africus: known only from Varro (*Ling.* 5.159), in Esquiliae, said to be so called because hostages from Africa were kept there under guard during the Punic wars.

Vicus Anici: the reading proposed by Valentini and Zucchetti (VZ 1.43) to replace Vicus Valeri, listed in Regio XIII on the Capitoline Base (*CIL* 6.975 = *ILS* 6073). See also Horrea Aniciana.

Vicus Antistianus: known from a single inscription (*AE* 1960.58) and of unknown location.

Vicus Apollinis: a street in Regio X known from the Capitoline Base (*CIL* 6.975 = *ILS* 6073), presumably in the vicinity of the Temple of Apollo Palatinus (see Apollo Palatinus, Aedes).

Vicus Armilustri: see **Armilustrium.**

Vicus Bellonae: known from a single inscription (*CIL* 6.2235), presumably either the street along the east flank of the Temple of Bellona (see Bellona,

Aedes) or that along its back, but listed in Pomponio Leto in Regio VI (VZ 1.216) and argued by Palmer to be near Porta Collina.
MEFRA 87 (1975): 653–65 (R. E. A. Palmer).

Vicus Brutianus: in Regio XIV, known from the Capitoline Base (*CIL* 6.975 = *ILS* 6073) but presumably connected with the Campus Bruttianus of the regionary catalogues. The origin of the name is unknown.

Vicus Caeseris: known from a single inscription (*CIL* 6.9492 = *ILS* 7556a), without further topographical identification.

Vicus Caeseti: known from the Capitoline Base, listed in Regio XIII (*CIL* 6.975 = *ILS* 6073). This may possibly have derived its name from Caesetius Rufus, a senator whose house Fulvia, the wife of Antony, coveted (Val. Max. 9.5.4; Appian, *BellCiv* 4.29). See Domus, Caesetius Rufus.

Vicus Camenarum: listed first in Regio I on the Capitoline Base (*CIL* 6.975 = *ILS* 6073), presumably the short street running roughly north/south from Porta Capena to Vicus Trium Ararum in the direction of the Palatine. See Camenae.

Vicus Canarius: mentioned in a single inscription (*IGUR* 1659) and in the acts of the Christian martyrs and located by the *Mirabilia* (Jordan 2.615; VZ 3.24) near S. Giorgio in Velabro. It may be that this should be connected with the Temple of Hercules in the Forum Boarium that neither dogs nor flies were believed to enter (Pliny, *HN* 10.79). See Hercules Victor, Aedes (1) and Jordan 2.588.
RendPontAcc 61 (1988–89): 353–56 (L. Moretti).

Vicus Capitis Africae: mentioned by Probus (Keil, *Gramm. Lat.* 4.198) and identified by G. Gatti (*AdI* 54 [1882]: 191–220) as the ancient street under Via della Navicella leading from the Ludus Magnus to Porta Caelimontana, or perhaps only the relatively level upper stretch of this. See Caput Africae.
CEFR 98 (1987): 653–85 (C. Pavolini).

Vicus Capitis Canteri: listed on the Capitoline Base in Regio XIII (*CIL* 6.975 = *ILS* 6073); it might have taken its name from a mule's head used as a device on a street fountain or something similar.

Vicus Caprarius: a street mentioned in a bull of Pope Paschal II of A.D. 1104 as being in Regio V of papal Rome (and cf. the forged bull of Pope John III given in Jordan 2.669–70, where it is called Viculus Capralicus). From this it appears to have run south from the line of the Aqua Virgo at the point where it bent sharply west just south of Piazza Trevi, and ancient paving blocks found under Via Lucchesi are thought to have belonged to it. It is undoubtedly to be connected with the Aedicula Capraria (q.v.).

HJ 459–60.

Vicus Castrorum: known from Probus (Keil, *Gramm. Lat.* 4.198) and of uncertain location.

Vicus Ceios: in Regio XII, listed on the Capitoline Base (*CIL* 6.975 = *ILS* 6073), but otherwise unknown. The interpretation of the name is quite uncertain.

Vicus Censori: known from the Capitoline Base (*CIL* 6.975 = *ILS* 6073) and two other inscriptions (*CIL* 6.451 = *ILS* 3619, 821), which locate it on the Tiber island in Regio XIV, the only vicus known on the island and perhaps the only one there. It seems to have been named for a family of which the earliest known representative is C. Censorius Niger of the time of Hadrian.

Vicus Collis Viminalis: known from two inscriptions (*CIL* 6.2227, 2228 = *ILS* 6076), believed to be the ancient street known to have run the length of the ridge of the Viminal from near the Gallinae Albae (q.v.) to Porta Viminalis in the Servian Walls. Its upper stretch may have been somewhat modified at the time of the construction of the Thermae Diocletiani (q.v.). Whether the continuation of this street from Porta Viminalis to Porta Chiusa in the Aurelian Walls was called by the same name is unknown but seems likely.

Vicus Columnae Ligneae: known only from the Capitoline Base, listed in Regio XIII (*CIL* 6.975 = *ILS* 6073). Because wooden columns cannot have been uncommon in Rome, we should perhaps think of a conspicuous votive column. The numerous ancient sanctuaries on the Aventine make it difficult to identify one as likelier than another.

Vicus Compiti Pastoris: known only from the Capitoline Base, listed in Regio XII (*CIL* 6.975 = *ILS* 6073).

Vicus Cornicularius: in Regio III, known only from two inscriptions of the vicomagistri belonging to a compital shrine located near the Ludus Magnus in the direction of S. Giovanni in Laterano. The name may allude either to the low-ranking military officer so called or to a worker in horn as a material.

The inscriptions date from the middle of the first century after Christ.

ArchCl 10 (1958): 231–34 (L. Moretti).

Vicus Cuprius (often spelled **Cyprius**): an important street leading northeast from the Forum Romanum along the northwest slope of the Oppius, in later antiquity represented by the street cutting through the north corner of the Basilica Constantini. Into it fed a short street leading down from the Tigillum Sororium (q.v.) on the extension of Sacra Via that ran to the Oppius (Dion. Hal. 3.22.8), and at its highest point it was crossed by the Clivus Orbius (q.v.), which, following the desecration of her father's corpse by Tullia, was divided between the Clivus Orbius (from the Argiletum to the Vicus Cuprius) and the Vicus Sceleratus (from the Vicus Cuprius southeast across the Oppius) (Livy 1.48.6–7). Varro (*Ling.* 5.159) derives the name from the Sabine word for "good" and would have it that the Sabines settled there when they were admitted to citizenship, but the manuscripts give the spelling for this as *ciprum* (or *cyprum*), which would yield rather the sense "copper," and all other early associations of the Sabines are with the Quirinal and Capitoline.

Journal of Indo-European Studies 1 (1973): 368–78 (R. E. A. Palmer).

Vicus Curiarum: a street in Regio X (*CIL* 6.975 = *ILS* 6073) probably deriving its name from the Curiae Veteres (q.v.) and to be located a little south of the northeast corner of the Palatine. It is even possible that the street commonly called Via Triumphalis (under Via S. Gregorio) is the Vicus Curiarum and ran between the Curiae Veteres and the Curiae Novae.

Vicus Curvus: known from the Vicocorvenses of *CIL* 6.31893 d8, a fragment of the fourth-century decree of Tarracius Bassus, located in Esquiliae (2) (q.v.).

Vicus Cyclopis: known from an inscription (*CIL* 6.2226 = *ILS* 6077) and there located in Regio I, therefore to be associated with the Antrum Cyclopis (q.v.) of Regio II. The Lugli and Gismondi map locates this as the street leading to Porta Metrovia in the Aurelian Walls, the boundary between Regio I and Regio II here, but there is no proof.

MemPontAcc, ser. 3.7 (1944): 157 (A. M. Colini).

Vicus Dianae: known from the Capitoline Base, listed in Regio XII (*CIL* 6.975 = *ILS* 6073), but otherwise unknown. It may have been near the church of S. Saba (see *CIL* 6.3677 = 30853).

Vicus Drusianus: a street in Regio I (*CIL* 6.975 = *ILS* 6073) probably named from the Arcus Drusi (1) (q.v.), which spanned Via Appia a little north of the point where Via Latina diverged from Via Appia. An important street ran almost straight to the northeast from Piazza Numa Pompilio (at the east corner of the Thermae Antoninianae) to Piazza S. Giovanni, from the boundary between Regio I and Regio XII across Regiones I and II and into V. Today it is represented by Via Druso and Via Amba Aradam. This may have been Vicus Drusianus.

Vicus Epicteti (?): see **Epictetinses.**

Vicus Fabrici: the last street listed in Regio I on the Capitoline Base (*CIL* 6.975 = *ILS* 6073), associated with the Compitum Fabricium (q.v.), which is located on the western slope of the Caelian near the Curiae Novae. Identification of the vicus as the street along the southwest front of the Temple of Divus Claudius (so on the Lugli and Gismondi map) is entirely conjectural and not likely to be correct.

Vicus Fanni: known from a single inscription (*CIL* 6.7542) without further indication of location.

Vicus[. . .]ionum Ferrariarum: known only from an inscription found near the church of S. Pancrazio on the Janiculan hill (*CIL* 6.9185). It seems possible to complete the missing word in many ways, but none suggests itself as clearly what is required.

Vicus Fidi: known from the Capitoline Base, listed first in Regio XIII (*CIL* 6.975 = *ILS* 6073), otherwise unknown.

Vicus Fontis Salientis: the reading proposed by Valentini and Zucchetti (VZ 1.45) to replace VICO [. . .]ANI SALIENTIS in Regio XII on the Capitoline Base (*CIL* 6.975 = *ILS* 6073).

Vicus Fortunae Dubiae: known from the Capitoline Base, listed last in Regio XIII (*CIL* 6.975 = *ILS* 6073), otherwise unknown. The great number of shrines to Fortuna known to have existed in Rome includes some with very strange epithets. This might well have been a compital shrine.

Vicus Fortunae Mammosae: known from the Capitoline Base, listed in Regio XII (*CIL* 6.975 = *ILS* 6073) and to be associated with a shrine listed in the regionary catalogues (see Fortuna Mammosa), but with no more precise location.

Vicus Fortunae Obsequentis: known from the Capitoline Base, listed in Regio I (*CIL* 6.975 = *ILS* 6073), presumably named from the shrine ascribed by Plutarch (*De fort. Rom.* 10, *Quaest. Rom.* 74) to Servius Tullius. The same epithet is given to Venus (see Venus Obsequens) with a temple ad Circum Maximum, and Fortuna was often identified with Venus.

Vicus Fortunae Respicientis: known from the Capitoline Base, listed in Regio X (*CIL* 6.975 = *ILS* 6073) and to be associated with the shrine of Fortuna Respiciens listed in the regionary catalogues in Regio X between the Curiae Veteres and the Septizodium, so probably to be located on the southeast slope of the Palatine Hill.

Vicus Fortunati: known from the Capitoline Base, listed in Regio XIII (*CIL* 6.975 = *ILS* 6073), but otherwise unknown. Fortunatus was an extremely common cognomen in all periods.

Vicus Frumentarius: known from the Capitoline Base, listed in Regio XIII (*CIL* 6.975 = *ILS* 6073), so presumably in the area southwest of the Aventine where warehouses clustered behind the Emporium and presumably a street where dealers in grain were concentrated, but it cannot be more precisely located.

Vicus Gemini: known from the Capitoline Base, listed first in Regio XIV after the Vicus Censori on the island (*CIL* 6.975 = *ILS* 6073), so presumably near the river and the bridgeheads. Geminus is a well-attested cognomen.

Vicus Honoris et Virtutis: known from the Capitoline Base, listed in Regio I (*CIL* 6.975 = *ILS* 6073) and to be associated with the well-known Temple of Honos et Virtus (1) just inside Porta Capena on the slope of the Caelian near the church of S. Gregorio Magno. It may have been the street branching from the Clivus Scauri and running south and then southeast along the brow of the Caelian that the Lugli and Gismondi map shows as the boundary between Regiones I and II. The name recurs on the epistyle of a compital shrine to the Lares and Genii Caesarum of A.D. 83 (*CIL* 6.449 = *ILS* 3617), which also gives the date of the first vicomagistri of this vicus as 9 B.C. Unfortunately the find spot of this block is unknown. See also *Doxa* 2 (1949): 72–73 (A. Degrassi) = *AE* 1949.170.

Vicus Huiusce Diei: known from the Capitoline Base, listed last in Regio X (*CIL* 6.975 = *ILS* 6073) and possibly named for a shrine or altar of the same Fortuna to whom Catulus built a temple in the Campus Martius (see Fortuna Huiusce Diei, Aedes). Because Catulus is known to have built himself a magnificent house on the Palatine, probably after the victory over the Cimbri (Pliny, *HN* 17.2), it may well be that the name of the vicus began as derisive of Catulus and his ostentation, as well as of his claim to a triumph for that victory (see Domus, Catulus).

Vicus Iani: mentioned only by Porphyrion in a note on Horace, *Epist.* 1.20.1 and explained as where there was an arch consecrated to Janus, but without more precise location.

Vicus Ianuclensis: known from the Capitoline Base, listed in Regio XIV (*CIL* 6.975 = *ILS* 6073) and from its name probably to be associated with the top of the Janiculan ridge close to the point where the Via Aurelia ran out from Porta Aurelia on a narrow neck between valleys to either side. It is probably at least the upper stretch of the road running parallel to Via Aurelia through the Transtiberim and climbing the slope south of S. Pietro in Montorio that converges with Via Aurelia at the top a little inside the gate.

Vicus Insteius (Livy 24.10.8), **Insteianus** (Varro, *Ling.* 5.52): on the Collis Latiaris, the southwestern extremity of the Quirinal, the site of an *auguraculum* (q.v.) and a place where a spring erupted in 214 B.C. with such violence that it tumbled before it the dolia that happened to be there. This end of the Quirinal is exceptionally rich in water, the Fons Cati (now known as the Acqua S. Felice) being the source of the Petronia Amnis and other water having been encountered with great frequency in building operations (LA 236), so it is not surprising that on the lowest lobe of the hill such a phenomenon should have occurred. No ancient street is known on the hill proper, but as Varro puts the auguraculum *in summo vico*, it is likely to be the street that led past the great basilical hall of the Mercati di Traiano from the Via Biberatica eastward to a juncture with the street coming south from Alta Semita in the vicinity of Piazza (Largo) Magnanapoli. The name is a relatively uncommon Roman gentilicial name.

Vicus Iovis Fagutalis: a street on the Oppius known only from a single inscription of A.D. 109 (*CIL* 6.452 = *ILS* 3620) commemorating the restoration of a compital shrine. It derived its name from the sacellum of Iuppiter Fagutalis (see Fagutal) at the top of the Clivus Pullius (Solinus 1.26). It may be the ancient street crossing Piazza S. Pietro in Vincoli from northwest to southeast.

Vicus Isidis: mentioned casually by Tertullian (*Idol.* 20.2) without a more precise location.

Vicus Iugarius (Fig. 19): listed in the regionary catalogues in Regio VIII, the street along the shoulder of the Capitoline Hill above the Forum Romanum linking the foot of the Quirinal with the Porta Carmentalis (cf. Livy 35.21.6) and, because it was a very old street, always a vital part of the road system bringing those in quest of salt from the Via Salaria and Alta Semita to the ferry landing at the mouth of the Cloaca in the Forum Boarium. Where the Vicus Iugarius began and ended in the early period is open to question; after the construction of the Servian Walls, it probably was thought to extend only to Porta Carmentalis (Livy 24.47.15). The beginning was destroyed by the construction of the Forum Traiani, if not earlier, but, like the line of the Servian Walls, the road must have kept to the highest ground and shortest route available in the crossing from Quirinal to Capitoline and probably ran not far from the southwest façade of the Basilica Ulpia. Because this would have brought it into conjunction with the so-called Clivus Argentarius, which was probably also a very old track leading out to the Campus Martius, we may think of the Vicus Iugarius as once beginning at that juncture. In the imperial period it was probably not thought of as extending beyond the Area Volcani, and Festus (370L) has it begin at the Lacus Servilius adjacent to the Basilica Iulia. For purposes of definition, then, we may say that it began behind the Rostra Augusti, ran between the Temple of Saturn and Basilica Iulia, and followed the base of the Capitoline Hill (Livy 35.21.6) along the line of the modern Via della Consolazione and Vico Iugario, ending just short of Via del Teatro di Marcello (Via del Mare).

The Vicus Iugarius is said to have got its name from the Altar of Iuno Iuga erected there (Paulus *ex Fest.* 92L), but more likely the name prompted erection of the altar of Juno as patroness of marriage. Nor is it likely that there were ever yoke makers there or that it was conceived as linking the Forum Romanum and Forum Boarium, or other places. More likely the name simply means the road "following the ridge" or "following the heights," as distinct from the other roads in the vicinity. In later times it took on new importance as the main artery between the Forum Romanum and the lower Campus Martius. It seems always to have been the road by which triumphs and similar processions first entered the forum (Livy 27.37.14).

Nash 2.514; *BullCom* 84 (1974-75): 149-72 (P. Virgili).

Vicus Laci Fundani: known from an inscription (*CIL* 1².1.721 = 6.1297 = *ILS* 872 = *ILLRP* 352, a dedication by the vicus to Sulla) and clearly deriving its name from the Lacus Fundani (q.v.). It lay in the saddle between the Quirinal and the Capitoline (Tacitus, *Hist.* 3.69) and was probably obliterated by the construction of the Forum Traiani.

Vicus Laci Miliari: known only from the Capitoline Base, listed in Regio XIII (*CIL* 6.975 = *ILS* 6073). A watering trough at a milestone would not be uncommon outside the city, but in Regio XIII the only road with milestones was probably that along the Tiber with the distances measured from the Porta Trigemina (a branch of Via Ostiensis). We can locate this vicus, then, in the district of warehouses behind the Emporium.

Vicus Laci Restituti: known from the Capitoline Base, listed in Regio XIV (*CIL* 6.975 = *ILS* 6073). Restitutus is probably the cognomen of the man responsible for establishing this watering place.

Vicus Laci Tecti: known from the Capitoline Base, listed in Regio XII (*CIL* 6.975 = *ILS* 6073), otherwise unknown.

Vicus Larum Alitum: known from the Capitoline Base, listed in Regio XIII (*CIL* 6.975 = *ILS* 6073), presumably named for a compital shrine. But winged Lares are an anomaly, and Wissowa (Roscher 2.1885) conjectures that here images of winged divinities (possibly Erotes) were simply substituted for proper Lares.

Vicus Larum Iu(ga)lium (?): the restoration by Valentini and Zucchetti (VZ 1.46) of the name of a street listed on the Capitoline Base in Regio XIV (*CIL* 6.975 = *ILS* 6073). The reading is far from certain, but because this is followed by the Vicus Ianuclensis and Vicus Brutianus (qq.v.) in the list, it may have been on the outskirts of the city. G. Gatti proposed the reading: Vicus Larum Curialium.

Vicus Licinianus: known only from a sepulchral inscription (*CIL* 6.9871 = *ILS* 7585) found on Via Tiburtina 4 miles from Rome and without further indication of location.

Vicus Longi . . . Aquilae: known from the Capitoline Base, listed in Regio XIV (*CIL* 6.975 = *ILS* 6073) and presumably the district of the Aquilenses of the fourth-century edict of Tarracius Bassus (*CIL* 6.31893.a6 = *ILS* 6072). The genitive is probably to be read as a proper name. R. E. A. Palmer (*PAPS* 125 [1981]: 369–70) would read Longus and identify this as the first part of Via Campana/Portuensis.

Vicus Longus: located by an inscription (*AE* 1964.126) in Regio VI, the street running southwest/

northeast up the valley between the Quirinal and the Viminal and originally joining Alta Semita a short distance inside Porta Collina, probably at the point where modern Via Quintino Sella joins Via XX Settembre. The Vicus Longus is first mentioned by Livy (10.23.6) in connection with the foundation of the sacellum of Pudicitia Plebeia in 296 B.C. (cf. Festus 270L). There was a Temple of Febris *in summa parte* (Val. Max. 2.5.6) and an altar of Fortuna Euelpis, or perhaps Spei Bonae (Plutarch, *De fort. Rom.* 10). The Vicus Longus is mentioned in at least two inscriptions (*CIL* 6.9736 = *ILS* 7618, 10023). Its pavement was found during construction of Via Nazionale in front of the Banca d'Italia, in front of the Palazzo delle Esposizioni, and at a number of points between here and the Thermae Diocletiani. For the construction of the Thermae a considerable stretch of the vicus was destroyed and a new cross street created running from Alta Semita to Vicus Collis Viminalis, into which Vicus Longus then debouched. Its termination at its southwest end is less certain.

Vicus Lorari or **Lorarius:** a street known from one sepulchral inscription (*CIL* 6.9796 = *ILS* 7604) from the Via Appia. The name is presumably in allusion to harness makers or whip makers who were concentrated here, but the form of the adjective is odd. One expects *Lorariorum*, which may have been found to be an awkward mouthful.

Vicus Loreti Maioris, Minoris: see **Loretum.**

Vicus Luc . . . ii: a street in Regio XIV listed on the Capitoline Base (*CIL* 6.975 = *ILS* 6073). This might be restored as Vicus Lucceii; there seems to have been more than one Vicus Lucceius in Rome.
BullCom 85 (1976-77): 135-38 (R. E. A. Palmer).

Vicus Mamuri: see **Clivus Mamuri.**

Vicus Materiarius: a street in Regio XIII (*CIL* 6.975 = *ILS* 6073) presumably named for a concentration of lumberyards along it and to be located in the warehouse district behind the Emporium. However, Hülsen would put it on the summit of the Aventine because of its place in the list (HJ 170).

Vicus Minervi: known from an altar of Stata Mater Augusta set up by the vicomagistri, found in a cemetery just outside Porta Pinciana (*CIL* 6.766 = *ILS* 3309). This locates the vicus in Regio VII. PA suggests that it ran northeast from the gate, presumably meaning the street labeled on the Lugli and Gismondi map Via Salaria Vetus, but that would take Regio VII farther east than seems advisable, and there are extensive cemeteries here (HJ 437). The name seems to allude to a shrine of Minerva otherwise unknown, possibly compital.

Vicus Mundiciei: a street known from the Capitoline Base, listed in Regio XIII (*CIL* 6.975 = *ILS* 6073). Mundicius is a rare but well attested gentilicial name.

Vicus Novus: known from the Capitoline Base, in Regio XIII (*CIL* 6.975 = *ILS* 6073).

Vicus Orbius: see **Clivus Orbius.**

Vicus Pac(r)ae: known from the Capitoline Base, in Regio XIV (*CIL* 6.975 = *ILS* 6073; VZ 147); the name has not been satisfactorily restored.

Vicus Padi: known from the Capitoline Base, listed first in Regio X, before the Vicus Curiarum (*CIL* 6.975 = *ILS* 6073) and therefore conjectured to belong on the east slope of the Palatine. The meaning of the name is unknown.

Vicus Pallacinae: see **Pallacinae.**

Vicus Panispernae: probably the ancient name of a district (likely a vicus) around the church of S. Lorenzo in Panisperna near the southwest end of the Viminal. This name for the church appears only about A.D. 1000; earlier it was called S. Laurentii in Formoso or ad (in) Formosum, after its builder (HCh 292-93). The question of whether this is a corruption of the original name is complicated by the existence in the near neighborhood of the locality Gallinae Albae (q.v.), which increases the likelihood of a joke name. Attempts to derive the name from the ancient cognomen Perperna (Perpenna) are now generally recognized to be mistaken.

Vicus Patricius: one of the oldest and most important streets in Rome, running straight from the Argiletum up the valley between Cispian and Viminal to the Porta Viminalis in the Servian Walls following the line of modern Via Urbana and Via d'Azeglio. Roman antiquarians believed that the name went back to the regal period (Festus 247L), and it persisted in use into the early Middle Ages. It is generally regarded as the boundary separating this part of Regio IV from Regio VI. Beyond Porta Viminalis it probably continued for some distance (see Isis Patricia), and part of it was known, though perhaps only relatively late, as Clivus Patricius (LPD 1.221 [Innocent I, A.D. 401-417]; VZ 2.236). It is mentioned by Martial (7.73.2, 10.68.2) and Plutarch (*Quaest.*

Rom. 3). There were few shrines along its length; only one of Diana (Plutarch, *Quaest. Rom.* 3) and that of Isis already cited are known. It is given as the location of the church of S. Euphemia in the Einsiedeln itinerary 1.12 (Jordan 2.646; cf. HCh 249-50).

Vicus Pauli: known only from the Capitoline Base, listed in Regio XIV (*CIL* 6.975 = *ILS* 6073). Paulus was a fairly common cognomen.

Vicus Piscinae Publicae: the street, or part of the street, between Porta Raudusculana and the street leading in from Porta Capena to the Septizodium (Amm. Marc. 17.4.14). It separated the Aventinus Maior from the Aventinus Minor following the line of modern Viale Aventino and was part of the boundary between Regio XII and Regio XIII but is listed in XII (*CIL* 6.975 = *ILS* 6073). It was named for the Piscina Publica (q.v.), which also gave its name to Regio XII.

Vicus Platanonis: not listed on the Capitoline Base but conjectured from the occurrence of the genitive *platanonis* listed in the regionary catalogues in Regio XIII between the Mappa Aurea and Horrea Galbae et Aniciana. On that evidence it should be near the Porta Lavernalis.

Vicus Ploti: known from the Capitoline Base, listed in Regio XIV (*CIL* 6.975 = *ILS* 6073) but otherwise unknown. Ploti could be either a cognomen or a nomen.

Vicus Portae Collinae: a name given in an inscription (*CIL* 6.450 = *ILS* 3618) of A.D. 98-99. Presumably this was the stretch of Alta Semita (q.v.) just inside Porta Collina, but there is no indication of where the point of distinction occurred.

Vicus Portae Naeviae: known only from the Capitoline Base, listed next to last in Regio XII (*CIL* 6.975 = *ILS* 6073). This must be the street connecting Vicus Piscinae Publicae and Porta Naevia, running south, then southeast over the Aventinus Minor.

Vicus Portae R(a)udusculanae: known from the Capitoline Base (where it is spelled Rudusculanae), listed in Regio XII (*CIL* 6.975 = *ILS* 6073) just before Vicus Portae Naeviae. This is usually taken to be the street connecting Porta Raudusculana and Porta Ostiensis in the Aurelian Walls, but other streets named for gates lead to those gates, not out of them. Therefore, it is better to take this as the final stretch of the street known as Vicus Piscinae Publicae, perhaps the southwest stretch beyond the juncture with Vicus Portae Naeviae.

Vicus Pulverarius: known from the Capitoline Base, listed in Regio I (*CIL* 6.975 = *ILS* 6073). This has been taken to refer to the great beds of pozzolana *(pulvis Puteolanus)* known to have lain outside Porta Appia (HJ 219), but because the obvious and convenient route of access to these was the Appia itself, this would have to be a branch road leading off it somewhere in the vicinity of these. It might allude also to dealers in pozzolana (cf. Clivus Argentarius).

Vicus Quadrati: known from the Capitoline Base, listed in Regio XIV (*CIL* 6.975 = *ILS* 6073) and from an inscription from the sanctuary of Diana Nemorensis of Aricia (*CIL* 14.2213). Quadratus was a fairly common cognomen.

Vicus Raciliani Maioris, Minoris: streets in Regio XIV listed on the Capitoline Base (*CIL* 6.975 = *ILS* 6073). The wife of Cincinnatus was named Racilia, and Cincinnatus is known to have had a small farm in the Transtiberim, in the Prata Quinctia (q.v.) opposite the Navalia. There might be a connection. However, a L. Racilius was tribunus plebis in 56 B.C., so the family did not die out. A Collegium Iuvenum Racilianensium *(RendPontAcc,* ser. 3.4 [1925-26]: 394-95 [O. Marucchi]) must belong in the same area.

Vicus Rostratae: listed on the Capitoline Base in Regio XIV (*CIL* 6.975 = *ILS* 6073), third in the regio. R. E. A. Palmer (*PAPS* 125 [1981]: 369) would supply *columnae* for the missing element, but this seems a strange location for what necessarily would be a triumphal monument.

Vicus Sabuci: a street in Regio III known from an inscription (*CIL* 6.801 = *ILS* 3305), a dedication to Vulcan found in Via Merulana near S. Martino ai Monti. If this was in situ, the only ancient street lacking a name in this neighborhood is that leading from the axis of the Thermae Traiani northeast to Porta Esquilina, a relatively unimportant street with no known monuments along it. *Sabucus* (or *sambucus*) is the Latin word for the elder tree.

Vicus Salutaris: known as the name of two streets, one on the Palatine in Regio X, one in the Transtiberim in Regio XIV, both listed on the Capitoline Base (*CIL* 6.975 = *ILS* 6073). That on the Palatine is

listed just before the Vicus Apollinis and might be connected with the Temple of Apollo Palatinus.

Vicus Salutis: known only from a fragmentary inscription (*CIL* 6.31270 = *ILS* 128 = *ILLRP* 434) and, if the reading is correct, probably the relatively level stretch of Clivus Salutis (q.v.) on the Quirinal (Collis Salutaris).

Vicus Sandaliarius: one of the best-known streets of Rome, in Regio IV (see Apollo Sandaliarius). It must have taken its name from an early concentration of shoemakers and sandal makers here; in the time of Aulus Gellius (18.4.1) it was the place *par excellence* of booksellers and scholars. Because these had earlier been concentrated along the lower Argiletum (q.v.) and must have been displaced by the construction of the Forum Nervae (Transitorium), it seems likely that the Vicus Sandaliarius was the street running along the northeast side of Templum Pacis (called Vicus Cuprius on the Lugli and Gismondi map). Augustus erected the statue of Apollo Sandaliarius here (Suetonius, *Aug.* 57.1). The Vicus Sandaliarius is mentioned in three inscriptions (*CIL* 6.448 = *ILS* 3614, 761 = *ILS* 3308, *BullCom* 5 [1877]: 162-63 [R. Lanciani], 18 [1890]: 132 [R. Lanciani]).
HJ 329.

Vicus Saufei: known only from the Capitoline Base, listed in Regio XIV (*CIL* 6.975 = *ILS* 6073). Saufeius is a gentilicial name commoner in the republic than in the empire.

Vicus Scauri: known from a single inscription (*CIL* 6.9940 = *ILS* 7619), probably the part of Clivus Scauri on the summit of the Caelian.

Vicus Sceleratus: see **Clivus Orbius.**

Vicus Sergi: known only from the Capitoline Base, listed in Regio XIV (*CIL* 6.975 = *ILS* 6073). Sergius is a well-known gentilicial name.

Vicus (Sil)ani Salientis: see **Vicus Fontis Salientis.**

Vicus Sobrius: a street in Rome said by Festus (382-83L) to be so called because there Mercury was offered milk rather than wine. This appears to be the same as the Mercurius Sobrius mentioned in two inscriptions (*CIL* 6.9483, 9714 = *ILS* 7510). A compital shrine of Augustan date dedicated to Mercury was found on the Esquiline near Torre Cantarelli in

1888 (*BullCom* 16 [1888]: 221-39 [G. Gatti]; *CIL* 6.30974 = *ILS* 92); this has been suggested to be the Mercury in question (HJ 334-35), but there is no hard evidence.

Vicus Stablarius: a reconstruction. Rodriguez Almeida proposes to restore the inscription VI[. . .] BLARIVS on fragments of the Marble Plan as Vicus Stablarius; others had proposed Vicus Bublarius (Rodriguez 1.149-50 and pl. 33, fragments 37, 40). The vicus is located in the Campus Martius southwest of the Theatrum Pompeii in an area bounded by the Lungotevere Tebaldi, Via dei Pettinari, Via de'Giubbonari, Via del Giglio, and Piazza Farnese, or roughly from the river to the Theater of Pompey and from Ponte Sisto to Piazza Farnese. The city blocks here are by and large regular and rectangular and seem to have been chiefly shops and workshops with dwellings above. If we restore *Stablarius*, the known existence of the stabula (q.v.) of several of the circus factions in the neighborhood might account for the name, or it could have the sense "public house," "inn."

Vicus (S)tabuli Proconsulus: mentioned by Probus (Keil, *Gramm. Lat.* 4.198), otherwise unknown.

Vicus Statae Matris: a street on the Caelian in Regio II known from the inscription on a compital altar (*CIL* 6.36809). It is unlikely that this was the same as the dedication to Stata Mater in the Forum Romanum mentioned by Festus (416L) in the past tense and said to have been set up after the forum was paved by Cotta (?). Dedications to Stata Mater are relatively common in Rome (cf., e.g., *ILS* 3306-9), and the epithet Augusta that appears in a number of these seems to allude to Augustus's reorganization of the regiones of the city and the vigiles (cf., e.g., *CIL* 6.761 = *ILS* 3308, 802 = *ILS* 3306). In a city where fire was a constant danger, the goddess credited with the power to stop fires is apt to have been widely worshiped at compital shrines. As Festus says, once the image had been established in the Forum Romanum, the people took her worship to their own neighborhoods. Unfortunately, we seem to have no identifiable likeness of Stata Mater.

Vicus Statae Siccianae: a street in the Transtiberim known from the Capitoline Base (*CIL* 6.975 = *ILS* 6073).

Vicus Statuae Valerianae: in the Transtiberim; see **Statua Valeriana.**

Vicus Statuae Verris: a name proposed for the street running through the north corner of the Basilica Constantini on the evidence of a mutilated inscription that must be heavily restored.

RendPontAcc 51-52 (1978-79): 111-36 (R. E. A. Palmer).

Vicus Strobili: mentioned by Probus (Keil, *Gramm. Lat.* 4.198), otherwise unknown. The allusion may be to a fountain in the form of a pine cone like the famous one in the Cortile delle Pigna in the Vatican (Helbig[4] 1.478).

Vicus Sulpicii or **Sulpicius:** given as the location of the Baths of Caracalla (S.H.A. *Heliogab.* 17.8-9) and listed on the Capitoline Base in Regio I with a division into a Vicus Sulpici Ulterior and a Vicus Sulpici Citerior (*CIL* 6.975 = *ILS* 6073). Because the baths were in Regio XII, the vicus has been identified (PA s.v., HJ 208-9) as the street running along the southwest side of the peribolus of the baths, the dividing line between Regio I and Regio XII, with the Via Appia the boundary between the Vicus Citerior to the northeast and the Vicus Ulterior to the southwest. This is all simply hypothetical, and the terms *citerior* and *ulterior* indicate rather a direction perpendicular to that proposed. It may be that the construction of the bath complex entailed displacement and reorientation of the vicus. Lanciani (LA 268) would have the two vici the continuations of the streets flanking the peribolus of the baths on the southeast and northwest on the northeast side of Via Appia (the former identified on the Lugli and Gismondi map as Vicus Drusianus, the latter nameless) and place the Vicus Drusianus closer to Porta Capena. This seems possible, if we allow the stretch connecting the two (and Porta Metrovia) to have been originally part of Vicus Sulpici Citerior. The street is also named on an altar of the republican period (*CIL* 1[2].1002 = 6.2221 = *ILS* 6078 = *ILLRP* 702) that mentions *magistri de duobus pagis et Vici Sulpici.* See also Via Nova (2).

Vicus Summi Choragi: known from a fragment of the Marble Plan (*FUR* 61 and pl. 15.3; Rodriguez 1.57 and pl. 1). The placing of this, which is only slightly uncertain given its small size and other physical characteristics, identifies the Vicus Summi Choragi as the short street just east of the church of S. Clemente. See Summum Choragium.

Vicus Tiberini: known from the Capitoline Base, listed last in Regio XIV (*CIL* 6.975 = *ILS* 6073). On the basis of its name and place in the list, Lanciani (LFUR sheet 28) has tentatively identified this as a street found under modern Via della Lungaretta between Viale di Trastevere and the river, the first stretch of what would become Via Aurelia and the street into which the Pons Aemilius and Pons Cestius led. This seems possible, but if there was a second vicus on the island, that would be a preferable identification. Presumably the Vicus Tiberini took its name from a sacellum dedicated to the god of the river.

Vicus Triari: known from the Capitoline Base, listed in Regio XII (*CIL* 6.975 = *IL* 6073), presumably the same as the Clivus Triarius (q.v.). The name is a cognomen of the Gentes Valeria and Pomponia, but rare.

Vicus Trium Ararum: known from the Capitoline Base, listed in Regio I (*CIL* 6.975 = *ILS* 6073), and from a compital dedication found in front of S. Gregorio Magno (*CIL* 6.453 = *ILS* 3616). The vicus is therefore probably the street running in front of S. Gregorio from the Clivus Scauri to the street in from Porta Capena, and the altars were connected with the sanctuaries of the Camenae and Honos et Virtus. See also Clivus Scauri.

Vicus Trium Viarum: known from the Capitoline Base, listed in Regio XIII (*CIL* 6.975 = *ILS* 6073). A fork of three streets is so common a feature in urban planning that one looks for some more conspicuous oddity. The confluence in the elongated wedge between the Horrea Galbae and the "Porticus Aemilia" might be what is meant, but there is no proof.

Vicus Turarius: a name that late commentators mistakenly give for the Vicus Tuscus, stemming almost certainly from someone's misreading or misunderstanding of *Tuscus* to mean incense was sold here, perhaps because a blot obliterated the last three letters of the word in his source (Porphyrion on Horace, *Epist.* 1.20.1, 2.1.269; pseudo-Asconius *ad Cic. Verr.* 2.1.154 [Stangl 255]). Incense may, of course, have been sold there, but this is a misnomer.

Vicus Tuscus: the street running southwest out of the Forum Romanum between the Temple of Castor and the Basilica Iulia that emerged in the Velabrum and presumably was the main street leading to the Porta Flumentana. It was the main route between the Forum Romanum and lower Forum Boarium, and hence to the Circus Maximus (Livy 27.37.15). Originally it must have run along the left bank of the Cloaca and presumably crossed it at the site of the Ianus Quadrifrons of the Velabrum. It was joined before reaching the Ianus by the Clivus Victoriae descending from the Palatine.

The street supposedly received its name from a settlement of Etruscans there, variously explained as a contingent that came to aid Romulus against Titus Tatius (Varro, *Ling.* 5.46; Servius *ad Aen.* 5.560; Propertius 4.2.49–52), remnants of Porsenna's army after the Battle of Aricia (Livy 2.14.9; Festus 486–87L; Dion. Hal. 5.36.4), or supporters of Tarquinius Priscus (Tacitus, *Ann.* 4.65). It is more likely that it got its name from being the main route from the Forum Romanum and Palatine to the Etruscan bank of the Tiber by first the Cloaca ferry and later the Pons Sublicius. The only shrine that is known to have been there was that of the Etruscan god Vortumnus (see Signum Vortumni) behind the Temple of Castor; this was believed to be very old.

It was always a very busy street in which there were shops of many sorts, but especially of fine clothing (Martial 11.27.11 [*serica*]; *CIL* 6.9976, 33923 = *ILS* 7575 [*vestiarius tenuiarius*], 37826, 14.2433 = *ILS* 7597 [*purpurarius*]). Early on it had a bad reputation (Plautus, *Curc.* 482), probably especially for the high prices asked by the merchants there (Horace, *Sat.* 2.3.228).

Jordan 1.1.273–74; Nash 2.315.

Vicus Unguentarius: listed in the *Notitia* in Regio VIII, but without further indication of its location. One is inclined to put it in the neighborhood of the Vicus Tuscus (q.v.), where there is known to have been a concentration of shops dealing in luxuries.

RivIstArch, ser. 3.8–9 (1985–86): 111–17 (E. Rodriguez Almeida).

Vicus V[aler]i (?): see **Vicus Anici.**

Vicus Veneris Almae: a street in Regio XII listed first in that regio on the Capitoline Base (*CIL* 6.975 = *ILS* 6073) and probably the district of the Venerenses of the fourth-century edict of Tarracius Bassus (*CIL* 6.31901). Very likely this should be connected with the Temple of Venus Obsequens and/or the Temple of Venus Verticordia (see Venus Obsequens, Aedes and Venus Verticordia, Aedes) near the southeast end of the Circus Maximus, but no known ancient street suggests itself as a candidate. The fact that the epithet of Venus is not that of any known shrine to this goddess may indicate that the allusion was rather to a compital shrine.

Vicus Vestae: a street in Regio VIII known from an inscription, a fragmentary dedication to the Lares Augusti (*CIL* 6.30960 = *ILS* 3621) of the time of Alexander Severus. This must be either the ramp and stair connecting the Nova Via with the Forum Romanum that debouches between the Temple of Vesta and the Temple of Castor (Ovid, *Fast.* 6.395–98) or the short street at the east end of the Atrium Vestae that connects the Sacra Via and Nova Via. The latter is to be preferred in view of the use of the term *vicus* (cf. Asconius *in Cic. Scaur.* 45 [Stangl 27], and see Domus, Scaurus).

Jordan 1.2.297–98.

Vicus Victoriae: known from a single sepulchral inscription (*MAAR* 36 [1980]: 239 [S. Panciera]); it was the site of a *portus olearius* and might have been a continuation of the Clivus Victoriae of the Palatine (q.v.).

Vicus Victoris: known only from the Capitoline Base, listed last in Regio XII after the Vicus Portae Naeviae (*CIL* 6.975 = *ILS* 6073), so perhaps somewhere beyond Porta Naevia.

Vicus Viridari: a street named in the sepulchral inscription for a magister of this vicus (*CIL* 6.2225) reported to have been found on Via Praenestina (Gabina). A *viridarium* being a small, usually enclosed, garden, this cannot be identified.

Vicus Vitrarius: a street in Regio I listed in the regionary catalogues but not on the Capitoline Base, presumably named for a concentration of glass workers there, but there is no indication where it might be.

Vigiles: see **Cohortes Vigilum, Stationes.**

Villa Coponiana: mentioned by Cicero in a letter to Atticus (*Att.* 12.31.2) and described as being an old house of no great size with a splendid wooded park. Because of Cicero's association of this with the villas of Silius and Cotta on Via Ostiensis (see *Att.* 12.23.3, 12.27.1), this is probably to be located there too. Because it is called a *villa*, it may have been some distance from Rome.

Villa Publica: originally a large park on the edge of the Campus Martius just beyond the Petronia Amnis, containing the only building in the campus in the early republic. According to Livy (4.22.7), the censors C. Furius Paculus and M. Geganius Macerinus created the Villa Publica in 435 B.C. expressly for the purpose of taking the census of the Roman people. Whether the Villa Publica contained any building at first may be doubted, but possibly shortly thereafter one might have been built to house the census lists while these were in the process of being compiled, though in the first century B.C. they seem to have been kept in the Temple of the Nymphs (see Nymphae, Aedes). In 194 B.C. there is a record of a rebuilding and enlargement of both the Villa Publica and the Atrium Libertatis (Livy 34.44.5). Varro (*Rust.* 3.2.3–6) describes the Villa Publica as simple

and without luxuries yet adorned with a wealth of pictures and statues and a well-shaded retreat from the sun, but designed to serve for levies of the army held by a consul, inspection of arms, and the census. One gathers from this that it was an essentially open area planted with trees and with porticoes around its boundaries where pictures were displayed. No part of it was farmed, but it was near, probably originally adjacent to, the Saepta (Cicero, *Att.* 4.16.14[17.7]; Varro, *Rust.* 3.2.1), which was at one time called the Ovile (q.v.) in allusion to its physical layout and place in the context of a villa.

Much has been made of the fact that in 82 B.C. the senate, while meeting in the Temple of Bellona, could hear the cries of the prisoners taken in the Battle of Porta Collina as they were slaughtered by Sulla's orders in the Villa Publica (Livy, *Epit.* 88; Val. Max. 9.2.1; Strabo 5.4.11 [249]; Seneca, *Clem.* 1.12.2; Florus 2.9.24; [Aur. Vict.,] *De Vir. Ill.* 75.10; Cass. Dio 30–35 frag. 109.5–8). The point of the story is that the prisoners were taken to the Villa Publica under the impression that they were to be enrolled in the army in a regular levy, and the senate was meeting in the Temple of Bellona as if to discuss a triumph. Generals awaiting a senatorial decision with respect to a triumph and foreign ambassadors were often, perhaps regularly, lodged in the Villa Publica (Livy 30.21.12, 33.24.5; Josephus, *BellIud* 7.5.4).

The Villa Publica is shown on a coin of P. Fonteius Capito of ca. 59–55 B.C. (*B. M. Coins, Rom. Rep.* 1.479 nos. 3856–60; Crawford 429/2). It appears as a section of a colonnade in two storeys, the lower storey arcuated, the upper not, with a sloping roof. The inscription seems to refer to a restoration by T. Didius (cos. 98 B.C.), and it is conjectured that Fonteius himself restored it, but that is hardly likely. Its area was eroded by the building programs of Julius Caesar and Augustus, and it is hard to say what its original boundaries may have been. On the east it cannot have extended beyond Via Lata (Via Flaminia), and on the west the Saepta Iulia covered land that probably once all belonged to it. On the south the Petronia Amnis, later buried under Vicus Pallacinae, seems a convenient limit, and on the north it probably did not extend beyond the line of the Aqua Virgo, although whether that followed its boundary is unclear. It lost territory first to the Porticus Minucia in 110 B.C., then to the Saepta Iulia and Diribitorium beginning in 54 B.C. The Saepta and Diribitorium were followed by the Theatrum and Crypta Balbi dedicated in 13 B.C. The Isaeum Campense is probably of the time of Caligula, and the great rusticated building (Porticus Minucia Frumentaria?) along Via Lata, probably Claudian. Valerius Maximus, writing in the later years of the reign of Tiberius, refers to the Villa Publica in the past tense, but Josephus's account of the triumph of Vespasian and Titus in A.D. 71 shows that at least some part of it still retained its original character and purpose at that time. After the fire of Titus in A.D. 80 destroyed most of the lower Campus Martius from the Pantheon to the Porticus Octaviae and from the scaena of the Theatrum Pompeii to the Temple of Iuppiter Optimus Maximus, what was left of the Villa Publica seems to have been rebuilt by Domitian as the Divorum, a rectangular parklike square planted with trees and surrounded by porticoes, very much what it had been earlier but now including temples to Divus Vespasianus and Titus just inside its northern limit.

L. Bonfante and H. von Heintze, eds., *In Memoriam Otto J. Brendel* (Mainz 1976), 159–63 (L. Richardson, "The Villa Publica and the Divorum"); *CEFR* 98 (1987): 211–34 (S. Agache).

Viminalis Collis (Fig. 72): always the least important of the hills making up the traditional seven hills of Rome, and relatively small, a tongue of high ground projecting to the southwest from the plateau of the Campagna, separated from the Cispian on the southeast by the valley up which ran the Vicus Patricius (now the Via Urbana) and from the Quirinal on the northwest by the valley up which now runs the Via Nazionale. It was, like the Quirinal, called collis, not mons, and with the Quirinal made up the Regio Collina of Rome of the Four Regions (see Regiones Quattuor). However, the Viminal does not seem to have shared the Sabine character of the Quirinal and had no temples of importance that we know of. When the Servian Walls were built, the gate spanning the extension of the Vicus Collis Viminalis to which Vicus Patricius also ran was called Porta Viminalis, but it is not clear how great the importance of this road may have been or where it led; it was never a major artery, and the gate in the Aurelian Walls through which it ran is nameless and was early walled up (Porta Chiusa). In the Augustan reorganization of Rome, the Viminal was included with the Quirinal in Regio VI, Alta Semita.

The Viminal was commonly supposed to have received its name from willow copses (*vimineta*) or the osiers (*vimina*) cut from these (Festus 516–17L; Juvenal 3.71), but Varro (*Ling.* 5.51) holds that it got its name from Iuppiter Viminus (q.v.), whose altar was there. This accords with Varro's further statement that all five of the hills of the Regio Collina were named from sanctuaries and seems clearly the preferable derivation. The meaning of the epithet is then obscure.

HJ 372–93; Jordan 2.261–62; Roscher 2.653 (E. Aust); *BullCom* 92 (1987–88): 109–26 (F. De Caprariis), 127–36 (M. Sediari); *QITA* 10 (1988): 29–44 (F. De Caprariis).

Vinea Publica: known from a boundary stone of A.D. 75 (*CIL* 6.933 = *ILS* 249; cf. *CIL* 6.31208). The inscription records a reclaiming of public land by Vespasian through the agency of the pontifices and was found outside the Aurelian Walls between "Porta Ardeatina" and Porta Appia, outside the Bastione del Sangallo. The suggestion is that the wine from this vineyard was used for pontifical libations; how it came to be invaded by private citizens is therefore puzzling.

Virgo Caelestis: A shrine of this divinity, essentially Punic and a patroness of Carthage (= Astarte) has been conjectured to have stood on the northern lobe of the Capitoline and to have been responsible for the name of the church of S. Maria in Aracoeli. This is based on an inscription (*CIL* 6.37170 = *ILS* 4438) honoring a priestess and describing the goddess as *numen loci montis Tarpei*. It was found near the Monument of Victor Emanuel and is dated A.D. 259. The goddess seems to have been introduced into Rome in the time of Elagabalus (Herodian 5.6.4). But more probably the church, earlier known as S. Mariae in (or de) Capitolio, got its name through a misreading of an inscription on the medieval high altar. Cf. HCh 323–24.

Virtus: a shrine said by Plutarch (*De fort. Rom.* 5) to have been built by Scipio Numantinus. Plutarch mistakenly dates M. Claudius Marcellus's Temple of Honos et Virtus after Scipio's, a curious error. Because there is no other mention of this shrine, it seems likely to have been relatively modest, but we have no idea where it was located. It may be connected with the statue of the next entry.

Virtus, Signum: a statue known from a dedicatory inscription (*CIL* 6.3735 = 31061) found in Via XX Settembre during construction of the Ministero delle Finanze, probably just outside Porta Collina and probably the same one referred to by Cassius Dio (48.43.4). The proximity of this to the ancient Temple of Honos extra Portam Collinam (see Honos, Aedes) suggests that Virtus was associated with Honos here, as elsewhere.

HJ 414–15; Wissowa, *RK* 149–51.

Vivarium: an enclosure, or set of enclosures, in which wild animals that were to be shown in amphitheatral games were kept (A. Gellius 2.20). It was near the Porta Praenestina, and a *custos vivari* is mentioned in one inscription (*CIL* 6.130 = *ILS* 2091) of A.D. 241. It is described in some detail by Procopius (*BellGoth* 1.22.10, 23.13–23). It formed the most vulnerable part of the Aurelian Walls, the Romans having built it at a point where the ground was very level, and because it was not strengthened with towers or battlements. This suggests that the Vivarium was essentially a stoutly built enclosure, probably rectangular, that Aurelian had made part of his fortification system without modification. The lack of battlements made the Vivarium especially vulnerable, and a gate, or gates, on the city side would be easily taken by an enemy once it had penetrated to the interior. All this is clear, but its location is not. The wish to locate the Vivarium in the area outside Porta Maggiore using the walled-up arches of the Aqua Claudia as its southern wall and the line of Via Labicana as its northern boundary (HJ 365–67; Nash 2.516) entails enormous difficulties. First, the Vivarium existed before the Aurelian Walls, and the use of an aqueduct line in animal enclosures seems unthinkable before that time. Second, there was another important aqueduct line in this area, a line that would have run right through the pens, with problems of pollution as well as maintenance. It seems best, then, to locate the Vivarium to the north of Porta Praenestina. In either location it must be presumed that Belisarius's rebuilding of the walls after the Gothic ravages has obliterated all trace of the Vivarium.

In the later Middle Ages the Castra Praetoria was called Vivarium (*Vivaio*) and an annex south of it Vivariolum (*Vivaiolo*). The origin and meaning of these terms is obscure, but the difficulties with locating the Vivarium where others wished led Lanciani to believe the building south of the camp had been the original Vivarium. However, this flies in the face of its date relative to the Aurelian Walls, as well as the explicit information given by Procopius.

Nash 2.516.

Volcanal: probably the same as the Area Volcani, an area adjacent to the Forum Romanum where there was an altar of Vulcan supposed to have been erected by Titus Tatius (Dion. Hal. 2.50.3; Varro, *Ling.* 5.74). The Volcanal was distinctly higher than the forum (Dion. Hal. 2.50.2; A. Gellius 4.5.4) and the Comitium (Festus 370L), and in the regal period and early republic the kings and magistrates transacted public business there (Dion. Hal. 2.50.2), and public assemblies were regularly held there (Dion. Hal. 6.67.2, 7.17.2, 11.39.1). The Volcanal was also big enough to include a bronze aedicula of Concordia, dedicated there in 304 B.C. All this taken together indicates that originally the Volcanal covered

the lower slope of the Capitoline along the stair that extended the line of the Sacra Via up the hill, an area later covered by the Temple of Concordia. The Volcanal was large enough for rains of blood to be observed there (Livy 39.46.5, 40.19.2) and for numerous dedications to have found place there.

The earliest of the dedications was a bronze quadriga supposed to have been offered by Romulus (Dion. Hal. 2.54.2). There was also a statue of Horatius Cocles, originally erected in the Comitium, but moved after lightning struck it (A. Gellius 4.5.1–4; [Aur. Vict.,] *De Vir. Ill.* 11.2; Plutarch, *Poplic.* 16.7), as well as a statue of a player killed in the circus that was mounted on a column over his grave (Festus 370L). There grew there a lotus tree and a cypress of great age, the former so big that its roots extended to the Forum Iulium (Pliny, *HN* 16.236). A base dedicated to Vulcan by Augustus in 9 B.C. was found near the church of S. Adriano (*CIL* 6.457 = *ILS* 93). The cult must have existed until the time of Pliny, although the Area Volcani must by then have shrunk through erosion of its boundaries to a small plot immediately around the altar, perhaps in the area to one side of the stair of the Temple of Concordia. The latest public assembly we hear of there was one that Appius Claudius the decemvir called in 450 B.C., the last rain of blood one in 181 B.C. (Livy 40.19.2). The festival of Vulcan was the Volcanalia on 23 August, at which time he was worshiped here, together with Maia (Degrassi 500–501), and offerings of live fish were made on his altar (Festus 276L).

Volcanus, Aedes : a temple in the Campus Martius supposed to have been built by Romulus (Plutarch, *Rom.* 27.5, *Quaest. Rom.* 47) and certainly very old. Lightning struck it in 214 B.C. (Livy 24.10.9) and again in 197 (Livy 32.29.1). Near it *(propter)* Verres had gilded equestrian statues of himself set up, supposed to be offerings of the Sicilian planters (Cicero, *Verr.* 2.2.150). We know virtually nothing about the history of the temple, and there is no record of a restoration. Its anniversary was the Volcanalia, 23 August (Degrassi 500–501). It is located in Campo by Livy (24.10.9) and in Circo Flaminio by the Fasti Vallenses; the latter location is to be preferred as more precise and in keeping with the tradition of a Romulean foundation. Finding a place for it around the Circus Flaminius is a problem, because it antedated the creation of the circus and was thought by Plutarch to have been built possibly so that Romulus could confer with the senate in a secluded place. This suggests that it stood off by itself in some way, not one of a row of temples. Might it possibly be the enigmatic building on the very edge of the Tiber shown on the Marble Plan under Circus Flaminius (*FUR* pl. 56 frag. 614; Rodriguez pl. 24; M. Conticello de'Spagnolis, *Il tempio dei Dioscuri nel Circo Flaminio* [Rome 1984], 51–56)?

Volupia, Sacellum: near Porta Romana (Romanula) in Nova Via (Varro, *Ling.* 5.164); that is, where the Nova Via emerged in the Velabrum (Varro, *Ling.* 6.24). On the authority of Masurius Sabinus, Macrobius (*Sat.* 1.10.7–8) says a likeness of Angerona with bound and sealed mouth embellished the altar of Volupia (cf. Pliny, *HN* 3.65; Solinus 1.6), and the pontifices sacrificed to her on 21 December, known as the Divalia Angeronae or Angeronalia (Degrassi 541–42). Varro (*Ling.* 6.23) says the Angeronalia was celebrated in the Curia Acculeia. It appears that the Sacellum Volupiae and Curia Acculeia were identical, or the sacellum was in the curia, and the proximity of the tomb of Acca Larentia (see Sepulcrum Accae Larentiae) enhances this probability. Volupia appears to be simply another name for Angerona (perhaps another aspect), because hers is the only worship reported here. Because a curia was a place where priests attended to religious obligations (Varro, *Ling.* 5.155), an ancient compital shrine might have kept that designation in some sources. We can locate this shrine with some confidence at the foot of the Palatine at its west corner, just before the conjunction of Nova Via and Clivus Victoriae.

If Angerona had two names and by her gesture enjoining silence or her gagged mouth was believed to exercise a sort of guardianship over the secret name of Rome, then her festival's occurrence at the winter solstice may be thought to have significance. It was an occasion for looking to the future and assuring that the new year began auspiciously. The doubling of names may have been a further gesture in that direction.

For a completely different interpretation of the evidence, one that takes the Velabrum up to the edge of the Forum Romanum, see Coarelli 1983, 227–98, especially 255–61. See also Wissowa, *RK* 241.

Vortumnus, Aedes: a temple in the Vicus Loreti Maioris (see Loretum) on the Aventine in which there was a portrait of M. Fulvius Flaccus dressed as triumphator in the toga picta (Festus 228L). Because Fulvius Flaccus triumphed over the Volsinians in 264 B.C., and Vortumnus was regarded as especially a Volsinian divinity (Propertius 4.2.1–4), it seems likely that Flaccus built the temple as a victory offering following an evocatio during the siege of the city. The day of dedication was 13 August (Degrassi 494–95). Hülsen (HJ 162–63) puts the Armilustrium and Loretum near the middle of the Aventine, but PA prefers a location for the temple toward the northwest, where it would overlook the route of the triumph. It is tempting to see it as a close neighbor to, and rival of, T. Papirius Cursor's Temple of Consus (see Consus, Aedes) of a few years earlier, but the evidence is insufficient.

X
Z

Xenodochium Aniciorum: a medieval hospital mentioned twice in extant literature (Gregorius Magnus, *Registrum Epistularum* 9.8; LPD 2.25 ch. 81 [Leo III, A.D. 795–816]; VZ 2.303). The letter mentions an oratory of S. Lucia that must be S. Lucia de Calcarario or de Apothecis Obscuris (HCh 301, 306), because a monumental inscription of the fifth century after Christ in the Via delle Botteghe Oscure (*CIL* 6.1676) puts a Domus Aniciorum in that vicinity. Presumably the hospital simply took over the insula of the Anicii, and in due course the oratory grew to become an important church.

HJ 549n.118.

Xenodochium Belisarii: a hospital that Belisarius built in the sixth century *in Via Lata et in Via Flaminia* (LPD 1.296 [Vigilius, A.D. 537–555]; VZ 2.248) next to the monastery of S. Iuvenalis. The site is that of S. Maria in Trivio (earlier S. Mariae in Sinodochio) in Via Poli between Via del Tritone and the Fontana di Trevi (HCh 365–66). If the hospital covered the area between the church and the Via Flaminia, it was very large.

HJ 459n.36.

Xenodochium S. Gregorii Iuxta Gradus S. Petri:
a hospital built by Saint Gregory the Great by the steps of the basilica of S. Pietro. It is known from a single passage (Petrus Mallius, *De Basilica Vaticana*, 4) written in the twelfth century and dedicated to Pope Alexander III (1159–1181), and consequently its existence has been questioned, but cf. Gregorius Magnus, *Registrum Epistolarum* 9.63.

LPD 2.195 (Stephanus V, A.D. 885–871); VZ 2.330. Cf. D. M. Cerrati, *De basilicae Vaticanae antiquissima et nova structura* (*Studi e Testi* 26, Rome 1914) 23, 130–31.

Xenodochium Valeriorum: see **Domus, Valerii.**

Xenodochium de Via Nova: a hospital mentioned once in the sixth century (Gregorius Magnus, *Registrum Epistolarum* 1.42.210). It is uncertain which Via Nova is meant, but it is more probably that parallel to Via Appia in Regio XII than that at the foot of the Palatine.

Zater[. . . nses]: the fragmentary reading of an item of the fourth-century edict of Tarracius Bassus (*CIL* 6.31901), presumably designating those living in a street or neighborhood of Rome, but closer identification is impossible.

434

Glossary

Acroterion. A sculptural figure or conventional ornament (usually floral) mounted on the apex or corner of a pediment, enclosure wall, or sarcophagus.

Adventus. The ceremony with which a returning general or governor was welcomed at the city gate.

Aedicula. A small shrine, usually mounted on a base, framed with columns and surmounted by a pediment.

Aedituus. A temple attendant, or sacristan, who probably always lived adjacent to the shrine for which he was responsible.

Africano. A breccia quarried at Teos in Asia Minor (Ionia). It is a smoky black in color, mottled with purplish gray, and profusely veined and splotched with bright red and white. It came into use in Rome about 50 B.C. and was called *marmor Luculleum*.

Amazonomachy. A battle between Amazons and Greeks, usually in two-figure compositions, the Amazon mounted, the Greek nude and on foot, popular as a subject for sculptured friezes and metopes.

Amorino. *See* **Eros.**

Amphora. A large earthenware jar with two handles and an elongated body, used for shipping and storage, especially for wine and foodstuffs. The base usually terminates in an elongated foot intended to be sunk in the earth to hold it upright.

Ancile (pl. **Ancilia**). A shield of archaic form, shaped like a broad figure eight, but only slightly contracting at the waist. The sacred shields of Mars carried by the Salii were of this form.

Angiportus. A narrow lane or alley, essentially public but often a cul-de-sac. It might lead back to a house entrance or even several entrances.

Anio Tufa. A lithoid tufa of even quality and medium density, brick red in color, quarried especially in the neighborhood of the confluence of the Anio and Tiber rivers, but available in deep strata throughout Rome and its vicinity. It comes into use especially after the Second Punic War and is the commonest tufa in use in the time of the empire. It is also called *lapis ruber*.

Antefix. An ornament covering the end of a file of *imbrices* (cover tiles) along the eaves of a building. In the republican period these commonly show heads of divinities or Maenads and satyrs. Under the empire antefixes are likelier to be palmettes. They may be terracotta or marble, rarely bronze.

Anthemion. An architectural ornament in which lilies alternating with palmettes are joined in a chain by looping stems, often reversing S spirals. The designs have great variety, and often palmettes of several different forms are included.

Aplustre. The stern ornament of a ship, especially a warship, usually a re-curved fan of small timbers resembling a half-palmette, sometimes bound at the base with a band secured with a large boss or shield. Aplustria, as well as rostra, were often displayed as trophies.

Aquila. The main standard of a legion, orginally one of four animals, but after the second consulship of Marius in 104 B.C. the only one. It showed an eagle with spread wings at relatively small scale in silver or bronze. It was mounted on a base on a tall pole to make it readily visible.

Araeostyle. Having intercolumniations wider than three lower diameters of the columns, a characteristic of Roman and Etruscan wooden-roofed architecture until the first century B.C..

Arcosolio. A large low niche, usually with bowed ceiling, let into a tomb wall to receive a body or sarcophagus.

Ashlar. Masonry of squared stone in regular courses with fine joints, especially masonry in which the courses are successively staggered, with the vertical joints falling at the midpoints of the blocks above and below them.

Balteus. A relatively broad passage around the cavea of a theater or amphitheater to divide one zone of seating from another and facilitate the movement of crowds, in Greek called *diazoma*.

Batter. A perceptible slope to the outer face of a wall, especially a terrace wall or fortification.

Biga. A two-horse chariot.

Boustrephedon. An inscription in which the lines run alternately from left to right and right to left, like the plowing of oxen.

Bucrania. Ox skulls or heads, often decked with fillets, mounted in a sanctuary. They became a common sculptural motif for metopes and friezes, often combined with garlands.

Bustum. A simple burial plot, for either an individual or a family, surrounded by a wall. The body was burned on a pyre erected here and the ashes collected and buried in an urn within the enclosure, the spot often marked with a small inscription let into the surrounding wall. This was the regular form of burial in the republican period, but gradually died out in the early empire.

Caementum (pl. **Caementa**). The small material, usually broken stone or terracotta, added to the mixture of lime and pozzolana to make Roman concrete. By careful grading of *caementa* of different weight, domes could be constructed with heavy bases and light crowns. *See also* **Opus Caementicium.**

Camillus. A young attendant of a priest at a sacrifice, an acolyte.

Cappellaccio. The poor granular tufa that covers the tops of the hills of Rome. It is dark gray and speckled with occasional black-and-white scoriae. It is soft enough to be dug out with a mattock and an unsatisfactory building stone, but used extensively for terracing and foundations through the fifth century B.C. In such work it usually appears in large rectangular slabs.

Carceres. The stalls behind the starting gates of a circus. They were built on a shallow curve to give all the contestants an equal distance to the *linea alba* (starting line), and all could be opened simultaneously.

Castellum (**Aquae**). A terminal building of an aqueduct from which the water was distributed in several channels that could be opened and closed individually to ensure fair distribution and public utility.

Cavea. The spectator seating of a theater or amphitheater, usually divided by horizontal passageways (*baltei*) into zones, which were assigned to different social classes, and by vertical stairs into wedge-shaped sectors (*cunei*). Individual places were numbered, and theater tickets were inscribed with zone, sector, and seat numbers.

Chryselephantine. Descriptive of statuary in which the flesh was represented by ivory, sometimes tinted, and the drapery of gold or gilded bronze.

Cipollino. Carystian stone from southeastern Euboea of thin layers of varying pale green color, so when cut it resembles onionskin.

Cippus. A stone block or stele used as a marker of any sort, often inscribed on at least one face to indicate its purpose.

Clivus. A Roman street running up an incline. This distinction from a level vicus was strongly felt, and a street name sometimes changed, when, after running level, it began to ascend a slope.

Collegium. An association of individuals with a common interest of any sort, from a priestly college to a burial fraternity, but especially a professional organization.

Comitia Centuriata. The assembly of Roman citizens in their military units, the organization in which they elected their chief magistrates, passed legislation, and held important trials. Such assemblies were always held outside the pomerium, usually in the Campus Martius.

Comitia Tributa. The assembly of Roman citizens in their tribes, the organization in which they elected the lesser magistrates, passed plebiscites, and held minor trials. Such comitia might be held anywhere within a mile of the city, but usually met in the Campus Martius for elections.

Compitum. A crossroads where the vicomagistri offered sacrifice to the Lares Compitales on behalf of the neighborhood. This was a very old tradition, the foundation of the Compitalia being ascribed to Tarquinius Priscus, and it was especially fostered by Augustus, who created the Augustales to attend to this worship. The compital shrines were of modest size, but might be very elegant.

Contio. An assembly of the Romans convened by a magistrate or priest for any purpose other than elections or legislation, often simply a political rally.

Cryptoporticus. A passage, either underground or behind an outer portico, lit by apertures in the shoulder of a vaulted ceiling, by skylights, or by windows to the portico next to it. It was usually a corridor of more than one wing, often a continuous rectangle. Cryptoporticus served especially as refuges from the summer heat and were not infrequently adjuncts of fora. They became popular only about the middle of the first century B.C. and do not go beyond the end of the second century after Christ.

Cuniculus. A small tunnel of any sort, but especially a drain. An extensive system of such cuniculi of unusual size under the main square of the Forum Romanum seems to have been constructed about the time of Sulla and to have drained into the Cloaca. It is provided with manholes in a regular pattern.

Damnatio Memoriae. Originally a consequence of condemnation on the crime of *maiestas*, but later a decree by which the senate took revenge on its enemies even after death and rid Rome of embarrassing memories. The name of the offender was expunged from all public records and documents and erased from his buildings and inscriptions, and statues and pictures of him were pulled down and destroyed. Nero and Domitian offer signal examples of this treatment.

Decastyle. Having ten columns on the principal façade. Hadrian's Temple of Venus et Roma is the only decastyle temple in Rome.

Decennalia. Celebration of the tenth anniversary of the rule of a princeps.

Denarius. A Roman silver coin introduced in the late third century B.C., first equivalent in value to ten bronze asses and afterward sixteen, equivalent to the Attic drachma. In the late republic it was much used by moneyers as a vehicle for political propaganda, and this continued under the principate.

Diaeta. A small room for use in the daytime for study or lounging, more or less isolated and of relatively open architecture; a summerhouse.

Diastyle. Having columns spaced three lower diameters apart.

Diploma (pl. **Diplomata**). A document of a pair of bronze tablets showing that a soldier had been honorably discharged after service and was entitled to certain privileges. This was prominently posted in a sanctuary, at first usually within the Area Capitolina in Rome, later near the Temple of Divus Augustus, and its place specified. Such *diplomata militaria* were first given in the time of Claudius to the auxiliaries and marines and, beginning under Vespasian, to the praetorians and urban cohorts. The latest known is dated A.D. 306.

Dolium. A very large storage jar, often as tall as a man, of thick walls and globular shape, usually sunk up to its neck or shoulder in the ground. Dolia seem to have been used for many purposes, even occasionally as ornaments.

Equirria. Horse races in honor of Mars held in the Campus Martius on 27 February and 14 March. Romulus is supposed to have established them.

Eros (pl. **Erotes**). A small bird-winged divinity, usually shown as a child two or three years old, one of a great number of such spirits attendant on Venus and shown with various of her attributes (torch, scepter, girdle) or engaged in games, trades, or ceremonies; also called an *amorino* or *putto*.

Euripus. An artificial channel for water, usually bordered with a walk and often provided with bridges, fountains, and sculptures along its length. A euripus is often a feature of a garden and may be used for breeding fish.

Exauguration. The process of deconsecrating a shrine by promising the incumbent divinity an equal or better shrine elsewhere. Only an augur could perform this.

Exedra. A room or alcove open across the whole of one side to a lobby or court.

Favisa (**Favissa**). An underground storeroom or pit in a sacred precinct in which was deposited material that had been dedicated but was damaged or superfluous. Those connected with the Temple of Iuppiter Optimus Maximus Capitolinus could not be altered.

Ferculum. A handbarrow carried by two or four men on which were displayed, for public admiration, the spoils of a successful campaign, allegorical images of rivers and geographical landmarks, and similar appurtenances of triumphs and religious processions.

Fetial. A priest of a Roman college charged with performing the ceremonies of demanding satisfaction before formal declaration of war and concluding and sanctifying the treaty of peace at a war's conclusion. The rituals were elaborate and had to be performed with great care and punctiliousness. The college was believed to have been founded by Numa Pompilius.

Fidenae Tufa. A poor volcanic tufa characterized by its bright yellow color and very large black scoriae, quarried in the vicinity of Fidenae, where the Cremera joins the Tiber. It is little used in Rome because of its quality, and what blocks of it do appear are thought to have been plundered from Fidenae after its sack in 426 B.C.

Fornix. An arch or, more properly, a passageway through an arch.

Gabine Stone. *See* **Sperone.**

Giallo Antico. A fine breccia quarried at Chemtou in modern Tunisia. It contains large pebbles of deep yellow color in a matrix of dark red, or white pebbles in a matrix of deep yellow. It first appeared in Rome in the time of Sulla and was called *marmor Numidicum.*

Grotta Oscura Tufa. A fine-grained volcanic tufa of yellowish gray color quarried along the Tiber in the vicinity of Veii and much used in construction at Veii. Its use in Rome follows the sack of Veii at the beginning of the fourth century B.C., and it then continues to be the favorite stone for construction for more than a century, perhaps because it was easy to quarry and could be shipped to Rome on barges. It is the characteristic stone of the Servian Walls.

Hexastyle. Having six columns on the principal façade.

Horreum. A storehouse, especially a granary.

Horti. A house in town with the characteristics of a house designed for pleasure in the country, especially gardens, parterres, plantations of trees, fountains, and ornamental waters.

Hypaethral. Of a temple having no roof, open to the heavens.

Hypocaust. A system in which heat is circulated in a low chamber under the floor of a room, the floor being raised on a grid of pillars. The firebox is usually in a pit adjacent to the rooms to be so heated, and the walls are usually hollow to permit further circulation of the heat.

Imago Clipeata. A fairly common pictorial convention of the Romans in which a head or bust is framed in a deep circular border resembling a shield. The head may or may not be a portrait, and the border is usually richly ornamented.

Insula. A large building in which there were living units for a number of families. Also one of these units. Usually there were multiple storeys, the ground floor being taken up with shops and workshops of one or two rooms, often with living quarters in mezzanine balconies, while the floors above were divided into more spacious apartments of a half-dozen rooms, the same plan being repeated from floor to floor. Usually there was also a central courtyard, but a city block might be made up of a number of insulae.

Laconicum. A dry sweat bath, almost always a round room, either a separate facility or, in a bath complex, an addition to the usual sequence of frigidarium, tepidarium, and caldarium. In such complexes it is accessible from the tepidarium, not the caldarium.

Lacus. A public watering place, either a spring or a watering trough for animals.

Lectisternium. A religious celebration, usually extraordinary and often expiatory, in which dining couches were elaborately prepared for the gods and their images or symbols publicly displayed on these, while a sumptuous feast was served in their honor. This might last for several days.

Libertina. A freedwoman, often used as synonymous for a prostitute of the better sort.

Lituus. The curved staff of the augur, his badge of office and used in laying out his templum when taking augury. It was inherited from the Etruscans and seems to have somewhat changed shape over time, but always resembled a crosier.

Loculus. A place for the deposit of valuables, especially a small chamber in the base of a temple, accessible from the exterior and closed by a metal door. Individuals could rent space. The Temple of Castor on the Forum Romanum was ringed with loculi. Also a niche in a tomb for the deposit of a cinerary urn.

Loricate. Wearing a cuirass, used to describe a statue in military dress.

Ludus. A training school, especially a *ludus gladiatorius*, an establishment in which gladiators were kept in military discipline under a *lanista* (master) and gave exhibitions. Domitian established four such *ludi* in the vicinity of the Colosseum.

Lunate. Used of a pediment with a bowed, rather than triangular, shape.

Lustrum. Properly the sacrifice that a censor performed at the close of the census, a purification of the Roman people as a whole by lustration. Because this occurred only once every five years under the republic, it came to be synonymous with the period between lustrations.

Macellum. A food market, more particularly a building in which a central courtyard was surrounded by a portico in which space or booths could be rented and mechandise displayed. Often there are other shops surrounding this on the exterior. In the center of the courtyard there was regularly a tholus piped with water for fishmongers, and butchers might have a place with marble counters assigned to them. These buildings were often architecturally handsome and lavishly decorated, public benefactions. The word is supposed to be of Punic origin.

Maenianum. A balcony, especially one above the shops around a forum from which spectators might watch the ceremonies, gladiatorial shows, and games offered there. These were not infrequently cantilevered.

Meta. A tall, tapering form, a curvilinear cone, used in groups of three for the turning posts at the ends of the spina of a circus. Also anything of this general shape, such as the Meta Sudans (q.v.), or the domed shape in which ivy was trained in ancient gardens.

Monopteros (adj. **Monopteral**). A ring of columns supporting a roof or dome, making a circular pavilion without walls.

Monteverde Tufa. A volcanic tufa quarried at the southern end of the Janiculan ridge on the right bank of the Tiber. It is stone of medium grain in use as early as the middle of the fourth century B.C. and often found in conjunction with Grotta Oscura tufa. But because it had to be hauled upstream from the quarries, it was more sparingly used and especially only for facing. It was most popular in 125–75 B.C. and went out of use about the middle of the first century B.C., being replaced by Anio tufa. It is olive brown in color, with a thick sprinkling of small black-and-brown scoriae.

Natatio. An open-air swimming pool.

Naumachia. An artificial body of water intended especially for the mounting of mock naval engagements as a public amusement. We know little about them, but Augustus offered one in which Greeks were matched against Persians, presumably a reenactment of the Battle of Salamis. The earliest one we hear of was created by Julius Caesar in 46 B.C., the latest one that of Philippus Arabs in A.D. 247, which may have been a restoration of that of Augustus.

Niobids. The children of Niobe falling mortally wounded by the arrows of Apollo and Diana, a popular subject in Greek and Roman art.

Nymphaeum. An artificial grotto or architectural construciton of any sort designed to be the setting for a display of water in motion. Nymphaea took many forms and were regularly embellished with statuary, both fountain figures and ornamental, columns of colored marble, and mosaic. A favorite form for public nymphaea was the scaenae frons (see Scaena) in several storeys. The earliest private ones seem to have been of the first century B.C., and they became a regular feature of horti and pleasure villas.

Octastyle. Having eight columns on the principal façade.

Oculus. A central opening in the crown of a dome. That of the Pantheon is 9 m in diameter.

Omphalos. A copy of the omphalos stone of Delphi. A half-egg covered with a network of fillets, thought of as either the tomb or the egg of the Pytho and the navel of the world. This was commonly used for boundary stones and markers, as well as a cult object.

Opus Caementicium. Roman concrete, a mixture of slaked lime and pozzolana, ground fine, with an aggregate of broken stone or terracotta in small chunks, poured between faces of carefully constructed masonry or into wooden forms, the latter being used for foundations and vaults. Its earliest securely dated use is in the Temple of Castor of 117 B.C.

Opus Incertum. Facing of stone broken into irregular fist-sized chunks with one relatively flat face and fitted with narrow joints, but without any attempt at coursing. It is regularly quoined with masonry of small rectangular blocks. This is used to face Roman concrete walls from the last quarter of the second century B.C. until the time of Augustus, overlapping with *opus quasi-reticulatum* and *opus reticulatum.* The stone is regularly either tufa or limestone, depending on the locale and the nature of the construction.

Opus Mixtum Vittatum. Facing of Roman concrete walls in opus reticulatum quoined with brick or alternate courses of brick and small rectangular stone blocks, in which bands of brick running through the wall at regular intervals act as leveling courses and divide the reticulate into panels. This style was introduced in the late republic but is especially characteristic of the period from the Flavians to Antoninus Pius.

Opus Quadratum. Masonry of squared blocks of the same height, but not necessarily the same length, laid in regular courses. The Romans often laid alternate courses of all headers and all stretchers, a characteristic of the Servian Walls, but, because such masonry was built from the earliest period until the latest, there is enormous variety.

Opus Quasi-Reticulatum. Facing of Roman concrete walls in which the stones are only approximately pyramidal in shape, although they are set diagonally and approach reticulate in appearance. The beds of mortar are thicker than in reticulate, and quoining is in larger blocks, often tailed into the body of the wall. A late example of this can be seen in the remains of the Theater of Pompey.

Opus Reticulatum. Facing of Roman concrete in small blocks of tufa (rarely limestone) sawn to the form of truncated pyramids, often very precisely shaped, laid in diagonal lines in thin beds of mortar to make a network pattern. This is quoined at first with masonry in small rectangular blocks of stone (Julio-Claudian), later brick or a mixture of brick and small blocks. This does not seem to begin before the time of Julius Caesar, but then continues with some modification well into the Antonine period. It

is replaced by facing in brick, which first appears in the Flavian period.

Opus Sectile. The technique of cutting plates of colored stone into figures and geometric shapes and fitting these together to make richly patterned pavements and occasionally pictures. The stones especially favored were the harder ones, porphyry, serpentine, and the granites. Such work was rare under the Julio-Claudians but became increasingly popular beginning with Domitian.

Opus Signinum. *See* **Signinum.**

Orant. A figure in an attitude of prayer; for the Romans this was with face upturned toward heaven and hands outstretched palm-upward to show their purity.

Palaestra. For the Romans an exercise court, especially one attached to a bath complex in which an open area was bordered on one or more sides by a portico. Here many forms of exercise could find place, from simple ball games to violent contact sports. It was customary for the Romans to take some form of exercise before bathing.

Parodos. The lateral entrance to the orchestra of a theater connecting this directly to the exterior.

Patera. A shallow libation bowl, often richly embossed and chased, often with a central boss to facilitate grasping it with one hand (umbilical patera). It was especially the badge of the pontifices of Rome. It was a common decorative motif in religious contexts.

Pavonazzetto. A breccia from Phrygia in Asia Minor with large white pebbles or splotches in a matrix of rosy violet shading to dark purple. It first appeared in Rome about the middle of the first century B.C. and was much used in Augustan buildings. The quarries came at least in part under the control of Agrippa, who exploited them.

Peltate. Of the shape of the shield carried by an Amazon, *pelta*, a half-circle with the lower edge cut in two half-circles of half the diameter of the whole. This was much used in opus sectile and mosaic floors, flower beds, and the like.

Pentelic. Marble from Mount Pentelicus near Athens, a fine-grained white marble with a golden blush of varying intensity produced by deposits of iron. It was much admired in Rome and imported in quantity, the round temple by the Tiber being built of it, as were probably all marble temples until the opening of the quarries at Luna in the middle of the first century B.C..

Peperino. A very hard volcanic tufa of dark gray color peppered with small specks of black and white, the only tufa in the neighborhood of Rome that is suitable for carving and inscription. It was also prized for its resistance to fire. Its quarries were near modern Marino, and it was known as *lapis Albanus* in antiquity.

Peribolus. An enclosure, especially the ring of buildings around a temple precinct or the margin of one of the imperial bath complexes.

Peripteral. Having columns on all four façades.

Peripteral Sine Postico. Having columns on the principal façade and down either flank, but closed across the back with a solid wall, a favorite scheme for Roman temples.

Piscina. A tank for water, including everything from a small reservoir to a swimming pool.

Piscina Limaria. A tank near the end of an aqueduct that acted as a settling basin and, by interrupting the flow momentarily, drew off impurities carried in the water.

Pluteus. A low wall, usually about waist-high.

Porta Santa. A breccia quarried on the island of Chios in which the pebbles range from cream through yellow and vermilion and the matrix is salmon pink veined with gray. Its first securely dated uses are Augustan. It seems to have been prized for its hardness as well as its color and was much used in pavements, thresholds, baseboards, and the like.

Posterula. A postern gate in a fortification.

Pozzolana. A volcanic sand (pit sand) ranging from grayish yellow to dark red and black in color, which when mixed with slaked lime makes mortar of remarkable hydraulic property. It is the secret of the excellence of Roman concrete. It was first discovered at Puteoli on the Bay of Naples and therefore called *pulvis Puteolanus*; this was for a time imported to Rome. The superior Roman red variety was then discovered in the first century B.C. Vitruvius has a chapter (2.4) on the different types of pozzolana and their suitabilities.

Praecinctio. Vitruvius's term for the broad *balteus* (gangway) in a theater or amphitheater that separated one zone of seating from another.

Praefectus Praetorio. The commander of the praetorian guard, the personal bodyguard of the princeps, an office at first only military but, beginning with Sejanus under Tiberius, of increasingly extended power, so the praefectus praetorio became second only to the princeps. Beginning with Septimius Severus, the praefectus praetorio supervised all the departments of the state, including finances and law, and had his own court.

Praefectus Urbi. The chief magistrate of the municipal administration of Rome, an office revived and redefined by Augustus after it had fallen into insignificance under the republic. The new praefectus urbi saw to the peace and protection of the city, governed the police force, and oversaw provisioning and business activities. He had his own court, and its powers were gradually extended until they absorbed the functions of that of the praetor urbanus. At first he was appointed by the princeps for a period of years, sometimes for life, but after the middle of the third century after Christ (under Valerian) he seems to have been appointed annually and seldom was reappointed.

Proconnesian Marble. A large-grained white marble or a fine-grained white veined with black marble quarried on the island of Proconnesus in the western part of the Sea of Marmora. It was well-known and exported to the Aegean from an early period. It was known to Vitruvius but does not seem to have been imported to Rome before the beginning of the traffic in sarcophagi in the second century after Christ. Thereafter it became increasingly common.

Procurator. Anyone acting as steward for another in the management of property or business, especially an agent of the administration or of the princeps. Such officers often wielded considerable power.

Profectio. The ceremony of dispatching a governor or general on a mission abroad. He was escorted to the city gate by which he would depart by a company of officials, family, and friends, and vows were solemnly undertaken for his safe and successful return.

Pronaos. The porch of a temple preceding the cella, sometimes with lateral walls and columns in front that separated it from the pteron, but in Roman temples commonly open, simply a columnar porch, usually relatively deep and sometimes even as deep as the cella itself.

Propylaeum. The gateway to a sacred precinct given more or less elaborate architectural definition by columns and doors. It usually projects from the precinct wall on the exterior and may project on the interior as well.

Prostyle. Of a temple having columns only on the principal façade.

Pteron. A wing of the colonnade around a temple, but sometimes used for the whole colonnade.

Pulvinar. A box for the accommodation of the images or symbols of the gods in a theater, amphitheater, or temple precinct. Here dining couches or thrones were set out and sumptuously cushioned and draped and the images ceremonially ensconced for games, *lectisternia*, and ceremonies in their honor.

Pulvinus. A bolster, especially the carved roll at the end of an altar table or the volute member of an Ionic capital.

Pycnostyle. Having intercolumniations of one and one-half lower diameters of the columns, a relatively tight spacing that emphasizes verticality.

Quadriga. A four-horse chariot.

Quinaria. The Roman measure for the size of an aqueduct, being the size of a pipe with a diameter of one and one-quarter (five-fourths) digits, the digit being one-sixteenth of a foot. Frontinus (*De aq.* 1.25) says this was introduced by either Agrippa or Vitruvius and was a measure of capacity, not volume.

Reticulate. *See* **Opus Reticulatum.**

Roman Concrete. *See* **Opus Caementicium.**

Rustication. The deliberate failure to finish the exposed faces of blocks and columns, especially in *opus quadratum*, so that they presented a quarry-hewn massiveness, an aesthetic particularly admired in the time of Claudius. Also the finish of walls with coarse bits of stone, mosaic, shells, and so forth to give the effect of grottoes.

Sacellum. A small shrine, usually independent and unroofed.

Sacrarium. A place for the deposit of sacred implements or material.

Salii. A very old Roman priesthood in the service of Mars and in charge of the *ancilia* kept in the *sacrarium Martis* in the Regia. There were two colleges of Salii, the Salii Palatina and the Salii Collini, each of which had twelve members.

Scaena. The stage building of a theater, usually essentially an independent structure consisting of a raised stage with a wing to either side and a wooden roof pitched back to throw the actors' voices toward the audience. The back wall was usually an elaborate confection of columns and statuary in profusion in two or three storeys that included three entrances, equally spaced, approached by stairs of a few steps. This was called the scaenae frons. Behind it was usually a shallow undifferentiated space running the whole width of the stage that served as a dressing room.

Scaenae Frons. *See* **Scaena.**

Schola. (*a*) An architectural form consisting of a semicircular, or nearly semicircular, bench where small groups could sit and converse. It was a common feature in sanctuaries, and it was a common form for tombs in the vicinity of city gates. (*b*) The headquarters of a *collegium* of any sort, but especially a professional organization. This could take many different forms but usually included provisions for meals that the collegium took in common and a shrine for the patron divinity or divinities.

Scyphos. A deep two-handled cup. The handles may take many forms but are attached to the rim, and the cup may or may not be given a foot.

Segmental. Descriptive of an arch or vault that is less than a full half-circle in development.

Selce. The modern name (derived from the Latin *silex*) for the lava quarried along the Via Appia near Rome to make the polygonal blocks that are the characteristic pavement of the streets of ancient Rome. It is a very heavy stone and useful as *caementa* in foundations, abundant, and sometimes used even for reticulate blocks.

Serpentine. *Lapis Lacedaemonicus*, sometimes called "green porphyry," a very hard stone, dark green, profusely flecked with lighter green crystals, quarried near Sparta. It became popular in Rome under the Flavians, especially for use in *opus* *sectile* pavements, and from then on was used regularly.

Sgraffito. Decoration produced by scratching with a point or by cutting away a surface to reveal a different colored surface beneath.

Signinum (Opus Signinum). A mixture of slaked lime with terracotta of different qualities ground to different consistencies, depending on the use for which it is intended. Very coarse signinum with an aggregate of ground roof tile and storage jars was used to make pavements; finer signinum was used as waterproofing in tanks and cisterns; and still finer signinum with an aggregate of powdered terra-cotta was used to face walls, especially in their lower parts.

Sleeper Wall. A relatively light wall, one of a series built at intervals from one another to support a superstructure or pavement.

Specus. The channel of an aqueduct both in a tunnel underground and in masonry supported on arches.

Spelaeum. In Mithraic worship the simulation of the cave in which Mithras slew the mystic bull, the symbol of life through death, and the place where his worshipers met at his rites and sacred banquets. It was usually tunnel-like, with benches for the diners along the sides and a representation of the slaying of the bull at one end. The amount of rustication varied, but it was always dimly lit and mysterious.

Sperone (Lapis Gabinus). A dark gray lithoid tufa resembling peperino, but slightly coarser and containing more scoriae, quarried in the neighborhood of Gabii. It could not be carved but was believed to be fire-resistant. Its earliest use in Rome was decorative, as the floor of the *specus* on bridges of the Aqua Marcia (144 B.C.), and it went out of use in the time of Nero.

Sphendone. The rounded end of a circus.

Spina. The divider down the middle of a circus around which the chariots raced, finished with *metae* at either end and usually embellished with statuary and dedications.

Stagnum. An artificial water of some size, but probably always chiefly ornamental and not very deep.

Suburbium. The immediate neighborhood of Rome, outside the pomerium but within the *ager Romanus*. It is hard to set limits for this; it would have included *pagi*, but not separate towns such as Antemnae.

Suovetaurilia. A sacrifice of a boar, a ram, and a bull, used especially in rites of lustration, at which time the victims were ritually caparisoned and driven around the object of the lustration before being sacrificed.

Suspensura. The support of pillars or columns on which the floor of a room heated by a hypocaust was raised. The support elements were regularly built of brick or of molded terracotta.

Sylloge. A collection of similar material, especially in a book.

Syzygium (Syzygy). An architectural form consisting of two columns carrying an epistyle or entablature, a common feature in depictions of rustic sanctuaries. Trophies and dedications might be attached to the columns and bronze vessels mounted on the cornice.

Taberna. A shop or office, usually a single room, often one of a series, with a large door, often the whole width, opening on a street or courtyard, not infrequently with a transom window over the door for light and ventilation when the door was shut. When a shop, the front part served as workshop and display area, and the back part for living quarters and storage. There might also be a mezzanine balcony (*pergula*) over the back part to provide more space.

Tali. Knucklebone dice, used in sets of four.

Temenos. A sacred precinct, with or without a temple building.

Tetrastyle. Having four columns on the principal façade.

Thiasos. A company of minor divinities and spirits in attendance on the epiphany of a major god. In the thiasos of Bacchus we find Pan and Eros, as well as Silenus, Maenads, and satyrs. In the marine thiasos of Venus we find erotes and nymphs riding on Tritons and hippocamps.

Tholus. A circular building of modest size, usually sacred and columnar, but not necessarily so.

Thymiaterion. An incense burner, often an elaborate affair like a candelabrum.

Togate. Describing a statue dressed in the toga, indicative of the subject's civilian status.

Travertine. A secondary limestone, formed when the streams from the Apennines hit the western coastal plain of Italy with its long volcanic fault and the lime in the water precipitates out, forming strata of new stone. This is coarse or fine depending on local conditions. The best is that formed around the abundant sulfur springs near Tivoli, where the water maintains a constant temperature throughout the year (*lapis Tiburtinus*). It is a hard white stone with occasional fine fissures, tinged with gold from deposits of iron. It is the best stone found near Rome for strength and texture and is used for the façades of the Theater of Marcellus and Colosseum. It appears in Rome early in the second century B.C., used only sparingly. Its first extensive use appears to have been in the Metellan Temple of Castor (117 B.C.).

Triskelion. A figure of three elements, especially legs, bent and joined at the center of a circle to make a wheel, the symbol of the island of Sicily.

Tufa. In Rome volcanic ash laid down in strata and subjected to pressure, usually under water, to produce stone of varying strength and weight. The color covers almost the whole spectrum, except for cream and white. Lithoid tufas are often treated as completely different from granular ones, such as cappellaccio. The tufas from the neighborhood of Rome were produced by eruptions of the Alban Hills and eruptions of the crater of Lago di Bracciano (Sabatini tufas). These are not to be confused with the limestone tufas of England and Greece (*poros*). Some authors' use of the word *tuff* to identify Roman tufa has further confused understanding.

Tympanum. The field, or back wall, of a pediment, either triangular or lunate, that may be filled with pedimental sculpture.

Venatio. A show of wild and exotic animals combined with a hunt of these put on usually in an amphitheater as part of public games. The hunters were usually both professional and amateur, and the privilege of participating was often eagerly sought. In games lasting three days, the hunt usually occupied the morning of the second day.

Vexillum. A military banner, a square of cloth suspended from a crossbar atop a pole. Various colors conveyed different signals, and each cohort within a legion had its own vexillum with a colored device woven into the cloth.

Via. A broad public road, especially one connecting one town with another, those radiating from Rome at first being named for the first town of importance along their course, later for their builder. Within Rome in the republican period only two streets carried this designation, the Sacra Via from the sacellum of Strenia on the Carinae to the top of the arx and the Nova Via from Porta Mugonia at the base of the Clivus Palatinus to the Velabrum, both, that is, of unusually long and complicated courses.

Vicennalia. Celebration of the twentieth anniversary of the rule of a princeps.

Vicus. (*a*) A street of ordinary width with a relatively flat course. (*b*) A neighborhood named for the most proment vicus within its limits. In the reform of Augustus, Rome was divided into vici for administrative purposes, each vicus having four vicomagistri, evidently responsible to the curatores of its regio. Their duties and privileges are not well understood.

Vomitorium. An exterior entrance for the public to a theater or amphitheater, usually numbered over the arch and the proper number recorded as the first item on the ticket of the spectator to facilitate his finding his seat.

Xenodochium. A hospital for the treatment of the ill and infirm, the earliest in Rome being no older than the late fifth century after Christ.

Xoanon. An archaic image of a divinity rudely carved in wood.

Xystus. A garden, usually adjoining a portico or enclosed by a peristyle, laid out with walks and plantations of trees to make a place to stroll and converse.

Chronological List of
Dated Monuments

753–717 B.C.	Reign of Romulus: Asylum; Circus Maximus established with games in honor of Consus; Altar of Consus; Temple of Iuppiter Feretrius; Temple of Iuppiter Stator; Lacus Curtius; Curiae Veteres; Temple of Vulcan. Reign of Titus Tatius: house on Capitoline on the site of the Temple of Iuno Moneta; altars to Ops, Flora, Vediovis and Saturn, Sol, Luna, Vulcan and Summanus, Larunda, Terminus, Quirinus, Vortumnus, Lares, Diana and Lucina.
715–672	Reign of Numa Pompilius: Auguraculum on Capitoline; house on Quirinal; Temple of Vesta; Aedicula Camenarum; Curia Saliorum (Palatinorum); Regia; Altar of Iuppiter Elicius; sacrarium Fidei (in Capitolio); sacrarium Termini; Ianus Geminus; sacraria Argeorum (?); Ara Martis (in Campo Martio).
672–640	Reign of Tullus Hostilius: Curia Hostilia; Curia Saliorum Collinorum; fanum of Pavor et Pallor.
640–616	Reign of Ancus Marcius: house at Summa Sacra Via; Pons Sublicius; Temple of Fors Fortuna (?); Temple of Iuppiter Feretrius enlarged; Carcer.
616–578	Reign of Tarquinius Priscus: house at Porta Mugonia; Temple of Iuppiter Optimus Maximus vowed; Circus Maximus laid out and places assigned to senators and equites where they might build seats (*fori*); forum surrounded with porticoes and tabernae; statue and puteal of Attus Navius in Comitium; city fortified; Cloaca dredged and regularized; Area Capitolina terraced and leveled for Temple of Iuppiter Optimus Maximus.
578–534	Reign of Servius Tullius: extends pomerium and fortifies the new city; Temple of Diana on the Aventine; temples of Mater Matuta and Fortuna (in Foro Boario); Temple of Fors Fortuna; shrines of Fortuna *Apotropaios*, Fortuna Brevis, Fortuna *Euelpis*, Fortuna Obsequens, Fortuna Primigenia (in Capitolio), Fortuna Privata, Fortuna Respiciens, Fortuna Virgo, Fortuna Virilis, Fortuna Viscata (?); Temple of Luna.
534–510	Reign of Tarquinius Superbus: Temple of Iuppiter Optimus Maximus constructed; seats constructed in Circus Maximus; work on the Cloaca continued.
511–493	Temple of Saturn dedicated.
509	Temple of Dea Carna vowed (and built some years later).
509–508	Temple of Iuppiter Optimus Maximus dedicated.
499	Temple of Castor vowed.
499–496	Temple of Ceres, Liber, and Libera vowed.

495	Temple of Mercury dedicated.
493	Temple of Ceres, Liber, and Libera dedicated.
485	House of Sp. Cassius razed (site of Temple of Tellus).
484	Temple of Castor dedicated.
before 476	Temple of Spes Vetus.
466	Temple of Semo Sancus dedicated.
456	Land on the Aventine given to the Plebs.
439	Columna Minucia.
438	Creation of the Aequimaelium.
435	Creation of the Villa Publica.
433–432	Temple of Apollo (Medicus) vowed.
431–430	Temple of Apollo (Medicus) dedicated.
396	Temple of Iuno Regina (on the Aventine) vowed.
395	Temple of Mater Matuta restored.
392	Temple of Iuno Regina (on the Aventine) dedicated.
after 391	Altar erected to Aius Locutius.
ca. 390	Sack of Rome by the Gauls and city burned, except for the Arx Capitolina.
388	Area Capitolina enlarged; Temple of Mars dedicated.
384	House of M. Manlius Capitolinus on the arx razed, and patricians forbidden in perpetuity to live on the Capitoline.
ca. 377–353	Servian Walls constructed.
375	Temple of Concordia vowed, but then not built.
353	Temple of Apollo (Medicus) restored.
345	Temple of Iuno Moneta vowed.
344	Temple of Iuno Moneta dedicated.
338	Columna Maenia; suggestus in Forum decorated with the rostra of Latin ships.
334	Via Latina extended as far as Cales.
329	First carceres constructed in the Circus Maximus.
325	Temple of Quirinus vowed.
after 312	Aqua Appia constructed; Via Appia constructed as far as Capua.
311	Temple of Salus vowed.
310	Gilded shields distributed to decorate the tabernae of the Forum for the celebration of a triumph.
306	Equus Tremuli.
305	Colossal statue of Hercules dedicated in Area Capitolina.
304	Aedicula Concordiae dedicated on Graecostasis.
302	Temple of Salus dedicated.

296   Quadriga of Jupiter on Temple of Iuppiter Optimus Maximus replaced; group of she-wolf and twins installed at Ficus Ruminalis; paved walk added along Clivus Martis; shrine of Pudicitia Plebeia dedicated; Temple of Bellona vowed.

295   Temple of Iuppiter Victor vowed and begun; Temple of Venus Obsequens begun.

294   Temple of Iuppiter Stator constructed; Temple of Victoria on the Palatine dedicated.

293   Colossus of Jupiter dedicated in Area Capitolina; Temple of Fors Fortuna; Temple of Quirinus dedicated.

291   Temple of Aesculapius established on Tiber island; Via Appia extended to Venusia.

290   House bestowed on M. Curius Dentatus at public expense.

287   Comitia centuriata held in Aesculetum.

281   Via Appia extended to Tarentum.

272   Contract for aqueduct of Anio Vetus let; Temple of Consus vowed or built on the Aventine.

268   Temple of Tellus vowed.

267   Temple of Pales.

ca. 264   Temple of Vortumnus on the Aventine.

264   Spoils dedicated in Area Sacra di Sant'Omobono by M. Fulvius Flaccus; Tabula Valeria added to Curia; Via Appia extended to Brundisium.

264–241   First Punic War: Temple of Spes in Forum Holitorium.

ca. 260   Columna Rostrata of C. Duilius (1) and (2); Templum of Ianus in Forum Holitorium.

259   Temple of Tempestates vowed.

ca. 255   Columna Rostrata of M. Aemilius Paullus.

after 249   Temple of Fides (in Capitolio).

241   Temple of Vesta burned; statue of quadrifrontal Janus brought to Rome from Falerii; Temple of Flora.

after 241   Temple of Iuturna in Campus Martius.

241–238   Clivus Publicius constructed and paved.

ca. 238   Temple of Libertas on the Aventine.

234   Temple of Honos (ad Portam Capenam) (traditional date).

231   Delubrum Fontis dedicated.

229   Taberna of Archagathus established at Compitum Acili.

221–220   Circus Flaminius created; Via Flaminia begun.

218–202   Second Punic War.

218   Temple of Concordia (in arce) vowed.

217   Temple of Concordia (in arce) begun; temples of Mens and Venus Erucina vowed; Servian Walls improved and strengthened.

216   Temple of Concordia (in arce) dedicated.

215   Temples of Mens and Venus Erucina (in Capitolio) dedicated.

214   Flood of water in Vicus Insteius; Atrium Publicum on Capitoline struck by lightning.

213   Fire destroys area from Porta Trigemina to Porta Carmentalis, including temples of Mater Matuta and Fortuna, and Spes outside Porta Carmentalis, which are immediately restored.

212   Servian Walls repaired.

210   Fire destroys the northeast side of the Forum from the Lautumiae to the Atrium Regium (Regia) and including the Forum Piscarium, but Curia and Comitium are spared and the Temple of Vesta saved.

209   Contract for rebuilding the macellum let (Forum Piscarium); Tabernae Septem rebuilt as Tabernae Quinque; statue of Hercules by Lysippus dedicated on the Capitoline.

208–205   Temple of Honos ad Portam Capenam rebuilt as Temple of Honos et Virtus.

207   Temple of Iuventas vowed.

204   Temple of Iuventas begun; Temple of Fortuna Primigenia (Fortunae Tres) vowed; black stone brought from Pessinus and contract for the Temple of Magna Mater let.

203   Clivus Publicius burned.

200   Temple of Vediovis vowed.

198   Temple of Vediovis (2) vowed.

197   Temple of Iuno Sospita vowed.

196   Temple of Faunus vowed; arches of Stertinius (Fornices Stertinii) erected in Forum Boarium and Circus Maximus.

194   Temple of Faunus dedicated; Temple of Vediovis (in insula) dedicated; Temple of Iuno Sospita dedicated; Temple of Fortuna Primigenia (Fortunae Tres) dedicated; atrium publicum rebuilt and enlarged; Villa Publica rebuilt.

193   Aedicula of Victoria Virgo dedicated; Tabernae Argentariae Novae constructed; Emporium established and portico constructed along it; Porticus Aemilia constructed from Porta Fontinalis to Ara Martis in Campus Martius; flood destroys two bridges.

192   Temple of Vediovis (in Capitolio) dedicated; Porticus inter Lignarios constructed.

191   Temple of Pietas vowed; Temple of Iuventas dedicated; Temple of Magna Mater dedicated.

190   Temple of Lares Permarini vowed; Arch of Cornelius Scipio along Clivus Capitolinus erected.

189   Temple of Muses vowed; statue of Hercules dedicated in Temple of Hercules Custos; statue of Pollentia erected in Circus Maximus; Clivus Martis cobbled.

187   Temple of Hercules Musarum built and Aedicula Camenarum removed to it by M. Fulvius Nobilior; Temple of Diana and Temple of Iuno Regina vowed by M. Aemilius Lepidus (later built in Circus Flaminius).

186   Temple of Ops struck by lightning and subsequently rebuilt.

184   Temple of Venus Erucina (extra Portam Collinam) vowed; Basilica Porcia constructed.

181   Temple of Pietas in Foro Holitorio dedicated; Temple of Venus Erucina at Porta Collina dedicated; tomb of Numa Pompilius discovered sub Ianiculo with empty sarcophagus and chest containing his writings.

180   Temple of Fortuna Equestris vowed.

179   Temples of Iuno Regina and Diana in Circo Flaminio dedicated; Temple of Lares Permarini dedicated; Area Capitolina cleared of dedications and walls and columns of the Temple of Iuppiter Optimus Maximus restuccoed; contract for Basilica Fulvia et Aemilia let; Forum Piscarium rebuilt as Macellum and enlarged; porticoes built post navalia, extra Portam Trigeminam, and post Spei; piers of Pons Aemilius built of stone with superstructure of wood.

174   Emporium remodeled and porticoes restored; Clivus Capitolinus paved and portico built from Temple of Saturn to Senaculum and beyond to Curia (Hostilia); Circus Maximus refurbished.

173   Temple of Fortuna Equestris dedicated.

172   Columna Rostrata of M. Aemilius Lepidus destroyed by lightning.

170   Basilica Sempronia constructed.

168   Porticus Octavia constructed.

167   Temple of Penates struck by lightning; ship shed built to house flagship of Perseus of Macedon.

159   Porticoes added to Area Capitolina by Scipio Nasica; P. Cornelius Scipio installs a water clock adjacent to the Basilica Fulvia et Aemilia.

after 150   Temple of Felicitas constructed.

148   Regia burned and restored.

after 146   Porticus Metelli constructed.

145   Temple of Hercules Victor vowed by Mummius; legislative assembly removed from the Comitium to the Forum.

144–140   Aqua Appia repaired; Anio Vetus aqueduct repaired; Aqua Marcia constructed by Q. Marcius Rex.

142   Temple of Hercules Victor dedicated; stone arches added to Pons Aemilius; ceiling of Temple of Iuppiter Optimus Maximus gilded.

ca. 133   Temple of Mars in Circo Flaminio constructed.

125   Aqua Tepula constructed.

121   Temple of Concordia constructed; Basilica Opimia constructed; Fornix Fabianus erected; house of C. Fulvius Flaccus on Palatine destroyed and Porticus Catuli built on its site after 101.

117   Temple of Castor rebuilt.

115–107   Temple of Fides and Temple of Mens in Capitolio restored by M. Aemilius Scaurus.

114   Temple of Venus Verticordia constructed.

111   Temple of Magna Mater burned and then restored by Metellus (Numidicus?).

ca. 110   Porticus Minucia (Vetus).

after 101   Porticus Catuli built on Palatine; Temple of Fortuna Huiusce Diei vowed.

100–90   Marius erects trophies celebrating his victories in the Area Capitolina and builds the Temple of Honos et Virtus Mariana; house of Marius built adjacent to Forum.

ca. 92   Ara Calvini.

91   Temple of Pietas struck by lightning.

90   Temple of Iuno Sospita restored.

87   Servian Walls repaired and strengthened.

83   Temple of Iuppiter Optimus Maximus burned and restoration undertaken by Sulla.

82–79   Dictatorship of Sulla: extends pomerium; repaves the Forum; may have done considerable work on the street system of Rome; probably refurbished the Atrium Vestae; probably restored the Temple of Hercules Custos; may have built a Temple of Hercules Sullanus.

80	Curia Hostilia restored and enlarged; statues of Pythagoras and Alcibiades removed from the corners of the Comitium.
78	Tabularium built by Q. Lutatius Catulus; Tumulus Sullae.
74	Gradus Aurelii in the Comitium.
63	Statue of Jupiter in the Area Capitolina turned to the east.
62	Cicero acquires house on the Clivus Victoriae on the Palatine; Pons Fabricius constructed.
ca. 62–28	Pons Cestius constructed.
before 60	Horti Luculliani.
58	Temple of Fides restored by M. Aemilius Scaurus; Theater of Scaurus.
57	Fornix Fabianus restored; Basilica Fulvia et Aemilia restored.
55	Theater of Pompey dedicated; Basilica Iulia begun; acquisition of land for Forum Iulium begun; Saepta Iulia planned; Tumulus Iuliae.
53	Theaters of Curio.
52	Temple of Venus Victrix in Theater of Pompey, with scaena, porticoes, and adjacencies dedicated; Curia Hostilia burned; Basilica Porcia burned.
51	Forum Iulium begun.
50–44	Dictatorship of Julius Caesar: begins redevelopment of Forum and Comitium; Rostra Caesaris; acquisition of land for theater (of Marcellus); Horti Caesaris.
49	Temple of Quirinus burned and restored.
48	Sacellum of Bellona on Capitoline destroyed; Temple of Isis and Serapis on Capitoline razed.
46	Forum Iulium and Temple of Venus Genetrix dedicated; Equus Caesaris; Circus Maximus enlarged and euripus dug in front of spectators; Naumachia Caesaris in Codeta Minor; Temple of Libertas decreed.
44	Temple of Clementia Caesaris decreed; Temple of Concordia Nova decreed; Curia Hostilia rebuilt; Temple of Felicitas projected; Temple of Pietas dismantled; altar and column erected to Julius Caesar and later removed.
43	Naumachis Caesaris filled in; Sepulcrum Hirtii and Sepulcrum Pansae in Campus Martius; Temple of Isis and Serapis voted.
42	Temple of Mars Ultor vowed; Temple of Divus Iulius begun; Rostra Augusti dedicated; Temple of Saturn rebuilt.
42–32	Temple of Neptune vowed and constructed by Cn. Domitius Ahenobarbus.
41	Expensive wall constructed around the grove of Iuno Lucina.
ca. 38	Atrium Libertatis reconstructed by Asinius Pollio; Bibliotheca Asinii Pollionis.
36	Regia burned and restored; Temple of Apollo Palatinus vowed; Columna Rostrata of Octavian erected.
34	Basilica Paulli dedicated; Villa Publica possibly restored by Fonteius Capito.
33	Agrippa undertakes to overhaul the water and sewer systems of Rome; Aqua Appia repaired; Aqua Marcia repaired; Aqua Iulia constructed and its water mixed with Aqua Tepula; Aqua Virgo begun; Gabine stone conduits of Cloaca and lower Petronia Amnis installed; Porticus Octavia restored.
32	Theater of Pompey restored.
31	Temple of Spes (in Foro Holitorio) burned and restored; Temple of Ceres, Liber, and Libera burned and restored; Circus Maximus burned and restored and Pulvinar added.

30   Columna Rostrata of Octavian and Agrippa.

29   Temple of Divus Iulius dedicated; Curia Iulia together with Chalcidicum dedicated and Altar of Victoria dedicated in Curia; Temple of Hercules Musarum restored together with Porticus Philippi; Amphitheater of Statilius Taurus constructed; Arch of Augustus (Octavian).

28-A.D.14   Principate of Augustus: Temple of Diana on Aventine restored by L. Cornificius; Temple of Flora (iuxta Circum Maximum) restored; Temple of Iuno Regina on Aventine restored; Temple of Minerva restored; Temple of Iuppiter Libertas on Aventine restored; Area Capitolina cleared of dedications, and statues moved to Campus Martius; Temple of Iuppiter Feretrius restored; Temple of Iuppiter Optimus Maximus restored; Temple of Lares restored; Temple of Penates restored; Arch of Octavius erected on Palatine; Lupercal restored; Basilica Iulia completed and Forum redeveloped; Shrine of Apollo Sandaliarius erected; Temple of Venus Erucina at Porta Collina restored; Porticus ad Nationes built; Macellum Liviae; Temple of Bona Dea Subsaxana restored by Livia.

28   Temple of Apollo Palatinus dedicated; Mausoleum Augusti; Stadium Augusti.

27   Pantheon of Agrippa; oak crown and pair of laurels added to house of Augustus.

26   Temple of Iuppiter Tonans vowed; Saepta Iulia dedicated.

25   Basilica Neptuni dedicated; house of Antony on Palatine burned.

25–12   Program of Agrippa in Campus Martius: Baths of Agrippa with Stagnum Agrippae and euripus; Campus Agrippae with Porticus Vipsania; Horti Agrippae; Pons Agrippae; also Horrea Agrippiana of Regio VIII.

23–21   Pons Fabricius repaired after being damaged by floods.

after 23   Porticus Octaviae with Temple of Iuppiter Stator and Temple of Iuno Regina, Bibliothecae Porticus Octaviae, Curia Octaviae, and Scholae.

22   Temple of Iuppiter Tonans on Capitoline dedicated.

20(?)   Milliarium Aureum in Forum.

19   Aqua Virgo completed; Parthian Arch of Augustus in Forum; Altar of Fortuna Redux.

16   Temple of Iuventas burned and restored; restoration of Temple of Quirinus together with porticoes completed.

15   House of Vedius Pollio presented to Augustus and razed.

14   Basilica Paulli burned and restored; Temple of Vesta burned and restored.

13   Ara Pacis Augustae decreed by senate; Theater and Crypta Balbi dedicated; Theater of Marcellus dedicated (13 or 11).

before 12   Sepulcrum C. Cestii (Pyramid of Cestius).

12   Horti Agrippae and Baths of Agrippa presented to Roman people with endowment for maintenance.

after 12   Campus Agrippae completed by Augustus; Domus Publica presented to Vestal Virgins for inclusion in Atrium Vestae; statue and altar of Vesta established on Palatine; Pons Aemilius restored and Fornix Augusti added.

11–4   Augustus repairs water system of Rome, especially Aquae Anio Vetus, Marcia, and Iulia; Aqua Augusta built to supplement Aqua Appia.

11   Statues of Salus Publica, Concordia, and Pax.

10   Obeliscus Augusti, Gnomon, brought from Egypt and erected as part of Horologium Augusti; Obeliscus Augusti brought from Egypt and erected on spina of Circus Maximus.

9   Ara Pacis Augustae dedicated.

after 9 Arcus Drusi (1).

8 Cohortes Vigilum organized and stationed throughout the city.

7 City of Rome reorganized into fourteen geographical regiones; Diribitorium opened; Porticus Liviae dedicated to Concordia; Campus Agrippae dedicated; Tiberius undertakes to rebuild the Temple of Concordia on the Forum.

5 Compitum Acili restored; aqueduct arch constructed over Via Tiburtina (Porta Tiburtina).

before 2 Aqua Alsietina constructed.

2 Forum Augustum dedicated, although still unfinished, together with Temple of Mars Ultor; Naumachia Augusti.

A.D. 2 Arcus Lentuli et Crispini.

3 Temple of Magna Mater restored.

ca. 3 House of Augustus burned and rebuilt; Horti Lamiani created (?).

6 Temple of Castor rebuilt and dedicated by Tiberius.

7 Altar of Ceres Mater et Ops Augusta dedicated.

10 Arcus Dolabellae et Silani.

10 or 12 Temple of Concordia completed and dedicated by Tiberius.

12 Basilica Iulia rebuilt and enlarged after a fire, dedicated in the names of Gaius and Lucius Caesar; shrine of Fortuna Augusta; statue of Stata Mater.

14 Aqua Iulia repaired.

14–37 Principate of Tiberius: Sacrarium Divi Augusti (ad Capita Bubula on Palatine); Templum Divi Augusti (Novum) with Bibliotheca Divi Augusti Novi; Domus Tiberiana on Palatine; Schola Xanthi in Forum.

15 Cura Riparum of Tiber instituted after a great flood.

16 Arcus Tiberii in Forum.

16 Temple of Ceres, Liber, and Libera dedicated after restoration; Temple of Flora dedicated after restoration; Temple of Fors Fortuna dedicated; Templum of Ianus (in Foro Holitorio) dedicated after restoration; Temple of Spes restored by Germanicus and dedicated.

19 Arcus Drusi et Germanici; Arcus (Fornix) Germanici (in Circo Flaminio).

20 Theater of Pompey burned and restored.

21–23 Castra Praetoria constructed.

22 Basilica Paulli restored by L. Aemilius Lepidus; Ara Pietatis vowed.

23 Arcus Drusi (2) decreed.

27 Mons Caelius devastated by fire.

28 Altars of Amicitia Tiberii and Clementia Tiberii decreed by senate.

30 Colossus of Tiberius erected near Temple of Venus Genetrix.

36 Parts of Circus Maximus toward Aventine burned and repaired.

37–41 Principate of Caligula: Templum Divi Augusti Novum dedicated; restoration of Theater of Pompey completed; Domus Tiberiana enlarged and bridge from this to Capitoline constructed; Gaianum created; Circus Gaii et Neronis begun and Obeliscus Vaticanus brought from Egypt and erected on spina; Amphitheatrum Caligulae begun in Campus Martius; Temple of Isis Campensis constructed (?).

38   Anio Novus and Claudia Aqueducts begun.

39–40   Façade of Carcer added.

41–54   Principate of Claudius: Amphitheatrum Caligulae demolished; Altar of Iuppiter Depulsor dedicated on Capitoline; Temple of Felicitas burned and apparently not restored; Temple of Salus burned and restored; Carceres of Circus Maximus rebuilt in marble; Theater of Pompey rededicated; Porticus Minucia Frumentaria constructed; statue of Diva Livia added in Temple of Divus Augustus.

43   Ara Pietatis Augustae dedicated.

46   Aqua Virgo repaired.

47   Aqua Claudia completed.

49   Pomerium extended with traditional ritual.

51–52   Arcus Claudii added to Aqua Virgo at crossing of Via Lata to celebrate victory in Britain.

52   Anio Novus aqueduct completed; Aqua Claudia dedicated; monumental arch to take aqueducts over Via Praenestina and Via Labicana.

54–68   Principate of Nero: Temple of Divus Claudius begun by Agrippina (before 64); Domus Transitoria connecting imperial properties on Palatine with Horti Maecenatiani on Esquiline; Arcus Caelimontani (Arcus Neroniani of Aqua Claudia); seating in Circus Maximus improved and euripus of Julius Caesar filled in; Atrium Vestae rebuilt before 64; Balneum Tigillini.

57   Amphitheatrum Neronis.

58   Arcus Neronis decreed.

59   Macellum Magnum on Caelian dedicated.

60   Thermae and Gymnasium Neronis in Campus Martius dedicated.

62   Arcus Neronis on Capitoline dedicated; trophies of Nero on Capitoline; Gymnasium Neronis struck by lightning and burned.

63   Temple of Fecunditas decreed.

64   Baths of Nero restored and rededicated; fire of Nero destroys Circus Maximus, Ara Maxima Herculis, Temple of Luna, Regia, Temple of Vesta, Amphitheatrum Statilii Tauri, Domus Transitoria.

64–68   Domus Aurea with Aedes Fortunae Seiani, Colossus Neronis, porticoes on Sacra Via (Porticus Miliariae), Stagnum Neronis; Temple of Divus Claudius transformed; Ara Maxima Herculis, Atrium and Temple of Vesta, and Circus Maximus restored; Pons Neronianus constructed.

68   Principate of Galba: Horrea Galbae enlarged and restored; contingent of German soldiers stationed in Atrium Libertatis.

69   Principate of Otho: continues construction of Domus Aurea.

69   Principate of Vitellius: Temple of Iuppiter Optimus Maximus burned.

69–79   Principate of Vespasian: Temple of Iuppiter Optimus Maximus rebuilt; sacellum of Iuppiter Conservator on Capitoline dedicated by Domitian; Stagnum Neronis drained and construction of Amphitheatrum Flavium begun on site; Temple of Divus Claudius completed as planned; Temple of Honos et Virtus restored; Colossus Neronis altered to Colossus Solis; Theater of Marcellus restored.

70   Aedicula Fontis (in Transtiberim).

71   Aqueducts repaired; Templum Pacis begun.

75   Pomerium extended; Templum Pacis dedicated.

before 79   Templum Divi Augusti Novum burned.

79–81   Principate of Titus: adds third and fourth storeys to the Amphitheatrum Flavium; begins construction of Temple of Divus Vespasianus; begins construction of Thermae Titi.

79   Aqua Marcia repaired.

80   Amphitheatrum Flavium dedicated with games; Thermae Titi dedicated; fire of Titus destroys Campus Martius from Pantheon to Porticus Octaviae and from scaena of Theater of Pompey to Temple of Iuppiter Optimus Maximus, including Baths of Agrippa, Basilica Neptuni, Saepta Iulia, Diribitorium, Temple of Isis, Theatrum and Crypta Balbi, Area Sacra di Largo Argentina, possibly Temple of Venus Genetrix and parts of Forum Romanum and Domus Tiberiana.

80–81   Aqua Claudia repaired; triple arch of Titus and Vespasian erected in Circus Maximus.

81–96   Principate of Domitian: Amphitheatrum Flavium completed; the so-called Arae Incendii Neronis erected; various Arcus Domitiani; Arcus Titi (2) erected; Atria Septem built; Templum Divi Augusti Novum restored; Balineum Charini; Balineum Claudii Etrusci; Balineum Lupi; Basilica Argentaria begun; Temple of Castor restored; Castra Misenatium established; Circus Maximus burned; Curia Iulia rebuilt; Templum Divorum constructed; Domus Tiberiana remodeled and vestibule complex on Forum added; Temple of Venus Genetrix rebuilt; Forum Transitorium (Nervae) created; Forum Traiani projected; Temple of Gens Flavia constructed; Horrea Agrippiana rebuilt; Horrea Piperataria constructed; Ianus Quadrifrons of Forum Nervae constructed; Temple of Isis Campensis restored; Porticus Octaviae and its two temples restored; Temple of Iuppiter Custos constructed; Temple of Iuppiter Optimus Maximus restored; four ludi for training of gladiators constructed around Amphitheatrum Flavium; Minerva Chalcidica constructed; Naumachia Domitiani constructed; Horologium Augusti raised and corrected; Odeum constructed; Temple of Divus Vespasianus completed; Porticus Minucia Vetus restored; Stadium Domitiani constructed; Theatrum and Crypta Balbi restored; Theater of Pompey restored; Baths of Agrippa restored; Horti Domitiae created.

89   Temple of Iuppiter Optimus Maximus dedicated.

90   Mica Aurea constructed.

91   Equus Domitiani erected.

ca. 92   Domus Augustiana on Palatine completed.

93   Temple of Fortuna Redux completed.

96   Meta Sudans constructed.

96–98   Principate of Nerva: work on Amphitheatrum Flavium continued; Atrium Libertatis restored; Horrea Nervae (?).

97   Forum Nervae dedicated.

98–117   Principate of Trajan: work on Amphitheatrum Flavium continued; Anio Novus aqueduct extended to better sources; Aqua Marcia extended to serve Aventine; Aqua Traiana constructed; Atrium Vestae renovated; Basilica Argentaria completed; Circus Maximus restored and seating capacity increased; Baths of Sura; Ludus Magnus rebuilt; Naumachia Traiani constructed; Pantheon struck by lightning and burned; Theatrum Traiani in Campus Martius; Temple of Fortuna; Altar of Pudicitia to Plotina; Odeum of Domitian restored; Arch of Trajan on Via Appia.

104   Domus Aurea burned and Baths of Trajan then built over ruins.

112   Basilica Ulpia dedicated.

113   Temple of Venus Genetrix dedicated after restoration; Forum Traiani dedicated; Columna Traiani dedicated.

117   Entrance arch of Forum Traiani made victory monument.

117–138   Principate of Hadrian: Aqua Marcia repaired; Arcus Divi Traiani erected; Templum Divi Traiani added to Forum Traiani; Athenaeum (Atrium Minervae?) constructed; aedicula Vestae constructed and Atrium Vestae improved; Basilica (Templum) Matidiae et Marcianae constructed; Basilica Neptuni restored; Temple of Bona Dea Subsaxana restored; Domus Tiberiana given new front on Sacra Via; Lavacrum Agrippinae restored; Pantheon rebuilt; Saepta Iulia restored; Baths of Agrippa restored; Temple of Divus Iulius restored; Forum Augustum restored; Auguratorium restored.

121   Entrance court of Domus Aurea destroyed and platform for Temple of Venus et Roma begun; pomerium restored.

ca. 128   Colossus Solis (Neronis) moved to stand near Amphitheatrum Flavium.

134   Pons Aelius completed.

ca. 135   Temple of Venus et Roma dedicated.

ca. 137   Altar of Diva Sabina.

138–161   Principate of Antoninus Pius: possibly completes Temple of Venus et Roma; Amphitheatrum Flavium restored; Templum Divi Augusti Novum restored; Graecostadium restored after fire; section of Circus Maximus collapses; Temple of Bacchus (on Sacra Via?) restored; Baths of Novatius.

139   Mausoleum Hadriani completed.

ca. 139–143 Balineum Mamertini.

after 141   Altar of Diva Faustina; Temple of Antoninus and Faustina on Sacra Via.

143   Curia Athletarum.

145   Temple of Divus Hadrianus dedicated.

147   Pons Agrippae restored.

152   Pons Cestius restored.

161–180   Principate of Marcus Aurelius: Columna Antonini Pii; Arcus Divi Veri; Temple of Mercury restored (?).

161   Rededication of Temple of Faustina to Divus Antoninus Pius and Diva Faustina.

after 175   Altar of Diva Faustina (Minor); Columna Marci Aurelii Antonini.

176   Arcus Marci Aurelii decreed.

176–181   Temple of Iuppiter Heliopolitanus of Lucus Furrinae rebuilt.

180–193   Principate of Commodus: Temple of Divus Marcus Aurelius constructed; Colossus of Sol (Nero) altered to portray Commodus with attributes of Hercules; cippi of *octroi* (customs) boundary.

183   Thermae Commodianae.

189   Bibliotheca Capitolina burned.

191   Fire of Commodus destroys Templum Pacis, Horrea Piperataria, and Temple of Vesta; shrine of Iuppiter Dolichenus on Esquiline enlarged and rededicated.

193–211   Principate of Septimius Severus: Templum Pacis restored; Temple of Divus Vespasianus restored; Tensa Iovis removed to Circus Maximus; Balinea Severi (in Transtiberim); Castra Nova Severiana Equitum Singularium constructed; Coriaria Septimiana (in Transtiberim); Domus Augustiana enlarged by new wing and exedra of hippodrome rebuilt; Equus Septimii Severi in Forum Romanum; Forum repaved; Rostra Augusti modified; Thermae Septimianae (in Transtiberim) and Thermae Severianae (in Regio I) constructed; Julia Domna remodels Atrium Vestae and restores Temple of Vesta.

196   Aqua Marcia repaired.

ca. 197   Domus Lateranorum presented; Septem Domus and Parthorum presented.

202   Pantheon restored.

203   Arcus Septimii Severi in Forum Romanum; Porticus Octaviae and its temples restored; Septizodium constructed.

ca. 203   Domus Cilonis presented.

204   Arcus Septimii Severi in Foro Boario.

209–211   Some restoration of Theater of Pompey.

211–217   Principate of Caracalla: Aqua Marcia repaired and Fons Antoninianus added to it to supply Thermae Antoninianae; Pons Aurelius constructed (?); *ianuae* of Circus Maximus enlarged; Via Nova constructed to serve baths.

216   Thermae Antoninianae dedicated; Arco di Druso probably constructed.

217   Amphitheatrum Flavium struck by lightning and severely damaged by fire.

218–222   Principate of Elagabalus: Sessorium palace ad Spem Veterem largely rebuilt, together with Amphitheatrum Castrense and Circus Varianus; repair of Amphitheatrum Flavium begun; part of peribolus of Thermae Antoninianae constructed; worship of Dea Virgo Caelestis introduced into Rome.

221   Temple of Elagabalus on Palatine dedicated; senaculum mulierum on Quirinal constructed.

222–235   Principate of Alexander Severus: Aqua Alexandrina constructed to supply his baths; Bibliotheca Panthei; Temple of Iuppiter Ultor (Victor) on Palatine restored; Diaetae Mammaeae created; Temple of Isis Campensis embellished; Temple of Dea Suria constructed; Basilica Alexandrina projected; Stadium of Domitian restored; shrine of Iuppiter Redux in Castra Peregrina.

223   Repair of Amphitheatrum Flavium continued.

226   Nymphaeum Alexandri.

227   Baths of Nero rebuilt and enlarged as Thermae Alexandrinae.

238   Principate of Gordians: Castra Misenatium enlarged; work on Thermae Surae; repair of Amphitheatrum Flavium completed.

247   Theater of Pompey and Hecatostylon burned; Naumachia of Philippus Arabs (Naumachia Augusti?).

249–251   Principate of Decius.

250   Amphitheatrum Flavium repaired after fire.

252   Baths of Decius.

252–268   Principate of Gallienus.

262   Arch of Gallienus.

268   Rule of the Thirty Tyrants: Quadrigae Pisonis.

270–275   Principate of Aurelian: extends pomerium; Castra Urbana in Campus Agrippae; adds Porticus Miliaria to Horti Sallustiani.

271–272   Muri Aureliani begun.

273   Temple of the Sun.

276–282	Principate of Probus: Muri Aureliani completed; Pons Probi.
282–284	Principate of Carinus: decoration of the stabulum of the Palatine palace.
283	Fire of Carinus destroys Basilica Iulia, Curia Iulia, Forum Iulium, Graecostadium, Porticus and Theatrum Pompeii.
284–305	Principate of Diocletian: restores Basilica Iulia, Curia Iulia, Forum Iulium, Porticus and Theatrum Pompeii (with Maximian); remodels Forum Romanum, adds new rostra and lines of columns carrying honorific statues; Aqua Antoniniana (Marcia) augmented to supply his baths; portion of Circus Maximus collapses.
303	Columns of Vicennalia in Forum Romanum.
303–304	Arcus Novus in Via Lata.
after 303	Umbilicus Romae.
305–306	Thermae Diocletiani on Quirinal.
306–312	Principate of Maxentius: baths added to Domus Augustiana; Basilica Nova (Constantini) begun; Muri Aureliani heightened and improved throughout circuit; Temple of Divus Romulus on Sacra Via.
307	Temple of Venus et Roma rebuilt after fire.
311	Secretarium Senatus restored.
312–337	Reign of Constantine: restores Atrium Vestae and Circus Maximus; encloses Meta Sudans with a new basin; constructs Ianus Quadrifrons in Forum Boarium and Porticus Constantini; repairs Aqua Virgo.
312	Castra Praetoria dismantled.
after 313	Thermae Constantini.
315–316	Arcus Constantini.
323–326	Baths of Helena restored.
328	Statio Aquarum restored.
ca. 331	Basilica Iunii Bassi.
334	Equus Constantini.
341	Temple of Iuppiter Heliopolitanus of Lucus Furrinae destroyed.
337–361	Reign of Constantius II.
344–345	Baths of Agrippa restored by Constantius and Constans.
352–353	Equus Constantii.
356	State visit of Constantius to Rome.
357	Obeliscus Constantii brought from Alexandria and erected on spina of Circus Maximus; Altar of Victoria removed from Curia.
ca. 358	Baths of Naeratius Cerialis.
360–363	Reign of Julian: Temple of Iuppiter Heliopolitanus of Lucus Furrinae rebuilt; Altar of Victoria restored in Curia.
363	Temple of Apollo Palatinus burned.
364–378	Macellum Liviae restored.
365–367	Valentinian I restores Pons Aurelius.
367	Porticus Deorum Consentium rebuilt by Vettius Praetextatus.

369	Pons Cestius rebuilt as Pons Gratianus.
ca. 374	Temple of Bonus Eventus and Porticus Boni Eventus constructed.
379–383	Arcus Gratiani, Valentiniani, et Theodosii.
ca. 380	Porticus Maximae.
381	Repair of Anio Novus.
382	Altar of Victoria removed from Curia by Theodosius; Mansiones Saliorum restored.
384–387	Pons Theodosii; Theater of Pompey restored.
395–423	Reign of Honorius: Theater of Pompey restored.
398	Quadriga of Arcadius and Honorius.
402–403	Muri Aureliani restored and gates extensively redesigned; Statuae Stilichonis.
404	Last gladiatorial games offered in Amphitheatrum Flavium.
after 405	Arcus Arcadii, Honorii, et Theodosii.
408	Earthquakes (?) for a week in Templum Pacis.
410	Sack of Alaric: Basilica Paulli burned; Horti Sallustiani devastated.
412	Secretarium Senatus repaired.
414	Baths of Sura restored.
416	Basilica Iulia restored by Gabinius Vettius Probianus.
442	Earthquake damages Forum Romanum, Amphitheatrum Flavium, and Porticus Nova (Pompeii?).
443	Baths of Constantine restored.
450	Forum Esquilinum restored.
463–483	Basilica Iunii Bassi converted into church.
470	Earthquake damages Amphitheatrum Flavium.
ca. 470	"Rostra Vandalica."
493–526	Reign of Theodoric: Forum Romanum repaired, Muri Aureliani repaired; Atrium Libertatis (Bibliotheca Ulpia?) restored; Stadium of Domus Augustiana repaired.
507–511	Theater of Pompey restored by Symmachus.
508?	Amphitheatrum Flavium repaired by prefect Basilius.
523	Last venationes offered in Amphitheatrum Flavium.
526–527	Temple of Divus Romulus converted into church.
535	Library established in "Domus Aniciorum" on Caelian by Pope Agapetus I.
537	Aqua Traiana cut by Goths of Vitiges; Rome sacked.
608	Columna Phocae in Forum Romanum.

Designed by Glen Burris
Set in Sabon by Graphic Composition, Inc.
Printed on 60-lb. Glatfelter Eggshell Offset by
The Maple Press Company

Tempio di Giove Tonante alle radici del Monte Capitolino, fù da Ottaviano Augusto fabbricato per voto, e
a lui per aver offerte vittime con altre Fabbriche del vicino Campid... ... restituite dall'Imp.r Adriano. Per ciò
... ... in questo insigne ... ... dell'Ambasciator Sberno tanto per la squisita delicatezza
... ... quante per ... ... a ... ... maestà della Fabbrica, egli suo meritam.te ammira

Veduta del Temp